CASES AND MATERIALS ON
EUROPEAN
UNION LAW
Third Edition

■ ■ ■

By
George A. Bermann
Jean Monnet Professor of European Union Law,
Walter Gellhorn Professor of Law and
Director, European Legal Studies Center,
Columbia University School of Law

Roger J. Goebel
Alpin S. Cameron Professor of Law and Director,
Fordham Center on European Union Law,
Fordham University School of Law

William J. Davey
Guy Raymond Jones Chair in Law Emeritus,
University of Illinois College of Law

Eleanor M. Fox
Walter J. Derenberg Professor of Trade Regulation,
New York University School of Law

AMERICAN CASEBOOK SERIES®

WEST®
A Thomson Reuters business

Mat #40637292

American Casebook Series is a trademark registered in the U.S. Patent and Trademark Office.

COPYRIGHT © 1993 WEST PUBLISHING CO.
© West, a Thomson business, 2002
© 2011 Thomson Reuters
   610 Opperman Drive
   St. Paul, MN 55123
   1–800–313–9378
Printed in the United States of America

ISBN: 978–0–314–18420–7

To my wife, Sandra, and to the children:
Sloan, Suzanne, Mark and Grant

G.A.B.

To the memory of my father, Frank L. Goebel,
and to the memory of my mother,
Anne M. Goebel

R.J.G.

To my mother, Jean M. Davey,
and to the memory my father,
Norman B. Davey

W.J.D.

To Jerry, and to my children
Doug, Margot and David, Randy and Tricia

E.M.F.

PREFACE

The study of European Union (or EU) law has steadily gained importance in recent years. The EU today consists of twenty-seven Member States with a complex institutional and constitutional structure. This casebook is intended to provide a basic understanding of the European Union and its predecessor, the European Community, including their structures, goals, fields of action, achievements and aspirations, providing a foundation for further research, analysis and legal writing.

There are many valid reasons to study European Union law. We present here three of the most important ones. The most pragmatic of them is that the EU has become the largest trading partner of the US, represents a major site of investment for US firms and is the principal site of overseas offices of American law firms. Indeed, its total Gross Domestic Product has recently surpassed that of the US. US law firms and international house counsel cannot afford to possess only a limited knowledge of Union structure, law-making processes and substantive law. European Union competition and trade law have long been staples of international practice. Today, the EU's harmonization of health, safety and technical standards, company, banking and securities law, environmental and consumer protection measures, and legislation in the field of employment law (to name just a sampling of sectors) represent matters of practical concern to American enterprises and their lawyers. The Economic and Monetary Union, with a single currency and a single monetary policy for a majority of EU States, is also of evident importance to the international business and legal world.

Second, European Union law is a rewarding field for comparative law study. This has long been true in competition and trade law, where academics and practitioners have found provocative points of comparison and contrast. A rich source of comparative study is also to be found in the EU programs for harmonization of laws. In some fields, as in environmental and consumer rights law, the EU has been significantly influenced by US models, but still strikes certain different notes. In other fields, such as banking, company law, employment law, and anti-discrimination law, the EU has taken quite a different path from the US. Constitutional comparisons and contrasts between the US and EU enrich legal analysis on both sides of the Atlantic.

Third, European Union law provides a laboratory for study of law formation: the development of an entire legal system in modern times. The study includes its evolving constitutional framework, its institutions, substantive legislation and judicial law, and the constant interplay of policy and politics in an evolving federal-type system, one comprised of twenty-seven nations having many common features, but also quite diverse legal and political systems, demographics and interests.

Students who take a basic EU law course for any or all of these reasons will find the casebook of great value. The book covers virtually all major fields of European Union law (except for certain technical fields, such as agriculture, transport, energy and public procurement). The notes and questions are intended to facilitate reflection on how and why the EU institutions, and especially the Court of Justice and Court of First Instance (now renamed the General Court) have reached their legal and policy conclusions. The text and notes make frequent comparisons with US law. The authors hope that students will thereby achieve not only a solid comprehension of European Union law, but also one permitting critical evaluation.

The casebook was written primarily for use in US law schools. It is suitable as well for law faculties in Europe and elsewhere. Our casebook follows traditional US teaching methods which give central attention to primary materials, notably the Treaty provisions, legislation and court judgments, inviting students to examine these materials critically through focused questions. Accordingly, Court judgments and EU legislation are subjected to the same kind of analytic review as US laws and Supreme Court opinions would be in a standard constitutional law casebook. We hope that European professors and students will find that the process of analytic examination of judgments and legislation through questions will assist in a more reflective comprehension of EU rules and judicial doctrines.

The entry into force on Dec. 1, 2009 of the Lisbon Treaty on European Union (TEU) and its accessory Treaty on the Functioning of the European Union (TFEU), which replaces the prior European Community Treaty (ECT), complicates to some extent current study of EU law. The Lisbon TEU's provisions include many innovations as compared to the prior Maastricht Treaty on European Union, in effect from Nov. 1, 1993. We have tried always to make clear to which TEU we are referring when discussing provisions in the casebook text. Moreover, although many TFEU articles only reiterate provisions of the ECT, some have significantly changed and all have been renumbered. We have customarily indicated the corresponding provisions of both the ECT and TFEU in the casebook text and the excerpted judgments. Over time the Lisbon TEU and TFEU provisions will become familiar, but currently some confusion is inevitable.

The Selected Documents, which accompanies the casebook, should prove quite helpful in this regard. It contains the Lisbon TEU, TFEU and the ECT (as most recently amended by the Treaty of Nice, effective Feb. 1, 2003), as well as a conversion table of article numbers between the TFEU and ECT. The Selected Documents also include the Charter of Fundamental Rights of the European Union, given Treaty legal force by the TEU, certain key Protocols, and a considerable number of secondary legislative measures that are important to the understanding of relevant casebook text. The accessibility of these documents should be helpful in research and writing.

Clearly there is more material in this casebook than can be responsibly covered in a single semester course. There is a range of possibilities. Teachers who wish especially to emphasize constitutional and institutional issues will find that Parts I and II of the book provide a comprehensive picture of the legal and institutional framework of the European Union, furnishing material for at least a full half-semester of teaching, thereby allowing constitutional and institutional themes to become the course's leitmotif. They may then assign substantive law chapters that best match their own and their students' interests. We recommend that any such substantive law selection include a very healthy dose of the material in Part III on the Internal Market, one or two basic chapters on competition policy (from Part IV), and one or two basic chapters on external relations and trade (from Part V) or economic and monetary union and free movement of capital (from Part VI).

Other teachers may wish to concentrate in a course or seminar on certain substantive aspects of Union law. Thus, a course might concentrate on the common market, or internal market, in Part III, perhaps with the addition of Part VI on free movement of capital and the Economic and Monetary Union, and some chapters from Part VII. Another likely course is one centered on competition law, the topic of Part IV, perhaps joined with coverage of external relations and trade law, the subject of Part V. Any of the assorted substantive law topics in Part VII—environmental protection, consumer rights, social policy, equal employment rights, and jurisdiction and judgments—might appropriately be covered either in a basic course or advanced seminar.

We hope that the casebook will prove easy to use while also highly instructive, and that it will stimulate further study and scholarship in the ever-widening fields of European Union law.

FOREWORD

It is a great pleasure to welcome the third edition of the Casebook written by Professors Bermann, Goebel, Davey, and Fox, which carries on the success of the two earlier ones. Bearing in mind the quality of its authors, it does not come as a surprise that the Casebook is an outstanding piece of scholarly work. A major revision has been undertaken to bring the previous edition up to date, by including many important new cases (such as *Mangold* and *Kadi*) and by taking account of the changes brought about by the Treaty of Lisbon, which entered into force on 1 December 2009.

The Casebook is divided into seven parts. Parts I and II examine the legal and institutional framework of the European Union (EU) and the reception and enforcement of EU law in the Member States, respectively. Parts III to VI look at the substantive law of the EU, i.e. fundamental freedoms, EU citizenship, competition policy, external relations and commercial policy, as well as EU economic and monetary union. Part VII is devoted to the most important specific policies of the EU, such as environmental law, consumer protection, social policy, equal employment rights and anti-discrimination policies, and litigation in civil and commercial matters. In a clear and entertaining style, the Casebook thus provides a comprehensive and innovative overview of EU law.

Like its predecessors, the third edition of the Casebook will be very much appreciated on both sides of the Atlantic. It exemplifies the important contribution of U.S. scholarship to the development of EU law, in terms of both teaching methodology and academic research. First, the structure of each chapter, which mirrors that of casebooks on U.S. Constitutional law, is suitable for the Socratic Method of teaching law, widely used in U.S. law schools but virtually unknown in continental Europe. Each chapter is structured as follows. It begins with an introduction which places the particular subject in its proper historical and/or normative context. Next, there is a selection of the most relevant case-law. The facts and legal issues raised by each case are summarised in an introductory paragraph, which is followed by the most salient passages of the European Court of Justice's (or, as the case may be, the European General Court's) ruling. A series of questions, notes and cross-references then provides a solid basis for discussion. Hence, by prioritizing the analysis of primary sources over academic commentary, the authors seek to stimulate and promote independent critical thinking. This is, in my view, an ideal way for readers to acquaint themselves with the key principles of EU law. Second, the Casebook contains many references to the case-law of the U.S. Supreme Court. Given my special interest in comparative law, I consider that this is one of the most valuable and distinctive features of the Casebook. By highlighting the convergences and divergences between the case-law of the ECJ and that of the U.S. Supreme Court, the Casebook encourages law students to learn to think unconventionally, as they encounter and compare different solutions (or indeed similar solutions based on a different rationale) to a particular legal issue. Last but not least, though U.S. law students are the primary target of the Casebook, I also believe that it will be particularly useful to European students and scholars. Throughout the Casebook, the authors often refer to U.S. legal concepts and examples in explaining how EU law operates. By drawing parallels with the U.S. legal order, not only does the Casebook facilitate the understanding of EU law by U.S. law students, but it also invites European students and scholars to discover the fascinating legal dynamics of another great legal order.

I find no better way of concluding than to quote the late Lord Slynn of Hadley, who excelled in writing the Foreword to the two previous editions. He rightly pointed out that 'Any student who masters this book, or specific sections of it, will have a profound and detailed knowledge of what European law is all about'.

Prof. dr. Koen Lenaerts,

Judge at the Court of Justice of the European Union.

ACKNOWLEDGMENTS TO THE FIRST EDITION

The authors of every project of this scope owe a multitude of debts to those who have inspired and assisted them along the way. While it is not possible to acknowledge all those who have helped us, a number of contributions deserve special mention.

We jointly give our thanks to those who have made suggestions that have helped to shape the coverage or text of this casebook. Preeminent among them are Bernhard Schloh of the Council Legal Service, Peter Oliver of the Commission Legal Service, and Professor Valentine Korah of University College, London.

George Bermann wishes to thank especially Professor Henry G. Schermers and Bernhard Schloh for their profound guidance in Community law over the years, as well as Judges Koen Lenaerts, Pierre Pescatore and Lord Gordon Slynn and Professor Meinhard Hilf for their helpful comments on his text. Mary Dominick, Lee Neuman, Carlin Stratton, April Tash and Sally Zelikovsky afforded essential research assistance. The secretarial help of Susan Martin and Kam Metcalf is also warmly appreciated.

Roger Goebel thanks the many members of the Court of Justice, the Council and the Commission who have enriched his knowledge of Community law, in particular Judge David Edward and former Judges Pierre Pescatore and Lord Gordon Slynn, Rafaello Fornasier, Hans–Joachim Glaesner and Bernhard Schloh of the Council Legal Service, Karen Banks, Daniel Calleja, Bernd Langeheine, Jörn Pipkorn, Rolf Wägenbaur and Richard Wainwright of the Commission Legal Service, Auke Haagsma, Helmut Schröder and John Temple Lang of DG IV, Christopher Cruickshank and Severine Israel of DG IV, and George Zavvos, Member of the European Parliament. Thanks are also due to Jacques Buhart, Stephen Spinks and Paulette Vander Schueren, his former colleagues at Coudert Brothers. He is most appreciative of the aid provided by his research assistants, Diane Duszak, Stephen Jones and Stewart Muglich, and the faculty secretaries, Carol DeVito and Mary Whelan.

William Davey would like to thank Professor Eric Stein for kindling his interest in EC law many years ago, as well as Judge Pierre Pescatore, Jacques Bourgeoise, Edwin Vermulst and his former colleagues at Cleary, Gottlieb, Steen and Hamilton in Brussels, Donald L. Holley, Dirk Vandermeersch and Marc Hansen, for comments on various draft chapters and for assisting in obtaining materials. He would also like to acknowledge the invaluable help of his research assistant, Gordon Wagner, and his secretary, Terri Macfarland.

Eleanor Fox would like to thank Professor Valentine Korah for her extraordinarily helpful comments on various drafts, and Professor Korah, Professor Barry Hawk, Donald L. Holley, and the dedicated staff and officials of the EC Competition Directorate for innumerable insightful conversations.

Also she wishes to acknowledge the valuable research assistance of James R. Farnsworth, Randall M. Fox, Robert Grundstein and Lene Skou and the dedicated assistance of her secretary, Linda Smalls.

We further wish to pay tribute to Professors Eric Stein, Peter Hay, Michel Waelbroeck and Joseph Weiler, whose earlier casebook representing a pioneering text from which we all profited when first teaching in this field.

Finally, we acknowledge the permission given by Sweet & Maxwell Ltd. for the use of excerpts from a number of national court judgments reported in the Common Market Law Reports, and thank the staff of the Court of Justice and of the information services of the EC Delegations in New York City and Washington, D.C., for their assistance in obtaining current materials.

ACKNOWLEDGMENTS TO THE SECOND EDITION

Professor Bermann acknowledges with special gratitude the research and editorial assistance of Richard H. Langan II and the research and secretarial assistance of Karina Rodriguez. Professor Bermann expresses thanks as well for the exceptionally valuable suggestions of Judge Koen Lenaerts of the Court of First Instance and Kurt Riechenberg, chef de cabinet of the President of the European Court of Justice.

Professor Goebel would like to thank his research assistant, Thomas Maeglin, together with Mary Whelan, Judy Haskell and Christian Steriti, members of the faculty secretariat, for their invaluable assistance.

Professor Davey would like to thank his research assistant, Valerie Demaret, and his administrative assistant, Ruth Manint.

Professor Fox expresses her appreciation for the research assistance of Krzysztof Kuik, David P. Herlihy, James Harvey and John Marco.

The authors wish to thank Duncan E. Alford, reference librarian at Columbia Law School, for his assistance in preparing the revised note on "Legal Sources and Citation Forms" (p. xvii).

ACKNOWLEDGMENTS TO THE THIRD EDITION

Professor Bermann wishes to thank his devoted team of research assistants from the Columbia Law School LLM class of 2009 for their diligent and cheerful research. Deep thanks, too, to Kieran Bradley of the Council Legal Service and Kurt Riechenberg of the European Court of Justice for their generous comments on prior drafts.

Roger Goebel thanks the many members of the Court of Justice who have enriched his knowledge of European Union law doctrines and leading judgments. Believing it appropriate only to cite the former members of the Court, he specifically expresses his gratitude to the late President, Ole Due, and Judges Pierre Pescatore and Gordon, Lord Slynn of Hadley; the retired Judges Sir David Edward, Fidelma Macken, John Murray, Jean–Pierre Puissochet, Leif Sevon, and Melchior Wathelet; and the retired Advocates–General Sir Francis Jacobs, Nial Fennelly, Carl–Otto Lenz and Walter Van Gerven; as well as Bo Vesterdorf, the former President of the Court of First Instance. He likewise thanks Jean–Claude Piris, the retiring Director–General of the Council Legal Service, and numerous former members of the Council and Commission Legal Services, notably Auke Haagsma, Marie–Jose Jonczy, Pieter Kuijper, Giuliano Marenco, Bernhard Schloh, John Temple Lang, Rolf Wagenbaur, and Richard Wainwright. Finally, he expresses his gratitude to his research assistant, Seth Bailey, and his secretaries, Alfred Bobek and Kim Holder.

Professor Davey would like to thank Professor Eric Stein for kindling his interest in EEC law many years ago at Michigan and his former colleagues at Cleary, Gottlieb in Brussels for helping to broaden his knowledge of the subject. He would also like to thank his research and faculty assistants at Illinois who have worked on the various editions of the casebook over the years—Gordon Wagner, Valerie Demaret, Terri Macfarland, Ruth Manint and Sue Carrell.

Professor Fox expresses great appreciation to Kevin Coates of the Competition Directorate of the European Commission for his generous and insightful comments, and to her assistant Linda Smalls for her dedicated work in helping to prepare the manuscript.

EU Law Research Guide

For resources and basic legal research methods for the law of the European Union, please consult **ASIL Guide to Electronic Resources for International Law: European Union** by Marylin J. Raisch.* This guide was prepared and is maintained with updated information under the Electronic Resource Guide section of the web site for the American Society of International Law at http://www.asil.org/eu1.cfm. As such, it is a publication of the American Society of International Law. ASIL electronic research tools are updated by the authors at least twice per year, in May and November, and this guide will remain posted at this link. Scheduled revision for the EU guide will include, for example, links provided by the new European e-Justice Portal, https://e-justice.europa.eu/home.do?&action=home&lang=en with its emphasis on guiding research in a cross-border context.

---

* Marylin J. Raisch, J.D., M.L.S., M.Litt. (Oxon.) is the Associate Law Librarian for International and Foreign Law, Georgetown Law Library, and head of its John Wolff International and Comparative Law Library. She is the author of several web-based research guides for topics in international and foreign law as well as recent publications available at http://ssrn.com/author=440837 and http://scholarship.law.georgetown.edu/ (under Raisch).

SUMMARY OF CONTENTS

PART 1. THE EUROPEAN UNION: LEGAL AND INSTITUTIONAL FRAMEWORK

TABLE OF CONTENTS

―――――

PART 1. THE EUROPEAN UNION: LEGAL AND INSTITUTIONAL FRAMEWORK

TABLE OF EU LAW CASES IN THE EUROPEAN COURT OF JUSTICE

The principal cases are in bold type. Cases cited or discussed in the text are in roman type. References are to pages. Cases cited in principal cases and within other quoted materials are not included.

TABLE OF EU LAW CASES IN THE GENERAL COURT (FORMERLY THE COURT OF FIRST INSTANCE)

The principal cases are in bold type. Cases cited or discussed in the text are roman type. References are to pages. Cases cited in principal cases and within other quoted materials are not included.

TABLE OF NATIONAL COURT DECISIONS

The principal cases are in bold type. Cases cited or discussed in the text are in roman type. References are to pages. Cases cited in principal cases and within other quoted materials are not included.

Table of European Commission Decisions

The principal cases are in bold type. Cases cited or discussed in the text are in roman type. References are to pages. Cases cited in principal cases and within other quoted materials are not included.

CASES AND MATERIALS ON
EUROPEAN
UNION LAW
Third Edition

PART 1

THE EUROPEAN UNION: LEGAL AND INSTITUTIONAL FRAMEWORK

■ ■ ■

The European Union—as did the European Community which, until the 2009 Treaty of Lisbon, formed a distinct part of the Union—performs a wide variety of functions across a vast regulatory domain. That domain can scarcely be defined, given its expansiveness across matters of both public and private law. The chapters that constitute Parts III through VII of this book will find the Union institutions addressing concerns ranging from market integration, to competition policy, to international trade and external relations more generally, to an ever-wider range of sectoral (e.g. labor, telecommunications) and non-sectoral (e.g. consumer and environmental protection) "policies." The evolution of the entity from European Economic Community, to European Community, and finally to European Union, like its development of an expansive and distinctive notion of "European citizenship," captures this remarkable phenomenon.

To accomplish its wide-ranging and important purposes, the European Union has need of viable legal and political systems that can generate and monitor their activities, while at the same time providing a continuity and stability that match the challenges they face. Part I of this book explores this stable, though often changing, legal and political framework, with special attention to the institutions of the Union, their objectives and their procedures,

After an historical introduction identifying the roots of European integration and the broad outlines of its institutional evolution (Chapter 1), Chapter 2 examines successively the basic treaty foundations of the "European project," as the entire enterprise is sometimes called, together with the political and judicial institutions that manage it. Because so much of this book deals with legal measures of various sorts, Chapter 3 describes the nature of those measures and analyzes the legislative and administrative processes from which they emerge.

The sphere of European Union law and policy, though vast, is not unlimited. Chapter 4 examines the various bounds on the "reach" of the Union and of Union law, including such aspects of the problem as implied

1

powers, "internal affairs," preemption and subsidiarity, as well as the curious notion of "enhanced cooperation."

The Union's judiciary plays the central role in determining the scope and meaning of Union law. Issues not only of interpretation but also of validity abound, and the courts of the Union—the Court of Justice, the General Court (formerly known as the Court of First Instance) and specialized tribunals—are equipped with a jurisdiction and a set of remedies designed to address them. Chapter 5 explores the role and function of these judicial institutions, while Chapter 6 traces the "fundamental rights" and "human rights" norms that increasingly inform their jurisprudence. The Union's own Charter of Fundamental Rights and the European Human Rights Convention play a vital role in this aspect of EU law.

A pervasive motif in this book is the relationship between Union and Member State law. The efficacy of European Union law depends heavily, not only on its taking precedence as a normative matter over national law and policy, but also on the effectiveness of the Member States' implementation of that law and policy. That jurisprudence continues to this day and is the subject of Chapter 7.

CHAPTER 1

THE HISTORY OF THE EUROPEAN COMMUNITY AND THE EUROPEAN UNION

■ ■ ■

In little more than 50 years, the European Community (EC), now absorbed into the European Union (EU), has achieved extraordinary results in economic, political, social and legal integration. The Community's architects sought to create on the historically fragmented continent of Europe an integrated economic market that would afford enterprise the benefits of harmonized regulation in a larger market with economies of scale, while bringing to the population as a whole a higher standard of living. Although principally designed to serve economic ends, the Community soon acquired political, social and cultural dimensions, with active programs in fields such as the harmonization of national technical and commercial rules, environmental, consumer and investor protection, employee rights, research and development, health, education and culture.

European integration has also always had a more purely political dimension. The notion of a political union of sorts was present in the minds of many of the Community's founders. The Preamble to the 1957 Treaty Establishing the European Economic Community set as one of its goals the achievement of "an ever closer Union among the peoples of Europe." In 1993, the Treaty of Maastricht (officially the Treaty on European Union) placed the Community within the framework of a broader European Union, which added new European integration initiatives while presenting to the world a unified European political face. The Treaty of Lisbon has now integrated the Community into the European Union, while revising its structure to enable the Union to operate more effectively and more democratically.

Given the traditional European commitment to the rule of law, it is not surprising that the European Community evolved into a highly structured and principled legal environment. Community law, and now Union law, is the product of political institutions operating through prescribed legal instruments. An independent Court of Justice interprets and applies the Treaties and legal measures adopted pursuant to them. It

3

is accordingly only natural that the international legal community should take a strong interest in this increasingly sophisticated legal law system.

The history of the European Union has been marked by differing combinations of "deepening" and "widening." Deepening signifies improving the efficiency of the operations of the political institutions and enhancing their democratic credentials, while achieving progress toward an integrated economic market bringing benefits to all its citizens. Widening suggests the addition of new Member States, enlarging the common market and introducing new political, social and cultural elements. Inevitably, widening also tends to strain the political institutions, leading to new pressure for deepening, especially through revisions of the treaties that regulate the EU's institutional structure. An appreciation of these successive cycles will considerably promote understanding of Chapter 2's presentation of the Union's institutions and the review of substantive law in later chapters.

In this historical depiction, we can only briefly note the contributions of political leaders of the Community, and later the Union, and of the Member States. It should be emphasized that the ability, energy and vision of these leaders have greatly marked the shaping of new structures, policies and programs.

This chapter presents some of the highlights of the progressive political, legal, economic and social evolution of the European Union. The successive treaties that amended the basic structure and the additions of new Member States will be given particular attention. Frequent references will be made to later chapters that elaborate on this initial presentation. Students interested in a more detailed and authoritative presentation should obtain Professor Desmond Dinan's Europe Recast: A History of the European Union (Lynne Rienner 2004).

A. THE POSTWAR MOVEMENT TOWARD EUROPEAN UNIFICATION

The vast destruction of life and property brought about by the Second World War, coupled with accompanying political instability, provided the background for a series of important steps toward European integration. The war had left a power vacuum in a Europe suffering from severe economic disarray. Moreover, the democracies of Western Europe felt increasingly threatened by the Soviet Union's taking control of the central and eastern European nations and of East Germany, its blockade of Berlin in 1949, and its development of an atomic bomb.

As early as September 1946, in a speech at Zurich University, Winston Churchill spoke in terms of a closer political union, calling for the construction of "a kind of United States of Europe," based on "a partnership between France and Germany." He made it clear that, although European leaders had geopolitical considerations in mind in developing their postwar arrangements, they were committed to economic integration under law and, above all, to the use of peaceful means and the principle of popular consent.

The creation of the Council of Europe in 1948 ushered in a period of close cooperation among the States of Western Europe across domains, including law. Its greatest legacy may well be the European Human Rights Convention of 1950, which figures importantly in Chapter 6 of this book.

US foreign policy in the postwar period encouraged precisely such political cooperation and development of new structures in Western Europe. To help coordinate the administration of Marshall Plan aid to the devastated nations of Western Europe, the US urged the sixteen recipient nations to create in 1948 a new intergovernmental body, called since 1960 the Organization for Economic Cooperation and Development (OECD). The OECD lacks formal lawmaking powers, but its reports, analyses and recommendations have significantly influenced national and European economic policies. In 1949, Canada, the US and a majority of Western European states set up the North Atlantic Treaty Organization (NATO) as a defensive military alliance, featuring an integrated military command structure and a collective decision-making mechanism. It is not surprising in this context that whenever European political leaders have proposed structures to achieve economic integration, the US has been supportive.

The European Coal and Steel Community (ECSC) was the first structure created for this economic integration. Its goal was to achieve the reconstruction and modernization of Europe's coal and steel resources. The political leaders concerned were also inspired by the belief that the ECSC would contribute to lasting peace among its members.

On May 9, 1950, the French government proposed the Schuman Plan, named after its foreign minister Robert Schuman. Under the plan, coal and steel production was to be regulated by a common High Authority composed of independent persons named by the participating national governments, but acting within an organization open to participation by other European countries. The High Authority would make decisions binding on the States without further national consent. The Treaty of Paris of April 18, 1951 created the European Coal and Steel Community among the three Benelux countries, France, Germany and Italy. Jean Monnet, a leading French advocate of European integration and advisor to Schuman, fittingly became the High Authority's first President.

Significantly, the ECSC Treaty created several new institutions to administer the ECSC, in addition to the High Authority. These were a Special Council of Ministers set up mainly to supervise the High Authority, a Common Assembly originally composed of members of the national parliaments and empowered to dismiss the High Authority and, finally, a Court of Justice to ensure implementation of the Treaty and of the secondary legislation expected to follow. The institutional shape of the ECSC and its concept of economic integration significantly influenced the structure of the later European Economic Community. The ECSC Treaty had a 50-year term. Upon its expiration, it was not renewed, and the European Community absorbed the ongoing programs of the ECSC.

As the cold war became more intense in the 1950's, Winston Churchill and other leaders called for the creation of a European defense force. France proposed this in the Pleven Plan, named after the French Minister of Defense. The six ECSC States signed the European Defense Community Treaty providing for a joint military force on May 27, 1952. However, a shift in sentiment caused the French Parliament to decline to ratify the treaty. Western Europe had to wait until the 1993 Treaty of Maastricht granted the European Union the power to coordinate military action in the Common Foreign and Security Policy in order to resume efforts to create a joint defense force.

B. THE EUROPEAN ECONOMIC COMMUNITY: 1958–69

Chancellor Konrad Adenauer, Germany's great post-war leader, and French Prime Minister Guy Mollet, together with the other ECSC political leaders, concluded in 1956 that the time was ripe to enter into some form of economic federation that might later lead to political union. They requested Paul–Henri Spaak, a former Belgian Foreign Minister, to propose the outline of a structure for a community to achieve a common economic market. After endorsing his report, the six States called an intergovernmental conference of Foreign Affairs ministers and their deputies in Brussels in the fall of 1956. Working with surprising speed, the conference, chaired by Spaak, drafted the European Economic Community (EEC) Treaty. The treaty was signed on March 25, 1957 in Rome, and hence is often called the Rome Treaty. Rapidly ratified, it entered into effect on January 1, 1958.

The intergovernmental conference also drafted the European Atomic Energy Community Treaty (often called the Euratom Treaty), likewise signed in Rome on March 25, 1957. Due to later frustration of the initial high hopes for civil energy exploitation of nuclear power, the Euratom Treaty has had only a minor impact and will not be further discussed in this book

The creation of the European Economic Community (EEC) prompted other west European nations, under the UK's leadership, to establish a free trade area, the European Free Trade Association (EFTA). EFTA, linking Austria, Denmark, Norway, Portugal, Sweden, Switzerland and the UK (the "outer seven" as opposed to the EEC's "inner six"), commenced in 1960. Unlike the EEC, which was committed to common external trade policies and a common internal market, EFTA was only a free trade area marked by certain loose forms of economic cooperation. Although the EEC and EFTA were popularly seen as rivals ("Europe at sixes and sevens"), in fact the two blocs enjoyed close and harmonious trade relations.

The Preamble to the EEC Treaty called for "common action to eliminate the barriers which divide Europe." Article 2, in its 1958 version, mandated the creation of a "common market" with a view to the harmonious development of economic activities, a continuous and balanced expansion, increased economic stability, a rise in the standard of living in Europe and closer relations among Member States. Article 3 prescribed as means to these ends the establishment of a common external tariff and commercial policy, the progressive elimination of barriers to the free movement of the principal factors of production (goods, persons, services and capital), the creation of a common Community policy in certain key sectors (notably agriculture, transport and competition), the coordination of economic and monetary policy, and the progressive harmonization of Member State laws in order to contribute to the proper functioning of the common market.

Drawing inspiration from the structure of the ECSC, the EEC operated through three political institutions, the Council, Commission and Parliament (initially designated as the Assembly), together with a judicial institution, the Court of Justice. Undoubtedly the most powerful body was the Council, commonly called the Council of Ministers because it consisted of each State's Minister of Foreign Affairs or another minister. The Council had the sole power to legislate and to set policy, usually by unanimity, which naturally meant that progress could be rapid when all the States saw the value of some form of action to achieve the common market, or slow, or indeed completely blocked, when action concerned sensitive sectors.

The Commission was composed of two commissioners each from France, Germany and Italy and one each from the Benelux States. The commissioners were senior civil servants, frequently former national ministers. The Commission rapidly assumed great importance in the planning of policies, the drafting of proposed legislation, and general administration.

Strong leadership was provided by the first President of the Commission, Walter Hallstein, a former German Secretary of State for Foreign Affairs and ally of Chancellor Konrad Adenauer. He was assisted by other prominent Commissioners, such as Paul Rey, Sicco Mansholt, and Hugo Van der Groeben. Rey and Mansholt later served as Commission Presidents. The Commission's energy and vision in drafting legislation and adopting policies to promote market integration and other Community goals led it to acquire its proud nickname, the "locomotive of the common market."

The Parliament, initially composed of delegations from the national parliaments, had little functional importance. The EEC Treaty provided that it should give advice in some fields, but in others it was not even required to be consulted. The Parliament soon began calling itself by that name, instead of Assembly, a change that had obvious democratic overtones, and pressed for a share in governance. Incidentally, the city of

Brussels offered to lease buildings suitable for use by the Commission and the Council. Without any formal decision, Brussels thus became the seat of these two political institutions. The Court of Justice had begun to function in Luxembourg in the ECSC at the invitation of the Luxembourg government, and remained there. Parliament held all of its plenary sessions in Strasbourg from 1952 to 1967, when it began holding half of its sessions in Luxembourg, a practice that in turn ended in 1981. Brussels eventually became Parliament's second seat.

The EEC Treaty provided a phased transitional period of twelve years, ending in 1969, for introducing the common external tariff and more generally the common market. The removal of internal tariffs and the creation of a common external tariff were accomplished ahead of schedule on July 1, 1968, rather than December 31, 1969, as envisaged. The Community began constructing a common commercial policy toward third countries, entering into trade and foreign aid agreements with many (e.g., Greece, Turkey, Yugoslavia), including former colonies. The Community also began representing the Member States in GATT, participating in the Kennedy Round of negotiations which successfully reduced tariff and other trade barriers in 1967.

Substantial progress was also made in attaining the common market. Framework action programs were adopted between 1960 and 1962 to facilitate the free movement of goods, workers, services and capital and the right of establishment. The principle of national treatment, or non-discrimination on the basis of nationality, was firmly established, and many significant interstate barriers were legislatively removed. For example, the first and second capital directives, adopted in 1961 and 1962, provided for the free movement of capital in most commercial and personal transactions, and established the principle of freedom of investment. Other sectors were marked by early progress. Directives harmonizing safety and technical standards began in 1962 with the foodstuffs sector, and continued during the 1960s and 1970s in fields like pharmaceuticals, cosmetics and dangerous products. A 1968 regulation legislated the virtually free movement of workers and their families, covering not only blue-collar and agricultural workers, but also skilled labor and management personnel.

Some sectors lagged behind. Little was done to remove state licensing barriers to the mobility of professionals or the regulatory barriers to trans-border banking, insurance or securities operations. Likewise little was achieved by way of a common transport policy.

Agriculture quickly became a priority sector for the Community, with the basic market organizations that still characterize the Common Agricultural Policy (CAP) already in place in the 1960s. The model was the market organization for cereals in 1962, followed some years later by market organizations for dairy products, wine and other commodities. Integrated European markets were created and farm income protected. Production was fostered to such an extent that by the 1970s the Community became a substantial net exporter of agricultural products and troublesome surpluses of certain commodities accumulated.

In the 1960s, the Community also launched a competition policy to implement the relevant EEC Treaty Articles. The Council enacted basic secondary legislation giving the Commission the power to issue regulations, to investigate and punish anti-competitive conduct, and to authorize conduct when justified by certain economic benefits. The Commission began to enforce the Treaty competition rules against cartels and market-partitioning license and distribution networks. The Commission's energetic pursuit of Community competition policy was largely endorsed by Court of Justice decisions starting in 1965.

As in the ECSC, the Court of Justice consisted of one judge appointed by each State for a six-year term, together with one additional judge to prevent tie votes, each named by common accord of all the States. The Court's initial membership merely continued from that of the ECSC court, and the Court followed its initial policy of deliberating and issuing judgments in French. In the continental tradition, the Court's judgments have always represented the collective views of the judges, without dissents.

The Court of Justice in the 1960s began to issue judgments in proceedings brought by the Commission against Member States for alleged infringements of Treaty obligations, and to respond to questions referred by national courts concerning the interpretation of Treaty provisions and secondary legislation. The Court also began to enunciate its fundamental doctrines concerning the nature and powers of the Community in judgments of seminal constitutional importance.

Thus, in 1964 in a landmark judgment, Costa v. ENEL, excerpted infra at page 245, the Court set forth its "new legal order" doctrine:

> By contrast with ordinary international treaties, the EEC Treaty has created its own legal system which, on the entry into force of the Treaty, became an integral part of the legal systems of the Member States and which their courts are bound to apply.

> By creating a Community of unlimited duration, having its own institutions, its own personality, its own legal capacity and capacity of representation on the international plane and, more particularly, real powers stemming from a limitation of sovereignty or a transfer of powers from the States to the Community, the Member States have limited their sovereign rights, albeit within limited fields, and have thus created a body of law which binds both their nationals and themselves.

The Court concluded that this new legal structure required the primacy of the Treaty over conflicting national rules. Later in the 1960s and 70s, the Court issued other judgments elaborating its doctrine of Treaty primacy and setting forth other fundamental principles, which were gradually accepted by national governments and supreme courts.

The rapid pace of progress described above was perceptibly slowed by a crisis in the fall of 1964. French President Charles De Gaulle would probably never have accepted the EEC had he been in power at the time, and he only reluctantly permitted its early evolution. In mid–1965, he reacted very negatively to proposals by Commission President Hallstein to enable the Community to have its own financial resources and to further implement the Common Agricultural Policy. De Gaulle ordered France's cessation of attendance at Council meetings for several months—resulting in the so-called "empty chair" policy—and effectively blocked Hallstein's re-election as President.

Finally, in a meeting of the foreign ministers of all the States in Luxembourg in January 1966, a compromise was reached. The ministers agreed that "when very important issues" concerned any State, the Council will strive to "reach solutions." They noted the French view that "unanimous agreement" had to be reached, but indicated that their "divergence of views" on this would not prevent the Council's work from resuming. Although this "Luxembourg Compromise" represented only an agreement to disagree, France resumed its place at the Council table. In 1984, President Mitterand renounced the claim that France should have a veto on important issues, but as a matter of practice the Council acted by unanimity (or consensus, including abstentions) until the adoption of the Single European Act. See Chapter 2B infra.

C. COMMUNITY SUCCESSES AND SETBACKS: 1970–83

1. THE ACCESSION OF NEW STATES AND MODIFICATIONS OF INSTITUTIONAL STRUCTURE

The Preamble to the EEC Treaty had foreseen that "other peoples of Europe" might join the Community, and its initial Article 237 laid down a procedure to enable other nations to accede to it. As early as 1961, British Prime Minister Macmillan initiated negotiations with a view to UK membership, but these ended, chiefly on account of French objections. In 1967, the UK again sought admission, along with Denmark, Ireland and Norway. Once again French President de Gaulle vetoed their accession. After President de Gaulle resigned, his successor, President Pompidou, proved to be favorably inclined to the expansion of the EEC. At the first important summit meeting of the political leaders of the Community at the Hague in December 1969, President Pompidou, German Chancellor Brandt and the other heads of government agreed to permit accession of the applicant States.

The UK's Conservative Prime Minister Edward Heath enthusiastically pressed for his country's membership despite considerable opposition, particularly from Harold Wilson, leader of the Labour Party. In launching the negotiations, the Community's leaders took a firm policy view that any nation seeking accession must accept the *"acquis communautaire,"* a French term, never easily translated, which essentially means the acceptance of the Community's political and legal structure, its basic policies and principles, and all of its legislation to date. In the initial and every subsequent accession, all candidate nations have had to accept the then *acquis communautaire.*

After nearly two years of negotiation, all four prospective members signed at Brussels a Treaty of Accession. Denmark, Ireland and the UK ratified the Treaty and entered the Community on January 1, 1973. However, a referendum in Norway produced a narrow majority against accession. The addition of three new Member States, all with reasonably solid economies, greatly increased the Community's market area and its financial sector.

After Greece, Spain and Portugal became free of right-wing dictatorships, they naturally applied for membership. Greece joined, effective January 1, 1981, followed five years later by Spain and Portugal, thus bringing membership to a total of twelve in what is often called the "second enlargement." Because Community structures and policies had by then become so complex, enlargement required extensive negotiations. Transition periods for phasing in various aspects of Community policy were as long as ten years in particularly sensitive areas like fishing rights and free movement of workers.

The most important institutional modification concerned the European Parliament. Although a Treaty provision foresaw that Parliament would be directly elected, for nearly thirty years (1952 to 1979) it was composed of representatives from national parliaments. One of the principal decisions of the Heads of State and Government at the Paris summit of December 1974 was to introduce the direct election of Parliament. After considerable debate over whether Members of Parliament could simultaneously sit in national parliaments (the so-called dual mandate, permitted until 2002) and other issues, the Council adopted the necessary legislation in 1976. The first popular election of Members of Parliament occurred in June 1979, with successive elections every five years thereafter. Parliament immediately acquired greater moral and political authority.

Throughout the 1960s, the Commission and Parliament had pressed for a system of financing to replace the initial mode of financial contributions from Member States. After the Member States finally agreed to this, the Community's so-called "own resources" system commenced in 1971. Under it, all customs duties and agricultural levies, as well as a share of each State's value added tax revenues, were assigned to the Community, thus rendering the Community more fiscally independent and less vulnerable to national political pressures.

2. THE EUROPEAN COUNCIL AND EUROPEAN POLITICAL COOPERATION

In December 1969, President Pompidou of France invited the other heads of government to convene at the Hague to discuss major policy issues affecting the Community. They reached agreement to open negotiations with the four nations that had applied for membership, and to provide the Community with its own resources, while also agreeing on agricultural and other issues. Subsequent summit meetings became commonly known as meetings of the "European Council," a term that generated (and continues to generate) confusion due to its similarity in name with the Council. Since 1974, the Heads of State or Government (accompanied by their foreign ministers) have met two to four times a year as the European Council. Because the French Constitution accords the President authority over foreign policy and the Prime Minister authority over economic affairs, both attend European Council meetings.

The European Council gradually assumed the role of providing important policy guidelines to the Commission and Council and deciding the essential nature of structural changes to the Community that would be made by Treaty amendments drafted by intergovernmental conferences. As we shall see, the role of the European Council received formal recognition in 1987 in the Single European Act.

Following the 1974 Paris summit, the European Council initiated a practice of cooperation among the Member States in foreign policy that became known as European Political Cooperation (EPC). At each summit the European Council adopted by consensus joint actions and declarations in foreign affairs. These have now become so commonplace that it is easy to assume, erroneously, that they were a Community feature from the very beginning.

3. PROGRESS AND SETBACKS IN THE COMMON MARKET

In the 1970s, the Council continued an active legislative program to promote market integration in various fields of the common market, adopting directives harmonizing company and securities law and, to a lesser extent, banking and insurance law. After the Court of Justice issued judgments promoting the right to provide trans-border services and the right of establishment, the Council also adopted directives harmonizing the rules for the mutual recognition of diplomas in the medical professions, and for architects and pharmacists. Prominent Court of Justice judgments promoted the free movement of goods, workers and services, as well as the enforcement of competition rules.

European Council policy declarations at the Paris summit in 1974 effectively added new fields of Community legislation. Although the Treaty contained provisions concerning social policy, virtually no legislative action had been taken until the European Council endorsed the 1974 Social Action Program. The French President Giscard d'Estaing, the German Socialist Chancellor Willy Brandt, and the UK's Labor Prime Minister Harold Wilson all strongly supported Community employment legislation. Not surprisingly, the Social Action Program yielded several significant measures in the field of employee protection and equal rights for women, as well as legislation to protect on-the-job health and safety. Supplemented by case law of the Court of Justice, social policy soon became one of the Community's more active though still controversial domains.

The 1974 Paris Summit also endorsed environmental and consumer protection as new fields for the Community, and programs commenced that year. Denmark, Germany and the Netherlands strongly advocated strict environmental protection legislation. Since the mid–1970s, the Community has adopted minimum standards for water and air quality, for limiting pollution and waste, and for protecting wildlife, and it has entered into many international agreements on these subjects. As for consumer rights, over a dozen harmonization directives were enacted in the 1970s and early 1980s on consumer information, labeling and advertising, and the elimination of unfair business practices in various fields.

The Commission headed during 1977–80 by President Roy Jenkins, a former Labor Chancellor of the Exchequer, proved to be particularly energetic. In addition to promoting new legislation in the fields of employment, company and securities law, and environmental and consumer protection, this Commission is noteworthy for its increased use of proceedings in the Court of Justice to challenge State barriers to inter-State trade and other infringements of the Treaty. President Jenkins was also particularly influential in promoting a new structure for monetary stability in the Community, the European Monetary System, described infra.

Despite this progress, the 1970s and early 1980s ushered in a sense of "Europessimism," fueled by the monetary crisis of 1971 and the oil crises later in that decade. Since adoption of most Community legislation required Council unanimity, measures were often slow to pass and in some cases watered down or totally blocked. The UK's Conservative Prime Minister Thatcher, first elected in 1979 and a pronounced Euroskeptic, caused the UK to oppose many policy and legislative proposals. The enormous complexity and expense of the common agricultural policy caused deep dissatisfaction, but political pressures from farming interests prevented reform. Meanwhile, the Community experienced chronic and severe budgetary problems, with wrangling in the Council and the Parliament over the Community budget becoming an annual affair. Business had the impression, founded or not, that non-tariff barriers to trade and other forms of protectionism had increased markedly in the late 1970s and were not effectively being addressed.

D. THE INTERNAL MARKET PROGRAM AND THE SINGLE EUROPEAN ACT: 1985–92

Jacques Delors, formerly the French Minister of the Economy, became President of the Commission in 1985, serving successive terms until 1995. Under his leadership and with the aid of the UK internal market commissioner, Lord Cockfield, the Commission issued the famous June 1985 White Paper on Completing the Internal Market. The White Paper set out a concrete plan for action, listing 279 proposals for measures to be adopted by December 31, 1992. After its endorsement by the European Council, the business sector and the media enthusiastically supported the program. By the 1992 deadline, 95% of the measures were adopted, with notable successes in fields previously blocked, such as banking, insurance, intellectual property, telecommunications and public procurement.

Enthusiasm for the internal market program catalyzed efforts to reform the Community's institutional structures. Parliament had been demanding a share in legislative power for years. Indeed, in 1984, the Parliament had issued a draft Treaty Establishing the European Union, which proposed substantial revisions in structure, including greater powers for the Parliament. The European Council was not inclined to endorse major revisions, but did call the Luxembourg Intergovernmental Conference (IGC) in fall 1985, which drafted the Single European Act (SEA). After ratification, the SEA became effective July 1, 1987.

The Single European Act consisted principally of modifications to the European Community Treaty. The SEA's central focus was on completing the single internal market by the end of 1992. A new Article 8a of the EEC Treaty (subsequently renumbered) set as a goal the removal of technical, legal and fiscal barriers to trade between Member States by that date. The SEA also formally authorized legislative action in the areas of environmental protection, occupational safety and health, research and technological development and regional development.

The SEA brought several significant institutional modifications: the introduction of a new legislative mode, called the cooperation procedure, which substantially enhanced Parliament's role in the legislative process; a broad increase in the number of fields where legislation could be adopted by a qualified majority vote of the Council instead of unanimity; and more extensive delegations of authority from the Council to the Commission. (Qualified majority voting, a complicated method of enabling legislative action to be taken by a large majority of States rather than unanimously, is described in Chapter 2B.) The expanded use of qualified majority voting was undertaken largely to make it easier to adopt legislation to complete the internal market by the 1992 deadline. The SEA substantially advanced economic and political integration within the Community, and its success generated a desire for still further reform.

The structural changes introduced by the SEA proved highly effective in practice. By the end of 1992, over 500 internal market measures had been adopted, promoting the harmonization and liberalization of rules and indeed revolutionizing commercial and financial law. In 1996, the Commission estimated that the internal market program had increased intra-Community trade by 20–30% and added measurably to the growth of GDP and levels of employment. For further discussion, see Chapter 14B on the internal market program.

As previously noted, the SEA formally recognized the nature and role of the European Council, making it an institution proper, though deliberately refraining from making it a *Community* institution and from granting it decision-making capacity, the SEA's Article D declared that the European Council would "define the general political guidelines" of the Community. Article D also prescribed that the President of the Commission join the heads of State or Government in comprising the European Council. The SEA's Title III set out the essential nature of Cooperation in Foreign Policy, which largely consisted of the ability to issue joint policy statements.

Finally, the SEA authorized the Council to create a court that would reduce the Court of Justice's increasingly heavy case load. The new Court of First Instance (CFI), set up in 1989, initially took over the burden of handling the many appeals from administrative decisions concerning the civil service staff of the Community. Soon recognizing its value, in the early 1990s the Council authorized the CFI to hear appeals from Commission decisions enforcing competition law. Appeals on the law, but not the facts, could then be taken to the Court of Justice. See Chapter 2F infra.

E.　THE MAASTRICHT TREATY AND THE EUROPEAN UNION: 1993–2002

Incited by proposals from the Commission, the Parliament and certain key leaders (notably German Chancellor Kohl, French President Mitterand, and Spain's Socialist Prime Minister Gonzalez), the European Council at its meeting in Dublin in June 1990 agreed to open, not one, but two intergovernmental conferences in Rome the following December. The first conference would deal with the proposal for a European Monetary Union and the second with institutional and procedural reform. The conferences reported to the Maastricht European Council in December 1991, which reached a compromise agreement on key unresolved issues. The Treaty of Maastricht was formally signed on February 7, 1992, and became effective November 1, 1993.

1.　ECONOMIC AND MONETARY UNION

Although the EEC Treaty from the start included chapters on economic and monetary coordination, little was achieved in the 1960s and the global monetary crises of the 1970s led to greater nationalism in economic and monetary policy. At a meeting in Bremen in 1978, Commission President Jenkins and German Chancellor Schmidt convinced the European Council to create a European Monetary System (EMS). Set up the following year, the EMS provided for joint support among Member States in case of serious monetary instability in any one of them and for increased cooperation among central banks. The EMS is best known for its structure to control exchange parities between national currencies and for its creation of an artificial currency unit, the ECU. Buoyed by the success of the EMS, Commission President Delors began to press for more substantial monetary integration. As a former French Minister of the Economy and banking expert, Delors was convinced that a monetary union with a central bank and a common currency would greatly promote economic integration.

At the invitation of the European Council meeting in Hanover, Germany in 1988, a committee of central bank directors and monetary experts chaired by Commission President Delors produced in April 1989 a report outlining the essential features of an Economic and Monetary Union (EMU). The European Council approved the Delors Report at its June 1989 meeting in Madrid. Working on the basis of proposals from the Commission's monetary experts and the central banks of Germany and the Netherlands, the IGC successfully drafted the complex treaty provisions for the creation of the EMU. In December 1991 at Maastricht, the European Council reached final agreement on the EMU. The Maastricht Treaty and related protocols committed the Member States over the course of the 1990s to bring about a convergence of their economic and monetary policies, and to reduce annual inflation and budget deficits to meet specific targets. The Treaty prescribed that a European Central Bank would take over the control of monetary policy within those States participating in a final stage of the Monetary Union, and a new currency would be created for the participating States. Separate Protocols enabled the UK and Denmark to opt out of that final stage.

2. POLITICAL UNION

In the political sphere, the Maastricht Treaty expanded the Community's fields of activity to include health, education, culture and consumer protection, thus endorsing the Community's longstanding informal involvement in these fields. The EEC Treaty was also amended to change the name "European Economic Community" ("EEC") to the simpler name "European Community" ("EC"), thus underscoring the Community's non-economic goals.

In the interest of democracy, the powers of the European Parliament were further enhanced. Under the Maastricht Treaty, Parliament won the right to approve the appointment of the Commission and its President and to request the Commission to initiate legislative proposals. Parliament's legislative role under the SEA's "cooperation procedure" was extended to new fields, while, more importantly, a new "codecision procedure" was introduced to adopt legislation designed to achieve the internal market. In the codecision procedure, Parliament received a nearly equal share in the process with the Council, with an effective veto over proposed legislation it opposed.

One of the Maastricht Treaty's most important innovations was to introduce a citizenship of the Union, which entailed civil rights for citizens, including the right to vote in local elections in one's place of residence, the right to travel and reside freely within the territory of the Union, and the right to petition the European Parliament. For a description of the impact of citizenship of the Union, see Chapter 16.

Besides amending the EC Treaty, the Treaty of Maastricht introduced a separate treaty among the member States, in the form of a Treaty on European Union (TEU), this being meant to represent a decisive step in political integration. Although the UK prevented use of the term "federal," the Member States accepted the concept of a "European Union," comprised of three "pillars": a "first pillar" consisting of the three existing European Communities (ECSC, EC and Euratom), a "second pillar" comprising the EU's system of a Common Foreign and Security Policy (CFSP), and a "third pillar" denoting a new sphere referred to obliquely as "Cooperation in Justice and Home Affairs" (JHA).

Title V, on Cooperation in Foreign and Security Policy, made quite clear that such cooperation was to take place outside the Community law framework—meaning outside the legal forms of Community law (regulations, directives, decisions), outside the scope of the Commission's enforcement powers as such, and outside the ambit of judicial review by the Court of Justice. Nonetheless, the complex provisions enabled the European Council by consensus to set common foreign policy positions, and the Council to implement them by joint action programs.

Title VI of the TEU inaugurated the "third pillar" on Cooperation in Justice and Home Affairs—fields declared by the TEU to be "matters of common interest." These included asylum policy, immigration policy, combat against drug addiction and international fraud, judicial cooperation in civil and criminal matters, and police cooperation in regard to terrorism, drug trafficking and other serious international crimes. Like the second pillar, this pillar operated outside the framework of Community law as such, and action under it remained basically intergovernmental. During the 1990's, action in the sphere of justice and home affairs consisted primarily of cooperative efforts, such as the creation of Europol, the drafting of conventions concerning asylum and immigration for adoption by the States, and the adoption of Council decisions intended to coordinate State efforts to combat terrorism and serious crime.

National processes for ratification of the TEU brought severe stresses to the surface. A June 1992 Danish referendum rejected the TEU, due to misgivings over the scale and pace of political integration and the dangers of excessive centralization. However, the Irish electorate soon thereafter gave its support to the Treaty and the French did likewise, albeit by a very slim majority. After winning certain concessions from the European Council, and declaring its intent to exercise its Protocol to opt out of the final stage of EMU, the Danish government achieved a successful result in a second referendum held in May 1993. Other States also encountered difficulties. After a bruising parliamentary debate, the UK's conservative government of Prime Minister Major narrowly succeeded in ratification. Germany ratified after its Constitutional Court's judgment concerning the Maastricht Treaty concluded that the new structures did not violate Germany's Constitution (see page 284, infra). The ratification process had plainly exposed popular concern over further movement toward European integration.

3. THE 1995 ACCESSION OF AUSTRIA, FINLAND AND SWEDEN

In the early 1990s, the EC and the EFTA nations agreed to form on January 1, 1993 a new entity known as the European Economic Area (EEA). Under the EEA Agreement, goods, persons, services and capital would flow freely among the participating States, on condition that the non-EU States accept virtually all Community harmonizing legislation, not only on trade, but also on a wider range of subjects including environmental and consumer protection, competition policy, company, securities, banking and insurance law and social policy. The prospect of being bound by EU rules without having participated in their making doubtless contributed to the readiness of Austria, Finland and Sweden to join the EU. After the 1995 EU enlargement, the only EEA members that remain outside the EU are Iceland, Liechtenstein and Norway. (Switzerland is neither an EU nor an EEA member.)

The accession of Austria, Finland and Sweden on January 1, 1995, bringing membership to 15 States, was undoubtedly the easiest enlargement. All three were solid democracies with strong economies, and they had been harmonizing their laws to those of the EC for several years. The Treaty of Accession was signed at the Corfu European Council meeting of June 1994. Referenda in all three nations easily approved accession. Although Norway had also negotiated for accession, a referendum in November 1994 again narrowly rejected accession.

While the accession of Austria, Finland and Sweden was achieved rather smoothly, and visibly augmented the Community's economic power by creating a still larger internal market, it also showed that enlargement inevitably made decisional processes more difficult, both by increasing the size of the institutions and by making the achievement of consensus among the Member States more problematic.

4. INTERNAL AND EXTERNAL DEVELOPMENTS: 1993–1999

The Commission headed by President Jacques Santer during 1995–99 devoted particular attention to establishing a monetary union and to launching negotiations with central and eastern European nations seeking to join the Union. Moreover, although 1992 marked the formal end of the internal market program, quite naturally the program continued with the adoption of new legislation in various fields. Especially noteworthy are the 1994 Community Trademark Regulation and the 1998 directive on the right of establishment of lawyers. Since 1996, the Commission has also undertaken to simplify and codify the existing complex corpus of legislation through the "Simpler Legislation in the Internal Market" (or "SLIM") project.

In tandem with progress toward achieving an integrated economic market, the Community in the 1990s initiated important developments in employee rights and employment policy. Building on the 1989 Social Charter of the Rights of Workers (endorsed by the European Council, with the exception of the UK, at its December 1989 meeting in Strasbourg), the Commission inaugurated a new Social Action Program. The Parliament and Council enacted a series of important new social policy directives, such as those mandating protection of adolescent workers and pregnant workers, limiting working time, and requiring consultation with workers on matters relating to employment conditions. The UK initially opted out of several of these measures by virtue of a Maastricht Treaty Protocol, but accepted them after Prime Minister Blair's Labor government was elected in May 1997. Due to the persistence of high unemployment levels through the 1990s, the 1994 Essen and later European Councils urged action programs, leading the Commission to propose a series of action plans to create new jobs, retrain workers, and better exploit information technology.

Substantial progress was achieved in creation of the Economic and Monetary Union. The second stage of evolution toward EMU began on January 1, 1994, marked by the establishment in Frankfurt of the transition European Monetary Institute (EMI), composed of a President and representatives of all States' central banks. Together with the Commission, the EMI helped coordinate Member State monetary policies and develop the legal framework necessary for the launch of the third and final stage of EMU. During the mid–1990s, every Member State made substantial (and in some cases quite surprising) progress toward achieving most of the "convergence criteria" established at Maastricht for entry into the third stage, i.e., lowered inflation and long-term interest rates, currency stability and reduced annual budget deficits. Accordingly, the Council in an extraordinary composition of Heads of State or Government (essentially the European Council), was able to decide in May 1998, based on reports by the Commission and the EMI, that all States other than Greece wishing to join the third stage of EMU were qualified to do so as of January 1, 1999. The Council subsequently decided, in June 2000, to endorse Greece's entry. Denmark and the UK invoked the Maastricht Treaty Protocol permitting them to "opt out," and Sweden, which deliberately persisted in a policy of not making its central bank independent, remained outside the final stage of EMU. The European System of Central Banks (ESCB) and its core structure, the European Central Bank (ECB), were then created. On January 1, 1999, the ECB took control of monetary policy for the States that had entered the third stage of EMU. See Chapter 31 for more details.

In the early 1990s the Community participated vigorously in the GATT negotiations which ultimately led in 1994 to the creation of the World Trade Organization. The negotiations necessitated major reforms of the Common Agricultural Policy. At the same time, they raised serious institutional issues due to the fact that the WTO Agreement dealt with intellectual property and external trade in services—areas (unlike external trade in goods) in which the Community did not have exclusive jurisdiction. In an important opinion by the Court of Justice on WTO accession, the Court of Justice held that the Community had to work together with the Member States in negotiating in certain fields that remained within the competence of the States, and in concluding any WTO Agreement. See Chapter 29B for discussion of the Court's opinion.

Clearly the WTO dispute settlement system, in effect since 1997, has exerted a major impact on Community policy. To mention highlights only, WTO panels have afforded victories to the EU in its complaints against the trade practices and policies of the US and other nations, but has upheld the US challenges to the Community's regulation of banana imports and ban on the importation of hormone-treated beef. The WTO has become a vital—though of course not the only—forum for sorting out EU–US economic relations.

In the aftermath of the fall of communist regimes in Central and Eastern Europe between 1989 and 1991, the EU entered into association agreements during the mid 1990s with all of the new democracies, commonly called "Europe Agreements." These agreements created an association between the EU and the individual countries, entailing political dialogue, expansion of trade and economic relations, a phased adoption of competition rules and most internal market measures, financial and technical assistance. The Europe Agreements greatly facilitated these countries' eventual integration into the EU.

The European Council in Copenhagen in June 1993 announced a series of criteria the candidate States had to satisfy before accession, essentially that they should become representative democracies practicing the rule of law and respect for human rights, should have developed free market economies, and should have adequate administrative infrastructures. The December 1994 European Council meeting in Essen outlined a "pre-accession strategy" and charged the Commission with producing a White Paper detailing it. The Commission then charted the course of enlargement in a White Paper on Preparation of the Associated Countries of Central and Eastern Europe for Integration into the Internal Market of the Union.

By 1996, ten central and eastern European nations as well as Cyprus and Malta had applied for accession. The Commission in July 1997 issued its recommendation that accession negotiations should be opened in 1998 with six applicant countries: Hungary, Poland, Estonia, the Czech Republic, Slovenia and Cyprus. Later that year the European Council agreed, but included all the applicant states in its "pre-accession strategy." Accession negotiations with the six began in March 1998. The process broke down the negotiation subjects into 31 chapters covering all aspects of membership obligations and the applicant States' readiness to assume them. The negotiations focused on the issues that had emerged as most problematic, including agriculture, the environment, free movement of persons and the security of external frontiers. The Commission subsequently produced annual country-by-country progress reports each November.

In October 1999, the Commission proposed that accession negotiations be opened with the remaining applicant states: Latvia, Lithuania, Slovakia, Romania, Bulgaria and Malta. In December, at Helsinki, the European Council agreed. At the same time, the European Council advised Turkey that, while it was ultimately capable of membership, negotiations would be postponed until Turkey improved its protection of basic rights and achieved better economic conditions. The Commission then devoted substantial efforts until 2003 in the complex negotiations with each of the applicant countries which were simultaneously working energetically to satisfy the Copenhagen criteria.

5. THE TREATIES OF AMSTERDAM AND NICE

Even at the time of the Maastricht Treaty, the Member States had foreseen the need to make some further improvements in the new Community and Union structures. Indeed, a specific TEU provision called for a new Intergovernmental Conference to be held in 1996, and one was held from March 1996 to June 1997. The election of Prime Minister Blair's Labor government in May 1997 enabled agreement to be reached on several contentious issues.

Signed in October 1997, the Treaty of Amsterdam entered into force on May 1, 1999 after a rather slow process of ratification. The Amsterdam Treaty's most important institutional revision was to augment the legislative power of the Parliament in two respects. First, it extended use of the codecision procedure to adopt legislation in the fields of social policy, transport, environmental and consumer protection. Second, it amended the EC Treaty's description of the codecision procedure to give the Parliament absolute equality with the Council.

Among the many amendments the Amsterdam Treaty made to the EC Treaty, those in two fields are especially noteworthy. As previously observed, the Member States were greatly concerned over persistently high levels of unemployment. They accordingly amended the Treaty to add a new Title VIII on Employment, with provisions requiring Community guidelines for action, and the adoption of incentive measures to promote employment. Moreover, the new UK Labor government's willingness to join the other States in adopting legislation concerning employment enabled a reformulation of the social policy chapter to authorize the use of the codecision procedure to adopt directives harmonizing employment law. Chapter 35A on Social Policy covers these developments.

The Amsterdam Treaty also shifted most of the fields of action in the TEU's third pillar, Cooperation in Justice and Home Affairs, over to the EC Treaty in a new Title on the Area of Freedom, Security and Justice. New provisions authorized the Community to adopt legislation concerning immigration from third countries, asylum, external border controls, and judicial cooperation in civil matters. The EU's third pillar survived in one important field, that of Police and Judicial Cooperation in Criminal Matters, in which only the Council could take action. Chapter 16G describes the Treaty modifications and some of the more important measures in this field.

Although no areas of the Common Foreign and Security Policy were transferred from pillar two into the Community law sphere, some amendments were made to facilitate action, notably the creation of a new post, the High Representative for Foreign and Security Policy, whose role was to assist in formulating policy and to represent the Council in the international arena. A prominent Spanish diplomat, Javier Solana, was promptly elected to a five-year term, subsequently renewed for a second term in 2004.

For all its complexity, the Treaty of Amsterdam failed to resolve certain basic institutional questions, most urgently, in light of prospective enlargement, the number and allocation of Commissioners and the weighting of votes in the Council for qualified majority voting purposes. A Protocol on the Institutions with the Prospect of Enlargement foresaw the need for another intergovernmental conference to deal with these contentious issues. With the prospect of adding so many new Member States, the need to modify the Community's institutional structure was all too apparent.

Almost immediately after the Treaty of Amsterdam entered into force on May 1, 1999, the fifteen Member States began work on a further treaty revision. An Intergovernmental Conference in 2000 produced a text covering the relatively non-controversial topics, but could not agree on the most contentious issues concerning changes in the Commission and Council. The European Council at Nice in December 2001, chaired by French President Chirac, agreed on a treaty embodying some essential compromises, but it was clear that the compromises were only provisional and that the basic issues would have to be reexamined later.

Because the Nice Treaty's amendments were often quite technical, and because Chapter 2 describes the institutions in some detail, we present here only highlights. The most controversial issue before the European Council at Nice was how to revise the system for qualified majority voting in the Council to accommodate the addition of the prospective new States. The European Council finally agreed upon a compromise that gave the smaller States substantial voting power, yet tried to protect the larger States, especially Germany, by requiring a "double majority," under which States voting for any action would also have to represent at least 62% of the Union's total population. The Treaty of Lisbon largely retained this formula. See Chapter 2B.

The Nice Treaty's Protocol on Enlargement required the number of Commissioners to be reduced out of a concern that a body of 27 would be too large for operational efficiency. The European Council, acting unanimously, was to adopt a system of rotation that would treat all States equally, regardless of population. This provision has proved quite controversial, because many States are unhappy with the prospect of being without a Commissioner at any time. The Treaty of Lisbon kept the requirement for the reduction, postponed to 2014, but it is currently uncertain whether the present structure of one Commissioner per State will ever be modified.

Because the Court of Justice continues to be composed of one judge per State, its functional efficiency could also be hampered by continuing to use the full court to decide some cases. Although chambers of three or five judges have handled the large majority of proceedings since the mid–1990's, the more important cases obviously need examination by a larger body. The Nice Treaty created a Grand Chamber of eleven judges to decide such cases, and made full court proceedings quite rare. This has proven highly beneficial, as the Court's operations in recent years have clearly been made more efficient through use of the Grand Chamber.

All the Member States except Ireland ratified the Treaty of Nice by parliamentary action, in most cases by comfortable majorities. An initial Irish referendum in June 2001 proved adverse, but after diligent efforts by the government, a second referendum in October 2002 produced a favorable 63% majority. The Treaty of Nice became effective on February 1, 2003, the last major modification of the treaties prior to the Treaty of Lisbon. The EC Treaty, as amended at Nice, is found in the Documents Supplement (doc. 8).

6. DEVELOPMENTS PRIOR TO ENLARGEMENT: 2000–03

During the period immediately preceding the central and eastern European enlargement, the event having the greatest resonance was the introduction of a common currency, the Euro, in January 2002 for the twelve States participating in the final stage of Monetary Union. The Commission and the European Central Bank collaborated to prepare the commercial world and the general public for the Euro's introduction. The momentous event went quite smoothly. Adequate quantities of the new currency came to be available, and by the end of January, 95% of cash transactions were taking place in Euros. Not only has the use of the Euro increased price transparency and reduced trans-border trade costs by eliminating currency exchange charges, but it has also become the most dramatic symbol of the Union in everyday life. As previously noted, Denmark, Sweden and the UK retained their national currencies. Following their accession in 2004, several new States were able to satisfy the conditions for entry into the final stage of EMU, so that today Cyprus, Estonia, Malta, Slovakia and Slovenia are all part of the "Euro-zone." For further information, see Chapter 33.

The Commission, headed by President Romano Prodi during 1999–2004, proved to be quite energetic. The Commission continued its program of codification of legislation in many internal market sectors, notably in banking and securities law. The European Council in March 2000 launched a major new policy program on "Employment, Economic Reform and Social Cohesion," popularly called the Lisbon Strategy, with the goal of achieving within ten years "the most competitive and knowledge-based economy in the world." The Prodi Commission vigorously supported the Lisbon Agenda with legislative proposals and studies.

The Prodi Commission also undertook a sweeping revision of the enforcement of Community competition rules, endorsed by the Council, which amended the basic regulation establishing Commission powers and procedures. The essential policy motivation for the revision was to greatly increase the enforcement responsibility of national competition authorities and lessen the Commission's regulatory burden.

International trade concerns also preoccupied the Commission. The WTO launched a new general round of negotiation at Doha in 2001. The Community quickly became a leader in the effort to liberalize trade in services, but found itself on the defensive against demands for reductions in its agricultural subsidies. However, negotiations have languished ever since.

Human rights advocates became understandably enthused when the European Council decided at Cologne in June 1999 to prepare a text on basic rights, and subsequently designated a body to draft the text. Chaired by former German President, Roman Herzog, a Convention of 62 members, principally delegates from the European Parliament and national parliaments, drafted a Charter of Fundamental Rights in early 2002. Although the European Council unanimously endorsed the Charter, it took no action to give it binding legal effect. Instead, the Presidents of the Parliament, Council and the Commission simply proclaimed the Charter at a ceremony at the Nice European Council session in December 2000. The Charter remained without binding legal effect, although its text has been cited by the Court of Justice as the source of specific rights. The Treaty of Lisbon has now given the Charter "the same legal value" as the Treaty. See Chapter 6 for further discussion. For the Charter's text, see Documents Supplement (doc. 6).

Naturally the Prodi Commission was greatly preoccupied with the final negotiations in preparation of the central and eastern European enlargement. The European Council periodically reviewed the progress and set deadlines for the conclusion of negotiations. The most difficult issues concerned agricultural subsidies in the new States, and establishing transitional restrictions on the free movement of persons. In October 2002, the Commission issued a report concluding that ten applicant States were ready for accession. The European Council at Copenhagen in December 2002 then set May 1, 2004 as the date for the accession of these States, and either January 1, 2007 or 2008 for Bulgaria and Romania.

F. THE CENTRAL AND EASTERN EUROPEAN ENLARGEMENT

The Accession Treaty of Athens of April 16, 2003 enabled ten nations to join the EU on May 1, 2004: Cyprus, the Czech Republic, Estonia, Hungary, Latvia, Lithuania, Malta, Poland, the Slovak Republic and Slovenia. The new States immediately began to participate in the Union and Community institutions and became subject to the basic Treaty rules. Indeed, the new States had to adopt all of the existing legislation of the Community prior to accession, nearly 2000 laws and other measures.

The Act of Accession annexed to the Treaty set out in detail numerous transitional arrangements. Thus, the Community provided the new States with only part of the agricultural subsidies that they ought to have received in comparison with the western States, and phased in progress toward the full amount over a ten-year period. The older Member States were permitted to keep their restrictions on migrant workers from the new States for up to seven years. Although the UK, Ireland and Sweden set no limits on such migrant workers, and received hundreds of thousands in 2004–06, the other States only gradually ended their restrictions. On their side, almost all the new States were permitted to retain their restrictions on foreign ownership of their agricultural and forest land for seven years.

Due to their weaker economic condition, Bulgaria and Romania were declared not ready to join the EU in 2004. The European Council in December 2004 set 2007 as the target date for accession. The Commission continued accession negotiations and assistance programs, ultimately concluding in a September 2006 report that both were ready to join. Pursuant to the Treaty of Luxembourg of April 25, 2005, Bulgaria and Romania acceded as of January 1, 2007. Both States have had difficulties since accession, however. Due to bitter disputes among its leading parties, Romania has had a succession of deadlocked governments, while Bulgaria has not made much progress in overcoming its serious political corruption.

Enlargement resulted in an increase from eleven to twenty in the number of working languages used in the EU for all legislation, Court judgments, Commission decisions, studies and reports, since all the new States except Cyprus added a new working language. Moreover, after their accession, Bulgaria and Romania added two more languages, and Ireland decided for the first time to require Irish as a working language, so that today there are twenty-three official languages. This obviously represents a substantial burden in added costs and reduced efficiency.

Although Turkey first applied to accede in 1987, and the US has always pressed for the accession of this crucial NATO member, the road to EU membership has been, and still is, a rocky one. The Community did enter into the Ankara Customs Union with Turkey in 1996, which has significantly reduced barriers to trade. The Commission's periodic reports on Turkey have criticized violations of human rights as well as noting serious economic issues. Periodic Parliament resolutions have also expressed concern about democratic weaknesses and human right violations, particularly with regard to the Kurdish minority.

In December 2004, the European Council declared Turkey to be "destined to join the Union," and the current Turkish government continues to press strongly for accession. However, Turkey's support for the Turkish government in northern Cyprus has proved to be an intractable problem. Despite UN negotiation efforts, the Greek Cyprus government and that of Turkish-controlled Cyprus have been unable to agree upon unification. Until that occurs, Cyprus blocks Turkish accession. Moreover, public opinion polls in western Europe regularly demonstrate that Turkish accession is highly unpopular. Consequently, when, if ever, Turkey will join the EU is quite uncertain.

Croatia applied for accession early in 2003, and received a favorable opinion from the Commission upon its readiness for accession. The European Council accepted Croatia as a prospective member in June 2004. In 2006, the Commission commenced accession negotiations, which have progressed fairly smoothly. Croatia must still improve its efforts to combat corruption. However, the Union political leaders postponed any accession until the Treaty of Lisbon entered into effect. Croatia is now likely to join the EU fairly soon.

Macedonia applied for accession in 2004, and the European Council declared it to be a suitable prospect in December 2005. However, the Commission evaluated Macedonia as requiring substantial political reforms and economic progress before negotiations could commence. Other south Balkan nations are definitely interested in accession, but without prospects in the near term.

G.   THE DRAFT CONSTITUTIONAL TREATY AND THE TREATY OF LISBON

1.   INSTITUTIONAL DEVELOPMENTS, 2004–09

In the summer of 2004, the European Council had some difficulty in the selection of a new Commission President, as several initial candidates either declined the post or were not acceptable to one or another large State. The European Council ultimately nominated Portugal's Conservative Prime Minister Jose Manuel Barroso, who was rapidly approved by

Parliament. President Barroso immediately worked with Member State governments in the nomination of the Commissioners, pressing particularly for a larger number of women to be named.

Both the June 2004 and June 2009 elections of Parliament revealed a voter preference for more conservative groups. The European People's Party is currently the largest party group, followed by the Socialist, Liberals, and Greens. The Parliament's desire to see a conservative political leader as head of the Commission influenced the choice of the Commission President in both years. Moreover, in November 2004, Parliament's threat to vote against the entire new Commission if it included a certain nominee for Commissioner disapproved in the Parliament's confirmation hearings occasioned the withdrawal of one nominee and a shift in prospective portfolios for two others.

Since 2000, the Commission, Parliament and Council have continued to work energetically on the simplification and codification of legislation. The codification of securities and banking law are prime examples. They also achieved agreement on comprehensive new legislation which liberalized the right of citizens of the Union to reside in any Member State, described in Chapter 16, and the right to provide trans-border services, discussed in Chapter 17. Also noteworthy are the new measures intended to promote an integrated financial market, such as the cross-border payments directive and the comprehensive money-laundering directive described in Chapter 30. In light of heightened concern over serious crimes and terrorist action following the London underground and Madrid railroad station bombings, the Council has adopted anti-terrorist measures and a regulation creating the European Arrest Warrant. The Union's absorption of twelve new States has clearly not impeded the adoption of important legislation.

Unfortunately, the unusually grave recession that struck the US also hit Europe in 2008 and continued into 2010, occasioning bank failures, sharp losses on the real estate and securities markets, a significant decline in production, the insolvency of some enterprises, and high unemployment. Although Ireland, Spain, Portugal, Hungary, Lithuania and Latvia—and, above all, Greece—were hardest hit, no Member State escaped the recession. This has naturally preoccupied the Union's political leaders and the European Central Bank, and restrained any significant new policy developments at the Union level.

After the June 2009 elections of the Parliament, the Member States easily agreed to nominate Commission President Barroso for the 2009–14 term, and Parliament readily endorsed him. The Member States then proceeded to nominate new, or retain former, Commissioners, who were allocated portfolios by President Barroso.

2. THE DRAFT CONSTITUTIONAL TREATY

Anticipating the central and eastern European enlargement, President Chirac of France, Chancellor Schroeder of Germany, Prime Minister

Aznar of Spain and other heads of government considered that a thorough review of Union structure was overdue. The European Council at Laeken, Belgium in December 2001 decided to convene a Convention for the purpose of improving the democracy, transparency and efficiency of the Union.

Former French President Giscard d'Estaing chaired the Convention, with former Belgian Prime Minister Dehaene and former Italian Prime Minister Amato as Vice-chairs. The convention consisted of 63 delegates, one designated by each State government, two by each parliament, sixteen members of the European Parliament, and two Commissioners. In addition, the applicant States also sent representatives of their governments and parliaments, who might present their views but not participate in any decisions taken. The Convention obviously represented far more diverse views than a traditional Intergovernmental Conference.

Inasmuch as most of the draft Constitutional Treaty's substantive provisions were replicated in the later Lisbon Treaty, it is unnecessary to discuss them here. Although the draft made significant structural changes to improve operational efficiency, and placed great emphasis on democratic values, incorporating the Charter of Fundamental Rights, it cannot be denied that its long, complicated text was difficult to understand even by experts.

A formal Intergovernmental Conference met in fall 2003, largely endorsing the draft Constitutional Treaty, but was unable to resolve several contentious issues. During the Irish European Council presidency in early 2004, Prime Minister Ahern employed patient diplomacy to lead to crucial compromises at the June 2004 European Council session. The Treaty was signed ceremonially at Rome on October 29, 2004.

The parliaments of eight States rapidly ratified the Constitutional Treaty and a Spanish referendum in February 2005 was decisively affirmative. But 55% of the French and 62% of the Dutch voters rejected it in referenda on May 29 and June 1, respectively. Although polls indicated that the unpopularity of both governments, opposition to Turkish accession and other unrelated issues influenced many voters, no one could deny that others simply opposed the complicated constitutional text. Despite further ratification by several more parliaments, the European Council soon realized that the draft Constitutional Treaty could not be adopted.

3. THE TREATY OF LISBON

After a period of reflection, in early 2007 the German presidency of recently elected Chancellor Angela Merkel resumed efforts toward a revision of the treaties. Her government undertook close contacts with the other Member State governments in order to develop a consensus on how to proceed. Under Chancellor Merkel's leadership, the European Council at Brussels in June 2007 agreed upon a modification of the existing EC Treaty and TEU that would retain virtually all of the substantive parts of the Constitutional Treaty, while jettisoning the name and those provisions symbolic of a Constitution. The Charter of Fundamental Rights was effectively incorporated into the new treaty. This led Prime Minister Blair of the UK to insist upon a Protocol that excluded application to the UK of certain interpretations of the Charter. Poland and the Czech Republic subsequently obtained more far-reaching Protocols on the Charter.

An Intergovernmental Conference rapidly drafted the final text which was signed ceremonially at Lisbon on October 22, 2007. This new Treaty of Lisbon substantially modified the TEU and replaced the European Community Treaty with a similarly detailed Treaty on the Functioning of the Union (or TFEU). The Community, merged into the Union, ceased to exist. Inasmuch as Chapter 2 and later chapters will present the main provisions of the Treaty of Lisbon, we will not review them here. The TEU, as amended by the Lisbon Treaty, and the TFEU are found in the Documents Supplement (docs. 1 and 2, respectively). So too is a "Conversion Table" showing the current treaty article numbers to which the pre-Lisbon TEU and EC Treaty articles cited throughout this book correspond (doc. 7).

Fortunately for proponents of the Lisbon Treaty, France's President Sarkozy and the Dutch Prime Minister Balkende decided that their countries could ratify by parliamentary action, instead of a referendum. Moreover, all the other Member States also concluded that parliamentary ratification was appropriate, except for Ireland. In most Member States, large majorities of the parliaments voted for ratification. Under Prime Minister Brown, who had succeeded Blair, the UK's government obtained a parliamentary majority to ratify despite the bitter opposition of the Conservatives.

Although the government and all of the Irish parties supported ratification, there was considerable anxiety as the Irish referendum approached. However, on October 2, 2009, the referendum produced a decisive 60% majority in favor. Within weeks, the presidents of Poland and the Czech Republic, both confirmed Euro-skeptics, accepted the inevitable after their parliaments had ratified, and they signed the Treaty. The Treaty of Lisbon accordingly entered into effect on December 1, 2009.

A special European Council meeting in late October selected Belgian Prime Minister Van Rompuy as the first President of the European Council and the UK's commissioner, Baroness Ashton, as the initial High Representative for Foreign and Security Affairs. Commission President Barroso, already chosen for a new term, then presented a new slate of Commissioners for 2009–14, together with their portfolios, to the Parliament for confirmation hearings. The new institutional structure of the Treaty of Lisbon thus commenced operations.

Further Reading

D. Dinan, Europe Recast: A History of the European Union (Lynne Rienner 2004)

D. Dinan, Ever Closer Union: An Introduction to European Integration (3d ed. Lynne Rienner 2005)

P. Kapteyn et. al. eds., The Law of the European Union and the European Communities (4th ed. Wolters Kluwer 2008).

CHAPTER 2

THE TREATIES AND THE UNION'S INSTITUTIONS

■ ■ ■

This chapter begins with a brief overview of the evolution of the EU's basic treaty framework. Thereafter, most of the chapter is devoted to describing the institutional structure of the European Union, indicating how the institutions have evolved up to the present Treaty of Lisbon. The EU's principal institutions are the Council, the European Council, the Parliament and the Commission, commonly called the political institutions, together with the Court of Justice. Each merits careful study. Although other bodies, such as the European Central Bank, and the Member State authorities also play a role in developing and implementing Union law and policy, the role of the political institutions and the Court of Justice is naturally preeminent.

A. THE TREATY FRAMEWORK OF THE EUROPEAN COMMUNITY AND THE EUROPEAN UNION

1. THE CONSTITUTIVE TREATIES

The European Economic Community was formed on January 1, 1958 by the Treaty Establishing the European Economic Community, often called the Treaty of Rome, because it was signed there on March 25, 1957. We previously noted in Chapter 1 that the earlier European Coal and Steel Community Treaty lapsed in 2002, as the European Community absorbed its programs, and the 1957 Euratom Treaty never achieved great importance.

Chapter 1's historical review indicated that the Single European Act (SEA), effective July 1, 1987, was the first major substantive modification of the EEC Treaty. The Treaty of Maastricht (formally the Treaty on European Union or TEU), effective November 1, 1993, substantially amended the initial Treaty, changing its name to the European Community Treaty (EC Treaty or ECT), and simultaneously created the European Union through the Treaty on European Union (TEU). Subsequent Treaties of Amsterdam, effective May 1, 1999, and Nice, effective February 1, 2003, amended significantly both the TEU and the ECT. Chapter 1 described the principal features of each of these successive treaties.

The Treaty of Amsterdam also renumbered all the articles of the TEU and the ECT, which created some confusion. More recently, the Lisbon Treaty did so again. In this text we will usually refer to Treaty articles as renumbered, providing the initial ECT or TEU article number only when useful to indicate an evolutionary development.

When created in 1993 by the TEU, the European Union consisted of the European Community, the ECSC and Euratom, commonly called the "first pillar," and two fields of purely intergovernmental action, the Common Foreign and Security Policy (CFSP or the "second pillar"), and Cooperation in Justice and Home Affairs (JHA or "third pillar"). Chapter 16 describes some important actions taken in the field of JHA, and Chapter 27 briefly notes the development of the CFSP.

However, the Treaty of Lisbon, effective December 1, 2009, substantially modified the EU, and absorbed the Community into it, ending the prior distinction between the two. The Treaty of Lisbon itself consists of a revised Treaty on European Union, which we will on occasion call the Lisbon TEU to differentiate it from the original Maastricht TEU, and the accessory Treaty on the Functioning of the European Union (TFEU), which replaced the EC Treaty. The post-Lisbon TEU and the TFEU may be found in the Documents Supplement, at docs. 1 and 2, respectively. The Treaty of Lisbon effectively abolishes the "pillar" distinction, as its TEU and TFEU encompass all EU operations. It also declares that the Union has "legal personality," which enables the Union to succeed to the Community in its network of international treaties, its ownership of land and other assets, and its employment of personnel, among other things.

Many provisions of the TFEU merely replicate provisions of the EC Treaty, although renumbering them. Because the vast majority of the primary materials in this casebook predate the Lisbon Treaty, the text will often refer to the pre-Lisbon numbering of the articles of the EC Treaty and the TEU, but always noting their renumbering by the Lisbon Treaty and any modification that Treaty may have made. To facilitate the task of identifying the current TEU and TFEU articles corresponding to the pre-Lisbon TEU and EC Treaty articles cited throughout the book, a "Conversion Table" is provided in the Documents Supplement, doc. 7.

As the recitals to the Lisbon Treaty's TEU indicate, the new Treaty continues "the process of creating an ever closer union among the peoples of Europe," a key goal of the original EEC Treaty. Further recitals demonstrate continuity with the prior treaties, such as the promotion of "economic and social progress," notably through achieving an integrated internal market and an economic and monetary union, the establishment of "a citizenship common to nationals of their countries," the implementation of a "common foreign and security policy," and the facilitation of free movement of persons by establishing "an area of freedom, security and justice." Another recital states the goal of furthering "the democratic and efficient functioning of the institutions" (presumably referring to new provisions such as those delimiting the competencies of the Union, and those augmenting the powers of the Parliament). This chapter will describe the modifications in institutional structure made by the Lisbon Treaty, and later chapters will indicate its impact in substantive fields of law.

An initial Lisbon TEU recital emphasized the Union's "attachment to the principles of liberty, democracy and respect for human rights and fundamental freedoms and the rule of law." This recital is the basis for some of the Lisbon Treaty's most significant innovations, namely the grant of Treaty force to the Charter of Fundamental Rights, the provisions describing the Union's adherence to basic democratic principles, and the addition of new fields to the scope of judicial review by the Court of Justice. Later chapters will describe these developments.

Distinguishing precisely between the nature and ambit of the European Community and the European Union prior to the Lisbon Treaty has not always been easy. In the vast majority of circumstances encountered in this book, the European institutions have taken the actions in question in pursuit of an objective set out in the EC Treaty and accordingly have invoked authority derived from a particular article of that treaty. To that extent we can properly speak of "a Community measure" or of "Community action." The proper reference after the Lisbon Treaty is Union, or EU, law.

The Treaties are commonly characterized as "constitutive" because they have created institutions and processes of law independent of the Member States. The fact remains, however, that the law and policies thereby generated are still a product of international agreements. In signing and ratifying the treaties, the national authorities were thus obliged to follow their own domestic constitutional procedures for treaty-making. In countries whose constitutions or legislation did not allow the transfer of competences contemplated by the Treaties, appropriate constitutional or legislative adaptations had to be made, or the Treaties had to be ratified by popular referenda.

Precisely because the Treaties are constitutive, they may receive a broader construction than international agreements typically receive. As we shall see in later chapters, the Court of Justice treats them as creating a "new legal order" which is governed by its own rules, rather than as ordinary international agreements construed according to conventional international law principles. In its 1991 European Area Opinion, discussed at page 1143 infra, the Court described the EC Treaty as the Community's "basic constitutional charter."

Besides the Treaties described above, the Member States entered into other agreements relating to the organization and functioning of the Community. Thus, in 1965 the Merger Treaty consolidated the political institutions that previously were separately structured under the EEC,

ECSC and Euratom Treaties. Later a 1970 Budgetary Treaty replaced the original system of financing the Community through contributions from the States by granting the Community its "own resources" from customs duties, agricultural levies and a share of national value added taxes.

When new countries join the EU, they do so through a Treaty of Accession, to which is annexed an Act of Accession setting out in detail any transitional provisions. These Accession Treaties necessarily modify the composition of all the institutions to make room for representatives from the new States.

2. THE PROCEDURE FOR TREATY AMENDMENTS AND THE PROCESS OF ACCESSION

Prior to the Lisbon Treaty, TEU Article 48 (replacing an earlier EC Treaty provision) governed the procedure for amending the treaties. The Council had the power to call an Intergovernmental Conference (IGC) composed of representatives of Member State governments to decide "by common accord" upon any amendments. (In practice, the European Council provided guidelines to the Council on the prospective agenda for each IGC.) The Treaty did not require the Council to act unanimously, and in fact the 1985 Luxembourg IGC was convened despite the opposition of Denmark, Greece and the UK, although they all participated once the IGC commenced.

The Lisbon TEU Article 48 authorizes the European Council to decide by simple majority to commence the "ordinary revision procedure" to be carried out either by an IGC or by a Convention. If a Convention is employed, it is to be composed of representatives of the States, of their national parliaments, and of the European Parliament and the Commission, and shall act "by consensus." Amendments proposed by a Convention must still go to an IGC for final action.

The new TEU Article 48 also authorizes the European Council to employ a "simplified revision procedure" to amend large portions of the TFEU (notably Part Three on Union policies and internal actions) by unanimity and after consultations. (All the Member States must also ratify the change.) In addition, the European Council may vote unanimously to substitute qualified majority voting for unanimity (or substitute the ordinary legislative process for a special legislative process) in any given case or area governed by the TFEU.

All of the EU's political institutions must collaborate in the process by which States accede to the Union. Article 49 of the Maastricht TEU, building on an earlier EC Treaty provision, made the Council the gatekeeper, deciding unanimously whether to accept an applicant State. In practice, however, the European Council took that decision, giving guidance to the Council. Both acted on the basis of a Commission opinion that examined in detail the suitability of a candidate State for membership. The Maastricht TEU provided Parliament with a veto power by requiring that it give its assent by an absolute majority vote of all its members. The Maastricht Treaty also set as a condition that candidate States must be democracies, with respect for human rights and the rule of law.

The Lisbon TEU's Article 49 has retained the existing accession procedure, adding that the European Council may set the "conditions of eligibility"—not an innovation, because it invariably did this in the past. The Lisbon TEU has, however, added an unusual feature: the right of a State to withdraw from the Union, set out in a new Article 50. This essentially provides that the withdrawing State shall negotiate "the arrangements for its withdrawal" with the Union. Given the severe adverse economic consequences that a withdrawing State is apt to encounter, a withdrawal does not seem very likely.

3.   OTHER SOURCES OF LAW

In the continental European tradition it is customary to identify the authoritative "sources" of law for any given legal system. Within the EU, the constitutive treaties, along with the other basic treaties we have identified, clearly constitute the primary sources of law. Secondary sources consist chiefly of the legally binding acts adopted by the EU institutions. As Chapter 3 explains, these acts include the many regulations, directives and decisions issued from time to time by the Council, the Parliament and the Council, or the Commission. Secondary sources also include the treaties to which the EU is a party, including trade and association agreements with third countries. Part V of this book deals with these international agreements and discusses their legal status. The EU has also acquired more and more "soft law," chiefly as a result of the informal lawmaking methods know as the "open method of coordination," discussed in Chapter Three.

Judgments of the Court of Justice and its accessory Court of First Instance (renamed the General Court by the Lisbon Treaty) also constitute important sources of EU law. See Chapters 5 and 6, which discuss the courts and the legal effect of their judgments. The Court of Justice considers the institutions and the Member States alike to be bound by the Court's interpretations of EU law and also by certain "general principles of law," such as the principles of proportionality and legitimate expectations (see Chapter 5 infra) and various fundamental rights which the Court has recognized in its case law (see Chapter 6 infra). These general principles not only constitute sources of EU law, but sources superior in rank to the EU's secondary legislation.

Does a convention among the Member States (to which the EU as such is not a party) have an EU law character merely because it deals with a subject related to the purposes of the Union? The answer is normally no, with the result that such treaties do not share the special legal force and effect of Union law within the Member States. (The exception would be agreements among the Member States on EU institutional matters specifically foreseen in the Treaties.)

Is the situation any different when the Treaties expressly contemplates the establishment of a given convention on a certain subject matter? EC Treaty Article 293 enabled the Member States "so far as is necessary" to negotiate various agreements including "the simplification of formalities governing the reciprocal recognition and enforcement of judgments of courts or tribunals and of arbitration awards." Pursuant to this provision, the Member States in 1968 concluded a Convention on Jurisdiction and Enforcement of Judgments in Civil and Commercial Matters, commonly known as the Brussels Convention. The Convention governed jurisdiction and the enforcement of foreign judgments in Member State courts. Shortly after signature of the Brussels Convention, the Member States entered into a Protocol conferring jurisdiction on the Court of Justice to render preliminary rulings on the interpretation of the Brussels Convention, in effect conceding that the Convention did not by itself constitute Community law. Moreover, the Acts of Accession to the EU have uniformly obligated new Member States "to accede to the conventions provided for in Article [293] . . . and to the protocols on the interpretation of those conventions by the Court of Justice."

The Brussels Convention was subsequently converted from an international agreement into EU legislation, by way of Council Regulation 44/2001 on Jurisdiction and the Recognition of Enforcement of Judgments in Civil and Commercial Matters (though the Convention remains intact for Denmark which opted out of the Regulation). We deal with the Convention, the Regulation and related matters in Chapter 36.

4. THE INSTITUTIONS ESTABLISHED BY THE TREATIES

Considering their scale of governance and range of concerns, the European Community initially, and later the European Union, have always had a very particular institutional structure.

Three of the EU institutions—the Council, the Commission and the European Parliament—share the political tasks of making and administering EU law at the European level. The fourth is the Court of Justice which, aided by the Court of First Instance (now named the General Court), represents the EU's judicial arm.

Although these institutions still bear some resemblance to those of the 1960s, they have undergone a distinct evolution in their respective powers and functions. Much of this evolution—e.g., the steady increase in the administrative power of the Commission and in the doctrinal authority of the Court of Justice—has been gradual. Other structural and procedural reforms were brought about by the Single European Act and the Treaties of Maastricht, Amsterdam and Nice, all of which notably increased the legislative power of Parliament.

Finally, the Treaty of Lisbon has formally added the European Council as an institution of the Union, thus recognizing a status that has effectively existed for many years, as well as the European Central Bank, in view of its control of the monetary policy of a majority of Member States. The remainder of this chapter describes each of these institutions except the European Central Bank, whose description is deferred to Chapter 31.

B. THE COUNCIL

1. INSTITUTIONAL ROLE AND COMPOSITION

The Council (or the Council of Ministers, as it is often called) does not have a perfect analogue among conventional government structures at the nation-state level. Since the Treaty of Maastricht, the Council's formal name is the Council of the European Union.

Prior to the Lisbon Treaty, EC Treaty Article 202 described the Council's role as to "ensure coordination of the general economic policies of the Member States," to "take decisions" and grant the Commission delegated powers of implementation. In fact, the Council's most important power has always been to adopt legislation, alone until the Single European Act, and thereafter jointly with the Parliament in many fields. The Council also decides external trade policies and concludes international agreements concerning trade, investment aid, fisheries, etc. The Lisbon TEU's Article 16 provides a good description: the Council shall "jointly with the Parliament, exercise legislative and budgetary functions," and, on its own, "carry out policy-making and coordinating functions." The Council's role in legislation is further described in Chapter 3, and in external affairs in Chapter 27.

Article 203 of the EC Treaty (now Lisbon TEU Article 16 (2)), states that the Council is to be composed of a representative of each Member State "at ministerial level" authorized to commit that Member State's government. Originally, Member States could be represented in the Council only by government ministers, but the term "representative ... at ministerial level" was introduced by the Maastricht Treaty so as to permit representatives of the German states or *Länder* to act in the name of Germany in the Council when Germany's federal structure so requires.

Often the Ministers of Foreign Affairs comprise the Council. When they meet as the Council on institutional or internal affairs, they are known as the "General Affairs Council," as distinct from the "External Relations Council," the name used when they meet for purposes of action under the Common Commercial Policy (i.e. external trade and economic relations) or the Common Foreign and Security Policy. When a meeting concerns a specialized subject, such as transport, agriculture or employment, the Council may consist of the relevant ministers (or pairs of ministers, when two distinct matters—foreign affairs and agriculture, for example—are involved). With the advent of Monetary Union, Council meetings of the economic and finance ministers (known for short as the Ecofin Council) became increasingly common. For operational efficiency, in June 2002, the European Council limited the number of Council compositions to nine.

Article 203 of the EC Treaty prescribed that the Presidency of the Council should rotate among Member States every six months, and the Lisbon TEU Article 16(9) retains this approach. Acting as President of a Council configuration has significant practical consequences, because the President largely sets the agenda for actions at meetings, which can be used to concentrate attention on a policy proposal or draft legislation of interest to the President or his or her State. The current Council President also chairs all Council meetings. A skillful chair can promote the efficiency of decision-making, while a chair lacking in skill may be unable to bring a meeting to a successful conclusion.

TFEU Article 236 confirms the prior practice by prescribing that the European Council sets the six-month rotation cycle. Thus, Spain and Belgium act as Council Presidents in 2010, and Hungary and Poland in 2011. Since the 1980's, a current Council President collaborates closely with his or her predecessor and successor to promote continuity in what is called a troika (the name of a Russian three-horse sleigh). Because many policy issues require Council attention for long periods of time, the use of troika cooperation is quite valuable.

The General Affairs Council meets almost every week, while other Council configurations meet when convened by their President to review policy or draft legislation, typically several times a year. Because all meetings require simultaneous translation, the Council meeting room must be extremely large. Accordingly, in recent years Council meetings have customarily been held in the Council's large building in Brussels, which has extensive facilities.

The Council's most important role is that of legislature. In a very few fields (notably in the CFSP), the Council alone legislates, although it must usually obtain the Parliament's views in the consultation procedure (see Chapter 3A). Thus, prior to the Lisbon Treaty, the Council alone adopted any legislation in the fields of agriculture and fisheries, taxation, competition, and cooperation in police and criminal justice.

Currently, the Council mostly legislates jointly with the Parliament, with each having an equal voice, in what the Lisbon Treaty denominates the "ordinary legislative procedure," previously called codecision (see Chapter 3B). Legislation to achieve the internal market, or to adopt most rules concerning employment or social policy, consumer protection, environmental protection, health, education and culture, are all adopted jointly by the Council and Parliament. The Lisbon Treaty added to this list agriculture and fisheries, as well as some other fields in which the Council had previously acted alone. Note also that, as will be seen below, the Commission plays a critical role in the legislative process, because in almost all fields the Treaty accords it the sole power of initiative to present the first draft, and subsequently to present successive drafts incorporating Council or Parliament amendments to the extent it chooses.

In international affairs, the Council plays a leading role. Not only does the Council ultimately enter into international agreements on behalf of the Union, but it establishes policy guidelines for the Commission in the latter's negotiation of agreements. The most important field is that of trade, but the EU also enters into many fisheries agreements, as well as agreements involving financial and technical assistance. The Treaty provisions concerning the final conclusion of international agreements are complex. See Chapter 27 for further discussion, particularly concerning the extent of involvement of Parliament and the possible necessity of joining with individual Member States in what are called "mixed agreements."

Whenever the European Council concludes that the Union should undertake a "common strategy" within the context of the Common Foreign Security Policy, it can provide guidelines to the Council, which can then take decisions to enable "joint actions" or "common positions" to implement them (see Maastricht TEU Articles 13–15, largely replicated in Lisbon TEU Articles 26–29). Through these provisions, for example, the Union was able to undertake action to adopt sanctions against Serbia and help end the civil war in Bosnia. For a further description see Chapter 27D.

The Amsterdam Treaty created the post of the High Representative for the CFSP, an office held by a prominent Spanish diplomat, Javier Solana, for two successive five-year terms, 1999–2009. The Lisbon Treaty has substantially augmented the authority and responsibilities of this official. Lisbon TEU Article 18 prescribes that the High Representative, named by the European Council by a qualified majority vote, shall preside over the Foreign Affairs Council (ending the rotation of that Council according to the six-month Presidencies) and shall "conduct the Union's common foreign and security policy." Moreover, the High Representative serves simultaneously as Vice-president of the Commission, with the foreign affairs portfolio. Inasmuch as the High Representative will head a new External Affairs Service, merging the prior services of the Commission and Council and responsible for all Union delegations to third states, the post will have substantially enhanced power. In November 2009, the European Council chose Baroness Ashton, formerly the Commissioner responsible for external affairs, as the High Representative.

The Council is greatly aided in its work by a body called the CORE-PER, an acronym for the French term for Committee of Permanent Representatives, which was recognized in EC Treaty Article 207(1) (now Lisbon TEU Article 16 (7)). COREPER, consisting of two representatives from each Member State customarily holding ambassadorial rank, usually meets weekly in two groups to review all draft legislation and other measures before their consideration by the Council itself. If COREPER is able to agree on a course of action, it recommends it to the Council, which usually endorses the recommendation with little or no debate. If CORE-PER is unable to agree, but believes certain policy issues concerning the proposed measure can be resolved by the Council, it will refer the issues to the Council for deliberation, and then accept the Council's views as the basis for further work. COREPER's work obviously greatly facilitates the taking of Council action. Note that the Court of Justice held in Commission v. Council (FAO fisheries agreement), Case C–25/94, [1996] ECR I–1469, that COREPER cannot itself take legally binding decisions.

The operational difficulty occasioned by the Union's many different languages merits mention at this point. Article 290 of the EC Treaty (now TFEU Article 342), authorizes the Council to determine, by unanimous action, the "rules governing the languages of the institutions" (except for the Court of Justice, which deliberates and drafts judgments in French, but otherwise follows the Council's language regime, publishing its judgments in all the languages). Not surprisingly, the Council requires that every Member State's official language or languages be used in publishing the text of all Treaties and Protocols, in preparing legislative drafts, and in publishing final legislation, decisions and other measures in the Official Journal or communicating them to interested parties. (Since they are not legal texts, studies and reports, even major ones, may not necessarily be published in every official language.) All the political institutions are bound by the Council language rules, as are the EU's agencies and other bodies unless specifically authorized otherwise (which is rare—see the Court judgment upholding the Council decision authorizing the Community Trademark Office to use four languages in its operations, infra, page 169).

Naturally this is extremely expensive and results in substantial time delays, especially since the number of official languages increased from twelve to twenty-three as a result of the 2004 and 2007 enlargements. (There are not twenty-seven official languages, because four States have official languages in common with other States.) Nonetheless it is not plausible to expect that any Member State government or people would accept being legally bound by Union rules that are not available in its official language. The Court of Justice has recently taken that position in holding that a Community customs regulation that had not been published in the Czech language version of the Official Journal had no binding force in the Czech Republic. See Skoma–Lux v. Olomouc Customs Office, Case C–161/06, [2007] ECR I–10841.

At all Council meetings, each minister's speech or comments must be simultaneously translated into all official languages. Media reports indicate that on occasion a minister has prevented a meeting from being held if the interpreter into his or her language is not available.

In view of its many roles, the Council's permanent staff of civil servants is relatively small, less than 3000. The Council has a Secretariat with departments dealing with main fields of Union affairs, e.g., external relations, agriculture, internal market, economy and finance. The Council Legal Service in principle reviews all draft legislation and decisions.

2. COUNCIL VOTING

The EEC Treaty had required the Council to act unanimously in some fields, but enabled it to act by a special majority vote, called qualified majority voting (QMV), in many others (and by way of great exception by simple majority vote, as on budgetary matters). As we observed in Chapter 1, President de Gaulle of France strongly objected to any significant Council action being taken other than by unanimity. As a result of the 1966 Luxembourg Compromise, the French government upheld this position until 1984, when President Mitterand declared in a speech to Parliament that France would respect normal Community voting procedures. However, as a matter of practice, other large States, particularly the UK, also took the view that achieving a consensus was appropriate whenever the Council acted upon a highly significant matter. Only after the launch of the internal market program in 1985 did the Council begin to adopt important legislation by QMV. Thus, Germany accepted being outvoted on automobile emission standards, and the UK on certain securities directives.

The Lisbon Treaty TEU's Article 24 continues to require Council unanimity for CFSP action. The TFEU also continues to require unanimity to adopt measures to harmonize taxation, sensitive environmental or social policy legislation, or measures pursuant to TFEU Article 352, the article relied on to adopt measures to achieve the common market when no Treaty provision expressly enables them. In a Union now consisting of 27 Member States, achieving unanimity in any of these is likely to be difficult. The Council is authorized to act by a simple majority of all Member States only when adopting its rules of procedure or requesting the Commission to prepare studies or proposals, pursuant to EC Treaty Articles 207–08 (now TFEU Articles 240–41).

QMV voting dates back to the original EEC Treaty. The essential idea is easy to understand. The Treaty stipulates that each State has a specific number of votes and then requires a stated total number of affirmative votes to take action on adopting policies, legislation or decisions by QMV. When there were only six Member States, the calculations were simple, and QMV voting operated smoothly, unless a State claimed a veto by virtue of the Luxembourg Compromise. This remained essentially true as the Community grew to fifteen States.

At the time of the European Council in Nice in December 2001, allocating votes to the current and prospective Member States and setting the formula to act via QMV proved one of the most difficult issues to resolve. The ultimate compromise is complicated. Although Germany has about one-third more people than France, Italy and the UK, all four states were allotted 29 votes, while Spain and Poland received 27. Going down in function of population, the Netherlands received 13 votes, Belgium 12, and so on down to the six States with the smallest population, which each received three (Malta), or four (the others). The QMV formula then required that 72% of the total weighted votes had to be affirmative to adopt a measure. In practice, this could mean that up to four of the six larger States could be outvoted. To prevent this, a so-called double majority vote was required: any State could request a calculation to determine whether States having 62% of the Union's population were in favor, and, if not, the proposed action would fail. Prior to the 2004 enlargement, Germany and another larger State, or three larger States not including Germany, could then be outvoted, but not more. Although complicated, this QMV system has operated satisfactorily. In practice, even when the Treaty stipulates QMV voting, the Council generally prefers to act by quasi-unanimity.

The Lisbon Treaty prescribes a new QMV system. Its TEU Article 16(4) requires for action the affirmative vote of 55% of all the ministers, (i.e. States) comprising at least fifteen of them, and representing 65% of the Union population. By requiring the concurrence of States having 65% of the Union population, the Lisbon Treaty slightly increases the influence of Germany and other large States and makes it less likely that they will be outvoted. However, Article 16(4) stipulates that a blocking minority must consist of at least four States. Moreover, due to opposition from smaller States, a Protocol on Transitional Provisions retains the Nice formula until November 1, 2014, and permits any State to invoke it until March 31, 2017.

In the 1990s, the Community began to adopt policies intended to make its operations, documents and decisions more transparent and available to the public, initially through codes of conduct and then by Treaty amendments. See Chapter 6D for discussion of this development. The Council accordingly began in 1993 to keep a public register of the votes of each State when the Council acted in a legislative capacity, annexing any relevant statements in the minutes. The Amsterdam Treaty amended EC Treaty Article 207 (now Lisbon TEU Article 16(8)), to make this mandatory. Voting on Council decisions and other action of a non-legislative nature remains confidential.

C.   THE EUROPEAN COUNCIL

We saw in Chapter 1 that the heads of state or government of the initial six Member States began to hold summit meetings, starting at the Hague in December 1968. Their success in resolving crucial policy issues led to a decision to hold regular meetings of the European Council, as the group became to be known, at least twice a year. Since the 1990's, the European Council has met regularly four times annually. The Presidents of the Council and the Commission are also members with full participation. Due to the French Constitution's division of power between the two officials, both the President and Prime Minister of France participate in European Council meetings, but with only one vote. The European Council met in the capital or another city of the State which held the rotating presidency of the Council, until 2004 when the increased number of Member States led to all sessions being held in the Council's Lipsius building in Brussels. Each State's minister for foreign affairs customarily assists the head of state or government, and the Lisbon TEU Article 15(2) adds the presence of the High Representative for Foreign and Security Affairs.

In 1987, the Single European Act first formally recognized the European Council as an informal policy-maker. Subsequently, the Maastricht TEU's Article 4 declared that the European Council shall "provide the Union with the necessary impetus for its development and define the general guidelines thereof." The European Council could not, however, take legally binding decisions, although its authoritative status enabled it in effect to direct the Council or Commission to do so.

Over the years, the European Council has resolved difficult policy issues that the Council lacked the political capacity to resolve. The European Council has set long-term policy guidelines for the Community, endorsed institutional reforms, embraced the idea of an Economic and Monetary Union (EMU), supported German reunification within the Community, set the criteria for accession of the central and eastern European states, scheduled successive intergovernmental conferences in contemplation of treaty amendments, commissioned and eventually endorsed the EU's Charter of Fundamental Rights, and of course, reached the agreement necessary to achieve the Treaty of Lisbon.

Among the European Council's most prominent functions is the coordination of Member State foreign policy, a process that evolved into the Common Foreign and Security Policy. The European Council may now unanimously establish guidelines which enable the Council of Ministers itself to take foreign policy decisions on a qualified majority voting basis. The CFSP is described in Chapter 27.

The European Council has never legally supplanted the Council which continues to take all the action necessary to carry out policy decisions of the European Council. But some confusion between the two did arise prior to the Lisbon Treaty. EC Treaty Article 99 authorized the European Council to set "broad guidelines" on the economic policies of Member States and the Community, guidelines that the Council of Ministers was then to implement. Still more significantly, EC Treaty Article 121 empowered the Council of Ministers, meeting as "Heads of State or of Government" (effectively the European Council), to take the decision whether and when to enter the final stage of Monetary Union, creating a European Central Bank and a single European currency. (See Chapter 33C.)

The Lisbon Treaty's designation of the European Council as an institution of the Union with the capacity to take binding decisions confirms its crucial policy-setting role. The Lisbon TEU's Article 15 retains the description of the European Council's composition, political guidance role, and meetings. Article 15 expressly bars the European Council from exercising any legislative functions. Its decisions are generally taken by consensus, but it can act by simple majority or qualified majority vote in certain decisions. Thus, TEU Article 48 enables the European Council to act by simple majority in deciding to launch a treaty amendment procedure, and TFEU Article 235 enables the European Council to act by qualified majority vote (using the Council mode of QMV) to nominate the President of the Commission, designate the High Representative, and fix the list of Council configurations and the rotation of the Council President. The President of the Commission has no vote in the European Council.

Naturally, the European Council remains a key actor in determining policy in the CFSP, where it defines the "general guidelines" and objectives, and may "adopt the necessary decisions" pursuant to Lisbon TEU Article 26. The TEU's Article 34 on the procedure for accession prescribes that the European Council sets "the conditions of eligibility" for applicant States, formalizing its customary practice up to then. Various TFEU Articles also give the European Council a policy-guidance role, e.g., in reviewing whether a State has satisfied the criteria necessary to enter the Euro-zone.

The Lisbon Treaty created a major new post, that of a full-time President of the European Council. Its TEU Article 15(6) states that the President shall serve a two-and-a-half year term, renewable once, with the European Council using a QMV vote under TFEU Article 235 to elect its President. In November 2009, the European Council chose Herman Van Rompuy, the Prime Minister of Belgium, as its first President.

The President of the European Council has several important duties: to chair the meetings and "drive forward" the European Council's work, to ensure continuity, to "endeavour to facilitate cohesion and consensus," and to report to Parliament after each meeting. The President also represents the Union externally in its common foreign and security policy, but "without prejudice" to the powers of the High Representative for Foreign Affairs and Security Policy.

Although the media has often called the post the "President of the European Union" instead of President of the European Council, it remains to be seen whether the President will become more of a spokesperson on Union affairs than is the President of the Commission. The basic idea behind creating the post was to promote continuity in European Council affairs by ending the shifts in views and emphasis due to the six-month rotation of the Council Presidency. Again, only time will tell whether the President of the European Council will be very successful in achieving this.

D. THE COMMISSION

The central administrative body of the Union, the European Commission, bears a striking but imperfect resemblance to a Government. Often referred to as the Community's executive organ, the Commission does in fact perform many tasks commonly identified with the executive: formulating a general legislative program, initiating the legislative process by drafting specific pieces of legislation, exercising regulatory powers delegated to it by the Council, taking administrative decisions, carrying out administrative policies and programs, and overseeing (and if need be enforcing) compliance with the law. The breadth of functions performed by the Commission will become even more apparent as the reader moves through the various substantive law chapters of this book.

We first review the role and powers of the Commission, its selection and possible revocation, then the role and powers of the Commission President, Commission operations, and the structure of the Commission civil service. Finally we will describe how the Commission exercises regulatory powers delegated by the Council.

1. THE COMMISSION'S ROLE AND POWERS

EC Treaty Article 211 described the role of the Commission in very general terms. Probably most important was "its own power of decision" and participation in the legislative process, indicating both the Commission's power to take administrative decisions in the implementation of agricultural and competition policy, and its right to initiate all legislative drafts. The Commission was also to "ensure that the provisions of this Treaty" are enforced, notably through its power to bring proceedings in the Court of Justice for infringements by Member States of the Treaty and its secondary law. The Commission often proudly refers to this as its role of "guardian of the Treaties."

Lisbon TEU Article 17 is more precise and detailed. It declares that the "Commission shall promote the general interest of the Union," "ensure the application of the Treaties," and oversee the application of Union law under the control of the Court of Justice. The Commission is also to exercise "coordinating, executive and management functions," executing the budget and managing programs, as well as providing the Union's "external representation" except in the CFSP.

Thus, the Commission plays a vital role in setting policy and drafting legislation, as well as in conducting operations and executing regulatory decisions. The Commission's significant monopoly on the initiation of legislation and the subsequent drafting of text throughout the legislative process, granted by EC Treaty Article 251 (now TFEU Article 294), enables it to set the legislative agenda. (The Parliament, Court and Member States have very limited rights to initiate legislation.) The Commission's delegated regulatory power and ability to take legally binding administrative decisions is particularly important in the fields of agriculture, fisheries, competition, technical standards, customs and trade. The Commission's regulation of agricultural policy is particularly complex, as it regulates product standards, marketing and prices for many different commodities at frequent intervals.

As noted in Chapter One, the Commission conducts membership negotiations with candidate States and reviews their progress toward accession. In the international arena, the Commission has the sole power to negotiate trade agreements (insofar as they deal with topics within EU competence), fisheries agreements, and investment and technical aid agreements.

Regarding the enforcement of Union laws, the Commission brings proceedings in the Court of Justice against Member States for maintaining barriers to trade, failing to implement EU legislation appropriately, or otherwise violating EU law obligations. The Commission also defends its administrative decisions when challenged before the Court, and provides amicus briefs in most other proceedings before the Court.

The Commission prepares the draft annual budget and multi-annual budget plan for action by the Council and Parliament, although each institution administers its own budget. The Commission owns and leases property on behalf of the Union and employs permanent or temporary staff. It provides annually numerous economic and social reports and studies, and a valuable annual general report on all Union activities, pursuant to EC Treaty Article 212 (now TFEU Article 249). Given this extraordinarily broad range of activities, the Commission early gained the appropriate nick-name, the "locomotive (or engine) of the common market."

The EC Treaty provided that the larger States (France, Italy, Germany, and later the UK and Spain) would each designate two Commissioners, while the smaller States would each name one. The Treaty of Nice eliminated the larger States' second Commissioner, and its Protocol required the Commission to be reduced in size after the central and eastern European enlargement in order to promote operational efficiency. The Commission currently consists of 27 Commissioners, certainly a very large body. The Lisbon Treaty's TFEU Article 244 states that the European Council shall unanimously decide upon a system of rotation, treating all States equally. However, several States are unhappy with the prospect of at any time being without a Commissioner. In an effort to encourage a favorable vote in the Irish referendum on the Lisbon Treaty in October 2009, the European Council in June 2009 indicated to Ireland that the rotation system would not be introduced. Presumably there will be a treaty amendment before 2014 to eliminate any rotation.

Some commentators have observed that providing each State with a Commissioner provides significant benefits that may offset the detriment of a large body. Commissioners understand what benefits or burdens proposed policies or legislation may bring to their home States and call attention to this in the decision-making. Commissioners also serve as a valuable conduit of information and interchange of ideas with their home State government. Finally, the fact that each State names one member of the Commission contributes to a general confidence in the Commission and acceptance of its decisions.

EC Treaty Article 213 (now TFEU Article 245) imposes a strong obligation of independence upon Commissioners. Member States are also bound by the Treaty not to influence Commissioners in the performance of their duties. Although this obligation is usually respected, Commission Presidents have had occasion to remind State governments that they should not try to pressure their Commissioners when the Commission is taking a decision on some controversial issue.

Originally Commissioners served a term of four years, but the Treaty of Maastricht extended the term to five years, beginning in November 1995, in order to enable the Parliament elected in June 1995 and at five-year intervals thereafter to have sufficient time to vote upon the nominees for Commissioner and the Commission President. Until the Maastricht Treaty, each State simply designated its Commissioner. After amendment by the treaties of Maastricht and Amsterdam, EC Treaty Article 214 (now TEU Article 17) provided that the States should first designate "by common accord" the President, who had to be "approved" by a Parliament vote. Then the States would nominate the other Commissioners "in common accord" with the President. Finally the Commission "as a body" would have to be approved by Parliament.

Although there is no reference to them in the Treaty, the Parliament began in 1995 to hold confirmation hearings on each Commissioner, examining their qualifications in committee. In 2004, after the Parliament conducted confirmation hearing on all nominees, it threatened to turn down the entire Commission if nomination of the prospective Italian Commissioner was not withdrawn, as the Parliament considered him unfit for the post. President Barroso was obliged to request Italy to reconsider, which the government did. Parliament accepted the new nominee, and voted in favor of the Commission as a body. Presumably this set an important precedent. In the future nominees not endorsed by the Parliament after confirmation hearings will probably be withdrawn, to avoid the risk that Parliament would reject the entire Commission. In January 2010, Rumiana Jeleva withdrew her candidacy as Commissioner named by Romania in the wake of parliamentary hearings that raised allegations of conflict of interest and serious doubts about the candidate's competence and judgment.

Lisbon TEU Article 17(7) retains the procedure for selection of the President and the other Commissioners set out in EC Treaty Article 214, except that it is the European Council, acting by qualified majority vote, that nominates the President, and the Council that, "in common accord" with the President, nominates the other Commissioners. The Lisbon Treaty's provision that the European Council nominates the President by qualified majority vote instead of the "common accord" previously required merits underlining. On several occasions in the past, able candidates for the Commission Presidency were vetoed by one or another larger State and ultimately a compromise candidate had to be chosen. This notably occurred in the designation of President Santer in 1995 and

President Barroso in 2004. While one may hope that vetoes will no longer be possible, only time will tell if this proves true.

Article 201 of the EC Treaty (now Lisbon TEU Article 17(8)) gives the Parliament a powerful weapon in its oversight of the Commission: by a two-thirds vote it may censure the Commission, which is then compelled to resign. On occasion the Parliament did threaten to censure the Commission, but never attained the requisite majority. However, in early 1999, after strong evidence of corruption by two members of the Santer Commission had arisen, and Parliament had threatened censure, the Commission itself named an independent three-member committee of experts to review the charges. In its report, the committee identified two Commissioners, among them former French prime minister Edith Cresson, as guilty of maladministration (a conclusion later upheld in a plenary judgment of the Court of Justice), and concluded that the Commission as a body had failed in oversight. Faced with a certain vote of censure, the Santer Commission resigned. (Note that the Commission could have resorted to EC Treaty Article 216, which authorizes it to request the Court of Justice to "retire" a commissioner for "serious misconduct.") The European Council accepted the resignation and accelerated the selection of the next President, Romano Prodi, and his Commission. The Prodi Commission promptly undertook administrative reforms to reduce the risk of any such future episode.

2. THE PRESIDENT OF THE COMMISSION

Over the years, starting with the first President, Walter Hallstein, Commission Presidents have shaped the Commission's agenda and often exerted great influence over Commission policy. This was decidedly the case with Jacques Delors, the former French Socialist Minister of Finance and President of the Commission between 1985 and 1995, who strongly promoted the Community's 1992 "internal market" program, the Monetary Union, and further steps toward political union. Several others— among them Roy Jenkins (1977–80), Romano Prodi (1999–2004), and current President José Manuel Barroso—have significantly promoted the EU's policies and programs.

The President's formal authority within the Commission has been progressively strengthened. As noted, he or she participates in the designation of the other Commissioners. Under EC Treaty Article 217 (now TEU Article 17(6)), the President is given the power to allocate and reallocate portfolios among the Commission's members and "lay down guidelines" for the Commission's work. Moreover, the President may require a Commissioner to resign, and the text does not indicate that this power is limited to cases of misconduct. (TFEU Article 247, like EC Treaty Article 216 before it, authorizes the Court of Justice to retire a Commissioner for serious misconduct on application by the Commission or the Council, acting by a simple majority.) Note that in 1999, if President Santer had then possessed the power to compel a Commissioner to resign he might well have done so, and have avoided the Commission's resignation.

Commission President Barroso set a precedent by exercising his power to allocate responsibilities among Commissioners both in 2004 and 2009, in some cases giving important portfolios to Commissioners from small States instead of larger States that customarily had obtained them. He also urged the States to nominate larger numbers of women as Commissioners, eight in 2004 and nine in 2009.

Probably the President's greatest influence on Commission operations is the ability to set the agenda for its program of action. Indeed, each January the President presents to the Parliament the Commission's agenda for the year. The President also chairs Commission meetings, setting their agenda as well. Another vital role of the President is to serve as the Commission's customary spokesman to the other institutions, the ECB, business sectors and the public at large. We have previously noted that the President is a member of the European Council, enabling him or her to present Commission views directly to the Union's highest political leaders and to participate in their deliberations. There is no question but that the Commission President has always been the most prominent leader and spokesperson of the EU up to the present time.

3. THE COMMISSION STRUCTURE

EC Treaty Article 219 (now TFEU Article 250) provides for the Commission to act by a majority of its members. However, it is generally believed that the Commission prefers to take any important decision by close to consensus, as does the Council. The Commission's Rules of Procedure, periodically updated, provide that the Commission shall "act collectively." Nonetheless, in view of the Commission's heavy workload, it has to be able to delegate the implementation of much EU law and policy to individual commissioners.

Thus, in Commission v. Germany (First company directive penalties), Case C–191/95, [1998] ECR I–5449, the Court held that the Commission had to collectively deliberate and take collective responsibility when initiating a proceeding before the Court to declare that a State had infringed the Treaty, but that it could delegate the final preparation of the necessary documentation to a single Commissioner. The Court concluded that:

[48] [While] the Commission's decision to issue a reasoned opinion and its decision to bring an [Article 226] action ... must be the subject of collective deliberation by the college of Commissioners [and] the information on which those decisions are based must therefore be available to the members of the college, [i]t is not ... necessary for the college itself formally to decide on the wording of the acts which give effect to those decisions and put them in final form.

The Court also observed that the principle of collegiality is based on the equal participation of the Commissioners in the adoption of decisions, so that "all members of the college of Commissioners should bear collective responsibility at political level for all decisions adopted" (¶ 39).

The Commission Rules provide that the President convenes the Commission to weekly meetings and sets their agendas. Although minutes must be kept, the meetings are strictly confidential. The Commission may delegate one or more Commissioners to take administrative acts. Indeed, due to the Commission's heavy workload, the Rules permit decisions to be taken by a form of written procedure, with proposals circulated to all Commissioners and then deemed to be approved after a stated period if no objection is raised. In practice most relatively non-controversial decisions are taken by this written procedure method.

The Commission's workload is always heavy. Its annual report to the Parliament indicates that it regularly proposes each year over 2000 legislative drafts, takes several hundred formal administrative decisions, and issues numerous reports and studies.

Structurally, the Commission has nineteen Directorates–General (DG), one for each major field of Union policy action, e.g., Agriculture, Competition, Economic and Financial Affairs, Employment and Social Affairs, Internal Market, and External Relations. A Commissioner supervises each DG, which is headed by a Director–General and his or her deputy. Due to the importance of their portfolios, several Commissioners in the 2009–14 Commission are frequently mentioned in the media, e.g., Michel Barnier, Internal Market; Joaquin Almunia, Competition; Ollie Rehn, Economic and Financial Affairs; and Karel de Gucht, External Commercial Relations. The DGs are sub-divided into directorates and then into units. In addition, the Commission has several internal services: Budget, Personnel, Legal Service and the Translation Office, each also supervised by a Commissioner. The Commission's permanent staff is around 18,000, surprisingly small for all of its operations.

The Commission headed by President Prodi adopted a White Paper on Reforming the Commission in March 2000, revising its personnel policies to emphasize promotion on merit and promoting equal opportunities for women, modernizing its financial management, and adopting a code of good behavior. The Prodi Commission also initiated a policy of rotating Directors–General and their deputies and other senior officials to new posts every five years in order to promote fresh approaches and thinking. Subsequently, in March 2004, the Commission adopted a new Staff Regulation that was supposed to improve entry and promotion procedures, enhance family leave provisions, and create better protection against discrimination and harassment. The Commission now sets annual gender balance targets for promotions to try to reduce the "glass ceiling" ' for women (which remains a serious problem even in 2010). After the enlargement in 2004, the Commission carried out a program to recruit staff, including senior civil servants, from the new Member States.

The Commission Legal Service, headed by its own Director–General, has a crucial role in its operations. The Commission's Rules of Procedure require that the Legal Service review all legislative drafts and proposed administrative decisions, and of course lawyers from the Service represent the Commission in proceedings before the Court of Justice and the Court of First Instance. The Legal Service currently has around 150 lawyers, divided into teams that concentrate on the different fields of Commission action.

The Commission's Translation Office is its largest unit, employing over 2000 translators and interpreters. Their burden was already great before the 2004 enlargement, and now is simply breath-taking. All draft and final legislation, administrative decisions, policy statements, and most reports and studies must be translated into each of the Union's 23 official languages. On an informal basis, the initial text is usually drafted either in French or English, and the Commission's staff is usually expected to be fluent in both.

4. THE COMMISSION'S DELEGATED REGULATORY POWER

As noted, and as is hardly surprising, the Commission exercises a substantial volume of rulemaking authority delegated to it by the Council, pursuant to Treaty provisions, especially in the fields of agriculture and fisheries, transport, environmental protection and energy—fields in which the value of flexibility and expertise is especially pronounced.

A question of basic importance is the scope of the regulatory power that the Council may delegate to the Commission. The question arose in ACF Chemiefarma NV v. Commission, Case 41/69, [1970] ECR 661. Acting under then EC Treaty Article 83 (now TFEU Article 103), which authorized it to enact legislation for the implementation of Community competition rules, the Council adopted Regulation 17, which in turn empowered the Commission to issue procedural rules for investigating suspected violations, holding hearings and fining violators. (Regulation 17 is described in Chapter 20.) A party that had been fined by the Commission under these rules challenged the action on the ground that Regulation 17 delegated powers to the Commission going beyond the "implementation" of Council rules. The Court rejected the argument that the Council was required by itself to exercise all the rulemaking authority that Article 83 confers on it. "[T]he rules laying down the procedure to be followed ..., however important they may be, constitute implementing provisions ..." [1970] ECR at 668.

The Council often delegates rulemaking powers to the Commission only on condition that the latter first submit its draft rules for an opinion from, and in some cases actual approval by, specialized committees representing the Member States. This was foreseen by EC Treaty Article 202 which expressly permitted the Council to impose conditions on the Commission's use of delegated powers in accordance with "principles and rules" to be established by the Council upon proposal by the Commission and advice by Parliament. In 1987, immediately upon entry into force of the Single European Act, the Council adopted a so-called Comitology Decision, which established a series of committee models (plus certain variants) for reviewing the Commission's exercise of delegated powers. That decision was updated by Council Decision 1999/468, O.J. L 184 (June 28, 1999), and supplemented by an agreement between the Parliament and Commission which guarantees that the Parliament will receive essential documents (e.g. draft agendas, draft measures) from the Commission at the same time as committee members do.

The most common procedure is the "management procedure," which entails a so-called "management committee," chaired by a non-voting Commission official, but composed of Member State representatives whose votes are weighted by State in the fashion of the Council itself. Under this system, the Commission's draft legislation is reviewed by the relevant management committee, and if the committee by qualified majority gives a favorable opinion of the legislation or expresses no opinion at all, the draft automatically becomes law. If, on the other hand, the committee by qualified majority disapproves the proposal, its effectiveness is postponed for one month, during which time the Council itself may act to reject it. However, only a vote of disapproval by the Council will prevent the measure from coming into effect; the management committee's disapproval alone is not sufficient.

Variations on the management committee system are the so-called "advisory" and "regulatory" committees. The former committees, as their name suggests, exercise purely consultative functions in that the Commission is bound to solicit and presumably consider their advice before finally adopting a measure pursuant to delegation; neither approval by the advisory committee nor by the Council itself is necessary in order for the delegated legislation to become effective. In contrast "regulatory committees" resemble the management committees, but actually go further in restricting the Commission's freedom of action. Under this system, formal committee opposition to a Commission proposal is not needed in order for implementation to be delayed. The measure may not legally come into force until it receives a favorable opinion from the regulatory committee (or the Council itself) acting by a qualified majority vote.

Under the current comitology system, the available committee models mirror the advisory, management and regulatory committees, operating as a menu from which the Council on any given occasion may freely select a pre-established mode of committee review. A 2006 reform introduced a new variant—"the regulatory procedure with scrutiny"—which allows the Parliament to block implementing measures that exceed what the basic instrument contemplated or that fail to respect the principles of subsidiarity or proportionality. Comitology serves to regularize the committee system and limit political debate over details of the review procedure to be incorporated by the Council in any given delegation of power.

The Court of Justice considered the legality of the management committee system in the case of Einfuhr- und Vorratsstelle fur Getreide und Futtermittel v. Köster, Berodt & Co., Case 25/70, [1970] ECR 1161, in which it ruled:

> ... The function of the Management Committee is to ensure permanent consultation in order to guide the Commission in the exercise of the powers conferred on it by the Council and to enable the latter to substitute its own action for that of the Commission. The Management Committee does not therefore have the power to take a decision in place of the Commission or the Council. ...[The] machinery enables the Council to delegate to the Commission an implementing power of appreciable scope, subject to its power to take the decision itself if necessary.

[1970] ECR at 1171. Does the Court's reasoning also support the validity of the regulatory committee system? The Court subsequently rejected the claim that such a system "[has] the effect of paralyzing the Commission" or has any other feature that would "affect [its] validity." Tedeschi v. Denkavit, Case 5/77, [1977] ECR 1555, 1579–80.

The procedure of delegating implementing powers of considerable importance in specific fields to specialized committees has become increasingly controversial in recent years. On the one hand, the procedure raises fears that sensitive decisions will be taken in secrecy and/or by persons lacking a broad and open perspective. Moreover the committees are largely free from democratic review and accountability. On the other hand, some issues require expert technical competence, and the fact that committee members customarily come from all the Member States provides broader perspectives. In a White Paper on Governance in 2002, the Commission called for reforms to achieve greater transparency in committee operations, without impairing their effectiveness.

The Lisbon Treaty has introduced a new TFEU Article 290, which authorizes a "legislative act" to delegate to the Commission the power to adopt "non-legislative acts of general application to supplement or amend certain non-essential elements of the legislative act." Either Parliament or the Council may revoke the delegation, and the delegated act (whose title must contain the word "delegated") enters into force only if neither the Council nor the Parliament, within a period set in the authorizing legislative act, votes to prevent this. Although Article 290 makes no reference to the committee delegation procedure, it provides for substantial democratic accountability by bringing Parliament into the authorization process for most fields in which committees are used. This is because the Lisbon Treaty has also transferred from the Council to the Parliament and Council the power to legislate by the ordinary legislative procedure in most fields where the delegated committee procedure is employed, such as agriculture and fisheries.

NOTES AND QUESTIONS

1. Although the management committee procedure presents some difficulties in principle, its use has occasioned very little conflict. A committee

referral to the Council tends to occur no more than once or twice in an entire year, if at all, even though hundreds of measures may be adopted under the management committee system during that time period.

2. The Court has taken a dim view of delegations of power to the Member States. In the leading case, the Council delegated authority to the Commission to take the measures needed to stabilize the sugar market, and the Commission in turn delegated that authority to Italy insofar as certain problems peculiar to the Italian market were concerned. The Italian government used this authority to impose a levy on stockholders of sugar. Upon challenge, the Court upheld the delegation to the Commission, but invalidated the subdelegation to Italy. Rey Soda v. Cassa Conguaglio Zucchero, Case 23/75, [1975] ECR 1279.

3. For a political science view on comitology, see Egan & Wolf, Regulation and Comitology: The EC Committee System in Regulatory Perspective, 4 Colum. J. Eur. L. 499 (1998).

4. The committee systems evoke in some respects the US "legislative veto," whereby Congress reserves the right to repudiate a federal agency rule promulgated under a prior delegation of authority to the agency. The legislative veto has been found unconstitutional to the extent that it allows Congress (or a house of Congress) to circumvent the usual constitutional ground rules for the enactment of legislation. See Immigration and Naturalization Service v. Chadha, 462 U.S. 919, 103 S.Ct. 2764, 77 L.Ed.2d 317 (1983).

E. THE EUROPEAN PARLIAMENT

The EEC Treaty's Article 189 had described the Parliament's role as purely "advisory and supervisory." Although the Council was required by the Treaty to consult the Parliament in some fields, Parliament had no power to make binding amendments, much less cast a veto. Indeed, the EEC Treaty originally designated the Parliament as the "Assembly," but almost at once it began to call itself the Parliament, and the SEA formally changed its name in 1987.

Until 1979, Parliament was composed of delegations drawn from national parliaments. The EEC Treaty foresaw that its members would be directly elected once the necessary provisions on electoral procedure were adopted unanimously by the Council. However, no progress was made toward achieving this in the 1960s, partly due to opposition from President de Gaulle. Only after the Paris summit of the European Council in December 1974 was agreement reached enabling the Council to enact rules governing Parliament's direct election. After several years of preparation, the first direct election was held in June 1979, with successive elections in June every five years thereafter.

All of the continental Member States employ a system of proportional representation to elect their Members of the European Parliament (MEPs). Thus, the MEPs are elected as a group either nationally or in large districts, with the victorious political parties allocated MEPs in accordance with each one's proportion of the total vote. The UK traditionally followed the mode it uses to elect its own members of the UK Parliament, electing each MEP in a district by a plurality of the votes in that district. Only in 2002 did the UK accept a Council decision that required it to elect its MEPs according to the vote in several multi-MEP districts. We noted in Chapter 1 that the initial 1976 Council act enabled members of national parliament to serve simultaneously as MEPs with a dual mandate. Over time MEPs with a dual mandate became increasingly rare, and in 2002 the Council forbid dual mandates.

Quite naturally, Parliament's size increased with each successive enlargement. After the accession of Portugal and Spain in 1986, Parliament numbered 518 MEPs, which increased to 626 after the accession of Austria, Finland and Sweden in 1995. In an effort to keep the Parliament's size within limits of operational efficiency, the Treaty of Nice set a maximum of 732 MEPs. The Treaty of Lisbon's TEU Article 14 makes the maximum 750 seats, and prescribes that the European Council shall decide on Parliament's composition, acting unanimously and with Parliament's consent.

Unlike the US House of Representatives, the number of MEPs allocated to each State does not closely correspond to its population. Traditionally the largest States have been underrepresented and the smaller ones overrepresented. This continues under the Lisbon TEU, whose Article 14(2) specifically prescribes that every State shall have at least six MEPs, with the largest limited to 96. Thus Germany is permitted only 96 MEPs, although its population would entitle it to around 40 more if MEPs were allocated purely on the basis of population. France, Italy, Poland, Spain and the UK are also substantially underrepresented, while Cyprus, Estonia, Luxembourg and Malta are guaranteed 6 MEPs, and many other smaller States are overrepresented as well.

MEPs are elected in the various Member States on the basis of their national political party affiliation. They then form coalitions to constitute party groups in the Parliament. From 1979 to 1994, the Socialists were the largest party, but in 1999 and subsequent elections the conservative group, the European Peoples Party, has been the largest group, averaging around 200 MEPs, while the Socialists average around 180, and the Liberals and Greens have 40–60. The remainder represent smaller left or right wing factions or are independent.

The Parliament elects its own President for a two-and-a-half year term, once renewable, by tradition alternating representatives of the two larger parties. Thus in 2004–09, the Spanish Socialist Bornell and the German Christian Democrat Pottering served successively as President, while in 2009, the former Polish Prime Minister Jerzy Buzek was elected President. The Parliament also elects 14 vice-presidents who join the President in the Bureau, which organizes Parliament's meetings and appoints the committees and their chairs. Most of Parliament's work is performed within the committees, with plenary sessions frequently merely voting to approve committee reports. Especially prominent committees are those on Economic Affairs, Legal Affairs, External Relations and the Budget. Unlike the US Congress, the Parliament has a rather small staff of around 5000, not counting accredited parliamentary assistants whom MEPs may hire and fire on their own.

One might expect a parliament to adopt all legislation and do so on its own. However, even today the European Parliament shares legislative power with the Council, as we shall see in detail in Chapter 3. Indeed, in some sensitive fields, such as taxation and competition, Parliament still only exercises the consultative role that it possessed originally, giving only advisory opinions to the Council. The Lisbon Treaty did give the Parliament an equal voice with the Council in adopting legislation concerning agriculture and fisheries, fulfilling a longstanding Parliament desire, and in a number of other fields, such as most measures concerning the Area of Freedom and Security.

Moreover, as we previously observed, it is the Commission that exercises the power of initiative in proposing legislation, although by virtue of a Maastricht Treaty amendment carried over in the Lisbon Treaty's TFEU Article 225, Parliament does have the right to request the Commission to propose specific legislation. In a July 2000 Inter-institutional Agreement, the Commission agreed to respond promptly to any such parliamentary request and to give close attention to any amendments Parliament proposes during the legislative process. (An Inter-institutional Agreement has the status of soft law, and is unlikely to be violated).

Apart from its part in the legislative process, Parliament gained over time an important role in the Union's international relations. In this sphere, the Parliament has the right of assent regarding the accession of new Member States under Maastricht TEU Article 49 (now Lisbon TEU Article 49, which uses the word consent rather than assent). In an assent (or consent) vote, the Parliament may either approve or veto, acting by an absolute majority of all of its members. Parliament also has the right of assent with regard to association agreements for close relations with third countries as well as agreements that entail substantial budgetary commitments or create institutional structures. See EC Treaty Article 300 (now TFEU Article 218). For other international agreements, Parliament has only a right to be consulted under TFEU Article 218, and to be kept informed in the field of the CFSP. For further details, see Chapters 27–28.

Following amendments by the Maastricht and Amsterdam Treaties, Parliament has progressively acquired a significant role in the process of designating the Commission and its President. Parliament must approve the nomination of Commission President and the appointment of the Commission, voting on the entire proposed slate of Commissioners. Moreover, as noted above in the section on the Commission, Parliament has conducted confirmation hearings since 1995 on each nominee for Commissioner, reviewing his or her specific qualifications. In November 2004 Parliament's threat to reject the entire slate for the Commission if a nominee it considered unqualified were not replaced was taken seriously, and the nominee was indeed replaced.

Parliament still does not, however, have the relationship to the Commission that one might expect in a parliamentary system. Commissioners are not chosen from among the members of Parliament, nor even in consideration of relative political party strengths in Parliament. The Lisbon TEU Article 17(7) does state that the European Council should take into account the results of the June parliamentary elections when nominating the Commission President, presumably because in 2004 and 2009 the European Peoples Party, which became the leading group in Parliament, urged that the President should come from a national conservative party. This did occur, Commission President Barroso having previously served as Prime Minister of a moderately conservative government in Portugal.

The European Parliament serves as a general forum for discussing and debating topics of interest to the peoples of the Member States, and for supervising the activities of the other institutions. EC Treaty Article 200 (now TFEU Article 233), calls upon the Parliament to discuss in open session the annual general report submitted to it by the Commission. Moreover, although the Treaty does not so require, every January the Commission President presents Parliament with the Commission's proposed program for that year.

Parliament has other means of supervising the Commission. EC Treaty Article 197 (now TFEU Article 230) requires the Commission to reply orally or in writing to questions put to it by Parliament or its members (while allowing Commissioners to attend and be heard at parliamentary meetings). "Question time," modeled after British parliamentary practice, is meant to offer Parliament a regular opportunity to question the Commission or its members and to debate publicly the answers given, though its use is uneven. Both questions and answers are recorded in the Official Journal. Parliamentary questions, asked in plenary session or committee, currently run into the hundreds annually. Through this "gadfly" function, MEPs may incite the Commission to act or at least to air information. Several thousand written questions are also addressed to the Commission and its somewhat more formal answers are likewise recorded in the Official Journal.

Since the European Council meeting at Stuttgart in June 1983, the Council of Ministers has also voluntarily submitted to parliamentary questioning, answering hundreds of questions annually. Each Council President, at the outset of the six-month presidency, presents the Council's program for the term, and also presents conclusions at the term's end. The President of the European Council likewise has appeared before Parliament at the start of each rotating Presidency. The Lisbon TFEU Article 15(6) requires the new President of the European Council to report to Parliament after every European Council meeting.

The Parliament may assemble a "Committee of Inquiry" to address emerging problems at the EU level. Borrowing a device that some Member States had found useful for reviewing government misconduct, the drafters of the Maastricht Treaty introduced EC Treaty Article 193 (now TFEU Article 226), allowing one-quarter of the MEPs to require the constitution of a committee to investigate "alleged contraventions or maladministration" by the Commission. Among its most high-profile uses was Parliament's inquiry into the Commission's handling of the "mad cow disease" crisis in 1997.

Already mentioned is the procedure under EC Treaty Article 201 (now TFEU Article 234), whereby Parliament may compel the Commission to resign as a body by adopting a motion of censure by a two-thirds majority of votes cast representing a majority of the membership. In the wake of certain fundamental policy differences with the Commission, motions of censure have on several occasions been tabled, but none has ever carried. Parliament came close to censuring the Santer Commission in 1997 in the wake of the "mad cow disease" episode. Moreover, we have previously noted that the Santer Commission resigned in March 1999 to avoid censure by the Parliament, following a committee report delivered by three experts chosen by the Santer Commission which concluded that the entire Commission had failed in its duty to prevent maladministration by two Commissioners.

Parliament would like to hold all of its committee meetings and plenary sessions in Brussels, in close proximity to the Council and Commission. However, a 1965 decision of the Member State governments required Parliament to hold its plenary sessions in Strasbourg or Luxembourg, and to have its secretariat in Luxembourg. A 1983 Court of Justice judgment held that Parliament was bound by the decision, but a subsequent 1991 judgment did accept that Parliament could hold its committee meetings in Brussels. The European Council at Edinburgh in December 1992 confirmed the 1965 decision, and an Amsterdam Treaty Protocol gave it treaty force, replicated in a Lisbon Treaty Protocol. In consequence, the Parliament is obliged to travel regularly almost every month to Strasbourg to hold plenary sessions at a cost estimated to exceed 100 million Euros annually. The Parliament also has a large modern building in both Brussels and Strasbourg, each costing around a billion euros.

Recent years have witnessed efforts to enable national parliaments to become more involved in EU affairs. Already in 1993 a Declaration annexed to the Maastricht Treaty urged this, and an Amsterdam Treaty Protocol on the Role of National Parliaments required the Commission to make its legislative proposals available to the national parliaments for comment at least six weeks before the proposal was placed on the Council agenda for action. The Lisbon TEU's Article 18 on the role of national parliaments requires that they be notified in advance of draft legislative acts, applications for accession, and any proposals for Treaty amendments. The Lisbon Treaty's Protocol on Subsidiarity (doc. supp., doc. 4) elaborates on this by increasing the minimum period for comment by national parliaments on draft legislation to eight weeks, and by enabling any national parliament to provide the Commission, Council and Parliament with a "reasoned opinion" whenever it believes that a proposal would violate the subsidiarity principle.

NOTES AND QUESTIONS

1.   For many years, Parliament complained of the Community's "democratic deficit," largely because it had such limited legislative powers. As Parliament has gained an equal voice with the Council in adopting most legislation, and a definite share in the process of designating the Commission and its President and in approving international agreements, it complains less often in that regard. What further changes do you think might be made to enhance Parliament's powers?

2.   Unlike some national legislatures, the European Parliament has no power under the relevant Treaty articles to censure an individual Commissioner, but only the Commission as a whole. Why do you suppose such a power was omitted, and what do you suppose are the consequences of the omission? Is it obvious why Parliament has no right of censure with respect to the Council?

3.   In 1996, in the wake of ever more intensive lobbying of MEPs, the Parliament adopted regulations governing that activity. In addition to requiring that ministerial staff members, private business and business association interests register before contacting members of Parliament and adhere to a code of conduct, the regulations require MEPs to make public an account of their financial interests and financial support provided by third parties.

NOTE ON THE OMBUDSMAN

Another innovation of the Maastricht Treaty was the creation of the office of Ombudsman, based on the Scandinavian model. See Treaty Article 195 (now TFEU Article 228). The Ombudsman reviews complaints of maladministration brought to it by MEPs or by any EU national or resident. He or she may compel the cooperation of any institution (except the Court of Justice) in an investigation, and ultimately makes findings and recommendations, supported by reports to the Parliament. Each new Parliament names an Ombudsman for the parliamentary term of office.

The Treaty requires that the Ombudsman be completely independent, neither seeking nor taking instructions from any body, and engaging in no other occupation while in office. In 1994, Parliament imposed as an eligibility requirement that the Ombudsman have the qualifications for exercising the highest judicial office in his or her country and possess "the acknowledged competence and experience to undertake the duties" of the office.

Any EU citizen or person resident or established in an EU Member State may complain to the Ombudsman, either directly or through an MEP, about maladministration on the part of the EU's political institutions. Any such complaint must be filed within two years of the underlying act and must show that efforts were made to remedy the problem through direct contact with the institution or body responsible. The filing of an application with the Ombudsman does not affect the time limits for bringing administrative or judicial challenges against the measure in question. Even without having received a complaint, the Ombudsman is free to conduct all the inquiries he or she deems necessary to "clarify" a possible instance of maladministration. The institution complained about is entitled to be informed immediately of the complaint; on the other hand, it is required to cooperate fully in furnishing information and files (except where needs of secrecy dictate otherwise) and in making officials available to testify. The Ombudsman has no means of enforcing its investigative powers, though Parliament may make representations on the Ombudsman's behalf. All information supplied to the Ombudsman is deemed confidential. If, however, information relates to possible criminal violations, it must be reported to the competent authorities. The Ombudsman may only examine acts of the EU institutions, and not of national institutions, even when the latter act in implementation of EU law.

If the Ombudsman finds there to be a prima facie case of maladministration, he or she must inform the institution or body and give it a period of three months in which to respond. Eventually, the Ombudsman issues a report to the Parliament (and to the institution in question, with notice to the complainant) as appropriate. The Ombudsman may propose (though not impose) corrective action. On the Ombudsman's significance in the development of legal norms, see Bonnor, The European Ombudsman: A Novel Source of Soft Law in the European Union, 25 Eur. L. Rev. 39 (2000).

F. THE EU JUDICIARY

Initially, the Court of Justice (ECJ) was the Community's sole court. Due to the Court's increasingly heavy caseload, the SEA authorized the Council to create an auxiliary Court of First Justice (CFI), which commenced operations in 1989. Subsequently, in 2006, the Civil Service Tribunal was created to reduce in turn the caseload of the CFI. The Treaty of Lisbon does not modify this court structure, although it changes the CFI's name to the "General Court." Since the Court of Justice remains by far the Union's most important judicial body, we concentrate on it.

1. THE COURT OF JUSTICE

The EC Treaty Article 220 (now Lisbon TEU Article 19(1)), never amended, stated: "The Court of Justice shall ensure that in the interpretation and application of this Treaty the law is observed." It should be immediately underlined that the Court's fundamental role is not simply to interpret and apply the Treaty and any secondary rules, but rather to ensure that "the law is observed" in doing so. "The law" has a deeper jurisprudential sense, derived from continental traditions that distinguish underlying fundamental legal principles from their articulation in statutes. The Court of Justice has relied upon Article 220's reference to the general principles of law which must be observed to enable it to recognize basic rights (see ¶ 4 of the *IHG* judgment, and ¶ 7 of *Stauder v. Ulm*, pages 160 and 191, respectively), to achieve a balance of power among the institutions (see ¶ 23 of Parliament v. Council (Post–Chernobyl), page 130), and to delimit the scope of judicial review under EC Treaty Article 230 (see ¶ 8 of IBM v. Commission, page 131).

The Court of Justice has four principal forms of jurisdiction and several secondary ones, all left intact by the Treaty of Lisbon. Perhaps the most important is EC Treaty Article 234 (now TFEU Article 267), which enables the Court to provide "preliminary rulings," i.e., answers to questions referred by a national court or tribunal concerning the interpretation of the Treaties, or the validity and interpretation of secondary legislation, administrative decisions or other legally binding acts of any EU institution or agency. Over half of the Court's judgments consist of replies to such national court questions. Because the Court's responses bind the national court that referred the question, this procedure effectively makes national courts a crucial means of achieving the enforcement of EU law. Many of the Court's most important doctrines were first enunciated or elaborated in answers to questions referred by national courts. Chapter 9 describes in detail the reference procedure.

EC Treaty Article 226 (now TFEU Article 258), authorizes the Commission to sue Member States whenever they violate a Treaty provision (e.g., by maintaining barriers to interstate trade) or fail to implement properly secondary legislation. If the Court of Justice concludes that a State has violated the Treaty, the State is bound to comply with the judgment. Chapter 11 describes this procedure.

The Court's third important form of jurisdiction is its power under EC Treaty Article 230 (now TFEU Article 263) to review the legality of legislative acts and of other legally binding acts of the EU institutions and agencies. Chapter 5 examines in detail this judicial review, including its standing requirements. The Court's fourth important type of jurisdiction is its appellate review of CFI judgments on issues of law only (see infra). On occasion, the Court, pursuant to EC Treaty Article 300(6) (now TFEU Article 218 (11)), also examines proposed international agreements to verify that their provisions are compatible with the Treaties.

Through its judgments, the Court plays a vital role in securing an EU legal order that is both effective and respectful of the rule of law and of individual rights. The Court's doctrinal contributions include the fundamental concepts of the direct effect of certain Treaty articles and the primacy of the Treaty over all national rules, described in Chapter 7. More generally, it has sought through its jurisprudence to clarify the Member States' responsibilities under EU law. At the same time, the Court is continually defining the freedom of action of the EU institutions themselves. On all such issues, the Court's understanding of the relevant EU legal norms is considered authoritative. This is why Court of Justice judgments figure so prominently throughout the substantive as well as the institutional chapters of this book.

The Court consists of one Judge per Member State and a stated number of Advocates General (currently eight), whose role is described below. (During periods when the EU had an even number of Member States, an additional judge, selected from one of the larger States on a rotating basis, was provided for as an eventual tie-breaker.) The Treaty is silent on the manner of judicial selection, but in practice each Member State effectively names its own judge after consultation with the other Member States.

TFEU Article 255 innovates by requiring that a panel of seven experts review the qualifications of persons nominated to serve as judges before they are confirmed as such. The Council appoints this panel from former judges, members of national supreme courts, and prominent lawyers. The Parliament proposes one of the experts. Parliament has on occasion suggested that it should be involved in the selection of judges, or be able to hold confirmation hearings, but neither proposal has met with support by the Court or by the Member States.

Judges and Advocates General serve six-year terms and may be reappointed, which frequently happens. Every three years, approximately half are appointed to start their term. This system of partial replacement provides a valuable measure of continuity in operations. EC Treaty Article 223 (now TFEU Article 253) requires members of the Court to be qualified for appointment to their highest court or to be "jurisconsults of recognized competence." Complete judicial independence is of course required, and States may not instruct their Judge or Advocate General or remove them during their term of office. Nor may judges hold any political or administrative office while in office. In practice, most Judges and Advocates General have previously served on a national supreme or appellate court, or been a high government official or prominent academic, and many are named to national supreme courts or become professors after their court service in Luxembourg.

Judicial neutrality is aided by certain practices not mandated by the Treaty, but nevertheless uniformly respected and in some respects required by the Statute of the Court. (For the Treaty Protocol on the Statute of the Court of Justice, see doc. supp., doc. 5). Thus, deliberations are held in private and the Court's decisions are signed by all judges sitting and deliberating in the proceeding, whatever their personal viewpoints may have been. Even after the accession of the UK and Ireland, concurring or dissenting opinions remain unknown. The position of the individual judge on a specific issue or case is accordingly not made public. On the other hand, some judges have done important and extensive academic writing while on the Court, and thus had unusual personal influence both on and off the Court.

The judges, and not the Member States, select their President for three-year terms, immediately after a new slate of judges is appointed. The President is frequently re-elected. Besides presiding in deliberations, the President has other important functions: the initial assignment of cases, issuance of orders to deal with requests for interim relief in case of urgency, and general administration of the Court's staff and finances. The Court's current President is Vassilios Skouris, first elected in 2003. Some of his prominent predecessors include Robert Lecourt, President 1967–76, Lord McKenzie Stuart, 1984–88, Ole Due, 1988–94, and Gil–Carlos Rodriguez Iglesias, 1994–2003.

Until the 1980s, the Court decided all cases in plenary session, and continued to use plenaries for most cases until 1995. Its growing caseload has compelled the Court to make use of three- or five-judge chambers. Anticipating the Court's increase in numbers after the 2004 enlargement to its present 27 judges, the Nice Treaty enabled it to act more efficiently by authorizing a Grand Chamber of 11 judges and making plenary sessions rare (e.g., in disciplinary proceedings concerning a Commissioner). The Court itself decides when a Grand Chamber is needed for a relatively important case, sometimes at the request of a chamber that initially dealt with it, and must use the Grand Chamber whenever an institution or a Member State that is a party to a proceeding requests it. Currently the Grand Chamber decides around 15–20% of all cases.

The Court's use of chambers for most proceedings enables it to handle a docket several times the size of that of the US Supreme Court. The Court issues on average 400 judgments every year, double the average prior to 1995. The principal fields for judgments are agriculture, value added taxation, free movement of goods, workers and services, customs, social security, environmental protection, and recently free movement of capital.

By tradition, the Court deliberates and initially drafts its judgments in French, which makes some facility with that language a virtual prerequisite to membership on the Court. All judgments must be translated into all of the EU's other languages. The "official" language of a case (that is, the language used in the pleadings, documents and oral hearings) is in principle the language of the claimant, except that in preliminary references and enforcement actions against a Member State, it is the language of the referring court or the defendant State, respectively. In all cases for which French is not the official language, the pleadings and documents will be translated into that language. Simultaneous translation is used at the oral hearings, but never in the Court's deliberations, which are always strictly confidential. The Court's translation of its judgment and all procedural documents into all the official languages is estimated to add at least six months to the time between filing a case and the judgment, which on average is around 18–21 months.

A Treaty Protocol establishes the Statute of the Court of Justice, prescribing the status of Judges and Advocates General, the Court's organization and formations, and the basic elements of the Court's procedure, both written and oral. (See doc. 5 in the documents supplement.) Until 2009, the Council alone could amend the Statute, but TFEU Article 281 now empowers the Parliament and the Council to do so by the ordinary legislative procedure. The Court itself establishes its Rules of Procedure which, subject to the approval of the Council, supplements provisions of the Statute.

Whether a case is heard in plenary session or in chamber, it is assigned to one judge, the reporting judge (*juge rapporteur*), who bears special responsibility for preparing the case. The reporting judge studies the file and presents a preliminary report to the Court on the issues of fact and/or law that appear to be in dispute. This will determine whether a preparatory inquiry into the facts is required. Prior to the oral proceeding, the reporting judge drafts a statement of the facts and of the parties' submissions. Upon completion of the oral hearing and after receiving the opinion of the Advocate General (see below), the reporting judge prepares a draft judgment, which will serve as the point of departure for the Court's deliberations. Depending on the outcome and reasoning adopted, the reporting judge in the end may have to rewrite the opinion so as to reflect the prevailing view. It should be emphasized that the reporting judge's judgment represents the views of the Court or chamber, not necessarily his or her own views. The use of largely written procedures, the "inquisitorial" style, the reliance on a reporting judge and the Court's collective decision-making may be familiar to students of French administrative law, which has in many ways served as the Court's procedural model.

The Advocate General (or AG), provided for in EC Treaty Article 222 (now TFEU Article 252) plays an especially important role in the Court's work. It is the Advocate General's duty, "acting with complete impartiality and independence," to make, in open court, reasoned submissions on cases. In this, the Advocate General is highly reminiscent of the *commissaire du gouvernement* before the French Conseil d'Etat.

At present there are eight Advocates General, who have the same rank as judges and are subject to the same rules with respect to appointment, qualification, term of office and removal. Every three years, four Advocates General are replaced, although they are often renewed for another term. By decision of the Member States, each of the five largest Member States appoints one Advocate General, while the other three AGs are named by the other States in rotation. A Declaration annexed to the Lisbon Treaty foresees that the number of Advocates General may be increased to 11, if the Court should request this, with Poland joining the five larger States in always naming one. In view of the Court's steadily increasing caseload, it appears likely that this will occur. Cases are distributed among the Advocates General by the first Advocate General, who is appointed by his or her colleagues for one year.

The function of the Advocate General is to examine the case independently on the basis of the file and the reporting judge's report. After the close of the pleadings and hearings, the Advocate General presents a detailed description of the facts, an analysis of the case and an indication of how it should be decided, with reasoning. In keeping with the French administrative law model, the parties do not comment on the AG's opinion and the Court is in no respect bound to follow it. Traditionally, however, the opinion carries great weight in the Court's deliberations and more often than not the Court will reach the same conclusion, though perhaps on different grounds. The opinion of the Advocate General is published in the official reports of the Court's decisions along with the judgment of the Court, is cited by academic writers, and is likely to influence later evolution of the case law. See N. Fennelly, Reflections of an Irish Advocate General, 5 Irish J. Eur. L. 5 (1996).

The office of Advocate General in the EU law system has given rise to "constitutional" doubt as a result of case law of the European Court of Human Rights. In Vermeulen v. Belgium, Case 58/1994/505/587, that Court ruled, 15–4, that participation by the *procureur-général* of the Belgian Court of Cassation in the adjudication of a civil case infringes Article 6(1) of the European Human Rights Convention, due to the fact that the *procureur-général* takes part in the court's deliberations (albeit without a vote) and that the private litigant has no right of reply to the *procureur-général's* submissions. Note that, while private litigants in the EU courts have no right of reply to the opinion of the Advocate General, the latter does not participate in the Court's deliberations as such. Should this make a difference? The situations have been further distinguished on the ground that the Belgian *procureur-général* intervenes in litigation before the Court of Cassation in the name of the Belgian public authorities, whereas the Advocate General represents in all respects an integral part of the EU judiciary and is correspondingly independent. See T. Tridimas, The Advocate General, 34 Common Mkt. L. Rev. 1349,1380–82 (1997).

The Court of Justice took an early opportunity to distinguish its Advocates General from the Belgian *procureur-général*, holding in Emesa Sugar (Free Zone) NV v. Aruba, Case C–17/98, [2000] ECR I–675, that since the opinion of the Advocate General "does not form part of the proceedings between the parties, but rather opens the stage of deliberation by the Court [and] is not therefore an opinion addressed to the judges or to the parties which stems from an authority outside the Court," the parties to a preliminary reference proceeding have no right (as both parties in the *Emesa Sugar* case had asserted) to submit written observations on the Advocate General's opinion.

Each Judge and Advocate General has at least three legal secretaries or *référendaires*, who perform duties similar to those of a judicial clerk in the US, but usually have had experience in government, academia or the judiciary. Besides a Registrar, the Court also has an extensive library of EU law, international law, comparative law and of course also Member

State law. Among the staff is at least one person from each Member State equipped to assist the Judges and their legal secretaries in the research of national law.

The Court receives submissions and hears oral argument from a wide variety of counsel. Counsel represent parties from both the public and the private sector. Lawyers in the service of both the EU institutions and the Member States (and their subdivisions and agencies) regularly participate and appear. The Commission Legal Service customarily provides the Commission's views to the Court in all preliminary reference proceedings. Counsel speak different languages and are trained, and practice, in a range of different legal cultures. (US lawyers who are admitted to a Member State bar may appear before the Court.) With this in mind, the Court has produced a comprehensive Note for Guidance of Counsel, covering matters ranging from pleadings and the availability of interim relief to the use of language and lawyerly dress.

Judgments of the Court, together with the corresponding Advocate General opinion, are published in the official court reports, though they are available much sooner in advance sheet form and on the Internet. Until 1994, the Court of Justice also published contemporaneously a "Report of the Hearing." Now that Report is available only in the official language of the case.

The drafters of the Treaties chose not to provide the Court of Justice with enforcement machinery of its own. According to EC Treaty Articles 244 and 256 (now TFEU Articles 280 and 299), enforcement of a Court judgment "shall be governed by the rules of civil procedure in force in the State in the territory of which it is carried out." Enforcement may be suspended only by a decision of the Court itself, except to the extent that there is a complaint about the irregularity of the method of enforcement.

2. THE COURT OF FIRST INSTANCE (THE "GENERAL COURT")

By the late 1980s, the Court of Justice found itself increasingly burdened by a large docket of cases, some of relatively secondary importance, and subject to lengthy delays in their review. The Court repeatedly requested the Council to alleviate its burden by creating a new tribunal to assist it. After the SEA authorized this, the Council rapidly created in 1988 the Court of First Instance (CFI), basing it in Luxembourg in part of the Court's building. The CFI began operations in 1989. The Lisbon Treaty makes no change in the CFI structure or operations, except to rename it the "General Court."

Initially, the Council transferred to the CFI all appeals in administrative proceedings concerning civil servants employed by the EU institutions and agencies, a substantial burden on the Court. Subsequently, after the Maastricht Treaty authorized the Council to do so, the Court transferred to the CFI appeals from Commission decisions in enforcing competition rules and from Council and Commission regulations imposing anti-dumping and anti-subsidy duties (trade protection measures discussed in Chapter 29 infra), cases whose factual details and complex legal issues tended to necessitate long and complicated judicial proceedings. Although the Council now also has the power to transfer certain categories of preliminary references to the CFI, it has not done so, apparently because the Court believes that preliminary questions can raise such important issues that only the Court should answer them, and also to avoid long delays that appeals to the ECJ would add to an already lengthy procedure.

CFI judges are named by the Member State governments acting by common accord; they must possess the same qualifications as required for appointment to judicial office in their own States, and they must be completely independent. They serve for six-year terms, renewable, and half the judges are selected every three years. The CFI ordinarily sits in chambers of three or five judges. It may also sit as an eleven-judge Grand Chamber, which it did, for example, to review Microsoft's appeal from a Commission decision that its marketing policies violated competition rules. (See page 913 infra.)

In 1999, the Council amended the decision establishing the CFI so as to permit that court to sit as a single judge, and the CFI amended its rules of procedure accordingly. In certain categories of actions, principally staff cases and tort actions against the Union, a single reporting judge may hear and decide the case provided it does not raise difficult questions of law or fact, is not especially important, and does not present other special circumstances. In 1999, a single CFI Judge issued the first judgment, but further single judge cases are not frequent, partly because of the subsequent transfer of staff cases to a new tribunal (see below).

The CFI judges elect a President for a three-year renewable term from among their members. As in the Court of Justice, the CFI President initially assigns cases to chambers, decides upon interlocutory relief applications, and handles staff and other administrative matters. The CFI's current president is Marc Jaeger. The CFI has no separately designated Advocates General. In agreement with the Court of Justice and with the approval of the Council, the CFI has established its own rules of procedure.

The CFI's decisions are made "subject to a right of appeal to the Court of Justice on points of law only," so as to enable the Court of Justice to ensure the correct interpretation of Union law. Article 51 of the Statute of the Court of Justice is still more explicit: appeals from the Court of First Instance are limited to issues of law, and more particularly to claims that the CFI lacked competence, committed a procedural violation or infringed a rule of EU law. In practice, appeals have become fairly frequent. They comprise about 15% of the Court's docket and represent about 25% of all CFI judgments.

The way the Statute formulates the scope of review sounds deceptively simple. Does a party raise an issue of law, for these purposes, when it claims that the CFI made an improper assessment of the evidence? When it claims that the CFI made an improper legal characterization of the facts?

The answer to the first of these questions is quite clear. In D v. Commission, Case C–89/95P, [1996] ECR I–53, the Court held that:

13   [A]n appeal may rely only on grounds relating to the infringement of rules of law, to the exclusion of any appraisal of the facts, and is therefore admissible only in so far as it is claimed that the decision of the Court of First Instance is incompatible with the rules of law the application of which it had to ensure.

14   The Court of Justice is no more competent, in principle, to examine the evidence accepted by the Court of First Instance in support of those facts than it is to find the facts themselves. In so far as the evidence was duly obtained and the rules and general principles of law relating to the burden of proof were observed, as well as the procedural rules in relation to the taking of evidence, it is for the Court of First Instance alone to assess the value which should be attached to the items of evidence produced to it.

15   Since the Court has no jurisdiction to review the assessment of the Court of First Instance, the appellant's arguments on that aspect ... must be rejected as manifestly inadmissible.

The answer to the second question is less clear. On the one hand, the Court has reiterated that "[once] the CFI has established or assessed the facts, the Court of Justice has jurisdiction ... to review the legal characterization of those facts by the Court of First Instance and the legal conclusions it has drawn from them." San Marco Impex Italiana Srl, Case C–19/95P, [1996] ECR I–4435 (¶ 39). But, as to the standard by which the Court of Justice conducts this review, the Court seems prepared, on most issues of importance, to accept the CFI's conclusions unless it finds them to be "manifestly erroneous." What is the difference between the CFI's "appraisal" of the facts (as to which there is in principle no review by the Court of Justice) and its "legal characterization of the facts" (as to which such review, albeit under a relaxed standard, is still available)? For a review of the Court's record as a court of appeals, see Sonelli, Appeals on Points of Law in the Community System: A Review, 35 Comm. Mkt. L. Rev. 871 (1998).

Occasionally a case raises an issue of the legality, not of an act of the political institutions, but of an act of the Court of First Instance itself. For a good example, see Ismeri Europa Srl v. Court of Auditors, Case C–315/99, [2001] ECR I–5281. The Court of First Instance had dismissed a management company's claim for damages against the Court of Auditors for losses resulting from criticism of it contained in a report made public by the Court of Auditors. On appeal, the company claimed that the CFI erred in refusing to hear certain witnesses, to which the Court of Justice replied:

19   [T]he Court of First Instance is the sole judge of any need for the information available to it concerning the cases before it to be supplemented. Whether or not the evidence before it is convincing is a matter to be appraised by it alone and is not subject to review by the Court of Justice on appeal, except where the clear sense of that evidence has been distorted or the substantive inaccuracy of the Court of First Instance's findings is apparent from the documents in the case-file.

20   No matter has been adverted to in the course of this appeal to lead the Court to believe that anything of that kind occurred in the present case.

While disappointed parties before the Court of First Instance have an appeal as of right to the Court of Justice, Article 119 of the ECJ's Rules of Procedure allow the Court to dismiss the appeal, even prior to opening the oral procedure, where the appeal is "clearly inadmissible or clearly unfounded." On appeal, the appellant will not be permitted to introduce for the first time "new pleas in law" or, evidently, new legal arguments.

If an appeal succeeds, the Court of Justice quashes the decision; it may then either give final judgment itself or remand the case to the CFI for judgment. The appeal does not as a general rule have suspensive effect, but the Court of Justice may in a given case suspend the effectiveness of a Court of First Instance judgment pending appeal (or prescribe other interim measures), if the circumstances so require.

In the last decade, the CFI has been burdened with a substantial overload, not only in volume but also in the complexity of issues in many competition and trade cases. Moreover, in the late 1990s, the CFI began to receive numerous appeals from the Trademark Office in Alicante concerning the issuance, rejection or revocation of EU trademarks (see Chapter 19D), which currently constitute around 25% of the CFI's docket.

Reacting to this problem, the Nice Treaty added to the EC Treaty a new Article 225a (now TFEU Article 257), empowering the Council to create, and "attach" to the CFI, specialized "judicial panels." The Council, acting unanimously, would then appoint the panel judges, who must meet the usual standards of qualification to serve on a national court and be independent. Decisions by a judicial panel could be appealed to the CFI on points of law.

In November 2004, the Council adopted Decision 2004/752, O.J. L 2004 333/7 (Nov. 2, 2004), to create the European Civil Service Tribunal. The new Tribunal is composed of seven judges, each serving for a six-year term, elected by the Council from a slate recommended by an independent advisory committee of lawyers. The Tribunal has its own President, initially Paul Mahoney. The Tribunal has been granted jurisdiction over all disputes between EU bodies and their employees. Appeals to the Court of First Instance are authorized essentially only for errors of law under conditions analogous to those for the present appeal procedure from the CFI to the Court of Justice.

The Civil Service Tribunal commenced operations in fall 2006 and already has a large caseload. Its judgments are only being issued in French. The efficiency of the General Court will certainly be promoted with the removal of staff cases from its workload. Moreover, the Council is currently considering the creation of a specialized tribunal for trademark cases.

NOTES AND QUESTIONS

1. Currently about half of the Court of Justice's docket consists of preliminary references from Member State courts, seeking interpretations of EU law as needed for disposing of those cases. The Council has the power to shift categories of references to the General Court (e.g., those concerning competition or customs rules), but has not acted, apparently because the Court of Justice is reluctant to transfer any references. One of the Court's concerns appears to be that references often involve issues other than those raised concerning a specified field and should therefore be handled only by the Court of Justice. What is your reaction?

2. A more radical solution would have been to create below the Court of Justice a system of regional EU courts, but the idea has gotten no traction and is largely abandoned. On these and other strategies, see J.–P. Jacqué & J. Weiler, On the Road to European Union—A New Judicial Architecture: An Agenda for the Intergovernmental Conference, 27 Common Mkt. L. Rev. 185 (1990); Editorial, The Future Development of the Community's Judicial System, 28 Common Mkt. L. Rev. 5 (1991).

3. For an insider's account of the workings of the Court of Justice, see David Edward, How the Court of Justice Works, 20 Eur. L. Rev. 539 (1995).

4. Based simply on this chapter's institutional description of the EU, how would you describe the separation of powers among its institutions? See generally K. Lenaerts, Some Reflections on the Separation of Powers in the European Community, 28 Common Mkt. L. Rev. 11 (1991).

3. THE COURT'S ROLE IN SPECIAL UNION SPHERES

Until 1987, the jurisdiction of the Court of Justice was co-extensive with the fields of action of the Treaties. When the SEA formally added cooperation in foreign policy, and the Treaty of Maastricht located this in the second pillar (as Cooperation in Foreign and Security Policy), the Court of Justice was excluded from any review of Council acts in that sphere. The Lisbon TEU retains the CFSP with its decidedly intergovernmental flavor, and TFEU Article 275 accordingly continues to exclude the Court from any review of European Council or Council acts in that sphere, except for Council decisions adopting "restrictive measures against natural or legal persons" (as in the terrorist asset sanction cases discussed in Chapter 27).

When the Maastricht Treaty inaugurated the third pillar, Cooperation in Justice and Home Affairs, the Court was likewise excluded from any jurisdiction. After the Treaty of Amsterdam transferred to the Community most of the JHA fields (e.g., visas, asylum, illegal immigration, residence rights of third state nationals, as well as civil justice), the Court acquired partial jurisdiction over any EU legislation or other Council acts. Pursuant to EC Treaty Article 68, the preliminary reference procedure of Article 234 was limited to questions raised by national supreme courts or other courts "against whose decisions there is no judicial remedy," and the Court could not rule on any measure or decision concerning "the maintenance of law and order and the safeguarding of internal security." TFEU Article 276 retains this reservation. The Lisbon Treaty transferred Police and Judicial Cooperation in Criminal Matters to the TFEU, ending its intergovernmental character, and accordingly making the Court's usual jurisdiction applicable, except that TFEU Article 276 bars Court review of the "validity or proportionality" of State police operations or State action to maintain law and order.

The Court of Justice has exercised the power to decide whether a Council act or decision should have been taken as an EU measure rather than under CFSP or the former JHA. Thus, in Commission v. Council (Airport transit arrangements), Case C–170/96, [1998] ECR I–2763, the Court ruled that a "joint action" that the Council had adopted pursuant to the then JHA provisions was appropriate, and could not have been adopted as a measure under the EC Treaty provision cited by the Commission.

The Treaty of Nice gave the Court a specific role in the Maastricht TEU's Article 46 which contemplates the sanctioning of States for violations of fundamental human rights. The Court has jurisdiction to review and enforce only "the purely procedural stipulations" of TEU Article 7, which authorizes the Council to determine whether there exists a clear risk of a serious breach of fundamental rights by a State, and, if so, to penalize the State by suspending its voting rights in the Council. TFEU Article 269 preserves this limited jurisdiction.

G. OTHER EU INSTITUTIONS AND BODIES

By far the most important of EU bodies other than the political institutions and the Court is the European Central Bank, created in 1998 in Frankfurt, which presently controls the monetary policy of a majority of Member States. Chapter 31 describes in detail its structures, role and operations. The Lisbon TEU adds the Bank to the list of Union institutions.

The Maastricht Treaty added the Court of Auditors, located in Luxembourg, to the list of Union institutions and prescribed its role as verifying all revenue and expenditure of the other institutions, agencies and bodies, while providing an audit report to the Parliament and Council. EC Treaty Articles 246–48 (now TFEU Articles 285–87) describe this Court's structure and functions.

The Economic and Social Committee (ECOSOC), located in Brussels, commenced at the start of the EU as a vehicle to provide advice during the drafting of legislation and policies from a broad range of social and economic perspectives. EC Treaty Articles 257–61 (now TFEU Articles 301–04) describe its structure and advisory role. Each Member State is allocated a number of ECOSOC members. After consulting the Commission, the Council appoints the members for four-year terms, renewable. (TFEU Article 302 extends the term to five years.) ECOSOC's advice is often quite influential in the preparation of internal market and agricultural sector measures.

The European Investment Bank (EIB), located in Luxembourg, was also created at the outset. Although probably of greater importance in the 1960s–70s, the EIB still provides useful support by financing infrastructure and other projects in less-developed regions (currently emphasizing central and eastern European projects) and "projects of common interest to several Member States" of dimensions that make it difficult for national institutions to finance them. The EIB provided a record 79 billion Euros in financing for projects in 2009. The EIB is described in EC Treaty Articles 266–67 (now TFEU Articles 308–09).

The Maastricht Treaty created a new institution, the Committee of the Regions, described in EC Treaty Articles 263–65, now TFEU Articles 305–07. Mirroring in some measure the Economic and Social Committee, this body performs essentially advisory functions, including the issuance of non-binding opinions to the Council, Commission and Parliament. Each Member State has a weighted number of seats on the Committee. The Committee of the Regions is composed of representatives of regional and local entities within the Member States, who cannot simultaneously serve in the European Parliament. Committee members are appointed by the Council for four-year renewable terms (extended to five years by the TFEU). Although enjoined to be independent and to act in accordance with the general EU interest, Committee members almost certainly function in part as representatives of their regions and thus promote more or less particular interests. The Lisbon Treaty sets its membership at no more than 350.

H. THE EU AGENCIES

Since the 1990s, the Community has created a number of European agencies to carry out particular tasks in more or less specialized policy fields, usually, but not always, in connection with the internal market. An EU agency is a public authority set up pursuant to secondary legislation, separate from the EU institutions proper and enjoying legal personality.

There are currently no fewer than nineteen agencies (with progressively more being established), based at locations assigned to them by the European Council as follows:

Community Fisheries Control Agency (Vigo)

Community Plant Variety Office (Angers)

European Agency for the Evaluation of Medicinal Products (London)

European Agency for Health and Safety at Work (Bilbao)

European Agency for Reconstruction (Thessaloniki)

European Aviation Safety Agency (Cologne)

European Center for Development of Vocational Training (Thessaloniki)

European Center for Disease Prevention and Control (Solna)

European Chemicals Agency (Helsinki)

European Environment Agency (Copenhagen)

European Food Safety Agency (Parma)

European Foundation for the Improvement of Living and Working Conditions (Dublin)

European Fundamental Rights Agency (Vienna)

European Maritime Safety Agency (Lisbon)

European Medicines Agency (London)

European Monitoring Centre for Drugs and Drug Addiction (Lisbon)

European Railway Agency (Valenciennes)

European Training Foundation (Turin)

Office for Harmonization in the Internal Market (Trademark and Designs) (Alicante)

While each agency has its own structure and functions, generally speaking they perform information gathering, information processing, research, coordination, and general administrative tasks in aid of the institutions, most notably the Commission. The European Environment Agency (EEA) may be taken as an example. The EEA is a monitoring center funded by the general Community budget, which began its operations in 1995. Its mission is to "collect and disseminate objective, reliable and comparable information at the European level enabling EU Member States to take measures to protect the environment, to assess the results of such measures and to ensure that the public is properly informed about the state of the environment and offer technical support."

The EEA is governed by a management board consisting of one representative per Member State, two Commission representatives, two representatives of the European Parliament and, in addition, one representative from each of the non-EU countries that participates in the work of the agency. On a proposal by the Commission, the board elects an Executive Director who serves for a renewable five-year term of office and is accountable to the board. The Director is assisted by a scientific committee which delivers opinions and publishes reports. The management board has broad discretion in further organizing the EEA, adopts the agency's annual and multi-annual work programs, and transmits the EEA's annual report to the Commission, Council and Parliament.

Two of the most significant agencies are the Office for Harmonization in the Internal Market (OHIM), which issues and administers Community Trademarks and Trade Designs, described in Chapter 19D, and the European Agency for the Evaluation of Medicinal Products, which reviews and authorizes pharmaceutical products on a Community-wide basis. Chapter 14E provides further information about this agency.

Largely due to their institutional separation from the Council, Commission and Parliament, as well as from the Member States, these agencies are commonly characterized as "independent." Unlike their US namesakes, however, they do not as a rule possess general regulatory power. Nevertheless, an important and controversial issue is the extent to which regulatory powers may eventually be delegated to them to the possible detriment of the Commission. See K. Lenaerts, Regulating the Regulatory Process: "Delegation of Powers" in the European Community, 18 Eur. L. Rev. 23 (1993); Editorial, 33 Common Mkt. L. Rev. 623 (1996).

Further Reading

N. Bacon & T. Kennedy, The Court of Justice of the European Communities (5th ed. Sweet & Maxwell 2000)

R. Corbett, F. Jacobs & M. Shackleton, The European Parliament (6th ed. Harper 2005)

P. Craig, EU Administrative Law (Oxford U. P. 2006)

P. Kapteyn, et. al., eds., The Law of the European Union and the European Communities (4th ed. 2008)

K. Lenaerts & P. Van Nuffel, Constitutional Law of the European Union (2d ed. Sweet and Maxwell 2005)

H. Wallace, W. Wallace & M. Pollock, eds. Policy–Making in the European Union (Oxford U. P. 2005)

M. Westlake & D. Galloway, The Council of the European Union (3rd ed. Harper 2004)

CHAPTER 3

LEGISLATION, THE LEGISLATIVE PROCESS, AND THE BUDGET

■ ■ ■

As we have seen, the political institutions of the Union have the power to adopt policies and take actions across an extraordinarily wide field. Not all of that policy and action takes the form of legally binding measures, but a great deal does. Foreseeing that, the Treaty drafters provided that the institutions might adopt certain species of "legal acts" and do so through a number of different pre-established "legislative procedures." As we have already seen, originally only the Council could adopt legislation, but over time the Parliament has acquired a large share of the legislative process, equal to the Council in most fields.

This chapter explores the nature of these acts and procedures not only as abstract notions, but also by way of concrete example. The chapter closes with a look at the budgetary system—the system by which the European institutions can "afford" their activities, legislative and non-legislative alike.

A. FORMS OF UNION ACTION

1. TYPES OF LEGAL ACTS

The EC Treaty defined the kinds of legal acts that the political institutions of the Community could take and the legal effects those acts would have. Article 249 stated that the Council, the Parliament acting jointly with the Council, and the Commission may, "in accordance with the provisions of this Treaty," issue regulations, directives, decisions, recommendations or opinions. The article went on to describe these instruments as follows:

> A regulation shall have general application. It shall be binding in its entirety and directly applicable in all Member States.

> A directive shall be binding, as to the result to be achieved, upon each Member State to which it is addressed, but shall leave to the national authorities the choice of form and methods.

A decision shall be binding in its entirety upon those to whom it is addressed.

Recommendations and opinions shall have no binding force.

TFEU Article 288 does not alter this basic structure of legally binding legislation and other acts. EC Treaty Article 253 (now TFEU Article 296) requires that regulations, directives and decisions state the reasons on which they are based and refer to whatever proposal or opinion the Treaty may have required the institutions to obtain before adopting them.

The terms "regulation" and "decision" are not in principle difficult to grasp. A regulation is a general rule of conduct applicable to all persons falling within its scope, like a statute or law in the US, while a decision relates only to the one or more persons specifically addressed in it. There is less certainty over precisely what the descriptions "binding" and "directly applicable" were meant to convey. At a minimum, however, a "binding" norm (in contrast to a mere recommendation or opinion) may be regarded as one that has the force of law, and a "directly applicable" norm as one that, once enacted at the EU level, becomes an effective part of the national legal order as well, even while retaining their character as EU law norms.

A directive is harder to understand, because there is no similar form of legal instrument either in the US or in any EU Member State. The initial Treaty drafters devised this kind of instrument as a way of giving States some discretion in deciding how to bring EU law norms into their domestic legal systems. A directive is stated to be "binding" only as to result, but not as to "the choice of form and methods." Directives are usually addressed to all the Member States, which must then take the legislative and/or administrative action needed to implement the rules set out in them. Although a directive does not have to be very detailed, in practice directives are often quite specific as to how they are to be implemented. The language of EC Treaty Article 249 (now TFEU Article 288) implies that directives, though "binding" on Member States, may not be "directly applicable." (This matter is taken up in Chapter 7A).

Legally binding acts—regulations, directives, and decisions, as well as international agreements—may be taken either by the Council alone, by the Council together with the Parliament, or by the Commission. Which body, or bodies, is competent to adopt a measure in any given circumstance, and what form that action must take, can only be determined by reference to the specific article of the Treaty involved. This is yet another way of underscoring the point that the constitutive treaties confer only limited decisional powers upon the institutions. These powers are limited not only because the relevant Treaty articles designate the institution that may act in any given case and the instruments it may employ in doing so, but also because—as this and later chapters will show—they prescribe, sometimes with remarkable specificity, various other procedural requirements as well as substantive conditions for action. This may have implications for judicial review, and in particular for deciding who may bring a legal challenge and indeed whether a legal challenge may be brought at all (questions largely taken up in Chapter 5A on judicial review).

One of the most important legal principles set out in the Treaty of Lisbon is the "principle of conferral" in TEU Article 5, which means that the Union "shall only act within the limits of the competences conferred upon it" by the Treaty. Chapter 4A is devoted to this principle.

EC Treaty Article 254 (now TFEU Article 297) provides that regulations, directives and decisions that are adopted under the codecision procedure, now renamed as the "ordinary legislative procedure," described in section C infra, are to be signed by the Presidents of the Parliament and Council and published in the *Official Journal* of the European Union, entering into force on the date they specify (or, absent a date, twenty days following their publication). Other regulations of the Council and Commission, as well as directives issued by them to all the Member States, are likewise required to be published in the *Official Journal*, with the same rules on entry into force. Other directives and decisions take effect upon notification to the persons addressed.

2. THE REQUIREMENT OF REASONS

EC Treaty Article 253 required that regulations, directives and decisions state the "reasons" on which they are based. TFEU Article 296 reiterates this obligation. The Court of Justice has held many times that the required statement must disclose in a clear and unequivocal fashion the reasoning that the institution or institutions followed, so that the persons concerned are aware of the reasons for the measure and may defend their rights, and so that the Court may exercise its supervisory jurisdiction. The following 1963 judgment demonstrates this. (Note that the very early ECJ opinions lack paragraph numbers.)

GERMANY v. COMMISSION

(Brennwein)
Case 24/62, [1963] ECR 63.

[The introduction of the common external tariff caused a sudden and significant increase in the import duties on the wine used to produce Brennwein (a low-priced wine-based alcoholic drink). The government of Germany, where Brennwein was chiefly produced, asked the Commission for approval to import 450,000 hectoliters of the wine at a lower rate of duty. The Commission allowed only 100,000 hectoliters to be imported at that rate, stating:

> On the basis of the existing information it has been possible to ascertain that the production of the wines in question within the Community is amply sufficient. The grant of a tariff quota of the volume requested might therefore lead to serious disturbances of the market in the products in question.

The Commission never specified the "existing information" on which it relied. Germany sued to have the decision set aside, in part on account of the insufficiency of the Commission's statement of reasons. The Court vindicated Germany's contentions, holding initially that although the Commission had discretion in setting the tariff quota in the context of working towards a Community common customs tariff, nonetheless it must provide a "statement of reasons" to justify its Decision in Germany's application.]

> In imposing upon the Commission the obligation to state reasons for its decisions, [EC Treaty Article 253, now TFEU Article 296] is not taking mere formal considerations into account but seeks to give an opportunity to the parties of defending their rights, to the Court of exercising its supervisory functions and to Member States and to all interested nationals of ascertaining the circumstances in which the Commission has applied the Treaty. To attain these objectives, it is sufficient for the Decision to set out, in a concise but clear and relevant manner, the principal issues of law and of fact upon which it is based and which are necessary in order that the reasoning which has led the Commission to its Decision may be understood. Apart from general considerations, which apply without distinction to other cases, or which are confined to repeating the wording of the Treaty, the Commission has been content to rely upon "the information collected", without specifying any of it, in order to reach a conclusion "that the production of the wines in question is amply sufficient".

> This elliptical reasoning is all the more objectionable because the Commission gave no indication, as it did belatedly before the Court, of the evolution and size of the surpluses, but only repeated, without expanding the reasons for it, the same statement "that there was no indication that the existing market situation within the Community did not allow these branches of the industry in the German Federal Republic a supply which is adequate in quantity and in quality".

* * *

> It follows from these factors that the inadequacy, the vagueness and the inconsistency of the statement of reasons for the Decision, both in respect of the refusal of the quota requested and of the concession of the quota granted, do not satisfy the requirements of Article [253].

> Those parts of the Decision which have been submitted to the Court must therefore be annulled.

NOTES AND QUESTIONS

1. In Groupement des Fabricants de Papiers Peints de Belgique v. Commission, Case 73/74, [1975] ECR 1491, the Commission imposed fines on several companies for price-fixing in the wholesale wallpaper market. The Court annulled the decision for insufficient reasoning because the Commission, in finding that the companies' conduct affected trade between Member

States, had significantly extended the principles of earlier decisions and thus should have given a more detailed statement of the grounds for its finding. The Court allowed that rulings fitting into "a well-established line of decisions" may be reasoned in a summary manner, "for example by a reference to those decisions." [1975] ECR at 1514. Had the decision merely followed established policy, reliance on previous decisions evidently would have passed muster.

2. Note that EC Treaty Article 253 (now TFEU Article 296) applies to regulations and directives as well as decisions. Is this surprising? The requirement of reasons accounts for the practice of introducing regulations and directives with a long series of recitals in the preamble to the text. The recitals often contain valuable indications of the motive for legislative act, its scope and its relation to other EU rules.

NOTE ON THE INTERPRETATION OF LEGISLATION

On many occasions, the Court of Justice has emphasized that the Treaties and EU legislation merit a broad and purposive interpretation, by which is meant an interpretation that will generously serve the Treaty's or legislation's underlying objectives. This mode of interpretation is not unlike the so-called teleological interpretation that continental courts commonly profess to give to their codes and to certain of their more basic statutes. At the same time, the Court has said that legislation should be interpreted, whenever possible, so as to conform to the Treaty and avoid illegality. "It is settled law that where the wording of secondary Community law is open to more than one interpretation, preference should be given to the interpretation which renders the provision consistent with the Treaty rather than the interpretation which leads to its being incompatible with the Treaty." Spain v. Commission (Motor vehicle aid), Case C–135/93, [1995] ECR I–1651 (¶ 37).

The Court has suggested that national authorities are under a similar obligation to give EU legislation a broad and purposive construction, and thus to extend that construction to national legislation enacted to implement EU law. Although this was thought at one time to create special difficulties for the English judiciary, accustomed to narrower and more circumscribed methods of statutory construction, most English judges (including members of the House of Lords) now have generally embraced the methodology for these purposes. See Litster v. Forth Dry Dock & Engineering Co. Ltd., [1990] 1 A.C. 546, [1989] 2 WLR 634, [1989] 1 All ER 1134, [1989] 2 CMLR 194, 201 (H.L., March 16, 1989) (per Lord Templeman). Lord Oliver, writing in the *Litster* case, was explicit:

> [If] legislation enacted to give effect to the United Kingdom's obligations under the EEC Treaty ... can reasonably be construed so as to conform with those obligations obligations—which are to be ascertained not only from the wording of the relevant directive but from the interpretation placed upon it by the European Court of Justice at Luxembourg—such a purposive construction will be applied even

though, perhaps, it may involve some departure from the strict and literal application of the words the legislature has elected to use.

[1989] 2 CMLR at 202–03. For earlier and somewhat different views from the UK courts, see Chapter 8G infra.

Indeed, EU legislation, once adopted, invariably requires interpretation. See Chapter 14C for further discussion of how the Court interprets legislation. A principal purpose of the preliminary reference mechanism is precisely to enable the Court of Justice to guide national courts in the proper interpretation of the EU law that is potentially applicable in cases before them. A good example of an interpretive question is whether a harmonization measure should be read as merely establishing *minimum* EU standards, thus enabling Member States to impose more exacting standards, or rather *uniform* standards that the Member States may not then vary, even in the direction of greater stringency. (This particular question will be further addressed in Chapter 14D.)

B. THE LEGISLATIVE PROCESS

One of the institutional features of the EU that has been modified most significantly over time is the legislative process. Under the EEC Treaty, the legislative process was originally quite simple. Certain legislative acts could only be adopted by the Council after receiving a non-binding opinion ("consultation") of the Parliament, while others could be adopted without any parliamentary input at all. Some specific Treaty articles required the Council to consult Parliament before adopting legislation or taking a formal decision, e.g., in agriculture, competition or the right of establishment. The Council was not obligated to consult Parliament in many fields, although it occasionally did so voluntarily.

As we shall see, in section C, the SEA's creation of the cooperation procedure, and even more the Maastricht Treaty's introduction of the codecision procedure in many fields of action, resulted in Parliament's obtaining an equal voice with the Council in most fields of EU legislation. Nonetheless the consultation procedure continued to apply in several important fields, such as agriculture, competition, state aids, harmonization of internal taxation, and some aspects of monetary union. Originally Parliament was not even consulted in action taken in the Maastricht Treaty's CFSP and JHA "pillars," but when most sectors of JHA were transferred to the Community sphere by the Amsterdam Treaty, Parliament gained the right to be consulted, or even became fully involved through codecision.

The Treaty of Lisbon has made the "ordinary legislative procedure" (the new name for codecision) applicable in several fields where consultation was previously used, notably in agriculture and fisheries. The consultation procedure, renamed by TFEU Article 89(2) as a "special legislative procedure," survives in several important fields, such as competition law, state aids, harmonization of internal taxation and monetary union. The

Lisbon TEU provisions on the CFSP still only require Parliament to be periodically informed, but not consulted.

Under the consultation procedure, the Commission initially delivers to the Council a proposal, which is published in the Official Journal. The proposal is sent for review to Parliament, which considers it first at the committee level, and then expresses its opinion by a vote in plenary session. Parliament often suggests amendments, which will be weighed seriously by the Commission. Indeed, the Commission commonly publishes a revised proposal in the Official Journal incorporating various parliamentary amendments. (Some proposals must also be reviewed at this stage by the Economic and Social Committee, and its suggestions too may be incorporated in the Commission revision.) This legislative phase, commonly called the "first reading," may take a year or two. Since the initial and all revised proposals are made public, private interests have substantial opportunities during this period to lobby both the Commission and Parliament.

Even while Parliament is being consulted, the Council begins taking up the Commission proposal in its own "first reading." The proposal is first dealt with by a Council working group, in contact with Member State experts, and then by COREPER. If COREPER approves a text unanimously, the Council often adopts it without further debate. If COREPER cannot reach an agreement, the Council will try to do so.

Council review in its "first reading," from initial working group to final adoption, usually takes months or even years, and lobbyists will once again be active, seeking to influence both the Member States and Council staff. (They will already have lobbied the Commission.) Of course, sometimes the Council cannot reach an agreement and draft proposals are then effectively tabled for years, and occasionally formally rejected. What is more, the Commission, as we shall see below, has the right to amend its proposal any time prior to adoption. If such an amendment occurs, it may occasion further delay.

If the Council votes, it does so either unanimously or by qualified majority, depending on the particular Treaty article under which the measure is being adopted. However, EC Treaty Article 250 (now TFEU Article 293) contains the important general rule that if the Council wishes to adopt a measure whose terms deviate from the terms of the Commission's proposed text as it then stands (perhaps revised to incorporate some amendments requested by the Parliament), then it must do so by unanimous vote, even if action on the subject matter ordinarily requires only a qualified majority vote in the Council. This rule has no effect if the Council must act unanimously anyway, but if the Treaty authorizes the Council to act by a qualified majority vote, and any Member State favors the Commission proposal, the Council is unable to amend it. Moreover, the same Treaty article gives the Commission the continuing prerogative power to amend its legislative proposals at any time prior to adoption.

Despite its apparent simplicity, the consultation procedure has occasionally given rise to difficulties.

ROQUETTE FRERES v. COUNCIL

(Isoglucose)
Case 138/79, [1980] ECR 3333.

[The Council, as required by EC Treaty Article 37 (now TFEU Article 43) had asked Parliament for its advice on a proposed regulation setting production quotas for isoglucose, a starch-based sweetener made from maize or corn (and known in the US as high fructose corn syrup). However, Parliament ended its final session shortly before Christmas holidays, without acting on the proposal, which was recommitted to its agriculture committee. Finally, some three and a half months after making its request to the Parliament, the Council adopted the regulation. The Council considered it vital to do so, since it considered a system of quotas to be essential and its predecessor regulation had been invalidated by the Court of Justice. The preamble to the regulation recited that Parliament had been consulted.

The Court initially held that Roquette Frères had standing to have the regulation annulled for violating an essential procedural requirement. Parliament intervened in its support. The Court invalidated the regulation.]

33   The consultation provided for in the third subparagraph of [EC Treaty Article 37(2), now TFEU Article 43(2)], as in other similar provisions of the Treaty, is the means which allows the Parliament to play an actual part in the legislative process of the Community. Such power represents an essential factor in the institutional balance intended by the Treaty. Although limited, it reflects at [the] Community level the fundamental democratic principle that the peoples should take part in the exercise of power through the intermediary of a representative assembly. Due consultation of the Parliament in the cases provided for by the Treaty therefore constitutes an essential formality disregard of which means that the measure concerned is void.

34   In that respect it is pertinent to point out that observance of that requirement implies that the Parliament has expressed its opinion. It is impossible to take the view that the requirement is satisfied by the Council's simply asking for the opinion....

35   The Council ... maintains ... that in the circumstances of the present case the Parliament, by its own conduct, made observance of that requirement impossible and that it is therefore not proper to rely on the infringement thereof.

36   Without prejudice to the questions of principle raised by that argument of the Council, it suffices to observe that in the present case ..., when the Council adopted [the regulation] without the opinion of the Assembly, the Council had not exhausted all the possibilities of obtain-

ing the preliminary opinion of the Parliament. In the first place the Council did not request the application of the emergency procedure provided for by the internal regulation of the Parliament although in other sectors and as regards other draft regulations it availed itself of that power at the same time. Further the Council could have made use of the possibility it had under [EC Treaty Article 196, now TFEU Article 229] to ask for an extraordinary session of the Assembly. . . .

NOTES AND QUESTIONS

1.   This is the first of many judgments in which the Court has supported Parliament in an inter-institutional dispute with the Council. Note in ¶ 33 the Court's reliance on the "institutional balance intended by the Treaty," a concept used by the Court in later judgments (see Parliament v. Council (Post–Chernobyl), infra page 130). Note that the Court also refers to "the fundamental democratic principle" which requires the participation of Parliament as a "representative assembly." In later years the Parliament has often claimed additional powers in order to remedy the "democratic deficit," because it is the only institution that directly represents the people.

2.   Often Parliament's delay is caused simply by the desire of its plenary sessions to have issues considered more carefully in committee, but occasionally it has deliberately refrained from providing an opinion. The Court judgment in the principal case led both Parliament and many academic commentators to believe consultation amounted to an *Isoglucose* veto." This view ended after the Court judgment in Parliament v. Council (Consultation of Parliament), Case C–65/93, [1995] ECR I–643. That case concerned a decision by the Council to adopt a preferential tariff arrangement before January 1, 1993, acting in the absence of an opinion of Parliament which had adjourned on December 18, 1992 without providing an opinion despite Council requests for urgent action since October. The Court held that the institutions had "mutual duties of sincere cooperation" which Parliament itself had violated (¶ 23), enabling the Council to take its decision without Parliament's opinion.

3.   Another interesting question is whether the right to be consulted on a proposal implies a right to be re-consulted if and when the proposal undergoes change prior to adoption. In Parliament v. Council (Passenger transport), Case C–388/92, [1994] ECR I–2067, the Court annulled a Council regulation allowing non-resident road transport firms to operate passenger service within a Member State, citing the fact that the Council failed to re-consult the Parliament after making major changes to the regulation as reviewed by the Parliament. The Council had modified the scope of the regulation from the broad category of all regular, chartered or shuttle services to the narrower category of services for the transport of workers and students in border areas. The Court ruled that this constituted a major change.

See also Parliament v. Council (Carriage of heavy goods), Case C–21/94, [1995] ECR I–1827, where the Court ruled that the Council had so significantly altered a draft directive on Member State taxation of vehicles for the carriage of heavy goods (notably by broadening the bases for exemption from the tax to such an extent that exemption could no longer be regarded as "exceptional" and by dropping language requiring the Council to adopt a harmonized system by a given date) that Parliament had a right to be re-consulted before the measure was adopted. For a case in which the amendments adopted by the Council were found by the Court *not* to be "substantial" for these purposes, see Parliament v. Council (Technical assistance to former Soviet States), Case C–417/93, [1995] ECR I–1185.

NOTE ON THE COOPERATION PROCEDURE

When adopting the Single European Act, the Member States responded to Parliament's demand for a stronger legislative voice by introducing into the Treaty a so-called "cooperation procedure" whose objective was to cause the Commission and Council to take Parliament's views more seriously into consideration. The procedure is detailed in EC Treaty Article 252.

Suffice it to say that the cooperation procedure enabled Parliament not merely to be consulted, but also to "reject" or seek to "amend" a Commission proposal that the Council had "provisionally" adopted in the form of a so-called "common position." By "rejecting" the common position, Parliament could not prevent the Council from enacting it into law, but could require that the Council enact it, if at all, by unanimity rather than by the usual qualified majority. Moreover, by seeking to "amend" the common position, Parliament in effect invited the Commission to revise its proposal in line with Parliament's thinking. (The procedure specifically gave the Commission the opportunity to do so.)

The Single European Act made the cooperation procedure immediately applicable in certain key Treaty articles, such as EC Treaty Article 95 (now TFEU Article 114), providing for harmonization of Member State law in furtherance of the internal market. Also subject to the procedure was legislation on the free movement of workers, the right of establishment, health and safety at work and the promotion of research and technological development.

When the Maastricht Treaty transferred the harmonization of laws under Article 95 to a still newer "codecision procedure," it also moved certain legislative fields into cooperation that had previously only been subject to consultation, such as environmental protection, vocational training and social policy. However, the Amsterdam Treaty subsequently reduced the scope of application of the cooperation procedure to use only in connection with certain measures adopted in monetary union. The Lisbon Treaty now eliminates it altogether in deference to the "ordinary legislative procedure," i.e., codecision.

C. THE CODECISION OR "ORDINARY LEGISLATIVE PROCEDURE"

Even after the SEA introduced the cooperation procedure, the Parliament sought to obtain a greater share in the legislative process, thereby furthering the democratic character of legislation. The Maastricht Treaty accordingly created a procedure for joint action by the Council and Parliament in the adoption of legislation to achieve the internal market and in certain other fields. The new procedure, called codecision, gave Parliament close to an equal voice with the Council. The Treaty of Amsterdam later amended EC Treaty Article 251, which sets out the codecision procedure, to give Parliament total equality with the Council. TFEU Article 294 renames it as the "ordinary legislative procedure," essentially retaining it, subject to some minor rewording.

The Maastricht Treaty replaced the cooperation procedure described above with codecision in the adoption of measures harmonizing national rules to achieve the internal market under EC Treaty Article 95 (now TFEU Article 114), as well as measures to promote the free movement of workers and the right of establishment. Codecision was also required to adopt the cooperative and incentive measures authorized by the Maastricht Treaty in the fields of education, culture and public health. The Treaty of Amsterdam subsequently replaced the cooperation procedure with codecision in all the other fields in which it was used (except for certain measures in monetary union), e.g., for measures in transport, environmental protection, visas, etc. The Lisbon Treaty has now authorized the ordinary legislative procedure in many other fields, notably in agriculture and fisheries, the promotion of freedom to provide transborder services, and most measures concerning visas, asylum, external borders, and cooperation in civil justice affairs.

Codecision is a complicated procedure with three successive stages. In its first phase, it actually mirrors the consultation procedure. The Commission drafts a proposed text which is published in the Official Journal. The Parliament in a "first reading" may suggest amendments, and the proposal, possibly amended by the Commission to win the requisite Council support as well as incorporate some of Parliament's amendments, is published in the Official Journal. The proposal, as amended, then receives a "first reading" by the Council, making use of its working groups and COREPER. This usually takes a year or longer.

Instead of finally approving the text (as in the consultation process), the Council merely adopts a "common position" or tentative approval, by a qualified majority of the Council. At any given time, only the then current Commission proposal may be adopted by the Council by QMV. Adoption of a different text requires unanimity in the Council. The common position, once adopted, is sent to the Parliament, along with a statement of reasons, thus starting a second legislative phase.

At this stage, Parliament has three months to conduct its "second reading." It has the choice, voting by absolute majority, among accepting the common position, rejecting it, or proposing amendments. If Parliament affirmatively accepts the text (or fails to take any action at all within the three months), the Council "shall" then definitively adopt the measure by qualified majority in its common position form.

Occasionally, the Parliament votes to reject the Council common position. This operates as a veto. The proposed text is then abandoned, although the Commission may decide to begin all over again with a new version. Requiring parliamentary assent for the enactment of legislation had simply come to be seen as a democratic imperative.

Most often the Parliament votes to make amendments to the Council's common position. The Council might then agree to the amendments by a qualified majority vote, leading to adoption of the text, or reject them, which opens the next stage in the process. (Alternatively, the Commission might have revised its proposed text, seeking to find a compromise between the Council and Parliament's views, which the Commission's power of legislative initiative enables it to do at any time. In that case, the Council may adopt this "reexamined proposal" by a qualified majority vote, or reject it.)

The real innovation, and benefit, of codecision commences at this point, enabling the impasse between the Council and Parliament to be broken. The different texts are sent to a Conciliation Committee, consisting of representatives of all the Council members and an equal number of MEPs, assisted by Commission representatives. The Committee has six weeks in which to try to find an acceptable compromise. A compromise text must be supported both by a qualified majority of the Council representatives on the Committee and by a majority of the MEPs on it. Such a text may be enacted into law if and only if both the Council (by a qualified majority) and the Parliament (by an absolute majority of votes cast) approve it in the "third reading" within the next six weeks. If either fails for any reason to do so—or if the Conciliation Committee never produces a compromise text in the first place—the draft measure once again lapses. In fact, Council and Parliament drafts are often brought into harmony, despite initial differences, thus avoiding the conciliation procedure.

When the cooperation procedure was first introduced by the SEA, it gave rise to fears of legislative delay and paralysis. Those fears on the whole have not materialized. Despite its complexity, the codecision procedure has worked reasonably well in practice, with the Council frequently accepting Parliament's proposed amendments and the Conciliation Committee on occasion achieving a breakthrough. Rarely is there a total roadblock to a proposal. The 1992 internal market program was chiefly legislated in this fashion.

In July 1994, the Parliament for the first time exercised its power to reject outright a common position adopted by the Council in the first phase of the co-decision procedure. The occasion was a vote on a new text liberalizing the European voice telecommunications market; Parliament found the proposal insufficiently protective of consumers. In March 1995, Parliament formally rejected a compromise text on protection of biotechnological inventions arrived at by a Conciliation Committee because a majority of MEPs found the text lacking in safeguards of animal welfare and limitations on the use of human genes and organs. More recently, in July 2001, a tie vote in the Parliament rejected the Conciliation Committee's compromise text on the draft Thirteenth Company Law Directive on takeovers. In all three cases the Commission issued new proposals which eventually were adopted (see Chapters 17D and 19D).

NOTES AND QUESTIONS

1. The Commission is intimately involved in the conciliation process. According to EC Treaty Article 251 (now TFEU Article 294), the Commission takes part in the proceedings and "shall take all the necessary initiatives with a view to reconciling the positions of the European Parliament and the Council." See generally, N. Foster, The New Conciliation Committee under Article 189b EC, 19 Eur. L. Rev. 185 (1994).

The codecision procedure diminishes the power of the Commission in at least one respect. Throughout the evolution of the legislative process, the Commission has enjoyed the privilege of requiring the Council to vote by unanimity whenever it sought to adopt a text in a form other than the one favored at that time by the Commission, even if the Council would normally have been able to adopt the Commission's proposal by qualified majority. Once a Conciliation Committee is convened under the codecision procedure, however, this rule is suspended. A joint text adopted by the Conciliation Committee may be adopted by the Council by qualified majority even over the Commission's objection. If Parliament also approves the measure in that form, it becomes law.

2. With a view to perfecting the codecision procedure, the Parliament, Council and Commission in May 1999 adopted a joint declaration on "practical arrangements" for its conduct. Bull. EU 5–1999. The declaration requires the institutions to endeavor to reconcile their positions on draft legislation as far as possible during the legislation's first reading. It calls on the Commission in particular to promote agreement between the Council and Parliament in a second reading, as well as in a Conciliation Committee. It prescribes various conciliation procedures (e.g. alternate hosting of meetings by the Council and Parliament and by their Presidents) in order to facilitate agreement in Committee.

3. Linked to pressures for greater transparency (see Chapter 6E infra) and respect for subsidiarity (see Chapter 4D infra) in the adoption of Union legislation has been a drive toward improving the quality of that legislation. (The Commission has spoken of "legislating less, but legislating better.") The Commission has undertaken periodically to simplify and consolidate existing legislation in the interest of greater clarity and consistency. See Timmermans, How Can One Improve the Quality of Community Legislation?, 34 Comm. Mkt. L. Rev. 1229 (1997). For further discussion, see Chapter 14B infra.

D. DISPUTES OVER THE CORRECT LEGAL BASIS FOR LEGISLATIVE ACTION

The introduction of the cooperation procedure, soon followed by codecision, occasioned frequent disputes between the Council, on the one hand, and the Commission, seeking to enhance the democratic character of legislation, on the other. Frequently the Commission would propose legislation to be adopted on the basis of a Treaty article that required either cooperation or codecision, but the Council preferred to be able to decide alone on the draft and accordingly changed the basis to a Treaty article requiring consultation, and then purported to adopt the legislation. The Commission would then bring suit against the Council and the Court would have to decide which legal basis was most appropriate.

The two most important early legal basis judgments both concerned environmental protection measures.

COMMISSION v. COUNCIL

(Titanium dioxide)
Case C–300/89, [1991] ECR I–2867.

[In 1989, the Council by unanimous vote enacted a directive harmonizing rules on the reduction of pollution caused by titanium dioxide waste, using EC Treaty Article 175 (now TFEU Article 192) which authorized the Council, acting alone, to adopt environmental legislation. The Commission, supported by Parliament, challenged the legality of the directive on the ground that the Council should have acted under EC Treaty Article 95 (now TFEU Article 114), which at the time called for the cooperation procedure and qualified majority voting.

The Commission and Parliament maintained that the directive, though contributing to environmental protection, was mainly concerned with improving competitive conditions in the titanium dioxide industry and was therefore an internal market measure within the meaning of Article 95. The Council, on the other hand, insisted that the "center of gravity" of the measure was reducing pollution caused by titanium dioxide production, hence environmental. The Court held that Article 95 represented the proper legal basis for the legislation.]

10   [I]n the context of the organization of the powers of the Community, the choice of the legal basis for a measure may not depend simply on an institution's conviction as to the objective pursued but must be based on objective factors which are amenable to judicial review. Those factors include in particular the aim and content of the measure.

11   As regards the aim pursued, Article 1 of [the directive] indicates that it is intended, on the one hand, to harmonize the programmes for the reduction and ultimate elimination of pollution caused by waste from

existing establishments in the titanium dioxide industry and, on the other, to improve the conditions of competition in that industry. It thus pursues the twofold aim of environmental protection and improvement of the conditions of competition.

12   As regards its content, [the directive] prohibits, or, according to strict standards, requires reduction of the discharge of waste from existing establishments in the titanium dioxide industry and lays down time-limits [for doing so. Thus it] conduces, at the same time, to the reduction of pollution and to the establishment of greater uniformity of production conditions and therefore of conditions of competition, since the national rules on the treatment of waste which the directive seeks to harmonize have an impact on production costs in the titanium dioxide industry.

13   It follows that according to its aim and content ... the directive is concerned, indissociably, with both the protection of the environment and the elimination of disparities in conditions of competition.

* * *

16   [T]he directive at issue displays the features both of action relating to the environment with which Article [175] of the Treaty is concerned and of a harmonizing measure which has as its object the establishment and functioning of the internal market, within the meaning of Article [95] of the Treaty.

17   As the Court [has previously] held, ... where an institution's power is based on two provisions of the Treaty, it is bound to adopt the relevant measures on the basis of the two relevant provisions. However, that ruling is not applicable to the present case.

18   ... In a case like this [in which one provision provides for parliamentary cooperation and the other for unanimous voting upon the mere consultation of Parliament], combining the two legal bases would tend to render the parliamentary cooperation procedure devoid of any substance.

* * *

20   The very purpose of the cooperation procedure, which is to increase the involvement of the European Parliament in the legislative process of the Community, would thus be jeopardized. As the Court stated in its judgments [in, among others, the *Roquette Frères* case, supra page 82], that participation reflects a fundamental democratic principle that the peoples should take part in the exercise of power through the intermediary of a representative assembly.

21   It follows that in the present case recourse to the dual legal basis of Articles [95 and 175] is excluded and that it is necessary to determine which of those two provisions is the appropriate legal basis.

22   It must be observed in the first place that, pursuant to the second sentence of Article [175(2)] of the Treaty, "environmental protection

requirements shall be a component of the Community's other policies.'' That principle implies that a Community measure cannot be covered by Article [175] merely because it also pursues objectives of environmental protection.

23   Secondly, as the Court [has previously] held, provisions which are made necessary by considerations relating to the environment and health may be a burden upon the undertakings to which they apply and, if there is no harmonization of national provisions on the matter, competition may be appreciably distorted. It follows that action intended to approximate national rules concerning production conditions in a given industrial sector with the aim of eliminating distortions of competition in that sector is conducive to the attainment of the internal market and thus falls within the scope of Article [95]....

24   Finally, it must be observed that Article [95] requires the Commission, in its proposals for measures for the approximation of the laws of the Member States which have as their object the establishment and functioning of the internal market, to take as a base a high level of protection in matters of environmental protection. That provision thus expressly indicates that the objectives of environmental protection may be effectively pursued by means of harmonizing measures adopted on the basis of Article [95]....

25   [Accordingly] the contested measure should have been based on Article [95] ... and must therefore be annulled.

COMMISSION v. COUNCIL

(Waste directive)
Case C–155/91, [1993] ECR I–939.

[In 1991, the Commission relied on EC Treaty Article 95 (now TFEU Article 114) on internal market harmonization as the basis for a proposed amendment to a 1995 directive on waste disposal, which had originally been adopted under a rule of unanimity, as required under the only then-available treaty bases. When finally adopting the amendment as Directive 91/156, the Council, rather than citing Article 95, relied on Article 175 (now TFEU Article 192) on the environment, which at the time still required unanimity. The Commission challenged the measure as having been adopted on the wrong legal basis.]

8   As for the aim pursued by Directive 91/156, the ... preamble state[s] that, in order to achieve a high level of environmental protection, the Member States must take measures to restrict the production of waste and to encourage the recycling of waste and its re-use as raw materials, and they must become self-sufficient in waste disposal and reduce movements of waste.

9   As for the content of the directive, it requires the Member States, in particular, to encourage the prevention or reduction of waste production and waste recovery and disposal without endangering human

health and without harming the environment, and to prohibit the abandonment, dumping and uncontrolled disposal of waste (Articles 3 and 4). Accordingly, the directive requires the Member States to establish an integrated and adequate network of disposal installations which will enable the Community as a whole and the Member States individually to become self-sufficient in waste disposal, with the waste being disposed of in one of the nearest installations (Article 5). In order to attain those objectives, the Member States are to draw up waste management plans and may prevent movements of waste which are not in accordance with those plans (Article 7). Lastly, the directive requires the Member States to subject disposal undertakings and establishments to rules providing for permits, registration and inspections (Articles 9 to 14) and confirms, in the field of waste disposal, the 'polluter pays' principle (Article 15).

10 It appears from the above particulars that, according to its aim and content, the directive at issue has the object of ensuring the management of waste, whether it is of industrial or domestic origin, in accordance with the requirements of environmental protection.

* * *

16 The Commission ... argues that the directive leads to the approximation of legislation inasmuch as Article 1 introduces a single, common definition of waste and related activities. ... [The Commission] refers in particular to the ... preamble to the directive, according to which any disparity between Member States' laws on waste disposal and recovery can affect the quality of the environment and interfere with the functioning of the internal market.

* * *

18 Admittedly, it must be acknowledged that some provisions of the directive, in particular the definitions set out in Article 1, affect the functioning of the internal market.

19 However ... the mere fact that the establishment or functioning of the internal market is affected is not sufficient for [Article 95] of the Treaty to apply. It appears from the Court's case-law that recourse to [Article 95] is not justified where the measure to be adopted has only the incidental effect of harmonizing market conditions within the Community.

20 That is the case here. The harmonization provided for in Article 1 of the directive has as its main object to ensure, with a view to protecting the environment, the effective management of waste in the Community, regardless of its origin, and has only ancillary effects on the conditions of competition and trade. As a result, it differs from [the directive at issue in the *Titanium dioxide* case], which ... is intended to approximate national rules concerning production conditions in a given industrial sector with the aim of eliminating distortions of competition in that sector.

21 Accordingly, the contested directive must be deemed to have been validly adopted on the sole basis of [Article 175] of the Treaty.

NOTES AND QUESTIONS

1. Are the *Titanium dioxide* and *Waste directive* judgments consistent? Can it be said, as the Council argued, that the waste directive was concerned exclusively with the management of waste treatment and disposal, and had nothing to do either with the free movement of goods or conditions of competition?

In any case, the Court appears to have abandoned its suggestion in *Titanium dioxide* that where an institution's power is based on two Treaty provisions, it ordinarily must adopt the relevant measures in compliance with both of them (the "double legal basis" theory). The approach adopted by the Court in the *Waste directive* case is commonly likened to a "center of gravity" test. Is this an apt description?

2. The Commission generally cited the importance of parliamentary participation in the legislative process in pressing for cooperation or, later, codecision. Bearing in mind that those procedures also entailed QMV in the Council rather than unanimity, can you see any other reason why the Commission would take the legal basis issue so seriously as to bring suit to challenge the adoption of a measure it had itself initially proposed?

3. For still more recent applications of the Court's approach in an environmental case, see Spain v. Council (Danube Convention), Case C–36/98, [2001] ECR I–779; Parliament v. Council (Waste movement), Case C–187/93, [1994] ECR I–2857.

4. In Parliament v. Council (Post–Chernobyl), discussed at page 130 infra, the Court held that the Parliament also had a right to challenge a Council act, although at the time EC Treaty Article 230 (now TFEU Article 263) did not expressly give it that right. In 1987, the Commission proposed and the Council adopted a so-called "Post–Chernobyl" regulation on maximum radiation levels, acting unanimously under the Euratom Treaty rather than through cooperation and qualified majority voting under then EC Treaty Article 100a (later EC Treaty Article 85, and now TFEU Article 114). Parliament sued, claiming that the Euratom Treaty provision should not have been used since it applied only to protection against direct injury from the use of nuclear energy and not against "secondary radiation," and that the cooperation procedure had been improperly circumvented.

Parliament won a landmark ruling to the effect that it enjoyed an implied right to sue under Article 230, in order to protect its "prerogatives" (using the "institutional balance" concept), even though it lost on the merits, where the Court held that the Post–Chernobyl regulation had only an "incidental" effect on the free movement of goods and did not constitute an internal market measure within the meaning of the then Article 100a. (As we shall see in Chapter 5A, the EC Treaty was amended in two steps, first in the Maastricht Treaty to give Parliament a right to sue but only to protect its prerogatives, and then in the Nice Treaty, to eliminate the restriction.).

A noted instance in which Parliament subsequently challenged successfully the Council's choice of legal basis is Parliament v. Council (Government procurement), Case C–360/93, [1996] ECR I–1195. There the Court invalidated a 1993 Council decision approving the conclusion of a Memorandum of Understanding with the US on government procurement that was intended to promote EU–US trade in sales to government entities. The Council adopted that decision on the basis of EC Treaty Article 133 on external trade (now TFEU Article 207), which then entailed qualified majority voting upon a Commission proposal but without consultation of Parliament. When the Parliament challenged this legal basis, the Court ruled that, to the extent that the agreement dealt with the provision of services that are not supplied across frontiers, the Council decision approving the agreement could not be based on Article 133 of the Treaty alone. Unable to craft a partial annulment, the Court annulled the Council decision approving the agreement in its entirety.

5. The choice of legal basis is of course not only of concern to the institutions. Member States may likewise have an interest in one legislative procedure being followed rather than another. This has mostly to do with differences in Council voting requirements. The phenomenon arose at an early point in regard to several agricultural measures whose adoption had been prompted in part by non-agricultural considerations. At that time, most agricultural measures could be taken by qualified majority voting under the EC Treaty Article 37 (now TFEU Article 43), whereas other policies—such as consumer protection, for example—could only be pursued through treaty articles requiring unanimity in the Council. The latter included implied powers under Article 308 (now TFEU Article 352) or pre-SEA harmonization under the then EC Treaty Article 94.

For example, in United Kingdom v. Council (Agricultural hormones), Case 68/86, [1988] ECR 855, the UK and Denmark objected to the fact that the Council used the then EC Treaty Article 43 rather than the then Article 100 in adopting its ban on the use of hormones for fattening livestock. At the time, which was prior to the Single European Act, harmonization legislation could only be adopted under Article 100 (renumbered by the Amsterdam Treaty as Article 94) which required unanimity in the Council. The claimant States asserted that the ban was a consumer protection, not an agricultural policy measure, thus governed by Article 100 and not Article 43. The Court sustained the measure, finding that qualified majority voting was the appropriate procedural course. For a similar situation and result, see United Kingdom v. Council (Laying hens), Case 131/86, [1988] ECR 905.

Undoubtedly the most prominent legal basis suit brought by a Member State was the UK's challenge to the controversial Working Time directive.

UNITED KINGDOM v. COUNCIL

(Working time directive)
Case C–84/94, [1996] ECR I–5755.

[In this action for annulment, the UK challenged the legality of Council Directive 93/104, commonly known as the "Working Time Directive." The directive, which the Council had adopted on the basis of the then Article 118a of the EC Treaty (an article whose provisions, as amended, were renumbered by the Amsterdam Treaty as EC Treaty Article 137, and are now found in TFEU Article 153), laid down certain minimum standards for working time in both the public and private sectors, including periods of daily and weekly rest on the job, annual leave, maximum work week, and special protection for night workers and shift workers. (See Chapter 36D for a fuller description of the Working Time Directive.)

The UK had opposed the directive, but was outvoted in the Council. It claimed, among other things, that the Council wrongly relied on Article 118a, enabling the Council to act by a qualified majority vote, when it should have used either the then Article 100 on harmonization to achieve the common market or the then Article 235 (now TFEU Article 352, the implied powers provision), both of which required unanimity in the Council.]

The scope of Article 118a

13   [The UK] argues ... that [Article 118a] permits the adoption only of directives which have a genuine and objective link to the "health and safety" of workers. That does not apply to measures concerning, in particular, weekly working time, paid annual leave and rest periods, whose connection with the health and safety of workers is too tenuous. That interpretation is borne out by the expression "working environment" used in Article 118a, which implies that directives based on that provision must be concerned only with physical conditions and risks at the workplace.

* * *

15   There is nothing in the wording of Article 118a to indicate that the concepts of "working environment," "safety" and "health" as used in that provision should, in the absence of other indications, be interpreted restrictively, and not as embracing all factors, physical or otherwise, capable of affecting the health and safety of the worker in his working environment, including in particular certain aspects of the organization of working time. On the contrary, the words "especially in the working environment" militate in favour of a broad interpretation of the powers which Article 118a confers upon the Council for the protection of the health and safety of workers. . . .

* * *

18   [Further], the applicant argues that, in the light of previous directives based on Article 118a, that provision does not authorize the Council to adopt directives, such as that in dispute here, which deal with the question of health and safety in a generalized, unspecific and unscientific manner. [The Court then cited several Council directives that clearly focus upon a specific health or safety problem in a specific situation.]

* * *

22 [W]here the principal aim of the measure in question is the protection of the health and safety of workers, Article 118a must be used, albeit such a measure may have ancillary effects on the establishment and functioning of the internal market. . . .

The choice of legal basis for the directive

* * *

26 As regards the aim of the directive, the applicant argues that it represents a continuation . . . of a series of earlier initiatives at Community level concerned with the organization of working time in the interests of job creation and reduced unemployment. It is in reality a measure concerned with the overall improvement of the living and working conditions of employees and with their general protection, and is so broad in its scope and coverage as to be capable of classification as a social policy measure, for the adoption of which other legal bases exist.

* * *

29 The approach taken by the directive, viewing the organization of working time essentially in terms of the favourable impact it may have on the health and safety of workers, is apparent from several recitals in its preamble. Thus, for example, the eighth recital states that, in order to ensure the safety and health of Community workers, they must be granted minimum rest periods and adequate breaks and that it is also necessary in that context to place a maximum limit on weekly working hours. In addition, the eleventh recital states that "research has shown that . . . long periods of night work can be detrimental to the health of workers and can endanger safety at the workplace", while the fifteenth recital states that specific working conditions may have detrimental effects on the safety and health of workers and that the organization of working according to a certain pattern must take account of the general principle of adapting work to the worker.

30 While, in the light of those considerations, it cannot be excluded that the directive may affect employment, that is clearly not its essential objective.

31 As regards the content of the directive, the applicant argues that the connection between the measures it lays down, on the one hand, and health and safety, on the other, is too tenuous for the directive to be based on Article 118a of the Treaty.

32 In that respect, it argues that no adequate scientific evidence exists to justify the imposition of a general requirement to provide for breaks where the working day is longer than six hours (Article 4), a general requirement to provide for a minimum uninterrupted weekly rest period of twenty-four hours in addition to the usual eleven hours' daily rest (Article 5, first sentence), a requirement that the minimum rest period must, in principle, include Sunday (Article 5, second

sentence), a general requirement to ensure that the average working time for each seven-day period, including overtime, does not exceed forty-eight hours (Article 6(2)), and a general requirement that every worker is to have a minimum of four weeks' paid annual leave (Article 7).

[At this point, the Court focused on the specific requirement in the directive that the mandatory weekly rest period is normally to comprise a Sunday. Finding that the Council had failed to explain why Sunday, as a weekly rest day, was more closely connected with the health and safety of workers than any other day of the week, and finding this requirement to be severable from the rest of the directive, the Court annulled this particular provision.]

38   The other measures laid down by the directive, which refer to minimum rest periods, length of work, night work, shift work and the pattern of work, relate to the "working environment" and reflect concern for the protection of "the health and safety of workers"....

* * *

45   Since it is clear from the above considerations that, in terms of its aim and content, the directive has as its principal objective the protection of the health and safety of workers by the imposition of minimum requirements for gradual implementation, neither Article 100 nor Article 100a could have constituted the appropriate legal basis for its adoption.

* * *

48   Finally, as regards Article 235 of the Treaty, it is sufficient to point to the Court's case-law, which holds that that article may be used as the legal basis for a measure only where no other Treaty provision confers on the Community institutions the necessary power to adopt it.

49   It must therefore be held that the directive was properly adopted on the basis of Article 118a, save for the [Sunday weekly rest requirement,] which must accordingly be annulled.

NOTES AND QUESTIONS

1. To fully understand how strongly the conservative UK government of Prime Minister Major opposed becoming subject to the Working Time Directive, one needs to know that this government had insisted upon a Maastricht Treaty Social Protocol that provided that the UK would not be bound by any employment law or other social policy directives except for those adopted pursuant to the then Article 118a. See Chapter 35A concerning this Protocol, which was eliminated by the Amsterdam Treaty after Prime Minister Blair's Labor government took office in 1997. Prime Minister Major presumably believed that the other States deliberately misused Article 118a when adopting the Working Time Directive. In any case, what, for example, does the adequacy of the available scientific evidence (¶ 32) have to do with the correctness of the legal basis used?

2. As we shall see in Chapter 14, directives harmonizing the rules for specific products or types of products frequently enable States to ban products, whether imported or domestic, when a serious health or safety risk arises from their use. When, after long controversy during its drafting, the General Product Safety Directive was finally adopted, Germany challenged its Article 9 concerning the Commission's power to compel States to take specific protective measures to cope with newly discovered health and safety risks.

GERMANY v. COUNCIL

(General product safety directive)
Case C–359/92, [1994] ECR I–3681.

[Germany sought the annulment of article 9 of Council Directive 92/59 harmonizing Member State laws on general product safety, which the Council had adopted as an internal market measure under EC Treaty Article 100a (renumbered by the Amsterdam Treaty as EC Treaty Article 95, and now TFEU Article 114). Article 9 authorized the Commission, upon learning that a product raises a serious and immediate risk to consumer health, and that two or more States have reacted by taking substantially different protective measures, to take decisions requiring the Member States concerned to impose uniform temporary protective measures with respect to that product. Germany maintained that Article 9 of the Directive lacked any legal basis in the EC Treaty, while the Council and Commission insisted that Article 100a furnished an adequate basis.]

30 Under the scheme established by the directive, it is possible, even likely, that differences may exist between the measures taken by Member States. As the preamble states, such differences may "entail unacceptable disparities in consumer protection and constitute a barrier to intra-Community trade".

* * *

32 The Community legislature therefore considered it necessary, in order to cope with a serious and immediate risk to the health and safety of consumers, to provide for an adequate mechanism allowing, in the last resort, for the adoption of measures applicable throughout the Community, in the form of decisions addressed to the Member States. . . .

* * *

34 As is apparent from the . . . preamble to the directive and from the structure of Article 9, [Article 9's] purpose . . . is to enable the Commission to adopt, as promptly as possible, temporary measures applicable throughout the Community with respect to a product which presents a serious and immediate risk to the health and safety of consumers, so as to ensure compliance with the objectives of the directive. The free movement of goods can be secured only if product safety requirements do not differ significantly from one Member State to another. A high level of protection can be achieved only if danger-

ous products are subject to appropriate measures in all the Member States.

* * *

[37] Such action is not contrary to Article 100a(1) of the Treaty. The measures which the Council is empowered to take under that provision are aimed at "the establishment and functioning of the internal market". In certain fields, and particularly in that of product safety, the approximation of general laws alone may not be sufficient to ensure a unified market. Consequently, the concept of "measures for the approximation" of provisions must be interpreted as encompassing the Council's power to lay down measures relating to a specific product or class of products and, if necessary, individual measures concerning those products.

NOTES AND QUESTIONS

1. Basically Germany was contending that each State should have discretion in establishing protective measures for new safety risks, and that the Council did not have the power under the then Article 100a to give the Commission the final say on protective measures, because such a power went beyond the Council's right under that article to harmonize national rules on products. Do you agree with the Court's reasoning?

2. Germany also advanced the argument that, by regulating a matter within the constitutional competence of the German states, or *Länder,* rather than the German federal government, Article 9 impermissibly interfered with principles of German federalism. The response of the Court of Justice to this argument was simple:

[38] [I]t must be borne in mind that the rules governing the relationship between the Community and its Member States are not the same as those which link the [German federal state] with the *Länder.* Furthermore, the measures taken for the implementation of Article 100a of the Treaty are addressed to Member States and not to their constituent entities. Nor do the powers conferred on the Commission by Article 9 of the directive have any bearing upon the division of powers within the Federal Republic of Germany.

NOTE ON "NEW GOVERNANCE" AND "THE OPEN METHOD OF COORDINATION"

The European Council, meeting in Lisbon in 2000, set as a major objective improving the EU's competitive position in the world economy, notably vis-à-vis the US. The initiative had a strong process dimension. It sought to privilege, as against traditional "top-down" governance, a new more "open" set of decisional processes that included greater use of guidelines as opposed to prescriptive mandates, involvement of different level of government and sectors of society (including NGOs and civil society generally), use of qualitative and quantitative benchmarks and "best practices," and periodic monitoring and evaluation. The underlying concept was to develop and utilize techniques of mutual learning, which seemed especially appropriate for a dynamic EU of diverse membership, at least in certain domains. These tools were also seen as promoting greater and more meaningful public participation, and thus transparency and democracy.

Economic policy and employment were the first two fields to become the subject of this open method of coordination (or OMC), but its use was extended to welfare, health care, social policy, education, and information technology, among others. By its nature, including its flexibility, the new governance and OMC are best appreciated in the various regulatory contexts in which they have been used. They will be particularly salient in Part VII of this book, where a number of specific substantive EU policies are sampled.

E.   EU FINANCES AND THE BUDGET

No picture of the Union institutions and activities would be complete without some understanding of the EU's financial and budgetary system. This system has changed over time with a view both to enhancing the EU's financial independence and strengthening the role of the Parliament in budgetary matters.

Initially, the European Community derived its revenue from Member State contributions. As seen in Chapter 1, at a 1969 meeting of the heads of state and government at the Hague, the Member States agreed to place Community finances on a more secure and independent footing. The following year, the Council brought into being a system of so-called "own resources" for the Community. However, not all the machinery of that system was put in place until the end of that decade.

Under the "own resources" system, the EU receives all revenues from customs duties and levies on imported agricultural products. These are collected by the Member States, which keep a percentage of the proceeds to cover their collection costs, remitting the balance to the EU. The third and largest source of EU revenue is a share of each Member State's collection of value added tax, a share currently set at 1.4% of the value of the products subject to the tax. Severe and chronic budgetary problems of the 1980s, accompanied by actual talk of Community bankruptcy, finally led in 1988 to the addition of a new and important revenue source, namely a direct levy on the Member States calculated in proportion to their Gross National Products (GNPs).

The creation of this additional own resource for the Community ("the fourth resource"), based on the Gross National Product of the Member States, was necessary to ensure adequate funding for the EU and its activities. But having a GNP-based component of the budget made it necessary to reinforce the comparability and reliability of GNP aggregates by harmonizing the definition of GNP and the method of its calculation. This was effectuated by Council Directive 89/130/EC on the harmonization of the compilation of gross national product at market prices, O.J. L 49 (Feb. 21, 1989).

Concerned about future budgetary demands, especially in view of the 2004 enlargement, a 1998 Commission report reviewed the own resources system. The March 1999 Berlin European Council then requested the Commission to propose revisions to the Council, which adopted a new Own Resources Decision 2001/597, O.J. L 253/42 (Oct. 7, 2000). Its main features are that the own resources ceiling remains at 1.27% of the Union's GNP; the amount retained by Member States to cover their costs of collecting the "own resources" rises from 10% to 25%; the maximum EU share of VAT is reduced to 0.50% from 2004; and the costs of the longstanding budgetary rebate to the UK are shifted as among the other Member States.

Throughout most of the history of the EU, subsidies to farmers and other agricultural expenses represented over half the Community budget, despite periodic efforts by some States, notably the UK and the Netherlands, to rein in the expenditures. France has always been the principal beneficiary of agricultural aid and naturally its chief advocate. Pressure upon the EU to reduce its subsidies in GATT and in the WTO Doha Round negotiations resulted in some diminution of CAP expenditures, which currently represent about 43% of the total budget.

The second largest budget item is regional aid. For years the principal beneficiaries were Greece, Ireland, Italy, Portugal and Spain. Since the mid–1990s, financial aid for infrastructure and other projects to the central and eastern European countries has become a significant expenditure factor. Even after their accession, these States receive substantial amounts of regional aid, since their annual GNPs and average income levels remain much lower than those prevailing in western Europe.

Financial assistance to less developed countries, especially the former European colonies in Africa, represents another significant budget item. Chapter 28 describes the successive Conventions entered into with these nations and the nature of commodity support and other aid. Finally, the financing of the administrative expenses of the EU institutions and agencies average less than 10%, currently around 7%, of the total budget.

Since 1988, decisions on budgetary discipline, together with inter-institutional agreements on budgetary discipline, have brought about a stable relationship between the European Union's commitments and its own resources. The Delors Commission initiated a policy of drafting seven-year budget plans subscribed to between the Council, Parliament and the Commission in order to provide a multi-annual framework for improved budgetary discipline. The current framework budget covers 2007–2013. In this context, the Council issued a regulation on September 26, 2000 on budgetary discipline, O.J. L 244, (Sept. 29, 2000), containing provisions on monetary reserves, the reserve relating to EU loans and loan guarantees to non-member countries, and the reserve for emergency aid, as well as specifications for the method of calculating the agricultural guidelines. It also provides for additional measures to strengthen and simplify the rules on the application of budgetary discipline.

Prior to the Lisbon Treaty, the EU's complicated budget planning and approval process was set out in EC Treaty Articles 269 to 279. The Commission drafted a preliminary budget, submitting it to the Council no later than September 1, and in practice during the month of July. The draft budget was reviewed and adopted by the Council and then by the Parliament, followed by a second examination by both institutions. By December 31, the President of the Parliament would need to declare the budget adopted. The EC Treaty gave the Council the final decision on expenditures required by the Treaty, including agricultural policy. Parliament had the final voice (within a fixed "maximum rate of increase") on so-called discretionary expenditures such as certain administrative expenses. Since most expenditures are deemed to be compulsory for these purposes, the Council had the larger share of power in budgetary decision-making.

The Community's awkward budgetary process reflected contention between the Council and Parliament over their respective shares of power in the process and over substantive budgetary issues. As early as 1980 (its first year as a directly elected body), Parliament sought to reject the draft budget in its entirety, and twice in the early 1980s and once again in the early 1990s, the two institutions went before the Court of Justice to resolve their differences. One of Parliament's principal substantive claims has been that agricultural spending should be reduced and amounts spent on regional development and research and development funding increased.

The Treaty of Lisbon has significantly modified the prior Treaty provisions in favor of the Parliament. TFEU Article 311 prescribes that the Council, acting unanimously and after consulting the Parliament, shall decide upon the EU's system of own resources. Article 312 requires a "multi-annual financial framework" of at least five years, set by the Council after obtaining Parliament's consent. In contrast, the process for adopting the annual budget under TFEU Article 314 requires a conciliation committee whenever the Council and Parliament cannot agree, and ultimately grants Parliament the decisive voice, provided 60% of the votes cast by an absolute majority of its members endorse an approach on disputed budget items. The Commission implements the budget, pursuant to TFEU Article 317. For several years, the annual budget has exceeded 100 billion Euros.

Budgetary politics can produce divisions along Member State lines. In the early 1980s, the UK, under the leadership of Prime Minister Thatcher, strongly contended that the budget should be adjusted to reflect the fact that Britain (not being a major agricultural producer) paid much more into Community revenues than it received. The European Council finally agreed at its 1984 Fontainebleau meeting to give the UK a rebate of a portion of the amount by which its contribution to Community revenue exceeded its receipts. Since that time, the UK has in fact become a major recipient of EC regional development aid, especially for Scotland and Wales. The budgetary breakthrough was a factor in the Community's emergence from the period of "Europessimism" referred to in Chapter 1.

Once the budget is adopted, the Commission has responsibility for administering the receipt of revenues, the control of cash flow and the disbursement of expenditures. Its administration of EU finances is reviewed by the Court of Auditors, described at page 71, supra. The Court of Auditors in effect carries out an annual audit and reports to the Council and the Parliament.

Fraud, especially in payments under the Common Agricultural Policy, has become a serious problem. EC Treaty Article 280 (now TFEU Article 325) enjoins the Member States and the EU to make serious efforts to combat it. For its part, the Commission has launched its own program of investigation, chiefly through its anti-fraud unit known as OLAF. The Commission's annual reports count many thousands of incidents entailing hundred of millions of euros implicated, mostly in connection with agricultural supports under the Common Agricultural Policy and in regional aid. As noted, the Santer Commission's failure to act energetically to combat fraud in these areas helped fuel the critique that eventually led to the Commission's forced resignation. A significant portion of the EU budget is now devoted to detecting and preventing fraud.

CHAPTER 4

THE SPHERE OF EU LAW AND POLICY

■ ■ ■

When in 1993 the Treaty of Maastricht removed the word "economic" from the title of the European Economic Community Treaty, it underlined the fact that the Community had greatly expanded its initial fields of activity and had acquired political, social and cultural dimensions. The EEC Treaty's Article 2, stating the Community's basic objectives, has been frequently amended over time to add new Treaty goals, such as the achievement of the internal market and monetary union, but also social, environmental and political goals.

The Lisbon Treaty's TEU Article 3 not only expressly states additional goals, but does so with greater precision, and merits reading at this point (see the Documents Supplement, doc. 1). Article 3 first states the goal of promoting the Union's democratic and basic rights values set out in Article 2, a topic dealt with in Chapter 6. Article 3 then gives priority to promoting the rights of Union citizens within the "area of freedom, security and justice without internal frontiers." Thereafter Article 3 sets out the economic goals of an internal market and monetary union, full employment and social progress, a high level of environmental protection, cultural and linguistic diversity, and the promotion of a variety of global concerns in international relations, including respect for the principles of the UN Charter.

The present chapter is devoted to describing the sphere of Union law and policy within the context of the promotion of its goals. We begin by observing that the EU may act within its many fields of action only in accordance with the principle of conferred or enumerated powers. We will then discuss the wide extent of its implied powers, noting that the Court of Justice has occasionally imposed limits on such implied powers. Next, we will review how a Member State law or regulation may be invalidated or narrowed in scope through application of the preemption doctrine when the State rule conflicts with the Treaty or secondary EU law. Somewhat in contrast, we will discuss the principle of subsidiarity as another mode for delimiting Union authority. We will then consider how the internal affairs doctrine results in the conclusion that certain Member State rules have no meaningful inter-State impact and are therefore not of EU law concern.

Finally, we will discuss how the Union permits some Member States to pursue closer cooperative arrangements, while other States voluntarily exclude themselves from such arrangements. These are all, each in its own way, aspects of the definition of the EU law sphere.

A. UNION COMPETENCES AND THE PRINCIPLE OF CONFERRAL

The EEC Treaty's Article 3 had listed fields of Community activity principally related to achieving an integrated common market: the elimination of customs duties between States; the removal of obstacles to the free movement of goods, persons, services and capital; the creation of a common commercial policy; the development of common policies in agriculture, competition and transport; and a policy in the social sphere. In 1987, the SEA added environmental protection, and in 1993 the Maastricht Treaty added as fields consumer protection, promotion of research and development, cooperative action in health, education and culture, energy, and tourism.

In view of this lengthy list of fields of activity, it is not surprising that the Maastricht Treaty also introduced into EC Treaty Article 5 an enumerated powers clause: "The Community shall act within the limits of the powers conferred upon it by this Treaty and the objectives assigned to it therein." The Lisbon Treaty's TEU Article 5 (2) maintains the principle, terming it the "principle of conferral." Elaborating upon this, TFEU Article 2 distinguishes between exclusive Union competences, in which States can only act if empowered by the Union to do so, and shared competences, where States can adopt legally binding acts to the extent that the Union does not do so. Article 2 also identifies a third category of Union competence to "support, coordinate or supplement" State actions, without any power to harmonize legislation or otherwise enact binding law.

TFEU Article 3 lists only five fields as falling within exclusive Union competence: the customs union, the common commercial policy, monetary policy within the monetary union, competition policy, and the conservation of marine biological resources. Article 4 lists as shared competences almost all the other fields of action previously listed in EC Treaty Article 3, while Article 6 lists health, industry, culture, tourism, education, youth and sport and civil protection as fields for Union support and coordination only. Article 5 adds that the EU may provide guidelines for Member States in their coordination of economic and employment policies.

The TEU, as introduced by the Maastricht Treaty recognized two new fields of intergovernmental action: the Common Foreign and Security Policy (CFSP) and Cooperation in Justice and Home Affairs (JHA). As the TEU's pillars two and three, they fell within the EU's, but not the Community's, sphere of action. The Lisbon TEU retains CFSP as a field of special intergovernmental action, albeit not in a separate pillar. Most of the JHA was transferred to the Community sphere by the Treaty of Amsterdam, and the Lisbon Treaty's TFEU Article 4 transfers the remaining parts of the JHA, now called the Area of Freedom, Security and Justice, to the list of shared competences. Of course, under the Lisbon Treaty, the pillars themselves are no more.

As we shall observe in subsequent chapters, wherever a Treaty article authorizes the EU to take action, it specifies substantive and procedural requirements for doing so. One of the roles of the Court of Justice is to ensure compliance with these requirements.

NOTES AND QUESTIONS

1. Paradoxically perhaps, some Euroskeptics regard the principles of conferral and reserved powers, while ostensibly limiting the scope of Union competences, as suggestive of a move toward a "federal state." Only a federal state, it is argued, has need of such a clause; international treaty regimes have no need of it, due to the obvious premise that powers not conferred on international organizations continue to reside with the signatory states. Do you agree?

2. Some commentators view discussions of competences as basically artificial and even misleading, in that no delimitation of competences, however precise, can possibly capture the true nature of "who does what"—if only because governance at both levels is simply too closely linked. Do you agree? Have other countries with a federal-type government—the US, Germany, and Switzerland, for example—succeeded in meaningfully delimiting competences? For a comparison of the delimitation of competences in the European Union and the United States, see G. Bermann & N. Kalypso, "Basic Principles for the Allocation of Competence in the United States and the European Union" in The Federal Vision: Legitimacy and Levels of Governance in the United States and the European Union (K. Nicolaidis & R. Howse, eds. 2001).

B. IMPLIED POWERS

1. THE GENERAL TREATY PROVISION ON IMPLIED POWERS

The drafters of the EEC Treaty proved remarkably prescient in foreseeing the need for an "implied powers clause" that would enable the Council to adopt legislation or take decisions in order to achieve a Treaty objective when no specific Treaty article authorized the action. EC Treaty Article 308 (initially numbered and well-known as Article 235) reads as follows:

> If action by the Community should prove necessary to attain, in the course of the operation of the common market, one of the objectives of the Community and this Treaty has not provided the necessary powers, the Council shall, acting unanimously on a proposal from the Commission and after consulting the European Parliament, take the appropriate measures.

Sometimes called an "elastic" or "necessary and proper" clause because of its functional similarity to the US constitutional provision interpreted to grant the Congress implied legislative powers, this Treaty article has proved its worth in enabling the Council at various times to adopt highly beneficial legislation, e.g., the initial environmental protection directives, the directive requiring equal treatment for men and women in employment, and the Community Trademark Regulation (see Chapters 32, 34 and 19, respectively). Subsequent Treaty amendments have inserted articles that specifically authorize legislation in the fields of environmental protection, social policy and the creation of intellectual property rights, so that reliance on implied powers is unnecessary.

Despite its obvious functional value, Article 308 had a serious procedural flaw in terms of democratic legitimacy: Parliament was only consulted. Not surprisingly, the Lisbon Treaty's new version—TFEU Article 352—requires that Parliament consent to a proposed Council measure, with the unusual feature that it may vote in favor or veto, but not amend, as in the ordinary legislative procedure. The new text also prevents Article 352 from being used to harmonize laws in fields of cooperative action where other Treaty articles forbid harmonization. Likewise, TFEU Article 352 cannot be used to take action to achieve the objectives of the CFSP.

2. IMPLIED POWERS UNDER SPECIFIC TREATY ARTICLES

Inevitably issues would arise over whether the Council, or later the Council together with the Parliament, could expansively interpret specific Treaty articles in order to adopt legislation by the means prescribed in those articles, rather than unanimously under Article 308. The Court of Justice occasionally has had to delimit the meaning of the treaty articles in these "fringe" cases.

Indeed the issue even arose in interpreting the ECSC Treaty. In Fédération Charbonnière v. High Authority (Fédéchar), Case 8/55, [1954–1956] ECR 245, the Court of Justice held that the ECSC High Authority had the implied power to fix the prices of Belgian coal producers temporarily to prevent them from excessively benefiting from ECSC subsidies, although no ECSC Treaty article expressly granted a price-fixing power.

In view of the broad reach of the power to harmonize national legislation to achieve the internal market pursuant to EC Treaty Article 95 (initially numbered as 100a and now TFEU Article 114), described in Chapter 14B, cases requiring the delimitation of this legislative power were bound to arise and attract attention.

SPAIN v. COUNCIL

(Medicinal product certificates)
Case C–350/92, [1995] ECR I–1985.

[In 1992, in order to compensate pharmaceutical manufacturers for delays in the marketing of patented drugs occasioned by the lengthy pharmaceutical review process, the Council adopted Regulation 1768/92 creating a supplementary protection certificate for medicinal products, which extended the same rights as the basic patent for a period of time up to an absolute maximum of five years. The regulation was adopted under the then Article 95 (now TFEU Article 114), which authorized harmonization to achieve the internal market and at the time required parliamentary cooperation and qualified majority voting in the Council.

Spain, supported by Greece, challenged the regulation as "a grave infringement of the sovereignty of Member States," because the EC Treaty did not give the Community legislative power to create patent rights, or indeed any other form of intellectual property rights. Spain also argued that if legislative competence existed at all, it could only be by virtue of Article 308 and not 95, thus requiring unanimous voting. The Council argued that it could legislate in the field of intellectual property under Article 95 where necessary to achieve the internal market.]

26 Article [308] may be used as the legal basis for a measure only where no other provision of the Treaty gives the Community institutions the necessary power to adopt it.

* * *

33 [H]armonizing measures [adopted under Article 95] are necessary to deal with disparities between the laws of the Member States in so far as such disparities are liable to hinder the free movement of goods within the Community.

34 The contested regulation is intended precisely to establish a uniform Community approach by creating a supplementary certificate which may be obtained by the holder of a national or European patent under the same conditions in each Member State, and by providing, in particular, for a uniform duration of protection.

35 The regulation thus aims to prevent the heterogeneous development of national laws leading to further disparities which would be likely to create obstacles to the free movement of medicinal products within the Community and thus directly affect the establishment and the functioning of the internal market.

36 The Council rightly emphasizes that differences in the protection given in the Community to one and the same medicine would give rise to a fragmentation of the market, whereby the medicine would still be protected in some national markets but no longer protected in others.

* * *

40   It follows from the above that the regulation was validly adopted on the basis of Article [95] of the Treaty, and did not therefore have to be adopted on the basis of . . . Article [308].

NOTES AND QUESTIONS

1. Note that the EC Treaty has never been amended to provide any specific legislative competence to harmonize national laws in the field of intellectual property. Such legislation must be rationalized in terms of achieving the internal market and based on Article 95 (now TFEU Article 114). Do you find the Court's reliance on Article 95 persuasive? Should it have relied on Article 308 instead?

2. The Court subsequently used similar reasoning to uphold the use of Article 95 to adopt the Biotechnological Patent Directive, which represented an even more far-reaching innovation. See the excerpt at page 119 infra. Note that TFEU Article 118 authorizes the Council to create new intellectual property rights, such as the Community Trademark, but not to harmonize existing national rights.

3. In a rare judgment, in 2000 the Court invalidated a 1998 directive restricting tobacco advertising because it covered forms of advertising that had no cross-border impact. This important judgment is excerpted at page 144. That it was exceptional is evidenced by the Court's subsequent endorsement of the use of Article 95 to adopt a later directive that contained all the restrictions on advertising except those that the Court had specifically held not to have a cross-border impact. Moreover, in 2002 the Court endorsed the use of Article 95 to adopt a directive setting maximum limits on the amount of nicotine and tar in cigarettes and mandatory large health warnings on the packages. See the *British American Tobacco* judgment, excerpted at page 120 infra.

In a recent judgment with considerable practical impact, the Court held that the EU enjoyed the implied power to require Member States to impose criminal sanctions in order to adequately achieve the aims of a legislative act.

COMMISSION v. COUNCIL

(Criminal sanctions for environmental measures)
Case C–176/03, [2005] ECR I–7879.

[The Commission, supported by Parliament, contended that a Council Framework Directive requiring States to adopt criminal penalties for a number of serious environmental offences should have been adopted under the then EC Treaty Article 175(1) (now TFEU Article 192(1)), authorizing environmental legislation, rather than under the then TEU's pillar 3 on cooperative measures in police and criminal affairs. The Court exercised its line-drawing power to determine whether a measure should properly be adopted under the EC Treaty or the TEU.]

41   [P]rotection of the environment constitutes one of the essential objectives of the Community. In that regard, Article 2 EC states that the Community has as its task to promote "a high level of protection and

improvement of the quality of the environment" and, to that end, Article 3(1)(*l*) EC provides for the establishment of a "policy in the sphere of the environment".

42   Furthermore, in the words of Article 6 EC, "[e]nvironmental protection requirements must be integrated into the definition and implementation of the Community policies and activities," a provision which emphasises the fundamental nature of that objective and its extension across the range of those policies and activities.

43   Articles 174 EC to 176 EC comprise, as a general rule, the framework within which Community environmental policy must be carried out. In particular, Article 174(1) EC lists the objectives of the Community's action on the environment and Article 175 EC sets out the procedures to be followed in order to achieve those objectives. The Community's powers are, in general, exercised in accordance with the procedure laid down in Article 251 EC [the codecision procedure], following consultation of the Economic and Social Committee and the Committee of the Regions.

* * *

46   As regards the aim of the framework decision, it is clear both from its title and from its first three recitals that its objective is the protection of the environment. The Council was concerned "at the rise in environmental offences and their effects which are increasingly extending beyond the borders of the States in which the offences are committed", and, having found that those offences constitute "a threat to the environment" and "a problem jointly faced by the Member States", concluded that "a tough response" and "concerted action to protect the environment under criminal law" were called for.

47   As to the content of the framework decision, Article 2 establishes a list of particularly serious environmental offences, in respect of which the Member States must impose criminal penalties. Articles 2 to 7 of the decision do indeed entail partial harmonisation of the criminal laws of the Member States, in particular as regards the constituent elements of various criminal offences committed to the detriment of the environment. As a general rule, neither criminal law nor the rules of criminal procedure fall within the Community's competence.

48   However, the last-mentioned finding does not prevent the Community legislature, when the application of effective, proportionate and dissuasive criminal penalties by the competent national authorities is an essential measure for combating serious environmental offences, from taking measures which relate to the criminal law of the Member States which it considers necessary in order to ensure that the rules which it lays down on environmental protection are fully effective.

49   [I]n this instance, although Articles 1 to 7 of the framework decision determine that certain conduct which is particularly detrimental to the environment is to be criminal, they leave to the Member States

the choice of the criminal penalties to apply, although . . . the penalties must be effective, proportionate and dissuasive.

50   The Council does not dispute that the acts listed in Article 2 of the framework decision include infringements of a considerable number of Community measures, which were listed in the annex to the proposed directive. Moreover, it is apparent from the first three recitals to the framework decision that the Council took the view that criminal penalties were essential for combating serious offences against the environment.

51   It follows from the foregoing that, on account of both their aim and their content, Articles 1 to 7 of the framework decision have as their main purpose the protection of the environment and they could have been properly adopted on the basis of Article 175 EC.

* * *

55   In the light of all the foregoing, the framework decision must be annulled.

NOTES AND QUESTIONS

1.   The principal case builds upon prior judgments such as *Von Colson & Kamann* and *Marshall II*, infra pages 356 and 359, respectively, which required States to impose effective and dissuasive civil penalties. However, this judgment is the first to hold that the EU may be competent to require criminal penalties as a means of ensuring the effective application and enforcement of EU law. Are you persuaded by the Court's reasoning, or do you think that a Treaty amendment should have been required?

2.   In ¶ 52 (not excerpted above), the Court observes that EC Treaty Article 135 (now TFEU Article 33), which authorizes the Council to adopt measures to strengthen customs cooperation, and EC Treaty Article 280(4) (now TFEU Article 325(4)), which authorizes the Council to adopt measures to reduce fraud effecting the Union, both bar the Council from requiring States to adopt criminal measures. Do these provisions indirectly support the Court's holding?

3.   The Commission promptly issued a Communication on the judgment's implications, COM (2005) 583, noting at once that the Court's reasoning may be relied upon not just with regard to environmental protection legislation, but any EU legislation where there exists "a clear need to combat shortcomings" and "to ensure full effectiveness." However, the Commission must carefully examine the necessity of criminal sanctions in "observance of the principles of subsidiarity and proportionality." In an Annex, the Commission listed existing measures which potentially required amendment, notably the Money Laundering Directive, discussed at page 1232, and several proposed directives which needed to be re-examined.

4.   In Commission v. Council (Ship source pollution), Case C–440/05, [2007] ECR I–9097, the Commission sought to annul the Council's Frame-

work Decision 2005/67, which required States to provide for a minimum level of criminal sanctions in cases of pollution caused by ships. The Commission considered that EC Treaty Article 80(2) (now TFEU Article 100(2)), which empowered the Council to adopt rules concerning sea transport, should have been used. The Court quoted ¶ 48 of its judgment in Commission v. Council, supra, and agreed that the Council could have validly used EC Treaty Article 80(2) to adopt criminal penalties to impose environmental protection (¶ 69), but then held that "the determination of the type and level of the criminal penalties to be applied does not fall within the Community's sphere of competence" (¶ 70). What importance does this judgment have in practice? Is it simply an application of the principle of subsidiarity?

C. PREEMPTION OF MEMBER STATE LAW

In a federal system, federal and state governments may each adopt regulations in a particular sector. Often such regulations may coexist without difficulty, or the federal regulation may even expressly authorize complementary state regulation. Sometimes, however, the federal courts may conclude that the state regulation conflicts directly or indirectly with the federal, or that the federal regulation is so comprehensive that it is not desirable to have any state regulation at all. In that case the federal courts will invalidate totally, or narrowly apply, the state regulation in the field.

In the US, we use the term preemption to refer to the ability of federal law to restrict or invalidate conflicting state law. In the EU, the Court of Justice does not use that term, but applies a parallel analysis in examining whether EU and Member State rules may coexist or not. When the Court invalidates Member State rules which it considers to conflict with EU law, it is in effect applying the principle of the primacy of the Treaty and secondary Community rules. See Chapter 7B for analysis of this crucial Court doctrine.

Preemption issues arise most often in relation to EU legislation harmonizing national rules to achieve the internal market. We will discuss leading judgments in Chapter 14C infra. However, preemption issues also may arise in the sectors of agriculture and competition law, and the earliest leading precedents arose in those fields.

WILHELM v. BUNDESKARTELAMT

(Walt Wilhelm)
Case 14/68, [1969] ECR 1.

[In 1967, the Commission began proceedings to enforce its relatively recent competition rules against several dyestuffs manufacturers, including four German companies, for allegedly fixing the prices of aniline in violation of then EC Treaty Article 81 (ex 85 and now TFEU Article 101). Later that year, the German Federal Cartel Office imposed fines on those German companies under the 1957 German law against restraints of competition. The companies challenged the Cartel Office decision before a Berlin court, which sought a preliminary ruling from the Court of Justice on the question whether the Cartel Office could take action concerning conduct that at the same time was the subject of proceedings before the Commission.]

2   [T]he national court asks whether, when a procedure has already been initiated by the Commission [to enforce EC competition rules], it is compatible with the Treaty for the national authorities to apply to the same facts the prohibitions laid down by the national law on cartels. This request is elaborated [by a] question, relating to the risk of a different legal assessment of the same facts and to the possibility of distortions of competition in the common market to the detriment of those subject to the said national law.

3   Community and national law on cartels consider cartels from different points of view. Whereas Article [81] regards them in the light of the obstacles which may result for trade between Member States, each body of national legislation proceeds on the basis of the considerations peculiar to it and considers cartels only in that context. It is true that as the economic phenomena and legal situations under consideration may in individual cases be interdependent, the distinction between Community and national aspects could not serve in all cases as the decisive criterion for the delimitation of jurisdiction. However, it implies that one and the same agreement may, in principle, be the object of two sets of parallel proceedings, one before the Community authorities under Article [81] ..., the other before the national authorities under national law.

4   Moreover this interpretation is confirmed by the provision in Article [83(2)(e), now TFEU Article 103(2)(e)], which authorizes the Council to determine the relationship between national laws and the Community rules on competition; it follows that in principle the national cartel authorities may take proceedings also with regard to situations likely to be the subject of a decision by the Commission. ... However, if the ultimate general aim of the Treaty is to be respected, this parallel application of the national system can only be allowed in so far as it does not prejudice the uniform application throughout the Common Market of the Community rules on cartels and the full effect of the measures adopted in implementation of those rules.

5   While the primary object [of the Treaty's competition rules] is to eliminate the obstacles to the free movement of goods within the common market and to confirm and safeguard the unity of that market, it also permits the Community authorities to carry out certain positive, though indirect, action with a view to promoting a harmonious development of economic activities within the whole Community, in accordance with Article 2 of the Treaty. Article [83(2)(e)], in conferring on a Community institution the power to determine the relationship

between national laws and the Community rules on competition, confirms the supremacy of Community law.

* * *

7   It follows from the foregoing that should it prove that a decision of a national authority regarding an agreement would be incompatible with a decision adopted by the Commission at the culmination of the procedure initiated by it, the national authority is required to take proper account of the effects of the latter decision.

* * *

9   Consequently, ... national authorities may take action against an agreement in accordance with their national law, even when an examination of the agreement from the point of view of its compatibility with Community law is pending before the Commission, subject however to the condition that the application of national law may not prejudice the full and uniform application of Community law or the effects of measures taken or to be taken to implement it.

[The German court's second question to the Court was whether any general Community law principle prohibits exposing enterprises to the risk of a "double sanction." The Court answered in the negative, but suggested that principles of "natural justice" might prevent the imposition of consecutive sanctions or at least require that a previous sanction be taken into account in fixing a second sanction for the same conduct.]

MASTERFOODS LTD. v. HB ICE CREAM LTD.
Case C–344/98, [2000] ECR I–11369.

[HB, a leading Irish ice cream producer, sued in an Irish court to prevent Masterfoods from inducing retailers to breach their contractual undertaking to display only HB products in the freezer cabinets supplied to them by HB. In the same court, Masterfoods sought a declaration that the exclusivity clause was null and void under both Irish and EU competition law. The Irish court found in favor of HB, and issued the requested injunction. Masterfoods appealed to the Irish Supreme Court and at the same time lodged a competition law complaint with the Commission. When the Commission found HB's policy to infringe EU competition law, HB sought review in the Court of First Instance. At this point, the Irish Supreme Court asked the Court of Justice whether it was required to stay Masterfoods' appeal, pending the result of the CFI appeal and any further appeal to the Court of Justice.]

49   It is ... clear from the case-law of the Court that the Member States' duty [of sincere cooperation] under Article [10] of the EC Treaty [now Lisbon TEU Article 4(3)] to take all appropriate measures, whether general or particular, to ensure fulfilment of the obligations arising from Community law and to abstain from any measure which could jeopardise the attainment of the objectives of the Treaty is binding on

all the authorities of Member States including, for matters within their jurisdiction, the courts.

* * *

56   [A]pplication of the Community competition rules is based on an obligation of sincere cooperation between the national courts, on the one hand, and the Commission and the Community Courts, on the other. . . .

57   When the outcome of the dispute before the national court depends on the validity of the Commission decision, it follows . . . that the national court should, in order to avoid reaching a decision that runs counter to that of the Commission, stay its proceedings pending final judgment in the action for annulment by the Community Courts, unless it considers that, in the circumstances of the case, a reference to the Court of Justice for a preliminary ruling on the validity of the Commission decision is warranted.

NOTES AND QUESTIONS

1.   *Walt Wilhelm* establishes that the EU and the Member States share, albeit unequally, the ability to set and to enforce competition law norms. The relationship between national and EU competition law is taken up in detail in Chapter 20 infra. The Court's crucial holding is in paragraph 9 of the judgment to the effect that national law may not be permitted to "prejudice the full and uniform application of Community law or the effects of measures taken or to be taken to implement it." This is a clear application of the principle of Treaty primacy.

2.   In *Masterfoods*, the Commission initially found that HBs policy had an impact on inter-State trade so that Article 81 applied, and then concluded that the policy violated Article 81. Unless the CFI reverses the Commission, the Commission decision would bind Irish courts on account of EU law primacy, which attaches to Commission decisions as well as to regulations and directives. Do you see why the Court of Justice held in ¶ 57 that the Irish Supreme Court should postpone action on the Irish appeal?

The Court has not been as tolerant of concurrent competences in all fields of EU law governance. The following agricultural policy case illustrates the point, but the reader should also be sensitive to the preemption question in cases throughout the substantive law chapters of this book. For a general discussion, see Soares, Pre-emption, Conflicts of Powers and Subsidiarity, 23 Eur. L. Rev. 132 (1998).

PIGS MARKETING BOARD v. REDMOND
Case 83/78, [1978] ECR 2347.

[Legislation in Northern Ireland required producers to sell certain categories of pigs through a Pigs Marketing Board which was empowered to regulate price and other conditions of sale. Under the law, transporting pigs without authorization by the Board subjected a producer to criminal sanctions and forfeiture of the livestock. Redmond was charged with transporting pigs without Board authorization.]

11   The defendant argued in his defense [in national court] that the provisions of the Pigs Marketing Scheme ... were incompatible with the provisions of Community law, in particular with the regulations on the common organization of the market in pigmeat....

* * *

56   [O]nce the Community has, pursuant to Article [34] of the Treaty [now TFEU Article 40], legislated for the establishment of the common organization of the market in a given sector, Member States are under an obligation to refrain from taking any measure which might undermine or create exceptions to it.

57   With a view to applying that statement in the case of the Pigs Marketing Scheme it should be borne in mind that ... the common organization of the market in pigmeat, like the other common organizations, ... is based on the concept of an open market to which every producer has free access and the functioning of which is regulated solely by the instruments provided for by that organization.

58   Hence any provisions or national practices which might alter the pattern of imports or exports or influence the formation of market prices by preventing producers from buying and selling freely within the State in which they are established, or in any other Member State, [on] conditions laid down by Community rules ... are incompatible with the principles of such organization of the market.

59   Any action of this type, which is brought to bear upon the market by a body set up by a Member State and which does not come within the arrangements made by Community rules cannot be justified by the pursuit of special objectives of economic policy, national or regional; the common organization of the market ... is intended precisely to attain such objectives on the Community scale [on] conditions acceptable for the whole of the Community and taking account of the needs of all its regions....

60   Any intervention by a Member State or by its regional or subordinate authorities in the market machinery apart from such intervention as may be specifically laid down by the Community regulation runs the risk of obstructing the functioning of the common organization of the market and of creating unjustified advantages for certain groups of producers or consumers to the prejudice of the economy of other Member States or of other economic groups within the Community.

* * *

65   [A] marketing system [of the sort presented here is] to be considered as incompatible with the requirements of Articles [28 and 29 and the regulation] on the common organization of the market in pigmeat.

NOTES AND QUESTIONS

1. *Pigs Marketing Board* is only one of many cases holding that Member States may not establish national systems restricting business in a sector specifically covered by a common market organization adopted by the EU. According to these cases, once the EU exercises its legislative power to install such an organization, national power to regulate various stages of production and distribution within that market is preempted. This corresponds to the notion of "field preemption" in US law.

2. The fact that a matter is not preempted by EU legislation does not of course mean that the national measure in question necessarily comports with EU law. For example, Germany was able to show that the EU's common organization of the dairy market did not preempt its regulation of imitation milk products, but it nevertheless failed to show that the regulation in question was a justifiable restriction on the free movement of goods under EC Treaty Articles 28 and 30 (now TFEU Articles 34 and 36). Commission v. Germany (Milk substitutes), Case 76/86, [1989] ECR 1021.

3. Directives may on occasion either expressly authorize or forbid national rules concerning a given matter. Thus, in Republic v. Di Pinto, Case C–361/89, [1991] ECR I–1189, a national court asked the Court of Justice whether Council Directive 85/577, protecting consumers from contracts "negotiated away from business premises," precluded States from extending its protection of consumers to traders seeking to sell an ongoing business, a type of sale which would not usually be considered as covered by the directive. The Court relied on Article 8 of the directive which stated that the directive "shall not prevent Member States from adopting or maintaining more favourable provisions to protect consumers in the field which it covers."

In contrast, Directive 65/65 on the marketing of proprietary medicines expressly provides that "authorization ... shall not be refused, suspended or revoked except on the grounds set out in this Directive." Such language may be regarded as conclusive evidence of preemption. See Pierrel SpA v. Ministero della Sanita, Case C–83/92, [1993] ECR I–6419.

4. Treaty provisions occasionally expressly authorize complementary State rules. Thus EC Treaty Article 137 (now TFEU Article 153), which authorizes the harmonization of employment law, provides in ¶ 5 that EU legislation "shall not prevent any Member State from maintaining or introducing more stringent protective measures compatible with this Treaty." EC Treaty Articles 176 on environmental protection and Article 153 on consumer protection (now TFEU Articles 193 and 169, respectively) contain comparable language. Such express non-preemption language makes it clear that EU standards in these areas constitute a floor on Member State regulation and not a ceiling. However, the Articles cited do require that any such "more stringent" State measures must still be "compatible with this Treaty."

D. THE SUBSIDIARITY PRINCIPLE

As section A demonstrates, the EU's fields of action represent enumerated or conferred areas of competence. The Lisbon Treaty reinforces this through its TEU and TFEU provisions on the principle of conferral. There remains, however, an important question: how broadly or narrowly may the political institutions of the Union legislate or otherwise take legally binding action in exercising the powers conferred upon them?

The Maastricht Treaty amended the EC Treaty to insert Article 5 (now Lisbon TEU Article 5) which sets out the principle of subsidiarity. After the initial paragraph states the principle of conferral, the second reads as follows:

> In areas which do not fall within its exclusive competence, the Community shall take action, in accordance with the principle of subsidiarity, only if and insofar as the objectives of the proposed action cannot be sufficiently achieved by the Member States and can therefore, by reason of the scale or effects of proposed action, be better achieved by the Community.

The third paragraph of Article 5 adds the principle of proportionality: Community action "shall not go beyond what is necessary to achieve the objectives of this Treaty." We will discuss in Chapter 5 the principle of proportionality, which can be used to limit or restrictively apply not only EU law measures, but also national rules creating barriers to the achievement of the internal market.

The term, "subsidiarity," does not appear in US constitutional analysis, although the application of the Tenth Amendment and the "states' rights" doctrine does present certain analogies. The concept of subsidiarity is therefore not so easy to grasp. The basic notion behind subsidiarity is that the EU should not exercise a legislative or other power shared with the Member States if, upon examination, the underlying purpose can be achieved as well, or perhaps even better, by the Member States. EU action must be shown to be more effective or efficient than Member State action. Moreover, the reference to Member State action does not indicate only national action, but includes also regional or local action, which should often be preferred in order to keep government closer to the people.

Undoubtedly, the drafters of the Maastricht Treaty saw Article 5 as a kind of corrective to the expansion of EU powers and to the Treaty amendments that had made it easier to adopt EU legislation. The principle of subsidiarity had in fact first appeared in the Single European Act as a limitation on the adoption of environmental protection legislation, but the express reference there was deleted as superfluous in view of the general subsidiarity provision in the Maastricht Treaty. Commission President Delors strongly endorsed the subsidiarity principle, which the Commission did not view as preventing appropriate legislative action.

On October 25, 1993, the Commission, Council and Parliament joined in an Inter-institutional Declaration on Democracy, Transparency and Subsidiarity, Bull. EC 10/93, at 118, which conveyed the Commission's intention to apply the principle of subsidiarity when proposing new legislation. Both the final Delors Commission and the Santer Commission accordingly withdrew a number of draft texts and narrowed the scope of others. However, protests from the Parliament caused the Commission to reintroduce a draft directive on the protection of animals in zoos, which was ultimately adopted; to broaden again the proposed comparative advertising amendments to the unfair advertising directive, also ultimately adopted; and to retain other draft directives, particularly in the environmental field. The Commission now customarily includes a recital in each draft directive affirming that the text satisfies the principle of subsidiarity.

The UK's conservative government of Prime Minister Major particularly championed the new Treaty principle. The European Council meeting at Edinburgh in December 1992 issued a statement amplifying upon the principle. This led ultimately to the drafting of the Amsterdam Treaty's Protocol on Subsidiarity.

The Treaty of Lisbon has reaffirmed the principle of subsidiarity. Its TEU Article 5(3) essentially replicates the text of the former EC Treaty Article 5 and the Lisbon Treaty retains the Protocol on Subsidiarity and Proportionality that had appeared with the Nice Treaty. See document 4 in the Documents Supplement, and the Note on the national parliaments' role in this regard, infra, page 113.

Member States can and do invoke the subsidiarity principle in their political opposition to various legislative proposals at the European level. But to what extent should the Court of Justice entertain challenges to EU legislation brought by Member States on the ground that the legislation seeks to advance objectives that could just as well be attained at the national level? In other words, is the subsidiarity principle justiciable? The following case considers that key question.

GERMANY v. PARLIAMENT AND COUNCIL

(Deposit-guarantee schemes)
Case C–233/94, [1997] ECR I–2405.

[Germany challenged an EU directive which required the Member States to set up a "deposit guarantee system" to ensure that every bank or other credit institution would guarantee its customers' deposits in the event of the bank's insolvency. The Council, acting on the basis of EC Treaty Article 47(2) (now TFEU Article 53), had adopted the measure over Germany's opposition. Germany claimed, among other things, that the Council and Parliament had failed to comply with the requirement of a statement of reasons under the then Article 253 of the Treaty (now TFEU Article 296). Germany contended that an adequate statement must necessarily address the principle of subsidiarity. More specifically, it maintained that the institutions had to "indicate in a detailed way why the Community may be considered as alone capable of taking action on the matter in question [or why] the objectives [of the measure] could not sufficiently be achieved through action taken at the level of the Member States." The Court held that the directive complied with the principle of subsidiarity.]

26   [T]he Parliament and the Council stated in the ... preamble to the Directive that "consideration should be given to the situation which might arise if deposits in a credit institution that has branches in other Member States became unavailable" and that it was "indispensable to ensure a harmonized minimum level of deposit protection wherever deposits are located in the Community". This shows that, in the Community legislature's view, the aim of its action could, because of the dimensions of the intended action, be best achieved at Community level. The same reasoning appears [elsewhere in the preamble], from which it is clear that the decision regarding the guarantee scheme which is competent in the event of the insolvency of a branch situated in a Member State other than that in which the credit institution has its head office has repercussions which are felt outside the borders of each Member State.

27   Furthermore, in the [preamble] the Parliament and the Council stated that the action taken by the Member States in response to the Commission's Recommendation has not fully achieved the desired result. The Community legislature therefore found that the objective of its action could not be achieved sufficiently by the Member States.

28   Consequently, it is apparent that ... the Parliament and the Council did explain why they considered that their action was in conformity with the principle of subsidiarity and, accordingly, that they complied with the obligation to give reasons as required under Article [253] of the Treaty. An express reference to that principle cannot be required.

NOTES AND QUESTIONS

1.   The Court refers in ¶ 27 to the Commission's earlier Recommendation that all States should adopt a deposit guarantee scheme. The Commission proposed the directive only after the Recommendation failed to get all the States to act. Does this sequence suggest that the directive satisfied the principle of subsidiarity?

2.   Rather than charge the institutions with violating the principle of subsidiarity, Germany charged them with failing to state reasons that demonstrated their compliance with the principle. Can you explain this? What is the difference? What is to prevent the institutions from satisfying the requirement of reasons through merely conclusory statements about the need for EU-wide action? Consider that, in a recent reference to subsidiarity, the Court held that the institutions' compliance with the principle "is necessarily implicit" in recitals in the preamble to the challenged directive to the effect that "in the absence of action at Community level, the development of the

laws and practices of the different Member States impedes the proper functioning of the internal market." See Netherlands v. Parliament and Council (Biotechnological inventions), Case C–377/98, [2001] ECR I–7079.

3.   What are the understandings about subsidiarity in the US, which, like the EU, is a divided-power system in which federal jurisdiction depends heavily on the notion of interstate commerce, and in which maintaining the proper balance of power between the states and federal government is considered to be of utmost importance? For a comparative discussion of EU subsidiarity and US federalism, see G. Bermann, Taking Subsidiarity Seriously: Federalism in the European Community and the United States, 94 Colum. L. Rev. 331 (1994).

A claim that EU legislation violates the principle of subsidiarity is often raised in connection with legislation adopted under EC Treaty Article 95 (now TFEU Article 114) on harmonization to achieve the internal market. The following case is best known for the Court's holding that the Council and Parliament had the power to act pursuant to Article 95, subsidiarity notwithstanding.

THE QUEEN v. SECRETARY OF STATE FOR HEALTH EX PARTE BRITISH AMERICAN TOBACCO

Case C–491/01, [2002] ECR I–11453.

[In 2001, Parliament and Council adopted Directive 2001/37 on the manufacture, presentation and sale of tobacco products, using EC Treaty Articles 95 and 133 (now TFEU Articles 114 and 207) to enact far stricter rules than those initially adopted in 1989 and 1990 directives. Two British tobacco product manufacturers challenged the UK's obligation to transpose the directive into domestic law before the domestic courts. They questioned whether the directive infringed the principle of subsidiarity. The Court upheld the directive.]

174   The claimants in the main proceedings maintain that the principle of subsidiarity is applicable to measures relating to the internal market such as the Directive ... and that the Community legislature [had] no need to adopt the Directive, since harmonised rules had already been established by Directives 89/622 and 90/239 for the purpose of eliminating barriers to trade in tobacco products. Furthermore, they argue that no evidence has been adduced to show that the Member States could not adopt the measures of public health protection they considered necessary.

175   The Belgian Government and the Parliament maintain that the principle of subsidiarity does not apply to the Directive, inasmuch as that principle is applicable only in those areas in which the Community does not have exclusive competence, whereas the Directive, being adopted for the purpose of attaining the internal market, comes within one of those areas of exclusive competence... In any event, even if it were accepted that that principle applied to the Directive, it

was complied with in the circumstances, since the action undertaken could not have been satisfactorily achieved at Member State level.

176 The United Kingdom, French, Netherlands and Swedish Governments, and the Council and Commission, submit that the principle of subsidiarity is applicable in the present case and was complied with by the Directive.... According to the Netherlands Government and the Commission, where the conditions for the use of Article 95 EC have been satisfied, the conditions for Community action under the second paragraph of Article 5 EC [the subsidiarity principle] are also satisfied, since it is clear that no Member State acting alone can take the necessary measures to prevent any divergence between the laws of the Member States having an impact on trade.

179 It is to be noted, as a preliminary matter, that the principle of subsidiarity applies where the Community legislature makes use of Article 95 EC, inasmuch as that provision does not give it exclusive competence to regulate economic activity on the internal market, but only a certain competence for the purpose of improving the conditions for its establishment and functioning, by eliminating barriers to the free movement of goods and the freedom to provide services or by removing distortions of competition....

180 As regards the question whether the Directive was adopted in keeping with the principle of subsidiarity, it must first be considered whether the objective of the proposed action could be better achieved at Community level.

181 [T]he Directive's objective is to eliminate the barriers raised by the differences which still exist between the Member States' laws, regulations and administrative provisions on the manufacture, presentation and sale of tobacco products, while ensuring a high level of health protection, in accordance with Article 95(3) EC.

182 Such an objective cannot be sufficiently achieved by the Member States individually and calls for action at Community level, as demonstrated by the multifarious development of national laws in this case....

183 It follows that, in the case of the Directive, the objective of the proposed action could be better achieved at Community level.

* * *

185 It follows from the foregoing conclusions ... that the Directive is not invalid by reason of infringement of the principle of subsidiarity.

NOTES AND QUESTIONS

1. Note that the Court rejects in ¶ 179 the view that establishing the internal market under Article 95 is a field of exclusive Community competence, which would have made the principle of subsidiarity irrelevant. The Lisbon Treaty's TFEU Article 4 also considers action to achieve the internal market a field of shared powers.

2.   Does the *British American Tobacco* judgment resolve the issue of the justiciability of subsidiarity claims? Has the Court in effect indicated that a goal would be "better achieved" by EU action, satisfying the subsidiarity principle, whenever action is necessary under Article 95 to remove disparities in national law that hinder inter-State trade, as the Commission argued in ¶ 176?

3.   In discussing the ambit of the doctrine of preemption, we previously noted Masterfoods Ltd. v. HB Ice Cream Ltd., supra page 113, in which the Court essentially held that the doctrine's application required Irish courts to suspend proceedings concerning a competition law dispute between two private parties until the Commission had issued a decision applying its competition regulatory rules to the circumstances of the same dispute. After the Commission subsequently held that HB's contract clause violated competition rules, HB appealed to the Court of First Instance, claiming that the Commission violated the principle of subsidiarity by taking a decision concerning a dispute between two Irish companies concerning retail sales of Irish products when the dispute was in the process of being settled by litigation in Irish courts. The CFI rejected the claim:

198   The issues dealt with in the contested decision had a wider Community importance, in particular in light of the fact that various national courts and competition authorities were dealing with parallel cases raising similar issues to those in the present case.... In those circumstances, the adoption of the contested decision by the Commission was appropriate in order to ensure that the Community competition rules would be applied coherently ... to the various forms of exclusivity practised by ice-cream manufacturers throughout the Community.

199   The Commission is ... entitled to adopt, at any time, individual decisions applying Articles [81] and [82] of the Treaty, even though it shares competence to apply [these Articles] with the national courts, and even where an agreement or practice has already been the subject of a decision by a national court and the decision contemplated by the Commission conflicts with the national court's decision....

NOTE ON NATIONAL PARLIAMENTS' SUPERVISION OF THE SUBSIDIARITY PRINCIPLE

As previously noted, the Lisbon Treaty's revised Protocol on Subsidiarity (doc. 4 in the doc. supp.) provides a structured mode of review of draft legislation by national parliaments. When the Commission has produced a draft text and sends it to the Council and Parliament, it must simultaneously send it to all the national parliaments. The Parliament and Council are also required to send to the national parliaments resolutions and common positions developed during the legislative process. This "early warning system" puts domestic political actors, who are frequently unaware of developments in Brussels, on notice of proposed legislation sufficiently in advance to allow them to participate in the process.

Upon review of a proposal, any national parliament (or chamber of a national parliament) is permitted within eight weeks to send the Presidents of the Parliament, Council, and Commission "a reasoned opinion" explaining its position that the proposal violates the principle of subsidiarity, which the institutions must consider.

In the most innovative aspect of the monitoring system, the Protocol establishes a threshold for subsidiarity-based opposition by national parliaments. For "voting" purposes, each chamber of a national parliament in a bicameral national system has one vote (i.e., two votes per State), while national parliaments of Member States having unicameral legislatures have two, thus preserving Member State equality. In most instances, if at least one third of these national parliamentary "votes" challenges a proposal's compliance with subsidiarity, the legislative process is suspended and the Commission must review its proposal. Upon reexamination, the Commission is free to maintain, amend, or withdraw the proposal, but it must state its reasoning. If, however, the opposition amounts to a simple majority of the votes allotted to national parliaments, and the proposal is made within the ordinary legislative procedure, the consequences are more stringent. Not only will the Commission have to justify maintaining the proposal, but the Council (with a 55% majority) or Parliament (with a simple majority) may decide to block the proposal permanently.

Finally, jurisdiction is conferred on the Court to entertain claims of the infringement of the principle of subsidiarity brought by Member States "or notified by [the Member States] in accordance with their legal order on behalf of their national parliament or a chamber of it." (Although the quoted language is ambiguous, the most likely interpretation is that the national parliaments, or their chambers, do not themselves have standing, but merely the possibility of asking the Member State to mount a challenge on their behalf.)

The Protocol's provisions according the national parliaments a voice in the monitoring of subsidiarity reflects a generally broader view of the desirability of involving the national parliaments in EU affairs. See also the separate Protocol on the Role of National Parliaments in the European Union (doc. supp., doc. 3), which codifies prior understandings about the national parliaments' right to be kept informed on EU legislative initiatives.

E. THE INTERNAL AFFAIRS DOCTRINE AND REVERSE DISCRIMINATION

On occasion, when questions are referred to the Court of Justice pursuant to the preliminary reference procedure, the Court holds that no issues are presented that involve EU law, and informs the referring court that it should only apply national law. This scenario is commonly said to illustrate the internal affairs doctrine. Moreover, because the applicable national law rules may be less liberal or more restrictive than EU rules, in some cases this has the consequence that nationals of a State are disadvantaged when compared with non-nationals who can legitimately invoke a European Union rule of law. This result is often called reverse discrimination.

Court judgments have applied the internal affairs doctrine in a variety of contexts. Thus, in Criminal proceedings against Bekaert, Case 204/87, [1988] ECR 2029, a French national and resident operating a supermarket in France was prosecuted for giving false information in his application for a permit to enlarge his business premises. He claimed that the French permit requirement violated EU legislation on competition and the right of establishment. The Court of Justice gave the French criminal court the following preliminary ruling:

> [EC Treaty Article 43 (now TFEU Article 49) and the directives that implement it] do not apply to situations which are purely internal to a Member State, such as that of a national of a Member State who has never resided or worked in any other Member State.

[1988] ECR at 2039. For a comparable judgment in which the Court rejected an alleged violation of the right of free movement of workers, see Moser v. Land Baden–Württemberg, Case 180/83, [1984] ECR 2539, excerpted at page 614 infra.

Similarly in Ministère Public v. Aubertin, Joined Cases C–29–35/94, [1995] ECR I–301, French hairdressers (none of whom claimed to have obtained any professional qualifications in another Member State) were charged with operating hair salons without being in possession of the necessary French professional diploma. They claimed "reverse discrimination" on the ground that French law, implementing an EC directive, permitted nationals of other Member States to operate hair salons in France without any diploma, provided they had lawfully operated a salon in another Member State for a specified length of time. The Court could not find a "connecting factor between [their] situations and ... those contemplated by Community law, so that the Treaty rules on freedom of establishment are inapplicable." The Court noted that the directive in question did not aim to harmonize the conditions laid down by national law for pursuit of the hairdressing profession. If the directive had had such an aim, would that have changed the result or would the cases still be purely "internal"? See Chapter 18 D.

The Court has on occasion found that exercise of a Treaty-based right can invalidate a State's claim that the internal affairs doctrine applies.

KNOORS v. SECRETARY OF STATE FOR ECONOMIC AFFAIRS
Case 115/78, [1979] ECR 399.

[Knoors, a Dutch national, who resided and conducted a heating and plumbing business in Belgium, sought to provide services regularly in the Netherlands as well. Dutch law ordinarily forbid conduct of such a business in the Netherlands without a local license. Directive 64/427 on the freedom of establishment and freedom of services in respect of self-employed persons authorized various craftsmen to provide services in other States from their State of residence, but the Netherlands contended that a Dutch national resident abroad could not rely on the directive. An administrative court referred the issue to the Court of Justice.]

9   Directive No. 64/427 is intended to facilitate the realization of freedom of establishment and of freedom to provide services in a large group of trade activities relating to industry and small craft industries.

* * *

11   Article 3 of the directive provides that, where, in a Member State, the taking up or pursuit of any activity referred to in the directive is dependent on the possession of certain qualifications, "that Member State shall accept as sufficient evidence of such knowledge and ability the fact that the activity in question has been pursued in another Member State".

* * *

17   Directive No. 64/427 is based on a broad definition of the "beneficiaries" of its provisions, in the sense that the nationals of all Member States must be able to avail themselves of the liberalizing measures which it lays down, provided that they come objectively within one of the situations provided for by the directive, and no differentiation of treatment on the basis of their residence or nationality is permitted.

18   Thus the provisions of the directive may be relied upon by the nationals of all the Member States who are in the situations which the directive defines for its application, even in respect of the State whose nationality they possess.

19   This interpretation is justified by the requirements flowing from freedom of movement for persons, freedom of establishment and freedom to provide services.

20   In fact, these liberties, which are fundamental in the Community system, could not be fully realized if the Member States were in a position to refuse to grant the benefit of the provisions of Community law to those of their nationals who have taken advantage of the facilities existing in the matter of freedom of movement and establishment and who have acquired, by virtue of such facilities, the trade qualifications referred to by the directive in a Member State other than that whose nationality they possess.

NOTES AND QUESTIONS

1. Do you agree with the Court's reasoning in *Knoors*? If a Belgian residing in Belgium (or a German residing in Belgium) can rely upon the directive to provide services in the Netherlands, why shouldn't a Dutch citizen residing in Belgium? See also Broekmeulen v. Huisarts Registratie Commissie, Case 246/80, [1981] ECR I–2311, noted at page 332, infra.

2. Even if a person has never exercised the right of free movement, the fact that he or she possesses dual nationality may bar the application of the

internal law of a State. See Garcia–Avello v. Belgium, noted at page 623 infra, where the Court held that Belgium could not rely on the internal affairs doctrine in requiring the use of a customary Belgian form of registering a family surname when an applicant possessing dual Belgian and Spanish citizenship preferred the registration of the customary Spanish form.

3.   In Case C–212/06, Government of the French Community v. Flemish Government, the French Community in Belgium challenged a Flemish care insurance scheme which was open only to Flemish residents in the Flanders region of Belgium (and not, for example, to those working in Flanders but residing in French-speaking Wallonia). An internal affair of Belgium, as a federal state, or a matter for EU law? The Court held that "Community law clearly cannot be applied to such purely internal situations" (§ 38). The Court further held that "citizenship of the Union is not intended to extend the material scope of the Treaty to internal situations which have no link with Community law" (¶ 39).

F.   FLEXIBILITY AND "CLOSER COOPERATION"

Until the late 1980s, it was taken for granted that EU law and policy would apply equally in all the Member States. As proposals were advanced for the EU's expansion into new fields, it was apparent that some States were reluctant to participate in certain of those initiatives. The idea that the EU might commence operations in new fields but permit some States to opt out of them is often called a "two-tier" or "two-speed" or multi-speed Europe, or a "Europe of variable geometry."

The Treaty of Maastricht could not have been signed or ratified without this approach. As we have seen in Chapter 1, the crucial compromise for the inclusion of the monetary union provisions in the Treaty was the acceptance of Protocols enabling Denmark and the UK to opt out. Similarly, in order to enable all the other States to move ahead in adopting employment legislation, the Maastricht Social Protocol again enabled the UK to opt out. As an inducement to the Danish people to ratify the Maastricht Treaty in a referendum, Denmark was permitted to opt out of the defense aspects of the CFSP. Finally, most States joined in the complex Schengen arrangements to achieve free movement of people and remove frontier controls, but the UK and Ireland did not.

The Treaty of Lisbon, building on provisions of the EC Treaty, provides a general scheme for an Enhanced Cooperation Procedure in its TEU Article 20. The article authorizes a minimum of nine Member States to enter into enhanced cooperation arrangements in a sphere of non-exclusive competences (i.e., competences other than the ones specified in TFEU Article 3) in order to "further the objectives of the Union, protect its interests, and reinforce its integration process." As previously, enhanced cooperation should be a "last resort."

TFEU Articles 326–34 provide some detailed rules governing any efforts to use enhanced cooperation. Article 326 naturally requires the cooperation arrangements to comply with Union law and not create any barriers to trade between States or otherwise "undermine" the internal market.

The process of actually creating some form of enhanced cooperation is governed by TFEU Article 329. The States desiring to create one must notify the Commission, which may then submit a proposal for it to the Council (but may also refuse to submit a proposal, giving reasons for this). The Council must act unanimously to approve enhanced cooperation and the Parliament must give its consent. In view of the obvious difficulty in satisfying these procedural requirements, it may be doubted that any future type of enhanced cooperation will develop, although there have been proposals that harmonization of tax legislation and measures in the matrimonial field might be agreed upon by some States by use of enhanced cooperation.

CHAPTER 5

JUDICIAL REVIEW OF EUROPEAN UNION ACTS

■ ■ ■

This chapter treats the subject of direct judicial review in the Court of Justice of legal acts, both legislative and administrative, taken by the political institutions and other bodies and agencies of the European Union. Until the creation in 1989 of the Court of First Instance (renamed the General Court by the Lisbon Treaty), the Court of Justice alone was responsible for judicial review at the EU level. A growing case load, exacerbated by the fact that the ECJ decides every case before it without the benefit of a certiorari mechanism, led of course to creation of the Court of First Instance. With the Council having largely transferred to the CFI the task of judicial review of all administrative acts during the 1990s, the Court of Justice now exercises direct judicial review in challenges to legislative acts and upon appeal from the General Court.

That the drafters of the EC Treaty would give the Court of Justice express authority to review legislative acts of the institutions was not to be lightly assumed. The US Constitution contains no such express grant of authority and an important chapter of early US constitutional history concerns the Supreme Court's successful efforts to develop this implied power. Moreover, in several Member States, judicial power to review legislative acts is either limited or non-existent. In contrast, the drafters of the EC Treaty clearly regarded direct review of Community acts in the Court of Justice as an important protection against abuses of authority by the Community political institutions.

The principal focus of this chapter is upon EC Treaty Article 230 (now TFEU Article 263) which regulates the substance and procedure of judicial review of EU legal acts. We will examine the standing of the institutions, the Member States and private parties to seek judicial review, and any limits on that standing. Much of the chapter will be devoted to the grounds for judicial review stipulated in Article 230.

Several other topics closely related to judicial review are also covered in this chapter. We will briefly examine EC Treaty 232 (now TFEU Article 265), which authorizes judicial review of the claim that a political institution failed to take action despite a duty to do so. The chapter also treats the relatively rare application of EC Treaty Article 241 (now TFEU Article 277) concerning illegality of EU law as a defense, as well as EC Treaty Article 235 (now TFEU Article 268), concerning suits for damage against the EU.

This chapter deals mostly with procedural issues, such as who may seek judicial review, by what means and on what grounds? However, since a principal ground for review is the violation of EU rules of law, this chapter will also deal with the Court's concept of legality. One aspect of legality is, of course, respect for fundamental rights, including human rights. The rapidly expanding developments in that area warrant separate treatment in Chapter 6.

A. INSTITUTIONAL ASPECTS OF JUDICIAL REVIEW IN THE COURT OF JUSTICE

1. ROLES OF THE POLITICAL INSTITUTIONS AND THE MEMBER STATES

EC Treaty Article 230 (now TFEU Article 263) provides that the political institutions, Member States and other qualified parties may challenge the validity of EU measures directly in the Court of Justice. If successful, the Court may declare the act concerned to be void, pursuant to Article 231 (now TFEU Article 264). This remedy is derived from the *action en recours pour excès de pouvoir*, central to the French and other continental systems of administrative law. As Article 231 suggests, judgments of the Court in actions for annulment are essentially declaratory. However, Article 233 (now TFEU Article 266) specifically provides that when an act of an EU institution is declared void, that institution must "take the necessary measures to comply with the judgment of the Court."

The original EEC Treaty permitted direct judicial review only of acts taken by the Council and the Commission, because the drafters envisioned only those institutions as capable of taking legally binding acts. Naturally, once the Parliament began to join the Council in adopting legislation by codecision, Article 230 was amended to include judicial review of such legislation as well. Likewise, when the Maastricht Treaty provided for the creation of the European Central Bank, its legal acts were made reviewable. Thus, in Commission v. European Central Bank (OLAF), Case C–11/00, [2003] I–1651, the Court invalidated an ECB decision setting up an internal anti-fraud body instead of accepting the jurisdiction of OLAF, a Union-wide body that had been empowered to investigate charges of fraud and corruption.

The Lisbon Treaty's TFEU Article 263 amends the initial paragraph of EC Treaty Article 230 to provide that legally binding acts of the European Council may also be reviewed by the Court of Justice, as may the acts of any "bodies, offices or agencies of the Union intended to produce legal effects vis-à-vis third parties." See Chapter 2C concerning the power of the European Council to adopt legally binding decisions (but not legislation) and Chapter 2G on agencies and other bodies.

The EC Treaty originally only authorized the Council, Commission or a Member State to request judicial review under Article 230. They could challenge a reviewable act without demonstrating any particular "interest" in doing so and are therefore often called "privileged applicants." Thus, in Italy v. Council, Case 166/78, [1979] ECR 2575, the Court held that a Member State may sue to challenge a measure even though it had voted in favor at the time the Council adopted the measure.

Shortly after becoming directly elected, Parliament began militating in favor of institutional standing—alongside the Council and Commission—to challenge reviewable acts taken by the other institutions. The issue became especially live when the Single European Act introduced the parliamentary cooperation procedure and Parliament had reason to insist that the Commission and Council follow that procedure whenever applicable. Initially, in Parliament v. Council (Comitology), Case 302/87, [1988] ECR 5615, the Court of Justice was unwilling to permit Parliament to challenge a Council decision in the absence of an express reference to Parliament as a plaintiff in Article 230. Subsequently however, when Parliament sued to challenge a Council regulation adopted by use of a Euratom Treaty article permitting the Council to act alone rather than pursuant to an EC Treaty article granting Parliament a legislative role, the Court concluded that Parliament ought to be able to seek judicial review to protect one of its own "prerogatives." The Court essentially ruled that institutional balance was so critical to the EU's legitimacy that Parliament had to be able to vindicate its prerogatives in the ECJ:

23　The Court, which under the treaties has the task of ensuring that in the interpretation and application of the treaties the law is observed, must therefore be able to maintain the institutional balance and, consequently, review the observance of the Parliament's prerogatives when called upon to do so by the Parliament, by means of a legal remedy which is suited to the purpose which the Parliament seeks to achieve.

* * *

26　The absence in the treaties of any provision giving the Parliament the right to bring an action for annulment may constitute a procedural gap, but it cannot prevail over the fundamental interest in the maintenance and observance of the institutional balance laid down in the treaties establishing the European Communities.

27　Consequently, an action for annulment brought by the Parliament against an act of the Council or the Commission is admissible provided that the action seeks only to safeguard its prerogatives and that it is founded only on submissions alleging their infringement.

Parliament v. Council (Post–Chernobyl), Case C–70/88, [1990] ECR I–2041.

Although this judgment might be regarded as an instance of judicial activism, the Member States accepted the Court's view, amending Article 230 by the Maastricht Treaty in 1993 to expressly enable the Parliament, the ECB and the Court of Auditors to sue to protect "their prerogatives." Subsequently, the Treaty of Nice further amended Article 230 to remove Parliament's limited standing to sue only to protect its prerogatives, while retaining that limitation for the other two bodies. The Lisbon TFEU Article 263 does not change this, but adds the Committee of the Regions as yet another body entitled to sue to protect its prerogatives.

In keeping with the French administrative law model, Article 230's fifth paragraph requires a request for review to be brought within a very short time period, in principle two months from publication or notification of the challenged measure. The sixth paragraph of TFEU Article 263 retains this short statute of limitations. This requirement is justified on grounds of judicial orderliness and legal security. An EU act that has not been challenged within this short time period may not thereafter be directly challenged in the Court of Justice. (However, as we shall see, the validity of such a measure may nevertheless be called into question as an incidental issue in litigation before Member State courts. The preliminary reference procedure under EC Treaty Article 234 (now TFEU Article 267) allows and, under certain circumstances, requires a national court to put the issue before the Court of Justice as the occasion arises, even long after the limitations period has passed.)

2. WHAT ACTS MAY BE CHALLENGED DIRECTLY IN THE COURT OF JUSTICE?

Students of American administrative law will be familiar with the threshold problems of defining an "act" whose legality may be challenged and of determining whether a particular party has standing to bring such a challenge. A well-known competition law judgment provides a standard for determining when an act should be considered to produce legal effects capable of receiving judicial review.

IBM v. COMMISSION
Case 60/81, [1981] ECR 2639.

[After several years' investigations, the Commission initiated proceedings against IBM for abuse of a dominant position in violation of EC Treaty Article 82 (now TFEU Article 102). The Director General for Competition sent IBM a "statement of objections" indicating the claims against it and inviting a reply in writing, assuring IBM that it also had the right at a later stage to an oral hearing. IBM immediately challenged the proceedings, raising numerous procedural and substantive objections. When the Commission declined to terminate the proceedings, IBM brought suit under EC Treaty Article 230.]

8 According to Article [230] of the Treaty proceedings may be brought for a declaration that acts of the Council and the Commission other than

recommendations or opinions are void. That remedy is available in order to ensure, as required by [EC Treaty Article 220, now Lisbon TEU Article 19], that in the interpretation and application of the Treaty the law is observed. . . .

9 In order to ascertain whether the measures in question are acts within the meaning of Article [230] it is necessary, therefore, to look to their substance. [A]ny measure the legal effects of which are binding on, and capable of affecting the interests of, the applicant by bringing about a distinct change in his legal position is an act or decision which may be the subject of an action under Article [230] for a declaration that it is void. However, the form in which such acts or decisions are cast is, in principle, immaterial as regards the question whether they are open to challenge under that article.

10 In the case of acts or decisions adopted by a procedure involving several stages, . . . in principle an act is open to review only if it is a measure definitively laying down the position of the Commission or the Council on the conclusion of that procedure, and not a provisional measure intended to pave the way for the final decision.

* * *

14 [The Commission's dispatch of a statement of objections is a procedural step] designed to enable the undertakings concerned to communicate their views and to provide the Commission with the fullest information possible before it adopted a decision affecting the interests of an undertaking. Its purpose is to create procedural guarantees for the benefit of the latter and . . . to ensure that the undertakings have the right to be heard by the Commission.

* * *

19 A statement of objections does not compel the undertaking concerned to alter or reconsider its marketing practices and it does not have the effect of depriving it of the protection hitherto available to it against the application of a fine. . . . Whilst a statement of objections may have the effect of showing the undertaking in question [that] it is incurring a real risk of being fined by the Commission, that is merely a consequence of fact, and not a legal consequence which the statement of objections is intended to produce.

20 An application for a declaration that the initiation of a procedure and a statement of objections are void might make it necessary for the Court to arrive at a decision on questions on which the Commission has not yet had an opportunity to state its position and would as a result anticipate the arguments on the substance of the case, confusing different procedural stages, both administrative and judicial. It would thus be incompatible with the system of the division of powers between the Commission and the Court and of the remedies laid down by the Treaty, as well as the requirements of the sound administration of

justice and the proper course of the administrative procedure to be followed in the Commission.

21 It follows from the foregoing that neither the initiation of a procedure nor a statement of objections may be considered, on the basis of their nature and the legal effects they produce, as being decisions within the meaning of Article [230] Treaty which may be challenged in an action for a declaration that they are void. . . .

Notes and Questions

1. The *IBM* case raises questions that are commonly associated with the problems of ripeness and finality in US administrative law, that is questions of timing. Do you agree that IBM's complaints were premature? Naturally, as the Court observed in ¶ 4, if the Commission ultimately decides that IBM violated competition rules, the decision can be appealed.

2. Can you imagine any challenges to Commission antitrust proceedings that would be considered "ripe" at the stage at which IBM brought suit? In AKZO Chemie BV v. Commission, Case 53/85, [1986] ECR 1965, a company against which the Commission had brought competition law charges objected to the disclosure of certain confidential business documents to the party that had complained to the Commission. Although the Commission proceedings were still in progress, the Court considered that the decision to disclose confidential information was ripe for review. It held that AKZO's grievance was independent of the competition law charge and, if founded, would not adequately be redressed through review of the final Commission decision. Do you agree?

3. Internal administrative guidelines usually do not have the "legal effects" necessary for judicial review under EC Treaty Article 230. As the Court noted in Spain v. Commission, Case C–443/97, [2000] ECR I–2415, "in principle, internal guidelines have effects only within the administration itself and give rise to no rights or obligations on the part of third parties. They do not therefore constitute acts adversely affecting any person, against which, as such, an action for annulment can be brought under Article [230] of the Treaty." In accord is Reynolds Tobacco v. Commission, Case C–131/03, [2006] ECR I–7795, where the Court held that acts "not producing legal effects which are binding on and capable of affecting the interests of the individual, such as confirmatory measures and implementing measures . . ., mere recommendations and opinions . . . and, in principle, internal instructions" cannot be challenged under Article 230.

4. France has frequently challenged various "soft" Commission instruments, obliging the Court to decide whether the "soft" legal instrument in question was an act subject to review under Article 230. See France v. Commission (State aid communication), Case C–325/91, [1993] ECR I–3283 ("Communication" to the Member States on application of state aid policy to public undertakings in the manufacturing sector held reviewable because it creates additional obligations); France v. Commission (Pension funds), Case C–57/95, [1997] ECR I–1627 (Commission communication on an internal

market for pension funds lays down specific obligations going beyond the Treaty's free movement provisions and is a reviewable act).

3.　PRIVATE PARTY STANDING TO SEEK JUDICIAL REVIEW

Prior to the entry into force of the Lisbon Treaty, paragraph 4 of EC Treaty Article 230 read as follows:

> Any natural or legal person may, under the same conditions [as set out in connection with institutional standing], institute proceedings against a decision addressed to that person or against a decision which, although in the form of a regulation or a decision addressed to another person, is of direct and individual concern to the former.

Obviously the provision's principal purpose was to enable private parties to challenge a legally binding action taken against them in the form of a decision. A clear example would be an appeal from the imposition of a fine in a Commission competition decision. The paragraph, however, also allowed judicial review in some cases by a party who is *not* the addressee of the decision in question, though only if the decision is "of direct and individual concern" to that party. The text went even a step further, allowing a private party to challenge a regulation, provided it too is "of direct and individual concern" to the party or, as the matter is sometimes put, represents for the party "a disguised decision."

Without question, most appeals by private parties under EC Treaty Article 230 have been against decisions specifically addressed to them. As previously noted, the Court of First Instance has taken over from the Court of Justice all challenges to administrative acts raised by private parties.

Occasionally, however, a private party does challenge a decision addressed to another party or to a Member State as one that has "direct and individual concern" to the plaintiff, and on rare occasion a regulation may be attacked on the same basis. Then the Court, or now the CFI, must initially address the issue of whether the plaintiff has the requisite standing. The focus tends to be on whether a given measure is "of individual concern" to the plaintiff. See generally A. Arnull, Private Applicants and the Action for Annulment under Article 173 of the EC Treaty, 32 Comm. Mkt. L. Rev. 7 (1995). We begin with standing to challenge decisions addressed to others, before turning to standing to challenge regulations, a matter as to which the Lisbon Treaty brings significant change.

a. Private Party Standing to Challenge Decisions Addressed to Other Parties

METRO–SB–GROSSMARKTE v. COMMISSION

(Metro I)

Case 26/76, [1977] ECR 1875.

[SABA, a German electronics manufacturer, notified the Commission of its complicated contractual system of selling products through carefully selected wholesalers and retailers, commonly called a selective distribution system, as required under EU competition rules. After several years of careful review, the Commission issued a decision of December 15, 1975, addressed to SABA, permitting the distribution system. Metro, a discount wholesaler that had complained to the Commission about SABA's refusal to allow Metro to participate in the system, had provided the Commission with material adverse to SABA for use in its review. The Commission ultimately wrote to Metro on January 14, 1976, notifying it of the December 15 decision favorable to SABA. Metro then challenged the decision in the Court of Justice.]

6   Since the contested decision was not addressed to Metro it is necessary to consider whether it is of direct and individual concern to it.

7   Metro is a so-called self-service wholesale trading undertaking [whose mode of] marketing is ... characterized both by special sales methods and by the nature of the customers sought by the wholesaler.

8   When the applicant applied to SABA for recognition as a wholesaler ... SABA refused because the applicant would not agree to a number of conditions to which SABA subjects the grant of the status of a SABA wholesaler and which, the applicant maintains, are not compatible with the structure of the self-service wholesale trade as Metro engages in it.

[The Court then outlined the Commission's proceedings with respect to SABA, describing certain changes in the distribution system agreed to by SABA at the Commission's request.]

12   Since Metro considered that the distribution system thereby approved retained features unlawfully preventing its appointment as a SABA wholesaler it lodged this application.

13   The abovementioned facts establish that the contested decision was adopted in particular as the result of a complaint submitted by Metro and that it relates to the provisions of SABA's distribution system, on which SABA relied and continues to rely as against Metro in order to justify its refusal to sell to the latter or to appoint it as a wholesaler, and which the applicant had for this reason impugned in its complaint.

14   It is in the interests of a satisfactory administration of justice and of the proper application of [EC Treaty Articles 81 and 82, now TFEU Articles 101–102] that natural or legal persons who are entitled to request the Commission to find an infringement of Articles [81 and 82] should be able, if their request is not complied with either wholly or in

part, to institute proceedings in order to protect their legitimate interests.

15 In those circumstances the applicant must be considered to be directly and individually concerned ... by the contested decision and the application is accordingly admissible.

[On the merits, the Court sustained the Commission decision.]

NOTES AND QUESTIONS

1. The implications of *Metro I* are unclear. Metro was adversely affected by the Commission's approval of the SABA network. Is that in itself sufficient to allow Metro to appeal the SABA decision? Or is appeal only allowed when the appellant a) formally complained to the Commission prior to the decision, and/or b) provided relevant information and participated in the proceeding? Does *Metro* suggest that all persons who unsuccessfully petition the Commission for action will have standing in the Court of Justice to challenge the Commission decision denying that action?

2. In Timex Corporation v. Council and Commission, Case 264/82, [1985] ECR 849, the EU imposed an antidumping duty on importers of watches at the request of the European industry association. Timex, the largest UK watch producer and member of the association, provided the Commission with a good deal of information in its investigation. Timex considered the antidumping duty to be too low and was found to have standing to sue to press that claim. See Chapter 29 on the standing of competitors to challenge Commission or Council regulations imposing antidumping duties.

b. Private Party Standing to Challenge a Regulation

As seen in Chapter 3A, regulations are essentially laws that are generally applicable, and hence presumptively not directly subjected to challenge by individuals in the EU courts. That presumption was spelled out early on by the Court in the case of a challenge to an agricultural regulation by an association of fruit and vegetable producers, in Confédération Nationale des Producteurs de Fruits et Légumes v. Council, Cases 16, 17/62, [1962] ECR 471. The Court held that "a regulation, being essentially of a legislative nature, is applicable not to a limited number of persons, defined or identifiable, but to categories of persons viewed abstractly and in their entirety." The Court did accept that "if a measure entitled [as] a regulation contains provisions which are capable of being not only of direct but also of individual concern to certain natural or legal persons, it must be admitted that ... those provisions do not have the character of a regulation and may therefore be [challenged] by those persons." Finding that the regulation addressed "objectively determined situations" and applied to "categories of persons viewed in a general and abstract manner," the Court concluded that the claimant was not individually concerned.

The judgment was a major precedent, not only because of its treatment of the notion of a disguised decision, but also because of its practical impact. The Common Agricultural Policy entails literally thousands of Council and Commission regulations in the administration of the market organizations for different products. These regulations are very detailed, often affect private interests quite specifically and are frequently amended. If they were easily challenged by private parties, the administration of the CAP would be gravely impaired and the EU courts would be seriously burdened. The following recent judgment illustrates the Court's continuing reluctance to treat an agricultural regulation as a disguised decision.

FRANCE v. COMAFRICA SpA AND DOLE FRESH FRUIT EUROPE LTD. & CO.

Case C–73/97, [1999] ECR I–185.

[Two banana producers brought suit in the Court of First Instance for annulment of Commission Regulation 3190/93 which established a complex system for calculating quotas for imports of bananas in 1994. The CFI described the measure, though denominated a regulation, as "properly construed as a collection of individual decisions addressed to each operator," and granted standing to the producers to challenge it.

On appeal, the Court of Justice reversed, declaring the producers' claim inadmissible. The Court observed that the calculation system is a multi-step affair, with the operators first supplying prior years' marketing information to the national authorities and the authorities then verifying the accuracy of the information supplied, applying a weighted coefficient to the reported quantities, and sending all this information to the Commission (but not necessarily to the operators). At that point, the Commission sets a mode of calculating imports for each category of operator. The Court continued:]

30　[T]he figures notified by the operators ... may be altered several times in the course of the procedure before the reduction coefficient is fixed, without the alterations made by the competent authorities or the Commission being brought to the attention of the operators concerned.

31　Consequently, an operator is not able to ascertain, on the basis of either the figures notified by it to the national competent authority or the provisions of Regulation 3190/93 the reference quantity [of bananas] to which the reduction coefficient is to be applied [to calculate the import quotas].

[The Court distinguished the instant case from an earlier case in which reference quantities of beef and veal had been based on the exact quantities shown on the operators' quota applications, without adjustment, so that the operators themselves could multiply a quantity known to them by a reduction coefficient laid down in the relevant regulation.]

38 The Court of Instance was therefore wrong to conclude ... that Regulation 3190/93, properly construed, was a collection of individual decisions addressed to each operator effectively informing him of the precise quantities [of bananas] which he would be entitled to import in 1994.

NOTES AND QUESTIONS

1.   One important field in which the Court of Justice has found regulations to be disguised decisions is that of antidumping or protective trade measures. For discussion of cases in which the Court recognized the standing of private persons who are affected by antidumping regulations to challenge them under Article 230, see Chapter 29 infra.

2.   In 2002, the Court of First Instance issued a controversial judgment, which would have greatly expanded private party standing to challenge regulations if it had not been reversed by the Court of Justice.

JEGO–QUERE v. COMMISSION

Case T–177/01, [2002] ECR II–2365.

[A French company conducting fishing operations off Ireland challenged a Commission regulation fixing minimum net sizes in order to safeguard an endangered fish species. The CFI found that Jégo–Quéré had standing:]

50 [In view of] the fact that the EC Treaty established a complete system of legal remedies and procedures designed to permit the Community judicature to review the legality of measures adopted by the institutions, the strict interpretation, applied until now, of the notion of a person individually concerned according to the fourth paragraph of Article 230 EC [now TFEU Article 263], must be reconsidered.

51 [I]n order to ensure effective judicial protection for individuals, a natural or legal person is to be regarded as individually concerned by a Community measure of general application that concerns him directly if the measure in question affects his legal position, in a manner which is both definite and immediate, by restricting his rights or by imposing obligations on him. The number and position of other persons who are likewise affected by the measure, or who may be so, are of no relevance in that regard.

52 In the present case, obligations are indeed imposed on Jégo–Quéré by the contested provisions. The applicant, whose vessels are covered by the scope of the regulation, carries on fishing operations in one of the areas in which, by virtue of the contested provisions, such operations are subjected to detailed obligations governing the mesh size of the nets to be used.

53 It follows that the contested provisions are of individual concern to the applicant.

54 Since those provisions are also of direct concern to the applicant, the objection of inadmissibility raised by the Commission must be dismissed and an order made for the action to proceed.

The Court of Justice clearly thought that the CFI went too far, and reversed it in a straightforward judgment.

COMMISSION v. JEGO–QUERE & CIE

Case C–263/02P, [2004] ECR I–3425.

33 [I]t is not appropriate for an action for annulment before the Community Court to be available to an individual who contests the validity of a measure of general application, such as a regulation, which does not distinguish him individually in the same way as an addressee, even if it could be shown, following an examination by that Court of the particular national procedural rules, that those rules do not allow the individual to bring proceedings to contest the validity of the Community measure at issue. Such an interpretation would require the Community Court, in each individual case, to examine and interpret national procedural law. That would go beyond its jurisdiction when reviewing the legality of Community measures.

* * *

36 Although the condition that a natural or legal person can bring an action challenging a regulation only if he is concerned both directly and individually must be interpreted in the light of the principle of effective judicial protection by taking account of the various circumstances that may distinguish an applicant individually, such an interpretation cannot have the effect of setting aside the condition in question, expressly laid down in the Treaty. . . .

37 That applies to the interpretation [given by the Court of First Instance] to the effect that a natural or legal person is to be regarded as individually concerned by a Community measure of general application that concerns him directly if the measure in question affects his legal position, in a manner which is both definite and immediate, by restricting his rights or by imposing obligations on him.

38 Such an interpretation has the effect of removing all meaning from the requirement of individual concern set out in the fourth paragraph of Article 230 EC.

NOTES AND QUESTIONS

1. What do you think motivated the CFI to attempt to broaden private party standing in this respect? The CFI seemed concerned that there might never be a proper "case or controversy" permitting individual challenge. Even if there might be, should persons who can prove an individual injury be made to wait for relief until such time as they violate the measure and the measure is "enforced" against them? How do efficiency considerations cut? Are there

valid case load concerns? (Remember that the two-month statute of limitations continues to apply.)

Note also the Court of First Instance's view that there is no compelling reason to read a requirement of differentiation into the term "individual concern" within paragraph four of Article 230. In fact, in US law, a claimant ordinarily needs to show ascertainable individual injury to him or her, but not necessarily his or her uniqueness in that respect.

2. A large number of Members of the European Parliament sought to challenge a regulation requiring MEPs to cooperate in certain ways with investigations conducted by OLAF, the EU's anti-fraud unit. They claimed that, while none of them was affected in ways that would distinguish them from MEPs in general, they nevertheless formed a "closed" set of individuals whose identity could at any given time be specifically ascertained, and that each was therefore individually as well as directly affected. The Court held that established standing principles required that the claim be dismissed, and it reminded the MEPs that they still would have "a posteriori" opportunities for judicial review. Rothley v. Parliament, Case C–167/02, [2004] ECR I–3149. What do you suppose those opportunities might be?

3. The Treaty of Lisbon importantly reformulates the fourth paragraph of ECT Article 230 in what is now TFEU Article 263:

> Any natural or legal person may, under the conditions laid down in the first and second paragraphs, institute proceedings against an act addressed to that person or which is of direct and individual concern to them, and against a regulatory act which is of direct concern to them and does not entail implementing measures.

The TFEU text does not change the "direct and individual concern" standard's application when a private party seeks to challenge a decision addressed to another party. However, the reformulation significantly changes the handling of private party attacks upon regulations by specifically granting standing when the regulation is "of direct concern and does not entail implementing measures." Individual concern is not any longer required. The Court of Justice will presumably have to interpret the reformulation, but it appears to grant standing to a party in circumstances analogous to those in *Jégo–Quéré*.

c. Private Party Standing to Challenge Decisions Addressed to Member States

ALFRED TÖEPFER AND GETREIDE–IMPORT GESELLSCHAFT v. COMMISSION.

Cases 106–107/63, [1965] ECR 405.

[On October 1, 1963, two German grain dealers filed applications with the German authorities to import maize (or corn) from France. Because the import levy at that time happened to be zero, the dealers stood to realize exorbitant profits. The German authorities therefore invoked certain "safeguard" measures against grave market disturbances caused by low-priced imports, and temporarily suspended import applications. The Commission subsequently raised the rate of the levy (effective October 2). Then, on October 3, the Commission issued a decision to the German government authorizing it to reject all applications filed from October 1 through 4 inclusive. The dealers sued the Commission in the Court of Justice for the annulment of that decision.]

> It is clear from the fact that on 1 October 1963 the Commission took a decision fixing new free-at-frontier prices for maize imported into the Federal Republic as from 2 October that ... the only persons concerned by the said measures were importers who had applied for an import licence during the course of the day of 1 October 1963. The number and identity of these importers had already become fixed and ascertainable before 4 October, when the contested decision was made. The Commission was in a position to know that its decision affected the interests and the position of the said importers alone.

> The factual situation thus created differentiates the said importers, including the applicants, from all other persons and distinguishes them individually just as in the case of the person addressed.

> Therefore the objection of inadmissibility which has been raised is unfounded and the applications are admissible.

[The Court concluded on the merits that the Commission was wrong in finding that the maize imports in question were capable of causing grave market disturbances, a finding required to justify use of a safeguard measure.]

NOTES AND QUESTIONS

1. Why didn't the plaintiffs in *Töpfer* bring their action in national court against the German agency? Bear in mind that the Commission decision merely authorized the action of the national authorities. It did not direct it.

2. One class of decisions addressed to Member States that private parties have a definite interest in challenging is a Commission decision on whether or not a State subsidy, tax reduction or other aid to private enterprises violates EU rules governing such state aids or subsidies. Philip Morris Holland v. Commission, Case 730/79, [1980] ECR 2671, is a good example. The Dutch government, intending to grant financial assistance to Philip Morris to expand its cigarette production facilities, notified the aid to the Commission as required under EC Treaty Articles 87 and 88 (now TFEU Articles 107 and 108) governing state aids. The Commission wrote to the Dutch government denying permission to grant the aid, and Philip Morris (not the Dutch government) brought suit in the Court of Justice. The Commission conceded that Philip Morris, as the prospective recipient of the aid, had standing to sue. (Philip Morris lost the case on the merits.)

Competitors of the recipients of state aid have also been held to be entitled to challenge decisions addressed to Member States authorizing them to grant aid. See COFAZ v. Commission, Case 169/84, [1986] ECR 391; Association of Sorbitol Producers (ASPEC) v. Commission, Case T–435/93,

[1995] ECR II–1281. Is the extension justified? Should standing be limited to rivals who participated in the procedures leading up to the grant of aid?

3. Does Flanders, as a region of the federal State of Belgium, have standing to challenge a Commission decision addressed to Belgium? The Commission decision had invalidated as an improper State subsidy an interest-free loan from Flanders to an airline based in Antwerp. In Het Vlaamse Gewest (Flemish Region) v. Commission, Case T–214/95, [1998] ECR II–717, the CFI held that Flanders had the status of a legal person entitled to judicial review under EC Treaty Article 230, and was directly and individually affected by the decision. Because Flanders is not a State, the CFI held that it, rather than the Court of Justice, should handle the appeal. On the merits, the CFI upheld the Commission decision.

NOTE ON INTERIM RELIEF

Actions before the Court of Justice do not normally have suspensive effect. However, according to EC Treaty Articles 242 and 243 (now TFEU Articles 278 and 279), the Court may, "if it considers that circumstances so require," suspend application of the challenged act or order other necessary interim measures. The Court is commonly called upon by applicants to order interim relief, and its Statute and Rules of Procedure lay down some simple guidelines for this purpose. Thus Article 83(2) of the Court Rules requires applicants for interim relief to state the subject matter of the proceedings, the reasons for the urgency of relief (typically a risk of serious and irreparable damage), and the elements of law and fact that create a prima facie case for the grant of such relief.

Decisions on interim relief applications are made by the President of each court, with several being made each year. Appeals from interim relief decisions by the President of the CFI are taken directly to the President of the Court of Justice. If either President considers that review by the full court is warranted, the President may refer the interim relief request directly to the court.

Under the case law of the Court, applicants for interim relief must show not only that the relief sought is prima facie justified in law and in fact, but also that the interim relief must be ordered and produce its effects before a decision is reached in the main action in order to avoid serious and irreparable damage to the applicant's interests. The Court will also take into account the prejudice that the interim relief sought would cause to the public interest and other private interests. Commission v. Atlantic Container Line, Case C–149/95, [1995] ECR I–2165 (¶ 22).

Article 86(4) of the Court Rules (reiterating Article 36 of the Statute) confirms that the issuance of an order of interim relief is without prejudice to the ultimate decision of the Court. As a corollary, the Court's President seeks to avoid issuing any order that may "prejudge the points of law or fact in issue or neutralize in advance the effects of the decision subsequently to be given in the main action" (id., ¶ 23).

Undoubtedly the most prominent request for interim relief came in United Kingdom v. Commission (Mad cow disease), Case C–180/96, [1996] ECR I–3903, which the President referred to the full Court in view of its importance. The Commission had banned the export of British beef due to evidence that some beef transmitted to humans BSE, or "mad cow disease." The UK sought the ban's interim suspension. The UK's claims were comprehensive: that the ban was not justified by any serious hazard to human or animal health, that it infringed the principles of proportionality, non-discrimination and legal certainty (discussed later in this chapter), that it unlawfully impeded the free movement of goods within the internal market, that it conflicted with the objectives of the common agricultural policy as set out in the Treaty, that it was inadequately reasoned, and that it represented a misuse of power since it was adopted for economic rather than public health reasons.

The Court canvassed all the factors bearing upon the justification or non-justification of the ban, including particulars about the disease and its incidence. It focused primarily on the question "whether it is necessary to make a provisional ruling in order to avoid the occurrence of serious and irreparable harm as a result of [the immediate] application of the measure." Although the Court did not doubt the severity of the economic impact on British beef producers, it pointed to various measures the EU institutions had adopted to compensate those producers, at least in part. Above all, the Court concluded, in light of the magnitude of the risk to human health, that "a balancing of interests would, on any view, favour maintaining the Commission's decision, inasmuch as the interest in having the contested decision maintained is not really comparable to the applicant's interest in having its operation suspended." Even admitting that much of the damage suffered by the UK interests would be irreparable were the UK ultimately to prevail in the action, the Court found that "[t]hat damage cannot . . . outweigh the serious harm to public health which is liable to be caused by suspension of the contested decision, and which could not be remedied if the main action were subsequently dismissed."

Did the Court avoid prejudging the merits? Note that the Court ultimately sustained the ban in United Kingdom v. Commission (Mad cow disease), Case C–180/96, [1998] ECR I–2265.

B. THE SCOPE OF JUDICIAL REVIEW

The second paragraph of EC Treaty Article 230 (now TFEU Article 263) sets out four distinct grounds for invalidating Community measures. These grounds are lack of competence, infringement of an essential procedural requirement, infringement of the Treaty or implementing law, and misuse of powers. Most continental administrative law authorities recognize these or similar grounds for challenging national regulations, so that it was natural for the Treaty drafters to cite them. (When the Court reviews the validity of a Union act by way of preliminary reference from a national court, it may do so on the same four grounds.) Although these grounds for review bear an affinity to the principles governing judicial review of administrative action in the US, they also present certain distinctive features that warrant a closer look.

1. LACK OF COMPETENCE

Claims of lack of competence (or jurisdiction) may raise either or both of two related questions. The first question is whether the particular institution that took the challenged measure or action was the competent authority to do so. A leading decision of this kind is France v. Commission (Antitrust agreement with the US), Case C–327/91, [1994] ECR I–3641. Here, the Commission was found lacking in competence to enter into a binding agreement with the United States for mutual cooperation and assistance in antitrust enforcement. The Court held that the Commission's attempted arrangement constituted an international agreement that under EC Treaty Article 300 (now TFEU Article 218) only the Council had the authority to make. The Council subsequently did enter into the arrangement. See page 864 infra.

More recently, France challenged the Commission's decision to conclude a general agreement with the US setting out "Guidelines on Regulatory Cooperation and Transparency." The Guidelines were negotiated between the relevant Commission services and their counterparts in the US Department of Commerce and US Trade Representative under the aegis of the 1995 Transatlantic Economic Partnership. In this case, the Court found the Guidelines to be "voluntary," both in letter and spirit and not covered by the requirement of Council action. France v. Commission (Regulatory cooperation with US), Case C–233/02, [2004] ECR I–2759.

A second competence question is whether the Union (or previously the Community) as a whole, rather than a particular institution, has the power to take the measure or action being challenged. A good example of a broad *ultra vires* claim of this sort is a challenge by foreign producers to the Commission's alleged attempt to apply competition rules extraterritorially, as in the *Wood pulp* case, infra page 859. Often the issue is framed in terms of whether a given Treaty article authorizes the action taken. The cases in Chapter 4B demonstrated the Court of Justice's willingness to interpret expansively grants by the Treaty of authority to legislate at the EU level. What follows is a rare but prominent exception.

GERMANY v. PARLIAMENT AND COUNCIL
(Tobacco Advertising I)
Case C–376/98, [2000] ECR I–8419.

[Germany sought to annul Directive 98/43/EC of the Council and Parliament on "the approximation of the laws, regulations and administrative provisions of the member States relating to the advertising and sponsorship of tobacco products." Adopted on the basis of the then EC Treaty Articles 47(2) on freedom of establishment (now TFEU Article 53), 55 on freedom of services (now TFEU Article 62), and 95 on harmonization to achieve the internal market (now TFEU Article 114), the directive basically banned all advertising and sponsorship of tobacco products in the EU. "Sponsorship" was defined as "any public or private contribution to an event or activity with the aim or the direct or indirect effect of promoting a tobacco product."

The Court noted that EC Treaty Article 152(4) (now TFEU Article 168(5)) on public health specifically excluded the harmonization of Member State laws designed to protect and improve human health, and that the national measures to be harmonized by the directive did in fact chiefly pursue public health objectives. On the other hand, according to the Court, this did not mean that harmonization measures could not have any impact on the protection of human health; indeed Article 152(1) (now TFEU Article 168(1)) stated that health needs should be a component of the Community's other policies—provided, the Court stressed, that "[o]ther articles of the Treaty ... not ... be used as a legal basis in order to circumvent [Article 152(4)'s] express exclusion of harmonisation" of public health law. Against this background, the Court turned to the institutions' choice of Treaty articles to provide a legal basis for the directive. The Court initially quoted Article 95 as well as the definition of the "internal market" in Article 14 (now TFEU Article 26).]

83   [It is] clear that the measures referred to in Article [95(1)] of the Treaty are intended to improve the conditions for the establishment and functioning of the internal market. To construe that article as meaning that it vests in the Community legislature a general power to regulate the internal market would not only be contrary to the express wording of the provisions cited above but would also be incompatible with the principle embodied in Article [5] of the EC Treaty [now TEU Article 5] that the powers of the Community are limited to those specifically conferred on it.

84   Moreover, a measure adopted on the basis of Article [95] of the Treaty must genuinely have as its object the improvement of the conditions for the establishment and functioning of the internal market. If a mere finding of disparities between national rules and of the abstract risk of obstacles to the exercise of fundamental freedoms or of distortions of competition liable to result therefrom were sufficient to justify the choice of Article [95] as a legal basis, judicial review of compliance with the proper legal basis might be rendered nugatory. The Court would then be prevented from discharging the function entrusted to it by Article [220] of the EC Treaty [now TEU Article 19] of ensuring that the law is observed in the interpretation and application of the Treaty.

85   So, in considering whether Article [95] was the proper legal basis, the Court must verify whether the measure whose validity is at issue in fact pursues the objectives stated by the Community legislature.

86 It is true ... that recourse to Article [95] as a legal basis is possible if the aim is to prevent the emergence of future obstacles to trade resulting from multifarious development of national laws. However, the emergence of such obstacles must be likely and the measure in question must be designed to prevent them.

* * *

The Directive

90 In the ... preamble to the Directive, the Community legislature notes that differences exist between national laws on the advertising and sponsorship of tobacco products and observes that, as a result of such advertising and sponsorship transcending the borders of the Member States, the differences in question are likely to give rise to barriers to the movement of the products which serve as the media for such activities and the exercise of freedom to provide services in that area, as well as to distortions of competition, thereby impeding the functioning of the internal market.

* * *

95 It therefore is necessary to verify whether the Directive actually contributes to eliminating obstacles to the free movement of goods and to the freedom to provide services, and to removing distortions of competition.

Elimination of obstacles to the free movement of goods and the freedom to provide services.

96 It is clear that, as a result of disparities between national laws on the advertising of tobacco products, obstacles to the free movement of goods or the freedom to provide services exist or may well arise.

97 In the case, for example, of periodicals, magazines and newspapers which contain advertising for tobacco products, it is true, as the applicant has demonstrated, that no obstacle exists at present to their importation into Member States which prohibit such advertising. However, in view of the trend in national legislation towards ever greater restrictions on advertising of tobacco products, reflecting the belief that such advertising gives rise to an appreciable increase in tobacco consumption, it is probable that obstacles to the free movement of press products will arise in the future.

98 In principle, therefore, a Directive prohibiting the advertising of tobacco products in periodicals, magazines and newspapers could be adopted on the basis of Article [95] of the Treaty with a view to ensuring the free movement of press products ...

99 However, for numerous types of advertising of tobacco products, the prohibition under Article 3(1) of the Directive cannot be justified by the need to eliminate obstacles to the free movement of advertising media or the freedom to provide services in the field of advertising.

That applies, in particular, to the prohibition of advertising on posters, parasols, ashtrays and other articles used in hotels, restaurants and cafés, and the prohibition of advertising spots in cinemas, prohibitions which in no way help to facilitate trade in the products concerned.

* * *

105 In those circumstances, it must be held that the Community legislature cannot rely on the need to eliminate obstacles to the free movement of advertising media and the freedom to provide services in order to adopt the Directive on the basis of Articles [95, 47(2) and 55] of Treaty.

[The Court then considered whether the Directive could be justified because it eliminated an "appreciable distortion of competition," but concluded that that was not the case. The Directive's impact on advertising agencies was deemed to be "remote and indirect" (¶ 109).

While acknowledging that a directive prohibiting certain forms of advertising and sponsorship of tobacco products could have been validly adopted under Article 95, the Court thought that, given the deliberate generality of the prohibition, partially annulling the directive would amount to amending it, which is the province of the Community's political branches. The Court accordingly annulled the entire directive (¶ 118).]

GERMANY v. PARLIAMENT AND COUNCIL

(Tobacco Advertising II)
Case C–380/03, [2006] ECR I–11573.

[After the Court's initial judgment, the Parliament and Council relied on EC Treaty Article 95 to adopt Directive 2003/33/EC, forbidding most types of advertising and sponsorship of tobacco products. However, Article 3 permits a limited form of advertising in the press and other printed publications i.e., advertising in publications intended exclusively for professionals in the tobacco trade and publications which are printed and published in third countries, where those publications are not principally intended for the EU market. Article 4 actually goes beyond the initial directive because it prohibits all forms of radio advertising for tobacco products and sponsorship of radio programmes by tobacco companies. (Note that the Television Broadcasting Directive 89/552, discussed at page 685 infra, already forbid the advertising of tobacco products on television.) Germany again attacked the directive, contending that Article 95 could not authorize its provisions. The Court upheld the reformulated directive.]

37 While a mere finding of disparities between national rules is not sufficient to justify having recourse to Article 95 EC, it is otherwise where there are differences between the laws, regulations or administrative provisions of the Member States which are such as to obstruct the fundamental freedoms and thus have a direct effect on the functioning of the internal market. . . .

* * *

41   [W]hen there are obstacles to trade, or it is likely that such obstacles will emerge in the future, because the Member States have taken, or are about to take, divergent measures with respect to a product or a class of products, which bring about different levels of protection and thereby prevent the product or products concerned from moving freely within the Community, Article 95 EC authorises the Community legislature to intervene by adopting appropriate measures, in compliance with Article 95(3) EC and with [applicable] legal principles, in particular the principle of proportionality.

* * *

53   The market in press products, like the radio market, is a market in which trade between Member States is relatively sizeable and is set to grow further as a result, in particular, of the link between the media in question and the internet, which is the cross-border medium par excellence.

54   [T]he movement of newspapers, periodicals and magazines is a reality common to all the Member States and is not limited only to States sharing the same language. The proportion of publications from other Member States may even in certain cases come to more than half of the publications on the market, according to information provided at the hearing . . . which was not challenged. It is necessary to include, in that intra-Community trade in press products on paper, trade made possible by information society services, especially the internet which enables direct access in real time to publications distributed in other Member States.

55   Also, . . . several Member States already prohibited advertising of tobacco products, . . . while others were about to do so. Consequently, disparities existed between the Member States' national laws and, contrary to the applicant's submissions, those disparities were such as to impede the free movement of goods and the freedom to provide services.

* * *

60   Finally, the risk that new barriers to trade or to the freedom to provide services would emerge as a result of the accession of new Member States was real.

61   The same finding must be made with regard to the advertising of tobacco products in radio broadcasts and information society services. Many Member States had already legislated in those areas or were preparing to do so. Given the increasing public awareness of the harm caused to health by the consumption of tobacco products, it was likely that new barriers to trade or to the freedom to provide services were going to emerge as a result of the adoption of new rules reflecting that development and intended to discourage more effectively the consumption of tobacco products.

* * *

69   It remains to determine whether, in the fields covered by Articles 3 and 4 of the Directive, those articles are in fact designed to eliminate or prevent obstacles to the free movement of goods or the freedom to provide services or to remove distortions of competition.

79   This conclusion is not called into question by the applicant's line of argument that the prohibition laid down in Articles 3 and 4 of the Directive concerns only advertising media which are of a local or national nature and lack cross-border effects.

[The Court then observed that it had already decided in *Tobacco Advertising I* that a general ban on advertising in periodicals, magazines and newspapers could be adopted on the basis of Article 95 to eliminate barriers caused by different national rules, including an appropriate exception for advertising in publications intended for professionals in the tobacco trade. Citing the example of the Television Broadcasting Directive, the Court reached the same conclusion with regard to the directive's ban on tobacco advertising on radio.]

80   Recourse to Article 95 EC as a legal basis does not presuppose the existence of an actual link with free movement between the Member States in every situation covered by the measure founded on that basis. As the Court has previously pointed out, to justify recourse to Article 95 EC as the legal basis what matters is that the measure adopted on that basis must actually be intended to improve the conditions for the establishment and functioning of the internal market.

81   Accordingly, it must be held that ... Articles 3 and 4 of the Directive are intended to improve the conditions for the functioning of the internal market.

[Germany further claimed an infringement of the then EC Treaty Article 152(4), which authorized cooperative and incentive measures to promote public health, but forbade harmonization of national rules in that field.]

93   Article 95(3) EC explicitly requires that, in achieving harmonisation, a high level of protection of human health should be guaranteed.

94   The first subparagraph of Article 152(1) EC provides that a high level of human health protection is to be ensured in the definition and implementation of all Community policies and activities.

95   While it is true that Article 152(4)(c) EC excludes any harmonisation of laws and regulations of the Member States designed to protect and improve human health, that provision does not mean, however, that harmonising measures adopted on the basis of other provisions of the Treaty cannot have any impact on the protection of human health.

96   With regard to the applicant's argument that public health protection largely prompted the choices made by the Community legislature when adopting the Directive, in particular so far as concerns Articles 3 and 4, suffice it to state that the conditions for recourse to Article 95 EC were met in this instance.

97   The Community legislature therefore did not infringe Article 152(4)(c) EC by adopting Articles 3 and 4 of the Directive on the basis of Article 95 EC.

NOTES AND QUESTIONS

1. *Tobacco advertising I* is the first instance in which the Court of Justice ruled that provisions of a directive adopted under EC Treaty Article 95 could not validly be regarded as an internal market harmonization measure within the meaning of that Article. The crux of the Court's judgment is that Article 95 does not grant "a general power to regulate the internal market" (¶ 83). Note that the Court accepted most of the directive's prohibitions of tobacco advertising, striking down only relatively secondary prohibitions in ¶ 99. This made it easy for the Council and Parliament to revise the directive and adopt in its place Directive 2003/33. Note ¶¶ 53–61 in *Tobacco Advertising II* which provide the Court's justification for holding that actual or likely barriers to interstate trade permitted using Article 95 to adopt the 2003 Directive.

2. Note that in both judgments the Court held that EC Treaty Article 152(4)(c) excluded any harmonization of laws and regulations of the Member States designed to protect and improve human health, but did not bar harmonization measures adopted on the basis of other provisions of the Treaty from promoting the protection of human health? Do you agree with the Court's distinction? (The Lisbon Treaty replaced Article 152(4)(c) with TFEU Article 168. While Article 168 does not expressly bar harmonization in public health, it implies that the EU should confine itself to coordinating and supporting activities in that area.)

3. As in ¶ 8 of the *IBM* judgment, supra page 131, in ¶ 84 of *Tobacco Advertising I* the Court relies on Article 220 of the EC Treaty (now TEU Article 19) to justify the scope of its review and its invalidation of the directive? Does Article 220 support that result?

4. It was widely believed that the Court would follow *Tobacco Advertising I* in subsequent judgments. However, in addition to *Tobacco Advertising II*, the Court upheld the reliance on Article 95 to justify strict rules on the composition and packaging of tobacco products in The Queen v. Secretary of State for Health ex parte British American Tobacco, excerpted at page 120, and harmonization of patent rules in Netherlands v. Parliament and Council, excerpted at page 119.

5. In European Parliament v. Council and Commission, Joined Cases C–317 & 318/04, [2006] ECR I–4721, the ECJ annulled Council Decision 2004/496/EC on the conclusion of an Agreement between the European Community and the US on the processing and transfer of Passenger Name Record (PNR) data by Air Carriers to the US Department of Homeland Security, Bureau of Customs and Border Protection. The European Parliament claimed that EC Treaty Article 95 was not the correct choice as legal basis since Decision 2004/496 did not have as the objective of improving the functioning of the internal market, but rather of permitting the processing of personal data required in the sphere of national security and criminal law

enforcement, and were accordingly excluded from the scope of Directive 95/46 on the protection of personal data.

6.   Interestingly, US courts have shown a reawakened interest in setting constitutional limits on federal legislative jurisdiction. Thus, the Supreme Court ruled 5–4, in the case of United States v. Lopez, 514 U.S. 549, 115 S.Ct. 1624, 131 L.Ed.2d 626 (1995), that the Federal Gun–Free School Zones Act (making it a federal offense to possess a firearm on school grounds or within 1000 feet of them) was unconstitutional as in excess of Congress' power to legislate under the Interstate Commerce Clause. See, more recently, United States v. Morrison, 529 U.S. 598, 120 S.Ct. 1740, 146 L.Ed.2d 658 (2000). In addition, in New York v. United States, 505 U.S. 144, 112 S.Ct. 2408, 120 L.Ed.2d 120 (1992), and in Printz v. United States, 521 U.S. 898, 117 S.Ct. 2365, 138 L.Ed.2d 914 (1997), the Supreme Court declared it unconstitutional for federal authorities (including Congress) to "commandeer" state legislative or administrative powers. The Court has also severely curtailed Congress' use of its legislative powers under the 14th Amendment. See United States v. Morrison, supra; City of Boerne v. Flores, 521 U.S. 507, 117 S.Ct. 2157, 138 L.Ed.2d 624 (1997).

2. INFRINGEMENT OF AN ESSENTIAL PROCEDURAL SAFEGUARD

The EC Treaty and, now, the TFEU are fairly specific about the procedures that the institutions are to follow in taking the various measures they are authorized to take. Whether a measure's validity depends on observance of those procedures is a somewhat different question. The Court of Justice has ruled that the violation of a procedural requirement justifies setting aside the resulting measure only if the requirement in question is an "essential" one.

An example of a procedural norm generally held to be essential is the requirement of prior consultation of a designated advisory body, including of course the requirement to consult the Parliament, as in Roquette Frères v. Council (Isoglucose), supra page 82. We have already seen that the Treaty is replete with consultation requirements. Typically, failure to perform a required consultation will be regarded as reason enough for a measure's annulment. One might also regard the requirement of reasons, as set forth in EC Treaty Article 253 (now TFEU Article 296), as procedural in nature; in any event, it too is considered to be by definition essential.

Procedural norms are not only to be found in the Treaties, but also in secondary legislation. Indeed, in one case, Germany won the annulment of a Commission decision establishing procedures for testing the conformity of construction products to specifications because the Commission, upon consulting the Standing Committee on Construction prior to adopting the decision, failed to send the Member States a notice and agenda of the Committee meeting, the draft decision and the relevant working papers in German (rather than merely in English), as required by the Committee's rules of procedure. Germany v. Commission (Construction products), Case C–263/95, [1998] ECR I–441.

The Court of Justice has frequently had occasion to examine procedural issues in Commission proceedings to enforce competition law and has gradually developed a body of "procedural due process" case law.

TRANSOCEAN MARINE PAINT v. COMMISSION
Case 17/74, [1974] ECR 1063.

[As will be seen in Chapter 20, the Commission has the regulatory power under EC Treaty Article 81(3) (now TFEU Article 101(3)) to decide that certain anti-competitive agreements may be permitted in view of their beneficial features. In the present case, the Commission had granted an Association of medium-sized maritime paint producers a competition law exemption under Article 81(3) for the producers' agreement to coordinate manufacturing and marketing practices. When the exemption expired, the Association requested its renewal. After review, in July 1973, the Commission notified the Association of certain new conditions that the producers would have to satisfy in order to have the exemption renewed, and it gave the Association an opportunity to comment and a hearing.

When, in December the Commission finally renewed the exemption, it did so subject to an additional condition (concerning the reporting of interlocking relations with non-Community paint manufacturers) of which the Association had not had prior notice and on which it had not commented. The Association objected to the new condition strictly on substantive grounds, and asked the Court to annul the decision granting the exemption to the extent that it carried this condition. Advocate–General Warner discerned a procedural due process issue in the case, and the Court addressed it.]

8   The applicants claim that at no time could they infer from [the Commission's statements during its review] that the Commission intended to impose on them a condition ... to which they would not be able, by reasons of its breadth, to adhere and which, without good reason, would harm their interests. If they had been in a position to realize the Commission's intentions they would not have failed to make known their objections on this matter so as to draw the Commission's attention to the inconvenience which would result from the obligation in issue and to the illegality by which it is vitiated. Since they were not given this opportunity, they allege that the Decision, insofar as the obligation in issue is concerned, must be annulled since it is vitiated by a procedural defect.

* * *

11 [According to Council Regulation 17], the Commission, before taking decisions ..., shall give the undertakings or associations of undertak-

ings concerned the opportunity of being heard on the matters to which the Commission has taken objection. . . .

* * *

[15] It is clear both from the nature and objective of the procedure for hearings, and from [Regulation 17], that this regulation . . . applies the general rule that a person whose interests are perceptibly affected by a decision taken by a public authority must be given the opportunity to make his point of view known. This rule requires that an undertaking be clearly informed, in good time, of the essence of conditions to which the Commission intends to subject an exemption and it must have the opportunity to submit its observations to the Commission. This is especially so in the case of conditions which, as in this case, impose considerable obligations having far-reaching effects.

[19] [T]he minutes of the hearing . . . show that at no time was the general condition later contained in the Decision the subject of an exchange of points of view. This fact confirms the applicants' assertion that they were convinced that the obligation as stated in the "notice of objections" concerned only the mutual relations between members of the Association and not such links as might exist with outside undertakings, including those operating outside the Common Market and concerned with the manufacture of paints other than marine paints.

[20] Accordingly, the [added] condition . . . was imposed in breach of procedural requirements and the Commission must be given the opportunity to reach a fresh decision on this point after hearing the observations or suggestions of the members of the Association.

NOTES AND QUESTIONS

1. *Transocean Marine Paint* is one of the first judgments in which the Court seems to have drawn upon English law principles in developing its jurisprudence. Discussion of British "natural justice" figured prominently in the conclusions of Advocate General Warner, though not to the exclusion of analogous doctrines in the other Member States. [1974] ECR at 1082, 1088.

2. The *Transocean* judgment guarantees a certain measure of what might be called procedural due process to "a person whose interests are perceptibly affected by a decision taken by a public authority" (¶ 15). This language leaves open several questions. How important must an individual's interests be, and how specifically and dramatically must they be affected, in order to trigger the due process requirement? Assuming due process is triggered, what precise procedural safeguards might due process entail?

NOTE ON "ADMINISTRATIVE DUE PROCESS"

While the Treaties and secondary legislation commonly impose procedural requirements on the EU decision-making process, the EU has no general code of administrative procedure. Accordingly, the procedural protections of private parties stemming from EU law have become largely a matter for determination by the Court of Justice and the Court of First Instance, through the notion of unwritten general principles of law. This case law has arisen from disputes in which the EU courts have been called upon to review the legality of the measures that ultimately emerge across a broad range of field—e.g. competition law, anti-dumping, state aids, trademarks, anti-fraud activities, financial assistance programs—in which the EU institutions rather than the Member States are the primary decisionmakers. The ultimate question is whether complaining parties enjoyed a "fair hearing." See Lenaerts & Vanhamme, Procedural Rights of Private Parties in the Community Administrative Process, 34 Common Mkt. L. Rev. 531 (1997).

Under the case law of the Court, a fair hearing (or, as it is sometimes called, the "right of defense") is in principle required for proceedings which are initiated against a person and are liable to culminate in a measure adversely affecting that person. Commission v. Lisrestal, Case C–32/95P, [1996] ECR I–5373.

What exactly does a fair hearing entail? An important incident of fair procedure is access to, and the opportunity to comment upon, essential documents—particularly documents upon which the institutions intend to rely in reaching their adverse decision. The right of access to documents is discussed more generally in Chapter 6E infra, but that right clearly takes on procedural due process dimensions when the requesting party is the one against whom the authorities intend to make an adverse decision. See Solvay v. Commission, Case T–30/91, [1995] ECR II–1775, a competition case in which the Court of First Instance invoked "the general principle of equality of arms [which] presupposes that in a competition case the knowledge which the undertaking concerned has of the file used in the proceeding is the same as that of the Commission." To the Commission's argument that the documents withheld would not have been exculpatory, the Court replied that "where . . . difficult and complex economic appraisals are to be made, the Commission must give the advisers of the undertaking concerned the opportunity to examine documents which may be relevant so that their probative value for the defence can be assessed."

Due process also entails the availability of an independent and impartial tribunal. While it is sometimes complained that the Commission combines rulemaking, prosecutorial and quasi-adjudicatory functions, the Court of Justice has found no constitutional infirmity in that situation. Crucial to this conclusion is, of course, the availability to legitimately aggrieved persons of an independent and impartial tribunal, in the form of the Court of First Instance and the Court of Justice. Naturally, the efficacy of such review in the courts depends in turn on its scope and on the courts' degree of scrutiny of administrative decisions, as well as the stringency with which the courts enforce the requirement of reasons set out in EC Treaty Article 253 (now TFEU Article 296).

NOTE ON PROCEDURAL RIGHTS IN COMPETITION LAW PROCEEDINGS

The Commission's investigative and enforcement activities in the competition law area have understandably given rise to a large number of procedural due process issues. For example, in SA Musique Diffusion Francaise v. Commission (Pioneer), Cases 100–103/80, [1983] ECR 1825, European distributors and their Japanese supplier complained about a variety of irregularities in the Commission's decisional process that culminated in fines for their anticompetitive behavior, including (in addition to the Commission's combination of the functions of judge and prosecutor) (a) insufficiency of the statement of objections, (b) failure to notify the full extent of the period of violation claimed, (c) failure to state the basis for the proposed fine, and (d) failure to disclose certain documents on which the Commission relied. The Court found two procedural violations: failure to disclose certain documents (as a result of which the Court ruled that those documents could not be relied upon) and failure to notify the full extent of the period of violation claimed (as a result of which the Commission's fine had to be reduced by more than 50%).

In BASF v. Commission (Low-density polyethylene), Joined Cases T–80–112/89, [1995] ECR II–729, the Court of First Instance was called upon to review the Commission's imposition of fines in excess of $49 million for fixing prices in, and partitioning the market for, low-density polyethylene used in the production of film and plastic packaging. The CFI annulled the decisions due to the Commission's alteration of those decisions after their adoption, excessive delegation of authority to an individual commissioner, and failure to authenticate the measures in all the necessary languages on a timely basis. The Commission subsequently amended its rules in 1999 to make its delegation procedures more precise.

Among the most notable procedural rights cases in the competition law field are those concerning companies' privacy and related interests in Commission investigations. In National Panasonic (UK) Ltd. v. Commission, Case 136/79, [1980] ECR 2033, the company contested the Commission's failure to give advance notice of an on-site search and seizure of company files (or an opportunity to be heard before the decision to conduct such a search and seizure was taken). While conceding that fundamental rights limit the Commission's procedural freedom, the Court did not consider surprise raids (commonly called "dawn raids," because they are conducted early in the morning) disproportionate to the Commission's aim to determine whether a competition law infringement had occurred or otherwise violative of the right to privacy under Article 8 of the European Human Rights Convention.

In Hoechst AG v. Commission, Case 46/87 & 227/88, [1989] ECR 2859, the Court further clarified the Commission's powers in conducting investigations by holding that, subject to compliance with the requirements of Regulation 17, and absent manifest unconstitutionality, the Commission could conduct a search, seek documents without specifically identifying them, enlist the assistance of national law enforcement officers in accordance with national search warrant requirements, and fine a company for refusing to submit to the investigation.

In Roquette Frères SA v. Directeur général de la concurrence, Case C–94/00, [2002] ECR I–9011, the Court of Justice faced the fact that developments in the field of protection of human rights since *Hoechst* had created some uncertainty as to the scope of the principle established in that case, namely, "the need for protection against arbitrary or disproportionate intervention by public authorities in the sphere of the private activities of any person, whether natural or legal" (¶ 27). The Court essentially reaffirmed *National Panasonic* and *Hoechst*, but provided in a single numbered paragraph 9 the following very specific guidelines concerning the authorization by the relevant national court for the Commission's on-site investigation:

9   In accordance with the general principle of Community law affording protection against arbitrary or disproportionate intervention by public authorities in the sphere of the private activities of any person, whether natural or legal, a national court having jurisdiction under domestic law to authorise entry upon and seizures at the premises of undertakings suspected of having infringed the competition rules is required to verify that the coercive measures sought in pursuance of a request by the Commission for assistance ... are not arbitrary or disproportionate to the subject-matter of the investigation ordered. Without prejudice to any rules of domestic law governing the implementation of coercive measures, Community law precludes review by the national court of the justification of those measures beyond what is required by the foregoing general principle.

Community law requires the Commission to ensure that the national court in question has at its disposal all the information which it needs in order to carry out the review which it is required to undertake. In that regard, the information supplied by the Commission must in principle include:

— a description of the essential features of the suspected infringement, that is to say, at the very least, an indication of the market thought to be affected and of the nature of the suspected restrictions of competition;

— explanations concerning the manner in which the undertaking at which the coercive measures are aimed is thought to be involved in the infringement in question;

— detailed explanations showing that the Commission possesses solid factual information and evidence providing grounds for suspecting such infringement on the part of the undertaking concerned;

— as precise as possible an indication of the evidence sought, of the matters to which the investigation must relate and of the powers conferred on the Community investigators; and

— in the event that the assistance of the national authorities [e.g. assistance by the local police] is requested by the Commission as a precautionary measure, in order to overcome any opposition on the part of the undertaking concerned, explanations enabling the national court to satisfy itself that, if authorisation for the coercive measures were not granted on precautionary grounds, it would be impossible, or very difficult, to establish the facts amounting to the infringement.

Paragraph 9 further indicates that the national court is not entitled to review the Commission's evidentiary file prior to acting, and that a national court must notify the Commission of any difficulties foreseen, and may deny the authorization only if it considers that "the coercive measures envisaged" are "arbitrary or disproportionate."

In *AM & S* Europe Ltd. v. Commission, Case 155/79 [1982] ECR 1575, the company refused to tender certain documents to the Commission on account of attorney-client privilege, though it agreed to disclose enough of the documents to satisfy the inspectors that they were indeed privileged. The Commission demanded the documents in full so as to be able to determine itself the applicability of the privilege. The Court found that all Member States recognize an attorney-client privilege, though of differing scope. It accordingly concluded that the Commission had to respect the confidentiality of written communications between lawyer and client, where the communications were made in the interest of the client's defense and where the lawyer enjoyed independence from the client.

The Court further held that a firm does not need to reveal the contents of the communications in question in order to assert their confidentiality; it need only provide material sufficient to demonstrate the applicability of the privilege. If the Commission is not persuaded, and continues to contest the applicability of the privilege, it may order production and fine subsequent non-production, though the issue of the validity of such an order and fine could presumably then be brought before the EU courts for an independent determination. As to the case at hand, the Court concluded that most of the documents in question met the conditions for application of the attorney-client privilege. American and other non-EU lawyers were greatly upset by the Court's stipulation that only communications with lawyers qualified in EU States were privileged, but have been subsequently assured by senior Commission Competition Directorate General officials that their communications would also be privileged. Note that house counsel are not considered to be independent.

Faced with a claim of privilege against self-incrimination in Orkem, SA v. Commission, Case 74/87, [1989] ECR 3283, the Court could not find such a privilege in the constitutional traditions of the Member States, as it had with the attorney-client privilege. (The States generally limited the privilege to natural persons charged with committing a criminal offense.) Moreover, the Court could not find any broader privilege under either the European Human Rights Convention or the 1966 International Covenant on Civil and Political Rights. The Court nevertheless found the right against self-incrimination to be necessary to safeguard the "rights of the defence" fundamental to the Community legal order (¶ 32). Thus, "the Commission may not compel an undertaking to provide it with answers which might involve an admission on its part of the existence of an infringement which it is incumbent on the Commission to prove" (¶ 35). In the event, the Court found that some of the Commission's informational demands were subject to the privilege and others were not. For a recent application by the Court of First Instance of the *Orkem* rule, see Mannesmannrohren–Werke AG v. Commission, Case T–112/98, [2001] ECR II–729.

Future competition law cases may be expected to raise still other aspects of the right to be heard and procedural due process more generally. If anything, the Court and the CFI may become more rigorous in protecting procedural rights as a result of the Lisbon Treaty's grant of legal force to the Charter of Fundamental Rights (doc. 6 in doc. supp.). The Charter's Article 41(2) specifically grants a right of hearing before any Union institution, body or agency takes a measure that adversely affects a party, and Article 47 provides a right to a fair trial. See Chapter 6 for further discussion.

3. INFRINGEMENT OF THE TREATY OR ANY RULE OF LAW RELATING TO ITS APPLICATION

The third ground for review under EC Treaty Article 230 (now TFEU Article 263)—"infringement of [the] Treaty or of any rule of law relating to its application"—commonly covers claims of a substantive character. Some claims assert that an EU act violates a Treaty article, a provision of secondary legislation or an international agreement entered into by the EU. Others, and they are among the most interesting, involve claims that an EU act violates some "general principle of law" or some basic right recognized by the Court's own case law.

In contending that the Council or Commission has acted in violation of law, a claimant typically means to say that the institution failed to satisfy the substantive conditions set out in the Treaty or legislative provisions governing such action. For the Court to determine whether the applicable legal conditions for action are met may be a simple matter of verification. If, however, verification is not easy (as is often the case with the application of legal norms to social or economic facts), the Court will have to decide how closely to review the Council's or Commission's exercise of discretion. Specifically, when should the Court substitute its independent judgment for that of the Council or Commission in taking the action in question? When instead should the Court show deference to the judgment that the Council or Commission has brought to the matter, and how should such deference be expressed?

Article 33 of the ECSC Treaty (which expired in 2002) had sought to address these questions as follows:

> The Court may not ... examine the evaluation of the situation, resulting from economic facts or circumstances, in the light of which

the High Authority took its decisions or made its recommendations, save where the High Authority is alleged to have misused its powers or to have manifestly failed to observe the provisions of this Treaty or any rule of law relating to its application.

This provision appears to embody a distinction between more or less purely factual questions of an economic or other nature, on which the Court of Justice owes no particular deference to EU decisionmakers, and questions entailing the characterization or evaluation of those facts, on which deference may be due. The distinction between mistakes in the "material existence" of the facts, on the one hand, and in their "legal characterization," on the other, is recognized in French and other European systems of administrative law, and has roughly the same significance. See G. Bermann, The Scope of Judicial Review in French Administrative Law, 16 Colum. J. Transnat'l L. 195 (1977).

Although the EC Treaty contained no analogous provision, the Court's attitude toward the standard of judicial review under that Treaty was very much the same. The Court has frequently remarked that the Commission enjoys a wide discretion in evaluating complex economic situations and that its exercise of discretion should not be set aside unless clearly erroneous or otherwise manifestly abusive. See EEC Seed Crushers' and Oil Processors' Federation (FEDIOL) v. Commission, Case 187/85, [1988] ECR 4155; Philip Morris Holland v. Commission, discussed *supra*. In Société Arcelor Atlantique et Lorraine v. Premier Ministre, Case C–127/07, [2008] ECR I–9895, the Court acknowledged that the EU legislature has a broad discretion where its action involves political, economic and social choices and where it is called on to undertake complex assessments and evaluations. Where it is called on to restructure or establish a complex system, the legislature is entitled to have recourse to a step-by-step approach and to proceed in the light of the experience gained.

Recently the CFI has proved especially rigorous in reviewing Commission competition law enforcement decisions, especially the Commission's evaluation of complex economic factual situations in permitting or forbidding mergers. In several prominent 2002 judgments, the CFI reversed the Commission due to "manifest error" in its factual evaluation.

Thus, in Airtours Plc v. Commission, excerpted at page 1026 infra, the CFI concluded that "the decision, far from basing its prospective analysis on cogent evidence, is vitiated by a series of errors of assessment as to factors fundamental to any assessment of whether a collective dominant position might be created" (¶ 294). Similarly, in Tetra Laval BV v. Commission, Case T–5/02, [2002] ECR II–4381, the CFI held that the Commission failed to establish "to the requisite legal standard that the modified merger would give rise to significant anti-competitive conglomerate effects.... It must therefore be concluded that the Commission committed a manifest error of assessment in prohibiting the modified merger on the basis of the evidence relied on in the contested decision relating to the foreseen conglomerate effect" (¶ 336). The Court of Justice affirmed. See page 1035 infra. The CFI also found that the Commission had made grave errors of assessment in Schneider Electric SA v. Commission, Case T–310/01, [2002] ECR II–4071.

The Commission was reportedly, and understandably, stung by this series of rulings, and Competition Commissioner Monti expressed his determination to ensure that the Commission's merger ruling showings would be more convincing in the future.

Thus far the approach taken by the Court of Justice as a reviewing court is not especially remarkable. However, the Court also has developed some more far-reaching doctrines that allow it greater scope in securing the rule of law within the EU. These doctrines include a number of unwritten "general principles of law" of sweeping application, mostly derived from norms of continental administrative law.

a. The Principle of Proportionality

By far the most important "general principle of law" is the principle of proportionality, which applies not only as a limit on the scope of Community or Union regulation, but also on Member State rules that restrict or impact adversely the achievement of the common or internal market. As we shall see in the substantive law chapters, the Court of Justice invariably applies the principle of proportionality in evaluating whether a national rule infringes EU law or not. The principle of proportionality has several strands: the measure must be rationally related to a legitimate objective; its costs must not be excessive in light of its benefits; and it must represent the least restrictive alternative available and avoid unnecessary incidental constraints.

The principle of proportionality has traditionally been recognized and applied in French, German and other continental systems of continental law. It is not especially well known by that name in the UK or other common law systems. Nonetheless, do you think that its several strands are common to US constitutional and administrative law?

The Court applies the principle of proportionality in its review of all fields of EU law, but it first became prominent in its review of agricultural regulations. The Court's 1970 *IHG* judgment is still one of the best-known articulations of the principle.

INTERNATIONALE HANDELSGESELLSCHAFT mbH v. EINFUHR– UND VORRATSSTELLE FUR GETREIDE UND FUTTERMITTEL

Case 11/70, [1970] ECR 1125.

[A 1967 Council regulation made the grant of export licenses for certain agricultural products conditional on the prior payment of a deposit which was to be forfeited if the export was not made. A German exporter challenged enforcement of the regulation on the ground that it violated the principle of "proportionality" (*Verhältnismässigkeit*) recognized in

German public law. According to the German view of the principle, a governmental measure must be reasonably related, and not "out of proportion," to the public good sought to be achieved. The German administrative court seriously questioned the regulation's proportionality and referred the issue to the Court of Justice.]

2   According to the evaluation of the [administrative court], the system of deposits is contrary to certain structural principles of national constitutional law which must be protected within the framework of Community law, with the result that the primacy of supranational law must yield before the principles of the German [Constitution, or Basic Law]. More particularly, the system of deposits runs counter to the principles of freedom of action and of disposition, of economic liberty and of proportionality arising in particular from Articles 2(1) and 14 of the Basic Law. The obligation to import or export resulting from the issue of the licences, together with the deposit attaching thereto, constitutes an excessive intervention in the freedom of disposition in trade. . . .

The Protection of Fundamental Rights in the Community Legal System

3   Recourse to the legal rules or concepts of national law in order to judge the validity of measures adopted by the institutions of the Community would have an adverse effect on the uniformity and efficacy of Community law. The validity of such measures can only be judged in the light of Community law. In fact, the law stemming from the Treaty, an independent source of law, cannot because of its very nature be overridden by rules of national law, however framed, without being deprived of its character as Community law and without the legal basis of the Community itself being called in question. Therefore the validity of a Community measure or its effect within a Member State cannot be affected by allegations that it runs counter to either fundamental rights as formulated by the constitution of that State or the principles of a national constitutional structure.

4   However, an examination should be made as to whether or not any analogous guarantee inherent in Community law has been disregarded. In fact, respect for fundamental rights forms an integral part of the general principles of law protected by the Court of Justice. The protection of such rights, whilst inspired by the constitutional traditions common to the Member States, must be ensured within the framework of the structure and objectives of the Community. It must therefore be ascertained, in the light of the doubts expressed by the [administrative court], whether the system of deposits has infringed rights of a fundamental nature, respect for which must be ensured in the Community legal system.

* * *

6   According to the ... preamble to [the challenged regulation], "the competent authorities must be in a position constantly to follow trade movements in order to assess market trends and to apply the measures

... as necessary" and "to that end, provision should be made for the issue of import and export licenses accompanied by the lodging of a deposit guaranteeing that the transactions for which such licences are requested are effected." [Thus,] the system of deposits is intended to guarantee that the imports and exports for which the licences are requested are actually effected in order to ensure ... precise knowledge of the intended transactions.

7   This knowledge ... is essential to enable the competent authorities to make judicious use of the instruments of intervention ... which are at their disposal for guaranteeing the functioning of the system of prices instituted by the regulation, such as purchasing, storing and distributing [products and] applying protective measures.... This is all the more imperative in that the implementation of the common agricultural policy involves heavy financial responsibilities for the Community and the Member States.

8   It is necessary, therefore, for the competent authorities to have available not only statistical information on the state of the market but also precise forecasts on future imports and exports. ... [A] forecast would lose all significance if the licences did not involve the recipients in an undertaking to act on them. And the undertaking would be ineffectual if observance of it were not ensured by appropriate means.

* * *

10   A system of mere declaration of exports effected and of unused licences, as proposed by the plaintiff in the main action, would, by reason of its retrospective nature and lack of any guarantee of application, be incapable of providing the competent authorities with sure data on trends in the movement of goods.

* * *

13   The principle of the system of deposits cannot therefore be disputed.

* * *

16   The costs involved in the deposit do not constitute an amount disproportionate to the total value of the goods in question and of the other trading costs. It appears therefore that the burdens resulting from the system of deposits are not excessive and are the normal consequence of a system of organization of the markets conceived to meet the requirements of the general interest. ...

17   The plaintiff in the main action also [contends] that forfeiture of the deposit in the event of the undertaking to import or export not being fulfilled really constitutes a fine or a penalty which the Treaty has not authorized the Council and the Commission to institute.

18   This argument is based on a false analysis of the system of deposits which cannot be equated with a penal sanction, since it is merely the guarantee that an undertaking voluntarily assumed will be carried out.

* * *

20 It follows from all these considerations that the system of licenses . . . does not violate any right of a fundamental nature. The machinery of deposits constitutes an appropriate method for carrying out the common organization of the agricultural markets. . . .

NOTES AND QUESTIONS

1. Although it upheld the regulation's validity, the Court was eager to demonstrate its willingness to subject EU legislation to "constitutional" review and to describe the principle of proportionality as a basic right that EU measures must respect. However, the ruling did not prevent the German Constitutional Court from later conducting a similar review of the regulation under German constitutional law principles. For the result of that inquiry, see the German court's own *Internationale Handelsgesellschaft* ruling in Chapter 6A, infra page 279.

2. On what authority does the Court of Justice invoke and apply general principles of law? Note that the Court's language in ¶ 4 echoes that of EC Treaty Article 220 (now Lisbon TEU Article 19), which states that the fundamental role of the Court is to ensure that "the law is observed." See Chapter 2F supra.

3. The Court's discussion of the necessity of a deposit system raises some questions. Why should an exporter be expected to export what it is no longer sound to export? Does inducing the exporter to do so help "assess market trends" (¶ 6)? On the other hand, what fundamental right of the exporter is at stake? Is there a fundamental right to freedom of trade, or to freedom from restrictions on trade that are not justified by the public good? Are you satisfied with the Court's reasoning? Do you think the Court's doctrine represents undue judicial activism?

4. The Court has on several occasions held "that there is no such thing as a general principle of objective unfairness under Community law [or any] legal basis . . . for exemption [from Community law obligations] on grounds of natural justice." Nor is there a general principle "that a Community provision . . . may not be applied by a national authority if it causes the person concerned hardship which the Community legislature would clearly have sought to avoid if it had envisaged [it]." Hoche v. Bundesanstalt für landwirtschaftliche Marktordnung, Case C–174/89, [1990] ECR I–2681, 2711. Does this still leave room for an inquiry into the proportionality of EU law measures?

5. A proportionality claim succeeded in the later case of Buitoni v. Fonds d'orientation, Case 122/78, [1979] ECR 677. When Buitoni sought to recover from the French authorities the security it had deposited upon applying for a license to import tomato concentrate, it learned that while the imports were timely, its application to recover the security was not. A Commission regulation required the importer, within six months following expiry of the license, to submit proof to the authorities that all import formalities had been completed. Because it failed to apply in time, Buitoni was denied its recovery and it brought suit in French court. Responding to a preliminary reference, the Court of Justice held the forfeiture penalty to be "excessively severe in

relation to the objectives of administrative efficiency." It objected to the fact that the failure to apply promptly for the refund was essentially punished as heavily as the failure to import, and ruled that only a "considerably less onerous" penalty than forfeiture of the whole security would be commensurate with the administrative inconvenience caused. Do you agree? What would be a "proportionate" penalty?

We have examined at page 93 supra the UK's unsuccessful legal basis challenge to the Working Time Directive (described in Chapter 36C infra) as having been adopted on an incorrect legal basis. The UK also raised serious proportionality issues.

UNITED KINGDOM v. COUNCIL

(Working time directive)
Case C–84/94, [1996] ECR I–5755.

The plea of breach of the principle of proportionality

50   The applicant points out that the Council may adopt on the basis of [EC Treaty Article 137, now TFEU Article 153] only "minimum requirements for gradual implementation, having regard to the conditions and technical rules obtaining in each of the Member States." ...

51   [The UK argues that] not all measures which may "improve" the level of health and safety protection of workers constitute minimum requirements. In particular, ... global reductions in working time or global increases in rest periods, whilst having a certain beneficial effect on the health or safety or workers, do not constitute "minimum requirements" within the meaning of Article [137].

52   Second, a provision cannot be regarded as a "minimum requirement" if the level of health and safety protection of workers which it establishes can be attained by measures that are less restrictive and involve fewer obstacles to the competitiveness of industry and the earning capacity of individuals. In the applicant's submission, ... the directive [does not] provide any explanation as to why the desired level of protection could not have been achieved by less restrictive measures, such as, for example, the use of risk assessments if working hours exceeded particular norms.

53   Third, the conclusion that the measures envisaged will in fact improve the level of health or safety protection of workers must be based on reasonable grounds. In its view, the present state of scientific research in the area concerned falls far short of justifying the contested measures.

* * *

57   As regards the principle of proportionality, the Court has held that, in order to establish whether a provision of Community law complies with that principle, it must be ascertained whether the means which it employs are suitable for the purpose of achieving the desired objective and whether they do not go beyond what is necessary to achieve it.

58   As to judicial review of those conditions, however, the Council must be allowed a wide discretion in an area which, as here, involves the legislature in making social policy choices and requires it to carry out complex assessments. Judicial review of the exercise of that discretion must therefore be limited to examining whether it has been vitiated by manifest error or misuse of powers, or whether the institution concerned has manifestly exceeded the limits of its discretion.

59   So far as concerns the first condition, it is sufficient that ... the measures on the organization of working time [with the exception of the designation of Sunday as the mandatory weekly day of rest, supra page 96], contribute directly to the improvement of health and safety protection for workers within the meaning of Article [137], and cannot therefore be regarded as unsuited to the purpose of achieving the objective pursued.

60   The second condition is also fulfilled. Contrary to the view taken by the applicant, the Council did not commit any manifest error in concluding that the contested measures were necessary to achieve the objective of protecting the health and safety of workers.

61   In the first place, Article 4, which concerns the mandatory rest break, applies only if the working day is longer than six hours. [Furthermore,] that provision may be the subject of several derogations [specified in Article 17 of the directive].

62   Second, the minimum uninterrupted weekly rest period of twenty-four hours provided for by the first sentence of Article 5, plus the eleven hours' daily rest referred to in Article 3, may be the subject of the same derogations as those authorized in relation to Article 4, referred to above....

63   Third, as regards Article 6(2), which provides that the average working time for each seven-day period is not to exceed forty-eight hours, Member States may lay down a reference period not exceeding four months, which may in certain cases be extended to six months ... or even to twelve months [by derogations in Articles 16–18].

64   Fourth, in relation to Article 7 concerning paid annual leave of four weeks, Article 18(1)(b)(ii) authorizes Member States to allow a transitional period of three years, during which workers must be entitled to three weeks' paid annual leave.

65   Finally, as to the applicant's argument that adoption of the contested directive was unnecessary since [an existing directive] already applies to the areas covered by the contested directive, it is sufficient to note that [the earlier directive] merely lays down, in order to encourage improvements in the health and safety of workers at work, general principles, as well as general guidelines for their implementation, concerning the prevention of occupational risks, the protection of health and safety, the elimination of risk and accident factors.... It is not therefore apt to achieve the objective of harmonizing minimum

rest periods, rest breaks and a maximum limit to weekly working time, which form the subject-matter of the contested directive.

66 It follows that, in taking the view that the objective of harmonizing national legislation on the health and safety of workers, while maintaining the improvements made, could not be achieved by measures less restrictive than those that are the subject-matter of the directive, the Council did not commit any manifest error.

67 In the light of all the foregoing considerations, the plea of breach of the principle of proportionality must also be rejected.

NOTES AND QUESTIONS

1. Do you find the Court's proportionality analysis convincing? Note that most of the derogations referred to by the Court were inserted by the Council in an unsuccessful effort to make the directive more acceptable to the UK. The Court's *Working time directive* ruling created a major stir in the UK. Prime Minister Major denounced the ruling as an attempt to restrain Britain's free-market economy, and threatened renewed "non-cooperation" in the Council unless the UK were exempted from it. (The UK clearly could not be exempted from the ruling as such, though it could of course seek, by legislative amendment, to be exempted from the directive.) The Blair Labor government, elected in 1997, soon after the judgment, endorsed the working time directive.

2. Issues of proportionality and subsidiarity likewise arose in Germany's challenge to the General Product Safety Directive, discussed on page 97 supra. Regarding proportionality, Germany argued that the Commission could adequately attain its objectives by pursuing infringement proceedings against a Member State under EC Treaty Article 226 (now TFEU Article 258) for its failure adequately to protect public health. The Court held that:

48 [E]ven if Member States are required to adopt certain specified measures under the directive, the Commission would be obliged to bring proceedings for failure to fulfil its obligations against every Member State that had not adopted such measures, inevitably rendering the procedure more cumbersome.

* * *

50 In particular, the infringement procedure would not enable consumer protection to be secured in the shortest possible time. ... Furthermore, a declaration that a Member State has failed to fulfil its obligations would, in the circumstances envisaged, presuppose a cautious appraisal, scarcely compatible with urgency of the need to adopt a particular measure....

3. In Queen v. Secretary of State for the Environment, ex parte Standley, Case C–293/97, [1999] ECR I–2603, UK farmers complained in the High Court that by fixing a ceiling of 50 mg per liter on nitrate concentrations in waters found to be "nitrate vulnerable," Council Directive 91/676 on water pollution by nitrates from agricultural sources offended the principle of proportionality and the right of property. The farmers essentially argued that

while agricultural producers were not solely responsible for the nitrate concentration in those waters, because the pollution might well come in part from other sources, they were nevertheless being made solely responsible for ensuring that the nitrate ceiling was not exceeded. Replying to a preliminary reference, the Court of Justice found that the directive was sufficiently flexible so as to allow Member States to take account of other sources of pollution when implementing its provisions and to avoid imposing disproportionate costs on farmers or any other single pollution source.

Is the Court in effect shifting the burden of ensuring respect for the principle of proportionality under EU law from the EU institutions that enacted that law to the national regulators and courts that are compelled to implement it?

b.   The Principles of Equal Treatment and Non–Discrimination

A prominent feature of the original EEC Treaty and every subsequent version of it is EC Treaty Article 10 (formerly EC Article 5, and now TFEU Article 18) which forbids "any discrimination on grounds of nationality" within the scope of application of the Treaty. The Court of Justice has had occasion to apply this fundamental right in an extraordinary variety of contexts in the substantive chapters of this casebook.

The Court not only readily strikes down direct discrimination based on nationality, but frequently invalidates indirect discrimination, such as national rules that discriminate on the basis of residence (see *Clean Car Auto Service*, infra page 565), or require discriminatory fees for access to education from students from other States (see *Gravier*, infra page 626), or discriminate against the providers or recipients of trans-border services (see *Bickel & Franz*, infra page 622).

Apart from enforcing the Treaty prohibition of discrimination based on nationality, the Court has enunciated a principle of equal treatment in contexts where nationality is not the issue.

BELA–MUHLE JOSEF BERGMANN KG v. GROWS–FARM GmbH

(Skimmed-milk powder)
Case 114/76, [1977] ECR 1211.

[In an effort to reduce the accumulated surplus of skimmed-milk powder in the EU, the Council adopted Regulation 563/76 requiring animal feed producers to use skimmed-milk powder (held in stock by the Member State agencies) as the protein ingredient in their product. A purchaser of feed refused to pay its supplier for the resulting increase in the price of raw materials (as required by their contract) on the ground that Regulation 563/76, which had occasioned the increase, was invalid. It maintained that the regulation required use of a form of protein several times more expensive than the protein element (soya) that producers customarily used, and was therefore unreasonably burdensome. The case reached the Court of Justice on preliminary reference from the German civil court hearing the main contract action.]

5   The validity of these arrangements has been contested on grounds of conflict in particular with the objectives of the common agricultural policy as defined in Article [33] of the Treaty [now TFEU Article 39], the prohibition of discrimination laid down in the second subparagraph of Article [34(2)] [now TFEU Article 40(2)] and the principle of proportionality between the means employed and the end in view. Because of the close connection between these grounds of complaint, it will be appropriate to consider them together.

6   Under Article [33], the objectives of the common agricultural policy are to be the rational development of agricultural production, the assurance of a fair standard of living for the whole of the agricultural community, the stabilization of markets and the availability of supplies to consumers at reasonable prices. . . . Furthermore, [Article 34(2)] lays down that the common organization of the markets "shall exclude any discrimination between producers or consumers within the Community."

7   The arrangements made by Regulation (EEC) No. 563/76 [entailed] the imposition not only on producers of milk and milk products but also, and more especially, on producers in other agricultural sectors of a financial burden which took the form, first, of the compulsory purchase of certain quantities of an animal feed product and, secondly, of the fixing of a purchase price for that product at a level three times higher than that of the substances which it replaced. The obligation to purchase at such a disproportionate price constituted a discriminatory distribution of the burden of costs between the various agricultural sectors. Nor, moreover, was such an obligation necessary in order to attain the objective in view, namely, the disposal of stocks of skimmed-milk powder. It could not therefore be justified for the purposes of attaining the objectives of the common agricultural policy.

8   In consequence, the answer must be that Council Regulation No. 563/76 is null and void.

NOTES AND QUESTIONS

1. As the first occasion on which the Court invalidated a significant agricultural regulation, the Skimmed-milk powder case generated some controversy. Note that the Court relied substantially on the prohibition in EC Treaty Article 34 (now TFEU Article 40) against discrimination in agricultural policy. What made the discrimination between dairy farmers, on the one hand, and the chicken and hog farmers required to bear the higher animal feed costs, on the other, an unjustified one? Did the regulation also impermissibly discriminate against soy bean producers?

2. The judgment also invokes the principle of proportionality. To the extent that it relies on that principle, does the Court find that the regulation

(a) is not a rational means of achieving a legitimate objective, (b) is a manifestly less advantageous (or more drastic) means of achieving its objective than others that were available, or (c) entails costs outweighing the regulation's benefits?

3.   DVK v. OHIM, excerpted at page 793 infra, raises an important issue concerning equal treatment of languages in the operations of a Union body. When the Community Trademark Office was created, the Council authorized it to conduct its operations in five languages (apart from an applicants's own language, which is always used for an application). When a Dutch lawyer challenged the failure to use Dutch as one of the operational languages, both the CFI and the Court of Justice held that a Union citizen or entity had no right to require that all Union official languages be used in every Union body, when efficiency and cost considerations make that inadvisable.

4.   The Treaty from the start established a right to equal pay in employment for men and women. Subsequently, a directive adopted in 1977 under the implied power provision, EC Treaty Article 308 (now TFEU Article 352), established a right of equal treatment for men and women in all employment circumstances. Chapter 34 covers the abundant Court case law applying the two directives. Just as an immediate illustration of the Court's liberal approach in this sector, the Court has frequently held that an employer must provide a sufficient objective justification for lower pay or benefits to part-time workers as compared to full-time employees, because the large majority of part-time workers are women. With regard to equal treatment, the Court held in a prominent judgment, Kreil v. Germany, infra page 1416, that Germany could not restrict women in its military services from all military posts involving the use of arms.

Moreover, after the Treaty of Amsterdam authorized the Council to adopt directives that prohibited discrimination on the basis of race, ethnic origin, religion, age, disability and sexual orientation, the Council adopted in 2000 two directives to achieve that goal. See Chapter 34 for a description of the directives and some significant recent judgments interpreting them.

c.   Legal Certainty, Legitimate Expectations, and Non-retroactivity

A general principle of law that has found fertile ground in the EU law sphere is that of "legal certainty," derived from general principles of French and German public law, *sécurité juridique* and *Rechtssicherheit*, respectively. This principle posits, within limits of course, that the political institutions should not disturb settled legal relationships, and should state rules that affect private parties in a clear manner to enable their proper compliance (or a challenge to the rules).

Besides laying the basis for a suit to annul a regulation, and/or obtain relief in damages, the principle of legal certainty may also operate as a rule of interpretation. Thus, when the French authorities and the Commission sought to interpret a tariff exemption narrowly, contrary to its normal reading, the Court disagreed, stating that: "The principle of legal certainty requires that rules imposing charges on the taxpayer must be clear and precise so that he may know without ambiguity what are his rights and obligations and may take steps accordingly." Administration des Douanes v. SA Gondrand Frères, Case 169/80, [1981] ECR 1931, 1942.

An aspect of the principle of legal certainty is the protection of legitimate expectations (*Vertrauensschutz* or *la protection de la confiance légitime,* as it is known in German and French law, respectively). The idea is to protect a private party's reliance on current EU rules when that party could reasonably have expected those rules to remain in force. The very nature of the Council's and Commission's regulatory tasks suggests that traders will frequently claim loss due to unexpected changes in EU rules. The Court's protection of legitimate expectations is well illustrated in the following judgment.

MULDER v. MINISTER VAN LANDBOUW EN VISSERIJ

Case 120/86, [1988] ECR 2321.

[In return for a non-marketing premium made available pursuant to a 1977 Council regulation, a Dutch farmer agreed not to market milk for five years, 1979 to 1984. When he decided in 1984 to re-enter the dairy business, he applied for a milk production quota, but was denied one on the ground that such quotas were, according to a 1984 regulation, to be issued on the basis of 1983 production of which he had none. The Dutch court in which the farmer sued made a preliminary reference. The Court squarely addressed the question of the farmer's legitimate expectations:]

23 [A] producer who has voluntarily ceased production for a certain period cannot legitimately expect to be able to resume production under the same conditions as those which previously applied and not to be subject to any rules of market or structural policy adopted in the meantime.

24 [However,] where such a producer ... has been encouraged by a Community measure to suspend marketing for a limited period in the general interest and against payment of a premium he may legitimately expect not to be subject, upon the expiry of his undertaking, to restrictions which specifically affect him precisely because he availed himself of the possibilities offered by the Community provisions.

* * *

26 [T]otal and continuous exclusion ... for the entire period of application of the regulations ..., preventing the producers concerned from resuming the marketing of milk at the end of the five-year period, was not an occurrence which those producers could have foreseen when they entered into an undertaking, for a limited time, not to deliver milk. ... Such an effect therefore frustrates those producers' legitimate expectations that the effects of the system to which they had rendered themselves subject would be limited.

* * *

28   [T]he [1984 regulation] is invalid in so far as it does not provide for the allocation of a reference quantity for producers who, pursuant to an undertaking entered into under [the 1977 regulation], did not deliver milk during the reference year. . . .

Note that the Court did not invalidate the 1984 regulation in its entirety, but merely held that it could not validly be applied by its terms under the circumstances of a case like this.

The principle of legitimate expectations protects only justifiable expectations and reasonable reliance, presumably measured by the objective standard of an ordinarily prudent person in the plaintiff's situation. However, these notions necessarily have a subjective component. In a particularly interesting judgment, the Court invalidated a Council regulation imposing a customs duty on Austrian products (Austria not yet being an EU Member State) on the basis of the principle of legitimate expectations, because the regulation was adopted less than a month before the European Economic Area Agreement between the Community and Austria would have become effective, prohibiting any new customs duties. See Opel Austria GmbH v. Council, Case T–115/94, [1997] ECR II–39, discussed at page 1114 infra.

The principle of "non-retroactivity" is an important manifestation of the notion of legal certainty. The Court has ruled that the EU institutions may not in principle apply regulations retroactively, if doing so would cause private parties serious economic loss that they cannot avoid by adjusting their conduct. In most cases, the temporal effect of a measure is not specified. When that is the case, the retroactivity or non-retroactivity of a measure becomes a matter of interpretation. Based on considerations of legal certainty and reliance, EU regulations are commonly interpreted "as applying to situations existing before their entry into force only in so far as [that] clearly follows from their terms, objectives or general scheme." Openbaar Ministerie v. Bout, Case 21/81, [1982] ECR 381, 390.

NOTE ON THE RETROACTIVE EFFECT OF COURT OF JUSTICE RULINGS

Discussion of legal certainty is a suitable context in which to consider the retroactive effect of the Court of Justice's own rulings on EU law. The Court's general view is that such rulings merely clarify what was always the proper interpretation of a rule of law, and thus date back to the coming into effect of the rule of the law in question. In Procureur de la République v. Waterkeyn, Cases 314–16/81 & 83/82, [1982] ECR 4337, a French court inquired about the temporal effect of a recent Court of Justice judgment striking down aspects of French legislation on the advertising of alcohol because they discriminated against imported products in violation of EC Treaty Article 28 (now TFEU Article 34). Pending before the French court were several prosecutions for violation of the same French law. The Court of Justice reasoned that the invalidity of the French legislation flowed from Article 28, and not from the Court's decision, and that the French courts therefore could not continue any prosecutions under the French law even if the conduct in question occurred prior to the Court's decision.

By the same general reasoning, the Court has required States to make back benefit payments available to claimants where the regulations on the basis of which such payments had been refused were invalidated by the Court, and to give refunds to parties who had made payments pursuant to regulations later declared invalid. Thus, in Commission v. France (Frontier worker pensions), discussed at page 578 infra, the Court held that France would have to make substantial back pension benefits (ca. $35,000,000) to Belgian frontier workers employed in France.

In exceptional circumstances, the Court has decided that its judgments should not have retroactive effect, invoking precisely the notion of legal certainty. The most famous example is Defrenne v. Société Anonyme Belge de Navigation Aérienne Sabena, excerpted infra page 240. The Court there discarded a widely-held assumption that the principle of equal pay for women in the then EC Treaty Article 119 (later EC Article 141, and now TFEU Article 157) was not legally effective until implemented by Member State legislation. Holding that Article 119 had horizontal direct effect, the Court permitted discrimination victims to claim damages from employers. Fearing that claims for back pay dating back to 1962 (when Article 119 became effective for the original Member States) might be so substantial as to create a risk of bankruptcy for some employers, the Court held that the ruling would not have retroactive effect, except for those few plaintiffs who had already filed suits:

> [I]t is appropriate to take exceptionally into account the fact that, over a prolonged period, the parties concerned have been led to continue with practices which were contrary to Article 119, although not yet prohibited under their national law.

* * *

> In these circumstances ... important considerations of legal certainty affecting all the interests involved, both public and private, make it impossible in principle to reopen the question as regards the past.

The Court concluded that, except for claims already then filed, "the direct effect of Article 119 cannot be relied on in order to support claims concerning pay periods prior to the date of this judgment." [1976] ECR at 480–81.

The Court again invoked the principle of non-retroactivity to deny claims for employer pension benefits earned prior to the Court's 1990 *Barber* ruling (page 1432 infra) that the ban on gender discrimination in pay applies to pension benefits. The Court limited the retroactive effect of the ruling to persons who had initiated legal proceedings or their equivalent under national law prior to the time of the 1990 ruling. Ten Oever v. Stichting Bedrijfspensioenfonds, Case C–109/91, [1993] ECR I–4879. The result spared European employers billions of dollars in potential liability.

Similarly, in Blaizot v. University of Liège, infra page 627, the Court decided that a discriminatorily higher Belgian university fee for students from other Member States violated the Treaty article on equal access to vocational training, but only allowed those students who had already filed claims for reimbursement to avail themselves of the ruling. In view of the fact that the fees were relatively small, so that the aggregate amount of any reimbursement would have been nowhere near the sums in question in the equal pay judgments, do you agree with the result?

Significantly, in a related case, the Court held that a Member State may not itself enact a law restricting the retroactive effect of a Court of Justice ruling unless that ruling expressly so provides. Barra v. Belgium and City of Liège, Case 309/85, [1988] ECR 355. "The fundamental need for a general and uniform application of Community law implies that it is for the Court of Justice alone to decide upon the temporal restrictions to be placed on [its judgments]." Id. at 375.

The issue of fairness in the retroactive application of new legal principles has also vexed the US Supreme Court. A divided Court has insisted that newly-announced principles, particularly constitutional ones, receive retroactive application even if they result in very heavy new liabilities. Harper v. Virginia Department of Taxation, 509 U.S. 86, 113 S.Ct. 2510, 125 L.Ed.2d 74 (1993).

4. MISUSE OF POWERS

Misuse of powers—the fourth general ground for annulment of EU law measures—is an English rendition of a traditional concept of French administrative law known as *détournement de pouvoir*. A misuse of power in this sense occurs when authority is exercised for purposes other than those for which it was conferred. In EU law, as in French administrative law, misuse of power is said to denote a "subjective" wrong, in contrast with the other grounds for review which are intrinsically "objective." More specifically, it entails an inquiry into the motives or purposes behind an act rather than the act itself or, as the matter is sometimes put, into the act's "internal" as opposed to "external" aspects. See F. Schockweiler, La notion de détournement de pouvoir en droit communautaire, [1990] Actualité Juridique, Droit Administratif 435.

The following case illustrates the misuse of power concept.

GIUFFRIDA v. COUNCIL
Case 105/75, [1976] ECR 1395.

[Giuffrida was an unsuccessful applicant for a high administrative post in the Directorate–General for regional policy. When the appointment was given to someone else, Giuffrida brought suit alleging that the competition was not genuine. He contended that the post had been reserved in advance for his competitor, one Emilio Martino. The Court annulled the Council's appointment of Martino.]

5   Article 27 of the Staff Regulations state that "Recruitment shall be directed to securing for the institution the services of officials of the highest standard of ability, efficiency and integrity. . . ."

6   In addition, Article 29 of the Staff Regulations lays down the necessary recruitment procedures—which, in paragraph 1(b), include the internal competition—so that vacant posts may be filled by officials chosen on the basis of objective criteria and only in the interests of the service.

* * *

10   It is clear from the [admissions made by the Council's Secretary General] that [the competition] was organized by the appointing authority for the sole purpose of remedying the anomalous administrative status of a specific official and of appointing that same official to the post declared vacant.

11   The pursuit of such a specific objective is contrary to the aims of any recruitment procedure, including the internal competition procedure, and thus constitutes a misuse of powers.

12   The existence of [a] misuse of powers in this instance is moreover confirmed by the fact that one of the conditions for admission to the competition was that the successful candidate must have held the secretariat for meetings of Council working parties or committees on regional policy for at least four years.

13   It is not disputed that such a restrictive condition corresponds exactly to the duties performed by Emilio Martino in his previous post.

14   Furthermore, none of the information provided by the defendant shows why it was necessary in the interests of the service to lay down such a specific condition as regards the duration of the duties referred to.

15/16   Furthermore . . . a memorandum [from] the Secretary–General . . . provided, in particular, that "in order to ensure the equal treatment of all officials internal competitions will take place on the basis of qualifications and tests offering the same guarantees of selection as open competitions although adapted to the internal nature of the competition and the types of post to be filled".

17   Whether or not the memorandum in question was at that time in the nature of a decision, the fact remains that . . . the appointing authority should have regarded itself as under a moral obligation to comply with it and, therefore, to organize the competition in question on the basis not only of qualifications but of tests also.

18   On these grounds it must be concluded that the decision to make the appointment in question involves a misuse of powers and must therefore be annulled.

NOTES AND QUESTIONS

1.   Would there have been anything wrong with requiring experience as a working group secretary if two or more candidates possessed that credential? In other words, was fixing this qualification for the post "objectively" wrong or only "subjectively" wrong? Do you find it helpful to draw such lines?

2.   Claims of misuse of powers rarely result in the annulment of EU law measures. (Advocate General Warner began his opinion in *Giuffrida* with the words, "Misuse of power [is] often pleaded but seldom proved. . . . [I]n this case, it has been proved." [1976] ECR at 1405.) One of the reasons for this rarity was alluded to in the previous note. Consider the problem also from a remedial angle. What should the Court of Justice do if it concludes that an EU official has made a decision based on his or her private interest, or on an "incorrect" public interest, but that the same decision could have been justified in terms of the "correct" public interest? The Court has held, much as the French administrative courts have done, that an "error" in motive should be deemed harmless unless the mistaken purpose was in fact the dominant one or otherwise substantially affected the outcome.

BOOSS AND FISCHER v. COMMISSION

Case T–58/91, [1993] ECR II–147.

[Booss (a German) and Fischer (a Dutchman) had served since 1984 on the agriculture and fisheries team of the Commission Legal Service. In 1990, the Commission reorganized the Directorate General for Fisheries, publishing three vacancy notices for directors' posts. In a first round limited to applicants seeking promotion from within the Commission, none of the candidates (including Booss and Fischer) was found to be qualified, although Booss had been President of the International Convention for the North Atlantic Fisheries. The Commission proceeded to a second "outside" round at the end of which Monreal, a Spanish national, and Mastracchio, an Italian national, were selected for directors' posts. Booss and Fischer complained that the results of the competition had been prearranged in violation of staff regulations and in an abuse of procedure. They also claimed that neither of the successful candidates possessed the required knowledge of the fisheries policy called for in the vacancy notices. Unsuccessful, they sued. In their suit, they raised for the first time the claim that the posts had been reserved for candidates on the basis of nationality. In fact, Article 27 of the Staff Regulations forbids reserving posts for nationals of any specific Member State, unless required for the proper functioning of the service.

The Court found that neither Monreal nor Mastracchio had the thorough knowledge of Community fisheries policy called for by the vacancy notice. Regarding Monreal, the Court also noted that in the hearing before the Court, the Commission's representative stated that the Spanish Government had urged, with obvious reference to its great interest in fisheries policy, that the Court "not be oblivious to certain political realities." The Court annulled the appointments.]

95   ... It is apparent [that] the Spanish Government considered, in the light of the vacancies which had arisen in 1990, that, politically speaking, it was "owed" a director's post. It is apparent that, by accepting the "Spanish" application presented to it, the Commission accepted, at least by implication, the "political reality" to which its representative referred at the hearing. ... It is also apparent that, without any need to await the results of the consideration of the internal applications, the Commission already knew, at least in June 1990, that the Spanish Government's candidate would in any event be appointed.

96   Consequently, ... the post in question had been reserved, within the Commission and on the basis of at least an implied agreement, for the only candidate of Spanish nationality, and ... it had been so reserved before the decisions rejecting the applicants' candidatures had been adopted. The Commission agreed to accept a "less ideal" candidate for the purpose of assigning the post to the only candidate of Spanish nationality. That decision was motivated by the "political reality" pleaded before the Court, whilst considerations concerning the proper functioning of the service ... within the meaning of ... Article 27 of the Staff Regulations played no part.

* * *

100   [T]he circumstances indicate that the [second] post in question was regarded as an "Italian post", even though no contacts with the Italian Government were established. ... [T]he Court finds that ... the post [in Directorate D also] was reserved within the Commission for a candidate of a predetermined nationality. Once again, without its being necessary to await the results of the consideration of the internal applications, the Commission and Mr. Mastracchio already knew in June 1990 that only an "Italian" application had any prospect of being accepted. ... Considerations regarding the proper functioning of the service ... once again played no part.

NOTES AND QUESTIONS

1. Note that, while Booss and Fischer alleged an "abuse of procedure" as such, the Court decided the case on grounds of violation of Staff Regulations. This may illustrate an aversion to deciding cases on "misuse" or "abuse" of power grounds, when violation of an applicable rule of law will do. Is it not obvious, though, that the Court thought that an abuse of procedure had occurred?

2. We learn that in staff recruitment, or promotion, positions cannot be reserved in advance for particular nationalities. Does this mean that nationality is an altogether impermissible consideration in the filling of positions? Should it be an impermissible consideration in a political entity such as the European Union? In fact there is no question that a fair representation of different nationalities in positions within the institutions is sought, even in

bodies like the Commission which are sworn to independence from the Member States. Thus, after the Central and Eastern European enlargement in 2004, the Commission publicly carried out a program of recruitment of nationals of the new Member States. Where and how would you draw the line between fair representation and nationality favoritism?

Note on the Scope of Review in the Maastricht Treaty's Second and Third Pillars

As noted in Chapter 1's historical review, the Treaty of Maastricht created two fields of intergovernmental action, commonly called the second and third "pillars," in which only the Council and the European Council could adopt policies or measures, without any judicial review by the Court of Justice.

Although the Lisbon Treaty abolishes the pillars as such, the Common Foreign and Security Policy, as laid out in the TEU, retains its essentially intergovernmental character. The Court of Justice continues to be almost totally without a role. Thus, TFEU Article 275(1) declares that the Court of Justice of the EU shall not have jurisdiction with respect to the provisions relating to the common foreign and security policy nor with respect to acts adopted on the basis of those provisions. However, the Court may still, even without reviewing the merits of common foreign and security policy actions, act to ensure that those actions do not intrude upon the Union's other competences, in effect through use of an improper legal basis.

When the Treaty of Amsterdam moved to the Community sphere most of the fields previously assigned to intergovernmental action under the third pillar (Cooperation in Justice and Home Affairs, or JHA), it stipulated special forms of judicial review and renamed the sector the Area of Freedom, Security and Justice. Under the Lisbon Treaty, the Area of Freedom, Security and Justice is dealt with in the TFEU's Title V. The Court enjoys limited jurisdiction over proceedings, brought in accordance with the conditions laid down in TFEU Article 263(4), and may review the legality of Council decisions laying down restrictive measures against natural or legal persons in relation to border checks, asylum and immigration. The role of the Court in this domain is dealt with in some detail in Chapter 16F.

The Amsterdam Treaty left only the field of police and judicial cooperation in criminal matters within the TEU as distinct from the EC. The then TEU Article 35, as amended by the Amsterdam Treaty, made the action to annul available only insofar as it targeted "framework decisions," confining standing to the Commission and the Member States (thus not to Parliament or private parties), and it excluded judicial review altogether of the validity or proportionality of operations carried out by the police or other law enforcement services of a Member State or the exercise of the responsibilities incumbent upon Member States in maintaining law and order and safeguarding internal security. Under the Lisbon Treaty, TFEU Article 276 provides that "[i]n exercising its powers the Court of Justice of the European Union shall have no jurisdiction to review the validity or proportionality of operations carried out by the police or other law-enforcement services of a Member State or the exercise of the responsibilities incumbent upon Member States with regard to the maintenance of law and order and the safeguarding of internal security."

C. COMPLAINT FOR FAILURE TO ACT

EC Treaty Article 232 authorized all the EU political institutions and the Member States to bring an action against the Parliament, the Council or the Commission should any of them, by an omission to act, violate an EC Treaty obligation. French administrative law calls this an *action en carence*, that is, a complaint for failure to act. The Maastricht Treaty amended Article 232 to include the European Central Bank as a possible defendant. The Treaty of Lisbon's TFEU Article 265 reformulates the text to include the European Council as well as any "institution, body, office or agency of the Union" as potential defendants.

In theory, the failure to fulfill a duty can be as harmful as a malperformance of the duty. In practice, however, courts tend to defer to exercises of administrative discretion as to when and how a duty should be performed. Not surprisingly, complaints of failure to act rarely meet with success.

In any event, the complaint for failure to act is subject to a kind of exhaustion of remedies requirement. The complainant must first call upon the defendant institution to act, giving it two months in which to "define its position." If at the end of that period the complainant is dissatisfied, it has a further two months within which to sue for inaction. If successful, the suit results in a declaration that the institution's failure to act is contrary to the Treaty. Curiously, although an Article 232 (now TFEU Article 265) suit must be brought within two months after the failure to act is established, the prior request itself is not apparently subject to a time limitation. For an indication that the request nevertheless must be made within a "reasonable time" following the circumstances giving rise to the infringement, see Netherlands v. Commission (Aids to iron and steel industry), Case 59/70, [1971] ECR 639.

Probably the best known Article 232 case is Parliament v. Council (Transport policy), Case 13/83, [1985] ECR 1513. One of the Community's most conspicuous failures in the early 1980s was the absence of a Common Transport Policy, even though the initial EC Treaty's Article 74 made it a goal and authorized the Council to adopt measures to achieve the policy. In 1983, Parliament brought an action against the Council for its failure to act on long-pending Commission proposals for a transport policy or to take action to secure freedom to provide transport services. A threshold question was whether Parliament was authorized under the language of the predecessor of Article 232 to bring such a suit. The Court found Parliament to be an "institution of the Community" within the meaning of the article.

However on the merits, the Court held that then Article 74 did not impose a sufficiently precise obligation on the Council with respect to adoption of a common transport policy to justify a ruling in Parliament's favor. On the other hand, the Court condemned the Council's failure to take action to secure freedom to provide transport services, action that the Court found to be sufficiently well-defined in the relevant Treaty articles, and clearly overdue. Although Parliament did not prevail on the transport policy claim, the case doubtless added to the pressure to develop transport policy measures and may help account for the Council's adoption in the late 1980s of some key transport legislation.

Private parties may also sue under what is now TFEU Article 265 for a failure to act, but they must be able to show not only that the institution failed to act, but also that the institution's duty to act was a duty owed to them. As the following case shows, this may be difficult.

LORD BETHELL v. COMMISSION
Case 246/81, [1982] ECR 2277.

[Lord Bethell was a member of the European Parliament and of the House of Lords, a regular user of scheduled air passenger services within the EU and an advocate of greater airline competition. After a lengthy correspondence, he formally asked the Commission to take action against certain airlines for price fixing and other concerted practices in violation of EC Treaty Articles 81 and 82 (now TFEU Articles 101 and 102). The Commission wrote to Lord Bethell promising to study the matter further and to take action if justified. The Commission also stated that it would notify the Member States that government-fixed fares must not be so excessive as to constitute an abuse of a dominant position. The Commission further indicated that it was drafting a directive to the Member States on criteria for airfare approvals. Dissatisfied with this response, Lord Bethell brought suit under both EC Treaty Articles 230 and 232.]

13   It appears from [Articles 230 and 232] that the applicant, for his application to be admissible, must be in a position to establish either that he is the addressee of a measure of the Commission having specific legal effects with regard to him, which is, as such, capable of being declared void, or that the Commission, having been duly called upon to act . . . has failed to adopt in relation to him a measure which he was legally entitled to claim by virtue of the rules of Community law.

* * *

15   The principal question to be resolved in this case is whether the Commission had, under the rules of Community law, the right and the duty to adopt in respect of the applicant a decision in the sense of the request made by the applicant to the Commission in his letter of 13 May 1981. It is apparent from the content of that letter and from the explanations given during the proceedings that the applicant is asking

the Commission to undertake an investigation with regard to the airlines in the matter of the fixing of air fares with a view to a possible application to them of the provisions of the Treaty with regard to competition.

16   It is clear therefore that the applicant is asking the Commission, not to take a decision in respect of him, but to open an inquiry with regard to third parties and to take decisions in respect of them. No doubt the applicant, in his double capacity as a user of the airlines and a leading member of an organization of users of air passenger services, has an indirect interest . . . in such proceedings and their possible outcome, but he is nevertheless not in the precise legal position of the actual addressee of a decision, which may be declared void under the second paragraph of Article [230], or in [the precise legal position] of the potential addressee of a legal measure which the Commission has a duty to adopt with regard to him, as is [the] position under the third paragraph of Article [232]

17   It follows that the application is inadmissible from the point of view of both Article [230] and Article [232].

The Court's judgment in *Lord Bethell* suggests that whether a party has standing to challenge a failure to act may depend upon whether that party would have had standing to challenge the act if it had in fact been taken. Thus, if a private person asks that a regulation be adopted, and the request is not acted upon, for standing purposes the private party's right to challenge the failure to act depends on whether he could have challenged an adopted regulation. As we have seen, normally a private party cannot make such a challenge.

NOTE ON COMMISSION "INACTION" ON COMPETITION LAW COMPLAINTS

Given the multitude of complaints that the Commission receives about private anti-competitive conduct, it is small wonder that the Commission's alleged non-response to some complaints, has given rise to "failure to act" case law. An important threshold question in this respect is whether the Commission is accused of refusing to act on a complaint or, rather, of ignoring a complaint altogether. Presumably the Commission is not permitted to ignore a complaint altogether, and if it were to do so, an action for failure to act under Article 232 would lie. Such was the case in United Parcel Service Europe SA v. Commission, Case T–127/98, [1999] ECR II–2633, where the Court of First Instance ruled that the Commission failed in its duties to UPS by not taking a position on UPS' four-year old complaint that Germany's subsidization of Deutsche Post AG violated EU competition law.

More commonly the Commission declines to act, in which case the complainant's remedy is presumably a suit to annul a "negative" act. In Schmidt v. Commission, Case 210/81, [1983] ECR 3045, Schmidt, a retailer, complained that his exclusion from the Revox selective distribution network amounted to anticompetitive conduct by Revox in violation of Article 81 (now TFEU Article 101). After reviewing the matter, the Commission decided not to take action against Revox and so notified Schmidt. Upon suit by Schmidt, the Court ruled that the Commission had made a negative decision which was reviewable under Article 230 (now TFEU Article 263), rather than merely failed to act under Article 232 (now TFEU Article 265). (Schmidt lost on the merits.)

When the Commission positively declines to act (rather than ignores a request to do so), the principal question becomes the scope of judicial review of such a decision. The Court of First Instance established its framework of analysis in the case of Automec Srl. v. Commission, Case T–24/90, [1992] ECR II–2223. In *Automec*, an Italian car dealer complained to the Commission about BMW's termination of its distributorship contract. The Commission declined to investigate whether BMW had committed a competition law violation and the dealer brought suit. The Court of First Instance held that "the Commission cannot be required to give a ruling [on a competition law infringement] unless the subject-matter of the complaint is within its exclusive remit," which it was not. Moreover, since the Commission is not obligated to issue a ruling, "it [also] cannot be compelled to conduct an investigation, because this could have no purpose other than to seek evidence of the existence or otherwise of an infringement, the existence of which it is not required to establish." The Court emphasized the Commission's prerogative to decide for itself how best to spend its time and resources. "[F]or an institution performing a public-interest task, the power to . . . settl[e] priorities in the framework laid down by law, where those priorities have not been settled by the legislature, is an inherent part of the work of administration."

The Court in *Automec* did not, however, treat the Commission's exercise of investigatorial discretion as wholly unreviewable. If challenged, the decision to close the files on a complaint without further investigation is subject to judicial review on the question whether the Commission "evaluat[ed] with all the requisite care the [complaint's] factual and legal aspects," whether the Commission gave proper reasons (duly allowing for its right to set priorities), and whether the Commission committed "a mistake in law or a manifest error of assessment or . . . a misuse of powers."

D.   THE PLEA OF ILLEGALITY

Article 241 of the EC Treaty permitted a challenge to a regulation adopted by the Council, the Parliament together with the Council, the Commission or the European Central Bank as an incidental issue in the course of some other proceeding brought on a proper and timely basis in an EU court. TFEU Article 277 reformulates the text to permit a challenge to any legal act of the political institutions, which now includes the European Council, or any other body, office or agency of the Union.

The significance of the plea of illegality lies in the fact that, by its terms, it allows a regulation to be challenged indirectly even after the time for bringing a direct challenge has expired. This so-called "plea of illegality" derives from French administrative law, more particularly the *exception d'illégalité*. The usual scenario is one in which a party seeks the annulment of an individual decision addressed to it, in whole or in part because the decision in turn is based on an illegal regulation. If two months have passed since the regulation's effective date, the regulation itself may no longer be challenged directly, even by a party that otherwise would have had standing under EC Treaty Article 230 or, now, TFEU Article 263. However, an action to annul the individual decision implementing the regulation may still be timely, and EC Treaty Article 241 and, now, TFEU Article 265 expressly allow the regulation to be collaterally attacked in that proceeding.

If the TFEU Article 265 claim in our example is successful, the regulation will not be formally annulled. However, since it cannot serve as the legal basis for the challenged decision, the decision itself will be annulled. Although the institutions could conceivably continue in the future to take action on the basis of the regulation (precisely because it has not been annulled), they are unlikely to do so. The Court of Justice itself maintains that a ruling on the legality of an EU law measure made under the plea of illegality procedure in a preliminary reference from a national court, though addressed only to that court, constitutes "sufficient reason for any other national court to regard that [measure] as void." SpA International Chemical Corporation v. Amministrazione delle Finanze dello Stato, Case 66/80, [1981] ECR 1191.

Simmenthal v. Commission (Simmenthal III), Case 92/78, [1979] ECR 777, is a well-known Article 241 case. The Italian intervention authorities solicited bids for the purchase of some of their stock of frozen beef, and the Simmenthal firm submitted one. Before action on the bid could be taken, the Commission addressed a decision to the Member States fixing maximum quantities and minimum prices for beef sales by national intervention agencies. The Italian authorities accordingly rejected Simmenthal's tender as falling outside the allowable limits. Simmenthal brought a direct action for annulment of the Commission decision. (Simmenthal was found to have standing because the decision, though addressed to the Member States, was of direct and individual concern to it.)

Simmenthal invoked Article 241, arguing that the Commission guidelines which formed the basis of the decision limiting Member States beef sales were themselves invalid. The Court found the decision and the guideline to be invalid, annulled the limitation on beef sales that was based on them, and remanded the matter to the Commission and the Italian authorities.

According to the Court in *Simmenthal III*, Article 241 permits the collateral attack of prior measures only if the party bringing the attack "was not entitled under Article [230] ... to bring a direct action challenging those measures." The Court cited a "need to provide those persons who are precluded by ... Article [230] from instituting proceedings directly in respect of general acts with the benefit of a judicial review of [those acts] at the time when they are affected by ... decisions [implementing those acts.]'' [1979] ECR at 800.

A similar result obtained in National Farmers' Union v. Secretariat général du gouvernement, Case C–241/01, [2002] ECR I–9079, where the Court held that France could not, in proceedings before the French courts, question the validity of two Commission decisions setting out the terms under which imports of beef from the United Kingdom could resume, due to the fact that France had not sought to annul those decisions in a timely fashion.

There is every reason to suppose that national courts likewise will permit the indirect challenge of an EU law measure. The preliminary reference mechanism plainly contemplates that in the course of litigation before them, national courts may encounter questions about the validity of EU law acts, and may (and in some cases must) refer those questions to the Court of Justice.

On the other hand, as we shall see in Chapter 7 (and more particularly in the *Foto–Frost* case, infra page 253), national courts may not themselves invalidate an EU law measure. If they question the validity of such an act, they must make a preliminary reference to the Court of Justice.

E. DAMAGE ACTIONS AGAINST THE UNION

This chapter has thus far dealt with various ways of contesting EU law measures directly in the courts of the EU. Parties, however, are not always content with rulings that merely "declare" EU law measures invalid or "call upon" the offending institution to set matters right. They may seek more tangible and immediate benefit in the form of monetary relief against the institutions.

Article 235 of the EC Treaty (now TFEU Article 268) vests the Court of Justice with jurisdiction over damage actions against the EU, taking the scope of liability from TFEU Article 340, which is identical in wording to EC Treaty Article 288(2), and reads as follows:

> In the case of non-contractual liability, the Union shall, in accordance with the general principles common to the laws of the Member States, make good any damage caused by its institutions or by its servants in the performance of their duties.

This section deals with the scope of TFEU Article 340, first as a basis for the EU's tort liability, and then as a basis of liability for the legal actions of the institutions.

1. THE EU'S LIABILITY IN TORT

The language of EC Treaty Article 288(2), and now TFEU Article 340, suggests that the EU can become liable in tort, and that this liability may include vicarious liability. Interestingly, very few tort actions have been brought against the Community or EU on account of the acts of its "servants." That damage suits are more commonly brought on account of institutional acts is due to the fact that the EU normally acts through legal measures rather than through physical conduct on the part of specifically identifiable persons.

Another reason for the paucity of cases is the Court's own initial response to the central question in vicarious liability, namely whether the tortious conduct falls within the employee's "scope" of employment.

SAYAG v. LEDUC

Case 9/69, [1969] ECR 329.

[A businessman sued a Euratom engineer in Belgian court for injuries suffered in an automobile accident during a visit to certain Euratom installations. The engineer had been instructed to conduct the visit and was specifically given a travel order to use his own car. On preliminary reference from the highest Belgian court, the Court of Justice gave an exceedingly restrictive definition of the term "in the performance of their duties" in the provision of the Euratom Treaty which paralleled EC Treaty Article 288(2)]

> By referring at one and the same time to damage caused by the institutions and to that caused by the servants of the Community, [the Treaty] indicates that the Community is only liable for those acts of its servants which, by virtue of an internal and direct relationship, are the necessary extension of the tasks entrusted to the institutions.

* * *

> A reference to a servant's private car in a travel order does not bring the driving of such car within the performance of his duties, but is basically intended to enable any necessary reimbursement of the travel expenses involved in the use of this means of transport to be made in accordance with the standards laid down for this purpose.

> Only in the case of force majeure, or in exceptional circumstances of such overriding importance that without the servant's using private means of transport the Community would have been unable to carry out the tasks entrusted to it, could such use be considered to form part of the servant's performance of his duties, within the meaning of the ... Treaty.

[1969] ECR at 335–36. The plaintiff's only option was thus the suit he had also brought against the engineer in Belgium. Is this a sound result?

Adams v. Commission, Case 145/83, [1985] ECR 3539, is a rare case in which the Court awarded damages on account of the personal conduct of EU officials, rather than the institutions' legal acts. Stanley Adams, an employee of the Swiss pharmaceutical firm Hoffmann–LaRoche, reported to the Commission certain corporate activities he thought to be in violation of EU competition law, and the Commission eventually issued a decision unfavorable to the company. Although the Commission at Adams' request did not disclose his identity as informant, documents that the Commission supplied to Hoffmann–LaRoche enabled the company to identify Adams as the whistle-blower and have him arrested and prosecuted under Swiss law for betraying his former employer's economic secrets. Following a period of solitary confinement and news of his wife's suicide in the wake of the police investigation, Adams confessed to having been the informant, a fact that the Commission then confirmed. After receiving a one-year suspended sentence, Adams sued the Commission for failing to protect his identity. The Court held the Commission liable in tort for breach of its duty to protect Adams' identity, though it reduced Adams' recovery by half by reason of his own negligence in allowing his identity to become known and exposing himself to arrest.

Article 340(2) fixes the EU's vicarious liability by reference to "the general principles common to the laws of the Member States." In practice, French administrative tort law appears to have had singular influence over this aspect of EU law. Under that law, the EU basically may be held liable for its officials' fault committed within the scope of office, including negligence or bad faith or conduct contrary to instructions or law.

General principles of law are also consulted on narrower issues of substance in the field of tort. In Grifoni v. Euratom, Case C–308/87, [1990] ECR I–1203, for example, a contracting party was awarded damages for Euratom's failure to maintain safe physical conditions at a meteorological installation at which the claimant was making improvements. The Court found Euratom at fault for failing to comply with the local Italian legislation governing the prevention of industrial accidents.

2. LIABILITY FOR THE EU'S LEGAL ACTS

Considering the functions they characteristically perform, the institutions of the EU are not often charged with the kind of "garden variety" torts—negligent driving, poor maintenance of premises, police misconduct and the like—commonly associated with government tort liability. More usual are claims for economic relief from EU law measures shown to be illegal on one or more of the grounds for review discussed previously. This kind of claim may not be a very promising one in the US, due to the statutory exemptions for policy or discretionary decisions typically found in American government tort claim statutes. In the EU, however, damage actions for economic injury are increasingly common, though, for reasons to be explored in the cases that follow, not very often successful.

Turning then to the substantive dimension, when is it proper for the Court to award damages against the EU? The Court sought to address that question in principle in Aktien-Zuckerfabrik Schöppenstedt v. Council, Case 5/71, [1971] ECR 975, where a German sugar producer objected to a Council regulation that compensated sugar producers who were adversely affected by price changes under a new common market organization in that commodity, but that expressly excluded German firms producing white or raw sugar (of which the plaintiff was one). The Council considered such firms to be only "marginally" affected by the changes. The plaintiff argued that the excluded producers were affected more than marginally and claimed damages on account of the discrimination. The Court set a high standard for any liability in damages:

> Where legislative action involving measures of economic policy is concerned, the Community does not incur noncontractual liability for damage suffered by individuals as a consequence of that action [under] Article [288] . . . of the Treaty, unless a sufficiently flagrant violation of a superior rule of law for the protection of the individual has occurred.

[1971] ECR at 984. The quoted language has become known as the "*Schöppenstedt* formula." The Court concluded in the case that under the circumstances the exclusion was not discriminatory and thus no violation of a "superior rule of law" had occurred.

Among the best-known judgments in this area is the following:

BAYERISCHE HNL VERMEHRUNGSBETRIEBE GmbH v. COUNCIL AND COMMISSION.

(Second Skimmed-milk powder case)
Cases 83, 94/76 & 4, 15, 40/77, [1978] ECR 1209.

[It will be recalled that in the initial Skimmed-milk powder case, supra page 167, the Court struck down as discriminatory and "disproportionate" a regulation requiring animal feed producers to use skimmed-milk powder as the protein ingredient in their product, thus forcing poultry farmers to buy more expensive feed. In the present case, producers of poultry and eggs sought damages from the Council and Commission for losses due to the higher feed prices they had to pay until the regulation was invalidated. The Court first recalled the grounds on which it had invalidated the regulation and then turned to the damages question.]

4   The finding that a legislative measure . . . is null and void is . . . insufficient by itself for the Community to incur non-contractual liability for damage caused to individuals. . . .

5   In the present case there is no doubt that the prohibition on discrimination . . . is in fact designed for the protection of the individual, and that it is impossible to disregard the importance of this prohibition in the system of the Treaty. . . . Although [the principles in the legal systems of the Member States governing the liability of public authorities for damage caused to individuals by legislative measures] vary considerably from one Member State to another, it is however possible to state that the public authorities can only exceptionally and in special circumstances incur liability for legislative measures which are the result of choices of economic policy. This restrictive view is explained

by the consideration that the legislative authority ... cannot always be hindered in making its decisions by the prospect of applications for damages whenever it has occasion to adopt legislative measures in the public interest which may adversely affect the interests of individuals.

6   It follows from these considerations that individuals may be required ... to accept within reasonable limits certain harmful effects on their economic interests as a result of a legislative measure without being able to obtain compensation from public funds even if that measure has been declared null and void. In a legislative field such as the one in question, in which one of the chief features is the exercise of a wide discretion essential for the implementation of the Common Agricultural Policy, the Community does not therefore incur liability unless the institution concerned has manifestly and gravely disregarded the limits on the exercise of its powers.

7   This is not so in the case of a measure of economic policy such as that in the present case. ... [T]his measure affected ... all buyers of compound feeding-stuffs containing protein, so that its effects on individual undertakings were considerably lessened. Moreover, the effects of the regulation on the price of feeding-stuffs as a factor in the production costs of those buyers were only limited since that price rose by little more than 2%. ... The effects of the regulation on the profit-earning capacity of the undertakings did not ultimately exceed the bounds of the economic risks inherent in the activities of the agricultural sectors concerned.

8   In these circumstances the fact that the regulation is null and void is insufficient for the Community to incur liability under ... Article [288] of the Treaty.

NOTES AND QUESTIONS

1. A broadly similar result occurred in the damage actions arising out of the Court's isoglucose cases. After the Court invalidated a tax on isoglucose producers as in violation of the principle of equal treatment, three isoglucose manufacturers brought separate actions for many millions of dollars in damages, due largely to massive lost investments in isoglucose production. The three were the EU's only significant producers and each had allegedly suffered grievously, one of them going into bankruptcy as a result. Recovery was nevertheless denied. The Court did not dispute the seriousness of the plaintiffs' loss, but found that the Commission's error in adopting the illegal measure was not a grave one, holding that although the Commission had imposed "manifestly unequal" burdens and thus acted illegally, it did not "manifestly or gravely disregard the limits on its discretion." Koninklijke Scholten–Honig NV v. Council and Commission, Case 143/77, [1979] ECR 3583. Does this make sense to you?

2. In the following relatively rare judgment, the Court held that the plaintiff could obtain damages due to the Commission's violation of the principle of legitimate expectations discussed previously.

SOFRIMPORT S.A.R.L. v. COMMISSION

Case C–152/88, [1990] ECR I–2477.

[In April 1988, the Commission adopted regulations suspending the issuance of import licenses for dessert apples from Chile. By this time Sofrimport, a French importer of fresh fruit, had already shipped a cargo of Chilean apples to France, the ship reaching Marseille one week after the suspension of licenses took effect. The French authorities refused to issue the necessary import papers and Sofrimport brought an action for annulment of the regulations as applied and for damages.

The Court ruled that the regulations were of both direct and individual concern to Sofrimport. On the merits, it found that if the regulations were applied to apples already in transit, they would impermissibly disappoint an importer's legitimate expectations, particularly since the Council regulation that initially set up the market organization in fruits and vegetables required that the Commission "take account of the special position of products in transit" (art. 3(3)). The Court then turned to Sofrimport's claim for damages due to its inability to market the apples until June 1988 when the suspension was lifted.]

25   ... According to [our previous rulings] the Community does not incur liability on account of a legislative measure which involves choices of economic policy unless a sufficiently serious breach of a superior rule of law for the protection of the individual has occurred.

26   [T]he purpose of ... Article 3(3) of [the Council regulation] is to protect traders who import goods covered by that regulation into the Community from the unfavourable consequences of protective measures which might be adopted by the Community institutions. That provision thus gives rise to a legitimate expectation the disregard of which constitutes a breach of that superior rule of law.

27   Secondly, it must be held that by failing completely to take account of the position of traders such as Sofrimport, without invoking any overriding public interest, the Commission committed a sufficiently serious breach of Article 3(3).

28   Thirdly, the damage alleged by Sofrimport goes beyond the limits of the economic risks inherent in the business in issue inasmuch as the purpose of that provision is precisely to limit those risks with regard to goods in transit.

29   Consequently, the Community must make good the damage caused to Sofrimport by the adoption of the contested regulations.

NOTES AND QUESTIONS

1. Were the regulations in *Sofrimport* "legislative measures which involve choices of economic policy?" Why did the principle of legitimate expectations make a difference?

2. Another issue in cases of liability in tort for the EU's legal acts is the *extent* of liability. In Mulder and Heinemann v. Council and Commission,

Joined Cases C–104/89 & C–37/90, [1992] ECR I–3061, the Court ruled that recoverable damages should include all relevant forms of lost income. At the same time, the Court inferred from the general principles common to the laws of the Member States a requirement that the injured party make all reasonable efforts to mitigate its damages, and bear its own losses to the extent that it fails to do so.

CHAPTER 6

FUNDAMENTAL RIGHTS, THE CHARTER OF RIGHTS, DEMOCRATIC VALUES AND TRANSPARENCY

■ ■ ■

One of the most remarkable recent developments in European Union law is the gradual elaboration of its protection of fundamental or basic rights. This chapter tells the story of that evolution.

As early as the 1970s, the Court of Justice declared that implicit in its function of judicial review was protection of fundamental rights. From that time to the present the Court has rendered a series of landmark judgments protecting a variety of rights. The initial part of this chapter surveys the most important of these judgments. But the Court did not proceed in a vacuum. Not only was it prompted by pressures emanating from Member state constitutional courts, but it was equally encouraged by political developments. The chapter's second and third parts describe in particular the Treaty of Amsterdam's contributions to respect for the rule of law and fundamental rights, and the Charter of Fundamental Rights of the European Union, drafted in 2000, proclaimed at Nice, and given legal force by the Lisbon Treaty, which takes further steps toward solidifying the Union's adherence to democratic values. The last section of this chapter treats the related issues of transparency in governance, including public access to documents.

The drafters of the original EEC Treaty had not included any comprehensive, much less entrenched, statement of basic or fundamental rights, even though by that time the German, Italian and other post-war European national constitutions contained many specific human rights protections. This may have been due to the fact that Community law was expected to be implemented in the main by Member State officials, who were themselves subject to national and international human rights constraints. The United Nations General Assembly had adopted the Universal Declaration of Human Rights in 1948, and all the initial six Member States had signed the European Convention on Human Rights, drafted in 1950 under the auspices of the Council of Europe.

The EEC Treaty did contain a few express provisions reflecting basic rights. Most important was the principle of non-discrimination based on nationality in all fields of Community action, set out in EC Treaty Article 12 (now in TFEU Article 18). The Treaty's provisions on the free movement and residence rights of workers may also be regarded not only as essential to achieving the internal market, but also as aspects of basic rights. EEC Treaty Article 117 further expressly prohibited gender discrimination in pay. Clearly, though, these rights were limited in scope.

This Chapter links to the preceding and next chapters. Chapter 5 showed how the Court of Justice progressively elaborated doctrines of proportionality, equal treatment, legal certainty, and the protection of legitimate expectations as limitations on legislative and administrative actions. Chapters 7 and 8 will show how the Court gradually developed its doctrine of the primacy, or supremacy, of the Treaty over national (and even over national *constitutional*) law. The Constitutional Courts of Germany and Italy in particular made their acceptance of the primacy of EU law conditional on the Community's readiness to clearly and adequately protect human rights, which created an incentive for the Court to firmly demonstrate its commitment to the protection of fundamental rights.

One basic rights topic is reserved for treatment in Chapter 16. The Maastricht Treaty introduced the concept of citizenship of the Union. Subsequent legislation and Court judgments have generated extremely broad rights of free movement and residence for citizens of the Union, meriting separate coverage in that chapter.

A.   THE COURT OF JUSTICE'S PROTECTION OF BASIC RIGHTS

1.   JUDICIAL PROTECTION OF BASIC RIGHTS AT THE EU LEVEL

It could not be foreseen in the 1960s that the Court of Justice would take upon itself the task of establishing basic rights at the EU level. Its commitment was primarily to enforcing the specific Treaty-based rights of free movement of goods, workers and services and the right of establishment. General principles such as proportionality and legitimate expectations did not figure prominently in early decisions such as Geitling v. High Authority, Cases 36–38/59, [1960] ECR 423, and Sgarlata v. Commission, Case 40/64, [1965] ECR 215.

The landmark case of Stauder v. City of Ulm, Case 26/69 [1969] ECR 419, marked a change. The issue there was whether persons entitled to the social benefit of cheaply priced butter could invoke a right of privacy to avoid having to identify themselves by name upon purchasing butter. To decide this question, the Court first had to interpret a Commission decision whose crucial text varied according to the national language version. (The Court's approach to this issue of interpretation of varying language texts is discussed at pages 533–35 infra.) The Court held that the decision should receive in this regard its "most liberal interpretation" (¶ 4). The Court explained:

6   [T]he provision in question must be interpreted as not requiring—although it does not prohibit—the identification of beneficiaries by name. The Commission was thus able to publish on 29 July 1969 an amending decision to this effect. Each of the member States is accordingly now able to choose from a number of methods by which the coupons may refer to the person concerned.

7   Interpreted in this way the provision at issue contains nothing capable of prejudicing the fundamental human rights enshrined in the general principles of Community law and protected by the Court.

Paragraph 7 is the first time the Court declared that it would protect fundamental rights. Note the Court's reference to "the general principles of Community law" which is evocative of EC Treaty Article 220 (now TEU Article 19), according to which the Court's responsibility is to ensure, in the interpretation and application of the Treaty, "that ... the law is observed." By giving "law" a deeper jurisprudential meaning, the Court managed to bring unwritten fundamental rights into the corpus of Community law.

In 1970, the Court rendered its seminal judgment in the *Internationale Handelsgesellshaft* case (supra page 160), which held that the principle of proportionality constituted a basic right that Community law measures had to respect and which in ¶ 4 reiterated that "respect for fundamental rights forms an integral part of the general principles of law protected by the Court of Justice." The Court went on to indicate that it would draw inspiration in this regard from "the constitutional traditions common to the Member States."

2. THE RIGHT OF PROPERTY AS A FUNDAMENTAL EU LAW RIGHT

NOLD v. COMMISSION

Case 4/73 [1974] ECR 491.

[An ECSC regulation intended to rationalize and modernize coal production and distribution required the German national coal producer, Ruhrkohle, to sell only to wholesalers capable of entering into large two-year supply contracts. Nold, a small wholesaler, unable to buy in such quantities, contended that the regulation deprived him of the ability to continue in business, thus violating his right to property and right to freely engage in a profession.]

13   [F]undamental rights form an integral part of the general principles of law ... In safeguarding these rights, the Court is bound to draw inspiration from constitutional traditions common to Member States,

and it cannot therefore uphold measures which are incompatible with fundamental rights recognized and protected by the Constitution of those States.

Similarly, international treaties for the protection of human rights on which the Member States have collaborated, or of which they are signatories, can supply guidelines which should be followed within the framework of Community law.

[However, the Court underscored that the rights asserted by Nold were less than absolute.]

14   If rights of ownership are protected by the constitutional laws of all the Member States and similar guarantees are given in respect of their right freely to choose and practice their trade or profession, the rights thereby guaranteed, far from constituting unfettered prerogatives, must be viewed in the light of the social function of the property and activities protected thereunder. For this reason, rights of this nature are protected by law, subject always to limitations laid down in accordance with the public interest.

Within the Community legal order it likewise seems legitimate that these rights should, if necessary, be subject to certain limits justified by the overall objectives pursued by the Community, on condition that the substance of these rights is left untouched.

As regards the guarantees accorded to a particular undertaking, they can in no respect be extended to protect mere commercial interests or opportunities, the uncertainties of which are part of the very essence of economic activity.

15   ... It was for the applicant, confronted by the economic changes brought about by the recession in coal production, to acknowledge the situation and itself carry out the necessary adaptations.

NOTES AND QUESTIONS

1. The Court's position that property rights are always subject to limits in accord with "the public interest" is not an uncommon one. The European Convention on Human Rights also declares that a State may regulate property "in accordance with the general interest." Does Nold's "economic freedom" argument today seem somewhat outmoded?

2. The Court's reference to common constitutional traditions was probably intended to reassure the German and other constitutional courts that the ECJ was prepared to embrace their most fundamental human rights principles. On the other hand, the reference to "international treaties" was presumably to the European Convention on Human Rights to which all the then Member States were signatories.

3. In its famous 1974 *"Solange I"* judgment, discussed at page 279 infra, the German Constitutional Court undertook to review the same agricultural regulation that figured in the *Internationale Handelsgesellshaft* judgment, supra page 160. The German Constitutional Court insisted that it have the

final word on the compatibility of EU law, as implemented in Germany, with fundamental rights guaranteed by the German Constitution. This attitude would continue "so long as" (*solange*) the Court of Justice's protection of basic rights was limited in character and the EC lacked both a catalogue of fundamental rights and a directly elected Parliament.

HAUER v. LAND RHEINLAND–PFALZ

Case 44/79 [1979] ECR 3727.

[Liselotte Hauer wanted to plant a vineyard on a parcel of land that she claimed was suitable for that purpose. The German authorities denied her permission to do so, citing a Council regulation that sought to deal with the Community's wine surplus by prohibiting for three years all new cultivation of vines. Hauer brought suit in a German court, which asked the Court of Justice whether the regulation violated her fundamental rights to property and the free pursuit of commerce.]

14   As the Court declared in ... Internationale Handelsgesellschaft ..., the question of a possible infringement of fundamental rights by a measure of the Community institutions can only be judged in the light of Community law itself. The introduction of special criteria for assessment stemming from the legislation or constitutional law of a particular Member State would, by damaging the substantive unity and efficacy of Community law, lead inevitably to the destruction of the unity of the Common Market and the jeopardizing of the cohesion of the Community.

15   ... [F]undamental rights form an integral part of the general principles of the law, the observance of which it ensures. In safeguarding those rights, the Court is bound to draw inspiration from constitutional traditions common to the Member States, so that measures which are incompatible with the fundamental rights recognized by the constitutions of those States are unacceptable in the Community. Similarly, international treaties for the protection of human rights on which the Member States have collaborated or of which they are signatories, can supply guidelines which should be followed within the framework of Community law. That conception was later recognized by the joint declaration of the European Parliament, the Council and the Commission of 5 April 1977, which, after recalling the case-law of the Court, refers on the one hand to the rights guaranteed by the constitutions of the Member States and on the other hand to the European Convention for the Protection of Human Rights and Fundamental Freedoms of 4 November 1950.

* * *

17   The right to property is guaranteed in the Community legal order in accordance with the ideas common to the constitutions of the Member States, which are also reflected in the first Protocol to the European Convention for the Protection of Human Rights.

18   Article 1 of that Protocol provides as follows:

"Every natural or legal person is entitled to the peaceful enjoyment of his possessions. No one shall be deprived of his possessions except in the public interest and subject to the conditions provided for by law and by the general principles of international law.

The preceding provisions shall not, however, in any way impair the right of a State to enforce such laws as it deems necessary to control the use of property in accordance with the general interest or to secure the payment of taxes or other contributions or penalties."

19   [I]t is incontestable that the prohibition on new planting cannot be considered to be an act depriving the owner of his property, since he remains free to dispose of it or to put it to other uses which are not prohibited. On the other hand, there is no doubt that that prohibition restricts the use of the property. In this regard, the second paragraph of Article 1 of the Protocol ... accepts in principle the legality of restrictions upon the use of property, whilst at the same time limiting those restrictions to the extent to which they are deemed "necessary" by a State for the protection of the "general interest".

* * *

20   [As for] the constitutional rules and practices of the nine Member States, ... those rules and practices permit the legislature to control the use of private property in accordance with general interest. Thus some constitutions refer to the obligations arising out of the ownership of property (German Grundgesetz, Article 14(2), first sentence), to its social function (Italian constitution, Article 42 (2)), to the subordination of its use to the requirements of the common good (German Grundgesetz, Article 14(2), second sentence, and the Irish constitution, Article 42.2.2), or of social justice (Irish constitution, Article 43.2.1). In all Member States, numerous legislative measures have given concrete expression to that social function of the right to property. Thus in all the Member States there is legislation on agriculture and forestry, the water supply, the protection of the environment and town and country planning, which imposes restrictions, sometimes appreciable, on the use of real property.

21   More particularly, all the wine-producing countries of the Community have restrictive legislation ... concerning the planting of vines, the selection of varieties and the methods of cultivation. In none of the countries concerned are those provisions considered to be incompatible in principle with the regard due to the right of property.

* * *

23   However, [e]ven if it is not possible to dispute in principle the Community's ability to restrict the exercise of the right to property ..., it is still necessary to examine whether the restrictions introduced by the provisions in dispute in fact correspond to objectives of general

interest pursued by the Community or whether, with regard to the aim pursued, they constitute a disproportionate and intolerable interference with the rights of the owner, impinging upon the very substance of the right to property. . . .

24   The provisions of Regulation No. 1162/76 must be considered in the context of the common organization of the market in wine which is closely linked to the structural policy envisaged by the Community in the area in question. . . .

25   Within the framework of the guidelines laid down by [the Treaty], [the common organization of the wine market] seeks to achieve a double objective, namely, on the one hand, to establish a lasting balance on the wine market at a price level which is profitable for producers and fair to consumers and, secondly, to obtain an improvement in the quality of wines marketed. In order to attain that double objective of quantitative balance and qualitative improvement, the Community rules relating to the market in wine provide for an extensive range of measures which apply both at the production stage and at the marketing stage for wine . . .

27   Regulation [No. 1162/76] . . . fulfills a double function: on the one hand, it must enable an immediate brake to be put on the continued increase in the surpluses; on the other hand, it must win for the Community institutions the time necessary for the implementation of a structural policy designed to encourage high-quality production, whilst respecting the individual characteristics and needs of the different wine-producing regions of the Community, through the selection of land for grape growing and the selection of grape varieties, and through the regulation of production methods.

* * *

29   Seen in this light, the measure criticized does not entail any undue limitation upon the exercise of the right to property. Indeed, the cultivation of new vineyards in a situation of continuous over-production would [only increase] the volume of the surpluses [and make] more difficult the implementation of a structural policy at the Community level. . . .

30   Therefore . . . the restriction imposed upon the use of property by the prohibition on the new planting of vines introduced for a limited period by Regulation No. 1162/76 is justified by the objectives of general interest pursued by the Community and does not infringe the substance of the right to property . . . protected in the Community legal order.

[Using essentially the same analysis, the Court also concluded that Hauer's fundamental right to pursue her professional activities freely was not violated.]

NOTES AND QUESTIONS

1. In what ways does the Court's analysis in *Hauer* represent an advance over its analysis in *Nold*? Are you convinced by it?

The *Hauer* judgment may have helped convince the German Constitutional Court in its "*Solange II*" judgment of 1986, described at page 281 infra, that the Court of Justice would adequately protect fundamental rights, thereby permitting the German Constitutional Court to accept the primacy of the Treaty.

2. Judge Pierre Pescatore, who served on the Court of Justice from 1968 to 1984 and wrote frequently on constitutional issues, once conceptualized fundamental rights as derived from a "common background of ideas of order, justice and reason that underlie the legal culture to which the member states belong." How thoroughly did the ECJ analyze the constitutional culture and traditions of the Member States?

3. In order to accommodate agricultural market rules to constantly changing circumstances, Council regulations and Commission implementation decisions frequently impose restrictions on agricultural producers. When the producers challenge these as a violation of their property rights, the Court generally follows *Hauer* in concluding that the EU institutions may properly limit the property rights to serve the public interest concerns applied in the agricultural sector. See, e.g., The Irish Farmers Association v. Minister for Agriculture, Case C–22/94, [1997] ECR I–1809, ¶¶ 26–29.

In one unusual circumstance, the Court held that agriculture firms in Scotland raising fish were not entitled to compensation when the Scottish health authorities followed an EU directive requiring the destruction of all fish exposed to contagious parasites. The Court held that the destruction of the fish without compensation was justified by a legitimate public interest and did not constitute a disproportionate interference with property rights (¶ 68). The Court noted that fish farmers bear the commercial risk of loss when a fish disease breaks out, a risk "inherent in the business of risking and selling livestock" (¶ 83). See Booker Acquaculture v. Scottish Ministers, Joined Cases C–20 & 64/00, [2003] ECR I–7411.

4. The EU's enforcement of international trade sanctions has given rise to some high-profile property rights cases. In Bosphorus v. Ireland, excerpted at page 1126, infra, the Court held that an EU regulation adopted in pursuance of UN sanctions against Serbia during the Bosnian civil war properly authorized the seizure of a Serbian airline plane leased to a Turkish air cargo company and used for purposes that did not benefit Serbia. The Court specifically found that the innocent Turkish airline's loss of the aircraft during the lease did not constitute a disproportionate invasion of its property rights in view of the highly important public interest in pressuring Serbia to end its interference in the conflict in Bosnia (¶¶ 25–26).

The focus of the more recent Kadi v. Council and Commission case, excerpted at page 1130 infra, was on whether the fact that the EU regulations were issued in implementation of UN sanctions against terrorists made a difference in the analysis. We defer that issue to a later chapter, confining the excerpt that follows to the question whether Kadi's property rights had been violated in the first place.

KADI v. COUNCIL AND COMMISSION
Joined Cases C–402/05P & C–415/05P, [2008] ECR I–6351.

357   Next, it falls to be examined whether the freezing measure provided by the contested regulation amounts to disproportionate and intolerable interference impairing the very substance of the fundamental right to respect for the property of persons who, like Mr Kadi, are mentioned in the list set out in Annex I to [the Council] regulation.

358   That freezing measure constitutes a temporary precautionary measure which is not supposed to deprive those persons of their property. It does, however, undeniably entail a restriction of the exercise of Mr Kadi's right to property that must, moreover, be classified as considerable, having regard to the general application of the freezing measure and the fact that it has been applied to him since 20 October 2001.

359   The question therefore arises whether that restriction of the exercise of Mr Kadi's right to property can be justified.

360   [A]ccording to the case-law of the European Court of Human Rights, there must exist a reasonable relationship of proportionality between the means employed and the aim sought to be realised. The Court must determine whether a fair balance has been struck between the demands of the public interest and the interest of the individuals concerned. In so doing, the Court recognises that the legislature enjoys a wide margin of appreciation, with regard both to choosing the means of enforcement and to ascertaining whether the consequences of enforcement are justified in the public interest for the purpose of achieving the object of the law in question.

361   As the Court has already held [in *Bosphorus*], the importance of the aims pursued by a Community act is such as to justify negative consequences, even of a substantial nature, for some operators, including those who are in no way responsible for the situation which led to the adoption of the measures in question, but who find themselves affected, particularly as regards their property rights.

362   [T]he restrictive measures laid down by the contested regulation contribute to the implementation, at Community level, of the restrictive measures decided on by the Security Council against Usama bin Laden, members of the Al–Qaeda organisation and the Taliban and other individuals, groups, undertakings and entities associated with them.

363   With reference to an objective of general interest as fundamental to the international community as the fight by all means, in accordance with the Charter of the United Nations, against the threats to international peace and security posed by acts of terrorism, the

freezing of the funds, financial assets and other economic resources of the persons identified by the Security Council or the Sanctions Committee as being associated with Usama bin Laden, members of the Al–Qaeda organisation and the Taliban cannot per se be regarded as inappropriate or disproportionate [citing *Bosphorus*].

364   [Moreover,] the contested regulation ... provides ... that, on a request made by an interested person, and unless the Sanctions Committee expressly objects, the competent national authorities may declare the freezing of funds to be inapplicable to the funds necessary to cover basic expenses, including payments for foodstuffs, rent, medicines and medical treatment, taxes or public utility charges....

365   [Also,] the resolutions of the Security Council to which the contested regulation is intended to give effect provide for a mechanism for the periodic re-examination of the general system of measures they enact and also for a procedure enabling the persons concerned at any time to submit their case to the Sanctions Committee for re-examination....

366   It must therefore be found that the restrictive measures imposed by the contested regulation constitute restrictions of the right to property which might, in principle, be justified.

[It was at this point that the Court turned from the claimed deprivation of property as such to the procedural context in which it occurred.]

368   [T]he applicable procedures must afford the person concerned a reasonable opportunity of putting his case to the competent authorities. In order to ascertain whether this condition, which constitutes a procedural requirement inherent in Article 1 of Protocol No 1 to the ECHR, has been satisfied, a comprehensive view must be taken of the applicable procedures.

369   The contested regulation, in so far as it concerns Mr Kadi, was adopted without furnishing any guarantee enabling him to put his case to the competent authorities, in a situation in which the restriction of his property rights must be regarded as significant, having regard to the general application and actual continuation of the freezing measures affecting him.

370   [Therefore,] the imposition of the restrictive measures laid down by the contested regulation in respect of Mr Kadi, by including him in the list contained in Annex I to that regulation, constitutes an unjustified restriction of his right to property.

371   The plea raised by Mr Kadi that his fundamental right to respect for property has been infringed is therefore well founded.

Kadi is a rare judgment holding that an EU measure violates the right of property, and significant since commentators had sometimes queried whether the Court was truly serious about protecting property rights, since it usually upheld the EU law measure questioned against that charge.

3. JUDICIAL PROTECTION OF NON–ECONOMIC FUNDAMENTAL RIGHTS

Staff cases have given the Court of Justice ample opportunities to develop its protection of basic rights outside the field of property rights. Thus, in Maurissen v. Court of Auditors, Case C–193, 194/87, [1990] ECR I–95, the Court ruled that the institutions may not prohibit their officials from joining a trade union or participating in trade union activities. The Court found that freedom of union activity guarantees union leaders the right to time off from work to help the Commission prepare employment-related proposals to be submitted to the Council. The Court also held that it guarantees the Union leaders the right to disseminate union literature at work, but it does not require the institutions to make their own messenger services available for this purpose.

Freedom of religion surfaced in the 1976 decision in Prais v. Council, Case 130/75, [1976] ECR 1589, in which the plaintiff complained that a competitive recruitment examination had been scheduled on a Jewish holiday, and sought to annul the examination result as a violation of the principle of equal treatment. The Court held that the Council must schedule examinations to avoid conflicts with religious holidays to the extent administrative considerations permitted, but it declined to annul the examination since the plaintiff had failed to give notice of the conflict within a reasonable time before the examination.

The Court also has had occasion to examine the right of privacy in staff cases. In X v. Commission, Case C–404/92P [1994] ECR I–4737, the Commission used various medical tests to review whether an applicant was physically fit for employment, concluding that he was not after certain tests suggested AIDS-related issues. These tests were undertaken after the applicant refused the usual direct test for the AIDS virus. Reversing the CFI, the Court accepted that the applicant had a right of privacy to decline the usual AIDS test, but that the Commission could not "be obliged to take the risk of recruiting" an applicant who refuses a test that the medical officer considers essential for the examination. In view of the result, do you consider the Court adequately protected the right of privacy?

Freedom of expression claims were inevitable. In Commission v. De Bry, Case C–344/05P, [2006] ECR I–10915, a staff member asserted that his right to a fair hearing was violated by the Commission's failure to warn him in advance of the criticism leveled at his job performance in a regular bi-annual performance review. The CFI held that advance warning was required to enable the staff member "to effectively defend his inter-est." But the Court of Justice reversed, holding that while a staff member has a right to "defend himself against any criticism of his conduct" during the performance review, he has no right to receive any prior warning (¶ ¶ 39–43). Do you agree with the Court or the CFI?

CONNOLLY v. COMMISSION

Case C–274/99, [2001] ECR I–1611.

[During a leave of absence granted for personal reasons, Connolly, a senior Commission official in the Directorate of Monetary Affairs, published a book entitled "The Rotten Heart of Europe: The Dirty War for Europe's Money." Upon dismissal following a disciplinary proceeding for undermining the dignity of his post and the interests of the institution (as well as for failing to obtain the prior clearance which the Staff Regulation required for a publication related to his Commission activities), Connolly brought suit in the Court of First Instance. The CFI recognized the principle of freedom of expression, as guaranteed by the European Human Rights Convention, but found that Connolly's dismissal did not offend it. Connolly appealed. The Court of Justice quoted TEU Article 6(2), introduced by the Maastricht Treaty, and continued.]

39   As the Court of Human Rights has held, "Freedom of expression constitutes one of the essential foundations of [a democratic society], one of the basic conditions for its progress and for the development of every man. Subject to paragraph 2 of Article 10 [of the ECHR], it is applicable not only to 'information' " or 'ideas' " that are favourably received or regarded as inoffensive or as a matter of indifference, but also to those that offend, shock or disturb; such are the demands of that pluralism, tolerance and broadmindedness without which there is no 'democratic society'."

40   Freedom of expression may be subject to the limitations set out in Article 10(2) of the ECHR, in terms of which the exercise of that freedom, "since it carries with it duties and responsibilities, may be subject to such formalities, conditions, restrictions or penalties as are prescribed by law and are necessary in a democratic society, in the interests of national security, territorial integrity or public safety, for the prevention of disorder or crime, for the protection of health or morals, for the protection of the reputation or rights of others, for preventing the disclosure of information received in confidence, or for maintaining the authority and impartiality of the judiciary."

41   Those limitations must, however, be interpreted restrictively. According to the Court of Human Rights, the adjective "necessary" involves, for the purposes of Article 10(2), a "pressing social need" and, although "[t]he contracting States have a certain margin of appreciation in assessing whether such a need exists", the interference must be "proportionate to the legitimate aim pursued" and "the reasons adduced by the national authorities to justify it" must be "relevant and sufficient".

42   Furthermore, the restrictions must be prescribed by legislative provisions which are worded with sufficient precision to enable interested parties to regulate their conduct, taking, if need be, appropriate advice.

43   As the Court has ruled, officials and other employees of the European Communities enjoy the right of freedom of expression even in areas falling within the scope of the activities of the Community institutions. That freedom extends to the expression, orally or in writing, of opinions that dissent from or conflict with those held by the employing institution.

44   However, it is also legitimate in a democratic society to subject public servants, on account of their status, to obligations such as those contained in Articles 11 and 12 of the Staff Regulations. Such obligations are intended primarily to preserve the relationship of trust which must exist between the institution and its officials or other employees.

45   [T]he scope of those obligations must vary according to the nature of the duties performed by the person concerned or his place in the hierarchy. . . .

46   In terms of Article 10(2) of the ECHR, specific restrictions on the exercise of the right of freedom of expression can, in principle, be justified by the legitimate aim of protecting the rights of others. The rights at issue here are those of the institutions that are charged with the responsibility of carrying out tasks in the public interest. Citizens must be able to rely on their doing so effectively.

47   That is the aim of the regulations setting out the duties and responsibilities of the European public service. So an official may not, by oral or written expression, act in breach of his obligations under the regulations . . . towards the institution that he is supposed to serve. That would destroy the relationship of trust between himself and that institution and make it thereafter more difficult, if not impossible, for the work of the institution to be carried out in cooperation with that official.

48   In exercising their power of review, the Community Courts must decide, having regard to all the circumstances of the case, whether a fair balance has been struck between the individual's fundamental right to freedom of expression and the legitimate concern of the institution to ensure that its officials and agents observe the duties and responsibilities implicit in the performance of their tasks.

* * *

[The Court then examined Connolly's case in particular.]

60   The Court of First Instance referred . . . not only to Mr Connolly's high-ranking grade but also to the fact that the book at issue "publicly expressed . . . the applicant's fundamental opposition to the Commission's policy, which it was his responsibility to implement, namely bringing about economic and monetary union, an objective which is, moreover, laid down in the Treaty".

* * *

62   The foregoing observations of the Court of First Instance ... make it clear that Mr Connolly was dismissed not merely because he had failed to apply for prior permission, contrary to the requirements of ... Article 17 of the Staff Regulations, or because he had expressed a dissentient opinion, but because he had published, without permission, material in which he had severely criticised, and even insulted, members of the Commission and other superiors and had challenged fundamental aspects of Community policies which had been written into the Treaty by the Member States and to whose implementation the Commission had specifically assigned him the responsibility of contributing in good faith. In those circumstances, he committed "an irremediable breach of the trust which the Commission is entitled to expect from its officials" and, as a result, made "it impossible for any employment relationship to be maintained with the institution".

64   It follows that the Court of First Instance was entitled to conclude ... that the allegation of breach of the right to freedom of expression ... was unfounded.

NOTES AND QUESTIONS

1. The Court cited not only the text of the European Human Rights Convention, but also specific rulings of the European Court of Human Rights (ECHR). Although the Court of Justice has never conceded being bound by ECHR precedents, it is obviously heavily influenced by them.

2. In Commission v. Cwik, Case C–340/00 P, [2001] ECR I–10269, the Commission refused Cwik, an economist in a relatively secondary post in the Monetary Union directorate, permission to deliver a lecture concerning the possible impact of the Monetary Union on fiscal and wage policies, relying on a Staff Regulation that authorized a refusal if a presentation "is liable to prejudice the interest of the Communities." Cwik challenged the refusal. The CFI sustained his challenge, holding that the refusal was unwarranted because he held no management post and was addressing a specialist audience, and because the Commission had not as yet set a definitive policy on the issues concerned. The Court of Justice affirmed, holding that the Commission had made a manifest error of assessment. In view of the importance of freedom of expression, only a "real risk of serious prejudice to the interests of the Communities" would justify the denial of permission (¶ 23).

NOTE ON THE EUROPEAN CONVENTION FOR THE PROTECTION OF HUMAN RIGHTS

The Court of Justice has commonly taken inspiration concerning fundamental rights (as in *Hauer, Kadi* and *Connolly*) from the Council of Europe's 1950 Convention for the Protection of Human Rights and Fundamental Freedoms (ECHR), of which all the Member States are signatories, often expressly citing it.

The Convention both lays down important human rights principles and establishes a serious enforcement regime. Until 1988, a European

Commission of Human Rights operated as a sort of gatekeeper, screening individual petitions to the Court of Human Rights in Strasbourg. Only if the Commission determined that a claimant had exhausted all available domestic remedies would he or she be permitted to proceed further. With the ratification of Protocol No. 11 to the Convention, effective November 1, 1998, the Commission was abolished, leaving substantive responsibility to a new, single permanent European Court of Human Rights (ECHR) (sometimes called the "Strasbourg Court" to distinguish it from the Court of Justice in Luxembourg).

The ECHR is an extremely busy tribunal, receiving between 50,000 and 60,000 petitions for review every year, and issuing decisions in some 1600 of them. Each nation that is a party to the Convention designates one judge, for a current total of 47. Most decisions are rendered by 7–judge chambers, although some important cases go to a 17–judge Grand Chamber. Dissents are permitted.

Countries that become parties to the Convention agree to accept and be bound by the judgments of the Strasbourg Court, although the Court has no power to impose sanctions on a nation that does not comply with its decisions. In fact most members of the Council of Europe, including all EU Member States, have incorporated the Convention into their domestic legal systems. As a result of the UK Human Rights Act of 1998 (discussed in Chapter 8G infra), this is now true even of the UK, which until then had resisted incorporation, due to the time-honored doctrine of parliamentary sovereignty according to which no Parliament could bind its successors.

Not only is the Court of Justice strongly influenced in its fundamental rights judgments by the case law of the ECHR, but as early as 1977 the Parliament, Council and Commission issued a Joint Declaration proclaiming their attachment to "the protection of fundamental rights, as derived in particular from the constitutions of the Member States and the European [Human Rights] Convention," as well as their intention to respect those rights.

Throughout the 1980s, the Commission and the European Parliament urged that the Community formally accede to the Convention, thus rendering the Convention's catalogue of basic rights directly binding on the institutions. The Maastricht Treaty, while not taking this step, did introduce TEU Article 6 which, echoing judgments like *Nold* and *Hauer*, required the European Union to respect fundamental rights as guaranteed by the Convention and as recognized in the Member States' common constitutional traditions. Technically speaking, this did not compel the EU to abide by the Convention or its interpretation by the ECHR. However, as we have seen, both the Convention and the ECHR decisions serve as sources of inspiration for the EU courts.

In April 1994, the Commission sought an opinion from the Court of Justice on whether the Community could legally accede to the Convention. In Opinion 2/94, [1996] ECR I–1759, the Court acknowledged that, since respect for human rights is in any event a condition of the lawfulness of all Community acts, accession to an international human rights regime could not be considered as going beyond the scope of Community powers. However, it found that formal accession "would entail the entry of the Community into a distinct international institutional system as well as integration of all the provisions of the Convention into the Community legal order." Consequently,

35   [s]uch a modification of the system for the protection of human rights in the Community, with equally fundamental institutional implications for the Community and the Member States, would be of constitutional significance and would therefore be such as to go beyond the scope of [Article 308, now TFEU Article 352]. It could be brought about only by way of Treaty amendment.

36   [T]herefore . . ., as Community law now stands, the Community has no competence to accede to the Convention.

A certain consequence of the Opinion was the impetus for the EU to adopt its own catalogue of rights, which now exists in the form of the Charter of Fundamental Rights proclaimed at Nice and made legally binding by the Lisbon Treaty.

B. THE AMSTERDAM TREATY AND FUNDAMENTAL RIGHTS

As indicated in Chapter 1's historical survey, the Treaty of Amsterdam was principally intended to make essential treaty modifications in view of the prospective accession of the Central and Eastern European States. When the European Council meeting at Copenhagen in June 1993 set the conditions which those States would have to satisfy in order to accede to the Union, the first and crucial condition was that of "stability of institutions guaranteeing democracy, the rule of law, human rights and respect for and protection of minorities." Throughout the 1990s, the Commission's negotiations with the applicant nations entailed a review of their creation of independent judiciaries, guarantees of constitutional rights, free elections and measures to achieve equal rights for various minorities (notably the Russian minority in the Baltic nations and the Roma people in Bulgaria, Romania and elsewhere).

Accordingly, the Amsterdam Treaty inserted into the Maastricht TEU an Article 6(1) declaring that the "Union is founded on the principles of liberty, democracy, respect for human rights and fundamental freedoms, and the rule of law." The Amsterdam Treaty then amended TEU Article 49 to make respect for the principles of Article 6 a condition for accession to the EU. To ensure that these obligations are respected, the Amsterdam Treaty also introduced TEU Article 7, establishing a system of sanctions against a State that violates human rights, notably through a suspension of the State's voting rights within the institutions. The procedure contemplates that the European Council (here called the Council in its composition of heads of state or government) will decide, acting unanimously (except for the accused State's leader) upon a proposal from the Commission or one-third of the Member States, and after receiving Parliament's assent, whether a serious breach has occurred. TEU Article 7 was later broadened by the Treaty of Nice so that even a clear risk of a serious breach would suffice to trigger the sanctions procedure—a change undoubtedly occasioned by the controversy surrounding Jorg Haider's Freedom Party joining an Austrian coalition government. The sanctions regime was clearly meant as a "nuclear bomb" threat, so serious that no State would ever seriously violate Article 6's principles.

The Lisbon Treaty carries forward all of these protections, replacing the Maastricht TEU's Articles 6(1), 7 and 49 with new TEU Articles 2, 7 and 49, respectively. Article 10 of the Lisbon TEU declares that the "functioning of the Union shall be founded on representative democracy," with the Parliament primarily serving that function at the Union level, while at the national level Member State leaders in the European Council or Council are "democratically accountable either to their national Parliaments, or to their citizens."

The Treaty of Amsterdam introduced EC Treaty Article 13, authorizing the Council, acting unanimously on a Commission proposal, after consulting the Parliament, to adopt measures "to combat discrimination based on sex, racial or ethnic origin, religion or belief, disability, age or sexual orientation." The Irish commissioner for social policy, Padraig Flynn, initially proposed the provision in a Commission White Paper on Social Policy in 1994, and the Irish government inserted Article 13 when, as President of the Council, Ireland prepared in 1996 the initial draft Amsterdam Treaty text. The Lisbon Treaty carries forward this provision in TFEU Article 19, which replicates EC Treaty Article 13, but changes the Council's obligation to consult Parliament upon adopting anti-discrimination measures to a requirement to obtain Parliament's consent.

The Council acted with surprising speed to adopt in 2000 two directives, one forbidding discrimination based on race or ethnic origin in any Union context, and the second forbidding discrimination in employment on any of the other grounds specified in Article 13. See Chapter 34 for an account of these directives, and several recent Court judgments interpreting and applying them. To provide an illustration of the impact of the directives in furthering fundamental rights, we provide here the most prominent of those judgments, concerning discrimination based on age.

MANGOLD v. HELM
Case C–144/04, [2005] ECR I–9981.

[Helm, a German lawyer, employed Mangold, also a German lawyer, then aged 56, under a fixed-term employment contract. The German law governing fixed-term contracts sets conditions to prevent their abuse, including the requirement of an objective justification. However, the law established a derogation from the requirement of an objective justification in the case of employees who have already reached the age of 52. The Munich Labour Court was uncertain whether this provision was compatible with Directive 2000/78/EC establishing a general framework for equal treatment in employment and occupation. According to its Article 6, Member States may provide that differences of treatment in employment and occupation on grounds of age shall not constitute discrimination, if they are objectively justified by a legitimate aim, including a legitimate employment policy, and by labor market and vocational training objectives, and if the means of achieving that aim are appropriate and necessary.]

64   [A]pplication of [the German] legislation ... leads to a situation in which all workers who have reached the age of 52, without distinction, whether or not they were unemployed before the contract was concluded and whatever the duration of any period of unemployment, may lawfully ... be offered fixed-term contracts of employment which may be renewed an indefinite number of times. This significant body of workers, determined solely on the basis of age, is thus in danger, during a substantial part of its members' working life, of being excluded from the benefit of stable employment which ... constitutes a major element in the protection of workers.

65   In so far as such legislation takes the age of the worker concerned as the only criterion for the application of a fixed-term contract of employment, when it has not been shown that fixing an age threshold, as such, regardless of any other consideration linked to the structure of the labour market in question or the personal situation of the person concerned, is objectively necessary to the attainment of the objective which is the vocational integration of unemployed older workers, it must be considered to go beyond what is appropriate and necessary in order to attain the objective pursued. Observance of the principle of proportionality requires every derogation from an individual right to reconcile, so far as is possible, the requirements of the principle of equal treatment with those of the aim pursued.... Such national legislation cannot, therefore, be justified under Article 6(1) of Directive 2000/78.

[The Court then adverted to its longstanding position that, even though the period for the transposition of a directive into domestic law had not yet expired, Member States must refrain from taking any measures liable seriously to compromise the attainment of the directive's objectives.]

75   The principle of non-discrimination on grounds of age must thus be regarded as a general principle of Community law. Where national rules fall within the scope of Community law, which is the case with [the German law in question], ... and reference is made to the Court for a preliminary ruling, the Court must provide all the criteria of interpretation needed by the national court to determine whether those rules are compatible with such a principle....

[76] Consequently, observance of the general principle of equal treatment, in particular in respect of age, cannot as such be conditional upon the expiry of the period allowed the Member States for the transposition of a directive intended to lay down a general framework for combating discrimination on the grounds of age. . . .

* * *

[78] . . . Article 6(1) of Directive 2000/78, must be interpreted as precluding a provision of domestic law such as that at issue in the main proceedings which authorises . . . the conclusion of fixed-term contracts of employment once the worker has reached the age of 52.

NOTES AND QUESTIONS

1. Why did the Court in *Mangold* rely, in ¶ 75, on the status of the principle of non-discrimination on grounds of age as a general principle of EU law if the directive alone justified the Court's result? The Court also could have cited Article 21(1) of the EU's Charter of Fundamental Rights, which prohibits discrimination based on age, but it did not do so. Can you explain why?

2. Does the Court's holding that the principle of non-discrimination on grounds of age is a fundamental right mean that it applies in any context governed by EU law, and not only in employment, the subject of Directive 2000/78?

C. THE CHARTER OF FUNDAMENTAL RIGHTS

As the European Community, and later the European Union, steadily gained increasing political, economic and social powers in the 1980s and 1990s, it seemed increasingly anomalous that its "constitution" lacked any bill of rights. Although the Court of Justice repeatedly took inspiration from the European Convention of Human Rights, its Opinion 2/94 of 1996 barred accession to the Convention, absent a Treaty amendment authorizing such a step.

Prompted by the German Presidency, the European Council decided at Cologne in 1999 to prepare a Charter of its own that would set forth the fundamental rights applicable at the Union level. At its Tampere meeting the following October, the European Council resolved to empanel a committee to prepare the draft Charter. Chaired by Roman Herzog, the former President of Germany, this body consisted of fifteen representatives of the Member States, one representative of the President of the Commission, sixteen MEPs, and two national parliamentarians per Member State. This committee, calling itself a Convention, began meeting in Brussels in December 1999, working independently of the intergovernmental conference that was at the same time preparing the Treaty of Nice. Considering the sensitivity of some of the issues, extraordinary progress was made, with a complete first draft available by July 2000. After receiving critical comments from Parliament, organized labor and non-governmental organizations, the Convention presented a second draft in September 2000.

The European Council unanimously endorsed the Charter of Fundamental Rights of the European Union at its meeting in Biarritz in September 2000, and the Presidents of the Parliament, the Council and the Commission then endorsed it on the occasion of the December 2000 European Council meeting in Nice (which explains why the instrument is commonly referred to as the Nice Charter). For the Charter's text, see the Selected Documents, document 6.

The Charter sets out a concise, yet comprehensive statement of fundamental rights, divided among six chapters corresponding to six fundamental values: dignity, freedoms, equality, solidarity, citizens' rights and justice. The chapter on dignity declares the inviolability of human dignity, forbids the death penalty and outlaws trafficking in human beings. It also establishes innovative, if vague, guarantees against the abuse of genetic engineering and biotechnology, for example expressly prohibiting "the reproductive cloning of human beings." The chapter on freedoms proclaims, among other things, the right of privacy (including data privacy protection), freedom of expression and assembly, pluralism of the media, the right of property, the right to education and freedom to choose an occupation. Conspicuous in the chapter on equality are prohibitions of discrimination on the basis of "sex, race, colour, ethnic or social origin, genetic features, language, religion or belief, political or other opinion, membership of a national minority, property, birth, disability, age or sexual orientation," as well as the inclusion of provisions on the rights of children and the elderly, and the right to cultural diversity. The chapter on solidarity provides for various rights of employees, the right to health care, and the goals of high levels of environmental and consumer protection. Citizens' rights in chapter five include the right of access to documents and the right of petition. Chapter six on justice promises, among other things, the right to a fair trial and an effective remedy, as well as certain rights for criminal defendants.

The Charter, according to its Article 51, is specifically addressed to the institutions and bodies of the EU and to the Member States when implementing EU law. To underscore that the Charter does not make human rights protection as such an EU competence, Article 51 specifically disclaims "extend[ing] the field of application of Union law beyond the powers of the Union or establish[ing] any new power or task for the Union, or modify[ing] powers and tasks as defined in the Treaties."

As for the Charter's relationship to the European Human Rights Convention, Article 52 specifies that the "meaning and scope" of the rights it proclaims are to be the same as those of any rights guaranteed by the Convention. Similarly, rights in the Charter resulting from the constitutional traditions common to the Member States are to be interpreted consistently with those traditions. More generally, Article 53 of the Charter asserts that it is not to be understood as restricting any human rights or fundamental freedoms otherwise recognized by EU law, international law, domestic constitutional law, or international agreements to which the Union or the Member States are party. On the other hand, according to Article 54, no right given by the Charter may be abused, in the sense of justifying "any activity or . . . any act aimed at the destruction of any of the rights and freedoms recognised in this Charter or at their limitation to a greater extent than is provided for [by the Charter]."

The Charter's principal weakness has been that the Protocol annexing it to the Nice Treaty expressly declared it to be judicially unenforceable. In applauding the Charter, both then President Romano Prodi of the Commission and President Nicole Fontaine of the Parliament cited this as a serious shortcoming. However, the Lisbon Treaty now gives the Charter legal force. See page 214 infra.

Notes and Questions

1. The Charter proclaims far more rights, and proclaims them in much greater detail, than the European Convention on Human Rights had done. Some critics contend that too many of the Charter's provisions are vague and questionable, and that often rather than enunciate rights, they merely express aspirations. Consider respect for "academic freedom" (art. 13), "legal, economic and social protection" of the family (art. 33), "right of access to preventative health care" (art. 35), and "high-level" environmental and consumer protection (arts. 37 and 38).

A related critique is that the Charter does a better job of enumerating and classifying rights than in indicating how they are to be balanced against other interests and indeed against each other. To still others, the Charter may simply go too far in establishing rights that are more appropriate for legislation than for a constitutional document. A U.S. reader might find it excessive for employee rights as detailed in Articles 27–32 (such as management's obligation to consult with employee representatives on many issues affecting the workforce, or limits on employees' daily, weekly and annual work-time) to have found their way into the Charter. However, the Charter of the Rights of Workers, described in Chapter 35, endorsed by all the Member State governments (including the UK, after the election of Prime Minister Blair's Labor government), also contained rights of this kind.

According to a different critique, portions of the Charter are not relevant to the EU. For example, Article 1 safeguards human dignity. However, in *Omega Spielhallen*, excerpted at page 695 infra, the Court of Justice accepted human dignity, protected in the German Constitution, as a public interest justifying a limitation on the right to receive services. Article 5 of the Charter prohibits trafficking in human beings, which might seem irrelevant, but in 2002 the Council adopted a Framework Decision on combating trafficking in human beings, O.J. L 203/1 (Aug. 1, 2002) (see Chapter 16F). Article 2 forbids the death penalty, but this is considered a condition for accession, and currently poses a difficult issue for Turkey, which punishes certain serious offences with the death penalty.

For general appraisals of the Charter, see K. Lenaerts & de Smijter, A 'Bill of Rights' for the European Union, 38 Common Mkt. L. Rev. 273 (2000); G. De Burca, The Drafting of the European Union Charter of Fundamental Rights, 26 Eur. L. Rev. 126 (2001).

2.   Article 17 on the right of property indicates that a "public interest" may justify the deprivation of a person's "possessions," but then adds that this is "subject to fair compensation." Note that the European Convention on Human Rights' Protocol on the right to property does not provide for "fair compensation," so that the Charter language is quite significant. Now that the Charter has binding legal force, should compensation be required in circumstances such as those described in *Booker Acquaculture* or *Bosphorus*, in the notes supra page 197?

3.   Article 8 of the Charter states a "right to protection of personal data." This too may not strike all as meriting fundamental rights status. But its inclusion reflects a long-standing view in the EU. Not only did Directive 95/46 on the protection of personal data, described in Chapter 16A, establish a high level of protection for such data, but the Treaty of Amsterdam introduced into the EC Treaty Article 286, which requires EU institutions and bodies to protect personal data and mandates the Council and Parliament to create an independent supervisory body to monitor this protection. The Lisbon Treaty's TFEU Article 16 largely replicates Article 286, adding that the Council and Parliament may also adopt rules for the protection of personal data when Member States carry out activities within the scope of EU law.

The personal data protection directive has now been interpreted in several cases. In Criminal Proceedings against Lindquist, Case C–101/01, [2003] ECR I–8419, the Court held that a member of a parish violated the directive by publishing on the internet personal data, including a reference to a physical injury, concerning other parish members. Because the defendant claimed that she was exercising her freedom of expression in attempting to promote religious life, apparently in good faith, the Court informed the national court that it must balance the interests concerned, particularly in determining the sanction it might impose on the defendant.

Germany sought to combat serious crime by maintaining a register of all resident foreign nationals containing substantial amounts of personal data (such as marital status, last place of residence in the country of origin, any criminal record, arrest warrants, suspected violation of drugs or immigration rules or involvement in terrorist activities). In Huber v. Germany, Case C–524/06, [2008] ECR I–9705, an Austrian national challenged the practice as a violation of data privacy protected by Directive 95/46. The Court of Justice held that maintaining a special register of foreign nationals, containing data necessary to verify whether a foreign national met the requirements for legal residence was in itself permissible (¶ 58), and could be used for statistical purposes (¶¶ 63–64). On the other hand, systematic processing of personal data of citizens of other Member States for the purpose of fighting crime, when Germany maintained no comparable register for its own nationals, violated the principle of non-discrimination on the basis of nationality (¶¶ 75–81).

PARLIAMENT v. COUNCIL

(Family reunification)
Case C–540/03, [2006] ECR I–5769.

[Article 4(1) of Directive 2003/86 on family reunification requires Member States to permit minor children who are third state nationals to enter the EU and reside with their parents, provided the parents are lawfully resident in a Member State. The directive permits Member States to set limits on this family reunification for minors over 12 years old who arrive independently from the rest of their families. A recital declares that the directive "respects the fundamental rights" in the European Convention and the Charter. The Parliament challenged the exception for minors over 12 as a violation of these fundamental rights. The Court chiefly invoked family reunification principles derived from the European Convention and the ECHR case law, but also, in the paragraphs quoted below, the Charter of Fundamental Rights.]

38   The Charter was solemnly proclaimed by the Parliament, the Council and the Commission in Nice on 7 December 2000. While the Charter is not a legally binding instrument, the Community legislature did, however, acknowledge its importance by stating, in the second recital in the preamble to the Directive, that the Directive observes the principles recognised not only by Article 8 of the ECHR but also in the Charter. Furthermore, the principal aim of the Charter, as is apparent from its preamble, is to reaffirm "rights as they result, in particular, from the constitutional traditions and international obligations common to the member states, the Treaty on European Union, the Community Treaties, the [ECHR], the Social Charters adopted by the Community and by the Council of Europe and the case-law of the Court ... and of the European Court of Human Rights".

* * *

58   The Charter recognises, in Article 7, the same right to respect for private or family life [as the European Convention]. This provision must be read in conjunction with the obligation to have regard to the child's best interests, which is recognised in Article 24(2) of the Charter, and taking account of the need, expressed in Article 24(3), for a child to maintain on a regular basis a personal relationship with both his or her parents.

59   These various instruments stress the importance to a child of family life and recommend that states have regard to the child's interests but they do not create for the members of a family an individual right to be allowed to enter the territory of a state and cannot be interpreted as denying member states a certain margin of appreciation when they examine applications for family reunification.

61   The final subparagraph of Article 4(1) of the Directive has the effect, ... where a child aged over 12 years arrives independently from the rest of the family, of partially preserving the margin of appreciation of the member states by permitting them, before authorising entry and residence of the child under the Directive, to verify whether he or she meets a condition for integration provided for by the national legislation in force on the date of implementation of the Directive.

62   In doing so, the final subparagraph of Article 4(1) of the Directive cannot be regarded as running counter to the right to respect for family life. In the context of a directive imposing precise positive obligations on the member states, it preserves a limited margin of appreciation for those states which is no different from that accorded to them by the European Court of Human Rights, in its case-law relating to that right, for weighing, in each factual situation, the competing interests.

* * *

64   Note should also be taken of Article 17 of the Directive which requires member states to take due account of the nature and solidarity of the person's family relationships and the duration of his residence in the member state and of the existence of family, cultural and social ties with his country of origin. Such criteria correspond to those taken into consideration by the European Court of Human Rights when it reviews whether a state which has refused an application for family reunification has correctly weighed the competing interests.

* * *

71   Consequently, the final subparagraph of Article 4(1) of the Directive cannot be interpreted as authorising the member states, expressly or impliedly, to adopt implementing provisions that would be contrary to the right to respect for family life.

* * *

73   Nor does it appear that the Community legislature failed to pay sufficient attention to children's interests. The content of Article 4(1) of the Directive attests that the child's best interests were a consideration of prime importance when that provision was being adopted and it does not appear that its final subparagraph fails to have sufficient regard to those interests or authorises member states which choose to take account of a condition for integration not to have regard to them. On the contrary, ... Article 5(5) of the Directive requires the member states to have due regard to the best interests of minor children.

NOTES AND QUESTIONS

1. The *Family reunification* judgment is an early instance of the ECJ's citation to the Charter prior to the Charter yet having binding legal force. (Note, though, that the Council had itself cited the Charter in the directive's

preamble.) The practice should not surprise. The Court had for decades cited the ECHR to which the EU was not even a party. In fact, the CFI had begun citing the Charter in its judgments from as early as 2002. Note that the Court first discusses the impact of the European Convention and ECHR judgments before referring to the Charter. Now that the Charter has been declared legally binding by the Lisbon Treaty, does the Court have warrant to continue relying on the Convention and the constitutional traditions of the Member States?

2.   The Court of Justice has applied the principle of family unification in several other important recent judgments, such as *Baumbast* and *Zhu and Chen*, infra pages 586 and 641, which granted parents who were not citizens of the Union derivative rights to residence together with their minor children who were nationals of a Member State. Likewise, in *Orfanopoulos*, infra page 596, the Court held that a court must consider whether the expulsion by German authorities of an Italian migrant worker after a jail sentence could violate the principle of family unity when the worker's spouse and children legally resided in Germany.

3.   More generally, the Court of Justice has cited the Charter as a source of rights in such key recent judgments as *Laval*, infra page 214, concerning union rights, and *Kadi*, supra page 198, on property rights and the enforceability of sanctions against alleged terrorists. The Court cited the Charter's Article 49, on the principles of legality and proportionality in criminal law, in Advocaten voor de Wereld v. Leden van de Ministerrad, Case C–303/05, [2007] ECR I–3633. When a Belgian lawyer's association challenged a Belgian law implementing the Council's 2002 Framework Decision on the European Arrest Warrant as including among offenses justifying extradition ones that were too "vague and imprecise," the Court held that the offenses had to be determined by Member State courts in accordance with the "principle of the legality of criminal offences and penalties" guaranteed by the Charter and the European Convention (¶ 49).

4.   The political institutions have taken steps to make the Charter both better known and more effective. Thus, in 2007 a Fundamental Rights Agency was created, replacing an earlier Monitoring Center for Racism and Xenophobia. The Center, sited in Vienna, produces reports, studies and opinions. The Commission also created in 2002 a group of independent experts on fundamental rights which likewise produces reports and studies. Finally, as previously observed, the Commission commonly inserts references to the Charter in recitals to draft legislation when relevant, as in the case of Directive 2003/109, on long-term residence rights for third state nationals, and Council Framework Decision 2002/475 on combating terrorism (both described in Chapter 16G).

D.   THE CONTRIBUTION OF THE LISBON TREATY

The Treaty of Lisbon's TEU Article 6(1) finally gives the Charter of Fundamental Rights (doc. 6 in the Documents Supplement) "the same legal value as the Treaties," while adding that this "shall not extend in any way the competences of the Union." The Charter having "legal value" presumably means that its provisions have become binding on the courts of the EU and the Member States. The number and breadth of the rights enumerated, and the complex balancing of values they require, guarantee that the EU courts will shoulder a substantial interpretive burden. Not to be overlooked is the fact that, as the price for winning their assent to the Lisbon Treaty, Poland, the Czech Republic and the UK secured via Protocols certain protections against the invalidation of laws and other measures as "inconsistent" with a fundamental right stated in the Charter. These represent very serious provisos whose practical import remains to be seen.

The Lisbon Treaty did not content itself with rendering the Charter legally binding and enforceable. TEU Article 6(2) further provides that the "Union shall accede to the European Convention for the Protection of Human Rights and Fundamental Freedoms." This may prove to be procedurally complicated. When that occurs, the EU will effectively have two charters of fundamental rights, each entrusted primarily to a different court: one in Luxembourg, the other in Strasbourg. Theoretically, the European Court of Human Rights could take a decision contrary to that of the Court of Justice concerning the same issues, and even the same case. However, a collision is unlikely, since the two Courts have a record of showing considerable deference to each other's judgments.

We already know that the Strasbourg Court is averse to reviewing a Court of Justice judgment that has taken seriously issues of fundamental rights common to cases before the two courts. Nine years after the Court decided in the *Bosphorus* case, supra page 197, that the innocent Turkish company's property rights were outweighed by the public interest in sanctioning Serbia to secure its cooperation in ending the Bosnian civil war, the European Court of Human Rights was confronted, in a suit against Ireland, with exactly the same issue under exactly the same facts. It ruled that Ireland could act in reliance on the Court of Justice's own *Bosphorus* judgment:

155   ... State action taken in compliance with ... legal obligations [under international treaties establishing international organizations] is justified as long as the relevant organisation is considered to protect fundamental rights, as regards both the substantive guarantees offered and the mechanisms controlling their observance, in a manner which can be considered at least equivalent to that for which the Convention provides ... By "equivalent" the Court [of Human Rights] means "comparable" ": any requirement that the organisation's protection be "identical" could run counter to the interest of international co-operation pursued. However, any such finding of equivalence could not be final and would be susceptible to review in the light of any relevant change in fundamental rights' protection ...

156   If such equivalent protection is considered to be provided by the organisation [the EC], the presumption will be that a State has not

departed from the requirements of the Convention when it does no more than implement legal obligations flowing from its membership of the organisation. However, any such presumption can be rebutted if, in the circumstances of a particular case, it is considered that the protection of Convention rights was manifestly deficient. In such cases, the interest of international co-operation would be outweighed by the Convention's role as a "constitutional instrument of European public order" in the field of human rights . . ."

The ECHR then examined the history and nature of judicial protection in the EU.

165   [T]he Court finds that the protection of fundamental rights by Community law can be considered to be, and to have been at the relevant time, "equivalent" (within the meaning of paragraph 155 above) to that of the Convention system. Consequently, the presumption arises that Ireland did not depart from the requirements of the Convention when it implemented legal obligations flowing from its membership of the European Community . . .

Moreover, the Court found that the presumption stated in the immediately preceding paragraph had not been rebutted. Bosphorus Hava Yollari Turizm ve Ticaret Anonim Sirketi v. Ireland, no. 45036/98, [2005] ECHR 440.

In the unlikely event, after accession, of an irreconcilable conflict between the two courts, would the Court of Justice be bound to follow the ECHR decision?

E. APPLICATION OF EU FUNDAMENTAL RIGHTS PRINCIPLES TO MEMBER STATE MEASURES

The Court of Justice considers as subject to fundamental rights protection not only the institutions of the EU, but also the Member States whenever there is a sufficient nexus between a Member State measure and EU law itself. (Of course, even in the absence of a sufficient nexus, Member State measures will still be subject to fundamental rights protection emanating from domestic constitutional law and from international law, as received by national courts.)

But under what circumstances is a sufficient nexus present or may a Member State be said to be acting in implementation of EU law? The issue has presented itself to the Court from time to time, but more frequently with the heightened attention to fundamental rights in the EU. It will certainly arise under the Charter which expressly confines its application to Member State measures to situations in which a State is implementing EU law. In some cases the answer will be clear. In Rutili v. Minister for the Interior, a 1975 judgment excerpted at page 591 infra, the Court held that French rules restricting the right of residence of a citizen of another Member State were limited by fundamental rights principles inspired by the European Convention. In other cases, the answer is less clear.

VEREINIGTE FAMILIAPRESS v. HEINRICH BAUER VERLAG

Case C–368/95, [1997] ECR I–3689.

[Familiapress, an Austrian newspaper publisher, asked a Vienna commercial court for an order requiring a German newspaper publisher, Bauer, to cease marketing publications in Austria that offered readers the chance to play games for prizes, in violation of the Austrian law on Unfair Competition which bars offering consumers free gifts linked to the sale of goods or supply of services. German competition law imposes no such prohibition.

The Court readily found that the ban on the imported periodicals with games of chance infringed the free movement of goods under EC Treaty Article 28 (now TFEU Article 34), and turned to Austria's argument that the infringement could be justified in the overriding public interest in maintaining press diversity. Austria cited fierce competition among publishers to offer games and drawings for ever larger prizes, with small publishers unable to compete in this marketing practice.]

26   A prohibition on selling publications which offer the chance to take part in prize games competitions may detract from freedom of expression. Article 10 of the [EHRC] does, however, permit derogations from that freedom for the purposes of maintaining press diversity, in so far as they are prescribed by law and are necessary in a democratic society.

27   [I]t must therefore be determined whether a national prohibition such as that in issue in the main proceedings is proportionate to the aim of maintaining press diversity and whether the objective might not be attained by measures less restrictive of both intra-Community trade and freedom of expression.

28   To that end, it should be determined, first, whether newspapers which offer the chance of winning a prize in games, puzzles or competitions are in competition with those small press publishers who are deemed to be unable to offer comparable prizes and whom the contested legislation is intended to protect and, second, whether such a prospect of winning constitutes an incentive to purchase capable of bringing about a shift in demand.

29   It is for the national court to determine whether those conditions are satisfied on the basis of a study of the Austrian press market.

30   In carrying out that study, it will have to define the market for the product in question and to have regard to the market shares of individual publishers or press groups and the trend thereof.

31   Moreover, the national court will also have to assess the extent to which, from the consumer's standpoint, the product concerned can be replaced by papers which do not offer prizes, taking into account all the circumstances which may influence the decision to purchase, such as the presence of advertising on the title page referring to the chance of winning a prize, the likelihood of winning, the value of the prize or the extent to which winning depends on a test calling for a measure of ingenuity, skill or knowledge.

[Finally, the Court required that consideration be given to the availability and efficacy of less restrictive means of achieving Austria's objective, such as removing the relevant newspaper page in copies intended for Austria or including a notice that readers in Austria are ineligible to win a prize.]

NOTES AND QUESTIONS

1. Courts in Europe tend to hold that restrictions on commercial advertising are more easily justified than those on political speech or expression. Do you agree with the Court's acceptance of Austria's concern for maintaining press diversity as a possible justification on its ban on games of chance or puzzles with prizes inserted in newspapers or magazines? Were there less restrictive but still adequate alternatives available to Austria?

The question of the extent to which commercial advertising can be limited without violating freedom of expression also arose in Herbert Karner Industrie–Auktionen v. Troostwijk, Case C–71/02, [2004] ECR I–3025. The Austrian Unfair Competition Law forbids misleading advertising. In Austria, it is commonly supposed that when an insolvency administrator sells the goods of an insolvent estate, those goods will be sold cheaply. When Troostwijk advertised an auction sale of an insolvent estate without indicating that this was not a sale by an insolvency administrator, a trial court enjoined the sale. Among the issues raised on preliminary reference to the Court of Justice was whether Troostwijk's advertising was protected by freedom of expression. The Court held that a restriction on commercial advertising to achieve the goals of consumer protection and fair trading was reasonable and proportionate (¶ 52).

2. Freedom of expression cases before the ECJ, though typically raising market integration issues, can—like First Amendment cases in the US—have a strong political dimension. Two cases excerpted later in the book make the point. In Schmidberger v. Austria, excerpted at page 491 infra, the Court approved a decision by Austrian regional authorities to permit an environmental protection group to block the trans-Alpine highway between Germany and Italy for 28 hours to protest pollution, despite the obvious serious interference with the free movement of goods caused by the blockade. In a very different context, the Court in Laval v. Byggnands, excerpted at page 681 infra, held that a Swedish union's blockade of a work-site of a Latvian contractor violated the contractor's right to provide trans-border services, and was not justified by the union's desire to compel the contractor to pay its Latvian employees the prevailing Swedish construction workers' wage while they were temporarily working in Sweden. Although the Court recognized the

Swedish union's social right to take collective action, it considered the blockade to be disproportionate in the absence of a Swedish law mandating a minimum wage for such construction workers.

Still, the internal affairs doctrine discussed in Chapter 3 can on occasion cause EU fundamental rights principles to be inapplicable to measures taken under national law. The following case nicely illustrates the point.

KREMZOW v. AUSTRIA
Case C–299/95 [1997] ECR I–2629.

[In December 1982, Kremzow, a retired Austrian judge, confessed to the murder of an Austrian lawyer, but subsequently retracted his confession. In 1984, the Court of Assizes found Kremzow guilty of murder and unlawful possession of a firearm, sentencing him to a term of 20 years' imprisonment. On appeal, Kremzow specifically advanced an EU law claim, namely that his unlawful imprisonment infringed his right as an EU citizen under EC Treaty Article 18 (now TFEU Article 21) to move freely throughout the Union.]

15　[W]here national legislation falls within the field of application of Community law, the Court, in a reference for a preliminary ruling, must give the national court all the guidance as to interpretation necessary to enable it to assess the compatibility of that legislation with the fundamental rights as laid down in particular in the Convention ... However, the Court has no such jurisdiction with regard to national legislation lying outside the scope of Community law.

16　The appellant ... is an Austrian national whose situation is not connected in any way with any of the situations contemplated by the Treaty provisions on freedom of movement for persons. Whilst any deprivation of liberty may impede the person concerned from exercising his right of free movement, the Court has held that a purely hypothetical prospect of exercising that right does not establish a sufficient connection with Community law to justify the application of Community provisions.

17　Moreover, Mr. Kremzow was sentenced for murder and for illegal possession of a firearm under provisions of national law which were not designed to secure compliance with rules of Community law.

18　It follows that the national legislation applicable in the main proceedings relates to a situation which does not fall within the field of application of Community law.

NOTES AND QUESTIONS

1.　*Kremzow* illustrates the more general idea that free movement principles may not be invoked in cases lacking a meaningful cross-border dimension. See, as another example, the *Moser* case, discussed at page 124 supra.

2.　The need to delimit Member State implementation of EU law from their enforcement of domestic law is not unique to issues of fundamental rights. EU law from the start barred discrimination by Member States against nationals of other Member States while acting within the sphere of EU law. Given the expansiveness of EU law, it is proving more and more difficult for States to escape EU law scrutiny by claiming to be acting outside the EU law sphere. See, for example, the case of Hayes v. Kronenberger GmbH, Case C–323/95, [1997] ECR I–1711.

3.   Return to the case of Stauder v. City of Ulm, supra page 191. Note the Court's remark (¶ 6) that, while the Commission program of offering subsidized butter for certain classes of persons did not require beneficiaries to identify themselves by name when purchasing butter, it did not bar Member States from requiring them to do so. Having read the cases in this section, do you think that is an accurate statement under current law?

F.   TRANSPARENCY AND ACCESS TO DOCUMENTS

In addition to its TEU Article 2 on Values Underpinning the Union and its TEU Articles 9–12 on Democratic Principles, the Lisbon Treaty reiterates in TEU Article 10(3) the Maastricht Treaty's injunction that "decisions shall be taken as openly and as closely as possible to the citizen."

Transparency lay behind the Treaty of Amsterdam's requirement in EC Treaty Article 207 that whenever the Council acts in its legislative capacity, "the results of votes and explanations of votes as well as statements in the minutes shall be made public," though its decisions on non-legislative matters and any votes concerning them could remain confidential. The Lisbon Treaty's TEU Article 16(8) retains this distinction between the public nature of legislative sessions and the private character of other discussions. (Because the Lisbon Treaty does not authorize the European Council to adopt legislation, it does not require European Council votes to be made public.)

Even before that, Declaration No. 17 to the Maastricht Treaty had specifically called for a right of access to information. The first formal step in that direction was the Commission's and Council's adoption in December 1993 of a "Code of Conduct" on public access to documents, promising "the widest possible access to documents held by the Commission and the Council," whether through on-site inspection or through delivery of photocopies. Code of Conduct Relating to Access to Documents within the Community, O.J. L 340/41 (Dec. 31, 1993). The notion of "document" was sweeping, covering in principle even internal preparatory documents and notes.

The Code of Conduct erected a strong presumption of openness, authorizing refusal of access to documents only to the extent required in the interest of individual privacy, commercial secrecy, the Community's financial interest, confidentiality of the institutions' proceedings, the confidentiality interest of the supplier of the information, or other stated interests (public security, international relations, monetary stability, or the integrity of judicial proceedings, inspections or investigations).

The Council and the Commission each adopted the Code by formal decisions in 1993 and 1994, respectively, and the Parliament adopted a similar one in 1997. The right of access to documents acquired Treaty force when the Treaty of Amsterdam introduced EC Treaty Article 255 (now TFEU Article 15), which established that right and mandated that the Council and Parliament adopt legislation under the codecision procedure, to effectuate it. The institutions accordingly adopted Regulation 1049/2001 on public access to Parliament, Council and Commission documents, O.J. L 145/43 (May 31, 2001).

The 2001 Regulation (commonly referred to as the "Access Regulation") applies to all documents relating to the policies, activities and decisions of the three institutions within their sphere of responsibility, whatever their form (paper, electronic, recordings). The Commission's draft text had provided for a categorical exclusion for internal memoranda, discussion documents, and informal messages, but the Parliament deleted this during the legislative process. Disclosure is subject to a "harm test," meaning that access must be granted unless disclosure would seriously harm one of a series of specified interests in Article 4(1), e.g., public security, international relations, or the integrity of court proceedings. Article 7 of the regulation provides that the right of access applies equally to documents relating to the CFSP and the Area of Freedom, Security and Justice.

The access regulation applies to all documents "held" by the institutions, thereby bringing within the scope of the right of access documents not actually drawn up by the institutions, but emanating from third parties (including Member States) and merely found in the institutions' files. This extension, urged by both the Parliament and the Ombudsman, actually aligns the EU's documents policy with existing access to documents legislation in most Member States. The regulation's grounds for refusal of access apply equally to documents drawn up by third parties, though where there is doubt about the applicability of an exception, the institution must first consult the document's author. (If the author fails to reply, the institutions may proceed to disclose.)

Ever since the initial Codes of Conduct, the media, non-governmental organizations and academics have filed frequent requests for documents, particularly from the Commission, which receives well over a thousand requests each year. All three political institutions usually respond favorably to requests, though on occasion they reject them or delete material claimed to be confidential.

Parties denied requests in whole or in part have occasionally appealed to the Court of First Instance, with further appeals possible to the Court of Justice.

NETHERLANDS & VAN DER WAL v. COMMISSION

Joined Cases C–174/98P & C–189/98P, [2000] ECR I–1.

[Van der Wal, a lawyer specializing in competition law, requested copies of Commission replies to questions received from national courts (referred to in the Commission's 1994 annual competition report). Pleading the protection of the public interest in the confidentiality of replies to a [national] court," the Commission declined to produce the documents. On appeal, the CFI agreed, concluding that the guarantee of a fair trial in the European Convention on Human Rights required a respect for the confidentiality of documents produced solely for purposes of a particular court proceeding. The Court of Justice reversed.]

20   In order to determine under what conditions, in the context of its cooperation with national courts with a view to the application by them of [EC Treaty Articles 81 and 82, now TFEU Articles 101 and 102], the Commission must refuse access to documents which it holds, on the ground that the protection of the public interest ... may be undermined, it is necessary to consider the manner in which such cooperation works in practice.

21   [As the 1993 Commission Notice on cooperation between national courts and the Commission in applying EC competition rules shows, national] courts may need information of a procedural nature "to enable them to discover whether a certain case is pending before the Commission, whether a case has been the subject of a notification, whether the Commission has officially initiated a procedure or whether it has already taken a position through an official decision or through a comfort letter sent by its services. If necessary, national courts may also ask the Commission to give an opinion as to how much time is likely to be required for granting or refusing individual exemption for notified agreements or practices, so as to be able to determine the conditions for any decision to suspend proceedings or whether interim measures need to be adopted."

22   According to ... the Notice, national courts may also consult the Commission on points of law where the application of Articles [81 and 82] causes them particular difficulties....

23   Lastly, ... national courts can obtain information from the Commission regarding factual data: statistics, market studies and economic analyses.

24   It follows ... that documents supplied by the Commission to national courts are often documents which it already possesses or which, although drafted with a view to particular proceedings, merely refer to the earlier documents, or in which the Commission merely expresses an opinion of a general nature, independent of the data relating to the case pending before the national court. In relation to those documents,

the Commission must access in each individual case whether they fall within the exceptions listed in the code of conduct . . .

25   Documents supplied by the Commission may also contain legal or economic analysis, drafted on the basis of data supplied by the national court. In those cases, the Commission acts as a legal or economic adviser to the national court and documents drafted in the exercise of that function must be subject to national procedural rules in the same way as any other expert report, in particular as regards disclosure.

26   In those cases, national law may preclude the disclosure of those documents and compliance with that law may be regarded as a public interest worthy of protection under the exceptions provided for by Decision 94/90.

27   That is, however, not enough to exonerate the Commission entirely from its obligation to disclose those documents. In so far as they are held by the Commission, such documents fall within the scope of Decision 94/90, which provides for the widest public access possible. Any exception to that right of access must therefore be interpreted and applied strictly.

28   Consequently, the Commission does not discharge its duty merely by refusing any request for access to the documents in question. Compliance with national procedural rules is sufficiently safeguarded if the Commission ensures that disclosure of the documents does not constitute an infringement of national law. In the event of doubt, it must consult the national court and refuse access only if that court objects to disclosure of the documents.

NOTES AND QUESTIONS

1. Do you agree with the Court of Justice or the CFI? The Court of Justice places upon the Commission the burden of distinguishing between those replies to national courts that are confidential under national law and those that are not.

2. As noted, the right of access to documents also applies to documents generated by the institutions acting under the Maastricht Treaty's second and third pillars. The CFI first reached that conclusion in Svenska Journalistforbundet v. Council, Case T–174/95, [1998] ECR II–2289, with regard to Justice and Home Affairs (JHA). The CFI held that when the Council's 1993 decision endorsing the Code of Conduct made "all Council documents" available, subject to listed exceptions, the Council implicitly included also JHA documents. The CFI then held that the Council had failed to provide a sufficient reason for its refusal to furnish the documents, which related to the Council's creation of Europol, the European Police Office.

3. In Hautala v. Council, Case C–353/99P, [2001] ECR I–9565, Hautala, a member of the European Parliament, asked the Council for a report from its Working Group on Conventional Arms Exports. The Court held that the 1993

Council decision endorsing the Code of Conduct requires the EU courts to consider giving partial access to documents even if some portions must remain confidential. On the other hand, the Court invoked the principle of proportionality to hold that the Council could decline to supply the document if the administrative burden involved in excising confidential material outweighed the benefit of providing only a fragmentary report. The Court came to much the same conclusion in Mattila v. Council, Case C–353/01P, [2004] ECR I–1073, where it held that the Council must review certain documents concerning the EU's foreign relations with Russia and the Ukraine to consider the possibility of providing partial access to non-confidential portions.

SWEDEN v. COUNCIL

(Turco)

Cases C–39/05P & C–52/05P, [2008] ECR I–4723.

[In 2002, Turco requested the Council to provide documents relating to a Justice and Home Affairs Council meeting, notably an opinion of the Council's Legal Service concerning a draft directive on minimum standards for the reception of asylum applicants. The Council refused access to the opinion, citing its interest in obtaining internal legal advice. On appeal by Sweden, acting on Turco's behalf, the CFI held that, while a legal opinion as such did not automatically qualify for an exception to disclosure under Regulation 1049/2001, in this case the legal opinion's disclosure could give rise to doubts concerning the lawfulness of the draft directive. The Court of Justice reversed the CFI.]

36   In view of the objectives pursued by Regulation No. 1049/2001, [any] exceptions must be interpreted and applied strictly.

37   As regards the exception relating to legal advice laid down in the second indent of Article 4(2) of Regulation No. 1049/2001, the examination to be undertaken by the Council when it is asked to disclose a document must necessarily be carried out in three stages, corresponding to the three criteria in that provision.

38   First, the Council must satisfy itself that the document which it is asked to disclose does indeed relate to legal advice and, if so, it must decide which parts of it are actually concerned and may, therefore, be covered by that exception.

39   The fact that a document is headed "legal advice/opinion" does not mean that it is automatically entitled to the protection of legal advice ensured by ... Regulation No. 1049/2001. Over and above the way a document is described, it is for the institution to satisfy itself that that document does indeed concern such advice.

40   Second, the Council must examine whether disclosure of the parts of the document in question which have been identified as relating to legal advice "would undermine the protection" of that advice.

41   In that regard, it must be pointed out that neither Regulation No. 1049/2001 nor its *travaux préparatoires* [drafts] throw any light on the

meaning of "protection" of legal advice. Therefore, that term must be interpreted by reference to the purpose and general scheme of the rules of which it forms part.

42　Consequently, the exception relating to legal advice ... must be construed as aiming to protect an institution's interest in seeking legal advice and receiving frank, objective and comprehensive advice.

43　The risk of that interest being undermined must, in order to be capable of being relied on, be reasonably foreseeable and not purely hypothetical.

44　Third and last, if the Council takes the view that disclosure of a document would undermine the protection of legal advice as defined above, it is incumbent on the Council to ascertain whether there is any overriding public interest justifying disclosure despite the fact that its ability to seek legal advice and receive frank, objective and comprehensive advice would thereby be undermined.

45　In that respect, it is for the Council to balance the particular interest to be protected by non-disclosure of the document concerned against, *inter alia*, the public interest in the document being made accessible in the light of the advantages stemming, as noted in recital 2 of the preamble to Regulation No. 1049/2001, from increased openness, in that this enables citizens to participate more closely in the decision-making process and guarantees that the administration enjoys greater legitimacy and is more effective and more accountable to the citizen in a democratic system.

46　Those considerations are clearly of particular relevance where the Council is acting in its legislative capacity, as is apparent from recital 6 of the preamble to Regulation No. 1049/2001, according to which wider access must be granted to documents in precisely such cases. Openness in that respect contributes to strengthening democracy by allowing citizens to scrutinize all the information which has formed the basis of a legislative act. The possibility for citizens to find out the considerations underpinning legislative action is a precondition for the effective exercise of their democratic rights.

47　[U]nder the second subparagraph of Article 207(3) EC, the Council is required to define the cases in which it is to be regarded as acting in its legislative capacity, with a view to allowing greater access to documents in such cases. Similarly, Article 12(2) of Regulation No. 1049/2001 acknowledges the specific nature of the legislative process by providing that documents drawn up or received in the course of procedures for the adoption of acts which are legally binding in or for the Member States should be made directly accessible.

* * *

49　If the Council decides to refuse access to a document which it has been asked to disclose, it must explain, first, how access to that document could specifically and effectively undermine the interest protected by an exception laid down in Article 4 of Regulation No. 1049/2001 relied on by that institution and, secondly ... whether or not there is an overriding public interest that might nevertheless justify disclosure of the document concerned.

50   It is, in principle, open to the Council to base its decisions in that regard on general presumptions which apply to certain categories of documents, as considerations of a generally similar kind are likely to apply to requests for disclosure relating to documents of the same nature. However, it is incumbent on the Council to establish in each case whether the general considerations normally applicable to a particular type of document are in fact applicable to a specific document which it has been asked to disclose.

[The Court then applied these general principles to the circumstances being reviewed.]

57   ... [T]he Court of First Instance did not require the Council to have checked whether the reasons of a general nature on which it relied were in fact applicable to the legal opinion whose disclosure was requested. Secondly, ... the Court of First Instance erred in holding that there was a general need for confidentiality in respect of advice from the Council's legal service relating to legislative matters.

59   As regards, first, the fear expressed by the Council that disclosure of an opinion of its legal service relating to a legislative proposal could lead to doubts as to the lawfulness of the legislative act concerned, it is precisely openness in this regard that contributes to conferring greater legitimacy on the institutions in the eyes of European citizens and increasing their confidence in them by allowing divergences between various points of view to be openly debated. It is in fact rather a lack of information and debate which is capable of giving rise to doubts in the minds of citizens, not only as regards the lawfulness of an isolated act, but also as regards the legitimacy of the decision-making process as a whole.

* * *

62   As regards, secondly, the Council's argument that the independence of its legal service would be compromised by possible disclosure of legal opinions issued in the course of legislative procedures, it must be pointed out that ... the exception provided for in the second indent of Article 4(2) of Regulation No. 1049/2001 ... seeks specifically to protect an institution's interest in seeking legal advice and receiving frank, objective and comprehensive advice.

* * *

65   As regards the Commission's argument that it could be difficult for an institution's legal service which had initially expressed a negative opinion regarding a legislative act in the process of being adopted subsequently to defend the lawfulness of that act if its opinion had

been published, it must be stated that such a general argument cannot justify an exception to the openness provided for by Regulation No. 1049/2001.

66 In view of those considerations, there appears to be no real risk that is reasonably foreseeable and not purely hypothetical that disclosure of opinions of the Council's legal service issued in the course of legislative procedures might undermine the protection of legal advice within the meaning of the second indent of Article 4(2) of Regulation No. 1049/2001.

* * *

69 That finding does not preclude a refusal, on account of the protection of legal advice, to disclose a specific legal opinion, given in the context of a legislative process, but being of a particularly sensitive nature or having a particularly wide scope that goes beyond the context of the legislative process in question. In such a case, it is incumbent on the institution concerned to give a detailed statement of reasons for such a refusal.

NOTES AND QUESTIONS

1. Lawyers understandably believe that it is in the public interest for legal opinions provided to a client in the context of representing it in a court proceeding to be protected by a confidentiality privilege. Here, the Council's legal advisor was providing an opinion concerning draft legislation on asylum, a decidedly sensitive field. Do you agree with the CFI that the opinion should be exempt from access by the party requesting it, or with the Court of Justice's view that the Council must specifically justify the denial of access?

2. Denmark and Finland supported Sweden in its appeal of the CFI judgment. The three Scandinavian States have traditionally advocated broad access to EU documents. On the other hand, the Commission and the UK supported the Council. The Commission may in particular be concerned that the far more numerous internal opinions of its legal service may now be accessible to the public upon request. Would you support an amendment of Regulation 1049/2001 to make the legal opinions delivered to the Commission and Council by their respective legal services exempt from access along the lines of the CFI judgment?

3. Compare the *Turco* judgment with Sison v. Council, Case C–266/05, [2007] ECR I–1233. There, the Council denied a request for access to Council documents relating to the Council's decision to place Sison on the list of alleged terrorists whose assets were frozen pursuant to the Council's 2001 regulation authorizing measures to combat terrorism (see Chapter 16G infra). The Court affirmed the CFI's denial of access, holding that the public security exception in Article 4(1) of Regulation 1049/2001 permitted the Council "wide discretion" and "a margin of appreciation" (¶¶ 34–36). The Court emphasized that the documents fell within the scope of Council action in CFSP, and not under the EC Treaty (¶ 42).

4. Article 4(5) of the Access Regulation provides that if a party requests from one of the institutions a document furnished to the institution by a Member State, the Member State must be notified and allowed to ask that the document not be released. The Regulation does not state whether the Member State must justify its request for non-disclosure (or on what grounds) or whether its request must be honored by the institution. Germany made such a request in relation to documents it had submitted to the Commission in connection with the latter's approval of a construction project in an environmentally sensitive location, and the Commission complied. The environmental NGO that had requested the document challenged the Commission's refusal to produce the document in the Court of First Instance, which upheld the refusal on the ground that the Regulation entitled the State that supplied the document to veto its disclosure, to do so in reliance on national law and policy, and to refrain from giving reasons. Sweden, supported by Finland, brought an appeal against the CFI ruling. The Court ruled that while Member States such as Germany have the right to request non-disclosure, they must give reasons and furthermore those reasons must correspond to one or more of the grounds for denial of access set out in the Regulation. It further held that the Member State must be willing to enter into dialogue with the institution as to whether non-disclosure would be justified in terms of the Regulation's exceptions to the duty to disclose. Sweden v. Commission (Access to German documents), Case C–64/05P, [2007] ECR I–11389.

CHAPTER 7

THE RELATIONSHIP BETWEEN UNION
AND MEMBER STATE LAW

■ ■ ■

What is the legal relationship between national law and Union (or, before that, Community) law? This question is of utmost importance, given that EU law and policy are to a very substantial extent implemented by national administrative authorities and courts. Not surprisingly, the Court of Justice gave the question early and authoritative attention to the issues involved.

Due to their constitutional importance, this chapter deals chiefly with two of the Court' most fundamental doctrines: the doctrine of direct effect and the doctrine of EU law primacy. The first two sections of this chapter deal with these topics.

Soon after addressing the direct effect and primacy of the Treaties themselves, the Court was asked to consider the more complex prospect of giving direct effect to EU secondary legislation, notably directives. The third section of the chapter covers this topic, which has manifest practical importance.

The courts of the Member States have understandably claimed a voice of their own in determining the force and effect of EU law in their own domestic legal orders. Precisely because the EU relies pervasively on national authorities to effectuate EU law and policy, their attitudes cannot be ignored. Developments on this front, which naturally differ from State to State, are presented in Chapter 8.

A. THE DIRECT EFFECT OF CERTAIN
TREATY PROVISIONS

Almost immediately upon establishment of the EEC, the question arose whether Treaty provisions needed to be transposed into national law to have legal effect, or whether they might have legal effect, in whole or part, on their own. If they had immediate effect, Treaty articles might then enable private parties to assert rights against their governments that Member State courts and administrative authorities would be obligated to respect. The issue came later to be captured by the term "vertical direct effect," denoting the vertical relationship between the State and private parties.

The answer the Court gave to that question soon enough caused parties to assert that Treaty articles also could have "horizontal direct effect" in the sense of giving them rights assertable against private parties.

A subsidiary but fundamental question inhered in both of these questions, namely who would have the authority to make these determinations.

Due to the intrinsic interest of these questions from both a legal and political point of view, they attracted an enormous amount of attention in early scholarship on Community law. Beyond that, enterprising lawyers began asserting EU law-based claims in litigation before national courts, which in turn were prompted to refer questions to the Court under the preliminary reference procedure of Article 234 (now TFEU Article 267). These questions pertained not only to the meaning of a particular Treaty article or provision of secondary legislation, but also to the fundamentals of the relationship between EU and Member State law. As shown by the cases that follow, the Court seized these early opportunities to establish basic and novel principles for defining that relationship. The principles that the Court discerned are ones that distinctly tend, as the Court put it, to promote *l'effet utile* of EU law, i.e., its effectiveness within the national legal orders.

NOTE ON THE DIRECT APPLICABILITY OF EU LAW

Despite its prominence in EU law and practice, the term "direct effect" appears nowhere in the Treaties. It is largely a construction of the European Court of Justice.

The original EEC Treaty and its successors (including the TFEU in its Article 288) refer instead to regulations as being "directly applicable." The relationship between direct applicability and direct effect has given rise to some confusion. When TFEU Article 288 describes regulations as directly applicable, it means to say that they become a part of the national legal order upon their enactment and entry into force at the EU level. (The term directly applicable, as used in this sense, has an obvious affinity with the term "self-executing" as used to describe certain treaties in US international law.) EU regulations do not require transposition into domestic law. (In that sense, federal law in the US is also directly applicable in the states.) The term direct applicability served well to distinguish between regulations and directives (terms examined in some depth in Chapter Three of this book), since while regulations were deemed to produce their intended effect throughout the EU upon their entry into force, directives by definition required transposition. They "directed" Member States to introduce or change their law; they did not themselves bring about that introduction or change.

The fact that a norm is directly applicable (i.e., part of domestic law without separate transposition) does not mean, however, that the norm is "directly effective," as defined above, i.e., that it gives rise to individual rights that agencies and courts of Member States are obligated to recognize and effectuate. And yet it is the latter—direct effect—upon which the *effet utile* of EU law ultimately depends, for unless private parties have access to Treaty rights in the only legal channels that are normally open to them (namely national administrations and national courts), and unless those fora make appropriate remedies available, the purposes of EU law stand to be frustrated. This will of course explain the substantially greater emphasis given to direct effect, as compared to direct applicability, in both the case law of the Court and in the literature. Significantly, the term the Court of Justice used in the landmark case, *Van Gend en Loos*, infra page 232, was "direct effect" rather than "direct applicability." The Court sometimes appears to use the two terms interchangeably (see, for example, *Defrenne*, infra page 240, ¶ 24), and at other times not. In this book, the term direct effect will consistently be used to designate those provisions that are clear, precise and unconditional enough to create rights for private parties, and not merely obligations for the Member States. The practical consequence is that private parties can then enforce these rights against the Member States in national courts, the latter guided as necessary by the Court of Justice through preliminary rulings.

However, the term directly applicable is not without significance, for it importantly dispenses with any necessity of "domesticating" Treaty articles in order for them to become an element of the national legal order. In fact, the Court considers it wrong and dangerous for Member States to incorporate Treaty articles and even regulations into domestic law in ways that might obscure their EU law origin and status. In the Court's view, EU law rules directly engage the Member States as, when and to the extent those rules themselves provide. However, some Member States, as we shall see, considered it necessary upon joining the EU to adopt a constitutional or legislative text doing away with the need for the separate incorporation of the Treaties or secondary legislation into the domestic legal order. The implication is that in these States, absent the constitutional or legislative language adopted, each EU law instrument would have had to be separately transposed by some national enactment in order to become directly applicable domestically.

Finally, does it follow from the fact that regulations are by definition directly applicable that they necessarily also have direct effect? Some of the Court's language suggests that this may be the case. In Variola SpA v. Amministrazione Italiana delle Finanze, Case 34/73, [1973] ECR 981, a Trieste court sought to know whether certain "administrative" and "statistical" duties imposed by Italian customs officials were charges equivalent to customs duties in violation of Council regulations purporting to abolish such duties. It asked the Court of Justice both to interpret the regulations and to decide if they have direct effect. The Court's ruling and reasoning are strikingly simple:

Article [249] of the Treaty [provides that] a Regulation "shall have general application" and "shall be directly applicable in all Member States."

Accordingly, owing to its very nature and its place in the system of sources of Community law, a Regulation has immediate effect and, consequently, operates to confer rights on private parties which the national courts have a duty to protect.

[1973] ECR at 990. More likely, whether a directly applicable measure such as a regulation is also directly effective, in the sense of being capable of creating individual rights that a national court must recognize, will depend at least in part on the language of the instrument itself. See De Sociale Voorzorg Mutual Insurance Fund v. Bertholet, Case 31/64, [1965] ECR 81, 86.

1. VERTICAL DIRECT EFFECT

VAN GEND EN LOOS v. NEDERLANDSE ADMINISTRATIE DER BELASTINGEN

Case 26/62, [1963] ECR 1.

[Van Gend en Loos, a Dutch importer of ureaformaldehyde, objected to the imposition by Dutch customs authorities of an 8% tariff on a quantity of the product imported from Germany. It claimed that when Dutch law reclassified ureaformaldehyde under a new tariff category, resulting in an increase in the applicable rate of duty, it violated the then EEC Treaty Article 12, which required Member States to "refrain from ... increasing [the customs duties on imports] which they already apply in their trade with each other." The Dutch Tariff Commission referred two questions to the Court of Justice, asking whether an individual may invoke Article 12 before a national court or tribunal, and whether reclassifying ureaformaldehyde at a higher customs duty level constituted a violation of Article 12.]

The First Question

A. Jurisdiction of the Court

The Government of the Netherlands and the Belgian Government challenge the jurisdiction of the Court on the ground that the reference relates not to the interpretation but to the application of the Treaty in the context of the constitutional law of the Netherlands, and that in particular the Court has no jurisdiction to decide ... whether the provisions of the EEC Treaty prevail over Netherlands legislation ...

However in this case the Court is not asked to adjudicate upon the application of the Treaty according to the principles of the national law of the Netherlands, which remains the concern of the national courts, but is asked, in conformity with ... Article [234] of the Treaty [now TFEU

Article 267], only to interpret the scope of Article 12 of the said Treaty within the context of Community law and with reference to its effect on individuals. This argument has therefore no legal foundation.

* * *

[I]n order to confer jurisdiction on the Court in the present case it is necessary only that the question raised should clearly be concerned with the interpretation of the treaty. It appears from the wording of the questions referred that they relate to the interpretation of the treaty. The Court therefore has the jurisdiction to answer them.

* * *

B.   On the Substance of the Case

The first question ... is whether Article 12 of the Treaty has direct application in national law in the sense that nationals of Member States may on the basis of this Article lay claim to rights which the national court must protect.

To ascertain whether the provisions of an international treaty extend so far in their effects it is necessary to consider the spirit, the general scheme and the wording of those provisions.

The objective of the EEC Treaty, which is to establish a Common Market, the functioning of which is of direct concern to interested parties in the Community, implies that this Treaty is more than an agreement which merely creates mutual obligations between the contracting states. This view is confirmed by the preamble to the Treaty which refers not only to governments but to peoples. It is also confirmed more specifically by the establishment of institutions endowed with sovereign rights, the exercise of which affects Member States and also their citizens.

In addition the task assigned to the Court of Justice under Article [234], the object of which is to secure uniform interpretation of the Treaty by national courts and tribunals, confirms that the states have acknowledged that Community law has an authority which can be invoked by their nationals before those courts and tribunals.

The conclusion to be drawn from this is that the Community constitutes a new legal order of international law for the benefit of which the states have limited their sovereign rights, albeit within limited fields, and the subject of which comprise not only Member States but also their nationals. Independently of the legislation of Member States, Community law therefore not only imposes obligations on individuals but is also intended to confer upon them rights which become part of their legal heritage. These rights arise not only where they are expressly granted by the Treaty, but also by reason of obligations which the Treaty imposes in a clearly defined way upon individuals as well as upon the Member States and upon the institutions of the Community.

The wording of Article 12 contains a clear and unconditional prohibition which is not a positive but a negative obligation. This obligation, moreover, is not qualified by any reservation on the part of states which would make its implementation conditional upon a positive legislative measure enacted under national law. The very nature of this prohibition makes it ideally adapted to produce direct effects in the legal relationship between Member States and their subjects.

The implementation of Article 12 does not require any legislative intervention on the part of the states. The fact that under this Article it is the Member States who are made the subject of the negative obligation does not imply that their nationals cannot benefit from this obligation.

In addition the argument based on Articles [226 and 227] of the Treaty [now TFEU Articles 258 and 259] put forward by the three Governments which have submitted observations to the Court . . . is misconceived. The fact that these Articles of the Treaty enable the Commission and the Member States to bring before the Court a State which has not fulfilled its obligations does not mean that individuals cannot plead these obligations, should the occasion arise, before a national court. . . .

A restriction of the guarantees against an infringement of Article 12 by Member States to the procedures under Articles [226 and 227] would remove all direct legal protection of the individual rights of their nationals. . . .

The vigilance of individuals concerned to protect their rights amounts to an effective supervision in addition to the supervision entrusted by Articles [226 and 227] to the diligence of the Commission and of the Member States.

It follows from the foregoing considerations that, according to the spirit, the general scheme and the wording of the Treaty, Article 12 must be interpreted as producing direct effects and creating individual rights which national courts must protect.

The Second Question

[The wording of the Dutch Tariff Commission question appeared to require the Court to examine the tariff classification of ureaformaldehyde imported into the Netherlands, which would have been outside the jurisdiction conferred upon the Court of Justice by the preliminary reference procedure. The Court however considered that the real meaning of the question put by the Dutch Tariff Commission was whether, in law, an effective increase in customs duties charged on a given product as a result of a new classification of the product contravened the prohibition in Article 12. The Court addressed that issue on the merits, holding that Article 12 is violated by a customs reclassification of products that results in an increase in the applicable rate of customs duty.]

NOTES AND QUESTIONS

1. Although almost 50 years old, *Van Gend en Loos* remains one of the Court's most forceful statements on the legal nature of the Community and

now the Union. The Court's reference to "a new legal order" in which "the states have limited their sovereign rights" has become the Court's classic legal conception of the EU. Note the words, "of international law," following the "new legal order" language. Those words do not appear in later Court references to the new legal order concept. See, e.g., *Costa v. ENEL,* infra page 245 (second excerpted paragraph). Is that significant?

Like the Treaty itself, the Court in *Van Gend en Loos* refrains from using the terms federation or confederation to describe the EU. Why? (In 1991, the UK prevented the Treaty on European Union drawn up at Maastricht from being called the Treaty on European Federal Union, or from using the term "federal" at all, even though use of the term was strongly urged by Germany, France and other States.)

2. Note that the Court in *Van Gend en Loos* describes Article 12 as having "direct effect" or "immediate effect." It appears to assume that they were in any event directly applicable, as defined above. Why do you think it did so? Whether a Treaty provision has direct effect apparently depends in turn on whether it is "clear and unconditional" or instead "require[s] legislative intervention by the States." Does the quoted language of Article 12 in your judgment satisfy this test? Note that the Court did not merely establish the test for direct effectiveness, but proceeded to decide whether Article 12 satisfied it, rather than leave that operation to the national court.

There is no reason to believe that the provisions of the TFEU articles, many of which do no more than substitute the term "Union" for "Community," will have any less direct effect than their EC Treaty counterparts. Note that the articles of the Maastricht TEU were never held to have direct effect, and it is unlikely that the Court of Justice will hold the Lisbon Treaty's TEU articles to have direct effect either. The Lisbon TEU consists of provisions setting out general principles, democratic values, essential institutional structure, and the nature and operations of the CFSP. None of these are apt to be deemed suitable for direct legal effect.

3. Note the Court's rejection of the argument that the availability of enforcement actions under EC Treaty Articles 226 and 227 rendered direct effect unnecessary. Do you agree with the Court's endorsement of "the vigilance of individuals" in protecting their rights? US courts have adopted a similar view in implying private party enforcement of certain federal civil rights and securities law provisions.

4. In what respect does *Van Gend en Loos* remind you of early constitutional law decisions of the US Supreme Court? Note the reference (in ¶ 5) to the Preamble of the Treaty and the admonition (in ¶ 4) "to consider the spirit [and] the general scheme" as well as the "wording" of the Treaty.

COSTA v. ENTE NAZIONALE PER L'EENERGIA ELETTRICA (ENEL)
Case 6/64, [1964] ECR 585.

[Italy nationalized its electricity production and distribution industries in 1962, transferring their property to a new organization, ENEL. Costa, an Italian lawyer, deliberately refused to pay a $3 electric bill, apparently so as to generate a dispute on the basis of which he might challenge the act of nationalization that created ENEL. Costa argued that the nationalization act violated the Italian Constitution and several articles of the EEC Treaty. The Milan court sought preliminary rulings both from the Italian Constitutional Court on the relevant questions of Italian constitutional law and from the Court of Justice on the proper interpretation of the relevant Treaty articles. The Italian Government maintained that only the Italian Constitutional Court could set aside a national statute, and even then only by reference to the Italian Constitution, so that a preliminary reference should have been made to it, and it alone.

The Court dealt first with Italy's contention that by finding that a Treaty provision has direct effect in national law the Court might in effect declare a national law invalid, which is not its province. The Court insisted that it could determine the direct effectiveness and meaning of a Treaty provision, and still not "apply the Treaty to a specific case or . . . decide upon the validity of a provision of domestic law in relation to the Treaty." The Court also rejected the notion that a Member State court is bound to apply national law even if it violates the Treaty. For this discussion, see page 245. The Court then turned to the direct effect and meaning of the Treaty articles Costa had invoked.]

On the Interpretation of Article [97] [now TFEU Article 119]

Article [97] provides that, where "there is reason to fear" that a provision laid down by law may cause "distortion", the Member State desiring to proceed therewith shall "consult the Commission"; the Commission has power to recommend to the Member States the adoption of suitable measures to avoid the distortion feared.

This Article, placed in the chapter devoted to the "Approximation of Laws", is designed to prevent the differences between the legislation of the different nations with regard to the objectives of the Treaty from becoming more pronounced. By virtue of this provision, Member States have limited their freedom of initiative by agreeing to submit to an appropriate procedure of consultation. By binding themselves unambiguously to prior consultation with the Commission in all those cases where their projected legislation might create a risk, however slight, of a possible distortion, the States have undertaken an obligation to the Community which binds them as States, but which does not create individual rights which national courts must protect. . . .

On the Interpretation of Article 88 [now TFEU Article 108]

Under [Articles 88(1) and (2), now TFEU Articles 108(1) and (2)], the Commission, in cooperation with member States, is to "keep under constant review all systems of aid existing in those States" with a view to the adoption of appropriate measures required by the functioning of the Common Market.

By virtue of Article [88(3)], the Commission is to be informed, in sufficient time, of any plans to grant or alter aid, the Member State concerned not being entitled to put its proposed measures into effect until the Community procedure, and, if necessary, any proceedings before the Court of Justice, have been completed.

These provisions . . . are designed, on the one hand, to eliminate progressively existing aids and, on the other hand, to prevent the individual States . . . from introducing new aids . . . which are likely directly or indirectly to favour certain undertakings or products in an appreciable way, and which threaten, even potentially, to distort competition. By virtue of Article [87], the member States have acknowledged that such aids are incompatible with the Common Market and have thus implicitly undertaken not to create any more, save as otherwise provided in the Treaty; in Article [88], on the other hand, they have merely agreed to submit themselves to appropriate procedures for the abolition of existing aids and the introduction of new ones.

By so expressly undertaking to inform the Commission "in sufficient time" of any plans for aid, and by accepting the procedures laid down in Article [88], the States have entered into an obligation with the Community, which binds them as States but creates no individual rights except in the case of the final provision of Article [88(3)], which is not in question in the present case.

* * *

On the Interpretation of Article 53 [since repealed]

By Article 53 [since repealed] the Member States undertake not to introduce any new restrictions on the right of establishment in their territories of nationals of other Member States, save as otherwise provided in the Treaty. The obligation thus entered into by the States simply amounts legally to a duty not to act, which is neither subject to any conditions, nor . . . to the adoption of any measure either by the States or by the Commission. It is therefore legally complete in itself and is consequently capable of producing direct effects on the relations between Member States and individuals. Such an express prohibition which came into force with the Treaty throughout the Community, and thus became an integral part of the legal system of the Member States, forms part of the law of those States and directly concerns their nationals, in whose favor it has created individual rights which national courts must protect.

[The Court proceeded to interpret Article 53 as barring a Member State from introducing measures subjecting the establishment of nationals of other Member States to more severe rules than those that the State prescribes for its own nationals. (Freedom of establishment is dealt with in Chapter 17 infra.)]

On the Interpretation of Article [31] [now TFEU Article 37]

Article [31(1)] provides that Member States shall progressively adjust any "State monopolies of a commercial character" so as to ensure that no discrimination regarding the conditions under which goods are procured and marketed exists between nationals of Member States. By Article

[31(2)], the Member States are under an obligation to refrain from introducing any new measure which is contrary to the principles laid down in Article [31(1)].

* * *

Article [31(2)] contains an absolute prohibition: not an obligation to do something but an obligation to refrain from doing something. This obligation is not accompanied by any reservation which might make its implementation subject to any positive act of national law. This prohibition is essentially one which is capable of producing direct effects on the legal relations between Member States and their nationals.

Such a clearly expressed prohibition which came into force with the Treaty throughout the Community, and so became an integral part of the legal system of the Member States, forms part of the law of those States and directly concerns their nationals, in whose favor it creates individual rights which national courts must protect.

[The Court then interpreted Article 31 as prohibiting any new commercial monopolies giving rise to national discrimination in the procurement or marketing of goods, and left it to the national court to decide whether these conditions were satisfied in the given case.]

NOTES AND QUESTIONS

1. Do you agree with the Court that it was able to determine the direct effectiveness and meaning of the Treaty provisions in question without presuming to apply those provisions to the specific case or passing on the validity of national law?

2. Why did the Court conclude that Article 31 and former Article 53 were directly effective, but that Articles 88 and 97 were not? What criteria did it use? Are the holdings consistent? Are they the same as the criteria identified in *Van Gend en Loos* and were they properly applied here?

VAN DUYN v. HOME OFFICE
Case 41/74, [1974] ECR 1337.

[The British government, considering the Church of Scientology to be socially harmful and a threat to public welfare, instituted a policy of denying admission into the UK of any foreign national seeking to study or work at the Church's UK headquarters. There were no restrictions on British nationals seeking to practice scientology. Van Duyn, a Dutch national, was refused entry into Britain because she intended to work as a secretary at a college of the Scientology Church. She brought an action against the Home Office claiming a violation, among other things, of EC Treaty Article 39 (initially, EEC Treaty Article 48, now TFEU Article 45) guaranteeing the free movement of workers. The High Court asked the Court of Justice whether Article 39 was directly effective.]

5   It is provided, in Article [39(1) and (2)], that freedom of movement for workers ... shall entail "the abolition of any discrimination based on

nationality between workers of Member States as regards employment, remuneration and other conditions of work and employment."

6 These provisions impose on Member States a precise obligation which does not require the adoption of any further measure on the part either of the Community institutions or of the Member States and which leaves them, in relation to its implementation, no discretionary power.

7 Paragraph 3 [of Article 39], which defines the rights implied by the principle of freedom of movement for workers, subjects them to limitations justified on grounds of public policy, public security or public health. The application of these limitations is, however, subject to judicial control, so that a Member State's right to invoke the limitations does not prevent the provisions of Article [39], which enshrine the principle of freedom of movement for workers, from conferring on individuals rights which are enforceable by them and which the national courts must protect.

8 The reply to the first question must therefore be in the affirmative.

NOTES AND QUESTIONS

1. Do you agree with the Court's remark (¶ 6) that the principle as stated in Articles 39(1) and (2) imposes a "precise" obligation and leaves Community and Member State authorities "no discretionary power" as to its implementation? Do you agree with its remark (¶ 7) that because a Member State's resort to the "public policy, public security or public health" exception in Article 39(3) is subject to judicial review, the exception does not prevent the quoted language in Article 39 from having direct effect?

2. Since the 1970s, the Court has had occasion to decide whether many EC Treaty articles have direct effect, in whole or in part. Some of these cases will appear in later chapters of this book. For example, the Court has held that provisions of EC Treaty Articles 23 and 28 (now TFEU Articles 28 and 34) on the free movement of goods, 43 (now TFEU Article 49) on the right of establishment, 49 (now TFEU Article 56) on the right to perform trans-border services, and 56 (now TFEU Article 63) on the free movement of capital all have vertical direct effect. There is no reason to believe that they will not continue to have direct effect under the Lisbon Treaty.

3. Hurd was headmaster of the European School at Culham, Oxfordshire, UK. Although the Board of Governors of the European Schools had decided that a portion of the teachers' salaries (namely the "European supplement," or amount needed to bring the Member State's national teacher salary up to a standard salary level fixed by the Board) was not to be taxed under national law, the British tax authorities indeed sought to tax that portion of Hurd's salary. The British Income Tax Commissioners, hearing Hurd's objections, asked the Court of Justice for a preliminary ruling. The Court held that the UK's taxation of the supplement constituted a drain on Community resources and thus jeopardized the attainment of the Treaty's objectives in violation of EC Treaty Article 10 (now TEU Article 4(3)), which

imposes on the Member States a "duty of genuine cooperation and assistance" toward the Community.

Hurd was nevertheless found not to be entitled under EU law to avoid payment of the disputed tax in the British courts. Was that because the language of Article 10 does not qualify for direct effect? If so, do you agree? See Hurd v. Jones, Case 44/84, [1986] ECR 29.

4. Not surprisingly, the Court ruled that the statement of Community objectives in Article 2 of the EC Treaty did not create privately enforceable obligations for the Member States. See Alsthom Atlantique v. Sulzer, Case 339/89, [1991] ECR I–107.

5. The question whether international treaties entered into by the EU are capable of having direct effect is best deferred to Part V of this book. Suffice it here to say that the Court of Justice has held that the provisions of the GATT, by virtue of the GATT's "spirit, general scheme and terms," are not capable of having direct effect. See Amministrazione delle Finanze dello Stato v. Chiquita Italia SpA, Case C–469/93, [1995] ECR I–4533. (On the other hand, the Court found in that case that certain pertinent provisions of the Lomé Convention did have direct effect.) The Court has subsequently held that provisions of the 1994 WTO agreements do not have direct legal effect in the Community legal order either, although some may be used in the interpretation and application of the EU's trade regulation measures. See Chapter 29.

2. HORIZONTAL DIRECT EFFECT

DEFRENNE v. SOCIETE ANONYME BELGE DE NAVIGATION AERIENNE SABENA

Case 43/75, [1976] ECR 455.

[Defrenne, a flight attendant with Sabena Airlines since 1951, was required by her contract to cease employment as a crew member when she reached a specific age, though Sabena did not require male flight attendants to retire at that age. She brought several actions against Sabena in a Belgian labor court for losses resulting from alleged gender discrimination in salary, severance pay and pension rights, invoking the right to equal pay for equal work under then EC Treaty Article 119 (later renumbered Article 141, and now found in TFEU Article 157). On appeal from a dismissal of certain of her claims, a preliminary reference was made to the Court of Justice regarding the effect of Article 119 in the Belgian courts.]

7   The question of the direct effect of Article 119 must be considered in the light of the nature of the principle of equal pay, the aim of this provision and its place in the scheme of the Treaty.

8   Article 119 pursues a double aim.

9   First, in the light of the different stages of the development of social legislation in the various Member States, the aim of Article 119 is to avoid a situation in which undertakings established in States which have actually implemented the principle of equal pay suffer a competi-

tive disadvantage in intra-Community competition as compared with undertakings established in States which have not yet eliminated discrimination against women workers as regards pay.

10   Secondly, this provision forms part of the social objectives of the Community, which is not merely an economic union, but is at the same time intended, by common action, to ensure social progress and seek the constant improvement of the living and working conditions of their peoples. . . .

* * *

12   This double aim, which is at once economic and social, shows that the principle of equal pay forms part of the foundations of the Community.

* * *

18   [A] distinction must be drawn within the whole area of application of Article 119 between, first, direct and overt discrimination which may be identified solely with the aid of the criteria based on equal work and equal pay referred to by the article in question and, secondly, indirect and disguised discrimination which can only be identified by reference to more explicit implementing provisions of a Community or national character.

* * *

21   Among the forms of direct discrimination which may be identified solely by reference to the criteria laid down by Article 119 must be included in particular those which have their origin in legislative provisions or in collective labor agreements and which may be detected on the basis of a purely legal analysis of the situation.

22   This applies even more in cases where men and women receive unequal pay for equal work carried out in the same establishment or service, whether public or private.

23   [I]n such a situation the court is in a position to establish all the facts which enable it to decide whether a woman worker is receiving lower pay than a male worker performing the same tasks.

24   In such [a] situation, at least, Article 119 is directly applicable and may thus give rise to individual rights which the courts must protect.

[The Court then rejected the argument that use of the term "principle" in Article 119 shows that the Article was to be considered only "a vague declaration." It held that, on the contrary, the term showed the "fundamental nature" of the provision. The Court further rejected an argument based on the fact that Article 119 only refers expressly to "Member States." The Court held that the direct effect of a provision is not excluded by the fact that it is formally addressed to the Member States, because such a circumstance "does not prevent rights from being conferred at the same time on any individual who has an interest in the performance of the duties thus laid down" (¶ 31).]

32   The very wording of Article 119 shows that it imposes on States a duty to bring about a specific result to be mandatorily achieved within a fixed period.

33   The effectiveness of this provision cannot be affected by the fact that the duty imposed by the Treaty has not been discharged by certain Member States and that the [Council and Commission] have not reacted sufficiently energetically against this failure to act.

34   To accept the contrary view ... would not be consistent with the task assigned to the Court by Article [220] of the Treaty [now TEU Article 19].

35   Finally, in its reference to "Member States", Article 119 is alluding to those States in the exercise of all those of their functions which may usefully contribute to the implementation of the principle of equal pay.

* * *

37   Therefore, the reference to "Member States" in Article 119 cannot be interpreted as excluding the intervention of the courts in direct application of the Treaty.

* * *

39   [S]ince Article 119 is mandatory in nature, the prohibition on discrimination between men and women applies not only to the action of public authorities, but also extends to all agreements which are intended to regulate paid labor collectively, as well as to contracts between individuals.

40   The reply to the first question must therefore be that the principle of equal pay contained in Article 119 may be relied upon before the national courts and that these courts have a duty to ensure the protection of the rights which this provision vests in individuals, in particular ... in cases in which men and women receive unequal pay for equal work which is carried out in the same establishment or service, whether private or public.

[However, "considerations of legal certainty affecting all the interests involved" caused the Court to hold that Article 119 should not be given direct effect retroactively in support of claims for periods of work prior to the date of the Court's judgment (except for claims that by then had already been filed).]

NOTES AND QUESTIONS

1. Since most of the Treaty provisions impose obligations on the Member States rather than on private parties, direct effect was initially conceived of as pertaining to legal claims directed against Member State authorities, thus having vertical direct effect. *Van Gend en Loos, Costa v. ENEL* and *Van Duyn* typify such claims. Defrenne, however, invoked Article 119 in support of

a claim for damages due to employment discrimination in a private law employment relationship. Even if Sabena might arguably have been considered a public entity, note that the Court in *Defrenne* deliberately extended the direct effect of the equal pay right in Article 119 to all establishments or services "whether public or private" (¶ 40). To the extent that Treaty articles are found to establish rights in private legal relationships, they are commonly described as having horizontal direct effect. As we will see later in Chapter 34, since *Defrenne,* Article 119 has regularly been applied horizontally to purely private sector employment relationships.

What if anything in the language of EEC Treaty Article 119 led the Court to give the provision horizontal direct effect? Few other provisions of the Treaty have been found by the Court to give rise to direct horizontal effect. The most prominent are the competition law Articles 81 and 82 (now TFEU Articles 101 and 102), forbidding private commercial agreements in restraint of trade and abuses by enterprises of a dominant position. Often a party to a contractual arrangement (e.g., a license or distribution agreement) has occasion to challenge a provision of the contract as a violation of Article 81. Thus, in Courage Ltd. v. Crehan, Case C–453/99, [2001] ECR I–6297, the Court observed that the "principle of automatic nullity [of anti-competitive contractual obligations under Article 81] can be relied on by everyone, and the courts are bound by it" (¶ 22). More generally, to the extent that private parties seek a direct remedy against others for anti-competitive conduct as urged by the Commission (see Chapter 20C infra), they make direct horizontal use of EU law.

In an important development, the Court has held that the prohibition of discrimination on the basis of nationality set forth in EC Treaty Article 39 (now TFEU Article 45) on the free movement of workers applies to discrimination by private parties as well, thus giving that aspect of Article 39 horizontal direct effect. See Angonese v. Cassa di Risparmio di Bolzano SpA, as excerpted at page 572 infra. Does the language of the Treaty article justify this result?

2.   In light of its requirement that Member States "ensure and subsequently maintain" the principle of equal pay for men and women, how could then EC Treaty Article 119 be said to be unconditional or not to require implementing legislation? In ¶¶ 31–37, the Court ruled that the fact that certain Member States had failed to implement Article 119 by the end of 1962, as required by the initial article text, and that the Council had to issue a 1975 directive on equal pay to promote compliance, did not detract from the Article's direct effect. What purpose does the equal pay directive serve after *Defrenne*? See Chapter 34B. Note that the Court in ¶ 34 cites its role under EC Treaty Article 220 (now TEU Article 19) to ensure that "the law" is observed as a justification for its holding that the right to equal pay is directly effective.

3.   The Court in *Defrenne* (¶¶ 18–24) confined the direct effect of Article 119 to cases of "direct" as opposed to "indirect" discrimination or, to be more precise, discrimination "which may be identified solely by reference to the criteria laid down by Article 119." Does this seem sound to you? In Chapter

34, we will see that the Court subsequently held that Article 119 could also be relied upon to prohibit indirect discrimination.

4. At the end of the judgment in *Defrenne*, the Court went on to rule (¶ 75) that Article 119 should not be given "retroactive" direct effect, that is, be applied to claims for pay periods prior to the date of judgment (except for claims that by then had already been filed). As we have already seen in Chapter 5, as a general rule the Court treats its judgments recognizing the direct effect of a Treaty article as applying retroactively. *Defrenne* is an exception to the rule. Is non-retroactivity consistent with the very notion of direct effect? Does ¶ 75's holding of non-retroactivity mean that Member State agencies and courts are actually *barred* from providing pay discrimination relief based on Article 119, or does it merely mean that Community law *does not require* them to give Article 119 direct effect to that extent?

B. THE DOCTRINE OF PRIMACY OF EU LAW

The fact that the Treaties and regulations are directly applicable and may have direct effect does not in itself tell us the rank that they occupy vis-à-vis domestic law within the national legal orders. EU law could have direct applicability and direct effect without necessarily trumping inconsistent Member State law. Unsurprisingly, the Court of Justice was not prepared to leave the question of primacy to chance. It has held, practically unreservedly, that the Treaties and any secondary legislation enacted pursuant to them prevail over any contrary provision of Member State law, and done so without the benefit of a Supremacy Clause such as Article VI of the US Constitution, declaring the Constitution, acts of Congress and treaties to take precedence over contrary state law.

The closest thing in the original EEC Treaty to a supremacy clause was Article 5 (subsequently renumbered as EC Treaty Article 10 by the Treaty of Amsterdam), which essentially declares that Member States have an obligation of loyalty to the Community:

> Member States shall take all appropriate measures, whether general or particular, to ensure fulfillment of the obligations arising out of this Treaty or resulting from action taken by the institutions of the Community. They shall facilitate the achievement of the Community's tasks. They shall abstain from any measure which could jeopardize the attainment of the objectives of this Treaty.

The Lisbon TEU retains the language of the former EC Article 10, incorporating it into TEU Article 4(3) as one of the basic principles of the Union, and adds to it a duty of "sincere cooperation" between the Union and the Member States.

Significantly, the Draft Treaty Establishing a Constitution for Europe did contain an express supremacy provision (albeit expressly limited to measures taken by the institutions within their scope of competence). But it was among the casualties of the Constitutional Treaty's defeat in national referenda. The drafters of the Lisbon Treaty chose to include no such text. On the other hand, Declaration No. 17 to the Treaty refers to a Council Legal Service opinion affirming that the absence of such a clause does not lessen the primacy of EU law, which remains a "cornerstone principle of Community law."

In the absence of any express affirmation in the Treaties, the question whether and to what extent Community law would prevail over conflicting Member State law was left to the Court of Justice itself.

COSTA v. ENTE NAZIONALE PER L'ENERGIA ELETTRICA (ENEL)

Case 6/64, [1964] ECR 585.

[For the facts of the case and part of the Court's judgment, see page 235 supra. As noted there, the Milan court had also referred the nationalization law to the Italian Constitutional Court for a ruling on its validity under the Italian Constitution. (Under Italian procedure, a court having doubts about the constitutionality of an Italian statute must refer the question to the Constitutional Court for an authoritative ruling. No other court may declare an Italian statute invalid.) The Italian Constitutional Court ruled that the EC Treaty ranked as a law in the Italian legal order because Italy had ratified it by a simple statute, and that the Treaty was therefore subordinate to any subsequent Italian legislation.

The Court of Justice was well aware of the Italian Constitutional Court ruling when it decided *Costa v. ENEL*. Advocate General Lagrange sharply criticized it as having "disastrous consequences [for] the very future of the Common Market" and as threatening to "undermine the very foundations of the Treaty." [1964] ECR at 605–06. He suggested that a State whose Constitution prevents national courts from giving immediate application to Community law over a conflicting domestic statute has "only two courses of action ...: either to amend its Constitution ... or to renounce the Treaty itself." Id. at 606. The opinion of the Court of Justice on the primacy question follows.]

> By contrast with ordinary international treaties, the [EC] Treaty has created its own legal system which, on the entry into force of the Treaty, became an integral part of the legal systems of the Member States and which their courts are bound to apply.
>
> By creating a Community of unlimited duration, having its own institutions, its own personality, its own legal capacity and capacity of representation on the international plane and, more particularly, real powers stemming from a limitation of sovereignty or a transfer of powers from the States to the Community, the Member States have limited their sovereign rights, albeit within limited fields, and have thus created a body of law which binds both their nationals and themselves.
>
> The integration into the laws of each Member State of provisions which derive from the Community, and more generally the terms and

the spirit of the Treaty, make it impossible for the States, as a corollary, to accord precedence to a unilateral and subsequent measure over a legal system accepted by them on a basis of reciprocity. Such a measure cannot therefore be inconsistent with that legal system. The executive force of Community law cannot vary from one State to another in deference to subsequent domestic laws, without jeopardizing the attainment of the objectives of the Treaty set out in [Article 10(2), now TEU Article 4(3)] and giving rise to the discrimination prohibited by [Article 12, now TFEU Article 18].

The obligations undertaken under the Treaty establishing the Community would not be unconditional, but merely contingent, if they could be called in question by subsequent legislative acts of the signatories [citing Treaty articles].... Applications by Member States for authority to derogate from the Treaty are subject to a special authorization procedure [citing other Treaty articles], which would lose its purpose if the Member States could renounce their obligations by means of an ordinary law.

The precedence of Community law is confirmed by [EC Treaty Article 249, now TFEU Article 288], whereby a regulation "shall be binding" and "directly applicable in all Member States". This provision, which is subject to no reservation, would be quite meaningless if a State could unilaterally nullify its effects by means of a legislative measure which could prevail over Community law.

It follows from all these observations that the law stemming from the Treaty, an independent source of law, could not, because of its special and original nature, be overridden by domestic legal provisions, however framed, without being deprived of its character as Community law and without the legal basis of the Community itself being called into question.

The transfer by the States from their domestic legal system to the Community legal system of the rights and obligations arising under the Treaty carries with it a permanent limitation of their sovereign rights, against which a subsequent unilateral act incompatible with the concept of the Community cannot prevail. Consequently [EC Treaty Article 234, now TFEU Article 267] is to be applied regardless of any domestic law, whenever questions relating to the interpretation of the Treaty arise.

[Having decided that Community law had primacy over conflicting Member State law, the Court turned to the question whether the relevant EC Treaty articles had direct effect in the national legal orders. For that discussion, see page 235 supra.]

NOTES AND QUESTIONS

1. The Italian Government initially urged the Court of Justice not to answer the questions put by the Milan judge because it considered them to be

improperly motivated by political opposition to the nationalization. The Court categorically refused to examine the judge's motives in making the reference, and its willingness to answer almost all questions that national courts refer to it is now a firm rule in preliminary reference proceedings. See Chapter 9.

2. Do you consider this portion of *Costa v. ENEL* to be justified in terms of "original intent" or is it an example of judicial activism comparable to early US Supreme Court assertions of federal power? In any event, do you agree with the Court as a matter of interpretation and policy? See M. Puder, Supremacy of the Law and Judicial Review in the European Union: Celebrating Marbury v. Madison with Costa v. ENEL, 36 Geo. Wash. Int'l. L. Rev. 567 (2004).

3. Upon receiving the Court's ruling in *Costa*, the Milan judge found the Italian nationalization to violate EC Treaty Article 31 (now TFEU Article 37) and the then Article 53 (a standstill provision prohibiting new restrictions on the right of establishment, since repealed). This decision was ultimately appealed to the Italian Supreme Court which held that Costa lacked standing to challenge the nationalization through an action contesting his electric bill! Thus the Italian litigation ended without a result on the merits.

4. The Italian Constitutional Court's views on the relationship between the EC Treaty and Italian legislation have evolved significantly since the early 1960s, as successive judgments have effectively recognized aspects of the primacy doctrine. For a discussion, see Chapter 8D infra.

5. *Costa* involved the relationship between EU law and national *legislation*. Recall that in 1970, in the case of *Internationale Handelsgesellschaft*, supra page 160, the Court directly addressed the question whether Community legislation also enjoys primacy over national *constitutional* norms, and held in ¶ 3 that it does. This was a momentous step for States accustomed to thinking of the national constitution as "the supreme law of the land."

C. EU LAW PRIMACY AND ITS COROLLARIES

AMMINISTRAZIONE DELLE FINANZE DELLO STATO v. SIMMENTHAL SpA

(Simmenthal II)
Case 106/77, [1978] ECR 629.

[Simmenthal, an Italian importer of beef from France, disputed charges imposed by the local authorities for veterinary and public health inspection of such beef. The local court asked the Court of Justice to decide whether the charges violated the principle of the free movement of goods as set out in EC Treaty Article 28 (now TFEU Article 34). The Court ruled in Simmenthal S.p.A. v. Italian Minister for Finance, Case 35/76, [1976] ECR 1871, that the charges indeed were invalid. When the national court then ordered the Italian Finance Ministry to repay the charges with interest, the Ministry appealed, arguing that an Italian statute had authorized the charges and that a national court could not, under longstanding Italian constitutional procedure, treat an Italian stat-

ute as invalid—and refuse to apply it—on account of its conflict with a
higher norm. Instead, the national court had to suspend proceedings and
refer the constitutional question to the Italian Constitutional Court,
resuming its proceedings only after receiving the Constitutional Court's
answer, which it would be bound to follow. (This mechanism was of course
a model for the EU's own preliminary preference procedure.) Accordingly,
only the Constitutional Court could invalidate an Italian statute and
authorize its non-application. The Italian judge then sought a further
ruling from the Court of Justice on the proper course to follow.]

14   Direct applicability ... means that rules of Community law must be
fully and uniformly applied in all the Member States from the date of
their entry into force and for so long as they continue in force.

15   These provisions are therefore a direct source of rights and duties for
all those affected thereby, whether Member States or individuals, who
are parties to legal relationships under Community law.

16   This consequence also concerns any national court whose task it is as
an organ of a Member State to protect, in a case within its jurisdiction,
the rights conferred upon individuals by Community law.

[The Court then clearly reiterated the principle of Community law primacy.]

18   [A]ny recognition that national legislative measures which encroach
upon the field within which the Community exercises its legislative
power or which are otherwise incompatible with the provisions of
Community law had any legal effect would amount to a corresponding
denial of the effectiveness of obligations undertaken unconditionally
and irrevocably by Member States pursuant to the Treaty and would
thus imperil the very foundations of the Community.

* * *

21   [E]very national court must, in a case within its jurisdiction, apply
Community law in its entirety and protect rights which the latter
confers on individuals and must accordingly set aside any provision of
national law which may conflict with it, whether prior or subsequent
to the Community rule.

22   Accordingly any provision of a national legal system and any legislative, administrative or judicial practice which might impair the effectiveness of Community law by withholding from the national court
having jurisdiction to apply such law the power to do everything
necessary at the moment of its application to set aside national
legislative provisions which might prevent Community rules from
having full force and effect are incompatible with those requirements
which are the very essence of Community law.

* * *

24   [Thus] a national court which is called upon, within the limits of its
jurisdiction, to apply provisions of Community law is under a duty to

give full effect to those provisions, if necessary refusing of its own motion to apply any conflicting provision of national legislation ... and it is not necessary for the court to request or await the prior setting aside of such provision by legislative or other constitutional means.

NOTES AND QUESTIONS

1. Note that the Ministry of Finance did not question the primacy of Community law as such, but only the method of enforcing the principle within Italy. Certainly Member State procedural rules do not normally fall within the province of the Court of Justice. Is it appropriate for the Court to insist that a Member State trial court apply EU law at once in preference to national legislation, without first seeking the judgment of the national Constitutional Court on whether the two are indeed in conflict? What factors may explain the Court of Justice's strictness? Concern over procedural delay? Concern over disparate treatment of litigation in the courts of different States? Concern that supreme or constitutional courts of a Member State might be less willing than lower courts to make preliminary references?

The Italian Constitutional Court ultimately accepted the position of the Court of Justice on the procedural question at issue in *Simmenthal II*. See the note on Italy, infra page 284.

2. *Simmenthal II* raises a more general question of the minimum procedural protection that Member State courts must make available to litigants who assert EU law-based claims. Put differently, it suggests that the primary principle may have important procedural corollaries. For a fuller discussion of *Simmenthal II's* implications in this regard, see Chapter 10A.

3. Recall the judgment in Masterfoods Ltd. v. HB Ice Cream Ltd, discussed at page 113 supra. The Court there held that, once the Commission had issued a decision condemning HB for a competition law violation in the form of a contractual restraint of trade, the Irish Supreme Court could not exercise its appellate jurisdiction to sustain a lower court judgment awarding HB contract damages for violation of the contract provision in question. Should this too be regarded as a simple application of the primacy principle?

4. The *Simmenthal* principle was extended in Larsy v. INASTI, Case C–118/00, [2001] ECR I–5063, and in Consorzio Industrie Fiammiferi v. Autorità Garante della Concorrenza e del Mercato, Case C–198/01, [2003] ECR I–8055, where the Court ruled that not only national courts but also national administrative agencies—namely, the national social insurance institution and the competition authority, respectively—had to decline to apply conflicting national legislation, without reference to the Italian Constitutional Court, in order to give effect to the primacy of EU law.

THE QUEEN v. SECRETARY OF STATE FOR TRANSPORT, EX PARTE FACTORTAME LTD.

(Factortame I)

Case C–213/89, [1990] ECR I–2433.

[In 1988, the UK amended its Merchant Shipping Act quite deliberately to prevent Spanish fishing interests from taking a share of the fishing quota allotted to the UK under the Common Fisheries Policy. The amendment effectively prevented Spanish-owned fishing vessels from being registered as UK vessels. (In order to prevent so called "quota hopping," even vessels owned by a UK company were to be deemed non-British if less than 75% of the company's shares were owned by persons resident and domiciled in the UK or if less than 75% of its directors were persons of that description.) A group of UK companies and their directors and shareholders brought suit challenging the 1988 amendment. All of the companies had a majority of Spanish directors and shareholders and the 95 UK registered vessels they owned were therefore ineligible under the amendment to fish against the UK quota.

The UK trial court thought it probable that the plaintiffs would prevail on the merits and issued an interim order suspending application of the 1988 Act as to the plaintiffs. The Court of Appeal reversed, holding that under UK constitutional tradition, a court may never enjoin an Act of Parliament.

The House of Lords found that the plaintiffs would suffer irreparable damage if interim relief were denied and they were ultimately to win the case, but it agreed that British law barred the relief sought. Because they thought that Community law might require a different result, the Law Lords referred questions to the Court of Justice asking whether national courts had the power or the obligation to grant interim relief against an Act of Parliament that might violate Community law.]

17   [T]he preliminary question raised by the House of Lords seeks essentially to ascertain whether a national court which, in a case before it concerning Community law, considers that the sole obstacle which precludes it from granting interim relief is a rule of national law must disapply that rule.

18   [In the *Simmenthal II* case, supra] the Court held that directly applicable rules of Community law "must be fully and uniformly applied in all the Member States from the date of their entry into force and for so long as they continue in force" and that ... "provisions of the Treaty and directly applicable measures of the institutions ... render automatically inapplicable any conflicting provision of ... national law."

19   In accordance with [this] case law of the Court, it is for the national courts, in application of the principle of co-operation laid down in [EC

Treaty Article 10, now TEU Article 4(3)] to ensure the legal protection which persons derive from the direct effect of provisions of Community law.

20   The Court has also held that any provision of a national legal system and any legislative, administrative or judicial practice which might impair the effectiveness of Community law by withholding from the national court having jurisdiction to apply such law the power to do everything necessary at the moment of its application to set aside national legislative provisions which might prevent, even temporarily, Community rules from having full force and effect are incompatible with those requirements, which are the very essence of Community law.

21   [T]he full effectiveness of Community law would be just as much impaired if a rule of national law could prevent a court seized of a dispute governed by Community law from granting interim relief in order to ensure the full effectiveness of the judgment to be given on the existence of the rights claimed under Community law. It follows that a court which in those circumstances would grant interim relief, if it were not for a rule of national law, is obliged to set aside that rule.

22   That interpretation is reinforced by the system established by [EC Treaty Article 234, now TFEU Article 267] whose effectiveness would be impaired if a national court, having stayed proceedings pending the reply by the Court of Justice to the question referred to it for a preliminary ruling, were not able to grant interim relief until it delivered its judgment following the reply given by the Court of Justice.

23   Consequently ... Community law must be interpreted as meaning that a national court which, in a case before it concerning Community law, considers that the sole obstacle which precludes it from granting interim relief is a rule of national law must set aside that rule.

NOTES AND QUESTIONS

1. Do you think the Court gave sufficient consideration to the weight of the British constitutional tradition at stake? Note that the Court did not even mention the UK's constitutional tradition that courts may not enjoin acts of Parliament. Instead, in ¶¶ 20–23, the Court essentially treated the issue as if it were merely one of civil procedure.

2. The House of Lords accepted the Court's answer and granted the interim injunction. Regina v. Secretary of State for Transport ex parte Factortame, [1991] 1 All ER 70, [1990] 3 CMLR 375 (Oct. 11, 1990). For Lord Bridge's forceful acceptance of the primacy doctrine, see page 315 infra.

3. The trial court in *Factortame* had also referred questions to the Court of Justice, but they were on the merits. The Court of Justice gave its answers to those questions a year after issuing its judgment above. The Court held that the 1988 amendment at issue in the principal case violated EC Treaty

Article 43 (now TFEU Article 49) in so far as it required direct or indirect owners of British-registered fishing vessels to be either UK citizens or resident in the UK. See The Queen v. Secretary of State for Transport, ex parte Factortame (Factortame II), excerpted at page 707 infra. The Spanish fishing vessel owners subsequently sought damages from the UK, which occasioned another notable decision by the Court. See *Brasserie du Pecheur*, page 374 infra.

Like direct applicability and direct effect, the primacy principle is addressed not only to national courts, but also to the legislative and executive arms of the Member States. The emphasis on judicial enforcement of the principle simply reflects the fact that Member State courts are the legal arenas in which battles of this sort are authoritatively resolved.

The obligation to give precedence to EU law is sweeping. It does not matter whether a national law precedes or follows the EU law with which it conflicts. It does not matter where in their respective legal hierarchies the national and EU law provisions are situated. (In principle, according to the Court, a mere Commission decision trumps a provision of a national constitution.) In the event of conflict, the EU law norms always prevail. See Rewe v. Hauptzollamt Kiel, Case 158/80, [1981] ECR 1805. As we shall see in Chapter 11, the responsibility of Member State governments for violations of EU law is not lessened by virtue of the fact that it might be the national legislature rather than the national government or courts, or a regional or local government rather than the central government, that committed the violation, and that they alone may be constitutionally able to remedy the situation.

The Court of Justice's uncompromising assertion of the primacy of EU law can only be fully understood in light of its attachment to legal certainty and uniformity. In the Court's view, unless EU law at all times prevails throughout the Member States, EU law's effectiveness and integrity will be at risk. This belief has led the Court of Justice to perhaps a still more fundamental claim, namely that *the Court itself* determines the legal relationship between EU and national law, and draws the specific procedural and substantive consequences. Decisions of the Court from *Van Gend en Loos* and *Costa v. ENEL* down through *Simmenthal II* and *Factortame* amply illustrate this. Evidently, even longstanding constitutional traditions in the Member States will not be allowed to stand in the way.

The only basis, consistent with this view, upon which a Member State court might plausibly claim the right to withhold application of a rule of EU law is that the latter itself violates a higher EU law norm. One might argue that the very logic that mandates giving direct effect and primacy to EU law within the national legal orders also dictates that Member State courts prefer higher over lower EU law norms where the two are themselves in conflict. However, that raises the issue of the extent to which, if at all, a national court can assert the power to invalidate an EU law measure, however lowly in the EU law hierarchy of norms. The following decision by the Court of Justice decisively addresses that issue.

FIRMA FOTO–FROST v. HAUPTZOLLAMT LUBECK–OST

Case 314/85, [1987] ECR 4199.

[Foto–Frost raised a challenge in German court to a Commission decision denying it a "post clearance recovery of duties" under an EU customs regulation. Foto–Frost maintained that it satisfied all the conditions that the regulation laid down for the recovery of duty and that the Commission should have granted the request. The German court asked the Court of Justice whether it had competence to declare the Commission decision invalid as contrary to the EU regulation.]

14   [National] courts may consider the validity of a Community act and, if they consider that the grounds put forward before them by the parties in support of invalidity are unfounded, they may reject them, concluding that the measure is completely valid. By taking that action they are not calling into question the existence of the Community measure.

15   On the other hand, those courts do not have the power to declare acts of the Community institutions invalid. . . . [T]he main purpose of the powers accorded to the Court by [EC Treaty Article 234, now TFEU Article 267] is to ensure that Community law is applied uniformly by national courts. That requirement of uniformity is particularly imperative when the validity of a Community act is in question. Divergences between courts in the Member States as to the validity of Community acts would be liable to place in jeopardy the very unity of the Community legal order and detract from the fundamental requirement of legal certainty.

16   The same conclusion is dictated by consideration of the necessary coherence of the system of judicial protection established by the Treaty. In that regard it must be observed that requests for preliminary rulings, like actions for annulment, constitute means for reviewing the legality of acts of the Community institutions. . . .

17   Since [EC Treaty Article 230, now TFEU Article 263] gives the Court exclusive jurisdiction to declare void an act of a Community institution, the coherence of the system requires that where the validity of a Community act is challenged before a national court the power to declare the act invalid must also be reserved to the Court of Justice.

18   It must also be emphasized that the Court of Justice is in the best position to decide on the validity of Community acts. Under Article [23] of the Protocol on the Statute of the Court of Justice, Community institutions whose acts are challenged are entitled to participate in the proceedings in order to defend the validity of the acts in question. Furthermore, under the second paragraph of Article [24] of that Protocol, the Court may require the Member States and institutions which are not participating in the proceedings to supply all information which it considers necessary for the purposes of the case before it.

19 It should be added that the rule that national courts may not themselves declare Community acts invalid may have to be qualified in certain circumstances in the case of proceedings relating to an application for interim measures; however, that case is not referred to in the national court's question.

20 The answer to the ... question must therefore be that the national courts have no jurisdiction themselves to declare that acts of Community institutions are invalid.

NOTES AND QUESTIONS

1. *Foto–Frost* holds that national courts may not purport to invalidate EU law measures even on account of their conflict with higher EU law. Does it follow that they also may not withhold application of such measures on account of their invalidity? May a national court, in referring a question of validity to the Court of Justice at least state its view that a particular EU law measure is invalid?

2. The Court in *Foto–Frost* expressly observed that a national court may reject a party's challenge to the validity of an EU law measure and uphold the measure's validity, because in so doing it is "not calling the existence of the Community measure into question" (¶ 14). Do you find this convincing? Do you believe it to be sound policy?

3. As we shall see in Chapter 8, winning assent to the proposition that only the Court of Justice may invalidate an EU law measure required a belief on the part of the Member States (and particularly their constitutional courts) that the Court of Justice would in fact enforce certain fundamental "constitutional" claims against the institutions. The Court went a long way toward securing that belief through its case law on the general principles of law and on basic rights (including the *Internationale Handelsgesellschaft, Nold* and *Hauer* judgments) treated in Chapter 6 supra.

4. Suppose, following *Foto–Frost,* a national court refers a question to the Court of Justice on the validity of an EU law measure, but is asked to award interim relief suspending the measure's application (the question left open in ¶ 19 of the judgment). Is a national court free to do so? For discussion of what has become a complex area of Community law, see Chapter 9G infra.

NOTE ON PRIMACY AND THE "ABUSE OF RIGHTS" DOCTRINE

Most civil law jurisdictions recognize a general "abuse of rights" principle, whereby the exercise of a right (even a clearly recognized legal right) is not permitted when it is exercised under circumstances that render it "abusive," as that term is defined in the relevant jurisdiction. Article 281 of the Greek Civil Code, for example, declares that "the exercise of a right is prohibited where it manifestly exceeds the bounds of good faith or morality or the economic or social purpose of that right." In the *Pafitis* case, discussed in another context at page 270 supra, a Greek court wondered whether the exercise of a right conferred by Community law—in that case, the right of shareholders under an EU law directive to vote upon a proposed increase in company capital—could be limited by Article 281.

What do you think the Court's response should and would be? In fact, the Court avoided deciding the question because it found that the exercise of the right in question could not, in any event, be considered abusive. The Court was nevertheless quite dubious about the application of national "abuse of rights" principles:

68 [A]s to whether it is permissible, under the Community legal order, to apply a national rule in determining whether a right conferred by the provisions of Community law at issue is being exercised abusively, the fact remains that, in any event, the application of such a rule must not detract from the full effect and uniform application of Community law in the Member States.

69 It must be borne in mind ... that it is for the Court of Justice, in relation to rights relied on by an individual on the basis of Community provisions, to verify whether the judicial protection available under national law is appropriate.

This is not to say that the Court is insensitive to allegations of the abuse of EU law rights, as indicated in the following case.

BRENNET AG v. PALETTA

Case C–206/94, [1996] ECR I–2357.

[Italian migrant workers, resident and working in Germany, sought disability payments from their German employer, Brennet, on account of their incapacity to work. Brennet, suspicious of the Italian certificates of disability furnished by the workers, refused to pay. When a German labour court ordered Brennet to pay, the latter appealed. The case reached the German Supreme Labour Court, which sought guidance on what national authorities are permitted to do in the event of a suspected abuse of Community law rights. The Court of Justice had this to say:]

24 As to whether the national courts may, where there has been an abuse by the worker concerned, query the certification of incapacity for work ..., the Court has consistently held that Community law cannot be relied on for the purposes of abuse or fraud [citing various judgments of the Court limiting claims of the free movement of goods, persons and services].

25 Although the national courts may, therefore, take account—on the basis of objective evidence—of abuse or fraudulent conduct on the part of the worker concerned in order, where appropriate, to deny him the benefit of the provisions of Community law on which he seeks to rely, they must nevertheless assess such conduct in the light of the objectives pursued by those provisions.

26 However, the [German] case-law referred to by the Supreme Labour Court, according to which the worker must produce additional evi-

dence that the medically certified incapacity for work is genuine, in cases where the employer argues on the basis of adequate supporting evidence that there are serious grounds for doubting the existence of the alleged incapacity, is not compatible with the objectives pursued by [Community legislation]. A worker whose incapacity for work arises in a Member State other than the competent Member State would, as a result, be confronted with difficulties involved in obtaining evidence which the Community rules in fact seek to eliminate.

27 On the other hand, that provision does not preclude employers from adducing evidence to support, where appropriate, a finding by the national court of abuse or fraudulent conduct on the part of the worker concerned, in that, although he may claim to have become incapacitated for work, such incapacity having been certified in accordance with the Community legislation, he was not sick at all.

Does this mean that there is an EU law "abuse of rights" doctrine? If so, how would you formulate it? Consider the express "abuse of rights" provision (art. 54) of the Charter of Fundamental Rights, quoted at page 210 supra.

Even in the absence of a full-fledged EU law abuse of rights doctrine, the rule that national law must not impair the full effect and uniform application of EU law gives the Court of Justice an opportunity to police application of the domestic law abuse of rights notion by national courts. A good example is Kefalas v. Greece, Case C–367/96, [1998] ECR I–2843, where a Greek court wondered whether a shareholder "abuses" the Second Company Law directive at issue in the *Pafitis* case, supra, by voting against a capital increase that was adopted and actually improved the company's economic situation, or by declining to exercise his preemptive, or preferential, right to acquire new shares.

The Court took the occasion to interpret the purposes of the directive so as to preclude the national court from treating the shareholder's claim as abusive. It held squarely that "a shareholder cannot be deemed to be abusing the right ... merely because the increase in capital contested by him has resolved the financial difficulties threatening the existence of the company concerned and has clearly enured to his economic benefit or because he has not exercised his preferential right ... to acquire new shares issued [up]on the increase in capital." It explained that although the "very nature" of a capital increase is to improve a company's financial situation, a shareholder's decision not to exercise his preferential rights to subscribe to the capital increase merely reflected the shareholder's disagreement with the increase, which he is entitled to express.

Should the Court not just go ahead and declare that EU law-based claims are subject exclusively to an EU law abuse of rights analysis?

D. THE DIRECT EFFECT OF EC DIRECTIVES AND DECISIONS

The question whether directives could be capable of having direct effect in the national legal orders was a problematic one. EC Treaty Article 249 stated that "the national authorities [have] the choice of form and methods" by which directives are implemented, which clearly implies that States must adopt legal acts in order to make them effective in the national legal order. (Note that the Lisbon TFEU Article 288 on Union legislation largely replicates ECT Article 249, making no change in the description of the nature of directives.)

Nonetheless, there is no doubt that attributing direct effect to directives would enhance the overall effectiveness of EU law, especially as the Council and Parliament customarily use directives as the vehicle for harmonizing national laws to achieve the internal market under EC Treaty Article 95 (now TFEU Article 114) (see Chapter 14B). Therefore, the question arises whether certain provisions of directives could properly be given direct effect and whether such effect, if given, might run horizontally as well as vertically.

It is important to note at the outset that the Court does not have to hold that an entire directive has direct effect, i.e., constitutes a disguised regulation. It can decide that the language used in certain articles, or parts of articles, of directives appropriately receive direct legal effect, even if other parts do not.

The following cases laid the foundations for treating provisions of directives as capable of having vertical direct effect in the national legal order, notwithstanding the language of EC Treaty Article 249. Note that the Court had no difficulty in reconciling the original criteria for direct effect—precision, unconditionality, the absence of Member State discretion, and the absence of a need for implementing measures—with the particular nature of directives.

1. VERTICAL DIRECT EFFECT

VAN DUYN v. HOME OFFICE

Case 41/74, [1974] ECR 1337.

[For the facts of the case and the Court's judgment establishing the direct effect of EC Treaty Article 39 (now TFEU, Article 45), see page 238 supra. The English High Court also asked the Court of Justice whether Article 3(1) of Directive 64/221, which sets out substantive and procedural rules elaborating upon the public policy, public security and public health exception to the free movement of workers contained in Article 39 (see Chapter 15 infra), was directly effective.]

[10] [T]he only provision of the Directive which is relevant is ... Article 3(1) which provides that "measures taken on grounds of public policy

or public security shall be based exclusively on the personal conduct of the individual concerned."

11   The United Kingdom observes that, since [EC Treaty Article 249, now TFEU Article 288] distinguishes between the effects ascribed to regulations, directives and decisions, it must therefore be presumed that the Council, in issuing a directive rather than making a regulation, must have intended that the directive should have an effect other than that of a regulation and accordingly that the former should not be directly applicable.

12   If, however, by virtue of the provisions of Article [249] regulations are directly applicable and, consequently, may by their very nature have direct effects, it does not follow from this that other categories of acts mentioned in that Article can never have similar effects. It would be incompatible with the binding effect attributed to a directive by Article [249] to exclude, in principle, the possibility that the obligation which it imposes may be invoked by those concerned. In particular, where the Community authorities have, by directive, imposed on Member States the obligation to pursue a particular course of conduct, the useful effect [*l'effet utile*] of such an act would be weakened if individuals were prevented from relying on it before their national courts and if the latter were prevented from taking it into consideration as an element of Community law. [EC Treaty Article 234, now TFEU Article 267], which empowers national courts to refer to the Court questions concerning the validity and interpretation of all acts of the Community institutions, without distinction, implies furthermore that these acts may be invoked by individuals in the national courts. It is necessary to examine, in every case, whether the nature, general scheme and wording of the provision in question are capable of having direct effects on the relations between Member States and individuals.

13   By providing that measures taken on grounds of public policy shall be based exclusively on the personal conduct of the individual concerned, Article 3(1) of Directive No. 64/221 is intended to limit the discretionary power which national laws generally confer on the authorities responsible for the entry and expulsion of foreign nationals. First, the provision lays down an obligation which is not subject to any exception or condition and which, by its very nature, does not require the intervention of any act on the part either of the institutions of the Community or of Member States. Secondly, because Member States are thereby obliged, in implementing a clause which derogates from one of the fundamental principles of the Treaty in favor of individuals, not to take account of factors extraneous to personal conduct, legal certainty for the persons concerned requires that they should be able to rely on this obligation even though it has been laid down in a legislative act which has no automatic direct effect in its entirety.

[14] If the meaning and exact scope of the provision raise questions of interpretation, these questions can be resolved by the courts, taking into account also the procedure under Article [234] of the Treaty.

[On the merits, the court gave an interpretation of Article 39 and Directive 64/221 that allowed the UK to exclude Van Duyn from entry on public policy grounds. *See* Chapter 15D infra.]

NOTES AND QUESTIONS

1. Note that the Court in ¶ 13 uses the same formula to determine whether Article 3(1) of the directive has direct effect that it used in deciding whether a Treaty Article has direct effect. Also note that the Court only holds that Article 3(1), a part of one article of the directive, has direct effect, not the entire directive.

2. How can the Court find that Directive 64/221 contains a provision precise enough to have direct effect if it believes (¶ 14) that Member State courts may have such doubts about the provision's meaning as to need preliminary rulings from the Court of Justice? Should the Court's ability to give guidance to national courts, referred to in ¶ 14, always enable vague provisions in directives to have direct effect?

3. The Court strongly reaffirmed its position on the direct effect of directives in Becker v. Finanzamt Münster–Innenstadt, Case 8/81, [1982] ECR 53. Becker, a self-employed credit negotiator, claimed an exemption from certain "turnover" taxes on income she received from March to June 1979 in the form of commissions, basing the exemption on a May 1977 Council directive (the Sixth Value Added Tax Directive) which required the Member States by January 1, 1979 to exempt from turnover taxation all income earned from credit negotiation. However, since Germany had not yet implemented the directive (and in fact did not do so until January 1, 1980), the German tax law contained no exemption on which Becker could rely, and the authorities accordingly assessed a turnover tax on her commission income for the period in question. The German tax court to which Becker appealed asked the Court of Justice whether the provision of the directive granting the tax exemption was "directly applicable" in Germany. Echoing *Van Duyn,* the Court of Justice held:

> [W]herever the provisions of a directive appear . . . to be unconditional and sufficiently precise, those provisions may, in the absence of implementing measures adopted within the prescribed period, be relied upon as against any national provision which is incompatible with the directive. . . . [1982] ECR at 71.

In a similar case several years later, the Supreme Tax Court of Germany refused to follow the *Becker* decision and continued to deny direct effect to the Sixth VAT Directive. For discussion of that judgment (*Kloppenburg*) and the German Constitutional Court's disapproval of it, see page 283 infra.

4. In Comitato di Coordinamento per la Difesa della Cava v. Regione Lombardia, Case C–236/92, [1994] ECR I–483, the Court held that Council Directive 75/442 on the prevention, recycling and processing of waste lacks

direct effect, and that individuals may not therefore rely on any of its provisions to challenge the region's approval of a solid urban waste facility as abridging their rights to protection of the environment. It interpreted the directive as establishing a framework for action to be taken by the Member States on waste treatment, and not as in itself requiring the adoption of specific measures or the adoption of a particular waste disposal method. Is the Court looking so much at statutory language in making this determination as looking at legislative intent? Many environmental protection directives take the form of "framework" directives and, by this reasoning, also ordinarily lack direct effect. However, if an environmental directive contains a provision setting out a specific obligation, such as carrying out an environmental impact assessment prior to taking action that affects the environment, then that provision may have direct effect. See World Wildlife Fund v. Autonome Provinz Bozen, Case C–435/ 97, (1999) ECR I–5613.

5. The case of Marks & Spencer v. Customs and Excise Commissioners, Case C–62/00, [2002] ECR I–6325, adds a new dimension to the direct effect of provisions of directives. Marks & Spencer sued the UK tax authorities for a refund of value-added tax which had been erroneously paid. After the English Court of Appeal requested a preliminary ruling on how sums unduly paid should be refunded, the Court held that, even though a directive has been correctly transposed into a national legal system, EU law continues to provide individuals with rights directly derived from a directive. In this case, the UK had transposed the directive correctly, but arguably the UK legislation had been incorrectly applied. The Court held that:

27 [T]he adoption of national measures correctly implementing a directive does not exhaust the effects of the directive. Member States remain bound actually to ensure full application of the directive even after the adoption of those measures. Individuals are therefore entitled to rely before national courts, against the State, on the provisions of a directive which [are] unconditional and sufficiently precise whenever the full application of the directive is not in fact secured, that is to say, not only where the directive has not been implemented or has been implemented incorrectly, but also where the national measures correctly implementing the directive are not being applied in such a way as to achieve the result sought by it.

In other words, directives need to be properly applied as well as properly transposed.

PUBBLICO MINISTERO v. RATTI

Case 148/78, [1979] ECR 1629.

[An Italian solvent and varnish manufacturer, represented by Ratti, decided to package and label its products in accordance with two Community law directives, 73/173 (on solvents) and 77/728 (on varnishes), even though the directives had not yet been implemented in Italy. Ratti was prosecuted for not including labeling information that was required by the Italian law then in force, but not required under the directives. At the time the goods were marketed, Italy's deadline for implementing Directive 73/173 on solvents had passed, but the deadline for implementing Directive 77/728 on varnishes had not. Ratti raised the directives in his defense, and the Criminal Court of Milan asked the Court of Justice several questions about the enforceability of the penalties prescribed by Italian law.]

A. The Interpretation of Directive No. 73/173

[The Court repeated its language in *Van Duyn* and *Becker* on the capacity of directive provisions to have direct effect.]

[22] Consequently a Member State which has not adopted the implementing measures required by the directive in the prescribed periods may not rely, as against individuals, on its own failure to perform the obligations which the directive entails.

* * *

[24] Therefore the answer to the first question must be that after the expiration of the period fixed for the implementation of a directive, a Member State may not apply its internal law—even if it is provided with penal sanctions—which has not yet been adapted in compliance with the directive, to a person who has complied with the requirements of the directive.

[The Court then found that the labeling provisions of the 1973 solvents directive preempted the Italian law. This aspect of the case is treated at page 542 infra.]

B. The Interpretation of Directive No. 77/728

[39] [T]he national court asks whether Council Directive No. 77/728 [on varnishes] . . . is immediately and directly applicable with regard to the obligations imposed on Member States to refrain from action as from the date of notification of that directive in a case where a person, acting upon a legitimate expectation, has complied with the provisions of that directive before the expiry of the period within which the Member State must comply with the said directive.

* * *

[41] Article 12 of that directive provides that Member States must implement it within 24 months of its notification, which took place on 9 November 1977.

[42] That period has not yet expired and the States to which the directive was addressed have until 9 November 1979 to incorporate the provisions of Directive No. 77/728 into their internal legal orders.

[43] It follows that, for the reasons expounded in the grounds of the answer to the national court's first question, it is only at the end of the prescribed period and in the event of the Member State's default that the directive . . . will be able to have the effects described in the answer to the first question.

44   Until that date is reached the Member States remain free in that field.

* * *

46   In conclusion, since a directive by its nature imposes obligations only on Member States, it is not possible for an individual to plead the principle of "legitimate expectation" before the expiry of the period prescribed for its implementation.

47   Therefore the answer to the [present] question must be that Directive No. 77/728 . . . cannot bring about with respect to any individual who has complied with the provisions of the said directive before the expiration of the adaptation period prescribed for the Member State any effect capable of being taken into consideration by national courts.

NOTES AND QUESTIONS

1.   The Court in *Ratti* (¶ 46) concluded that it was "not possible" for a person to avoid criminal liability under Member State law by invoking the Community directive on varnishes, since Italy still had time to implement it. Does this mean that Italy was actually *barred* from exempting Ratti from liability in this case, or was simply *not required* to exempt him from such liability? Which would be the better rule? Note that the Court also rejected the defendant's claim that it had relied on the doctrine of 'legitimate expectations,' discussed in Chapter 5C supra. Why do you suppose the doctrine does not apply here?

2.   Criminal charges were brought against a restaurant in Arnhem, the Netherlands, for offering for sale a beverage that it called mineral water but that was in fact only carbonated tap water. The charges were brought under a municipal ordinance that prohibited marketing for human consumption goods of unsound composition. The prosecution cited a Council directive requiring the Member States to take the measures necessary to ensure that only certified natural mineral waters were marketed as such, but that the Dutch government at the time of the events in question was overdue in implementing.

May a criminal charge be based on the Council directive under the principle of direct effect? The Court held that it could not. See Criminal Proceedings against Kolpinghuis Nijmegen, Case 80/86, [1987] ECR 3969, where the Court specifically held that "a directive cannot" of itself and independently of a law adopted for its implementation, have the effect of determining or aggravating the liability in criminal law of persons who act in contravention of the provisions of that directive." The Court cited the "principles of legal certainty and non-retroactivity" as justifying this conclusion. See Chapter 4C supra. To the same effect, see Criminal Proceedings against Niselli, Case C–457/02, [2004] ECR I–10853. Do you see the logic and policy behind this rule? Would you extend the rule to non-criminal (i.e. civil) actions by the government against private parties, at least if they impose fines or other penalties?

3.   In Inter–Environnement Wallonie ASBL v. Region Wallonne, Case C–129/96, [1997] ECR I–7411, the Walloon regional executive issued an order on

hazardous waste that allegedly violated an unimplemented directive whose period for transposition had not fully elapsed at the time the Walloon order was issued. In answer to a question put by the Belgian Conseil d'Etat, which was hearing a legal challenge to the order, the Court of Justice ruled that, as of the time a directive is adopted—and throughout the period set for implementation by the States—Member States are precluded from adopting any national measures contrary to that directive.

According to the Court, a directive has legal effect vis-à-vis the Member States from the moment it is addressed to them, which means that during the implementation period States must take the measures necessary to ensure that the prescribed result is achieved by the end of that period. (The Court derived this conclusion from EC Treaty Articles 249 and 251 (now TFEU Articles 288 and 294) in conjunction with EC Treaty Article 10 (now TEU Article 4(3)). The Court accepted that a State could take implementing action in stages rather than all at once (¶ 49). But the introduction during the implementation period of any measure that might seriously compromise a State's ability to achieve the intended result by the appointed time would be inconsistent with its obligations. (For a recent affirmation of the point, see the case of Mangold v. Helm, excerpted at page 206 supra).

4. Are Commission and Council *decisions* addressed to Member States also capable of having direct effect so as to give rise to privately enforceable rights? Decisions, like regulations, are directly applicable, but EC Treaty Article 249 (now TFEU Article 288) provides that they can be binding only on those to whom they are addressed (whether they be Member States, legal entities, or individuals).

The question arose in the case of Grad v. Finanzamt Traunstein, Case 9/70, [1970] ECR 825, where the Court held that certain decisions can be directly effective, providing they fulfill the *Van Gend en Loos* criteria. Grad, a long-distance hauler based in Austria, refused to pay a German tax for long distance travel on German roads, claiming that the tax violated a 1965 Council decision requiring the Member States to introduce a value added tax by January 1, 1972, and barring them after that point from collecting any other turnover taxes on imports or exports between Member States. Germany enacted its value added tax on January 1, 1968, but the next year introduced the long-distance travel tax contested by Grad. The Court ruled as follows:

5   It would be incompatible with the binding effect attributed to decisions by [Article 249, now TFEU Article 288] to exclude in principle the possibility that persons [not as such addressed by a decision but nevertheless] affected may invoke the obligation imposed by [the] decision.... [T]he effectiveness (*"l'effet utile"*) of [a Community decision imposing an obligation on a Member State] would be weakened if the nationals of that State could not invoke it in the courts and the national courts could not take it into consideration as part of Community law.... [I]n each particular case, it must be ascertained whether the nature, background and wording of the provision in question are capable of producing direct effects in the legal relationships between the addressee of the act and third parties.

In *Grad,* the decision was not only addressed to Member States, but also bore some resemblance to a regulation.

2. HORIZONTAL DIRECT EFFECT
OF DIRECTIVES

Giving vertical direct effect to unimplemented directives was a bold move, given the fact that the Treaty drafters evidently did not even view directives as directly applicable, as earlier defined. The move could be justified, as the *Ratti* judgment suggests, not only by the notion of *effet utile*, but also by the precept that a State should not be permitted to benefit from its own legal failings. Giving directives horizontal direct effect was more problematic, and the Court of Justice clearly had reservations about doing so, as shown by the case of Marshall v. Southampton and South–West Hampshire Area Health Authority, Case 152/84, [1986] ECR 723.

Marshall was employed by a UK regional Health Authority from June 1966 until March 1980, when she was dismissed solely because she had passed the compulsory retirement age (60) that the Health Authority applied to women. Because the Authority's retirement age for men was 65, Marshall claimed that she was the victim of sex discrimination in violation of Directive 76/207 on equal work conditions for men and women. The Employment Appeal Tribunal found that the UK had simply not adequately implemented the directive and that the directive itself, having effectively remained unimplemented, could not be relied on in national court. The Court stated clearly that an unimplemented directive could not be invoked against a private party.

48   ... [A]ccording to [EC Treaty Article 249, now TFEU Article 288], the binding nature of a directive, which constitutes the basis for the possibility of relying on the directive before a national court, exists only in relation to "each Member State to which it is addressed". It follows that a directive may not of itself impose obligations on an individual and that a provision of a directive may not be relied upon as such against such a person....

Fortunately for Marshall, however, the Court treated the situation as vertical rather than horizontal, on account of her employer being the State:

49   [W]here a person involved in legal proceedings is able to rely on a directive as against the State he may do so regardless of the capacity in which the latter is acting, whether employer or public authority. In either case it is necessary to prevent the State from taking advantage of its own failure to comply with Community law.

The Court was not impressed by the UK's argument (¶ 51) that to treat the employment relationship as a vertical one "would give rise to an arbitrary and unfair distinction between the rights of State employees and those of private employees." Such discrimination, the Court said, could easily be avoided if the Member State concerned correctly implemented the directive in national law.

The result in *Marshall* incidentally raised an interesting choice of law issue. Is the question whether an entity is an instrumentality of the State or other public authority, as opposed to being merely a state-owned commercial entity (hence, private), to be determined by reference to EU or national law rules? Given the great disparity between the classification of state-owned enterprises in Member States, this was a question of some importance. In Foster v. British Gas, Case C–188/89 [1990] ECR I–3313, the Court opted for an EU definition, holding that a State agency or entity that provides "a public service under the control of the State" is deemed to be a public authority for this purpose, but that holding left the status of state-owned commercial enterprises (e.g. railroads or airlines) in some doubt. On that basis, the House of Lords then concluded that British Gas was a public entity against which the directive could be given direct effect. [1991] 2 WLR 1075, [1991] 2 CMLR 217 (H.L., April 18, 1991).

MARLEASING v. LA COMERCIAL INTERNACIONAL DE ALIMENTACION

Case C–106/89, [1990] ECR I–4135.

[Marleasing sued La Comercial in a Spanish court to have declared null and void the articles of incorporation of La Commercial on the ground that they lacked "cause" (a requirement for a contract's validity under the Spanish Civil Code) and also had been procured through misrepresentation and fraud. Specifically, Marleasing claimed that La Commercial had been formed by a third company, Barviesa, for the sole purpose of placing Barviesa's assets beyond the reach of its creditors, one of whom was Marleasing. All three companies were incorporated in Spain.

Under Spanish law, misrepresentation or fraud ordinarily would justify a court in declaring such a contract null, but La Commercial claimed that the availability of relief was governed by the company law rules set out in Council Directive 68/151 (the First Company Law Directive, described at page 717 infra). Article 11 of Directive 68/151 provided that companies could be declared null and void only for the specific reasons set out in that article. The unlawfulness of the corporate purposes or their violation of public policy were included among the listed reasons, but not fraud or misrepresentation toward the creditors of the founding shareholders. However, at the time in question, implementation of the directive in Spain had yet to occur and was in fact overdue. The Spanish court asked the Court of Justice whether it could nullify La Comercial's incorporation for reasons other than those mentioned in Article 11 of the Directive.]

6   [A]s the Court has consistently held, a directive may not of itself impose obligations on an individual and, consequently, a provision of a directive may not be relied upon as such against such a person [citing *Marshall*].

7   However, it is apparent ... that the national court seeks in substance to ascertain whether a national court hearing a case which falls within

the scope of Directive 68/151 is required to interpret its national law in the light of the wording and the purpose of that directive in order to preclude a declaration of nullity of a public limited company on a ground other than those listed in Article 11 of the directive.

8   [T]he Member States' obligation arising from a directive to achieve the result envisaged by the directive and their duty under [EC Treaty Article 10, now TEU Article 4(3)] to take all appropriate measures, whether general or particular, to ensure the fulfillment of that obligation, is binding on all the authorities of Member States including, for matters within their jurisdiction, the courts. It follows that, in applying national law, whether the provisions in question were adopted before or after the directive, the national court called upon to interpret it is required to do so, as far as possible, in the light of the wording and the purpose of the directive in order to achieve the result pursued by the latter and thereby comply with the third paragraph of Article [249] of the Treaty.

9   [Accordingly,] Article 11 of Directive 68/151 precludes the interpretation of provisions of national law relating to public limited companies in such a manner that the nullity of a public limited company may be ordered on grounds other than those exhaustively listed in Article 11 of the directive in question.

Notes and Questions

1. *Marleasing* requires Member State courts to interpret national legislation in a way that renders it consistent with EU directives even if those directives have not been implemented. Professor Paul Craig calls what the Court requires in *Marleasing* "indirect effect." P. Craig, Directives: Direct Effect, Indirect Effect, 22 Eur. L. Rev. 519 (1997). In *Marleasing*, the time period for Spain's implementation had ended. Suppose it had not yet fully lapsed. Should national courts in that period likewise be bound by *Marleasing*'s interpretive obligations? The Court has ruled that they are bound. Criminal Proceedings against Kolpinghuis Nijmegen BV, Case 80/86, [1987] ECR 3969.

2. Notice that the directive in *Marleasing* was not simply transposed incorrectly; it was not transposed at all. Moreover, the Spanish law that was the subject of interpretation was the Spanish Civil Code, the fundamental private law text in Spain, dating to 1889. Does it surprise you that the Court expects such a text—which has been the subject of well over a century of decided cases in Spain—to now be interpreted as in keeping with a late Twentieth Century directive?

3. A number of prominent Advocates General have urged the Court to overrule *Marshall* to the extent that it denies horizontal direct effect to directives. Following the Court's judgment in *Marshall*, Advocate General Francis Jacobs argued in his opinion in Vaneetveld v. Le Foyer, Case C–316/93, [1994] ECR I–763, as follows:

29   There are sound reasons of principle for assigning direct effect to directives without any distinction based on the status of the defendant. It would be consistent with the need to ensure the effectiveness of Community law and its uniform application in all the Member States. It would be consistent, in particular, with the recent emphasis in the Court's case-law on the overriding duty of national courts to provide effective remedies for the protection of Community rights.... Distortions will obviously result, both between and within Member States, if directives are enforceable, for example, against employers or suppliers of goods or services in the public sector but not in the private sector. It is no answer to suggest that such distortions will be removed if the directive is properly implemented; the situation which has to be envisaged is one in which the directive has not been properly implemented.

Advocate General Carl–Otto Lenz made essentially the same argument in his opinion in the following case, invoking in ¶ 53 of his opinion the principle of equal treatment as underscored by the Maastricht Treaty. The Court declined to follow his views.

FACCINI DORI v. RECREB Srl

Case C–91/92, [1994] ECR I–3325.

[While at the Milan railroad station, Faccini Dori signed a contract with the provider of an English-language correspondence course. Four days later she wrote to the company, attempting to cancel the contract. Litigation ensued, at the end of which Faccini Dori was found liable for the sum due under the contract. Directive 85/577 on the protection of consumers in respect of contracts negotiated away from business premises required that consumers be given the right to cancel a contract, be informed of that right, and have seven days after signing a contract in which to give notice of cancellation. Italy did not implement the directive until 1992, five years after it should have done so. If Italy had implemented it on time, Faccini Dori would presumably not have been held liable. When Faccini Dori asked the Italian court to vacate its order, the court made a preliminary reference to the Court of Justice. The Court first concluded that the directive's provisions on the right of cancellation were sufficiently precise and unconditional to have vertical direct effect and then turned to the issue of horizontal direct effect.]

19   The second issue raised by the national court relates ... to the question whether, in the absence of measures transposing the directive within the prescribed time-limit, consumers may derive from the directive itself a right of cancellation against traders with whom they have concluded contracts and enforce that right before a national court.

* * *

22   [A]s is clear from the judgment in *Marshall*, the case-law on the possibility of relying on directives against State entities is based on the fact that under [Article 249, now TFEU Article 288]] a directive is

binding only in relation to "each Member State to which it is addressed." That case-law seeks to prevent "the State from taking advantage of its own failure to comply with Community law."

23   It would be unacceptable if a State, when required by the Community legislature to adopt certain rules intended to govern the State's relations—or those of State entities—with individuals and to confer certain rights on individuals, were able to rely on its own failure to discharge its obligations so as to deprive individuals of the benefits of those rights...

24   The effect of extending the case-law to the sphere of relations between individuals would be to recognize a power in the Community to enact obligations for individuals with immediate effect, whereas it has competence to do so only where it is empowered to adopt regulations.

25   It follows that, in the absence of measures transposing the directive within the prescribed time-limit, consumers cannot derive from the directive a right of cancellation as against traders with whom they have concluded a contract or enforce such a right in a national court.

NOTES AND QUESTIONS

1.   What are the rationales used by the Court for denying horizontal direct effect to directive provisions that satisfy the test for vertical direct effect? Do you agree with its conclusion in ¶ 24 of *Faccini Dori*, or with the views of Advocates General Jacobs and Lenz?

2.   It is in consumer protection cases like *Faccini Dori* that the Court's refusal to grant horizontal direct effect to directives seems most harsh. For a further example, consider El Corte Ingles v. Blazquez Rivero, Case C–192/94, [1996] ECR I–1281. Claiming that the travel arrangements made by her travel agency, Viajes El Corte Inglés, were substandard, a Spanish tourist refused to repay in full a loan that she had taken out to finance the holiday travel abroad. The finance company that had financed the trip (El Corte Inglés) was a close corporate affiliate of the travel agency and had the exclusive contractual right to extend credit to the agency's customers. The finance company brought suit in a Seville trial court for the outstanding loan balance. If Spain had timely and properly transposed Council Directive 87/102, harmonizing Member State laws on consumer credit, the tourist would have had a defense against the finance company. However, Spain had not done so and the period for doing so had expired.

Marleasing notwithstanding, the Spanish court felt unable to interpret the existing Spanish law in such a way as to attain the directive's objectives. The court nevertheless wondered whether the intervening entry into force of Article 153 of the EC Treaty (now TFEU Article 169), requiring the Community to pursue "a high level of consumer protection," justified reaching a different result. The Court of Justice thought not:

18   Article [153] of the Treaty cannot alter that case-law, even if only in relation to directives on consumer protection.

* * *

20   In so far as it merely assigns an objective to the Community and confers powers on it to that end without also laying down any obligation on Member States or individuals, Article [153] cannot justify the possibility of clear, precise and unconditional provisions of directives on consumer protection which have not been transposed into Community law within the prescribed period being directly relied on as between individuals.

3.   In a portion of the *Faccini Dori* judgment excerpted at page 371, infra, the Court raised the possibility of affording Faccini Dori an alternative remedy in damages.

4.   Perhaps due to misgivings over the impact of the horizontal direct effect case law on innocent parties, whom unimplemented directives were precisely meant to protect, the Court has allowed some inroads to be made in its jurisprudence, though their contours are far from clear. The most salient of these is the recognition of certain exceptional "triangular cases" in which horizontal direct effect may be allowed, as in the following case.

WELLS v. SECRETARY OF STATE FOR TRANSPORT AND LOCAL GOVERNMENT

Case C–201/02, [2004] ECR I–3923.

[Delena Wells purchased a house near a quarry that had been long dormant. Later, the quarry's owners sought to re-commence mining by reactivating a mining permission that had been granted over 40 years earlier. After imposing new planning conditions on the existing permission, the authorities granted approval. Wells objected, relying in part on Council Directive 85/337, which requires Member States to conduct environmental impact assessments prior to granting development consents. No such assessment had been performed.]

57   Mere adverse repercussions on the rights of third parties, even if the repercussions are certain, do not justify preventing an individual from invoking the provisions of a directive against the Member State concerned. . . .

58   In the main proceedings, the obligation on the Member State concerned to ensure that the competent authorities carry out an assessment of the environmental effects of the working of the quarry is not directly linked to the performance of any obligation which would fall, pursuant to Directive 85/337, on the quarry owners. The fact that mining operations must be halted to await the results of the assessment is admittedly the consequence of the belated performance of that State's obligations. Such a consequence cannot, however, as the United Kingdom claims, be described as 'inverse direct effect' of the provisions of that directive in relation to the quarry owners.

NOTES AND QUESTIONS

1.   The Court in *Wells* observed in ¶ 56 that directives do not have horizontal direct affect so as to enable private parties to enforce obligations

falling upon other private parties, citing *Marshall*. Hence the plaintiff could not have sued, for example, to compel the quarry miners to respect health and safety requirements imposed by an environmental directive. Here, however, the plaintiff only sought to compel the UK authorities to carry out an environmental impact assessment in accordance with the directive, even though doing so would temporarily, and possibly even permanently, prevent the quarry miners from operating.

2. Pafitis v. Trapeza Kentrikis Ellados AE, Case C–441/93, [1996] ECR I–1347, is another illustration. The original shareholders of a Greek bank brought suit against the bank and its new shareholders who acquired their shares through a capital increase ordered by the Greek bank supervisory authorities in order to confront the risk of a possible bank insolvency. The plaintiffs contended that the capital increase violated Article 25 of the Second Company Law Directive 77/91 because that Article required any capital increase to be approved at a general meeting of shareholders. In a preliminary ruling, the Court of Justice held that Article 25 precluded the capital increase ordered by the bank authorities. In other words, absent the appropriate shareholder vote, the national court had to deny legal effect to a national law requiring an increase in capital. While it is true that the target of the challenge was an act of the public authorities, the fact remains that the challenge directly affected the shareholders' private legal relationship—indeed, it ended the claim of the purported new shareholders to hold any shareholding interest in the company, because it invalidated the capital increase.

Cases like *Wells* and *Pafitis* are sometimes described as entailing "triangular" relationships to distinguish them from the bilateral relationships said to be involved in the horizontal direct effect cases discussed previously. In what sense can they be considered as triangular scenarios? Are the results consistent with the principle that directives lack horizontal direct effect?

3. Commentators have discerned three species of "triangular" relationships. See Lackhoff & Nyssens, Direct Effect of Directives in Triangular Situations, 23 Eur. L. Rev. 397 (1998). First, a directive may grant a private party the right to demand action (or inaction) from a public authority, with the action (or inaction) necessarily imposing a burden on another private party. In this scenario, the horizontal direct effect may be described as "incidental." Second, national authorities may have failed to comply with a directive which required them to impose a burden on a private party, and a third (private) party may bring an action against the authorities to compel them to do so. In the third type of situation, the directive calls upon the State to confer a particular right or benefit on a private party. If, by conferring some right or benefit on a private party, the State denies a different private party the right or benefit conferred by the directive, that party may bring an action the effect of which would be to adversely affect the third party. In all these cases, a private party's claim against the State has a necessarily adverse effect on another private party—hence "triangular." Is this analysis defensible? helpful? workable?

PART 2

THE RECEPTION AND ENFORCEMENT OF EUROPEAN LAW IN THE MEMBER STATES

■ ■ ■

In exploring the framework of European Union law (and the law of the European Community that became absorbed into the Union with the 2009 Lisbon Treaty), Part I of this book—and particularly Chapters 6 and 7—drew heavily on the perspective of the European Court of Justice. In doing so, it necessarily put to one side the question of whether and to what extent national authorities share that perspective. The fact remains, however, that national authorities enjoy considerable opportunity to determine how completely and how well European Union law will be integrated into and implemented as the Member State level and below, where the great bulk of the administration of Union law in fact occurs. Chapter 8 in a sense presents the corresponding "view from the States," focusing on those States, such as Germany, whose courts have given these issues the most deliberate and sustained attention.

This is by no means to suggest that the European authorities are prepared to leave to the Member States themselves the task of determining the correctness of the Member States' understandings of EU law or the adequacy of their implementation of that law. The very existence of the preliminary reference mechanism, and the obligations for Member States courts that it entails, demonstrate that fact. Given the importance of preliminary references and rulings on Union law, both as to their interpretation and validity, we devote a separate chapter—Chapter 9—to this mechanism.

Precisely because Member States participate so intensively in the legislative, executive and judicial implementation of Union law, their legislative practices and their administrative and judicial remedies go a long way in determining the effectiveness of Union law in the national legal orders. The matter is complicated by the fact that the legislative, executive and judicial systems in each Member State present their own peculiarities. Consequently, questions about the adequacy of these remedies arise with great frequency, making their way to the Court of Justice

271

both by preliminary references and through direct actions of various sorts. The highly complex and subtle "remedies" case law that has resulted is the subject of Chapter 10.

Finally, we consider in Chapter 11 the direct enforcement mechanisms with which the Treaty on European Union has equipped the Union. Their role in essence is to permit the Union institutions—notably the Commission and the Court of Justice—to ascertain whether Member State authorities have failed in their obligations under EU law and, if so, to determine the consequences.

CHAPTER 8

THE RECEPTION OF EUROPEAN UNION LAW IN THE MEMBER STATES

■ ■ ■

The previous chapter explored the notions of direct effect and supremacy as the doctrinal pillars of EU law. These are largely creations of the Court of Justice. However, because the architects of the Union, and of the Communities before it, chose to leave basic responsibility for implementing EU law in the hands of the Member States, the attitudes and practices of national institutions also require consideration. These are the subject of the present chapter.

Member State courts have expressed diverse views on the place of EU law in their legal orders. Moreover, national attitudes have evolved significantly over time. The starting point for discussion is a reminder that the European Communities grew out of an international treaty and not in a vacuum, and the EU does as well. Member State attitudes toward the integration of EU law norms into the domestic legal order have therefore been influenced by their more general understandings about the effect of treaty law within the national legal systems.

A distinction is commonly drawn between so-called monist and dualist attitudes toward international law. Under a monist view, domestic and international (including treaty) law are said to constitute a single integrated legal system. Although treaties initially become effective in a given State only when entered into in accordance with domestic constitutional procedures, once effective, they become a source of law within that State. Under a monist view, therefore, treaties are normally directly applicable in the national legal orders, without need of legislative implementation or other act of incorporation. Moreover, while monism does not logically imply the superiority of international over national law in the event of conflict, it is commonly associated with that principle.

The monist perspective has obvious appeal to the Court of Justice, since it obviates the question of direct applicability and leaves the direct effect of EU law norms to be determined largely by the Court itself. As noted, monism also creates a doctrinal setting that is hospitable to the supremacy of EU over national law. If direct applicability, direct effect and supremacy are assumed to attach not only to the Treaties, but also to the secondary legislation adopted by the institutions those Treaties create, then monism goes a long way toward giving EU law the full supranational effect championed by the Court of Justice.

By contrast, a dualist approach to international law is said to view domestic and international law as separate and distinct spheres, with different purposes and different constituencies. Under this view, a treaty may engage a State in its international relations (notably by creating obligations to other States), but does not of itself affect internal legal relationships except to the extent that domestic law provides.

Dualism presents certain obvious disadvantages from the EU point of view. First, it seems by definition to deny EU law's direct applicability, as that term is used in this book. To require each EU law instrument to be separately incorporated into national law before acquiring binding force domestically is essentially to foreclose direct applicability. Moreover, if EU law is not of its own force directly applicable within the Member States, it can hardly exert direct effect of its own force either, much less claim legal supremacy over domestic law norms.

A Member State that subscribes to the dualist view may still, of course, confer a privileged status on EU law within the national legal order. Thus, primary and secondary EU law alike may be entrenched in national law through an express constitutional amendment or other special enactment to that effect. Depending on the instrument and language used, EU law may accordingly enjoy direct applicability, direct effect and even supremacy within the domestic legal order.

A common though somewhat confusing way of describing these arrangements is to say that the relevant constitutional or legislative texts have effected a limited "transfer" of Member State sovereignty to the EU institutions. Sometimes reference is made to a partial "delegation" of legislative authority. In either event, the extent to which direct applicability, direct effect or supremacy of EU law is achieved depends on the language of the transfer or delegation, its interpretation, and of course the extent to which the transfer or delegation is constitutionally entrenched. Unfortunately, Member States sometimes employ language that is ambiguous as to the conditions on which they have made a transfer or delegation of power. This ambiguity has helped fuel doubts over the willingness of certain Member States to accept fully the Court's supranationalist tenets.

Whether and to what extent a Member State meets the normative demands of EU law ultimately depends on the practices of countless national and local administrative officers—tax, customs, immigration and a host of different regulatory and enforcement officials—throughout the national territory. However, the attitudes of these officers are in turn likely to be shaped by the positions that the national judiciaries adopt. Although the Court of Justice has constructed a powerful set of doctrinal tools for ensuring the primacy and immediacy of EU law, the Member State judiciaries also have well-developed constitutional procedures and modes of constitutional analysis of their own, and these are the courts that ultimately shape and manage the legal framework within which the conflicting demands of domestic and EU law are resolved on a daily basis. This chapter highlights both the objections and the accommodations that the high courts of various Member States have made in the face of EU law's weighty normative imperatives.[1]

With the growth in EU membership, this book can no longer afford to follow a State-by-State approach to the matter. The present chapter is accordingly organized around a distinction between qualified and unqualified supremacy of EU law. As we shall see, the qualifications that Member States place on the supremacy of EU law do not all sound the same. And in at least one State—the United Kingdom—the position of the courts remains difficult to characterize.

A. THE UNQUALIFIED SUPREMACY OF EU LAW

EU LAW IN BELGIUM

Though Belgium is generally regarded as in the monist tradition, the language of its Constitution is not especially clear as to the place that EU law occupies in that country's legal order. The 1831 Constitution was amended in 1970 to provide that "the exercise of given powers may be conferred by a treaty or by a law on institutions created under public international law" (art. 34). But even today, the Constitution does not speak to EU law's direct applicability or direct effect, much less its supremacy in the Belgian legal order.

Under these circumstances, ready acceptance of all of the Court of Justice's supranational tenets could not have been taken for granted. The 1971 *Fromagerie "Le Ski"* decision of the Belgian Cour de Cassation, the highest civil court in Belgium, is therefore especially striking. After the ECJ ruled in 1964 that certain Belgian decrees of 1958 violated Article 12 of the then-EEC Treaty by introducing import duties on dairy products, Belgium eliminated the duties. However, a 1968 Belgian statute declared that the imposition of past duties under the decrees was not subject to judicial review of any kind, and that duties once paid could not be recovered. Fromagerie "Le Ski" nevertheless sued to recover duties it had paid. Before the Cour de Cassation, the Belgian Government argued that since Belgium had ratified the EEC Treaty by statute, it took effect in Belgium simply as a statute and could be superseded by later national legislation such as the 1968 statute. (Note that the *Costa v. ENEL* judgment of the Court of Justice, supra page 245, had by then squarely rejected this argument). Second, Belgium argued that the courts could not

---

1. For a general review by the Court of Justice of the Member State judiciaries' compliance with Community law obligations, see the report, "Apercu sur l'application du droit communautaire par les juridictions nationales" (Direction Bibliothèque, Recherche et Documentation, report 01/008, Feb. 2001).

in any event annul a Belgian statute because Article 97 of the national Constitution vested that authority exclusively in the Belgian Parliament.

The Belgian Procureur Général, obviously influenced by *Costa v. ENEL*, argued as follows:

> The [Community] Treaties ... have in relation to conventional international treaties special features [making] the relationship between Community law and national legislation ... a special one.
>
>   * * *
>
> First, by their agreement on the transfer of their rights and obligations under the Treaty to the Community legal system, the States definitively limited "their sovereign rights", or to put it more accurately, "the exercise of their sovereign powers." ...
>
>   * * *
>
> Secondly, Community law is a specific and autonomous law which is binding on the courts of Member States and makes it impossible to set against it any domestic law whatsoever. The very nature of the legal system instituted by the Treaties of Rome confers on that primacy its own foundation, independently of the constitutional provisions in States. This specific character of Community law stems from the objectives of the Treaty which are the establishment of a new legal system to which are subject not only States but also the nationals of those States. It also stems from the fact that the Treaty has set up institutions having their own powers and especially that of creating new sources of law.

[1972] CMLR at 352, 355–56.

The Belgian Cour de Cassation largely agreed, holding that if a domestic statute conflicts with a treaty introduced into national law by statute, it is nevertheless to be regarded as conflicting with the treaty. It concluded:

> The rule that a statute repeals a previous statute in so far as there is a conflict between the two does not apply in the case of a conflict between a treaty and a statute.
>
> In the event of a conflict between a norm of domestic law and a norm of international law which produces direct effects in the internal legal system, the rule established by the treaty shall prevail. The primacy of the treaty results from the very nature of international treaty law.
>
> This is *a fortiori* the case when a conflict exists, as in the present case, between a norm of internal law and a norm of Community law.
>
> The reason is that the treaties which have created Community law have instituted a new legal system in whose favor the Member States have restricted the exercise of their sovereign powers in the areas determined by those treaties.

Etat Belge, Ministre des Affaires Economiques v. SA Fromagerie Franco–Suisse "Le Ski," [1971] Pasicrisie Belge 886, [1972] CMLR 330, 373 (Belgian Cour de Cassation, first chamber, May 21, 1971). Observing that the then Article 12 was directly effective and conferred rights on individuals that national courts must uphold, the Cour de Cassation held that the Belgian courts were permitted—and indeed required—not to enforce the 1968 Belgian statute. The court maintained that refusing to enforce a national statute (that is, "finding that its effects are stopped") does not amount to declaring the statute null and void. Although *Le Ski* entailed conflict between a Belgian statute and the EEC Treaty, the result would apparently have been no different if the conflict had been with a piece of secondary EU legislation instead.

The Belgian Conseil d'Etat (the Supreme Administrative Court) has had no difficulty following the Cour de Cassation's line of reasoning. Even before the *Le Ski* case, the Belgian Conseil d'Etat had ruled that directly applicable treaties are a source of administrative law and a basis upon which to review not only the validity of administrative regulations and decisions, but also the enforceability of national legislation, even if enacted subsequently. In a later case, however, the Conseil d'Etat was asked to go a step further.

ORFINGER v. BELGIUM

Belgian Conseil d'Etat
Case no. 62.9222, A.61.059/VI–12.193, 2000 Comm.
Mkt. L. Rep. 612 (2000) (Nov. 5, 1996).

[Orfinger challenged a 1994 royal decree on recruitment criteria for the Belgian civil service. Article 1(3) of the decree required applicants to be Belgian nationals or nationals of another EU Member State. Orfinger objected to making EU nationals other than Belgians eligible for civil service positions, invoking Article 10(2) of the Constitution which provides that "Belgians ... are the only ones eligible for civil and military service, but for the exceptions provided for by law." Orfinger maintained that international law does not authorize States to make treaties contrary to their own Constitution and that a constitutional amendment was needed before Belgium could ratify a treaty contrary to the Constitution. He also argued that for the EU judiciary to dictate the eligibility of candidates for the Belgian civil service would violate the principle of subsidiarity.]

* * *

5. ... The problem [in this case] is that of the compatibility between the Constitution and the interpretation of one of the provisions of the Treaty, long after its ratification, by the authorities established under this Treaty for the purpose of ensuring a uniform interpretation of its own provisions valid in all the Member States of the Union.

6. Article 34 of the Constitution allows the exercise of specific powers to be conferred through a treaty or a statute to public international law

bodies. Although [Article 34] is posterior to the ratification of the EC Treaty, ... it provides a constitutional basis for the institutional mechanisms which the Treaty established with a particular view to guaranteeing its uniform interpretation in all Member States of the European Union. [Article 34] in no way determines the powers that can be attributed, and therefore puts no limit on them.

* * *

8. In case of conflict between a rule of national law and a rule of international law of direct effect in the national legal order, the rule established by the Treaty must prevail. According to the established case law of the European Court of Justice, relying on provisions of national law with a view to limiting the effect of the Community law would result in undermining the unity and efficiency of Community law and therefore cannot be accepted, even where the provisions of national law are those of the Constitution. Under Belgian constitutional law, the authority conferred upon the Court of Justice's interpretation of the Treaty of Rome is based on Article 34 of the Constitution, even where such interpretation would result in blocking the effects of certain parts of Articles 8 and 10 of the Constitution.

9. This conclusion is not in contradiction with any of the principles on which the applicant has based his action. The application of all the provisions of the EC Treaty, and their interpretation by the European Court of Justice, is the result of Belgium's membership of the European Union and this application could possibly be set aside following an initiative by the Belgian authorities to either denounce their membership or renegotiate the conditions thereof. As long as such an initiative has not taken place, the principle of the rule of law requires that Community law be fully applied. Although it may be recommended, as did the Conseil d'Etat's Legislation Division, that the text of the Constitution should be amended to meet the requirements of European law, the application of that law cannot be subject to an amendment of the Constitution to meet the requirements of European law which is mandatory even in the absence of such an amendment.

NOTES AND QUESTIONS

1. On the reception of EU law in Belgium, see K. Lenaerts & P. Foubert, Belgian Law and the European Community: 1993–1996, 22 Eur. L. Rev. 599 (1997); K. Lenaerts & K. Coppenholle, The Application of Community Law in Belgium: 1989–1992, 17 Eur. L. Rev. 447 (1992); P. Wytinck, The Application of Community Law in Belgium: 1986–1992, 30 Common Mkt. L. Rev. 981 (1993).

2. A number of other Member States, like Belgium, consider EU law to prevail over contrary provisions of national law, arguably even law of a constitutional nature. Among others, these apparently include Luxembourg, the Netherlands, the Slovak Republic, Bulgaria, Romania, the Baltic States (Estonia, Latvia and Lithuania), Cyprus and Malta.

3. How do you assess the price paid by States like Belgium for their strict adherence to the supremacy of EU law?

B.   THE QUALIFIED SUPREMACY OF EU LAW

According to a view that has gained ascendancy in recent years, EU law is supreme, but not unconditionally so. The conditions imposed vary from country to country, but some patterns recur.

1.   EU LAW IN GERMANY

Upon Germany's entry into the European Communities in 1957, the seemingly relevant provisions of the Grundgesetz (GG or Basic Law of 1949), which is functionally the German Constitution, were the following:

Article 24 (Entry into a collective security system)

(1) The Federation may by legislation transfer sovereign powers to intergovernmental institutions. . . .

Article 25 (International law integral part of federal law)

The general rules of public international law shall be an integral part of federal law. They shall take precedence over the laws and shall directly create rights and duties for the inhabitants of the federal territory.

Despite this constitutional language, the German courts from early on voiced reservations about the categorical supremacy of EU law asserted by the European Court of Justice. The first major pronouncement was Internationale Handelsgesellschaft mbH v. Einfuhr- und Vorratsstelle für Getreide und Futtermittel (*Solange I*), Case 2 BvL 52/71, 37 BVerfGE 271, [1974] 2 CMLR 540 (Fed. Const'l Court, second senate, May 29, 1974). This case arose out of the same circumstances as the 1970 Court of Justice judgment of the same name, supra page 160. Following the ECJ ruling, which upheld the forfeiture feature of the EU's export license regulation, the German administrative court turned to the German Federal Constitutional Court for a preliminary ruling on the conformity of the same EU regulation with the fundamental human rights provisions of the German Constitution.

The majority opinion of the Court first laid down the premise that "Community law is neither a component part of the national legal system nor international law, but forms an independent system of law flowing from an autonomous legal source." From that it deduced that while the competent European institutions (notably the European Court of Justice) rule on the construction and binding force of EU law, the competent national organs (notably the German Constitutional Court itself) rule on the construction and binding force of German constitutional law. This, the Court asserted, "does not lead to any difficulties as long as the two systems of law do not come into conflict with one another in their substance...."

The majority then turned specifically to the "basic rights" set out in the German Constitution:

4.   The part of the Constitution dealing with fundamental rights is an inalienable essential feature of the valid Constitution of the Federal Republic of Germany and one which forms part of the constitutional structure of the Constitution. Article 24 of the Constitution does not without reservation allow it to be subjected to qualifications. In this, the present state of integration of the Community is of crucial importance. The Community still lacks a democratically legitimated parliament directly elected by general suffrage which possesses legislative powers and to which the Community organs empowered to legislate are fully responsible on a political level; it still lacks in particular a codified catalogue of fundamental rights, the substance of which is reliably and unambiguously fixed for the future in the same way as the substance of the Constitution. ... As long as this legal certainty, which is not guaranteed merely by the decisions of the European Court of Justice, favorable though these have been to fundamental rights, is not achieved in the course of the further integration of the Community, the reservation derived from Article 24 of the Constitution applies.

* * *

The majority's much-quoted conclusion was:

7.   ... As long as the integration process has not progressed so far that Community law also receives a catalogue of fundamental rights decided on by a parliament and of settled validity, which is adequate in comparison with the catalogue of fundamental rights contained in the Constitution, a reference by a court in the Federal Republic of Germany to the [German Constitutional Court] following the obtaining of a ruling of the European Court under [EC Treaty Article 177, later renumbered as Article 234, and now TFEU Article 267] of the Treaty, is admissible and necessary if the German court regards the rule of Community law which is relevant to its decision as inapplicable in the interpretation given by the European Court, because and in so far as it conflicts with one of the fundamental rights in the Constitution.

Turning to the merits, the court ruled that the Council regulation, as interpreted by the European Court of Justice, did not conflict with the principle of proportionality or any other guarantee of fundamental rights in the German Constitution.

The decision is known as *Solange I* (*solange* meaning "as long as") because of its conditional holding. Note that neither the majority nor minority considered as alternatives: (a) permitting national courts to review the conformity of EU law with basic rights, on condition that the latter are defined by reference to EU rather than national constitutional norms, or (b) permitting review by the Court of Justice under *both* EU and national constitutional norms.

Three members of the Court dissented, finding the reference to the Court inadmissible. In their view, the Court of Justice had amply recognized fundamental rights (including the principle of proportionality that was relevant to the case at hand), and the Treaty's system of remedies adequately safeguarded them. While individual standing in the Court of Justice was very limited, the preliminary reference mechanism enabled national courts to obtain a ruling from the Court of Justice on the conformity of EU law to fundamental rights whenever that law furnishes the basis of a national implementation measure. In the years following *Solange I*, the Constitutional Court has never found an EU law measure violative of fundamental rights under German law.

Twelve years later, in an otherwise unremarkable opinion, the Constitutional Court revisited the principle it had stated in *Solange I*. The case was In re Application of Wünsche Handelsgesellschaft, Case 2 BvR 197/83, 73 BVerfGE 339, [1987] 3 CMLR 225 (Fed. Const'l Court, second senate, Oct. 22, 1986), otherwise known as *Solange II*. Wünsche, a German importer, was denied a license to import mushrooms from Taiwan under an import license system dating back to 1974. Wünsche claimed that the market disturbances that originally prompted the adoption of that system no longer existed, and that there was in fact a shortage of mushrooms, both domestic and imported. At Wünsche's request, Germany's supreme administrative court referred the question of the system's legality to the European Court of Justice, which upheld the system as a reasonable exercise of the Commission's discretion. The German court refused, however, to refer Wünsche's further constitutional claims (including the right to a fair hearing) either to the Court of Justice or to the German Constitutional Court. Maintaining that this refusal in itself was a deprivation of its constitutional rights, Wünsche then brought a constitutional complaint directly to the German Constitutional Court.

In its unanimous judgment, the Court affirmed its position in *Solange I* that Article 24(1) of the German Constitution does not allow Germany "to surrender ... the identity of the prevailing constitutional order [or] undermine essential structural parts of the Constitution [such as] fundamental rights," but then revisited the question of how those fundamental rights are to be protected:

> (d) In the judgment of this Chamber, a measure of protection of fundamental rights has been established [since 1974] within the sovereign jurisdiction of the European Communities which in its conception, substance and manner of implementation is essentially comparable with the standards of fundamental rights provided for in the Constitution. All the main institutions of the Community have since acknowledged in a legally significant manner that in the exercise of their powers and the pursuit of the objectives of the Communi-

ty they will be guided as a legal duty by respect for fundamental rights, in particular as established by the constitutions of Member States and by the European Convention on Human Rights. There are no decisive factors to lead one to conclude that the standard of fundamental rights which has been achieved under Community law is not adequately consolidated. . . .

(aa) This standard of fundamental rights has in the meantime, particularly through the decisions of the European Court, been formulated in content, consolidated and adequately guaranteed. [The court here made reference to several Court of Justice rulings on fundamental rights discussed in Chapters 5 and 6 supra.]

(bb) The European Parliament, the Council and the Commission of the Community adopted the . . . joint declaration on 5 April 1977 [to the effect that] "in the exercise of their powers and in pursuance of the aims of the European Communities they respect and will continue to respect these rights."

The Court concluded:

(f) In view of those developments, it must be held that, so long as the European Communities, and in particular . . . the case law of the European Court, generally ensure an effective protection of fundamental rights as against the sovereign powers of the Communities which is to be regarded as substantially similar to the protection of fundamental rights required unconditionally by the Constitution, and in so far as they generally safeguard the essential content of fundamental rights, the Federal Constitutional Court will no longer exercise its jurisdiction to decide on the applicability of secondary Community legislation cited as the legal basis for any acts of German courts or authorities within the sovereign jurisdiction of the Federal Republic of Germany, and it will no longer review such legislation by the standard of the fundamental rights contained in the Constitution. . . .

(g) The question [referred to the Court] must therefore remain unanswered. . . .

NOTES AND QUESTIONS

1. Note the Court's deliberate use of the language "so long as" in paragraph (f). This explains the common reference to this judgment as *Solange II*.

2. Might a party seek to enjoin the German government on constitutional grounds from participating in the adoption of EU legislation in the Council? In M GmbH v. Bundesregierung, Case 2 BvQ 3/89, [1990] 1 CMLR 570 (Federal Constitutional Court, May 12, 1989), such an effort was rebuffed on the ground that the plaintiffs, a group of German tobacco companies opposed to a draft Council directive on tobacco product labeling, lacked standing to press a claim in the Constitutional Court that the directive would infringe their fundamental rights of free expression, property and freedom of com-

merce. The Court also suggested that the claim was unripe and should in no event be heard until the directive is adopted and implemented: "The Federal Government's participation ... is only a contribution to the creation of a directive, which does not adversely affect the applicants until it has come into force and is implemented into national law." [1990] 1 CMLR at 574.

Suppose the tobacco companies eventually challenge the German implementing statute. To what extent and by what means may the statute's validity be questioned? In *M GmbH* the German Constitutional Court stated:

> ... The question whether the applicants' constitutional ... rights are infringed in the implementation of the directive ... is one which is open to constitutional judicial review in all respects.

> In so far as the directive may infringe the basic constitutional standards of Community law, the European Court of Justice ensures legal protection of rights. If the constitutional standards laid down as unconditional by the German Constitution should not be satisfied by this route, recourse can be had to the Federal Constitutional Court.

Id. Is the Court's position in *M GmbH* consistent with its position in *Wünsche Handelsgesellschaft?*

3. In *Solange II,* the Constitutional Court confined itself to the question of the supremacy of Community over national law. Does the opinion also imply that the German courts will regard themselves as bound to give an EC directive direct effect once the Court of Justice interprets that directive as having direct effect?

The Bundesfinanzhof, the highest German tax court, did not initially take that view. In 1985, it ruled that a German taxpayer could not claim a tax exemption for 1978 income from certain credit transactions by invoking a 1977 Council Directive (the Sixth VAT Directive) that required the Member States to provide such an exemption by January 1, 1978. Its reason was that the Sixth VAT Directive had not been implemented in Germany by 1978. (The directive was in fact not implemented until 1980). The Bundesfinanzhof so held, even though the Court of Justice had already twice ruled in 1981 and 1982 (Becker v. Finanzamt Münster–Innenstadt, supra page 259; R.A. Grendel GmbH v. Finanzamt für Körperschaften in Hambourg, Case 255/81, [1982] ECR 2301) that the directive had direct effect. In fact, the lower court had earlier requested a preliminary ruling from the Court of Justice on the same question, and the Court of Justice had reaffirmed its 1981 rulings. Kloppenburg v. Finanzamt Leer, Case 70/83, [1984] ECR 1075, 1087. The Bundesfinanzhof's decision was thus all the more striking, and it produced a constitutional complaint by the taxpayer to the German Constitutional Court.

The Constitutional Court held that the Bundesfinanzhof had indeed violated the taxpayer's constitutional rights. According to the Court, her constitutional right to her "lawful judge" (under Article 101(1) of the German Constitution) was infringed when the tax court knowingly disregarded the Court of Justice's rulings on the direct effect of the Sixth VAT Directive instead of asking the Court of Justice to reconsider its position. In re Application of Frau Kloppenburg, Case 2 BvR 687/85, 75 BVerfGE 223, [1987] EurR 333, [1988] 3 CMLR 1 (Federal Constitutional Court, second senate,

April 8, 1987). For a more recent reaffirmation, see In re Application of Frau R, Case 1 BvR 1036/99 (Jan. 9, 2001).

4. The positions taken by the German Constitutional Court have resonated in other Member States, old and new. For an analogous holding by the Italian Constitutional Court, see Frontini v. Ministero delle Finanze, [1974] 2 CMLR 372 (Constitutional Court); Spa Fragd v. Amministrazione delle Finanze, 72 RDI (1989). In the case of SpA Granital v. Amministrazione delle Finanze, [1984] 21 CMLR 756, the Italian Constitutional Court effectively embraced the position on the relation between EU law and national constitutional law that the ECJ had taken in the *Simmenthal* case discussed at page 247 supra. For comparable Polish case law, see the case of Polish Membership of the European Union (Accession Treaty), K18/04 (May 11, 2005).

BRUNNER AND OTHERS v. THE EUROPEAN UNION TREATY

(The Maastricht Judgment)
German Constitutional Court, Second Senate
Case 2 BvR 2134/92 & 2159/92, [1994] 1 CMLR 57, 1993 WL 965303 (Oct. 12, 1993).

[Following Germany's signature of the Maastricht Treaty, twenty separate lawsuits were filed against the bill of ratification, one of them by Manfred Brunner, the former chief of staff to EC Commissioner Martin Bangemann. The essence of the complaints was that approval of the TEU would violate the principle that all state power emanates from the people—a principle implicit in the requirement of Article 38 of the German Basic Law that members of the Bundestag (the principal legislative chamber, which elects the Federal Chancellor and exercises political control over the Government) be elected through "general, direct, free, equal, and secret elections" and function as "representatives of the whole people." Other claims were that ratification of the TEU would infringe the basic rights enshrined in the German Constitution (notably Articles 1(1), 2(1), 5(1), 9(1) in conjunction with 21(1), 12(1), 14(1), and 20(4)), as well as principles of German federalism.]

B.

* * *

(a) Articles 38(1) and (2) of the Constitution guarantee to Germans entitled to vote the individually assertable right to participate in the election of deputies to the German Bundestag. In the act of voting, the power of the state proceeds from the people. The Bundestag then exercises state power as a legislative body, which also chooses the Federal Chancellor and controls the government (Article 20(2), first and second sentences).[2] Article 38 not only contains a safeguard to ensure that the citizen is accorded the right to elect the German Bundestag and that in the election the constitutional principles of electoral law will be upheld; the

---

2. "All state authority emanates from the people. It is ... exercised by the people through elections and voting and by specific organs of the legislature, the executive power and the judiciary."

safeguard also extends to the fundamental democratic content of that right: what is guaranteed to Germans entitled to vote is the individually assertable right to participate in the election of the Bundestag and thereby to co-operate in the legitimation of state power by the people at federal level and to have an influence over its exercise. . . .

* * *

The complainant's right arising from Article 38 of the Constitution can . . . be infringed if the exercise of the powers within the competence of the Bundestag is transferred to an institution of the European Union or European Communities formed by the Member States' governments to such an extent that the minimum requirements, which under Article 20(1) and (2) in conjunction with Article 79(3)[3] may not be dispensed with, for the democratic legitimation of the sovereign power exercised in respect of citizens are no longer satisfied.

(b) The complainant . . . submits that at present already nearly 80 per cent of regulations in the economic sphere are determined by Community law and nearly 50 per cent of all German legislation is occasioned by Community law. He says that the [TEU] will now substantially extend these areas of competence of the Council as an executive organ with legislative power, and will deprive the Bundestag of decision-making competence over a wide range. . . . For these purposes the Treaty establishes the majority principle in the Council for a range of competences, and thus allows legislation by the executive as regards Germany even against the will of the German organs concerned. In the monetary union, monetary policy will be withdrawn from any parliamentary influence and other democratic legitimation. The powers and competences of the Bundestag will finally become devoid of all substance as a result of [then] Article F(3) of the Union Treaty, which gives the Union a power to extend its own powers, since it enables it to provide itself with any necessary powers and competences.

* * *

(c) In the event, it appears possible on the arguments set out above that the Act of Accession to the [TEU] is an infringement of the complainant's rights under Article 38 of the Constitution.

C.

In so far as the first complainant's constitutional complaint is admissible it is unfounded. . . . The content of [Article 38] is not infringed by the Act of Accession, as appears from the content of the Treaty: the Treaty establishes a European federation of states, which is based on the Member States and respects their identities; it concerns Germany's membership of supra-national organizations, not its belonging to a European state. The

---

3. Article 79(3) excludes any amendment to the Constitution that would affect the basic rights in Articles 1 and 20 of the Constitution, or the division of the German state into *Länder* or the participation of the *Länder* in legislation.

functions of the European Union and the powers granted for their implementation are regulated in a sufficiently foreseeable manner, because the principle of limited individual powers is adhered to, no power to extend its powers is conferred on the European Union, and the claiming of further functions and powers by the European Union and the Communities is made dependent on supplementation and amendment of the Treaty, and is therefore subject to the affirmative decision of the national parliaments. The scope of the functions and powers granted to the European Union and to the institutions of the European Communities and the means of formation of political intentions laid down by the Treaty do not at present have the effect of reducing the content of the decision-making and supervisory powers of the Bundestag to an extent which infringes the democratic principle in so far as it is declared by Article 79(3) of the Constitution to be unassailable.

... The conferring of sovereign powers has the consequence that their exercise no longer depends solely on the will of one Member State all the time. [But] to see that as a breach of the constitutional principle of democracy would not only contradict the openness of the Constitution to integration, which was intended, and stated expressly, by the makers of the Constitution in 1949; it would also entail a conception of democracy that would make every democratic state incapable of any integration going beyond the principle of unanimity.... The conferring of sovereign powers which ... Articles [23 and 24] authorize, requires a prior legislative resolution. The requirement of a statute gives the political responsibility for conferring sovereign rights to the Bundestag (together with the Bundesrat) as the national representative body; it has to debate the wide-ranging consequences (not least for the competences of the Bundestag itself) bound up with the assent to such a course, and has to reach a decision on them. In the statute assenting to accession to a community of States is found the democratic legitimation both of the existence of the community of States itself and of its powers to take majority decisions which are binding on the Member States ...

(b) The democratic principle thus does not prevent the Federal Republic of Germany from becoming a member of a community of States (organized on a supra-national basis). ...

(c) The exercise of sovereign power through a federation of States like the European Union is based on authorizations from States which remain sovereign and which in international matters generally act through their governments and control the integration process thereby. It is therefore primarily determined governmentally. If such a community power is to rest on the political will-formation which is supplied by the people of each individual State, and is to that extent democratic, that presupposes that the power is exercised by a body made up of representatives sent by the Member States' governments, which in their turn are subject to democratic control. The passing of European legal regulations, too, may (without prejudice to the consequent need for a democratic control of the governments) lie with an institution composed of representatives of the Member

States' governments, that is to say, on an executive basis, to a greater extent than would be constitutionally acceptable at national level.

3.

* * *

There is ... a breach of Article 38 of the Constitution if an Act that opens up the German legal system to the direct validity and application of the law of the (supra-national) European Communities does not establish with sufficient certainty the powers that are transferred and the intended program of integration. If it is not clear to what extent and degree the German legislature has assented to the transfer of the exercise of sovereign powers, then it will be possible for the European Communities to claim functions and powers that were not specified. That would be equivalent to a general enablement and would therefore be a surrender of powers, something against which Article 38 of the Constitution provides protection.

... What is decisive is that Germany's membership and the rights and duties that follow therefrom ... have been defined in the Treaty so as to be predictable for the legislature and are enacted by it in the Act of Accession with sufficient certainty. That also means that subsequent important alterations to the integration program set up in the [TEU] and to the Union's powers of action are no longer covered by the Act of Accession to the present Treaty. Thus, if European institutions or agencies were to treat or develop the [TEU] in a way that was no longer covered by the Treaty in the form that is the basis for the Act of Accession, the resultant legislative instruments would not be legally binding within the sphere of German sovereignty. The German state organs would be prevented for constitutional reasons from applying them in Germany. Accordingly the Federal Constitutional Court will review legal instruments of European institutions and agencies to see whether they remain within the limits of the sovereign rights conferred on them or transgress them.

II.

The [TEU] satisfies the above-stated requirements ...

* * *

2.

The [TEU] satisfies the requirements of certainty because it lays down the future course of implementation, that is to say, the possible uses to be made of the sovereign powers granted, in a manner which is sufficiently predictable: that establishes that the Act of Accession adheres to the requirements of parliamentary responsibility. There are no grounds for the complainant's concern that the European Community will be able, because of its widely set objectives, to develop into a political union having unspecified sovereign rights without a renewed parliamentary instruction for its laws to apply. The [TEU] adopts the principle of limited individual empowerment, which already applied to the European Communities, and strengthens it. . . .

* * *

(c) The Member States have given the European Union objectives in Article B [now Article 2] of the Union Treaty, and laid down that these may only be achieved as provided in the Treaty. In addition they have defined the tasks and powers of the three European Communities in detail and confined the European institutions and agencies to carrying them out. Any alterations and extensions of those definitions of tasks and powers are subject to their prior formal agreement, which restricts the possibilities for further legal developments on the basis of the existing Treaty. . . . But any such alterations or extensions of the Treaty presuppose that the Member States give their consent in accordance with their rules of constitutional law. . . .

* * *

Any further development of the European Union cannot escape from the conceptual framework set out above. The legislature in amending the Constitution took that into account in connection with this Treaty by the insertion of Article 23 into the Constitution, since express mention is made there of the development of the European Union, which is subject to the principles of democracy and the rule of law, social and federal principles, and the subsidiarity principle. What is decisive, therefore, from the viewpoint both of the Treaties and of constitutional law, is that the democratic bases of the Union will be built up in step with the integration process, and a living democracy will also be maintained in the Member States as integration progresses.

NOTES AND QUESTIONS

1. The *Maastricht* judgment essentially sustained the German law of ratification of the TEU as constitutional, thus empowering the Federal President to sign the Maastricht Treaty. However, the Court's reasoning has led commentators to view it as giving to the TEU not a simple "yes," but rather a "yes but."[4] Would you agree? For an excellent analysis, see M. Herdegen, Maastricht and the German Constitutional Court: Constitutional Restraints for an "Even Closer Union," 31 Comm. Mkt. L. Rev. 235 (1994).

2. The *Maastricht* ruling is especially interesting for its assumptions about the nature of the European Union. It specifically characterizes the European Union as an association or union of European states (*Staatenverbund*), which retain their separate national identities, rather than as a Federal State (*Bundesstaat*), having its own national identity.

3. To what extent does the *Maastricht* ruling distance the German Constitutional Court's views on the primacy of EU law over national constitu-

---

4. See H. G. Crossland, Three Major Decisions Given by the Bundesverfassungsgericht (Federal Constitutional Court), 19 Eur. L. Rev. 202, 212 (1994).

tional law and on the exclusive role of the Court of Justice in determining the validity and effectiveness of EU law from those espoused in ECJ case law? The ruling has spawned a rich literature on democracy and representation in the EU, on the existence of a European *demos*, and on the relationship between the European Court of Justice and the Member States' domestic guardians of fundamental rights. See, for example, M. Kumm, Who is the Final Arbiter of Constitutionality in Europe?: The German Federal Constitutional Court and the European Court of Justice, 36 Comm. Mkt. L. Rev. 351 (1999). That the issues remain sharply contested, at least in Germany, is shown by the following note.

4.   The Constitutional Court revisited the supremacy question in a case arising out of a famous dispute over international trade in bananas. (On the controversy generally, see Everling, Will Europe Slip on Bananas? The *Bananas* Judgment of the Court of Justice and National Courts, 33 Comm. Mkt. L. Rev. 401 (1996).) In the case, a group of banana importers were classified under Regulation 404/93 as Category A operators and allotted a provisional quota of imports for the third quarter of 1993. Objecting to the limitation on imports, they brought an action in the Frankfurt administrative court for a declaration that the regulation infringed EU law. References to the ECJ resulted in a preliminary ruling on the availability of interim relief in national court against EU law measures (see page 347 infra), as well as a preliminary ruling reaffirming the validity of Regulation 404/93. Atlanta Fruchthandelsgesellschaft GmbH v. Bundesamt für Ernährung und Forstwirtschaft, Cases C–465 & C–466/93, [1995] ECR I–3761. The Frankfurt court then referred to the German Constitutional Court the question whether enforcing Regulation 404/93 in Germany would infringe Articles 3(1), 12(1), 14(1) or 23(1), sentence 1, of the German Constitution.

The German Constitutional Court declared the reference inadmissible because the referring court had failed to show "that the European evolution of law, including the rulings of the European Court of Justice, has resulted in a decline below the required standard of fundamental rights," as required under *Solange II*, to justify the Court's examining the conformity of EU law with the German Constitution. According to the Court, the referring court misunderstood the *Maastricht* ruling if it regarded that ruling as undermining *Solange II*. "[T]he assumption of a contradiction between the *Solange II* and the *Maastricht* decisions lacks a sound basis." Order of the Second Senate of the Constitutional Court on the Constitutionality of the Application of the European Union's Common Market for Bananas in Germany (Banana ruling), German Constitutional Court, second senate, 2 BvL 1/97 June 7, 2000. For commentary on the *Banana* judgment, see U. Elbers & N. Urban, The Order of the German Federal Constitutional Court of 7 June 2000 and *Kompetenz–Kompetenz* in the European Judicial System, 7 Eur. Pub. L. 21 (2001).

5.   Article 2(A) of the Hungarian Constitution provides that Hungary "in its capacity as a Member State of the European Union, may exercise certain constitutional powers jointly with other Member States *to the extent necessary* in connection with the rights and obligations conferred by the Treaties on the foundation of the European Union and the European Communities" (emphasis added). It remains to be seen whether the Hungarian Constitutional Court

will follow the German Court's *solange* approach in interpreting the expression "to the extent necessary."

EUROPEAN ARREST WARRANT CASE

German Constitutional Court, second senate
Case 2 BvR 2236/04 (July 18, 2005).

[In 2003, Germany received a request from Spain for the extradition of Darkazanli, a citizen of both Germany and Syria, so that he could be tried on charges of terrorist activity. According to the allegations, he had given financial and other aid to Al–Qaeda. Spain initially sought extradition on the basis of an international arrest warrant. The Hamburg judicial authorities initially refused, citing Darkazanli's German nationality. However, after the entry into force in 2004 of the German European Arrest Warrant Act, by which Germany implemented the EU's Framework Decision on the European Arrest Warrant, the German judicial authorities agreed to arrest him. Darkazanli sued in German court to halt the extradition proceedings and to obtain a ruling from the Federal Constitutional Court on the constitutionality of the German European Arrest Warrant Act.

Unsuccessful, Darkazanli initiated a constitutional complaint in the German Constitutional Court which, at the suspect's request, temporarily enjoined extradition pending the outcome of the constitutional challenge. In the action, Darkazanli invoked, among other things, Article 16 of the German Constitution, according to which:

> (2) No German may be extradited to a foreign country. The law may provide otherwise for extraditions to a member state of the European Union or to an international court, provided that the rule of law is observed.

The Court addressed the constitutional issue as follows.]

64.   1.   German citizens are protected from extradition by the fundamental right under Article 16.2 [of the Constitution]. Pursuant to the second sentence of this provision, the protection can, however, be restricted by law in specific cases ... [But] the legislature is subject to constitutional commitments. ... When pursuing public interests, the constitution-restricting legislature is obliged to preserve the extent of protection provided by the fundamental right as far as possible; the constitution-restricting legislature may therefore restrict it only in compliance with the principle of proportionality and is to observe other constitutional commitments, such as the guarantee of legal protection under Article 19.4 of the Basic Law[5].... The European Arrest Warrant Act does not comply with these constitutional requirements ...

* * *

---

5. Article 19.4 states: "Should any person's rights be violated by public authority, he may have recourse to the courts. If no other jurisdiction has been established, recourse shall be to the ordinary courts...."

70.   b) The encroachment upon the scope of protection of Article 16.2 sentence 1 of the Basic Law is justified exclusively under the prerequisites set out in Article 16.2 sentence 2 of the Basic Law [which] permits, under certain conditions, the extradition of a German citizen to a Member State of the European Union. . . .

* * *

80.   The particular bar mentioned in Article 16.2 sentence 2 of the Basic Law does not, however, replace the limits of the Constitution that exist for every law that restricts fundamental rights. In turn, the law that restricts fundamental rights must comply with all commitments to constitutional law, may not tolerate conflicts with other provisions of the constitution and must implement the encroachment in a considerate manner, complying with the precept of proportionality.

* * *

84.   . . . When adopting the Act implementing the Framework Decision on the European arrest warrant, the legislature was obliged to implement the objective of the Framework Decision in such a way that the restriction of the fundamental right to freedom from extradition is proportionate. . . . [T]he legislature has to take into account that the ban on extradition is precisely supposed to protect, inter alia, the principles of legal certainty and protection of public confidence as regards Germans who are affected by extradition. The reliability of the legal system is an essential prerequisite for freedom, i.e. for a person's self-determination over his or her own concept of life and its implementation. . . .

* * *

88.   . . . [S]pecific weighing of the individual case is required if the act has been committed entirely or partly in Germany but the result has occurred abroad. What must be weighed and correlated in such cases are the gravity of the alleged offence and the possibilities of effective prosecution on the one hand and the prosecuted person's interests that are protected by fundamental rights on the other hand, taking into account the objectives connected with the creation of a single European judicial area.

89.   To the extent that the legislature does not make use of the latitude provided to it by . . . the Framework Decision on the European arrest warrant by specifying constituent elements of offences, it has to ensure through its programme of legal examination that the authorities that implement the Act will engage in a specific weighing of the conflicting legal positions. . . . As regards the extradition of persons, in particular of a state's own citizens, the Basic Law demands in each individual case a specific examination of whether the prosecuted person's corresponding rights are guaranteed. . . .

90.   d) The European Arrest Warrant Act does not meet these constitutional requirements. The manner of achieving the Framework Decision's objectives that the law has chosen encroaches upon the freedom from

extradition under Article 16.2 of the Basic Law in a disproportionate manner.

* * *

95. The legislature could have chosen an implementation that shows a higher consideration in respect of the fundamental right concerned without infringing the binding objectives of the Framework Decision because the Framework Decision contains possibilities for exceptions that permit the Federal Republic of Germany to take account of the fundamental-rights requirements that follow from Article 16.2 of the Basic Law....

* * *

97. cc) The European Arrest Warrant Act's infringement of the fundamental right to protection from extradition and of the principles of the rule of law that are applicable in this context would have been avoided by exhausting the margins afforded by the framework legislation when incorporating it into national law. The legislature was not entitled to refrain in this context from exhausting the latitude afforded to it, not even taking into account the legislature's freedom of drafting. The legislature did not correctly perform the weighing, which it is called upon to conduct by Article 16.2 of the Basic Law in connection with the principle of the rule of law, between the European interest in cross-border prosecution and the claim to protection that follows from the rights that stem from a person's status as a German. The legislature has already failed to see the mandate for weighing that follows from the special proviso of legality of Article 16.2 of the basic Law; in any case, it factually has not carried it out by providing a sufficient extent of protection from extradition.

* * *

102. 2. The lack of voidability of the decision [editors note: the term "voidability" as used here means "access to judicial review"] on the application for a grant of extradition in proceedings concerning extradition to a Member State of the European Union ... infringes Article 19.4 of the Basic Law. Admittedly, legal practice and legal literature have up to now rejected the possibility of recourse to the courts to void the decision on the application for a grant of extradition in extradition proceedings because its foreign-policy and general-policy aspects belong to the core area of executive power. This can, however, no longer apply if the decision on the application for a grant of extradition puts the legal restriction of a fundamental right in concrete terms.

103. a) Article 19.4 of the Basic Law guarantees a fundamental right to effective protection provided by the courts from acts of public authority (aa) to the extent that they encroach upon the rights of the person affected (bb).

104. aa). ... The guarantee provided by the Basic Law comprises access to the courts, the examination of the relief sought in formal

proceedings and the binding decision of the court. The citizen has a substantial claim to judicial review that is as effective as possible.

105. An integral part of the guarantee of effective legal protection is above all that the judge has sufficient authority to review ... the factual and legal aspects of a dispute so that he or she can remedy a violation of the law. The precept of effective legal protection does, however, not exclude that, depending on the type of measure that is to be examined, the concession of scope for drafting, discretion and assessment can result in differences regarding the completeness of judicial review.

* * *

114. ... The decision on the grant of extradition, which is to be taken on the basis of the weighing of facts and circumstances, serves to protect the prosecuted person's fundamental rights and may not be removed from judicial review ... To the extent that the legislature is constitutionally obliged to regulate other elements that are to be taken into account in a decision on extradition, Article 19.4 of the Basic Law also requires that the decision on extradition is subject to judicial review in this respect.

* * *

117. The European Arrest Warrant Act is void; an interpretation in conformity with the Constitution or a ruling that establishes the Act's partial voidness is excluded because the German legislature must be in a position to decide again, in normative freedom and taking into account the constitutional standards, about the exercise of the qualified legal proviso in Article 16.2 sentence 2 of the Basic Law ... As long as the legislature does not adopt a new Act implementing Article 16.2 sentence 2 of the Basic Law, the extradition of a German citizen to a Member State of the European Union is inadmissible.

* * *

126. The order of the [court] has been issued on the basis of an unconstitutional law and cannot be upheld for this reason alone.

127. Also the decision on the application of a grant of extradition is based on unconstitutional law and is overturned already for this reason.

NOTES AND QUESTIONS

1. Is the *Arrest warrant* decision surprising, in light of the previous German constitutional case law? Does it matter that the ruling targets the German implementing legislation rather than the Framework Decision itself?

2. The *Arrest warrant* decision was not in fact unanimous. One judge found the German legislation contrary to the principle of subsidiarity, as enshrined in the German Constitution. Another, while agreeing with the result, found the holding to be overbroad. A third flatly dissented on the ground that the majority violated the precept that Member State law should be interpreted if at all possible in such a way as not to violate EU law and that the German legislation could have been so interpreted.

3. For a broadly similar invalidation of national legislation implementing the European arrest warrant, see the Polish Constitutional Court's Decision No. P 1/05 of April 27, 2005, 43 CMLR 1181 (2006). On the many issues spawned by the European arrest warrant, see Elspeth Guild (ed.), Constitutional Challenges to the European Arrest Warrant (2006); R. Blekxtoon & W. van Ballegooij, Handbook on the European Arrest Warrant (2004).

THE *LISBON* JUDGMENT OF THE GERMAN CONSTITUTIONAL COURT

The issues raised by the *Maastricht* and *Arrest warrant* cases returned to the German Constitutional Court in a big way when a coalition of conservative and leftist members of Parliament challenged Germany's ratification of the Treaty of Lisbon as unconstitutional. High-profile individuals made their views known in the proceedings. Addressing the court in Karlsruhe, the German Foreign Minister, Frank–Walter Steinmeier, said the Treaty would boost democracy in Europe and enhance the role of national parliaments in the EU legislative process, while Interior Minister Wolfgang Schaeuble said the Treaty did not compromise German sovereignty. Opponents depicted the Treaty as part of a federalist agenda threatening national sovereignty, and scarcely any different from the ill-fated EU Constitution that French and Dutch voters had rejected in 2005.

The resulting *Lisbon* judgment (Case 2 BvE 2/08, June 30, 2009) follows broadly the lines of the *Maastricht* ruling. After a lengthy historical introduction and survey of the Lisbon Treaty's principal features, the Court framed the central issues as whether the German ratifying legislation entailed "a violation of the principle of democracy, the loss of statehood of the Federal Republic of Germany and a violation of the principle of the social state."

On the principle of democracy, the Court observed that it "is not amenable to weighing with other legal interests, . . . is inviolable . . . [and constitutes] an insurmountable boundary to any future political development" (¶ 216). However:

> The elaboration of the principle of democracy by the Basic Law is open to the objective of integrating Germany into an international and European peaceful order. The new shape of political rule which is thereby made possible is not schematically subject to the requirements of a constitutional state applicable on the national level and may therefore not be measured without further ado against the concrete manifestations of the principle of democracy in a Contracting State or Member State. The empowerment to embark on European integration permits a different shaping of political opinion-forming than the one that is determined by the Basic Law for the German constitutional order" (¶ 219).

Nevertheless, according to the Court, conformity with the principle of democracy requires that certain safeguards of democracy be in place. Thus, to the extent that Germany confers power on the European institutions, that conferral must be embodied in a democratically voted act of the legislature and must be expressed in terms that are sufficiently precise and determinate (¶¶ 236, 246). Beyond that, Germany must not transfer sovereign powers to European institutions in such a way that the latter can independently establish additional competences for themselves or even determine their own competence.

In a highly significant portion of the judgment, the Court identified certain fields of law that must remain national—for example, public safety and order, the use of military force, fundamentals of criminal procedure, fiscal matters, social policy, legal issues of family, religion and education (¶¶ 251–52). Even more widely-remarked than the enumeration was the rhetoric with which it was explained. Some salient passages follow:

> 253.   As regards the preconditions of criminal liability as well as the concepts of a fair and appropriate trial, the administration of criminal law depends on cultural processes of previous understanding that are historically grown and also determined by language, and on the alternatives which emerge in the process of deliberation which move the respective public opinion. . . . The penalisation of social behaviour can . . . only to a limited extent be normatively derived from values and moral premises that are shared Europe-wide. Instead, the decision on punishable behaviour, on the rank of legal interests and the sense and the measure of the threat of punishment, is to a particular extent left to the democratic decision-making process. . . . [T]he Member States must, in principle, retain substantial space of action in this context. . . .

> 254–55.   A similarly determined limit is drawn by the Basic Law as regards decisions on the deployment of the German *Bundeswehr* (army). With the exception of the state of defence, the deployment of the *Bundeswehr* abroad is only permitted in systems of mutual collective security, with the specific deployment mandatorily depending on the approval of the German Bundestag. . . . Even if the European Union were further developed into a peacekeeping regional system of mutual collective security within the meaning of Article 24.2 of the Basic Law, a supranationalisation with a primacy of application with a view to the specific deployment of German armed forces would be inadmissible in this area due to the precept of peace and democracy, which precedes the empowerment for integration of Article 23.1 of the Basic Law in this respect. The mandatory requirement of parliamentary approval for the deployment of the *Bundeswehr* abroad is not amenable to integration. . . .

> 256.   A transfer of the right of the Bundestag to adopt the budget and control its execution by the government which would violate the principle of democracy and the right to elect the German Bundestag in its essential content would take place if the determination of the character and the amount of the levies affecting the citizen were supranationalised to a considerable extent. The German Bundestag must decide in a manner that may be accounted for vis-à-vis the

people, on the total amount of the burdens placed on the citizens. The same applies correspondingly as regards essential expenditure of the state ... What is decisive is, however, that the overall responsibility, with sufficient space for political discretion, can still be assumed in the German Bundestag.

257. The principle of the social state establishes the obligation on the part of the state to ensure a just social order. The state must fulfil this mandatory responsibility on the basis of a broad scope of discretion ...

258. ... It is true that pursuant to Article 23.1 sentence 1 of the Basic Law, Germany's participation in the process of integration depends, *inter alia*, on the European Union's commitment to social principles. Accordingly the Basic Law not only safeguards social tasks for the German state union against supranational demands in a defensive manner but wants to commit the European public authority to social responsibility in the spectrum of tasks accorded to it....

259. Accordingly, the essential decisions in social policy must be made by the German legislative bodies on their own responsibility. In particular the securing of the individual's livelihood, which is a responsibility of the state that is based not only on the principle of the social state but also on Article 1.1 of the Basic Law, must remain a primary task of the Member States, even if coordination which goes as far as gradual approximation is not ruled out. This corresponds to the legally and factually limited possibilities of the European Union for shaping structures of a social state.

The Court's insistence on German particularity comes through most powerfully here:

260. Finally, democratic self-determination especially depends on the possibility of realising oneself in one's own cultural area as regards decisions that are made in particular concerning the school and education system, family law, language, part of the provisions governing the media, and the status of churches and religious and ideological communities. The activities of the European Union in these areas that are already perceivable intervene in society on a level that is the primary responsibility of the Member States and their component parts. The manner in which curricula and the content of education and, for instance, the structure of a multi-track school system are organised are fundamental policy decisions which bear a strong connection to the cultural roots and values of every state. Like the law on family relations and decisions on issues of language and the integration of the transcendental into public life, the manner in which school and education are organised particularly affects grown convictions and concepts of values which are rooted in specific historical traditions and experiences. Here, democratic self-determination requires that the respective political community that is connected by

such traditions and convictions remain the subject of democratic legitimisation.

Echoing its earlier *Maastricht* ruling, the Court reserved to itself the right to determine whether an EU measure is ultra vires, and reaffirmed that acts that are found to be ultra vires will be ineffective and unenforceable at the national level. Germany must also reserve a right of withdrawal from the Union (¶¶ 233–35, 240–41). In short, the Member States must "permanently remain masters of the Treaties" (¶ 231). The European Union, the Court emphasized, is not a federal state and is not governed by a federal constitution. The Bundestag must remain "the focal point of an interweaved democratic system" (¶ 277). According to the eminent constitutional law authority and former Constitutional Court judge, Dieter Grimm, the decisions gives a "negative answer to the question of whether the Basic Law permits the transformation of the EU into a federal state—a question that had been left open in the Maastricht decision." Dieter Grimm, Comments on the German Constitutional Court's Decision on the Lisbon Treaty: Defending Sovereign Statehood against Transforming the European Union into a State, 5 Eur. Const'l L. Rev. 353 (2009).

According to the Court, the organization and functioning of the European Union must itself comply with democratic principles, although not necessarily in the same fashion as at the national level. "An increase of integration can be unconstitutional if the level of democratic legitimisation is not commensurate to the extent and the weight of supranational power" (¶ 262). Legitimacy at the EU level results from the political responsiveness of the Council to the people of the several Member States and from the direct election of the European Parliament. At the international level, democratic legitimacy may be derived also from strengthened citizens' and associations' opportunities for participation in a transparent environment (¶ 290). Key to the Court's analysis is the role of national parliaments in ensuring respect for the principle of subsidiarity (¶ 305). The Court found it not incompatible with the principle of democracy at the international level that the Member States and their peoples do not have equal representation in the European institutions, or that EU law within its proper sphere enjoys primacy over Member State law.

The one serious obstacle to ratification, in the Court's view, was the failure of the ratifying legislation to require a vote by the German Parliament before Germany could cast a vote in the Council in favor of modification of the Treaties through the Lisbon Treaty's simplified amendment procedure or "bridging" procedure. Such steps would be fundamental enough to require specific national authorization. The German act of ratification was subsequently amended to so provide and to permit German ratification.

In the end the democratic character of the European Union does not, in the Court's assessment, meet the democratic criteria of a State, but neither is it so inadequate as to bar German ratification of the Treaty.

Notes and Questions

1. In November 2008, some six months before the German *Lisbon* judgment came down, the Constitutional Court of the Czech Republic rendered an opinion addressing many of the same issues as the German Constitutional Court would treat in its *Lisbon* judgment. The Czech Court concluded that the amendments brought about by the Lisbon Treaty were not so radical as to result in an unacceptable loss of national sovereignty. It found that the transfer of powers to the EU neither destroyed the essence of the Czech Republic as an independent democratic state, in violation of Articles 1(1), 9(2) and 10 of the Constitution, nor permitted the EU to expand its powers at will. However, it made clear that in the event of a conflict between EU law and the Czech Constitution that cannot be avoided by interpretation, the Constitution must prevail.

2. Germany and the Czech Republic are the only States whose courts entertained direct constitutional challenges to ratification of the Lisbon Treaty. However, suit was brought in the UK for a declaration that the Government was legally bound, by an election promise made in the context of the Constitutional Treaty, to hold a referendum. The claim was rejected.

2. EU LAW IN FRANCE

At the time of French entry into the European Communities, the then new 1958 French Constitution provided as follows:

Article 54

If the Constitutional Council, when consulted by the President of the Republic, the Prime Minister, or the president of one of the houses of Parliament, declares that an international treaty or agreement contains a clause contrary to the Constitution, the Constitution must be revised before the treaty or agreement can be ratified or approved.

Article 55

Once published, properly ratified or approved treaties or agreements have priority over municipal law, provided that the other contracting parties fully apply them.

Article 61

Institutional Acts, before their promulgation, private members' bills mentioned in article 11 before they are submitted to referendum, and the rules of procedure of the Houses of Parliament shall, before coming into force, be referred to the Constitutional Council, which shall rule on their conformity with the Constitution. . . .

Although Article 55 of the Constitution appeared to privilege treaties in the French legal order, the exact contours of the supremacy of EU law had to be worked out by the courts. Article 54 complicated the picture, however, by requiring that in the event the Conseil Constitutionnel declares a treaty to be contrary to the Constitution, it may not be ratified until either it or the Constitution has been duly amended to eliminate the inconsistency. To that extent, the constitutionality of a treaty is dealt with much like the constitutionality of statutes is handled under the French Constitution. Article 61 of the Constitution authorizes the Conseil Constitutionnel, at the request of a small number of individuals, to review ex ante the constitutionality of a statute prior to its promulgation. If the statute is contrary to the Constitution, it too may not be promulgated until it or the Constitution has been amended appropriately.[6]

In June 1992, Articles 88–1 and 88–4 were added to the French Constitution, following a ruling by the Conseil Constitutionnel that without those amendments, France could not constitutionally ratify the Maastricht Treaty and thereby become a party to the Treaty on European Union. Decision No. 92–554 of April 9, 1992, [1993] 3 CMLR 345, paras. 21852–54. Those articles read as follows:

Article 88–1

The French Republic participates in the European Communities and in the European Union, which are composed of States that have chosen freely, pursuant to the treaties that have constituted these entities, to exercise certain of their competences in common.

Article 88–4

The Government shall submit all proposed Community measures containing provisions of a legislative character to the National Assembly and to the Senate at the same time that those proposed measures are transmitted for action to the Council of the Communities.

During legislative sessions as well as outside of them, resolutions within the scope of this article may be adopted according to procedures determined by the rules of each assembly.

The situation in France has been complicated by the division of the judiciary into two court systems functioning independently of one other. While a system of ordinary, or judicial, courts deals primarily with civil, commercial and criminal matters, most disputes over the exercise of public authority in France are decided in separate administrative courts. The latter, though formally part of the administrative rather than judicial branch of government, operate in practice as courts completely independent of the executive. Each of the two systems has its own court of last resort, the Cour de Cassation for the ordinary courts and the Conseil d'Etat for the administrative courts. A further complication stems from the creation in 1958 of a separate Conseil Constitutionnel (Constitutional Council) whose functions include deciding the constitutionality of treaties and new legislation when challenged.

---

6. The French Constitution was amended in 2008 to permit the country's supreme courts (the Cour de Cassation and Conseil d'Etat) to refer questions of the constitutionality of statutes to the Conseil Constitutionnel if they arise in litigation before them. The lower courts may not do so.

The Conseil d'Etat initially ruled that it would not give priority to an EU regulation over a prior French statute with which it was in conflict, since to do so would effectively be to judge the constitutionality of legislation, which the judiciary (at least since the French Revolution) is forbidden by law and tradition to do.[7] Matters took a different turn when, in 1975, the Conseil Constitutionnel in a ruling on the constitutionality of an abortion reform stated the view that, Article 55 notwithstanding, reviewing a statute's conformity with a treaty is a fundamentally different exercise than reviewing a statute's conformity with the Constitution.[8] This position was then taken by the Cour de Cassation in the case that follows as a signal that it could reject application of a statute due to its inconsistency with a treaty without being seen as questioning the validity of the statute, much less invalidating it.

ADMINISTRATION DES DOUANES v. SOCIETE CAFES JACQUES VABRE

French Cour de Cassation (combined chambers)
[1974] cass. ch. mix. 6, [1975] 2 CMLR 336 (May 24, 1975).

[Vabre, a coffee importer, claimed that a French consumption tax levied on Dutch coffee imported for resale in France violated the EC Treaty's prohibition of discriminatory taxation. The tax was levied under the 1966 French Customs Code. Vabre sued for a refund, plus damages.

The lower courts ruled in favor of Vabre, observing that, under Article 55 of the French Constitution, the Treaty takes precedence over a contrary French statute, even one of a later date. The customs authorities, having been ordered to pay the refund plus damages, appealed to the Cour de Cassation.]

It is . . . complained that the judgment below invalidated the internal consumption tax established by . . . the Customs Code as a consequence of its incompatibility with the provisions of [EC Treaty Article 90, now TFEU Article 110] on the ground that by virtue of Article 55 of the Constitution the latter has an authority higher than that of internal statute, even if the statute be later in time. According to the appeal, a court may judge the legality of regulations laying down a tax which is challenged, but cannot without exceeding its powers discard the application of an internal statute on the pretext that it is unconstitutional. [According to the appeal], the provisions of the Customs Code . . . were enacted by [an] Act of 14 December 1966 which conferred on them the absolute authority which belongs to legislative provisions and which are binding on all French courts.

But the [Treaty], which by virtue of [Article 55] of the Constitution has an authority greater than that of statutes, institutes a separate legal order integrated with that of the Member States. Because of that separate-

---

7. See Syndicat général des Fabricants de semoules de France (1968). [1970] CMLR 395 (March 1, 1968).

8. Décision No. 75–54, Jan. 15 1975, Rev. Droit Pub. 1975.165.

ness, the legal order which it has created is directly applicable to the nationals of those States and is binding on their courts. Therefore the [lower court] was correct and did not exceed its powers in deciding that Article 95 of the Treaty was to be applied in the instant case, and not the Customs Code, even though the latter was later in date. It follows that the [claim] must be dismissed.

It is also complained that the judgment applied Article 95 of the [Treaty] when, according to the appeal, Article 55 of the Constitution expressly subjects the authority which it gives to treaties ratified by France to the condition that they should be applied by the other party. The judge at first instance was not therefore able validly to apply this constitutional provision without investigating whether the State (Holland) from which the product in question was imported has met this condition of reciprocity.

But in the Community legal order the failings of a Member State ... to comply with the obligations falling on it by virtue of the [Treaty] are subject to the [Member State enforcement] procedure laid down by Article 170 of that Treaty [now TFEU Article 259] and so the plea of lack of reciprocity cannot be made before the national courts. It follows that this ground must be dismissed.

NOTES AND QUESTIONS

1. Under the Court's approach in *Cafés Jacques Vabre*, when a statute is not enforced due to its inconsistency with a treaty, it is not invalidated, but merely "disapplied." Does that distinction make sense to you? Note that even before *Cafés Jacques Vabre*, the French civil courts were prepared to disregard a French statute if it conflicted with Community measures of a *later* rather than *earlier* date. See, for example, von Kempis v. Geldof, [1975] cass. civ. 3e 282 (no. 373), [1976] 2 CMLR 152, 176–77 (Dec. 15, 1975). But that was regarded as a simple application of the *lex posterior derogate legi priori* principle.

2. Nearly fifteen years after *Cafés Jacques Vabre*, the Conseil d'Etat revisited the supremacy issue. In *Nicolo*, [1989] Recueil Lebon 190, [1990] 1 CMLR 173 (Oct. 20, 1989), the Conseil d'Etat implied its willingness to reconsider its position, and one year later, in *Boisdet*, 1991 1 CMLR 3 (Sept. 24, 1990), it for the first time actually denied effect to a French statute on account of its conflict with an earlier EU law instrument. It confirmed the principle of supremacy in SA Rothmans International France and SA Philip Morris France, Rec. Leb. 1992.81, [1993] 1 CMLR 253, 255 (C.E., Feb. 28, 1992).

The Conseil d'Etat had more difficulty with the notion of the direct effect of directives. This is due to the nature of directives, which contemplate further normative action on the part of Member States to achieve the objectives of the directive. In Ministre de l'interieur v. Cohn–Bendit, [1980] 1 CMLR 543 (Dec. 22, 1978), the Conseil d'Etat stated that "... national authorities alone have the authority to choose how to execute the directives and to establish for themselves, under national judicial control, the proper means of giving them effect in domestic law. Therefore, irrespective of the provisions that they may address to the Member States, directives may not be invoked by nationals of these States in support of legal claims directed against an individual administrative act." The Conseil d'Etat has since nuanced that position, by holding that a statute may be denied application for inconsistency with a directive if the statute was meant to implement the directive "and even when the directive has not yet been transposed into national law."[9] As for the Conseil Constitutionnel, it ruled in its decision of June 10 and July 1, 2004 (Nos. 2004/496 and 2004/497) that it lacked jurisdiction to review the conformity with EU law of an act that transposes an EU directive into national law.

3.   The Conseil Constitutionnel has been asked on numerous occasions to determine whether the enactment of legislation required by EU law necessitated an amendment to the French Constitution. For example, a challenge was brought to a law allowing non-French EU nationals to enter the French civil service. (The Conseil Constitutionnel declined to decide the case on the ground that it lacks jurisdiction to decide the compatibility of a French statute with a treaty. Decision No. 91–293 of July 23, 1991.) Another challenge was brought to the French law authorizing ratification of the Schengen Convention (infra page 638). On this claim, the Conseil Constitutionnel reached the merits, concluding that the Convention violated nothing in the French Constitution. Decision No. 91–294 of July 25, 1991. However, the Constitutional Council did declare unconstitutional the French law, enacted pursuant to the Schengen Agreement, that made individual asylum decisions by other Contracting States binding on France, as violative of the French constitutional right of asylum. Decision No. 93–325 of August 13, 1993. The result was yet another French constitutional amendment, of November 1993, adding a new Article 53–1 to the Constitution.

4.   In Sarran et Lavacher, [1998] Rev. Fr. dr. adm. 1081 (1998), [1998] A.J.D.A. 1039 (1998) (Oct. 30, 1998), the Conseil d'Etat in plenary session ruled that international treaties do not enjoy a status superior to that of the French Constitution within the national legal order. What implications does this have for the supremacy of EU law in France?

SOCIETE ARCELOR ATLANTIQUE ET LORRAINE v. PREMIER MINISTRE
Conseil d'Etat N°287110
February 8, 2007.

[Following on the Kyoto Protocol, the EU adopted Directive 2003/87/EC, creating a system of greenhouse gas emission allowance trading. The Directive was designed to apply initially only to certain activities (listed in Annex I) and to certain greenhouse gases (listed in Annex II). Firms covered by the directive, such as Société Arcelor (a steel producer), were

---

9. See Judgment of July 8, 1991, Palazzi (1991); Judgment of Feb. 28, 1992, Rothmans International France and Arizona Tobacco Products (1992); Judgment of Feb. 6, 1998, Tête et. al. (1998). See generally Koen Lenaerts & Piet van Nuffel, Constitutional Law of the European Union 682 (2d ed. 2006).

required under the EU scheme to obtain a permit to emit greenhouse gases and to surrender allowances equal to the total emissions from their installations during a specified period, on pain of financial penalties. If the emissions from an installation exceeded the quantities allocated to the operator pursuant to a national allowance allocation plan, the operator was required to obtain additional allowances.

Arcelor asked the French authorities to repeal the provision of the implementing decree that extended the scheme to the steel sector, arguing that the exclusion from the scheme of the chemical and non-ferrous metal sectors, such as the plastics and aluminium sectors, was an unwarranted discrimination among producers in violation of the right to property, freedom to carry on a business, and the principle of equal treatment. As its request remained unanswered, Arcelor brought an action before the Conseil d'État challenging the implied decision rejecting its request.]

Annex I of the Directive subjects the production and processing of ferrous metals to the greenhouse gas allowance trading scheme and its language is repeated verbatim in the Annex to the [French] implementing decree. The Directive excludes the possibility for a Member State to remove activities mentioned in Annex I from the scheme's field of application.

* * *

The applicant companies claim that Article 1 of the decree violates several principles having constitutional value [in France].

Although the text of Article 55 of the Constitution provides that "once published, properly ratified or approved treaties or agreements have priority over municipal law, provided that the other contracting parties fully apply them," the supremacy thereby accorded to international agreements does not prevail, within the internal legal order, over the principles and rules of constitutional value. In regard to the provisions of Article 88–1 of the Constitution . . . , from which there results a constitutional duty to transpose directives, review of the constitutionality of the implementing acts that makes this transposition is to be exercised in particular ways when the rules to be transposed are precise and unconditional. Therefore, subject to pertinent rules of jurisdiction and procedure, it is for the administrative court, presented with a claim of violation of a rule or principle of [French] constitutional value, to determine whether there exists a rule or a general principle of Community law that, in view of its nature and scope, as understood under current Community case law, guarantees . . . respect for the rule or constitutional principle invoked. If so, the administrative court has reason, for purposes of guaranteeing the decree's constitutionality, to determine whether the directive that the decree transposes is itself in conformity with the [relevant] rule or general principle of Community law. Absent a serious issue in this regard, the court may reject the argument invoked. Otherwise, the judge makes a preliminary reference to the European Court of Justice, in accordance with Article 234 of the EC Treaty [now TFEU Article 267]. Conversely, if there exists no rule or general principle of Community law that effectively guarantees respect for the [French] rule or constitutional principle invoked, the administrative court is competent to directly examine the constitutionality of the challenged implementing measure.

* * *

[T]he claimants maintain that Article 1 of the challenged decree infringes the principle of equal treatment since companies that belong to the competing sectors, notably plastics and aluminium—and that emit similar quantities of greenhouse gas—are not subject to the allowance trading scheme.

The principle of equal treatment, which is a norm of [French] constitutional value, constitutes a general principle of Community law. It appears from current Court of Justice case law that violation of this principle occurs when comparable situations are treated differently, provided the difference in treatment is not objectively justified. The scope of this general principle of Community law ensures, as to this argument, effective respect for the [French] constitutional principle in issue. Accordingly, the Conseil d'Etat is competent to determine whether the directive, insofar as it includes steel companies within its field of application, infringes the general principle of Community law to which it is subject.

The record shows that plastic and aluminium companies emit greenhouse gases identical to those whose emission the directive aims to limit. These industries produce materials that are partially substitutable for those produced by the steel industry and that are thus in a competitive relationship with it. They are not currently covered by the greenhouse gas allowance trading scheme, and are not indirectly subject to it unless they have combustion facilities having a heating power in excess of 20 megawatts. If the decision not to include plastic and aluminium companies in the scheme at this time has been taken on account of their relative share in the total emissions of greenhouse gas and of the need to ensure a gradual implementation of an overall policy, the question whether the directive's difference in treatment is objectively justified raises a serious issue. Therefore, the Conseil d'Etat is competent to stay these proceedings ... until the Court of Justice has decided the preliminary question of the conformity of the directive with the principle of equal treatment, insofar as it applies the greenhouse gas allowance trading scheme to installations in the steel sector, but not within the aluminium and plastic industries.

* * *

[The Court decides] to stay the proceedings ... until the Court of Justice rules on the conformity of the directive with the principle of equal treatment, insofar as it applies the greenhouse gas allowance trading scheme to installations in the steel sector, but not within the aluminium and plastic industries....

NOTES AND QUESTIONS

1.   In *Arcelor*, the Conseil d'Etat found that EU law contained a principle analogous to the French constitutional principle of equal treatment, which permitted the court to rely on the Court of Justice to ensure respect for it. Suppose, however, the French constitutional principle allegedly breached by the implementing legislation is specific to the French Constitution, and has no EU law counterpart (such as, the principle of *laicité*, or secularism). What result then? For an assessment of the *Arcelor* decision, see Oreste Pollicino, The Conseil d'Etat and the relationship between French internal law after Arcelor: Has something really changed?, 45 CMLR 1519 (2008).

2.   In its subsequent preliminary ruling, the Court of Justice found no violation of the principle of equal treatment. Société Arcelor Atlantique et Lorraine v. Premier Ministre, Case C127/07, [2008] ECR I–9895. It reasoned that the allowance trading scheme's novelty and complexity required that a limit be placed initially on the number of participants. Arcelor subsequently brought an unsuccessful direct challenge to the scheme in the Court of First Instance. Arcelor SA v. Parliament and Council, Case T–16/04, [2010] ECR II––––.

3.   France has company in the EU in subjecting to constitutional review domestic legislation that faithfully implements directives or other EU law. On the position of the Polish courts, see Krystyna Kowalik–Bańczyk, Should we polish it up? The Polish Constitutional Tribunal and the idea of supremacy of EU law, 6 German L. J. 1355 (2005); on the position of the Italian courts, see Paul Craig & Gráinne de Búrca, European Union Law 363–65, (4th ed., 2008). Spain is more difficult to classify. Rafael Leal–Arcas, The Reception of Community law in Spain, 1 Hanse Law Review 18 (2005).

3.   EU LAW IN DENMARK

On no occasion have the Danish courts seriously questioned the direct applicability, direct effect or supremacy of an EU law measure as interpreted by the Court of Justice. The case of Carlsen v. Rasmussen, Case I 361/1997 (1988), UfR 1998.800, para. 9.6, [1999] 3 CMLR 854 (1999) (April 6, 1998), however, suggests that judicial acceptance of these principles in Denmark is not unqualified. In that case, twelve Danish citizens brought suit challenging the prime minister's signature of the Maastricht Treaty. They claimed that the Treaty's delegation of sovereignty was on such a scale as to be inconsistent with the Danish Constitution's premise of a democratic form of government. More specifically, they objected to the Treaty's having retained the then Article 235 [now TFEU Article 352] on implied powers, thereby violating Article 20(1) of the Constitution which permits the parliament to delegate sovereignty to international organizations only "to an extent specified by statute."

The Court had this to say:

15.   The demand for specification in section 20(1) precludes [leaving it] to the international organization to make its own specification of its powers.

16. [On the other hand,] the term "to an extent specified by statute" cannot be interpreted to the effect that powers which are vested in the authorities of [Denmark] can be entrusted to an international organization only to a limited—i.e. minor—extent.

* * *

24. It appears from the wording of Article 235 [now TFEU Article 352] that the fact that action by the Community is considered necessary in order to attain one of the objectives of the Community does not in itself constitute [a] sufficient [basis] for applying the provision. It is a further condition that the intended action is "in the course of the operation of the common market." . . .

25. The stated interpretation of Article 235 must be taken as the basis, even though prior to the amendment of the Treaty the provision may have been applied on the basis of a wider interpretation.

26. A legislative act, which does not go any further than to confer powers to issue legislative acts or decide upon other measures in accordance with the interpretation of Article 235 stated above, does not constitute a violation of the demand for specification in section 20 of the Constitution.

27. The adoption of any measure pursuant to Article 235 must be unanimous. Therefore the Government may prevent the provision from being applied to any adoption which is beyond the stated scope of Denmark's delegation of powers to the EC. . . . [Given the purpose of Article 235], it is unavoidable that the precise delimitation of the scope of application of the provision may give rise to doubts. [This means] that the Act of Accession grants the Government a not insignificant margin [of judgment].

* * *

30. The fact that the detailed determination of the powers vested in the institutions of the Community may give rise to doubts, and that the jurisdiction to give rulings [on such questions] is transferred to the European Court of Justice, cannot in itself be regarded as incompatible with the requirement of specification in section 20 of the Constitution.

* * *

31. The appellants have pleaded that the jurisdiction of the European Court of Justice under the Treaty [in light of the principle of supremacy of EC law] implies that Danish courts of law are prevented from enforcing the limits for the surrender of sovereignty [made] by the Act of Accession. . . .

32. [T]he power to test the validity and legality of EC acts lies with the European Court of Justice. This implies that Danish courts of law cannot hold that an EC act is inapplicable in Denmark, without the question of its compatibility with the Treaty having been tried by the

European Court of Justice. . . . However, the . . . demand for specification in section 20(1) of the Constitution [implies] that the [Danish] courts of law cannot be deprived of their right to try questions as to whether an EC [legal] act exceeds the limits for the surrender of sovereignty made by the Act of Accession. Therefore, Danish courts must rule that an EC act is inapplicable in Denmark if the extraordinary situation should arise that it can be established with the required certainty that an EC act [whose validity] has been upheld by the European Court of Justice is based on an application of the Treaty which lies beyond the surrender of sovereignty [made by] the Act of Accession. . . .

* * *

34.   [Against this background], the Supreme Court finds that neither the additional powers that have been delegated to the Council in pursuance of Article 235, nor the law-making activities of the Court of Justice, can be regarded as incompatible with the demand for specification in section 20(1) of the Constitution.

It has been suggested that the Danish *Maastricht* ruling "may be evidence of a horizontal dynamic whereby the highest courts in member states will be influenced by each other in the warnings issued to the European Court and the reasoning adopted in doing so [and that] such concerted action will increase the pressure on the European Court to act within its competence." S. Weatherill & P. Beaumont, EU Law 451 (3d ed. 1999).

For an in-depth treatment of the Danish decision, see K. Heogh, The Danish Maastricht Judgment, 24 Eur. L. Rev. 80 (1999).

4.   EU LAW IN IRELAND

Article 29(4)(3) of the 1937 Irish Constitution, added in 1972, provides a basis for Irish membership in the EU:

The State may become a member of the [ECSC, EEC and Euratom]. No provision of this Constitution invalidates laws enacted, acts done or measures adopted by the State necessitated by the obligations of membership of the Communities or prevents laws enacted, acts done or measures adopted by the Communities, or institutions thereof, from having the force of law in the State.

The 1972 European Communities Act (no. 27, Dec. 6, 1972) followed. In a suit brought to prevent Irish ratification of the Single European Act, the Irish Supreme Court held Article 29(4)(3) of the Constitution to be broad enough to authorize Irish ratification of the Single Act's provisions on qualified majority voting, on the new Court of First Instance and on the introduction of new EU competences. However, it found that Title III (art. 30) of the Single Act, on European Political Cooperation (EPC), was not covered by Article 29(4)(3) since it altered "the essential scope and objectives of the Communities," chiefly by envisioning "a form of European political union between the Member States ... as an addition to the existing economic union between them." [1987] 2 CMLR at 729–30. The Irish Supreme Court accordingly ruled that the government needed the fresh assent of the Irish people in order to curtail Ireland's freedom of action in foreign policy, and the SEA's entry into force was in fact postponed from January 1, 1987 to July 1, 1987 to permit a referendum and a constitutional amendment to that effect. Crotty v. An Taoiseach, [1987] ILRM 400, [1987] 2 CMLR 666 (April 9, 1987). On the other hand, Chief Justice Finlay chose to affirm in *Crotty* that decisions of the Council have "primacy" over domestic law and that decisions of the Court of Justice "take precedence" both over domestic law and over national court rulings on the meaning of the Community Treaties.

The case of Murphy v. Bord Telecom Eireann, [1989] ILRM 53, [1988] 2 CMLR 753 (April 11, 1988), is revealing. Following a preliminary ruling from the Court of Justice (Murphy v. Bord Telecom Eireann, Case 157/86, [1988] ECR 673), to the effect that the principle of equal pay under EC Treaty Article 119 (later renumbered 141, and now TFEU Article 157) applies not only to cases in which women are paid less than men for equal work, but also to cases in which they are paid less than men for work of higher value), the Irish High Court issued a remand to the Labor Court, which had previously held that in such cases men and women are not engaged in "like work." In the remand, the High Court provided the Labor Court the following instruction:

> 1. Article 119 of the [EC] Treaty is part of the domestic law of the State by virtue of ... the European Communities Act 1972. So too is Article 177 [later renumbered 234, and now TFEU Article 267], which enables a judge of a national court to obtain a ruling on the interpretation of any Article of the Treaty, which ruling once obtained is binding on the national court.

* * *

> 5. The interpretation of [the relevant Irish legislation], in accordance with the canons of construction normally applied in Irish courts, has in the present case yielded a result which is in conflict with Article 119 of the Treaty as interpreted by the Court of Justice....

> 6. Where such a conflict exists, national law must yield primacy to Community law....

> 7. Where such a conflict arises, the national law is, accordingly, inapplicable.

[1988] 2 CMLR at 755. In striving to interpret Irish legislation as not in contradiction with EU law, the Irish courts acknowledge adopting a teleological approach to the interpretation of national measures implementing EU law. Lawlor v. Minister for Agriculture, [1988] ILRM 400, [1988] 3 CMLR 22 (High Court, Oct. 2, 1987).

The language in the *Crotty, Murphy* and other cases would suggest that EU law is securely anchored in the Irish legal order. Commentators largely agree. See N. Travers, Community Directives: Effects, Efficiency, Justiciability, 1998 Irish J. Eur. L. 165. But neither of those cases pitted EU law against claims based on fundamental individual rights guaranteed by the Irish Constitution. The following case, however, did.

SOCIETY FOR THE PROTECTION OF UNBORN CHILDREN (IRELAND) LTD. v. GROGAN

Irish Supreme Court
[1989] IR 753, [1990] 1 CMLR 689 (Dec. 19, 1989).

[Article 40.3.3 of the Irish Constitution protects the right to life of unborn children and prohibits abortions. The plaintiff organization sought an interlocutory and permanent injunction prohibiting certain student unions and their officers from publishing handbooks with the names and addresses of abortion clinics in the UK, where abortions were legal. The defendants argued that EU law, notably the principle of free movement of services, protected their right to publish such information. When the Irish High Court asked the Court of Justice for a preliminary ruling on the issue, the plaintiff immediately appealed to the Irish Supreme Court. It claimed that the lower court's failure to award interim relief pending the Court of Justice's ruling amounted to unconstitutionally enjoining enforcement of the right to life.

The Irish Supreme Court began its analysis by citing its own prior decision that assisting pregnant women in Ireland to travel abroad to obtain abortions violated Article 40.3.3 of the Constitution and could be enjoined.]

FINLAY, C.J.:

This application for an interlocutory injunction ... consists of an application to restrain an activity which has been clearly declared by this Court to be unconstitutional and therefore unlawful and which could assist, and is intended to assist, in the destruction of the right to life of an unborn child, a right acknowledged and protected under the Constitution.

That constitutionally guaranteed right must be fully and effectively protected by the Courts.

If and when a decision of the European Court of Justice rules that some aspect of European Community law affects the activities of the defendants impugned in this case, the consequence of that decision on these constitutionally guaranteed rights and their protection by the Courts will then fall to be considered by these Courts.

Having regard to that duty of the Court, it is clearly quite inappropriate to approach the exercise of the discretion to grant or refuse an interlocutory injunction upon the basis of a supposed *status quo ante* consisting of activities which are constitutionally forbidden acts.

* * *

With regard to the issue of the balance of convenience, I am satisfied that where an injunction is sought to protect a constitutional right, the only matter which could properly be capable of being weighed in a balance against the granting of such protection would be another competing constitutional right.

I am quite satisfied that in the instant case where the right sought to be protected is that of a life, there can be no question of a possible or putative right which might exist in European law as a corollary to a right to travel so as to avail of services, counterbalancing as a matter of convenience the necessity for an interlocutory injunction.

[The Chief Justice also rejected the defendants' claim that, before granting an interlocutory injunction, the court was required to refer to the Court of Justice for a preliminary ruling the question whether granting such a remedy was permissible and appropriate under EU law.]

NOTES AND QUESTIONS

1. In the awaited ruling, the Court of Justice held that medical termination of pregnancy that is lawful where performed is a service within the meaning of EC Treaty Article 50 (now TFEU Article 57), but that the link between the students' activities in *Grogan* and the availability of UK abortion services was "too tenuous" to render interference with those activities a restriction on freedom of services. For the Court's opinion, see Society for the Protection of Unborn Children Ireland Ltd. v. Grogan, Case C–159/90, [1991] ECR I–4685, infra page 697.

2. Following receipt of the preliminary ruling in *Grogan*, the Irish High Court (per Judge Morris) issued a permanent injunction forbidding the student leaders from distributing the abortion information in question. Society for the Protection of Unborn Children Ireland Limited (SPUC) v. Grogan, [1994] 1 IR 46, [1993] 1 CMLR 197 (Aug. 4, 1992). The Court evidently also referred the students' alleged breaches of the prior interlocutory injunction to the Director of Public Prosecutions. See The Irish Times, Aug. 8, 1992, pp. 1, 4.

3. Do you agree that the link in *Grogan* was "too tenuous"? Suppose, as actually happened in one case, the Irish authorities physically prevented a young girl from leaving Ireland for the UK to obtain an abortion? Would the link to the free movement of services still be "too tenuous"? When that case arose, the Irish Supreme Court avoided the conflict by holding that the young girl's threat to commit suicide if forced to give birth placed her within the exception to the Irish prohibition on abortion for real and substantial risk to the mother's life. Attorney General v. X, [1992] 2 CMLR 277 (March 5, 1992).

C. THE CASE OF THE UNITED KINGDOM

The ultimate place of EU law in the UK defies easy summary. The UK has no written constitution. It was therefore not possible to base EU membership on a constitutional provision or amendment as in the other

Member States. Moreover, the UK maintains a dualist approach to international law, which prevents treaties from taking effect in domestic law unless implemented by national legislation. The English Court of Appeal remarked in a decision rendered just after British accession: "Even though the Treaty of Rome has been signed, it has no effect, so far as these Courts are concerned, until it is made an Act of Parliament. Once it is implemented by an Act of Parliament, these Courts must go by the Act of Parliament. Until that day comes, we take no notice of it." McWhirter v. Attorney General, [1972] CMLR 882 (C.A., June 30, 1972).

EUROPEAN COMMUNITIES ACT OF 1972
(1972 ch. 68).

Sec. 2.   General implementation of Treaties.

(1) All such rights, powers, liabilities, obligations and restrictions from time to time created or arising by or under the Treaties, and all such remedies and procedures from time to time provided for by or under the Treaties ... are without further enactment to be given legal effect or used in the United Kingdom, shall be recognised and available in law, and be enforced, allowed and followed accordingly; and the expression "enforceable Community right" and similar expressions shall be read as referring to one to which this subsection applies.

(2) [Subject to stated exceptions], at any time after its passing Her Majesty may by order in Council, and any designated Minister or department may by regulations, make provision (a) for the purpose of implementing any Community obligation of the United Kingdom, or enabling any such obligation to be implemented, or of enabling any rights enjoyed or to be enjoyed by the United Kingdom under or by virtue of the Treaties to be exercised; or (b) for the purpose of dealing with matters arising out of or related to any such obligation or rights or the coming into force, or the operation from time to time, of subsection (1) above; ...

* * *

(4) [A]ny enactment passed or to be passed, other than one contained in this Part of this Act, shall be construed and have effect subject to the foregoing provisions of this section, but except as may be provided by any Act passed after this Act.

* * *

Sec. 3.   Decisions on, and proof of, Treaties and Community instruments, etc.

(1) For the purposes of all legal proceedings any question as to the meaning or effect of any of the Treaties, or as to the validity, meaning or effect of any Community instrument, shall be treated as a question of law (and, if not referred to the European Court, be for determination as such

in accordance with the principles laid down by any relevant decision of the
European Court).

NOTES AND QUESTIONS

1. Does Section 2(1) of the European Communities Act establish the
direct effectiveness of EU law in the UK? Does it at least provide a standard
for determining whether a particular EU law measure is to have direct effect?
Does Section 3 help?

2. Parliamentary sovereignty is said to mean that Parliament has perfect freedom to legislate except that it cannot limit its future legislative
freedom. (Consider Section 2(4) of the Act.) If that is so, how could the
European Communities Act possibly establish the supremacy of EU law?

3. Mr. Albert Blackburn thought that any British statute effective to
implement the European Treaties in the UK would necessarily surrender
British sovereignty, and on that account he sued to prevent the UK from
acceding to the EU. The Court of Appeal dismissed the suit as premature. On
the question whether the courts would refuse to enforce a British statute that
was squarely in conflict with existing Community legislation, Lord Denning,
in his opinion, remarked that "we will wait till that day comes." Blackburn v.
Attorney General, [1971] 2 All ER 1380, [1971] CMLR 784, 790 (C.A., civ. div.,
Feb. 27 & May 10, 1971). As shown by the House of Lords' ruling in the
Factortame case, infra page 315, that day has come.

MACARTHY'S LTD. v. SMITH

English Court of Appeal (civil division)
[1979] 3 All ER 325, [1979] 3 CMLR 44 (May 23–25, July 25, 1979).

[Smith successfully sued Macarthys under UK sex discrimination
legislation intended to implement EC Treaty 119 (later numbered 141,
now TFEU Article 157) on the ground that Macarthys paid her only £50 a
week, while it had paid £60 a week to the male employee she was hired to
replace. Macarthys argued on appeal that Smith's recovery contravened
the plain meaning of the British statute which by its terms only covered
discrimination between persons employed by the same employer for the
same work at the same time. Lord Denning, for the Court of Appeal,
referred several questions of interpretation to the Court of Justice, but in
doing so had this to say.]

DENNING, L.J.:

[T]he United Kingdom has passed legislation with the intention of giving
effect to the principle of equal pay. It has done it by the Sex Discrimination Act [of] 1975. . . .

* * *

. . . In construing our statute, we are entitled to look to the Treaty as an
aid to its construction; but not only as an aid but as an overriding force. If
on close investigation it should appear that our legislation is deficient or is

inconsistent with Community law by some oversight of our draftsmen, then it is our bounden duty to give priority to Community law. Such is the result of § 2(1) and (4) of the European Communities Act [of] 1972.

I pause here, however, to make one observation on a constitutional point. Thus far I have assumed that our Parliament, whenever it passes legislation, intends to fulfill its obligations under the Treaty. If the time should come when our Parliament deliberately passes an Act with the intention of repudiating the Treaty or any provision in it or intentionally of acting inconsistently with it and says so in express terms, then I should have thought that it would be the duty of our courts to follow the statute of our Parliament. I do not however envisage any such situation.

[Lord Denning found that the Treaty article clearly applied "not only to cases where the woman is employed on like work at the same time with a man in the same employment, but also when she is employed on like work in succession to a man." He conceded that the UK's 1970 equal pay legislation (adopted prior to EC membership) required employment "at the same time." However, he thought that UK law could and should be interpreted as not imposing it, thus reaching "this very desirable result ... that there is no conflict between ... the Treaty and [the UK legislation]." He continued.]

Now my colleagues take a different view. They are of [the] opinion that [the UK legislation] should be given its natural and ordinary meaning, and that is, they think, that it is confined to cases where the woman is employed *at the same time* as a man.

* * *

[A]s my colleagues think that Article 119 is not clear on the point, I agree that reference should be made to the European Court at Luxembourg to resolve the uncertainty in that article.

LAWTON, L.J.:

In my judgment the grammatical construction of [the UK statute] is consistent only with a comparison between a woman and a man in the same employment at the same time. The words, by the tenses used, look to the present and the future but not to the past. They are inconsistent with a comparison between a woman and a man, no longer in the same employment, who was doing her job before she got it.

* * *

As the meaning of the words ... is clear, ... under our rules for the construction of Acts of Parliament the statutory intention must be found within those words. It is not permissible to read into the statute words which are not there....

* * *

Being in doubt as to the ambit of {the Treaty article] and being under an obligation ... to apply that article in our courts, ... a decision is necessary as to [its] construction....

... I consider myself under a judicial duty not to guess how [the Court of Justice] would construe it but to find out how it does.

[The opinion of CUMMING-BRUCE L.J., agreeing substantially with that of LAWTON L.J., is omitted.]

NOTES AND QUESTIONS

1. Does *Macarthys* base the primacy of EU law on the European Communities Act of 1972 or treat it as an imperative of EU law itself? Does it matter?

2. Lord Denning employed a teleological interpretation of EU law. That approach, he has written, "is not really so alarming as it sounds." Under it, judges go "not ... by the literal meaning of the words or by the grammatical structure of the sentence, [but] by the design or purpose which lies behind it. When they come upon a situation which is to their minds within the spirit— but not the letter—of the legislation, ... they interpret the legislation so as to produce the desired effect. This means that they fill in gaps, quite unashamedly...." James Buchanan & Co., Ltd. v. Babco Forwarding & Shipping (U.K.) Ltd., [1977] Q.B. 208, 213, [1977] 2 CMLR 455, 458–59 (Dec. 2, 1976). On the other hand, the House of Lords, on appeal from Lord Denning's opinion, suggested that British courts are not bound to follow a teleological approach to interpreting national statutes that implement Community law. Buchanan v. Babco, [1978] A.C. 141, [1978] 1 CMLR 156 (H.L., Nov. 9, 1977).

More recent comments from the House of Lords suggest that Lord Denning's attitude may now be winning favor. In Webb v. EMO Air Cargo (UK) Ltd., [1992] 4 All ER 929, [1993] 1 WLR 49 (Nov. 26, 1992), the House of Lords acknowledged that UK courts have the responsibility to "construe domestic legislation in any field covered by a Community directive so as to accord with the interpretation of the directive as laid down by the European Court, if that can be done without distorting the meaning of domestic legislation," and that this is so whether the domestic legislation predates or postdates the directive. However, Lord Keith of Kinkel, delivering the judgment on behalf of the court, underscored that national courts only need to construe domestic legislation in conformity with a directive insofar as the law is open to an interpretation consistent with it. And, indeed, the House of Lords subsequently concluded that the UK legislation at issue (section 1(1)(a) of the Sex Discrimination Act 1975) could be interpreted in conformity with the European Court's ruling in *Webb*. Webb v. EMO Air Cargo (UK) Ltd. *(Webb 2)*, [1995] 4 All ER 577, [1995] 1 WLR 1454 (Oct. 19, 1995),

Lord Templeman has put the matter this way: British courts are "willing and anxious" to find UK legislation to be consistent with EU law. Duke v. GEC Reliance Ltd., [1988] A.C. 618, 638, [1988] 2 WLR 359, [1988] 1 All ER 626 (H.L., Feb. 11, 1988). Particularly when a statute is passed to implement an EU directive, Parliament will be presumed to have meant to satisfy its obligations, and the statute will if possible be interpreted accordingly.

3. The question of the primacy of EU law over a subsequent act of Parliament finally arose sharply in connection with the Court of Justice's preliminary ruling in the *Factortame* case, discussed at page 250 supra. The House of Lords had implicitly accepted the primacy doctrine by asking the Court of Justice whether a UK court should temporarily enjoin enforcement of an act of Parliament as in probable violation of EU law. The issue would have been irrelevant if a subsequent British statute necessarily prevailed over EU law. But the same case, at a later stage, demanded a more direct answer.

REGINA v. SECRETARY OF STATE FOR TRANSPORT EX PARTE FACTORTAME LTD.

House of Lords
[1991] 1 All ER 70, [1990] 3 CMLR 375 (Oct. 11, 1990).

LORD BRIDGE OF HARWICH:

Some public comments on the [Court of Justice's] decision [in *Factortame I*] ... have suggested that this was a novel and dangerous invasion by a Community institution of the sovereignty of the United Kingdom Parliament. But such comments are based on a misconception. If the supremacy ... of Community law over the national law of Member States was not always inherent in the EEC Treaty it was certainly well established in the jurisprudence of the European Court of Justice long before the United Kingdom joined the Community. ... Under the terms of the [European Communities] Act of 1972 it has always been clear that it was the duty of a United Kingdom court, when delivering final judgment, to override any rule of national law found to be in conflict with any directly enforceable rule of Community law. ... Thus there is nothing in any way novel in according supremacy to rules of Community law in those areas to which they apply and to insist that, in the protection of rights under Community law, national courts must not be inhibited by rules of national law from granting interim relief in appropriate cases is no more than a logical recognition of that supremacy.

[Lord Bridge then concluded that under English principles an interim injunction should be ordered. All of the Lords reached the same conclusion, though the opinion of Lord Goff ([1990] 3 CMLR at 382) provides the fullest analysis.]

NOTES AND QUESTIONS

1. Immediately after making the excerpted remarks, Lord Bridge added that "the judgment of the ... Court of Justice does not fetter our discretion to determine whether an appropriate case for the grant of interim relief has been made out." [1991] 1 All ER at 108, [1990] 3 CMLR at 380. Do you agree? For discussion of the latitude national courts enjoy in deciding whether to issue orders of interim relief in aid of EU law claims, see Chapter 10A infra.

2. As will be seen (page 707 infra), the Court of Justice later ruled that the 1988 amendments to the UK Merchant Shipping Act at issue in *Factortame* violated the EU principle of freedom of establishment.

3. More as a response to its obligations under the European Convention on Human Rights than under EU law as such, the UK in 1998 enacted the Human Rights Act, effective October 2, 2000. Section 6 makes it unlawful for "public authorities," as defined in Section 10, to "act in a way which is incompatible with a Convention right." Claimants may either bring a direct action against the relevant authority or invoke the Act in the context of other ongoing proceedings (section 7). In order to bring suit, a claimant must be deemed capable of qualifying as a "victim of an unlawful act," for purposes of instituting an action in the European Court of Human Rights.

Section 3 of the Act requires that primary and subordinate legislation must be read and given effect, if at all possible, in a way that is compatible with the Convention. UK courts and tribunals must take into account any prior judgment or advisory opinion of the European Court of Human Rights. If a court is satisfied that a provision of primary legislation is incompatible with a Convention right, it still must give effect to that legislation; a court must do the same with subordinate legislation even if, despite all efforts to construe it otherwise, the court finds the legislation to be in breach of Convention rights. However, in these situations, the higher UK courts—and they alone—may make a "declaration of incompatibility," which has no direct legal effect but sets in motion a "fast-track" mechanism for parliamentary amendment of the offending legislation. Section 10 permits the amendment of primary legislation by subordinate legislation where there are "compelling reasons" for not seeking the full consent of Parliament.

Where a public authority has breached a Convention right, the court may make any order or grant any relief or remedy within its powers that it considers just and appropriate. However, an award of damages may be made only if the court finds that such a remedy is necessary to afford the victim "just satisfaction."

For more on the UK Act, see Oliver, The Human Rights Act and the Public Law/Private Law Divides, 2000 Eur. Human Rts. L. Rev. 343 (2000).

THOBURN v. SUNDERLAND CITY COUNCIL

(Metric martyrs case)
Queens Bench Division, Divisional Court.
[2003] QB 151, [2002] CMLR 50 (Feb. 18, 2002).

[Thoburn and the other appellants, sellers of fruits and vegetables, were charged with pricing fruits and vegetables according to their weight as measured in pounds. While the UK Weights and Measurements Act of 1963 had permitted both imperial and metric units to be used, Council Directive 80/181 (the "Metrification Directive"), as amended, made the use of metric weights and measures compulsory, subject to a long transition period. In 1985, the UK enacted a statute expressly permitting continued use of the imperial measurement system. The directive itself was subsequently amended to extend the transition period through December 31, 1999, for loose produce in bulk. The conduct with which appellants were charged took place in early 2000, just after the end of the revised transition period. They were accordingly in violation of the amended directive. However, that directive had been transposed into UK law in 1994 by regulation, rather than legislation, as expressly permitted by Section 2(2) of the European Communities Act of 1972 [ECA]. (Section 2(2) ECA permitted UK legislation to be modified by secondary legislation (i.e. regulation) if the latter's purpose was to enable the UK to comply with EU law.) Appellants took the position that the 1985 statute, being later in time than the 1972 ECA, impliedly repealed Section 2(2) ECA as concerns weights and measures, so that the implementing regulations (on the basis of which appellants had been charged) were invalid and unenforceable. Opposing counsel advanced several arguments, but the pertinent one here was that EU law, not UK law, determined the effect of the amended directive in the UK.]

Lord Justice Laws:

53. [Counsel for the City Council] submitted that the EC treaty was not like other international treaties. It created a new and so far unique legal order, supreme above the legal systems of the Member States, so that upon accession to the Community by force of the ECA, the United Kingdom bowed its head to this supremacy. One consequence was that while the Parliament of the United Kingdom retained the legal power to repeal the ECA by express legislation, it could not do so impliedly....

54. In support of her overall position as to ... the impossibility of implied repeal of the ECA, [counsel] relied in particular on two seminal decisions of the Court of Justice, decided in the relatively early days of the Community [citing *Van Gend en Loos*, supra page 232, and *Costa v. ENEL*, supra page 245]

55. Plainly, any treaty not incorporated into domestic law takes its place on the international plane only.... So far as a treaty is so incorporated, its effect in domestic law must depend upon the terms of its incorporation. In drawing the contrast she did, I take [Counsel for the City Council] to deny this latter proposition's application in the case of the EC Treaty; or at any rate she would say that is not the whole story. She would submit that the EC Treaty's effect in domestic law does not depend, merely at least, upon the terms of its incorporation by the ECA, but, in part at least (and to a decisive extent), upon principles of EU law itself. ...

56. ... [Counsel] submits that all this reasoning as to the supremacy of EC law became part of the law of England by force of the ECA, notably ss. 2(1) and (4), and 3(1). The effect of her submission is that by the ECA Parliament entrenched EC law in the domestic law of the United Kingdom, subject only ... to the possibility of withdrawal from the EU by express repeal of the ECA. And if that were to be contemplated, Parliament's hand would not be free. There would have to be consultations and negotiations first. And here, I think, is the critical proposition for her purpose: though it was done by means of the ECA, EC law is said to have been entrenched, rather than merely incorporated, not by virtue of any principle of domestic constitutional law, but by virtue of principles of

Community law already established in cases such as *Van Gend en Loos* and *Costa v. ENEL*.

57.   [According to this reasoning], (i) everything that is already or will become part of the corpus of EU law ipso facto is already or will become part of the corpus of the law of England; (ii) there can be no implied repeal or abrogation of any such law, nor of any of the principal measures contained in the ECA ..., and this is by virtue of EU law itself; (iii) any legislative initiative to withdraw, entirely or partially, from the EU would be subject to the fulfillment of compulsory preconditions. Since we are dealing here with the strict legal position, and not with the realpolitik of the thing, I am not entirely sure why [Counsel] does not go the further mile and submit that Parliament could not legislate tomorrow to withdraw from the EU at all. Such a state of affairs might be said to be vouchsafed by the reasoning in *Costa v. ENEL* ("permanent limitation of their sovereign rights") as readily as the more modest propositions which I have enumerated at (i)–(iii). At all events, her argument appears to me to entail the proposition that the legislative and judicial institutions of the EU may set limits to the power of Parliament to make laws which regulate the legal relationship between the EU and the United Kingdom.

58.   Thus baldly stated, that proposition is in my judgment false. [Counsel's] submissions forget the constitutional place in our law of the rule that Parliament cannot bind its successors, which is the engine of the doctrine of implied repeal. Here is her argument's bare logic. (1) The ECA incorporated the law of the EU into the law of England. (2) The law of the EU includes the entrenchment of its own supremacy as an autonomous legal order, and the prohibition of its abrogation by the Member States. Therefore (3) that entrenchment, and that prohibition, are thereby constituted part of the law of England. The flaw is in step (3). It proceeds on the assumption that the incorporation of EU law effected by the ECA (step (1)) must have included not only the whole corpus of European law upon substantive matters such as (by way of example) the free movement of goods and services, but also any jurisprudence of the Court of Justice, or other rule of Community law, which purports to touch the constitutional preconditions upon which the sovereign legislative power belonging to a Member State may be exercised.

59.   Whatever may be the position elsewhere, the law of England disallows any such assumption. Parliament cannot bind its successors by stipulating against repeal, wholly or partly, of the ECA. It cannot stipulate as to the manner and form of any subsequent legislation. It cannot stipulate against implied repeal any more than it can stipulate against express repeal. Thus there is nothing in the ECA which allows the Court of Justice, or any other institutions of the EU, to touch or qualify the conditions of Parliament's legislative supremacy in the United Kingdom. Not because the legislature chose not to allow it; because by our law it could not allow it. ... This is, of course, the traditional doctrine of sovereignty. If it is to be modified, it certainly cannot be done by the incorporation of external texts. The conditions of Parliament's legislative

supremacy in the United Kingdom necessarily remain in the United Kingdom's hands. . . .

[At this point, Mr. Justice Laws therefore tested the implied repeal argument under UK, not EU, law.]

60.   The common law has in recent years allowed, or rather created, exceptions to the doctrine of implied repeal: a doctrine which was always the common law's own creature. There are now classes or types of legislative provision which cannot be repealed by mere implication. These instances are given, and can only be given, by our own courts, to which the scope and nature or Parliamentary sovereignty are ultimately confided. . . .

* * *

62. . . . In the present state of its maturity, the common law has come to recognise that there exist rights which should properly be classified as constitutional or fundamental . . . And from this a further insight follows. We should recognise a hierarchy of Acts of Parliament: as it were "ordinary" statutes and "constitutional" statutes. . . . In my opinion a constitutional statute is one which (a) conditions the legal relationship between citizen and State in some general, overarching manner, or (b) enlarges or diminishes the scope of what we would now regard as fundamental constitutional rights. . . . Examples are the Magna Carta, the Bill of Rights 1689, the Act of Union, the Reform Acts which distributed and enlarged the franchise, the HRA, the Scotland Act 1998 and the Government of Wales Act 1998. The ECA clearly belongs in this family. It incorporated the whole corpus of substantive Community rights and obligations, and gave overriding domestic effect to the judicial and administrative machinery of Community law. It may be [that] there has never been a statute having such profound effects on so many dimensions of our daily lives. The ECA is, by force of the common law, a constitutional statute.

63.   Ordinary statutes may be impliedly repealed. Constitutional statutes may not. For the repeal of a constitutional Act or the abrogation of a fundamental right to be effected by statute, the court would apply this test: is it shown that the legislature's actual—not imputed, constructive or presumed—intention was to effect the repeal or abrogation? I think the test could only be met by express words in the later statute, or by words so specific that the inference of an actual determination to effect the result contended for was irresistible. The ordinary rule of implied repeal does not satisfy the test. Accordingly, it has no application to constitutional statutes. . . .

64.   This development of the common law regarding constitutional rights and . . . constitutional statutes is highly beneficial. It gives us most of the benefits of a written constitution, in which fundamental rights are accorded special respect. But it preserves the sovereignty of the legislature and the flexibility of our uncodified constitution. . . . Nothing is plainer than

that this benign development involves . . . the recognition of the ECA as a constitutional statute.

[Mr. Justice Laws concluded that the 1985 statute could not therefore impliedly repeal the ECA, and that the regulations that were enacted under Section 2(2) ECA, and that appellants were charged with violating, were valid. Their convictions were accordingly upheld.]

Notes and Questions

1. The significance of the *Thoburn* ruling is apparent. According to it, the UK Parliament may derogate from its EU law obligations, though only if it does so expressly. Subject to this proviso, Parliament enjoys final authority to determine which legal norms are effective in the UK. To what extent is the position taken in *Thoburn* consistent with the House of Lords' position in *Factortame*?

Mr. Justice Laws sought as follows to reconcile his reasoning in *Thoburn* with Lord Bridge's opinion for the House of Lords in *Factortame*:

> As Lord Bridge makes crystal clear, [the] context [of *Factortame*] was the requirement . . . stated by the Court of Justice . . . that the courts of member states must possess the power to override national legislation, as necessary, to enable interim relief to be granted in protection of rights under Community law. . . . [That] case is concerned with the primacy of [Community law's] *substantive* provisions. It has no application where the question is, what is the legal *foundation* within which those substantive provisions enjoy their primacy, and by which the relation between the law and institutions of the EU law and the British State ultimately rests. The foundation is English law.

Do you find the distinction persuasive?

2. *Thoburn* occasioned massive academic commentary. According to a commonly held view, "[t]he reaction of our national courts to such an unlikely eventuality remains to be seen. Either they could choose to follow the latest will of Parliament, thereby preserving some remnant of traditional orthodoxy on sovereignty. Or they could argue that it is not open to our legislature to pick and choose which obligations to subscribe to while still remaining within the Community. . . ." Paul Craig, Britain in the European Union, in J. Jowell & D. Oliver (eds.), The Changing Constitution (6th ed., 2007).

3. The appellants in *Thoburn* filed an appeal, but the House of Lord denied leave to appeal. At that point, they filed a claim in the European Court of Human Rights under Article 6 of the European Human Rights Convention, charging that the House of Lords denied them an opportunity to make their case and complaining that Mr. Justice Laws acted fundamentally unfairly by failing to draw counsel's attention to the cases he relied on in his discussion of "constitutional statutes." The Court declared the application inadmissible. Thoburn v. United Kingdom, application no. 30614/02 (2004).

CHAPTER 9

THE PRELIMINARY REFERENCE

■ ■ ■

In many ways, the most important basis in the Treaty for the Court of Justice's exercise of judicial authority is the preliminary reference procedure, provided for in TFEU Article 267 (formerly EC Treaty Article 234). Article 267 states in its first paragraph that the Court of Justice has jurisdiction to issue rulings on the interpretation of the Treaties or on the validity or meaning of acts of the institutions or other bodies of the Union, whenever a Member State court or tribunal "considers that a decision on the question is necessary to enable it to give judgment" in a pending case, and accordingly refers the question to the Court.

Questions sent to the Court under TFEU Article 267, as previously under EC Treaty Article 234, are commonly known as "preliminary references" or "referrals" and the judgments the Court renders as "preliminary rulings." The idea of preliminary references comes from Germany and Italy, whose courts are required to refer constitutional questions to a separate constitutional court when an answer to those questions is necessary for the decision of a pending case.

TFEU Article 267 contains two further paragraphs:

Where such a question is raised before any court or tribunal of a Member State, that court or tribunal may, if it considers that a decision on the question is necessary to enable it to give judgment, request the Court of Justice to give a ruling thereon.

Where any such question is raised in a case pending before a court or tribunal of a Member State against whose decisions there is no judicial remedy under national law, that court or tribunal shall bring the matter before the Court of Justice.

The second of these paragraphs places an obligation to refer such questions upon a national supreme or constitutional court (or upon a lower court, if no appeal from its judgment is possible in the national legal order). By contrast, the preceding paragraph permits, but does not require any lower court or tribunal to refer questions to the Court of Justice. As we shall see, in practice most questions come from the lower courts or tribunals.

Apart from replacing the word "Community" in EC Treaty Article 234 by the word "Union," the Lisbon TFEU Article 267 only adds a final paragraph that obliges the Court to "act with the minimum of delay" to questions referred that concern "a person in custody."

The preliminary reference procedure is the critical link between the Member State judiciaries and the Court of Justice. It is widely viewed (and has been described by the Court of Justice) as a crucial form of "cooperation" between the EU and the national judiciaries. In the first place, it enables national courts and tribunals to secure an authoritative ruling from the Court of Justice on the interpretation and validity of EU law whenever the proper solution of a case before them so requires. Since 1989, when staff cases were transferred to the Court of First Instance (or "General Court," under the Lisbon Treaty), references have represented around one-half of all cases on the Court's docket. This is not surprising. Since EU law in most sectors is enforced chiefly by Member State rather than EU bodies, disputes over its meaning normally surface in national litigation.

Second, referrals provide the Court with a continuous opportunity to develop substantive EU law, whether by clarifying the meaning of its legal instruments or by formulating and applying general principles of law. The distinguished former Judge Pierre Pescatore of the Court of Justice has written: "The decisions of the Court which have made the most conspicuous contribution to the development of Community law have been delivered [by preliminary ruling]: . . . the direct effect of Community law, its primacy over national law, the protection of fundamental rights, the principles relating to the common market and the law of competition [and] the social dimension of the Community." P. Pescatore, References for Preliminary Rulings under Article 177 (EC Off'l Pub. Office, 1986), at 11.

Third, preliminary references must be seen as an important, albeit indirect, way for individuals to bring their EU claims to the Court of Justice. Enterprising lawyers before national courts and tribunals increasingly raise claims that are based on EU law rights and obligations. Although these claims have to be adjudicated in a national forum, preliminary rulings enable the Court of Justice to supply the forum with the applicable legal principles.

The success of the preliminary reference is evidenced by the fact that the relevant EC Treaty provision was never amended prior to the Lisbon Treaty, and even then only slightly. (As noted, a final paragraph was added enjoining the Court of Justice to act with a minimum delay in the issuance of preliminary rulings if the case from which the reference came concerned a person being held in custody.) This continuity demonstrates that the EU leadership is satisfied that this mode of enforcing EU law is effective. The alternative approach of creating lower Union courts, similar to federal courts in the US, was advanced in the past, but never seriously considered.

The Treaty of Nice added a new Article 225(3) to the EC Treaty authorizing the Council to transfer specific categories of preliminary references from the Court of Justice to the Court of First Instance, subject to "exceptional" appeals to the Court of Justice, and TFEU Article 256(3) retains this possibility. The Council has requested both courts to provide their views on the advisability of such a change, but because the Court of Justice is likely to prefer to retain all preliminary references, Council action appears unlikely, at least at the present time.

Finally, it should by now be clear that the concept of direct effect, which in a sense is the cornerstone of supranationalism, depends utterly on the preliminary reference mechanism. When national courts refer EU law questions to the Court of Justice, secure guidance through the Court's preliminary rulings, and then follow those rulings, they engage in a vital form of EU law enforcement.

A. THE REFERENCE PROCEDURE

The national court itself, not the parties before it, has the authority to decide that a preliminary ruling will be sought. Although courts usually refer questions raised by a party, sometimes they decide to refer a question entirely on their own. Thus a preliminary reference differs fundamentally from an appeal. The extent to which a judge relies on counsel to help formulate the questions for referral depends entirely on that judge's inclination and on judicial traditions in his or her State. (Reliance on counsel is common in the UK and Ireland, much less so on the Continent.) In any event, the national courts are the ones to decide whether, when and what to refer.

There are wide discrepancies in the incidence of preliminary references from national courts. Recent Court statistics indicate that Germany and Italy lead in absolute terms, averaging around 60 and 35 references a year, respectively; the Netherlands, France, the UK and Belgium follow. Courts and tribunals in Austria, Ireland, Spain and the Scandinavian States occasionally refer questions, but those in over half the States rarely do so. The Court of Justice would obviously like to stimulate the courts in these States to refer questions, but there is no legal or political means of achieving this.

In a preliminary reference, the referring court sends the Court of Justice the file of the case, including the facts to the extent then ascertained. It also provides a summary of the procedure to that point, the parties' claims, the relevant national law, the court's reasons for making the reference and the specific questions of EU law presented. The Registrar of the Court of Justice then notifies the Member States, the Commission, the Council, and the Parliament, each of which may submit written observations and appear at an oral hearing. The Commission invariably does so, and its views are treated rather like those of the US Justice Department acting through the Solicitor General as *amicus curiae*. The Council and Parliament, in contrast, normally participate only if the validity, and not merely the interpretation, of one of their own acts is called into question. Otherwise, only parties to the national court proceeding (or persons who have been granted to leave by the national court to intervene in those proceedings) may participate in the preliminary reference procedure in Luxembourg. Others may not do so, even if they claim to have an "interest" in the question being referred. Biogen Inc. v. Smithkline Beecham Biological S.A., Case C–181/95, [1996] ECR I–357.

Prior to the mid–1990s, the Court customarily handled reference proceedings in plenary session, but an increase in the number of judges and in caseload has led it to deal with the large majority in chambers, with only the most important cases going to the Grand Chamber. Following presentation of the Advocate General's opinion, the Court renders judgment in the usual way, discussing the questions presented and giving reasoned rulings on them. (Since the Court amended its Rules of Procedure in 2008, an accelerated procedure is possible for questions concerning the area of freedom, security and justice.) In theory, the Court does not decide questions of fact or apply the relevant EU law to the facts. However, in practice its answers often indicate quite clearly how the national court should approach and even decide these matters.

Although the reference procedure enables the Court of Justice to clarify EU law for the benefit of national courts and tribunals, the latter are ultimately responsible for applying the Court's guidance to the cases out of which preliminary references grow. Because, in principle, the Court of Justice simply rules on the questions of EU law submitted to it, without itself applying that law or otherwise deciding the case, it neither overrules decisions of the national courts nor invalidates national legislation. It does not even pass explicitly on the compatibility of national law with EU law, though it often makes its views on this matter so clear that the question is all but answered. Needless to say, the Court does not in any event rule on the meaning of national law as such.

The logic of the preliminary reference would suggest that referring courts are bound to follow preliminary rulings of the Court in the cases that occasion them, and the Court has so held. Benedetti v. Munari, Case 52/76, [1977] ECR 163; Milch-, Fett- und Eierkontor GmbH v. Hauptzollamt Saarbrücken, Case 29/68, [1969] ECR 165. Moreover, though preliminary rulings only answer the questions put by a national court in a particular case, they are cast in somewhat general or abstract terms and have been held by the Court also to apply to future cases. Thus, despite the absence of a formal rule of *stare decisis* binding the Court of Justice itself, preliminary rulings constitute binding precedents for national courts in later cases. Like other Court of Justice rulings, they allow EU law to acquire a determined meaning throughout the territory of the EU, and thus promote legal certainty and unity.

This principle applies *a fortiori* to the Court's preliminary rulings that invalidate rather than merely interpret EU legislation, Commission decisions or other legal acts. The Court held in SpA International Chemical

Corporation v. Amministrazione delle Finanze dello Stato, Case 66/80, [1981] ECR 1191, that if the Court declares an EU law measure to be invalid, any national court should thereafter consider the measure to be null and void. The Court did note that a further reference may be necessary "if questions arise as to the grounds, the scope and possibly the consequences of the invalidity established earlier." Id. at 1215.

If a national court disagrees with a Court of Justice ruling on the meaning of EU law, or otherwise would like the Court to reconsider the ruling in a subsequent case, the court always has the right to resubmit the question in the expectation or simple hope that the Court will change its mind, or give a more nuanced ruling.

Do referring courts follow the answers provided by the Court of Justice? While there is no assurance that they will apply a preliminary ruling properly in the pending case, there is every indication that they try to do so. Judge Pescatore has stated: "Only in wholly exceptional cases have national courts misunderstood the rulings or showed reluctance to implement them." P. Pescatore, op. cit., at 23.

Despite its benefits, the preliminary reference mechanism entails a price, namely the delay in awaiting the Court's response before resumption of the national court proceedings. As a result of its heavy caseload, exacting procedures, and translation delays (remember that the Court uses 23 official languages), proceedings for a preliminary ruling from the Court currently average around 17 months. This time must be added to delays already present in the national court system.

In its reflection papers provided to the Council in preparation for the inter-governmental conferences that drafted the Treaties of Amsterdam and Nice, the Court of Justice firmly rejected any proposal that would prevent trial courts or any other specific courts or tribunals from referring questions. The Court did raise the prospect of its being given a certiorari-type of power to decline to answer questions deemed to be trivial or already answered. This proposal has not borne fruit, but three other Court proposals have been implemented.

First, by an amendment in May 2000 to the Court's Rules of Procedure, the Court may respond to questions by a brief reasoned Order when it considers the answer to be provided by prior case law or "admits of no reasonable doubt." Orders are used in a growing number of cases. Secondly, the Court may request a clarification of imprecise or ambiguous questions from the referring court of tribunal, and occasionally does so. Finally, the Court may apply an accelerated procedure when the questions have "exceptional urgency." Thus, in Jippes v. Minister van Landbouw, Case C–189/01, [2001] ECR I–5689, the Court used an accelerated procedure to answer questions relating to action to combat "foot and mouth" disease outbreaks among animals in the Netherlands.

NOTES AND QUESTIONS

1. What do you suppose motivated the drafters of the Treaties to adopt a reference mechanism rather than an EU trial court system? Why has a system of appeals from national supreme courts to the Court of Justice, an idea that has occasionally been suggested and that has a US analogue, never been adopted? An analogy to the preliminary reference may be found in the US system, but in reverse direction. A majority of states allow federal courts, when dealing with state law, to refer questions on that law to the highest state court, but that opportunity is not widely used. Why do you suppose that is the case?

2. In view of the delay caused by preliminary references, do you think the Council should transfer some categories of referred questions, such as those concerning customs or competition law issues, to the General Court (formerly the CFI) or a specialized court? Or do you think that might create too much legal uncertainty?

B. FRAMING THE REFERENCE AND THE RULING

National courts, especially trial courts, are often not expert in EU law and may not know exactly how to formulate their questions. References may be imprecise or verbose; they may address the wrong parts of the Treaty or secondary legislation; they may confuse EU law concepts. Moreover, a referring court may be mistaken in its belief that an answer to an EU law question is really necessary for resolving the case before it.

The Court of Justice understands these difficulties. From its earliest judgments, the Court has followed a policy of answering questions whether or not the answers are truly essential to the national litigation, while at the same time reformulating the questions if they are imprecise or confused. Moreover, since its *Costa v. ENEL* ruling, supra pages 246–47, the Court has in principle declined to examine the motives that may have caused a national court to make a reference.

There are, however, certain limitations on the Court's willingness to answer all questions asked of it. For example, the Court may refuse to give its preliminary ruling in cases where the questions referred are not articulated clearly enough for it to be able to give any meaningful response, or where the questions raised are wholly irrelevant to the resolution of the substantive action in the national court. The cases that follow illustrate both the Court's desire to answer referred questions whenever possible, but also the limitations on its doing so.

PRETORE DI SALO v. PERSONS UNKNOWN

Case 14/86, [1987] ECR 2545.

[An Italian magistrate was investigating possible criminal liability for water pollution under the Italian law that implemented a 1978 Council framework directive on the protection of fresh water quality and fish life. He first asked the Court of Justice whether Italian water pollution rules were "consistent with the principles and quality objectives" set out in the 1978 directive. His second question was extremely obscure, asking whether the directive called for "rules . . . capable of ensuring a constant flow [of water and thus] preserving the minimum volume . . . essential for the development of fish species." Italy argued that the questions were premature, since no criminal proceeding had as yet been begun. The Commission also considered the questions inappropriate.]

10   [I]f the interpretation of Community law is to be of use to the national court, it is essential to define the legal context in which the interpretation requested should be placed. In that perspective, it might be convenient in certain circumstances for the facts of the case to be established and for questions of purely national law to be settled at the time when the reference is made to the Court of Justice so as to enable the latter to take cognizance of all the matters of fact and law which may be relevant to the interpretation of Community law which it is called upon to give.

11   However, as the Court has already held . . ., those considerations do not in any way restrict the discretion of the national court, which alone has a direct knowledge of the facts of the case and of the arguments of the parties, which will have to take responsibility for giving judgment in the case, and which is therefore in the best position to appreciate at what stage of the proceedings it requires a preliminary ruling from the Court of Justice. The decision at what stage in proceedings a question should be referred to the Court of Justice for a preliminary ruling is therefore dictated by considerations of procedural economy and efficiency to be weighed only by the national court and not by the Court of Justice.

* * *

16   [Furthermore, the] Court . . . may extract from the wording of the questions formulated by the national court, and having regard to the facts stated by the latter, those elements which concern the interpretation of Community law for the purpose of enabling that court to resolve the legal problems before it. In this case, however, in view of the generality of the question and the absence of any specific elements which would make it possible to identify the doubts entertained by the national court, it is not possible for the Court to reply to the question referred to it.

NOTES AND QUESTIONS

1. The Court of Justice in *Pretore di Salo* (¶ 11) emphasized its duty to respect the views of national courts in their assessment of "procedural economy and efficiency" in deciding when to make a preliminary reference. Certainly, Member State judges have a greater knowledge of the facts, the issues and the posture of a case, and ultimately are the ones responsible for delivering a judgment. Nonetheless, the Court emphasized in ¶ 10 that the national courts frequently ought to ascertain the facts and resolve purely national law issues before making a reference. Note that the Court ultimately declined to answer the Pretore's question. Why?

2. In ¶ 16 of *Pretore di Salo*, the Court indicated that its policy is to reformulate questions that are ambiguous or imprecise in order to state the legal issues that it perceives to be really at stake. A noted instance in which the Court reformulated questions put to it is Pigs Marketing Board v. Redmond, supra page 114. The Northern Ireland magistrate before whom a prosecution was pending for the unlicensed sale of hogs referred pages of questions on the nature of the Pigs Marketing Board and its regulatory powers in the light of virtually all the Treaty provisions on agriculture. Perhaps embarrassed by the questions' volume and hopeless mixing of facts and law, the UK urged the Court not to answer them. However, the Court ruled that it could still extract the critical EU law issues in the "improperly formulated" questions, and, in doing so, provided important early guidance on the principle of preemption. The Court frequently reformulates referred questions.

3. The Court of Justice has also stated that it will reject a reference "if it is quite obvious that the interpretation of Community law ... sought by [a national] court bears no relation to the actual nature of the case or to the subject matter of the main action." Salonia v. Poidomani, Case 126/80, [1981] ECR 1563, 1576–77. Since determining whether EU law is not relevant to a case for preliminary reference purposes naturally presupposes some understanding of the scope of EU law, the Court may find itself anticipating to some extent the merits of the case. A striking example is Grado and Bashir, Case C–291/96, [1997] ECR I–5531. When applying to a local court for a summary punishment order against an Italian national for committing a traffic offense in Germany, the local prosecutor deliberately omitted from his petition the courtesy title, "Herr," which he ordinarily would have used in charging a German male. The German court itself asked the Court of Justice for a ruling on the compatibility with EU law of this manner of proceeding. The Court refused, regarding such a discrimination in the context of prosecuting traffic offenses as falling outside the scope of EU law. The Italian national concerned was a migrant worker, yet the Court considered that the prohibition on discrimination on the basis of nationality applicable to migrant workers was not involved. Do you agree?

4. Starting in the 1990s, the Court occasionally held that a valid preliminary reference requires the national court to define the factual and legislative background to the case (or at least the factual hypotheses on the basis of which the reference was made) and that in the absence of such

information, the reference will be deemed inadmissible. Telemarsicabruzzo SpA v. Circostel, Joined Cases C–320–22/90, [1993] ECR I–393; Banco de Fomento e Exterior SA v. Martins Pechim, Case C–326/95, [1996] ECR I–1385.

As previously observed, an amendment to the Court's Rules of Procedure in 2000 enables the Court to request the referring court or tribunal to clarify its questions. The Court makes frequent use of this provision. Furthermore, in a non-binding Information Note on References by National Courts for a Preliminary Ruling O.J. C 143/1 (June 11, 2005), the Court admonishes that preliminary references should state succinctly but completely the reasons, so as to give the Court of Justice, the Member States, the institutions, and interested parties "a clear understanding of the factual and legal context of the main proceedings" and enable the Court to give an answer that will be of assistance to the national court.

5. The Court frequently states that, in rendering a preliminary ruling, it does no more than clarify the scope and meaning of the EU law provision in question, and refrains from deciding whether or how that provision applies to the facts of the case at hand:

> The Court has no power in the context of [preliminary reference] proceedings . . . either to interpret provisions of national law or to rule on their possible incompatibility with Community law. However, in the context of the interpretation of Community law, it may provide the national court with the criteria enabling it to deal with the action before it. . . .

Enka v. Inspecteur der Invoerrechten en Accijnzen, Case 38/77, [1977] ECR 2203, 2213; Rustica Semences SA v. Finanzamt Kehl, Case C–438/92, [1994] ECR I–3519. Despite these statements, when reading some judgments later in the book, you may have occasion to wonder whether the Court does in fact follow this policy.

6. Common law commentators sometimes complain that the Court's preliminary rulings are too abstract, too devoid of factual references and too literal in responding to the questions presented. As you read the many preliminary rulings in this book, reflect on whether you agree, or whether you think the critics are simply accustomed to the lengthy, detailed and fact-oriented style of common law judgments, which civil law lawyers sometimes find confusing.

C. WHAT IS A "COURT OR TRIBUNAL"?

Only a "court or tribunal" of a Member State may make a preliminary reference to the Court of Justice. Whether a referring body is a "court or tribunal" for these purposes is normally not an issue, but occasionally is. Each Member State has not only a variety of courts, some of which (like certain commercial and labor courts) consist of both judges and lay persons, but also administrative and quasi-judicial tribunals whose members rarely are judges. Which of these bodies may refer questions to the Court?

The Court of Justice has given a generally expansive definition of "court or tribunal," with a view to enabling a broad range of official bodies to avail themselves of the preliminary reference mechanism. It has not required that a court be composed entirely of judges, provided its members in fact adjudicate disputes. Even the latter condition is broadly construed. The Italian magistrate in *Pretore di Salo*, who conducted preliminary investigations before a criminal trial, was allowed to make a reference. The Court of Justice considered the *pretore* to be a judge for these purposes because he was in the business of "judging, independently and in accordance with the law, cases coming within the jurisdiction conferred on [him] by law." [1987] ECR at 2567. The Court may have been influenced by the fact that similar magistrates exist in most continental states, and are regarded as members of the judiciary.

In contrast, the Court has held that an Italian public prosecutor (*Procura della Repubblica*) is not empowered to make preliminary references, since the role of that officer is "not to rule on an issue in complete independence but, acting as prosecutor in the proceedings, to submit that issue, if appropriate, for consideration by the competent judicial body." See Procura della Repubblica v. X, Joined Cases C–74 & 129/95, [1996] ECR I–6609.

It appears that the Court, in determining whether a national body is a court or tribunal for the purpose of making preliminary references, considers both the body's status (is it a public authority or at least formally authorized to act on behalf of a public authority?) and its functions (does it perform judicial or quasi-judicial tasks?) The Court has accordingly treated as "tribunals" a number of different tariff and customs, social security, immigration and tax appeal bodies, whatever their official title.

On the other hand, administrative agencies performing ordinary executive functions do not qualify as courts or tribunals for these purposes, even though they obviously have occasion to apply EU law, possibly on a daily basis. Thus, in Corbiau v. Administration des Contributions, Case C–24/92, [1993] ECR I–1277, the Court held that the Director of Taxation of Luxembourg could not be considered a court or tribunal when conducting a proceeding to determine whether a taxpayer was entitled to obtain repayment of an over-withholding of income tax. The Court ruled that a court or tribunal for preliminary reference purposes must stand in a third party relationship with the body that took the decision being challenged. Since the Director headed the tax administration and was organizationally linked to the department that made the contested calculation, he did not meet that requirement.

More recently, the Court has set out a catalogue of factors relevant to deciding the "court or tribunal" question: whether the referring body is established by law, whether it is permanent, whether its jurisdiction is compulsory, whether its procedures are *inter partes*, whether it applies rules of law, and whether it is independent of the administration. In recent judgments applying these criteria (some of them quite detailed on the issue), the Catalonian Regional Economic–Administrative Tribunal and the German federal public procurement awards supervisory board were found to meet the test. See Gabalfrisa SL v. Agencia Estatal de Administracion Regional de Cataluna, Joined Cases C–110–147/98, [2000] ECR I–1577; and Dorsch Consult Ingenieurgesellschaft mbH v. Bundesbaugesellschaft Berlin mbH, Case C–54/96, [1997] ECR I–4961.

By contrast, in Synetairismos Farmakopoion Aitolias & Akarnanias (Syfait) v. GlaxoSmithKline, Case C–53/03, [2005] ECR I–4609, the Court held that the Greek Competition Commission was not a tribunal due to (i) its supervision by the Minister for Development, (ii) the lack of safeguards against dismissal of its members, (iii) the fact that its president coordinates policy for and is the immediate superior of the personnel of the secretariat, and (iv) the fact that the Greek Competition Commission may be relieved of its competence by a decision of the European Commission when the latter decides to adjudicate the very same case.

Advocate General Ruiz–Jarabo Colomer has expressed dissatisfaction with the Court's criteria for identifying a "court or tribunal." In his opinion in a 2001 case, he argued:

14 The result is case-law which is too flexible and not sufficiently consistent, with the lack of legal certainty which that entails. The profound contradictions noted between the solutions proposed by Advocates General in their Opinions and those adopted by the Court of Justice in its judgments illustrate that the path is badly signposted and [that] there is therefore a risk of getting lost. The case-law is casuistic, very elastic and not very scientific....

[The Advocate General proposed a much simpler test.]

86 [A] body which does not form part of the national court system and has not been granted the power to state the law by interpreting and applying the law in judicial proceedings must not be considered a court or tribunal.

87 Only as an exception should the Court of Justice accept questions referred for a preliminary ruling by a body which does not form part of the national court system, namely when the referring body, although outside the judicial framework, has the last word in the national legal order, because its decision may not be not be contested. In those circumstances, the purpose and *raison d'etre* of the preliminary gruing procedure make it essential for the Court of Justice to accept and reply to the questions put to it.

88 However, such situations, as well as being exceptional, are virtually non-existent, thanks to the recognition of the right to effective legal protection, which requires the abolition of areas exempt from judicial review....

In its judgment, the Court of Justice made no reference to the Advocate General's Opinion and simply reaffirmed its prior case law, including the list of relevant criteria. It found (as the Advocate General would not have) that an administrative body responsible for handling the appeals of taxes imposed by the region of Brussels should be considered as a national tribunal for preliminary reference purposes. De Coster v. College des Bourgmestre et Echevins, Case C–17/00, [2001] ECR I–9445.

The standing of self-governing professional bodies to refer questions has been particularly problematic. The Court has accepted referrals from bodies of that kind when they exercise quasi-judicial authority (as in professional licensing or discipline), but has refused referrals arising out of those bodies' more purely administrative tasks.

Broekmeulen v. Huisarts Registratie Commissie, Case 246/80, [1981] ECR 2311, is a leading case. The Royal Netherlands Society for the Promotion of Medicine has the authority under Dutch law to certify licensed doctors for the treatment of patients covered by national health insurance. Its appeals committee asked the Court of Justice questions about the Council directive on the mutual recognition of Member State diplomas (see Chapter 18F infra).

The Court held that the appeals committee was a tribunal for preliminary references purposes. It was influenced by the fact that, practically-speaking, registration with the Society was "essential" to becoming established as a doctor in the Netherlands, that the appeals committee operated with the consent of the public authorities, that no case could be found in which an adverse decision by the committee had been challenged in the ordinary courts, and that the committee itself followed adversarial procedures in reaching decisions. The Court thought it "imperative" that it be in a position to guide such a body in its application of Community law. [1981] ECR at 2328. As we shall see later in Chapter 18, the Court has also on several occasions permitted a national or local bar association to refer questions concerning the licensing of lawyers.

More dubious is the status of arbitral bodies, typically called tribunals. If such bodies are accessory to the state judicial system, as in compulsory commercial or labor arbitration, they may well qualify as courts or tribunals. Most arbitrations, however, are based upon provisions in private contracts and are conducted by designated private arbitrators or arbitration tribunals.

NORDSEE DEUTSCHE HOCHSEEFISCHEREI GmbH v. REEDEREI MOND HOCHSEEFISCHEREI NORDSTERN AG

Case 102/81, [1982] ECR 1095.

[Three German shipping groups contracted for the joint construction of freezer ships and sought financial aid for the project from the EU's European Agricultural Guidance and Guarantee Fund (EAGGF). Learning that funds would be available for some but not all ships they planned to build, the companies entered into a secret "pooling" agreement to share the available financial aid equally among themselves, in proportion to the number of ships each actually built and irrespective of which ships the

EAGGF had seen fit to fund. Subsequently, in a dispute between two of the groups, one sought arbitration pursuant to a clause in the pooling agreement. The clause named as arbitrator the president of the highest court in the state of Bremen. The German Procedure Code requires arbitrators to apply German civil procedure, makes arbitral awards definitive and provides for judicial enforcement of awards, subject to certain challenges. The arbitrator decided that the validity of the agreement under German law depended on whether or not pooling was permissible under EU law (which was unlikely, in view of Commission guidelines), and he sought a preliminary ruling from the Court of Justice on that question.]

7   Since the arbitration tribunal ... was established pursuant to a contract between private individuals the question arises whether it may be considered as a court or tribunal of one of the Member States within the meaning of [EC Treaty Article 234, now TFEU Article 267].

* * *

10   [T]here are certain similarities between the activities of the arbitration tribunal in question and those of an ordinary court or tribunal inasmuch as the arbitration is provided for within the framework of the law, the arbitrator must decide according to law and his award has, as between the parties, the force of res judicata, and may be enforceable if leave to issue execution is obtained. However, those characteristics are not sufficient to give the arbitrator the status of a "court or tribunal of a Member State"...

11   The first important point to note is that when the contract was entered in 1973 the parties were free to leave their disputes to be resolved by the ordinary courts or to opt for arbitration by inserting a clause to that effect in the contract. From the facts of the case it appears that the parties were under no obligation, whether in law or in fact, to refer their disputes to arbitration.

12   The second point to be noted is that the German public authorities are not involved in the decision to opt for arbitration, nor are they called upon to intervene automatically in the proceedings before the arbitrator....

13   [Accordingly,] the link between the arbitration procedure in this instance and the organization of legal remedies through the courts in the Member States in question is not sufficiently close for the arbitrator to be considered as a "court or tribunal of a Member State"...

NOTES AND QUESTIONS

1.   The Commission in *Nordsee* argued that German procedural law sufficiently governed the arbitration to justify allowing a preliminary reference. The UK and Italy argued the contrary. What do you think? Would it have made any difference to the Court if the contract had stipulated that EU law as well as German law governed any dispute arising under it?

2. Why do you think the Court declined the opportunity to enlarge the circle of institutions authorized to seek rulings on Community law? Consider that private arbitrations in commercial matters are increasingly favored in Europe. In May 1994, Parliament adopted a resolution calling for greater use of arbitration—and for the enactment of a uniform set of arbitral procedures—for the resolution of disputes arising out of transactions within the EU, O.J. C 205/457 (July 25, 1994). The Commission has voiced particular concern that arbitrators deciding competition law claims (which they often do) may misconstrue EC competition law principles, and possibly disregard them entirely. Does this concern justify amending TFEU Article 267 to allow arbitrators to refer questions to the Court of Justice?

3. Elsewhere in its judgment, the Court indicated that EU law issues could be raised in national court proceedings ancillary to the arbitration. The Court has accepted preliminary references from national courts hearing an action to annul an arbitral award. In Gemeente Almelo v. Energiebedrijf Ijsselmij NV, Case C–393/92, [1994] ECR I–1477, the Court did so even though the arbitration agreement provided for the arbitrator to decide the case not according to a national body of law, but rather according to what is "fair and reasonable."

D. WHEN SHOULD A COURT REFER A QUESTION?

TFEU Article 267, like EC Treaty Article 234 before it, states that the test for deciding when a preliminary reference, whether discretionary or mandatory, is appropriate is whether a decision on the question is "necessary" to enable the national court to give judgment. While seemingly simple, this requirement has given rise to disparate Member State practices. As previously observed some state courts—notably those of Italy, Germany, the UK, Belgium and the Netherlands—seem much more inclined than others to refer questions to the Court.

At a minimum, the EU law issue must be relevant to the disposition of the case at hand. Absent relevance, a decision on the issue can scarcely be said to be necessary. But how much more than bare relevance might have to be shown? The only Member State in which appellate courts have tried to set precise guidelines for deciding when a reference is "necessary" is the UK.

Much of the discussion in the UK was prompted by the celebrated opinion by Lord Denning in the case of H.P. Bulmer Ltd. v. J. Bollinger S.A., [1974] 2 Ch. 401, [1974] 3 WLR 202, [1974] 2 All ER 1226, [1974] 2 CMLR 91 (Ct. of Appeal, May 22, 1974). Bollinger and other French champagne producers sought in 1970 to enjoin Bulmer from marketing English cider under the names "champagne cider" and "champagne perry," claiming that "champagne" was a protected designation of origin. After the UK entered the Community in 1973, the French producers amended their complaint to include claims based on the protection of designations of origin under Community agricultural regulations. The

French producers asked the trial court to refer to the Court of Justice not only the substantive question, but also the question whether such a question should even be referred. When the trial court refused to make a reference, the French producers appealed.

Before addressing the referral issue, Lord Denning made the often-quoted remark that "when we come to matters with a European element, the Treaty is like an incoming tide. It flows into the estuaries and up the rivers. It cannot be held back." Noting that under the European Communities Act of 1972, supra page 311, British courts must "without more ado" give EU law effect in the UK, Lord Denning conceded that the Court of Justice is the supreme authority on the meaning of that law. However, he proceeded to lay down guidelines for lower courts to follow in deciding whether to seek rulings from the Court.

One suggestion was that the national court should find a precedent of the Court of Justice on substantially the same issue and simply follow it. Another is that the national court should consider deciding the facts first, in order to be certain that the EU law issue is truly necessary. In Irish Creamery Milk Suppliers Association v. Ireland, Cases 36, 71/80, [1981] ECR 735, the Court held that national courts might find it convenient to establish both the facts and the applicable national law before referring a question to it, but it emphasized that the trial judge is in the best position to decide at what stage a preliminary ruling should be had.

Other guidelines include Lord Denning's suggestion that to be "necessary," the ruling that is requested must pertain to an EU law issue that is "conclusive" in the sense of determining the outcome one way or another, that national courts should be concerned about the length of time before receiving the Court's reply, and finally that national courts should "hesitate" to seek a ruling if either party to the proceeding opposes the reference.

Lord Denning also suggested in *Bulmer* that UK courts should make use of the *acte clair* doctrine, derived from French law. The essential idea is that a national court need not refer an EU law question to the Court of Justice if the national court considers the answer to that question to be clear. The doctrine makes considerable sense, but also is subject to abuse, particularly by courts of last resort, if invoked to avoid otherwise proper references. The Court of Justice eventually had occasion in the *CILFIT* case, infra page 337, to set limits on national court use of the *acte clair* doctrine.

NOTE ON UK APPELLATE COURT ATTITUDES TO REFERENCES

Whatever weight Lord Denning's guidelines in *Bulmer* might have carried at the time, they are no longer authoritative or reliable. Thus in Polydor Ltd. v. Harlequin Record Shops Ltd., [1980] FSR 362, [1980] 2 CMLR 413, 426 (May 15, 1980), the Court of Appeals (per Templeman, L.J.), in full knowledge of the *Bulmer* guidelines, referred a question to the Court of Justice at an interlocutory stage of a case well before the facts had been found. Concurring in the result, Ormond, L.J. pointedly interpreted the term "necessary" in Article 234 to mean "reasonably necessary" rather than "unavoidable." [1980] 2 CMLR at 428.

In 1987, Lord Justice Kerr of the English Court of Appeal remarked as follows:

> [The *CILFIT* case, infra,] makes it clear that the principle of "acte clair" is . . . applicable . . . where there can be no doubt about the correct answer. However . . . our courts should hesitate long before reaching such a conclusion. . . .

* * *

> [I]n Polydor Ltd. v. Harlequin Record Shops Ltd., Ormrod and Templeman L.JJ. expressed strong views in this Court about the apparently clearly correct answer to a question of Community law which had been raised before them. But they nevertheless referred the case to the Court of Justice, and [its] ultimate decision was in fact the other way.

Regina v. Statutory Committee of the Pharmaceutical Society of Great Britain, [1987] 3 CMLR 951, 969, 971 (C.A., July 30, 1987).

The Court of Appeal took a fresh look at Lord Denning's guidelines in the case of Regina v. International Stock Exchange [1993] 1 All ER 420, [1993] 2 CMLR 677 (Oct. 16, 1992). There, three shareholders of a company sought judicial review of the Stock Exchange's decision to cancel the company's listing. When the High Court referred questions concerning the application of a directive on stock exchange listings to the Court of Justice, the Stock Exchange appealed. Speaking through Bingham, M.R., the Court of Appeal stated that, once the facts have been clarified, the decision to refer or not should depend on whether the EU law provision in question is critical to the outcome of the case and whether the national court can resolve the question of its interpretation with complete confidence. Even if the answer to the first question is yes, according to Bingham, M.R., the national court should "ordinarily" make the reference if the answer to the second question is no. In other words, while discretion still plays a role, references are under those circumstances to be preferred. According to a leading comment on the case, "the discretion is subject to a presumption in favour of referral at the outset. The court will be under an obligation to refer unless there are some exceptional circumstances sufficient for it to decide otherwise." D. Walsh, The Appeal of an Article 177 EEC Referral, 56 Mod. L. Rev. 881 (1993).

An official "Practice Direction on References to the European Court of Justice by the Court of Appeal and the High Court" issued in 2000 does not echo any of the *Bulmer* restrictions.

SRL CILFIT v. MINISTRY OF HEALTH (I)
Case 283/81, [1982] ECR 3415.

[Several Italian textile firms claimed that an Italian health inspection levy on the import of wool violated a 1968 EU agricultural regulation. The firms lost in the lower courts, which felt that the levy so clearly conformed to EU rules that a preliminary reference was unnecessary. On appeal to the Italian Supreme Court, the firms argued that the absence of any further judicial remedy under national law rendered a preliminary reference obligatory. The Supreme Court evidently was not so certain about this, since, rather than make a reference on the merits, it made one on the question of its duty to make references at all when EU law seems to be clear beyond "a reasonable interpretative doubt."]

13   [T]he Court [has] ruled that: "Although the third paragraph of [EC Treaty Article 234] unreservedly requires courts or tribunals of a Member State against whose decisions there is no judicial remedy under national law ... to refer to the Court every question of interpretation raised before them, the authority of an interpretation under Article [234] already given by the Court may deprive the obligation of its purpose and thus empty it of its substance. Such is the case especially when the question raised is materially identical with a question which has already been the subject of a preliminary ruling in a similar case." [The Court's quotation is from Da Costa v. Nederlandse Belastingadministratie, Cases 28–30/62, [1963] ECR 31].

14   The same effect ... may be produced where previous decisions of the Court have already dealt with the point of law in question, irrespective of the nature of the proceedings which led to those decisions, even though the questions at issue are not strictly identical.

15   However, it must not be forgotten that in all such circumstances national courts and tribunals remain entirely at liberty to bring a matter before the Court of Justice if they consider it appropriate to do so.

16   Finally, the correct application of Community law may be so obvious as to leave no scope for any reasonable doubt as to the manner in which the question raised is to be resolved. Before it comes to the conclusion that such is the case, the national court or tribunal must be convinced that the matter is equally obvious to the courts of the other Member States and to the Court of Justice. Only if those conditions are satisfied may the national court or tribunal refrain from submitting the question to the Court of Justice and take upon itself the responsibility for resolving it.

17   However, the existence of such a possibility must be assessed on the basis of the characteristic features of Community law and the particular difficulties to which its interpretation gives rise.

18   To begin with, it must be borne in mind that Community legislation is drafted in several languages and that the different language versions are all equally authentic. An interpretation of a provision of Community law thus involves a comparison of the different language versions.

19   It must also be borne in mind, even where the different language versions are entirely in accord with one another, that Community law uses terminology which is peculiar to it. Furthermore, it must be emphasized that legal concepts do not necessarily have the same meaning in Community law and in the law of the various Member States.

20   Finally, every provision of Community law must be placed in its context and interpreted in the light of the provisions of Community law as a whole, regard being had to the objectives thereof and to its state of evolution at the date on which the provision in question is to be applied.

NOTES AND QUESTIONS

1.   As *CILFIT* makes plain in ¶ 13, as early as 1963, in the *Da Costa* case cited there, the Court had held that national courts prepared to follow Court of Justice precedents are free to avoid a reference on a "materially identical" issue. (The Court of Justice precedent relied upon in *Da Costa* was in fact the *van Gend en Loos* decision, supra page 232). However, a number of national courts, including the French Conseil d'Etat (as illustrated in the *Cohn–Bendit* case, supra page 301), have considered themselves free not to make a referral whenever *they* feel that EU law is clear. Sometimes they then proceed to misconstrue or misapply EU law. Advocate General Capotorti in his opinion in *CILFIT* sharply criticized this practice and urged that the Italian Supreme Court be told to refer otherwise necessary questions except when Court of Justice precedent makes a reference unnecessary. The Court of Justice did not follow his view. Should it have?

2.   The Court's approval of the *acte clair* doctrine in *CILFIT* is obviously highly conditional. Look especially at ¶¶ 16–20. Do the conditions imposed adequately address the risks that the doctrine poses? For the view that the Court actually went too far in constraining Member State courts in their use of *acte clair,* see H. Rasmussen, The European Court's Acte Clair Strategy in CILFIT, 9 Eur. L. Rev. 242 (1984).

3.   After *CILFIT,* the Supreme Court of Italy decided to refer its questions about the 1968 regulation to the Court of Justice for a ruling on the merits. See Srl CILFIT v. Ministry of Health (II), Case 77/83, [1984] ECR 1257, where the Court issued a long ruling on the merits. What does that tell you about the risks of the *acte clair* doctrine?

4.   The Court underscored a further limit on the *acte clair* doctrine in Gaston Schul Douane-expediteur BV v. Minister van Landbouw, Case C–461/03, [2005] ECR I–10513. The national court queried whether it could declare invalid a provision in an agricultural regulation that was similar to one in another regulation that the Court had invalidated. In its response, the

Court cited *Foto–Frost*, supra page 253, and held that the national court could not rely upon the similarity of the two provisions in order to invalidate the one before it. The Court held that "careful examination may show that a provision whose validity is in question is not comparable to a provision which [the Court] has declared invalid" (¶ 20). The Court also observed that saving time in the national proceedings "cannot serve as a justification for undermining the sole jurisdiction of the Community courts to rule on the validity of Community law" (¶ 23). The Court then concluded by invalidating the agricultural regulation provision at stake in the national court proceeding.

5.   The German Constitutional Court has placed its own limits on the *acte clair* doctrine. We previously noted the Constitutional Court's *Kloppenburg* ruling, supra page 283. In the case of Re Patented Feedingstuffs, Case 2 BvR 808/82, [1988] NJW 1456, [1989] 2 CMLR 902 (second senate, Nov. 9, 1987), the Constitutional Court went further, squarely holding it to be a violation of due process under the German Constitution for a court of last resort to "give no consideration at all" to referring a question that the court itself considers relevant to the case at hand and on which it "entertains doubts as to the correct answer." The Constitutional Court also stated in *Feedingstuffs* that a court of last resort acts unconstitutionally when, in a case where a Court of Justice precedent is not clear-cut, it refuses to make a reference, if in so doing it "exceed[s] to an indefensible extent the scope . . . of discretion which it must necessarily have in such cases." [1989] 2 CMLR at 909.

Certain civil law systems recognize the right of lower courts to "resist" a ruling of a higher court, not only in analogous cases but possibly even in the case that generated the ruling. Such resistance may be viewed as a form of judicial dissent that might cause the higher court to reconsider and modify its views. Is there any room under EU law for national courts to adopt a similar attitude of "resistance" to precedents of the Court of Justice? Note ¶ 15 of *CILFIT*.

6.   Suppose that after *CILFIT* a national court declines to refer a question on *acte clair* grounds and proceeds to misconstrue EU law in the case before it. Judge Pescatore considers that this may sometimes be "merely a cloak for the resistance of certain highly placed courts to the authority of Community law, or for their desire not to give the Court an opportunity to clarify certain problems." P. Pescatore, References for Preliminary Rulings under Article 177 (EC Off'l Pub. Office, 1986) at 28, citing *Cohn–Bendit* (supra page 301) and the ruling of the Supreme German Tax Court in *Kloppenburg*. Can anything be done in such cases? See the discussion in Chapter 11B(2) infra.

7.   It is assumed that whether to make a preliminary reference, and what reference if any to make, is a matter for the national court, usually after discussion with the parties. For an interesting account of national governments' growing role in these determinations, however, see M.–P. Granger, When Governments Go To Luxembourg: The Influence of Governments on the Court of Justice, 29 Eur. L. Rev. 3 (2004), showing how governments' participation in the decision to refer and in the reference proceeding that may

follow has become a means of attempting to influence the direction of case law.

E. DISCRETIONARY AND MANDATORY REFERENCES

In regard to preliminary references, the Treaty draws a distinction between courts that may refer questions to the Court of Justice and those that must do so whenever a preliminary ruling would be appropriate. For most courts, the decision to make a preliminary reference (or not) is a discretionary one. However, TFEU Article 267, like EC Treaty Article 234 before it, makes preliminary references mandatory for courts "against whose decisions there is no judicial remedy under national law." This formula is in fact ambiguous. Under one interpretation, only courts that are hierarchically designated as of last resort, or supreme, must refer matters to the Court when the conditions for a reference are met; under the second, the last available court of appeal in any given case, irrespective of its general place in the judicial hierarchy, has that obligation. In 1982 the Court of Justice ruled that the purpose behind making references mandatory from the highest available national court is to prevent the development of a body of national case law that is contrary to the principles of EU law. See Morson and Jhanjan v. Netherlands, Cases 35, 36/82, [1982] ECR 3723, 3734. This would suggest that the second interpretation is the right one.

In most Member States the question lacks practical importance because appeal to the highest national court is of right, so that the question simply does not arise. Under British procedure, however, either the Court of Appeal or the House of Lords may grant leave to appeal to the House of Lords. Suppose the Court of Appeal declines to refer a question. Unless the House of Lords grants leave to appeal and then decides to refer a question, no English court will have been bound to refer. The Court of Appeal has ruled that it will consider itself to be a court of last resort for preliminary purposes only when "there is no possibility of any further appeal from it." Regina v. Statutory Committee of the Pharmaceutical Society, [1987] 3 CMLR 951, 969 (C.A., July 30, 1987). See F. Jacobs, Which Courts and Tribunals Are Bound to Refer to the European Court?, 2 Eur. L. Rev. 119 (1977).

In Criminal Proceedings against Lyckeskog, Case C–99/00, [2002] ECR I–4839, the Court of Justice brought some clarity to this issue. Lyckeskog had been found guilty of attempted smuggling by a Swedish District Court and appealed that decision to the Court of Appeal for Western Sweden. Under Swedish law, judgments of the latter court may be appealed to the Supreme Court, but the Supreme Court must declare the appeal "admissible" before it actually reviews the case. (The procedure appears to be analogous to the US Supreme Court's certiorari procedure.)

The Court of Appeal filed a preliminary reference asking whether "a national court or tribunal which in practice is the last instance in a case, because a declaration of admissibility is needed in order for the case to be reviewed by the country's supreme court, is a court or tribunal within the meaning of the third paragraph of Article 234 EC." The Court of Justice answered as follows:

16   Decisions of a national appellate court which can be challenged by the parties before a supreme court are not decisions of a 'court or tribunal of a Member State against whose decisions there is no judicial remedy under national law' within the meaning of Article 234. The fact that examination of the merits of such appeals is subject to a prior declaration of admissibility by the supreme court does not have the effect of depriving the parties of a judicial remedy.

Is this a sound solution? May we assume that, if the Supreme Court does not declare the appeal "admissible," the Court of Appeal may then still make the preliminary reference itself? Should it not be obligated to do so?

The Court has, however, answered the important question whether a preliminary reference is mandatory in an action in Member State court for provisional relief (such as a preliminary injunction) when the grant or denial of such relief is not subject to appeal. A reference might be thought to be mandatory in such a case. However, the Court of Justice has ruled that, when the merits of the application for provisional relief are essentially the same as the merits of the main action for permanent relief, and when such a subsequent proceeding will take place, the court deciding on provisional relief is not a court of last resort within the meaning of Article 234, and is not bound to make a preliminary reference. Hoffmann–La Roche AG v. Centrafarm, Case 107/76, [1977] ECR 957.

F.   "PUT UP" QUESTIONS AND INAPPROPRIATE REFERRALS

The Court of Justice has on rare occasion faced the question whether to entertain preliminary references arising out of disputes that the parties in national court appear to have contrived (or "put up") for no reason other than to secure a preliminary ruling. It might be said in such a case that the parties do not have a "real" case or controversy (i.e. are not really "opposed.").

This scenario is exemplified in Foglia v. Novello (I), Case 104/79, [1980] ECR 745. Two Italian wine dealers included in their contract for the sale of Italian wine a provision barring any charge to the buyer (Novello) for French or Italian taxes or duties that were contrary to the EC Treaty provisions on the free movement of goods. The seller (Foglia) in turn put a disclaimer of liability for such taxes or duties in his contract with the French transport carrier that was chosen to receive the shipment and deliver it to Novello. The obvious purpose of these contract provisions was to make it possible for the French excise tax to be challenged in an Italian court. When the transporter paid a French excise tax and included that amount in its bill to Foglia, Foglia claimed reimbursement from Novello, who refused to pay. Foglia then sued Novello in an Italian court. Both parties urged the court to ask the Court of Justice certain questions about the legality of the French tax under EC Treaty Articles 90 and 92 (now TFEU Articles 110 and 112) which set limits on internal taxes on goods. The Italian court referred those questions, but the Court of Justice declined to rule on them, maintaining that the dispute was not a genuine one. Novello then returned to the Italian court.

FOGLIA v. NOVELLO (II)

Case C–244/80, [1981] ECR 3045.

[Novello argued that the Court of Justice's refusal to answer violated its customary deference to the national court's determination that an EU law question needed to be answered, and prevented the national court from deciding the case before it. The Italian court, obviously sympathetic to this view, submitted a new round of questions to the Court of Justice on the division of authority between referring courts and the Court of Justice. The Court maintained its refusal to answer the questions referred, stating that:]

18   [T]he duty assigned to the Court by Article [234] is not that of delivering advisory opinions on general or hypothetical questions but of assisting in the administration of justice in the Member States. It accordingly does not have jurisdiction to reply to questions of interpretation which are submitted to it within the framework of procedural devices arranged by the parties in order to induce the Court to give its views on certain problems of Community law which do not correspond to an objective requirement inherent in the resolution of a dispute. A declaration by the Court that it has no jurisdiction in such circumstances does not in any way trespass upon the prerogatives of the national court but makes it possible to prevent the application of the procedure under Article [234] for purposes other than those appropriate for it.

[The Court seemed most disturbed by the prospect of private parties "putting up" a question in a court of one Member State calling into question the validity of the law of another Member State, as in the situation at hand:]

29   ... [T]he possibility arises that the conduct of the parties may ... make it impossible for the State concerned to arrange for an appropriate defence of its interests by causing the question of the invalidity of its legislation to be decided by a court of another Member State. Accordingly, in such procedural situations, it is impossible to exclude the risk that the procedure under Article [234] may be diverted by the parties from the purposes for which it was laid down by the Treaty.

30   The foregoing considerations as a whole show that the Court of Justice for its part must display special vigilance when, in the course of proceedings between individuals, a question is referred to it with a view to permitting the national court to decide whether the legislation of another Member State is in accordance with Community law.

NOTES AND QUESTIONS

1. Do you agree with the Court that it was inappropriate for the French tax law to be challenged in an Italian court? What difference does it make whether the question reaches the Court from an Italian or a French court? In any case, the most that the Italian court can achieve is to obtain a Court of Justice ruling that the transporter might later attempt to rely on in a French court to recover the French tax paid. How should the Italian court go about interpreting the relevant EU law norms if the Court of Justice refuses to provide a ruling? Could it decline to decide the case at all, since deprived of the benefit of a preliminary ruling? (Advocate General Sir Gordon Slynn stated in his opinion that the Court should have answered the questions put to it in *Foglia*.)

In Bacardi–Martini SAS v. Newcastle United Football Co., Ltd., Case C–318/00, [2003] ECR I–905, the Court of Justice received a reference from the UK High Court questioning whether a French law prohibiting television advertising of alcoholic beverages violated the free movement of services if it prevented the broadcast in France of a televised UK sports event because a stadium billboard advertised a French alcoholic beverage. The Court ruled that it had to display "special vigilance" when the validity of a law of one Member State is called into question by a reference from another State's court. Rather than exclude such references, the Court said that it needed more than the usual detail as to the referring court's reasons for considering a preliminary ruling to be necessary. The Court of Justice ultimately declined to answer the High Court's questions because the High Court was unable to show that a reply was necessary to resolve the dispute before it.

What is your view as to whether the Court should answer references concerning one State's national law when they are referred by a court in another State?

2. Note the apparent contradiction between the result (and reasoning) in *Foglia* with the Court's often-repeated claim that it does not inquire into a national court's reasons for referring a question. By the test that it used in *Foglia*, should the Court have answered the questions put to it in *Costa v. ENEL*, supra page 235? Recall that Costa challenged Italy's nationalization of certain electric utilities by contesting a roughly $3.00 electric bill before an Italian small claims court, and the Court of Justice accepted the referral. See also Firma Anton Dürbeck v. Hauptzollamt Frankfurt am Main–Flughafen, Case 112/80, [1981] ECR 1095, where the Court agreed to rule on the validity of EU law quotas on apples in an obvious test case involving the importation from Chile of only two boxes of apples.

The passage of time has shown that *Foglia* is very much the exception that proves the rule that the Court of Justice almost invariably answers questions that are put to it. The rule stated in *Foglia* was heavily criticized at the time. Subsequent judgments show that the Court is unlikely to follow it. Thus, in Firma Eau de Cologne & Parfümerie–Fabrik Glockengasse No. 4711 v. Provide SRL, Case C–150/88, [1989] ECR 3891, a German court referred questions about the conformity of Italian legislation to Council directives on the labeling of cosmetic products. The questions arose in a contract dispute over an Italian distributor's refusal to accept delivery from a German manufacturer of a product that did not meet the requirements of the Italian legislation. Although Italy formally objected to the referral, citing *Foglia*, the Court of Justice gave a ruling on the merits anyway. The Court said that a court of one Member State may examine the conformity to EU law of another State's legislation, provided the underlying dispute is genuine. To the same effect, see Walter Rau Lebensmittelwerke v. De Smedt, Case 261/81, [1982] ECR 3961, 3971.

In a subsequent case, French broadcasters refused to air an advertisement for fuel sold by a French importer in its supermarkets, citing a French law that prohibited televised advertising by the distribution sector. The importer sued, alleging that the French law violated both the EC Treaty and the 1989 television broadcasting directive. Both the broadcasters and the importer asked the French commercial court to refer this question to the Court of Justice, and indeed to broaden it by questioning the validity of the French ban on televised advertising in all the sectors to which the French ban applied (viz., alcoholic beverages, literary publications, cinema and the press).

The Court answered the question insofar as the ban on televised advertising by the distribution sector was concerned. However, the Court positively refused to answer the question in terms of any of the other sectors because, to that extent, "the interpretation of Community law has no connection whatever with the circumstances or purpose of the main proceedings." (On the merits, it ruled that the ban violated neither the free movement of goods nor the television broadcasting directive.) Société d'Importation Edouard Leclerc–Siplec v. TF1 Publicité, excerpted at page 499 infra.

3. Apart from the issue of "put-up" questions, occasionally the Court of Justice declines to furnish an answer to an otherwise relevant question of EU law because it does not consider a reply to be appropriate, for one reason or another.

One scenario arises when a party had standing to bring a direct challenge in the EU courts to a decision addressed to it (or, exceptionally, to a regulation or a decision addressed to another party, as indicated in Chapter 5B supra) but failed to do so, or to do so within the time limit allowed. May that party later on raise the question of the validity of the decision in a national court proceeding and thereby secure a preliminary ruling from the Court of Justice on the question?

In Nachi Europe GmbH v. Hauptzollamt Krefeld, Case C–239/99, [2001] ECR I–1197, a Council regulation imposed anti-dumping duties on ball bearings produced by three named Japanese manufacturers. Two of the three manufacturers (NTN and Koyo Seiko) appealed the regulation insofar as it imposed duties on their products. They were successful in the CFI and, on appeal, in the ECJ, at which point the Commission published a notice entitling importers of those products to refunds from national customs authorities. Nachi Europe, an importer, then sought reimbursement from the German authorities of duties it had paid on the import of ball bearings produced by the third Japanese manufacturer, which happened to be Nachi Europe's Japanese parent company, Nachi Fujikoshi. Upon refusal, Nachi Europe brought a refund suit in a German tax court, which asked the Court of Justice whether it could award the refund sought.

The Court of Justice ruled that Nachi could not obtain a refund in the German court, because neither it nor its parent had made an appeal to the CFI within the time period set in EC Treaty Article 230 (now TFEU Article 263). See Chapter 5A. According to the Court, Nachi Europe "undoubtedly" could have sought annulment of the regulation in a direct action in the CFI insofar as it imposed duties on Nachi Fujikoshi products (¶ 38), but having failed to do so, it could not subsequently plead the invalidity of the duty in the tax court (¶ 40). The Court wanted to foreclose use of a preliminary reference as an indirect mode of challenging the anti-dumping duty.

Is this a sound result, especially considering that Nachi Europe probably would have been successful in challenging the invalidity of the anti-dumping duties if the Court had entertained the reference? If Nachi Europe is at this point estopped from obtaining a preliminary ruling from the Court, is the German court likewise barred from doing so *sua sponte*?

The Court cited its judgment in TWD Textilwerke Deggendorf v. Germany, Case C–188/92, [1994] ECR I–833, in which it held that where the Commission has denied a Member State's request to make a state aid available to an enterprise, and the enterprise failed to challenge that denial in the Community courts when it had standing to do so under EC Treaty Article 230, the enterprise cannot thereafter indirectly challenge the denial in national court and thereby obtain a preliminary ruling on its validity.

4. Questions regarding state aids or subsidies constitute a second category of EU law questions that, though relevant, may be "off-limits" to the preliminary reference process. Consider Proceedings against Déménagements–Manutention Transport SA, Case C–256/97, [1999] ECR I–3913. Belgian law allowed the State, through its Social Security Office, to grant a grace period to financially troubled employers for collecting social security contributions. The Tribunal de Commerce, which had to approve the grant, asked the Court of Justice (a) whether such a grant constituted a state aid and (b) if so, whether it was compatible with the common market. The Court answered the first question (basically in the affirmative), but refused to answer the second, on the grounds that the Treaty provision on state aids authorized the Commission to review them and take the initial decision as to whether they are compatible with the common market. Accordingly, it would be premature for the Court to examine the legality of the state aid until the Commission acted. Any Commission decision could, of course, be appealed to the Court.

By contrast, in a third scenario, the Court considered a preliminary reference to be admissible even though it questioned the validity of an EU directive prior to the final date for its implementation. The Court quickly dismissed the view that a reference under those circumstances should not be admissible:

40   The opportunity open to individuals to plead the invalidity of a Community act of general application before national courts is not conditional upon that act's actually having been the subject of implementing measures adopted pursuant to national law. In that respect, it is sufficient if the national court is called upon to hear a genuine dispute in which the question of the validity of such an act is raised indirectly.

The Queen v. Secretary of State for Health ex parte British American Tobacco Ltd, discussed at page 120, supra.

G. THE APPEALABILITY OF PRELIMINARY REFERENCES AND REFUSALS TO REFER

It is unrealistic to assume that the national litigation from which a preliminary reference arises will be "frozen" until the Court's ruling is received, and only resume thereafter. After all, a trial court's decision to refer may be subject to interlocutory appeal. (The successful appeal to the Conseil d'Etat in *Cohn–Bendit,* supra page 301, from the lower court's decision to refer illustrates this possibility.) A trial court's decision *not* to refer likewise may be appealed (as occurred in *Bulmer v. Bollinger,* supra page 334). These scenarios raise questions about the legal status and effect of a national court's decision to issue, or not issue, a preliminary reference.

The first question is whether and to what extent a decision to refer a question to the Court of Justice may be appealed. In Rheinmühlen–Düsseldorf v. Einfuhr- und Vorratsstelle für Getreide und Futtermittel, Cases 146, 166/73, [1974] ECR 33, 139, Advocate–General Warner argued that allowing an order for a preliminary reference to be appealed would violate the Treaty, which grants lower courts complete discretion to seek a preliminary ruling when they find that it is necessary and appropriate to do so. [1974] ECR at 43, 47. The Court, however, disagreed, holding that an order for a preliminary reference is subject to appeal to the same extent as similar interlocutory orders under national law. The Court of Justice has not, however, as yet decided whether EU law places any limits on a national court's right to set aside a lower court's decision to refer.

What effect should the pendency of an appeal have on the Court of Justice's jurisdiction to render a preliminary ruling? Doubtless, the appellant's hope in *Rheinmühlen,* supra, was that the Court would refrain from issuing a ruling until the appeal was decided. However, the Court held in that case that the lodging of an appeal does not deprive it of jurisdiction to decide the question referred or otherwise require it to suspend proceedings. As early as 1962, in de Geus v. Robert Bosch GmbH, Case 13/61, [1962] ECR 45, the Court recognized that the importance of a ruling by the Court might transcend the specific national litigation out of which the issue arose. An important exception is when an appeal from an order of reference has the effect *under national law* of suspending the effectiveness of the order. SA Chanel v. Cepeha Handelsmaatschappij NV, Case 31/68, [1970] ECR 404.

The net effect is that the appeal in a national court of a preliminary reference order and the Court of Justice's own preliminary reference proceedings may go on simultaneously. Though this may seem to be wasteful of resources, it does protect the autonomy of both the national and EU judicial systems. What should the Court of Justice do in the rare event that a preliminary reference order is reversed on appeal? In the *Rheinmühlen* case, the Court held that in those circumstances it will proceed no further and will refrain from issuing a ruling even if otherwise prepared to issue one. [1974] ECR at 47. In other words, the existence of a valid preliminary reference order is a continuing condition of the Court's preliminary reference jurisdiction.

Now suppose the national court refuses to refer a question to the Court of Justice and that decision is appealed. This scenario is a simpler one. The availability of an appeal and the standard of appellate review are once again presumably matters of national law. Whether EU law itself requires that Member States provide some sort of appellate remedy from a lower court's refusal to refer has never had to be decided. As for the Court of Justice's own freedom of action, the situation is clear: the Court cannot exercise preliminary reference jurisdiction unless and until it has received a valid preliminary reference from a national court.

NOTE ON PROVISIONAL RELIEF PENDING A PRELIMINARY RULING

The referring court may consider it appropriate to award some form of interim relief pending receipt of the ruling from Luxembourg. One circumstance in which interim relief may suggest itself is where a court suspects that a litigant has raised an EU law issue solely for delay or tactical advantage. See Portsmouth City Council v. Richards and Quietlynn Ltd., [1989] 1 CMLR 673 (C.A., Nov. 16, 1988).

The availability of provisional relief is presumptively a matter of domestic procedural law. However, we have already seen in the *Factortame* case, supra page 250, that the Court of Justice may regard a form of provisional relief as indispensable, at least in some circumstances, where the litigant is challenging a national measure as violative of EU law.

Consider a scenario in which the referring court questions the validity of secondary EU legislation, rather than a national law measure, under the Treaty or some other superior principle of EU law, such as fundamental rights. We know from the *Foto–Frost* case, supra page 253, that a national court may not treat the EU law measure as invalid, but must put the question to the Court of Justice. Thus the question has arisen whether, pending the Court's ruling, the national court may issue interim relief, for example, provisionally suspending enforcement of the national implementing measure.

Only recently have the Court's views on this emerged. Rather than categorically preclude provisional relief in these circumstances, the Court has offered up a more nuanced solution. Its first expression of views came in Zuckerfabrik Süderdithmarschen AG v. Hauptzollamt Itzehoe, Cases C–143/88 & C–92/89, [1991] ECR I–415. There the Court laid down a threshold requirement: an injunction is only proper if issued in connection with a "challenge that is based on *Community* law itself" (emphasis added). Does this mean that national courts may never enjoin the enforcement of a national measure implementing EU law on the ground that it violates *Member State* law? If so, is that a sound rule? Suppose a State, in implementing a directive, adopts a statute or rule in a manner contrary to basic rights principles, substantive or procedural, when the directive itself does not require implementation in that fashion?

The Court in *Süderdithmarschen* did not give national courts *carte blanche* to suspend the enforcement of national law implementing an EU law measure. An interim injunction may be issued only if (a) the measure's validity is seriously in doubt, (b) there is urgent need for relief to prevent serious and irreparable harm (which, according to the Court, is unlikely when the alleged harm is purely economic), and (c) the national judge immediately refers the question of the measure's validity to the Court of Justice. Finally, the Court admonished national courts to take fully into account the EU interest in not having a measure lightly set aside pending a ruling on its validity.

CHAPTER 10

NATIONAL REMEDIES FOR THE ENFORCEMENT OF EU LAW CLAIMS

■ ■ ■

Any discussion of EU law enforcement must forcefully convey the point that responsibility for this function is shared, though by no means evenly, between EU and Member State institutions.

Before turning in this chapter primarily to the role of Member States in the implementation of EU law, we need to recognize the range and importance of the Commission's own functions as EU law enforcer. Among the most prominent aspects of Commission law enforcement activity is the investigation and eventual "prosecution" under TFEU Article 258 (formerly EC Treaty Article 226) of Member State infringements of EU law. In the US, the federal government also undertakes some policing of state and local government action, as in the civil rights or environmental protection areas, but the Commission's enforcement role is far more general and pervasive. Chapter 11 infra is devoted to this species of enforcement.

The Commission also enforces EU law in the more general sense of implementing EU policy, often on a daily basis. Competition law is a prime example of this. The Commission, concurrently with authorities of the Member States, investigates allegedly anti-competitive behavior, decides whether or not to prosecute competition law violations and, eventually, to impose sanctions (and if so at what level). Implementation of EU competition law under TFEU Articles 101 and 102 (formerly EC Treaty Articles 81 and 82), as well as secondary legislation in that field, probably engages the Commission in its fullest range of administrative conduct, beginning as early as the gathering of information on possible breaches of competition policy through all enforcement stages. The procedural rules governing Commission activity in this area—as well as in the review of state aids under TFEU Article 108 (formerly EC Treaty Article 88)—are discussed in Part 4 of this book.

The Commission has still more general administrative powers. TEU Article 17(1) (formerly EC Treaty Article 211) provides that the Commission, besides exercising authority delegated by the Council, "shall ensure the application of the Treaties, and of measures adopted by the institutions pursuant to them [and] shall oversee the application of Union law." In addition, it "shall execute the budget and manage programs [and] exercise coordinating, executive and management functions, as laid down in the Treaties." The Commission also has the specific power to approve or disapprove the use that Member States make of the "safeguard clauses" that are found in certain Treaty articles and that permit them to avoid a specific obligation when exceptional circumstances so justify. An example is TFEU Article 114 (4)–(8) (formerly EC Treaty Article 95). The Commission's task in such cases is to determine whether a Member State's reliance on a safeguard clause is justified.

More significant than the Commission's relatively few Treaty-based powers of decision are the extensive decisional powers delegated to it by the Council and Parliament through secondary legislation. The Common Agricultural Policy (CAP) is an arena in which the Commission regularly makes important decisions by delegation. Agricultural regulations not only confer certain normative powers on the Commission, but specifically empower it to allow particular enterprises or Member States dispensation from the usual rules, provided a serious market disturbance or other threat to the CAP objectives has arisen.

There is in fact virtually no sphere of EU law in which the Commission does not exercise at least some type and measure of administrative function. The many decisions that the Treaty and secondary legislation call upon the Commission to make closely resemble action taken daily by US administrative agencies under the procedures of administrative law. Precisely because this kind of decisionmaking is best appreciated in context, it is taken up as appropriate in the various substantive law chapters that follow in this book.

All that having been said, the fact remains that the vast bulk of day-to-day enforcement of EU law and policy rests in the hands of Member State officials. EU rules on agriculture, customs, tariffs, tax, and cross-border inspections and formalities, for example, are virtually all entrusted to the same national bureaucracies that otherwise execute these bodies of law. This may seem obvious enough on core common market matters. But it is equally so in the many regulatory spheres, such as industrial standards, the environment, pharmaceutical licensing and occupational health, that have been harmonized by EU legislation. Where EU law takes the form of directives, the law that Member State officials administer, though shaped by EU standards, remains in all formal respects national law. In fact, those officials may not always realize that in administering *national law* they are actually implementing *EU policy*.

Primary enforcement of EU policy in the Member States takes place not only in national administrative agencies, but in some cases also directly in national courts. This will of course normally be the case for problems over which a Member State's courts, rather than its agencies, have primary enforcement responsibility. A good example is products liability. In 1985, a Council directive harmonized Member State law on products liability (see Chapter 33). Each Member State was then to adopt products liability legislation conforming to that directive, either through amendment of its Civil Code (if it had one) or through special enactment. Products liability actions are thus still brought directly through private litigation in Member State courts, though reflecting substantive EU law principles. In this way, national judges too can be primary EU law enforcers.

To the extent that EU policy is carried out through national decision-makers using domestic law means, its administration naturally takes on the institutional and procedural coloration of the various Member States. Each Member State has its own distinctive administrative institutions, as well as its characteristic processes for functions as diverse as inspection, licensing and taxation, not to mention adjudication. This book cannot, of course, enter into the details of national administrative law and procedure.

The essential point is that the EU has a significant interest in the adequacy of Member State enforcement, whether administrative or judicial. Questions of procedural adequacy surfaced earlier in Chapter 7 in connection with certain corollaries of the direct effect and supremacy doctrines. However, these questions have gained attention in their own right and they are taken up more systematically in Part A of the present chapter. In Part B, we turn to the question of the Member States' liability for their EU law failures.

A. THE ADEQUACY OF NATIONAL REMEDIES

If private parties are to enforce their EU law rights directly in Member States courts, then those courts must have and make available appropriate remedies. For national judges this means, first of all, identifying the domestic forms of relief that are available and suitable for the claims brought under the EU law banner. Second, it raises the question of whether national remedies ever need to be adapted to suit the requirements of EU law, and what is to be done in the event the available remedies cannot be. Obviously, the EU itself (particularly the Court of Justice) has a definite stake in ensuring the availability and adequacy of Member State remedies for enforcing EU law claims.

This issue plainly raises opportunities for dialogue between the national courts and the Court of Justice. As the following case reveals, the Court of Justice in principle requires the national procedural rules governing EU law claims to be no less favourable than those governing comparable domestic actions (the so-called "principle of equivalence") and not to render practically impossible or excessively difficult the exercise of rights conferred by EU law (the "principle of effectiveness").

REWE–ZENTRALFINANZ EG v. LANDWIRTSCHAFTS–
KAMMER FUR DAS SAARLAND

Case 33/76, [1976] ECR 1989.

[In 1968, two German companies paid charges for the phyto-sanitary inspection of apples imported from France. Some years later, the Court of Justice held such charges to be illegal under EU law. When the companies sought a refund with interest from the German authorities, they discovered that under German procedure their claim was time-barred. The case worked its way up to Germany's highest administrative court, which made a preliminary reference to the Court of Justice.]

5   The prohibitions laid down in [the Treaty and the regulation] have a direct effect and confer on citizens rights which the national courts are required to protect.

Applying the principle of cooperation laid down in [EC Treaty Article 10, now Lisbon TEU Article 4(3)], it is the national courts which are entrusted with ensuring the legal protection which citizens derive from the direct effect of the provisions of Community law.

Accordingly, in the absence of Community rules on this subject, it is for the domestic legal system of each Member State to designate the courts having jurisdiction and to determine the procedural conditions governing actions at law intended to ensure the protection of the rights which citizens have from the direct effect of Community law, it being understood that such conditions cannot be less favourable than those relating to similar actions of a domestic nature.

Where necessary, [EC Treaties Articles 94 to 97 EC, now TFEU Articles 114 to 117] and EC Treaty Article 308 [now TFEU Article 352] enable appropriate measures to be taken to remedy differences between the provisions laid down by law, regulation or administrative action in Member States if they are likely to distort or harm the functioning of the Common Market.

In the absence of such measures of harmonization the right conferred by Community law must be exercised before the national courts in accordance with the conditions laid down by national rules.

The position would be different only if the conditions and time-limits made it impossible in practice to exercise the rights which the national courts are obliged to protect.

This is not the case where reasonable periods of limitation of actions are fixed.

The laying down of such time-limits with regard to actions of a fiscal nature is an application of the fundamental principle of legal certainty protecting both the taxpayer and the administration concerned.

6   The answer to be given to the first question is therefore that in the present state of Community law, there is nothing to prevent a citizen

who contests before a national court a decision of a national authority on the ground that it is incompatible with Community law from being confronted with the defence that limitation periods laid down by national law have expired, it being understood that the procedural conditions governing the action may not be less favourable than those relating to similar actions of a domestic nature.

NOTES AND QUESTIONS

1. The Court in *Rewe–Zentralfinanz* held that States may freely fix the statute of limitations on tax refund claims, subject to satisfying the principles of equivalency and effectiveness (or adequacy). Bear in mind the formula generally used by the Court in this connection, namely that States may employ their own domestic rules, "provided, first, that such rules are not less favourable than those governing similar domestic actions . . . and, second, that they do not render virtually impossible or excessively difficult the exercise of rights conferred by Community law." Dilexport, Case C–343/96, [1999] ECR I–597). When might a limitations period make it impossible or excessively difficult to assert EU law rights? See Edilizia Industriale Siderurgica Srl v. Ministero delle Finanze, Case C–231/96, [1998] ECR I–4951.

In Vincenzo Manfredi v. Lloyd Adriatico Assicurazioni, Joined Cases C–295–298/04, [2006] ECR I–6619, the national rule provided that the limitations period for seeking damages for EU competition law violations began to run from the day on which the prohibited agreement or practice was adopted. The Court held that such a rule could make it practically impossible to exercise the right to seek compensation, particularly if that national rule also imposes a short limitation period which is not capable of being suspended. However, it remained the national court's task to determine whether such is the case.

2. Not surprisingly, the Court has also held that the Member States are free to decide which of their courts has jurisdiction to hear disputes involving individual rights derived from EU law, provided they ensure that those rights are in any event effectively protected. Bozzetti v. Invernizzi SpA and Ministero del Tesoro, Case 179/84, [1985] ECR 2301. However, if EU law requires Member States to ensure that individuals affected by a decision of a national regulatory authority have a right to appeal to an independent body, the body that would ordinarily be competent to perform that function must be empowered to do so, notwithstanding even a provision of national law explicitly excluding its competence. See Connect Austria, Case C–462/99, [2003] ECR I–5197.

3. Hans Just, a Danish importer of spirits, sued to recover the amount by which the Danish levy on imports exceeded the levy on domestic products, in violation of EC Treaty Article 90 (now TFEU Article 110). The authorities invoked a Danish rule, inspired by the principle of unjust enrichment, that sums unlawfully levied may not be recovered if they can be presumed to have been passed along to the consumer. May the national court apply such a principle in this case? Hans Just v. Danish Ministry for Fiscal Affairs, Case 68/79, [1980] ECR 501. In the case of Amministrazione delle Finanze dello

Stato v. SpA San Giorgio, Case 199/82, [1983] ECR 3595, the question was whether a Member State may make recovery of charges levied in breach of EU law conditional on the claimant's proving that the charges had not been passed on to third parties. The Court approved the rule, provided it was applied equally to claims for the recovery of improper charges under national law, and provided the requirements of proof were not such as to make recovery "virtually impossible or excessively difficult to secure."

In Société Comateb v. Directeur Général des Douanes et Droits Indirects, Joined Cases C–192–218/95, [1997] ECR I–165, the Court took a rather close look at national practices in the recovery of illegally levied charges. It not only ruled that a trader could be refused repayment only where it is proven that the illegal charge was borne entirely by someone else and that recovery by the trader would amount to unjust enrichment; it also ruled that the fact that a trader has a legal obligation (possibly with penalty) to build the charge into the cost price does not entitle a national court to assume that the entire charge has been passed on. On the other hand, the Court ruled that even if a charge is fully passed on, the trader might still have a claim for provable market losses in sales (and profits) on account of the increased price.

In still another twist on the principle of unjust enrichment, the Court of Justice was asked in effect to decide whether a UK court could apply the equitable principle that a person should not be allowed to benefit from his own illegal conduct to deny a party contract damages based on the breach of a contract contrary to EU competition law rules. Courage Ltd. v. Crehan, Case C–453/99, [2001] ECR I–6297 (¶¶ 17–18). Emphasizing the importance of EU competition law, the Court held that "any individual can rely on a breach of EC Treaty Article 81 (now TFEU Article 101) before a national court even where he is a party to a contract that is liable to restrict or distort competition within the meaning of that provision." Otherwise, "[t]he full effectiveness of [EC Treaty Article 81] . . . would be put at risk" (¶¶ 24–28).

On the other hand, "Community law does not prevent national courts from taking steps to ensure that the protection of the rights guaranteed by Community law does not entail the unjust enrichment of those who enjoy them. Similarly, provided that the principles of equivalence and effectiveness are respected, Community law does not preclude national law from denying a party who is found to bear significant responsibility for the distortion of competition the right to obtain damages from the other contracting party" (¶¶ 30–31). The factors relevant to this determination should include, notably, the respective bargaining power and conduct of the two parties (¶¶ 32–33).

How useful is this guidance to national courts? For a discussion of the case, see G.A. Cumming, Case Comment: Courage Ltd. v. Crehan, 23 Eur. Compet. L. Rev. 199 (2002).

4.   Does the Court's conditional tolerance of remedial differences among Member States raise the specter of forum-shopping and, if so, how serious is the problem? Would you favor the enactment of EU legislation prescribing the national law remedies (e.g., forms of relief, measurement of damages) that Member States must make available for vindicating EU law claims? If so, would you urge that the legislation also lay down uniform procedural rules (e.g., on standing) for asserting these remedies?

5. Must a Member State court give retroactive effect to a Court of Justice ruling even if a comparable ruling under national law would not be applied retroactively? See Carberry v. Minister for Social Welfare, [1990] 1 CMLR 29 (Irish High Court, April 28, 1989), giving retroactive effect to McDermott and Cotter v. Minister for Social Welfare (I), Case 286/85, [1987] ECR 1453. (In *McDermott I*, the Court ruled that after the implementation deadline for the EC directive on nondiscrimination in social security had passed, women could automatically claim the same advantages to which men in the same situation were entitled.)

The Court of Justice ruled in Kühne & Heitz NV v. Productschap voor Pluimvee en Eieren, Case C–453/00, [2004] ECR I–837, that a Member State administrative authority has an obligation upon request to review an administrative decision that has become final, due to an intervening Court of Justice ruling, provided: (a) national law gives the body the power to reopen the matter, (b) the administrative decision has become final "as a result of a judgment of a national court ruling at final instance," (c) the national judgment may be regarded, in light of the intervening ECJ ruling, as "based on a misinterpretation of Community law which was adopted without a question being referred to the Court for a preliminary ruling," and (d) the applicant complained to the administrative authority immediately upon becoming aware of the ECJ ruling.

The Court held that this result follows from "the principle of cooperation" set out in EC Treaty Article 10) (now TFEU 4(3)). On the other hand, the Court held in Kapferer v. Schlank & Schick GmbH, Case C–234/04, [2006] ECR I–2585, that EC Treaty Article 10 did not require a national court to "disapply" its internal rules of procedure in order to review and set aside a final judicial decision if that decision is contrary to EU law. The Court did not answer the question whether the principles laid down in *Kühne & Heitz* apply equally in the context of national judicial decisions.

6. Suppose that instead of levying a charge that is forbidden under EU law principles (as in *Rewe–Zentralfinanz*), Member State authorities refused to furnish plaintiff a remedy on the ground that the State had never implemented the Council directive mandating the remedy. Suppose also that the deadline for implementation has passed, but so has the ordinarily applicable domestic statute of limitations for challenging the refusal. Assuming the limitations period meets the two-part test set out in *Rewe–Zentralfinanz*, must the suit be dismissed? The Court of Justice has said no. "[U]ntil such time as a directive has been properly transposed, a defaulting Member State may not rely on an individual's delay in initiating proceedings against it in order to protect rights conferred … by the provisions of the directive and [the usual domestic limitations period] cannot begin to run before that time." Emmott v. Minister for Social Welfare, Case C–208/90, [1991] ECR I–4269. By what reasoning do you suppose the Court reached that result? For a case distinguishing Emmott on its facts, see Fantask A/S v. Industriministeriet, Case C–188/95, [1997] ECR I–6783.

However, the Court subsequently refused to extend the *Emmott* rule to the question of the length of time prior to the bringing of an employment discrimination action for which arrears of benefits are payable. In other words, the UK's failure to implement the directive did not prevent it, in entertaining the claim recognized by the directive, from applying the UK rule that back payment may be ordered only for the period of one year prior to the filing of a claim. Johnson v. Chief Adjudication Officer, Case C–410/92, [1994] ECR I–5483. Can *Emmott* and *Johnson* be reconciled? To the same effect as *Johnson,* see Steenhorst–Neerings v. Bestuur van de Bedrijfsvereniging voor Detailhandel, Case C–338/91, [1993] ECR I–5475.

VON COLSON AND KAMANN v. LAND NORDRHEIN–WESTFALEN

Case 14/83, [1984] ECR 1891.

[Two female social workers, von Colson and Kamann, complained to a local labor court that the German state of North Rhine–Westphalia refused to hire them for work in an all-male prison, hiring less well-qualified male candidates instead. They claimed that the state thereby violated their rights under Council Directive 76/207 on equal treatment in access to employment.

The labor court found that there had indeed been discrimination, but also found that the German Civil Code amendment implementing Directive 76/207 had limited damages in employment discrimination cases to losses resulting from the victim's reliance on there being no discrimination in hiring (in German, *Vertrauensschaden*). The court concluded that under that rule it could award Kamann nothing and von Colson only her 7.20 DM (i.e. $4–$5) job application fee. However, first it referred several questions to the Court of Justice concerning Directive 76/207.

On preliminary reference, the Court of Justice ruled that an employer who is guilty of discrimination is not necessarily required under the directive to conclude a contract of employment with the victim. But though the directive did not prescribe that, or any other, specific sanction, it did require Member States "to adopt measures which are sufficiently effective to achieve the objective of the directive and to ensure that those measures may in fact be relied on before the national courts by the persons concerned" (¶ 18). The Court continued.]

22   It is impossible to establish real equality of opportunity without an appropriate system of sanctions. That follows not only from the actual purpose of the directive but more specifically from Article 6 thereof which, by granting applicants for a post who have been discriminated against recourse to the courts, acknowledges that those candidates have rights of which they may avail themselves before the courts.

23   Although ... full implementation of the directive does not require any specific form of sanction for unlawful discrimination, it does entail that that sanction be such as to guarantee real and effective judicial protection. Moreover it must also have a real deterrent effect on the employer. It follows that where a Member State chooses to penalize the breach of the prohibition of discrimination by the award of

compensation, that compensation must in any event be adequate in relation to the damage sustained.

24 In consequence it appears that national provisions limiting the right to compensation of persons who have been discriminated against as regards access to employment to a purely nominal amount, such as, for example, the reimbursement of expenses incurred by them in submitting their application, would not satisfy the requirements of an effective transposition of the directive.

[The Court recalled that the Member States have a duty to achieve the results envisaged by directives and that this duty also binds the national courts. In language repeated in the *Marleasing* case, supra page 265, the Court held that national courts must interpret national law enacted to implement a directive "in the light of the wording and the purpose of the directive."

On the other hand, the Court found Directive 76/207 not to be sufficiently precise and unconditional so as to have direct effect, i.e., to create by itself (and apart from national implementing legislation) a right to specific compensation that individuals may assert in Member State court. The Court proceeded as follows.]

28 [But] although Directive [76/207] . . . leaves the Member States free to choose between the different solutions suitable for achieving its objective, it nevertheless requires that if a Member State chooses to penalize breaches of that prohibition by the award of compensation, then in order to ensure that it is effective and that it has a deterrent effect, that compensation must in any event be adequate in relation to the damage sustained and must therefore amount to more than purely nominal compensation such as, for example, the reimbursement only of the expenses incurred in connection with the application. It is for the national court to interpret and apply the legislation adopted for the implementation of the directive in conformity with the requirements of Community law, in so far as it is given discretion to do so under national law.

NOTES AND QUESTIONS

1. *von Colson and Kamann* (¶ 28) expressly left it to the national court to decide whether the relevant German implementing legislation could be construed to meet the Member States' obligations under Directive 76/207. Suppose the legislation could not be so construed. Considering that the Court found Directive 76/207 to lack direct effect, what then is going to be the result in German court for persons like von Colson and Kamann? full damages? nominal damages? no damages at all?

2. In Johnston v. Chief Constable of the Royal Ulster Constabulary, Case 222/84, [1986] ECR 1651, excerpted at page 1413 infra, a member of the constabulary challenged in UK court a police force policy of denying arms to female officers. She invoked the same directive (76/207) at issue in *von Colson*

and Kamann. The Court of Justice ruled on preliminary reference that Article 6 of the directive, which required Member States to introduce the measures needed to enable discrimination victims "to pursue their claims by judicial process" had direct effect in the national courts. It also ruled that the British implementing legislation, which exempted from judicial review any act taken to safeguard national security or public order, and which provided that the Secretary of State's certificate stating that a measure was taken for those purposes "shall be conclusive," ran afoul of the directive, and more specifically Article 6. The case shows how EU law may restrict a Member State's freedom to preclude judicial review of administrative action or to create irrebuttable legal presumptions.

By the same token, the Court has held that the principle of free movement of workers requires that a decision by the French authorities refusing to recognize a Belgian football-coaching diploma as equivalent to a French one must state its reasons and be subject to judicial review. Union nationale des entraineurs et cadres techniques professionnels du football v. Heylens, Case 222/86, [1987] ECR 4097.

3. When the Court condemned the UK under EC Treaty Article 226 (now TFEU Article 258) for failing adequately to implement certain social policy directives, it did so partly on account of remedial deficiencies in the UK implementing legislation. For example, the Court disapproved of the UK's implementation of the collective redundancies directive (75/129), in part because the UK measure permitted an employer to "set off" any amounts owed to a dismissed employee for failure to consult the latter's representatives, as required, against any sums payable to the employee under the employee's contract of employment or on account of its breach. The Court found that this mechanism largely deprived the UK sanction of its deterrent value. Commission v. United Kingdom (Collective redundancies), Case C–383/92, [1994] ECR I–2479. See also Commission v. United Kingdom (Transfer of undertakings), Case C–382/92, [1994] ECR I–2435, where the Court also rejected a feature of the UK legislation on employee rights in the event of transfers of undertakings, whereby an employer who failed to consult employee representatives, as required by Directive 77/187, could "set off" any amounts paid as a penalty against amounts it was required to pay for noncompliance with the consultation requirement in Directive 75/129 (see above) in the event of collective employee dismissals for redundancy. Was the UK rightly condemned in both cases? (Both cases are dealt with more fully in Chapter 35 on Social Policy.)

4. In Unibet (London) Ltd. v. Justitiekanslern, Case C–432/05, [2007] ECR–I 2271, a Swedish court asked the Court of Justice whether EU law requires Member States to make available a free-standing cause of action for a determination that national legislation contravenes EU law where there exist other legal remedies (such as a suit for damages or a challenge to an administrative act taken pursuant to the national legislation) in connection with which the issue could be ruled upon as a preliminary issue. The Court disclaimed any such requirement, though it rejected as an alternative remedy the mere possibility of raising the statute's illegality as a defense to an administrative or criminal enforcement proceeding by the State. Do you see why the Court rejected the latter alternative?

5. A recurring question has been whether EU law ever requires Member States, as a remedial matter, to criminalize private conduct. In Belgium v. Vandevenne, Case C–7/90, [1991] ECR I–4371, the Court (citing a prior case, Anklagemyndigheden v. Hansen & Soen I/S, Case C–326/88, [1990] ECR I–2911), ruled that when an EU regulation does not specify a penalty in case of breach, but refers to national provisions, Member States are free to refrain from imposing criminal penalties, provided they treat the EU law infringement in a procedural and substantive fashion comparable to similar infringements of national law, and provided that the treatment is in any event "effective, proportionate and dissuasive." See also Gallotti and Others, Joined Cases C–58, 75, 112, 119, 123, 135, 140, 141, 154 & 157/95, [1996] ECR I–4345.

MARSHALL v. SOUTHAMPTON AND SOUTH–WEST HAMPSHIRE AREA HEALTH AUTHORITY

(Marshall II)
Case C–271/91, [1993] ECR I–4367.

[This case is a sequel to the *Marshall* judgment at page 264 supra of the casebook. The industrial tribunal awarded Marshall £ 10,695 for financial losses, £ 1000 for injury to her feelings and £ 7710 in interest, in spite of the fact that the UK law implementing the equal treatment directive set a ceiling on recovery of £ 6250 and disallowed the payment of interest. On appeal, the House of Lords inquired of the Court of Justice whether EU law permitted UK courts to enforce the damages limitations established by UK law.]

22　Article 6 of the directive puts Member States under a duty to take the necessary measures to enable all persons who consider themselves wronged by discrimination to pursue their claims by judicial process. Such obligation implies that the measures in question should be sufficiently effective to achieve the objective of the directive and should be capable of being effectively relied upon by the persons concerned before national courts.

23　As the Court held in [*von Colson and Kamann*], Article 6 does not prescribe a specific measure to be taken in the event of a breach of the prohibition of discrimination, but leaves Member States free to choose between the different solutions suitable for achieving the objective of the directive, depending on the different situations which may arise.

24　However, the objective is to arrive at real equality of opportunity and cannot therefore be attained in the absence of measures appropriate to restore such equality when it has not been observed. As the Court stated in paragraph 23 in *von Colson and Kamann* . . . those measures must be such as to guarantee real and effective judicial protection and have a real deterrent effect on the employer.

25　. . . In the event of discriminatory dismissal contrary to Article 5(1) of the directive, a situation of equality could not be restored without either reinstating the victim of discrimination or, in the alternative, granting financial compensation for the loss and damage sustained.

26 Where financial compensation is the measure adopted in order to achieve the objective indicated above, it must be adequate, in that it must enable the loss and damage actually sustained as a result of the discriminatory dismissal to be made good in full in accordance with the applicable national rules.

* * *

29 The Court's interpretation of Article 6 as set out above provides a direct reply to the ... question relating to the level of compensation required by that provision.

30 It ... follows ... that the fixing of an upper limit of the kind at issue in the main proceedings cannot, by definition, constitute proper implementation of Article 6 of the directive, since it limits the amount of compensation *a priori* to a level which is not necessarily consistent with the requirement of ensuring real equality of opportunity through adequate reparation for the loss and damage sustained as a result of discriminatory dismissal.

31 With regard to the ... question relating to the award of interest, suffice it to say that full compensation for the loss and damage sustained as a result of discriminatory dismissal cannot leave out of account factors, such as the effluxion of time, which may in fact reduce its value. The award of interest, in accordance with the applicable national rules, must therefore be regarded as an essential component of compensation for the purposes of restoring real equality of treatment.

32 Accordingly, the reply to be given ... [is] that reparation of the loss and damage sustained by a person injured as a result of discriminatory dismissal may not be limited to an upper limit fixed *a priori* or by excluding an award of interest to compensate for the loss sustained by the recipient of the compensation as a result of the effluxion of time until the capital sum awarded is actually paid.

[Significantly, the Court then concluded that the pertinent provisions of the directive have direct effect:]

35 Accordingly, the combined provisions of Article 6 and Article 5 of the directive give rise, on the part of a person who has been injured as a result of discriminatory dismissal, to rights which that person must be able to rely upon before the national courts as against the State and authorities which are an emanation of the State.

* * *

37 It should be pointed out in that connection that ... the right of a State to choose among several possible means of achieving the objectives of a directive does not exclude the possibility for individuals of enforcing before national courts rights whose content can be deter-

mined sufficiently precisely on the basis of the provisions of the directive alone.

NOTES AND QUESTIONS

1. Does *Marshall II* in any sense overrule *von Colson and Kamann*? Would you answer the questions in note 1 following *von Colson and Kamann* any differently after *Marshall II*?

2. Does *Marshall II* go too far? Does it implicate the principle of subsidiarity? Note that Advocate General van Gerven opined in the case that the UK ceiling on damages could be accepted even if it meant "less than ... full" compensation, provided it permitted "adequate" compensation (adequacy to be determined in light of the most important components of damages traditionally taken into account in setting rules of liability). He thought the requirement of equivalence would in any event have to be satisfied.

3. The Court on occasion goes still further in determining what constitutes an adequate remedy. In National Pensions Office v. Jonkman, Joined Cases C–231–233/06, [2007] ECR I–5149, the Court held that in cases of discrimination in violation of EU law, Member States must, in addition to eliminating the violation, afford persons in the disadvantaged category the same advantages as those enjoyed by persons in the favored category.

VAN SCHIJNDEL AND VAN VEEN v. SPF
Joined Cases C–430, 431/93, [1995] ECR I–4705.

[van Schijndel and van Veen, Dutch physiotherapists, applied for exemption from compulsory membership in the Dutch "Pension Fund Foundation for Physiotherapists" (the "Fund"). According to the applicable rules, membership was not mandatory in cases where a physiotherapist practices the profession under a contract of employment and the employer makes pension insurance coverage available to all members of the profession whom it employs.

The Fund refused to exempt van Schijndel and van Veen on the ground that their company did not in fact make pension arrangements applicable to all members of the profession whom the company employed. The Fund thus ordered van Schijndel and van Veen to continue to make contributions, whereupon the two physiotherapists brought suit. Unsuccessful in court, they appealed to the Dutch Hoge Raad (the Supreme Court of the Netherlands). For the first time at this point, van Schijndel and van Veen argued that the lower court should have considered, "if necessary of its own motion," the compatibility of compulsory Fund membership with various articles of the then EC Treaty.

The Hoge Raad asked the Court of Justice whether a national court could or indeed must apply these EC Treaty articles even when the party having an interest in their application had failed to invoke them. Not surprisingly, the Court ruled that national courts have an obligation to apply these articles if domestic law permits national courts to do so under those circumstances.

The Court then considered whether the same result obtains when, in order to apply EC rules on its own initiative, "the court would have to abandon the passive role assigned to it by going beyond the ambit of the dispute defined by the parties themselves and/or by relying on facts and circumstances other than those on which the party to the proceedings with an interest in application of the provisions of the Treaty bases his claim." After reiterating its prior case law on the problem of remedial adequacy, the Court continued:]

19   For the purposes of applying those principles, each case which raises the question whether a national procedural provision renders application of Community law impossible or excessively difficult must be analysed by reference to the role of that provision in the procedure, its progress and its special features, viewed as a whole, before the various national instances. In the light of that analysis the basic principles of the domestic judicial system, such as protection of the rights of the defence, the principle of legal certainty and the proper conduct of procedure, must, where appropriate, be taken into consideration.

20   In the present case, the domestic law principle that in civil proceedings a court must or may raise points of its own motion is limited by its obligation to keep to the subject-matter of the dispute and to base its decision on the facts put before it.

21   That limitation is justified by the principle that, in a civil suit, it is for the parties to take the initiative, the court being able to act of its own motion only in exceptional cases where the public interest requires its intervention. That principle reflects conceptions prevailing in most of the Member States as to the relations between the State and the individual; it safeguards the rights of the defence; and it ensures proper conduct of proceedings by, in particular, protecting them from the delays inherent in examination of new pleas.

22   In those circumstances, the answer to the second question must be that Community law does not require national courts to raise of their own motion an issue concerning the breach of provisions of Community law where examination of that issue would oblige them to abandon the passive role assigned to them by going beyond the ambit of the dispute defined by the parties themselves and relying on facts and circumstances other than those on which the party with an interest in application of those provisions bases his claim.

NOTES AND QUESTIONS

1. Does *van Schijndel* represent a sound application of established legal principles? What was objectionable anyway about applying the usual Dutch rules to these two parties?

2. On the same day that it decided *van Schijndel,* the Court handed down judgment in Peterbroeck, van Campenhout & Cie., Case C–312/93,

[1995] ECR I–4599. Peterbroeck, a Belgian limited liability partnership, filed a complaint with the Belgian regional tax authorities on behalf of the Dutch company (CBT) that held an interest in the partnership. Specifically, Peterbroeck argued that the Belgian government erred in taxing CBT at the nonresident rate (44.9%), rather than the resident rate (at most 42%), on the income that CBT had withdrawn from the partnership. Unsuccessful in its complaint, Peterbroeck appealed to the Court of Appeal of Brussels, raising for the first time the argument that application of a higher tax rate to a Dutch company than a Belgian company was an infringement of EC Treaty Article 43 (now TFEU Article 49), guaranteeing freedom of establishment.

The Belgian government considered the argument inadmissible because it was raised beyond the time limit laid down in the Belgian Tax Code: under the code, "new" pleas, not raised in the initial complaint or considered by the authorities on their own motion, could only be raised within 60 days of the filing of the tax ruling. The Court of Appeal asked the Court of Justice whether the time bar could validly be applied in this case.

Noting that the 60–day deadline to file a new complaint was "not objectionable *per se*," the Court of Justice however distinguished the case from *van Schijndel*. First, the Cour d'Appel was the first court that could make a preliminary reference to the Court, as the Belgian regional tax Director to whom the initial complaint was filed did not qualify as a "court or tribunal." Second, as the limitations period started to run with the Director's lodging of a certified true copy of the contested decision, the period during which new pleas could be raised expired even before the hearing before the Cour d'Appel. Third, the Court of Justice noted that no higher Belgian court could of its own motion raise the question of compatibility. Thus, the national procedural rule could not be applied in this case.

3. In Van der Weerd v. Minister van Landbouw, Natuur en Voedselkwaliteit, Joined Cases C–222–225/05, [2007] ECR I–4233, the Court held that the rule of *van Schijndel* also applies in cases where, unlike in *van Schijndel*, the national court in question is the court of both first and last resort. That matter alone was found not to place the parties to the main proceedings in a special situation calling for a different result, and *Peterbroek* was distinguished as presenting the exceptional set of circumstances described in that judgment.

4. In a legal challenge in Dutch court against the government's approval of a "dyke reinforcement" project, the plaintiff neglected to raise the question whether the government should have prepared an environmental impact assessment, as required for certain public projects by a 1985 EC directive. The Dutch court accordingly included among its preliminary references to the Court of Justice the question whether, assuming an impact assessment for the project was required, it should enforce that requirement even though the plaintiff had failed to raise the issue.

The Court held that national law can not *prevent* national courts from raising an EU violation on their own motion. The Court also held that, if national courts are *required* by national law to raise points of domestic law, then they are likewise *required* to raise points of EU law. That left only the situation in which national law neither requires nor forbids courts to raise points of domestic law, but merely *permits* them to do so. As to this situation, the Court ruled that, while EU law did not demand that national courts raise the neglected issue in all cases, it did demand the availability of judicial review of the question whether, in choosing not to raise the issue, the national court exceeded its discretion. Aannemersbedrijf P.K. Kraaijeveld BV v. Gedeputeerde Staten van Zuid–Holland, Case C–72/95, [1996] ECR I–687.

5. In Heemskerk BV, Firma Schaap v. Productschap Vee en Vlees, Case C–455/06, [2008] ECR I–8763, the Court held that a Dutch court, when otherwise required to raise an issue of EU law on its own motion, may decline to do so on the basis of a Dutch legal principle (*reformation in pejus*), according to which a person bringing an action may not be placed in a less favorable position than if it had not brought the action in the first place.

ECO SWISS CHINA TIME LTD. v. BENETTON INTERNATIONAL NV

Case C–126/97, [1999] ECR I–4493.

[Benetton entered into a licensing agreement with Eco Swiss and Bulova Watch, which gave Eco Swiss the right to manufacture watches and clocks bearing the words "Benetton by Bulova" to be sold by Eco Swiss and Bulova. Eco Swiss could not sell the products in Italy, and Bulova could not sell them elsewhere in the EU. The contract provided for arbitration of disputes in the Netherlands. Five years into the agreement, Benetton terminated it, and Eco Swiss and Bulova initiated arbitration and prevailed.

Benetton sued in Dutch court to have the award set aside on the ground that it violated public policy because the underlying licensing agreement was null and void as anti-competitive under EC Treaty Article 81 (now TFEU Article 101), invoking the Dutch Civil Procedure Code provision for vacatur of awards contrary to public policy. However, by then the 3–month limitations period prescribed by Dutch law for vacatur actions had elapsed. Moreover, neither the parties nor the arbitrators had raised the Article 81 issue during the arbitration.

When the case reached the Dutch Supreme Court, the court held that Dutch law would not consider it contrary to public policy to enforce an arbitral award based upon a contract in violation of *Dutch* competition law. The Court also noted Benetton's twin failures to raise the competition law claim during the arbitration and to seek vacatur on a timely basis. (On the other hand, the referring court called attention to the *Nordsee* case, page 332 supra, holding that arbitral tribunals constituted pursuant to private contract cannot make preliminary references on EU law to the Court of Justice.) A preliminary reference ensued.

* * *

The second question

35 [I]t is in the interest of efficient arbitration proceedings that review of arbitration awards should be limited in scope and that annulment of

or refusal to recognise an award should be possible only in exceptional circumstances.

36 However, ... Article 81 EC constitutes a fundamental provision which is essential for the accomplishment of the tasks entrusted to the Community and, in particular, for the functioning of the internal market. The importance of such a provision led the framers of the Treaty to provide expressly, in Article 81(2) EC (ex Article 85(2)), that any agreements or decisions prohibited pursuant to that article are to be automatically void.

37 It follows that where its domestic rules of procedure require a national court to grant an application for annulment of an arbitration award where such an application is founded on failure to observe national rules of public policy, it must also grant such an application where it is founded on failure to comply with the prohibition laid down in Article 81(1) EC.

* * *

39 [Thus,] the provisions of Article 81 EC may be regarded as a matter of public policy....

40 Lastly ... arbitrators, unlike national courts and tribunals, are not in a position to request this Court to give a preliminary ruling on questions of interpretation of Community law. However, it is manifestly in the interest of the Community legal order that, in order to forestall differences of interpretation, every Community provision should be given a uniform interpretation, irrespective of the circumstances in which it is to be applied. It follows that, in the circumstances of the present case, unlike *van Schijndel and van Veen*, Community law requires that questions concerning the interpretation of the prohibition laid down in Article 81(1) EC should be open to examination by national courts when asked to determine the validity of an arbitration award and that it should be possible for those questions to be referred, if necessary, to the Court of Justice for a preliminary ruling.

41 [T]herefore ... a national court to which application is made for annulment of an arbitration award must grant that application if it considers that the award in question is in fact contrary to Article 81 EC, where its domestic rules of procedure require it to grant an application for annulment founded on failure to observe national rules of public policy

* * *

The fourth and fifth questions

43 [T]he referring court is asking essentially whether Community law requires a national court to refrain from applying domestic rules of procedure according to which [a final award] in respect of which no application for annulment has been made within the prescribed time-

limit acquires the force of *res judicata* and may no longer be called in question ... even if this is necessary in order to examine, in proceedings for annulment of the ... award, whether an agreement which the ... award held to be valid in law is nevertheless void under Article 81 EC.

[The Court determined that a 3–months limitations period did not make the exercise of rights under EU law excessively difficult or virtually impossible.]

[47] In those circumstances, Community law does not require a national court to refrain from applying such rules, even if this is necessary in order to examine, in proceedings for annulment of a subsequent arbitration award, whether an agreement which the interim award held to be valid in law is nevertheless void under Article 81 EC.

NOTES AND QUESTIONS

1. Having ruled that the Dutch court could enforce the national limitations period and treat the award as *res judicata*, the Court of Justice found it unnecessary to answer the other principal question referred, namely whether, if the vacatur action had been timely, Benetton's failure to raise the competition law defense during the arbitration could operate to estop it from invoking the violation of competition law as a public policy ground for vacatur.

How do you suppose the Court would have answered that question if it had reached it? Might the Court, for example, have ruled that, while the Dutch court *could* enforce the Dutch limitations period on the action to vacate the award, notwithstanding the public policy character of Article 81, it *could not* treat Benetton as having waived the claim by not raising it before the arbitrators?

2. Although the principle of equivalence is generally viewed as considerably more straightforward in application than the principle of effectiveness, the latter can nevertheless also raise challenging issues. In Transportes Urbanos y Servicios Generales SAL v. Administración del Estado, Case C–118/08, [2010] ECR–___, the question was whether if Spanish law, by way of exception, does not require exhaustion of remedies in damage actions for the legislature's breach of the Spanish Constitution, it must then also waive the exhaustion of remedies requirement in *Francovich* actions for the legislature's violation of EU law. What answer do you expect the Court of Justice gave to that question?

3. Recall the case of Pafitis v. Trapeza Kentrikis Ellados AE, discussed at page 254 supra, regarding application of national "abuse of rights" doctrine as a limitation on Community law-based claims.

4. For a thoughtful discussion of these issues, see John Temple Lang, The Duties of National Authorities under Community Constitutional law, 23 Eur. L. Rev. 109 (1998).

THE QUEEN v. SECRETARY OF STATE FOR TRANSPORT EX PARTE FACTORTAME LTD.

Case C–213/89, [1990] ECR I–2433.

[For the facts of the case and judgment of the Court, see page 250 supra.]

NOTES AND QUESTIONS

1. Why was it not sufficient for the UK to show that interim injunctive relief is not available in comparable domestic law cases against the Crown, and that EU law claims were therefore not being treated disadvantageously? Suppose interim relief was *never* available in British court, in any class of cases. Might EU law still require that it be available in EU law cases? That question finally came squarely before the Court in Unibet (London) Ltd. v. Justitiekanslern, Case C–432/05, [2007] ECR–I 2271, where the Court held that, irrespective of equivalency, interim relief must be made available if necessary to ensure the full effectiveness of the anticipated judgment.

Do the same considerations that require national courts to entertain petitions for interim injunctive relief in aid of EU law claims also limit their freedom in setting the standards for such relief or in deciding whether or not to grant it in any given case? The Court answered that question too in the *Unibet* case, supra, holding that national procedural rules govern the availability of provisional relief, but adding that the criteria used "cannot be less favourable than those applying to similar domestic actions and must not render practically impossible or excessively difficult the interim judicial protection of rights conferred by Community law" (¶ 82).

2. Most of the cases in this section involve private party claims against a Member State. Suppose, however, EU law gives Member States a claim against a private party and requires them to enforce that claim. Does EU law demand a minimally effective judicial remedy in this situation as well? The question has arisen concretely in connection with the requirement that Member States recover moneys (such as illegal state aids) improperly granted to private parties. See Lippische Hauptgenossenschaft v. Bundesanstalt für landwirtschaftliche Marktordnung, Cases 119, 126/79, [1980] ECR 1863; Ferwerda BV v. Produktschap voor Vee en Vlees, Case 265/78, [1980] ECR 617.

The typical case of Deutsche Milchkontor GmbH and others v. Germany, Joined Cases 205–15/82, [1983] ECR 2633, arose out of the German authorities' discovery that they had paid sums in aid to processors of foods that contained ingredients disqualifying them from aid under the applicable EU regulations. The basic regulation on financing the Common Agricultural Policy requires Member States to recover all funds erroneously disbursed, and the authorities accordingly demanded repayment. The recipient firms challenged the order in German court on various equitable grounds, and preliminary references to the Court of Justice ensued. In particular, the referring court asked whether EU law permitted it to take the legitimate expectations of the recipients into account in fixing the amounts to be repaid. (Under German law, the government may not recover public money unlawfully paid to a private party to the extent that the recipient relied upon the grant "and [that its] expectation, weighed against the public interest in revoking the decision, merits protection," or to the extent that the authorities knew or should have known that they had made the grant unlawfully.) The Court of Justice, noting that protection of legitimate expectations and legal certainty are principles of EU law as well, suggested that such national rules may be applied as long as in each case the EU's interest in revoking an illegal aid is also taken into account. As to whether recipients of aid may rely on the authorities' failure adequately to supervise the grant of aid as a defense to an action for recovery (a point the German firms obviously had pressed in the case), the Court merely observed that "in the present state of development of Community law those consequences are determined by national law and not by Community law." [1983] ECR at 2672. What do you think of these guidelines? Do you expect that they will put matters to rest?

The Court has taken a stricter position in regard to the recovery of illegal state aids, at least where the Member State granted the aid without notifying the Commission in advance, as required under EU law. In that circumstance, the State may not invoke the legitimate expectations of the recipient as an excuse for not complying with a Commission order to recover the aid. Commission v. Germany (State aid to BUG–Alutechnik), Case C–5/89, [1990] ECR I–3437. However, the Court has recognized an exception for circumstances where, "by reason of exceptional circumstances, repayment is inappropriate." Syndicat Français de l'Express International (SFEI) v. La Poste, Case C–39/34, [1996] ECR I–3547 (¶¶ 69–71).

3. Consider the case of Land Rheinland–Pfalz v. Alcan Deutschland GmbH, Case C–24/95, [1997] ECR I–1591. Following Germany's condemnation by the Court for failing to comply with a Commission order that it recover a state aid to Alcan, the state government of Rheinland–Pfalz revoked the aid and demanded repayment from Alcan of the 8 million DMs it had received. Alcan successfully challenged the order in German court on the ground that it violated a state administrative procedure act provision barring the revocation of administrative acts after one year from the time the government becomes aware of the facts justifying the revocation.

When the case reached the highest German administrative court, that court asked the Court of Justice whether EU law requires that the aid be revoked, notwithstanding the violation of state administrative law, as well as the violation of (a) the general German law principle of good faith, which arguably bars the government from suing to recover an aid for whose illegality it was itself primarily responsible and whose legality it had failed to bring in a timely way to the recipient's attention, and (b) the provision of the German Civil Code (sec. 818(3)) which precludes recovery where the gain arising from an unlawful administrative measure has ceased to exist. (Alcan argued that this provision applied because Alcan had in the intervening period closed the plant in question after incurring further losses.)

The Court squarely rejected the notion that the recipient of an unlawful aid could resist repayment on any of these national law grounds. Deciding otherwise "would seriously and adversely affect the Community interest and render practically impossible the recovery required by Community law" (¶ 41).

For an interesting comparative survey of Member State remedies for restitution of sums levied by national authorities in violation of EU law (as required by the *San Giorgio* case, discussed supra page 354, note 3), see A. Tatham, Restitution of Charges and Duties Levied by the Public Administration in Breach of European Community Law: A Comparative Analysis, 19 Eur. L. Rev. 146 (1994). See also L. Papadias, Interim Protection under Community Law before the National Courts: The Right to a Judge with Jurisdiction to Grant Interim Relief, 1994/2 Legal Issues of Eur. Integration 153; Note, Remedies for European Community Law Claims in Member States Courts: Toward a European Standard, 31 Colum. J. Transnat'l L. 377 (1993).

4. The US Supreme Court has ruled that a state must provide an adequate remedy to taxpayers against whom unconstitutional taxes have been levied. While stopping short of requiring that the state necessarily issue a refund of the money, and while allowing that the states have flexibility in fashioning a remedy, the Court insisted that if the state had not provided a full "pre-deprivation hearing," then it would have to provide "meaningful backward-looking relief to rectify any unconstitutional deprivation" or otherwise "create in hindsight a nondiscriminatory scheme." Harper v. Virginia Department of Taxation, 509 U.S. 86, 113 S.Ct. 2510, 125 L.Ed.2d 74 (1993).

B. DAMAGES FOR MEMBER STATE VIOLATIONS OF EU LAW

FRANCOVICH v. ITALY

Cases C–6/90, 9/90, [1991] ECR I–5357.

[Two Italian workers found themselves unable to collect salary owed to them by their bankrupt employers. They eventually sought recovery from the Italian Government for its failure to implement Council Directive 80/987, which had required the Member States to set up a system of salary protection for workers of bankrupt enterprises, a failure that the Court of Justice had previously condemned in Commission v. Italy (Worker protection directive), Case 22/87, [1989] ECR 143. A preliminary reference to the Court of Justice followed.

The Court first held that the unimplemented directive could not fairly be read to have direct effect in the sense of giving the plaintiffs a salary claim directly against Italy. It then turned to the question of Italy's possible liability in damages to the workers.]

30   [This] issue must be considered in the light of the general system of the Treaty and its fundamental principles.

[The Court recalled its landmark decisions on supremacy and direct effect, including *van Gend en Loos, Costa v. ENEL, Simmenthal* and *Factortame*].

33   The full effectiveness of Community rules would be impaired and the protection of the rights which they grant would be weakened if

individuals were unable to obtain redress when their rights are infringed by a breach of Community law for which a Member State can be held responsible.

34   The possibility of obtaining redress from the Member State is particularly indispensable where, as in this case, the full effectiveness of Community rules is subject to prior action on the part of the State and where, consequently, in the absence of such action, individuals cannot enforce before the national courts the rights conferred upon them by Community law.

35   It follows that the principle whereby a State must be liable for loss and damage caused to individuals as a result of breaches of Community law for which the State can be held responsible is inherent in the system of the Treaty.

36   A further basis for the obligation of Member States to make good such loss and damage is to be found in Article 4 TEU [ex Article 5 EC], under which the Member States are required to take all appropriate measures, whether general or particular, to ensure fulfilment of their obligations under Community law. Among these is the obligation to nullify the unlawful consequences of a breach of Community law.

37   It follows from all the foregoing that it is a principle of Community law that the Member States are obliged to make good loss and damage caused to individuals by breaches of Community law for which they can be held responsible.

[The Court then identified the three conditions under which a State would be liable in damages for failing to carry out its duties under a directive.]

40   The first of those conditions is that the result prescribed by the directive should entail the grant of rights to individuals. The second condition is that it should be possible to identify the content of those rights on the basis of the provisions of the directive. Finally, the third condition is the existence of a causal link between the breach of the State's obligation and the loss and damage suffered by the injured parties.

41   Those conditions are sufficient to give rise to a right on the part of individuals to obtain reparation, a right founded directly on Community law.

42   Subject to that reservation, it is on the basis of the rules of national law on liability that the State must make reparation for the consequences of the loss and damage caused. In the absence of Community legislation, it is for the internal legal order of each Member State to designate the competent courts and lay down the detailed procedural rules for legal proceedings intended fully to safeguard the rights which individuals derive from Community law.

43   Further, the substantive and procedural conditions for reparation of loss and damage laid down by the national law of the Member States must not be less favourable than those relating to similar domestic

claims and must not be so framed as to make it virtually impossible or excessively difficult to obtain reparation.

44   In this case, the breach of Community law by a Member State by virtue of its failure to transpose Directive 80/987 within the prescribed period has been confirmed by a judgment of the Court. The result required by that directive entails the grant to employees of a right to a guarantee of payment of their unpaid wage claims. As is clear from the examination of the first part of the first question, the content of that right can be identified on the basis of the provisions of the directive.

45   Consequently, the national court must, in accordance with the national rules on liability, uphold the right of employees to obtain reparation of loss and damage caused to them as a result of failure to transpose the directive.

NOTES AND QUESTIONS

1.   Do you agree that Member State liability to private parties for EU law violations is "inherent" in the EU law system (¶ 35)? What is the scope of this "inherent" liability? Does this mean that when they commit EU law violations, the Member States lose the sovereign immunity in tort they ordinarily enjoy under national law?

In a case arising out of facts similar to *Francovich*, the Court ruled that Directive 80/987 was intended to benefit members of the management of an undertaking with respect to salary arrears and that a Member State's exclusion of them from the benefit of the directive gave rise to a claim for compensation against the State for the damage suffered as a result. Miret v. Fondo de Garantía Salarial, Case C–334/92, [1993] ECR I–6911.

For a resounding affirmation of the *Francovich* principle, see Faccini Dori v. Recreb Srl, excerpted at page 267 supra. After determining that the "cooling-off period" provision of the consumer protection directive did not have direct horizontal effect, the Court instructed the Italian court to interpret national law "as far as possible" in its light. The Court continued as follows:

27   If the result prescribed by the directive cannot be achieved by way of interpretation, ... Community law [nevertheless] requires the Member States to make good damage caused to individuals through failure to transpose a directive [citing *Francovich* and restating its three conditions for liability].

28   The directive on contracts negotiated away from business premises is undeniably intended to confer rights on individuals and it is equally certain that the minimum content of those rights can be identified by reference to the provisions of the directive alone.

29   Where damage has been suffered and that damage is due to a breach by the State of its obligation, it is for the national court to uphold the right of aggrieved consumers to obtain reparation in accordance with national law on liability.

2. The Court in *Francovich* decided that the first two conditions of Member State liability were met. However, the Court effectively left it to the Italian courts to decide whether the third condition was met. Why? How free do you think are national courts to fix the rules on "the existence of a link of causality" (¶ 40) between the EU law violation and the injury suffered?

The UK Court of Appeal decision in Regina v. Secretary of State for the Home Department ex parte Gallagher, [1996] 2 CMLR 951 (June 10, 1996), shows that reserving issues of causation to Member State law can have an important effect on outcomes.

John Gallagher, an Irish national, was arrested in the UK and subjected to an exclusion order under the 1989 Prevention of Terrorism Act. The UK court in which Gallagher challenged that order made a preliminary reference to the Court of Justice, which ruled that EC Directive 64/221 prohibited the government from issuing an exclusion order until after the subject of that order has been interviewed by an independent authority and the report of that interview has been received. (See Queen v. Secretary of State for the Home Department ex parte Gallagher, Case C–175/94, [1995] ECR I–4253.) Parliament shortly thereafter amended the 1989 Act to bring it into conformity with the directive; meanwhile Gallagher, alleging that the government had failed to follow the procedures required by the directive, amended his complaint to seek damages.

The Court of Appeal was unpersuaded that Gallagher had shown a sufficiently serious violation of EU law to justify the imposition of liability, in part because the violation involved merely the mis-implementation, rather than non-implementation, of a directive. However, where the Court of Appeal chiefly parted ways with Gallagher was over the causation issue. It was unpersuaded "that the Home Secretary's decision would have been any different had he awaited receipt of Mr. Gallagher's representations and the report of the nominated person before making an exclusion order;" in fact, it considered it "probable that [had the proper procedures been followed] Mr. Gallagher would have been detained longer." [1996] 2 CMLR at 964–65.

3. *Francovich* has its sequel. After the ruling, the Italian government issued a decree transposing the insolvency directive into Italian law. The decree prescribed the terms of the salary guarantee to be paid to employees of insolvent employers and extended those terms to the calculation of damages to be paid by Italy to employees as a result of the belated transposition. Several Italian courts wondered about the compatibility of those terms with the directive as well as about the propriety of applying them retroactively to the calculation of *Francovich* damages. The Court ruled that the terms could be applied retroactively provided the directive has finally been properly transposed and provided those terms ensure adequate reparation for the loss suffered. Bonifaci and Berto v. Istituto Nazionale della Previdenza Sociale, Joined Cases C–94 & 95/95, [1997] ECR I–4006. In a companion case,[1] the Court disapproved of the Italian legislation's prohibition on the employee's

---

1. Maso and Gazzetta v. Istituto Nazionale della Previdenza Sociale, Case C–373/95, [1997] ECR I–4062. In another companion case, Palmisani v. Istituto Nazionale della Previdenza Sociale, Case C–261/95, [1997] ECR I–4037, the Court sustained as reasonable and non-discriminatory the decree's requirement that damage claims arising out of Italy's belated transposition of the insolvency directive be brought within one year of the decree's entry into force.

aggregating the compensation due under the directive with the job seeker's allowance (the latter being a general entitlement aimed at supporting an employee for three months following termination of employment).

4. What makes a breach of EU law "sufficiently serious"? The Court finds it to be present when, "in the exercise of its legislative power, a Member State has manifestly and gravely disregarded the limits on its discretion." An infringement meets that test when it "has persisted despite a judgment finding the infringement in question to be established, or a preliminary ruling or settled case-law of the Court on the matter from which it is clear that the conduct in question constituted an infringement." It is not a precondition to bringing a *Francovich* action in national court, that a court—either the ECJ or a national court—has previously rendered a judgment finding the State to be in breach of EU law. See Test Claimants in the Thin Cap Group Litigation v. Commissioners of Inland Revenue, Case C–524/04, [2007] ECR I–2107 (¶¶ 118–20).

5. Does it surprise you that the Court has required that the procedures national courts follow in *Francovich* liability cases (such as limitation periods) must themselves satisfy the principles of equivalence and effectiveness, as discussed at page 351 supra? See Danske Slagterier v. Germany, Case C–445/06, [2009] ECR I–2119.

6. In *Francovich*, Italy had failed to transpose the directive altogether. The Court evidently regarded such a total failure as *per se* a serious breach of EU law, and it has subsequently confirmed that view. See Dillenkofer v. Germany, Joined Cases C–178–79, 188, 190/94, [1996] ECR I–4845, a damage action against Germany by purchasers of package holidays and tours for Germany's failure to transpose into law an EC directive that required the Member States to enact legislation ensuring that package holiday and tour companies refund moneys and repatriate travelers in the event of insolvency.

Suppose a Member State, instead of failing altogether to implement a directive, simply implements it incorrectly. Under what circumstances is the State then liable to a private party that suffers economic loss as a result? In Robins v. Secretary of State for Work and Pensions, Case C–278/05, [2007] ECR I–1053, the Court held that where a directive allows Member States considerable discretion in transposing a directive, an incorrect transposition gives rise to liability only in the event of a State's manifest and serious disregard for the limits on its discretion.

The question of liability for mis-implementation, as opposed to non-implementation, arose in The Queen v. H.M. Treasury ex parte British Telecommunications plc, Case C–392/93, [1996] ECR I–1631. Council Directive 90/531, laying down procurement procedures (including reporting and disclosure requirements) for, *inter alia*, the telecommunications sector, applied to all private firms that "operate on the basis of special or exclusive rights granted by a competent authority of a Member State," notably the right to expropriate private property for telecommunication network purposes.

According to Article 8(1) of the directive, these procedures do not apply to "contracts which contracting entities ... award for purchases intended exclusively to enable them to provide one or more telecommunications services where other entities are free to offer the same services in the same geographical area and under substantially the same conditions." Article 8(2) required firms to notify the Commission of any services they regarded as covered by this exemption.

The 1992 regulations that transposed the directive in the UK specified that British Telecom (BT) did not satisfy the directive's criteria for exemption from the procurement rules, and BT challenged those regulations as having "incorrectly" transposed the directive. BT maintained that, in transposing the directive, the Member States were supposed to transpose the criteria quoted above rather than "apply" them to specific enterprises. BT claimed that this error imposed undue compliance costs on it and placed it at a competitive disadvantage vis-à-vis competitors. On preliminary reference, the Court of Justice agreed with BT that, under a proper interpretation of the directive, the UK's transposition was faulty. The Court then turned to the damages issue, observing that States have wide discretion in determining how statutorily to implement a directive and must not be hindered in the exercise of that discretion by the prospect of suits for damages due to the harm to that acts taken in the public interest may cause to private parties. The Court concluded that the UK had acted reasonably and in good faith, if mistakenly, in deciding to implement the directive as it did, and held that the error "cannot be regarded as a sufficiently serious breach of Community law" (¶ 45).

Was the Court in *British Telecom* correct in distinguishing between the faulty implementation and the non-implementation of a directive and suggesting that it would take a more indulgent look at the former than the latter?

BRASSERIE DU PECHEUR SA v. GERMANY
THE QUEEN v. SECRETARY OF STATE FOR TRANSPORT, EX PARTE FACTORTAME LTD.

(Brasserie du Pêcheur) and (Factortame III)
Joined Cases C–46, 48/93, [1996] ECR I–1029.

[Following the judgments of the Court in the *German beer* case (excerpted at pages 466 and 483 infra) and in *Factortame II* (excerpted at page 707 infra), the prevailing parties brought damage actions against Germany and Britain, respectively, in those countries' courts. Both actions provoked preliminary references to the Court of Justice on the scope of Member State liability under *Francovich*. The Court joined the two references.]

18   The German, Irish and Netherlands Governments contend that Member States are required to make good loss or damage caused to individuals only where the provisions breached are not directly effective: in *Francovich,* the Court simply sought to fill a lacuna in the system for safeguarding rights of individuals. . . .

19   That argument cannot be accepted.

20   The Court has consistently held that the right of individuals to rely on the directly effective provisions of the Treaty before national courts is

only a minimum guarantee and is not sufficient in itself to ensure the full and complete implementation of the Treaty. The purpose of that right is to ensure that provisions of Community law prevail over national provisions. It cannot, in every case, . . . avoid [individuals'] sustaining damage as a result of a breach of Community law attributable to a Member State. As appears from paragraph 33 of the judgment in *Francovich,* the full effectiveness of Community law would be impaired if individuals were unable to obtain redress when their rights were infringed by a breach of Community law.

* * *

22   It is all the more so in the event of infringement of a right directly conferred by a Community provision upon which individuals are entitled to rely before the national courts. In that event, the right to reparation is the necessary corollary of the direct effect of the Community provision whose breach caused the damage sustained.

23   In this case, it is undisputed that the Community provisions at issue, namely [EC Treaty Article 28, now TFEU Article 34] in [*Brasserie de Pêcheur*] and [EC Treaty Article 43, now TFEU Article 49] [in *Factortame*], have direct effect in the sense that they confer on individuals rights upon which they are entitled to rely directly before the national courts. Breach of such provisions may give rise to reparation.

24   The German Government further submits that a general right to reparation for individuals could be created only by legislation and that for such a right to be recognized by judicial decision would be incompatible with the allocation of powers as between the Community institutions and the Member States and with the institutional balance established by the Treaty.

25   It must, however, be stressed that the existence and extent of State liability for damage ensuing as a result of a breach of obligations incumbent on the State by virtue of Community law are questions of Treaty interpretation which fall within the jurisdiction of the Court.

* * *

27   Since the Treaty contains no provision expressly and specifically governing the consequences of breaches of Community law by Member States, it is for the Court, in pursuance of the task conferred on it by [EC Treaty Article 220, now TEU Article 19] of ensuring that in the interpretation and application of the Treaty the law is observed, to rule on such a question in accordance with generally accepted methods of interpretation, in particular by reference to the fundamental principles of the Community legal system and, where necessary, general principles common to the legal systems of the Member States.

* * *

29   The principle of the non-contractual liability of the Community expressly laid down in [EC Treaty Article 288, now TFEU Article 340] is

simply an expression of the general principle familiar to the legal systems of the Member States that an unlawful act or omission gives rise to an obligation to make good the damage caused. That provision also reflects the obligation on public authorities to make good damage caused in the performance of their duties.

* * *

[32] [T]hat principle holds good for any case in which a Member State breaches Community law, whatever be the organ of the State whose act or omission was responsible for the breach.

* * *

[35] The fact that, according to national rules, the breach complained of is attributable to the legislature cannot affect the requirements inherent in the protection of the rights of individuals who rely on Community law. . . .

* * *

Conditions under which the State may incur liability for acts and omissions of the national legislature contrary to Community law (second question in [Brasserie du Pêcheur] and first question in [Factortame])

[37] By these questions, the national courts ask the Court to specify the conditions under which a right to reparation of loss or damage caused to individuals by breaches of Community law attributable to a Member State is, in the particular circumstances, guaranteed by Community law.

* * *

[The Court stated that, in developing criteria, it would be guided by certain principles "inherent" in the EU legal order, notably the full effectiveness of EU rules, the effective protection of the rights that they confer, and the Member States' obligation of loyal cooperation. More particularly, the Court looked at its own case law on the non-contractual liability of the EU, which according to TFEU Article 340 (formerly EC Treaty Article 288) is in turn guided by "general principles common to the laws of the Member States." The Court noted that under its case law on the EU's non-contractual liability, attention is paid to "the complexity of the situations to be regulated, difficulties in the application or interpretation of the texts and, more particularly, the margin of discretion available to the author of the act in question" (¶ 43). The Court underscored the need both to avoid making public officials unduly fearful of liability to adversely affected private parties when acting in the public interest and to protect the wide discretion of policymakers. Accordingly, the EU "cannot incur liability unless the institution concerned has manifestly and gravely disregarded the limits on the exercise of its powers" (¶ 45).

The Court thus distinguished between situations in which the Member States are obligated to achieve a particular result, or to act or refrain from acting, on the one hand, and situations in which Member States are expected to exercise a wide discretion, much as the EU institutions often do, on the other. The Court then applied these criteria to the two cases before it.]

48   In [*Brasserie du Pêcheur*], the German legislature had legislated in the field of foodstuffs, specifically beer. In the absence of Community harmonization, the national legislature had a wide discretion in that sphere in laying down rules on the quality of beer put on the market.

49   As regards the facts of [*Factortame*], the United Kingdom legislature also had a wide discretion. The legislation at issue was concerned, first, with the registration of vessels, a field which, in view of the state of development of Community law, falls within the jurisdiction of the Member States and, secondly, with regulating fishing, a sector in which implementation of the common fisheries policy leaves a margin of discretion to the Member States.

50   Consequently, in each case the German and United Kingdom legislatures were faced with situations involving choices comparable to those made by the Community institutions when they adopt legislative measures pursuant to a Community policy.

51   In such circumstances, Community law confers a right to reparation where three conditions are met: the rule of law infringed must be intended to confer rights on individuals; the breach must be sufficiently serious; and there must be a direct causal link between the breach of the obligation resting on the State and the damage sustained by the injured parties.

* * *

[The Court found the first condition to be satisfied in both cases, since the Treaty provisions violated in *Brasserie du Pêcheur* on the free movement of goods and in *Factortame* on freedom of establishment give rise to rights for individuals which the national courts must protect. The Court turned to the second condition.]

55   As to the second condition, as regards both Community liability under [EC Treaty Article 288, now TFEU Article 340] and Member State liability for breaches of Community law, the decisive test for finding that a breach of Community law is sufficiently serious is whether the Member State or the Community institution concerned manifestly and gravely disregarded the limits on its discretion.

56   The factors which the competent court may take into consideration include the clarity and precision of the rule breached, the measure of discretion left by that rule to the national or Community authorities, whether the infringement and the damage caused was intentional or involuntary, whether any error of law was excusable or inexcusable, the fact that the position taken by a Community institution may have contributed towards the omission, and the adoption or retention of national measures or practices contrary to Community law.

57 On any view, a breach of Community law will clearly be sufficiently serious if it has persisted despite a judgment finding the infringement in question to be established, or a preliminary ruling or settled case-law of the Court on the matter, from which it is clear that the conduct in question constituted an infringement.

58 While, in the present cases, the Court cannot substitute its assessment for that of the national courts, which have sole jurisdiction to find the facts in the main proceedings and decide how to characterize the breaches of Community law at issue, it will be helpful to indicate a number of circumstances which the national courts might take into account.

[The Court drew a distinction in *Brasserie du Pêcheur* between (a) the German legislature's having kept in place provisions on beer purity that prohibited the marketing as "beer" imports from other Member States produced by different means than German beer and (b) the German legislature's ban on the import of beers containing additives. Given settled ECJ case law at the time the beer purity law was challenged, the Court was unwilling to consider the first violation as excusable error. However, it found the criteria governing the validity of the additives not to have been clearly settled. The Court similarly distinguished in *Factortame* between discrimination based on nationality, on the one hand, and residence and domicile, on the other. The first was clearly contrary to EU law, the second less so. The Court directed the national courts to take into account the kind of factors set forth in paragraph 56 of the judgment, as well as the allegation that the UK had failed to adopt the provisional measures that the Court had previously ordered in the *Factortame* case.]

65 As for the third condition, it is for the national courts to determine whether there is a direct causal link between the breach of the obligation borne by the State and the damage sustained by the injured parties.

66 The aforementioned three conditions are necessary and sufficient to found a right in individuals to obtain redress, although this does not mean that the State cannot incur liability under less strict conditions on the basis of national law.

67 [T]he State must make reparation for the consequences of the loss and damage caused in accordance with the domestic rules on liability, provided that the conditions for reparation of loss and damage laid down by national law must not be less favourable than those relating to similar domestic claims and must not be such as in practice to make it impossible or excessively difficult to obtain reparation.

[The Court posited that, in the absence of relevant EU law provisions, it is for the domestic legal system of each Member State to establish the criteria for determining the extent of compensation, provided they are not less favorable than those applicable to similar claims based on domestic law and do not make it impossible or excessively difficult to obtain recovery. In any event, compensation "must be commensurate with the loss or damage sustained so as to ensure the effective protection [of EU law] rights" (¶ 82).

Nevertheless, the Court proceeded, by way of answer to a series of specific questions posed by the referring courts, to pass judgment on certain of the national criteria for the imposition of liability. It found the following rules of liability and measure of damages unacceptable because apt to make obtaining effective compensation impossible or extremely difficult: (a) the German rule making compensation dependent upon the legislature's act or omission being referable to an individual situation rather than the public at large, (b) the English rule requiring proof of misfeasance in public office or abuse of power, (c) the German rule of civil law making the imposition of tort liability dependent on a finding of fault, whether intentional or negligent, (d) the German law rule limiting liability to compensation for damage to certain specifically protected individual interests, such as property, and excluding loss of profit, and (e) national law rules limiting liability to the damage sustained after the delivery of a judgment of the Court of Justice finding the infringement in question.

On the other hand, the Court accepted application to *Francovich* cases of national law rules on mitigation of damages and exhaustion of remedies. Punitive or exemplary damages, as known in English law, may be imposed, and indeed must be, if they would be imposed in the case of analogous domestic law claims.]

NOTES AND QUESTIONS

1. The Court in *Brasserie* concludes that a Member State bears liability for non-compliance with EU law even in cases in which the EU law measure in question has direct effect and may therefore be invoked directly in national court. Does this mean that, in such a case, the claimant may demand of the national court *both* that it give the measure direct effect *and* that it award damages against the State?

2. Suppose that a national court systematically finds that the Member State's breaches of EU law are not "sufficiently serious." What recourse, if any, might the EU institutions have?

3. When the *Factortame* case came back to it, the English High Court decided that the UK had committed a sufficiently serious breach of EU law intended to confer rights on individuals. It also decided that punitive damages could be withheld without violating the principle of equivalence between remedies for breaches of national law and breaches of EU law. The Court of Appeal affirmed. The House of Lords took a more nuanced view. In the principal opinion, Lord Slynn of Hadley (former Advocate General Slynn), distinguished among the nationality, domicile and residence requirements. He found the UK's imposition of the first two requirements to have been at the time a manifest breach of fundamental Treaty obligations. The residence requirement gave him greater pause, but he came to the same conclusion about it. Regina v. Secretary of State for Transport *ex parte* Factortame Ltd,

[1999] 4 All ER 906, [1999] 3 CMLR 597, [1999] 3 WLR 1062 (H.L., July 13–15, Oct. 28, 1999).

4. Predictably, the question of the seriousness of breaches of EU law has occasioned numerous preliminary references to the Court. Although the Court has said that it is for national courts to decide whether a breach is or is not sufficiently serious for liability purposes, it requires them to take into account the following factors: "the clarity and precision of the rule infringed, whether the infringement and the damage caused was intentional or involuntary, whether any error of law was excusable or inexcusable, and the fact that the position taken by a Community institution may have contributed towards the adoption or maintenance of national measures contrary to Community law." Haim v. Kassenzahnärztliche Vereinigung Nordrhein, Case C–424/97, [2000] ECR I–5123.

Moreover, the Court frequently gives its own view of the direction in which certain of these factors point. In *Haim*, for example, a German professional licensing agency was found to have infringed an Italian dentist's rights under the Treaty by not taking account, in applying the dentistry directive, of his prior practice in another Member State. On preliminary reference arising out of a subsequent damages claim, the Court noted that, while the rule of law violated in this case (freedom of establishment) was a directly applicable and longstanding Treaty provision, the facts of the case predated the judgment (*Vlassopoulou*, infra page 762) in which the Court first announced a rule requiring States to give full faith and credit to other Member States' equivalent tests and certifications.

On other occasions, the Court squarely decides by itself whether or not a breach is sufficiently serious. It did so in Rechberger, Greindl, Hofmeister and others v. Austria, Case C–140/97, [1999] ECR I–3499, where the question concerned Austria's implementation of the directive on package travel, holidays and tours. Article 7 of the directive required that tour organizers provide "sufficient evidence of security for the refund of money paid over and for the repatriation of the consumer in the event of insolvency." In transposing the directive, Austria limited the security guarantee to trips booked after January 1, 1995 (the effective date of Austria's accession) and having a departure date of May 1, 1995 or later. It also fixed the required security at a given percentage of the organizer's business turnover in the corresponding quarter of the previous calendar year. As a result, when a certain organizer went bankrupt, some disappointed travelers received no refund and others only a pro rata refund.

On preliminary reference, the Court ruled (¶¶ 51–52):

The Member State … enjoyed no margin of discretion as to the entry into force, in its own law, of the provisions of Article 7. That being so, the limitation of the protection … to trips with a departure date of 1 May 1995 or later is manifestly incompatible with the obligations under the Directive and thus constitutes a sufficiently serious breach of Community law.

The fact that the Member State has implemented all the other provisions of the Directive does not alter that finding.

5. The UK government denied Hedley Lomas authorization to export live sheep to Spain on the ground that Spain had failed to implement properly an EU directive governing the treatment of livestock in slaughterhouses. (In fact, for this reason, the UK had imposed a general ban on the export of livestock to Spain.) The UK also notified the Commission of its suspicions about the standards of Spanish slaughterhouses. When the Commission later decided, based on Spanish government assurances, not to bring an infringement action against Spain, it also advised the UK that any continuation of the export ban would violate the EC Treaty. The UK then lifted the ban.

At that point, Hedley Lomas sued the UK government for damages. On preliminary reference, the Court of Justice ruled that, in unilaterally determining that Spain was in breach of its duties of implementation, and in acting on that belief by barring exports to Spain, the UK had engaged in impermissible self-help and thus interfered with the free movement of goods. The Court found the first two conditions of liability to be satisfied (the latter because the UK "was not called upon to make any legislative choices and had only considerably reduced, or even no, discretion"), and left the causation factor to be considered by the national court. The Queen v. Ministry of Agriculture, Fisheries and Food ex parte Hedley Lomas (Ireland) Ltd., Case C–5/94, [1996] ECR I–2553. Is this the preliminary ruling that you would have recommended that the Court issue in this case?

6. Let us return to the bovine spongiform encephalopathy (BSE), or "mad cow disease," episode mentioned at several points in this book. After the Commission decided in 1999, based on scientific committee advice, to lift its 1996 ban on the export of British beef, the French food safety agency declared the step premature, and the French government announced that the embargo was still in effect. The Commission promptly issued a reasoned opinion and filed suit against France in the Court of Justice for infringing the free movement of goods. The Commission prevailed. Commission v. France (Ban on import of British beef), Case C–1/00, [2001] ECR I–9989. How likely is it that France has subjected itself to *Francovich* liability? to whom?

KOBLER v. AUSTRIA
Case C–224/01, [2003] ECR I–10239.

[Gerhard Köbler had been an Austrian university professor since 1986. In 1996, he applied to the relevant government authorities under Austrian salary legislation for a special "length-of-service" salary increment for university professors, which under that legislation required completion of 15 years' service as a professor at an Austrian university. Köbler could meet that requirement only if his years of service at universities in other Member States were taken into account. The administration's rejection of his claim was upheld by the Austrian Supreme Administrative Court on the ground that the program represented a "loyalty bonus," rather than salary, thus falling outside the scope of EU law. Köbler then sued Austria in a civil court of first instance for damages on account of the denial as upheld by the courts. Besides denying the violation, Austria contended that a decision of a national court of last resort cannot be the basis of a damages judgment against the State.

The Court rejected the notion that infringements of EU law attributable to a court decision cannot in principle give rise to *Francovich* liability. It was unconvinced by the position taken by several Member States in the case to the effect that the principle of legal certainty, *res judicata*, or the independence or authority of the judiciary stood in the way of imposing any such liability.]

39 [R]ecognition of the principle of State liability for a decision of a court adjudicating at last instance does not in itself have the consequence of calling in question that decision as *res judicata*. Proceedings seeking to render the State liable do not have the same purpose and do not necessarily involve the same parties as the proceedings resulting in the decision which has acquired the status of *res judicata*. The applicant in an action to establish the liability of the State will, if successful, secure an order against it for reparation of the damage incurred but not necessarily a declaration invalidating the status of *res judicata* of the judicial decision which was responsible for the damage. In any event, the principle of State liability inherent in the Community legal order requires such reparation, but not revision of the judicial decision which was responsible for the damage.

* * *

42 As to the independence of the judiciary, the principle of liability in question concerns not the personal liability of the judge but that of the State. The possibility that under certain conditions the State may be rendered liable for judicial decisions contrary to Community law does not appear to entail any particular risk that the independence of a court adjudicating at last instance will be called in question.

43 As to the argument based on the risk of a diminution of the authority of a court adjudicating at last instance owing to the fact that its final decisions could by implication be called in question in proceedings in which the State may be rendered liable for such decisions, the existence of a right of action that affords, under certain conditions, reparation of the injurious effects of an erroneous judicial decision could also be regarded as enhancing the quality of a legal system and thus in the long run the authority of the judiciary.

[The Court stated that the three requirements for *Francovich* liability— (a) breach of a rule intended to confer rights on individuals, (b) a sufficiently serious breach, and (c) a direct causal link between the breach and the injury—needed to be met in this situation as in any other. However, it had special remarks on the second condition in the context of liability on account of judicial action.]

53 [Here] regard must be had to the specific nature of the judicial function and to the legitimate requirements of legal certainty.... State liability for an infringement of Community law by a decision of a national court adjudicating at last instance can be incurred only in the

exceptional case where the court has manifestly infringed the applicable law.

54 In order to determine whether that condition is satisfied, the national court hearing a claim for reparation must take account of all the factors which characterise the situation put before it.

55 Those factors include, in particular, the degree of clarity and precision of the rule infringed, whether the infringement was intentional, whether the error of law was excusable or inexcusable, the position taken, where applicable, by a Community institution and non-compliance by the court in question with its obligation to make a reference for a preliminary ruling. . . .

56 In any event, an infringement of Community law will be sufficiently serious where the decision concerned was made in manifest breach of the case-law of the Court in the matter [citing *Brasserie du Pêcheur* and *Factortame*].

57 The three conditions mentioned [above] are necessary and sufficient to found a right in favour of individuals to obtain redress, although this does not mean that the State cannot incur liability under less strict conditions on the basis of national law.

[On the merits, the Court ruled that the Austrian regime, even if understood as a "loyalty bonus," clearly tended to impede the free movement of workers and could not be justified by pressing reasons of public interest. Regarding liability, the Court predictably focused on the second condition.]

120 It must therefore be examined whether that infringement of Community law is manifest in character having regard in particular to the factors to be taken into consideration for that purpose. . . .

* * *

122 Community law does not expressly cover the point whether a measure for rewarding an employee's loyalty to his employer, such as a loyalty bonus, which entails an obstacle to freedom of movement for workers, can be justified and thus be in conformity with Community law. No reply was to be found to that question in the Court's case-law. Nor, moreover, was that reply obvious.

123 . . . [T]he fact that the national court [did not make] a preliminary ruling . . . is not of such a nature as to invalidate that conclusion.

124 In those circumstances and in the light of the circumstances of the case, the infringement . . . cannot be regarded as being manifest in nature and thus as sufficiently serious.

NOTES AND QUESTIONS

1. Is this really a case of liability grounded on a judicial infringement of EU law, or rather the more usual case of legislative or executive infringement of EU law, which the national judiciary had simply failed to correct?

2.   The ECJ confirmed the *Köbler* judgment in Traghetti del Mediterraneo SpA v. Italy, Case C–173/03, [2006] ECR I–5177, stating that *Francovich* liability is not excluded merely because the infringement in question results from a court's interpretation of law or its assessment of facts or evidence.

3.   Do you expect the U.S. Supreme Court to find it "inherent" in the US constitutional system (as the ECJ did in the EU system) that the courts of the states are required to entertain damages actions by private parties against the states for the injury to the caused by the states' violations of federal law? See Alden v. Maine, 527 U.S. 706, 119 S.Ct. 2240, 144 L.Ed.2d 636 (1999).

CHAPTER 11

ENFORCEMENT PROCEEDINGS AGAINST MEMBER STATES

■ ■ ■

The European Union has a very real interest in ensuring that Member States properly carry out the tasks entrusted to them in applying and enforcing EU law. As we have seen, EC Treaty Article 10 announced a "duty of loyalty," enjoining Member States to "take all appropriate measures . . . to ensure fulfillment of [their] obligations" under EU law, to "facilitate the achievement of the Community's tasks" and to "abstain from any measure which could jeopardize the attainment of [Treaty] objectives." The Lisbon TEU Article 4(3) replicates this duty of loyalty, only replacing the term "Community" with "Union."

Negligence or inefficiency sometimes keeps a Member State from implementing EU law or policy in a timely and proper way. Not often does a State deliberately fail to comply with EU law, but that too has on occasion occurred.

Foreseeing this risk, the drafters of the original EEC Treaty empowered the Commission to "police" Member State compliance by drawing a State's attention to alleged defaults and, if necessary, bringing an "enforcement" or "infringement" action in the Court of Justice. (We use the two terms interchangeably.) EC Treaty Article 226 (initially EEC Treaty Article 169, and now TFEU Article 258) provides:

> If the Commission considers that a Member State has failed to fulfill an obligation under this Treaty, it shall deliver a reasoned opinion on the matter after giving the State concerned the opportunity to submit its observations.

> If the State concerned does not comply with the opinion within the period laid down by the Commission, the latter may bring the matter before the Court of Justice.

If the Court should find a Member State to be in default of its Treaty obligations, the Member State is required under TFEU Article 260(1) (formerly EC Treaty Article 228(1)) "to take the necessary measures to comply with the [Court's] judgment."

Reference will be made throughout this chapter to EC Treaty Article 226 even though, with the entry into force of the Lisbon Treaty in December 2009, this provision was superseded by TFEU Article 258. This is because all the enforcement judgments in this edition of the casebook predate the Lisbon Treaty, and the content of the provision has not changed.

Customarily, the Member States comply with Court judgments that they have violated their obligations, and take action to remedy the failings, although sometimes rather slowly. Occasionally a State's long delay in rectification, or its deliberate opposition to compliance, leads the Commission to return to the Court. To enforce Member State compliance, the Treaty of Maastricht added EC Treaty Article 228(2), which authorized the Commission to request that the Court order the Member State to pay a lump sum fine or on-going financial penalty. TFEU Article 260(2) replicates Article 228(2), with some minor rewording.

The original EEC Treaty also enabled one Member State to bring an action against another for the latter's alleged violation of its obligations under the Treaty. EC Treaty Article 227, which set forth this procedure, has now been replaced by TFEU Article 259 which, like TFEU Article 258, merely substitutes "the Treaties" for "this Treaty."

This chapter is principally devoted to proceedings under EC Treaty Article 226 (now TFEU Article 258), first providing in Section A an overview of the procedure, and then presenting in section B some significant Court judgments concerning the nature of State obligations and examining their defenses to alleged violations. Because the Court has now rendered several significant judgments imposing penalties on States under EC Treaty Article 228 (now TFEU Article 260), this is the subject of section C. A final section D deals with EC Treaty Article 227 (now TFEU Article 259), which has only rarely led to Court judgments.

A. AN OVERVIEW OF COMMISSION ENFORCEMENT PROCEEDINGS

Until the late 1970s, EC Treaty Article 226 (and its predecessor) received relatively little use. In 1977, however, the Commission under President Roy Jenkins decided to prosecute Member State infringements more vigorously, and Article 226 became an important enforcement weapon. Today, infringement actions are common, averaging 15–20% of the Court caseload; their number is exceeded only by that of preliminary references.

Initially the Statute of the Court of Justice required enforcement actions to be heard in plenary session if a Member State defendant so requested, and since States usually did, the burden on the Court was considerable. Article 16 of the Protocol on the Statute of the Court of Justice agreed upon at Nice in December 2000 authorized the Court to sit not as a full court but as a Grand Chamber whenever a Member State is a party to the proceeding and so requests. The corresponding Protocol to the Lisbon Treaty has not changed this provision. In practice, States now only occasionally make this request, so that most enforcement proceedings have been handled by chambers.

Although the Commission usually initiates infringement proceedings on its own initiative, they are often brought based on a complaint from a private party. Since the Commission has limited enforcement resources, it enjoys full discretion in choosing what actions to bring, and consequently, only relatively serious infringements are pursued by the Commission through this procedure.

Until the late 1980s, the largest number of enforcement actions by far (around 30% of the total) were brought against Italy. This was not due to Italy's hostility toward EU law or policy, but rather to institutional difficulties, particularly the conceded inefficiency of its parliament's legislative processes for implementing EU directives. Italy repeatedly tried to remedy the situation. In 1989, Italy put in place a new system providing for the enactment of an annual "Community Act" containing all the measures needed to implement European directives since the previous year's act. See R. Pettricione, A New Mechanism for the Implementation of Community Law, 14 Eur. L. Rev. 456 (1989). This reform substantially reduced the incidence of noncompliance. While enforcement proceedings have by no means abated, no single Member State stands out any longer as a particularly frequent target of such actions. Nowadays, the procedure also serves as an important tool for monitoring the reception of the *acquis communautaire* by the new Member States that acceded to the Union following the 2004 and 2007 enlargements. See Borissova, Enforcement Actions under EU Law—The New Member States, European Institute of Public Administration (2007).

The various stages of the enforcement procedure are clearly designed to encourage Member State compliance and to obviate the need for judicial recourse.

1. *Pre-contentious Stage.* If the Commission considers a Member State to be in default of its Treaty obligations, it will first give the State informal notice of the nature of the default. The State then has time to submit a right of reply, which must be long enough to be reasonable under the circumstances. Commission v. Belgium (University fees), Case 293/85, [1988] ECR 305. The reply may convince the Commission that a violation did not occur or has been ended, but the Commission frequently maintains its initial view.

2. *Formal Notification.* If the matter remains unresolved after the first stage, the Commission formally notifies the State by letter of the alleged infringement. The Member State usually has a two-month period in which to reply, which may be shorter in cases of urgency.

3. *Reasoned Opinion.* If the Commission remains unsatisfied with the Member State's reply to the formal notification letter, the Commission may issue a reasoned opinion, a technical term for a Commission commu-

nication that spells out the basis for its views and calls on the Member State to take remedial action within a specified period.

4. *Court filing.* If the Commission considers that the State has not taken adequate remedial action in time, it may file an action before the Court of Justice.

The Commission issues on average several thousand complaints to the States every year, often because the State has failed to implement a directive within the prescribed period for doing so, or because the Commission considers the State's implementation to be deficient in some manner. Sometimes the Commission complains about alleged State violations of a substantive Treaty provision or other EU law obligations that occur through negligence or poor administration. It is accordingly not surprising that a majority of the complaints are resolved by appropriate State action even before the Commission reaches the "reasoned opinion" stage. In fact, probably only 15–20% of the complaints result in a Court filing, and even then a majority are resolved before the Court issues a judgment.

As indicated in Chapter 2D, the Court held in Commission v. Germany (First company directive penalties), supra page 49, that the Commission must collectively deliberate and take collective responsibility when initiating an enforcement proceeding in court, but then may delegate the final preparation of the Court filing to a single commissioner. The Commission's Rules of Procedure permit such a delegation, which is obviously the only practical way of handling the numerous cases concerned.

Member States have occasionally challenged the Commission's reasoned opinion as unclear or insufficiently detailed. Usually the Court of Justice is not impressed with that complaint and proceeds to the merits. Rarely, the Court finds that the Commission was not precise enough as to what the Member State should or should not have done, and the Court will then decide in the State's favor because it views the Commission's failure as an essential procedural defect. See Commission v. Italy (Transit of live animals), Case 121/84, [1986] ECR 107. In no event may the Commission raise issues before the Court that were not fairly presented in the reasoned opinion. See, for example, Commission v. Denmark (Taxation of imported motor vehicles), Case C–52/90, [1992] ECR I–2187.

In enforcement actions, as in any other, the Court will entertain applications for interim relief. A notable example is Commission v. Germany (Charges for road use by heavy vehicles), Case C–195/90R, [1990] ECR I–3351. There, the Commission asked the Court to enjoin the German authorities temporarily from collecting a road tax on heavy vehicles that was then the subject of a Commission challenge before the Court. The Court ordered collection of the tax provisionally suspended on the ground that the tax was prima facie invalid and that its collection would cause serious and irreparable harm to the affected parties. In doing so, the Court rejected Germany's demand that the Commission put up some 500 million DM as security to cover the taxes that Germany might not later be able to recover if it won the action. The Court thought there was no reason to believe the Community could not or would not pay any damages that might be awarded against it.

The principal issue in an enforcement proceeding is typically the scope of a Member State's obligations under EU law. To this extent, enforcement proceedings are not unlike other actions before the Court, notably preliminary references. But unlike in preliminary references, the Court does not merely give guidance to other courts; it decides the case before it, with the Commission bearing the burden of proof. See, e.g., Commission v. Belgium (Pharmaceutical prices), Case C–249/88, [1991] ECR I–1275. Indeed, an infringement action is the only vehicle by which the Court rules directly on the compatibility of a provision of national law with EU law. Triveneta Zuccheri SpA v. Commission, Case C–347/87, [1990] ECR I–1083. In all other cases, the power to rule on the compatibility of national law with EU law belongs to the national courts, aided of course as needed by preliminary rulings from the Court of Justice.

In Commission v. Italy (Road haulage directive), infra page 400, the Court observed that it considers an enforcement action to be less a form of judicial review of the Commission's reasoned opinion than an adjudication of the Member State's alleged infringement. What significance might there be to this distinction?

The conduct of a Member State during enforcement proceedings may itself become a compliance issue. For example, the Court has sharply condemned Member States for refusing or failing to provide information to the Commission during the investigative stage. Thus, in Commission v. Greece (Olive oil trade restriction), Case 272/86, [1988] ECR 4875, the Court considered the Greek Government's refusal to supply requested documents to the Commission to be a violation of its duty of loyalty under EC Treaty Article 10 (now TEU Article 4(3)), since it hampered both the Commission in its duty to enforce the Treaty under Article 226 and the Court in its duty to enforce the law under EC Treaty Article 220 (now TEU Article 19). The Court called the refusal "a serious impediment to the administration of justice." See also Commission v. Belgium (Prices of crude oil and petroleum products), Case C–374/89, [1991] ECR I–367; Commission v. Greece (Obstacles to cereal imports), Case 240/86, [1988] ECR 1835.

The Commission prevails in the vast majority, almost 90%, of enforcement proceedings that reach the Court of Justice. The figure, however, is deceptive, since the Commission takes cases that far only very selectively. Moreover, a Member State government may mount only a pro forma defense if the reason for noncompliance, for example, is the national parliament's failure to implement a directive properly or on time, or inefficiency at some level of the administration. The Member State government may actually welcome the pressure for action coming from an adverse Court of Justice ruling. In any case, the utility of enforcement actions cannot be measured simply by the number of judgments rendered.

As seen, infringement actions have an administrative as well as a judicial phase, and Commission success at the former is certainly no less welcome than at the latter stage.

Since 1983, the Commission has issued annual reports on its monitoring of the application of EU law. Indeed, a Declaration of the European Council annexed to the Maastricht Treaty calls for these reports. The Commission accordingly indicates annually Member State infringements of the Treaties and regulations, and records the States' progress in implementing directives. The reports also contain various statistical analyses of the infringements noted.

As alluded to at various points in this casebook, the EC Treaty establishes a separate Commission enforcement regime in the state aid sector. EC Treaty Article 88 (now TFEU Article 108) directs the Commission, in cooperation with the Member States, to keep all existing systems of aid under review. More specifically, if the Commission finds, after giving the parties a chance to be heard, that a state aid that has been granted is not compatible with the rules governing them or is being misused, it may instruct the State to alter or abolish the aid. Should the State fail to do so within the prescribed time, the Commission or any other Member State may directly refer the matter to the Court of Justice.

The Treaty calls this procedure a "derogation" from the ordinary Commission enforcement procedures thus far described in this chapter. In fact, the main procedural difference seems to be the absence of a formal "reasoned opinion" phase, as well as the absence of any reference to sanctions or penalty payments as provided for in EC Treaty Article 228 (now TFEU Article 260), and discussed below. The state aid enforcement procedure is much used and has given rise to considerable Court case law.

NOTES AND QUESTIONS

1. A private party cannot challenge the Commission's failure to bring an infringement action against a State, even if the private party's complaint drew the Commission's attention to the alleged infringement. In Star Fruit v. Commission, Case 247/87, [1989] ECR 291, the Court held that the Commission had "a discretion which excluded the right for individuals to require" that it initiate enforcement proceedings (¶ 11). The Court emphasized that the Commission has a "right, but not a duty" to bring an action before the Court (¶ 12). See also Alfons Lütticke GmbH v. Commission, Case 48/65, [1966] ECR 19, where the Court decided that a private party has no cause of action for the Commission's express refusal to bring enforcement proceedings against an allegedly delinquent State.

2. Infringement actions occasionally result in judgments that expand our understanding of the scope of Member State obligations. An excellent example is Commission v. France (Produce imports), excerpted at page 450 infra, where the Court condemned France for "manifestly and persistently" failing to put an end to acts of violence by French farmers designed to prevent the import of less expensive produce from other Member States. The Court

effectively held that a Member State breaches its obligations under EC Treaty Article 10 (now TEU Article 4(3)), when it fails adequately to address repeated criminal conduct engaged in by its nationals or residents in violation of fundamental Treaty-based rights. Has the Court gone too far? Or is the judgment a proportionate response by the Court to an exceptionally urgent and intolerable situation? Query, how far does US law go in imposing a duty on governments to prevent private conduct that impairs other persons' fundamental rights? See DeShaney v. Winnebago County Department of Social Services, 489 U.S. 189, 195, 109 S.Ct. 998, 1003, 103 L.Ed.2d 249, 258 (1989), where a majority of the Court stated that "nothing in the language of the Due Process Clause itself requires the State to protect the life, liberty, and property of its citizens against invasion by private actors."

B.   WHAT CONSTITUTES AN INFRINGEMENT?

By definition, enforcement actions require the Court to determine whether a State has failed in an obligation under EU law. The rulings thus typically clarify what the relevant Treaty article, secondary legislation or general principle of EU law requires of States and determine whether the State has satisfied those requirements. The first of these inquiries ordinarily entails the direct interpretation of EU law. In fact, early judgments of the Court were the occasion for articulating important substantive principles of EU law.

The following case raised the more fundamental question of whether a State is necessarily responsible for situations in which the results intended by EU law have not been achieved.

COMMISSION v. FRANCE

(Municipal waste incineration).
Case C–60/01, [2002] ECR I–5679.

[The Commission sued France for failing to adopt the measures necessary and appropriate to ensure that all new municipal waste incineration plants operating in France complied with the specific combustion regulations laid down in Directives 89/369 and 89/429 on preventing pollution from such plants. France had adequately transposed the directive into French legislation, but according to reports that the Commission received from various sources, many plants in France were still not in compliance.]

23   The French Government contends that ... [f]rom the fact that a situation is not in conformity with the objectives laid down by a provision of a directive, the direct inference may not in principle be drawn that the Member State concerned has necessarily failed to fulfil its obligation under that provision. Furthermore, breach of a rule contained in a directive by a legal person independent of a Member State cannot constitute a failure by that State to fulfil its obligations.

* * *

25 However, Community legislative practice shows that there may be great differences in the types of obligations which directives impose on the Member States and therefore in the results which must be achieved.

26 Some directives require legislative measures to be adopted at national level and compliance with those measures to be the subject of judicial or administrative review.

27 Other directives lay down that the Member States are to take the necessary measures to ensure that certain objectives formulated in general and unquantifiable terms are attained, whilst leaving them some discretion as to the nature of the measures to be taken.

28 Yet other directives require the Member States to obtain very precise and specific results after a certain period.

* * *

30 Directives 89/369 and 89/429 form part of an overall Community strategy to protect the environment and reduce air pollution. Incineration plants were already covered by [a prior directive], under which the Member States were obliged to prescribe prior authorisation procedures and regular checks for their operation and gradually to adapt existing plants to the best available technology. Directives 89/369 and 89/429 supplemented that legislation by introducing detailed and precise requirements applicable to both new and existing municipal waste incineration plants.

* * *

32 Furthermore, Article 5(1) of both Directive 89/369 and Directive 89/429 specifies that the temperature and the oxygen content laid down are minimum values to be observed at all times when the plant is in operation.

33 It follows that Directives 89/369 and 89/429 impose on the Member States obligations, formulated in clear and unequivocal terms, to achieve a certain result, in order that their incineration plants meet detailed and precise requirements within the stated time-limits.

34 In those circumstances, contrary to the French Government's assertions, it is not therefore sufficient for a Member State to take all reasonably practicable measures to achieve the result imposed by Directives 89/369 and 89/249.

35 Furthermore, even assuming that absolute physical impossibility to perform the obligations at issue imposed by Directives 89/369 and 89/429 may justify failure to fulfil them, the French Government has not been able to establish such impossibility in the present case.

[The Court further rejected France's claim that the two directives did not allow sufficient time to bring the plants into compliance.]

NOTES AND QUESTIONS

1. France may have wanted the directives in question to be viewed as nothing more than "frameworks" for State action, as indeed many environmental protection directives are. How is one to know whether a directive commands a result or merely establishes a program of action?

2. France also raised pragmatic concerns of practicability and cost. These arguments are more in the nature of a defense against proven violations of EU law. As cases in the next section show, States may not plead administrative difficulties or costs to justify their failures to meet EU law obligations.

C. MEMBER STATE EXCUSES FOR NONCOMPLIANCE WITH EU LAW OBLIGATIONS

The discussion thus far suggests that the crucial issues in Commission enforcement proceedings usually concern the scope of a Member State's obligations under the Treaties, and the question of what constitutes a violation of those obligations. However, often States concede the existence of both the obligation and the violation, and seek only to "excuse" the violation. Sometimes States will plead in the alternative: they have not violated EU law, but even if they have, the violation is justified.

The Treaty does not acknowledge the existence of any such defenses, but that has not stopped Member States from advancing them. The Court in turn has wasted little time in rejecting virtually all Member state excuses or justifications for their infringements of EU law obligations.

COMMISSION v. LUXEMBOURG AND BELGIUM

(Milk products)
Cases 90, 91/63, [1964] ECR 625.

[In 1958, Belgium and Luxembourg introduced a new tax on the import of certain milk products. After several years of complaints, the Commission finally brought an enforcement action challenging the tax as a violation of then Article 12 of the EC Treaty, a subsequently-repealed "standstill" provision barring the introduction of new customs duties on intra-Community trade. (See the *van Gend en Loos* case, supra page 232.) Belgium and Luxembourg conceded their violation of Article 12, but argued that the tax was necessary to protect their markets, since the Community itself had failed to create in due time a market organization under the Common Agricultural Policy for the dairy products in question.]

Admissibility

The defendants ... complain that the Community failed to comply with the obligations falling on it ... and was thus responsible for the continuance of the alleged infringement of the Treaty. ... In their view, since international law allows a party, injured by the failure of another party to perform its obligations, to withhold performance of its own, the Commission has lost the right to plead infringement of the Treaty. However this relationship between the obligations of the parties cannot be recognized under Community law.

[T]he Treaty is not limited to creating reciprocal obligations between the different natural and legal persons to whom it is applicable, but establishes a new legal order which governs the powers, rights and obligations of the said persons, as well as the necessary procedures for taking cognizance of and penalizing any breach of it. Therefore, except where otherwise expressly provided, the basic concept of the Treaty requires that the Member States shall not take the law into their own hands. Therefore the fact that the Council failed to carry out its obligations cannot relieve the defendants from carrying out theirs.

* * *

The Substance

It is not disputed that the contested measures are customs duties on imports or charges having equivalent effect within the meaning of Article 12 of the Treaty.

* * *

Article 12 prohibits the introduction of new customs barriers, so as to facilitate the integration of national markets and the establishment of a common market. Without constituting of itself a measure removing economic protection, this prohibition of any new form of protection by way of customs duties constitutes an essential requirement both for the substitution of a common market for the different national markets and for the substitution of a common agricultural organization for the national organizations. Thus Article 12 constitutes a fundamental rule and any possible exception, which in any event must be strictly construed, must be clearly laid down.

* * *

... The Treaty expressly provides means and special procedures for remedying ... difficulties in [market effectiveness] under the supervision of the Community authorities or with their approval.

NOTES AND QUESTIONS

1.   Note that the Court in *Milk products* employed the "new legal order" language it had then only recently used in *van Gend en Loos*, supra page 232. The ruling formed part of the sequence of early Court judgments articulating the basic constitutional nature of the European Community.

2.   In *Milk products*, Belgium and Luxembourg invoked the *tu quoque* or "you too" principle of public international law: if one party to a treaty

violates it, the other party is justified in taking defensive measures. If this principle offers no defense, what recourse do Belgium and Luxembourg have within the "new legal order" to protect their dairy industry? The only plausible way was through adoption of an EU market organization for dairy products. As noted in Chapter 1, the creation of such agricultural product organizations was among the most difficult political decisions, and achievements, of the Community in the 1960s. As for the elimination of intra-Community customs duties, see Chapter 12A.

3.   Another plausible defense is that the EU law measure a State is accused of breaching is itself illegal because the measure violates a higher EU law principle. This is a species of the plea of illegality pursuant to EC Treaty Article 241 (now TFEU Article 277), discussed in Chapter 5E supra. As might be expected from the *Foto–Frost* judgment, supra page 253, the Court of Justice does not look favorably on such a defense.

COMMISSION v. FRANCE

(Mutton and Lamb)
Case 232/78, [1979] ECR 2729.

[Even by the late 1970s, political agreement had not been reached to create a common organization of the market in mutton and lamb, so that market was still regulated nationally. France sought to stabilize domestic prices by restricting the import of these products not only from non-EC nations, but also from the UK, by then an EU Member State. Following complaints from British trade and diplomatic circles, the Commission initiated infringement proceedings.]

6   The French Government does not dispute the fact that this system is incompatible with the Treaty provisions relating to ... the free movement of goods within the Community. However ... it puts forward in substance three arguments. First, it emphasizes the serious social and economic effects on the economy of certain economically less-favoured areas for which sheep-rearing is an important source of wealth of discontinuing the national organization of the market. Secondly, it draws attention to the [lack of] progress made in ... setting up a common organization of the market in mutton and lamb and stresses the harmful effects of interposing a phase of free trade between the discontinuance of the national organization and replacing it by a common organization. Finally it points to the inequality in the field of competition deriving from the fact that it would have to abolish its own organization of the market even though in the United Kingdom a national organization of the market, ... result[ing] in subsidizing exports of mutton and lamb to France, would remain intact....

7   Although the Court is aware of the genuine problems which the French authorities have to solve ... and of the desirability of achieving the establishment, in the shortest possible time, of a common organization of the market in mutton and lamb, it must again draw attention to the fact that ... after the expiration of the transitional period [i.e., Dec. 31,

1969] . . . a national organization of the market must no longer operate in such a way as to prevent the Treaty provisions relating to the elimination of restrictions on intra-Community trade from having full force and effect. . . . [A] decision to adopt [protective measures] can no longer be made unilaterally by the Member States concerned; they must be adopted within the Community system which is designed to guarantee that the general public interest of the Community is protected.

8   Consequently it is for the competent institutions and for them alone to adopt within the appropriate periods . . . [and] in a Community context . . . a comprehensive solution of the problem of the market in mutton and lamb and of the special difficulties which arise in this connection. . . . [T]he fact that this work has not yet been successful is not a sufficient justification for the maintenance by a Member State of a national organization of the market which includes features which are incompatible with the requirements of the Treaty relating to the free movement of goods. . . .

9   The French Republic cannot justify the existence of such a system with the argument that the United Kingdom has maintained a national organization of the market in the same sector. If the French Republic is of the opinion that that system contains features which are incompatible with Community law, it has the opportunity to take action, either within the Council, or through the Commission, or finally by recourse to judicial remedies with a view to achieving the elimination of such incompatible features. A Member State cannot under any circumstances unilaterally adopt . . . measures to protect trade designed to prevent any failure on the part of another Member State to comply with the rules laid down by the Treaty.

10   The Court must therefore conclude that the national organization of the market in mutton and lamb maintained by the French authorities is incompatible with the Treaty. . . .

NOTES AND QUESTIONS

1.   Reciprocity has never been successfully invoked as a defense to an infringement action, though the attempt has repeatedly been made. See, e.g., Steinike and Weinlig v. Germany, Case 78/76, [1977] ECR 595, and more recently, Commission v. Luxembourg, Case C–266/03 [2005] ECR I–4805. Note that some Member State constitutions excuse the nonperformance of an international treaty obligation if the other state parties to the treaty are themselves in breach. See, e.g., Article 55 of the French Constitution, supra page 298. Obviously, such provisions may not be invoked in the ECJ to justify a Member State's nonperformance of its EU law obligations.

2.   Nor has the Court permitted States to violate EU legislation on the basis of its invalidity—even its invalidity under EU law. The Court considers the Member States as bound to comply with all EU law measures unless and until annulled by the Court or suspended pending final judgment. Granaria

BV v. Hoofdproduktschap voor Akkerbouwprodukten, Case 101/78, [1979] ECR 623, 636.

3.   No more successful is a Member State's assertion that it has been treated less fairly, or indulgently, by the Commission than another Member State was treated. In Commission v. Spain (Bathing water), Case C–278/01, [2003] ECR I–14141, Spain argued that other Member States had been given a longer period of time in which to implement an environmental protection directive. The Court's answer was plain: "It was open to the Kingdom of Spain to request a transitional period for application of the Directive when it acceded to the European Communities. Since it did not make any such request, it cannot now rely on its failure to do so to claim a reduction in the penalty payment." The Court has also rejected as a defense a claim that a transitional period in an accession treaty had proved not to be sufficiently long. See Commission v. Spain (Midwives), Case C–313/19, [1991] ECRI–5231.

4.   A Member State's "selective prosecution" defense is also not accepted. In Commission v. Belgium, Case C–433/02, [2003], Belgium attempted to justify its failure to apply certain provisions of a Council directive on copyright rental rights in part on the ground that other Member States were also in default and had not been pursued. The Court's reply was equally plain: "[E]ven assuming that other Member States do not apply correctly the public lending right as provided for in the [Copyright Rental Right] Directive, it suffices to point out that, according to settled case-law, a Member State cannot justify its failure to perform its obligations under Community law by relying on the fact that other Member States are also in breach of their obligations" (¶ 21).

5.   Sometimes a Member State asserts that the Commission is estopped for one reason or another from pursuing an enforcement action—for example, due to its long-time tolerance of the practices complained of—or is accused of undue delay in taking action. See Commission v. France (Euratom supply agency), Case 7/71, [1971] ECR 1003; Germany v. Commission (Import duties on mutton), Cases 52, 55/65, [1966] ECR 159. Are these promising defenses?

6.   In the cases examined thus far, the defendant State sought to justify its noncompliance on some claim of justification. Following is a rare case in which a Member State deliberately refused as a matter of policy to enforce EU law rules. The Court reacted with unusually vigorous language.

COMMISSION v. ITALY
(Slaughtered cows II)
Case 39/72, [1973] ECR 101.

[Council Regulation 1975/69 attempted to deal with chronic surpluses of dairy products by 1) authorizing premiums to be paid to dairy farmers who slaughtered a portion of their dairy herd, and 2) creating a system of payments to farmers ("non-marketing premiums") for withholding dairy products from the market. The Member States were to set up the systems, notify farmers, verify that slaughter took place between February and May 1970, and pay the premiums. Italy failed to take any action in time, essentially because the government opposed the Regulation. Italy finally implemented the slaughtering premium system in October 1971. When the Commission brought an infringement proceeding, Italy argued that the issue was essentially moot, since the Council had terminated both programs in 1971.]

8   The defendant . . . claims that the pursuit of the action commenced by the Commission is no longer warranted because of the circumstances. The difficulties which had originally delayed the payment of the premiums for slaughtering having been overcome, the payment of these premiums is in process and therefore the *raison d'etre* of the proceedings instituted by the Commission has disappeared. . . .

9   The object of an action under Article [226] is established by the Commission's reasoned opinion, and even when the default has been remedied subsequent to the time limit prescribed by paragraph 2 of the same Article, pursuit of the action still has an object.

* * *

11   [I]n the face of both a delay in the performance of [one] obligation and a definite refusal [to perform another], a judgment by the Court under Articles [226 and 228] of the Treaty may be of substantive interest as establishing the basis of a responsibility that a Member State can incur as a result of its default, as regards other Member States, the Community or private parties.

12   The preliminary objection raised by the defendant must therefore be rejected.

* * *

2.   *As to the Premiums for Non-marketing*

19   The default in putting into operation the provisions of [the Regulation] with regard to premiums for non-marketing is due to a deliberate refusal by the Italian authorities. . . . [A]ccording to the Italian Government, measures intended to restrict the production of milk were inappropriate to the needs of the Italian economy, which is characterized by insufficient food production. . . .

[The Court then observed that Regulation 1975/69 had been validly enacted and was binding on the Member States.]

20   [I]t cannot be accepted that a Member State should apply in an incomplete or selective manner provisions of a Community Regulation so as to render abortive certain aspects of Community legislation which it has opposed or which it considers contrary to its national interests.

21   In particular . . . the Member State which omits to take, within the requisite time limits and simultaneously with the other Member States, the measures which it ought to take, undermines the efficacy of the [Regulation] decided upon in common, while at the same time taking an

undue advantage to the detriment of its partners in view of the free circulation of goods.

* * *

[24] In permitting Member States to profit from the advantages of the Community, the Treaty imposes on them also the obligation to respect its rules. For a State unilaterally to break, according to its own conception of national interest, the equilibrium between advantages and obligations flowing from its adherence to the Community brings into question the equality of Member States before Community law and creates discriminations at the expense of their nationals, and above all of the nationals of the State itself which places itself outside the Community rules.

[25] This failure in the duty of solidarity accepted by Member States by the fact of their adherence to the Community strikes at the fundamental basis of the Community legal order. It appears therefore that, in deliberately refusing to give effect on its territory to one of the systems provided for by [the Regulation], the Italian Republic has failed in a conspicuous manner to fulfil the obligations which it has assumed by virtue of its adherence to the European Economic Community.

NOTES AND QUESTIONS

1. Normally the Commission will not bring suit if a Member State ends its infringement during the preliminary phase of the enforcement proceeding. See Commission v. Italy (Public supply contracts), Case C–362/90, [1992] ECR I–2353. However, the fact that a period set for State action has expired will not necessarily cause the Court to consider the case moot, particularly if the case provides an opportunity to state an important principle for the future. *Slaughtered cows II* is a good example.

2. In ¶ 11, the Court suggested that its ruling might provide the basis for liability of a Member State to private parties injured by the infringement. Although the Court had not enunciated its doctrine to that effect at the time, it subsequently did so in the *Francovich* judgment, supra page 369. See also Commission v. Spain (Safety of work equipment), Case C–168/03, [2004] ECR I–8227.

3. The reporting judge in the principal case, Pierre Pescatore, may well have been responsible for the Court's strong language in condemning Italy's infringement. See ¶¶ 20–25. Note especially the Court's emphasis on each State's "duty of solidarity" in ¶ 25, and Italy's violation of "the fundamental basis of the Community legal order."

4. Clearly, opposition by people in a region to a national measure implementing an EU law directive—however strenuous—will not justify a Member State's failing to adopt such a measure. See Commission v. Greece (Kouroupitos pollution), Case C–45/91, [1992] ECR I–2525. The sequel to this case is excerpted at page 408, infra.

COMMISSION v. ITALY

(Road haulage directive)
Case 28/81, [1981] ECR 2577.

[Council Directive 74/561, adopted in November 1974, established generally stated requirements for engaging in the occupation of road haulage operator, including "good repute," "appropriate financial standing" and "professional competence." Italy did not implement the directive by the due date of January 1, 1977, and the Commission brought suit.]

3   The Italian Government ... explains that the directive in question has been included for implementation in a draft law which is now under consideration by the Chamber of Deputies. The draft was not tabled until 12 December 1980 owing to the detailed scrutiny to which it was first subjected by all the administrative authorities concerned. The Italian Government ... hopes to obtain approval within the shortest possible time [and therefore considers] that the object of the action has been eliminated in substance so that this application has become devoid of purpose.

4   Those circumstances do not expunge the failure of the Italian Republic to fulfil its obligations. According to well-established case law, a Member State may not plead provisions, practices or circumstances in its internal legal system in order to justify a failure to comply with obligations under Community directives.

5   [T]he Italian Government requested the Court to grant it an extension of the period allowed by the Commission pursuant to Article [226] of the Treaty for fulfilling the obligations under the directive in question.

6   The powers conferred on the Court ... under Article [226] of the Treaty do not include the power to substitute a different period for that laid down by the Commission ... in its reasoned opinion, although the legality of that opinion is subject to review by the Court. ... [I]t is for the Commission to decide whether such a request from a Member State is to be granted.

7   [T]he Italian Republic has failed to fulfil one of its obligations under the Treaty.

NOTES AND QUESTIONS

1.   The Court has consistently rejected the claim that constitutional or institutional difficulties within a Member State excuse its noncompliance with an EU law obligation. See, e.g., Commission v. Italy (Quality control of fruits and vegetables II), Case 69/86, [1987] ECR 773; Commission v. Italy (Administrative levy), Case 8/70, [1970] ECR 961. In many of these cases, a Member State government denies responsibility for the legislature's failure to act, a failure that may be attributed to parliamentary delay or inefficiency, or to political conflict (including possibly the fall of a government). Do you understand why the Court refuses to entertain such a defense? Suppose a Member State government fails to act as required by EU law because its courts have,

for reasons of domestic (possibly domestic *constitutional*) law, enjoined it from doing so. Would that make any difference? Remember the Court's application of its primacy doctrine in *Simmenthal II*, supra page 247.

2. Compare to the "horizontal" (or "separation of powers") problem the "vertical" (or "division of powers") situation in which a Member State claims to be powerless to remedy a violation for which a constituent state or local unit of government is exclusively responsible under the national constitution. Should such a case be treated differently? The Court evidently thinks not. See, for example, Germany v. Commission (Suckler cows), Case C–8/88, [1990] ECR I–2321, in which Germany unsuccessfully challenged its loss of certain agricultural funds on the ground that the German states, not the federal government, were responsible for the administrative lapses that had precipitated the sanction. See also *Casagrande*, infra page 581. Similarly, in Commission v. Italy (Toxic waste in Campania), Case C–33/90, [1991] ECR I–5987, the Court was wholly unsympathetic to Italy's claim that responsibility for noncompliance lay with "autonomous" regional authorities.

3. What if an offending State claims that an EU law requirement is too burdensome (as when Germany argued that the costs of enforcing penalties against companies that fail to publish their accounts as required by an EU directive were excessive and disproportionate to the directive's aims), or that it simply cannot afford the implementation costs (as when Ireland argued that it lacked the personnel and other resources to comply with a periodic reporting requirement on wholesale fish prices imposed by the Council)? The Court dismissed both defenses as legally insufficient. See Commission v. Germany (First Company Directive penalties), infra page 719; Commission v. Ireland (Fishery price information), Case C–39/88, [1990] ECR I–4271.

What if the defense in clothed in language of necessity or impossibility? In a very early decision, Italy sought to justify a ban on pork imports from other States, claiming that it had no other means of remedying the artificially low prices prevailing in the pigmeat sector and that general principles of public law entitle States to take emergency measures. The Court did not categorically rule out a necessity defense, but found that the Treaty provided its own emergency procedure that Italy had failed to use. Commission v. Italy (Pork import ban), Case 7/61, [1961] ECR 317.

But suppose, as has happened, a State claims that it could not implement an EU directive compelling data-gathering due to a terrorist bombing of the data processing center where the vital data was located. See Commission v. Italy (Transport statistics), Case 101/84, [1985] ECR 2629. The Court accepted that violations might in principle be excused on grounds of *force majeure*, and that a terrorist bombing might indeed constitute *force majeure*, but felt that under the circumstances Italy nevertheless had the time and wherewithal to re-collect and submit the data, and had failed to do so.

In fact the Court has suggested that impossibility may be the only defense available to a State, but it has also given notice that it will put the State to proof of impossibility and, in any event, require consultation with the Commission and best efforts at minimizing the effects of non-compliance:

[12]   The only defence available to a Member State in opposing an application by the Commission ... for a declaration that it has failed to fulfil its

Treaty obligations is to plead that it was absolutely impossible for it to implement the decision properly.

13 However, a Member State which, in giving effect to a Commission decision on State aid, encounters unforeseen and unforeseeable difficulties or becomes aware of consequences overlooked by the Commission, must submit those problems to the Commission for consideration, together with proposals for suitable amendments to the decision in question. In such cases, the Commission and the Member State must, by virtue of the rule imposing on the Member States and the Community institutions a duty of genuine cooperation which underlies, in particular, [EC Treaty Article 10, now TEU Article 4(3)], work together in good faith with a view to overcoming the difficulties whilst fully observing the Treaty provisions. . . .

Commission v. Italy (Aid to Aluminia), Case C–349/93, [1995] ECR I–343.

COMMISSION v. FRANCE

(French merchant seamen)
Case 167/73, [1974] ECR 359.

[Article 3(2) of the French Maritime Code of 1926 required that at least 75% of the crew of certain French vessels be composed of French nationals. The Commission complained that the French law violated EC Treaty Article 39 (now TFEU Article 45) on free movement of workers, and eventually invoked Article 226. The French government assured the Court that the Maritime Code provision was not and would not be applied to discriminate against other Member State nationals, and cited verbal instructions to the maritime authorities to treat nationals of all other Member States as if they were "French nationals." For its part, the Commission was unable to cite any instance in which the authorities had in fact treated EC nationals as "foreign" for these purposes.]

34 [T]he [French] Government . . . has sought to deny that a default exists . . . solely as a result of the maintenance in the national legal system of the law in dispute without taking into consideration the application which is made of it in practice.

[France contended that its administrative officials would accept that the provisions of Article 39 would render "all contrary provisions of internal law" inapplicable to seamen who are nationals of other Community States.]

* * *

41 [A]lthough . . . Article [39 is] directly applicable in the territory of the French Republic, nevertheless the maintenance in these circumstances of the wording of the Code . . . gives rise to an ambiguous state of affairs by maintaining, as regards those subject to the law who are concerned, a state of uncertainty as to the possibilities available to them of relying on Community law.

⁴² This uncertainty can only be reinforced by the internal and verbal character of the purely administrative directions to waive the application of the national law.

⁴³ The free movement of persons, and in particular workers, constitutes ... one of the foundations of the Community.

* * *

⁴⁷ The uncertainty created by the maintenance unamended of the [Code's] wording ... constitutes ... an obstacle [to achieving the free movement of workers].

⁴⁸ It follows that in maintaining [the Code provisions] unamended ... as regards the nationals of other Member States, the French Republic has failed to fulfil its obligations under Article 39 of the Treaty.

NOTES AND QUESTIONS

1. Do you regard the Court's position in the principal case as justifiable or formalistic? The case is not an isolated one. In Commission v. France (Waste oil directive), Case 173/83, [1985] ECR 491, the Court held that an administrative circular was insufficient to correct ambiguous legislation because the affected private interests were unlikely to know of it. Would the persons hiring a crew be apt to know that the Maritime Code provision should not and does not apply to nationals of other Member States?

2. Why did France not simply amend the code provision in question rather than defend the action all the way to the Court of Justice? In March 1996, the Court condemned France for still—22 years later—not having complied with the Court's judgment in the principal case! Commission v. France (Registration of vessels), Case C–334/94, [1996] ECR I–1307.

3. In 1983, in response to a written question from MEP Alan Tyrell, O.J.C. 268/25 (Oct. 6, 1983), the Commission indicated that it could "in principle" bring an infringement action against a Member State for erroneous decisions of national courts, but was reluctant to do because this would not be "the most effective basis for cooperation between national courts and the European Court of Justice." The Commission added that an enforcement action might be appropriate if "a court of last instance ... systematically and deliberately" fails to make proper use of the preliminary reference procedure. (The question was probably prompted by the French Supreme Administrative Court's practice of commonly deciding EU law issues on its own, often erroneously.)

COMMISSION v. ITALY

(Erroneous supreme court rulings)
Case C–129/00, [2003] ECRI–8003.

[An Italian statute established special procedural rules for the refund of various import duties and consumption taxes. The Court of Justice found the statute to be "in itself neutral in respect of EU law," but to have been construed by the Italian Supreme Court in a manner contrary to Community law.]

29   A Member State's failure to fulfil obligations may, in principle, be established under Article 226 EC whatever the agency of that State whose action or inaction is the cause of the failure to fulfil its obligations, even in the case of a constitutionally independent institution. . . .

30   The scope of national laws, regulations or administrative provisions must be assessed in the light of the interpretation given to them by national courts. . . .

* * *

32   [I]solated or numerically insignificant judicial decisions in the context of case-law taking a different direction, or still more a construction disowned by the national supreme court, cannot be taken into account. That is not true of a widely-held judicial construction which has not been disowned by the supreme court, but rather confirmed by it.

33   Where national legislation has been the subject of different relevant judicial constructions, some leading to the application of that legislation in compliance with Community law, [and] others leading to the opposite application, it must be held that, at the very least, such legislation is not sufficiently clear to ensure its application in compliance with Community law.

[The Court of Justice ultimately concluded in ¶ 35 that the Italian Supreme Court had issued erroneous judgments concerning refunds of duties and taxes invalidly collected and failed in its EU law obligations by failing to amend the relevant laws to overrule their mistaken construction (¶ 41).]

NOTES AND QUESTIONS

1.   The Court of Justice has no appellate power over a State supreme court and cannot of course reverse an erroneous judgment. That judgment may have the status of *res judicata* in the national legal order. Nor can the Court compel a national supreme court to change its attitude in future cases.

2.   As noted in Chapter 10B supra, the ECJ ruled in the *Francovich* case that under certain conditions a State could—and indeed must—be held liable in damages if its executive or legislative branches violate EU law in a manner that causes injury to private parties. Should the same principle apply if a national supreme court judgment causes harm to a private party? In *Kobler*, discussed in Chapter 10B, the Austrian government maintained that in no event could liability against the State be predicated on the adjudicatory acts of a national court of last resort.

The Court of Justice rejected that view, declaring to the contrary that:

59   . . . The principle that Member States are obliged to make good damage caused to individuals by infringements of Community law for which they are responsible is also applicable where the alleged infringement stems from a decision of a court adjudicating at last instance where the rule of Community law infringed is intended to confer rights on individuals, the

breach is sufficiently serious and there is a direct causal link between that breach and the loss or damage sustained by the injured parties.

However, the Court of Justice ruled on the merits that the Austrian Supreme Court had not committed "manifest error," so that Austria was not liable in damages.

3. The ECJ has yet to decide the politically sensitive issue whether a State may be prosecuted due to its supreme court apparently deliberately refraining from making preliminary references to the Court that, under EU law principles, it ought to make. In 2004 the Commission issued a reasoned opinion to Sweden, alleging the failure of its supreme court to refer questions to the Court as required under the Treaty, as well as the absence of any regulations in Sweden governing the procedure for making preliminary references. However, the Swedish government gave sufficient assurances of future conduct to dissuade the Commission from bringing an enforcement action before the Court.

D. MEMBER STATE NONCOMPLIANCE WITH ECJ RULINGS

As previously noted, Member States usually comply with Court judgments in infringement actions, although sometimes slowly due to administrative complications or political opposition. Naturally, the Commission exerts pressure to try to achieve compliance. Occasionally the delay becomes so great, or the political opposition so strong, that the Commission decides to return to the Court.

The original EEC Treaty did not provide any specific sanctions for Member State noncompliance with ECJ judgments. It was therefore not clear what either the Commission or the Court could or should do about that.

1. THE OBLIGATION TO COMPLY

COMMISSION v. ITALY

(Second art treasures)
Case 48/71, [1972] ECR 529.

[In 1968, in the *First art treasures* case, infra page 422, the Court held that an export duty levied on art and archaeological works leaving Italy violated the Treaty provisions guaranteeing free movement of goods. Italy failed to take corrective action, due principally to the fact that its parliament was unable to decide how otherwise to protect the works. The Commission then sued Italy again on the basis of the then EEC Treaty Article 171 (later renumbered as EC Treaty Article 228(1), and now TFEU Article 260(1)), according to which Member States must "take the necessary measures to comply with the [Court's judgment]." Italy's defense was that repeal of tax was "outside the control of the competent authorities" (i.e., the executive branch could not compel the parliament to act).]

5 Without having to examine the validity of such arguments, it suffices for the Court to observe that [in the *first Art treasures* judgment, it held that Italy's export duty violated the Treaty]....

6 Since it is a question of a directly applicable Community rule, the argument that the infringement can be terminated only by the adoption of measures constitutionally appropriate to repeal the provision establishing the tax would amount to saying that the application of the Community rule is subject to the law of each Member State and more precisely that this application is impossible where it is contrary to a national law.

7 In the present case the effect of Community law, declared as *res judicata* in respect of the Italian Republic, is a prohibition having the full force of law on the competent national authorities against applying a national rule recognized as incompatible with the Treaty and, if the circumstances so require, an obligation on them to take all appropriate measures to enable Community law to be fully applied.

* * *

10 It is therefore necessary to find that in not complying with the judgment of the Court [in the *first Art treasures* judgment] the Italian Republic has failed to fulfill the obligations imposed on it by Article 171 of the Treaty.

NOTES AND QUESTIONS

1. How does the judgment in *second Art treasures* enhance the enforcement of EU law as compared to the *first Art treasures* judgment? In any case, the judgment represents a significant decision on the primacy of EU law. In language that it was later to echo in the *Simmenthal II* case, supra page 247, the Court said:

> The attainment of the objectives of the Community requires that the rules of Community law ... are fully applicable at the same time and with identical effects over the whole territory of the Community without the Member States being able to place any obstacle in the way.

> The grant made by Member States to the Community of rights and powers [under] the Treaty involves a definitive limitation on their sovereign rights and no provisions whatsoever of national law may be invoked to override this limitation.

[1972] ECR at 532.

2. What should the Italian government do in view of the Court's judgment and the Italian legislature's continued inaction. Consider ¶ 7 of the judgment.

3. The *Mutton and lamb* case, excerpted supra page 395, proved to be an even more serious challenge to the Court's authority. France openly refused to follow the judgment of the Court striking down the French quotas and

charges on British lamb imports, thus creating a political crisis which received great publicity and contributed to some degree to the "Europessimism" of the early 1980s. The French government took the position that it would maintain its restrictions until the Council voted an agricultural support program favorable to French farmers and opposed at the time by the UK. The Commission then brought a new round of enforcement proceedings, but the Court declined to authorize interim relief against France, stating that France already had a duty to comply with the initial judgment (Cases 24, 97/80R, [1980] ECR 1319). After nearly a year of bitter dispute, the European Council resolved the crisis through a policy compromise of the agricultural and budgetary issues involved.

2.   SANCTIONS FOR MEMBER STATE NON-COMPLIANCE

Out of the not infrequent failures of Member States and the rare acts of outright defiance arose proposals to amend EEC Treaty Article 171 to provide for sanctions against delinquent and, even more so, recalcitrant States. The Maastricht Treaty, effective 1993, finally took that step. A new paragraph 2 was added to Article 171 authorizing the Commission, when faced with Member State non-compliance with an ECJ judgment in an enforcement action, to issue another reasoned opinion indicating how the State concerned had failed to comply with the initial Court judgment. If the State still did not "take the necessary measures" within a time period set by the Commission, the latter could return to the Court, recommending that a "lump sum or penalty payment" be imposed. If the Court agreed that the State has not complied with its judgment, it could then impose such a sanction. Article 171(2) was later renumbered by the Amsterdam Treaty as EC Treaty Article 228(2). TFEU Article 260(2) retains the provision, with some minor rewording.

A Commission Memorandum, O.J. C 242/6 (Aug. 21, 1996), set out its basic policy for determining when and how it would exercise its authority to request sanctions. The Commission stated that it would usually seek an ongoing penalty, setting the level in view of (a) the seriousness of the infringement (citing basic rights violations and environmental pollution as likely serious violations), (b) its duration, and (c) the need to ensure that the penalty is an effective deterrent to further infringement. Subsequently, in a Communication, O.J. C 63/2 (Feb. 28, 1997), the Commission indicated that its normal penalty would be set at 500 ecu per day, subject to increase for especially serious or longstanding infringements. (The ecu was an artificial Community currency that preceded the Euro.) Moreover, the Commission intended to multiply the normal penalty by a "co-efficient" fixed as a function of each State's GDP (running from 1 for Luxembourg to 26.4 for Germany).

In 2000 the Court rendered its first sanctions judgment.

COMMISSION v. GREECE

(Kouroupitos pollution II)
Case C–387/97, [2000] ECR I–5047.

[Following complaints of severe pollution of the Kouroupitos River in Crete caused by military, industrial and hospital waste, the Commission sued Greece and secured a 1992 Court judgment, Commission v. Greece (Kouroupitos pollution I), Case C–45/91, [1992] ECR I–2509. For several years the Commission sought unsuccessfully to obtain Greece's compliance with the judgment. In 1997, the Commission sued Greece again under EC Treaty Article 228(2) asking the Court to impose a daily penalty of 24,600 ecu from the date of the Court's judgment until Greece fully complied.

On the merits, the Court observed that Greece had admitted that the waste pollution was ongoing, that a new pollution-control installation was needed, and that it had not yet been built. Greece pleaded in defense public opposition and administrative and judicial challenges to the installation. Citing its doctrine that internal difficulties did not excuse violations, the Court rejected the argument. Although accepting that Greece had taken some remedial steps, the Court held that Greece had not complied with its 1992 judgment. This left the issue of sanctions.]

84 In the absence of provisions in the Treaty, the Commission may adopt guidelines for determining how the lump sums or penalty payments which it intends to propose to the Court are calculated, so as, in particular, to ensure equal treatment between the Member States.

[The Court then summarized the Commission's 1996 Memorandum and 1997 Communication.]

89 It should be stressed that these suggestions of the Commission cannot bind the Court. It is expressly stated in the third subparagraph of Article 171(2) of the Treaty that the Court, if it finds that the Member State concerned has not complied with its judgment . . . may impose a lump sum or a penalty payment on it. However, the suggestions are a useful point of reference.

* * *

92 [A]s the Commission has suggested, the basic criteria which must be taken into account in order to ensure that penalty payments have coercive force and Community law is applied uniformly and effectively are, in principle, the duration of the infringement, its degree of seriousness and the ability of the Member State to pay. In applying those criteria, regard should be had in particular to the effects of failure to comply on private and public interests and to the urgency of getting the Member State concerned to fulfil its obligations.

93 In the present case, having regard to the nature of the breaches of obligations, which continue to this day, a penalty payment is the means best suited to the circumstances.

94   As regards the seriousness of the infringements and in particular the effects of failure to comply on private and public interests, the obligation to dispose of waste without endangering human health and without harming the environment forms part of the very objectives of Community environmental policy as set out in [EC Treaty Article 174, now TFEU Article 191]. The failure to comply with the obligation resulting from Article 4 of Directive 75/442 could, by the very nature of that obligation, endanger human health directly and harm the environment and must, in the light of the other obligations, be regarded as particularly serious.

95   The failure to fulfil the more specific obligations of drawing up a waste disposal plan and drawing up, and keeping up to date, plans for the disposal of toxic and dangerous waste, imposed by Article 6 of Directive 75/442 and Article 12 of Directive 78/319 respectively, must be regarded as serious. . . .

* * *

98   As regards the duration of the infringement, suffice it to state that it is considerable, even if the starting date be that on which the Treaty on European Union entered into force and not the date on which the judgment in Case C–45/91 was delivered.

99   Having regard to all the foregoing considerations, Greece should be ordered to pay to the Commission, into the account [of] EC own resources, a penalty payment of 20,000 euros for each day of delay in implementing the measures necessary to comply with the judgment in Case C–45/91, from delivery of the present judgment until the judgment in Case C–45/91 has been complied with.

NOTES AND QUESTIONS

1.   *Kouroupitos pollution II* was the first occasion on which the Court imposed a fine under what is now TFEU Article 260(2). Note that the Court acknowledged the utility of the Commission guidelines for calculating sanctions on the basis of an infringement's duration and seriousness, and a State's ability to pay (¶ 92), but still insisted that only the Court itself could determine the sanctions that were called for (¶ 89). The Commission made two other applications to the court for fines (Commission v. France (Nightwork by women), Case C–224/99, and Commission v. Greece (Diploma recognition), Case C–197/98), but both cases were subsequently dropped.

2.   The next judgment imposing sanctions came in Commission v. Spain (Bathing water standards), Case C–278/01, [2003] ECR I–505, where the Court imposed a daily penalty payment upon Spain for failure to comply with a 1976 environmental protection directive that set quality standards for in-land bathing water (the British term for water suitable for swimming). Because quality standards under the directive are verified annually, the Court found it necessary to modify the usual penalty formula. The penalty was set at 624,150 euros per year for each 1% of in-land bathing water that did not meet the directive's standards.

In its next judgment, the Court heightened the impact of sanctions by holding that a lump sum payment and periodic penalties could be awarded concurrently.

COMMISSION v. FRANCE

(Sanctions for violation of fisheries rules)
Case C–304/02, [2005] ECR I–6263.

[In 1991, the Court ruled that France had failed to establish the controls needed to comply with Common Fishing Policy Regulations adopted in 1982 and 1987. In 1996, the Commission sent France a reasoned opinion alleging that it still had not put in place controls adequate to ensure that fishing nets met minimum mesh size standards and that undersized fish were not offered for sale. In 2000, after several years of further exchanges with France, the Commission sent France a supplementary reasoned opinion, reiterating its position and citing the inspections it has conducted and on which it was relying. In 2002, the Commission finally sued for sanctions.

The Court determined that the Commission had presented substantial and persuasive evidence from inspectors' reports that France had not complied with the initial judgment (¶¶ 47–62). The Court agreed with the Commission that France had not established a system of "penalties that are effective, proportionate and deterrent" (¶¶ 69–73), and that the failure continued to date (¶ 74).

The Court then turned to the sanctions issue. Because EC Treaty Article 228(2) referred to sanctions as a "lump sum or penalty payment," the question arose whether "or" was to be read as disjunctive, making the two sanctions alternative, or as permitting a cumulation of the two sanctions. Of course, the Court examined all of the language versions of the text (e.g., the French "*ou*", the German "*oder*"). France and twelve other Member States submitted briefs contending that "or" must be read as disjunctive, requiring the Court to choose between the two forms of sanctions, while the Commission and four States considered that they could be imposed concurrently.]

80   The procedure laid down in Article 228(2) EC has the objective of inducing a defaulting Member State to comply with a judgment establishing a breach of obligations and thereby of ensuring that Community law is in fact applied. The measures provided for by that provision, namely a lump sum and a penalty payment, are both intended to achieve this objective.

81   Application of each of those measures depends on their respective ability to meet the objective pursued according to the circumstances of the case. While the imposition of a penalty payment seems particularly suited to inducing a Member State to put an end as soon as possible to a breach of obligations which, in the absence of such a measure, would tend to persist, the imposition of a lump sum is based more on assessment of the effects on public and private interests of the failure

of the Member State concerned to comply with its obligations, in particular where the breach has persisted for a long period since the judgment which initially established it.

82   That being so, recourse to both types of penalty provided for in Article 228(2) EC is not precluded, in particular where the breach of obligations both has continued for a long period and is inclined to persist.

83   [The conjunction "or"] may, linguistically, have an alternative or cumulative sense and must therefore be read in the context in which it is used. In light of the objective pursued by Article 228 EC, the conjunction "or" ... must be understood as being used in a cumulative sense.

Imposition of a penalty payment

[The Court observed that the Commission had requested 316,500 euros per day as an on-going penalty payment until France complied adequately with the 1992 judgment, while France contended that it had already complied.]

* * *

104   [A]s the Commission has suggested in its communication of 28 February 1997, the basic criteria which must be taken into account in order to ensure that penalty payments have coercive force and Community law is applied uniformly and effectively are, in principle, the duration of the infringement, its degree of seriousness and the ability of the Member State to pay. In applying those criteria, regard should be had in particular to the effects of failure to comply on private and public interests and to the urgency of getting the Member State concerned to fulfil its obligations.

105   As regards the seriousness of the infringement and, in particular, the effects of failure to comply on private and public interests, it is to be remembered that one of the key elements of the common fisheries policy consists in rational and responsible exploitation of aquatic resources on a sustainable basis, in appropriate economic and social conditions. In this context, the protection of juvenile fish proves decisive for reestablishing stocks. Failure to comply with the technical measures of conservation prescribed by the common policy, in particular the requirements regarding the minimum size of fish, therefore constitutes a serious threat to the maintenance of certain species and certain fishing grounds and jeopardises pursuit of the fundamental objective of the common fisheries policy.

106   Since the administrative measures adopted by the French authorities have not been implemented in an effective manner, they cannot reduce the seriousness of the breach established.

107   Having regard to those factors, the coefficient of 10 (on a scale of 1 to 20) is therefore an appropriate reflection of the degree of seriousness of the infringement.

108   As regards the duration of the infringement, suffice it to state that it is considerable. . . . Accordingly, the coefficient of 3 (on a scale of 1 to 3) suggested by the Commission appears appropriate.

109   The Commission's suggestion of multiplying a basic amount by a coefficient of 21.1 based on the gross domestic product of the French Republic and on the number of votes which it has in the Council is an appropriate way of reflecting that Member State's ability to pay, while keeping the variation between Member States within a reasonable range.

110   Multiplying the basic amount of euros 500 by the coefficients of 21.1 (for ability to pay), 10 (for the seriousness of the infringement) and 3 (for the duration of the infringement) gives a sum of euros 316,500 per day.

111   As regards the frequency of the penalty payment, account should, however, be taken of the fact that the French authorities have adopted administrative measures which could [achieve adequate compliance with the 1992 judgment, but it is not possible for] their impact to be perceived immediately. It follows that any finding that the infringement has come to an end could be made only after a period allowing an overall assessment to be made of the results obtained.

112   Having regard to those considerations, the penalty payment must be imposed not on a daily basis, but on a half-yearly basis.

113   In light of all of the foregoing, the French Republic should be ordered to pay to the Commission, into the account "European Community own resources", a penalty payment of 182.5 x euros 316,500, that is to say of euros 57,761,250, for each period of six months from delivery of the present judgment at the end of which the judgment in Case C–64/88 Commission v. France has not yet been fully complied with.

Imposition of a lump sum

114   In a situation such as that which is the subject of the present judgment, in light of the fact that the breach of obligations has persisted for a long period since the judgment which initially established it and of the public and private interests at issue, it is essential to order payment of a lump sum.

115   The specific circumstances of the case are fairly assessed by setting the amount of the lump sum which the French Republic will have to pay at euros 20,000,000.

NOTES AND QUESTIONS

1.   The Court employed a teleological mode of interpretation to reach its conclusion, finding that the result it reached best comported with the objective of Article 228(2), namely to achieve compliance with Court judgments (¶ 83). Obviously, however, the Treaty drafters could have used an "and/or" (in French, "*et/ou*") formula, which would have disposed of the issue.

2.   The Court decision to impose a 20 million euro lump sum fine on top of an ongoing penalty of nearly 58 million euros every six months received great attention in the media. The Court may have been prompted not only by the fact of French inaction over a long period, but also by its concern over the fate of the EU's Common Fisheries Policy. The stock of many types of fish in the EU's fishing zone had fallen drastically in recent years, and protecting juvenile fish was considered crucial to restoring adequate supplies. The Commission finally concluded in November 2006 that France had taken the administrative measures necessary and ended the hefty periodic penalty (after collecting the penalty that had accrued).

3.   The Commission thought it necessary to issue a supplementary Communication in 2005, indicating that it would frequently request the Court to impose both forms of sanctions in an effort to induce States to comply more quickly with ECJ judgments. The Commission stated that it might in some cases request the Court to impose a lump sum penalty on a State even after it had finally complied, where the seriousness of the infringement and the prior delay warranted this.

4.   In the next judgment, Commission v. France (Penalties for tardy revision of product liability rules), Case C–177/04, [2006] ECR I–1931, the Court easily concluded that a 2004 French amendment to the Civil Code failed to comply fully with the Court's judgment of 2002 holding that France had not properly transposed a 1985 directive harmonizing Member State product liability rules. (For discussion of the directive, see Chapter 33 infra.) In fixing the sanctions, the Court decided that only an ongoing penalty was required because France had partially complied and the remaining infringement was not a particularly serious one. However, the Court increased the Commission's proposed penalty of 13,715 euros per day to 31,650 euros per day, in view of the length of time since the Court's initial judgment. Note that in ¶ 60 the Court refers to the possible imposition of a "penalty payment *and/or* a lump sum" (emphasis added).

COMMISSION v. FRANCE

(Sanctions for violation of GMO rules)
Case C–121/07, [2008] ECR I–9159.

[In 2001, the Parliament and Council adopted Directive 2001/18 harmonizing Member State rules regulating the use of genetically-modified organisms (GMOs) and the subsequent marketing of GMO-based food products. France failed to implement the directive on time, and the Commission in 2005 won a judgment against France on that account. Adoption of the necessary draft legislation by the French Parliament was delayed, in part due to substantial popular opposition. In 2007, the Commission took France back to the Court, upon which France almost immediately complied, enacting a series of decrees. Although the Commission initially regarded the decrees as unsatisfactory, at the oral hearing before the Court it accepted them. Due to France's eventual compliance, the Court declined to impose an ongoing penalty. On the other hand, the Court considered that France's delay in complying violated its duty under

EC Treaty Article 228(1) (now TFEU Article 260), and therefore turned to the possibility of imposing a lump sum penalty.]

64 If the Court decides to impose a penalty payment or lump sum payment, it must do so, in exercising its discretion, in a manner that is appropriate to the circumstances and proportionate both to the breach that has been established and the ability to pay of the Member State concerned. More specifically, as regards the imposition of a lump sum payment, the relevant factors to be taken into account include, in particular, factors such as how long the breach of obligations has persisted since the judgment which initially established it was delivered and the public and private interests involved.

* * *

66 First of all, ... as the Commission has observed, judgment has already been given against [France] in a number of cases, based on Article 226 EC, finding that it was in breach of its obligations as it had failed correctly to transpose directives adopted in [the specific field of GMOs].

* * *

69 As submitted by the Commission, where a Member State repeatedly engages in unlawful conduct in such a manner in a specific sector governed by Community rules, this may be an indication that effective prevention of future repetition of similar infringements of Community law may require the adoption of a dissuasive measure, such as a lump sum payment.

70 Secondly, with regard to the length of time for which the breach persisted after judgment was delivered in Case C–419/03, there is nothing ... that can justify the considerable delay that occurred ... in actually transposing Directive 2001/18, which, in essence, simply required national legislative provisions to be adopted.

* * *

72 As to [France's argument], that the outdoor cultivation of GMOs has provoked and continues to provoke violent demonstrations in France, entailing, *inter alia*, the uprooting of plants, and that the delay in implementing the judgment in Case C–419/03 was attributable, in particular, to the concern that guidance should be given to the Parliament in its work, ... according to settled case-law, a Member State cannot plead provisions, practices or situations prevailing in its domestic legal order to justify failure to observe obligations arising under Community law. In particular, even on the assumption that the social unrest referred to by the French Republic is in fact attributable in part to the implementation of Community rules, a Member State may not plead difficulties of implementation ..., including difficulties relating to opposition on the part of certain individuals, to justify a

failure to comply with obligations and time-limits laid down by Community law.

74   Moreover, . . . the rules laid down in that directive are based on the precautionary principle and the principle that preventive action should be taken, which are fundamental principles of environmental protection, as referred to in particular in [EC Treaty Article 174(2), now TFEU Article 191(2)].

77   As previously stated, where failure to comply with a judgment of the Court is likely to harm the environment and endanger human health, the protection of which is, indeed, one of the Community's environmental policy objectives, as is apparent from Article 174 EC, such a breach is of a particularly serious nature.

78   The same applies, in principle, where the free movement of goods continues to be hindered, in breach of Community law, notwithstanding the existence of a judgment of the Court establishing an infringement in that respect.

[The Court imposed a lump-sum fine of 10 million euros (¶ 87).]

NOTES AND QUESTIONS

1.   This was the first time the Court imposed a lump-sum fine even after a State had complied with a prior judgment. Not only in France, but elsewhere in Europe, there is great popular opposition to the marketing of agricultural products derived from GMO–modified plants (so-called "Frankenstein food"). Should the Court have considered this as a factor justifying a lower fine?

2.   Why do you suppose States persist in failing to comply with a judgment of the Court judgment when they risk steep fines in doing so? A State's executive branch cannot, of course, control the speed with which its parliament enacts legislation, especially when the text is complicated and controversial. Should the Court take this into consideration? Or is the Court's approach purely an application of the principle of Treaty primacy?

E.   MEMBER STATE ENFORCEMENT ACTIONS AGAINST OTHER MEMBER STATES

EC Treaty Article 227 (now TFEU Article 259) authorizes a Member State to initiate enforcement proceedings against another Member State. Enforcement actions by the Commission and other Member States do not however follow entirely parallel courses. A complaining State may not proceed formally in the Court of Justice without first "bring[ing] the matter before the Commission," and giving the latter three months in which to solicit the oral and written views of each of the States concerned and to issue a reasoned opinion. If the Commission finds that a violation has occurred, it may proceed to the Court of Justice just as if it had initiated the matter itself. On the other hand, if the Commission fails to issue a reasoned opinion within the prescribed time, concludes that no violation occurred, or otherwise fails to act, the complainant State is then free itself to go before the Court.

Thus far very few such actions have been brought. In the first, France v. United Kingdom, Case 141/78, [1979] ECR 2923, France complained that the UK had failed to enforce against British fishing interests an EU enactment regulating the dimensions of fishing net mesh. France, on whose side the Commission intervened, ultimately prevailed in its action against the UK. In the second, Belgium unsuccessfully sued Spain for violating free movement of goods rules by requiring that wine produced in Spain's La Rioja region be bottled only there (and not exported in containers for bottling in Belgium) in order to qualify as Rioja wine as a designation of origin. See Belgium v. Spain (Rioja wine), excerpted at page 770. In the third, Spain accused the UK of failing to fulfil its obligations relating to direct elections to the European Parliament (concerning the voting rights for Gibraltar residents), by enacting the "European Parliament (Representation) Act 2003." Spain v. United Kingdom, Case C–145/04, [2006] ECR I–7917. The Court found against Spain.

The relative paucity of State-to-State confrontations in the Court of Justice is understandable. Even without the required referral of Member State complaints to the Commission, it is all but certain that the Commission will become involved in controversies that pit Member States directly against one another on account of alleged Community law infringements. The Commission is very likely to respond favorably to Member State complaints that have substantial merit; perhaps more important, it has proved exceptionally adept at bringing about the amicable settlement of interstate disputes. An aggrieved Member State may of course actively support the Commission prosecution as, for example, the UK did in the Commission's action against France (supra page 381) for its continued ban on the import of British beef.

PART 3

THE COMMON MARKET, THE INTERNAL MARKET AND THE FOUR FREEDOMS

■ ■ ■

Part 3 presents the heart of the substantive law of the European Community, namely, the rules relating to the EC Treaty's initial goal of a common market, essentially based upon the well-known "four freedoms" (sometimes called the "pillars of the Community"): free movement of goods; free movement of persons (especially workers); freedom to provide commercial and professional services, together with the right of establishment; and free movement of capital. Each of the first three of the four freedoms is the subject of a chapter in Part 3 which sets out the relevant Treaty provisions, the influential Court of Justice doctrines, and key legislative measures. Later, in Part 6, a chapter on free movement of capital is presented in tandem with one on the Economic and Monetary Union (EMU).

The Lisbon Treaty has made almost no changes in the prior EC Treaty provisions on the "four freedoms," apart from replacing "Community" with "Union," and occasionally giving Parliament an equal share with the Council in the related legislative process.

One of the most important chapters in Part 3 is Chapter 14 on the internal market and its harmonization of laws program. As described in Chapter 1, the early 1980s were marked by diminished progress during the period of "Europessimism." Dynamic leadership by the Commission under the Presidency of Jacques Delors led to renewed legislative efforts in the internal market program from 1985 to 1992. The remarkable success of that program led in turn to the adoption of the Maastricht Treaty, which, i.a., further facilitated legislative efforts to achieve the internal market and created the EMU.

The Maastricht Treaty also introduced a vital new concept, citizenship of the Union. Chapter 17 describes the scope and consequences of citizenship of the Union, Court doctrines elaborating upon the concept, and recent legislation to promote rights of residence and equal treatment

417

for citizens. The Lisbon Treaty reiterated the prior Treaty provisions on citizenship of the Union. Chapter 17 also covers legislative measures to achieve an area of freedom, security and justice, added by the Treaty of Amsterdam in May 1999.

CHAPTER 12

FREE MOVEMENT OF GOODS: DUTIES, CHARGES, INTERNAL TAXES

■ ■ ■

Within the "four freedoms," the free movement of goods is undoubtedly the key concept. Not only is the free flow of commercial and industrial products throughout the Community the most tangible illustration of an integrated market, but the principles that have been elaborated in this field have significantly shaped those applicable to the free movement of persons, services and capital.

Free movement of goods itself can be analytically divided into two parts. This chapter's section A deals with the elimination of Member State customs duties and analogous charges. Section B then describes the elimination of discriminatory or protectionist internal taxes. Chapter 13 covers the elimination of non-tariff quantitative restrictions and the numerous analogous barriers to the free flow of goods.

In the US Constitution, the Interstate Commerce Clause serves a function analogous to that of the free movement of goods principle—analogous, but by no means precisely parallel. In the US constitutional framework, Congress has among its enumerated powers the ability "to regulate * * * commerce * * * among the several States." The US Constitution does not expressly set as a goal the free flow of goods between the states, but the power to regulate includes the power to facilitate interstate trade by limiting state restrictions upon it, and the Commerce Clause has historically served that purpose.

The central issue in European Union law is whether a Member State regulation or practice constitutes an impermissible restriction of free movement of goods. The analogous issue in the US, commonly referred to as that of the dormant or negative Commerce Clause, is whether restrictions on trade resulting from state regulation should be struck down because they impede free interstate commerce in a particular sector. Another major issue in US federal/state relations is the preemptive effect of federal legislation upon state legislation in the same area. This is also an important concern of EU law, and is analyzed in Chapter 15C.

419

A. CUSTOMS DUTIES AND CHARGES HAVING EQUIVALENT EFFECT

The Treaty coverage of free movement of goods begins with Article 9(1) in the 1957 European Economic Community Treaty, later renumbered in 1999 by the Treaty of Amsterdam as ECT Article 23, and now the Treaty of Lisbon's TFEU Article 28:

> The Community [now Union] shall be based upon a customs union which shall cover all trade in goods and which shall involve the prohibition between Member States of customs duties on imports and exports and of all charges having equivalent effect, and the adoption of a common customs tariff in their relations with third countries.

Note at the outset that the article regulates both external and internal trade. It mandates a "common customs tariff" for products coming from countries outside the Community. With regard to internal trade, the article requires the prohibition of import and export duties between Member States. EECT Article 9 was supplemented by EECT Article 10 (later ECT Article 24, and now TFEU Article 29), which provides that products imported into the Community "shall be considered to be in free circulation" as soon as import formalities are completed and customs duties paid. In articles now deleted, the Treaty initially set a transitional period of twelve years for the removal of customs duties between States. Whenever new Member States have joined the Community later, similar transitional periods were set for certain products by each Treaty of Accession, but all such periods have now expired.

The Lisbon TFEU has made virtually no change in the prior substantive provisions of the EC Treaty concerning the four freedoms. ECT Articles 23–25 are replicated in TFEU Articles 28–30, which only substitute "Union" for "Community." The Court judgments discussed hereinafter refer to the ECT Articles, but would undoubtedly reach the same result if a current case presented the same issue under the TFEU.

The removal of customs duties between Member States is inherent in the concept of a customs union. Less obvious is the prohibition of "all charges having equivalent effect" in ECT Article 25, now TFEU Article 30. This may well have been intended only to cover disguised duties, but, as will be seen, the Court of Justice has broadly construed this concept to eliminate virtually all charges, fees or costs imposed by Member States on goods in trade between the States.

1. WHAT IS A CHARGE EQUIVALENT TO A DUTY?

SOCIAAL FONDS v. SA CH. BRACHFELD

Cases 2 & 3/69, [1969] ECR 211.

[In 1962, Belgium required all importers of uncut diamonds to contribute to the diamond workers' social benefit fund, with the contribution calculated as 0.33% of the value of the uncut diamonds. When the fund took action against 200 importers to collect unpaid contributions, they challenged the 1962 law. The trial court in a preliminary reference proceeding asked the Court of Justice whether the 1962 Belgian law constituted a charge equivalent to a duty in violation of ECT Articles 23 and 25 (now TFEU Article 28 and 30).]

7/10 The position of [Article 23] at the beginning of that Part of the Treaty reserved for the "Foundations of the Community" * * * is sufficient to show the fundamental role of the prohibitions laid down therein.

11/14 In prohibiting the imposition of customs duties, the Treaty does not distinguish between goods according to whether or not they enter into competition with the products of the importing country. Thus, the purpose of the abolition of customs barriers is not merely to eliminate their protective nature, [but] to ensure the free movement of goods. It follows from the system as a whole and from the general and absolute nature of the prohibition of any customs duty applicable to goods moving between Member States that customs duties are prohibited independently of any consideration of the purpose for which they were introduced and the destination of the revenue obtained therefrom. The justification for this prohibition is based on the fact that any pecuniary charge—however small—imposed on goods by reason of the fact that they cross a frontier constitutes an obstacle to the movement of such goods.

15/18 * * * Consequently, any pecuniary charge, however small and whatever its designation and mode of application, which is imposed unilaterally on domestic or foreign goods by reason of the fact that they cross a frontier, and which is not a customs duty in the strict sense, constitutes a charge having equivalent effect within the meaning of Articles [23 and 25] of the Treaty, even if it is not imposed for the benefit of the State, is not discriminatory or protective in effect or if the product on which the charge is imposed is not in competition with any domestic product.

19/21 It follows * * * that the prohibition of new customs duties or charges having equivalent effect, linked to the principle of the free movement of goods, constitutes a fundamental rule which, without prejudice to the other provisions of the Treaty, does not permit of any exceptions. * * *

22/23   The provisions of the Treaty laying down the abovementioned prohibitions impose precise and clearly-defined obligations on Member States which do not require any subsequent intervention by Community or national authorities for their implementation. For this reason, these provisions directly confer rights on individuals concerned.

24/26   [The prohibition] of any new pecuniary charge to goods circulating within the Community when they cross a frontier [applies] irrespective of the nationality of the traders who might be placed at a disadvantage by such measures. Thus, * * * there is no justification for a distinction to be made according to whether the measures in question adversely affect certain Member States and their nationals, or all the citizens of the Community, or only the nationals of the Member State which was responsible for the measures in question.

NOTES AND QUESTIONS

1.   How broad is the definition of a "charge equivalent to a duty"? Wouldn't one normally think a charge to benefit retired or injured diamond cutters has nothing to do with a duty? Why did the Court consider it immaterial that this charge did not bring in revenues to Belgium or protect a Belgian industry, the two usual motives for adopting a customs duty?

2.   Belgium does not have diamond mines. If Belgium produced a significant quantity of diamonds, and the benefit fund contribution was imposed both on imported and domestic uncut diamonds, should it be evaluated under ECT Article 23? After reading section B, consider whether the contribution might violate ECT Article 90 (now TFEU Article 110).

3.   Another leading judgment is Commission v. Italy (First art treasures), Case 7/68, [1968] ECR 423, which involved a charge equivalent to an export duty, forbidden by ECT Article 25. Since 1939, Italy had imposed a substantial charge upon the export of works of art and archaeological treasures, as a means of encouraging their retention in Italy. The Court of Justice held that Italy's motive and the absence of a revenue-raising intent were both irrelevant, since the charge operated as a restriction on exports.

The judgment also defined the term "goods" upon which duties fall. Italy had argued that this meant consumer or commercial goods, and therefore wouldn't cover works of art. The Court held that "goods" meant any "products which can be valued in money and which are capable, as such, of forming the subject of commercial transactions." [1968] ECR at 428.

4.   Undoubtedly the most important type of "charge equivalent to a duty" is the fee charged for the health inspection of imports of slaughtered meat, fruits and vegetables, or living animals and plants. Assuming for the moment that such an inspection itself does not violate the Treaty (an issue covered on page 447), the question is whether a fee charged for the inspection violates the free movement of goods.

This has given rise to a complex body of case law. In 1972, the Court held that health inspection fees levied only on imported products constituted a charge in violation of ECT Article 23, even though some other inspection fee was levied on similar domestic products. SpA Marimex v. Italian Finance Administration, Case 29/72, [1972] ECR 1309. Later, the Court held that a State could not justify the fee on the ground that the inspection is necessary to protect general health, stating that the public should bear the cost and not the importer. Bresciani v. Amministrazione Italiana delle Finanze, Case 87/75, [1976] ECR 129.

In many sectors, the Community has set up a system of Community-wide health and safety inspections for animals, plants and meat or plant products. In Bauhuis v. Netherlands, Case 46/76, [1977] ECR 5, the Court held that a fee for the health inspection of bovine animals, required by a Community agricultural regulation before export to another State, did not constitute an illegal charge equivalent to an export duty, provided the fee covered only the actual cost of the inspection.

CARBONATI APUANI v. COMMUNE DI CARRARA

Case C–72/03, [2004] ECR I–8027.

[The municipality of Carrara in Italy imposed a tax on the export of its famous marble outside the municipality, but not on its use within the municipality. A buyer of marble challenged the tax as one equivalent to an export duty. The court asked the Court of Justice whether this should be the case.]

18   [T]he tax at issue is applied to Carrara marble when it is transported across the territorial boundaries of the Comune di Carrara. The chargeable event thus consists of the crossing of those boundaries. Marble used within the Comune di Carrara is exempt from the tax, precisely because it is used locally and not on account of objective criteria that might apply equally to marble transported out of the municipality. Because of those factors, the tax at issue cannot be described as internal taxation within the meaning of Article 90 EC [see section B infra].

19   The next question to be considered is whether a tax such as the marble tax constitutes a charge having effect equivalent to a customs duty for the purposes of Article 23 EC.

* * *

22   [T]he justification for the prohibition of customs duties and charges having equivalent effect is that any pecuniary charges imposed on goods by reason of the fact that they cross a frontier constitutes an obstacle to the movement of such goods. The very principle of a customs union, as provided for by Article 23 EC, requires the free movement of goods to be ensured within the union generally, not in trade between Member States alone, but more broadly throughout the territory of the customs union. If Articles 23 EC and 25 EC make express reference only to trade between Member States, that is because the framers of the Treaty took it for granted that there were no

charges exhibiting the features of a customs duty in existence within the Member States.

23   Again, it is to be borne in mind that in 1986 the Single European Act added to the EEC Treaty Article [14], which set as an aim the establishment of an internal market before 31 December 1992. Article 14(2) EC defines the internal market as 'an area without internal frontiers in which the free movement of goods, persons, services and capital is ensured', without drawing any distinction between inter-State frontiers and frontiers within a State.

NOTES AND QUESTIONS

1.   This is a relatively rare case in which a charge on exports, rather than imports, is considered to be one equivalent to a customs duty. Note that the Court considered it irrelevant that the tax was imposed on marble exported elsewhere in Italy, as well as to other States, and relied in ¶ 23 upon the definition of the internal market set out in ECT Article 14(2), now in TFEU Article 26 (2). The Court also considered it to be "immaterial" that the tax was imposed by a municipality, rather than Italy.

2.   Later in the judgment the Court considered the municipality's request to limit the retroactivity of the judgment out of its concern for the "serious financial consequences" of many refunds. The Court accepted the request only in part, barring only refund claims prior to July 16, 1992. The Court held that a judgment on that date, Legros, Case C–163/90, [1992] ECR I–4625 constituted a precedent that should have enabled the municipality to realize that its tax violated ECT Article 23. For a general discussion of the retroactivity of Court judgments, see Chapter 5B.

2.   ARE EMERGENCY DUTIES PERMISSIBLE?

How absolute is the ban on intra-community tariffs? Can ECT Article 25 be construed to allow an exception when a Member State, allegedly on an emergency basis, temporarily imposes a customs duty on goods from other Member States?

SOCIÉTÉ LES COMMISSIONAIRES RÉUNIS v. RECEVEUR DES DOUANES

Cases 80 & 81/77, [1978] ECR 927.

[In 1975, France imposed an emergency duty on Italian wine. France claimed it had the power to do so under the Community agricultural policy Regulation 816/70 governing the market in wine. That regulation contained a national safeguard clause which authorized Member States, in order to "avoid disturbances on their markets, to take measures that may limit imports from another Member State."

Following a Commission complaint, France repealed its decree. Plaintiffs had paid the duty on Italian wine while the decree was in force and sued for a refund. The trial court asked the Court of Justice, in an Article 234 proceeding, whether the safeguard clause of Regulation 816/70 was "contrary to the rules of the Treaty on the free movement of goods."]

14　The first question asks in substance whether Article 31(2) of Regulation No. 816/70 is valid in so far as it authorizes producer Member States to prescribe and to levy * * * charges having an effect equivalent to customs duties in intra-Community trade on a product * * *, in the present case table wine.

15　The answer to this question requires the interpretation of Article [32(2)] of the EEC Treaty which reads: "Save as otherwise provided in Articles [33 to 40], the rules laid down for the establishment of the Common Market shall apply to agricultural products."

* * *

17　[I]n the view of the Government of the French Republic, having regard to the place of agriculture in the Common Market, its characteristics and the specific objectives of the Common Agricultural Policy, this provision allows the Council to derogate from the rules of the Treaty in general and those on the free movement of goods in particular when such derogations are based on Articles [33 to 40] of the Treaty.

* * *

22　Article 2 of the EEC Treaty provides that it is by establishing a common market and progressively approximating the economic policies of Member States that the Community must promote throughout the Community development of economic activities, the raising of the standard of living and closer relations between the Member States.

23　As is stressed by Article [32(1)] of the Treaty, placed at the head of the title devoted to the Common Agricultural Policy, the Common Market shall extend to agriculture and trade in agricultural products.

24　The abolition between Member States of customs duties and charges having equivalent effect constitutes a fundamental principle of the Common Market applicable to all products and goods with the result that [citing prior cases] "any possible exception, which in any event must be strictly construed, must be clearly laid down". * * *

26　Therefore in order that the exception provided for in Article 32(2) should apply to the introduction of charges having an effect equivalent to customs duties in intra-Community trade at the end of the transitional period, it is necessary to find in Articles [33 to 40] a provision which either expressly or by necessary implication provides for or authorizes the introduction of such charges.

27　Articles [33 to 40] contain no provision of this nature.

* * *

29 Under Article [37(3)(b)] each common organization of the market "ensures conditions for trade within the Community similar to those existing in a national market".

* * *

35 It is clear * * * that the extensive powers, in particular of a sectorial and regional nature, granted to the Community institutions in the conduct of the Common Agricultural Policy must be exercised from the perspective of the unity of the market to the exclusion of any measure compromising the abolition between Member States of customs duties and quantitative restrictions or charges or measures having equivalent effect.

* * *

38 Therefore, Article 31(2) of Regulation No. 816/70 in so far as it authorizes producer Member States to prescribe and levy, in intra-Community trade in [wine], charges having an effect equivalent to customs duties, is incompatible with Article [25] * * * and is consequently invalid.

NOTES AND QUESTIONS

1. The Common Agricultural Policy (CAP), is certainly an important sphere of Community action. Does this case show that free movement of goods is more important than the CAP, or is the Court merely trying to interpret two Treaty chapters in a harmonious fashion? Can there ever be any basis for an emergency duty?

2. This is a "Treaty primacy" judgment in its important holding that the Council of Ministers cannot adopt legislation contrary to a Treaty provision. This "Treaty primacy" doctrine parallels the US Supreme Court's constitutional interpretation which invalidates laws of Congress when they violate the Constitution. Note that this aspect of "Treaty primacy" is not a self-evident principle. In fact, Advocate General Warner took the contrary view that the Council had the power to adopt the safeguard clause. This judgment complements those on Treaty primacy over Member State legislation in Chapter 7. We will note in later cases that the Court occasionally has repeated its doctrine that legislation cannot violate Treaty provisions. There is no reason to believe that the adoption of the Treaty of Lisbon will change this.

3. In striking contrast is Prudential Ins. Co. v. Benjamin, 328 U.S. 408, 66 S.Ct. 1142, 90 L.Ed. 1342 (1946), in which the Supreme Court held that Congress had the power to authorize a discriminatory state tax on insurance which was levied only upon out-of-state insurers, and not domestic insurers. The opinion held that the McCarren Act implicitly permitted state taxes on insurance operations to be discriminatory, and specifically stated that the Commerce Clause "enables Congress not only to promote but also to prohibit interstate commerce." Id. at 434, 66 S.Ct. at 1157. The Supreme Court first took this view in Wilkerson v. Rahrer, 140 U.S. 545, 11 S.Ct. 865, 35 L. Ed.

572 (1891), which held that Congress validly enacted a statute permitting a 'dry' state to prohibit the importation of alcohol from another state, observing that the Constitution did not guarantee freedom of inter-state commerce. Does the difference in language ("regulate commerce" versus ensuring "free movement of goods") account for the difference in attitude between the Court of Justice and the Supreme Court? Or do you suspect that the two courts are also influenced by their impression of how far market integration has been achieved in the US as compared to the Community?

B. DISCRIMINATORY OR PROTECTIVE INTERNAL TAXATION

Although both ECT Article 90 and its replacement TFEU Article 110 are located in a later chapter of the Treaty entitled "Tax Provisions," each one's obvious role is to further free movement of goods. In fact, ECT Article 90, which was inspired by corresponding GATT provisions, was intended to prevent Member States from replacing customs duties with protectionist indirect taxes. Article 90 states that:

> No Member State shall impose, directly or indirectly, on the products of other Member States any internal taxation of any kind in excess of that imposed directly or indirectly on similar domestic products.

> Furthermore, no Member State shall impose on the products of other Member States any internal taxation of such a nature as to afford indirect protection to other products.

Thus, the first paragraph prohibits discriminatory internal taxation and the second forbids protectionist internal taxation. TFEU Article 110 replicates both paragraphs of ECT Article 90.

Like ECT Article 25, Article 90 has been held to have direct effect. In Alfons Lütticke GmbH v. Hauptzollamt Saarlouis, Case 57/65, [1966] ECR 205 at 210, the Court said that the prohibition in paragraph one of Article 90 is "complete, legally perfect and consequently capable of producing direct effects on the legal relationships between the Member States and persons within their jurisdiction." The Court subsequently held in Firma Fink–Frucht GmbH v. Hauptzollamt Munchen, Case 27/67, [1968] ECR 223, that the second paragraph of Article 90 likewise had direct effect. This means that private parties can invoke both parts of Article 90 in national litigation to challenge a State's internal tax system. This is certainly also true for TFEU Article 110.

1. BASIC APPLICATION OF ECT ARTICLE 90 (NOW TFEU ARTICLE 110)

The most common types of internal taxes relating to goods and services are value added taxes levied at stages in the production and sale of most consumer products (analogous to sales taxes levied by U.S. states), and excise taxes on alcohol, tobacco, jewelry, cars and other products.

HUMBLOT v. DIRECTEUR DES SERVICES FISCAUX

Case 112/84, [1985] ECR 1367.

[France imposed a tax on the purchase of all new cars. For low-and medium-level horsepower cars, the tax was levied at a progressively increasing rate depending on the horsepower level, up to a ceiling of F1100. For the most powerful cars, at or above 16 CV (horsepower rating), a special flat-rate tax of F5000 was imposed. All cars at or above 16 CV were imported, chiefly from Germany and the UK. Humblot, purchaser of a 16 CV car, claimed that the special tax violated Article 90. The issue was referred by the French court under Article 234.]

7   [T]he essence of the question is whether Article [90] prohibits the charging on cars exceeding a given power rating * * * of a special fixed tax the amount of which is several times the highest amount of the progressive tax payable on cars of less than the said power rating for tax purposes, where the only cars subject to the special tax are imported * * *.

8   Mr. Humblot argues that * * * vehicles of 16 CV or less and vehicles exceeding 16 CV are completely comparable as regards their performance, price and fuel consumption. As a result, he contends that the French State, by subjecting imported vehicles alone to a special tax much greater in amount than the differential tax, has created discrimination contrary to Article [90] of the Treaty.

9   [T]he French Government * * * argues that the special tax is charged solely on luxury vehicles, which are not similar, within the meaning of the first paragraph of Article [90], to cars liable to the differential tax. Moreover, whilst the French Government concedes that some vehicles rated [above and below] 16 CV are in competition and so subject to the second paragraph of Article [90], it maintains that the special tax is not contrary to that provision, since it has not been shown that the tax has the effect of protecting domestic products. It argues that there is no evidence that a consumer who may have been dissuaded from buying a vehicle of more than 16 CV will purchase a car of French manufacture of 16 CV or less.

10 The Commission considers that the special tax is contrary to the first paragraph of Article [90] of the Treaty. It argues that all cars, irrespective of their power rating for tax purposes, are similar * * *. That being so, it is no longer possible for a Member State to create discrimination between imported and domestically-produced vehicles. The only exception is where a Member State taxes products differently—even identical products—on the basis of neutral criteria consistent with objectives of economic policy which are compatible with the Treaty. * * * The Commission contends, however, that [France's] power rating for tax purposes, is not geared to an economic policy objective, such as heavier taxation of luxury products or vehicles with high fuel consump-

tion. Accordingly, the Commission considers that the special tax, which is almost five times the highest rate of differential tax and affects imported vehicles only * * * is contrary to the first paragraph of Article [90] of the Treaty.

* * *

12 It is appropriate in the first place to stress that as Community law stands at present the Member States are at liberty to subject products such as cars to a system of road tax which increases progressively in amount depending on an objective criterion, such as the power rating for tax purposes * * *.

13 Such a system of domestic taxation is, however, compatible with Article [90] only in so far as it is free from any discriminatory or protective effect.

14 That is not true of a system like the one at issue in the main proceedings. Under that system there are two distinct taxes: a differential tax which increases progressively and is charged on cars not exceeding a given power rating for tax purposes and a fixed tax on cars exceeding that rating which is almost five times as high as the highest rate of the differential tax. Although the system embodies no formal distinction based on the origin of products it manifestly exhibits discriminatory or protective features contrary to Article [90], since the power rating determining liability to the special tax has been fixed at a level such that only imported cars, in particular from other Member States, are subject to the special tax whereas all cars of domestic manufacture are liable to the distinctly more advantageous differential tax.

15 In the absence of considerations relating to the amount of the special tax, consumers seeking comparable cars as regards such matters as size, comfort, actual power, maintenance costs, durability, fuel consumption and price would naturally choose from among cars above and below the critical power rating laid down by French law. However, liability to the special tax entails a much larger increase in taxation than passing from one category of car to another in a system of progressive taxation embodying balanced differentials * * *. The resultant additional taxation is liable to cancel out the advantages which certain cars imported from other Member States might have in consumers' eyes over comparable cars of domestic manufacture, particularly since the special tax continues to be payable for several years. In that respect the special tax reduces the amount of competition to which cars of domestic manufacture are subject and hence is contrary to the principle of neutrality with which domestic taxation must comply.

NOTES AND QUESTIONS

1. Was the high horsepower car tax discriminatory or protectionist or both? What is meant by the "principle of neutrality," cited by the Court in ¶ 15, and frequently applied as a guiding principle in later cases?

2. In contrast to *Humblot* is Commission v. Greece (Car tax), Case C–132/88, [1990] ECR I–1567. Greece's consumption tax on cars was substantially higher for high horsepower cars than for intermediate or low horsepower cars. Greece manufactured only low horsepower cars. The Court held that the tax appeared to be motivated by social policy considerations (presumably meaning that it constituted an indirect tax on wealth). The Court further held that the Commission had not proved that the Greek tax incited consumers to buy domestic cars rather than intermediate or low horsepower imports. Is this result compatible with *Humblot?*

3. In Commission v. Denmark (Car tax), Case C–47/88, [1990] ECR 4509, the Commission contended that a Danish car registration tax on new cars, imposed at rates of 105–180% of the purchase price, violated Article 90. Denmark maintained that the tax could not violate Article 90 because no cars are produced in Denmark. The Commission argued that the rate was so high that it substantially impeded car sales and hence the importation of cars. The Court held that high taxes as such were neither discriminatory nor protectionist in the absence of domestic car production. Subsequently, in De Danske Bilimportorer v. Skatteministeriet, Case C–383/01, [2003] ECR I–6065, the Commission contended that the Danish tax was so high that it impeded the importation of cars and hence violated Article 23's prohibition of measures equivalent to quantitative restrictions. The Court rejected the Commission view and held that Article 23 was inapplicable to a challenge to an internal tax.

4. In Commission v. Denmark (Car tax), *supra*, the Court also held that Denmark's imposition of a 90% registration tax on imported used cars, when no tax was imposed on sales of used cars already in Denmark, was discriminatory and violated Article 90. The Court reached the same conclusion in later reviews of used car tax systems in other States. In Brzezinski v. Director of the Warsaw Customs Office, Case C–313/05, [2007] ECR I–513, the Court held that "Art. 90EC seeks to ensure the complete neutrality of internal taxation" as between imported second-hand vehicles and domestically sold vehicles. The national court was accordingly instructed to review the complex national car registration tax system to ensure that was the case.

WEST LYNN CREAMERY, INC. v. HEALY

512 U.S. 186, 114 S.Ct. 2205, 129 L.Ed.2d 157 (1994).

[Massachusetts levied a 'premium payment' on milk sold by distributors, with the proceeds used for a subsidy for Massachusetts dairy farmers. Most of the milk subject to the "premium payment" came from other states. The Massachusetts Supreme Judicial Court held that the charge was not discriminatory and that the incidental burden on interstate commerce was outweighed by the benefit to the local dairy industry. The Supreme Court reversed, 7–2, with Justice Stevens writing for five justices.]

The 'negative' aspect of the Commerce Clause prohibits economic protectionism—that is, regulatory measures designed to benefit in-state economic interests by burdening out-of-state competitors * * * unless the discrimination is demonstrably justified by a valid factor unrelated to economic protectionism.

* * *

The "premium payments" are effectively a tax which makes milk produced out of State more expensive. Although the tax also applies to milk produced in Massachusetts, its effect on Massachusetts producers is entirely (indeed more than) offset by the subsidy provided exclusively to Massachusetts dairy farmers. Like an ordinary tariff, the tax is thus effectively imposed only on out-of-state products.

* * *

A pure subsidy funded out of general revenue ordinarily imposes no burden on interstate commerce, but merely assists local business. The pricing order in this case, however, is funded principally from taxes on the sale of milk produced in other States. By so funding the subsidy, [Massachusetts] not only assists local farmers, but burdens interstate commerce.

* * *

Finally, Massachusetts argues that any incidental burden on interstate commerce "is outweighed by the 'local benefits' of preserving the Massachusetts dairy industry. [Massachusetts contends that] to save an industry from collapse, is not protectionist." If we were to accept these arguments, we would make a virtue of the vice that the rule against discrimination prohibits. Preservation of local industry by protecting it from the rigors of interstate competition is the hallmark of the economic protectionism that the Commerce Clause prohibits.

NOTES AND QUESTIONS

1. *West Lynn Creamery* is a good example of US cases in which state taxes or charges have been invalidated as providing a commercial advantage to local business at the expense of out-of-state competitors. Another leading case is New Energy Co. of Indiana v. Limbach, 486 U.S. 269, 108 S.Ct. 1803, 100 L.Ed.2d 302 (1988), invalidating as discriminatory under the Commerce Clause an Ohio statute that granted a tax credit to fuel dealers for the sale of ethanol produced in Ohio, but not generally for ethanol produced out-of-state.

2. ALCOHOL EXCISE AND CONSUMPTION TAXES

A series of cases significantly increased the use of ECT Article 90 as a weapon to foster free movement of goods. In the late 1970s, the Commission brought several Treaty infringement proceedings against Member States challenging their alcohol excise tax systems. The Commission urged the Court of Justice to broaden the concept of the relevant product market within which the domestic and imported alcohols could be said to be competing.

COMMISSION v. FRANCE

(Alcohol excise tax)
Case 168/78, [1980] ECR 347.

[France had a substantially higher excise tax on strong alcohol derived from grain (whisky, rum, gin, vodka) than on those derived from wine or fruit (cognac, armagnac, calvados). France produced negligible quantities of grain-based alcohol, but substantial quantities of wine or fruit-based alcohol. The Commission challenged this tax structure in a Treaty infringement proceeding as a violation of ECT Article 90.]

4   As the Commission has correctly stated, Article [90] must guarantee the complete neutrality of internal taxation as regards competition between domestic products and imported products.

5   The first paragraph of Article [90], which is based on a comparison of the tax burdens imposed on domestic products and on imported products which may be classified as "similar", is the basic rule in this respect. This provision * * * must be interpreted widely so as to cover all taxation procedures which conflict with the principle of the equality of treatment of domestic products and imported products; it is therefore necessary to interpret the concept of "similar products" with sufficient flexibility. * * * [I]t is necessary to consider as similar products which "have similar characteristics and meet the same needs from the point of view of consumers". It is therefore necessary to determine the scope of the first paragraph of Article [90] on the basis not of the criterion of the strictly identical nature of the products but on that of their similar and comparable use.

6   The function of the second paragraph of Article [90] is to cover * * * indirect tax protection in the case of products which, without being similar within the meaning of the first paragraph, are nevertheless in competition, even partial, indirect or potential, with certain products of the importing country. * * * [I]t is sufficient for the imported product to be in competition with the protected domestic production by reason of one or several economic uses to which it may be put, even though the condition of similarity for the purposes of the first paragraph of Article [90] is not fulfilled.

[The Court reviewed the characteristics of spirits and considered that they had "common generic features" since they were all produced by distillation and all had high alcohol content. On the other hand, spirits did come from a variety of raw materials (wine, fruit or cereals), had different odors and tastes, and were consumed in different modes (neat, diluted, or with mixes).]

12   Two conclusions follow from this analysis of the market in spirits. First, there is * * * an indeterminate number of beverages which must be classified as "similar products" within the meaning of the first paragraph of Article [90], although it may be difficult to decide

this in specific cases, in view of the nature of the factors implied by distinguishing criteria such as flavour and consumer habits. Secondly, even in cases in which it is impossible to recognize a sufficient degree of similarity between the products concerned, there are nevertheless, in the case of all spirits, common characteristics which are sufficiently pronounced to accept that in all cases there is at least partial or potential competition.

13 It appears from the foregoing that Article [90], taken as a whole, may apply without distinction to all the products concerned.

* * *

The Application of the Contested Tax System

* * *

29 [T]he Commission observes that the French tax system is adjusted so as to place at a disadvantage spirits obtained from cereals which are almost exclusively imported from other Member States, whereas domestic production of those products is insignificant. * * * [Thus, the tax system affords] an indirect competitive advantage to national production.

* * *

32 As regards the criteria which may be used for the classification of the products, the French Government considers that it is the "flavour" of the distillate, in other words, a number of organoleptic properties combining taste, aroma and smell, which, from the point of view of satisfying the needs of the consumer, forms the basis of the classification of products which are neither similar nor even interchangeable or competing within Article [90].

33 [France further argues that its] tax legislation is based on the distinction between "digestives" on the one hand, in other words beverages consumed at the end of the meal including in particular spirits obtained from the distillation of wine and fruit, such as cognac, armagnac and calvados, and "aperitifs" on the other, which are beverages drunk before meals including above all grain-based spirits, most frequently consumed diluted with water, such as whisky [and] gin. * * *

* * *

36 [T]he Court [does not] think it is possible to adopt as a relevant classification the distinction advocated by the French Government between "aperitifs" and "digestives". * * * [T]he distinction between aperitifs and digestives does not take into account many circumstances in which the products in question may be consumed before, during or after meals or even completely unrelated to such meals; * * * according to consumer preferences the same beverage may be used indiscriminately as an "aperitif" or "digestive". Therefore it is impossible

to recognize * * * the distinction upon which French tax practice is based.

37   The same observation applies to the criterion for distinction based on the flavour of the various spirits for the purpose of * * * the application of tax legislation. There is no question of denying the reality of and the shades of difference in the flavour of the various alcoholic products; it is necessary however to bear in mind that this criterion is too variable in time and space to supply by itself a sufficiently sound basis for distinction * * *. The same applies to consumer habits which also differ from region to region and even according to social environment, so that they cannot supply appropriate differentiating criteria for the purpose of Article [90].

* * *

39   After considering all these factors the Court deems it unnecessary for the purposes of solving this dispute to give a ruling on the question whether or not the spirituous beverages concerned are wholly or partly similar products within the meaning of the first paragraph of Article [90] when it is impossible reasonably to contest that without exception they are in at least partial competition with the domestic products * * * and that it is impossible to deny the protective nature of the French tax system within the second paragraph of Article [90].

BACCHUS IMPORTS, LTD. v. DIAS
468 U.S. 263, 104 S.Ct. 3049, 82 L.Ed.2d 200 (1984).

[Hawaii imposed a 20% excise tax on sales of liquor, but exempted Okolehao (brandy made from a Hawaiian shrub) and pineapple wine from the tax. When challenged as a violation of the dormant Commerce Clause, the Hawaiian Supreme Court held the tax exemptions "rationally related to the State's legitimate interest in promoting domestic industry." The U.S. Supreme Court reversed.]

A cardinal rule of Commerce Clause jurisprudence is that "[n]o State, consistent with the Commerce Clause, may impose a tax which discriminates against interstate commerce ... by providing a direct commercial advantage to local business." Boston Stock Exchange v. State Tax Comm'n, 429 U.S. 318, 329 (1977).

* * *

The State relies in part on statistics showing that for the years in question sales of Okolehao and pineapple wine constituted well under one percent of the total liquor sales in Hawaii. It also relies on the statement by the Hawaii Supreme Court that "[w]e believe we can safely assume these products pose no competitive threat to other liquors produced elsewhere and consumed in Hawaii." * * * However, neither the small volume of sales of exempted liquor nor the fact that the exempted liquors do not constitute a present "competitive threat" to other liquors is dispositive of the question whether competition exists between the locally produced beverages and foreign beverages; instead, they go only to the extent of such competition. It is well settled that "[w]e need not know how unequal the Tax is before concluding that it unconstitutionally discriminates."

* * *

No one disputes that a State may enact laws pursuant to its police powers that have the purpose and effect of encouraging domestic industry. However, the Commerce Clause stands as a limitation on the means by which a State can constitutionally seek to achieve that goal. One of the fundamental purposes of the Clause "was to insure . . . against discriminating State legislation." Welton v. Missouri, 91 U.S. 275, 280 (1876).

* * *

[Hawaii contends that its law was intended] "to subsidize nonexistent (pineapple wine) and financially troubled (okolehao) liquor industries peculiar to Hawaii." However, we perceive no principle of Commerce Clause jurisprudence supporting a distinction between thriving and struggling enterprises under these circumstances, and the State cites no authority for its proposed distinction. In either event, the legislation constitutes "economic protectionism" in every sense of the phrase.

NOTES AND QUESTIONS

1. What is the Court of Justice's test for determining "similar products" in the *French alcohol excise tax* case? What did you think of the French argument that these products aren't similar because cereal-based alcohol tends to be consumed as an aperitif while wine or fruit-based alcohol tends to be consumed as a digestif? Why isn't the distinction between aperitifs and digestives a valid indication of consumer views in France?

2. Although most of the *French alcohol excise tax* judgment is devoted to the "similar products" issue, at the end the Court switches to Article 90 paragraph 2. Why? Were you convinced by the Court's analysis? How can dissimilar products still be competitive? What is meant by saying imported and domestic spirits are in "partial competition"? When later you have read Part IV of this casebook on Competition Policy, consider whether this judgment accords with the product market analysis made there.

3. In *Bacchus* the tax discrimination is evident. Do you agree that neither of Hawaii's arguments for its discriminatory tax exemption are justified? Would the Court of Justice rule the same way on analogous facts? Would the Supreme Court find that a state's excise tax discrimination between types of alcohol in circumstances parallel to those in the *Alcohol excise tax* case violate the dormant Commerce Clause?

4. Although in the *French alcohol excise tax* case, the Court concentrated its analysis of "similar products" on the consumer's views, in other cases another criterion, that of objective physical characteristics, has been decisive. Thus, in Commission v. Denmark (Wine tax), Case 106/84, [1986] ECR 833,

the Court considered the beverage's production process, taste and alcohol content, as well as consumer preferences, in finding that normal grape wine and other fruit-based wines constituted similar products. The Court then found that a tax rate on imported grape wine that was 50% higher than that on domestic fruit-based wines constituted discriminatory treatment under Article 90 paragraph 1. However, in John Walker & Sons Ltd. v. Ministeriet for Skatter, Case 243/84, [1986] ECR 875, the Court held that distillation, the production process for Scotch whiskey, as well as its stronger alcohol content and taste, made Scotch whiskey an intrinsically different product from Danish fruit liqueurs under Article 90 paragraph 1. Do you agree with the result in these cases?

5. In F.G. Roders BV v. Inspecteur der Invoerrechten, Cases C–367 to 377/93, [1995] I–2229, eleven Dutch sellers of wine made from grapes challenged under Article 90 the Dutch excise tax levied from 1976 to 1992 on such wine, because no excise tax was levied on wine made from fruit other than grapes. The Court held that ordinary grape table wine was "similar" to wine made from other fruit, applying the criteria used in the *Danish wine tax* case, *supra*. It further held that sherry, madeira, vermouth and champagne were not "similar," but that the national court should review whether they might still be in competition with other fruit-based wine under the second paragraph of Article 90.

6. In a rare modern case, in Commission v. France (Tobacco tax), Case C–302/00, [2002] ECR I–2055, the Court held a 1998 French Finance Law violated Article 90 by setting a higher tax rate for light-tobacco cigarettes, largely imported, than on dark-tobacco cigarettes, largely domestic made. Although dark-tobacco cigarettes must contain 60% tobacco, and are stronger, the Court applied its consumer-view point test, and held that the two types of cigarettes were similar in organoleptic characteristics, i.e., their taste and smell (¶¶ 23–23). The difference in excise tax rates accordingly violated Article 90(1).

COMMISSION v. UNITED KINGDOM

(Wine and beer taxes)
Case 170/78, [1983] ECR 2265.

[The United Kingdom excise tax on light wine was about five times that levied on beer, calculated per gallon, and represented about 38% of the consumer sale price for light wine, versus 25% for beer. The UK produces almost no wine, but substantial amounts of beer. The Commission challenged the UK's wine tax as a violation of Article 90. The Court first reiterated its findings in a prior interlocutory judgment in the case.]

Competitive Relationship Between Wine and Beer

8   As regards the question of competition between wine and beer, the Court considered that, to a certain extent at least, the two beverages in question were capable of meeting identical needs, so that it had to be acknowledged that there was a degree of substitution for one another. * * * [F]or the purpose of measuring the possible degree of substitu-

tion, attention should not be confined to consumer habits in a Member State or in a given region. Those habits, which were essentially variable in time and space, could not be considered to be immutable; the tax policy of a Member State must not therefore crystallize given consumer habits so as to consolidate an advantage acquired by national industries concerned to respond to them.

9   The Court nonetheless recognized that, in view of the substantial differences between wine and beer, it was difficult to compare the manufacturing processes and the natural properties of those beverages * * *. For that reason, the Court requested the parties to provide additional information with a view to dispelling the doubts which existed concerning the nature of the competitive relationship between the two products.

10   The Government of the United Kingdom did not give any opinion on that question in its subsequent statements. * * *

11   The Italian Government contended * * * that it was inappropriate to compare beer with wines of average alcoholic strength or, *a fortiori,* with wines of greater alcoholic strength. In its opinion, it was the lightest wines with [low alcoholic content], that is to say the most popular and cheapest wines, which were genuinely in competition with beer. * * * [T]hose wines should be chosen for purposes of comparison where it was a question of measuring the incidence of taxation on the basis of either alcoholic strength or the price of the products.

12   The Court considers that observation by the Italian Government to be pertinent. In view of the substantial differences in the quality and, therefore, in the price of wines, the decisive competitive relationship between beer, a popular and widely consumed beverage, and wine must be established by reference to those wines which are the most accessible to the public at large, that is to say, generally speaking, the lightest and cheapest varieties.

* * *

Determination of an Appropriate Tax Ratio

19   It is not disputed that comparison of the taxation of beer and wine by reference to the volume of the two beverages reveals that wine is taxed more heavily than beer in both relative and absolute terms. Not only was the taxation of wine increased substantially in relation to the taxation of beer when the United Kingdom replaced customs duty with excise duty * * *, but it is also clear that during the years to which these proceedings relate, namely 1976 and 1977, the taxation of wine was, on average, five times higher, by reference to volume, than the taxation of beer; in other words, wine was subject to an additional tax burden of 400% in round figures.

[Applying the criteria for comparison based upon the relative alcoholic strength of beer and wine and upon the price of beer and cheaper types of wine, the Court concluded that in each case imported cheap wine was taxed more heavily than beer to a substantial degree.]

27   It is clear, therefore, following the detailed inquiry conducted by the Court—whatever criterion for comparison is used, there being no need to express a preference for one or the other—that the United Kingdom's tax system has the effect of subjecting wine imported from other Member States to an additional tax burden so as to afford protection to domestic beer production. * * * Since such protection is most marked in the case of the most popular wines, the effect of the United Kingdom tax system is to stamp wine with the hallmarks of a luxury product which, in view of the tax burden which it bears, can scarcely constitute in the eyes of the consumer a genuine alternative to the typical domestically produced beverage.

28   It follows from the foregoing considerations that, by levying excise duty on still light wines made from fresh grapes at a higher rate, in relative terms, than on beer, the United Kingdom has failed to fulfill its obligations under the second paragraph of Article [90] of the EEC Treaty.

NOTES AND QUESTIONS

1. Did the UK tax violate ECT Article 90 paragraph 1 or paragraph 2? Should attention be paid to UK consumer habits or Community-wide consumer habits? Why was the Italian intervention helpful to the Court's conclusion? Note in ¶ 8 the Court's statement that tax policies must not "crystalize given consumer habits," which the Court has frequently repeated in other judgments concerning free movements of goods.

2. The cumulative effect of these Treaty infringement proceedings against Member State alcohol excise tax systems has been quite substantial, since States have had to re-examine their excise tax systems to see whether they constitute indirect barriers to Community trade, and in some cases have decided to modify the systems.

3. How sizable must a tax differential be in order to be considered protectionist? Where should the line be drawn? In Commission v. Sweden (Wine vs. Beer taxes), Case C–167/05, [2008] ECR I–2127, the Court repeated its view that light wine could be said to be in competition with beer in applying Article 90. However, given the customary higher retail price of wine, twice that of beer, Sweden's higher tax on wine only marginally affected the post-tax retail price of each. Accordingly, the Court held that the Commission had not proven that the Swedish tax rates produced a protective effect for beer, largely domestic, versus wine, an imported product. Contrast Commission v. Greece (Alcohol excise tax), Case C–230/89, [1991] ECR I–1909 where the Court found a 36% value added tax on whisky, gin, rum, etc. (largely imported) to have a protectionist effect, since only a 16% rate was imposed on ouzo and brandy (largely domestic).

4. On several occasions, the WTO Appellate Body has confirmed panel findings that Japan, Korea and Chile have violated GATT rules by imposing

higher excise taxes on imported alcoholic beverages than on domestically produced beverages. See Chapter 28. Thus, in March 2001 the Community agreed not to contest Chile's reduction of excise taxes on imported whisky, gin and cognac to levels closer to the excise tax on Chile's own pisco (a type of hard alcohol). Chile acted to comply with a December 1999 WTO ruling.

3.   HARMONIZATION OF INTERNAL TAXES

EC Treaty Article 93 (replicated in TFEU Article 113) authorizes the Council to "adopt provisions for the harmonization of legislation concerning turnover [i.e., value added] taxes, excise duties and other forms of indirect taxation." There are, however, two significant limitations on the exercise of this legislative grant. First, the Council must act unanimously, which gives every State veto power over a proposal. Moreover, the Council may only adopt legislation "necessary to ensure the establishment and functioning of the internal market," a limitation which enables States hostile to a proposal to launch a policy debate as to the proposal's necessity.

The Council made use of Article 93 principally to harmonize the substantive coverage and the procedural operation of national value added tax systems. (Value added taxes are imposed on most products at every stage of production and distribution, and are ultimately paid by consumers when buying the products.) The Council deemed this harmonization indispensable, because the Community takes a percentage share of the value added tax collected by each State. This share of national value added tax represents a large part of Community revenues, so naturally the base and mode of collection must be essentially the same in each State. Building upon several earlier measures, the Sixth Value Added Tax Directive 77/388 on a uniform basis of assessment, O.J. L 145/1 (June 13, 1977), sets out the harmonized provisions in elaborate detail. Nonetheless, the application of the Sixth Directive requires interpretation. Each year the Court of Justice decides ten to fifteen cases interpreting its provisions.

Since the late 1980s, the Commission has frequently urged proposals to harmonize the rates at which both value added taxes and excise taxes are levied on specific fields of products. The obvious goal is to achieve a more nearly level impact of taxation on commercial transactions throughout the Community. These efforts have largely failed, because indirect taxation constitutes a sensitive political sector, representing a large part of the global revenues of many States. In 1992, the Council was able to achieve a modest degree of success by adopting several directives to require Member States to set minimum (but not maximum) rates for tobacco, petroleum and alcoholic beverages.

Although amending the Treaty to enable the Council to use a qualified majority vote in harmonizing internal taxes would seem to be desirable in order to achieve the internal market, this is highly unlikely. Tax harmonization continues to be sensitive. The Treaty of Lisbon does not modify the requirement for Council unanimity nor grant the Parliament any co-decision veto. This is perhaps not very surprising—would Congress ever seriously undertake to harmonize the rates of state sales taxes or excise taxes?

CHAPTER 13

FREE MOVEMENT OF GOODS: QUANTITATIVE RESTRICTIONS

■ ■ ■

This chapter continues the topic of free movement of goods, but deals with a different sort of barrier: quantitative restrictions and measures equivalent to them. The Court's interpretation of what constitute "measures equivalent" has evolved considerably over time. Moreover, the case law on the extent to which certain State measures restricting free movement of goods are permitted is both voluminous and complex. The doctrines developed by the Court of Justice are among the core principles of Community law today.

The principal EC Treaty article intended to promote free movement of goods was ECT Article 28 (initially Article 30 in the 1957 European Economic Community Treaty) which prohibits "quantitative restrictions on imports and all measures having equivalent effect." ECT Article 29, which prohibits "quantitative restrictions on exports, and all measures having equivalent effect," parallels Article 28. However, restrictions on exports are far less common than those on imports, so that Article 29 has been infrequently applied. The Treaty of Lisbon replicates ECT Articles 28 and 29 in TFEU Articles 34 and 35.

What is the meaning of a "quantitative restriction"? The obvious sense is a quota, a numerical limitation on products in inter-state trade. In fact, the initial EEC Treaty Article 32, now deleted, used the word "quota" as though it were synonymous with quantitative restriction, and the initial Article 33, also now deleted, contained a lengthy description of how intra-Community quotas should be progressively eliminated. The term "quantitative restriction" comes from GATT Article XI, which generally prohibits "quotas, import or export licenses or other measures," subject however to various exceptions.

Given this rather clear sense of quantitative restrictions, one might think that "measures having equivalent effect" would have a fairly narrow meaning, referring to some form of state licensing or other express limit on trade. Instead, as we will see, the Court of Justice has given this innocuous-seeming phrase an extraordinarily expansive interpretation, and it has become a powerful weapon in the efforts to achieve market integration within the European Union.

The Commission's role in expanding the meaning of "measures having equivalent effect" has also been significant. The Commission has made aggressive use of ECT Article 226 (now TFEU Article 258) to challenge a variety of Member States measures having equivalent effect, and often provides briefs in support of private parties challenging government rules through preliminary reference proceedings under ECT Article 234 (now TFEU Article 267).

The Treaty contains an express exception to the general abolition of quantitative restrictions and measures equivalent thereto. ECT Article 30 (initially EECT Article 36, and now TFEU Article 36) allows States to maintain such restrictions for a number of specifically enumerated policy reasons, which will be considered in detail later in this chapter. Many of the cases brought before the Court involve the proper demarcation of these specified exceptions.

Attacking the many varied barriers to Community trade through Court proceedings alone would be a laborious and piecemeal method of achieving free movement of goods. The Commission and the Council accordingly commenced a program of legislative action in the 1960s to harmonize national rules which could adversely affect intra-Community trade. This program received substantial new impetus through the Single European Act's commitment to the goal of completing the internal market by 1992. We will postpone to Chapter 14 the description of harmonization of law and the internal market program. However, it should be emphasized that the Court of Justice case law described in this chapter evolved in tandem with the legislative program discussed in Chapter 14 and that the two reciprocally influenced one another.

Finally, mention should be made of ECT Article 31 (now TFEU Article 37), which deals with "State monopolies of a commercial character," i.e., state-owned or controlled agencies, bodies or enterprises. Article 31 forbids state monopolies to discriminate in any way against any nationals or entities of Member States in the procurement or supply of goods. Public procurement was identified as a sector requiring priority action in the 1985 Commission White Paper on Completing the Internal Market. Since the late 1980s, a series of legislative measures have been adopted for the purpose of removing barriers to Community trade in public procurement, but unfortunately space constraints prevent coverage of this topic. For helpful reviews, see C. Bovis, Public Procurement in the European Union (2005); B. Drijber & H. Stergiou, Public Procurement Law and Internal Market Law, 46 Common Mkt. L. Rev. 805 (2009).

A. QUANTITATIVE RESTRICTIONS AND MEASURES HAVING EQUIVALENT EFFECT

EECT Article 30, later renumbered as ECT Article 28, and now TFEU Article 34, prohibits "quantitative restrictions on imports and all measures having equivalent effect." Because the prohibition is clear and unconditional, ECT Article 28 was an obvious candidate for treatment as a Treaty article which has direct effect. The Court of Justice so held in Ianelli & Volpi SpA. v. Meroni, Case 74/76, [1977] ECR 557, 575, referring to the prohibition as "mandatory and explicit," and therefore creating "individual rights which national courts must protect."

A quantitative restriction's usual sense is that of a quota, a numerical limitation on imported products in some form. But suppose a State totally bans the import of products for some policy reason. This occurred in *Regina v. Henn & Darby, infra,* where the United Kingdom totally banned the importation of indecent or obscene literature. The UK Court of Appeal considered that a total ban does not violate Article 28 because, in literal terms, a ban does not limit imports to a certain quantity. The Court of Justice took the more common sense view that the prohibition of quantitative restrictions also covers a total ban of products. The Court has taken the same position on bans on imports for health and safety reasons, e.g., the Dutch prohibition of the sale of Italian apples with a residue of a specific pesticide, the issue in *Prosecutor v. Heijn, infra.*

1. WHAT ARE "MEASURES HAVING EQUIVALENT EFFECT"?

The concept of "measures having equivalent effect" to quantitative restrictions is obviously a highly indefinite term. In an effort to provide guidance as to its meaning, the Commission issued Directive 70/50 of December 22, 1969, on the abolition of measures which have an effect equivalent to quantitative restrictions on imports. The initial EECT Article 33(7), now deleted, gave the Commission a rare power to issue guideline directives in this area. At this point, read carefully the directive's text, Document 9 in the Selected Documents.

NOTES AND QUESTIONS

1. Observe the Commission's definition of "measures" in the first recital, and its attempt to define generically "measures having equivalent effect" to quantitative restrictions in article 2(1) and (2). Is a protectionist intent necessary? What is the Commission trying to achieve by adopting such an expansive definition?

2. Note that in article 2(1), the Commission does not forbid State measures that are "applicable equally to domestic or imported products," i.e., that do not discriminate against imported products, unless their "restrictive

efforts" are disproportionate, pursuant to article 3. As we shall see in analyzing the *Cassis de Dijon* judgment in section C, the Court of Justice has rejected the Commission's view on this point.

3. When reading the illustrative list in Directive 70/50, try to think of concrete examples. Even though non-exhaustive, this list indicates the great variety of measures affecting Community trade forbidden by Article 28 and is a valuable summary of prohibited measures. Since 1969, the Court of Justice has delivered judgments concerning national measures representative of virtually every item on this list. Thus, in Commission v. Germany (Pharmaceutical representatives), Case 247/81, [1984] ECR 1111, the Court held that Germany could not require exporters of pharmaceutical products from other States to Germany to have a branch or agent in Germany, despite Germany's alleged health justification, citing the Directive's article 2(3)(g). A leading authority, Peter Oliver, provides a list of judgments identifying diverse measures violating Article 28 in P. Oliver, Free Movement of Goods in the European Community ¶¶ 7.03–7.94 (4th ed. 2003).

More authoritative than the Commission's view is the Court of Justice's definition of "measures having equivalent effect." We turn to the leading cases on this subject.

PROCUREUR DU ROI v. DASSONVILLE

Case 8/74, [1974] ECR 837.

[A 1934 Belgian law not only required importers to furnish a certificate of origin for certain types of hard liquor, but further stipulated that the certificate must come from the country of origin. A Belgian firm was prosecuted for importing Scotch whisky bought in France, providing evidence of its Scotch origin derived from a French register instead of the required certificate of origin from Scotland. The trial court asked the Court of Justice whether the Belgian law violated ECT Article 28.]

4 [A] trader, wishing to import into Belgium Scotch whisky which is already in free circulation in France, can obtain such a certificate only with great difficulty, unlike the importer who imports directly from the producer country.

5 All trading rules enacted by Member States which are capable of hindering, directly or indirectly, actually or potentially, intra-Community trade are to be considered as measures having an effect equivalent to quantitative restrictions.

6 In the absence of a Community system guaranteeing for consumers the authenticity of a product's designation of origin, if a Member State takes measures to prevent unfair practices in this connexion, it is however subject to the condition that these measures should be reasonable and that the means of proof required should not act as a hindrance to trade between Member States and should, in consequence, be accessible to all Community nationals.

* * *

9   Consequently, the requirement by a Member State of a certificate of authenticity which is less easily obtainable by importers of an authentic product which has been put into free circulation in a regular manner in another Member State than by importers of the same product coming directly from the country of origin constitutes a measure having an effect equivalent to a quantitative restriction as prohibited by the Treaty.

NOTES AND QUESTIONS

1.   Compare the Court's definition of "measures having equivalent effect" with that of the Commission in Directive 70/50. Which is broader? The Court's expansive definition of what could have been treated as a narrow, quota-related term is a clear illustration of the Court's "activist" interpretation of the Treaty, applauded by most commentators but sharply criticized by some. What do you suppose motivated the Court of Justice in its approach? Is it a justifiable instance of judicial rulemaking?

2.   If the Court had concluded with ¶ 5, a State could never have "trading rules" which hinder Community trade, except when allowed to do so by ECT Article 30. Can one draw from ¶ 6 the inference that ¶ 5 is subject to a "reasonableness" test? We will return to this point when discussing *Cassis de Dijon* in section C. In 1993, the *Keck* judgment significantly limited *Dassonville's* broad definition of "measures equivalent" to measures relating to products, excluding measures relating to the merchandising of products. For clarity, *Keck* and the case law applying its doctrine will be postponed to section D.

COMMISSION v. GERMANY

(Sekt and Weinbrand)
Case 12/74, [1975] ECR 181.

[A 1971 German law permitted the use of the word "Sekt" only for German sparkling wine and "Weinbrand" only for German brandy distilled from wine, while imported sparkling wine had to be called "Schaumwein" and imported wine-brandy "Branntwein aus Wein". The apparent purpose was to create consumer recognition of the German products in a fashion analogous to that for the French products "champagne" and "cognac," which are protected appellations of origin. The Commission brought a Treaty infringement proceeding to challenge the law, arguing that "Sekt" and "Weinbrand" should not qualify as appellations of origin, and that the German law adversely affected intra-Community trade in violation of ECT Article 28.]

5   The Common Market is based upon the free circulation of goods within the Community.

* * *

7   Whatever the factors which may distinguish them, registered designations of origin and indirect indications of origin * * * always describe

at the least a product coming from a specific geographical area. To the extent to which these appellations are protected by law they must satisfy the objectives of such protection, in particular the need to ensure not only that the interests of the producers concerned are safeguarded against unfair competition, but also that consumers are protected against information which may mislead them.

These appellations only fulfil their specific purpose if the product which they describe does in fact possess qualities and characteristics which are due to the fact that it originated in a specific geographical area. As regards indications of origin in particular, the geographical area of origin of a product must confer on it a specific quality and specific characteristics of such a nature as to distinguish it from all other products.

8   The German legislation on vine products provides that the appellations "Sekt" and "Weinbrand" shall describe products originating in the Federal Republic of Germany or [Austria].

An area of origin which is defined on the basis either of the extent of national territory or a linguistic criterion cannot constitute a geographical area * * * capable of justifying an indication of origin, particularly as the products in question may be produced from grapes of indeterminate origin. In this instance, it is not disputed that the area of origin referred to by the legislation on vine products does not show homogeneous natural features which distinguish it in contrast to adjacent areas * * *. The German Government maintains, however, that the products covered by the appellations "Sekt" and "Weinbrand" are clearly distinguished from all other products as a result of the particular method of manufacture used in Germany which confers on them a typical flavour * * *.

9   In the case of vine products, the natural features of the area of origin, such as the grape from which these products are obtained, play an important role in determining their quality and their characteristics. Although the method of production used for such products may play some part in determining their characteristics, it is not alone decisive, independently of the quality of the grape used, in determining its origin.

* * *

14   * * * Under the terms of Article 2(3)(s) of Directive No 70/50/EEC of the Commission, measures which "confine names which are not indicative of origin or source to domestic products only" are to be regarded as prohibited * * *.

By reserving these appellations to domestic production and by compelling the products of the other Member States to employ appellations which are unknown or less esteemed by the consumer, the legislation on vine products is calculated to favour the disposal of the domestic product on the German market to the detriment of the products of other Member States. Thus, this legislation on vine products involves measures having an effect equivalent to quantitative restrictions on imports * * *.

For the purposes of this prohibition it is not necessary to show that such measures actually restrict imports of the products concerned but, in accordance with Article 2(1) of the abovementioned Directive, that they may merely hinder "imports which could otherwise take place".

NOTES AND QUESTIONS

1. On its face, does the German law appear to be protectionist, or rather designed to achieve a consumer interest goal? Does the German motivation matter? Note also the Court's conclusion in ¶ 14 that the German law violated Article 28 even if it could not be proved that it actually reduced imports. Why?

2. In Commission v. France (Alcohol advertising), Case 152/78, [1980] ECR 2299, the Commission challenged a French law regulating alcohol advertising. Wine and beer (produced domestically and imported, both in substantial volumes) could be freely advertised; advertising of brandy, calvados and other fruit-based liquors (largely domestic products) was partially restricted, while no advertising at all was allowed for whisky, gin and vodka (imported products). France defended its law as intended to combat alcoholism. Is the law a measure equivalent to a quantitative restriction? If it is, can the French categories of restrictions on advertising be justified?

3. In the preceding chapter, we discussed the status under ECT Article 25 of fees for health inspections of slaughtered meat, fruits and vegetables, live animals and plants. Are such inspections themselves a measure equivalent to a quantitative restriction? See Rewe–Zentralfinanz v. Landwirtschaftskammer, Case 4/75, [1975] ECR 843, which held that a health inspection of apples imported into Germany constituted a measure equivalent to a quantitative restriction, but was justified as a health protection measure under ECT Article 30, because the inspection sought to prevent the spread of insect pests not present in Germany.

2. WHAT ARE "MEASURES"?

Thus far, we have assumed that we know the meaning of the word "measure." But do we? Clearly, a measure means at least any state law, regulation or administrative practice. Does it have a wider sense?

COMMISSION v. IRELAND
(Buy Irish)
Case 249/81, [1982] ECR 4005.

[Troubled by an unfavorable balance of trade and domestic unemployment, in 1978 Ireland launched a program to promote Irish products. The Irish Goods Council organized a major publicity campaign to urge consumers to buy domestic products and encouraged the use of a "Guaranteed

Irish" symbol for Irish products. The Irish Goods Council was a private company, but its Management Committee was appointed by Ireland's Minister for Industry and Commerce. Moreover, Ireland provided a subsidy to finance most of the Irish Goods Council's activities. In a Treaty infringement proceeding, the Commission claimed that Ireland had violated ECT Article 28. After reviewing the facts, the Court concluded:]

15   It is thus apparent that the Irish Government appoints the members of the Management Committee of the Irish Goods Council, grants it public subsidies which cover the greater part of its expenses and, finally, defines the aims and the broad outline of the campaign conducted by that institution to promote the sale and purchase of Irish products. In the circumstances the Irish Government cannot rely on the fact that the campaign was conducted by a private company in order to escape any liability it may have under the provisions of the Treaty.

* * *

The Application of Article [28] of the Treaty

20   The Commission maintains that the "Buy Irish" campaign and the measures taken to prosecute the campaign must be regarded, as a whole, as measures encouraging the purchase of domestic products only. * * * The Commission refers to Article 2(3)(k) of Commission Directive No 70/50/EEC stating that measures which encourage the purchase of domestic products only must be regarded as contrary to the prohibitions contained in the Treaty.

21   The Irish Government maintains that the prohibition against measures having an effect equivalent to quantitative restrictions in Article 28 is concerned only with * * * binding provisions emanating from a public authority. * * *

22   The Irish Government goes on to emphasize that the campaign has had no restrictive effect on imports since the proportion of Irish goods to all goods sold on the Irish market fell from 49.2% in 1977 to 43.4% in 1980.

23   The first observation to be made is that the campaign cannot be likened to advertising by private or public undertakings, * * * to encourage people to buy goods produced by those undertakings.

* * *

25   Whilst it may be true that the two elements of the programme which have continued in effect, namely the advertising campaign and the use of the "Guaranteed Irish" symbol, have not had any significant success in winning over the Irish market to domestic products, it is not possible to overlook the fact that, regardless of their efficacity, those two activities form part of a government programme which is designed to achieve the substitution of domestic products for imported

products and is liable to affect the volume of trade between Member States.

* * *

27   In the circumstances the two activities in question amount to the establishment of a national practice * * * the potential effect of which on imports from other Member States is comparable to that resulting from government measures of a binding nature.

28   Such a practice cannot escape the prohibition laid down by Article [28] of the Treaty solely because it is not based on decisions which are binding upon undertakings. Even measures adopted by the government of a Member State which do not have binding effect may be capable of influencing the conduct of traders and consumers in that State and thus of frustrating the aims of the Community * * *.

* * *

30   Ireland has therefore failed to fulfil its obligations under the Treaty by organizing a campaign to promote the sale and purchase of Irish goods within its territory.

NOTES AND QUESTIONS

1.   Is this a natural or an excessively elastic interpretation of "measure"? Is a State responsible in this context for the acts of every private firm which receives substantial state subsidies? Or for the acts of firms or associations whose management the State designates? Where should the line be drawn?

2.   Cf. Apple & Pear Development Council v. K.J. Lewis Ltd., Case 222/82, [1983] ECR 4083, where the Court of Justice held that a UK body's advertising campaign to encourage British consumers to buy British apples and pears constituted a measure having equivalent effect to a quantitative restriction. Suppose the state of Washington financed a Washington Apple Growers Association, whose board is also named by the Governor. Suppose then that the Association launched a publicity campaign to urge Washington residents to consume domestic apples, rather than apples grown elsewhere in the US. Would this violate the dormant Commerce Clause?

3.   Building upon the Court's doctrine in leading cases, the Commission frequently issues policy guidelines intended to assist courts, lawyers and business managers to comply with Community rules. Thus, the Commission Guidelines for Member States' Involvement in Promotion of Agricultural and Fisheries Products, issued in 1986 and updated in O.J. C 252/5 (Sept. 12, 2001), gave examples both of promotional actions which are permissible (e.g., advertising products in a generic manner without reference to national origin), as well as promotional actions which violate Article 28 (e.g., campaigns intended to disparage the quality or discourage the purchase of products from other States).

COMMISSION v. FRANCE

(Produce Imports)
Case C–265/95, [1997] ECR I–6959.

[For over a decade and especially in 1993–95, French farmers engaged in an organized campaign to reduce the importation of vegetables and fruits, notably strawberries, from Spain. In addition to threats against retailers marketing these products, on repeated occasions some farmers blocked the movement of trucks carrying Spanish produce, destroyed the truck cargos, and committed acts of violence against the truck drivers. The French police rarely took any action to prevent these incidents, even though often present at the scene. Public prosecutors investigated, but rarely prosecuted anyone. After Commission protests proved unavailing, the Commission launched a Treaty infringement proceeding against France. In its defense, France claimed that it had a public policy discretion in executing police action in the face of serious public unrest and that the "commando-type" operations of the farmers were difficult to combat. France also contended that it had paid FF 17,000,000 in compensation to victims of the offences.]

30   As an indispensable instrument for the realization of a market without internal frontiers, Article [28] does not prohibit solely measures emanating from the State which, in themselves, create restrictions on trade between Member States. It also applies where a Member State abstains from adopting the measures required in order to deal with obstacles to the free movement of goods which are not caused by the State.

31   The fact that a Member State abstains from taking action or * * * fails to adopt adequate measures to prevent obstacles to the free movement of goods that are created by actions by private individuals on its territory aimed at products originating in other Member States is just as likely to obstruct intra-Community trade as is a positive act.

32   Article [28] therefore requires the Member States not merely themselves to abstain from adopting measures or engaging in conduct liable to constitute an obstacle to trade but also, when read with Article [10] of the Treaty, to take all necessary and appropriate measures to ensure that the fundamental freedom is respected on their territory.

33   [T]he Member States, which retain exclusive competence as regards the maintenance of public order * * *, unquestionably enjoy a margin of discretion in determining what measures are most appropriate to eliminate barriers to the importation of products in a given situation.

34   It is therefore not for the Community institutions to act in place of the Member States and to prescribe for them the measures which they must adopt and effectively apply in order to safeguard the free movement of goods on their territories.

35   However, it falls to the Court, taking due account of the discretion referred to above, to verify, in cases brought before it, whether the

Member State concerned has adopted appropriate measures for ensuring the free movement of goods.

* * *

38   The acts of violence committed in France and directed against agricultural products originating in other Member States, such as the interception of lorries transporting those products, the destruction of their loads and violence towards drivers, * * * unquestionably create obstacles to intra-Community trade in those products.

* * *

43   [T]he French authorities had ample time to adopt the measures necessary to ensure compliance with their obligations under Community law.

44   Moreover, notwithstanding the explanations given by the French Government, which claims that all possible measures were adopted in order to prevent the continuation of the violence and to prosecute and punish those responsible, it is a fact that, year after year, serious incidents have gravely jeopardized trade in agricultural products in France.

* * *

48   Moreover, it is not denied that when such incidents occurred the French police were either not present on the spot, despite the fact that in certain cases the competent authorities had been warned of the imminence of demonstrations by farmers, or did not intervene, even where they far outnumbered the perpetrators of the disturbances. Furthermore, the actions in question were not always rapid, surprise actions by demonstrators who then immediately took flight, since in certain cases the disruption continued for several hours.

49   Furthermore, it is undisputed that a number of acts of vandalism were filmed by television cameras, that the demonstrators' faces were often not covered and that the groups of farmers responsible for the violent demonstrations are known to the police.

50   Notwithstanding this, only a very small number of the persons who participated in those serious breaches of public order has been identified and prosecuted.

* * *

52   In the light of all the foregoing factors, the Court, while not discounting the difficulties faced by the competent authorities in dealing with situations of the type in question in this case, cannot but find that, having regard to the frequency and seriousness of the incidents cited by the Commission, the measures adopted by the French Government were manifestly inadequate to ensure freedom of intra-Community trade in agricultural products on its territory by preventing and

effectively dissuading the perpetrators of the offences in question from committing and repeating them.

* * *

56   [T]he Member State concerned, unless it can show that action on its part would have consequences for public order with which it could not cope by using the means at its disposal, [must] adopt all appropriate measures to guarantee the full scope and effect of Community law so as to ensure its proper implementation in the interests of all economic operators.

* * *

59   As regards the fact that the French Republic has assumed responsibility for the losses caused to the victims, this cannot be put forward as an argument by the French Government in order to escape its obligations under Community law.

60   Even though compensation can provide reparation for at least part of the loss or damage sustained by the economic operators concerned, the provision of such compensation does not mean that the Member State has fulfilled its obligations.

61   Nor is it possible to accept the arguments based on the very difficult socio-economic context of the French market in fruit and vegetables after the accession of the Kingdom of Spain.

62   It is settled case-law that economic grounds can never serve as justification for barriers prohibited by Article [28] of the Treaty.

* * *

66   Consequently, it must be held that, by failing to adopt all necessary and proportionate measures in order to prevent the free movement of fruit and vegetables from being obstructed by actions by private individuals, the French Government has failed to fulfil its obligations under Article [28], in conjunction with Article [10], of the Treaty.

NOTES AND QUESTIONS

1.   Do you consider that the conduct of the French police and prosecutors can be said to constitute an "administrative practice"? A governmental measure akin to that in the *Buy Irish* case? Can repeated or systemic inaction be deemed to be a governmental policy? Do you agree with the Court's ¶ 31?

2.   Advocate General Lenz in a carefully reasoned opinion concluded that ECT Article 28 could only be violated by a governmental measure, while in the *Produce imports* case only private individuals engaged in conduct obstructing the free movement of goods. He contended, however, that France had violated a duty of "due diligence" under ECT Article 10 (now the Lisbon TEU Article 4(3)) to carry out a policy protecting free movement of goods. Article 10 is frequently called the "duty of loyalty." Do you think the Court's reference to Article 10 in ¶ 32 is essential to its holding? Or is the reference

merely intended to add greater weight to a finding that French inaction violated Article 28? Note also the Court's statement in ¶ 62 that "economic grounds" cannot justify a limitation on the free movement of goods. This important doctrine also applies in the free movement of workers, services and capital.

3. Catalyzed by this judgment, the Council rapidly adopted Council Regulation 2679/98 on the functioning of the internal market in relation to the free movement of goods, O.J. L 337/8 (Dec. 12, 1998). The Regulation requires States to remove any obstacle to the free movement of goods, including action by private individuals to obstruct free movement, and forbids State inaction, defined as the failure to "take all necessary and proportionate measures" to remove the obstacle (article 1(2)).

B. JUSTIFIABLE NATIONAL LIMITS ON FREE MOVEMENT OF GOODS

The 1957 European Economic Community Treaty itself created an exception to the principle of free movement of goods in EECT Article 36, renumbered by the Treaty of Amsterdam in 1999 as ECT Article 30 (now TFEU Article 36):

> The provisions of Articles 28 and 29 [now TFEU Articles 34 and 35] shall not preclude prohibitions or restrictions on imports, exports or goods in transit justified on grounds of public morality, public policy or public security; the protection of health and life of humans, animals or plants; the protection of national treasures possessing artistic, historic or archaeological value; or the protection of industrial and commercial property. Such prohibitions or restrictions shall not, however, constitute a means of arbitrary discrimination or a disguised restriction on trade between Member States.

The text thus specifies several categories of interests which a Member State may protect even at the expense of free movement of goods. This section presents cases illustrating the scope of the exceptions for health and safety, public morality, public security and public policy. The exception for the protection of industrial and commercial property has given rise to an extensive and complex body of case law, treated in Chapter 19. In contrast, no case has raised issues concerning the protection of national treasures.

Note that the last sentence of ECT Article 30 (now TFEU Article 36) contains an exception to the exception. Generally speaking, Member States are sincerely motivated in adopting a measure to attain one of the Article 30 interests. Occasionally, however, a State is wholly or partially motivated by the desire to protect its own products and tries to use an Article 30 exception to mask its protectionism. A rare example is Commission v. United Kingdom (Christmas turkeys), Case 40/82, [1982] ECR 2793, in which the Court held that the UK did not have valid health reasons for banning the import of poultrymeat in fall 1981 following pressure from domestic poultry producers upset over substantial imports of turkeys and other poultry meat from France.

A major incentive for the harmonization of laws programs since the 1970s has been the desire to reduce the impact of Article 30 exceptions by the creation of Community-wide health and safety or other standards. See Chapter 14A. If the Community standards completely cover the field, then Member State rules and regulations are preempted. ECT Article 30 (and TFEU Article 36) then no longer justifies the State rules, which cease to be a barrier to trade. See Chapter 14C.

1. HEALTH AND SAFETY CASES

In the European Union, the Court of Justice frequently must decide whether a Member State rule can be deemed "justified [by] the protection of health and life of humans, animals or plants." The word, "justified," enables the Court to consider not only whether the rule is indeed intended to achieve a health and safety goal, as opposed to serving a disguised protectionist end, but also whether the rule is proportionate and narrowly tailored to its goal. Similar issues arise in the US when the Supreme Court or other courts must determine whether state health and safety rules are appropriate and do not violate the dormant Commerce Clause.

COMMISSION v. UNITED KINGDOM
(UHT milk)
Case 124/81, [1983] ECR 203.

[The Commission brought a Treaty infringement action against the UK, contending that it had failed to fulfill its obligations under Article 28 by placing restrictions on the importation of milk and cream treated by the Ultra Heat Treated (UHT) process and on the sale of those products in its territory. By use of the UHT process, which heats the product to over 100 degrees centigrade for a short time, milk and cream can be aseptically packed and kept in hermetically sealed containers for several months at room temperature. The Court summarized the UK rules as requiring: 1) all imported milk and cream to be authorized by an import license; and 2) UHT milk (whether domestic or imported) to be marketed in England, Wales and Scotland only by approved dairies or distributors holding a dealer's licence, certifying that the operator must pack the milk in a dairy approved by the competent local authority.]

The Requirement of a Specific Import Licence

9   The Court has already held that Article [28] precludes the application to intra-Community trade of national provisions which require, even as a pure formality, import licences or any other similar procedure.

* * *

12   However, those provisions, whilst constituting measures having an effect equivalent to quantitative restrictions, must be examined to see whether they are permissible under Article [30] of the Treaty * * *.

13 That article constitutes a derogation from the fundamental principle of the free movement of goods and must therefore be interpreted in such a way as not to extend its effects further than is necessary for the protection of the interests which it seeks to safeguard.

* * *

15 The United Kingdom stresses that cattle infected with foot-and-mouth disease may yield infected milk before the outward symptoms of the disease become evident and before the outbreak is discovered by the health authorities. [Thus], the milk, having undergone a treatment insufficient to inactivate the virus, might already be in transit or actually imported into the United Kingdom before the disease had been identified. It is therefore necessary [to be able] to trace the infected consignments and to destroy them before they reach the market. According to the United Kingdom, only a system of specific licences enabling consignments of imported milk to be identified and traced meets that requirement.

16 Whilst the protection of the health of animals is one of the matters justifying the application of Article [30], it must none the less be ascertained whether [the U.K. license system] constitutes a measure which is disproportionate in relation to the objective pursued, on the ground that the same result may be achieved by means of less restrictive measures * * *.

* * *

18 Even though * * * licences [may] be issued promptly and automatically, a system requiring the issue of an administrative authorization necessarily involves the exercise of a certain degree of discretion and creates legal uncertainty for traders. It results in an impediment to intra-Community trade which, in the present case, could be eliminated without prejudice to the effectiveness of the protection of animal health and without increasing the administrative or financial burden imposed by the pursuit of that objective. That result could be achieved if the United Kingdom authorities abandoned the practice of issuing licences and confined themselves to obtaining the information which is of use to them, for example, by means of declarations signed by the importers * * *.

19 It follows from the foregoing considerations that the requirement of import licences, which is incompatible with Article [28] of the Treaty, is not saved by the exception contained in Article [30].

The System of Dealers' Licences and the Requirement That Imported UHT Milk Be Packed on Premises Within the United Kingdom

20 [The UK regulations] which require [imported] UHT milk to be packed on premises within the United Kingdom, make it necessary to treat that milk again, since it is technically impossible to open the packs and

then repack the milk without causing it to lose the characteristics of "Ultra Heat Treated" milk.

21 Therefore, the need to subject that product to a second heat treatment causes delays in the marketing cycle, involves the importer in considerable expense and, moreover, is likely to lower the organoleptic qualities of the milk. In fact, the requirement of re-treatment and repacking constitutes, owing to its economic effects, the equivalent of a total prohibition on imports * * *.

* * *

23 The United Kingdom claims however, that in the present state of Community law such a prohibition is the only effective means of protecting the health of consumers and is therefore justified under Article [30].

24 The United Kingdom bases its view essentially on the disparities in the laws of the Member States relating to the production and treatment of UHT milk, on the varying degree of application of those different laws and on the impossibility of its exercising control over the production cycle of UHT milk in the other Member States from collection at the farm to packing and distribution.* * *

25 Those arguments cannot be upheld. In the first place, it is clear from the evidence before the Court * * * that the alleged disparities in the laws of the Member States are in truth limited. In fact * * * the production of UHT milk is carried on in the different Member States in accordance with very similar rules * * *.

26 Secondly, an analysis of the scientific and technical documents submitted by the parties for the Court's examination demonstrates that UHT milk is produced in the different Member States with machines manufactured by a very small number of firms in accordance with comparable technical characteristics and that the milk, having undergone identical controls, is of similar quality from the point of view of health.

* * *

28 Under those circumstances, the United Kingdom * * * could ensure safeguards equivalent to those which it has prescribed for its domestic production of UHT milk, without having recourse to the measures adopted, which amount to a total prohibition on imports.

29 To that end, the United Kingdom would be entitled to lay down the objective conditions which it considers ought to be observed as regards the quality of the milk before treatment and as regards the methods of treating and packing UHT milk of whatever origin offered for sale on its territory. The United Kingdom could also stipulate that imported UHT milk must satisfy the requirements thus laid down, whilst however taking care not to go beyond that which is strictly necessary for the protection of the health of the consumer. It would be able to ensure that such requirements are satisfied by requesting importers to produce

certificates issued for the purpose by the competent authorities of the exporting Member States.

31 [In addition,] the United Kingdom authorities [could carry] out controls by means of samples to ensure observance of the standards which it has laid down, or from preventing the entry of consignments found not to conform with those standards.

* * *

33 It follows from the foregoing considerations that the system of dealers' licences constitutes an impediment to the free movement of dairy produce which is disproportionate in relation to the objective pursued and is not therefore justified under Article [30] of the Treaty.

DEAN MILK CO. v. CITY OF MADISON

340 U.S. 349, 71 S.Ct. 295, 95 L.Ed. 329 (1951).

[A Madison ordinance forbid the sale of milk in the city unless it had been pasteurized and bottled at an authorized pasteurization plant within five miles of the city. Dean Milk, a distributor obtaining milk from dairy farms in northern Illinois, challenged the ordinance on Dormant Commerce Clause grounds. The Wisconsin Supreme Court upheld the ordinance as valid to achieve public health protection. Justice Clark spoke for six Justices in reversing.]

[W]e agree with appellant that the ordinance imposes an undue burden on interstate commerce.

* * *

[T]his regulation * * * in practical effect excludes from distribution in Madison wholesome milk produced and pasteurized in Illinois * * *. In thus erecting an economic barrier protecting a major local industry against competition from without the State, Madison plainly discriminates against interstate commerce. This it cannot do, even in the exercise of its unquestioned power to protect the health and safety of its people, if reasonable nondiscriminatory alternatives, adequate to conserve legitimate local interests, are available.

* * *

It appears that reasonable and adequate alternatives are available. If the City of Madison prefers to rely upon its own officials for inspection of distant milk sources, such inspection is readily open to it without hardship for it could charge the actual and reasonable cost of such inspection to the importing producers and processors.

* * *

[Alternatively, Madison could] determine the extent of enforcement of sanitary standards in the exporting area by verifying the accuracy of safety ratings of specific plants or of the milkshed in the distant jurisdiction through the United States Public Health Service, which routinely and on request spot checks the local ratings.

* * *

To permit Madison to adopt a regulation not essential for the protection of local health interests and placing a discriminatory burden on interstate commerce would invite a multiplication of preferential trade areas destructive of the very purpose of the Commerce Clause.

[Dissent by JUSTICE BLACK, speaking for two other Justices.]

This health regulation should not be invalidated merely because the Court believes that alternative milk-inspection methods might insure the cleanliness and healthfulness of Dean's Illinois milk.

* * *

No case is cited, and I have found none, in which a bona fide health law was struck down on the ground that some other method of safeguarding health would be as good as, or better than, the one the Court was called on to review. In my view, to use this ground now elevates the right to traffic in commerce for profit above the power of the people to guard the purity of their daily diet of milk.

If, however, the principle announced today is to be followed, the Court should not strike down local health regulations unless satisfied beyond a reasonable doubt that the substitutes it proposes would not lower health standards. I do not think that the Court can so satisfy itself on the basis of its judicial knowledge.

NOTES AND QUESTIONS

1. Do you think that the UK's rules in *UHT milk* were protectionist or motivated by a sincere desire to protect the health of humans and animals? Does the UK's motivation really matter? Why is the Court so rigorous in ¶¶ 9–13 in its appraisal of import licenses? How does the Court apply the principle of proportionality, expressed in ¶ 16? What health protection measures can the UK still take as to imported UHT milk? See ¶¶ 29–31.

2. Do you agree with Justice Clark or with Justice Black in *Dean Milk*? How would each have dealt with the issues presented in *UHT Milk*? Note that the Supreme Court frequently applies a principle of proportionality in evaluating state rules in dormant Commerce Clause cases, although it does not use that terminology.

ROSENGREN v. PUBLIC PROSECUTOR
Case C–170/04, [2007] ECR I–4071.

[The Swedish Alcohol Law not only grants the Systembolaget, a Swedish agency, a monopoly for the sale of alcoholic beverages by wholesalers and authorized retailers, but it also forbids the importation of alcohol other than through the agency. Rosengren challenged the import ban when his mail order of cases of Spanish wine was confiscated. The Court first held that the proper operation of the Swedish agency as a state monopoly under ECT Article 31 (now TFEU Article 37) consisted of the regulation of wholesale and retail trade, not the importation of alcohol. Inasmuch as a ban on alcohol imports by private parties obviously violated Article 28, the issue then became whether the ban was justified on health grounds. Although the Systembolaget did have a system for importing specific products upon a consumer's request, the Court held that this was not sufficient to justify a total ban on imports. Sweden also raised a health argument, arguing that only the Swedish monopoly agency could adequately check to ensure that buyers were at least 20 years old.]

50 [S]ince a ban such as that which arises from the national legislation at issue in the main proceedings amounts to a derogation from the principle of the free movement of goods, it is for the national authorities to demonstrate that those rules are consistent with the principle of proportionality, that is to say, that they are necessary in order to achieve the declared objective, and that that objective could not be achieved by less extensive prohibitions or restriction, or by prohibitions or restrictions having less effect on intra-Community trade.

51 The ban on imports * * * applies to everyone, irrespective of age. Accordingly, it goes manifestly beyond what is necessary for the objective sought, which is to protect younger persons against the harmful effects of alcohol consumption.

* * *

55 The question remains to be answered whether, in order to achieve that objective of protection of the health of young persons with at least an equivalent level of effectiveness, there are other methods less restrictive of the principle of free movement of goods and capable of replacing the method at issue.

56 In that regard, the Commission * * * submits, without being contradicted on that point, that age check could be carried out by way of a declaration in which the purchaser of the imported beverages certifies, on a form accompanying the goods when they are imported, that he or she is more than 20 years of age. The information before the Court does not, on its own, permit the view to be taken that such a method, which attracts appropriate criminal penalties in the event of noncompliance, would necessarily be less effective than that implemented by the Systembolaget.

57 Accordingly, it has not been established that the ban at issue in the main proceedings is proportionate for the purposes of attaining the objective of protecting young persons against the harmful effects of alcohol consumption.

NOTES AND QUESTIONS

1. Sweden regards alcoholism as a serious health problem—its creation of a state agency monopoly which tries to regulate the marketing and advertising of alcohol reflects this. The prevention of sales to young people is obviously a particularly serious concern. Do you think the Court is right in considering that age declarations by a purchaser will sufficiently protect against the risk of mail order sales to young people? Why is it important that the Court placed the burden of proof of proportionality upon Sweden?

2. Granholm v. Heald, 544 U.S. 460, 125 S.Ct. 1885, 161 L.Ed.2d 796 (2005), provides a useful comparison. In Justice Kennedy's opinion, he held that the ban on imported mail order wine by Michigan and New York was discriminatory and violated the dormant Commerce Clause. One of the states' justifications was to protect against sales to minors. Justice Kennedy held that the states had not provided concrete evidence to establish this, especially since minors are less likely to consume wine than beer or hard alcohol. He noted that the states could have required an adult's signature on mail orders as a less restrictive way of protecting minors.

DECKER v. CAISSE DE MALADIE DES EMPLOYES PRIVES

Case C–120/95, [1998] ECR I–1831.

[The Luxembourg health insurance program in its social security system provides a flat-rate sum reimbursement of spectacles (eyeglasses) with corrective lenses. The reimbursement is automatic for spectacles purchased from Luxembourg opticians, but is conditioned upon prior authorization for spectacles bought outside Luxembourg. When Decker used an ophthalmologist's prescription to buy spectacles in Belgium without a prior authorization, he was denied reimbursement. A Luxembourg social security tribunal referred several questions to the Court. The Court initially held that social security system rules must comply with ECT Article 28.]

34   [T]he rules at issue encourage persons insured under the Luxembourg social security scheme to purchase their spectacles from, and have them assembled by, opticians established in Luxembourg rather than in other Member States.

* * *

36   Such rules must be categorised as a barrier to the free movement of goods, since they encourage insured persons to purchase those products in Luxembourg rather than in other Member States, and are thus liable to curb the import of spectacles assembled in those States.

37   The Luxembourg Government submits, however, that the free movement of goods is not absolute and that the rules at issue * * * are justified [by the need to control health expenses].

* * *

39   * * * [A]ims of a purely economic nature cannot justify a barrier to the fundamental principle of the free movement of goods. However, it cannot be excluded that the risk of seriously undermining the financial balance of the social security system may constitute an overriding reason in the general interest capable of justifying a barrier of that kind.

40   But, as the Luxembourg Government acknowledged in reply to a question from the Court, it is clear that reimbursement at a flat rate of the cost of spectacles and corrective lenses purchased in other Member States has no effect on the financing or balance of the social security system.

41   The Belgian, German and Netherlands Governments have also submitted that the right of insured persons to have access to quality treatment constitutes a justification for the rules at issue, on the ground of the protection of public health * * *.

42   It must be observed that the conditions for taking up and pursuing regulated professions have been the subject of Council Directive 92/51/ EEC of 18 June 1992 on a second general system for the recognition of professional education and training.

43   This means that the purchase of a pair of spectacles from an optician established in another Member State provides guarantees equivalent to those afforded on the sale of a pair of spectacles by an optician established in the national territory.

44   Furthermore, in the present case the spectacles were purchased on a prescription from an ophthalmologist, which guarantees the protection of public health.

45   It follows that [the Luxembourg] rules are not justified on grounds of public health in order to ensure the quality of medical products supplied in other Member States.

NOTES AND QUESTIONS

1. We already encountered in *French Produce imports* the important doctrine that a State's economic concerns cannot justify a limitation on the free movement of goods. In ¶ 39 it indicates a certain nuance to this position. Why? Presumably because seven Member States had intervened to express concern that permitting persons to obtain medical goods (or services) outside their State of residence while obtaining health insurance reimbursement from that State would jeopardize the financial integrity of the health insurance system. *Decker* is an important precedent for the recent judgments on an individual's right to be reimbursed for hospital and medical services in other States covered in Chapter 17B.

2. How did the Court resolve the second public health issue, namely the concern about the qualifications of the Belgian optician who provided the spectacles? The Court's conclusion points up the utility of the harmonization of professional training and standards surveyed in Chapter 18.

CRIMINAL PROCEEDINGS AGAINST BLUHME

Case C–67/97, [1998] ECR I–8033.

[The Danish Minister for Agriculture may adopt measures to protect certain species of bees in defined areas. The Minister accordingly prohibited beekeeping of any bees other than the relatively rare sub-species Laeso brown bee on certain islands. When Bluhme was prosecuted for keeping a different species of bee, he contended that the Danish rule was an unjustifiable restriction on the importation of bees.]

33   [T]he Court considers that measures to preserve an indigenous animal population with distinct characteristics contribute to the maintenance of biodiversity by ensuring the survival of the population concerned. By so doing, they are aimed at protecting the life of those animals and are capable of being justified under Article [30] of the Treaty.

34   From the point of view of such conservation of biodiversity, it is immaterial whether the object of protection is a separate subspecies, a distinct strain within any given species or merely a local colony, so long as the populations in question have characteristics distinguishing them from others and are therefore judged worthy of protection either to shelter them from a risk of extinction that is more or less imminent, or, even in the absence of such risk, on account of a scientific or other interest in preserving the pure population at the location concerned.

* * *

36   Conservation of biodiversity through the establishment of areas in which a population enjoys special protection, which is a method recognised in the Rio Convention, especially Article 8a thereof, is already put into practice in Community law [in particular, by means of the special protection areas provided for in Council Directive 79/409/EEC on the conservation of wild birds* * *.]

37   As for the threat of the disappearance of the Læsø brown bee, it is undoubtedly genuine in the event of mating with golden bees by reason of the recessive nature of the genes of the brown bee. The establishment by the national legislation of a protection area within which the keeping of bees other than Læsø brown bees is prohibited, for the purpose of ensuring the survival of the latter, therefore constitutes an appropriate measure in relation to the aim pursued.

NOTES AND QUESTIONS

1. Note that in *Bluhme*, the Court treated a restriction on the entry of bees into certain islands, as opposed to a restriction on importation of bees into the entire State, as still constituting a measure equivalent to a quantitative restriction. Note also that the Court considered the restriction justified as protecting animals' health under ECT Article 30. The Court might alternatively have considered it justified as environmental protection—see section C3 infra.

2. Fearful of the spread of crayfish plague, Germany adopted a regulation in 1989 prohibiting the import of live crayfish for commercial purposes, whether for immediate consumption or for stocking fish farms. The regulation permitted the Food and Forestry Office to grant derogations to prevent "excessive hardships." In Commission v. Germany (Crayfish imports), Case C–131/93, [1994] ECR I–3303, the Court held that the German import ban was disproportionate, finding that Germany could require health certificates from an exporting State's authorities and then use spot checks to verify safety.

The US Supreme Court in Maine v. Taylor, 477 U.S. 131, 106 S.Ct. 2440, 91 L.Ed.2d 110 (1986), came to the opposite conclusion in reviewing a Maine law which prohibited the import of live bait fish based on a fear that imported fish might contain parasites that could spread to local wild fish. Justice Blackmun's majority opinion held that "Maine's unique and fragile fisheries * * * would be placed at risk by three types of parasites prevalent in out-of-state baitfish, but not common to wild fish in Maine." The Supreme Court upheld Maine's total interdiction of baitfish imports in a rare example of its acceptance of a compelling state interest as a justification for a discriminatory statute. Has the Court of Justice given sufficient importance to the wildlife health interest Germany tried to protect? Will the more proportionate measures the Court suggested adequately protect this interest?

3. National animal health safeguard measures can result in the partitioning of the Community market. To reduce this risk, Council Directive 91/67, O.J. L 46/1 (Feb. 19, 1991), set in place a Community-wide system to regulate the production and marketing of fish that can be raised by aquaculture, including administrative supervision, health precautions, and on-site checks.

CRIMINAL PROCEEDINGS AGAINST ALBERT HEIJN

Case 94/83, [1984] ECR 3263.

[A Dutch law bans the sale of foodstuffs or beverages that contain pesticide residue in excess of a level fixed by an administrative agency. For the pesticide vinchlozoline, usually no residue is allowed, although the agency permits a minor level on lettuce and endives. A retailer, Heijn, imported apples from Italy with vinchlozoline residue. Italy permits the residue on apples. A 1976 Directive fixes maximum levels for certain pesticides, but not this one.]

10 * * * [T]he German and Netherlands Governments contend that the prohibition in question is justified in the interests of the protection of public health, because pesticides are very dangerous substances *per se,* and that it is not necessary, before taking protective measures, to establish whether vinchlozoline on apples is dangerous.

11 Albert Heijn BV contends that such a prohibition is disproportionate in relation to the objective of protecting public health, since the

pesticide in question is known to the national authorities and is tolerated on certain fruits and vegetables.

12   In the Commission's view, it is necessary to reconcile the requirements of fruit and vegetable growing with the need to protect human and animal health, whilst taking account of the progress of scientific knowledge regarding pesticides and of the dietary habits of the population. * * *

[The Court then stated its conclusions.]

13   It is not disputed that pesticides constitute a major risk to human and animal health and to the environment * * *.

* * *

15   Member States must take account of the fact that pesticides are substances which are both necessary to agriculture and dangerous to human and animal health. The fact that the quantities absorbed by the consumer, in particular in the form of residues on foodstuffs, can neither be predicted nor controlled justifies strict measures intended to reduce the risks faced by the consumer.

16   In so far as the relevant Community rules do not cover certain pesticides, Member States may regulate the presence of residues of those pesticides on foodstuffs in a way which may vary from one country to another according to the climatic conditions, the normal diet of the population and their state of health. In that context, they may permit different levels of the same pesticide in respect of different foodstuffs.

17   National rules of that nature may thus form part of a general policy designed to prevent the presence of pesticide residues on foodstuffs.

18   The authorities of the importing Member State are however obliged to review the prescribed maximum level if it appears to them that the reasons which led to its being fixed have changed, for example, as a result of the discovery of a new use for such and such a pesticide.

19   The reply to the questions raised by the national court must therefore be that Articles [28 and 30] of the EEC Treaty do not prevent a Member State from prohibiting the importation of apples from another Member State on account of the presence in or on those apples of a quantity of vinchlozoline greater than that authorized by the legislation of the first Member State, even though the maximum permitted vinchlozoline content * * * differs from that laid down for other kinds of food and drink.

Notes and Questions

1. The presence of pesticide residue on fruits and vegetables certainly worries many health authorities and consumers, but in the absence of precise knowledge, how little is too much? It is obvious that strict standards can be a serious bar to imports, since States vary radically in their regulatory attitudes

toward pesticides. Note that the Netherlands allowed the pesticide in question in minor quantities on lettuce and endives, but not on apples. Shouldn't that have troubled the Court? Who should have the burden of proof as to a pesticide residue's safety?

2. In Criminal Proceedings against Brandsma, Case C–293/94, [1996] ECR I–3159, a Dutch supermarket chain was subject to penal charges in Belgium when its Belgian branch sold a tile cleanser intended to eliminate algae from walls and tiles. The cleanser contained a biocide authorized by the Dutch authorities, but the defendant had never requested an authorization from the Belgian authorities. The defendant argued that the Dutch approval should be recognized on mutual trust principles and that the Belgian government should have the burden of proof to show that the cleanser was dangerous to health under ECT Article 30. The Court accepted Belgium's contention that in the absence of harmonized rules, it was free to use its discretion in determining what biocides must obtain a Belgian authorization before retail sale.

CRIMINAL PROCEEDINGS AGAINST SANDOZ

Case 174/82, [1983] ECR 2445.

[A 1949 Dutch law prohibited the addition of vitamins to food without a Government authorization. Sandoz sought to import "muesli" bars and beverages, health foods containing Vitamins A and D, from Germany and Belgium, where they were lawfully marketed. When Sandoz was prosecuted for selling its imported products without an authorization, the trial court referred several questions in a preliminary reference procedure. After finding that the Dutch law violated ECT Article 28, the Court turned to Article 30.]

11   [V]itamins are not in themselves harmful substances but on the contrary are recognized by modern science as necessary for the human organism. Nevertheless excessive consumption of them over a prolonged period may have harmful effects, the extent of which varies according to the type of vitamin: there is generally a greater risk with vitamins soluble in fat than with those soluble in water. According to the observations submitted to the Court, however, scientific research does not appear to be sufficiently advanced to be able to determine with certainty the critical quantities and the precise effects.

12   It is not disputed that the concentration of vitamins contained in the foodstuffs of the kind in issue is far from attaining the critical threshold of harmfulness so that even excessive consumption thereof cannot in itself involve a risk to public health. Nevertheless such a risk cannot be excluded in so far as the consumer absorbs with other foods further quantities of vitamins which it is impossible to monitor or foresee.

* * *

16   [I]n so far as there are uncertainties at the present state of scientific research it is for the Member States, in the absence of harmonization,

to decide what degree of protection of the health and life of humans they intend to assure, having regard however for the requirements of the free movement of goods within the Community.

17 Those principles also apply to substances such as vitamins which are not as a general rule harmful in themselves but may have special harmful effects solely if taken to excess as part of the general nutrition, the composition of which is unforeseeable and cannot be monitored. In view of the uncertainties inherent in the scientific assessment, national rules prohibiting, without prior authorization, the marketing of foodstuffs to which vitamins have been added are justified on principle within the meaning of Article [30] of the Treaty on grounds of the protection of human health.

18 Nevertheless the principle of proportionality which underlies the last sentence of Article [30] of the Treaty requires that the power of the Member States to prohibit imports of the products in question from other Member States should be restricted to what is necessary to attain the legitimate aim of protecting health.

* * *

20 [Accordingly,] Community law permits national rules prohibiting without prior authorization the marketing of foodstuffs lawfully marketed in another Member State to which vitamins have been added, provided that the marketing is authorized when the addition of vitamins meets a real need, especially a technical or nutritional one.

* * *

23 [A]lthough the national authorities may* * *ask the importer to produce the information in his possession relating to the composition of the product, and the technical or nutritional reason for adding vitamins, they must themselves assess* * *whether authorization must be granted pursuant to Community law.

NOTES AND QUESTIONS

Why did the Court conclude that vitamin supplements could pose health risks? Did the Court go too far in ¶ 17 in giving a State discretion to ban vitamin-enriched food in the absence of serious evidence of risk? On the other hand, later in the judgment the Court states that a State must grant a product authorization when "compatible with the need to protect health" (¶ 18), and that the burden of proof as to safety cannot be placed on the importer (¶ 23). Why is that important?

COMMISSION v. GERMANY

(German beer)
Case 178/84, [1987] ECR 1227.

[A German law, dating back to the Reinheitsgebot (purity law) of 1516, requires that beer be manufactured only from malted barley, hops, yeast and water. The word "Bier" can only be used for beer produced in this manner. In other Member States, beer is also produced from rice and other cereals, with extensive use of additives. When the Commission challenged the German rules as violating ECT Article 28, Germany argued health grounds: some additives are dangerous, particularly since Germans consume far more beer per capita than other people do. The Court did not agree.]

The Absolute Ban on the Marketing of Beers Containing Additives

38 In the Commission's opinion the absolute ban on the marketing of beers containing additives cannot be justified on public-health grounds. It maintains that the other Member States control very strictly the utilization of additives in foodstuffs and do not authorize the use of any given additive until thorough tests have established that it is harmless. In the Commission's view, there should be a presumption that beers manufactured in other Member States which contain additives authorized there represent no danger to public health.* * * In any event, the rules on additives applying to beer in the Federal Republic of Germany are disproportionate in so far as they completely preclude the use of additives whereas the rules for other beverages, such as soft drinks, are much more flexible.

39 For its part, the German Government considers that in view of the dangers resulting from the utilization of additives whose long-term effects are not yet known and in particular of the risks resulting from the accumulation of additives in the organism and their interaction with other substances, such as alcohol, it is necessary to minimize the quantity of additives ingested. Since beer is a foodstuff of which large quantities are consumed in Germany, the German Government considers that it is particularly desirable to prohibit the use of any additive in its manufacture, especially in so far as the use of additives is not technologically necessary and can be avoided if only the ingredients laid down in the Biersteuergesetz are used. * * *

[The Court then stated its conclusions.]

41 The Court has consistently held that "in so far as there are uncertainties at the present state of scientific research it is for the Member States, in the absence of harmonization, to decide what degree of protection of the health and life of humans they intend to assure, having regard however to the requirements of the free movement of goods within the Community" [citing *Sandoz*].

42 * * * Community law does not preclude the adoption by the Member States of legislation whereby the use of additives is subjected to prior authorization granted by a measure of general application for specific additives, in respect of all products, for certain products only or for certain uses. Such legislation meets a genuine need of health policy,

namely that of restricting the uncontrolled consumption of food additives.

* * *

44 [However, in *Sandoz* and other prior judgments,] the Court inferred from the principle of proportionality underlying the last sentence of Article [30] of the Treaty that prohibitions on the marketing of products containing additives authorized in the Member State of production but prohibited in the Member State of importation must be restricted to what is actually necessary to secure the protection of public health. The Court also concluded that the use of a specific additive which is authorized in another Member State must be authorized in the case of a product imported from that Member State where, in view, on the one hand, of the findings of international scientific research, and in particular of the work of the Community's Scientific Committee for Food, the Codex Alimentarius Committee of the Food and Agriculture Organization of the United Nations (FAO) and the World Health Organization, and, on the other hand, of the eating habits prevailing in the importing Member State, the additive in question does not present a risk to public health and meets a real need, especially a technical one.

45 Secondly, * * * by virtue of the principle of proportionality, traders must also be able to apply, under a procedure which is easily accessible to them and can be concluded within a reasonable time, for the use of specific additives to be authorized by a measure of general application.

46 [Furthermore,] it must be open to traders to challenge before the courts an unjustified failure to grant authorization. Without prejudice to the right of the competent national authorities of the importing Member State to ask traders to produce the information in their possession which may be useful for the purpose of assessing the facts, it is for those authorities to demonstrate * * * that the prohibition is justified on grounds relating to the protection of the health of its population.

47 The German rules on additives applicable to beer result in the exclusion of all the additives authorized in the other Member States and not the exclusion of just some of them for which there is concrete justification by reason of the risks which they involve in view of the eating habits of the German population; moreover those rules do not lay down any procedure whereby traders can obtain authorization for the use of a specific additive in the manufacture of beer by means of a measure of general application.

48 [T]he German Government* * *maintains that it is important, for reasons of general preventive health protection, to minimize the quantity of additives ingested, and that it is particularly advisable to prohibit altogether their use in the manufacture of beer, a foodstuff consumed in considerable quantities by the German population.

49   However, it appears from the tables of additives authorized for use in the various foodstuffs submitted by the German Government itself that some of the additives authorized in other Member States for use in the manufacture of beer are also authorized under the German rules * * * for use in the manufacture of all, or virtually all, beverages. Mere reference to the potential risks of the ingestion of additives in general and to the fact that beer is a foodstuff consumed in large quantities does not suffice to justify the imposition of stricter rules in the case of beer.

* * *

53   Consequently, in so far as the German rules on additives in beer entail a general ban on additives, their application to beers imported from other Member States is contrary to the requirements of Community law as laid down in the case-law of the Court, since that prohibition is contrary to the principle of proportionality and is therefore not covered by the exception provided for in Article [30] of the EEC Treaty.

NOTES AND QUESTIONS

1.   Recall that the Court held in *Sandoz* that the burden of proof as to safety could not be placed on the importer. In *German beer,* where did the Court place the burden of proof as to whether certain additives constitute a health hazard? Why is an allocation of burden of proof so important? Note also the specific further procedural safeguards for importers required by the Court in ¶¶ 45–46. Why are they important? In recent ECT Article 30 cases, the Court has often expressly placed the burden of proof on the importing State and expressly required procedural safeguards for importers. In *Heijn,* supra, the Court did not place the burden of proof on the Netherlands. Should it have?

NOTE ON ADDITIVES TO FOOD

National parliaments and consumer advocate groups frequently press for strict health standards for foodstuffs, encouraging national administrative bodies to adopt authorization programs. The issue, once again, is the compatibility of the national health protection systems with the Community's goal of free movement of goods. The Court of Justice must then balance the interests.

In Commission v. Denmark (Vitamin additives), Case C–192/01, [2003] ECR I–9693, the Commission attacked a Danish administrative system that permitted the sale of foodstuffs with added vitamins or minerals only after specific authorization based upon whether the additives satisfied a health need in the Danish population. Denmark relied on *Sandoz* and the precautionary principle. The precautionary principle, initially employed to justify environmental protection measures (see ECT Article 174(2), now replaced by TFEU Article 191(2)), is now frequently cited by States in support of their health and safety standards, and occasionally also cited by the Community to support its rules. The Commission Communication on the Precautionary Principle, COM (2000) 1(Feb. 2, 2000), specifically states that it can be applied to support human, animal and plant health rules.

In the *Danish Vitamins* case, the Court accepted that Denmark had a wide discretion in protecting health, but insisted that marketing limits must be based on a "real risk* * * sufficiently established on the basis of the latest scientific data available" (¶ 48). Turning to Denmark's precautionary principle argument, the Court set the following standard:

51   A proper application of the precautionary principle presupposes, in the first place, the identification of the potentially negative consequences for health of the proposed addition of nutrients, and, secondly, a comprehensive assessment of the risk to health based on the most reliable scientific data available and the most recent results of international research.

52   Where it proves to be impossible to determine with certainty the existence or extent of the alleged risk because of the insufficiency, inconclusiveness or imprecision of the results of studies conducted, but the likelihood of real harm to public health persists should the risk materialise, the precautionary principle justifies the adoption of restrictive measures.

The Court ultimately concluded that Denmark's total ban of all foodstuffs with added vitamins and minerals until authorized was disproportionate (¶ 55). Other judgments reach similar results. In Commission v. France (Nutrient-added foods), Case C–24/00, [2004] ECR I–1277, the Court held that French rules requiring a specific authorization for all imported nutrient-enhanced foods were disproportionate. The Court held that the additives must pose "a genuine risk to public health" (¶ 27), and that the authorization procedures must be completed in a reasonable time. Two years to review the sports drink, "Red Bull", was held to be excessive. The Court also held that France could not ban nutrient-added foods if appropriate label warnings would suffice (¶ 75).

Once again, harmonization should be very helpful. Regulation 1925/2006, on common rules on the addition of vitamins, minerals and other substances to food, O.J.L. 404/9 (Dec. 30, 2006), sets minimum and maximum levels for such nutrients. Nutrients not listed in an annex (regularly updated) are prohibited. No nutrients may be added to fresh fruit, vegetables or meat.

2. PUBLIC MORALITY, PUBLIC POLICY AND PUBLIC SECURITY CASES

The Court of Justice has only infrequently had to interpret the scope of the public morality, public policy or public security exceptions in ECT Article 30 (now TFEU Article 36). Overall, it would appear that the Court is rather deferential to State rules based upon public morality or public security, but quite skeptical of a State claim that its rules are justified by public policy, probably because the latter concept can be so amorphous.

Cases raising public morality issues are rare. Regina v. Henn & Darby, Case 34/79, [1979] ECR 3795, attracted considerable attention, because it was the first time the Court of Justice examined a public morality issue and the first reference from the House of Lords. Henn and Darby were convicted of importing Danish sex films and magazines in violation of an 1876 customs law prohibiting the entry of "indecent or obscene" articles. As we noted earlier, the Court first held that a total ban on imports could constitute a measure equivalent to a quantitative restriction. The Court then held that "it is for each Member State to determine in accordance with its own scale of values and in the forum selected by it the requirements of public morality" (¶ 15). The Court finally held that the rules in different regions of the UK (England, Scotland, Wales), although not uniform in scope, "taken as a whole" did restrain or prohibit both the manufacture and marketing of indecent or obscene articles (¶ 21).

A later judgment, Conegate Ltd. V. H.M. Customs, Case 121/85, [1986] ECR 1007, distinguished *Henn & Darby* in holding that a customs prohibition of the import of erotic dolls from Germany did represent arbitrary discrimination under the second sentence of Article 30, because no UK law prohibited their manufacture and their sale was permitted in licensed sex shops.

The Court has recently considered a public morality issue in a case involving modern technology.

DYNAMIC MEDIEN VERTRIEBS v. AVIDES MEDIA
Case C–244/06, [2008] ECR I–505.

[Japanese cartoons in DVD or video cassette forms were rated by a UK film classification board as suitable for young persons over 15. When a firm sought to sell them by mail order into Germany, German authorities barred them until they should be rated by a German body and labelled accordingly. In an Article 234 proceeding, the Court initially held that the German rules requiring the new rating did not qualify as the regulation of 'selling arrangements' under the *Keck* doctrine, described in section D infra, because the review and labelling made the marketing of imports "more difficult and expensive" (¶ 34). The Court then observed that both the 1989 UN Convention on the Rights of the Child and article 24 of the Nice Charter of Fundamental Rights justify national rules for the protection of children.]

43   It is clear * * * that the national rules at issue in the main proceedings are designed to protect children against information and materials injurious to their well-being.

44   In that connection, it is not indispensable that restrictive measures laid down by the authorities of a Member State to protect the rights of the child * * * correspond to a conception shared by all Member States as regards the level of protection and the detailed rules relating to it. As the conception may vary from one Member State to another

on the basis of, inter alia, moral or cultural views, Member States must be recognised as having a definite margin of discretion.

* * *

47 There is no doubt that prohibiting the sale and transfer by mail order of image storage media which have not been examined and classified by the competent authority for the purpose of protecting young persons and which do not bear a label from that authority indicating the age from which they may be viewed constitutes a measure suitable for protecting children against information and materials injurious to their well-being.

48 As far as concerns the substantive scope of the prohibition concerned, the [German] Law on the protection of young persons does not preclude all forms of marketing of unchecked image storage media. It is clear from the decision making the reference that it is permissible to import and sell such image storage media to adults by way of distribution channels involving personal contact between the supplier and the purchaser, which thus ensures that children do not have access to the image storage media concerned. In the light of those factors, it appears that the rules at issue in the main proceedings do not go beyond what is necessary to attain the objective pursued by the Member State concerned

49 As regards the examination procedure established by the national legislature in order to protect children against information and materials injurious to their well-being, the mere fact that a Member State has opted for a system of protection which differs from that adopted by another Member State cannot affect the assessment of the proportionality of the national provisions enacted to that end. Those provisions must be assessed solely by reference to the objective pursued and the level of protection which the Member State in question intends to provide.

50 However, such an examination procedure must be one which is readily accessible, can be completed within a reasonable period, and, if it leads to a refusal, the decision of refusal must be open to challenge before the courts.

NOTES AND QUESTIONS

1. Do you agree with the Court view that Member States have a substantial degree of discretion in determining their "scale of values" and the level of protection of their moral interests? Should the Court try to set some Community standards, as it does when reviewing measures adopted to protect health or consumer interests? When we examine *Schindler* and later judgments concerning State regulation of forms of gambling in Chapter 17, we will observe a similar level of Court deference to State rules, unless they are found to be discriminatory in application.

CAMPUS OIL v. MINISTER FOR INDUSTRY AND ENERGY

Case 72/83, [1984] ECR 2727.

[Ireland has no domestic supply of crude oil. An Irish state-owned oil company owns the only oil refinery in Ireland. In 1982, an Irish Order required all oil importers to buy a certain percentage of their needs from this refinery, instead of from direct imports. Campus Oil challenged the law, which Ireland defended under the public policy and public security exceptions. The Court of Justice initially found the compulsory purchase obligation to constitute a quantitative restriction. Turning to ECT Article 30, the Court considered whether Ireland could continue to rely upon the public security exception after the Community had taken measures under the Common Energy Policy to protect Community interests in an energy crisis.]

The Justification of the Measures at Issue in the Light of Community Rules on the Matter

28   Certain precautionary measures have indeed been taken at Community level to deal with difficulties in supplies of crude oil and petroleum products. Council Directives 68/414/EEC and 73/238/EEC require Member States to maintain minimum stocks and to coordinate to a certain extent the national measures adopted for the purpose of drawing on those stocks, of imposing specific restrictions on consumption and of regulating prices. Council Decision 77/706/EEC provides for the setting of a Community target for a reduction in consumption in the event of difficulties in supply and for the sharing out between the Member States of the quantities saved.

* * *

30   Even though those precautions against a shortage of petroleum products reduce the risk of Member States being left without essential supplies, there would none the less still be real danger in the event of a crisis * * *.

31   Consequently, the existing Community rules give a Member State whose supplies of petroleum products depend totally or almost totally on deliveries from other countries certain guarantees that deliveries from other Member States will be maintained in the event of a serious shortfall in proportions which match those of supplies to the market of the supplying State. However, this does not mean that the Member State concerned has an unconditional assurance that supplies will in any event be maintained at least at a level sufficient to meet its minimum needs. In those circumstances, the possibility for a Member State to rely on Article [30] to justify appropriate complementary measures at national level cannot be excluded, even where there exist Community rules on the matter.

The Scope of the Public Policy and Public Security Exceptions

* * *

33   [T]he concept of public security * * * is the only one relevant in this case, since the concept of public policy is not pertinent * * *.

34   * * * [P]etroleum products, because of their exceptional importance as an energy source in the modern economy, are of fundamental importance for a country's existence since not only its economy but above all its institutions, its essential public services and even the survival of its inhabitants depend upon them. An interruption of supplies of petroleum products, with the resultant dangers for the country's existence, could therefore seriously affect the public security that Article [30] allows States to protect.

35   It is true that, as the Court has held on a number of occasions, * * * Article [30] refers to matters of a non-economic nature. A Member State cannot be allowed to avoid the effects of measures provided for in the Treaty by pleading the economic difficulties caused by the elimination of barriers to intra-Community trade. However, in the light of the seriousness of the consequences that an interruption in supplies of petroleum products may have for a country's existence, the aim of ensuring a minimum supply of petroleum products at all times is to be regarded as transcending purely economic considerations and thus as capable of constituting an objective covered by the concept of public security.

NOTES AND QUESTIONS

1. The Court of Justice justified the Irish legislation on public security grounds rather than public policy grounds, without giving any explanation for doing so. Perhaps the Court considers public policy to be a broader catch-all concept whose use should be avoided when a narrower ground can be applied. But is the public security rationale convincing? It seems strange that the Court of Justice, which usually presses so strongly for Community integration, should have allowed Ireland to adopt a unilateral energy protection policy, instead of relying on Community energy policy protection for all States in time of crisis. The judgment was sharply criticized for these reasons in L. Gormley, Prohibiting Restrictions on Trade Within the EEC 134–138 (North Holland 1985). Nonetheless, the Court considered *Campus Oil* to be an authoritative precedent in its recent series of *Golden share* cases surveyed in Chapter 32B.

2. In Commission v. Germany (Firefighter equipment), Case C–103/01, [2003] ECR I–5369, the Commission contended that certain German states' rules for personal protection equipment for firefighter helmets and safety belts created a barrier to imports. Germany argued that firefighter equipment falls within the competence of German states, which have the responsibility for "securing public safety or order." Do you think the German equipment standards qualify for an exception under the public policy or safety exception under Article 30? The Court drew a distinction between the role of firefighters

and that of "other forces whose main task is the maintenance of law and order" (¶ 36). Does this suggest that national rules regulating protective equipment intended to provide added safety to police officers might qualify for an ECT Article 30 exception?

C. THE COURT'S ELABORATION OF FREE MOVEMENT OF GOODS PRINCIPLES

1. THE CASSIS DE DIJON DOCTRINE

Thus far, we have dealt only with the interpretation and direct application of ECT Articles 28 and 30 (now TFEU Articles 34 and 36). The Court of Justice has however significantly elaborated on the Treaty text, making a major contribution to the achievement of the common market in this sphere. Going beyond the precise wording of ECT Article 28, the Court has enunciated the doctrine that national rules that are not discriminatory (somewhat awkwardly called "indistinctly applicable" rules) may nonetheless violate the basic principle of free movement of goods, but then accepted that national measures can be justified on grounds not listed in ECT Article 30. Perceiving the functional utility of this approach, the Commission has both publicized the Court doctrine and relied upon it in developing the internal market program, as we shall see in Chapter 14B.

REWE–ZENTRAL v. BUNDESMONOPOLVERWALTUNG FÜR BRANNTWEIN

(Cassis de Dijon)
Case 120/78, [1979] ECR 649.

[When Rewe–Zentral applied for a license to import French-produced "Cassis de Dijon," a popular fruit liqueur, for sale in Germany, the Federal Monopoly Administration for Spirits refused the license on the grounds that the fruit liqueur had too low an alcohol content to be lawfully sold in Germany. On appeal, the Hesse tax court referred questions concerning the application of ECT Articles 28 and 30 to the German rules.]

3   [German law requires] that the marketing of fruit liqueurs, such as "Cassis de Dijon", is conditional upon a minimum alcohol content of 25%, whereas the alcohol content of the product in question, which is freely marketed as such in France, is between 15 and 20%.

* * *

6   The national court is asking for assistance in the matter of interpretation in order to enable it to assess whether the requirement of a minimum alcohol content may be covered * * * by the prohibition on all measures having an effect equivalent to quantitative restrictions in

trade between Member States contained in Article [28] of the Treaty * * *.

* * *

8   In the absence of common rules relating to the production and marketing of alcohol * * * it is for the Member States to regulate all matters relating to the production and marketing of alcohol and alcoholic beverages on their own territory.

9   Obstacles to movement within the Community resulting from disparities between the national laws relating to the marketing of the products in question must be accepted in so far as those provisions may be recognized as being necessary in order to satisfy mandatory requirements relating in particular to the effectiveness of fiscal supervision, the protection of public health, the fairness of commercial transactions and the defense of the consumer.

* * *

10   As regards the protection of public health the German Government states that the purpose of the fixing of minimum alcohol contents by national legislation is to avoid the proliferation of alcoholic beverages on the national market, in particular alcoholic beverages with a low alcohol content, since, in its view, such products may more easily induce a tolerance towards alcohol than more highly alcoholic beverages.

11   Such considerations are not decisive since the consumer can obtain on the market an extremely wide range of weakly or moderately alcoholic products and furthermore a large proportion of alcoholic beverages with a high alcohol content freely sold on the German market is generally consumed in a diluted form.

12   The German Government also claims that the fixing of a lower limit for the alcohol content of certain liqueurs is designed to protect the consumer against unfair practices on the part of producers and distributors of alcoholic beverages.

This argument is based on the consideration that the lowering of the alcohol content secures a competitive advantage in relation to beverages with a higher alcohol content, since alcohol constitutes by far the most expensive constituent of beverages by reason of the high rate of tax to which it is subject.

13   However, this line of argument cannot be taken so far as to regard the mandatory fixing of minimum alcohol contents as being an essential guarantee of the fairness of commercial transactions, since it is a simple matter to ensure that suitable information is conveyed to the purchaser by requiring the display of an indication of origin and of the alcohol content on the packaging of products.

* * *

[14] In practice, the principal effect of requirements of this nature is to promote alcoholic beverages having a high alcohol content by excluding from the national market products of other Member States which do not answer that description.

* * *

There is therefore no valid reason why, provided that they have been lawfully produced and marketed in one of the Member States, alcoholic beverages should not be introduced into any other Member State; the sale of such products may not be subject to a legal prohibition on the marketing of beverages with an alcohol content lower than the limit set by the national rules.

[15] Consequently, * * * the concept of "measures having an effect equivalent to quantitative restrictions on imports" contained in Article [28] of the Treaty is to be understood to mean that the fixing of a minimum alcohol content for alcoholic beverages intended for human consumption by the legislation of a Member State also falls within the prohibition laid down in that provision where the importation of alcoholic beverages lawfully produced and marketed in another Member State is concerned.

NOTES AND QUESTIONS

1. In ¶ 9, the Court allowed "the defense of the consumer" and other "mandatory requirements" to restrict intra-Community trade. "Mandatory requirements" is an awkward translation of the French "exigences imperatives," which has been better translated in later judgments as imperative state or public interests. Note that the Court in ¶ 13 immediately applies the principle of proportionality to limit the German consumer interest claim.

2. What is the basis for the Court of Justice's acceptance of consumer protection as a state interest which can limit the free movement of goods? Is the Court in effect adding consumer rights and other major state interests to the exceptions listed in ECT Article 30? While that might seem plausible, the Court rejected such an interpretation in Commission v. Ireland (Irish souvenirs), Case 113/80, [1981] ECR 1625. A 1971 Irish law prohibited the sale of imported artifacts and jewelry representing motifs symbolic of Ireland (e.g., a shamrock or a wolfhound) unless the imported product indicated it was "foreign" or showed the country of origin. Ireland claimed this law protected consumer interests, and therefore fell under the public policy exception in ECT Article 30. The Court said that this was "mistaken" and the exceptions in Article 30 must be "interpreted strictly." Rather, the Court said, its established caselaw permitted consumer rights to be recognized as an interest which constituted an exception to Article 28 itself. Is this a distinction without a real difference? The Court's approach is often referred to as a "rule of reason" interpretation of Article 28. See L. Gormley, Prohibiting Restrictions on Trade Within the EEC 51–57 (North–Holland 1985).

3. The German minimum alcohol content law applied both to domestic and imported products. Would it have violated the guidelines of Commission

Directive 70/50 discussed above? No, because that directive says that national rules which are non-discriminatory are not measures having equivalent effect unless, pursuant to the directive's article 3, they are disproportionately restrictive. Yet in *Cassis de Dijon* the Court found the German law to be a measure equivalent to a quantitative restriction in violation of Article 28. After reviewing *Cassis,* the Commission has concluded that Directive 70/50 was flawed when it made an exception for non-discriminatory state measures. This is one of the instances where reading the Advocate General's opinion is helpful, since Advocate General Capotorti cited Directive 70/50 and concluded that the Commission was excessively prudent (a polite way of saying the Commission was wrong) in believing Member State measures did not violate Article 28 if they did not discriminate, but rather applied equally to domestic and imported goods (sometimes referred to as "indistinctly applicable" measures). [1979] ECR at 669–70.

NOTE ON THE COMMISSION 1980 COMMUNICATION ON CASSIS DE DIJON

The Commission has certainly read *Cassis de Dijon* as a landmark decision promoting the free movement of goods, rather than the reverse. On October 3, 1980, the Commission issued a policy Communication on the consequences to be drawn from *Cassis de Dijon*. This is Document 10 in the Selected Documents and merits careful reading.

Based upon the Court's language in ¶ 14, the Commission sees the main principle of *Cassis de Dijon* to be: "Any product lawfully produced and marketed in one Member State must, in principle, be admitted to the market of any other Member State." A corollary is that a State's commercial or technical rules may not take "an exclusively national viewpoint." This has been called the "mutual trust" principle: if one State's rules allow a product to be marketed, all other States should have confidence in the first State's judgment and likewise allow the product to be marketed. In later chapters, we will see how this concept is key to attaining an integrated internal market.

In its 1980 Communication, the Commission endorsed the Court of Justice's declaration that a State's protection of various "mandatory requirements (public health, protection of consumers or the environment, the fairness of commercial transactions, etc.)" constitutes a justifiable exception to ECT Article 28. This list is non-exhaustive; as we shall see, other imperative state interests are possible. Note that the Commission lists environmental protection as a state interest, although it was not mentioned by the Court in *Cassis*.

The Commission limits a State's protection of interests to measures which are "the most appropriate and at the same time least hinder trade." Consider the following cases:

In Criminal proceedings against Gilli, Case 788/79, [1980] ECR 2071, the defendant was prosecuted for importing apple vinegar from Germany in violation of an Italian law forbidding the marketing of vinegar made from anything other than wine, allegedly to protect consumers. The Court held that the ban on non-wine based vinegar was excessive, since a product labeling requirement would have been sufficient to protect consumer interests.

In Walter Rau Lebensmittelwerke v. De Smedt, Case 261/81, [1982] ECR 3961, a German producer of margarine packaged in a long rectangular shape challenged a Belgian law forbidding the sale of margarine in any form other than cubes, allegedly in order to prevent Belgian consumers from confusing butter with margarine. What result?

Before turning to later case law under *Cassis de Dijon,* a word on the US constitutional analogue, the dormant Commerce Clause. Because the US case law is so voluminous and the governing Supreme Court doctrines have evolved significantly in American constitutional history, it is quite difficult to draw many parallels with the Community rules. As noted in the previous chapter, American courts certainly strike down state laws found to be discriminatory or protectionist in effect, which does parallel Community doctrine. See, e.g., H.P. Hood & Sons v. Du Mond, 336 U.S. 525, 69 S.Ct. 657, 93 L.Ed. 865 (1949) (New York milk dealer licensing system found to protect New York producers at expense of exporter of milk to Massachusetts).

In most US cases, however, the state regulation is not clearly discriminatory or protectionist. The Supreme Court's modern "balancing" approach consists in analyzing whether there exists a "legitimate local public interest" which the state regulation seeks to protect, and then whether the burden on interstate commerce imposed by the local rule is "excessive in relation to the putative local benefits." Pike v. Bruce Church, Inc., noted at page 772 *infra.*

There is a certain resemblance between the *Pike* test and that of *Cassis de Dijon.* The analysis of whether there exists a "legitimate local public interest" corresponds to some degree with that of whether there exists a "mandatory requirement" or imperative state interest. Likewise, the Supreme Court's balancing analysis has some similarity to the proportionality examination made by the Court of Justice in reviewing whether the state rules are narrowly tailored and not excessive in relation to the end sought. However, the analytic approaches and the goals sought in the two systems are sufficiently different to make comparisons decidedly difficult. While reading the Community cases which follow, consider whether the US Supreme Court would have reached the same result under a dormant Commerce Clause analysis.

Finally, we should note that TFEU Article 36, which replicates ECT Article 30, does not add any public interests that could justify national law limits on the free movement of goods, not even the common ones of consumer protection and environmental protection. Presumably the drafters of the Lisbon Treaty felt it desirable to continue to allow the Court of Justice a free hand in deciding what interests should qualify under the *Cassis de Dijon* doctrine.

2. CONSUMER PROTECTION CASES

Without any doubt, consumer protection is the state interest which has most often generated issues in the application of the *Cassis de Dijon* doctrine. Just as in the United States, Member States enacted a flood of legislative and regulatory measures to protect consumer interests from the 1960s onward. Although usually non-discriminatory on their face, these consumer protection rules often could adversely affect intra-Community trade. Thus, the Court has frequently had to determine the importance of the consumer interest concerned, the proportionality of the measure taken, and the degree of adverse impact on intra-Community imports or exports. Not surprisingly, consumer protection has also become one of the most important fields of Community legislation since the mid–1970s—see Chapter 35.

COMMISSION v. UNITED KINGDOM
(Marks of origin)
Case 207/83, [1985] ECR 1201.

[A UK regulation, the 1981 Trade Descriptions Order, required that retailers ensure that certain types of products (clothing and textile goods, household electrical appliances, footwear and cutlery) have a "clear and legible" indication of their national origin. The Commission brought an Article 226 proceeding to challenge the Order.]

13   [The United Kingdom] contends that the Order is a national measure which applies to imported and national products alike [whose] effect * * * on trade between Member States is uncertain, if not non-existent. Secondly, it maintains that, in the case of the goods to which the Order applies, the requirements relating to indications of origin meet the requirements of consumer protection since consumers regard the origin of the goods which they buy as an indicator of their quality or true value.

* * *

16   It should first be observed, * * * that in order to escape the obligations imposed on him by the legislation in question the retailer will tend * * * to ask his wholesalers to supply him with goods which are already origin-marked. That tendency has been confirmed by complaints received by the Commission. Thus, the * * * [French Domestic Appliance Manufacturers' Association] informed the Commission that French manufacturers of domestic appliances who wish to sell their products on the United Kingdom market have had to mark such products systematically in response to pressure brought to bear on them by their distributors. The effects of the contested provisions are therefore liable to spread to the wholesale trade and even to manufacturers.

17   Secondly, * * * the purpose of indications of origin or origin-marking is to enable consumers to distinguish between domestic and imported

products and this enables them to assert any prejudices which they may have against foreign products. As the Court has had occasion to emphasize in various contexts, the Treaty, by establishing a common market and progressively approximating the economic policies of the Member States seeks to unite national markets in a single market having the characteristics of a domestic market. Within such a market, the origin-marking requirement not only makes the marketing in a Member State of goods produced in other Member States in the sectors in question more difficult; it also has the effect of slowing down economic interpenetration in the Community by handicapping the sale of goods produced as the result of a division of labour between Member States.

18   It follows from those considerations that the United Kingdom provisions in question are liable to have the effect of increasing the production costs of imported goods and making it more difficult to sell them on the United Kingdom market.

19   The second argument advanced by the United Kingdom is in effect that the contested legislation, applicable without distinction to domestic and imported products, is necessary in order to satisfy imperative requirements relating to consumer protection. It states that a survey carried out amongst United Kingdom consumers has shown that they associate the quality of certain goods with the countries in which they are made. They like to know, for example, whether leather shoes have been made in Italy, woolen knitwear in the United Kingdom, fashionwear in France and domestic electrical appliances in Germany.

20   That argument must be rejected. The requirements relating to the indication of origin of goods are applicable without distinction to domestic and imported products only in form because, by their very nature, they are intended to enable the consumer to distinguish between those two categories of products, which may thus prompt him to give his preference to national products.

21   [I]f the national origin of goods brings certain qualities to the minds of consumers, it is in manufacturers' interests to indicate it themselves on the goods or on their packaging and it is not necessary to compel them to do so. In that case, the protection of consumers is sufficiently guaranteed by rules which enable the use of false indications of origin to be prohibited. Such rules are not called in question by the EEC Treaty.

Notes and Questions

1. Although the UK may have had good intentions in adopting its label of origin rules, some UK consumers might well be inclined to buy domestic products rather than the identified foreign ones. Of course, as ¶ 31 indicates, some Community producers may want themselves to identify the State of origin if its products enjoy a high reputation. Note the Court's description of

the goal of "economic interpenetration" and the "division of labour" within the common market in ¶ 17.

2. In Commission v. Ireland (Hallmarking of precious metals), Case C–30/99, [2001] ECR I–4619, the Commission contended that Irish rules on the hallmarking of articles made from gold, silver and platinum to indicate their precious metal content violated Article 28. Ireland required domestic and imported articles to bear marks set by the Assay Office in Ireland or the UK, or a hallmark set by an approved office under an international convention. The Commission contended that the Irish rules required a second hallmarking for articles produced in some Member States that did not satisfy these rules. The Court held that Ireland could rely on consumer protection to justify hallmarking of such articles, but that the principle of proportionality required Ireland to accept hallmarked products from other States when the marks are "intelligible to consumers."

In ¶ 32, the Court applied its current standard: "the presumed expectations of an average consumer who is reasonably well informed and reasonably observant and circumspect." Note that this is not a low standard—not merely that of an "average consumer" who is casual, careless or ill-informed. The Court and the CFI also apply this standard in their recent trademark confusion judgments—see Chapter 19D.

HUNT v. WASHINGTON STATE APPLE ADVERTISING COMMISSION

432 U.S. 333, 97 S.Ct. 2434, 53 L.Ed.2d 383 (1977).

[A North Carolina regulation required all closed containers of apples shipped into or sold in the state to display only the U.S. Department of Agriculture (USDA) grade, but not state grades. Because 13 apple producing states had their own grading system, the ostensible purpose of the regulation was to eliminate deception and confusion. North Carolina did not have any state grades for its apples. The Washington State Apple Advertising Commission challenged the rule, observing that its apples are shipped in containers marked with its grades, which are equivalent to or superior to the USDA grades. Identifying and repacking or relabeling containers shipped to North Carolina would impose a substantial cost. The Supreme Court unanimously struck down the North Carolina regulation in an opinion by Chief Justice Burger.]

[A] finding that state legislation furthers matters of legitimate local concern, even in the health and consumer protection areas, does not end the inquiry.

* * *

Rather, when such state legislation comes into conflict with the Commerce Clause's overriding requirement of a national "common market," we are confronted with the task of effecting an accommodation of the competing national and local interests [citing *Pike v. Bruce Church*].

* * *

[T]he challenged statute has the practical effect of not only burdening interstate sales of Washington apples, but also discriminating against them.

* * *

[The discrimination] results from the fact that North Carolina apple producers, unlike their Washington competitors, were not forced to alter their marketing practices in order to comply with the statute. They were still free to market their wares under the USDA Grade or none at all as they had done prior to the statute's enactment. Obviously, the increased costs imposed by the statute would tend to shield the local apple industry from the competition of Washington apple growers and dealers who are already at a competitive disadvantage because of their great distance from the North Carolina market.

Second, the statute has the effect of stripping away from the Washington apple industry the competitive and economic advantages it has earned for itself through its expensive inspection and grading system.

NOTES AND QUESTIONS

1.　The Supreme Court early recognized that consumer protection rules represented a valid exercise of state police powers. In Plumley v. Massachusetts, 155 U.S. 461, 15 S.Ct. 154, 39 L.Ed. 223 (1894), the Court upheld a Massachusetts statute prohibiting the sale of oleomargarine colored yellow because the statute sought to "suppress false pretenses and to promote fair dealings." In *Hunt*, Chief Justice Burger accepted that states have "a substantial interest in protecting their citizens from confusion and deception in the marketing of foodstuffs," but considered that labelling rules on closed containers of apples did not really protect consumers, who buy apples which are removed from the containers at the retail level. Do you agree? How would the Court of Justice deal with a case parallel to *Hunt*?

COMMISSION v. GERMANY
(German beer).

[The excerpt of this judgment in the previous section considered whether Germany's prohibition of additives in the production of beer could be justified on public health grounds. The German law also had a consumer protection feature: it forbid imported beer to be labeled as "Bier," because consumers might be deceived into thinking that the imported product satisfied the German beer purity rules, when it did not.]

29　It is not contested that the [German law prohibiting the use of the word "Bier" for] beers from other Member States in whose manufacture raw materials other than malted barley have been lawfully used, in particular rice and maize, is liable to constitute an obstacle to their importation into the Federal Republic of Germany.

30　Accordingly, it must be established whether the application of that provision may be justified by imperative requirements relating to consumer protection.

31   The German Government's argument that [this provision of the beer law] is essential in order to protect German consumers because, in their minds, the designation "Bier" is inseparably linked to the beverage manufactured solely from the ingredients laid down in [the beer law] must be rejected.

32   Firstly, consumers' conceptions which vary from one Member State to the other are also likely to evolve in the course of time within a Member State. The establishment of the common market is, it should be added, one of the factors that may play a major contributory role in that development. Whereas rules protecting consumers against misleading practices enable such a development to be taken into account, legislation of the kind contained in [the beer law] prevents it from taking place. As the Court has already held in another context [in *the UK Wine and Beer case, supra* page 436], the legislation of a Member State must not "crystallize given consumer habits so as to consolidate an advantage acquired by national industries concerned to comply with them."

33   Secondly, in the other Member States of the Community the designations corresponding to the German designation "Bier" are generic designations for a fermented beverage manufactured from malted barley, whether malted barley on its own or with the addition of rice or maize. The same approach is taken in Community law as can be seen from heading No 22.03 of the Common Customs Tariff. * * *

34   The German designation 'Bier' and its equivalents in the languages of the other Member States of the Community may therefore not be restricted to beers manufactured in accordance with the rules in force in the Federal Republic of Germany.

35   It is admittedly legitimate to seek to enable consumers who attribute specific qualities to beers manufactured from particular raw materials to make their choice in the light of that consideration. However, * * * that possibility may be ensured by means which do not prevent the importation of products which have been lawfully manufactured and marketed in other Member States and, in particular, by the compulsory affixing of suitable labels giving the nature of the product sold. By indicating the raw materials utilized in the manufacture of beer "such a course would enable the consumer to make his choice in full knowledge of the facts and would guarantee transparency in trading and in offers to the public". It must be added that such a system of mandatory consumer information must not entail negative assessments for beers not complying with the requirements of [the beer law].

36   Contrary to the German Government's view, such a system of consumer information may operate perfectly well even in the case of a product which, like beer, is not necessarily supplied to consumers in bottles or in cans capable of bearing the appropriate details. That is borne out, once again, by the German legislation itself [which] provides for a

system of consumer information in respect of certain beers, even where those beers are sold on draught, when the requisite information must appear on the casks or the beer taps.

37 It follows from the foregoing that by [forbidding the use of the word "Bier" for] beers imported from other Member States which were manufactured and marketed lawfully in those States the Federal Republic of Germany has failed to fulfil its obligations under Article [28] of the EEC Treaty.

NOTES AND QUESTIONS

1. Although the Court's judgment was hardly surprising, it caused a popular outcry in Germany. The outcry was largely occasioned by the belief that the rigorous application of free movement of goods principles would lead to a lowering of quality standards on a domestic market which traditionally only has high quality products. Do you think that a genuine risk or only an imaginary one? Cf. 3 Glocken GmbH v. USL Centro–Sud, Case 407/85, [1988] ECR 4233, in which the Court struck down an Italian law requiring pasta to be made exclusively from durum wheat, because the Court found no health hazard in pasta made from common wheat, while consumer protection could be achieved by labeling.

2. Do most consumers pay much attention to ingredients listed on labels? Do you think the goal of Community market integration is sufficiently important to outweigh whatever risk there may be that free movement of goods might lower product quality in certain States? Or do you think the issue of concern for allegedly high quality domestic products is largely a red herring, and the real issue is whether national rules should be allowed to "crystallize" domestic tastes or customs? For a critical view, see H.–C. von Heydebrand, Free Movement of Foodstuffs, Consumer Protection and Food Standards in the European Community, 16 Eur.L.Rev. 391 (1991).

COMMISSION v. SPAIN

(Chocolate products)
Case C–12/00, [2003] ECR I–459.

[Directive 73/241 harmonized the rules on "the composition, manufacturing specifications, packaging and labelling of [chocolate] products in order to ensure their free movement." The fifth recital indicated that it was not yet possible to harmonize all provisions relating to cocoa and chocolate products. Article 14(2)(a) stated that the directive does not invalidate national laws "authorising or prohibiting the addition of vegetable fats other than cocoa butter to the chocolate products defined in Annex 1." Annex 1 set out the permissible ingredients for chocolate products, including a minimum of 18% cocoa butter.

In addition, article 5(1)(b) of Directive 79/112 on foodstuff labelling and advertising states that foodstuffs may be sold after importation using "the sales name under which the product is legally manufactured and marketed in the Member State of production". However, article 5(1)(c) permits the importing State to require a different name if necessary to achieve "correct information for consumers" because the comparable national food product is substantially different from the imported one.

A 1990 Spanish law forbid chocolate produced in Spain to use fats other than cocoa butter, and required imported products that do not fulfill this requirement to be marketed as "chocolate substitutes." Chocolate products produced in the UK and Scandinavian States use vegetable fats other than cocoa butter. After complaints, the Commission brought an Article 226 proceeding against Spain to challenge the obligation to call such imported products "chocolate substitutes." The Commission argued that the imported products qualified as "chocolate" under Directive 73/241, and the added vegetable fats did not "create confusion as to its basic characteristics." Spain contended that "the term, 'chocolate substitute,' is neutral and merely reflects an objective reality," because it follows the traditional views of Spanish consumers concerning the nature of chocolate.

The Court first held that "the wording and the scheme of Directive 73/241" established that it guaranteed free movement for chocolate products made with vegetable fats other than cocoa butter (¶¶ 55–69).]

79   [W]hile a prohibition such as that under the Spanish legislation, which entails the obligation to use a sales name other than that used in the Member State of production, does not absolutely preclude the importation into the Member State concerned of products originating in other Member States, it is nevertheless likely to make their marketing more difficult and thus impede trade between Member States.

80   In the present case, the prohibition on the use of the sales name 'chocolate' under which cocoa and chocolate products containing vegetable fats other than cocoa butter are lawfully manufactured in the Member State of production may compel the traders concerned to adjust the presentation of their products according to the place where they are to be marketed and consequently to incur additional packaging costs. It is therefore liable to obstruct intra-Community trade.

81   Moreover, even if, as the Spanish Government maintains, the obligation to change the sales name does not necessarily entail additional packaging costs, it is plain that the name 'chocolate substitute' required in this instance may adversely affect the customer's perception of the products in question, inasmuch as it denotes substitute, and therefore inferior, products.

* * *

84   [I]t is legitimate for a Member State to ensure that consumers are properly informed about the products which are offered to them, thus giving them the possibility of making their choice on the basis of that information.

85   In particular, the Court has consistently held that Member States may, for the purpose of protecting consumers, require those concerned to alter the description of a foodstuff where a product offered for sale under a particular name is so different, in terms of its composition or production, from the products generally understood as falling within that description within the Community that it cannot be regarded as falling within the same category.

86   However, where the difference is of minor importance, appropriate labelling should be sufficient to provide the purchaser or consumer with the necessary information.

87   It is therefore important to ascertain whether the addition to cocoa and chocolate products of vegetable fats other than cocoa butter substantially alters their composition, so that they no longer present the characteristics expected by consumers buying products bearing the name "chocolate" and that a label providing appropriate information as to their composition cannot be considered sufficient to avoid confusion in the minds of consumers.

* * *

90   The percentages set by Directive 73/241 are minimum contents which must be complied with by all chocolate products manufactured and marketed under the name 'chocolate' in the Community, independently of whether the legislation of the Member State of production authorises the addition of vegetable fats other than cocoa butter.

91   In addition, it must be pointed out that, since Directive 73/241 explicitly permits Member States to authorise the use, in the manufacture of cocoa and chocolate products, of vegetable fats other than cocoa butter, it cannot be claimed that the products to which those fats have been added, in compliance with that directive, are altered to the point where they no longer fall into the same category as those which do not contain such fats.

* * *

93   It follows that the inclusion in the label of a neutral and objective statement informing consumers of the presence in the product of vegetable fats other than cocoa butter would be sufficient to ensure that consumers are given correct information.

94   In those circumstances, the obligation to change the sales name of those products which is imposed by the Spanish legislation does not appear to be necessary to satisfy the overriding requirement of consumer protection.

NOTES AND QUESTIONS

1.   This case is the latest salvo in the "chocolate war" between most of the continental States, which prohibit the addition of vegetable fats other than cocoa butter, and the UK, Ireland and the Scandinavian States which

allow them. For nearly 30 years, the Council debated whether or not to amend Directive 73/241 to bar the use of vegetable fats other than cocoa butter. Finally, the Council and the Parliament agreed upon Directive 2000/36 which expressly permits the addition of a maximum of 5% of vegetable fats other than chocolate, and authorizes the marketing of such products throughout the Community, provided that the label conspicuously and clearly states that vegetable fats were added. Feelings run high on the issue of what is true chocolate. A prominent Parisian producer of quality chocolate draped his retail stores in black on the date the directive entered into effect.

2. Probably the most debatable issue in the case is whether the words, "chocolate substitute," are merely descriptive and neutral, within the context of traditional Spanish consumer habits, or may adversely affect consumers' perceptions, as the Court held. What is your view? Is the judgment apt to be contested by those who claim that Community harmonization rules tend to lower traditional national quality standards for food?

3. ENVIRONMENTAL PROTECTION CASES

The Court first specifically accepted that environmental protection constituted a legitimate exception to the free movement of goods under the *Cassis de Dijon* doctrine in Commission v. Denmark (Beverage containers), excerpted in Chapter 34C, which largely upheld Danish rules requiring the recycling of bottles and cans of beer and soft drinks. Several later judgments reached similar conclusions. Thus, in Aher–Waggon v. Germany, Case C–389/96, [1998] ECR I–4473, the Court held that German rules setting maximum noise emission standards to reduce noise from aircraft could be applied to prevent the registration in Germany of an aircraft previously registered in Denmark. Somewhat in contrast, in Commission v. Austria (Vehicle exhaust standards), Case C–524/07, [2008] ECR I–187 (Dec. 11, 2008), the Court held that an Austrian regulation which required imported used cars to meet standards for exhaust pollution set by the latest version of an EC directive, while permitting cars already registered in Austria to comply with the less strict standards of the prior directive on the subject, violated ECT Article 28. The Court interpreted the latest directive as requiring the stricter standard only for new cars, and held that if Austria opted to apply them to imported used cars, it must also do so for cars already registered in Austria.

AKLAGAREN v. MICKELSSON
Case C–142/05, [2009] ECR I–___ (June 4, 2009).

[A 1993 EC directive setting standards for recreational watercraft permitted States to regulate navigation in order to protect the environment and ensure the safety of navigable water. A Swedish law, effective July 1, 2004, defined a jet-ski as a type of craft with a water jet unit designed to be operated by a person standing, sitting or kneeling upon it. The law required local authorities to designate waterways where jet-skis could be used provided that the waters had little value for the environment, biodiversity, or fishing. However, as of Aug. 8, 2004, when Mikelsson was arrested for the illegal use of jet-skis, no local regulations had been issued.]

25   It is apparent from the file sent to the Court that, at the material time, no waters had been designated as open to navigation by personal watercraft, and thus the use of personal watercraft was permitted on only general navigable waterways. However, the accused and the Commission maintain that those waterways are intended for heavy traffic of a commercial nature making the use of personal watercraft dangerous* * *. The actual possibilities for the use of personal watercraft in Sweden are, therefore, merely marginal.

26   Even if the national regulations at issue do not have the aim or effect of treating goods coming from other Member States less favourably, which is for the national court to ascertain, the restriction which they impose on the use of a product in the territory of a Member State may, depending on its scope, have a considerable influence on the behaviour of consumers, which may, in turn, affect the access of that product to the market of that Member State.

27   Consumers, knowing that the use permitted by such regulations is very limited, have only a limited interest in buying that product.

28   In that regard, where the national regulations for the designation of navigable waters and waterways have the effect of preventing users of personal watercraft from using them for the specific and inherent purposes for which they were intended or of greatly restricting their use, which is for the national court to ascertain, such regulations have the effect of hindering the access to the domestic market in question for those goods and therefore constitute * * * measures having equivalent effect to quantitative restrictions on imports prohibited by Article 28 EC.

* * *

32   [A]ccording to settled case-law, national measures capable of hindering intra-Community trade may be justified by the objective of protection of the environment provided that the measures in question are proportionate to the aim pursued.

* * *

33   As the protection of the environment and the protection of health and life of humans, animals and plants are, in the present case, closely related objectives, they should be examined together in order to assess whether regulations such as those at issue in the main proceedings are justified.

34   It is not open to dispute that a restriction or a prohibition on the use of personal watercraft are appropriate means for the purpose of ensuring that the environment is protected. However, for the national regulations to be capable of being regarded as justified, it is also

incumbent on the national authorities to show that their restrictive effects on the free movement of goods do not go beyond what is necessary to achieve that aim.

38   [T]he wording of the national regulations themselves suggests that, on waters which must be designated by implementing measures, personal watercraft may be used without giving rise to risks or pollution deemed unacceptable for the environment. It follows that a general prohibition on using such goods on waters other than general navigable waterways constitutes a measure going beyond what is necessary to achieve the aim of protection of the environment.

39   [The national] regulations * * * may, in principle, be regarded as proportionate provided that, first, the competent national authorities are required to adopt such implementing measures, secondly, those authorities have actually made use of the power conferred on them in that regard and designated the waters which satisfy the conditions provided for by the national regulations and, lastly, such measures have been adopted within a reasonable period after the entry into force of those regulations.

40   * * *It is for the national court to ascertain whether those conditions have been satisfied in the main proceedings.

41   [I]n proceedings under Article 234 EC, which is based on a clear separation of functions between the national courts and the Court of Justice, any assessment of the facts in the case is a matter for the national court. However, in order to give the national court a useful answer, the Court may, in a spirit of cooperation with national courts, provide it with all the guidance that it deems necessary.

42   [T]he national regulations had been in force only for about three weeks [at the time of Mikelsson's arrest]. The fact that measures to implement those regulations had not been adopted at a time when those regulations had only just entered into force ought not necessarily to affect the proportionality of those regulations in so far as the competent authority may not have had the necessary time to prepare the measures in question, a matter which falls to be determined by the national court.

[The Court concluded by observing that if the local authorities should subsequently permit jet-ski operation on the waterway used by Mickelsson, then he should be subject only to "the most lenient penalty" for the offense (¶ 43).]

NOTES AND QUESTIONS

1.   Note first that in ¶¶ 26–28, the Court held that a restriction on the use of products could violate ECT Article 28, even if the national court found that the restriction did not affect imported products more than domestic ones. What reason did the Court give for this conclusion? Do you agree? The Court rejected the view of Advocate General Kokott, who proposed that national

restrictions on the use of products should be considered not usually to have an impact on intra-state trade, and therefore would not need to be examined by the Court under Article 28, by analogy to the national restrictions on marketing that escape Court review under the *Keck* doctrine (see section D infra).

2.　Do you agree with the Court that national limitations on where jet-skis can be used can be justified on environmental protection grounds (as well as safety concerns)? Might the skis' inevitable noise disturb persons who reside adjacent to waterways? What about their impact on fishermen, or persons in row boats or canoes? Note, however, the Court's emphasis on the authorities' need to apply the principle of proportionality to enable their use on at least some appropriate waterways.

4.　BASIC RIGHTS AS A CASSIS EXCEPTION

SCHMIDBERGER v. AUSTRIA

Case C–112/00, [2003] ECR I–5659.

[A 1953 Austrian law setting standards for the exercise of the right of free assembly requires prior notification to the authorities, who may forbid it if it is "likely to endanger public order or the common weal." On May 15, 1998, an association "to protect the biosphere in the Alpine region" notified its intent to hold a 28 hour demonstration on Friday–Saturday, June 12–13, that would block the Brenner highway. The Tirol state security authority permitted the demonstration, which was widely publicized in advance. Trans–Alpine truck traffic was accordingly blocked on the most widely used route between Germany and Italy.

Schmidberger, a German international transport service, sued Austria for damages occasioned by the delay in its truck traffic. The trial court asked the Court of Justice whether free movement of goods took precedence over the freedom of assembly and expression.]

57　[A]s an indispensable instrument for the realisation of a market without internal frontiers, Article [28] does not prohibit only measures emanating from the State which, in themselves, create restrictions on trade between Member States. It also applies where a Member State abstains from adopting the measures required in order to deal with obstacles to the free movement of goods which are not caused by the State [citing *French produce imports, supra* page 450].

58　The fact that a Member State* * *fails to adopt adequate measures to prevent obstacles to the free movement of goods that are created, in particular, by actions by private individuals on its territory aimed at products originating in other Member States is just as likely to obstruct intra-Community trade as is a positive act.

59　Consequently, Articles [28] and [29] of the Treaty require the Member States not merely themselves to refrain from adopting measures or engaging in conduct liable to constitute an obstacle to trade but also, when read with Article [10] of the Treaty, to take all necessary and appropriate measures to ensure that that fundamental freedom is respected on their territory. Article [10] of the Treaty requires the Member States to take all appropriate measures, whether general or particular, to ensure fulfilment of the obligations arising out of the Treaty and to refrain from any measures which could jeopardize the attainment of the objectives of that Treaty.

60 Having regard to the fundamental role assigned to the free movement of goods in the Community system* * *that obligation upon each Member State to ensure the free movement of products * * * applies without the need to distinguish between cases where such acts affect the flow of imports or exports and those affecting merely the transit of goods.

* * *

63 It should be added that that obligation of the Member States is all the more important where the case concerns a major transit route such as the Brenner motorway, which is one of the main land links for trade between northern Europe and the north of Italy.

64 In the light of the foregoing, the fact that the competent authorities of a Member State did not ban a demonstration which resulted in the complete closure of a major transit route such as the Brenner motorway for almost 30 hours on end is capable of restricting intra-Community trade in goods and must, therefore, be regarded as constituting a measure of equivalent effect to a quantitative restriction* * *.

Whether the restriction may be justified

* * *

69 It is apparent from the file that the Austrian authorities were inspired by considerations linked to respect of the fundamental rights of the demonstrators to freedom of expression and freedom of assembly, which are enshrined in and guaranteed by the ECHR and the Austrian Constitution.

* * *

71 According to settled case-law, fundamental rights form an integral part of the general principles of law the observance of which the Court ensures. For that purpose, the Court draws inspiration from the constitutional traditions common to the Member States and from the guidelines supplied by international treaties for the protection of human rights on which the Member States have collaborated or to which they are signatories. The ECHR has special significance in that respect [citing *Connolly*, supra page 201].

72 The principles established by that case-law were reaffirmed in* * *Article [6] of the Treaty on European Union.

73 It follows that measures which are incompatible with observance of the human rights thus recognised are not acceptable in the Community.

74 Thus, since both the Community and its Member States are required to respect fundamental rights, the protection of those rights is a legitimate interest which, in principle, justifies a restriction of the obligations imposed by Community law, even under a fundamental freedom guaranteed by the Treaty such as the free movement of goods.

78 [Although] the free movement of goods constitutes one of the fundamental principles in the scheme of the Treaty, it may, in certain circumstances, be subject to restrictions for the reasons laid down in Article [30] of that Treaty or for overriding requirements relating to the public interest, in accordance with the Court's consistent case-law since 'Cassis de Dijon'.

79 [Moreover] freedom of expression and freedom of assembly are also subject to certain limitations justified by objectives in the public interest* * *motivated by one or more of the legitimate aims under those provisions and necessary in a democratic society, that is to say justified by a pressing social need and* * *proportionate to the legitimate aim pursued [citing *Familiapresse*, supra page 217].

* * *

81 In those circumstances, the interests involved must be weighed* * *in order to determine whether a fair balance was struck between those interests.

* * *

85 [B]ecause of the presence of demonstrators on the Brenner motorway, traffic by road was obstructed on a single route, on a single occasion and during a period of almost 30 hours. Furthermore, the obstacle to the free movement of goods resulting from that demonstration was limited by comparison with both the geographic scale and the intrinsic seriousness of the disruption caused in the case giving rise to the judgment in [*French produce imports, supra*].

86 [I]t is not in dispute that by that demonstration, citizens were exercising their fundamental rights by manifesting in public an opinion which they considered to be of importance to society; it is also not in dispute that the purpose of that public demonstration was not to restrict trade in goods of a particular type or from a particular source. By contrast, in [*French produce imports, supra*], the objective pursued by the demonstrators was clearly to prevent the movement of particular products originating in Member States other than the French Republic, by not only obstructing the transport of the goods in question, but also destroying those goods in transit to or through France * * *.

87 [V]arious administrative and supporting measures were taken by the competent authorities in order to limit as far as possible the disruption to road traffic. Thus, * * *the police, the organisers of the demonstration and various motoring organisations cooperated in order to ensure that the demonstration passed off smoothly. Well before the date on which it was due to take place, an extensive publicity campaign had been launched by the media and the motoring organisations, both in Austria and in neighbouring countries, and various alternative routes had been designated, with the result that the economic operators concerned were duly informed of the traffic restrictions applying on the date and at the site of the proposed demonstration and were in a position timeously to take all steps necessary to obviate those restrictions. Furthermore, security arrangements had been made for the site of the demonstration.

* * *

89 Finally,* * *the competent national authorities were entitled to consider that an outright ban on the demonstration would have constituted unacceptable interference with the fundamental rights of the demonstrators to gather and express peacefully their opinion in public.

* * *

91 An action of that type usually entails inconvenience for non-participants, in particular as regards free movement, but the inconvenience may in principle be tolerated provided that the objective pursued is essentially the public and lawful demonstration of an opinion.

92 In that regard, the Republic of Austria submits [that] the alternative solutions* * *would have risked reactions which would have been difficult to control and would have been liable to cause much more serious disruption to intra-Community trade and public order, such as unauthorised demonstrations, confrontation between supporters and opponents of the group organising the demonstration or acts of violence* * *.

93 Consequently, the national authorities were reasonably entitled, having regard to the wide discretion which must be accorded to them in the matter, to consider that the legitimate aim of that demonstration could not be achieved in the present case by measures less restrictive of intra-Community trade.

NOTES AND QUESTIONS

1. Do you agree with the Court conclusion that freedom of assembly and freedom of expression should trump the free movement of goods in these circumstances? What of the doctrine of proportionality? The delay in truck traffic was increased because the Austrian traffic law forbids truck traffic on Saturday afternoon and Sunday, creating a 3 1/2 day blockage of truck traffic. Shouldn't the Court have considered whether the Austrian authorities ought

to have required the demonstration to be held earlier in the week? Suppose the biosphere association decides to hold demonstrations each month for six months. Should the balance shift then in favor of free movement of goods?

2. As previously indicated in Chapter 6C, the Lisbon TEU Article 6(2) mandates the Union to accede in an appropriate manner to the Strassbourg Convention on Human Rights. A vital issue then would become whether the Court of Justice or the Court of Human Rights should have the final decisive word on an issue such as a conflict between the free movement of goods and a fundamental human right's exercise. Does this judgment suggest that the question has more than merely theoretical importance?

D. THE ORIGIN AND EVOLUTION OF THE KECK DOCTRINE

1. FROM CASSIS TO KECK

The *Cassis de Dijon* doctrine that products legally produced and marketed in their State of origin should enjoy a presumption in favor of being marketed in other States has served the Union very well in its efforts to achieve true market integration. Not only has the Court of Justice used it in its case law to further free movement of goods, but, even more important, the approach became the basis for the "mutual recognition" principle that is at the heart of the internal market legislative program for both goods and services, described in later chapters.

In contrast, the *Cassis de Dijon* doctrine that Member State rules limiting free movement of goods must be justified by an imperative state interest, recognized as such by the Court of Justice, and then subject to the principle of proportionality, has turned out to be difficult to apply in many contexts. The approach worked rather well in the fields of consumer protection and environmental protection, both easily accepted and fairly well defined state interests. However, the Court found it increasingly hard to deal with State rules adopted to serve less precise social, cultural and economic interests. The Court's difficulties became evident in the Sunday trading cases.

In an early judgment, Proceedings against Oebel, Case 155/80, [1981] ECR 1993, German rules restricting the night working and delivery hours of bakeries were challenged as reducing export sales. The Court held that Germany had a legitimate state interest in protecting the health of workers. Later, in UDS v. Sidef Conforama, Case C–312/89, [1991] ECR 997, the Court held that a French labor law which guaranteed Sunday as a day of rest for employees was similarly justified.

Torfaen Borough Council v. B & Q, Case C–145/88, [1989] ECR 3851, concerned the 1950 UK Shops Act which generally forbid retail sales on Sunday in general, but allowed local authorities to permit certain retailers to sell a variety of products, e.g., newspapers and magazines, certain foodstuffs, alcoholic and tobacco products. When B & Q was prosecuted for selling do-it-yourself goods and garden tools on Sunday, the trial court

referred questions to the Court of Justice. Although the trial court stated
that the Shops Act reduced "the volume of imports," the Court of Justice
held that it was neutral in application, so that marketing of imported
products was not more difficult than marketing of domestic products
(¶ 11). The Court then held that the retail sales restrictions were justified,
citing *Oebel*, as reflecting "certain political and economic choices in so far
as their purpose is to ensure that working and non-working hours are so
arranged as to accord with national or regional socio-cultural characteristics* * *. Furthermore, such rules are not designed to govern the patterns
of trade between Member States" (¶ 14).

Although the Court cited *Oebel*, the Shops Act governs retail sales,
not employee work conditions. Moreover, the Commission had argued that
less restrictive means could be found to protect workers, i.e., by permitting employees to choose freely their days off. The Court's language
concerning the UK's public interest is decidedly vague. Is it economic?
Social? Socio-cultural? The original motivation for Sunday retail sales
restrictions was the preservation of the sabbath as a day of rest (they are
popularly called Sunday "blue laws"). In a modern pluralist society, that
justification is hard to defend. Advocate General van Gerven argued, at
¶ 29 of his opinion, that such a "prevention of offence to religious
convictions" could not fall within the ECT Article 30 public morality
exception.

In the next two years, English and Welsh courts reached quite
different conclusions in applying the Court's reply. When on appeal the
parties in *Torfaen* reached the House of Lords, it asked the Court of
Justice for further guidance on how to evaluate the UK rules in terms of
Article 28. In Council of the City of Stoke-on-Trent v. B & Q PLC, Case C–
169/91, [1992] ECR–I–6635, the Court responded initially by essentially
repeating its holding in *Torfaen*. Without any further analysis of the
proportionality of the UK Sunday trading rules to their "socio-cultural"
goals, the Court then ruled that they "were not excessive to the aim
pursued" (¶ 16), and did not violate ECT Article 28. The Court was
perhaps motivated by the view that political processes, not judges, should
make any desirable modifications in Sunday trading rules.

By 1993 the Court was ready to adopt a new doctrinal approach.

KECK AND MITHOUARD
Cases C–267 & 268/91, [1993] ECR I–6097.

[Two supermarkets in Alsace, managed by Keck and Mithouard, sold
French brands of beer and coffee at retail prices lower than their own
purchase price. When prosecuted for violation of a 1963 French law which
forbids merchants from selling products at prices lower than the acquisition cost, Keck and Mithouard contended that the French law violated
Article 28. The Strasbourg trial court asked the Court whether the French
rule violated "the principles of the free movement of goods" and "free

competition," particularly because it might distort "competition * * * in frontier zones."]

11　By virtue of Article [28], quantitative restrictions and all measures having equivalent effect are prohibited between Member States. The Court has consistently held that any measure which is capable of directly or indirectly, actually or potentially, hindering intra-Community trade constitutes a measure having equivalent effect to a quantitative restriction.

12　It is not the purpose of national legislation imposing a general prohibition on resale at a loss to regulate trade in goods between Member States.

13　Such legislation may, admittedly, restrict the volume of sales, and hence the volume of sales of products from other Member States, in so far as it deprives traders of a method of sales promotion. But the question remains whether such a possibility is sufficient to characterize the legislation in question as a measure having equivalent effect to a quantitative restriction on imports.

14　In view of the increasing tendency of traders to invoke Article [28] of the Treaty as a means of challenging any rules whose effect is to limit their commercial freedom even where such rules are not aimed at products from other Member States, the Court considers it necessary to re-examine and clarify its case-law on this matter.

15　In *"Cassis de Dijon"* it was held that, in the absence of harmonization of legislation, measures of equivalent effect prohibited by Article [28] include obstacles to the free movement of goods where they are the consequence of applying rules that lay down requirements to be met by such goods (such as requirements as to designation, form, size, weight, composition, presentation, labelling, packaging) to goods from other Member States where they are lawfully manufactured and marketed, even if those rules apply without distinction to all products unless their application can be justified by a public-interest objective taking precedence over the free movement of goods.

16　However, contrary to what has previously been decided, the application to products from other Member States of national provisions restricting or prohibiting certain selling arrangements is not such as to hinder directly or indirectly, actually or potentially, trade between Member States within the meaning of the *Dassonville* judgment, provided that those provisions apply to all affected traders operating within the national territory and provided that they affect in the same manner, in law and in fact, the marketing of domestic products and of those from other Member States.

17　Where those conditions are fulfilled, the application of such rules to the sale of products from another Member State meeting the requirements laid down by that State is not by nature such as to prevent their access to the market or to impede access any more than it impedes the access of domestic products. Such rules therefore fall outside the scope of Article [28] of the Treaty.

18   Accordingly, the reply to be given to the national court is that Article [28] of the EEC Treaty is to be interpreted as not applying to legislation of a Member State imposing a general prohibition on resale at a loss.

NOTES AND QUESTIONS

1.   In ¶ 15 the translation of this judgment has replaced the awkward term, "mandatory requirements," used in *Cassis de Dijon*, with the more understandable term, "public-interest objective." Unfortunately, ¶ 16 introduces another awkward translation, "selling arrangements," quite difficult to understand in English. The sense of the French original "modalites de vente," although not free from ambiguity either, would come across better if translated as "modes of marketing" or "merchandising methods," or simply "modalities of sale of products."

2.   The Court certainly intended its judgment to be a major precedent: the case was transferred from a chamber to a plenary proceeding, and the Court expressly stated that it was partially overruling *Dassonville*, one of its landmark judgments. Why do you think the Court felt the application of the *Dassonville* rule had gone too far? Is this a 'political' judgment, reacting in some measure to media criticism of 'activist' Court judgments during the ratification of the Maastricht Treaty? Several commentators suggest that the Court was influenced by the opinion of Advocate General Tessauro in a then pending case, Hunermund v. Baden–Wurttemberg Pharmacist Association, Case C–292/92, [1993] ECR I–6787, who argued that Article 28 should be considered to seek to achieve "a single integrated market, * * * not to strike down the most widely differing measures in order, essentially, to achieve the greatest possible expansion of trade" (¶ 28). The Court's judgment in *Hunermund* cited the *Keck* formula in declining to review a prohibition on advertising quasi-pharmaceutical products by pharmacists outside of their shop premises.

3.   Try to interpret ¶¶ 16–17. Do you find the new rule clear-cut and easy to apply? Even if you find it to be ambiguous, do you agree with the basic policy thrust or do you think *Dassonville* represents a better rule? Put another way, is it desirable for many national rules to be examined by the Court under the *Cassis de Dijon* public-interest analysis, requiring perhaps further multiplication of justifiable imperative interests, or is it preferable that many national rules should be treated as raising no free movement of goods issue at all?

4.   An article which may have influenced the Court's analysis in *Keck* is E. White, In Search of the Limits to Article 30, 26 Common Mkt. L. Rev. 235 (1989). Among the many initial commentaries on *Keck* are L. Gormley, Reasoning Renounced? The Remarkable Judgment in Keck & Mithouard, Eur. Bus. L. Rev. 63 (March 1994); and W. Wils, The Search for the Rule in Article 30 EEC: Much Ado About Nothing?, 19 Eur. L. Rev. 475 (1994). The late

Judge Rene Joliet advocated the *Keck* approach in Free Circulation of Goods: The Keck and Mithouard Decision, 1 Colum. J. Eur. L. 436 (1995).

2. POST–KECK: DISTINGUISHING REGULATION OF PRODUCTS FROM REGULATION OF SELLING ARRANGEMENTS

Although controversial from the outset, and seriously questioned by Advocates General van Gerven, Jacobs and Lenz as well as some academic commentators, the Court applied the *Keck* doctrine almost routinely in many late 1990 judgements. Its proper application, however, was not always easy. The chief difficulty occurred in properly demarcating the line between State rules regulating the sale, merchandising or promotion of products, which the Court would no longer examine (provided they were non-discriminatory in fact as well as in law), and State rules regulating products (together with their labels and packages), which the Court still must examine under the *Cassis de Dijon* imperative state interest analysis. At least, later judgments did make the concept of rules on "selling arrangements" more precise. They include principally restrictions on when goods may be sold (as in the Sunday trading cases), restrictions on where and how goods may be sold (as in *Keck*), and restrictions on advertising goods (as in *Leclerc–Siplec, infra*).

SOCIETE D'IMPORTATION EDOUARD LECLERC– SIPLEC v. TFI PUBLICITE

Case C–412/93, [1995] ECR I–179.

[A 1992 French law prohibits advertising on television for alcoholic beverages with a high alcohol content, literary works, cinema films, the press, and any form of sales distribution. Leclerc–Siplec, a gas station operator within a supermarket chain, sought to engage TFI, a French TV advertising company, to broadcast advertisements for its imported gasoline products. When TFI stated that the law prohibited this, Leclerc–Siplec sued TFI. Both parties asked the trial court to raise questions concerning the law's compatibility with ECT Article 28, which the court did. In the proceeding, France admitted that a major motive for the television advertising ban was to protect the advertising revenues of newspapers and magazines.

The Court initially held the questions referred to be admissible, even though both parties to the suit desired the same response. See the discussion of this issue in Chapter 9F *supra*. With regard to Article 28, the Court held:]

[19] A law or regulation such as that at issue in the main proceedings, which prohibits televised advertising in the distribution sector, is not designed to regulate trade in goods between member states. Moreover, such a prohibition does not prevent distributors from using other forms of advertising.

[20] Such a prohibition may, admittedly, restrict the volume of sales, and hence the volume of sales of products from other member states, in so far as it deprives distributors of a particular form of advertising their goods. . . .

[The Court then quoted the *Keck* doctrine.]

[22] A provision such as that at issue in the main proceedings concerns selling arrangements since it prohibits a particular form of promotion (televised advertising) of a particular method of marketing products (distribution).

[23] Furthermore, those provisions, which apply regardless of the type of product to all traders in the distribution sector, even if they are both producers and distributors, affect the marketing of products from other member states and that of domestic products in the same manner.

[24] The reply should accordingly be that on a proper construction art. [28] of the Treaty does not apply where a member state, by statute or by regulation, prohibits the broadcasting of televised advertisements for the distribution sector.

NOTES AND QUESTIONS

1. The Court's judgment is a strong endorsement of the *Keck* doctrine, rejecting the views of Advocate General Jacobs. His able and detailed opinion questioned the advisability of the *Keck* doctrine, but admitted that if it were applicable, the French prohibition of television advertising of distribution would fall outside of Article 28. He emphasized, however, the capital importance of television advertising for a foreign producer seeking to become a new market entrant. Advocate General Jacobs specifically suggested in ¶ 51 of his opinion that if a German beer producer should seek to use television advertising to launch the sale of beer not previously marketed in France, the *Keck* rules should not apply. Do you agree? Several academic authorities endorsed Advocate General Jacobs' market access exception to *Keck*. See S. Weatherill, After Keck: Some Thoughts on How to Clarify the Clarification, 33 Common Mkt. L. Rev. 879 (1996), and L. Idot's casenote on *Leclerc*, 33 Common Mkt. L. Rev. 113 (1996).

Indeed, suppose that a challenge to the French law is raised not by a German beer producer, but rather by a Belgian television station whose broadcasts reach France, seeking to carry out a Community-wide television advertising campaign for a new brand of beer. Can the French law be used to restrict such trans-border providing of advertising services? See the discussion of the non-applicability of the *Keck* doctrine to rules restricting trans-border services following the *Schindler* and related cases in Chapter 17B.

2. Other judgments holding challenged rules to concern "selling arrangements" and hence not to be reviewed by the Court were *Hunermund, supra* (rules forbidding pharmacists to advertize certain products outside shop premises); Boermans, Cases C–401 & 402/92, [1994] ECR I–2199 (rules requiring gas stations to close during the night); Criminal Proceedings against

Banchero, Case C–387/93, [1995] ECR I–4663 (rules restricting the sale of tobacco to licensed retailers); Commission v. Greece (Processed milk for infants), Case C–391/92, [1995] ECR I–1621 (rules requiring all processed milk for infants to be sold only in pharmacies); and Semeraro Casa Uno v. Sindaco del Commune, Cases C–418 to 421/93, [1996] ECR I–2975 (Italian Sunday retail trading rules).

In contrast, some judgments held the challenged rules to concern products, and therefore subject to review.

VERBAND SOZIALER WETTBEWERB v. CLINIQUE LABORATORIES

Case C–315/92, [1994] ECR I–317.

[Since the 1970s, Estée Lauder has sold cosmetics in Europe under the brand-name "Clinique," but substituted "Linique" in Germany because of a concern that use of the name, "Clinique," might raise an issue of non-compliance with the German Unfair Competition Law. In 1991, to save advertising and packaging costs, Estée Lauder decided to adopt "Clinique" for cosmetics in Germany. A German association created to help enforce the German Unfair Competition Law sued to enjoin sales under the name "Clinique" as deceptive of consumers. The Berlin trial court feared that some consumers might "attribute prophylactic or curative medical effects" to a cosmetic called "Clinique," but asked the Court of Justice whether such a concern was sufficient under ECT Articles 28 or 30 to bar a product "lawfully marketed under that name" elsewhere in the Community. The Court initially stated that neither Directive 76/768 on the packaging and labelling of cosmetic products, nor Directive 84/450 on the prevention of misleading advertising, contained a provision which precisely decided the issue.]

13 [T]he Court has recently ruled that Article [28] of the Treaty prohibits obstacles to the free movement of goods resulting from rules that lay down requirements to be met by such goods (such as requirements as to designation, form, size, weight, composition, presentation, labelling, packaging), even if those rules apply without distinction to all products, unless their application can be justified by a public-interest objective taking precedence over the free movement of goods (*Keck and Mithouard*).

* * *

19 The prohibition [under the German Unfair Competition Law] of the distribution within Germany of cosmetic products under the same name as that under which they are marketed in the other Member States constitutes in principle * * * an obstacle to intra-Community trade. The fact that by reason of that prohibition the undertaking in question is obliged in that Member State alone to market its products under a different name and to bear additional packaging and advertising costs demonstrates that this measure does affect free trade.

20   In order to determine whether, in preventing a product being attributed with characteristics which it does not have, the prohibition of the use of the name "Clinique" for the marketing of cosmetic products in Germany can be justified by the objective of protecting consumers or the health of humans, it is necessary to take into account the information set out in the order of reference.

21   [I]t is apparent from that information that the range of cosmetic products manufactured by the Estée Lauder company is sold in Germany exclusively in perfumeries and cosmetic departments of large stores, and therefore none of those products is available in pharmacies. It is not disputed that those products are presented as cosmetic products and not as medicinal products. It is not suggested that, apart from the name of the products, this presentation does not comply with the rules applicable to cosmetic products. Finally, according to the very wording of the question referred, those products are ordinarily marketed in other countries under the name "Clinique" and the use of that name apparently does not mislead consumers.

22   In the light of these facts, the prohibition of the use of that name in Germany does not appear necessary to satisfy the requirements of consumer protection and the health of humans.

23   The clinical or medical connotations of the word "Clinique" are not sufficient to make that word so misleading as to justify the prohibition of its use on products marketed in the aforesaid circumstances.

NOTES AND QUESTIONS

1. *Clinique* illustrates a product-related rule which continues to be analyzed under the *Cassis de Dijon* doctrine, rather than a rule governing modes of marketing, which would escape Article 28 altogether under the *Keck* doctrine. Do you find the distinction between product-related and marketing rules functionally useful and easy to apply, or relatively arbitrary and difficult to apply?

2. In ¶ 25 of his opinion in *Clinique*, Advocate General Gulmann concluded that "there may be specific differences in linguistic, social and cultural conditions which have the result that something which does not mislead consumers in one country may do so in another." He thought the Berlin court might properly take a market research survey to test the risk that German consumers could be misled. Do you agree with his view, or that of the Court? Subsequently, in Estee Lauder Cosmetics v. Lancaster Group, Case C–220/98, [2000] ECR I–117, the Court held that the trial court could consider "an expert opinion or a survey of public opinion" in deciding whether the name of a face cream conveyed deceptive public health promotion features (¶ 31). Do you think the product name, 'Monteil Firming Action Lifting Extreme Creme,' warranted the difference in approach?

3. In Verein gegen Unwesen in Handel v. Mars, Case C–470/93, [1995] ECR I–1923, Mars used wrappers for its ice cream bars marked with "+10%", to indicate that the bars were 10% larger than previously. A

consumer protection group challenged the use of the wrappers with their "+10%" as potentially deceiving consumers. The Court held that *Keck* did not apply, and that it could examine the German consumer protection rules because they were product-related, concerning packaging. On the merits, the Court then held that "+10%" would not deceive consumers into believing that retailers would not increase the previous price for such bars.

4. Another recent judgment has important basic right overtones. In Vereinigte Familiapress Zeitungsverlag v. Heinrich Bauer Verlag, *supra* page 217, an Austrian magazine publisher sought to enjoin the sale in Austria of a German magazine because it contained games of chance whose successful solution would entitle certain readers to prizes worth up to DM 5000. A 1993 Austrian law forbids magazines to contain games of chance. The Court of Justice initially concluded that the pages with the games formed a part of the magazine, so that the Austrian law affected the product and not a merchandising modality, even though the manifest intent of the games was to increase the magazine's circulation.

Applying the *Cassis de Dijon* doctrine, the Court recognized the need to ensure a diversity of publications ("pluralisme de la presse") as an imperative public interest, because it promotes a free press. However, when applying the principle of proportionality, the Court concluded that the Austrian law's absolute ban on the inclusion in magazines of games of chance affording minor prizes might limit too severely the freedom of the press.

The Court left to the trial court the task of determining whether the fact that Austria had an unusually small number of publishers could justify the Austrian law as a reasonable protection against the risk that rich foreign publishers might successfully use games of chance as a marketing device to gain a substantial competitive advantage. The trial court also had the duty to determine whether some measure less than a total ban on the sale of imported magazines containing games of chance could adequately protect the public interest. (Note that in the US, magazines containing similar games of chance customarily add notices indicating that residents of certain states may not participate in the games, due to legal restrictions in those states.)

3. POST–KECK: HOW VIABLE IS THE DOCTRINE CURRENTLY?

Since 2000, the *Keck* doctrine has continued to be challenged by several Advocates General and academic commentators. Presumably influenced by these views, the Court has narrowly applied *Keck* in recent judgments, but has never disavowed the doctrine. One approach is to question whether a national measure is truly "neutral in fact," if it significantly blocks access to the market. Advocate General Jacobs could not persuade the Court that market access might be a decisive factor in *Leclerc*, but his views had more success in the following case.

KONSUMENTOMBUDSMANNEN v. GOURMET INTERNATIONAL PRODUCTS

Case C–405/98, [2001] ECR I–1795.

[Swedish law provides that "in view of the health risks involved in alcohol consumption, alcoholic beverages should be marketed with particular moderation." It provides specifically that advertisements must not encourage alcohol consumption and totally prohibits advertising of alcoholic beverages on radio or television and in magazines and other periodicals. After Gourmet magazine published an issue for its subscribers (of whom 90% are retailers or merchants, but 10% are private individuals) containing three pages of advertisements for wine and whisky, the Swedish Consumer Ombudsman sued it, requesting a fine and an injunction. The trial court inquired whether the Swedish law violated ECT Article 28 and could be justified on public health grounds. The key issue presented was whether the law might discriminate "in fact" against imports.]

14   The Consumer Ombudsman [accepts] that the prohibition on advertising in Sweden affects sales of alcoholic beverages there, including those imported from other Member States, since the specific purpose of the Swedish legislation is to reduce the consumption of alcohol.

15   However, * * * the Consumer Ombudsman [contends] that the prohibition on advertising in issue in the main proceeding does not constitute an obstacle to trade between Member States, since it satisfies the criteria laid down by the Court in [*Keck*].

16   [Gourmet] contends that an outright prohibition [on alcohol advertising in magazines] does not satisfy those criteria. It argues that such a prohibition is, in particular, liable to have a greater effect on imported goods than on those produced in the Member State concerned.

* * *

18   [A]ccording to paragraph 17 in *Keck* and *Mithouard*, if national provisions restricting or prohibiting certain selling arrangements are to avoid being caught by Article [28] of the Treaty, they must not be of such a kind as to prevent access to the market by products from another Member State or to impede access any more than they impede the access of domestic products.

19   The Court has also held [in the *Swedish Consumer Ombudsman* case, *infra* page 687] that it cannot be excluded that an outright prohibition, applying in one Member State, of a type of promotion for a product which is lawfully sold there might have a greater impact on products from other Member States.

20   It is apparent that a prohibition on advertising such as that at issue in the main proceedings not only prohibits a form of marketing a product but in reality prohibits producers and importers from directing any

advertising messages at consumers, with a few insignificant exceptions.

21   Even without its being necessary to carry out a precise analysis of the facts characteristic of the Swedish situation, which it is for the national court to do, the Court is able to conclude that, in the case of products like alcoholic beverages, the consumption of which is linked to traditional social practices and to local habits and customs, a prohibition of all advertising directed at consumers in the form of advertisements in the press, on the radio and on television, the direct mailing of unsolicited material or the placing of posters on the public highway is liable to impede access to the market by products from other Member States more than it impedes access by domestic products, with which consumers are instantly more familiar.

22   The information provided by the Consumer Ombudsman and the Swedish Government concerning the relative increase in Sweden in the consumption of wine and whisky, which are mainly imported, in comparison with other products such as vodka, which is mainly of Swedish origin, does not alter that conclusion. First, it can not be precluded that, in the absence of the legislation at issue in the main proceedings, the change indicated would have been greater; second, that information takes into account only some alcoholic beverages and ignores, in particular, beer consumption.

* * *

25   A prohibition on advertising such as that at issue in the main proceedings must therefore be regarded as affecting the marketing of products from other Member States more heavily than the marketing of domestic products and as therefore constituting an obstacle to trade between Member States caught by Article [28] of the Treaty.

26   However, such an obstacle may be justified by the protection of public health, a general interest ground recognised by Article [30] of the Treaty.

27   In that regard, it is accepted that rules restricting the advertising of alcoholic beverages in order to combat alcohol abuse reflect public health concerns.

[The Court concluded that the trial court must evaluate the "circumstances of law and of fact" in order to determine whether the Swedish limits on alcohol advertising were proportionate to the public health goal. The Court noted that the Commission in its intervention had expressed doubt on the proportionality of an absolute ban on alcohol advertising, suggesting that advertising restrictions should only require the exercise of moderation in consumption.]

NOTES AND QUESTIONS

1. Advocate General Jacobs repeated in *Gourmet* his view that advertising restrictions may impact imports far more seriously than domestic products, noting that wine is essentially imported while there is a strong domestic beer production. His conclusion that the Swedish advertising limits accordingly "must have a greater adverse effect on [imported] new products" than on domestic products clearly influenced the Court's view in *Gourmet*. Do you agree?

2. How would you decide whether the alcohol advertising limits are proportionate to the public health goal? Is it relevant that Sweden has one of the highest alcoholism rates in the Community? Advocate General Jacobs noted that all Member States restrict alcohol advertising to some degree, but only Finland matches Sweden in the severity of its restrictions. He expressed concern that the Swedish restrictions might discourage switching of brands (e.g., from beer to wine), rather than reducing alcohol consumption. Would you accept the Swedish rules, or prefer restrictions that limit the nature of advertising e.g., forbidding advertising directed at young people, or advertising that associates alcohol with sophistication or sexual attraction?

DEUTSCHER APOTHEKERVERBAND v. 0800 DOC MORRIS

Case 322/01, [2003] ECR 14887.

[0800 Doc Morris, a licensed Dutch pharmacy staffed by qualified pharmacists, makes substantial sales in Germany via the internet, with arrangements for direct delivery to the customer at a border pharmacy or by courier. Doc Morris sells some pharmaceuticals that require a prescription in Germany and others that do not require a prescription there. For prescription medicine sales, the customer must provide Doc Morris with the original prescription, and can also obtain health advice from Doc Morris. When the German Association of Pharmacists sued to enjoin Doc Morris from internet sales and any advertising of such sales, the trial court referred questions to the Court of Justice.

The Court initially noted that a 2001 directive required all pharmaceuticals to be authorized for sale within the Community, but granted Member States discretion to decide which should be deemed likely to present a danger if used without medical supervision and hence should require a prescription. The Court then set out the elements of the *Keck* doctrine and noted the need to determine whether the German rules applied neutrally "in fact".]

71 In order to ascertain whether a particular measure affects in the same manner the 'marketing' of both domestic products and those from other Member States, the scope of the restrictive measure concerned must be ascertained.

72 The Court has accepted the relevance of the argument that a prohibition on television advertising deprived a trader of the only effective

form of promotion which would have enabled it to penetrate a national market [citing *Gourmet*].

73   [The German law] contains both a requirement that certain medicines be sold only in pharmacies and a prohibition on mail-order sales of medicines. It is true that such a prohibition on mail-order sales may be regarded as merely the consequence of the requirement for sales to be made exclusively in pharmacies. However, the emergence of the internet as a method of cross-border sales means that the scope and* * *the effect of the prohibition must be looked at on a broader scale than that suggested by the Apothekerverband, by the German, French and Austrian Governments and by the Commission.

74   A prohibition such as that at issue in the main proceedings is more of an obstacle to pharmacies outside Germany than to those within it [because domestic pharmacies can still sell in their shops]. For pharmacies not established in Germany, the internet provides a more significant way to gain direct access to the German market. A prohibition which has a greater impact on pharmacies established outside German territory could impede access to the market for products from other Member States more than it impedes access for domestic products. Accordingly, the prohibition does not affect the sale of domestic medicines in the same way as it affects the sale of those coming from other Member States.

Whether there is any justification for the prohibition on mail-order sales

[The Court first observed that a State's claim of a public health limit on free movement of goods must be examined by applying the principle of proportionality.]

Non-prescription medicines

112   None of the reasons which the Apothekerverband advances by way of justification can provide a valid basis for the absolute prohibition on the sale by mail order of non-prescription medicines.

113   [A]s regards the need to provide the customer with advice and information when a medicinal product is purchased, it is not impossible that adequate advice and information may be provided. Furthermore,* * *internet buying may have certain advantages, such as the ability to place the order from home or the office, without the need to go out, and to have time to think about the questions to ask the pharmacists, and these advantages must be taken into account.

114   * * * As regards incorrect use of the medicine, the risk thereof can be reduced through an increase in the number of on-line interactive features, which the customer must use before being able to proceed to a purchase. As regards possible abuse, it is not apparent that for persons who wish to acquire non-prescription medicines unlawfully,

purchase in a traditional pharmacy is more difficult than an internet purchase.

* * *

Prescription medicines

117   The supply to the general public of prescription medicines needs to be more strictly controlled. Such control could be justified in view of, first, the greater risks which those medicines may present * * *.

118   The fact that there might be differences in the way those medicines are classified by the Member States so that a particular medicinal product may be subject to prescription in one Member State but not in another, does not mean that the first Member State forfeits the right to take more stringent action with regard to that type of medicinal product. Given that there may be risks attaching to the use of these medicinal products, the need to be able to check effectively and responsibly the authenticity of doctors' prescriptions and to ensure that the medicine is handed over either to the customer himself, or to a person to whom its collection has been entrusted by the customer, is such as to justify a prohibition on mail-order sales.* * *Furthermore, the real possibility of the labelling of a medicinal product bought in a Member State other than the one in which the buyer resides being in a language other than the buyer's may have more harmful consequences in the case of prescription medicines.

NOTES AND QUESTIONS

1.   The principal importance of *Doc Morris* lies in the Court's holding that a ban on internet marketing will affect cross-border traders more than domestic ones, and accordingly is not neutral 'in fact'. Do you agree with the Court? The Court's further conclusion that Germany could ban cross-border sales of prescription medicines to consumers on health grounds is not surprising in view of the case law in section 13B above. The Court's conclusion that Doc Morris could sell non-prescription medicines in Germany is also not surprising, because the Court had reached essentially the same conclusion in Schumacher v. Hauptzollamt Frankfurt, Case 215/87, [1989] ECR 617, concerning mail order imports from France.

2.   In Commission v. Germany (Supply of hospitals by local pharmacies), Case C–141/07, [2008] I–6935, the Commission challenged German rules that in practice meant that only local pharmacies could supply hospitals with medical supplies (e.g., rules requiring that the pharmacy would agree to supply products in emergencies, would advise on product selection, and would check hospital stocks.) The Court held that the rules made it "more difficult and more costly" for pharmacies in other States to sell to German hospitals, and consequently did not satisfy *Keck's* condition that national rules apply neutrally "in fact" (¶ ¶ 35–36). However, the Court then concluded that the rules were justified by the public health concern that hospitals obtain phar-

maceutical products that are reliable, of good quality and quickly available (¶¶ 49–57).

3. In A. Punkt Schmuckhandels v. Schmidt, Case C–441/04, [2006] ECR I–2093, a 1994 Austrian law on fair trade practices prohibited marketing various goods, including jewelry and watches, at private homes. A German resident, Ms. Schmidt, operated a business in which she offers jewelry for sale at 'jewelry parties' in homes. After a jewelry store obtained an injunction preventing Schmidt's 'parties' in Klagenfurt, Austria, on appeal the appellate court referred questions to the Court of Justice. The Court held that the law applied to all traders in Austria, regardless of nationality, and thus satisfied *Keck's* initial condition for application. The Court then stated that the information provided to it did not enable a determination whether the Austrian law might affect marketing from other States more than marketing in Austria (¶ 25). The Court accordingly left the determination whether the law was 'neutral in fact' to the Austrian court.

It is hard to see on what basis the national court could conclude that cross-border traders are hindered more than domestic ones by a prohibition on sales at private homes. However, if the court does so conclude, note that consumer protection can justify a restriction on cross-border sales. The Court of Justice specifically referred to various risks to consumers in sales at homes, including a lack of information, the impossibility of comparing prices, and psychological pressure to buy (¶ 29).

The next judgment presents a relatively rare Court review of a State's rules aimed at protecting safety, rather than health. It has attracted attention because the State regulation limited use, not sale, of a product, and the Court declined to apply the *Keck* doctrine by analogy to State rules regulating the use of products.

COMMISSION v. ITALY

(Motorcycle-towed trailers)
Case C–110/05, [2009] ECR I–519.

[A 1992 Italian highway law permitted the use of cars and tractors, but not motorcycles, to draw trailers. In its ECT Article 226 infringement action against Italy, the Commission contended that Italy's prohibition of the use of motorcycles to draw trailers was not justified on safety grounds. A 1992 directive setting technical standards for motorcycles did not cover the issue, but contained a recital stating that the directive would not oblige States that forbid motorcycles to tow a trailer to change their rules. The Commission argued that the recital had no legal effect.

The Court first dealt with the preliminary issue of admissibility of the action. Italy and six other States contended that the *Keck* doctrine should apply to national rules concerning the use of products. The Court restated its holdings in *Cassis* and *Keck*, and then continued:]

49   In order to assess whether the Commission's complaint is well founded, it should be pointed out that * * * the national provision must be considered, in particular, from the angle of the restriction that it could

represent for free movement of trailers. Although it is not disputed that motorcycles can easily be used without a trailer, the fact remains that the latter is of little use without a motor vehicle that may tow it.

50 It is common ground that Article 56 of the Highway Code applies without regard to the origin of trailers.

* * *

55 In its reply to the Court's written question, the Commission claimed, without being contradicted by the Italian Republic, that, in the case of trailers specially designed for motorcycles, the possibilities for their use other than with motorcycles are very limited. It considers that, although it is not inconceivable that they could, in certain circumstances, be towed by other vehicles, in particular, by automobiles, such use is inappropriate and remains at least insignificant, if not hypothetical.

56 [A] prohibition on the use of a product in the territory of a Member State has a considerable influence on the behaviour of consumers, which, in its turn, affects the access of that product to the market of that Member State.

57 Consumers, knowing that they are not permitted to use their motorcycle with a trailer specially designed for it, have practically no interest in buying such a trailer. Thus, Article 56 of the Highway Code prevents a demand from existing in the market at issue for such trailers and therefore hinders their importation.

58 It follows that the prohibition laid down in Article 56 of the Highway Code, to the extent that its effect is to hinder access to the Italian market for trailers which are specially designed for motorcycles and are lawfully produced and marketed in Member States other than the Italian Republic, constitutes a measure having equivalent effect to quantitative restrictions on imports within the meaning of Article 28 EC, unless it can be justified objectively.

* * *

60 [T]he justification put forward by the Italian Republic relates to the need to ensure road safety, which, according to the case-law, constitutes an overriding reason relating to the public interest capable of justifying a hindrance to the free movement of goods.

61 In the absence of fully harmonising provisions at Community level, it is for the Member States to decide upon the level at which they wish to ensure road safety in their territory, whilst taking account of the requirements of the free movement of goods within the European Community.

* * *

63 [T]he Italian Republic contends that it introduced the measure because there were no type-approval rules, whether at Community level

or national level, to ensure that use of a motorcycle with a trailer was not dangerous. In the absence of such a prohibition, circulation of a combination composed of a motorcycle and an unapproved trailer could be dangerous both for the driver of the vehicle and for other vehicles on the road, because the stability of the combination and its braking capacity would be affected.

[64] In that regard, it must be held that the prohibition in question is appropriate for the purpose of ensuring road safety.

[65] With regard, second, to whether the said prohibition is necessary, account must be taken of the fact that in the field of road safety a Member State may determine the degree of protection which it wishes to apply in regard to such safety and the way in which that degree of protection is to be achieved. Since that degree of protection may vary from one Member State to the other, Member States must be allowed a margin of appreciation and, consequently, the fact that one Member State imposes less strict rules than another Member State does not mean that the latter's rules are disproportionate.

[66] [T]he Italian Republic contends * * * that the circulation of a combination composed of a motorcycle and a trailer is a danger to road safety. Whilst it is true that it is for a Member State which invokes an imperative requirement as justification for the hindrance to free movement of goods to demonstrate that its rules are appropriate and necessary to attain the legitimate objective being pursued, that burden of proof cannot be so extensive as to require the Member State to prove, positively, that no other conceivable measure could enable that objective to be attained under the same conditions.

[67] Although it is possible, in the present case, to envisage that measures other than the prohibition laid down in Article 56 of the Highway Code could guarantee a certain level of road safety for the circulation of a combination composed of a motorcycle and a trailer * * * the fact remains that Member States cannot be denied the possibility of attaining an objective such as road safety by the introduction of general and simple rules which will be easily understood and applied by drivers and easily managed and supervised by the competent authorities.

[69] In the light of those factors, it must be held that the prohibition on motorcycles towing trailers specially designed for them and lawfully produced and marketed in Member States other than the Italian Republic must be regarded as justified by reasons relating to the protection of road safety.

NOTES AND QUESTIONS

1. Because of the importance of the question whether national restrictions on a product's use should be considered to be exempt from Court of Justice review by analogy to the *Keck* doctrine, the case was transferred from

a chamber to the Grand Chamber. Advocate General Bot urged the Court to reject the *Keck* analogy, which it did in ¶¶ 56–58. Note that Advocate General Kokott's opinion in *Mickelsson*, supra page 488, advocated the *Keck* analogy to eliminate Court review of State restrictions on use, but the Court chamber in that case declined to follow her. Do you agree with the Court's reasoning in ¶¶ 56–58?

2. In its review of the Italian justification for its ban on motorcycle use to tow trailers, the Court observes that States may legitimately differ in their appraisal of safety risks (¶ 65), and that a State may apply "general and simple rules" for road safety (in this case, a ban) rather than more complicated ones that might permit some use of motorcycles (¶ 67). Again, do you agree?

3. In evaluating the evolving *Keck* doctrine, Peter Oliver concludes that "the Court has indeed ensured a high level of legal certainty and stability in this area of the law". P. Oliver, Free Movement of Goods in the European Community ¶ 6.69 (4th ed. Sweet & Maxwell 2003). In contrast, Professor Laurence Gormley asserts that "the ECJ should seriously consider renouncing *Keck*." L. Gormley, Silver Threads Among the Gold ... Fifty Years of the Free Movement of Goods, 31 Fordham Int'l L.J. 1637, at 1690 (2008). What is your view?

4. The latest edition of Peter Oliver's Free Movement of Goods in the European Community provides a detailed survey of all the topics treated in this chapter. Also valuable are these thoughtful articles analyzing the post-*Keck* case law: C. Barnard, Fitting the Remaining Pieces into the Goods and Persons Jigsaw? 26 Eur. L. Rev. 35 (2001); T. Connor, Accentuating the Positive: the "Selling Arrangement," the First Decade and Beyond, 54 Int'l & Comp. L. Q. 127 (2005); L. Gormley, Silver Threads Among the Gold, supra note 3; P. Oliver & S. Enchelmaier, Free Movement of Goods: Recent Developments in the Case Law, 44 Common Mkt. L. Rev. 649 (2007); and S. Weatherill, After Keck: Some Thoughts on How to Clarify the Clarification, 33 Common Mkt. L. Rev. 885 (1996).

Further Reading

Useful books containing material relevant to this chapter (and often relevant to Chapter 12) are:

C. Barnard, The Substantive Law of the EU: the Four Freedoms (Oxford 2004)

L. Gormley, EU Law of Free Movement of Goods and Customs Union (Oxford 2009)

P. Kapteyn & P. Verloren Van Themaat, The Law of the European Union and the European Communities (4th ed. Kluwer 2008)

P. Oliver, Free Movement of Goods in the European Community (4th ed. Sweet & Maxwell 2003)

S. Weatherill & P. Beaumont, European Community Law (3rd ed. Penguin 1999)

CHAPTER 14

THE COMMON MARKET, THE INTERNAL MARKET AND HARMONIZATION OF LAWS

■ ■ ■

A. THE COMMON MARKET AND HARMONIZATION OF LAWS

The 1957 European Economic Community Treaty declared in Article 2 that one of its prime goals was to establish a common market in order to achieve a variety of benefits, notably "a harmonious development of economic activities [and] an accelerated raising of the standard of living." A common market by its nature represents a high level of economic integration, far more than a free trade zone or a common customs area.

The scope of Community activities listed in Article 3 of the initial EEC Treaty suggest the principal dimensions of the common market: the elimination of obstacles to the free movement of goods, persons, services and capital (the "four freedoms"); common policies in the fields of agriculture, transport and competition; coordination of economic policies; and the approximation (or harmonization) of laws "for the proper functioning of the common market." The Lisbon Treaty's list of the Union's fields of action in its TFEU Articles 3 and 4 demonstrates that the Union continues to concentrate on the initial Community goals.

Chapters 12 and 13 have surveyed the vital role of the Court of Justice in removing barriers to the free movement of goods, and later chapters will describe the Court's important contributions to the achievement of the free movement of persons, services and capital. Indeed, the Court's role has always been crucial in stressing the fundamental nature of the four freedoms and articulating doctrines that have enabled both the Commission and private parties to sweep away many national barriers within the common market. Nonetheless the Court can only go so far towards achieving the common market goal, because it is always limited to enunciating doctrines based upon the particular circumstances that happen to be brought before the Court.

In contrast, Community legislation enabled the adoption of rules, more precise and uniform in character, throughout an entire field within the common market. As we shall see in later chapters, the Treaty makes specific grants of legislative power in many sectors of the common market, e.g., for the free movement of workers, the right of establishment, and for the free movement of services.

The first part of this chapter describes the legislative procedure for the harmonization of Member State laws, and reviews the dangerous substances and commercial agents directives as good examples of harmonized fields of law. Section B discusses the impact of the internal market program created through the 1987 Single European Act, together with its facilitation of harmonization legislation. Section C then reviews several prominent legal issues concerning such legislation, notably the scope of the legislative power to achieve the internal market, interpretation of legislation, and the preemption issue. The final section reviews the "new approach" to harmonization of rules in technical fields.

1. INITIAL HARMONIZATION OF LAWS

The grant of legislative power for the harmonization of laws to achieve the common market was contained in the initial 1957 European Economic Community Treaty Article 100 which declared:

> The Council shall, acting unanimously on a proposal from the Commission, issue directives for the approximation of such provisions laid down by law, regulation or administrative action in Member States as directly affect the establishment or functioning of the common market.

The success of the Community (and now the Union) depends in large measure on its ability to harmonize Member State laws. National health, safety and technical quality regulations, as well as rules to promote consumer interests or protect the environment, are the natural result of each State's independent effort to provide benefits to its citizens. Unfortunately, these Member State regulations become effective barriers to the free movement of goods or services when they impose specific technical product requirements and prevent the sale of imported products, or the performance of trans-border services, which do not conform to these requirements.

Such barriers make it difficult or more expensive for manufacturers to market throughout the Community, thus promoting the partition of national markets. Technical barriers also retard technological advance, since they divert capital from basic research to secondary development costs incurred to meet local market specifications. The benefits of free competition are diminished and consumers may be restricted in their freedom of choice. The creation of common rules and standards through harmonization therefore seeks to promote a Community market for products and services, while protecting the legitimate interests of consumers and the general public in a more uniform manner.

For the first thirty years of the Community, EECT Article 100 served as the chief legislative mode in adopting directives to remove barriers of trade in specific sectors in order to promote the common market. Article 100 had two deficiencies—it required the Council to act unanimously, creating the risk of delay or even veto by any Member State, and it gave the Parliament only a consultative, or advisory role, with no power of amendment. As we shall see in section B, the Single European Act introduced in 1987 an easier mode of legislation to achieve harmonization, EECT Article 100 a, which was subsequently amended by the Maastricht Treaty to augment Parliament's role in the legislative process. A good understanding of Article 100 is, however, essential to appreciating the initial success, and limits, of harmonization prior to 1987.

Article 100 authorized directives "for the approximation" of Member State laws or administrative acts. "Approximation" is a poor English translation of the terms used in the original Treaty languages, e.g. "rapprochement" in French, "Angleichung" in German. The Dutch version, the most precise, is "nader tot elkaar brengen," which translates into English as "to bring closer together." The English word "harmonization" conveys this better than "approximation" and is therefore customarily used by the Commission and commentators. Moreover, "harmonization" is the term used in some other initial Treaty articles concerning the specific fields of internal taxation and social policy, EECT Articles 99 and 117, as a synonym for "approximation."

Harmonization of laws does not require that Member State rules be made absolutely uniform. It merely requires that the rules be made similar. Harmonization directives accordingly set up a basic structure, with more or less detailed provisions, to which Member States must conform. Some directives make the Community rules the exclusive standard for all products, while others allow States to apply stricter standards, and a few make Community rules optional.

There was some debate, especially during the 1960s, over whether a harmonization directive's provisions had to be modeled on specific rules in one or more Member States. One could argue that, in strict logic, harmonization requires the alignment of some pre-existing set of national rules. However, policy considerations prevailed over logic. It became generally accepted that a harmonization directive may contain provisions that are innovations, not represented in any state's legal system, so long as the field is one appropriate for Community action. This sort of innovation is especially likely to occur in environmental protection legislation.

EECT Article 100 authorized directives, not regulations. Hence a harmonization measure adopted under Article 100 could not be passed as a regulation, with immediate force of law throughout the Community. Directives require implementing Member State laws or regulations within the time period specified (usually two years). As we have seen in prior chapters, the Commission frequently resorts to Treaty infringement proceedings against States that inadequately implement harmonization directives, or fail to adopt them on time. Moreover, applying the "direct effect" doctrine the Court of Justice has held some provisions of harmonization directives to be clear, precise and unconditional, so that individuals may rely upon them even when a State has failed to implement them, or implemented them improperly. For a good review of harmonization, see P. Slot, Harmonization, 21 Eur. L. Rev. 378 (1996).

Although some harmonization directives were adopted under Article 100 during the 1960s, widespread application started after the adoption of the General Program of May 28, 1969 for the elimination of technical barriers to trade, O.J. English Spec.Ed.2d Ser. 1974, at 25. By the mid–1980s, nearly 200 directives had been adopted pursuant to the technical barriers and related programs. The largest single sector was motor vehicles, where over 60 directives set technical regulations and standards for vehicle parts and equipment (e.g., brakes, doors, headlights, steering wheels, safety belts). Other important directives harmonized rules on the composition, labeling, packaging and review for safety of foodstuffs, cosmetics and pharmaceuticals, dangerous products of various kinds, electrical consumer goods, and mechanical products.

The adoption of the first environmental protection program in 1973 gave rise to an important new field of legislative harmonization. Initial environmental protection measures included directives to harmonize clean drinking and bathing water standards, automobile emission rules, clean air standards and wild bird protection. Chapter 34 describes the initial and on-going legislative programs for environmental protection.

2. A TYPICAL EARLY HARMONIZATION DIRECTIVE: DANGEROUS SUBSTANCES

At this point, it is helpful to analyze the structure and approach of a typical harmonization directive concerning dangerous products, adopted to facilitate the free movement of goods. Directive 92/32 on the approximation of laws relating to the classification, packaging and labeling of dangerous substances was initially adopted in 1967, with substantial amendments in 1979 and 1992 (see Document 11 in the Selected Documents).

This directive has five principal aspects. First, it defines a dangerous substance as one dangerous to man or the environment. Article 2 gives illustrations of "dangerous": explosive, flammable, toxic, carcinogenic, etc. Second, Member States must ensure that no dangerous substances are placed on the Community market until they have been reviewed and properly packaged and labeled. The directive does not, however, restrict or regulate the export of dangerous substances outside the Community.

Third, Article 6 of the directive requires a review process before marketing. The producer or importer must carefully investigate all relevant aspects of the substance, using laboratory tests "in compliance with the principles of good laboratory practice." Then, under article 7, the producer or importer must provide a technical file which evaluates the "foreseeable risks" and "unfavorable effects" of the product. Pursuant to articles 16–18, the competent national authority reviews this file in coordination with the Commission and comparable authorities in other States. Article 19 protects the producer's "commercially sensitive" information in this process.

Fourth, the national authority must approve an appropriate "strong and solid" package, so that the contents cannot escape. Since the 1979 amendment, the authority may require that the package be child-resistant or have a safety seal. Finally, the product must be "clearly and indelibly" labeled with a danger symbol, an indication of "special risks" and any "safety advice." Note that the danger symbol must be chosen from those in Annex II so as to be clearly recognizable throughout the Community, and must always be black on an orange-yellow background. (This approach of requiring that a single list of danger symbols be used in every State, so that the symbols will be recognizable to those who don't speak the local language, is also used for road safety and worksite safety signs.)

Notes and Questions

1. Observe the directive's article 30. The directive is intended not only to set acceptable minimum standards for the Community, but also to ensure that dangerous products, once reviewed by a national authority, may circulate freely throughout the Community. It illustrates the basic "mutual trust" principle, because importing States must rely on the exporting State's competent authority to perform its duties adequately. Only "in the light of new information" may a State temporarily prohibit an approved dangerous substance, subject to review by the Commission (article 31).

2. Article 24(5) allows Member States to require that imported products have labels in the importing state's official language or languages. This obviously represents an added expense and therefore a burden on trade. Do you think it is justified?

3. The dangerous substances directive was supplemented by Regulation 793/93 on the evaluation of risks of substances, O.J.L. 84/1 (Apr. 5, 1993), which requires the Commission and Member States to carry out an evaluation of the risks to workers, consumers and the environment of all dangerous substances being marketed. The dangerous substances directive was the model for several others, e.g., the directive on dangerous solvents, O.J. L 189/7 (June 4, 1973); on paints, varnishes, printing inks, etc., O.J. L 303/23 (Nov. 7, 1977); on pesticides, O.J. L 206/13 (June 26, 1978); on biocidal products, O.J. L 123/1 (Apr. 24, 1998). Analogous principles of prior review of a technical dossier, proper packaging and labeling (but without danger symbols) are found in the directive on cosmetic products, O.J. L 262/69 (July 27, 1976). All of the initial 1970s directives have been substantially amended, and sometimes codified.

3. THE COMMERCIAL AGENTS DIRECTIVE

Council Directive 86/653 on self-employed commercial agents, O.J. L 382/17 (Dec. 31, 1986), Document 12 in the Selected Documents, has considerable importance in the merchandising sector. Analysis of this directive, adopted to promote the right of establishment, helps illustrate how the Community harmonizes rules in a commercial field.

Commercial agents are intermediaries who either sell products, or negotiate contracts of sale to third parties on behalf of principals. (They are to be distinguished from distributors, who buy and sell products for their own account.) The sales contract is entered into directly between the principal and the third party. A commercial agent is remunerated by the principal through a fixed fee or commission or both. Commercial agents often perform other services for the principal, such as providing local advertising and market prospection, handling customs and sales tax, arranging for warehousing and transport of products, and handling after-sales service and repairs.

Prior to 1986, most continental European states had laws that protected commercial agents by granting them rights of notice and indemnities when terminated without cause by the principal. However, these laws varied widely in the scope of the rights and remedies of commercial agents, and the UK, Ireland and some other States did not provide any protection to commercial agents.

According to one of its whereas clauses, the goal of the commercial agent directive is to achieve equal conditions of competition in the common market by fixing uniform rules for commercial agents. The directive guarantees specific rights to commercial agents, notably to receive commissions at the level "customarily allowed" in the trade for all sales to the agent's customers, or for sales achieved through the agent's efforts; if the agent has a specific territory, then commissions are due on all contracts with buyers located within that territory (arts. 6–8). The directive further requires that commercial agents be given from one to three months' notice before termination of an indefinite term contract (art. 15). Agents are also entitled upon termination to indemnities for the value of the on-going customer relations, up to a ceiling of one year's remuneration (art. 17). The parties cannot by contract derogate from these rights (arts. 11, 15 & 19).

NOTES AND QUESTIONS

1. Do you agree that all States should provide this sort of protection to commercial agents in order to "achieve equal conditions of competition in the common market"? Is the goal of a level competitive playing field within the Community important enough to override a State's discretionary policy on whether or not to protect a particular type of commercial intermediary? Whether the need for a level competitive playing field requires all States to have the same substantive law in a given sector is an issue which frequently gives rise to heated debate when draft directives are being considered.

2. The policy rationale for protecting commercial agents is that they are usually small enterprises dealing at a disadvantage with economically powerful principals, so that it is appropriate that states should mandate that the agents receive certain economic benefits. (There is a definite analogy to the policy rationale for protection of employees in the event of dismissal. See Chapter 34B. Note the text of the directive's fifth whereas clause.) Do you think this policy should override the general free market principle of freedom of contract? If, in some cases, the consumer must pay a higher price to cover the economic cost of benefits to commercial agents, is that a desirable result?

3. Why should commercial agents be protected, but not distributors or franchisees? In the US, states do not have legislation protecting commercial agents. However, a majority of states have laws protecting franchisees, and some of the laws impose notice and indemnity requirements. The usual rationale given for protecting franchisees through these state laws parallels that given to justify protection of commercial agents in the Community. What factors might account for the fact that the Community protects commercial agents, but not franchisees, while some US states do the reverse? Might the impact of lobbying be the principal reason?

INGMAR GB v. EATON LEONARD TECHNOLOGIES

Case C–381/98, [2000] ECR I–9305.

[In 1989, Ingmar was appointed Eaton's commercial agent for the United Kingdom by a contract whose choice of law clause required the application of California law. After the contract was terminated in 1996, Ingmar sued for damages caused by termination pursuant to article 17 of the directive. The Court of Appeal asked the Court of Justice whether the directive's indemnity on termination provisions were mandatory in character, overriding the customary application of a choice of law clause.]

15   The parties to the main proceedings, the United Kingdom and German Governments and the Commission agree that the freedom of contracting parties to choose the system of law by which they wish their contractual relations to be governed is a basic tenet of private international law and that that freedom is removed only by rules that are mandatory.

16   However, their submissions differ as to the conditions which a legal rule must satisfy in order to be classified as a mandatory rule for the purposes of private international law.

* * *

21   The purpose of Articles 17 to 19 of the Directive, in particular, is to protect the commercial agent after termination of the contract. The regime established by the Directive for that purpose is mandatory in nature. Article 17 requires Member States to put in place a mechanism for providing reparation to the commercial agent after termination of the contract. Admittedly, that article allows the Member States to choose between indemnification and compensation for dam-

age. However, Articles 17 and 18 prescribe a precise framework within which the Member States may exercise their discretion as to choice of methods for calculating the indemnity or compensation to be granted.

22 The mandatory nature of those articles is confirmed by the fact that, under Article 19 of the Directive, the parties may not derogate from them to the detriment of the commercial agent before the contract expires.* * *

23 Second, it should be borne in mind that, as is apparent from the second recital in the preamble to the Directive, the harmonizing measures laid down by the Directive are intended, *inter alia*, to eliminate restrictions on the carrying-on of the activities of commercial agents, to make the conditions of competition within the Community uniform and to increase the security of commercial transactions.

24 The purpose of the regime established in Articles 17 to 19 of the Directive is thus to protect, for all commercial agents, freedom of establishment and the operation of undistorted competition in the internal market. Those provisions must therefore be observed throughout the Community if those Treaty objectives are to be attained.

25 [Therefore,] it is essential for the Community legal order that a principal established in a non-member country, whose commercial agent carries on his activity within the Community, cannot evade those provisions by the simple expedient of a choice-of-law clause. The purpose served by the provisions in question requires that they be applied where the situation is closely connected with the Community, in particular where the commercial agent carries on his activity in the territory of a Member State, irrespective of the law by which the parties intended the contract to be governed.

BELLONE v. YOKAHAMA
Case C–215/97, [1998] ECR I–2191.

[An Italian law required commercial agents to be entered on a register of commercial agents. Italian courts treated this obligation as mandatory and invalidated contracts entered into between principals and agents who did not inscribe themselves on the register. When Bellone, a non-registered agent, sought indemnities after her termination as a commercial agent by Yokahama, the trial court asked the Court of Justice whether the mandatory registration obligation was compatible with the directive.]

11 [T]he Directive does not deal with the question of registration of commercial agents.* * *It is therefore left to the Member States to require entry in the appropriate register if they consider it expedient so to do in order to satisfy certain administrative needs. As the Advocate General pointed out * * *, registration of commercial agents is required by law in a number of Member States.

* * *

13 [I]t should be borne in mind, first, that the Directive is designed to protect commercial agents, within the meaning of the Directive. According to Article 1(2), a commercial agent is 'a self-employed intermediary who has continuing authority to negotiate the sale or the purchase of goods on behalf of another person * * * or to negotiate and conclude such transactions on behalf of and in the name of that principal'. Since entry in a register is not referred to as a condition for protection under the Directive, it follows that protection under the Directive is not conditional upon entry in a register.

14 As regards, next, the form of the agency contract, Article 13(2) of the Directive * * * permits Member States to 'provide that an agency contract shall not be valid unless evidenced in writing'. It follows that the Directive starts from the principle that the contract is not subject to any formal requirement, whilst leaving it open to the Member States to require it to be in writing. [Moreover], as the Commission pointed out and the Advocate General noted * * *, by referring only to the requirement that the contract be in writing in order to be valid, the Community legislature dealt exhaustively with the matter in that provision. Member States may therefore not impose any condition other than requiring that a written document be drawn up.

15 That conclusion is confirmed by the fact that whenever the Directive allows the Member States to derogate from its provisions, express provision is made to that effect [citing examples]. If Article 13(2) of the Directive leaves it open to the Member States to require only that the document be in writing, it therefore follows that other derogations from the principle of freedom of form are contrary to the Directive. The entry of the agent in a register can therefore not be accepted as a condition for the validity of the contract.

16 That interpretation of the Directive is borne out by the fact that* * *the question of registration of agents had [been proposed] during the preparatory work, but was not taken up, since it was not considered necessary for agents to be registered in order to enjoy rights under the Directive.

NOTES AND QUESTIONS

1. Principals in the United States, where indemnities to commercial agents after a contract's termination are essentially unknown, naturally would like to contract out of an obligation to pay such indemnities to commercial agents in the Community. Choice of law clauses usually are accorded great respect by courts. Do you agree with the Court of Justice in *Ingmar* that the directive's indemnity provisions are mandatory, i.e., represent a strong public policy that overrides the choice of California law? Does the "level playing field" motive for the directive provide a justification for the Court's view?

2. Seven Member States required commercial agents to be listed on a register, but Italy was the only one that sanctioned non-registration with the

nullity of the contract; the other States imposed fines. Note that the *Bellone* judgement is a rare example of the use of legislative history by the Court in its interpretation of a directive. See Chapter 14C.

B. COMPLETION OF THE INTERNAL MARKET

1. THE WHITE PAPER OF JUNE 1985

As we observed in Chapter 1, in the early 1980s, the Community entered a period of "Europessimism" and "Eurostagnation." The process of harmonization of laws had appreciably slackened and there was widespread criticism of the slow pace of Community action. The difficulty in adopting legislation due to EECT Article 100's requirement of unanimity in Council votes was undoubtedly the principal cause, especially after new political leaders in some States were unenthusiastic about further Community measures.

The European Council discussed ways to reenergize the Community in several meetings during 1982–85. Notably, at its December 1984 meeting in Dublin, the European Council agreed that the Council "should take steps to complete the Internal Market." At its subsequent meeting in Brussels on March 29–30, 1985, the European Council "called upon the Commission to draw up a detailed program with a specific timetable" in order to "achieve a single large market by 1992."

A new Commission took office in January 1985, headed by President Jacques Delors, a leading French Socialist and former Minister of Finance. Much of the credit for the more dynamic Commission leadership since 1985 must be given to the vision and energy of President Delors. In response to the European Council's request, the Commission rapidly produced a White Paper. The principal author of this study was Lord Cockfield, a former Tory UK cabinet minister and adroit political leader, who was the Commissioner responsible for the internal market directorate-general.

THE WHITE PAPER COMPLETING THE INTERNAL MARKET

COM (85) 310 (June 1985).

3   [T]he Commission, which wholeheartedly shares the [European] Council's commitment [to the completion of the common market], sets out here the essential and logical consequences of accepting that commitment, together with an action program * * *.

* * *

5   [After initial Community achievements, in recent times] momentum was lost partly through the onset of the recession, partly through a lack of confidence and vision * * *.

6   [D]uring the recession, [non-tariff barriers] multiplied as each Member State endeavored to protect what it thought was its short term interests—not only against third countries but against fellow Member States as well. * * *

7   But the mood has begun to change, and the commitment to be rediscovered: gradually at first, but now with increasing tempo. * * * The time for talk has now passed. The time for action has come. That is what this White Paper is about.

* * *

8   [T]he objective of completing the internal market has three aspects:

— First, the welding together of the * * * individual markets of the Member States into one single market of 320 million people;

— Second, ensuring that this single market is also an expanding market—not static but growing;

— Third, to this end, ensuring that the market is flexible so that resources, both of people and materials, and of capital and investment, flow into the areas of greatest economic advantage.

* * *

10 For convenience the measures that need to be taken have been classified in this Paper under three headings:

— Part one: the removal of physical barriers

— Part two: the removal of technical barriers

— Part three: the removal of fiscal barriers.

11 The most obvious example of the first category are customs posts at frontiers. Indeed most of our citizens would regard the frontier posts as the most visible example of the continued division of the Community and their removal as the clearest sign of the integration of the Community into a single market. * * * Once we have removed [technical and fiscal] barriers, and found alternative ways of dealing with other relevant problems such as public security, immigration and drug controls, the reasons for the existence of the physical barriers will have been eliminated.

12 The reason for getting rid entirely of physical and other controls between Member States is not one of theology or appearance, but the hard practical fact that the maintenance of any internal frontier controls will perpetuate the costs and disadvantages of a divided market * * *.

13 * * * [T]he elimination of technical barriers * * * will give the large market its economic and industrial dimension by enabling industries to make economies of scale and therefore to become more competitive. An example of this second category—technical barriers—are the different standards for individual products adopted in different Member States for health or safety reasons, or for environmental or consumer protec-

tion. * * * The general thrust of the Commission's approach in this area will be to move away from the concept of harmonisation towards that of mutual recognition and equivalence. But there will be a continuing role for the approximation of Member States' laws and regulations.

[14] The removal of fiscal barriers may well be contentious and this despite the fact that the goals laid down in the Treaty are quite explicit* * *.

* * *

[17] This White Paper is not intended to cover every possible issue which affects the integration of the economies of the Member States of the community. It focuses on the Internal Market and the measures which are directly necessary to achieve a single integrated market* * *.

* * *

[20] There are many other areas of Community policy that interact with the Internal Market * * * and will benefit from the stimulus that will be provided by its completion. This is particularly true of transport, social, environment and consumer protection policy.

The White Paper urged new efforts in a number of sectors where progress had long been stalemated, such as the banking and insurance industries, internal tax harmonization, industrial and commercial property rights, and the free movement of professionals. The White Paper's Annex listed a total of 282 legislative measures, with a timetable for the drafting and adoption of each measure. The entire legislative process was to be completed by December 31, 1992. Incidently, the Commission adopted a traditional British practice in calling this a 'White Paper,' a term used for action programs. The Commission now also issues 'Green Papers,' comprehensive studies of particular fields for reflection on possible future action.

What in retrospect is so astonishing is that the White Paper did not remain just another interesting Commission study, but became in fact the blueprint for the tremendously successful program for achieving the "Europe of 1992." The European Council decisively endorsed the White Paper's program in Milan on June 28–29, 1985. The Commission's energetic development of proposed legislation and its continuous exertions for passage of the proposals certainly played a key role. The Parliament also gave its enthusiastic support. But perhaps equally important was the recognition and endorsement of the "Europe of 1992" goal by the media, leading industry and commercial groups, and by the general public, which stimulated the political will necessary in the difficult decision-making process. Lord Cockfield, The European Union–Creating the Single Market (Wiley Chancery 1994), is a fascinating description of the background of the White Paper and its success.

This endorsement of the "Europe of 1992" goal was reinforced by economic studies, notably the famous 1988 Cecchini report, made at the request of the Commission. This report consisted of 24 separate studies, including a survey of 11,000 business firms. The report estimated that the completed internal market would produce hundreds of billions of dollars in savings, and substantially increase investment and production. See P. Cecchini, The European Challenge (Gower 1988).

2. THE SINGLE EUROPEAN ACT'S ARTICLE 8a: ACHIEVING THE INTERNAL MARKET

Although the White Paper set the program for completing the internal market, this might well have been largely frustrated if the Single European Act had not introduced several structural Treaty improvements. Thus, the SEA's insertion of Article 8a into the EEC Treaty gave Treaty force to the policy goal of completing the internal market:

> The Community shall adopt measures with the aim of progressively establishing the internal market over a period expiring on 31 December 1992. * * *

> The internal market shall comprise an area without internal frontiers in which the free movement of goods, persons, services and capital is ensured in accordance with the provisions of this Treaty.

The definition of the internal market as "an area without internal frontiers" adds significantly to the attainment of the "four freedoms." EECT Article 8a's goal was to achieve a global market area in which the legal boundaries of Member States do not constitute functional limits on any of the "four freedoms." Moreover, Article 8a set a time frame with treaty force: the internal market legislative program is meant to be completed by Dec. 31, 1992. Article 8a was renumbered as ECT Article 14 by the Treaty of Amsterdam, and now as TFEU Article 26 by the Treaty of Lisbon.

Is EECT Article 8a one of those Treaty articles that can be given direct effect, and thus give rights to individuals, even in the absence of specified legislative measures? The Commission initially proposed to the Luxembourg Conference of Member State representatives, which prepared the SEA, that Article 8a expressly be given direct effect. The Conference declined to do so. Instead, the Conference adopted a "Declaration on Article 8a" which was annexed to the SEA, and expressly stated: "Setting the date of 31 December 1992 does not create an automatic legal effect."

Although some academic commentators contended that the Declaration on Article 8a had no binding legal force under public international law principles, it was always unlikely that the Court of Justice would ascribe direct effect to Article 8a. The Court has now definitively held that Article 8a does not have direct effect in *Wijsenbeek, infra* page 637, which permits States to retain border controls on persons.

Probably the best over-all analysis of the SEA is that by Claus–Dieter Ehlermann, the then-Director General of the Commission Legal Service, in The Internal Market Following the Single European Act, 24 Common Mkt. L. Rev. 361 (1987). For the views of Hans–Joachim Glaesner, the then-Director General of the Council Legal Service, see H. J. Glaesner, The Single European Act: Attempt at An Appraisal, 10 Fordham Int'l L. J. 446 (1987).

3. THE SINGLE EUROPEAN ACT'S ARTICLE 100a: LEGISLATION TO ACHIEVE THE INTERNAL MARKET

One of the principal reasons for the level of success in completing the internal market was the modification of the legislative process introduced by the SEA as Article 100a(1) of the EEC Treaty.

> By way of derogation from Article 100 and save where otherwise provided in this Treaty, the following provisions shall apply for the achievement of the objectives set out in Article 8a. The Council shall, acting by a qualified majority on a proposal from the Commission in co-operation with the European Parliament and after consulting the Economic and Social Committee, adopt the measures for the approximation of the provisions laid down by law, regulation or administrative action in Member States which have as their object the establishment and functioning of the internal market.

EECT Article 100a avoided the principal defects of Article 100. First, Article 100a permitted the adoption of measures by a qualified majority vote of the Council, instead of unanimity. Second, Article 100a gave the Parliament a substantial role in the legislative process, thus making the process more democratic. Article 100a introduced the use of the parliamentary cooperation procedure described in Chapter 3. Subsequently, the Treaty of Maastricht replaced the cooperation procedure with the legislative co-decision procedure, also described in Chapter 3. Thus Parliament has exercised essentially a veto power over internal market legislation since Nov. 1, 1993.

EECT Article 100a, as amended by the Maastricht Treaty, was renumbered as ECT Article 95(1) by the Treaty of Amsterdam. TFEU Article 114(1) replaces ECT Article 95(1), except to rename codecision as the ordinary legislative procedure.

Article 100a proved a decisive success. The psychology of Council operations significantly changed. Member States opposed to all or part of a proposal no longer remained inflexible in opposition, but tried to seek a compromise solution rather than see themselves outvoted. The process of deliberation thus accelerated. As for the Parliament, the Commission has observed in its annual General Reports that the Parliament's participation in the process has not significantly slowed the adoption of legislation and that about half of the Parliament's amendments are accepted by the Council.

EECT Article 100a did not totally replace Article 100. Article 100a(2) excluded from the scope of Article 100a measures relating to "fiscal provisions, * * * the free movement of persons [and] * * * the rights and interests of employed persons." These continued to be governed either by Article 100 or more specific articles, such as those authorizing legislation to achieve the free movement of workers and other persons, and those authorizing legislation to harmonize internal taxes. The Treaty of Amsterdam subsequently renumbered EECT Article 100a(2) as ECT Article 95(2), now replicated by TFEU Article 114(2). As a matter of fact, however, TFEU Article 114(2) now effectively only governs any proposal concerning the harmonization of taxation or other fiscal matters, because other Treaty provisions enable harmonization in the other two fields. EECT Article 100 survives in TFEU Article 115.

Article 100a(3) (renumbered as ECT Article 95(3)) required Commission proposals for legislation "concerning health, safety, environmental protection and consumer protection [to] take as a base a high level of protection." The Court of Justice has had occasion to cite Article 95(3) in examining whether Article 95 is an appropriate legal basis for legislation, as we shall see in section C. TFEU Article 114(3) replicates ECT Article 95(3).

In an unusual action, the European Council itself insisted on Article 100a(4), commonly called an "opt-out" provision. This enables a Member State to decline to adopt all or part of a harmonized measure if the State feels such an action justified by an Article 30 interest or by a need to protect the environment or the working environment. Article 100 (a) 4 was subsequently revised to provide for a complicated procedure to deal with a State's claim for a derogation, renumbered as ECT Article 95 (4) to (10), and further renumbered as TFEU Article 115(4) to (10) by the Treaty of Lisbon. P. Oliver, Free Movement of Goods in the European Community ¶¶ 12.45–58 (4th ed. 2003), provides a careful analysis of this complex procedure. In practice, Member States have rarely made use of this opt-out procedure.

4.　THE ONGOING INTERNAL MARKET PROGRAM AND THE LISBON STRATEGY

In any event, the White Paper has had a dramatic success. Its legislative agenda proved largely capable of attainment. In December 1992, the Edinburgh European Council "noted with particular satisfaction" the program's success, with the adoption of over 500 internal market measures, representing 95% of the White Paper list. Naturally, the internal market program did not end on Dec. 31, 1992. The Community continued to adopt important legislation in virtually all sectors to supplement the initial measures.

Perhaps the most significant initial internal market attainments were in the achievement of the free movement of capital, the harmonization of the essential rules in banking, insurance and securities law, the harmonization of traditional intellectual property rights, together with the creation of some new ones, the liberalization of public procurement and telecommunications, and further technical harmonization. Some of the more important legislative measures are described in later chapters. Highly useful measures to enable rights of residence for students and other persons were adopted in 1990, and sweeping rights of movement and residence have been adopted recently, removing virtually all frontier barriers to the free movement of persons. See Chapter 16 on Citizenship of the Union. However, to date little progress has been made upon initiatives to harmonize direct and indirect taxation.

Most of the measures adopted have been in the form of directives which require Member State implementation. For years some States lagged significantly behind in the implementation process, but the passage of time has alleviated this problem to some degree, even though the Commission regularly urges more rapid implementation of directives. Not surprisingly in view of the technical complexity of many directives, the Commission considers that some States have improperly implemented them, leading to large numbers of Treaty infringement proceedings, but, as usual, most of these are resolved satisfactorily before any Court action is required. However, many recent preliminary reference questions concern the interpretation of internal market directives.

The Commission issued a report on the economic impact and effectiveness of the single market on Oct. 30, 1996, COM (96) 520. The report concluded that the internal market program had increased intra-Community trade by 20–30%, created over 1% in added GDP growth annually, and stimulated the creation of 900,000 jobs.

The Commission's new emphasis on transparency, clarity and coherence in internal market measures, in part prompted by criticism of allegedly excessively detailed and abstruse Community legislation, has led it to improve its internal procedures. When the Commission joined the Council and the Parliament in the Interinstitutional Declaration on Democracy, Transparency and Subsidiarity on October 25, 1993, the Commission committed itself to "wider consultations before presenting proposals, ... publication of work programmes—and faster publication of Commission documents." The 1993 Interinstitutional Declaration also stated that "[i]n expressing its rights of initiative, the Commission shall take into account the principle of subsidiarity." The Commission now expressly covers this in the explanatory memorandum for each new proposal.

In May 1996 the Commission launched the SLIM program for "Simpler Legislation in the Internal Market," pressing for transparent and codified texts. The December 1996 Dublin European Council endorsed the SLIM project. The Community has made substantial progress in codifying legislation in some fields (e.g., cosmetic products, driving licenses, foodstuffs, professional rights, securities and banking law), but the process is slow and arduous.

The Commission has steadily continued its policy efforts toward achieving the internal market. By far the most important new initiative was the European Council's adoption in March 2000 of the Lisbon Strategy, a detailed policy statement entitled "Employment, Economic Reform and Social Cohesion," setting out a ten year program. Bull. EU 2000–3, at 8. Its "strategic goal" was to achieve "the most competitive and knowledge-based economy in the world, capable of sustained economic growth" and ensuring "more and better jobs and greater social cohesion." The principal focus was upon enhanced research and technology development, the removal of regulatory barriers to growth and the restructuring of fiscal policies, raising the quality of higher education, and the modernization of "the European social model."

The Prodi and Barosso Commissions enthusiastically supported the Lisbon Strategy program. However, in March 2005, the European Council's mid-term review observed that "the results are mixed" and urged a relaunching of efforts, Bull. EU 2005–3, at 8. Since 2005 the Commission adopts annual integrated Broad Economic Policy Guidelines and Employment Guidelines for the Member States. Although a Commission report in December 2007 reported satisfactory progress in the Lisbon Strategy program, the 2008–10 European recession has clearly slowed further progress.

The Department of Commerce and the Office of the US Trade Representative carefully followed the evolution of the Community legislative program and energetically urged the Commission and Council to modify proposals they considered to be harmful to US trade or investment. American industry groups also organized lobbying efforts to attempt to influence Community decisionmakers. During this dialogue, the Commission and other institutions were attentive to US views and in many cases modified proposals so as to reduce any adverse impact on the trade and investment interests of the US and the Community's other major trading partners. A good example was the change made to the reciprocity provision of the Second Banking Directive 89/646, discussed in Chapter 32C, after well-publicized protests by the US Government and banking community.

Inevitably, however, the Community's economic power substantially increased with the success of the internal market. The Community has now essentially attained a position of economic parity with the US, reflected in their relatively equal bargaining strength in the Uruguay Round GATT negotiations and currently within the WTO.

C. HARMONIZATION DIRECTIVES: ISSUES OF LEGISLATIVE POWER, INTERPRETATION AND PREEMPTION

1. LEGISLATIVE POWER

The Council and Parliament broadly applied ECT Article 95 (initially EECT Article 100a) in adopting legislation intended to achieve the internal market. The Court of Justice has usually upheld the use of EECT Article 100a, or the renumbered ECT Article 95 in challenges brought by Member States (often unhappy by being outvoted in the adoption of specific legislation.) Thus, the Court endorsed the adoption of a regulation to extend the term of certain patents through Article 95, although the Treaty contains no express power to legislate in the field of intellectual property. See Spain v. Council (Medical Products Certificate), supra page 107. Similarly the Court held that Article 95 was appropriate to adopt a directive enabling patents for biotechnological inventions in The Netherlands v. Council and Parliament, infra page 805.

In a rare judgment in 2000 setting limits to the use of ECT Article 95, Germany v. Parliament and Council (Tobacco advertising), excerpted at page 144 supra, the Court annulled Directive 98/43 on tobacco advertising, because it covered types of advertising (notably on posters, ashtrays, and parasols) that had no cross-border character. Subsequently in 2006 the Court endorsed the use of Article 95 to adopt a modified text, Directive 2003/33, which forbid tobacco advertising in newspapers, magazines and on the radio, but did not forbid the types of domestic advertising cited in the prior judgment. See Germany v. Parliament and Council, discussed at page 147 supra.

In the following judgment the Court endorsed the use of Article 95 to adopt a directive that may have a greater impact on smoking than the Tobacco Advertising Directive.

THE QUEEN v. SECRETARY OF STATE FOR HEALTH EX PARTE BRITISH–AMERICAN TOBACCO

Case C–491/01, [2002] ECR I–11453.

[Directive 2001/37, O.J.L. 194/26 (July 18, 2001) on the manufacture, presentation and sale of tobacco products, sets stringent rules for maximum limits on the amount of tar and nicotine in cigarettes in article 3. Under article 5, a general warning covering at least 30% of large surface of the cigarette package must be either "Smoking kills/Smoking can kill" or "Smoking seriously harms you and others around you." A variety of specific warnings (e.g., "Smoking causes fatal lung cancer" or "Smoking is highly addictive, don't start") is provided, and one must cover not less than 40% of the other large surface. Article 7 forbids the use of any text on the package "suggesting that a particular tobacco product is less harmful than others" (i.e., common terms such as "low-tar," "light" or "mild" are forbidden).

When leading UK tobacco producers challenged the directive's validity, contending that ECT Article 95 could not be used to adopt it, the question was referred to the Court of Justice. Eight Member State briefs argued for the directive's validity, while three contested this.]

61   [W]hile recourse to Article 95 EC as a legal basis is possible if the aim is to prevent the emergence of future obstacles to trade resulting from

multifarious development of national laws, the emergence of such obstacles must be likely and the measure in question must be designed to prevent them.

62   [P]rovided that the conditions for recourse to Article 95 EC as a legal basis are fulfilled, the Community legislature cannot be prevented from relying on that legal basis on the ground that public health protection is a decisive factor in the choices to be made. Moreover, the first subparagraph of Article 152(1) EC provides that a high level of human health protection is to be ensured in the definition and implementation of all Community policies and activity, and Article 95(3) EC explicitly requires that, in achieving harmonisation, a high level of protection of human health should be guaranteed.

64   The following considerations ought to be noted at the outset. First, as the Advocate General [Geelhoed] observed* * *, the market for tobacco products, especially cigarettes, in the Community is one in which trade between Member States represents a relatively large part. Second, national rules laying down the requirements to be met by products, in particular those relating to their designation, composition or packaging, are in themselves liable, in the absence of harmonisation at Community level, to constitute obstacles to the free movement of goods.

[The Court noted that prior directives, such as Directive 89/622 on the labelling of tobacco products, harmonized State laws only partially.]

* * *

66   On the one hand, some provisions contained in the Community harmonisation measures already adopted merely laid down minimal requirements, leaving the Member States a degree of discretion to adapt them. On the other hand, Directives 89/622 and 90/239 covered only certain aspects of the conditions for manufacture, presentation and sale of tobacco products, the Member States being free to adopt national rules in respect of those aspects not thereby covered.

67   [Because] the public is increasingly conscious of the dangers to health posed by consuming tobacco products, it is likely that obstacles to the free movement of those products would arise by reason of the adoption by the Member States of new rules intended more effectively to discourage consumption of those products by means of warnings and information appearing on their packaging or to reduce the harmful effects of tobacco products by introducing new rules governing their composition.

* * *

70   Similarly, the ninth recital in the preamble to the Directive states that differences had emerged between the laws of the Member States on the limitation of the maximum nicotine yield of cigarettes. Observations submitted show that three Member States had already intro-

duced such limitations and that several others were thinking of doing so * * * [creating a risk] of obstacles to trade.

72   In addition, the 19th and 22nd recitals in the preamble to the Directive refer to the fact that different Member States have different laws with regard to the presentation of warnings and indications of yields of harmful substances on the one hand and the ingredients and additives used in the manufacture of tobacco products on the other.

74   [U]nlike the directive at issue in the case giving rise to the tobacco advertising judgment, the Directive contains a provision, Article 13(1), which guarantees the free movement of products which comply with its requirements. By forbidding the Member States to prevent, on grounds relating to the matters harmonised by the Directive, the import, sale or consumption of tobacco products which do comply, that provision gives the Directive its full effect in relation to its object of improving the conditions for the functioning of the internal market.

75   It follows that the Directive genuinely has as its object the improvement of the conditions for the functioning of the internal market and that it was, therefore, possible for it to be adopted on the basis of Article 95 EC, and it is no bar that the protection of public health was a decisive factor in the choices involved in the harmonising measures which it defines.

* * *

79   With regard in particular to the protection of public health, it follows from Article 95(3) EC that the Community legislature, in harmonising the legislation, must guarantee a high level of protection, taking particular account of any new development based on scientific facts.

[The Court also rejected contentions that the directive violated the principles of proportionality and subsidiarity, or any intellectual property rights.]

NOTES AND QUESTIONS

1.   The Court's judgment is unusually long and detailed, perhaps to demonstrate how seriously it was examining the various objections to the directive's validity. That the Court upheld ECT Article 95 as the appropriate legal basis for all the stringent rules of the directive indicates that the first *Tobacco advertising* judgement was exceptional, rather than the precursor of frequent limitations on the scope of Article 95. Note the citation in ¶ 62 of Article 95(3)'s requirement of "a high level of protection of human health" in harmonization measures. Should the Court have occasion to examine the scope of TFEU Article 114, which replaced ECT Article 95, presumably it will continue the policy approach of liberal construction shown in the *BAT* judgment.

2.   The Court reached a similar conclusion in Alliance for Natural Health v. Secretary of State for Health, Case C–154/04, [2005] ECR I—6451, which

upheld the reliance on Article 95 to adopt Directive 2002/46 on food supplements, because of the likely emergence of barriers to trade caused by different national rules (¶¶ 29–38). To evidence the likelihood, the Court made an unusual citation of legislative history, noting the Commission's reference to complaints from 'economic operators' about differing rules in its Explanatory Memorandum for its proposal for the directive (¶ 37). The Court also accepted the precautionary principle (see page 470 *supra*) as a justification for technical decisions taken by the Scientific Committee on Food in declining to accept certain vitamins or mineral substances as safe in the Annex (¶¶ 66–68).

2. HOW SHOULD DIRECTIVES BE INTERPRETED

No matter how comprehensive and detailed harmonization directives may be, the Court of Justice is frequently called upon to interpret their provisions. This is inevitable for a variety of reasons. Thus, specific directive provisions may be imprecise, ambiguous text may have been inserted as a compromise during the drafting stage, issues may arise that were not envisaged during the legislative process, different language versions may not perfectly coincide, two different directives' provisions may overlap, etc. Does the Court of Justice have any guiding principle or principles in dealing with issues of interpretation?

In *Stauder*, previously discussed as a seminal judgment in basic rights protection (*supra* page 191), the Court had to reconcile substantially different official language versions of a Commission decision. The Court did not give priority to any language version, not even that used as a working draft during the administrative process.

STAUDER v. CITY OF ULM, SOZIALAMT
Case 29/69, [1969] ECR 419.

[In an attempt to reduce the Community's stock of surplus butter, a 1969 Commission decision authorized the Member States to make butter available to certain categories of social assistance recipients at a discount from the usual retail price. The decision required persons seeking to benefit from the program to present certain coupons to retailers. The German text of the decision provided for the coupon to identify the recipient. Stauder, a war victim who was entitled to participate in the program, objected to having to disclose his identity, characterizing the requirement as discriminatory and violative of his right to privacy guaranteed by the German Constitution. His suit in a German administrative court gave rise to the following preliminary ruling.]

2   The [Commission] decision is addressed to all the Member States and authorizes them, with a view to stimulating the sale of surplus quantities of butter on the Common Market, to make butter available at a lower price than normal to certain categories of consumers who are in receipt of certain social assistance. This authorization is subject to certain conditions designed, *inter alia*, to ensure that the product,

when marketed in this way, is not prevented from reaching its proper destination. To that end [the decision] stipulates in two of its versions, one being the German version, that the States must take all necessary measures to ensure that beneficiaries can only purchase the product in question on presentation of a "coupon indicating their names", whilst in the other versions, however, it is only stated that a "coupon referring to the person concerned" must be shown, thus making it possible to employ other methods of checking in addition to naming the beneficiary. It is therefore necessary in the first place to ascertain exactly what methods the provision at issue prescribes.

3   When a single decision is addressed to all the Member States, the necessity for uniform application and accordingly for uniform interpretation makes it impossible to consider one version of the text in isolation, but requires that it be interpreted on the basis of both the real intention of its author and the aim he seeks to achieve, in the light in particular of the versions in all four languages.

In a case like the present one, the most liberal interpretation must prevail, provided that it is sufficient to achieve the objectives pursued by the decision in question. It cannot, moreover, be accepted that the authors of the decision intended to impose stricter obligations in some Member States than in others.

* * *

6   It follows that the provision in question must be interpreted as not requiring * * * the identification of beneficiaries by name. The Commission was thus able to publish on 29 July 1969 an amending decision to this effect. Each of the Member States is accordingly now able to choose from a number of methods by which the coupons may refer to the person concerned.

7   Interpreted in this way the provision at issue contains nothing capable of prejudicing the fundamental human rights enshrined in the general principles of Community law and protected by the Court.

The Court's approach in *Stauder* is commonly described as teleological, interpreting a measure based upon the fundamental purpose it seeks to achieve. The Court's teleological approach is somewhat analogous to the US Supreme Court's frequent resort to its perception of congressional intent in its interpretation of imprecise or ambiguous statutes. There is, however, a major difference. The Supreme Court often carefully examines the legislative history of a statute in its effort to ascertain Congress' legislative intent. Although Advocates General may discuss the legislative history of a Community measure in their opinions, the Court only occasionally makes reference to a draft text or a Commission, Council or Parliament document, but rather interprets the language of the final version.

As we shall see in later chapters, the Court frequently employs this teleological approach in interpreting Treaty articles, notably in requiring that Member State rules that limit Treaty-based rights are objectively justified by important general good or public interest concerns. We also examined in Chapter 11 a prominent recent judgment, Commission v. France (Sanctions for violation of fisheries rules), supra page 410, where the Court held that it had the power to impose both a lump sum and an on-going penalty sanction upon a recalcitrant State in application of ECT Article 228. Using its teleological approach, the Court held that in the Treaty language, "lump sum or penalty payment," the word "or" ("ou" in French, "oder" in German, and the parallel word in other languages) should be read as permitting the cumulation of the two sanctions, rather than as a disjunctive conjunction.

In examining harmonization directives, the Court frequently interprets them liberally in order to better achieve the fundamental treaty goal in the sector concerned. In later chapters, we will see this clearly exemplified in the Court's broad interpretation of legislative measures to attain the free movement of workers or the free providing of services or the right of establishment. The following case illustrates this approach.

VEREIN GEGEN UNWESEN IN HANDEL KÖLN v. ADOLF DARBO

Case C–465/98, [2000] ECR 2297.

[Darbo manufactures strawberry jam in Austria in accordance with Austrian law. Its label calls the jam "naturrein" (naturally pure). A private consumer protection group sued to prevent the jam's sale in Germany, contending that the label reference was deceptive under the German foodstuff labeling law, which is intended to implement Directive 79/112 on the labeling, presentation and advertising of foodstuffs, O.J.L. 33/1 (Feb. 8, 1979). The directive's article 2(1) forbids labels that "could mislead the consumer to a material degree." The consumer group argued in particular that the jam contained traces of lead, cadmium and pesticides, so that the jam could not properly be called "naturally pure." When the Court of Justice was asked by the trial court to give guidance on the application of article 2(1), the Court began by indicating the proper standard to assess when consumers might be materially misled.]

20 As the Court has held on several occasions in relation to provisions similar to Article 2(1)(a) of the Directive, designed to prevent any deception of consumers * * *, it is for the national court to assess whether an appellation, brand name or advertising statement may be misleading, taking into account the presumed expectations of an average consumer who is reasonably well informed and reasonably observant and circumspect.

* * *

26 According to the Verein and the Finnish Government, use of the term 'naturally pure' is likely to create in the consumer's mind the impression the d'arbo jam is a pure and natural product, free of any impurity

or extraneous substance. However, the mere presence of residues of lead, cadmium and pesticides, whatever their respective amounts in the foodstuff, detracts from that description, which is therefore liable to mislead consumers as to the characteristics of the jam.

27   That argument cannot be upheld. It is common ground that lead and cadmium are present in the natural environment as a result, in particular, of air pollution and pollution of the aquatic environment * * *. Since garden fruit is grown in an environment of that kind, it is inevitably exposed to the pollutants present in it.

28   In those circumstances, even if it is assumed that, in certain cases, consumers might be unaware of that fact and thereby be misled, that risk remains minimal and cannot therefore justify a barrier to the free movement of goods [citing *Mars*, *supra* page 502].

29   The same conclusion is called for in relation to the presence of traces or residues of pesticides in Darbo jam. * * * [T]he use of pesticides, even by private individuals, is one of the most usual means of combating the presence of harmful organisms on vegetables and agricultural products. Thus, the fact that garden strawberries are grown 'naturally' does not in any event mean that they are free of pesticide residues.

[The Court concluded by noting that the traces of lead, cadmium and pesticides were well below the maximum levels permitted under either Community or national legislation, so that the "naturally pure" description did not violate Article 2(1) of the directive.]

NOTES AND QUESTIONS

1.   In order to interpret the somewhat general language of the Foodstuffs Directive's Article 2(1), the Court resorts to the "reasonably well informed and reasonably observant" consumer standard, which is the Court's modern standard in consumer protection cases, and is also used in trademark confusion cases (see Chapter 19E). We previously noted in Chapter 13C that this is a higher standard than the "average consumer." Has the Court's standard had an impact on its guidance to the Austrian Court?

2.   In Givane v. Secretary of State for the Home Department, Case C–257–00, [2003] ECR I–345, the Court had to interpret an article of Commission Regulation 1251/70 concerning the right of a spouse and children of a deceased migrant worker to continue to reside in a host State, when there existed different language versions of the article concerned. The English language text, cited by the referring court in the UK, was ambiguous, as were the Dutch, Spanish and other versions. In contrast, the French, Italian and German texts were quite clear in requiring the deceased migrant worker to have lived continuously in the host State for two years preceding death, and not continuously for two years at some other time during his life. The deceased worker and his family had only lived continuously in the UK for 21 months prior to his death.

The Court held that "all the language versions must, in principle, be recognized as having the same weight and this cannot vary according to the size of the population of the Member States using the language in question" (¶ 36). As in *Stauder*, the Court concluded that "the provision in question must be interpreted by reference to the purpose and general scheme of the rules of which it forms part" (¶ 37). The Court held the French, Italian and German version better served the Regulation's goal of ensuring that the family had become integrated into the Host State. Note that none of the parties discussed, nor did the Court consider, what might have been the evolution of the text during the drafting stage.

3.　THE ISSUE OF LOCAL LANGUAGE REQUIREMENTS

In reviewing the Dangerous Substances Directive, we noted that article 24(5) permits Member States to require that imported dangerous substances be labeled in the official national language(s). Such a provision is patently justified to ensure safe use of any product which is inherently dangerous. It is not surprising that article 20(6) of the recent Directive 98/8 on biocidal products, O.J.L. 123/1 (Apr. 24, 1998), makes the use of the national language(s) compulsory, and not merely optional, for labels.

In contrast, Directive 79/112 on the labeling, presentation and advertising of foodstuffs contained the following provision in the initial version of article 14 ¶ 2:

> "The Member States shall, however, ensure that the sale of foodstuffs within their own territories is prohibited if the particulars [required on the labels] do not appear in a language easily understood by purchasers, unless other measures have been taken to ensure that the purchaser is informed. This provision shall not prevent such particulars from being indicated in various languages."

Although certain foodstuffs may contain ingredients which are dangerous to consumers with allergies or other health problems, foodstuffs are not dangerous for the average consumer. The harmonization of labeling requirements in articles 3 and 4 of the directive is intended both to achieve "free circulation of these products" (first recital) and "to inform and protect the consumer" (sixth recital). Whether either goal has priority over the other has posed a difficult issue for the Court of Justice.

PIAGEME & ORRS v. PEETERS (PIAGEME I)
Case C–369/89, [1991] ECR I—2971.

[A 1986 Belgian decree intended to implement the Foodstuffs Directive required that labels "must at least appear in the language or languages of the linguistic region where the foodstuffs are offered for sale." Peeters sold in Flanders bottles of mineral water labeled in French and German, but not in Dutch. Piageme, an organization of French mineral water producers and their authorized Belgian distributors, sued to enjoin future sales by Peeters (presumably a parallel importer) on the basis of the Belgian decree. The trial court requested the Court of Justice to interpret Article 14(2).]

13   The only obligation [of Article14(2) is] to prohibit the sale of products whose labeling is not easily understood by the purchaser rather than to require the use of a particular language.

14   It is true that, according to a literal interpretation, art. 14 does not preclude a national law which allows, for the information of the consumer, only the use of the language or languages of the region where the products are sold, in so far as such a law would allow purchasers to understand easily the particulars appearing on the products. The language of the linguistic region is the language which seems to be the most "easily understood."

15   Such an interpretation of art. 14 fails, however, to take account of the aims of the directive. It follows from the first three recitals in the preamble that Directive 79/112 seeks in particular to eliminate the differences which exist between national provisions and which hinder the free movement of goods. It is because of that aim that art. 14 is limited to the requirement of a language easily understood by the purchaser and authorized where the relevant particulars do not appear in a language easily understood if "other measures have been taken to ensure that the purchaser is informed."

16   [Accordingly,] imposing a stricter obligation than the use of a language easily understood, that is to say, for example, the exclusive use of the language of a linguistic region and * * * failing to acknowledge the possibility of ensuring that the purchaser is informed by other measures, goes beyond the requirements of the directive. The obligation exclusively to use the language of the linguistic region constitutes a measure having equivalent effect to a quantitative restriction on imports, prohibited by art. [28] of the Treaty.

NOTES AND QUESTIONS

1.   The Court in ¶ 15 emphasizes the first goal of the directive, namely to promote the free movement of foodstuffs. What other measures could ensure that the "purchaser is informed?" Would a sign in Dutch adjacent to the products suffice? Widespread advertising? Note that the product here is mineral water, singularly unlikely to occasion health risks for any consumer. However, Belgium has strongly emphasized the status of the customary language in each of its regions in an effort to reduce social tensions. Is the Court's approach apt to be favorably received in Flanders? Should the cultural implications of the case influence the Court?

2.   Meyhui v. Schott Zwiesel Glaswerke, Case C–51/93, [1994] ECR I–3879, concerned the proper construction of Directive 69/493, which harmonized rules on the standards for the manufacture and labeling of crystal glass products. An Annex specified that the label description for a lower quality

product, crystalline, must be in the "languages of the country in which the goods are marketed." When a German producer refused to affix labels in French and Dutch for crystalline intended for sale in Belgium, a Belgian importer sued the producer.

The Court noted that a local language labeling obligation caused additional costs to a producer, thus representing "a barrier to intra-Community trade" (¶ 13). Nonetheless the Court found the local language provision justified to prevent consumer deception, particularly for the average consumer. The Court therefore concluded:

19   The fact that consumers in a Member State in which the products are marketed are to be informed in the language or languages of that country is therefore an appropriate means of protection. [T]he hypothesis referred to by the national court that another language may be easily comprehensible to the purchaser is of only marginal importance.

PIAGEME v. PEETERS NV (PIAGEME II)
Case C–85/94, [1995] ECR I–2955.

[The trial court obviously had difficulty in applying the Court's answers in *Piageme I* and referred further questions. The Court initially reiterated its position that the Belgian requirement to use "the official language" of a region could not automatically be substituted for the directive's requirement to use "a language easily understood by purchasers," because the latter phrase was "designed to ensure that the consumer is provided with information rather than to impose the use of a specific language." (¶ 15.) The Court then went on to give guidance on how the directive's customer information requirements should be satisfied:]

23   The aim of Article 14 [of the Directive] is to ensure that the consumer is given easy access to the compulsory particulars specified in the Directive.

24   In order to satisfy the need to inform and protect consumers, it is necessary for them always to have access to the compulsory particulars specified in the Directive, not only at the time of purchase, but also at that of consumption. That is particularly true as regards the date of minimum durability and any special storage conditions or conditions of use of the product.

25   It should also be borne in mind that the ultimate consumer is not necessarily the person who purchased the foodstuffs.

26   It follows that consumer protection is not ensured by measures other than labeling such as, for example, information supplied at the sales point or as part of wide-ranging advertising campaigns.

27   All the compulsory particulars specified in the Directive must appear on the labeling in a language easily understood by purchasers or by means of other measures such as designs, symbols or pictograms.

28   It is for the national court to determine in each individual case whether what appears on the labeling is such as to give consumers full information as to the compulsory particulars specified in the Directive.

29   It is also for the national court to determine in each individual case whether the compulsory particulars given in a language other than the language mainly used in the Member State or region concerned can be easily understood by consumers in that State or region.

30   As to that, various factors may be relevant, though not decisive in themselves; for example, the possible similarity of words in different languages, the widespread knowledge amongst the population concerned of more than one language, or the existence of special circumstances such as a wide-ranging advertising campaign or widespread distribution of the product, provided that it can be established that the consumer is given sufficient information.

31   The reply must therefore be that all the compulsory particulars specified in Directive 79/112 must appear on the labeling in a language easily understood by consumers in the State or region concerned or by means of other measures such as designs, symbols or pictograms. The ease with which the information supplied can be understood must be assessed in the light of all the circumstances in each individual case.

NOTES AND QUESTIONS

1. Do you think the Belgian court can now forbid the sale in Flanders of French and German mineral water that is not labeled in Dutch, based on a finding that this is necessary for consumer protection, rather than to protect its "official language"? Or is there enough leeway for alternative modes of informing the consumer in the Court's guidance that a trial court could hardly make such a finding? For a useful appraisal of the Court's approach, see the casenote by M. Verbruggen, 2 Colum. J. Eur. L. 164 (1995–96).

2. In *Geffroy*, Case C–366/98, [2000] ECR I–6579, Geffroy was subjected to substantial fines for offering for sale Coca Cola, Red Raw ginger ale and Merry Down cider labeled in English, in violation of a 1984 French decree that required all foodstuff labels to be in French. The court of appeals referred several questions on the application of Community law. Drawing upon *Piageme II*, the Court unequivocally declared that ECT Article 28 and the directive's article 14 precluded "a national rule . . . requiring the use of a specific language for the labeling of foodstuffs, without allowing for the possibility of using another language easily understood by purchasers or of ensuring that the purchaser is informed by other means." (¶ 28). Do you think Coca–Cola is so well known that it need not be labeled in French? Would you consider English labels for the other beverages to be easily understood in France? In Germany? In The Netherlands?

3. When the Commission proposed several technical amendments to the Foodstuffs Directive, Parliament insisted upon an amendment inserting a new Article 16. The first paragraph replicated the text of Article 14 ¶ 2, except that "consumer" replaced "purchaser"—a sensible change in view of *Piageme II*. Article 16 (2) states:

> 2. Within its own territory, the Member State in which the product is marketed may, in accordance with the rules of the Treaty, stipulate

that those labeling particulars shall be given in one or more languages which it shall determine from among the official languages of the Community.

The amended text gives a Member State the option to require that the label be in one or more of its official language(s). Does this represent sound policy? Would it change the result in *Piageme II* or in *Geffroy?* What is the effect of "in accordance with the rules of the Treaty"? The Foodstuffs Directive was reissued in a codified version, incorporating all amendments to date, in O.J. L 109/29 (May 6, 2000).

4. Article 6 of Directive 76/768 harmonising rules on cosmetic products requires that safety precautions and warnings be placed on the package or container label in legible and visible form. Article 7 requires that the precautions and warnings be supplied in the official language(s) of the State where the cosmetic products are marketed. However, Article 6 permits the warning to be provided in an enclosed leaflet, with abbreviated information on the package, when it is "impossible for practical reasons" to put the full warning on the label.

A German producer of hair dyes intended for use by professional hairdressers inserted warnings (concerning possible allergic reactions and the need to rinse eyes when splashed by the dyes) into leaflets, with reference to the leaflets on the container labels. The warnings were in the nine languages then commonly in use in the Community. When sued by a German consumer protection group, the producer contended that it was "impossible for practical reasons" to put the full warning on the label.

In Hans Schwarzopf GmbH v. Zentrale zur Bekampfung unlauteren Wettbewerbs, Case C–169/99, [2001] ECR I–5901, the Court initially held that the directive did not create any exception for products sold to professional users, as opposed to consumers. Although the Court recognized that producers faced operational problems in trying to supply warnings in different languages on packages, it stated that "the producer's or distributor's wish to facilitate the movement of his product within the Community is not sufficient ... to justify omitting the full obligatory warnings on the package label itself" (¶ 35). Do you agree with the Court's conclusion? Certainly a warning in one or two, or perhaps even three languages may fit on the package label but four or more seems unlikely. Thus, the producer will have to use several different packages for marketing in different States. Has the Court struck the right balance between protecting consumer safety and single market product integration?

4. PREEMPTION OF NATIONAL RULES BY COMPREHENSIVE HARMONIZATION

The most important legal issue raised by harmonization is the extent to which a harmonizing directive prevents a Member State from adopting supplementary regulation, whether stricter or simply different, in the field covered by the directive. (See the general review of preemption in Chapter 4.) The issue is particularly apt to arise when a Member State has prior legislation which the State does not repeal when it adopts the directive, or when a State subsequently passes new and stricter regulations to achieve a higher level of consumer protection or technical quality or health or safety.

In the US, the same issue has frequently arisen in application of the Interstate Commerce Clause and is characterized as one of possible preemption of state rules by a federal law. The test for determining when a federal law preempts state rules has evolved considerably in the last century. While formerly the Supreme Court was more inclined to develop various legal doctrines which justified preemption, its more modern view is that the principal test for preemption is whether "Congress has legislated comprehensively, thus occupying an entire field of regulation and leaving no room for the States to supplement federal law." Louisiana Public Service Com'n v. FCC, 476 U.S. 355, 368, 106 S.Ct. 1890, 1896, 90 L.Ed.2d 369 (1986). That the issue can be difficult is shown by the 5–3 division of the Court in Morales v. Trans World Airlines, Inc., 504 U.S. 374, 112 S.Ct. 2031, 119 L.Ed.2d 157 (1992) (state guidelines to prevent deceptive air fare advertising held to be preempted by the Airline Deregulation Act), and the 5–4 split in Cuomo v. Clearing House Association, ___ U.S. ___, 129 S.Ct. 2710, 174 L.Ed.2d 464 (National Bank Act grant of supervisory powers over national banks to Controller of the Currency does not preempt a state's enforcement of its fair-lending laws against banks).

Given the volume of harmonization directives now in force, it is not surprising that the Court of Justice has frequent occasion to rule on the validity of national regulations that differ somehow from a directive's terms. As in the US, one of the most common issues is whether the harmonization directive can be said to have fully harmonized the rules in a given sector, leaving accordingly no room for supplementary national rules.

PUBBLICO MINISTERO v. RATTI

Case 148/78, [1979] ECR 1629.

[For the facts of this case, see the excerpt at page 260. After deciding that the 1973 directive on dangerous solvents had direct effect, the Court went on to consider whether the directive preempted the 1963 Italian law.]

A. The Interpretation of Directive No 73/173

10 That directive proved necessary because dangerous substances and preparations were subject to rules in the Member States which displayed considerable differences, particularly as regards labeling, packaging and classification according to the degree of risk presented by the said products.

11 Those differences constituted a barrier to trade and to the free movement of goods and directly affected the establishment and functioning of the market in dangerous preparations such as solvents used

regularly in industrial, farming and craft activities, as well as for domestic purposes.

12   In order to eliminate those differences the directive made a number of express provisions concerning the classification, packaging and labeling of the products in question.

* * *

25   In the second question the national court asks, essentially, whether, in incorporating the provisions of the directive on solvents into its internal legal order, the State to which it is addressed may prescribe "obligations and limitations which are more precise and detailed than, or at all events different from, those set out in the directive", requiring in particular information not required by the directive to be affixed to the containers.

26   The combined effect of Articles 3 to 8 of Directive No 73/173 is that only solvents which "comply with the provisions of this directive and the annex thereto" may be placed on the market and that Member States are not entitled to maintain, parallel with the rules laid down by the said directive for imports, different rules for the domestic market.

27   Thus it is a consequence of the system introduced by Directive No 73/173 that a Member State may not introduce into its national legislation conditions which are more restrictive than those laid down in the directive in question, or which are even more detailed or in any event different, as regards the classification, packaging and labeling of solvents and that this prohibition on the imposition of restrictions not provided for applies both to the direct marketing of the products on the home market and to imported products.

* * *

33   Thus the answer to the national court must be that Directive No 73/173 must be interpreted as meaning that it is not permissible for national provisions to prescribe that containers shall bear a statement of the presence of ingredients of the products in question in terms going beyond those laid down by the said directive.

[The Italian court's final question was whether the supplemental labeling requirements could be justified in terms of the protection of health exception to free movement of goods under ECT Article 30. The Court responded:]

36   When Community directives provide for the harmonization of measures necessary to ensure the protection of the health of humans and animals and establish Community procedures to supervise compliance therewith, recourse to Article [30] ceases to be justified and the appropriate controls must henceforth be carried out and the protective measures taken in accordance with the scheme laid down by the harmonizing directive.

37 Directive No 73/173 provides that where a Member State established that a dangerous preparation, although satisfying the requirements of that directive, presents a health or safety risk, it may have recourse, temporarily and subject to the supervision of the Commission, to a protective measure provided for in Article 9 of the directive in accordance with the procedure laid down in that article.

38 It follows that national provisions going beyond those laid down in Directive No 73/173 are compatible with Community law, only if they have been adopted in accordance with the procedures and formalities prescribed in Article 9 of the said directive.

NOTES AND QUESTIONS

1. The hard issue presented in *Ratti* is whether Italy may enforce stricter health or consumer protection standards than those set down in a harmonizing directive. What has happened to Italy's powers under ECT Article 30? *Ratti* demonstrates a very important principle: when a harmonization directive is intended to deal completely with a health or safety issue, States can no longer rely on Article 30 (or its successor, TFEU Article 36). Do you think that this represents a sound policy? What is the trade-off for Italy's inability to protect its consumers at the higher level that it desires?

2. In Commission v. Germany (Pharmaceutical expiration dates), Case C–317/92, [1994] ECR I–2039, the Court held that when Directive 65/65 required all pharmaceutical product containers to indicate the "expiry date in plain language," Germany could not require the use of either June 30 or December 31 as the sole expiration dates. Although the German approach facilitated pharmacy staff checks of shelf life of products, this did not constitute a sufficiently high interest to justify the restriction on imports, which would have to be specially labeled for Germany.

3. In Commission v. Italy (Heater harmonization), Case C—112/97, [1999] ECR I—1821, the Court held that Directive 90/396 on appliances burning gaseous fuels constituted an exhaustive regulation of the field, replacing any national safety or health provisions, so that Italy's ban of a certain type of heater for alleged safety reasons was preempted. The Court noted that Italy had not made use of a directive provision that enabled a State to remove an appliance from the market temporarily for safety reasons, but required immediate notification of such an emergency safeguard to the Commission, which could then review the matter. As we observed in *Ratti*, article 9 of the dangerous solvents directive sets forth a parallel procedure.

4. In Roby Profumi v. Commune di Parma, Case C–257/06, [2008] ECR I–189, the question referred to the Court was whether an Italian law could require an importer of cosmetic products to notify to the authorities the name and registered address of the producer and a detailed list of the product's ingredients, under penalty of a fine. The Court held that Directive 76/768 on cosmetic products comprehensively covered the information required on product labels, but did not cover an importer's obligation to supply relevant information. The Court held that the Italian law was justified on health

protection grounds, because the authorities might need the information for medical treatment (¶¶ 23–24).

COMMISSION v. UNITED KINGDOM

(Dim-dip lighting)
Case 60/86, [1988] ECR 3921.

[Directive 70/156, O.J.–English Spec.Ed. 1970–I, 96, set up a system of type approval for parts of motor vehicles. This was supplemented by Directive 76/756 on lighting and light-signalling devices on motor vehicles, which harmonized national rules as to these vehicle parts. In 1984, the UK adopted a regulation requiring all vehicles manufactured after October 1, 1986 to have "dim-dip" headlights. The UK believed that requiring this device would significantly improve road safety.

In an Article 226 proceeding, the Commission argued that the directive does not permit Member States to require any lighting devices for vehicles except those authorized in its annex. The UK argued that the directive's language was ambiguous and permitted States to require lighting devices in addition to those authorized in the annex. The Court analyzed the 1976 directive's language and concluded that the list of authorized lighting devices in the annex was exhaustive and did not permit later additions by Member States. The Court then continued:]

10   It is clear from the documents before the Court that the reason for which dim-dip devices were not included in the provisions, even as optional devices, is that the technical committee of national experts did not consider them acceptable given the state of technical progress at the time. * * *

11   Such an interpretation of the exhaustive nature of the list of lighting and light-signaling devices set out in Annex I to the directive is consistent with the purpose of Directive 70/156/EEC which is to reduce, and even eliminate, hindrances to trade within the Community resulting from the fact that mandatory technical requirements differ from one Member State to another * * *.

12   It follows that the Member States cannot unilaterally require manufacturers who have complied with the harmonized technical requirements set out in Directive 76/756/EEC to comply with a requirement which is not imposed by that directive, since motor vehicles complying with the technical requirements laid down therein must be able to move freely within the common market.

13   It must therefore be declared that, by prohibiting, in breach of Council Directive 76/756/EEC the use of motor vehicles * * * which are not equipped with a dim-dip device, the United Kingdom has failed to fulfil its obligations under Community law.

1. Note that the judgment not only prevents the UK from requiring "dim-dip" headlights on vehicles imported into the UK, but also from requiring them for UK-manufactured vehicles. This is obviously because a substantial number of UK-produced cars are exported to other States which do not allow "dim-dip" lights.

2. Let us assume that "dim-dip" headlights are a desirable innovation which improves road safety (although Advocate General Mancini said that this UK view was "disputed in numerous quarters"). Obviously a 1976 harmonization directive with an exhaustive list of authorized devices freezes the technological state of the art. How can a Member State improve consumer protection when a superior device is invented? Since amending an existing directive is a slow and laborious process, it would be unfortunate if this were the only solution.

Council harmonization directives are indeed frequently amended. However, the slowness of the Council amendment process has prompted a different approach: some directives delegate to the Commission the power to amend the lists of devices or products contained in the annexes in order to adapt the directive to technical progress. The Commission obviously can act faster than the Council. This is one of the most important examples of the delegation of rule-making authority to the Commission.

5. EXPRESS OR IMPLIED AUTHORIZATION FOR SUPPLEMENTARY STATE RULES

Many harmonization directives, particularly in the fields of health protection, environmental protection, consumer protection, and employee rights, contain express provisions authorizing Member States to have stricter rules in order to achieve the directive's goal. Only occasionally do these require any Court interpretation. (The US Congress sometimes adopts similar provisions or even expressly authorizes supplemental state regulation, e.g., in antitrust and securities law.) In addition, some harmonization directives expressly declare that they represent only initial, or first stage, harmonization, which implicitly authorizes supplemental (but not contradictory) State rules. Finally, the language of particular clauses in some directives that would generally be considered to represent fairly exhaustive coverage of a field may implicitly permit State rules to go further in regulating to achieve the goal of the directive. The following cases illustrate each of these possibilities.

BUET v. MINISTÈRE PUBLIC
Case 382/87, [1989] ECR 1235.

[Directive 85/577 on contracts negotiated away from business premises (see Document 13 in the Selected Documents) contains various consumer protection provisions, notably in article 5 the consumer's right to cancel the contract within seven days. A 1972 French law forbids canvassing at home for the signature of contracts for a course of instruction. When the UK company, Encyclopedia Britannica, marketed a course of English language tapes at prospective buyers' homes, its French manager was fined and sentenced to a jail term. On appeal, the Paris Court of Appeal asked the Court of Justice questions as to the compatibility of the French law with the directive and ECT Article 28. The Court dealt summarily with the harmonization preemption issue.]

16 [W]hile the Council Directive requires Member States to ensure that consumers have the right to cancel a contract of sale concluded at their home, Article 8 allows the State to adopt or maintain more favourable provisions to protect consumers. In the last recital in the preamble to the directive the Council expressly recognized that Member States might introduce or maintain a total or partial prohibition on the conclusion of contracts away from business premises.

[The Court devoted most of the judgment to analyzing whether the total ban on the conclusion of contracts for instruction courses at a consumer's home was compatible with ECT Article 28.]

(A) The Existence of an Obstacle to the Free Movement of Goods

7 [T]o compel a trader either to adopt advertising or sales promotion schemes which differ from one Member State to another may constitute an obstacle to imports even if the legislation in question applies to domestic and imported products without distinction.

8 That finding applies *a fortiori* when the rules in question deprive the trader concerned of the possibility of using not a means of advertising but a method of marketing whereby he realizes almost all his sales.

9 Application of a prohibition on canvassing in order to sell foreign-language teaching material from another Member State must therefore be regarded as constituting an obstacle to imports.

(B) The Possibility of Justifying the Obstacle in Question by the Need to Protect Consumers

10 The Court has consistently held [citing *Cassis de Dijon*] that in the absence of common rules, obstacles to movement within the Community resulting from disparities between the national rules must be accepted, provided the rules are applied without distinction to domestic and imported products, as being necessary in order to satisfy mandatory requirements such as the protection of consumers and fair trading.

11 It is common ground that the French legislature adopted the prohibition of canvassing in question out of concern to protect consumers against the risk of ill-considered purchases. However, * * * such rules must be proportionate to the goals pursued, and if a Member State has at its disposal less restrictive means of obtaining the same goals, it is under an obligation to make use of them.

12 * * * To guard against [the risk of ill-considered purchases] it is normally sufficient to ensure that purchasers have the right to cancel a contract concluded in their home.

13 [However,] there is greater risk of an ill-considered purchase when the canvassing is for enrollment for a course of instruction or the sale of educational material. The potential purchaser often belongs to a category of people who, for one reason or another, are behind with their education and are seeking to catch up. That makes them particularly vulnerable when faced with salesmen of educational material who attempt to persuade them that if they use that material they will have better employment prospects. Moreover, as is apparent from the documents, it is as a result of numerous complaints caused by such abuses, such as the sale of out-of-date courses, that the legislature enacted the ban on canvassing at issue.

* * *

15 In those circumstances it is permissible for the national legislature of the Member State to consider that giving consumers a right of cancellation is not sufficient protection and that it is necessary to ban canvassing at private dwellings.

NOTES AND QUESTIONS

1. This 1985 "door-to-door" sales directive is a harmonization measure in the Community's consumer protection program. As Advocate General Tesauro observed, in this home sales technique "the consumer is exposed to a serious risk of fraud * * * especially if he is one of those who * * * may be more open to influence, such as the elderly, housewives or immigrant workers." [1989] ECR at 1240. Note that the French law is stricter than the directive, because it totally prohibits a type of home sales, namely, courses of instruction. However, the 1985 directive's preamble permits Member States to adopt a total or partial prohibition of home sales (see ¶ 16). The directive is thus an example of the type that allows States to go beyond the level of harmonization for the purpose of greater consumer protection.

2. Now for some review of Chapter 13 D. If *Buet* had been decided after the *Keck* judgment, would the Court still reach the conclusion it did in ¶¶ 7–9? After the *Gourmet* judgment, would the market access doctrine have to be considered in evaluating the French ban? *Buet* continues to be cited approvingly for the judgment's consumer interest analysis in ¶¶ 10–15.

3. In Schwarz v. Salzburg, Case C–366/04, [2005] ECR I–10139, Schwarz was convicted for the sale of chewing gum imported from Germany in a vending machine without a package. An Austrian law required confectionary or similar products to have wrapping when sold in vending machines. An EC directive on foodstuff hygiene set general hygiene conditions for vending machines, but did not make this specific requirement. The Court held that the Austrian law was justified by the public health concern for preventing the risk of damage to the product from moisture or insects, particularly ants.

THE QUEEN v. SECRETARY OF STATE FOR HEALTH EX PARTE GALLAHER

Case C–11/92, [1993] ECR I–3545.

[Directive 89/622 on the labeling of tobacco products provides that cigarette packages must display the warning, "Tobacco seriously damages health," on one large surface and a second specific health warning on the other large surface. One package side must display, in legible print in the language(s) of the country of sale, a precise indication of tar and nicotine yields. The warnings and the yield indication must cover "at least 4%" of the surface. The UK implementing regulation set the warnings and yield indication size at 6%, instead of 4%, for domestic cigarettes. Imported cigarettes were permitted if they satisfied the 4% requirement. When several UK tobacco producers challenged the UK regulation as implicitly forbidden by the Directive, the trial court referred the issue.]

10   [Directive 89/622] is designed to eliminate barriers to trade which might arise as a result of differences in national provisions on the labeling of tobacco products and thereby impede the establishment and operation of the internal market. With that end in view, the directive contains common rules concerning the health warnings to appear on the unit packet of tobacco products and the indications of the tar and nicotine yields to appear on cigarette packets.

11   These common rules are not always identical in nature.

12   Some of them give Member States no discretion to impose requirements stricter than those provided for in the directive, or even to impose more detailed or at any rate different requirements, with regard to the labeling of tobacco products.

13   Under Article 8(2), Member States still have the right to lay down * * * requirements concerning the import, sale and consumption of tobacco products which they deem necessary in order to protect public health, but only in so far as such requirements do not imply any changes to labeling as laid down in the directive.

14   Other provisions of the directive allow the Member States a degree of discretion to adapt the labeling of tobacco products to the requirements of public health protection. One such provision is Article 4(2), which allows the Member States to select the specific warnings which must appear on cigarette packets by choosing them from those listed in the annex to the directive. * * *

15   [The directive is in furtherance of] the Resolution of the Council * * * of 7 July 1986 on a programme of action of the European Communities against cancer to which the fifth recital in the preamble to the directive refers. Under that programme, the measures to be adopted by the Community with a view to limiting and reducing the consumption of tobacco were to be based on the practical experience gained in

the various Member States and were to contribute to increasing the effectiveness of national programmes and actions.

16 Member States which have made use of the powers conferred by the provisions containing minimum requirements cannot, according to Article 8 of the directive, prohibit or restrict the sale within their territory of products imported from other Member States which comply with the directive.

17 In order to reply to the question referred by the national court, it is therefore necessary to determine whether Articles 3(3) and 4(4) of the directive still allow the Member States a degree of latitude to require, with regard to domestic production, that the indications and warnings in question cover in each case more than 4% of the relevant surface area.

18 The applicants * * * consider that the rules in the directive requiring the indications and warnings to cover at least 4% of the relevant surface area must be incorporated as such by the Member States into their national law because the provisions in question confer on them no discretion. They argue that it is for manufacturers of tobacco products to decide whether the indications and warnings should cover a larger surface area. * * *

19 Those arguments cannot be accepted.

20 Articles 3(3) and 4(4) of the directive contain provisions directed to the Member States, to whom the directive is addressed, and not to the manufacturers of tobacco products, who have no interest in using a greater surface area for the indications and warnings in question. The expression 'at least' contained in both articles must be interpreted as meaning that, if they consider it necessary, Member States are at liberty to decide that the indications and warnings are to cover a greater surface area in view of the level of public awareness of the health risks associated with tobacco consumption.

21 The case-law on labeling cited by the applicants * * * concerns directives whose scope differs from that of Directive 89/622. So far as the decision in *Ratti* is concerned, the Court there ruled not on the interpretation of Article 6(1) of Directive 73/173, which also contains the expression 'at least', but on other provisions of that directive and on the nature of its provisions in general.

22 Admittedly, as the applicants * * * have pointed out, this interpretation of the provisions may imply less favourable treatment for national products in comparison with imported products and leaves in existence some inequalities in conditions of competition. However, those consequences are attributable to the degree of harmonization sought by the provisions in question, which lay down minimum requirements.

Notes and Questions

1. Unlike the directive examined in *Buet*, the tobacco labelling directive did not expressly state that it permitted stricter Member State regulation. Do you agree with the Court that the rather ambiguous words, "at least," implicitly permit States to go further? In a perceptive case note, 19 Eur. L. Rev. 55 (1994), Professor Weatherill views the Court's approach as a sharp shift from the classic preemption theory in *Ratti*. He wonders whether the judgment reflects a greater respect for the principle of subsidiarity, allowing Member States to experiment with innovative regulations, or whether it constitutes a "political" judgment, taken to avoid further UK criticism of Court doctrines. In any event, do you believe the Court's result represents good policy?

Note ¶¶ 16 and 22. Might the UK regulation indirectly promote cigarette imports? Why does the Court accept this potential competitive inequality? The judgment is a prime example of 'reverse discrimination', which occurs when a State sets stricter standards for domestic products than are possible for imports complying with a harmonization directive. Note that Directive 2001/37, upheld in the *BAT* judgment at page 530 *supra*, replaces Directive 89/662 with stricter rules. Moreover, the 2001 directive's recital 24 indicates that States may adopt "more stringent rules" to protect public health.

2. Suppose that the UK forbid outdoor advertising (e.g., billboards or signs) of cigarettes within a 1000 foot radius of a school or playground. Would such a rule be implicitly preempted by the tobacco labeling directive? In Lorillard Tobacco Co. v. Reilly, 533 U.S. 525, 121 S.Ct. 2404, 150 L.Ed.2d 532 (2001), Massachusetts had adopted such an outdoor advertising ban. Reversing the First Circuit, the Supreme Court held that the ban (and other restrictions on cigarette advertising) was preempted by the Federal Cigarette Labeling and Advertising Act, which mandates health warnings on cigarette packages and in advertising for cigarettes. The Supreme Court relied heavily on the Act's provision forbidding any state "prohibition based on smoking and health ... with respect to the advertising or promotion of cigarettes."

3. Valuable analyses of the Court doctrines on preemption in contrast with US views are provided by E. Cross, Preemption of Member State Law in the EEC, 29 Common Mkt. L. Rev. 447 (1992), and A. Goucha Soares, Preemption, Conflicts of Power and Subsidiarity, 23 Eur. L. Rev. 132 (1998).

D. THE "NEW APPROACH" TO TECHNICAL HARMONIZATION

In Chapter 13 C, we reviewed the Commission's 1980 Communication on Cassis de Dijon. In the Communication, the Commission declared that it intended to apply the Court's principle of mutual recognition of State standards as a means of reducing the future volume of harmonization directives. In January 1985, the new Commission under President Jacques Delors issued a major policy statement on this subject (Com (85) 19).

TECHNICAL HARMONIZATION AND STANDARDS: A NEW APPROACH

Bull. EC 1–1985.

1.3.2. It has to be acknowledged that:

● given the multiplicity of technical regulations and standards in all the Member States, the results in certain industrial fields are still almost negligible;

● technology is now developing too fast for there to be any hope that the harmonization procedures and the decision-making process in the Council will ever manage to bring us within reach of the "European continuum" * * *.

The Commission's New Approach

1.3.3. The new formula proposed by the Commission is based on [the following] fundamental principles;

(i) harmonization of laws will be restricted to the adoption of the essential safety requirements (or other requirements in the public interest) to which all products must conform if they are to be allowed to circulate freely within the Community;

(ii) the relevant industrial standardization bodies will be responsible for drawing up, with due regard to technological developments, the technical specifications that industry needs in order to produce and market products conforming to the essential requirements laid down by directive;

(iii) these technical specifications will not be mandatory: they will remain voluntary standards; * * *

1.3.4. * * * [When] a standard is approved by the Commission and published in the Official Journal, all Member States must accept goods which conform to it. Where a Member State disputes the conformity of a standard to the safety objectives set out in the Directive, it falls to that Member State to substantiate its contention. This reversal of the burden of proof means abandoning the rule of unanimity, which has been such a hindrance to the adoption of harmonization directives with extremely voluminous and detailed technical annexes.

1. THE NEW APPROACH IN PRACTICE

The Council approved the "new approach" by its Resolution of May 7, 1985, O.J. C 136/1 (June 4, 1985). The principal Community standardization bodies now being used in the new approach are the European Committee for Standardization (CEN) and the European Committee for Electrotechnical Standardization (CENELEC). Other specialized bodies exist for particular industries, e.g., the European Telecommunications Standards Institute (ETSI).

Thus, under the "new approach," product standards (national, European or international) are drawn up by bodies comprising representatives of industry, government, consumers and trade unions. In contrast to Council procedure, they are approved by a majority, which considerably accelerates and facilitates their preparation. Finally, they are essentially voluntary, so that a manufacturer who wishes to market a product without referring to an approved standard will remain free to do so; but he will bear the burden of proving that his product meets the safety requirements set out in any directive covering the relevant sector.

Although the "new approach" reduces the need for harmonization directives, it does not eliminate them. A smaller number of directives continue to be adopted, essentially as "frameworks" setting critical minimum health, safety and technical requirements, with details to be supplied by the Community standards bodies. Leading examples are Directive 88/378 of May 3, 1988 on the safety of toys, O.J. L 187/1 (July 16, 1988), and Directive 89/392 of June 14, 1989 on safety of machinery, O.J. L 183/9 (June 29, 1989), as amended, O.J. L 207/1 (June 22, 1998). The Commission has indicated general satisfaction with the new approach to technical harmonization in its annual General Reports and in the progress reports on the implementation of the White Paper.

From the point of view of US industry groups, the Community's progress in applying the "new approach" to facilitate technical harmonization of product standards throughout the Community market represented both an opportunity and a threat. It was an opportunity, because by adhering to the new standards, US producers could market on a Community-wide basis. On the other hand, the new approach was perceived as a threat to US interests to the extent that: 1) US producers do not participate in the European process of setting standards; 2) the new Community standards are different from those prevailing in the US. In May 1989, the Commission and the Department of Commerce agreed that US-manufactured products would be afforded equal access to Community certification procedures, and that ongoing negotiations should strive to achieve mutual recognition of standards between the US and the EEC. In June 1991, a further agreement permitted specified US certification laboratories to test the conformity of US products to Community standards. The arrangements do not remove all difficulties, however, because the US does not have many nationally recognized standards or standard setting bodies and US certification laboratories do not necessarily follow the same procedures as European ones.

One aspect of the TransAtlantic Economic Partnership, agreed between the US and the Community in London in May 1998, is further cooperation in science and technology. Pursuant to this, in November 1998, the Council authorized the Commission to negotiate with the US on the elimination of technical barriers to trade in industrial products. An earlier June 1997 mutual recognition agreement provided for the general mutual acceptance of standards and testing for telecommunication equipment, medical devices and most pharmaceutical products.

2.   PRIOR NOTIFICATION OF NEW STATE RULES

Despite the substantial number of technical rules and standards directives adopted, the volume of Member State technical barriers to trade has inexorably increased, due principally to the rapid rate of technological advances and to the demand for consumer and environmental protection legislation. The initial step taken to alleviate this situation was the adoption of Directive 83/89 on the provision of information on technical standards and regulations, O.J. L 109/8 (Apr. 26, 1983), amended and codified by Directive 98/34, O.J. L 204/37 (July 21, 1998). The purpose of this directive, sometimes called the "transparency" or "slow-down" directive, was to ensure a certain level of coordination between Member States and the Commission before a State adopted a new technical rule or standard.

The directive obligates a State to notify the Commission in advance of the adoption of any legally binding regulation which sets a "technical specification," defined as any product requirement as to quality, performance, safety, testing, packaging or labelling. The Commission must immediately notify all other States. The Commission or any other State may demand a six-month delay in the adoption of the proposed State regulation in order to consider possible amendments. The Commission may demand a year's delay if it decides to propose a harmonization directive in the sector involved.

The Commission believes that the notification system of this "transparency" directive is operating satisfactorily. After receiving comments from the Commission or other States, the notifying State frequently makes beneficial amendments when adopting the regulations. Nonetheless, obviously, the directive merely reduces the number of State technical barriers; it does not ensure Community-wide rules or standards. The Court has occasionally had to provide guidance on how to interpret or apply the directive, usually on what constitutes a "technical specification" that requires notification, but the cases are too fact-specific to merit mention here.

3.   THE CE MARK

Products certified by Community bodies as made in compliance with harmonization directives may be identified by an EC mark, "CE," which indicates a presumption in favor of their right to be marketed throughout the Community. A Member State may challenge the safety of an imported product bearing the mark, but must then justify its position to the Commission and a coordinating committee representing all the States.

The following judgment demonstrates that the CE mark may have important legal consequences.

CRIMINAL PROCEEDINGS AGAINST YONEMOTO

Case C–40/04, [2005] ECR I–7755.

[Directive 98/37 sets the essential health and safety requirements for machinery. Article 5 provides that machinery made in compliance with the directive may bear a CE mark and, accompanied by a certificate of conformity, circulate freely in the Community. An Annex requires that any instructions for safe use of the machinery must be translated into the language(s) of the State where it is used. A Finnish trial court found an importer to be criminally liable for physical injuries caused to a workman by an imported hydraulic press. On appeal, the appellate court referred questions concerning the effect of the CE mark.]

31   Directive 98/37 aims to ensure free movement of machinery in the internal market and to satisfy the imperative and essential health and safety requirements relating to that machinery by replacing national certification systems and conformity certification with a harmonised system. For that purpose, in particular in Article 3 and in Annex I, that directive lists the essential health and safety requirements that machinery and safety components manufactured in the Member States must satisfy. Under Article 4 of that directive, Member States may not restrict the placing on the market of machinery which complies with those essential requirements.

32   According to Article 5 of Directive 98/37, machinery bearing the CE marking and accompanied by the EC declaration of conformity is deemed to comply with that directive.

33   Article 8 (1) of that directive obliges the manufacturer or his authorised representative established in the Community to affix to the machine the CE marking and to draw up the EC declaration of conformity.

34   It is apparent from the 20th recital of Directive 98/37 that, as a general rule, manufacturers retain sole responsibility for certifying the conformity of their machinery to the essential health and safety requirements laid down by that directive.

* * *

41   [The trial court found] that the machine was dangerous in several respects, even though it bore a CE marking and was accompanied by an EC declaration of conformity. The main question which arises is that of whether, under Directive 98/37, the importer of that machine is liable for the consequences of that situation.

* * *

43   Article 7(3) of that directive provides that where machinery which does not comply bears the CE marking, the competent Member State is to take appropriate action 'against whom so ever has affixed the marking,' namely the manufacturer.

44   It would be inconsistent with the scheme of that directive and in particular Article 7 (3) thereof to increase the number of persons who could be held responsible for the conformity of machinery.

45   The essential objective of Directive 98/37 is to simplify the rules relating to the conformity of machinery so as to ensure as far as possible its free movement within the internal market. That objective would be impeded if operators downstream from the manufacturer, in particular importers of machinery from one Member State to another Member State, could also be held responsible for the conformity of that machinery.

46   Directive 98/37 thus precludes the application of national provisions requiring the importer in a Member State of a machine manufactured in another Member State, bearing the CE marking and accompanied by an EC declaration of conformity to ensure that that machinery meets the essential health and safety requirements laid down by that directive.

[Citing the directive's annex, the Court held that the importer could be required to translate the instructions for use into the language of the importing State. The Court added:]

52   Member States may require importers to cooperate concerning supervision of the market such as requiring them to pass on information. In the event of an accident such as giving rise to the main proceedings, a Member State may require the importer to provide all relevant information to ensure that similar accidents do not re-occur, in particular by cooperating with the competent authorities of that Member State for the purpose of adopting measures which those authorities might be prompted to take pursuant to Article 7 of Directive 98/37, such as the withdrawal of the machinery concerned from the market.

53   Such obligations to cooperate must not however amount to an obligation on the importer to verify himself that the machine complies with the essential requirements laid down by Directive 98/37, since such an obligation would be contrary to its scheme.

4.   SPECIALIZED TECHNICAL AGENCIES

No sector of Community technical regulations is more sensitive than pharmaceuticals, due to the manifest health and safety concerns and the traditional autonomy of State administrative agencies in the approval process. Community rules commenced with Directive 65/65, O.J. 1965–1966, Eng. Spec. Ed., p. 20, which required States to have agencies for the review of all pharmaceutical products, forbid marketing without authorization, and set initial standards for authorization. Although frequently amended, notably in 1975 and 1987, Directive 65/65 continues to supply the basic structure. State agency autonomy in deciding whether a drug is safe for marketing within that State remains the rule, although Directive 87/21, O.J. L 15/36 (Jan. 17, 1987), requires an "abridged" review procedure for a drug that has already been authorized in another State, permitting in particular reliance upon pharmacological, toxicological and clinical tests carried out in the State of first approval.

The merit of a single Community-wide authorization process, saving costs and time in a "one-step" approach, long advocated by the pharmaceutical industry, finally reached fruition in 1995. Council Regulation 2309/93, O.J. L 214/1 (Aug. 24, 1993) created the European Agency for the Evaluation of Medicinal Products and gave it the power to review and authorize proposed medications for marketing throughout the Community. The Agency commenced operation in London in 1995 and is considered to be functioning satisfactorily. Cooperative arrangements for the exchange of information and test results exist between the Agency and the US Food and Drug Administration. Regulation 726/2004, O.J. L 1361/1 (Apr. 30, 2004), amended the initial text, changing the agency name to European Medicines Agency and updating its administrative procedures.

The European Food Safety Authority (EFSA), operational since 2002, is another important agency whose creation was considered vital since the 'Mad Cow' disease was spread by contaminated beef exported from the UK in the 1990s. Regulation 178/2002, O.J. L 31/1 (Feb. 1, 2002), established general principles for food law and food safety, including acceptance of the precautionary principle in article 7. The EFSA, sited in Parma, Italy, principally serves as a center for scientific advice and technical information for Community institutions and States.

Another important technical body is the new European Chemicals Agency, sited in Helsinki and operational since June 2008. The agency will administer Regulation 1907/2006 on the registration, authorization and restriction of chemicals, O.J. L 396/1 (Dec. 30, 2006), which require the registration of over 30,000 chemical substances currently in use, and any future similar substances. Producers must assess any health and safety risks and provide appropriate information on safe use. Producers will also incur the burden of proof concerning the safe use of the chemical products. Due to strong opposition from producers who claimed the REACH Regulation would cause heavy compliance costs, the Regulation required several years for adoption.

Further Reading

C. Barnard & J. Scott, eds., The Law of the Single European Market (Hart 2002)

M. Egan, Constructing a European Market (Oxford U.P. 2001)

N. Nic Shuibhne, ed., Regulating the Internal Market (Edward Elgar 2006)

CHAPTER 15

FREE MOVEMENT OF WORKERS

■ ■ ■

The second of the fundamental "four freedoms" the Treaty seeks to achieve is the free movement of persons. This chapter concentrates on the free movement of workers. Initially, the chapter sets out the basic rights of workers in ECT Article 39 (now TFEU Article 45), and the early important Regulation 1612/68. Section B presents some prominent and decidedly liberal judgments of the Court concerning the rights of the migrant worker, his or her spouse and family. Section C describes the public policy and public service limits set by legislation and case law upon these rights. The final section deals with border-line cases concerning the status of migrant workers, their spouses and families. Note at once that the Treaty of Lisbon renumbers ECT Article 39 as TFEU Article 45 without any change except to replace "Community" by "Union."

In the post-World War II period, serious unemployment in most European countries led to the adoption of highly restrictive national employment policies. Foreign workers, commonly called migrant workers, were subject to restrictions in immigration and hiring, as well as discriminatory treatment once employed, in the state of employment (often called the host State). EECT Articles 48 and 49, the initial 1957 European Economic Community Treaty articles renumbered by the Treaty of Amsterdam in 1999 as ECT Articles 39 and 40, required the dismantling of this protectionist structure by the end of the transitional period, December 31, 1969.

Achieving the free movement of workers is one of the Union's most striking successes. The economic importance of unfettered mobility of labor should not be underestimated, since it enables employers to engage the most qualified personnel, regardless of nationality. Correlatively, it enables employees to seek better job opportunities or social advantages in other countries. States that have an insufficient work force for intensive physical labor or lower pay-scale employment (e.g., in agriculture, construction, heavy industry, hotels, restaurants or household help) can draw thousands of migrant workers from States with a surplus of labor. Moreover, the right of free movement covers not only blue collar workers, but also senior management and technically-skilled labor. The ability of multinational enterprises centered in the Union to develop a European-wide commercial outlook is substantially due to the mobility of senior and middle management, as well as technical staff, to or from headquarters, or from one part of the Union to another.

The free movement of workers also has major political, social and cultural dimensions. When people are employed and reside for long periods of time in other countries, they usually develop a broader social and intellectual outlook. As they attain levels of authority and influence in society, they tend to promote a European consciousness, with impact on both political affairs and the world of ideas.

Finally, if the children of migrant workers reside in the host State, they are usually educated in the host State school system, and when they become adults, often choose to work and reside in the host State. Moreover, labor mobility increases the number of marriages between people of different nationalities. However, in the EU, unlike the US, mobility of workers continues to be relatively low. A 2007 Commission report on progress under the Lisbon Strategy estimated that only 2% of working age persons worked in another State—presumably because of linguistic, social and cultural differences between States.

The Court of Justice has also recognized a social or "human" dimension in the concept of free movement of workers. The Court has treated this freedom as one of the fundamental rights of human beings and has expansively developed the social consequences of the right.

A. THE TREATY AND BASIC LEGISLATION

1. ECT ARTICLE 39 (NOW TFEU ARTICLE 45)

The EEC Treaty dealt with this topic in EECT Article 48, renumbered in 1999 as ECT Article 39, which reads as follows:

1. Freedom of movement for workers shall be secured within the Community [now Union].

2. Such freedom of movement shall entail the abolition of any discrimination based on nationality between workers of the Member States as regards employment, remuneration and other conditions of work and employment.

3. It shall entail the right, subject to limitations justified on grounds of public policy, public security or public health:

    (a) to accept offers of employment actually made;

    (b) to move freely within the territory of Member States for this purpose;

    (c) to stay in a Member State for the purpose of employment in accordance with the provisions governing the employment of nationals of that State laid down by law, regulation or administrative action;

(d) to remain in the territory of a Member State after having been employed in that State, subject to conditions which shall be embodied in implementing regulations to be drawn up by the Commission.

4. The provisions of this Article shall not apply to employment in the public service.

Although this text initially appears rather detailed, a closer look reveals that the term "worker" is not defined, nor is the full scope of free movement of workers indicated in subsections (2) and (3). As we shall see, the Court of Justice has defined the term "worker", and has expanded the scope of the rights of free movement and non-discrimination in employment. The exceptions to the right of free movement listed in (3) and (4) are important, but have been interpreted narrowly by the Court of Justice. Because TFEU Article 45 replicates ECT Article 39, we can safely assume that the Court caselaw has not been affected by the adoption of the Treaty of Lisbon.

When Greece, Spain and Portugal joined the Community, they had substantial unemployment and large numbers of their nationals were employed as migrant labor in the other Member States. Each accession treaty accordingly set a long transitional period (six or seven years) before full free movement was achieved. The free movement of workers was never an issue in the accession negotiations for Austria, Finland and Sweden. In contrast, it was one of the most sensitive topics in the accession negotiations with the Central European states, many of which had significant levels of unemployment.

The Treaty of Athens which enabled the accession of Cyprus, Malta and eight Central European States authorized the earlier Member States to retain any existing restrictions on employment and residence for nationals from the acceding States for a five year period (with a possible final two year extension). Only Ireland, Sweden and the UK initially allowed free entry of workers from the new States, receiving and satisfactorily employing hundreds of thousands. Gradually other States removed their restrictions, until by 2009 essentially only Austria and Germany retained theirs. When Bulgaria and Romania joined in 2007, the Treaty of Luxembourg permitted the other States to retain existing limitations on their workers for similar long transition periods, but Italy and Spain immediately allowed the entry of thousands of Romanian and Bulgarian migrant farm workers.

In 1994, the European Economic Area Agreement created a right of free movement of workers between the Community and Iceland, Norway and Liechtenstein. Although Swiss voters in a 1992 referendum rejected the EEA Agreement in part because of their concern about an influx of workers from adjacent Member States, Switzerland accepted an obligation to ensure free movement of persons in a series of treaties with the Community in June 1999. Also, some association treaties with adjacent States (e.g., Turkey and Morocco) grant their migrant workers some limited rights within the Community. But no such treaty exists with the US, and US citizens must therefore obtain permission to work on a country-by-country basis within the EU. While, generally speaking, Americans in senior management positions or with technical skills can obtain national work permits in Member States, other personnel (e.g., teachers, actors or secretaries) sometimes cannot. Directive 2003/109, recently effective in January 2006, grants third state national workers virtually permanent residence rights in a Member State once they have legally resided there for five years. See Chapter 16G.

The right of free movement of persons, commonly called the right to travel, is recognized by US law, although there is no express coverage of the topic in the Constitution. The Articles of Confederation contained a clause stating that "the people of each State shall have free ingress and egress to and from any other State, and shall enjoy therein all the privileges of trade and commerce * * * as the inhabitants thereof," but the Constitution is silent on the matter. The Supreme Court has concluded that the framers of the Constitution took the right for granted. The Fourteenth Amendment indirectly promotes the right by making any native born or naturalized citizens of the US likewise citizens "of the State wherein they reside." Citizens residing in one US state are free to travel to another state, take up employment and reside there. See *Hicklin* v. *Orbeck*, infra.

2. REGULATION 1612/68

ECT Article 40 supplemented Article 39 with a grant of legislative power (now contained in TFEU Article 46). The initial EECT Article 49, renumbered as ECT Article 40, authorized the Council to enact either regulations or directives to achieve the free movement of workers by a simple majority vote—one of the few instances of such voting in the Treaty. After the Single European Act, EECT Article 49 required a qualified majority vote in the Council, acting in cooperation with the Parliament. The Maastricht Treaty changed the mode of legislation to the co-decision procedure (renamed the ordinary legislative procedure by the Treaty of Lisbon).

Although earlier legislation adopted in 1961 and 1964 marked some progress toward free movement, decisive action came with Regulation 1612/68 of Oct. 15, 1968 on freedom of movement for workers, which is Document 14 in the Selected Documents.

Title I covers the basic right of free movement. Article 1 defines it as the "right to take up an activity as an employed person" in any Community State. A recital indicates that the Regulation covers seasonal workers, common in the agricultural and tourism sectors, and frontier workers, who live in one State and regularly cross a border to work in another. Article 2 describes the concomitant right to an employment contract under national law, without discrimination on grounds of nationality. Later articles seek to eliminate national legislation or administrative procedures which set quotas or other limits on foreigners, grant priority for nationals or discriminate against other Community nationals.

Although ECT Article 39 does not expressly limit the concept of "workers" to citizens of a Union State, article 1 of Regulation 1612/68 does so by limiting its grant of rights to nationals of Member States. Non–EU nationals accordingly have no right of free movement as workers under the Regulation.

Title II of Regulation 1612/68 amplifies the principle of non-discrimination in Article 39(2). Article 7 forbids discrimination in dismissal or re-hiring, as well as discrimination in conditions of employment. Article 7(2) adds the right to "enjoy the same social and tax advantages as national workers," a clause which the Court of Justice has interpreted broadly. Article 8 deals with trade unions and workers' representatives. Article 8 originally granted only the right to vote for employee representatives and union delegates, but it was amended in 1976 to enable migrant workers also to serve in such posts. Article 9 adds a right of equal treatment as to housing, including the right to own housing.

Finally, Title III accords rights to family members of the migrant worker. Although rights of family members are not mentioned in Article 39, a worker's ability to have his or her family live with the worker is manifestly a crucial element in promoting the mobility of labor. Title III creates a decidedly liberal framework of accessory rights for the worker's immediate family, defined as the spouse, children under 21 or otherwise dependent, and dependent parents or grandparents of the worker or spouse.

The rights granted to family members include notably the right to live with the worker (art. 10); the right of the spouse or children under 21, or otherwise dependent, to be employed in the same State, even if they are not nationals of any Member State (art. 11); and the right of children to admission on a nondiscriminatory basis to "general educational, appren-ticeship and vocational training courses" (art. 12). Article 12 is supple-mented by Directive 77/486 on the education of migrant workers' children, O.J. L 199/32 (Aug. 6, 1977), which requires special efforts to integrate such children into the host State's educational system, for example, through the teaching of the national language (art. 2), and of their "mother tongue and culture of the country of origin" (art. 3).

Over the years, Regulation 1612/68 strongly promoted the mobility of Community workers, in part because of its comprehensive coverage, but also due to its expansive interpretation by the Court of Justice. The Commission's 1985 White Paper on Completing the Internal Market cited free movement of workers as a sector already virtually complete.

Commission Regulation 1251/70 supplemented Article 39(3) by grant-ing workers the right to remain in the territory of a Member State after having been employed in that State. O.J. English Spec. Ed. 1970–II, 402. This enabled a migrant worker to retire in a host State, provided he or she had resided there continuously for more than three years and was continuously employed for the last year before reaching the host State's pensionable age (art. 2). The regulation also generally permitted the worker's family or surviving spouse to reside permanently in the host State after the worker's death (art. 3).

Recently the comprehensive Directive 2004/38, O.J. L 229/35 (Apr. 29, 2004), on the residence rights of EU citizens, has enhanced the scope of the rights previously covered by Regulation 1612/68 and Commission Regulation 1251/70. Effective Apr. 30, 2006, Directive 2004/38 not only liberalizes the residence and employment rights of workers and their families, but also those of all other EU citizens. The new directive is described in Chapter 16. However, all of the cases covered in the present chapter arose under the initial EECT Article 49, or its renumbered text, ECT Article 39, or Regulation 1612/68. For convenience, we will refer to the Treaty article as ECT Article 39.

B. RIGHTS OF THE MIGRANT WORKER, SPOUSE AND FAMILY

1. PROTECTION OF THE WORKER AGAINST DISCRIMINATORY TREATMENT

In Commission v. France (Merchant seamen), discussed at page 402, the Court of Justice held that ECT Article 39 had vertical direct effect. However, this has not proved very significant, because Regulation 1612/68 binds both States and private employers, and its terms are generally more detailed and far-reaching than ECT Article 39 itself. Most of the case law involves interpretation of Regulation 1612/68. The issue that arises most frequently is whether States may deny to migrant workers benefits which are extended to host State nationals. Occasionally, however, a State will bar non-nationals from a particular type of employment, or require certain employees to be residents.

Although section D is devoted to border-line cases on the definition of a worker, it is useful at the outset to have some Court guidelines on when a person is to be considered a worker for free movement purposes.

LAWRIE–BLUM v. LAND BADEN–WÜRTTEMBERG
Case 66/85, [1986] ECR 2121.

[Lawrie–Blum, a British national, obtained a teaching degree from a German university and applied to the Stuttgart teacher-training program. Teacher-training in Germany takes two years, consisting of further education and practice teaching in a high school for eleven hours a week, with a low salary in compensation for the teaching. Successful completion of this program is a prerequisite to becoming a German high school teacher. Lawrie–Blum was denied admission to the program because German law made high school teachers public officials and required German nationality. The Supreme German Administrative Court inquired in a preliminary reference whether a teacher-trainee should be considered a worker under ECT Article 39].

16   Since freedom of movement for workers constitutes one of the fundamental principles of the Community, the term "worker" in Article [39] may not be interpreted differently according to the law of each Member State but has a Community meaning. Since it defines the scope of that fundamental freedom, the Community concept of a "worker" must be interpreted broadly.

17   That concept must be defined in accordance with objective criteria which distinguish the employment relationship by reference to the rights and duties of the persons concerned. The essential feature of an employment relationship, however, is that for a certain period of time a person performs services for and under the direction of another person in return for which he receives remuneration.

18   In the present case, * * * during the entire period of preparatory service the trainee teacher is under the direction and supervision of the school to which he is assigned. It is the school that determines the services to be performed by him and his working hours and it is the school's instructions that he must carry out and its rules that he must observe. During a substantial part of the preparatory service he is required to give lessons to the school's pupils and thus provides a service of some economic value to the school. The amounts which he receives may be regarded as remuneration for the services provided and for the duties involved in completing the period of preparatory service. Consequently, the three criteria for the existence of an employment relationship are fulfilled in this case.

19   The fact that teachers' preparatory service, like apprenticeships in other occupations, may be regarded as practical preparation * * * is not a bar to the application of Article [39] if the service is performed under the conditions of an activity as an employed person.

20   Nor may it be objected that services performed in education do not fall within the scope of the EEC Treaty because they are not of an economic nature. All that is required for the application of Article [39] is that the activity should be in the nature of work performed for remuneration, irrespective of the sphere in which it is carried out. Nor may the economic nature of those activities be denied on the ground that they are performed by persons whose status is governed by public law since the nature of the legal relationship between employee and employer, whether involving public law status or a private law contract, is immaterial as regards the application of Article [39].

21   The fact that trainee teachers give lessons for only a few hours a week and are paid remuneration below the starting salary of a qualified teacher does not prevent them from being regarded as workers [citing *Levin*, infra page 602].

CLEAN CAR AUTO SERVICE v. LANDESHAUPTMANN VON WIEN

Case C–350/96, [1998] ECR I–2521.

[The 1994 Austrian Trade Code requires legal entities to have a manager resident in Austria. When the Clean Car company applied to be registered as a service station business, the Vienna authorities rejected the application because the proposed manager was then resident in Berlin, although seeking living accommodations in Vienna. On appeal, Clean Car contended that the residence requirement for a company manager violated ECT Article 39. The Supreme Administrative Court referred the issue to the Court of Justice, which first considered whether an employer, rather than the worker, could invoke Article 39. The Court held that Article 39 implicitly granted an employer standing to enforce its provisions, in order to make "truly effective" employee's rights (¶¶ 19–25). The Court then considered whether the residence requirement for company managers constituted indirect discrimination under Article 39.]

27 The Court has consistently held that the rules of equal treatment prohibit not only overt discrimination based on nationality but also all covert forms of discrimination which, by applying other distinguishing criteria, achieve in practice the same result.

28 It is true that [the Austrian law in question] applies without regard to the nationality of the person to be appointed as manager.

29 However,* * *national rules under which a distinction is drawn on the basis of residence are liable to operate mainly to the detriment of nationals of other Member States, as non-residents are in the majority of cases foreigners.

30 A requirement that nationals of other Member States must reside in the State concerned in order to be appointed managers of undertakings exercising a trade is therefore such as to constitute indirect discrimination based on nationality, contrary to Article [39(2)] of the Treaty.

31 It would be otherwise only if the imposition of such a residence requirement were based on objective considerations independent of the nationality of the employees concerned and proportionate to a legitimate aim pursued by the national law.

* * *

[Austria argued that the residence requirement was justified objectively by the need to ensure that the manager could "act effectively." The Court disagreed.]

35 [T]he fact that the manager resides in the Member State in which the undertaking is established and exercises its trade does not itself necessarily ensure that he will be in a position to act effectively as manager in the business. A manager residing in the State but at a

considerable distance from the place at which the undertaking exercises its trade should normally find it more difficult to act effectively in the business than a person whose place of residence, even if in another Member State, is at no great distance from that at which the undertaking exercises its trade.

NOTES AND QUESTIONS

1. In *Lawrie–Blum*, what are the three criteria in ¶ 17 that determine whether an employment relationship exists? How did the Court apply them to the status of a trainee-teacher? Do you find the Court's criteria helpful in analyzing border-line situations? The Court also held that a trainee for a secondary school teacher could not be considered to be in the State public service. See section C2 infra.

2. In *Clean Car*, the Court treats a company manager as it would any other employee for ECT Article 39 purposes, even though managers have legally specified powers and responsibilities for company law purposes. This is the first time that we encounter the important doctrine that a residence requirement, applied both to nationals and non-nationals, can constitute covert or indirect discrimination against non-national migrant workers. Do you agree with the Court's application of the approach with regard to managers? Is it any more operationally difficult for a manager of a Vienna business to be resident in Berlin than to be resident in Lindau, an Austrian town near Switzerland? Also, do you agree with the Court's conclusion that employers can rely on Article 39 in a proceeding against a State? Does it represent sound policy? Note that a prospective employee might not have the financial resources to seek administrative recourse in a case like *Clean Car*.

3. In Lyyski v. Umea Universitet, Case C–40/05, [2007] ECR I–99, a Swedish law authorized certain universities to carry out special teacher training programs which require practical work-place teaching under the supervision of a school principal. Lyyski, a Swedish national, was denied admission to the program because he sought to have the practice teaching take place in a Swedish speaking school in a Swedish-language region of Finland. The Court initially held that the rule disadvantaged prospective teachers who wished to exercise the right of free movement (¶ 37). The Court recognized that proper monitoring and assessment of practice teaching was essential (¶ 43), but left it to the referring court to determine whether under the principle of proportionality "the obstacles to completion of the practical part of the training course can be removed" (¶ 46).

4. German states require persons seeking to become lawyers to spend two years as trainees in law firms and as court clerks. In Kranemann v. Land Nordrhein–Westfalen, Case C–109/04, [2005] ECR I–2421, a trainee was denied reimbursement of his travel expenses to London where he worked as a trainee in a solicitor firm, although the state would have reimbursed travel expenses if he had worked for a law firm elsewhere in Germany. Should the Court of Justice find the denial a violation of Article 39? If the state had required all law firm training to concern German law in a German law firm, would that violate Article 39?

HICKLIN v. ORBECK

437 U.S. 518, 98 S.Ct. 2482, 57 L.Ed.2d 397 (1978).

[In 1972, concerned over a high level of unemployment, Alaska adopted the Local Hire under State Leases Act, which required all parties operating under Alaskan oil and gas leases or under Alaskan permits for oil and gas pipelines to give a hiring preference to Alaskan residents. The act set up a system of state issuance of "resident cards" to persons who had resided more than one year in Alaska. During the construction of the Trans–Alaska Pipeline in 1975, qualified non-resident job applicants challenged the Local Hire Act. The Alaskan Supreme Court sustained the Act's preference for hiring residents, but struck down the one year residence requirement as excessively long. On appeal, the US Supreme Court unanimously found the Local Hire Act unconstitutional in an opinion by Justice Brennan.]

Alaska Hire's discrimination against nonresidents cannot withstand scrutiny under the Privileges and Immunities Clause. For although the statute may not violate the Clause if the State shows "something to indicate that noncitizens constitute a peculiar source of evil at which the statute is aimed," certainly no showing was made on this record that nonresidents were "a peculiar source of the evil" Alaska Hire was enacted to remedy, namely, Alaska's "uniquely high unemployment." * * *. What evidence the record does contain indicates that the major cause of Alaska's high unemployment was not the influx of nonresidents seeking employment, but rather the fact that a substantial number of Alaska's jobless residents—especially the unemployed Eskimo and Indian residents—were unable to secure employment either because of their lack of education and job training or because of their geographical remoteness from job opportunities * * *.

Moreover * * * the discrimination the Act works against nonresidents does not bear a substantial relationship to the particular "evil" they are said to present. Alaska Hire simply grants all Alaskans, regardless of their employment status, education, or training, a flat employment preference for all jobs covered by the Act. A highly skilled and educated resident who has never been unemployed is entitled to precisely the same preferential treatment as the unskilled, habitually unemployed Arctic Eskimo enrolled in a job-training program. If Alaska is to attempt to ease its unemployment problem by forcing employers within the State to discriminate against nonresidents—again, a policy which may present serious constitutional questions—the means by which it does so must be more closely tailored to aid the unemployed the Act is intended to benefit. Even if a statute granting an employment preference to unemployed residents or to residents enrolled in job-training programs might be permissible, Alaska Hire's across-the-board grant of a job preference to all Alaskan residents clearly is not.

WÜRTTEMBERGISCHE MILCHVERWERTUNG–SÜDMILCH v. UGLIOLA

Case 15/69, [1969] ECR 363.

[German law required employers to treat the period which an employee must spend in compulsory military service as though it were employment for purposes of seniority and pension benefits. Ugliola, an Italian, worked in a German dairy for several years before being required to perform his compulsory Italian military service obligation. When his employer refused to treat the period of Italian military service as it would that of German military service, Ugliola sued. The Supreme German Labor Court made a preliminary reference.]

4   The fulfilment by migrant workers of an obligation for military service owed to their own State is liable to affect their conditions of work and employment in another Member State. * * *

5   A national law which is intended to protect a worker who resumes his employment with his former employer from any disadvantages occasioned by his absence on military service, by providing in particular that the period spent in the armed forces must be taken into account in calculating the period of his service with that employer falls within the context of conditions of work and employment. Such a law cannot therefore, on the basis of its indirect connexion with national defense, be excluded from the ambit of * * * Article 7 of EEC Regulation No 1612/68 on equality of treatment and protection for migrant workers "in respect of any conditions of employment and work".

6   Article [39] of the Treaty does not allow Member States to make any exceptions to the equality of treatment and protection required by the Treaty for all workers within the Community by indirectly introducing discrimination in favor of their own nationals alone based upon obligations for military service. * * *

7   Therefore, the abovementioned provisions entitle a migrant worker who is a national of a Member State and who has had to interrupt his employment with an undertaking in another Member State in order to fulfil his obligations for military service in the country of which he is a national, to have the period of his military service taken into account in the calculation of his seniority in that undertaking, to the extent to which the periods of military service in the country of employment are also taken into account for the benefit of national workers.

NOTES AND QUESTIONS

1.   Germany clearly has an interest in promoting its citizens' willingness to perform their military service duty. Why didn't this national defense argument prevail in *Ugliola*? Would the result be the same under ECT Article 39 alone, without Regulation 1612/68? Certainly a Member State could never adopt a local hire law granting an automatic employment preference to its residents. In *Hicklin*, the Supreme Court suggests that a hiring preference to

unemployed residents enrolled in job-training programs might perhaps be permissible. Would that be possible under the terms of Regulation 1612/68? For a U.S. case with analogies to *Ugliola,* see Attorney General of New York v. Soto–Lopez, 476 U.S. 898, 106 S.Ct. 2317, 90 L.Ed.2d 899 (1986), where Justice Brennan's plurality opinion struck down a New York law giving a civil service employment preference to veterans who had been residents of New York before their military service, on the basis that the preference given to New York residents violated the Equal Protection Clause and the right to travel.

2. In Kobler v. Austria, Case C–224/01, [2003] ECR I–10239, an Austrian law granted a special 'loyalty bonus' increase in their pension benefits to university professors after fifteen years of teaching in an Austrian university. The Court held that the Austrian law violated Article 39, both because it deterred Austrian professors from teaching elsewhere in the Community and it discriminated against professors from other States who secured a university post in Austria, because their prior university teaching could not be calculated in the seniority required by the bonus. *Kobler* is a well known judgment because the Court also held that a State could be liable in damages to private parties injured by a 'manifest' error of its supreme court in applying Community law. See the discussion at page 404 supra.

3. In Commission v. Greece (Ownership of housing), Case 305/87, [1989] ECR 1461, the Commission challenged a 1938 Greek law prohibiting foreigners from owning property in border areas and the islands, which amount to over 50% of Greek territory. It argued that the law constituted an indirect bar to free movement of workers, in violation of both Article 39 and Regulation 1612/68. How should the Court decide the case?

The final case in this section raises an intriguing issue: to what degree can a Member State require migrant workers in certain sectors to speak an official language of the State?

GROENER v. MINISTER FOR EDUCATION
Case C–379/87, [1989] ECR 3967.

[The Irish Constitution declares Irish to be the first official language. In 1979, the Ministry of Education issued a regulation requiring all lecturers in vocational education institutions to have a certificate of proficiency in the Irish language. Groener, a Dutch national, was employed in 1982 as a part-time art teacher in the Dublin College of Marketing and Design. She applied in 1984 for a permanent post, which the College wanted to grant, but she failed the Irish proficiency exam. When she sued the Ministry, the High Court asked the Court of Justice to interpret article 3(1) of Regulation 1612/68, which permits States to allow employment conditions "relating to linguistic knowledge required by reason of the nature of the post to be filled."]

[13] It is apparent from the documents before the Court that the obligation to prove a knowledge of the Irish language imposed by the national provisions in question applies without distinction to Irish and other Community nationals * * *.

14 [I]t is appropriate to consider first * * * whether the nature of a permanent full-time post of lecturer in art in public vocational education institutions is such as to justify the requirement of a knowledge of the Irish language.

15 According to the documents before the Court, the teaching of art, like that of most other subjects taught in public vocational education schools, is conducted essentially or indeed exclusively in the English language. It follows that * * * knowledge of the Irish language is not required for the performance of the duties which teaching of the kind at issue specifically entails.

16 However, that finding is not in itself sufficient to enable the national court to decide whether the linguistic requirement in question is justified "by reason of the nature of the post to be filled" * * *.

17 To apprehend the full scope of the second question, regard must be had to the special linguistic situation in Ireland, as it appears from the documents before the Court. By virtue of Article 8 of the "Bunreacht na hEireann" (Irish Constitution):

"(1) The Irish language as the national language is the first official language.

(2) The English language is recognized as a second official language.

(3) Provision may, however, be made by law for the exclusive use of either of the said languages for any one or more official purposes, either throughout the State or in any part thereof."

18 [A]lthough Irish is not spoken by the whole Irish population, the policy followed by Irish governments for many years has been designed not only to maintain but also to promote the use of Irish as a means of expressing national identity and culture.* * *Irish courses are compulsory for children receiving primary education and optional for those receiving secondary education. The obligation imposed on lecturers in public vocational education schools to have a certain knowledge of the Irish language is one of the measures adopted by the Irish Government in furtherance of that policy.

19 The EEC Treaty does not prohibit the adoption of a policy for the protection and promotion of a language of a Member State which is both the national language and the first official language. However, the implementation of such a policy must not encroach upon a fundamental freedom such as that of the free movement of workers. Therefore, the requirements deriving from measures intended to implement such a policy must not in any circumstances be disproportionate in relation to the aim pursued and the manner in which they are applied must not bring about discrimination against nationals of other Member States.

20 The importance of education for the implementation of such a policy must be recognized. Teachers have an essential role to play, not only through the teaching which they provide but also by their partic-

ipation in the daily life of the school and the privileged relationship which they have with their pupils. In those circumstances, it is not unreasonable to require them to have some knowledge of the first national language.

21   It follows that the requirement imposed on teachers to have an adequate knowledge of such a language must, provided that the level of knowledge required is not disproportionate in relation to the objective pursued, be regarded as a condition corresponding to the knowledge required by reason of the nature of the post to be filled within the meaning of the last subparagraph of Article 3(1) of Regulation No 1612/68.

* * *

23   Moreover the principle of non-discrimination precludes the imposition of any requirement that the linguistic knowledge in question must have been acquired within the national territory. It also implies that the nationals of other Member States should have an opportunity to retake the oral examination, in the event of their having previously failed it, when they again apply for a post of assistant lecturer or lecturer.

NOTES AND QUESTIONS

1. Advocate General Darmon informs us that only one-third of the Irish population claim fluency in Irish, that most of the teachers and students at the Dublin College of Marketing and Design habitually use English, and that Groener's proposed full-time duties would not significantly differ from the temporary duties which she successfully performed without any knowledge of Irish. [1989] ECR at 3981. In view of these factors, do you agree with the Court that Irish is "required by reason of the nature of the post to be filled"?

2. Advocate General Darmon later declares that: "The preservation of languages is one of those questions of principle which one cannot dismiss without striking at the very heart of cultural identity." "[E]very State has the right to determine the importance it wishes to attribute to its cultural heritage." Id. at 3982. *Groener* is a seminal judgment on the recognition of national culture as a legitimate limit on Community rules.

In an approving case comment, Professor McMahon concluded: "Cynics might say that the Court recognized the political necessity for such a decision and realised the cultural backlash which would have been inevitable if it had refused to recognise the legality of the Irish measures. * * * A more gracious and generous view, however, might be that we are here witnessing a real recognition of the legitimacy of national concerns in relation to national cultural heritage * * *." B. McMahon, Groener, 27 Common Mkt.L.Rev. 129, 139 (1990). Do you agree with the "cynics" or take the "more generous view"?

3. Suppose the regional authorities in Wales or in Brittany or in Catalonia required a Dutch teacher of art in a college to speak, respectively,

Welsh or Breton or Catalan. Would the result be the same? Why is the reference to the Irish language in the Irish Constitution so important?

4. The final issue in *Groener* is proportionality. Even if it is appropriate for Ireland to require primary school teachers to speak Irish, is it necessary for the preservation of the Irish language that an art teacher in a vocational training school be able to speak Irish? Do you agree with the Court on this? (Note that Irish law does not require teachers at the university level to be able to speak Irish.) Notice the procedural limits required of Ireland in ¶ 23. How helpful are they? Advocate General Darmon observed that Groener was the only one of six non-Irish candidates who failed the language exam when it was given. Is that significant or irrelevant?

2. HORIZONTAL DIRECT EFFECT

As already noted, the Court of Justice early concluded that ECT Article 39 had vertical direct effect, enabling workers to challenge state measures that discriminated on the basis of nationality. After *Defrenne*, supra page 240, accorded horizontal direct effect to then EEC Treaty Article 119, enabling individuals to challenge gender-based discrimination in pay committed by private sector employees, the question naturally arose whether Article 39 might also have horizontal direct effect. An indication that Article 39 could be considered to have horizontal direct effect came in *Bosman*, discussed in section D3 infra, when the Court held that private sports associations could not discriminate on the basis of nationality in their rules on members of sports teams. The issue has now been definitively resolved.

ANGONESE v. CASSA DI RISPARMIO DI BOLZANO
Case C–281/98, [2000] ECR I–4139.

[In Bolzano, a north Italian region where German is commonly spoken, a bank required its employees to be equally proficient in German and Italian. For this reason, it required applicants to obtain a certificate after passing a bilingual proficiency examination administered four times a year by the Bolzano authorities (who also used it for applications for public service employment). Angonese, an Italian citizen and resident of Bolzano, contested the bank's refusal to consider his application without having taken the examination, contending that his studies in the University of Vienna ought to be considered to prove his German proficiency. However, he had received no diploma from the University, and his formal studies there were in English, Polish, and Slovene.

When Angonese sued the bank, the trial court referred questions to the Court of Justice asking whether the requirement of the Bolzano examination constituted indirect discrimination on the basis of nationality. The Court first concluded that the fact that Angonese was an Italian citizen and resident did not mean that Community law was irrelevant to his suit, and left the trial court to decide the degree to which its responses to the questions referred were relevant. The Court then concluded that no provision of Regulation 1612/68 applied, so the issues were to be examined purely in terms of ECT Article 39.]

30   It should be noted at the outset that the principle of non-discrimination set out in Article [39] is drafted in general terms and is not specifically addressed to the Member States.

31   Thus, the Court has held that the prohibition of discrimination based on nationality applies not only to the actions of public authorities but also to rules of any other nature aimed at regulating in a collective manner gainful employment and the provision of services (citing *Walrave, infra* page 611).

32   The Court has held that the abolition, as between Member States, of obstacles to freedom of movement for persons would be compromised if the abolition of State barriers could be neutralized by obstacles resulting from the exercise of their legal autonomy by associations or organisations not governed by public law (citing *Walrave* and *Bosman*).

33   Since working conditions in the different Member States are governed sometimes by provisions laid down by law or regulation and sometimes by agreements and other acts concluded or adopted by private persons, limiting application of the prohibition of discrimination based on nationality to acts of public authority risks creating inequality in its application.

34   The Court has also ruled that the fact that certain provisions of the Treaty are formally addressed to the Member States does not prevent rights from being conferred at the same time on any individual who has an interest in compliance with the obligations thus laid down. The Court accordingly held, in relation to a provision of the Treaty which was mandatory in nature, that the prohibition of discrimination applied equally to all agreements intended to regulate paid labour collectively, as well as to contracts between individuals (citing *Defrenne*).

35   Such considerations must, *a fortiori*, be applicable to Article [39] of the Treaty, which lays down a fundamental freedom and which constitutes a specific application of the general prohibition of discrimination contained in Article [12] of the EC Treaty.

36   Consequently, the prohibition of discrimination on grounds of nationality laid down in Article [39] of the Treaty must be regarded as applying to private persons as well.

[The Court then considered the bilingual examination certificate requirement.]

38   According to the order for reference, the Cassa di Risparmio accepts only the Certificate as evidence of the requisite linguistic knowledge and the Certificate can be obtained only in one province of the Member State concerned.

39 Persons not resident in that province therefore have little chance of acquiring the Certificate and it will be difficult, or even impossible, for them to gain access to the employment in question.

40 Since the majority of residents of the province of Bolzano are Italian nationals, the obligation to obtain the requisite Certificate puts nationals of other Member States at a disadvantage by comparison with residents of the province.

41 That is so notwithstanding that the requirement in question affects Italian nationals resident in other parts of Italy as well as nationals of other Member States* * *.

* * *

43 The Court has ruled that the principle of non-discrimination precludes any requirement that the linguistic knowledge in question must have been acquired within the national territory (see *Groener* paragraph 23).

44 So, even though requiring an applicant for a post to have a certain level of linguistic knowledge may be legitimate and possession of a diploma such as the Certificate may constitute a criterion for assessing that knowledge, the fact that it is impossible to submit proof of the required linguistic knowledge by any other means, in particular by equivalent qualifications obtained in other Member States, must be considered disproportionate in relation to the aim in view.

45 It follows that, where an employer makes a person's admission to a recruitment competition subject to a requirement to provide evidence of his linguistic knowledge exclusively by means of one particular diploma, such as the Certificate, issued only in one particular province of a Member State, that requirement constitutes discrimination on grounds of nationality contrary to Article [39] of the EC Treaty.

NOTES AND QUESTIONS

1. Advocate General Fennelly had recommended that the case be considered not to raise a question of Community law, applying the internal affairs doctrine (see section D4 infra), because Angonese was an Italian citizen and resident of Bolzano and had not exercised any right of free movement to obtain a diploma in German studies at a foreign school or university. The Court's willingness to answer the referred question despite serious doubts that Angonese had standing to claim any Community rights may have been prompted in part by a desire to bring legal certainty to the resolution of the underlying issue of horizontal direct effect. Do you agree with the Court's view in ¶¶ 37–45 that the employer's requirement of the Bolzano bilingual proficiency examination constituted indirect discrimination on the basis of nationality?

2. Although Regulation 1612/68 covers most factual situations of discrimination, the horizontal direct effect of Article 39 can still have considera-

ble practical impact. Consider whether a small retail store owner could be sued for violation of Article 39 if he/she is proved to have dismissed an employee and expressed a clear bias against persons of the dismissed employee's nationality at the time of the firing. Could a factory in a city with high unemployment give a hiring preference to residents of that city? Could a retail store owner in a rural region hire exclusively salespersons who are nationals from that region in the belief that his/her rural customers are uncomfortable with salespersons from outside that region?

3. NON–DISCRIMINATION IN "SOCIAL ADVANTAGES"

MINISTÈRE PUBLIC v. MUTSCH

Case 137/84, [1985] ECR 2681.

[Mutsch, a Luxembourg national whose native language was German, resided and worked in a German-speaking community in Belgium. Belgian law permits Belgian nationals speaking German in certain designated German language regions to demand that any criminal proceedings against them be conducted in German. When accused of a crime, Mutsch claimed the benefit of this law. He was convicted *in absentia* and appealed. An appellate court referred the question raised by Mutsch's claim to the Court of Justice.]

12   Article [12] of the Treaty provides that "within the scope of application of this Treaty and without prejudice to any special provisions contained therein, any discrimination on grounds of nationality shall be prohibited". That provision must be applied in every respect and in all circumstances governed by Community law to any person established in a Member State. Similarly, * * * Article [39], on the status of workers, is likewise based on the principle that nationals of any Member State lawfully established in another Member State for the purpose of employment must be treated in the same way as nationals of that State.

13   It is therefore necessary to determine whether the right to require that legal proceedings take place in a specific language falls within the scope of the Treaty and must therefore be assessed in the light of the prohibition of discrimination set out in the provisions referred to above.

14   Since it appears from the documents before the Court that the accused is a worker (he describes himself as a roofer working in his father's firm), that question must be examined more particularly in the light of [Article 39] of the Treaty and * * * Regulation No 1612/68.

15   As is stated in the fifth recital in the preamble to Regulation No 1612/68, "the right of freedom of movement, in order that it may be exercised, by objective standards, in freedom and dignity, requires that equality of treatment shall be ensured in fact and in law in respect of all matters relating to the actual pursuit of activities as employed

persons and to eligibility for housing, and also that obstacles to the mobility of workers shall be eliminated, in particular as regards the worker's right to be joined by his family and the conditions for the integration of that family into the host country".

16   The right to use his own language in proceedings before the courts of the Member State in which he resides, under the same conditions as national workers, plays an important role in the integration of a migrant worker and his family into the host country, and thus in achieving the objective of free movement for workers.

17   In those circumstances that right must be held to fall within the meaning of the term "social advantage" as used in Article 7(2) of Regulation No 1612/68, according to which a worker who is a national of another Member State is entitled, in the host Member State, to "the same social and tax advantages as national workers". * * * [T]hat term covers all advantages "which, whether or not linked to a contract of employment, are generally granted to national workers primarily because of their objective status as workers or by virtue of the mere fact of their residence on the national territory".

18   [Therefore,] a worker who is a national of one Member State and habitually resides in another Member State [is] entitled to require that criminal proceedings against him take place in [German] if workers who are nationals of the host Member State have that right in the same circumstances.

REINA v. LANDESKREDITBANK BADEN–WÜRTTEMBERG

Case 65/81, [1982] ECR 33.

[The German state of Baden–Württemberg had a system of interest-free loans provided by the Landeskreditbank, a state bank, to parents to cover childbirth expenses. Only couples with at least one German spouse were eligible. The avowed policy was to promote German population growth and to reduce voluntary abortions. After having twins, an Italian migrant worker and his wife sued to obtain a loan. The trial court referred questions to the Court of Justice.]

9   In its first question, the national court asks in substance whether Article 7(2) of Regulation No 1612/68 * * * must be construed as meaning that the concept of "social advantage" referred to in that provision encompasses interest-free loans granted on childbirth by a credit institution incorporated under public law, on the basis of guidelines and with financial assistance from the State, to families with a low income with a view to stimulating the birth rate.

10   The Landeskreditbank contends in the first place that Article 7(2) may not be applied to the loans in question in view of the absence of any connection between the grant of the loan and the recipient's status as

a worker and on the ground that the refusal to grant the loan in no way hinders the mobility of workers within the Community.

* * *

12   * * * [T]he advantages which [Article 7(2) of Regulation 1612/68] extends to workers who are nationals of other Member States are all those which, whether or not linked to a contract of employment, are generally granted to national workers primarily because of their objective status as workers or by virtue of the mere fact of their residence on the national territory and the extension of which to workers who are nationals of other Member States therefore seems suitable to facilitate their mobility within the Community.

13   Consequently, childbirth loans such as those referred to by the national court satisfy in principle the criteria enabling them to be classified as social advantages to be granted to workers of all the Member States without any discrimination whatever on grounds of nationality, in particular in view of their aim which is to alleviate, in the case of families with a low income, the financial burden resulting from the birth of a child.

14   The Landeskreditbank disputes that conclusion by maintaining that childbirth loans * * * are granted principally for reasons of demographic policy in order to counteract the decline in the birth rate of the German population. It is therefore a measure adopted in the area of political rights, necessarily linked to nationality, and which as a result falls outside the ambit of Article [39] of the Treaty and [Regulation 1612/68].

15   [S]ince the Community has no powers in the field of demographic policy as such, the Member States are permitted, in principle, to pursue the achievement of the objectives of such a policy, even by means of social measures. This does not mean, however, that the Community exceeds the limits of its jurisdiction solely because the exercise of its jurisdiction affects measures adopted in pursuance of that policy. Accordingly, childbirth loans of that kind may not be considered as falling outside the scope of the rules of Community law relating to the free movement of persons and, more specifically, of Article 7(2) of Regulation No 1612/68, solely because they are granted for reasons of demographic policy.

NOTES AND QUESTIONS

1.   Does the result in *Mutsch* surprise you? Why do you think that the Court so expansively interpreted the term "social advantage"? Would an Italian worker in Belgium who spoke only Italian have the right to have criminal proceedings against him or her conducted in Italian? If not, could the worker claim the right to have an Italian interpreter? Article 6(e) of the European Convention on Human Rights requires an interpreter.

2.   In *Reina,* does the link between the status of a migrant worker and the childbirth loans stretch too far the concept of equal social advantages?

What is the policy rationale for the Court's decision? In accord with *Reina* is Commission v. Greece (Family subsidies), Case C–185/96, [1998] ECR I–6601 (Greece cannot refuse large family subsidies, granted on demographic policy reasons, to families of migrant workers from other Member States).

3. In Lair v. Universitat Hanover, infra page 606, Lair, a French national, worked in Germany as a bank clerk for two years. Subsequently she commenced studies in German and Romance languages at the University of Hanover. When she sued to obtain state financial aid to cover tuition and living expenses, the national court asked the Court of Justice whether these constituted a "social advantage" under Regulation 1612/68. The Court responded that a migrant worker had a non-discriminatory right "to all the advantages available to [national] workers for improving their professional qualifications and promoting their social advancements" (¶ 22). Accordingly, the Court concluded that financial aid to reimburse tuition at the university level is a "social advantage." However, the Court considered that financial aid for living expenses constituted a part of Germany's social welfare system, and accordingly was not a "social advantage" available to Lair. (Note that *Bidar*, infra page 632, partially reverses *Lair*.)

4. In Hendrix v. Raad van Bestuur van het UWV, Case C–287/05, [2007] ECR I–6909, Hendrix, a Dutch national, has a slight mental disability that restricts him to specially adapted work. After working for five years in Maastricht, Hendrix moved to Belgium while continuing to work in Maastricht. A Dutch social insurance agency had paid benefits to Hendrix, but ceased when he became a non-resident. Its rules permitted payments to non-residents only if necessary to avoid an 'unacceptable degree of unfairness.' In an Article 234 referral, the Court initially found Hendrix to be a migrant worker (a reverse frontier worker after his change of residence) (¶ 46), citing *Hartmann*, infra page 607. The Court then held that the Dutch rule requiring residence was objectively justified because the benefit was calculated in function of the Dutch minimum wage (¶ 55). However, the Court instructed the national court to decide whether the principle of proportionality required that Hendrix should receive the benefit to avoid unfairness, observing that the court should consider in particular that Hendrix "had maintained all of his economic and social links to the Member State of origin" (¶ 58).

5. France has a state fund that provides financial compensation to victims of crimes or accidents, or to their family upon their death. James Wood, a UK national, has lived and worked in France for 20 years. On the death of their daughter in a traffic accident, his wife, a French national, received compensation, but he was denied it because he was not French. Is this permissible? See Woods v. Fonds de Garantie, Case C–164/07, [2008] ECR I–4143.

6. The remedy for discrimination against migrant workers concerning benefits may be quite costly. In Commission v. France (Frontier worker pensions), Case C–35/97, [1998] ECR I–5325, the Court held that a complex French scheme of supplemental pension benefit to steel workers obliged to take early retirement discriminated against Belgian frontier workers, who resided in Belgium but worked in France. Because the discriminatory treatment dated back to 1979, France claimed that the liability might amount to

around F175,000,000 (ca. $35,000,000). The Court nonetheless denied France's request to limit the retroactive application of the judgement.

4. NON–DISCRIMINATION IN TAXATION

Article 7(2) of Regulation 1612/68 forbids discrimination with regard to "tax advantages." In 1994, the Commission issued a Recommendation concerning the tax treatment of non-resident workers, O.J. L 39/22 (Feb. 10, 1994). A typical example is a "frontier worker," living in one Member State, but crossing a border regularly, often daily, in order to work in another State. The Recommendation covers any worker earning more than 75% of his/her income in another State, including professionals, performing artists, and sports players as well as more typical employees. The State taxing the income of such non-resident workers is urged to provide any deductions, credits or benefits that would be accorded to its residents.

Presumably the Commission issued a recommendation instead of proposing a directive because any direct tax proposal would fall under Article 95(2) which requires a unanimous Council vote. The Commission's views have been reinforced by a series of Court judgements.

FINANZAMT KÖLN–ALTSTADT v. SCHUMACKER

Case C–279/93, [1995] ECR I–225.

[Schumacker, a Belgian national residing in Belgium with his wife and children, worked across the border in Germany in 1988–89. This employment provided his sole income and his wife was unemployed. German law taxes non-resident workers on their German income without giving them certain deductions and tax advantages granted to resident taxpayers. When Schumacker requested a more beneficial tax calculation mode granted only to married resident taxpayers, the tax court asked the Court of Justice whether ECT Article 39 forbids discrimination in taxing non-residents.]

21 Although, as Community law stands at present, direct taxation does not as such fall within the purview of the Community, the powers retained by the Member States must nevertheless be exercised consistently with Community law.

22 * * * Article [39(2)] of the Treaty requires the abolition of any discrimination based on nationality between workers of the Member States as regards, *inter alia*, remuneration.

23 [T]he principle of equal treatment with regard to remuneration would be rendered ineffective if it could be undermined by discriminatory national provisions on income tax. That is why the Council laid down the requirement in Article 7 of Regulation (EEC) No 1612/68 that workers who are nationals of a Member State are to enjoy, in the

territory of another Member State, the same tax benefits as nationals working there.

* * *

[The Court then considered whether denial of tax advantages to non-resident migrant workers might constitute indirect discrimination.]

26 The Court has consistently held that the rules regarding equal treatment forbid not only overt discrimination by reason of nationality but also all covert forms of discrimination.

27 It is true that the rules at issue in the main proceedings apply irrespective of the nationality of the taxpayer concerned.

28 However, national rules of that kind, under which a distinction is drawn on the basis of residence in that non-residents are denied certain benefits which are, conversely, granted to persons residing within national territory, are liable to operate mainly to the detriment of nationals of other Member States. Non-residents are in the majority of cases foreigners.

29 In those circumstances, tax benefits granted only to residents of a Member State may constitute indirect discrimination by reason of nationality.

* * *

38 In the case of a non-resident who receives the major part of his income and almost all his family income in a Member State other than that of his residence, discrimination arises from the fact that his personal and family circumstances are taken into account neither in the State of residence nor in the State of employment.

NOTES AND QUESTIONS

1. That ECT Article 39 forbids discriminatory tax treatment of resident migrant workers is not surprising, but that it also requires equal treatment of many non-resident workers is less evident. Do you agree with the Court, or do you think it should have deferred to Member State discretion in the sensitive field of direct taxation in the absence of harmonization? Note that Community legislation in the field of direct taxation can only be adopted by a unanimous Council vote under ECT Article 95(2), now TFEU Article 114(2), making such harmonization unlikely.

2. The Court has frequently followed *Schumacker* in a variety of contexts. See e.g., Ritter–Coulais v. Finanzamt Germersheim, Case C–152/03, [2006] ECR I–1711, where the Court held that a German worker living in France who received income only from employment in Germany was entitled to take an income tax reduction for a rental loss based on his house in France, inasmuch as such a deduction was possible for a dwelling in Germany. Similarly, in Zurstrassen v. Administration des Contributions Directes, Case C–87/99, [2000] ECR I–3337, the Court held that Luxembourg must grant a married Belgian couple residing in Belgium the benefits of a joint tax return

for the husband's income from work in Luxembourg, inasmuch as couples resident in Luxembourg could file a joint return.

3. For many years, New York City imposed an income tax on nonresident commuters employed in the city. When in 1999, the New York State legislature eliminated the tax on commuters resident in New York, it continued to authorize New York City to tax out-of-state commuters. Recalling *Hicklin*, supra page 567, do you think the income tax imposed only on out-of-state commuters violates the dormant Commerce Clause? See City of New York v. State of New York, 94 N.Y.2d 577, 709 N.Y.S.2d 122, 730 N.E.2d 920 (2000). Could the Belgian city of Antwerp impose an income tax on Dutch frontier workers employed in Antwerp: 1) if it imposed the tax only on Dutch frontier workers; or 2) if it imposed the same tax on commuters residing outside Antwerp, but within Belgium?

5. PROTECTION OF THE SPOUSE OR FAMILY AGAINST DISCRIMINATORY TREATMENT

As there is no mention of the worker's spouse or family in ECT Article 39, any grant of rights to them must either be based on Title III of Regulation 1612/68, or on the claim that rights given to the spouse or family further the migrant worker's ability to exercise his or her own rights. Both of these approaches figure in the case law.

CASAGRANDE v. LANDESHAUPTSTADT MÜNCHEN

Case 9/74, [1974] ECR 773.

[Bavaria gave a monthly grant to assist students from low income families, but restricted the grant to German nationals. Casagrande, an Italian secondary school student whose deceased father was an Italian migrant worker, resided in Munich and sued for the grant. In a preliminary reference, the national court inquired whether Regulation 1612/68, article 12, required Bavaria to grant the student aid to children of migrant workers.]

5   Under Article 12 "the children of a national of a Member State who is or has been employed in the territory of another Member State shall be admitted to that State's general educational, apprenticeship and vocational training courses under the same conditions as the nationals of that State, if such children are residing in its territory", and Member States are required to encourage "all efforts to enable such children to attend these courses under the best possible conditions".

6   According to the fifth recital of the Regulation, the latter was issued, *inter alia,* for the reason that "the right of freedom of movement, in order that it may be exercised, by objective standards, in freedom and dignity, requires * * * that obstacles to the mobility of workers shall be eliminated, in particular as regards the worker's right to be joined by his family and the conditions for the integration of that family into the host country".

[7] Such integration presupposes that, in the case of the child of a foreign worker who wishes to have secondary education, this child can take advantage of benefits provided by the laws of the host country relating to educational grants, under the same conditions as nationals who are in a similar position.

[8] It follows from the provision in the second paragraph of Article 12, according to which Member States are to encourage all efforts to enable such children to attend the courses under the best possible conditions, that the Article is intended to encourage special efforts, to ensure that the children may take advantage on an equal footing of the education and training facilities available.

[9] It must be concluded that in providing that the children in question shall be admitted to educational courses "under the same conditions as the nationals" of the host State, Article 12 refers not only to rules relating to admission, but also to general measures intended to facilitate educational attendance.

* * *

[11] In the Federal Republic of Germany [educational] policy is largely within the competence of the [German states], and therefore it must be asked whether Article 12 applies not only to the conditions laid down by laws emanating from the central power but also to those arising from measures taken by the authorities of a country which forms part of a Federal State, or of other territorial entities.

[12] Although educational and training policy is not as such included in the spheres which the Treaty has entrusted to the Community institutions, it does not follow that the exercise of powers transferred to the Community is in some way limited if it is of such a nature as to affect the measures taken in the execution of a policy such as that of education and training.

* * *

[14] As regards Article 12 of Regulation 1612/68, although the determination of the conditions referred to there is a matter for the authorities competent under national law, they must however be applied without discrimination between the children of national workers and those of workers who are nationals of another Member State who reside in the territory.

[15] Further, since Regulations, under Article [249] of the Treaty, have general application and are binding in their entirety and directly applicable in all Member States, it is irrelevant that the conditions in question are laid down by rules issued by the central power, by the authorities of a country forming part of a Federal State or of other territorial entities, or even by authorities which the national law equates with them.

NOTES AND QUESTIONS

1. Does any part of article 12 expressly or implicitly give any right to financial aid related to studies? Do you agree with the Court's approach? Why is the Court taking an expansive view of the rights of children of migrant workers?

2. *Casagrande* poses an interesting constitutional issue. Under the German constitution, education is exclusively a domain for the *Länder,* or states. Moreover, the EEC Treaty did not then include education as a specific field of Community action. How does the Court conclude that the Community can legislate with regard to education? Since the *Länder* did not sign the EEC Treaty, how are they bound to observe it? If Bavaria declined to follow the Court's opinion, could the Commission bring a Treaty infringement proceeding against Germany? Remember that in the dialogue between the Court of Justice and the German Constitutional Court described in Chapter 8, the Constitutional Court has always said it would, if necessary, safeguard the organic structure of the Federal Republic.

3. In accord are Michel S. v. Fonds national, Case 76/72, [1973] ECR 457 (mentally handicapped son of deceased Italian migrant worker, residing in Belgium, has right to benefits from Belgian fund to assist the mentally handicapped to obtain work); Alaimo v. Préfet du Rhône, Case 68/74, [1975] ECR 109 (daughter of Italian worker, residing in France, has right to financial aid granted by a French department to French students in a technical training school).

4. Germany offers training grants for certain higher education studies in other Community States. Di Leo, an Italian and the daughter of Italian migrant workers in Germany, was denied such a grant when she proposed to study medicine in Italy. Should children of migrant workers be entitled to receive foreign training grants for studies in medicine under article 12 of Regulation 1612/68? If so, does it matter whether the child wants to study in the State of which she is a national? See Di Leo v. Land Berlin, Case C–308/89, [1990] ECR I–4185.

5. The Court of Justice has interpreted article 7 of Regulation 1612/68 expansively to grant equal social advantages not only to the migrant worker, but also to the worker's spouse and family. Cristini v. SNCF français, Case 32/75, [1975] ECR 1085, is the leading case. A French regulation granted special railroad fare reductions to families with three or more children under 18, but restricted this to French nationals. The Italian widow of a deceased Italian migrant worker, mother of four children under 18, was held to have the right to the reduced fare. The Court first concluded that the reduced fare would be a social advantage if the worker himself were claiming it. The Court then held that Commission Regulation 1251/70 gave the widow and dependent children of a deceased migrant worker the right to continued residence in the host State and a right to equal treatment, which would entitle the widow to the benefit of equal social advantages.

6. Article 11 of Regulation 1612/68 grants a third-county national who is the spouse of a migrant worker a right to employment in the State where the

migrant worker is employed. In Mattern v. Ministre du Travail, Case C–10/05, [2006] ECR I–3145, a Luxembourg national claimed the status of a migrant worker in Belgium under *Lawrie–Blum* after she worked as a health care trainee there. Her husband then claimed the right to work in Luxembourg pursuant to article 11. How should the Court of Justice interpret the article?

6. RIGHT OF FREE ENTRY AND RESIDENCE

A right to work in other Community States must imply a right of free entry and residence. Although some frontier workers reside in their home State and commute to the State of employment, most migrant workers need to reside in the host State and wish to have their family live with them.

ECT Article 39(3) only specified certain "bare bones": the right of entry to accept employment and the right "to stay in a Member State for the purpose of employment." Council Directive 68/360 on the abolition of restrictions on movement and residence within the Community for workers of Member States and their families, set out the basic applicable rules until recently repealed in 2006 by the comprehensive Directive 2004/38, discussed in Chapter 16.

Directive 68/360 required the host State to permit the entry of workers and their family members with either an identity card or a passport (art. 3). Normally, the host State was required to issue the worker or family member an EC residence permit valid for five years, renewable automatically (art. 6). In order to obtain the EC residence permit, the worker only needed to provide his passport or home State identity card and proof of employment, while the family members only had to provide their passports or identity cards and proof of their relationship. The host State could not require the worker to obtain a labor permit. The residence permit could not be withdrawn when a worker became temporarily incapacitated or was dismissed by the employer (art. 7). Under article 8, residence permits were not required for frontier workers, for seasonal workers (e.g., migrant workers harvesting crops), or temporary stay workers expected to remain no more than three months.

How severely can a host State penalize migrant workers lacking the necessary residence permit? In Royer, Case 48/75, [1976] ECR 497, the Court held that the host State may not expel a worker who did not obtain a residence permit, as that sanction is too severe. In Regina v. Pieck, Case 157/79, [1980] ECR 2171, the Court held that a jail sentence is never an appropriate penalty. Finally, the Court held that Germany could not impose a maximum fine of DM 5000 upon nationals of other Member States for failure to hold a valid EC residence permit when the maximum fine on German nationals for failure to hold an identity card was only DM 1000. Commission v. Germany (Residence permit penalties), Case C–24/97, [1998] ECR I–2133.

Does a Community national have a temporary right of residence in a host State while looking for work and, if so, for how long? The issue is important, because looking for employment on the spot is generally more likely to prove successful than applying by mail or dealing through a distant employment agency. Member States have customarily allowed persons to reside temporarily for up to three months while ostensibly looking for work, in accord with a Council recommendation adopted along with Directive 68/360.

COMMISSION v. BELGIUM

(Temporary residence limits)
Case C–344/95, [1997] ECR I–1035.

[Belgium permits nationals of other Member States to stay no longer than three months while looking for employment. Belgium also requires short term or seasonal workers to obtain a residence certificate. The Commission challenged both rules. The Court began by stating that Article 39, as "one of the foundations of the Community * * * must be given a broad interpretation" (¶ 14). It then continued:]

15   [F]reedom of movement for workers entails the right for nationals of Member States to move freely within the territory of other Member States and to stay there for the purposes of seeking employment.

* * *

17   In the absence of Community provisions prescribing a period during which Community nationals who are seeking employment may stay in their territory, the Member States are entitled to lay down a reasonable period for this purpose. However, if after expiry of that period, the person concerned provides evidence that he is continuing to seek employment and that he has genuine chances of being engaged, he cannot be required to leave the territory of the host Member State.

18   In view of the foregoing, it is sufficient to state that the Belgian legislation infringes Community law in automatically requiring nationals of other Member States who are looking for employment to leave Belgium after expiry of the period laid down.

[With regard to the residence certificates required for short-term or seasonal workers, the Court declared that:]

31   Although Article 8(2) of the Directive provides that the competent authorities of the host Member State may require the worker to report his presence, * * * anything going beyond having to report one's presence and having the character of an authorization or a residence permit is not compatible with the Directive.

32   Furthermore, requiring a person to pay a charge when he reports his presence constitutes a financial obstacle to the movement of workers, which is also contrary to the Community rules.

NOTES AND QUESTIONS

1. The Court's conclusion in the *Belgian Temporary residence limits* case that a right to look for work in another State is implied in ECT Article 39 is not only plausible as an interpretation, but unquestionable on policy grounds. Why do you suppose the Court would not accept the three month period which the Council had initially recommended as a reasonable limit on a period of seeking employment? Will it be easy for a trial court to apply ¶ 17's approach?

2. In Collins v. Secretary of State for Work, Case C–138/02, [2004] ECR I–2703, Collins, an American citizen born and raised in the US, also possessed Irish nationality, although he never resided in Ireland. After several years of employment in the US, Collins came to the UK to seek work in social services. Collins sought a financial allowance that the UK granted to jobseekers. (As indicated in Chapter 16B, Collins, a dual national, may claim the rights of his Irish nationality even though he never resided in Ireland.) On its refusal, he appealed, and the appellate administrator referred questions to the Court. The Court held that Collins is entitled to enter the UK in order to seek work and reside there for a reasonable time while doing so (¶ 37). Then, in view of the Court's caselaw according "citizens of the Union lawfully resident in the territory of a host Member States" equal rights under ECT Treaty Article 12 in any situation falling within the scope of Community law (¶ 61), "it is no longer possible to exclude from the scope of Article 39 * * * a benefit of a financial nature intended to facilitate access to employment" in a host State (¶ 63). The UK authorities may, of course, verify whether Collins is genuinely seeking work (¶ 70). Although the judgment is hardly apt to be popular with the UK Treasury, do you consider it to represent desirable policy in promoting the interests of migrants seeking employment throughout the Community?

A right to temporary residence while looking for work is only an implied right, but certainly a very plausible one. The next judgment's implication of a derivative right to residence is much more surprising, but has proved to be seminal in inspiring further caselaw.

BAUMBAST AND R. v. SECRETARY OF STATE FOR THE HOME DEPARTMENT
Case C–413/99, [2002] ECR I–7091.

[In the first case, a German national, Baumbast, worked for several years in the UK. Although he has been employed since 1993 outside the European Union, his family has continued to reside in the UK. Baumbast's wife and her elder daughter are Columbian nationals while her younger daughter, Idanella, has German nationality.

In the second case, R, a US citizen, has resided since 1990 in the UK, initially with her husband, a French migrant worker. After a divorce in 1992, R has continued to reside in the UK with her two children, each of whom have French nationality. Although R's husband also lives in the UK, R has the primary custody of the children.

An immigration appeals tribunal inquired first, whether the children could have any right to reside in the UK under Article 12 of Regulation

1612/68, and second, whether the mothers then would have a derivative right of residence.]

50   In that respect, it must be borne in mind that the aim of Regulation No 1612/68, namely freedom of movement for workers, requires, for such freedom to be guaranteed in compliance with the principles of liberty and dignity, the best possible conditions for the integration of the Community worker's family in the society of the host Member State.

51   [F]or such integration to come about, a child of a Community worker must have the possibility of going to school and pursuing further education in the host Member State, as is expressly provided in Article 12 of Regulation No 1612/68, in order to be able to complete that education successfully.

52   In circumstances such as those in the Baumbast case, to prevent a child of a citizen of the Union from continuing his education in the host Member State by refusing him permission to remain might dissuade that citizen from exercising the rights to freedom of movement laid down in Article 39 EC and would therefore create an obstacle to the effective exercise of the freedom thus guaranteed by the EC Treaty.

* * *

54   In fact, to permit children of a citizen of the Union who are in a situation such as that of Mr Baumbast's children to continue their education in the host Member State only where they cannot do so in their Member State of origin would offend not only the letter of Article 12 of Regulation No 1612/68, which provides a right of access to educational courses for the children of a national of a Member State 'who is or has been employed' in the territory of another Member State, but also its spirit.

* * *

56   As to whether the fact that the children are not themselves citizens of the Union can affect the answer to the first question, suffice it to state that, under Article 10 of Regulation No 1612/68, the descendants of a Community worker who are under the age of 21 or are dependants, irrespective of their nationality, are to be regarded as members of his family and have the right to install themselves with that worker and that, accordingly, they have the right to be admitted to the school system in accordance with Article 12 of that regulation.

57   Furthermore, the right of 'his spouse and their descendants who are under the age of 21 years or are dependants' to install themselves with the migrant worker must be interpreted as meaning that it is granted both to the descendants of that worker and to those of his spouse. To give a restrictive interpretation to that provision to the effect that only the children common to the migrant worker and his spouse have the

right to install themselves with them would run counter to the aim of Regulation No 1612/68 noted above.

58 As regards, second, the R case, the children concerned enjoy, as members of the family of a worker who is a national of one Member State and who is employed in the territory of another Member State, a right of residence and a right to pursue their education under Articles 10 and 12 of Regulation No 1612/68.

* * *

60 Even though R and her first husband have meanwhile divorced, it is apparent from the file that he continues to pursue an activity as an employed person in the United Kingdom and therefore enjoys the status of a worker who is a national of one Member State and who is employed in the territory of another Member State for the purposes of Articles 1 and 10 of Regulation No 1612/68.

* * *

62 The fact that the children of R's first husband do not live permanently with him does not affect the rights which they derive from Articles 10 and 12 of Regulation No 1612/68. In providing that a member of a migrant worker's family has the right to install himself with the worker, Article 10 of that regulation does not require that the member of the family in question must live permanently with the worker, but, as is clear from Article 10(3), only that the accommodation which the worker has available must be such as may be considered normal for the purpose of accommodating his family.

63 In the light of the foregoing, the answer to the first question must be that children of a citizen of the European Union who have installed themselves in a Member State during the exercise by their parent of rights of residence as a migrant worker in that Member State are entitled to reside there in order to attend general educational courses there, pursuant to Article 12 of Regulation No 1612/68. The fact that the parents of the children concerned have meanwhile divorced, the fact that only one parent is a citizen of the Union and that parent has ceased to be a migrant worker in the host Member State and the fact that the children are not themselves citizens of the Union are irrelevant in this regard.

64 By its second question, the national tribunal seeks essentially to ascertain whether, where children have the right to reside in a host Member State in order to attend general educational courses pursuant to Article 12 of Regulation No 1612/68, that provision must be interpreted as entitling the parent who is the primary carer of those children, irrespective of his nationality, to reside with them in order to facilitate the exercise of that right notwithstanding the fact that the parents have meanwhile divorced or that the parent who has the status of citizen of the European Union has ceased to be a migrant worker in the host Member State.

65   According to R and the Baumbast family, the provisions of Community law must be interpreted broadly so that the rights granted are effective, particularly where a right as fundamental as the right to family life is concerned. They thus submit that, in the case of minor children who have spent all their life living with their mother and continue to do so, the refusal to afford her a right of residence during the continuation of the children's education is an interference with their rights which impairs the exercise of those rights. They also submit that such a refusal is a disproportionate interference with family life, contrary to Article 8 of the European Convention for the Protection of Human Rights and Fundamental Freedoms.

[The UK, supported by the Commission, argued that no derivative right of residence should be accorded to the mothers.]

68   First, Article 12 of Regulation No 1612/68 and the rights which flow from it must be interpreted in the context of the structure and purpose of that regulation. It is apparent* * *that in order to facilitate the movement of members of workers' families the Council took into account, first, the importance for the worker, from a human point of view, of having his entire family with him and, secondly, the importance, from all points of view, of the integration of the worker and his family into the host Member State without any difference in treatment in relation to nationals of that State.

71   In circumstances such as those of the main proceedings, where the children enjoy, under Article 12 of Regulation No 1612/68, the right to continue their education in the host Member State * * *, it is clear that if those parents were refused the right to remain in the host Member State during the period of their children's education that might deprive those children of a right which is granted to them by the Community legislature.

72   Moreover, * * * Regulation No 1612/68 must be interpreted in the light of the requirement of respect for family life laid down in Article 8 of the European Convention. That requirement is one of the fundamental rights which, according to settled case-law, are recognised by Community law.

73   The right conferred by Article 12 of Regulation No 1612/68 on the child of a migrant worker to pursue, under the best possible conditions, his education in the host Member State necessarily implies that that child has the right to be accompanied by the person who is his primary carer and, accordingly, that that person is able to reside with him in that Member State during his studies. To refuse to grant permission to remain to a parent who is the primary carer of the child exercising his right to pursue his studies in the host Member State infringes that right.

NOTES AND QUESTIONS

1. The Court's judgment in *Baumbast* is certainly an extremely liberal one. Do you agree with the Court that children of a migrant worker have a right of residence while obtaining an education in the host State even after the migrant worker no longer works or has any other right to reside there? Or is this stretching too far the language of article 12 of Regulation 1612/68? May the children reside in the UK while pursuing post-graduate education? If the children should become employed in the UK during the period of education, does article 10 grant them a further right of residence? Does it make a difference whether a child has the nationality of a Member State, or not?

2. Do you agree with the Court that the two mothers should enjoy a right of residence derived from that of the children? If R's ex-husband had the custody of their children and she only enjoyed a right of visitation, should she be entitled to reside in the UK? If the children finish their education at age 18, would their mothers' right of residence end at that point? (For Baumbast's own right of residence in the UK as a citizen of the Union, see page 639 infra.)

3. In Eind v. Minister voor Vreemdelingenzaken, Case C–291/05, [2007] ECR I–10719, the Court recognized that a migrant worker's right to return to his home State carried derivative rights for members of his family. While Eind, a Dutch national, worked in the UK, his 11 year old daughter, a Surinamese national, joined him and received a UK resident permit. When Eind and his daughter returned to the Netherlands, the immigration authorities denied her a residence permit. In an ECT Article 234 reference proceeding, the Court held that a worker's willingness to be employed in a host State could be deterred if family members could not return with him to his home State, even if the family members first joined the migrant in the host State (¶¶ 39–40). The Court cited *Baumbast*, and referred to "the importance of ensuing protection for the family life" of migrant workers (¶ 44).

C. ARTICLE 39'S EXCEPTIONS TO FREE MOVEMENT

1. THE PUBLIC POLICY AND PUBLIC SECURITY EXCEPTIONS

ECT Article 39(3) allows Member States to limit the right of free movement on grounds of public policy, public security or public health. In order to give substantive content to these terms, as well as to set procedural safeguards, in 1964 the Council adopted Directive 64/221 (Document 15 in the Selected Documents), which merits careful reading. The comprehensive Directive 2004/38 on residence rights, described in Chapter 16, essentially replicates the terms of Directive 64/221, repealed in 2006.

Directive 64/221 applies both to self-employed persons and to workers, as well as their family members. It covers situations where a State invokes public policy, public security or public health either to deny entry, to deny the issuance or renewal of a residence permit, or to expel a person (art. 2). Important substantive limits placed upon a State's recourse to Article 39(3) include requiring a State to take action on public policy or public security "exclusively on the personal conduct of the individual concerned," and forbidding action based exclusively on past criminal convictions (art. 3). As for public health, a State may not refuse entry or a residence permit except for a disability or disease listed on an annex, and a State may never expel a person for a disability or disease occurring after he or she has received a residence permit (art. 4).

Procedural rights granted by Directive 64/221 include notice to the person concerned of the grounds for the adverse decision "unless this is contrary to the interests or the security of the State involved" (art. 6); a right of administrative recourse (art. 8); and some form of judicial or administrative appeal (art. 9).

There have been a surprising number of cases interpreting the concept of public policy and the procedural rights outlined in Directive 64/221. States have a natural tendency to invoke the rather vague concept of public policy in order to expel or otherwise restrict individuals whose views or conduct are considered inimical to the public interest. The Court of Justice has been steadily limiting the use of public policy for this purpose and protecting the rights of migrant workers and their families. The Court's respect for basic human rights figures strongly in its judgments, especially in the following landmark case.

RUTILI v. MINISTER FOR THE INTERIOR

Case 36/75, [1975] ECR 1219.

[Rutili, an Italian national, resident in France since his birth, had his residence permit revoked in 1968 because of his alleged leftist trade union activities and participation in the May 1968 riots. French authorities granted him an EEC residence permit in 1970, but with a restriction preventing him from living in Alsace–Lorraine, his customary residence. French law permits barring French nationals from residing in certain regions after conviction of serious crimes or during a state of emergency. Rutili sued to challenge the restriction placed on his residence permit and the administrative court referred several questions to the Court of Justice.]

8   The first question asks whether the expression "subject to limitations justified on grounds of public policy" in Article [39] of the Treaty concerns only the legislative decisions which each Member State has decided to take in order to limit within its territory the freedom of movement and residence for nationals of other Member States or whether it also concerns individual decisions taken in application of such legislative provisions.

* * *

17   Inasmuch as the object of the provisions of the Treaty and of second-
      ary legislation is to regulate the situation of individuals and to ensure
      their protection, it is also for the national courts to examine whether
      individual decisions are compatible with the relevant provisions of
      Community law.

                              * * *

19   This conclusion is based in equal measure on due respect for the rights
      of the nationals of Member States, which are directly conferred by the
      Treaty and by Regulation No 1612/68, and the express provision in
      Article 3 of Directive No 64/221 which requires that measures taken
      on grounds of public policy or of public security "shall be based
      exclusively on the personal conduct of the individual concerned".

20   It is all the more necessary to adopt this view of the matter inasmuch
      as national legislation concerned with the protection of public policy
      and security usually reserves to the national authorities discretionary
      powers which might well escape all judicial review if the courts were
      unable to extend their consideration to individual decisions taken
      pursuant to the reservation contained in Article [39(3)] of the Treaty.

                              * * *

22   The second question asks what is the precise meaning to be attributed
      to the word "justified" in the phrase "subject to limitations justified
      on grounds of public policy" in Article [39(3)] of the Treaty.

23   In that provision, the words "limitations justified" mean that only
      limitations which fulfil the requirements of the law, including those
      contained in Community law, are permissible with regard, in particu-
      lar, to the right of nationals of Member States to freedom of move-
      ment and residence.

24   In this context, regard must be had both to the rules of substantive
      law and to the formal or procedural rules subject to which Member
      States exercise the powers reserved under Article [39(3)].

                              * * *

*Justification of Measures Adopted on Grounds of Public Policy From
the Point of View of Substantive Law*

26   By virtue of the reservation contained in Article [39(3)], Member
      States continue to be, in principle, free to determine the requirements
      of public policy in the light of their national needs.

27   Nevertheless, the concept of public policy must, in the Community
      context * * *, be interpreted strictly, so that its scope cannot be
      determined unilaterally by each Member State without being subject
      to control by the institutions of the Community.

28   Accordingly, restrictions cannot be imposed on the right of a national
      of any Member State to enter the territory of another Member State,

to stay there and to move within it unless his presence or conduct constitutes a genuine and sufficiently serious threat to public policy.

29   In this connexion Article 3 of Directive No 64/221 imposes on Member States the duty to base their decision on the individual circumstances of any person under the protection of Community law and not on general considerations.

30   Moreover, Article 2 of the same directive provides that grounds of public policy shall not be put to improper use by being "invoked to service economic ends".

31   Nor, under Article 8 of Regulation No 1612/68, which ensures equality of treatment as regards membership of trade unions and the exercise of rights attaching thereto, may the reservation relating to public policy be invoked on grounds arising from the exercise of those rights.

32   Taken as a whole, these limitations placed on the powers of Member States in respect of control of aliens are a specific manifestation of the more general principle, enshrined in Articles 8, 9, 10 and 11 of the Convention for the Protection of Human Rights and Fundamental Freedoms, signed in Rome on 4 November 1950 and ratified by all the Member States, and in Article 2 of Protocol No 4 of the same Convention, signed in Strasbourg on 16 September 1963, which provide, in identical terms, that no restrictions in the interests of national security or public safety shall be placed on the rights secured by the above-quoted articles other than such as are necessary for the protection of those interests "in a democratic society."

Measures Adopted on Grounds of Public Policy: Justification From the Procedural Point of View

[The Court cited the procedural safeguards detailed in articles 6, 8 and 9 of the directive.]

37   [A]ny person enjoying the protection of the provisions quoted must be entitled to a double safeguard comprising notification to him of the grounds on which any restrictive measure has been adopted in his case and the availability of a right of appeal.

38   It is appropriate to state also that all steps must be taken by the Member States to ensure that this double safeguard is in fact available to anyone against whom a restrictive measure has been adopted.

39   In particular, this requirement means that the State concerned must, when notifying an individual of a restrictive measure adopted in his case, give him a precise and comprehensive statement of the grounds for the decision, to enable him to take effective steps to prepare his defense.

The Justification for, in Particular, a Prohibition on Residence in Part of the National Territory

41   [T]he Government of the French Republic stated that such measures may be taken in the case of its own nationals either in the case of

certain criminal convictions, as an additional penalty, or following the declaration of a state of emergency.

* * *

49   [I]n the case of partial prohibitions on residence, limited to certain areas of the territory, persons covered by Community law must, under Article [12] of the Treaty* * *be treated on a footing of equality with the nationals of the Member State concerned.

50   It follows that a Member State cannot, in the case of a national of another Member State covered by the provisions of the Treaty, impose prohibitions on residence which are territorially limited except in circumstances where such prohibitions may be imposed on its own nationals.

NOTES AND QUESTIONS

1.   *Rutili* is a leading precedent on the direct effect of ECT Article 39 and Directive 64/221. *Rutili* is also a leading basic rights case in its application of the 1950 European Human Rights Convention, and is frequently cited for its emphasis on protecting human rights in a democratic society. For discussion of Community basic rights protection, see Chapter 6.

2.   Why is it important that the Court held "public policy" to have a Community law content rather than one based on national law concepts? Note the Court's emphasis on the procedural rights granted by Directive 64/221. In view of the Court's "equal treatment" analysis, may France bar Rutili from living in Alsace–Lorraine? See ¶ 41.

3.   In Commission v. Spain (Private security firms), Case C–114/97, [1998] I–6717, the issue was whether Spain could justifiably require that all managers and staff of private security firms (i.e., enterprises engaged in the protection of persons or property, or the installation and maintenance of surveillance and alarm systems) must be Spanish nationals. The Court held that private security firms were not engaged in ensuring public security and that Article 39(3) could not be used to exclude a private economic sector from the duty of non-discrimination on the basis of nationality.

4.   What is the meaning of the "personal conduct" requirement in article 3 of Directive 64/221? In Bonsignore v. Oberstadtsdirektor Köln, Case 67/74, [1975] ECR 297, Bonsignore, an Italian worker, accidentally killed his brother with a pistol for which he had no permit. Although he was found guilty of negligent homicide, no penalty was imposed. The German authorities apparently sought to deport Bonsignore as a warning to others, even though there appeared to be no risk that he would repeat his conduct. In a preliminary reference proceeding, the Court held that "a deportation order may only be made for breaches of the peace and public security which might be committed by the individual affected." Id. at 307. The Court rejected any deportation "for the purpose of deterring other aliens." Ibid.

However, in Regina v. Bouchereau, Case 30/77, [1977] ECR 1999, Bouchereau, a French auto mechanic residing in London, was convicted twice for possessing small quantities of illegal drugs (marijuana and "pep" pills) for personal use. A deportation proceeding gave rise to a preliminary reference. Although the Court cited Directive 64/221's language that "previous criminal convictions" are not as such sufficient to warrant deportation, the Court stated that the convictions could be considered as evidence of personal conduct which might constitute a "propensity to act in the same way in the future." Id. at 2013. The Court was perhaps influenced by Advocate General Warner's argument that an alien's conduct can cause "such deep public revulsion" that he can be deported, just as a houseguest may be thrown out for offensive behavior. Id. at 2022.

ADOUI v. BELGIUM

Cases 115 & 116/81, [1982] ECR 1665.

[Adoui and Cornuaille, French citizens, were refused residence permits in Liège, Belgium on public policy grounds. They worked as bar waitresses, allegedly scantily dressed, and on occasion would entertain customers privately. A 1948 Belgian law prohibited brothels, pimping and public solicitation, but not prostitution itself. The city of Liège prohibited streetwalking and public displays by prostitutes, but not prostitution. Adoui and Cornuaille appealed the refusal of residence permits and the national court made a preliminary reference.]

5   [The initial question is] whether a Member State may, by virtue of the reservations contained in [Article 39], expel from its territory a national of another Member State or deny him access to that territory by reason of activities which, when attributable to the former State's own nationals, do not give rise to repressive measures.

6   [P]rostitution as such is not prohibited by Belgian legislation, although the Law does prohibit certain incidental activities, which are particularly harmful from the social point of view, such as the exploitation of prostitution by third parties and various forms of incitement to debauchery.

7   The reservations contained in [Article 39] permit Member States to adopt, with respect to the nationals of other Member States * * *, measures which they cannot apply to their own nationals, inasmuch as they have no authority to expel the latter from the national territory or to deny them access thereto.* * *

8   [R]eliance by a national authority upon the concept of public policy presupposes the existence of * * * * "a genuine and sufficiently serious threat affecting one of the fundamental interests of society". Although Community law does not impose upon the Member States a uniform scale of values as regards the assessment of conduct which may be considered as contrary to public policy, it should nevertheless be stated that conduct may not be considered as being of a sufficiently serious nature to justify restrictions on the admission to or residence within the territory of a Member State of a national of another Member State in a case where the former Member State does not adopt, with respect

to the same conduct on the part of its own nationals, repressive measures or other genuine and effective measures intended to combat such conduct.

* * *

10 In the tenth question, the national court asks whether the action taken by a Member State which, "anxious to remove from its territory prostitutes from a given country because they could promote criminal activities, does so systematically, declaring that their business of prostitution endangers the requirements of public policy and not taking the trouble to consider whether the persons concerned may or may not be suspected of contact with the 'underworld' ", constitutes a measure of a general preventive nature within the meaning of Article 3 of Directive No 64/221.

11 Article 3(1) of the directive provides that measures taken on grounds of public policy or of public security are to be based exclusively on the personal conduct of the individual concerned. In that regard it is sufficient to refer to the judgment [in *Bonsignore,* supra], in which the Court held that "measures adopted on grounds of public policy and for the maintenance of public security against the nationals of Member States of the Community cannot be justified on grounds extraneous to the individual case" * * *.

NOTES AND QUESTIONS

1. What does the Court mean when it speaks of the need for a State to "adopt, with respect to the same conduct on the part of its nationals, repressive measures or other genuine and effective measures intended to combat such conduct"? May deportation be ordered for conduct that a State deems socially undesirable, or must the conduct be illegal? Must the State actively enforce the law against the illegal conduct? Concretely, may Belgium expel Adoui? May a State that makes the use of marijuana illegal, but does not systematically enforce the law, deport a migrant worker who habitually uses marijuana?

ORFANOPOULOS v. LAND BADEN–WURTTEMBERG

Case C–482/01, [2004] ECR I–5257.

[German law enables the expulsion of a non-national after he has been sentenced to imprisonment after a violation of the narcotics laws, but requires "serious grounds of public security" if the offender has a family relation with a German national. A Greek national, Orfanopoulos, is married to a German spouse, with three children. He is a drug addict, only occasionally employed, and has been convicted nine times for narcotics offences and acts of violence. While imprisoned, in 2001, an administrative tribunal ordered his expulsion to Greece, citing his past offences and the real risk of future ones, due to his drug addiction. An appellate body asked the Court whether the expulsion was possible under ECT Article 39 and Directive 64/221.]

92   In the present case, it seems, at first sight, that in spite of family circumstances being taken into account, the system of expulsion described in the order for reference contains an element of automatism or, in any event, a presumption that the person should be expelled. [The Court cites specific provisions of the German law.]

93   If the system in question does indeed have such an effect, that means that the expulsion of a national of another Member State who has received a particular sentence for specific offences is ordered, in spite of family considerations being taken into account, on the basis of a presumption that that national must be expelled, without proper account being taken of his personal conduct or of the danger he represents for the requirements of public policy.

94   [S]uch a system is contrary to Article 39 EC and Article 3 of Directive 64/221.

95   So far as the question referred by the national court is concerned, it must be pointed out that the examination on a case-by-case basis by the national authorities of whether there is personal conduct constituting a present threat to the requirements of public policy and, if necessary, of where lies the fair balance between the legitimate interests in issue must be made in compliance with the general principles of Community law.

96   It is for the competent national authority to take into account, in its assessment of where lies the fair balance between the legitimate interests in issue, the particular legal position of persons subject to Community law and of the fundamental nature of the principle of the free movement of persons [citing *Bouchereau*].

97   Moreover, it is necessary to take into account the fundamental rights whose observance the Court ensures. Reasons of public interest may be invoked to justify a national measure which is likely to obstruct the exercise of the freedom of movement for workers only if the measure in question takes account of such rights.

98   [T]he importance of ensuring the protection of the family life of Community nationals in order to eliminate obstacles to the exercise of the fundamental freedoms guaranteed by the Treaty has been recognised under Community law. It is clear that the removal of a person from the country where close members of his family are living may amount to an infringement of the right to respect for family life as guaranteed by Article 8 of the ECHR, which is among the fundamental rights, which, according to the Court's settled case-law, are protected in Community law.

99   Finally, the necessity of observing the principle of proportionality must be emphasised. To assess whether the interference envisaged is proportionate to the legitimate aim pursued, in this instance the

protection of public policy, account must be taken, particularly, of the nature and seriousness of the offences committed by the person concerned, the length of his residence in the host Member State, the period which has elapsed since the commission of the offence, the family circumstances of the person concerned and the seriousness of the difficulties which the spouse and any of their children risk facing in the country of origin of the person concerned [citing an ECHR judgment].

NOTES AND QUESTIONS

1. This case demonstrates the difficulty confronting a national tribunal in deciding when a non-national drug-addict can be expelled. The Court's ¶¶ 97–99 certainly suggest that someone married with a family should not be deported. Would you agree? In contrast, can one infer that an addict without a family could be deported on this record of offences? Although the Court cites *Bouchereau* in ¶ 96, do you think a consumer of small amounts of marijuana and 'pep pills' could be deported in view of ¶ 99?

2. THE EXCEPTION FOR PUBLIC SERVICE

The term "public service" is unfortunately an ambiguous one, differing significantly in scope among the various Member States. Should it be given a Community sense? Should it be interpreted broadly or restrictively? Should it cover only employees of the national government, or also employees of regional and local government? What about employees of State-owned post offices, utilities, railroads, or commercial enterprises?

COMMISSION v. BELGIUM

(Public service I)
Case 149/79, [1980] ECR 3881.

[The Commission brought a Treaty infringement action against Belgium because it required Belgian citizenship for employment in certain posts with the city of Brussels and other local governments, and with the Belgian national railways. Belgium argued that its Constitution allowed only Belgian nationals to be admitted to State civil and military posts.]

10 Article [39(4)] removes from the ambit of Article [39(1) to (3)] a series of posts which involve direct or indirect participation in the exercise of powers conferred by public law and duties designed to safeguard the general interests of the State or of other public authorities. Such posts in fact presume on the part of those occupying them the existence of a special relationship of allegiance to the State and reciprocity of rights and duties which form the foundation of the bond of nationality.

11 * * * [D]etermining the sphere of application of Article [39(4)] raises special difficulties since in the various Member States authorities acting under powers conferred by public law have assumed responsi-

bilities of an economic and social nature or are involved in activities which are not identifiable with the functions which are typical of the public service yet which by their nature still come under the sphere of application of the Treaty. In these circumstances the effect of extending the exception contained in Article [39(4)] to posts * * * which do not involve any association with tasks belonging to the public service properly so called, would be to remove a considerable number of posts from the ambit of the principles set out in the Treaty and to create inequalities between Member States according to the different ways in which the State and certain sectors of economic life are organized.

12   * * * [There are] problems of appraisal and demarcation in specific cases. [The proper] classification depends on whether or not the posts in question are typical of the specific activities of the public service in so far as the exercise of powers conferred by public law and responsibility for safeguarding the general interests of the State are vested in it.

13   Where, in the case of posts which, although offered by public authorities, are not within the sphere to which Article [39(4)] applies,* * *a worker from another Member State [cannot]be debarred from those posts simply on the grounds of his nationality.

* * *

16   The Belgian Government further [cites] Article 6 of the Belgian Constitution by which "Belgians * * * only shall be admitted to civil and military posts save in special cases for which exception may be made" [and similar provisions in other states' constitutions]. The Belgian Government has itself stated that it does not deny that "Community rules override national rules" but it believes that the similarity between the constitutional laws of those Member States should be used as an aid to interpretation to cast light on the meaning of Article [39(4)]* * *.

* * *

19   [R]ecourse to provisions of the domestic legal systems to restrict the scope of the provisions of Community law would have the effect of impairing the unity and efficacy of that law and consequently cannot be accepted. That rule, which is fundamental to the existence of the Community, must also apply in determining the scope and bounds of Article [39(4)] of the Treaty.

NOTES AND QUESTIONS

1. Note that Belgium did not challenge the primacy of Community law over its Constitution. Belgium argued instead that common constitutional traditions in several States should help in the interpretation of "public service." Why isn't it appropriate to look to common constitutional traditions for this purpose, even though the Court does look to such traditions in developing a Community doctrine of fundamental rights?

2.   Is the Court's test in ¶¶ 10–12 for deciding when employment falls in the public service too broad or too narrow or about right? Does it open many posts in State employment to migrant workers? The Court instructed the Commission and Belgium to apply its test to the contested posts, but they were unable to agree, so the issue returned to the Court in Commission v. Belgium (Public service II), Case 149/79, [1982] ECR 1845. After reviewing factual material provided with regard to the nature of the posts, the Court held that nurses, electricians, and gardeners employed by local governments, and drivers, signalmen, canteen staff, workshop hands and nightwatchmen employed by the State railway, were not engaged in public service employment. On the other hand, architects and supervisors employed by local governments were to be considered as employed in the public service.

3.   In Commission v. France (Status of nurses), Case 307/84, [1986] ECR 1725, France permitted foreign nationals to take temporary employment as nurses in public hospitals, but denied them permanent employment. The Commission contended that Community nationals should be allowed such permanent employment. At the time, 89,000 nurses were employed in French public hospitals, of whom about 150 were foreigners. Should public hospital nurses be considered to be employed in the public service?

4.   In a March 1988 statement, the Commission urged Member States to remove nationality restrictions for posts for which they are generally inappropriate. In the Commission's view, employment in State-owned airlines, public transport, utilities, post and telecommunications, and public health services should not be restricted to nationals. The Commission considered that nationality requirements were appropriate for high State offices, the judiciary, the armed forces, the police and tax authorities. In other sectors, such as regional and local governments and lower national government posts, an examination of the functions required for the post must be made to decide whether a nationality requirement is permissible. Obviously, drawing the line is not an easy task. Do you think the Commission's approach reasonably follows the Court's guidelines, or is it too broadly or narrowly conceived? For a careful analysis, see J. Handoll, Article 48(4) EEC and Non–National Access to Public Employment, 13 Eur.L.Rev. 223 (1988).

5.   In McCarthy v. Philadelphia Civil Service Commission, 424 U.S. 645, 96 S.Ct. 1154, 47 L.Ed.2d 366 (1976), a per curiam opinion of the Supreme Court upheld Philadelphia's requirement that city workers must be residents of the city, holding that the Equal Protection Clause was not applicable to such a rule. Many US cities have such residence requirements for particular categories of employees, notably policemen, firemen and administrative staff. Would similar city residence requirements be permitted by the Court of Justice, or would it consider them to constitute indirect discrimination based on nationality?

One of the largest categories of state employees is that of teachers, from the primary school through the university level. Most Member States have traditionally treated all teachers in public schools as state officials and reserved the position to their own nationals. Whether this was permissible after *Commission v. Belgium* soon became a major issue.

ALLUÉ v. UNIVERSITÀ DI VENEZIA

Case 33/88, [1989] ECR 1591.

[In 1986, the University of Venice, a public university, refused to extend Allué's employment contract as a Spanish language lecturer. She had been employed since 1980, but an Italian decree set six years as the maximum period for the employment of a foreign language instructor. Allué sued to obtain permanent employment, and the national court asked whether the post of foreign language instructor at the university level should be considered to be one in "public service."]

7   [A] teaching post does not involve direct or indirect participation in the exercise of powers conferred by public law and in the discharge of functions whose purpose is to safeguard the general interests of the State or of other public authorities and which therefore require a special relationship of allegiance to the State on the part of persons occupying them and reciprocity of rights and duties which form the foundation of the bond of nationality.

* * *

9   [T]herefore * * * employment as a foreign-language assistant at a university is not employment in the public service within the meaning of Article [39(4)] of the EEC Treaty.

10   [In] the second question the national court seeks essentially to establish whether Article [39(2)] of the EEC Treaty precludes the application of a provision of national law which imposes a limit on the duration of the employment relationship between universities and foreign-language assistants where there is in principle no such limit for other workers.

11   [T]he principle of equal treatment of which Article [39(2)] is one embodiment prohibits not only overt discrimination based on nationality but all covert forms of discrimination which, by applying other distinguishing criteria, in fact achieve the same result * * *.

12   [A]lthough it applies regardless of the nationality of the worker concerned, the time-limit imposed by the legislation in question on working as a foreign-language assistant in a university essentially concerns workers who are nationals of other Member States. According to the statistics supplied by the Italian Government, only 25% of foreign-language assistants are Italian nationals.

13   In order to justify the legislation at issue in the main proceedings, the Italian Government claims that it is the only means of ensuring that universities have foreign-language assistants with an up-to-date knowledge and experience of the mother tongue which they teach.

14   [T]he danger of their losing contact with their mother tongue is slight, in the light of the increase in cultural exchanges and improved communications, and in addition it is open to the universities in any event to check the level of assistants' knowledge.

NOTES AND QUESTIONS

1. In Bleis v. Ministère de l'Education Nationale, Case C–4/91, [1991] ECR I–5627, the Court held that secondary school teachers in the French educational system did not constitute a post in "public service." *Allué* and *Bleis* have a far-reaching impact, since States employ hundreds of thousands of teachers in primary, secondary and university level education. Migrant workers may qualify in virtually any educational field, provided of course, they possess the requisite credentials, including the capacity to speak the host State language. May, however, a State reserve administrative or supervisory posts in education, such as principals or deans, to its own nationals?

2. In Commission v. Luxembourg (Public service employment), Case C–473/93, [1996] ECR I–3207, the Court rejected Luxembourg's claim that all posts in public health, the railroad and urban transport, posts and telecommunication, and water, gas and electricity supply required Luxembourg nationality as a rule. Luxembourg made a specific defense of its nationality requirement for teachers, contending that "in order to transmit traditional values," the nationality requirement was an essential condition for preserving Luxembourg's national identity. (¶ 32.) How should the Court react to this argument? Is Luxembourg's policy of hiring only nationals as teachers as justifiable as Ireland's policy of requiring its teachers to speak Irish, discussed in *Groener*, supra?

D. WHO IS A WORKER, SPOUSE OR FAMILY MEMBER?

Thus far we have assumed that we knew what is meant by a worker, a spouse, or a dependent family member. Border-line cases have arisen, however, occasioning some difficulty in defining these terms, and therefore in determining the persons who are entitled to the rights described in ECT Article 39 and Regulation 1612/68.

1. DEFINITION OF A WORKER

LEVIN v. STAATSSECRETARIS VAN JUSTITIE
Case 53/81, [1982] ECR 1035.

[Levin, a UK national and the wife of a non-Community national, applied in 1978 for a Dutch residence permit. When her application was denied because she was not a "worker," Levin then took a low-paying but regular part-time job and reapplied. The Dutch authorities again refused her a residence permit, maintaining that her part-time employment earnings were insufficient for self-support and that her true motive was improper, since it was really to enable her husband to live in the Netherlands. On appeal, a preliminary reference was made.]

6   In its first and second questions, * * * the national court is essentially asking whether the provisions of Community law relating to freedom of

movement for workers also cover a national of a Member State whose activity as an employed person in the territory of another Member State provides him with an income less than the minimum required for subsistence within the meaning of the legislation of the second Member State. In particular the court asks whether those provisions cover such a person where he either supplements his income from his activity as an employed person with other income so as to arrive at that minimum or is content with means of support which fall below it.

* * *

9   [T]he terms "worker" and "activity as an employed person" are not expressly defined [in the Treaty or any legislation]. It is appropriate, therefore, in order to determine their meaning, to have recourse to the generally recognized principles of interpretation, beginning with the ordinary meaning to be attributed to those terms in their context and in the light of the objectives of the Treaty.

10   The Netherlands and Danish Governments have maintained that the provisions of Article [39] may only be relied upon by persons who receive a wage at least commensurate with the means of subsistence considered as necessary by the legislation of the Member State in which they work, or who work at least for the number of hours considered as usual in respect of full-time employment in the sector in question. * * *

11   That argument cannot, however, be accepted. As the Court has already stated in Case 75/63 *Hoekstra,* [1964] ECR 1977, the terms "worker" and "activity as an employed person" may not be defined by reference to the national laws of the Member States but have a Community meaning. If that were not the case, the Community rules on freedom of movement for workers would be frustrated, as the meaning of those terms could be fixed and modified unilaterally, without any control by the Community institutions, by national laws which would thus be able to exclude at will certain categories of persons from the benefit of the Treaty.

12   Such would, in particular, be the case if the enjoyment of the rights conferred by the principle of freedom of movement for workers could be made subject to the criterion of what the legislation of the host State declares to be a minimum wage, so that the field of application *ratione personae* of the Community rules on this subject might vary from one Member State to another. The meaning and the scope of the terms "worker" and "activity as an employed person" should thus be clarified in the light of the principles of the legal order of the Community.

13   In this respect it must be stressed that these concepts define the field of application of one of the fundamental freedoms guaranteed by the Treaty and, as such, may not be interpreted restrictively.

* * *

15 * * * Since part-time employment, although it may provide an income lower than what is considered to be the minimum required for subsistence, constitutes for a large number of persons an effective means of improving their living conditions, the effectiveness of Community law would be impaired and the achievement of the objectives of the Treaty would be jeopardized if the enjoyment of rights conferred by the principle of freedom of movement for workers were reserved solely to persons engaged in full-time employment * * *.

16 It follows that the concepts of "worker" and "activity as an employed person" must be interpreted as meaning that the rules relating to freedom of movement for workers also concern persons who pursue or wish to pursue an activity as an employed person on a part-time basis only and who, by virtue of that fact obtain or would obtain only remuneration lower than the minimum guaranteed remuneration in the sector under consideration. In this regard no distinction may be made between those who wish to make do with their income from such an activity and those who supplement that income with other income, whether the latter is derived from property or from the employment of a member of their family who accompanies them.

17 It should however be stated that whilst part-time employment is not excluded from the field of application of the rules on freedom of movement for workers, those rules cover only the pursuit of effective and genuine activities, [but not] activities on such a small scale as to be regarded as purely marginal and ancillary.

* * *

19 The third question essentially seeks to ascertain whether the right to enter and reside in the territory of a Member State may be denied to a worker whose main objectives * * * are different from that of the pursuit of an activity as an employed person * * *.

20 Under Article [39(3)] of the Treaty the right to move freely within the territory of the Member States is conferred upon workers for the "purpose" of accepting offers of employment actually made. By virtue of the same provision workers enjoy the right to stay in one of the Member States "for the purpose" of employment there.

* * *

21 However, these formulations merely [indicate] that the advantages which Community law confers in the name of that freedom may be relied upon only by persons who actually pursue or seriously wish to pursue activities as employed persons * * *.

22 Once this condition is satisfied, the motives which may have prompted the worker to seek employment in the Member State concerned are of no account and must not be taken into consideration.

NOTES AND QUESTIONS

1. Why is it important that "worker" have a Community law sense rather than a meaning based on national law concepts? Note the Court's emphasis in *Levin* on giving the term a broad meaning because freedom of movement of workers is a fundamental freedom. In this context, do you agree that a person's motive in taking employment is unimportant? Concretely, assume that Levin moved to the Netherlands and took a trivial part-time job only to enable her husband, who is not a Community national, to obtain an EEC residence permit there, when the UK would not have granted him a residence permit. Do you agree with the Court that both Levin and her husband should obtain rights of residence under Article 39?

2. Observe the social and economic importance of *Levin*. Any person who works part-time in "effective and genuine activities" has a right to residence in the host State. The Netherlands, supported by Denmark, had argued that only persons who earned a minimum wage for subsistence should qualify as workers. These two States were probably concerned that their reputation for being agreeable places to live might attract persons who lack substantial means of support and who choose to earn little in order to enjoy maximum leisure. States may fear that such persons pay low taxes and are not likely to be very productive economic participants in society, yet may become a substantial burden on the public health and social security systems. If this concern is a valid one (which is a debatable proposition), do you consider the right of free movement important enough to outweigh it? Note in the next chapter that the 1990 directives on rights of residence for students, retired persons and the unemployed require that such persons have sufficient resources to avoid becoming a burden on the host State.

3. *Levin* creates a *de minimis* rule for part-time workers, excluding "marginal and ancillary" activities. Presumably babysitting for two hours a week would not qualify one for worker status. There are, however, several interesting cases on the borderline.

In Kempf v. Staatssecretaris van Justitie, Case 139/85, [1986] ECR 1741, a German musician resided in the Netherlands for a year. He worked initially as a part-time music teacher, giving twelve lessons a week, and earning less than $500 per month. Because of low earnings, he received public assistance benefits. He later became ill and unable to work, receiving health, unemployment and public assistance benefits. At this point, his application for an EEC residence permit was refused. On appeal, the court asked the Court of Justice whether a person whose part-time earnings have to be supplemented by public assistance funds can be considered a worker. What would you answer?

In Steymann v. Staatssecretaris van Justitie, Case 196/87, [1988] ECR 6159, a German member of the Bhagwan sect lived in the sect's community center in the Netherlands. The sect provided him with food, clothing and housing. He engaged in cleaning, plumbing and other household tasks, as well as working in the sect's disco-lounge, but received only pocket-money for minor personal expenses. In an Article 234 reference, the Court held that

Steymann satisfied the *Lawrie–Blum* criteria for a worker and was entitled to a residence permit.

In contrast, in Trojani v. Centre Public d'Aide Sociale, Case C–456/02, [2004] ECR I–7573, Trojani, a French national, lived in a Salvation Army hostel where he worked in odd jobs for 30 hours a week and received a room, meals and pocket money as part of a socio-occupational reintegration program. Considering that he did not qualify as a worker, Belgian authorities denied him a minimum subsistence allowance. In a reference, the Court held that the national court should determine whether Trojani's work could be considered "part of the normal labour market," in order to decide whether his work constituted "real and genuine" employment (¶¶ 23–24). In contrast, if the national court should decide that his work represented "merely a means of rehabilitation," then it would not satisfy the "real and genuine" condition.

LAIR v. UNIVERSITAT HANOVER
Case 39/86, [1988] ECR 3161.

[Lair, a French national, became a student in 1984 at the University of Hanover, studying German and Romance languages and literature. Her request for state financial aid to cover tuition and living expenses was denied because Germany provides such aid only to German nationals, the children of migrant workers, and to migrant workers who have been regularly employed in Germany for the previous five years. Lair had worked in Germany as a bank clerk for two years. After her dismissal, she had only brief periods of employment for the next three years. When she sued to obtain the aid, an appellate court inquired whether Lair qualified as a "worker."]

The concept of worker

31 Although [Article 39 and Regulation 1612/68] do not provide an express answer to [the] question, there is nevertheless a basis in Community law for the view that the rights guaranteed to migrant workers do not necessarily depend on the actual or continuing existence of an employment relationship.

* * *

33 Persons who have previously pursued in the host Member State an effective and genuine activity as an employed person as defined by the Court [citing *Levin*] but who are no longer employed are nevertheless considered to be workers under certain provisions of Community law.

[The Court cited Directive 68/360, supra page 584, and Commission Regulation 1251/70, supra page 562, each of which grant workers certain rights to continued residence in the host State after ceasing employment.]

35 Furthermore, Article 7(3) of Regulation No 1612/68 guarantees migrant workers access, by virtue of the same right and under the same conditions as national workers, to training in vocational schools and retraining centres. That right to specific training, guaranteed by

Community legislation, does not depend on the continued existence of an employment relationship.

36   It is therefore clear that migrant workers are guaranteed certain rights linked to the status of worker even when they are no longer in an employment relationship.

37   [S]uch a link between the status of worker and * * * the pursuit of university studies does, however, presuppose some continuity between the previous occupational activity and the course of study; there must be a relationship between the purpose of the studies and the previous occupational activity. Such continuity may not, however, be required where a migrant has involuntarily become unemployed and is obliged by conditions on the job market to undertake occupational retraining in another field of activity.

38   Such a conception of freedom of movement for migrant workers corresponds, moreover, to current developments in careers. Continuous careers are less common than was formerly the case. Occupational activities are therefore occasionally interrupted by periods of training or retraining.

39   The answer to the [referred] question should therefore be that a national of another Member State who has undertaken university studies in the host State leading to a professional qualification, after having engaged in occupational activity in that State, must be regarded as having retained his status as a worker and is entitled as such to the benefit of Article 7(2) of Regulation No 1612/68 * * *.

[The Court concluded by rejecting an argument that the prior employment in Germany must have been pursued for some minimum period of time, striking down Germany's condition of five years' employment.]

NOTES AND QUESTIONS

1.   Do you agree that a migrant worker who voluntarily gives up employment in order to pursue higher education should still be considered a worker for the purpose of securing equal treatment in the receipt of financial aid for the studies? How will studying German and Romance languages and literature enhance Lair's credentials for future employment?

2.   Ninni–Orasche is an Italian national, legally resident in Austria as the wife of an Austrian. In 1995 she worked for ten weeks as a waitress-cashier under a fixed term contract. In 1996 she began studying Romance languages at an Austrian university. In an appeal from the authorities' denial of financial aid, the Austrian court inquired whether she qualified as a worker, which would usually entitle her to aid. Citing *Levin* and *Lair*, the Court held that the period of work was sufficiently long to qualify her as a worker, and that the fact that it was a fixed-term contract was irrelevant so long as the work was real and genuine. Ninni–Orasche v. Bundesminister fur Wissenschaft, Case C–413/01, [2003] ECR I–13187.

3.   Can there be a 'reverse frontier worker?' In Hartmann v. Freistaat Bayern, Case C–212/05, [2007] ECR I–6303, a German national working in

Germany moved to Austria to reside with his Austrian spouse. When Mrs. Hartmann was refused a German child raising allowance, in an Article 234 reference the Court held that Hartmann qualified as a frontier migrant worker (¶¶ 18–20). The Commission had supported Germany in arguing the contrary. The Court then held that the child-raising allowance constituted a 'social advantage' to which Mrs. Hartmann was entitled, derivatively from her husband.

2. DEFINITION OF "SPOUSE" AND "DEPENDENT"

Issues have also arisen as to the ability of a person to claim the status of a spouse or dependent under Regulation 1612/68. To resolve these issues, the Court of Justice has had, to some extent, to concern itself with family law.

THE NETHERLANDS v. REED

Case 59/85, [1986] ECR 1283.

[Ms. Reed, a UK national, lived since 1981 with Mr. W, an unmarried UK national, who worked and resided in the Netherlands. Although not herself a worker, she obtained a residence permit in 1982. Her application for a renewal was denied, because she was neither a worker nor the spouse of a worker. When she sued, the court held that an unmarried companion should be treated as a spouse under Regulation 1612/68. The appellate court affirmed, but on the principle of nondiscrimination, since under Dutch administrative rules the unmarried companion of a Dutch national would receive a residence permit, provided the two persons live together as one household and possess adequate housing and means of support. The supreme court referred questions to the Court of Justice.]

9 Miss Reed argues that, in the light of legal and social developments, in applying Article 10 of Regulation No 1612/68, and in particular the word "spouse" in that article, * * * unmarried companions must in so far as is possible be treated as spouses.

10 The Netherlands Government points out that [Article 10 must] be interpreted in the Community context. The Community legislature used the word "spouse" in the sense given to that word in family law. When, in support of a dynamic interpretation, reference is made to developments in social and legal conceptions, those developments must be visible in the whole of the Community; such an argument cannot be based on social and legal developments in only one or a few Member States. There is no reason, therefore, to give the term "spouse" an interpretation which goes beyond the legal implications of that term, which embrace rights and obligations which do not exist between unmarried companions.

11 The Commission points out that there is no provision of Community law which defines the terms "spouse" and "marital relations". In the

Community as it now stands it is impossible to speak of any consensus that unmarried companions should be treated as spouses.

* * *

[13] [A]n interpretation given by the Court to a provision of [Regulation 1612/68] has effects in all of the Member States, and any interpretation of a legal term on the basis of social developments must take into account the situation in the whole Community, not merely in one Member State.

* * *

[15] In the absence of any indication of a general social development which would justify a broad construction, * * * it must be held that the term "spouse" in Article 10 of the Regulation refers to a marital relationship only.

* * *

[18] [Miss Reed further argues] that Netherlands policy with regard to the unmarried companions of workers who are nationals of another Member State * * * results in discrimination in relation to Regulation No 1612/68, inasmuch as it authorizes a Netherlands national to bring to the Netherlands a companion of foreign nationality whereas that possibility is not open to a national of another Member State.

* * *

[24] Article 7(2) of Regulation No 1612/68 provides that in the host State a worker who is a national of another Member State must "enjoy the same social and tax advantages as national workers".

* * *

[28] [T]he possibility for a migrant worker of obtaining permission for his unmarried companion to reside with him, where that companion is not a national of the host Member State, can assist his integration in the host State and thus contribute to the achievement of freedom of movement for workers. Consequently, that possibility must also be regarded as falling within the concept of a social advantage for the purposes of Article 7(2) of Regulation No 1612/68.

NOTES AND QUESTIONS

1. While declining to treat Reed as a sort of common-law spouse, the Court of Justice granted her a derivative right of residence through another expansive interpretation of the term "social advantages" in Regulation 1612/68. Do you agree with the Court? Suppose Reed receives her residence permit, but thereafter she and W quarrel and she ceases to be his companion. May the Netherlands then deport Reed? Suppose Reed is the companion of a migrant worker who is a woman? Do the answers to both questions turn on the nondiscrimination principle only?

2. In Diatta v. Land Berlin, Case 267/83, [1985] ECR 567, Diatta, a Senegalese national, married a French national who resided and worked in Berlin. She resided with him from February to August 1978, and then separated from him allegedly with the intention of securing a divorce, but never obtained one. Diatta's application to renew her residence permit was denied because she did not live "with the worker" within the meaning of article 10 of Regulation 1612/68. Replying to questions from the national court, the Court of Justice held that Regulation 1612/68 did not require the spouse of a migrant worker to live with the worker. The Court added that "the marital relationship cannot be regarded as dissolved so long as it has not been terminated by the competent authority." Id. at 590. Do you agree?

3. In a striking indication of the evolution of social views, the comprehensive Directive 2004/38 on residence rights, discussed in Chapter 16, includes as a family member a "partner with whom the Union citizen has contracted a registered partnership," provided the host State treats such partnerships as equivalent to marriage (art. 2(2)). The Directive also grants a continued right of residence to a former spouse after divorce or annulment, and to the former partner after termination of the registered partnership, provided he or she is a national of a Member State, and in some circumstances even if he or she is a third State national (art. 13). The status of an unmarried companion who is not a partner in a registered partnership, or who resides in a State that does not recognize a registered partnership as equivalent to marriage, presumably continues to be controlled by *Reed*. Article 35 of the Directive authorizes Member States measures to combat abuse of rights or fraud, such as a 'marriage of convenience,' entered into only for the purpose of obtaining residence rights.

4. When is a migrant worker's child over 21 still to be considered a dependent with a right of residence under Regulation 1612/68, article 10? In Centre public d'aide sociale v. Lebon, Case 316/85, [1987] ECR 2811, the 25–year–old daughter of a French migrant worker residing in Belgium applied for social welfare assistance. The Court held that a child over 21, not herself a worker, generally is not entitled to rights accorded under Regulation 1612/68. However, a dependent child over 21 would still have the right to social welfare assistance, since this would constitute a "social advantage" for the migrant worker. The Court further held that the test for determining whether a child over 21 is dependent is whether the worker in fact provides the child with basic support, regardless of the motive for the support or whether the child is disabled or otherwise incapable of self-support. Do you agree with the Court?

3. PLAYERS ON PROFESSIONAL SPORTS TEAMS

Many European sports teams (e.g., soccer, football, basketball, hockey) represent cities or countries in various leagues or national or international competitive events. Should Article 39 be applied to set aside the rules of many national or international sports federations which require teams to be exclusively composed of a state's nationals, or limit the number of non-nationals? Are professional sports team players to be considered "workers" in terms of ECT Article 39? Moreover, how can a sports federation or a specific sports team be considered to be bound by Article 39 when they are part of the private sector and the discriminatory rules are not set by State law? All these issues had to be confronted.

Initially, in Walrave v. Union Cycliste Internationale, Case 36/64, [1974] ECR 1405, the Court of Justice held that Article 39 applied to limit not only public authorities, but also any national or international body's rules "aimed at collectively regulating gainful employment and services." Id. at 1421. The Court went on to hold that the rules of an international bicycle riding sports federation could not discriminate against Community nationals in the hiring of employees of bicycle riders. The Court did allow a federation to have rules which allow only nationals as competitors for "sports teams, in particular national teams, the formation of which is a question of purely sporting interest," but did not define "purely sporting interest."

Not surprisingly, sports federations resisted compliance with this case law. The Commission attempted for years to enforce the non-discrimination principle in direct discussions with certain federations, but with little success. Then came a 1995 judgement that attracted more media attention than any other that year.

UNION ROYALE BELGE DES SOCIETES DE FOOTBALL v. BOSMAN

Case C–415/93, [1995] ECR I–4921.

[Bosman, a Belgian football player, wanted to sign a contract with a French football club at the end of his two-year contract with the Belgian Liege club. However, the Belgian Football Association rules required his prospective French club employer to pay to the Belgian club a substantial transfer fee that could attain 14 times the annual salary. If agreement cannot be reached on paying the transfer fee, a player must enter into a new contract with his prior club; if not, he is suspended from professional play. In Bosman's case, the proposed transfer fee was 4.8 million Belgian francs (ca.$150,000), and the Liege club declined agreement out of concern that the French club's economic condition didn't assure payment. Bosman refused a new contract for lower pay with the Liege club, was suspended, and sued for damages and to enjoin interference with his transfer.

The Liege tribunal asked the Court of Justice not only whether the transfer fee system violated Article 39, but also whether the national and international sport federation rules limiting the number of non-national players violated it as well. The Belgian federation belongs to both the European football association (UEFA), and the international football association (FIFA), and the Belgian rules in question were set in accordance with UEFA and FIFA rules. The 1991 UEFA rules, set after discussion with the Commission, essentially limited the number of non-national active professional players to five per club.

The first important issue was whether Article 39 governed rules of private federations in the field of sports. The sports federations, supported by Germany, argued for "the autonomy of sport," claiming that Liege and most clubs "carry on an economic activity only to a negligible extent." Germany also argued that sport formed a part of national culture which should be respected. The Court rejected this view.]

73 [S]port is subject to Community law only in so far as it constitutes an economic activity within the meaning of Article 2 of the Treaty.

* * *

75 Application of Article [39] of the Treaty is not precluded by the fact that the transfer rules govern the business relationships between clubs rather than the employment relationships between clubs and players. The fact that the employing clubs must pay fees on recruiting a player from another club affects the players' opportunities for finding employment and the terms under which such employment is offered.

76 As regards the difficulty of severing the economic aspects from the sporting aspects of football, the Court has held that the provisions of Community law concerning freedom of movement of persons and of provision of services do not preclude rules or practices justified on non-economic grounds which relate to the particular nature and context of certain matches. It stressed, however, that such a restriction on the scope of the provisions in question must remain limited to its proper objective. It cannot, therefore, be relied upon to exclude the whole of a sporting activity from the scope of the Treaty.

* * *

82 Once the objections concerning the application of Article [39] of the Treaty to sporting activities such as those of professional footballers are out of the way, it is to be remembered that, Article [39] not only applies to the action of public authorities but extends also to rules of any other nature aimed at regulating gainful employment in a collective manner (citing *Walrave*).

* * *

84 [W]orking conditions in the different Member States are governed sometimes by provisions laid down by law or regulation and sometimes by agreements and other acts concluded or adopted by private persons. Accordingly, if the scope of Article [39] of the Treaty were confined to acts of a public authority there would be a risk of creating inequality in its application (see *Walrave*). That risk is all the more obvious in a case such as that in the main proceedings in this case in that * * * the transfer rules have been laid down by different bodies or in different ways in each Member State.

* * *

87 Article [39] of the Treaty therefore applies to rules laid down by sporting associations such as URBSFA, FIFA or UEFA, which determine the terms on which professional sportsmen can engage in gainful employment.

[The Court then concluded that the transfer fee system constituted an indirect restriction of free movement in ¶¶ 105–113, the Court rejected the arguments made to justify the transfer rules. The Court then turned to the non-national players restriction, noting first that article 4 of Regulation 1612/68 forbids any national rules which set quotas on employment by migrant workers.]

119   The same principle applies to clauses contained in the regulations of sporting associations which restrict the right of nationals of other Member States to take part, as professional players, in football matches.

120   The fact that those clauses concern not the employment of such players, on which there is no restriction, but the extent to which their clubs may field them in official matches is irrelevant. In so far as participation in such matches is the essential purpose of a professional player's activity, a rule which restricts that participation obviously also restricts the chances of employment of the player concerned.

[The Court then rejected the justifications for the nationality clauses advanced by the sports federations.]

123   [The sports federations and several governments argued that the] clauses serve to maintain the traditional link between each club and its country, a factor of great importance in enabling the public to identify with its favourite team and ensuring that clubs taking part in international competitions effectively represent their countries.

* * *

129   [T]he nationality clauses cannot be deemed to be in accordance with Article [39] of the Treaty, otherwise that article would be deprived of its practical effect and the fundamental right of free access to employment which the Treaty confers individually on each worker in the Community rendered nugatory * * *.

131   [A] football club's links with the Member State in which it is established cannot be regarded as any more inherent in its sporting activity than its links with its locality, town, [or] region* * *.

NOTES AND QUESTIONS

1.   Advocate General Lenz's remarkably detailed and analytical opinion undoubtedly greatly influenced the Court. In particular, he urged that the Court answer the question on the nationality clause, although the issue arguably had little relevance to Bosman's lawsuit, because of the importance of the issue and the limited likelihood that it would be raised again.

2.   Do you sympathize with the German government's view that sports teams ought to be able to restrict the number of non-nationals as an aspect of

the "cultural" tradition of States? (Advocate General Lenz noted that foreign players were often among the most popular ones on specific teams, citing examples.) For a strong endorsement of the Court's view (and admiration for Advocate General Lenz's opinion), noting its revolutionary consequences for the sport, see the casenote by S. Weatherill, 33 Common Mkt. L. Rev. 991 (1996).

Would you support Community legislation to exempt sports federations rules from the ambit of ECT Article 39? Could the Council and Parliament validly adopt such legislation? *Bosman* is a good example of the type of case that popular opinion finds hard to understand, and that can accordingly lead to hostility toward the Court and Treaty rules. Lobbying to try to obtain a treaty amendment to exclude sport from Treaty rules failed, but the Amsterdam Treaty did annex a Declaration on Sports urging that the views of sports federations be seriously considered.

4. THE INTERNAL AFFAIRS DOCTRINE

In Chapter 4E, we discussed the Court of Justice's internal affairs doctrine, which holds that Community law does not apply to factual situations which are considered to involve only internal state affairs. On occasion, when personal rights of free movement and residence are involved, parties claim that failure to apply Community law gives rise to reverse discrimination. Thus, when a particular right has been recognized for migrant workers in applying ECT Article 39, Regulation 1612/68 or some relevant directive, may a national of a Member State residing within that State claim the same right, on the basis of the principle of nondiscrimination of nationality stated in Article 39?

MOSER v. LAND BADEN–WÜRTTEMBERG

Case 180/83, [1984] ECR 2539.

[Moser, a German national, applied for admission to a teacher-training program in Baden–Württemberg, but was refused because he was a member of the Communist party. When he appealed, the national court asked the Court of Justice whether Moser should be considered a worker and therefore protected by the nondiscrimination provision in Article 39(2).]

12 [The German labor court] asks essentially whether [Moser] may rely on Article [39] to prevent the application to him of legislation, such as that in force in the *Land,* by virtue of which persons as regards whose loyalty to the Basic Law there is insufficient certainty are denied access to the vocational training necessary to enable them to become teachers in primary and secondary education.

* * *

15 [T]he provisions of the Treaty concerning the free movement of workers and particularly Article [39] cannot be applied to situations

which are wholly internal to a Member State, in other words where there is no factor connecting them to any of the situations envisaged by Community law.

16 The case described by the national court concerns * * * a German national who has always lived and maintained his residence in the Federal Republic of Germany and who contests the refusal by the German authorities to allow him access, under the legislation of that State, to a particular kind of vocational training.

17 In order to establish a connection with the Community provisions, Mr. Moser claimed * * * that the application to him of the German legislation in question, by making it impossible for him to complete his training as a teacher, entails the result that he is precluded from applying for teaching posts in schools in the other Member States.

18 That argument cannot be upheld. A purely hypothetical prospect of employment in another Member State does not establish a sufficient connection with Community law to justify the application of Article [39] of the Treaty.

NOTES AND QUESTIONS

1. For other cases applying the internal affairs doctrine despite claims of reverse discrimination, see Morson v. The Netherlands, Cases 35 & 36/82 [1982] ECR 3723 (Surinamese nationals, parents of Dutch nationals, cannot claim rights under Regulation 1612/68 as family members because their children are not migrant workers, so no Community law issue is involved); and Land Nordrhein–Westfalen v. Uecker, Case C–64/96, [1997] ECR I–3171 (Norwegian spouse of a German national, who has never exercised the right of free movement, cannot challenge under Article 39 the terms of her contract as a Norwegian language instructor at the University of Munster, because there is no factor linking her complaint to Community law).

2. Does the internal affairs doctrine as applied in *Moser* and similar cases represent sound policy? Since the Court has stressed repeatedly its respect for basic rights, among which the principle of non-discriminatory treatment clearly figures, why doesn't the Court consider that nationals (or their family members) should receive as favorable treatment by a Member State as a migrant worker would in similar circumstances? What about the argument that if there is no real Community law issue, the Court of Justice has no jurisdiction to provide any relief? The issue is certainly troublesome, because in the absence of Community law recourse, some national courts may be able to apply national constitutional principles to avoid reverse discrimination in these cases, but others will be unable to do so.

In Steen v. Deutsche Bundespost II, Case C–132/93, [1994] ECR I–2715, when a German trial court was told by the Court of Justice that a German national's claim against the German post office raised no Community law issue, the trial court referred a second question, namely, what relief might be given if a German national cannot claim rights in Germany that another Member State migrant worker would enjoy? The Court replied: "Community law does not preclude a national court from examining the compatibility with its constitution of a national rule which, in a situation unconnected with * * * Community law, treats national workers less favorably than nationals from other Member States." Presumably the Court's answer represents a helpful endorsement of a national court's use of its own constitutional equal treatment principles.

Further Reading

C. Barnard, The Substantive Law of the EU: The Four Freedoms (2d ed. Oxford 2007)

P. Kapteyn & P. Verloren van Themaat, The Law of the European Union and the European Communities (4th rev. ed. Kluwer 2009)

N. Rogers & R. Scannell, Free Movement of Persons in the Enlarged European Union (Sweet & Maxwell 2004)

F. Weiss & F. Woolridge, Free Movement of Persons within the European Community (2d ed. Kluwer 2007)

R. White, Workers, Establishment and Services in the European Union (Oxford 2004)

CHAPTER 16

CITIZENSHIP OF THE UNION AND THE FREE MOVEMENT OF PERSONS

■ ■ ■

Citizenship of the Union is a vital symbol with far-reaching legal and practical impact. Created by the Treaty of Maastricht in 1993, citizenship of the Union has steadily increased in importance, particularly as the Court of Justice has progressively expanded the rights of citizens in an extraordinary variety of situations. See sections A and B. Early judgments of the Court recognizing migrant students' rights of access to vocational training and higher education, with concurrent rights of residence, influenced later judgments on the rights of citizens in general. Section C deals with this topic. We will then examine in sections D and E some of the strikingly liberal Court judgments granting rights of residence and non-discrimination to citizens, and narrowly applying public policy limits on these rights.

The Parliament and Council have furthered citizenship rights through adoption of Directive 2004/38, described in section F, which now comprehensively covers the free movement and residence rights. Recent legislation also accords new rights to third state nationals after long-term residence in the Union. Section G covers this development, and concludes with a brief final review of the Area of Freedom, Security and Justice, notably measures concerning asylum and cooperation in criminal and police affairs.

We can deal only summarily with citizenship of the Union despite its intrinsic importance, because the legislation is highly technical in character and the Court's case law is very extensive. At least this chapter, like those on free movement of workers, social policy and equal rights, provides a feeling for the human dimension of the European Union.

The evolution of the rights of citizens of the Union enables interesting comparisons with US constitutional law, especially with regard to access to social benefits. The Supreme Court does not permit a state to restrict social welfare benefits to persons by requiring a long period of residence within the state. Thus, in Shapiro v. Thompson, 394 U.S. 618, 89 S.Ct. 1322, 22 L.Ed.2d 600 (1969), the Supreme Court struck down a state law that granted social welfare benefits only to persons who had resided one year within the state. Justice Brennan's majority opinion did not specify whether the right to the benefits was founded on the Privileges and Immunities Clause, or the Commerce Clause, or both. Recently, in Saenz v. Roe, 526 U.S. 489, 119 S.Ct. 1518, 143 L.Ed.2d 689 (1999), Justice Stevens' majority opinion reaffirmed *Shapiro* in striking down a California law restricting welfare assistance to new residents during their first year of residence to the lower level of the assistance benefits of the state from which they had moved. The Court held that equal treatment of new residents is required by the Fourteenth Amendment's Privileges and Immunities of citizens clause.

For a valuable comparative study of US and EU cases, see F. Strumia, Citizenship and Free Movement, 12 Colum. J. Eur. L. 713 (2006). As we analyze issues in this chapter under Community law, consider also how they might be resolved under US principles.

A. THE PEOPLE'S EUROPE PROGRAM

The idea that there should be a status of citizenship of the Community was initially proposed by the Belgian Prime Minister Tindemanns in the 1970s. When in early 1984 a committee of experts recommended to the European Council a program designed to bring the Community's policies closer to the people, they included a proposal to create such citizenship. In June 1984, the European Council meeting at Fontainebleau reacted favorably to the report, resolving it was "essential that the Community should respond to the expectations of the people of Europe by adopting measures to strengthen and promote its identity and its image both for its citizens and for the rest of the world." Bull. EC 1985–7 Supp. 5. Before discussing citizenship of the Union itself, the People's Europe program merits brief description because to some degree it prepared the way for the creation of citizenship rights.

To implement the People's Europe program, the Commission proposed measures to grant rights of residence throughout the Community to persons who are neither employed nor self-employed, to recognize the equivalence of higher education diplomas, and to further student interchange and cooperation between educational institutions. All these initiatives soon bore fruit. The Council's adoption of the directives on rights of residence in 1990 represents one of the principal successes of the People's Europe program. The residence directives and the student exchange programs will be discussed in section C, and the diploma recognition directive in Chapter 18A.

Several People's Europe measures produce considerable benefits in daily life. The Community introduced a Community passport in 1985, which has now replaced all national passports. Postal rates for mail within the Community are now charged on the same basis as domestic mail. A 1992 Council decision introduced 00 as the standard telephone access code for international calls, replacing a variety of international access numbers. Periodically, a directive sets common summertime (daylight savings time) standards for all the Member States (except that the United Kingdom and Ireland are one hour earlier). Largely for its symbolic effect, in 1986 the Council authorized a Community flag (a circle of twelve gold stars on a blue background), which is flown in front of the buildings housing Community institutions and at conferences and meetings.

Of considerable practical importance is Directive 91/439, 1991 O.J. L 237/1 (Aug. 24, 1991), which sets minimum standards for drivers' tests and medical examinations, and requires that any license issued by one State be recognized in all others. A more comprehensive text, Directive 2006/126, O.J.L. 403/18 (Dec. 30, 2006), establishes a Community model form for driver's licenses, prescribes anti-forgery measures, and sets standards for licenses to drive various types of vehicles (cars, trucks, tractors, motorcycles, etc.), while retaining the principle of mutual recognition.

Another directive intended to provide concrete benefits in daily life is Directive 95/46 on the protection of individuals with regard to the processing of personal data, O.J. L 281/31 (Nov. 23, 1995), commonly called the data privacy directive. The stated goal of the directive is to "protect the fundamental rights and freedoms of natural persons, and in particular their right of privacy" with respect to the processing of personal data (art. 1).

The data privacy directive contains detailed provisions on the circumstances under which personal data can be processed (usually only when the subject "has unambiguously given his consent" or is under a legal obligation to provide the data) (art. 7) and generally prohibits the processing of sensitive data, e.g., "revealing racial or ethnic origin, * * * religious or philosophical beliefs," or "data concerning health or sex life" (art. 8). Further provisions govern the data subject's right of access to data concerning him or her (art. 12), and a right to object to use of the data, particularly for "direct marketing" (art. 14). Member States must provide judicial remedies and suitable sanctions for the breach of rights (arts. 22–24).

The data privacy directive also prohibits the transfer of personal data to a third country unless the country "ensures an adequate level of protection" (art. 25). This article provoked difficult negotiations with the United States, where there are few regulatory modes of protection of personal data and where the collection and use of such data, especially for direct marketing, has become a substantial business. In July 2000, the Commission and the Commerce Department reached a "safe harbor" arrangement under which US entities that desire to receive personal data from the Community should undertake to obtain the consent of the data subject and otherwise essentially follow the directive's requirement.

Note that the Treaty of Amsterdam subsequently introduced ECT Article 286 (now TFEU Article 16), which requires Community institutions to protect personal data, and Article 8 of the Nice Charter of

Fundamental Rights states a "right to protection of personal data." See Chapter 6C.

B. CITIZENSHIP OF THE UNION— BASIC NOTIONS

1. TREATY PROVISIONS

After the European Council at Dublin in April 1990 had urged its creation, the Treaty of Maastricht created citizenship of the Union and its attendant rights in a series of articles, EECT Article 8 to 8e, which were renumbered by the Treaty of Amsterdam as ECT Articles 17–22. ECT Article 17 makes every national of a Member State a "citizen of the Union," and states that such citizenship shall "complement and not replace national citizenship." TFEU Article 20(1) replaces Article 17, without change.

Who are "nationals" of Member States who then become citizens of the Union? A declaration annexed to the Treaty on European Union states that that question is to be "settled solely by reference to the national law of the Member State concerned." The Court of Justice declined to set any Community law constraints on such a Member State determination of its own nationality in the Queen v. Secretary of State for the Home Department ex parte Kaur, Case C–192/99, [2001] ECR I–1237, permitting the United Kingdom to refuse residence rights to British Overseas Citizens (certain persons from former UK colonies who were granted UK citizenship in 1948, but without a right to reside in the UK).

What about dual nationals? In Micheletti v. Delegacion del Gobierno, Case C–369/90, [1992] ECR 1–4239, the Court held that the Spanish authorities must deliver a Community residence permit to Micheletti, an Argentine–Italian dual national, even though he had apparently spent most of his life in Argentina and resided there immediately before coming to Spain. Spain could not apply its law treating dual nationals as essentially having only the nationality of the country of principal or most recent residence. We noted in *Collins,* supra page 586, that the UK authorities had to treat a dual national seeking employment in the UK as Irish, although he had been born and raised in the US and never lived in Ireland.

The most important identified right of a citizen of the Union is set out in ECT Article 18(1) (initially EECT Article 8a), which guarantees "the right to move and reside freely within the territory of the Member States," subject to any conditions set elsewhere in the Treaty or implementing legislation. This reference to conditions preserves the public policy, public security and public health limitations on free movement of workers in ECT Article 39(3) and the parallel limitations on free movement of the self-employed in ECT Articles 46 and 55. ECT Article 18(2) authorizes the Parliament and Council to act by means of the co-decision procedure in order to facilitate the rights of movement and residence, but requires the Council to act unanimously. The Lisbon Treaty renumbers ECT Article 18 as TFEU Article 21, but eliminates the requirement of Council unanimity. Directive 2004/38, described in section F, now comprehensively covers movement and residence rights.

ECT Article 19 permits every Union citizen resident in another State to "vote and to stand as a candidate at municipal elections," as well as in elections for the European Parliament in that State. Under ECT Article 21, citizens of the Union also have the right to petition Parliament and to bring complaints to the Community Ombudsman. The Lisbon Treaty replaces ECT Articles 19 and 21 with TFEU Articles 22 and 24.

Directive 93/109, O.J. L 329/34 (Dec. 30, 1993), sets out the conditions for voting or standing as a candidate for the European Parliament. Parallel in approach, but somewhat more detailed, is Directive 94/80, O.J. L 368/38 (Dec. 31, 1994), stating the rights of citizens of the Union to vote or run for office in municipal elections in the State in which they reside.

Although the two directives grant voting and candidacy rights which had existed previously in only a few States, the rights are still rather limited in nature. Directive 94/80 covers only municipal elections, not national or even regional ones, and article 5(3) permits States to continue to reserve the chief executive office (or collegial executive board) of a municipality to its own nationals. Both directives also grant a derogation to a State if the total number of voting age nationals of other Union States exceeds 20% of the total voting age population. This was intended for Luxembourg, where almost 30% of the voting age population is comprised of nationals of other States, in part because so many Union institutions are located there. Most of the Member States had to amend their Constitutions in order to comply with the directive.

Although the right to vote in local elections is certainly of some value, a far greater contribution to Member State nationals residing long-term or even permanently in other States would be to permit them to vote in national elections. This, however, is not yet on the horizon. Moreover, since some States do not permit absentee voting in national elections, one may wonder why there has been no proposal to legislate to require this for migrant workers who often do not have the time or means to return to their home State to vote. For a thoughtful analysis of the issues, see D. Kochenov, Free Movement and Participation in the Parliamentary Elections in the Member State of Nationality, 16 Maastricht J. Eur. L. 197 (2009).

2. NON-DISCRIMINATION BASED ON NATIONALITY

CRIMINAL PROCEEDINGS AGAINST BICKEL AND FRANZ

Case C–274/96, [1998] ECR I–7637.

[Under Italian law, German speaking citizens of the Province of Bolzano (where most of the German speaking minority in Italy live) are entitled to have judicial proceedings involving them conducted in German. Bickel, an Austrian national and resident was arrested for driving his truck in Bolzano under the influence of alcohol. Franz, a German national and resident, was arrested while he was a tourist in Bolzano for possession of a knife prohibited by law. Each stated that he spoke no Italian and requested that the criminal proceedings be conducted in German. The trial court asked the Court of Justice whether either should be accorded that right pursuant to ECT Articles 12 and 18.]

[20]   In the submission of Mr. Bickel and Mr. Franz, if any discrimination contrary to Article [12] of the Treaty is to be avoided, the right to have proceedings conducted in German must be extended to all citizens of the Union, since it is already available to nationals of one of the Member States.

[21]   The Italian Government contends that the only nationals upon whom the right in question is conferred are those who are both residents of the Province of Bolzano and members of its German-speaking community, the aim of the rules in issue being to recognize the ethnic and cultural identity of persons belonging to the protected minority.

* * *

[25]   Even on the assumption that, as the Italian Government maintains, German speaking nationals of other Member States who are resident in the Province of Bolzano may rely on the rules in issue and submit their pleadings in German—so that there is no discrimination on grounds of nationality as between residents of the region—Italian nationals are at an advantage by comparison with nationals of other Member States. The majority of Italian nationals whose language is German are in a position to demand that German be used throughout the proceedings in the Province of Bolzano, because they meet the residence requirement laid down by the rules in issue; the majority of German-speaking nationals of other Member States, on the other hand, cannot avail themselves of that right because they do not satisfy that requirement.

[26]   Consequently, rules * * * which make the right, in a defined area, to have criminal proceedings conducted in the language of the person being resident in that area, favour nationals of the host State by comparison with nationals of other Member States exercising their

right to freedom of movement and therefore run counter to the principle of non-discrimination laid down in Article [12] of the Treaty.

* * *

29   The Italian Government's contention that the aim of those rules is to protect the ethno-cultural minority residing in the province in question does not constitute a valid justification in this context. Of course, the protection of such a minority may constitute a legitimate aim. It does not appear, however, from the documents before the Court that that aim would be undermined if the rules in issue were extended to cover German-speaking nationals of other Member States exercising their right to freedom of movement.

30   Furthermore, it should be recalled that Mr. Bickel and Mr. Franz pointed out at the hearing, without being contradicted, that the courts concerned are in a position to conduct proceedings in German without additional complications or costs.

NOTES AND QUESTIONS

1. *Bickel and Franz* is an important precedent because it indicates that the Court is willing to imply a right of nondiscrimination based on nationality to any citizen of the Union who moves for any reason into the territory of a host State. Advocate General Jacobs urged that non-discrimination on the basis of nationality in criminal proceedings flowed directly from ECT Article 18, without any need to find a link to a specific Treaty right (e.g. here, to the right to provide or receive services).

2. Although Shakespeare queried, 'what's in a name', their choice of their family name mattered a great deal to those concerned in Garcia Avello v. Belgium, Case C–148/02, [2003] ECR I–11613. Garcia Avello, Spanish, and Weber, Belgian, married and resided in Belgium where they had two minor children, who possess dual Spanish and Belgian nationality. The Belgian Register of Births recorded the children's family name as Garcia Avello, while the parents registered them with the Spanish consulate under Garcia Weber in accordance with the Spanish custom of combining the parents' names. After the parents sued to compel the Belgian authorities to replace Garcia Avello with Garcia Weber for the children's family name, the issue came to the Court of Justice in a reference proceeding. The Court held that Belgium must respect the children's preference for use of the family name customary in Spain, inasmuch as they were dual Spanish–Belgian nationals (¶¶ 26–29). Note that the parents acted on behalf of the minor children—what would happen if either child, on becoming an adult, should prefer to be called Garcia Avello?

D'HOOP v. OFFICE NATIONAL DE L'EMPLOI
Case C–224/98, [2002] ECR I–6191.

[Belgium grants young people a tideover allowance while seeking their first job after completing their secondary education. Ms. D'Hoop, Belgian, completed her secondary education in France in 1991, and then studied at a Belgian university until 1995. She was denied the tideover allowance because the Belgian rules permitted only the children of migrant workers residing in Belgium to have their secondary education take place elsewhere in the Community.]

28   Union citizenship is destined to be the fundamental status of nationals of the Member States, enabling those who find themselves in the same situation to enjoy within the scope *ratione materiae* of the Treaty the same treatment in law irrespective of their nationality, subject to such exceptions as are expressly provided for [citing *Grzelczyk, infra* page 631].

29   The situations falling within the scope of Community law include those involving the exercise of the fundamental freedoms guaranteed by the Treaty, in particular those involving the freedom to move and reside within the territory of the Member States, as conferred by Article [18] [citing *Bickel and Franz* and *Grzelczyk*].

30   [A] citizen of the Union must be granted in all Member States the same treatment in law as that accorded to the nationals of those Member States who find themselves in the same situation. [Accordingly,] it would be incompatible with the right of freedom of movement were a citizen, in the Member State of which he is a national, to receive treatment less favourable than he would enjoy if he had not availed himself of the opportunities offered by the Treaty in relation to freedom of movement.

31   Those opportunities could not be fully effective if a national of a Member State could be deterred from availing himself of them by obstacles raised on his return to his country of origin by legislation penalising the fact that he has used them.

32   That consideration is particularly important in the field of education. The objectives set for the activities of the Community include, in Article 3(p) of the EC Treaty, a contribution to education and training of quality. That contribution must, according to the second indent of [Article 149(2)], be aimed, *inter alia,* at encouraging mobility of students and teachers.

33   [The Belgian] legislation introduces a difference in treatment between Belgian nationals who have had all their secondary education in Belgium and those who, having availed themselves of their freedom to move, have obtained their diploma of completion of secondary education in another Member State.

34   By linking the grant of tideover allowances to the condition of having obtained the required diploma in Belgium, the national legislation thus places at a disadvantage certain of its nationals simply because they have exercised their freedom to move in order to pursue education in another Member State.

35   Such inequality of treatment is contrary to the principles which underpin the status of citizen of the Union, that is, the guarantee of the same treatment in law in the exercise of the citizen's freedom to move.

NOTES AND QUESTIONS

1. Why could not D'Hoop claim non-discrimination rights under ECT Article 39? Because, by definition, she is not yet a worker. *D'Hoop* is a crucial precedent for the Court's expansive interpretation of the implications of citizenship of the Union. Note that the internal affairs doctrine discussed in Chapter 4E does not bar this Belgian citizen from claiming rights against Belgium, because she exercised her right of free movement in order to study abroad.

2. Most personal tax cases that come to the Court involve workers or the self-employed. In contrast, Proceedings re Turpeinen, Case C–520/04, [2006] ECR I–10685, concerned a Finnish woman who had retired to live in Spain. Finland charged her a 35% withholding tax on her retirement pension, whereas she would have paid 28% had she continued to live in Finland. Citing *D'Hoop*, the Court held that she could not be placed at a disadvantage by exercising her right to residence abroad under ECT Article 18 (¶¶ 20–23). Citing *Shumacker,* supra page 579, the Court then held that, because the pension constituted her sole income, her income tax should not be higher than that of a Finnish resident (¶¶ 26–29).

3. In Commission v. Germany (Housing subsidies), Case C–152/05, [2008] ECR I–39, Germany granted housing subsidies to income taxpayers who build or buy a dwelling for their personal residence within Germany. Germany's motive was to ensure an adequate supply of housing for its population. The Commission contended that granting the subsidy only for German housing violated Article 18 because it might deter citizens from moving their personal residence to another State while remaining German taxpayers. What should the Court decide?

C.   STUDENTS, EDUCATION AND CULTURE

The initial Treaty of Rome contained no provision on education as such, but EECT Article 128, within the Title on Social Policy, authorized the Council to "lay down general principles for implementing a common vocational training policy" for the benefit of the common market. Presumably the intent was to facilitate skilled employment. The Court of Justice, however, expansively applied this text, in conjunction with the principle of non-discrimination on the basis of nationality, to develop a right of free movement for students in higher education.

1.   STUDENT ACCESS TO HIGHER EDUCATION

May Community nationals claim the right of equal treatment with host State nationals in access to higher education? With regard to financial assistance for tuition and fees? With regard to social assistance during studies? How does the Court's doctrine on the rights of students to access to higher education differ from that of the US Supreme Court?

GRAVIER v. CITY OF LIÈGE

Case 293/83, [1985] ECR 593.

[A 1983 Belgian regulation required all state schools to charge enrollment fees to foreign students whose parents are not resident in Belgium. Belgian students were not charged any comparable fee. Gravier, a French student whose parents resided in France, sued to demand enrollment in the Liège fine arts academy without payment of an annual enrollment fee (ca. $600). Gravier intended to study strip cartoon art. The trial court asked the Court of Justice whether ECT Article 12 granted the right of non-discrimination based on nationality to students following vocational training courses and whether strip cartoon art study could be considered vocational training.]

12 The Belgian State * * * argued before the Court that the reason why foreign students in Belgium are required to contribute to the financing of education is the imbalance which has existed since 1976 between the number of foreign students studying in Belgium and the number of Belgian students living abroad. Since that imbalance had serious consequences for the national education budget the Belgian Government was compelled to ask students who are nationals of other Member States and who normally do not pay taxes in Belgium to make a proportional contribution to the cost of education. Far from being discriminatory, such a contribution puts foreign students on the same footing as Belgian nationals.

13 The Commission provided the Court with figures showing that the mobility of students within the Community is limited in scope but that Belgium is the Member State in which the percentage of students who are nationals of other Member States, in relation to the total number of students, is the highest. The information provided also shows that Belgium is the only Member State which requires foreign students to pay an enrolment fee * * *.

14 [I]t is clear * * * that the cost of higher art education is not borne by students of Belgian nationality, whereas foreign students must bear part of that cost. The inequality of treatment is therefore based on nationality * * *.

15 Such unequal treatment based on nationality must be regarded as discrimination prohibited by Article [12] of the Treaty if it falls within the scope of the Treaty.

* * *

19 [A]lthough educational organization and policy are not as such included in the spheres which the Treaty has entrusted to the Community

institutions, access to and participation in courses of instruction and apprenticeship, in particular vocational training, are not unconnected with Community law.

[The Court then noted that EECT Article 128 authorized the Council to "lay down general principles" for vocational training policy, and that the Council had accordingly adopted guidelines in 1971.]

25   It follows from all the foregoing that the conditions of access to vocational training fall within the scope of the Treaty.

26   [Accordingly,] the imposition on students who are nationals of other Member States, of a charge * * * as a condition of access to vocational training, where the same fee is not imposed on students who are nationals of the host Member State, constitutes discrimination on grounds of nationality contrary to Article [12] of the Treaty.

27   In its second question the national court wishes to know what criteria must be used in deciding whether courses in strip cartoon art constitute vocational training.

* * *

29   The general guidelines laid down by the Council in 1971 state that "in view of the constantly changing needs of the economy the aim" of vocational training "should be to offer everyone the opportunity of basic and advanced training and a continuity of in-service training designed, from a general and vocational point of view, to enable the individual to develop his personality and to take up a career".

30   It follows from those statements that any form of education which prepares for a qualification for a particular profession, trade or employment or which provides the necessary training and skills for such a profession, trade or employment is vocational training, whatever the age and the level of training of the pupils or students, and even if the training programme includes an element of general education.

BLAIZOT v. UNIVERSITY OF LIÈGE

Case 24/86, [1988] ECR 379.

[Blaizot, a French national studying veterinary medicine, sued for reimbursement of enrollment fees paid prior to the date of judgment of *Gravier*. The trial court asked the Court of Justice whether university studies leading to a doctorate in veterinary medicine were to be considered vocational training. Belgium argued that vocational training should be defined in its traditional sense of apprenticeship and technical training for certain trades and professions.]

17   [N]either the provisions of the Treaty, in particular Article [150], nor the objectives which these provisions seek to achieve, in particular those relating to freedom of movement for persons, give any indication that the concept of vocational training is to be restricted so as to

exclude all university education. It is accepted in all the Member States that some university studies are indeed intended to provide students, at the academic level, with certain knowledge, training and skills as preparation for specific occupations. It should be added that Article 10 of the European Social Charter, to which most of the Member States are contracting parties, treats university education as a type of vocational training.

* * *

[19] With regard to the issue whether university studies prepare for a qualification for a particular profession, trade or employment * * *, that is the case not only where the final academic examination directly provides the required qualification for a particular profession, trade or employment but also in so far as the studies in question provide specific training and skills, that is to say where a student needs the knowledge so acquired for the pursuit of a profession, trade or employment, even if no legislative or administrative provisions make the acquisition of that knowledge a prerequisite for that purpose.

[20] In general, university studies fulfil these criteria. The only exceptions are certain courses of study which, because of their particular nature, are intended for persons wishing to improve their general knowledge rather than prepare themselves for an occupation.

* * *

[23] [Accordingly,] university studies in veterinary medicine fall within the meaning of the term "vocational training", and consequently a supplementary enrolment fee charged to students who are nationals of other Member States and wish to enrol for such studies constitutes discrimination on grounds of nationality contrary to Article [12] of the EEC Treaty.

VLANDIS v. KLINE

412 U.S. 441, 93 S.Ct. 2230, 37 L.Ed.2d 63 (1973).

[Connecticut required non-resident students to pay substantially higher state university tuition than that paid by state residents. Connecticut defined a non-resident as anyone whose "legal address" was outside Connecticut at any time within one year prior to admission. A non-resident could not acquire the status of a resident for tuition purposes during the period of university studies. Plaintiff Kline was a California resident when she was accepted as a student by the University of Connecticut, but subsequently married a Connecticut resident. The Klines had a home in Connecticut and the plaintiff obtained a Connecticut driver's license and registered as a Connecticut voter. Justice Stevens, speaking for a majority of five, struck down the Connecticut statute.]

Statutes creating permanent irrebuttable presumptions have long been disfavored under the Due Process Clauses of the Fifth and Fourteenth Amendments.

* * *

It may be that most applicants to Connecticut's university system who apply from outside the State or within a year of living out of State have no real intention of becoming Connecticut residents and will never do so. But it is clear that not all of the applicants from out of State inevitably fall in this category. Indeed, [Kline possesses] many of the indicia of Connecticut residency, such as year-round Connecticut homes, Connecticut drivers' licenses, car registrations, voter registrations, etc.; and [was] found by the District Court to have become [a bonafide resident] of Connecticut before the 1972 spring semester. Yet, under the State's statutory scheme, [she was not] permitted any opportunity to demonstrate the bona fides of her Connecticut residency for tuition purposes, [nor will she] ever have such an opportunity in the future so long as she remains a student.

[Justice Stevens rejected Connecticut's arguments that higher fees on initial non-residents were justified in order to equalize public education costs between residents and non-residents, to reward past taxpayers and to achieve administrative certainty.]

Our holding today should in no wise be taken to mean that Connecticut must classify the students in its university system as residents for purposes of tuition and fees, just because they go to school there. Nor should our decision be construed to deny a State the right to impose on a student, as one element in demonstrating bona fide residence, a reasonable durational residency requirement, which can be met while in student status. We fully recognize that a State has a legitimate interest in protecting and preserving the quality of its colleges and universities and the right of its own bona fide residents to attend such institutions on a preferential tuition basis.

We hold only that a permanent irrebuttable presumption of nonresidence—the means adopted by Connecticut to preserve that legitimate interest—is violative of the Due Process Clause, because it provides no opportunity for students who applied from out of State to demonstrate that they have become bona fide Connecticut residents.

[CHIEF JUSTICE BURGER dissented, together with JUSTICE REHNQUIST.]

A state university today is an establishment with capital costs of many millions of dollars of investment. Its annual operating costs likewise may run into the millions. Parents and other taxpayers willingly carry this heavy burden because they believe in the values of higher education. It is not narrow provincialism for the State to think that each State should carry its own educational burdens. Until we redefine our system of government—as we are free to do by constitutionally prescribed means—the States may restrict subsidized education to their own residents.

NOTES AND QUESTIONS

1. *Gravier* is another judgment demonstrating the Court of Justice's tendency to construe broadly Treaty articles and secondary legislation. The Court's application of ECT Article 12 to vocational studies owes a great deal to its emphasis on basic rights protection. Are you persuaded by the Court's analysis or do you consider such an "activist" approach to be excessive in this case? Note that, at the time, Belgium was the only Member State which experienced a serious budgetary problem due to the large number of foreign students. Why should Belgian taxpayers bear the burden of educating Community nationals from other States? For a favorable review of *Gravier*, see J. Lonbay, Education and Law: The Community Context, 14 Eur. L. Rev. 363 (1989).

2. *Blaizot* effectively expands the scope of ECT Article 12's protection against discrimination on the basis of nationality to most forms of higher education. What fields of study would not qualify as vocational training, using the Court's analysis? Do you agree with the Court's broad conception of vocational training? Obviously, university studies in architecture, engineering or law would qualify, but what about traditional liberal arts studies in history, literature or philosophy?

3. In *Vlandis*, although the Supreme Court required states to treat former non-resident students as residents for university tuition purposes once they have provided sufficient evidence of a change of residence, the Court majority did not question the ability of a state to charge non-resident students higher tuition. Indeed, the Court previously affirmed without opinion a district court decision allowing Minnesota to charge university students from other states higher tuition until they had completed one year's residence in Minnesota. Starns v. Malkerson, 401 U.S. 985, 91 S.Ct. 1231, 28 L.Ed.2d 527 (1971), affirming 326 F.Supp. 234 (D.Minn.1970). The district court had stressed that access to higher education was not one of the "basic necessities of life," unlike social welfare assistance. The Court of Justice and the Supreme Court obviously hold sharply contrasting views on the right of access by non-residents to higher education. As a matter of policy, with which court do you agree?

4. France limits the number of students enrolled in university studies of medicine. As a result, universities in the French-speaking part of Belgium, receive large numbers of French students seeking to study medicine and veterinary science. The government accordingly adopted a 2006 decree that largely limited enrollment to students who have a right to permanent residence in Belgium. A ceiling was fixed for non-resident students, who were chosen by lot out of all non-resident applicants. Denied admission, a non-resident French student sued. In Bressol v. Gouvernement de la Communaute Francaise, Case C–73/08, [2010] ECR–I ___ (Apr. 13, 2010), the government of the French-speaking region argued that its medical and veterinary faculties could adequately train only a specific number of students each year and that

it feared that not enough qualified doctors and veterinarians would remain in its territory to satisfy public health needs. The Court accepted this justification in principle (¶¶ 67–68), but instructed the referring court to require the authorities to supply "an objective, detailed analysis * * * capable of demonstrating, with solid and consistent data, that there are genuine risks to public health" (¶ 71). The Court incidentally queried whether selecting the non-resident students by lot, rather than based on their "aptitude," was suitable (¶ 81).

5.   Like France, Germany limits the number of students commencing university studies, accepting only the highest-ranked secondary students. Not surprisingly, many young Germans then seek university studies, especially in medicine, in Austria. However, an Austrian regulation required prospective students from outside Austria to satisfy the entrance requirements for the desired field of study set in their home State, thus largely blocking German applicants. In Commission v. Austria (Access to universities), Case C–147/03, [2005] ECR I–5969, the Court held that the Austrian rule constituted indirect discrimination on the basis of nationality in violation of ECT Article 12, particularly harmful because of the Community goal of "encouraging mobility of students and teachers" (¶ 44). Austria's justification was that it would incur "structural, staffing and financial problems" if it admitted the foreign students (¶ 50). The Court rejected this, noting that Advocate General Jacobs had suggested the alternative of a special entry exam or minimum grade level (¶ 61). Austrian Chancellor Schussel criticized the judgment, and in 2006 a new law reserved almost 75% of available places for Austrians seeking access to university studies. A case note by C. Rieder, 43 Common Mkt. L. Rev. 1711 (2006), reports this and believes the new law to violate Article 12. Would you agree? Do you have some sympathy for Austria, which must expand its university programs to provide sufficient access to both Austrian and German students, due to Germany's refusal to expand its universities?

2.   THE STUDENT RESIDENCE DIRECTIVE AND STATE BENEFITS

Following the Court's initial judgments, the Council adopted Directive 93/96 on the right of residence for students, O.J.L. 317/59 (Dec. 18, 1993), Document 16 in the Selected Documents, which grants a right of residence for vocational studies, but permits the host State to limit the residence permit to the duration of studies. The directive grants an accessory residence right to the student's spouse and dependent children, even if not a Member State national. However, article 1 sets two important conditions: the student must provide evidence that he or she has "sufficient resources to avoid becoming a burden on the social assistance system," and be covered by "sickness insurance in respect of all risks", both during the period of residence. (Directive 2004/38, infra, now replaces this directive.)

After the Treaty of Maastricht introduced citizenship of the Union, it was predictable that the Court might narrowly apply the sufficient resources condition. In Grzelczyk v. Centre Public d'aide Sociale, Case C–

184/99, [2001] ECR I–6193, Grzelczyk, a French national, was denied the Belgian minimum subsistence allowance when he applied for it during his fourth year of study at Louvain University. Answering referred questions, the Court held that because a Belgian student could obtain the allowance, denial of it to Grzelczyk constituted discrimination on the basis of nationality in violation of ECT Article 12 (¶¶ 29–30). Interpreting Directive 93/96 liberally, the Court held that its article 1 does not prohibit a migrant student from receiving financial assistance, but only requires him to provide truthfully initial evidence of his ability to avoid becoming a burden on the social assistance system (¶¶ 39–20). The Court noted that a student's financial situation may change over time (¶ 45).

A subsequent judgment went further, granting migrant students a right to obtain on a non-discriminatory basis a State's financial benefits for students.

THE QUEEN EX PARTE BIDAR v. LONDON BOROUGH OF EALING

Case C–209/03, [2005] ECR I–2119.

[In 1998, Bidar, a French national, came to the UK and lived with his grandmother while finishing his secondary education. In 2001, after starting studies at the University of London, he applied for a student loan from a government agency, which denied it because he was not "settled" in the UK. A family member of a migrant worker does not have to be "settled" but must have lived in the UK for three years prior to university studies. Bidar satisfied the three year residence condition, but was not a member of a migrant worker's family. After he sued, the trial court made an ECT Article 234 reference.]

35 As is apparent from *D'Hoop*, a national of a Member State who goes to another Member State and pursues secondary education there exercises the freedom to move guaranteed by Article 18 EC.

36 Furthermore, a national of a Member State who, like the claimant in the main proceedings, lives in another Member State where he pursues and completes his secondary education, without it being objected that he does not have sufficient resources or sickness insurance, enjoys a right of residence on the basis of Article 18 EC and Directive 90/364.

[The Court noted that in *Lair*, supra page 606, it had held that migrant students were not entitled to maintenance allowances.]

39 However, since judgment was given in *Lair* * * *, the Treaty on European Union has introduced citizenship of the Union into the EC Treaty and added [Articles 149 and 150 on] education and vocational training.

40 Thus Article 149(1) EC gives the Community the task of contributing to the development of quality education by encouraging cooperation

between Member States and, if necessary, by supporting and supplementing their action* * *.

41　Under paragraphs 2 and 4 of that article, the Council may adopt incentive measures * * * and recommendations aimed in particular at encouraging the mobility of students and teachers (see *D'Hoop*, paragraph 32).

42　In view of those developments * * *, it must be considered that the situation of a citizen of the Union who is lawfully resident in another Member State falls within the scope of application of the Treaty within the meaning of the first paragraph of Article 12 EC for the purposes of obtaining assistance for students, whether in the form of a subsidised loan or a grant, intended to cover his maintenance costs.

[In ¶¶ 44–45, the Court accepted that students who move to another State in order to pursue higher education studies, and commence residence at that time, are barred from receiving maintenance grants pursuant to Article 3 of Directive 93/96.]

46　However, Article 3 of Directive 93/96 does not preclude a national of a Member State who * * * is [already] lawfully resident in the territory of another Member State where he intends to start or pursue higher education from relying * * * on the fundamental principle of equal treatment enshrined in the first paragraph of Article 12 EC.

* * *

56　[Nonetheless,] a Member State [may] ensure that the grant of assistance to cover the maintenance costs of students from other Member States does not become an unreasonable burden which could have consequences for the overall level of assistance which may be granted by that State.

57　In the case of assistance covering the maintenance costs of students, it is thus legitimate for a Member State to grant such assistance only to students who have demonstrated a certain degree of integration into the society of that State.

59　[T]he existence of a certain degree of integration may be regarded as established by a finding that the student in question has resided in the host Member State for a certain length of time.

60　With respect to [the UK] Regulations, the guarantee of sufficient integration into the society of the host Member State follows from the conditions requiring previous residence in the territory of that State, in this case the three years' residence required* * *.

NOTES AND QUESTIONS

1. In *Lair*, supra page 606, the Court held that the migrant student could claim the German financial aid to cover university fees, citing *Blaizot*. However, the Court held that aid for living expenses fell within general social assistance, not subject to Community law. Citizenship of the Union enables

the Court to reverse *Lair* and require the UK to provide the maintenance subsidy for students from other States who are already legally resident in the UK (¶ 46). The Court did accept that the UK could set a three year residence requirement for the maintenance aid, to demonstrate "integration into the society" (¶ 57). In view of that rather long residence requirement, it is obvious that not many migrant students will qualify for the UK maintenance aid. *Bidar* will, however, benefit migrant students in States that provide financial maintenance grants but do not require such a lengthy period of residence.

3. EDUCATION, VOCATIONAL TRAINING AND CULTURE

The promotion of the mobility of university students and cooperation between higher education institutions were two of the goals of the People's Europe program. After its endorsement by the European Council, in 1987 the Council adopted Erasmus, the well-known acronym for the European Action Scheme for the Mobility of University Students, Council Decision 87/327, O.J. L 166/20 (June 25, 1987). Erasmus encouraged cooperation between academic institutions on courses of study and research and provided direct financial aid to students who engaged in studies in other States for up to one year. Although the financial aid grants were moderate in amount, Erasmus encouraged the home State institution to give full academic credit for the foreign studies and also required that students studying abroad continue to receive any grants to which they were entitled from their home institution.

Erasmus proved an immediate success. During the academic year 1990–91, 1200 institutions engaged in academic cooperation and 59,000 students received financial assistance in the academic year 1990–91. A later Commission study in January 2000 showed that four-fifths of the Erasmus exchange students were the first members of their family to study abroad. Stimulated by Erasmus, some universities created new masters degree and summer study programs designed principally for foreign students. In fact, some Belgian, Dutch and German universities decided to offer certain courses for all students in English in order to facilitate studies by Erasmus exchange students. Since 2004, Erasmus has been supplemented by the Erasmus Mundus program, which encourages student and teacher exchange and joint masters' degrees with universities in the US, Canada and some other countries.

Probably no other Community program has enjoyed greater popularity and appreciation than Erasmus. The Member States presumably intended to build upon its success in inserting Article 149 into the EC Treaty as one of the Maastricht amendments. Article 149 expressly gives the Community competence to act for "the development of quality education," but, in accord with the principle of subsidiarity, the article guarantees that the Member States' principal role in determining "the content of teaching and the organization of educational systems and their cultural and linguistic diversity" should be respected. The Lisbon TFEU Article 165 largely replicates ECT Article 149.

Community (and now Union) action is essentially to encourage cooperation among Member States and to adopt "incentive measures, excluding any harmonization of the laws". ECT Article 149 (2) lists as spheres of possible action: "developing the European dimension in education, particularly through the teaching and dissemination of the languages of the Member States; encouraging mobility of students and teachers, inter alia by encouraging the academic recognition of diplomas and periods of study; and promoting cooperation between educational establishments." For an analytical study of the education competence of the Community, see K. Lenaerts, Education in European Community Law after Maastricht, 31 Common Mkt. L. Rev. 7 (1994). TFEU Article 165(2) only adds to the above fields "developing the European dimension in sport, by promoting * * * cooperation between bodies responsible for sports."

Since Article 149 became effective in 1993, the Community has steadily expanded the scope and diversity of its educational programs. Article 149 is not limited to higher education, although the principal emphasis in Community action has been at that level. Measures are also now in place to encourage cooperation among primary and secondary schools, especially in partnership programs, including exchanges of teaching staff and pupils. The Nice European Council in December 2000 endorsed an Action Plan for Mobility, declaring that increasing the mobility of "all those being educated and their teachers in Europe is a major political goal" and that "it is through education that Europeans will acquire the shared cultural references that are the basis of European citizenship and of a political Europe." E.U. Bull. 12/2000, at 28–29.

The current action program is set out in Decision 1720/2006 of the Parliament and Council on Lifelong Learning, O.J. L 327/45 (Nov. 24, 2006). This covers student exchange and educational cooperation in higher education under the Erasmus program; partnership, exchange and other cooperation in primary and secondary education under the Comnenius program; exchange and cooperative projects in vocational training under the Leonardo da Vinci program, and designated research centers and professorships under the Jean Monnet program. Statistics from the 2006–07 academic year indicate that about 160,000 students and 26,000 teachers were in Erasmus exchanges, over 12,000 schools and 870,000 pupils benefitted from Comnenius programs; and almost 800 professors held Jean Monnet chairs. The consolidated programs will have a seven billion Euro budget for 2007–13.

The Commission commenced programs for European cultural initiatives in the 1980s. The Maastricht Treaty amendments to the EC Treaty included a new Article 151 which declares that the Community shall "contribute to the flowering of the cultures of the Member States." Just as for education, Community action is limited to promoting cooperation among Member States and adopting incentive measures. Moreover, Article

151 (4) requires the Community to "take cultural aspects into account in its actions" in other fields. TFEU Article 167 largely replicates ECT Article 151. Probably the most prominent cultural initiative is the annual designation of several cities as Cultural Capitals, sites of special artistic and cultural programs for that year. Also worthy of note is the Council Work Plan for Culture 2008–10, O.J. L 143/06 (June 10, 2008), which encourages national promotion of the mobility of artists, cultural events and creative industries.

The most significant legislation in the cultural field is undoubtedly Directive 93/7 on the return of cultural objects unlawfully removed from the territory of another Member State, O.J. L 74/74 (Mar. 27, 1993), supplemented by Council Regulation 3911/92, O.J. L 395/1 (Dec. 9, 1992), which requires licenses for the export of cultural goods to third countries. The increasingly grave problem of the theft of art and archaeological treasures prompted the directive, whose scope covers "cultural objects classified as national treasures." The directive creates a right to obtain the return of the unlawfully removed cultural object and contains a long annex intended to indicate the variety of cultural objects concerned. For a longer description, see V. Vitrano, Protecting Cultural Objects in an Internal Border–Free EC, 17 Fordham Int'l L.J. 1164 (1994).

D. PROMOTING FREE MOVEMENT AND RESIDENCE RIGHTS

1. BORDER CONTROLS

Ever since the 1985 White Paper on Completing the Internal Market described border controls as "the obvious manifestation of the continued division of the Community," the European Council and the Commission have pressed for their abolition. However, the United Kingdom, under both Conservative and Labor governments, is convinced that the elimination of border controls poses too great a risk that terrorists, illegal immigrants and asylum seekers, and drug traffickers would move freely over its borders. Because legislation to remove border controls requires Council unanimity, the UK exercises an effective veto power.

The Court of Justice has, however, set standards for the manner in which border controls can be carried out. In Commission v. Belgium (Border controls), Case 321/87, [1989] ECR 997, the Court held that Belgium could not carry out any systematic border check other than to establish that a person held a Member State passport or identity card. In Commission v. The Netherlands (Border controls), Case 68/89, [1991] ECR 2637, the Court held that the Netherlands could not question Community nationals crossing the frontier about the purpose and duration of their journey and the financial means at their disposal.

In 1999, a frontal attack on the legitimacy of internal border controls came to the Court.

CRIMINAL PROCEEDINGS AGAINST WIJSENBEEK

Case C–378/97, [1999] ECR I—6207.

[On arriving at Rotterdam airport, which receives flights only from sites within the Community, Wijsenbeek, a Dutch national, refused to show a Dutch passport or identity card to the police officer at the border control post. Wijsenbeek claimed that ECT Articles 14 and 18 conferred on citizens of Member States the right to move freely in the interior of the European Union without presenting a passport. The trial court requested the Court of Justice to interpret the two articles.]

40   Article 14 cannot be interpreted as meaning that, in the absence of measures adopted* * *to abolish controls of persons at the internal frontiers of the Community, that obligation automatically arises from expiry of that period. * * *.

42   [A]s long as Community provisions on controls at the external borders of the Community, which also imply common or harmonized rules on, in particular, conditions of access, visas and asylum, have not been adopted, the exercise of those rights presupposes that the person concerned is able to establish that he or she has the nationality of a Member State.

43   At the time of the events in question in the main proceedings, there were no common rules or harmonized laws of the Member States on, in particular, controls at external frontiers and immigration, visa and asylum policy. Consequently, even if, under Article [14] or Article [18] of the Treaty, nationals of the Member States did have an unconditional right to move freely within the territory of the Member States, the Member States retained the right to carry out identity checks at the internal frontiers of the Community, requiring persons to present a valid identity card or passport * * * in order to be able to establish whether the person concerned is a national of a Member State, thus having the right to move freely within the territory of the Member States, or a national of a non-member country, not having that right.

NOTES AND QUESTIONS

1. *Wijsenbeek* answers the question, long debated in academic circles, whether ECT Article 14 (initially EECT Article 8a) could be said to have direct effect when it required the completion of the internal market, "an area without internal frontiers," by December 31, 1992, at least with regard to the elimination of border controls on persons. See Chapter 14B. The Commission and all the intervening States argued that Article 14 did not have direct effect, and Advocate General Cosmos also supported this view.

2. The United States, of course, has no border controls at state lines, although it has large numbers of illegal immigrants who move rather easily throughout the country. From a policy point of view, do you think the benefits in ending internal border controls in the Community outweigh the risks, or not? For a thoughtful analysis of *Wijsenbeek* and later developments, see H.

Toner, Passport Controls at Borders Between Member States, 25 Eur. L. Rev. 415 (2000).

3.   In fact, border controls have largely been ended among the States that comprise what is popularly called Schengenland. In 1985, the Benelux States, France, Germany and Italy signed the Schengen Accord to enable the ultimate elimination of frontier controls by harmonizing key aspects of their immigration and visa policies, as well as coordinating their combat of illegal traffic in drugs and weapons. Over time, all of the Member States except Denmark, the United Kingdom and Ireland have joined in the Schengen Accord, as have Iceland and Norway by a 1996 agreement. The implementation procedure was complicated, but the accord is largely operational in most States. The current border crossing rules are set out in Regulation 562/2006, O.J. L 105/1, (Apr. 9, 2006). Accordingly, persons traveling across frontiers within "Schengenland" by car, rail, plane or boat are no longer automatically stopped for passport or other frontier checks, although they may be occasionally for spot checks. The Schengen Accord States have also instituted a central computer system in Strasbourg to aid in the identification of suspected drug dealers, terrorists and other criminals. The Amsterdam Treaty's Schengen Protocol incorporates legal measures adopted under the Schengen Accord into the Community legal system in a rather complicated manner. A Lisbon Treaty Protocol 19 now replaces the prior Schengen Protocol.

2. PROMOTION OF RIGHTS OF RESIDENCE

For over fifteen years, two 1990 directives set out the rights of residence for all those not covered by the directives granting such rights to migrant workers, students and the self-employed.

The directives were adopted through use of the implied legislative power provision, ECT Article 308 (now TFEU Article 352), which requires unanimous Council action, because the Council considered that no specific Treaty grant of legislative power authorized the directives. The first, Directive 90/365, O.J. L 180/28 (July 13, 1990), grants a right of residence to all "persons who have ceased their occupational activity," which essentially means formerly employed or self-employed persons who have retired or become disabled. The second, Directive 90/364 O.J. L 180/26 (July 13, 1990), grants a right of residence in any Member State to nationals of other States who do not enjoy a right of residence under any other provision of Community law. Both directives are now replaced by Directive 2004/38.

The directives grant an accessory right of residence to the spouse of the person covered by the directive, and any dependent descendants or ancestors of either spouse, even if the person involved is not a Community national (art. 2). They thus parallel the right of residence granted to family members of workers by Regulation 1612/68. On the other hand, article 1 of each directive sets an important condition on the residence right. Both require the person concerned to have sufficient resources to "avoid becoming a burden on the social security system of the host Member State," and be covered by all-risk health insurance. "Sufficient resources" is defined in the directives as an amount higher than the level at which host State nationals may obtain state social assistance.

Referring directly to the residence rights of citizens of the Union under ECT Article 18, the Court has now reduced the impact of the "sufficient resources" condition.

BAUMBAST AND R v. SECRETARY OF STATE FOR THE HOME DEPARTMENT

Case C–413/99, [2002] ECR I–7091.

[Baumbast, a German national employed in the UK for several years in the 1990s, presently is employed outside the European Union. His wife and children continue to reside in the UK (see the judgment excerpt at page 586) and Baumbast considers this to be his home. When Baumbast requested a UK residence permit, the administrative tribunal asked the Court whether he was entitled to one as a citizen of the Union and, if so under what conditions.]

81   Although, before the Treaty on European Union entered into force, the Court had held that that right of residence, conferred directly by the EC Treaty, was subject to the condition that the person concerned was carrying on an economic activity within the meaning of Articles [39, 43 and 49], since then, Union citizenship has been introduced into the EC Treaty and Article 18(1) EC has conferred a right, for every citizen, to move and reside freely within the territory of the Member States.

82   Under Article 17(1) EC, every person holding the nationality of a Member State is to be a citizen of the Union. Union citizenship is destined to be the fundamental status of nationals of the Member States [citing *Grzelczyk*].

83   Moreover, the Treaty on European Union does not require that citizens of the Union pursue a professional or trade activity, whether as an employed or self-employed person, in order to enjoy the rights provided on citizenship of the Union. Furthermore, there is nothing in the text of that Treaty to permit the conclusion that citizens of the Union who have established themselves in another Member State in order to carry on an activity as an employed person there are deprived, where that activity comes to an end, of the rights which are conferred on them by the EC Treaty by virtue of that citizenship.

84   [T]he right to reside within the territory of the Member States under Article 18(1) EC * * * is conferred directly on every citizen of the Union by a clear and precise provision of the EC Treaty. Purely as a national of a Member State, and consequently a citizen of the Union, Mr. Baumbast therefore has the right to rely on Article 18(1) EC.

85   Admittedly, that right for citizens of the Union to reside within the territory of another Member State is conferred subject to the limita-

tions and conditions laid down by the EC Treaty and by the measures adopted to give it effect.

* * *

[87] Article 1(1) of Directive 90/364 provides that Member States can require of the nationals of a Member State who wish to enjoy the right to reside within their territory that they themselves and the members of their families be covered by sickness insurance in respect of all risks in the host Member State and have sufficient resources to avoid becoming a burden on the social assistance system of the host Member State during their period of residence.

[88] [I]t is clear from the file that Mr. Baumbast pursues an activity as an employed person in non-member countries for German companies and that neither he nor his family has used the social assistance system in the host Member State. In those circumstances, * * * Mr. Baumbast satisfies the condition relating to sufficient resources imposed by Directive 90/364.

[The UK claimed that Baumbast's German health insurance might not cover emergency treatment in the UK. Applying the principal of proportionality, the Court held that to deny Baumbast his right of residence solely on this ground "would amount to a disproportionate interference with the exercise of that right" (¶ 93).]

NOTES AND QUESTIONS

1. The judgement in *Baumbast* is the first time that the Court held that ECT Article 18(1) had direct effect, so that citizens of the Union could rely upon it against State measures. Previously the Court had cited Article 18 but relied upon the general non-discrimination language of ECT Article 12. Since 2002, the Court regularly cites *Baumbast* in its judgments concerning the residence rights of citizens. *Baumbast* is also important for its use of the proportionality principle to interpret narrowly the effect of the conditions set in the residence directives. Presumably the Court of Justice will hold that the correlative language of the Lisbon TEU Article 4(3) and TFEU Article 21(1), which replace ECT Articles 12 and 18(1), have direct effect.

2. In Commission v. Belgium (Sufficient resources for residence), Case C–408/03, [2006] ECR I–2647, the Court cited *Baumbast* for its holding that Article 18 had direct effect (¶ 34), and then held that Belgium could not require a citizen of the Union to have sufficient resources when someone else will provide the resources, citing the example of a Portuguese national who lived with her long-standing unmarried partner, a Belgian national. The Court rejected Belgium's contention that the person supporting the citizen must have some legal relationship with the citizen (¶ 46), but observed that Belgium could monitor whether the support continued in the future (¶ 50).

ZHU AND CHEN v. SECRETARY OF STATE FOR THE HOME DEPARTMENT

Case C–200/02, [2004] ECR I–9925.

[Mrs. Chen, a Chinese national, went to Belfast in 2000 in order to give birth to her daughter, Catherine Zhu, who acquired Irish nationality by being born on the island of Ireland. Although Northern Ireland is a part of the UK, Catherine did not acquire UK nationality by being born there. Mrs. Chen then moved with Catherine to reside in Cardiff. Mrs. Chen and her husband are both employed by a Chinese company, but Mr. Chen does not reside in the UK. Through her employment, Mrs. Chen has ample resources for herself and Catherine, as well as private sickness insurance. After Mrs. Chen's application for a UK residence permit for herself and Catherine was denied, an appellate tribunal asked the Court of Justice whether Catherine and Mrs. Chen had rights of residence under EU law. The Court initially cited *Baumbast* and held that Article 18(1)'s grant of a residence right had direct effect (¶ 26). The Court then turned to the "sufficient resources" condition of Directive 90/364.]

28   It is clear from the order for reference that Catherine has both sickness insurance and sufficient resources, provided by her mother, for her not to become a burden on the social assistance system of the host Member State.

29   The objection raised by the Irish and United Kingdom Governments that the condition concerning the availability of sufficient resources means that the person concerned must, in contrast to Catherine's case, possess those resources personally and may not use for that purpose those of an accompanying family member, such as Mrs. Chen, is unfounded.

30   According to the very terms of Article 1(1) of Directive 90/364, it is sufficient for the nationals of Member States to 'have' the necessary resources, and that provision lays down no requirement whatsoever as to their origin.

31   The correctness of that interpretation is reinforced by the fact that provisions laying down a fundamental principle such as that of the free movement of persons must be interpreted broadly.

* * *

34   The United Kingdom Government contends [that] Mrs. Chen's move to Northern Ireland with the aim of having her child acquire the nationality of another Member State constitutes an attempt improperly to exploit the provisions of Community law. * * * It is, in their view, settled case-law that Member States are entitled to take measures to prevent individuals from improperly taking advantage of provisions of Community law or from attempting, under cover of the rights created by the Treaty, illegally to circumvent national legislation.* * *

35   That argument must also be rejected.

36   It is true that Mrs. Chen admits that the purpose of her stay in the United Kingdom was to create a situation in which the child she was expecting would be able to acquire the nationality of another Member State in order thereafter to secure for her child and for herself a long-term right to reside in the United Kingdom.

37   Nevertheless, under international law, it is for each Member State, having due regard to Community law, to lay down the conditions for the acquisition and loss of nationality [citing *Micheletti* and *Kaur*, supra page 620].

38   None of the parties that submitted observations to the Court has questioned either the legality, or the fact, of Catherine's acquisition of Irish nationality.

[The Court then considered whether Mrs. Chen had a right of residence.]

45   [A] refusal to allow the parent, whether a national of a Member State or a national of a non-member country, who is the carer of a child to whom Article 18 EC and Directive 90/364 grant a right of residence, to reside with that child in the host Member State would deprive the child's right of residence of any useful effect. It is clear that enjoyment by a young child of a right of residence necessarily implies that the child is entitled to be accompanied by the person who is his or her primary carer and accordingly that the carer must be in a position to reside with the child in the host Member State for the duration of such residence (see, *mutatis mutandis*, in relation to Article 12 of Regulation No 1612/68, *Baumbast and R*, paragraphs 71 to 75).

46   For that reason alone, where * * * Article 18 EC and Directive 90/364 grant a right to reside for an indefinite period in the host Member State to a young minor who is a national of another Member State, those same provisions allow a parent who is that minor's primary carer to reside with the child in the host Member State.

NOTES AND QUESTIONS

1. That the Court of Justice decided this extraordinary case in a plenary session underlines its importance. Do you agree with the Court's conclusion in ¶¶ 34–36 that Mrs. Chen's motive in choosing Belfast as Catherine's birthplace in order to obtain Irish citizenship for her daughter is irrelevant? Why isn't this an abuse of right? The Court, citing *Kaur*, held that full respect had to be given to Ireland's nationality legislation (¶ 37). The Court might also have cited *Levin*, supra page 620, on the lack of relevance of Mrs. Chen's motive. Moreover, isn't Catherine, who enjoys Irish nationality and thus is a citizen of the Union, a totally innocent holder of the rights? On a comparative note, federal circuit opinions have authorized the deportation of parents who are not US citizens when they have minor children who are citizens, even though the minor child needs parental care and must leave with the parents.

See Gonzalez–Cuevas v. INS, 515 F.2d 1222 (5th Cir. 1975); Aalund v. Marshall, 461 F.2d 710 (5th Cir. 1972).

2. Mrs. Chen's derivative right to reside with Catherine as her primary caretaker is inevitable in view of the Court's conclusions in *Baumbast and R*, supra page 586. Her derivative residence right would normally end when Catherine becomes an adult, but it is possible that Article 3(2) of Directive 2004/58 would enable her to continue to reside with Catherine as a family member. For a thoughtful analysis of the issues, see the case comment by K. Vanvoorden, 12 Colum. J. Eur. L. 305 (2005–06).

E. PUBLIC POLICY AND PUBLIC SECURITY LIMITS

The free movement and residence right accorded by ECT Article 18 to citizens of the Union is expressly made "subject to the limitations and conditions laid down in this Treaty and by the measures adopted to give it effect." For workers and the self-employed, ECT Articles 39 and 46 expressly enable public policy, public security and public health limits. The Court of Justice by analogy applies these, and the terms of Directive 64/221, to all citizens of the Union.

Expulsion is a Member State's most severe sanction for forbidden behavior by nationals of other States. Not surprisingly, the Commission has on several occasions brought ECT Article 226 proceedings against States whose regulations are so broadly drafted as to appear to make it possible that a citizen of the Union might be automatically expelled after conviction of a serious criminal offence. Thus, in Commission v. Netherlands (Expulsion rules), Case C–50/06, [2007] ECR I–4383, the Court referred to the substantive and procedural safeguards set out in Directive 64/221 as applying to all citizens of the Union (¶¶ 34–40). The Court then held that the public policy exception must be interpreted strictly, in accordance with its holding in *Rutili* that the State must establish that an individual's conduct represents "a genuine and sufficiently serious threat to one of the fundamental interests of society" (¶ 43). The Court accordingly invalidated the Dutch rules. The Court reached the same conclusion in Commission v. Spain (Expulsion rules), Case C–503/03, [2006] ECR I–1097.

The following case provides a more vivid example of the Court's limitation of the sanction expulsion.

OLIVERI v. BADEN–WURTTEMBERG
Case C–493/01, [2004] ECR I–5257.

[Oliveri, an Italian national, was born in Germany and has always resided there with his parents. He is a drug addict, convicted often for the sale of narcotics. In 2000, while in prison, the administrative authorities ordered his expulsion on the basis of his serious criminal record, and the risk of further offences due to his drug addiction. In an appeal, the appellate court learned that Oliveri was gravely ill with HIV and chronic hepatitis. The court then asked the Court of Justice whether expulsion was warranted under these circumstances. The Court initially noted that the record did not clearly show that Oliveri could claim the status of a worker, but that he could be treated as a citizen of the Union (¶¶ 52–53).]

66 Concerning measures of public policy, it is clear from Article 3 of Directive 64/221 that, in order to be justified, they must be based exclusively on the personal conduct of the individual concerned. It is stated in the same provision that previous criminal convictions cannot in themselves justify those measures. As the Court has held, * * * the concept of public policy presupposes the existence * * * of a genuine and sufficiently serious threat to the requirements of public policy affecting one of the fundamental interests of society.

67 While it is true that a Member State may consider that the use of drugs constitutes a danger for society such as to justify special measures against foreign nationals who contravene its laws on drugs, the public policy exception must, however, be interpreted restrictively, with the result that the existence of a previous criminal conviction can justify an expulsion only in so far as the circumstances which gave rise to that conviction are evidence of personal conduct constituting a present threat to the requirements of public policy [citing *Calfa,* infra page 695].

* * *

77 For the purposes of deciding whether a national of another Member State may be expelled under the exception based on reasons of public policy, the competent national authorities must assess, on a case-by-case basis, whether the measure or the circumstances which gave rise to that expulsion order prove the existence of personal conduct constituting a present threat to the requirements of public policy * * *.

78 [C]ircumstances may arise between the date of the expulsion order and that of its review by the competent court which point to the cessation or the substantial diminution of the threat which the conduct of the person ordered to be expelled constitutes to the requirements of public policy.

79 [D]erogations from the principle of freedom of movement for workers must be interpreted strictly, and thus the requirement of the existence of a present threat must, as a general rule, be satisfied at the time of the expulsion.

80 While it is for the domestic legal system of each Member State to lay down the detailed procedural rules governing actions for safeguarding rights which individuals derive from Community law, the fact remains that those rules must not be such as to render virtually impossible or excessively difficult the exercise of rights conferred by Community law.

81   A national practice such as that described in the order for reference is liable to adversely affect the right to freedom of movement to which nationals of the Member States are entitled and particularly their right not to be subjected to expulsion measures save in the extreme cases provided for by Directive 64/221. That is especially so if a lengthy period has elapsed between the date of the decision to expel the person concerned and that of the review of that decision by the competent court.

NOTES AND QUESTIONS

1.   *Oliveri* is actually a companion case to *Orfanopoulos*, concerning a Greek migrant worker, supra page 596. The Court clearly suggests that the referring court should prevent Oliveri's deportation. Do you agree? Do you think Germany could expel a drug addict imprisoned for criminal offences who is not seriously ill? Presumably Germany could expel someone, addict or not, convicted repeatedly for selling narcotics, who is not seriously ill.

2.   Remember that the directives on residence rights for different categories of non-working citizens of the Union required financial resources sufficient to avoid becoming a burden on the host State social assistance system. Although the Court has narrowly interpreted that condition, it has never invalidated it. Thus, in *Trojani*, supra page 606, the Court held that if it was determined that Trojani's work at the Salvation Army hostel did not constitute real and genuine employment, then Belgium could deport him, although the Court did note that "recourse to the social assistance system by a citizen of the Union may not automatically entail such a measure" (citing *Grzelczyk*) (¶ 45).

3.   Ministerul Administratiei v. Jipa, Case C–33/07, [2008] I–5157, is a rare case concerning restriction on leaving, rather than entering, a Member State. In 2006, Belgium deported Jipa, a Romanian citizen, due to his illegal residence there. A 1995 agreement between Belgium and Romania required Romania to readmit any deported Romanians. In 2007, the Romanian Ministry for Administration sought to bar Jipa from leaving Romania to travel to Belgium for three years. The court hearing Jipa's challenge to the bar asked the Court of Justice whether the exit ban violated ECT Article 18. Not surprisingly, the Court held that the right of free movement under Article 18 included a right to leave the home State (¶ 18). Although public security interests could limit the right, the home State had to make a specific assessment of Jipa's personal conduct to determine whether it satisfied the *Rutili* standard of a "genuine, present and sufficiently serious threat to one of the fundamental interests of society" (¶ 23). As Romania had admitted this was not the case, presumably Jipa would be free to travel to Belgium.

F. DIRECTIVE 2004/38: THE COM-PREHENSIVE CITIZENS' RES-IDENCE DIRECTIVE

Directive 2004/38 on the movement and residence rights of citizens of the Union and their family members, O.J.L. 158/77 (Apr. 30, 2004), now comprehensively covers the field, repealing some provisions in Regulation 1612/68, the 1990s residence directives, Directive 64/221, etc., effective as of Apr. 30, 2006. We can here present only the key features of this long and detailed text, which is Document 17 in the Documents Supplement. Overall, the directive is significantly more liberal than prior directives, especially in granting more extensive and ultimately permanent rights of residence to citizens and their family members, and in requiring equal treatment with Host State nationals. A key recital declares that "Union citizenship should be the fundamental status of nationals of Member States" and that the directive is intended to "simplify and strengthen the right of free movement and residence of all Union citizens."

Article 2 naturally makes any Member State national a citizen of the Union, in accord with Treaty Article 17. The definition of a 'family member' of citizens replicates article 10 of regulation 1612/68, but adds a partner in a registered partnership of a Member State, provided that this status is recognized in the host State in which rights are being asserted. All of these family members enjoy all the rights accorded by Directive 2004/38. In addition, article 3(2) states that host States are urged to facilitate entry and residence for "any other family members" who "are dependents or members of the household of the Union citizen," as well a "partner with whom the Union citizen has a durable relationship."

These provisions have already been interpreted in Metock v. Minister for Justice, Case C–127/08, [2008] ECR I–6241, which concerned the refusal of Ireland to grant residence rights to four men who had initially been denied asylum, but who had married non-Irish citizens of the Union during the rather lengthy asylum proceedings. The Court held that all four were entitled to residence derivatively from their spouses, who were migrant workers in Ireland. Citing the importance of "a normal family life" (¶ 62), and the need to encourage the mobility of citizens of the Union, the Court held that the husbands did not have to be married to the citizens of the Union prior to their movement to Ireland. The Court noted that Ireland could refuse to recognize "marriages of convenience" pursuant to article 35 of the Directive (¶ 75), but Ireland accepted that all of the four marriages concerned were valid.

Under article 6, citizens and their family members (citizens or not) have a short-term right of residence for up to three months in a host State so long as they possess a valid identity card or passport. A right of residence for more than three months is set out in article 7, but, as in the prior residence directives, those citizens who are not workers or self-employed must have sufficient resources to avoid becoming a burden on the host State social assistance system, and possess sickness insurance.

One of the most liberal provisions of the directive is that citizens and their family members residing with them (including third state nationals) acquire a right of permanent residence in a host State after five years of continuous residence (art. 16). They then no longer need to satisfy the condition of possession of sufficient financial resources. They are also entitled to receive a document certifying the right of permanent residence (arts. 19–20). The right of permanent residence may be lost through a continuous absence of two years (art. 16(4)).

The directive no longer requires citizens to obtain an EU residence permit from the host State, although they must register with the authorities (art. 8). The authorities may require a valid passport or identity card, proof of employment or self-employment, and proof of a relationship from spouses, registered partners, or family members. Any family members who are third state nationals must obtain a Residence Card from the host State, valid for five years (arts. 10–11). A citizen's spouse and family members may have continued rights of residence after the death of the citizen, or after divorce or termination of a registered partnership, subject to the condition of possessing sufficient financial resources and sickness insurance, and to various other conditions for those who are third state nationals (arts. 12–13).

One of the most important rights granted by the directive in article 24 is that of a citizen's right of equal treatment with host State nationals, thus incorporating the Court's application of EC Treaty Article 12 in some precedents. Likewise following Court doctrine, article 24(2) enables the host State to limit access to social assistance during the first three months of residence.

The directive contains a series of articles setting out a host State's power to limit entry or residence on the grounds of public policy, public security or public health which largely replicate the substantive provisions and the procedural rights accorded by Directive 64/221. Article 27(2) incorporates the Court's doctrine that "the personal conduct of the individual concerned must represent a genuine, present and sufficiently serious threat affecting one of the fundamental interests of society" in order to justify deportation on any of these grounds.

The Court of Justice has already had occasion to interpret Directive 2004/38 in several judgments. Following is the most prominent one, which re-examines some of the issues raised in *Baumbast and R*, supra page 586.

TEIXEIRA v. LONDON BOROUGH OF LAMBETH
Case C–480/08, [2010] ECR ___ (Feb. 23, 2010).

[Ms. Teixeira, a Portuguese national, came to the UK in 1989 with her migrant worker husband. Although now divorced, she has resided continuously in the UK since then, intermittently working, but unemployed since 2005. She is the primary caretaker of her daughter, Patricia, born in 1991. When Ms. Teixeira applied for the UK social welfare benefit of housing assistance, her application was denied. On appeal, she contended that she was lawfully resident as the primary caretaker of her daughter who was then, in 2007, receiving secondary education, pursuant to the Court's judgment in *Baumbast and R*. The referring court inquired whether she had a right of residence and the right to the housing assistance on various factual grounds pursuant to Directive 2004/38. The Court initially reiterated its conclusions in *Baumbast and R* (¶¶ 36–39).]

44   First, the right of children of migrant workers to equal treatment in access to education, under Article 12 of Regulation No 1612/68, applies only to children who are residing in the Member State in which one of their parents is or has been employed.

45   Access to education thus depends on the child first being installed in the host Member State. Children who have installed themselves in the host Member State in their capacity of members of the family of a migrant worker, [as well as] children of a migrant worker who, like Ms. Teixeira's daughter * * * have resided since birth in the Member State in which their father or mother is or was employed, may rely on the right of access to education in that State.

46   Contrary to the submissions of the London Borough of Lambeth and the United Kingdom and Danish Governments, Article 12 of Regulation No 1612/68, as interpreted by the Court in *Baumbast and R*, allows a child to have an independent right of residence in connection with the right of access to education. In particular, the exercise of the right of access to education was not conditional on the child retaining, throughout the period of education, a specific right of residence under Article 10(1)(a) of that regulation * * *.

[The Court then noted that article 38 of Directive 2004/38 did not repeal the text of Regulation 1612/68's article 12 (see Chapter 15A), even though it repealed its article 10 concerning derivative residence rights of family members of workers.]

49   It follows that, once the right of access to education derived by the child from Article 12 of that regulation has been acquired * * *, the right of residence is retained by the child and can no longer be called into question because the conditions which were set out in Article 10 of that regulation are not satisfied.

50   Second, the right of children to equal treatment in access to education does not depend on the circumstance that their father or mother retains the status of migrant worker in the host Member State. As is apparent from the very wording of Article 12 of the regulation, that right * * * applies also to children of former migrant workers.

* * *

54   That independence of Article 12 of Regulation No 1612/68 from Article 10 of that regulation, which has since been repealed, formed the basis

of the [*Baumbast and R* judgment], and was not called into question by the entry into force of Directive 2004/38.

* * *

56   [T]here is nothing to suggest that, when adopting Directive 2004/38, the legislature intended to alter the scope of Article 12 of that regulation, as interpreted by the Court, so as to limit its normative content from then on to a mere right of access to education.

* * *

60   Finally, it should be noted that, according to recital 3 in the preamble to Directive 2004/38, the aim of that directive is inter alia to simplify and strengthen the right of free movement and residence of all Union citizens * * *.

61   [Accordingly,] a national of a Member State who was employed in another Member State in which his or her child is in education may, in circumstances such as those of the main proceedings, claim, in the capacity of primary carer for that child, a right of residence in the host Member State on the sole basis of Article 12 of Regulation No 1612/68, without being required to satisfy the conditions laid down in Directive 2004/38.

[The Court then turned to the UK authorities' contention that Directive 2004/38's provision requiring "sufficient resources" meant that Ms. Teixeira did not satisfy a crucial condition for legal residence.]

67   [S]ince the Court pointed out, in *Baumbast and R*, that in view of the context and the objectives of Regulation No 1612/68, in particular Article 12, that provision cannot be interpreted restrictively and must not be rendered ineffective, it cannot be argued on the basis of that judgment that the granting of the right of residence at issue is conditional on self-sufficiency, as the Court did not base its reasoning even implicitly on such a condition.

68   The interpretation that the right of residence in the host Member State of children who are in education there and the parent who is their primary carer is not subject to the condition that they have sufficient resources and comprehensive sickness insurance cover is supported by Article 12(3) of Directive 2004/38, which provides that the departure or death of the citizen of the Union does not entail the loss of the right of residence of the children or the parent who has actual custody of them, irrespective of their nationality, if the children reside in the host Member State and are enrolled at an educational establishment for the purpose of studying there, until the completion of their studies.

69   While that provision is not applicable in the main proceedings, it illustrates the particular importance which Directive 2004/38 attaches to the situation of children who are in education in the host Member State and the parents who care for them.

[70] The answer to Question 2(b) is therefore that the right of residence in the host Member State of the parent who is the primary carer of a child exercising the right to pursue his or her education in accordance with Article 12 of Regulation No 1612/68 is not conditional on that parent having sufficient resources not to become a burden on the social assistance system of that Member State during the period of residence and having comprehensive sickness insurance cover there.

NOTES AND QUESTIONS

1. The Court's judgment clearly demonstrates that it intends to interpret Directive 2004/38 liberally, just as it always did in interpreting Regulation 1612/68. Note the Court's stress in ¶ 60 on the Directive's third recital whose full text is: "Union citizenship should be the fundamental status of nationals of the Member States when they exercise their right of free movement and residence." It is not surprising that the Court should reiterate its conclusions in *Baumbast and R.* The Court goes beyond that precedent in holding that Teixeira does not have to fulfill the Directive 2004/38's requirement of "sufficient resources" because her right to residence stems from her role as primary caregiver of a child with residence rights (¶¶ 67–70). Do you agree?

2. Note that Directive 2004/38 expressly only repeals articles 10 and 11 of Regulation 1612/68 (because they are replaced by other provisions in the directive), but not article 12 or the rest of the regulation. Thus, all of the other provisions described in Chapter 14A, and the interpretative caselaw in 14B, remain fully effective.

3. The Court also dealt with the UK contention that Teixeira's derivative residence right should end when her daughter becomes an adult, at the age of 18 in the UK, which in fact occurred while the judgment was pending. In ¶¶ 79–80, the Court held that the daughter's rights under article 12 continued during higher education, and in ¶ 86 that a caregiver's role might continue until the child completes his or her education. Would you agree?

G.   TOWARD AN AREA OF FREEDOM, SECURITY AND JUSTICE

1.   FROM THE MAASTRICHT TREATY'S CJHA TO THE TREATY OF LISBON

The Treaty of Maastricht inserted Article 100c into the EC Treaty, authorizing the Council to "determine the third countries whose national must be in possession of a visa when crossing the external borders of the Member States." Article 100c was intended to be the first step in harmonizing Member State rules on external border controls. A common visa policy ensures mutual trust among the States concerning the status of non-Community nationals moving into the Union on a short term basis. A common visa policy obviously facilitates the adoption of measures concerning rights of free movement and residence of legal immigrants.

In 1995, the Council adopted Regulation 1683/95 on the introduction of a common format for visas, O.J.L. 164/1 (July 14, 1995), which not only governs the visa format, but also requires that visas contain secret specifications set by the Commission to reduce the risk of counterfeit visas. Article 5 prescribes that the usual maximum term for a visa is three months. Updating and slightly revising an initial 1995 text, Council Regulation 1932/2006, O.J.L. 405/23 (Dec. 30, 2006), determines the third countries whose nationals must possess a visa, with an Annex listing 100 such countries.

The Maastricht Treaty created the "third pillar" of the European Union, Cooperation in Justice and Home Affairs (CJHA), set out in then Article K of the Treaty on European Union. Article K.1. identified a number of areas of "common interest," notably immigration and asylum policies, control of frontiers with third countries, police cooperation and judicial cooperation. Under Article K.2, the Council might propose Conventions, adopt joint actions or propose cooperative measures to the Member States. Both the Commission and Member States might propose initiatives, and the Council usually had to act unanimously. Parliament was only to be kept informed. By the time of the 1996 Intergovernmental Conference which drafted the Treaty of Amsterdam, most Member States were prepared to move beyond the inter-governmental cooperation in CJHA. Considerable credit goes to the Irish and Dutch presidencies, which made this a priority matter.

The Treaty of Amsterdam, effective since May 1, 1999, introduced into the EC Treaty a new Title IV on Visas, Asylum, Immigration and Other Policies Related to Free Movement of Persons, thereby largely eliminating the "third pillar." ECT Article 61 set as a goal the progressive establishment of "an area of freedom, security and justice." ECT Article 63(3) authorized the Council to adopt measures setting "standards on procedures for the issue by Member States of long term visas and residence permits, including those for the purpose of family reunion," and measures that would enable third state nationals legally resident in one Member State to take up residence in another State.

Generally speaking, the Council was to act unanimously after consulting Parliament. By three Protocols, Denmark, Ireland and the United Kingdom do not participate in the legislative process and have no obligation to comply with measures adopted under the Title. However, the Protocols enabled each State to "opt in" with regard to specific measures, in whole or in part. A "two-tier" Union thus exists in this sphere. P.J. Kuijper, Some Legal Problems Associated With the Communitarization of Policy on Visas, Asylum and Immigration Under the Amsterdam Treaty, 37 Common Mkt. L. Rev. 345 (2000), provides an expert analysis of the provisions.

The Lisbon Treaty's Title V Area of Freedom, Security and Justice significantly revises the former Title IV. TFEU Article 67(1) begins by declaring: "The Union shall constitute an area of freedom, security and justice with respect for fundamental rights and the different legal systems and traditions of Member States." This clearly moves beyond the former goal of "progressively establishing" the area.

Title V's twenty-two articles provide in much greater detail for measures to achieve the removal of border controls for persons, the adoption of common policies on asylum, immigration and external border control, the mutual recognition of civil judgments, and cooperation in police and criminal matters. A major change is that the Parliament and Council act jointly through the ordinary legislative process, replacing the requirement for unanimous Council action in some legislative fields, such as the adoption of measures concerning visas, external border controls, common asylum rules, and common immigration policies (TFEU Articles 77–79). Denmark, Ireland and the United Kingdom have kept their Protocols providing that they will not participate in the legislative process or be bound by measures adopted pursuant to Title V, unless they opt otherwise.

2. LONG TERM RESIDENCE RIGHTS FOR THIRD STATE NATIONALS

The European Council at Tampere, Finland in October 1999 called for action to create long-term residence rights for third state nationals. Directive 2003/109 on long-term residents, O.J. L 16/44 (Jan. 23, 2004) achieved this, becoming effective Jan. 23, 2006. Like Directive 2004/38, the long-term residence rights directive substantially liberalizes prior rules. However, the directive is not in effect in Denmark, Ireland or the UK because these States exercised their Protocol-based right to opt-out of measures adopted under ECT Article 63(3).

Third-state nationals (including, of course, American citizens) obtain the status of long-term residents in a Member State after five years of continuous legal residence (art. 4) and can then obtain a residence permit valid for at least five years, automatically renewable (art. 8). The principal condition for residence is that the national and his/her family must have sufficient financial resources to avoid recourse to the social assistance system (art. 5). The host State may, of course, deny or terminate long-term residence on grounds of public policy or public security (art. 6).

Long-term residents will enjoy equal treatment with nationals as to access to employment or self-employment, access to education or vocational training, receipt of social assistance or social security, taxation, etc. (art. 11). They may be expelled only after a proceeding determines (with right of judicial appeal) that the resident "constitutes an actual and sufficiently serious threat to public policy or public security" (art. 12).

One of the most important new rights accorded to long-term residents is that of movement to reside in another Member State, either for employment, study, or "other purposes" (e.g., retirement) (art. 14). The new host State may require the new resident to have sufficient financial resources to maintain himself or herself and dependent family members (art. 15). The new residents will enjoy the right of equal treatment with host State nationals (art. 21).

Supplementing this extremely liberal directive is Directive 2004/114 on the admission of third-state nationals for studies, O.J. L 375/12 (Dec. 23, 2004), effective Jan. 24, 2007. Although the principal beneficiaries are students admitted to college or university study, the directive also covers pupils in secondary school exchange programs and trainees in vocational training (arts. 2–3). Students must have sufficient resources for their studies, maintenance and return travel (art. 7), but may be employed for 10 hours per week, or more if the host State permits it (art. 17). Note that Denmark, Ireland and the UK are not bound by this directive, in view of the Protocols mentioned above.

Finally, a recent directive establishes a 'blue card' system intended to attract highly skilled third state nationals. Directive 2009/50, O.J. L 155/17 (June 18, 2009), requires Member States to facilitate the entry of highly qualified persons who will be granted a Blue Card residence permit for one to four years. This is an initiative within the context of the Lisbon Strategy discussed in Chapter 14B. As noted above, the directive does not apply to Denmark, Ireland and the UK.

3. ASYLUM AND REFUGEES

The European Council session at the Hague in November 2004 set a series of priority objectives in the area of freedom, security and justice, followed by a five-year Commission Action Plan in 2005, O.J. C 198/1 (Aug. 12, 2005). A recent Commission Communication provides an evaluation of the process in the Hague Program, COM (2009) 263.

Action to achieve common standards and policies concerning asylum and refugees is an important priority. Directive 2003/9, O.J. L 31/18 (Feb. 6, 2003), set minimum standards for the reception of asylum seekers, covering not only the initial review, but also minimum health care, schooling for minors, standards for any housing provided by the host State, etc. Subsequently, Directive 2005/85, O.J. L 326/13 (Dec. 13, 2005), set minimum standards on procedures for granting refugee status. The directive is extremely detailed, covering the rights of a personal interview, access to interpreters and legal advisers, rapid decisions and administrative or court appeal. Council Decision 2002/463, O.J. L 161/11 (June 19, 2002), authorized an action program for national administrative cooperation in the fields of external border controls, asylum and immigration. A recent Commission Communication appraises the need for further cooperative action on asylum, COM (2008) 360. Note finally that the Nice Charter of Fundamental Rights, which now has legal effect by the Lisbon Treaty, contains articles 18–19 on asylum rights.

A Council Framework Decision on preventing illegal immigration and residence, O.J. L 328/1 (Dec. 5, 2002), provides for stronger enforcement and penalties to combat illegal immigration. The EU is a natural magnet for illegal refugees from Africa and Asia. Italy and Spain have particularly severe problems in coping with boatloads of African refugees seeking to land in their territory.

4. POLICE AND JUDICIAL COOPERATION IN CRIMINAL MATTERS

The Treaty of Amsterdam did not completely eliminate the TEU's third pillar. It retained provisions enabling police and judicial cooperation in criminal matters, notably the combatting of "racism and xenophobia," terrorism, offenses against children, illegal drug and arms traffic, corruption and fraud (ECT Article 29). Complex provisions on the types of measures and decisions, as well as on conventions, and the process for taking action, were taken over from the former Maastricht TEU Article K. ECT Article 35 provided for limited forms of Court jurisdiction analogous to the EC Treaty Articles 226 and 234.

Although such an intergovernmental approach is inherently slow-moving and cumbersome, it did prove reasonably successful in launching some important initiatives. Priority attention was given to the creation of a European Police Office (Europol), headquartered in the Hague. The Council proposed the Europol Convention to the Member States in 1995, O.J. C 316/1 (Nov. 27, 1995), and, after long debate, a Protocol permitted States to opt to refer questions interpreting or applying the Protocol to the Court of Justice, O.J. C 299/1 (Oct. 9, 1996). The Hague Europol office began operations in 1995 as a center of information and intelligence, assisting national police efforts to combat drug traffic, money laundering, illegal immigration networks and trade in stolen vehicles.

In March 2000, the Council adopted an Action Plan on Organized Crime, with a variety of proposals to boost the role of Europol and enhance inter-state cooperation. One result was Council Decision 2000/799/JHA creating a Judicial Cooperation Unit (Eurojust), O.J. L 324/1 (Dec. 12, 2000), which was recently amended by Council Decision 2009/426/JHA, O.J. L 138/14 (June 4, 2009), in order to strengthen its staff and operating procedures. Similarly, the Europol Convention has been replaced by Council Decision 2009/371/JHA, O.J.L. 121/37 (May 15, 2009), effective Jan. 1, 2010, which makes Europol a Union entity funded out of the general budget, improves its structure and operating procedures, and specifies its relations with third states, Interpol and other organizations.

After the tragic destruction of the World Trade Center and the attack upon the Pentagon on Sept. 11, 2001, the European Council held an emergency session in Brussels on Sept. 21 to declare the Union's solidarity with the US in the combat of terrorism. The European Council instructed the Council of Justice Ministers to act expeditiously on concrete measures. The Council accordingly adopted the Framework Decision on combating terrorism, O.J. L 164/3 (June 22, 2002), which defined terrorism as action intended to seriously intimidate people, or seriously destabilize political, economic or social structures, notably by physical attacks, kidnaping or hostage taking, causing extensive destruction to facilities, manufacture, supply or use of explosives or weapons, etc. (art. 1), and mandated Member States to adopt effective criminal penalties for terrorist offences (art. 5). A 2008 amendment requires States to criminalize also recruitment or training for terrorism, and aiding and abetting terrorists.

Since 2002, the Council has adopted a number of measures in the field of cooperation against crime, notably the Framework Decision on combating trafficking in human beings, O.J. L 203/1 (Aug. 1, 2002); the Framework Decision on exchanging information and intelligence in law enforcement, O.J. L 386/89 (Dec. 29, 2006); and the Council Decision on cross-border cooperation in combating terrorism and crime, O.J. L 210/1 (Aug. 6, 2008).

Undoubtedly the most important measure is the Framework Decision on the European arrest warrant, O.J. L 190/1 (July 18, 2002), which replaces a prior Convention. The decision was intended to simplify, better structure, and speed up national procedures for the arrest and extradition of persons to other Member States, either to stand trial for offences punishable by prison for at least three years, or to serve such a sentence. The decision lists 32 offences, many obvious (e.g., murder, kidnaping, drug-dealing armed robbery, terrorism), others less so and somewhat vague (e.g., facilitation of unauthorized entry or residence, forgery of administrative documents) (art. 2).

The decision describes in detail the content of the warrant (art. 8), the right to counsel and a hearing due to an arrested person (arts. 11–14), time limits for arrest and execution of the warrant (art. 17), and provisions for the surrender of the person arrested to the requesting State (arts. 23–25). The decision's provisions are made expressly subject to the respect for fundamental rights (art. 1). A Commission report, COM(2007)407, indicated that the decision had nearly doubled such arrest warrants, reduced the time for execution from a year to about five weeks, and resulted in 1770 arrests in 2005. The Court of Justice upheld the decision in Advocaten voor de Wereld v. Leden van de Ministerraad, Case C–303/05, [2007] ECR–I 3633, concluding that the Council had the power to act by a decision instead of a convention, and that the list of offences was not so "vague and imprecise" as to violate human rights, because there could be "interpretative assistance given by the courts" (§§ 48–50).

We previously observed that the Treaty of Lisbon significantly amended Title V on the Area of Freedom, Justice and Security. The Maastricht TEU's Title VI on Police and Judicial Cooperation in Criminal Matters has been absorbed into the Lisbon's TFEU Title V, although retaining some of the unusual features of the former third pillar provisions. TFEU Articles 82 and 83 promote judicial cooperation in criminal matters, authorizing the Parliament and Council to adopt through the ordinary legislative procedure directives for the mutual recognition of criminal judgments and to establish minimum rules for the definition of offences and sanctions for serious crimes with a cross-border dimension. However, in both cases a Member State may request that the proposed measure be referred to the European Council for consideration, with the suspension of the legislative procedure until the European Council, acting by consensus, decides to refer the draft back to the Council.

TFEU Articles 85 and 86 now specifically govern Eurojurist's structure and operations. TEFU Article 87 provides for cooperation among Member States's police and other law enforcement services, and Article 88 governs the structure, tasks and operation of Europol.

Further Reading

E. Guild, Legal Elements of European Identity: EU Citizenship and Migration Law (Kluwer 2005)

S. Peers, EU Justice and Home Affairs Laws (Oxford 2006)

J. Shaw, The Transformation of Citizenship in the European Union (Cambridge 2007)

N. Walker (ed.), Europe's Area of Freedom, Security and Justice (Oxford 2004)

CHAPTER 17

RIGHT OF ESTABLISHMENT AND RIGHT TO PROVIDE SERVICES

■ ■ ■

The right of establishment and the related right to provide trans-border services are crucial to achieving the internal market. These two rights facilitate the optimal allocation of factors of production and the efficient operation of commercial and financial entities throughout the Union. Moreover, recent statistics indicate that the total value of the market for services exceeds that of the market for goods in the EU.

An integrated internal market is impossible unless commercial and financial enterprises can conduct their business freely, either through cross-border services or through the operation of firms, subsidiaries and branches anywhere in the Union. This enables enterprises to exploit production capacity in regions where the costs of production are low, to market their products or services from regional or local centers, and to adapt their operations readily to the needs of a local market. Naturally, Union-wide commercial and financial operations also lead to substantial economies of scale and promote the development of larger, more sophisticated enterprises better able to compete in the global marketplace.

The two rights are also essential to individuals engaged as entrepreneurs in business or exercising a craft, because they allow personal mobility and free choice of a site from which to conduct business. Accessory rights of personal residence, access to housing and eligibility for social benefits become important insofar as they facilitate personal mobility.

This chapter initially reviews in section A the nature of the Treaty rights and the dimensions of the legislative program intended to enforce them. We will analyze in some detail in section B the Court's doctrines on the right of commercial and financial enterprises to provide and also to receive services, with particular attention to "general good" or public interest concerns which may justify Member States in limiting the right. Section B also reviews the 1989 television broadcasting directive and surveys the recent comprehensive services directive, adopted in 2006. Section C describes the Court doctrine that persons and enterprises also enjoy the right to receive trans-border services, subject to public interest limits. Section D concentrates upon the right of establishment, especially with regard to corporations. Section E provides a review of the most important directives harmonizing company law.

The directives and Court doctrines concerning the right of lawyers and other professionals to provide trans-border services and establish themselves throughout the Union are quite distinct from those concerning commercial services, and are accordingly covered in Chapter 18.

A. TREATY PROVISIONS AND LEGISLATIVE PROGRAMS

1. THE NATURE OF THE TREATY RIGHTS

Commentators frequently consider the right of establishment, and the right to provide trans-border services, to be two aspects of the same right, namely, the right to conduct freely commercial, financial or professional activities throughout the Community, and find the line of demarcation between the two difficult to discern. There is a great deal of truth to this observation. Implementing legislation and interpretative case law sometimes apply to the exercise of both rights, without any distinction drawn between them. However, in general, a State has greater latitude to demand that an established person or entity should respect its rules than it has to require a trans-border service provider to do so.

The chapter on establishment begins with ECT Article 43 (now TFEU Article 49):

> [R]estrictions on the freedom of establishment of nationals of a Member State in the territory of another Member State shall be prohibited. Such prohibition shall also apply to restrictions on the setting up of agencies, branches or subsidiaries by nationals of any Member State established in the territory of any Member State.
>
> Freedom of establishment shall include the right to take up and pursue activities as self-employed persons, and to set up and manage undertakings, in particular companies or firms * * * under the conditions laid down for its own nationals by the law of the country where such establishment is effected * * *.

The text thus identifies three aspects of the right of establishment, namely 1) to set up agencies, branches and subsidiaries, 2) to conduct activities as a self-employed person, and 3) to set up and manage companies and firms. ECT Article 43 is the renumbered text of the 1957 EECT Article 52, and is in turn replaced by TFEU Article 49, without any substantive change.

The right of establishment is not unlimited. It essentially guarantees only national treatment, i.e., the same treatment that nationals of the host State enjoy. Because some conditions imposed by a State on the conduct of a business or profession can, for various reasons, be more easily satisfied by a national than a non-national, the text may still permit an indirect impairment of the right of establishment. To minimize this, the

Community adopted measures in many fields to harmonize the standards and conditions for the conduct of business. Moreover, the Court of Justice has held that in order to fully achieve the right of establishment, Member State rules that restrict the conduct of a business or profession must be justified by a serious public interest.

ECT Article 44 (now TFEU Article 50) provides that legislation to achieve the right of establishment shall be adopted by codecision, i.e., the ordinary legislative procedure. Under the initial EEC Treaty Article 54, the Council needed only to consult Parliament. Article 44(2) lists certain areas of concentration for the legislative program. Paragraph (g), which calls for the coordination of Member State rules intended to protect members (usually partners or shareholders) of companies and firms, is important for the harmonization of company law and rules regulating securities and the financial industries

ECT Article 47 (now TFEU Article 53) authorizes legislation for the mutual recognition of diplomas and for the harmonization of the conditions that Member States may impose on the exercise of business or professional activities by self-employed persons. This article will be discussed in the next chapter. ECT Article 48 (now TFEU Article 54) stipulates that companies or firms are to be treated as having the same rights of establishment as natural persons. ECT Article 294 (now TFEU Article 55) is also relevant: it grants national treatment in any Member State to Union nationals who participate in "the capital of companies and firms."

The initial EEC Treaty placed only two express limits on the right of establishment, which have been carried over in the EC Treaty and now the TFEU without change. ECT Article 45 permitted Member States to restrict establishment rights with regard to activities "connected, even occasionally, with the exercise of official authority", and Article 46 allowed them to restrict the right on grounds of public policy, public security or public health. ECT Article 46 paralleled ECT Articles 30 and 39(3) which permitted similar limits on the free movement of goods and workers, respectively. As we shall see, the Court of Justice has narrowly interpreted the scope of both Articles 45 and 46. The Treaty of Lisbon renumbers ECT Articles 45–46 as TFEU Articles 51–52, without any substantive change.

Turning to the chapter on services, ECT Article 49 (now TFEU Article 56) states:

> [R]estrictions on freedom to provide services within the Community shall be prohibited in respect of nationals of Member States who are established in a State of the Community other than that of the person for whom the services are intended.

> The Council may, acting by a qualified majority on a proposal from the Commission, extend the provisions of the Chapter to nationals of a third country who provide services and who are established within the Community.

ECT Article 50 (now TFEU Article 57) then defines services to include industrial, commercial and professional services and the activities of artisans, to the extent that they are "normally provided for remuneration." The remuneration need not, however, be provided by the recipient of the service. For example, a TV station broadcast constitutes a service to all persons who receive the program even though the station's remuneration comes from advertisers or public subsidies.

ECT Article 50 also enables the person providing a service to "temporarily pursue his activity" within another State. This raises the issue of drawing the line between service providing accompanied by a temporary residence and long-term residence considered to constitute establishment. As we shall see, the Court of Justice has provided some guidelines on where to draw the line. ECT Articles 49 and 50 were originally numbered as EECT Articles 59 and 60. TFEU Articles 56 and 57 replicate ECT Articles 49 and 50, except to replace "Community" with "Union."

ECT Article 52 enabled the Council to adopt directives to achieve liberalization of services, acting by qualified majority vote after consulting the Parliament. TFEU Article 59, which replaces ECT Article 52, prescribes that the Parliament and Council shall use the ordinary legislative procedure to adopt directives to liberalize services. Note finally that ECT Article 55 (initially EECT Article 66, and now TFEU Article 62) carries over to the field of services the "official authority" exception of ECT Article 45 and the public policy, security and health limitations of ECT Article 46.

At this point, a comparative note with the United States is of interest. Neither a right of establishment nor a right to provide services freely in other states is expressly mentioned in the Constitution, but both are treated as implicit in the Privileges and Immunities Clause and the Interstate Commerce Clause. There is abundant case law striking down state laws that discriminate against persons or entities from other states when providing services or seeking to create or operate branches or subsidiaries. Non-discriminatory state laws have also been examined under the balancing of interests approach of the dormant Commerce Clause. See generally J. Nowak & R. Rotunda, Constitutional Law Ch. 8 (8th ed. West 2010).

Nonetheless, the states regulate many spheres of corporate, commercial, and financial activity, with only limited intervention by the federal government. They have thus adopted the laws creating and governing corporations and partnerships, and regulations of state banking and insurance. Except for national banking and the securities sector, there has been little attempt to "federalize" these fields or to harmonize the diverse state systems. In contrast, the European Union has extensively harmonized Member State legislation in these areas.

2. LEGISLATION TO IMPLEMENT ECT ARTICLES 43 AND 49 (NOW TFEU ARTICLES 49 AND 56)

A moment's reflection reveals that the removal of Member State barriers to the right of establishment and the right to provide cross-border services is a tall order. Although some Member States had protectionist regulations designed to restrict foreign persons or enterprises from activities on their market, most barriers resulted from State regulation of particular business or financial sectors to achieve goals perceived as advancing legitimate local interests. The difficulty and added cost involved in complying with such local regulations inevitably reduced foreign participation in each national market. Opening each sector of the Community market accordingly required Community legislation not only to end express discrimination, but also to coordinate or harmonize the national rules regulating that sector.

Community action began in 1962 when the Council adopted the General Program for the abolition of restrictions on freedom of establishment, and the General Program for the abolition of restrictions on freedom to provide services, O.J. English Spec.Ed. 1974, IX, at 3 (Document 18 in the Selected Documents). These programs did not have the force of law, as they are neither regulations nor directives. However, they have served as guidelines for the adoption of legislation and have been cited by the Court of Justice in the interpretation of Treaty-based rights.

The purpose of the General Program on Establishment was to set a timetable for legislative action before December 31, 1969, the end of the transitional period set by the initial 1957 European Economic Community Treaty. The General Program's continuing value lies in its long list of the types of discriminatory national regulations or practices that are deemed to violate ECT Article 43, or now TFEU Article 49. This serves as the same sort of useful checklist of prohibited rules as Directive 70/50's list of prohibited measures equivalent to quantitative restrictions on the free movement of goods.

Some notable examples of discriminatory rules are those which require non-nationals to obtain a special authorization or permit, or which impose specific taxation or other financial burdens upon non-nationals. A companion list prohibited the imposition of conditions or limitations upon foreign nationals or enterprises only. These include limitations on the ability of Community nationals to enter into contracts; to obtain licenses or authorizations, or State subsidies; to acquire or use real estate, personal property or intellectual property rights; to enjoy access to loans or credit; or to be a party to litigation or administrative proceedings. The General Program on Services essentially parallels that on establishment.

The two programs also foresaw an end to restrictions on rights of residence for the self-employed. This was largely achieved by Directive 73/148 of May 21, 1973 on the abolition of restrictions on movement and residence, O.J. L 172/14 (June 28, 1973). The terms of this directive essentially paralleled those set down for workers in Directive 68/360, described in Chapter 15B. Council Directive 64/221 on the application of public policy, public security or public health limits on residence rights, described in Chapter 15C, applied to self-employed persons as well as to workers. These initial directives have been replaced by Directive 2004/38, described in Chapter 16F.

The legislative process to facilitate enjoyment of establishment and service rights, sector by sector, concentrated in the 1960s and 1970s on agriculture, the crafts and general business and commercial fields. Over 50 directives eliminated discriminatory rules, practices and conditions in such diverse fields as agriculture, forestry, fisheries, mining, the hotel, restaurant and tavern industries, film production and distribution, real estate brokerage, and general wholesale and retail operations. In the context of the SLIM program for the simplification and codification of legislation (see Chapter 14B), a recent directive sets out a general mechanism for the recognition of qualifications in crafts, O.J.L. 201/77 (July 31, 1999), consolidating in one text 35 directives adopted between 1963 and 1982.

The company law harmonization program began in 1968, and that for securities law harmonization in 1977. Insurance law harmonization started with reinsurance in 1964 and the first banking directive came in 1973, but in both fields progress was initially quite limited.

The 1985 White Paper on Completing the Internal Market expressed dissatisfaction with the level of progress in attaining service and establishment rights and in facilitating Community-wide operations in the financial services, information and audio-visual industries. The White Paper urged a new approach based on mutual recognition, a concept carried over from the free movement of goods. As previously indicated, the internal market program dramatically changed the legislative picture, and harmonization efforts in these fields have largely been crowned with success. The legislative program in the financial services sector is described in Chapter 30C.

B. CASE LAW ON FREEDOM TO PROVIDE SERVICES

1. THE RIGHT TO PROVIDE CROSS-BORDER SERVICES

When discussing the subject of free movement of goods, we noted that Community legislation and Court of Justice case law had evolved in tandem, with reciprocal influence on one another. That is likewise the situation with the freedom to provide services.

An issue that was bound to arise was whether EECT Article 59, later renumbered as ECT Article 49, could have direct effect. The Commission and legal commentators initially regarded this as not likely, because they considered it necessary to implement the right through Council legislation. In an early leading judgment, the Court of Justice held that EECT Article 59, later ECT Article 49, did have direct effect, and also stated for the first time the important doctrine that a "general good" interest might limit the right to provide trans-border services.

VAN BINSBERGEN v. BESTUUR VAN DE BEDRIJFSVERENIGING
Case 33/74, [1974] ECR 1299.

[Kortmann, a Dutch legal representative, was engaged by van Binsbergen to represent him in a Dutch administrative proceeding. The Dutch authorities refused to allow Kortmann to continue to act in the matter after he became a Belgian resident, because Dutch law required legal representatives to reside in the Netherlands. Kortmann appealed this decision. The Supreme Court for Social Security Affairs inquired whether ECT Articles 49 and 50 had direct effect.]

23   Article [49] * * * expresses the intention to abolish restrictions on freedom to provide services * * *.

* * *

25   The provisions of that article abolish all discrimination against the person providing the service by reason of his nationality or the fact that he is established in a Member State other than that in which the service is to be provided.

26   Therefore, as regards at least the specific requirement of nationality or of residence, Articles [49] and [50] impose a well-defined obligation, the fulfilment of which by the Member States cannot be delayed or jeopardized by the absence of provisions which were to be adopted in pursuance of powers conferred under Articles [52 and 55].

[The Court then considered whether a State can require residence as a condition to perform the services in question.]

11   [A] requirement that the person providing the service must be habitually resident within the territory of the State where the service is to be provided may * * * have the result of depriving Article [49] of all useful effect, in view of the fact that the precise object of that Article is to abolish restrictions on freedom to provide services imposed on persons who are not established in the State where the service is to be provided.

12   However, * * *, specific requirements imposed on the person providing the service cannot be considered incompatible with the Treaty where they have as their purpose the application of professional rules justified by the general good—in particular rules relating to organization, qualifications, professional ethics, supervision and liability—which are binding upon any person established in the State in which

the service is provided, where the person providing the service would escape from the ambit of those rules being established in another Member State.

13 Likewise, a Member State cannot be denied the right to take measures to prevent the exercise by a person providing services whose activity is entirely or principally directed towards its territory of the freedom guaranteed by Article [49] for the purpose of avoiding the professional rules of conduct which would be applicable to him if he were established within that State * * *.

14 In accordance with these principles, the requirement that persons whose functions are to assist the administration of justice must be permanently established for professional purposes within the jurisdiction of certain courts or tribunals cannot be considered incompatible with the provisions of Articles [49] and [50], where such requirement is objectively justified by the need to ensure observance of professional rules of conduct connected, in particular, with the administration of justice and with respect for professional ethics.

15 That cannot, however, be the case when the provision of certain services in a Member State is not subject to any sort of qualification or professional regulation and when the requirement of habitual residence is fixed by reference to the territory of the State in question.

16 [In that case], the requirement of residence within that State constitutes a restriction which is incompatible with Articles [49] and [50] of the Treaty if the administration of justice can satisfactorily be ensured by measures which are less restrictive, such as the choosing of an address for service.

NOTES AND QUESTIONS

1. *Van Binsbergen's* conclusion that ECT Articles 49 and 50 had direct effect followed by a few months the Court's conclusion in *Reyners*, infra page 728, that ECT Article 43 on the right of establishment had direct effect. There is no doubt that the Court will hold TFEU Articles 56 and 57, the successors to ECT Articles 49 and 50, likewise to have direct effect, if the issue ever arises. In the next Chapter, we shall see that the Court's judgements in the two cases catalyzed the Council into adopting a series of harmonization directives in the professional services sector.

2. We have already seen that the Court often treats a State's residency requirement for obtaining some particular right or benefit as an indirect mode of discrimination on the basis of nationality in the context of free movement of workers. *Van Binsbergen's* ¶ 11 is, however, the earliest instance of this analytical approach. *Van Binsbergen's* conclusion in ¶ 12 that States may impose limits on trans-border service providers in order to protect a "general good" interest is also seminal. Do you agree that national professional qualification and ethics rules constitute a "general good" interest? Why is Kortmann nonetheless permitted to provide legal services in the Netherlands?

3. *Van Binsbergen* is also seminal in setting out an exception in ¶ 13. When may a State legitimately restrict or forbid persons from providing transborder services? A good example is Vereniging Veronica v. Commissariaat voor de Media, Case C–148/91, [1993] ECR I–487, in which a Dutch company was accused of setting up and financing a Luxembourg television station intended to broadcast programs in Dutch by cable into the Netherlands, when the broadcasts would not comply with the Dutch law limiting advertising in television broadcasting. The Court first held that State rules requiring broadcasters to follow a pluralist and non-commercial cultural policy could constitute a general good interest. The Court then held that the Netherlands could forbid television broadcasts from Luxembourg into the Netherlands if the television station could be shown to have been established in order to circumvent the Dutch broadcasting rules. A useful casenote is by W. Hins, 31 Common Mkt. L. Rev. 901(1994).

NEW HAMPSHIRE v. PIPER

470 U.S. 274, 105 S.Ct. 1272, 84 L.Ed.2d 205 (1985).

[Piper, a resident of Vermont, passed the New Hampshire bar examination, but was denied admission to the bar because New Hampshire required its lawyers to be residents. Piper lived 400 yards from New Hampshire. She was married and owned a house with her husband in Vermont. When her challenge of the residence requirement reached the Supreme Court, Justice Powell, speaking for eight Justices, held that the residence requirement violated the Privileges and Immunities Clause.]

Derived * * * from the Articles of Confederation, the Privileges and Immunities Clause was intended to create a national economic union. It is therefore not surprising that this Court repeatedly has found that "one of the privileges which the Clause guarantees to citizens of State A is that of doing business in State B on terms of substantial equality with the citizens of that State" [quoting *Toomer* v. *Witsell, infra* note 1].

There is nothing in [our precedents] suggesting that the practice of law should not be viewed as a "privilege" under Art. IV, § 2. Like the occupations considered in our earlier cases, the practice of law is important to the national economy. As the Court noted in *Goldfarb* v. *Virginia State Bar*, 421 U.S. 773, 788, 95 S.Ct. 2004, 2014, 44 L.Ed.2d 572, the "activities of lawyers play an important part in commercial intercourse."

The lawyer's role in the national economy is not the only reason that the opportunity to practice law should be considered a "fundamental right." We believe that the legal profession has a noncommercial role and duty that reinforce the view that the practice of law falls within the ambit of Privileges and Immunities Clause. Out-of-state lawyers may—and often do—represent persons who raise unpopular federal claims. In some cases, representation by nonresident counsel may be the only means available for the vindication of federal rights.

* * *

Because a lawyer is not an "officer" of the State in any political sense, there is no reason for New Hampshire to exclude from its bar nonresidents. We therefore conclude that the right to practice law is protected by the Privileges and Immunities Clause.

Our holding in this case does not interfere with the ability of the States to regulate their bars. The nonresident who seeks to join a bar, unlike the *pro hac vice* applicant, must have the same professional and personal qualifications required of resident lawyers. Furthermore, the nonresident member of the bar is subject to the full force of New Hampshire's disciplinary rules.

[Justice Powell then rejected New Hampshire's arguments that non-resident lawyers might be less familiar with its rules and procedures, less apt to behave ethically, or less likely to be available for court proceedings.]

[Justice Rehnquist dissented]

The [Court's] decision will be surprising to many, because it so clearly disregards the fact that the practice of law is—almost by definition—fundamentally different from those other occupations that are practiced across state lines without significant deviation from State to State. The fact that each State is free, in a large number of areas, to establish *independently* of the other States its own laws for the governance of its citizens, is a fundamental precept of our Constitution that, I submit, is of equal stature with the need for the States to form a cohesive union.

* * *

The reason that the practice of law should be treated differently is that law is one occupation that does not readily translate across state lines. Certain aspects of legal practice are distinctly and intentionally *nonnational*; in this regard one might view this country's legal system as the antithesis of the norms embodied in the Art. IV Privileges and Immunities Clause. Put simply, the State has a substantial interest in creating its own set of laws responsive to its own local interests, and it is reasonable for a State to decide that those people who have been trained to analyze law and policy are better equipped to write those state laws and adjudicate cases arising under them.

* * *

A State similarly might determine that * * * those citizens trained in the law are likely to bring their useful expertise to other important functions that benefit from such expertise and are of interest to state governments—such as trusteeships, or directorships of corporations or charitable organizations, or school board positions, or merely the role of the interested citizen at a town meeting.

NOTES AND QUESTIONS

1. Justice Powell in *Piper* declared that the Privileges and Immunities Clause was intended by its draftsman, Charles Pinckney, to express the ideas of the Articles of Confederation, which stated in article four: "the people of each State shall have free ingress and regress to and from any other State, and shall enjoy therein all the privileges of trade and commerce, subject to the same duties, impositions and restrictions as the inhabitants thereof." *Piper* continues a line of cases in which the Privileges and Immunities Clause or the dormant Commerce Clause were used to invalidate state laws charging salesmen or peddlers selling out-of-state goods substantially higher state license fees than persons selling products of the state, e.g., in Ward v. Maryland, 79 U.S. (12 Wall.) 418, 20 L.Ed. 449 (1871), and Welton v. Missouri, 91 U.S. (1 Otto) 275, 23 L.Ed. 347 (1875). In a modern analogue, in Toomer v. Witsell, 334 U.S. 385, 68 S.Ct. 1156, 92 L.Ed. 1460 (1948), the Court relied on the Privileges and Immunities Clause to invalidate a South Carolina law imposing a $2,500 license fee on nonresident shrimp fishermen, in contrast to a $25 fee for resident fishermen.

2. In *Piper*, would you agree with Justice Powell or Justice Rehnquist? Note that both the Court in *Van Binsbergen* and Justice Powell in *Piper* declare that the host State may impose its professional rules on the non-resident lawyer. In the next chapter we will consider whether that approach can produce difficulties, especially when the lawyer only occasionally provides trans-border services.

CRIMINAL PROCEEDINGS AGAINST WEBB

Case 279/80, [1981] ECR 3305.

[Dutch law forbids persons to engage in the supply of personnel for temporary help without a license, which is granted after review of whether the applicant's operations "might harm good relations in the labour market" or insufficiently safeguard the interests of the personnel supplied. A UK company, the International Engineering Services Bureau (IESB), and its manager, Webb, were prosecuted for supplying technical staff on a temporary basis to Dutch firms without a Dutch license. The staff remained employees of IESB. IESB held a license granted by UK authorities for personnel supply services, but never obtained a Dutch license, even though its principal business was in the Netherlands. After conviction, IESB and Webb appealed. The Dutch Supreme Court asked the Court of Justice to rule on whether the supply of personnel constituted a service and, if so, whether the Dutch license requirements complied with ECT Article 50, especially since IESB had a UK license.]

16   The principal aim of the third paragraph in Article [50] is to enable the provider of the service to pursue his activities in the Member State where the service is given without suffering discrimination in favour of the nationals of that State. However, it does not mean that all national legislation applicable to nationals of that State and usually

applied to the permanent activities of undertakings established therein may be similarly applied in its entirety to the temporary activities of undertakings which are established in other Member States.

[17] * * * [T]he freedom to provide services is one of the fundamental principles of the Treaty and may be restricted only by provisions which are justified by the general good and which are imposed on all persons or undertakings operating in the said State in so far as that interest is not safeguarded by the provisions to which the provider of the service is subject in the Member State of his establishment.

[18] [T]he provision of manpower is a particularly sensitive matter from the occupational and social point of view. * * * [P]ursuit of such a business directly affects both relations on the labour market and the lawful interests of the workforce concerned. * * *

[19] [I]t is * * * a legitimate choice of [State] policy pursued in the public interest, to subject the provision of manpower within its borders to a system of licensing in order to be able to refuse licences where there is reason to fear that such activities may harm good relations on the labour market or that the interests of the workforce affected are not adequately safeguarded. * * * [T]he Member State in which the services are to be supplied has unquestionably the right to require possession of a licence issued on the same conditions as in the case of its own nationals.

[20] Such a measure would be excessive in relation to the aim pursued, however, if the requirements to which the issue of a licence is subject coincided with the proofs and guarantees required in the State of establishment. In order to maintain the principle of freedom to provide services the first requirement is that in considering applications for licences and in granting them the Member State in which the service is to be provided may not make any distinction based on the nationality of the provider of the services or the place of his establishment; the second requirement is that it must take into account the evidence and guarantees already furnished by the provider of the services for the pursuit of his activities in the Member State of his establishment.

PROCEEDINGS AGAINST SCHNITZER

Case C–215/01, [2003] ECR I–14847.

[German law requires that skilled trade craftsmen must be enrolled on a Skilled Trade Register, which then authorizes them to carry out their craft. Schnitzer, manager of a Portuguese company, employed Portuguese plasterers to do plastering for several buildings in Bavaria during three years. When he was prosecuted for violating the law, the trial court asked the Court of Justice whether the company's activities in Germany during these years constituted trans-border service providing or an establishment, and whether temporary service providers could be compelled to enroll on the Register.]

28   The Court has held that the temporary nature of the activity of the person providing the service in the host Member State has to be determined in the light not only of the duration of the provision of the service but also of its regularity, periodical nature or continuity. The fact that the activity is temporary does not mean that the provider of services within the meaning of the Treaty may not equip himself with some form of infrastructure in the host Member State (including an office, chambers or consulting rooms) in so far as such infrastructure is necessary for the purposes of performing the services in question [citing *Gebhard,* infra page 734].

* * *

30   Thus, 'services' within the meaning of the Treaty may cover services * * * which are provided over an extended period, even over several years, where, for example, the services in question are supplied in connection with the construction of a large building. * * *

31   No provision of the Treaty affords a means of determining, in an abstract manner, the duration or frequency beyond which the supply of a service or of a certain type of service in another Member State can no longer be regarded as the provision of services within the meaning of the Treaty.

* * *

33   In the main proceedings, although this is a matter for the national court to determine, the Portuguese undertaking does not appear to have an infrastructure in Germany allowing it to be regarded as established in that Member State, or to be seeking illegitimately to evade the obligations imposed by that Member State's national legislation.

34   So far as concerns entry on the trades register, * * * the requirement imposed on an undertaking established in one Member State which wishes, as a provider of a service, to carry on a skilled trade activity in another Member State to be entered on the latter's trades register constitutes a restriction within the meaning of Article 49 EC.

35   While a restriction on freedom to provide services may admittedly be justified by overriding requirements relating to the public interest, such as the objective of guaranteeing the quality of skilled trade work and of protecting those who have commissioned such work, the application of national rules to providers of services established in other Member States must be appropriate for securing attainment of the objective which they pursue and must not go beyond what is necessary in order to attain it.

36   In consequence, the authorisation procedure set up by the host Member State must neither delay nor complicate exercise of the right of persons established in another Member State to provide their services on the territory of the first State if examination of the conditions governing access to the activities concerned has been carried out [in the home State] and it has been established that those conditions are satisfied.

37 Once those conditions are satisfied, any entry required on the trades register of the host Member State cannot be other than automatic, and that requirement cannot constitute a condition precedent for the provision of services, result in administrative expense for the person providing them or give rise to an obligation to pay subscriptions to the chamber of trades.

38 That applies not only to providers of services who intend to supply services in the host Member State only occasionally, or even a single time, but also to those who supply or wish to supply services in a repeated or more or less regular manner.

39 At the moment when a provider of services envisages supplying services in the host Member State and examination of the conditions governing access to the activities concerned is carried out, it is often difficult to say whether those services are going to be supplied just once or very occasionally or whether, on the other hand, they will be supplied in a repeated or more or less regular manner.

NOTES AND QUESTIONS

1. The national rules in *Webb* and *Schnitzer* were applied both to domestic persons and firms and to those providing services from other States. Accordingly, they did not violate the obligation not to discriminate on the basis of nationality. Already in 1981 in ¶ 17 of *Webb*, the Court went beyond that obligation and enunciated the doctrine that State rules restricting services are compatible with the Treaty only if they are justified by a general good interest. As we shall see, this doctrine is not only crucial in the area of free movement of services, but has now been carried over to the right of establishment. What was the general good interest that the Court accepted in *Webb*? What consideration must the Netherlands give to IESB's UK license?

2. In *Webb* and in *Schnitzer* the Court applied the mutual recognition principle we previously saw as integral to the *Cassis de Dijon* doctrine in the free movement of goods: the host State should accept the home State's examination of the qualifications of the service provider. In *Schnitzer* the Court also applied the principle of proportionality to conclude that foreign craftsmen providing services in Germany must be entered on the Skilled Trade Register automatically based on their home State credentials, and cannot be obliged to pay any fees for the entry. Germany has a strong tradition of demanding high quality workmanship in its crafts and undoubtedly felt the Register entry system provided beneficial guarantees to the public. There is a certain analogy between the German policy here and that behind its quality standards in *German beer*, supra page 483.

3. As previously mentioned, it is often difficult to determine when transborder activities go beyond temporary service providing and become an establishment, which the host State may regulate to a greater degree. Not

only skilled workers, but construction workers, financial service providers, performing artists and others may come quite regularly to provide services in a host State. Is the Court's guidance on line drawing helpful? Would you prefer, or not, a bright-line test of a number of years, or a maximum number of visits? The Court relies heavily on *Gebhart*, a seminal case on lawyers' trans-border services, infra page 734.

COMMISSION v. GERMANY

(German insurance)
Case 205/84, [1986] ECR 3755.

[The Commission brought a Treaty infringement proceeding against Germany for violation of ECT Articles 49 and 50 and for improper implementation of three directives adopted in the 1970s to partially coordinate national rules on the regulation of cross-border insurance services. The proceeding involved many distinct issues, and occasioned a long, complex judgment. Our concern here is with perhaps the two most important issues: 1) could Germany require Community insurers to obtain an authorization, and 2) could it require a permanent establishment in Germany in order to carry out the cross-border insurance operations permitted by the directives. The Court initially set out its doctrine on the general good or public interest limit to the providing of trans-border services.]

27   [T]he freedom to provide services, as one of the fundamental principles of the Treaty, may be restricted only by provisions which are justified by the general good and which are applied to all persons or undertakings operating within the territory of the State in which the service is provided in so far as that interest is not safeguarded by the provisions to which the provider of a service is subject in the Member State of his establishment. In addition, such requirements must be objectively justified by the need to ensure that professional rules of conduct are complied with and that the interests which such rules are designed to safeguard are protected.

28   [T]he requirements in question in these proceedings, namely that an insurer who is established in another Member State, authorized by the supervisory authority of that State and subject to the supervision of that authority, must have a permanent establishment within the territory of the State in which the service is provided and that he must obtain a separate authorization from the supervisory authority of that State, constitute restrictions on the freedom to provide services inasmuch as they increase the cost of such services in the State in which they are provided, in particular where the insurer conducts business in that State only occasionally.

29   It follows that those requirements may be regarded as compatible with Articles [49 and 50] of the EEC Treaty only if it is established that in the field of activity concerned there are imperative reasons relating to the public interest which justify restrictions on the freedom to provide

services, that the public interest is not already protected by the rules of the State of establishment and that the same result cannot be obtained by less restrictive rules.

(a) The Existence of an Interest Justifying Certain Restrictions on the Freedom to Provide Insurance Services

30 As the German Government [argued], the insurance sector is a particularly sensitive area from the point of view of the protection of the consumer both as a policy-holder and as an insured person. This is so in particular because of the specific nature of the service provided by the insurer, which is linked to future events, the occurrence of which, or at least the timing of which, is uncertain at the time when the contract is concluded. An insured person who does not obtain payment under a policy following an event giving rise to a claim may find himself in a very precarious position. Similarly, it is as a rule very difficult for a person seeking insurance to judge whether the likely future development of the insurer's financial position and the terms of the contract, usually imposed by the insurer, offer him sufficient guarantees that he will receive payment under the policy* * *.

31 [Also,] in certain fields insurance has become a mass phenomenon. Contracts are concluded by such enormous numbers of policy-holders that the protection of the interests of insured persons and injured third parties affects virtually the whole population.

32 Those special characteristics, which are peculiar to the insurance sector, have led all the Member States to introduce legislation making insurance undertakings subject to mandatory rules both as regards their financial position and the conditions of insurance which they apply, and to permanent supervision to ensure that those rules are complied with.

33 [Accordingly, in the field of insurance,]there are imperative reasons relating to the public interest which may justify restrictions on the freedom to provide services, provided, however, that the rules of the State of establishment are not adequate in order to achieve the necessary level of protection and that the requirements of the State in which the service is provided do not exceed what is necessary in that respect.

[The Court next considered whether Germany could require an authorization or license in order to protect these consumer interests.]

(c) The Necessity of an Authorization Procedure

44 [I]n all the Member States the supervision of insurance undertakings is organized in the form of an authorization procedure * * *. An undertaking which sets up branches and agencies in [other States] must therefore obtain an authorization from the supervisory authority of each of those States.

* * *

46   [T]he German Government's argument to the effect that only the requirement of an authorization can provide an effective means of ensuring the supervision which * * * is justified on grounds relating to the protection of the consumer both as a policy-holder and as an insured person, must be accepted. Since a system such as that proposed in the draft for a second [insurance] directive, which entrusts the operation of the authorization procedure to the Member State in which the undertaking is established, working in close cooperation with the State in which the service is provided, can be set up only by legislation, it must also be acknowledged that, in the present state of Community law, it is for the State in which the service is provided to grant and withdraw that authorization.

47   It should however be emphasized that the authorization must be granted on request to any undertaking established in another Member State which meets the conditions laid down by the legislation of the State in which the service is provided, that those conditions may not duplicate equivalent statutory conditions which have already been satisfied in the State in which the undertaking is established and that the supervisory authority of the State in which the service is provided must take into account supervision and verifications which have already been carried out in the Member State of establishment. * * *

* * *

(d) The Necessity of Establishment

52   If the requirement of an authorization constitutes a restriction on the freedom to provide services, the requirement of a permanent establishment is the very negation of that freedom. It has the result of depriving Article [49] of the Treaty of all effectiveness * * *.

53   In that respect, the German Government points out in particular that the requirement of an establishment in the State in which the service is provided makes it possible for the supervisory authority of that State to carry out verifications in *situ* and to monitor continuously the activities carried on by the authorized insurer * * *.

54   [C]onsiderations of an administrative nature cannot justify derogation by a Member State from the rules of Community law. * * * [I]t is therefore not sufficient that the presence on the undertaking's premises of all the documents needed for supervision * * * may make it easier for [the German]authorities to perform their task. It must also be shown that those authorities cannot, even under an authorization procedure, carry out their supervisory tasks effectively unless the undertaking has in the aforesaid State a permanent establishment at which all the necessary documents are kept.

55   That has not been shown to be the case. * * * [I]t appears to the Court that such supervision may be effected on the basis of copies of balance sheets, accounts and commercial documents, including the conditions of insurance and schemes of operation, sent from the State

of establishment and duly certified by the authorities of that Member State. It is possible under an authorization procedure to subject the undertaking to such conditions of supervision by means of a provision in the certificate of authorization and to ensure compliance with those conditions, if necessary by withdrawing that certificate.

56 It has therefore not been established that the considerations acknowledged above concerning the protection of policy-holders and insured persons make the establishment of the insurer in the territory of the State in which the service is provided an indispensable requirement.

NOTES AND QUESTIONS

1. Observe that the Court of Justice in *German insurance* adopted in ¶ 29 the *Cassis de Dijon* rule of reason approach to ECT Article 28 (see Chapter 13C) as equally applicable to ECT Articles 49 and 50. Although the Court quotes the *van Binsbergen* general good doctrine in ¶ 27, subsequent judgments have generally used the public interest formula. The Commission had suggested that the Court adopt the language used in *Cassis de Dijon* in order to promote a common doctrinal approach.

2. After *van Binsbergen,* the *German insurance* case is undoubtedly the most influential judgment in the services field. The Court provided guidelines on the public interest in the insurance sector which substantially influenced the Commission's drafting of later insurance harmonization directives and the Second Banking Directive. See Chapter 30C. Given the substantial consumer interests that need protection, the Court holding that Germany can require the foreign insurer to obtain an authorization is not surprising.

3. The judgment's holding that even the protection of highly important public interests cannot justify a host State requirement that the service provider have an establishment is an important precedent and often cited. Thus, in Commission v. Italy (Stockbroker rules), Case C–101/94, [1996] ECR I–2691, the Court invalidated Italy's 1991 regulation requiring stockbrokers dealing in "transferable securities" on Italian stock markets to be constituted as an Italian stock corporation, allegedly to be certain that the brokers could be effectively supervised by the Italian authorities. The Court held that ECT Article 43's right of establishment should enable foreign stockbrokers to operate by an agency or branch, supplying whatever documents or information the authorities required (§§ 12, 21–22). Italy could, however, require the foreign stockbrokers to provide local financial guarantees of their solvency (§ 23).

4. In Commission v. Belgium (Private security firms), Case C–355/98, [2000] ECR I–1221, a Belgian law required all firms providing security services intended to safeguard persons and property to have a place of business within Belgium, and all service firm managers to reside in Belgium. The Commission challenged these rules as covert discrimination based on nationality. Should the Court agree?

2. WHAT PUBLIC INTERESTS CAN LIMIT THE PROVIDING OF CROSS–BORDER SERVICES?

COMMISSION v. FRANCE

(Tour guides)

Case C–154/89, [1991] ECR I–659.

[A 1975 French law required all tour guides to possess a French license in order to conduct groups of French and foreign tourists in museums and historical monuments and on public transport. The license was accorded after passage of an examination on the history, culture and economy of France, with part of the oral examination conducted in French. The Commission brought a Treaty infringement proceeding against France, contending that a license requirement for guides who conducted groups from other Member States violated ECT Article 49. The Commission did not contest a license obligation for guides in museums or monuments whose rules of entry required a specialized professional guide.]

12   Articles [49 and 50] of the Treaty require not only the abolition of any discrimination against a person providing services on account of his nationality but also the abolition of any restriction on the freedom to provide services imposed on the ground that the person providing a service is established in a Member State other than the one in which the service is provided. In particular, the Member State cannot make the performance of the services in its territory subject to observance of all the conditions required for establishment; were it to do so the provisions securing freedom to provide services would be deprived of all practical effect.

13   The requirements imposed by the * * * French legislation amount to such a restriction. By making the provision of services by tourist guides accompanying a group of tourists from another Member State subject to possession of a specific qualification, that legislation prevents both tour companies from providing that service with their own staff and self-employed tourist guides from offering their services to those companies for organized tours. It also prevents tourists taking part in such organized tours from availing themselves at will of the services in question.

* * *

15   [T]hose requirements can be regarded as compatible with Articles [49 and 50] of the Treaty only if it is established that with regard to the activity in question there are overriding reasons relating to the public interest which justify restrictions on the freedom to provide services, that the public interest is not already protected by the rules of the State of establishment and that the same result cannot be obtained by less restrictive rules.

16   The French Government contends that the French legislation in question seeks to ensure the protection of general interests relating to the proper appreciation of places and things of historical interest and the widest possible dissemination of knowledge of the artistic and cultural heritage of the country. According to the French Government, those interests are not adequately safeguarded by the rules to which the provider of the services, in this case the tour company, is subject in the Member State in which it is established. Several States require no occupational qualifications for tourist guides or demand no special knowledge of the historical and cultural heritage of other countries.
* * *

17   The general interest in the proper appreciation of places and things of historical interest and the widest possible dissemination of knowledge of the artistic and cultural heritage of a country can constitute an overriding reason justifying a restriction on the freedom to provide services. However, the requirement in question contained in the French legislation goes beyond what is necessary to ensure the safeguarding of that interest inasmuch as it makes the activities of a tourist guide accompanying groups of tourists from another Member State subject to possession of a licence.

18   The service of accompanying tourists is performed under quite specific conditions. The independent or employed tourist guide travels with the tourists and accompanies them in a closed group; in that group they move temporarily from the Member State of establishment to the Member State to be visited.

19   In those circumstances a licence requirement imposed by the Member State of destination has the effect of reducing the number of tourist guides qualified to accompany tourists in a closed group, which may lead a tour operator to have recourse instead to local guides employed or established in the Member State in which the service is to be performed. However, that consequence may have the drawback that tourists who are the recipients of the services in question do not have a guide who is familiar with their language, their interests and their specific expectations.

20   Moreover, the profitable operation of such a group tour depends on the commercial reputation of the operator, who faces competitive pressure from other tour companies; the need to maintain that reputation and the competitive pressure themselves compel companies to be selective in employing tourist guides and exercise some control over the quality of their services.

21   It follows that in view of the scale of the restrictions it imposes, the legislation in issue is disproportionate in relation to the objective pursued, namely to ensure the proper appreciation of places and things of historical interest and the widest dissemination of knowledge of the artistic and cultural heritage of the Member State in which the tour is conducted.

NOTES AND QUESTIONS

1. The Court accepted that France had a genuine public interest concern in an accurate depiction of its culture and history in the *French tour guides* judgement. Why then did the Court refuse to permit France to require a license for tour guides accompanying groups from other States? The Commission won parallel cases against Greece and Italy. Advocate General Lenz's analytical opinion notes that for tour groups and their guides, the provider of services and the recipients of services will be physically together in the same State, but enjoy Treaty rights because they are both exercising a right of free movement to a host State.

HER MAJESTY'S CUSTOMS AND EXCISE v. SCHINDLER

Case C–275/92, [1994] ECR I–1039.

[The 1976 United Kingdom Lotteries and Amusements Act prohibits lotteries, but makes an exception for small-scale lotteries for charitable purposes. The Act also forbids the importation of tickets for foreign lotteries, or the transfer abroad of money to acquire foreign lottery tickets. Schindler was an independent agent for the sale of tickets on behalf of the SKL, a public body organizing lotteries for four south German states. After Schindler sent invitations to buy tickets in an SKL lottery from the Netherlands to the UK, he was prosecuted for violation of the Act. When Schindler raised Treaty issues in his defense, the trial court asked the Court of Justice whether lottery tickets constituted goods, or their sale represented a service, and whether the Act could be justified under the Treaty exceptions to free movement of goods or services.

The Court first concluded that the mailing of application forms and tickets was entirely accessory to the participation in a lottery, so that the proper Treaty focus was upon ECT Articles 49 and 50. The Court next found that the sale of lottery tickets constituted a service for remuneration (the price of the ticket) and the trans-border mailing fell under Article 49. The Court then examined whether the UK rules could be considered to be justified.]

49   The Commission and the defendants * * * argue * * * that legislation such as the United Kingdom lotteries legislation is in fact discriminatory [because it] prohibits large lotteries [but] permits the simultaneous operation by the same person of several small lotteries, which is equivalent to one large lottery and further the operation of games of chance which are comparable in nature and scale to large lotteries, such as football pools or "bingo".

* * *

51   However, even though the amounts at stake in the games so permitted in the United Kingdom may be comparable to those in large-scale lotteries and even though those games involve a significant element of

chance they differ in their object, rules and methods of organization from * * * large-scale lotteries * * *.

52   In those circumstances legislation such as the United Kingdom legislation cannot be considered to be discriminatory.

* * *

57   [T]he United Kingdom legislation, before its amendment by the 1993 Act establishing the national lottery, pursued the following objectives: to prevent crime and to ensure that gamblers would be treated honestly; to avoid stimulating demand in the gambling sector which has damaging social consequences when taken to excess; and to ensure that lotteries could not be operated for personal and commercial profit but solely for charitable, sporting or cultural purposes.

* * *

60   [I]t is not possible to disregard the moral, religious or cultural aspects of lotteries, like other types of gambling, in all the Member States. The general tendency of the Member States is to restrict, or even prohibit, the practice of gambling and to prevent it from being a source of private profit. Secondly, lotteries involve a high risk of crime or fraud, given the size of the amounts which can be staked and of the winnings which they can hold out to the players, particularly when they are operated on a large scale. Thirdly, they are an incitement to spend which may have damaging individual and social consequences. A final ground which is not without relevance, although it cannot in itself be regarded as an objective justification, is that lotteries may make a significant contribution to the financing of benevolent or public interest activities such as social works, charitable works, sport or culture.

61   [Accordingly] national authorities [have] latitude to determine what is required to protect the players and, more generally, in the light of the specific social and cultural features of each Member State, to maintain order in society, as regards the manner in which lotteries are operated, the size of the stakes, and the allocation of the profits they yield. [The Member States may] assess not only whether it is necessary to restrict the activities of lotteries but also whether they should be prohibited, provided that those restrictions are not discriminatory.

62   When a Member State prohibits in its territory the operation of large-scale lotteries * * *, the prohibition on the importation of materials intended to enable nationals of that Member State to participate in such lotteries organized in another Member State cannot be regarded as a measure involving an unjustified interference with the freedom to provide services. Such a prohibition on import is a necessary part of the protection which the Member State seeks to secure in its territory in relation to lotteries.

63 Accordingly, * * * the Treaty provisions relating to freedom to provide services do not preclude legislation such as the United Kingdom lotteries legislation, in view of the concerns of social policy and the prevention of fraud which justify it.

NOTES AND QUESTIONS

1. *Schindler* was decided four months after *Keck*, page 496 supra, which introduced the new doctrine that non-discriminatory rules regulating "selling arrangements" do not violate ECT Article 28. The Court did not follow that approach in applying ECT Article 49. Do you see any reason why the Court might conclude that the *Keck* doctrine should not carry over to the field of services?

2. The Court's ultimate conclusion is based on a general good or public interest analysis. Certainly the prevention of fraud represents a legitimate consumer interest. But is there really any risk of fraud in the sale of tickets in a German state lottery by an authorized agent? The Court in *Schindler* also refers to social and cultural interests as a justification of the Act. What examples were given by the Court? Do you agree that these are important enough to justify the Act? For useful information on the extent of gambling in the UK, and a critical review of the judgment, see the casenotes by L. Gormley, 19 Eur. L. Rev. 644 (1994), and V. Hatzopoulos, 32 Common Mkt. L. Rev. 841 (1995).

3. Ironically, the UK established a national lottery in 1993, while judgment was pending. Having created its own national lottery, could the UK today bar the sale of German state lottery tickets? Would that not represent discriminatory treatment of a foreign provider of services? Note the final clause in ¶ 61.

4. Portugal requires the operation of games of chance and gambling to take place only in casinos licensed by the government, with specified exceptions for lotteries, bingo, contests and certain other games. When the rules were challenged, the trial court asked the Court of Justice whether they violated Article 49. Citing *Schindler*, the Court held that a Member State's concern for consumer protection and "the maintenance of order in society" (¶ 73), as well as "the prevention of fraud" (¶ 75), justified the limitation on Article 49. The Court further held that the fact that other States had less restrictive regulation did not invalidate the Portuguese rules, because each State can "arrange for the appropriate legislation to govern gaming, in the light of [its] specific social and cultural features" (¶ 78). Anomar v. Portugal, Case C–6/01, [2003] ECR I–8621. An earlier judgment, concerning Finnish regulation of establishments operating slot machines, reached the same conclusion. See Laara v. District Prosecutor of Finland, Case C–124/97, [1999] ECR I–6067.

5. As suggested in note 2 supra, State rules forbidding or restricting a type of gambling cannot discriminate against trans-border service providers. In Criminal proceedings against Gambelli, Case C–243/01, [2003] ECR I–13031, Gambelli was prosecuted for enabling an English bookmaker, Stanley International Betting, to take bets over the internet on Italian sporting

events. Italian law restricts the collecting of bets on sporting events to licensed operators, but Stanley operated under a license granted by UK authorities. The Court initially held that betting over the internet between the UK and Italy constituted a trans-border providing of service. Citing *Schindler*, the Court accepted that Italy could regulate betting, but informed the Italian court that it must verify whether Italy's restriction of betting to national licensees was intended to secure more license fee revenue (¶ 68), and whether periodic checks on a betting operator licensed in another Member State was not a more proportionate way to protect against fraud (¶ 74). The national court was also informed that it should consider whether criminal penalties to enforce the Italian law should not be deemed disproportionate in this context (¶ 72).

6. In Liga Portuguesa de Futebol v. Departmento de Jogos de Santa Casa, Case C–42/07, [2009] ECR I–___ (Sept. 8, 2009), the Court was requested to decide whether a Portuguese law that granted a charitable organization exclusive rights to carry out internet gambling on sports events violated the right of a private betting enterprise sited in Gibraltar to conduct internet sports gambling in Portugal. The Court held that "the fight against crime" justified a State in creating a monopoly for internet sports betting, noting that the sector had "a high risk of crime or fraud" (¶ 63). The Court then found that Santa Casa, a charitable organization that operated in the public interest and was subject to effective government supervision, constituted an appropriate body to hold the monopoly (¶¶ 64–67). The Court further held that a private operator in another State could not provide a "sufficient assurance" of eliminating the risk of fraud or crime in view of the difficulties in supervising the "integrity of operators" (¶ 69).

NOTE ON POSTING OF WORKERS

Contractors who erect large buildings and factories, or construct bridges, railroads, etc. constitute a major service industry. When there are substantial disparities between States in pay levels for construction workers, contractors can make good profits by bringing in workers from a State whose pay levels are comparatively low. Germany's wage levels for construction workers are high. After re-unification with East Germany in 1991, the reconstruction of East German infra-structure proved a magnet for UK, Portugese and other contractors who brought in their lower paid workers for months or even years. Not surprisingly, Germany adopted regulations to protect the interests of German construction workers, who risked losing employment opportunities and/or being compelled to accept lower pay scales, while the UK in particular criticized the rules as violating free market competition.

In an initial judgment, Criminal proceedings against Arblade and Leloup, Case C–369 & 376/96, [1999] ECR I–8453, the Court held that Belgium could require French contractors to comply with Belgian worker health and safety standards and to pay the higher Belgian minimum wage, but could not require various documents concerning the status and pay of employees to be kept in Belgium when they were readily accessible from France.

Shortly thereafter Directive 96/71 on the posting of workers, O.J. L 18/1 (Jan. 21, 1997), became effective. Although an employment relationship is generally regulated by the rules of the home State of the employer and employee, the directive enables the host State where workers are posted to regulate health, safety, and protective measures for young workers and pregnant workers; maximum work periods and minimum rest periods; minimum paid holidays; and minimum pay rates, including overtime (art.3) The host State rules must be set either by government action or collective bargaining agreements universally applicable in an industry sector.

Cases concerning the posting of workers continued to occasion Court judgments. In Portugaia Construcoes, Case C–164/99, [2002] ECR I–787, the issue was whether the German law setting minimum wages for the construction industry was indeed intended to provide social protection to workers. Noting that the referring court had cited the law's recitals of the need to protect against 'social dumping' resulting from an influx of low-wage labour, the Court instructed the referring court to determine whether the law represented a disguised "protection of domestic businesses" (¶ 26), in which case it could not be applied to set the wages of the Portuguese construction workers. However in Commission v. Germany (Translation of documents), Case C–490/04, [2007] ECR I–6095, the Court held that Germany could properly require documents concerning the pay of posted workers to be translated into German in order to monitor their compliance with worker protection rules.

By far the most prominent recent judgment posed a conflict between fundamental social rights and the free movement of services.

LAVAL v. BYGGNADS

Case C–341/05, [2007] ECR I–11767.

[Laval, a Latvian contractor, took 35 of its workers to Sweden in order to construct a school. Laval tried to negotiate an agreement concerning the pay of the workers with Byggnads, the Swedish construction workers union, but the negotiations were unsuccessful. The union also demanded that Laval pay 8% of gross wages to the union for various administrative charges. The union then carried out a blockade of the construction site, preventing Laval's workers from entering. Laval had to abandon the project and return its workers to Latvia. When Laval sued the construction workers union for damages due to its interference, the trial court referred questions to the Court of Justice.

After observing that Sweden had no law setting minimum pay scales, and that no universally applicable collective bargaining agreements set them (¶ 67), the Court concluded that the Posting of Workers directive did not "justify an obligation on [trans-border] service providers to comply with rates of pay such as those which the trade unions seek" (¶ 70), and that none of the directive's other terms permitted the unions to require

Laval to pay the administrative charges they demanded (¶ ¶ 83–84). The Court then turned to the union's use of collective action, noting that the right to take collective action is recognized both in the Charter of the Fundamental Rights of Workers (see Chapter 36A) and the Nice Charter of Fundamental Rights (¶ 90).]

93   [T]he Court has already held that the protection of fundamental rights is a legitimate interest which, in principle, justifies a restriction of the obligations imposed by Community law, even under a fundamental freedom guaranteed by the Treaty, such as the free movement of goods [citing *Schmidberger*, supra page 491] or freedom to provide services [citing *Omega,* infra page 695].

* * *

96   It must therefore be examined whether the fact that a Member State's trade unions may take collective action in the circumstances described above constitutes a restriction on the freedom to provide services, and, if so, whether it can be justified.

* * *

98   Furthermore, compliance with Article 49 EC is also required in the case of rules which are not public in nature but which are designed to regulate, collectively, the provision of services. The abolition, as between Member States, of obstacles to the freedom to provide services would be compromised if the abolition of State barriers could be neutralised by obstacles resulting from the exercise of their legal autonomy by associations or organisations not governed by public law [citing *Walrave* and *Bosman*, supra page 611].

99   In the case in the main proceedings, it must be pointed out that the right of trade unions of a Member State to take collective action by which undertakings established in other Member States may be forced to sign the collective agreement for the building sector—certain terms of which * * * establish more favourable terms and conditions of employment [than those covered in] Directive 96/71 and others relate to matters not referred to in [the directive]—is liable to make it less attractive, or more difficult, for such undertakings to carry out construction work in Sweden, and therefore constitutes a restriction on the freedom to provide services within the meaning of Article 49 EC.

* * *

103   [T]he right to take collective action for the protection of the workers of the host State against possible social dumping may constitute an overriding reason of public interest within the meaning of the case-law of the Court which, in principle, justifies a restriction of one of the fundamental freedoms guaranteed by the Treaty.

104   [A]ccording to Article 3(1)(c) and (j) EC, the activities of the Community are to include not only an 'internal market characterised by the abolition, as between Member States, of obstacles to the free move-

ment of goods, persons, services and capital', but also 'a policy in the social sphere'. Article 2 EC states that the Community is to have as its task, inter alia, the promotion of 'a harmonious, balanced and sustainable development of economic activities' and 'a high level of employment and of social protection'.

105 Since the Community has thus not only an economic but also a social purpose, the rights under the provisions of the EC Treaty on the free movement of goods, persons, services and capital must be balanced against the objectives pursued by social policy, which include * * * proper * * * social protection and dialogue between management and labour.

* * *

107 [I]n principle, blockading action by a trade union of the host Member State which is aimed at ensuring that workers posted in the framework of a transnational provision of services have their terms and conditions of employment fixed at a certain level, falls within the objective of protecting workers.

108 However, as regards the specific obligations, linked to signature of the collective agreement for the building sector, which the trade unions seek to impose on undertakings established in other Member States by way of collective action * * *, the obstacle which that collective action forms cannot be justified with regard to such an objective. * * *

109 Finally, as regards the negotiations on pay which the trade unions seek to impose, by way of collective action such as that at issue in the main proceedings, on undertakings, established in another Member State which post workers temporarily to their territory, it must be emphasised that Community law certainly does not prohibit Member States from requiring such undertakings to comply with their rules on minimum pay by appropriate means [citing *Arblade*].

110 However, collective action such as that at issue in the main proceedings cannot be justified * * * where the negotiations on pay * * * form part of a national [legal] context characterised by a lack of provisions, of any kind, which are sufficiently precise and accessible that they do not render it impossible or excessively difficult in practice for an undertaking [providing services from another State] to determine the obligations with which it is required to comply as regards minimum pay.

[The Court also answered a question concerning the impact of Laval's agreement with its workers under Latvian law.]

116 In that regard, it must be pointed out that national rules, such as those at issue in the case in the main proceedings, which fail to take into account * * * collective agreements to which undertakings that post workers to Sweden are already bound in the Member State in which they are established, give rise to discrimination against such undertakings * * *.

NOTES AND QUESTIONS

1. The Court's judgment provoked considerable criticism in the Swedish media and indignation among Swedish labor leaders. Would you agree with the priority given to free movement of services in these specific circumstances? Suppose that Swedish law did set minimum pay levels for construction workers, and Laval's pay scales were below them. Would that change the outcome? If Laval then agreed to pay to workers the requisite minimum pay, could it further be required to pay Byggnands the 8% of gross pay administrative charges?

2. Note an important part of the Court's judgment: the Court held in ¶ 98 that Article 49 has horizontal direct effect, just as Article 39 does (see *Angonese*, supra page 572). It is true that an individual or a single enterprise is unlikely to have sufficient economic power to frustrate an effort to provide trans-border services, but a collective body, such as the group of labor unions in this case, or perhaps a group of companies or banks, is able to do so.

3. In Ruffert v. Land Niedersachsen, Case C–346/06, [2008] ECR I–1989, the Court followed *Laval* in holding that a German state could not require a Polish contractor to pay its workers on a German prison construction project the pay scales customary in that state when these were neither set by law nor fixed by a universally applicable collective agreement.

3. CROSS–BORDER SERVICES PROVIDED BY TECHNOLOGICAL MEANS

Some types of services are provided across borders without physical movement by either the provider or the recipient. The best example is radio and television broadcasting, but cross-border services can also be provided by modern telecommunications or computer networks (e.g., transmission of messages or information by telex, fax, or computer software). Does ECT Article 49 cover these technological transmissions?

Already in 1974 the Court held in Sacchi, Case 155/73, [1974] ECR 490, that the broadcasting of television across frontiers fell within the scope of free movement of services. A series of cases in the 1980's dealt with questions raised when national rules restricted trans-border television broadcasting. Thus, in Procureur du Roi v. Debauve, Case 52/79, [1980] ECR 833, the Court held that Belgium, which then prohibited advertising in television broadcasts, could forbid a cable television retransmission of programs from other States that contained advertising. The Court stated that the Belgian law was justified by "grounds of general interest" (¶ 15), without defining the interest.

The Court's conclusion that television broadcasting across frontiers constituted a cross-border service prompted the Commission to propose rules for television broadcasting appropriate for the common market. Council Directive 89/552 on the coordination of rules concerning television broadcasting activities, O.J. L 298/23 (Oct. 17, 1989), Document 19 in the

Selected Documents, often called the Television Without Frontiers Directive, sought to create a common television program production and distribution market. The directive requires Member States to ensure freedom of reception and retransmission of television broadcasts from other Member States (art. 2(2)). The State from which television is broadcast is responsible for ensuring that all programs broadcast comply with the directive's rules.

The heart of the directive is its regulation of television advertising and sponsorship. Advertising must be readily recognizable; subliminal or surreptitious advertising is forbidden (art. 10). The frequency of advertising breaks and the total advertising share of daily broadcast time is restricted (arts. 11 and 18). Sponsors of programs must be clearly identified and may not influence the "editorial independence" of the broadcaster (art. 17).

Advertising for all tobacco products and for prescription medication is prohibited (arts. 13–14) and advertising for alcoholic beverages is restricted (art. 15). Advertising may not involve discrimination on grounds of race, sex or nationality, be "offensive to religious or political beliefs," or "encourage behavior prejudicial to the protection of the environment" (art. 12). Moreover, the directive permits Member States to have more detailed or stricter rules regulating advertising.

Apart from the regulation of advertising, the directive requires that programs not "seriously impair the physical, mental or moral development of minors, in particular [by display of] pornography or gratuitous violence" (art. 22). Programs which might have this effect are to be broadcast at times when minors would normally not be watching television.

A directive recital emphasizes the role of television in promoting culture. Implicitly taking the view that there is a common European culture, the directive's most controversial feature is the requirement that a "majority proportion" of broadcast time, apart from news and sports, be devoted "where practicable" to "European works" (art. 4(1)). "European works" were defined to include not only those produced in Member States, but, under certain conditions, those produced in other European states. The "European works" requirement was motivated by concern over the dominance of non-European (usually US) feature films, comedies and serials. Estimates vary, but in 1989 in some States non-European production probably amounted to 70% of total broadcasts.

US producers of motion picture films and films made for television vehemently criticized the European content provision in the draft directive and the US Government strongly urged its elimination. The US film industry feared a significant decline in its European revenues, estimated at around one billion dollars in 1989, representing a 500% increase since 1980. A US House of Representatives resolution denounced the directive as "trade restrictive." Despite vigorous efforts, the US was unable to have the WTO agreement, concluded in 1994 at the end of the Uruguay Round, forbid national quotas or preferences for feature film or television film distribution. Thus, the US has no ability to secure recourse through a WTO panel. See Chapter 29.

Directive 97/36, O.J. L 202/60 (July 30, 1997), made a series of amendments to the Television Without Frontiers Directive. The principal modifications make more precise the jurisdiction provisions and enable the directive to cover the field of telemarketing, which had recently become popular in Europe. The most heated debate came over a new article 3a, proposed by Parliament, which permits States to designate certain sporting events, and other events of "major importance for society" (e.g., the Olympic games, the Derby or the Tour de France), for which exclusive broadcast rights cannot be granted and access by the general viewing public must be ensured.

Directive 2007/65, O.J. L 332/27 (Dec. 18, 2007) substantially amends the Television Broadcasting Directive and changes its name to the Audiovisual Media Services Directive (art. 1). Member States were obligated to implement the new provisions by Dec. 19, 2009. As the name change suggests, the directive now covers "on-demand audiovisual media services," which are defined as those provided by a server by an electronic communications network to users who request programs selected from a catalog supplied by the server (art. 1(g)), notably pay-per-view programs.

The Audiovisual Media Services Directive requires the State in which the service provider is established (usually where its head office and editorial center are located) to ensure compliance with the directive's rules (art. 2). The public policy limits on types of advertising and special protection for minors are essentially the same as in the Television Broadcasting Directive (art. 3e). Although surreptitious and subliminal advertising continue to be forbidden, the new directive liberalizes the prior rules on total advertising time and frequency and permits new forms of advertising (e.g., split screen or interactive advertising).

NOTES AND QUESTIONS

1. The Television Without Frontiers Directive not only facilitates cross-border broadcasting, but also sets the basic rules for all broadcasting. It is thus a far-reaching example of harmonization. On the whole, what is your reaction? Are its rules well-founded and fair? Would you like to see some of these rules (apart from European content) adopted in the US? Might First Amendment concerns make it difficult to adopt some rules?

2. Do you think that the Community's concern over protection of European culture is genuine or merely veils economic protectionism? Assuming the concern is genuine, do you think it justifies this type of provision? In May 1995, the Commission proposed to amend the Television without Frontiers Directive by the deletion of the qualification, "where practicable," before the majority content requirement. Although President Chirac of France pressed vigorously for this approach at the June European Council meeting in Cannes, the UK and several other States opposed the deletion. In the fall, the Parliament endorsed the deletion by a majority vote, but not by the absolute

majority required to keep the amendment under discussion in the codecision process. The words, "where practicable," accordingly remain as a qualification. However, the Commission in a July 2000 report monitoring the effect of the directive indicated that almost all States were respecting the majority European works content clause and that the major television channels' broadcasts of European works averaged between 53% and 82% of the total broadcast time.

The television broadcasting directive has now been interpreted in several leading cases, some of which influenced the clarificatory amendments mentioned above.

KONSUMENTOMBUDSMANNEN v. DE AGOSTINI (SVENKSA) FORLAG

Cases C–34 to 36/95, [1997] ECR I–3843.

[In the first preliminary reference from Sweden, questions were raised concerning the propriety of the Consumer Ombudsman's efforts to enjoin advertisements initially broadcast by TV3, a UK broadcaster, and retransmitted by satellite for broadcast in Sweden. In two cases, the Ombudsman sought to prevent TV-Shop Europe from making allegedly unsubstantiated health and therapeutic claims and deceptive comparative prices for a skin-care product, and from claiming that a detergent was "environmentally friendly" and "biodegradable" without having proof of these claims.

In a third case, an Italian magazine publisher advertised "Everything about Dinosaurs," a children's magazine series that featured the inclusion of dinosaur model parts that could be assembled by purchase of the entire series. The Ombudsman contended that this violated the Swedish Broadcasting law prohibiting advertising directed at children less than 12 years old. Besides questions on the interpretation of Directive 89/552, the referring court inquired whether the Swedish law might violate ECT Article 49.

The Court began by indicating that Directive 89/552 accorded the home State the responsibility for the supervision of broadcasters on its territory to ensure compliance with the Directive's substantive rules, including those on advertising. However, the Court noted that the Directive's 17th recital stated that its provisions were "without prejudice to existing or future Community acts of harmonization, in particular to satisfy overriding considerations of consumer protection, fair trading and competition." (¶ 28.) The Court continued:]

32   Consequently, it follows that, as regards the activity of broadcasting and distribution of television programmes, the Directive, whilst coordinating provisions laid down by law, regulation or administrative action on television advertising and sponsorship, does so only partially.

* * *

35   Consequently, where a Member State's legislation * * *, for the purpose of protecting consumers, provides for a system of [restrictions] on advertisers, enforceable by financial penalties, application of such legislation to television broadcasts from other Member States cannot be considered to constitute an obstacle prohibited by the Directive.

36   According to De Agostini, TV–Shop and the Commission, the principle that broadcasts are to be controlled by the State having jurisdiction over the broadcaster would be seriously undermined in both its purpose and effect if the Directive were held to be inapplicable to advertisers. They argue that a restriction relating to advertising has an impact on television broadcasts, even if the restriction concerns only advertising.

37   In response to that objection, it is sufficient to observe that Council Directive 84/450/EEC * * * concerning misleading advertising, which provides * * * that Member States are to ensure that adequate and effective means exist for the control of misleading advertising in the interests of consumers as well as competitors and the general public, could be robbed of its substance in the field of television advertising if the receiving Member State were deprived of all possibility of adopting measures against an advertiser and that this would be in contradiction with the express intention of the Community legislature.

38   [Accordingly,] a Member State [may take] pursuant to general legislation on protection of consumers against misleading advertising, measures against an advertiser in relation to television advertising broadcast from another Member State, provided that those measures do not prevent the retransmission, as such, in its territory of television broadcasts coming from that other Member State.

* * *

As regards Article [49] of the Treaty

50   Provisions such as those in question in the main proceedings, where they restrict the possibility for television broadcasters established in the broadcasting State to broadcast television advertising specifically directed at the public in the receiving State, involve a restriction on freedom to provide services.

* * *

53   [A]ccording to settled case-law, fair trading and the protection of consumers in general are overriding requirements of public interest which may justify restrictions on freedom to provide services [citing *Alpine Investments,* infra page 1236].

54   [Accordingly,] on a proper construction of Article [49] of the Treaty, a Member State is not precluded from taking, on the basis of provisions of its domestic legislation, measures against an advertiser in relation to television advertising. However, it is for the national court to

determine whether those provisions are necessary for meeting overriding requirements of general public importance * * *, whether they are proportionate for that purpose and whether those aims or overriding requirements could be met by measures less restrictive of intra-Community trade.

The second question

55   By its second question the [Swedish court] asks the Court for an interpretation of Community law with regard to a provision of a domestic broadcasting law which provides that advertisements broadcast during commercial breaks on television must not be designed to attract the attention of children under 12 years of age.

56   Application of such a domestic provision to advertising broadcast by a television broadcaster established in the same State cannot be contrary to the Directive since Article 3(1) of that provision does not contain any restriction as regards the interests which the Member States may take into consideration when laying down more strict rules for television broadcasters established in their territory. However, the situation is not the same where television broadcasters established in another Member State are concerned.

57   In Articles 16 and 22, the Directive contains a set of provisions specifically devoted to the protection of minors in relation to television programmes in general and television advertising in particular.

58   The broadcasting State must ensure that those provisions are complied with.

59   This certainly does not have the effect of prohibiting application of legislation of the receiving State designed to protect consumers or minors in general, provided that its application does not prevent retransmission, as such, in its territory of broadcasts from another Member State.

60   However, the receiving Member State may no longer, under any circumstances, apply provisions specifically designed to control the content of television advertising with regard to minors.

61   If provisions of the receiving State regulating the content of television broadcasts for reasons relating to the protection of minors against advertising were applied to broadcasts from other Member States, this would add a secondary control to the control which the broadcasting Member State must exercise under the Directive.

62   It follows that the Directive is to be interpreted as precluding the application to television broadcasts from other Member States of a provision of a domestic broadcasting law which provides that advertisements broadcast in commercial breaks on television must not be designed to attract the attention of children under 12 years of age.

NOTES AND QUESTIONS

1. In the Swedish *Consumer Ombudsman* case, note that in ¶ 36 the Commission supported the defendants' argument that only the State of initial broadcasting should monitor claims of false and misleading advertising. Obviously, there is a clash between the goal of promoting an internal market in TV broadcasting and that of protecting local consumer interests. The Court rejected the Commission's views, instead deciding in favor of permitting the supervision of misleading advertising claims by the State receiving the broadcast. Would you agree? The Court's view imposes a substantial cost on the UK advertiser to check for compliance with the consumer protection rules in every State into which the program is broadcast. On the other hand, giving the monitoring role only to the State of initial broadcast may make it both costly and procedurally difficult for consumers in States receiving the broadcast to get adequate recourse against misleading advertising. If TV3 were to broadcast from the UK a program in Swedish for a Swedish audience, could the UK authorities easily apply UK misleading advertising rules to review the advertising?

2. Since the Court permitted Sweden to apply its misleading advertising rules, why did it prevent Sweden from enforcing its rule against advertising directed at children under 12? The judgement applies the preemption rules described in Chapter 14C. Do you agree? On policy grounds, would you support the amendment of the television broadcasting directive to incorporate the Swedish rule? Would such a rule be desirable, or legally feasible in the US?

3. In Commission v. Belgium (Cable TV transmission), Case C–11/95, [1996] ECR I–4115, the Court held that the French and Flemish regional rules requiring a system of prior review for cable broadcasts from other Member States violated the directive's article 2, which gives jurisdiction to the State of initial broadcast to ensure compliance with the directive. Belgium's claim that its review was necessary to protect cultural interests and "pluralism in the audiovisual field" was rejected. The Court followed this precedent in Criminal Proceedings against Denuit, Case C–14/96, [1997] ECR I–2785, informing the trial court that it should not penalize a Belgian rebroadcaster of the Turner Cartoon Network prosecuted because of an alleged failure to respect the directive's majority European content rules. As the cartoon broadcasts originated in the UK, the Court held that it was the UK's responsibility to monitor compliance with the European content rules, noting that Belgium could bring an ECT Article 227 proceeding against the UK if it considered that the UK was not carrying out its responsibilities. See Chapter 11D.

4. Mediakabel offers pay-per-view programming in the Netherlands to subscribers who select films from Mediakabel's catalog, pay to see them, and receive a key to unscramble the encoded film. In Mediakabel v. Commissariat voor de Media, Case C–89/04, [2005] ECR I–4891, the Court initially held that the Television Broadcasting Directive did cover pay-per-view broadcasting (¶ 45). The Court then held that Mediakabel must comply with the directive's

majority European content rule in selecting films for its catalog, although its subscribers would ultimately decide which films they want to view (¶ 51).

5. In UTECA v. Administracion General, Case C–222/07 [2009] ECR I–1407 (Mar. 5, 2009), a television producers' federation challenged a Spanish law that, i.a., required that they spend 60% of at least 5% of their prior year's operating revenue to produce cinema and television films in one of the official languages of Spain. The Court accepted Spain's claim that the requirement was justified by a cultural interest, namely the protection of its official languages (¶¶ 26–29), and further held that 3% of the operating budget (60% of 5%) did not represent a disproportionate expenditure (¶ 31). Would you agree? Is the judgment reminiscent of *Groener*, supra page 569?

4. THE 2006 GENERAL SERVICES DIRECTIVE

Proposed by the Commission in January 2004, the initial draft soon encountered serious resistance from France, Germany and other States, largely due to concerns that a directive might produce 'social dumping,' i.e., service providing by entities that had competitive advantages due to a more cheaply paid workforce or that operated with lower quality standards. On several occasions labor unions organized protest marches of thousands of workers. The Commission's initial principle that the country of origin of a provider should essentially regulate the services provided in a host State was removed by the Parliament in its first reading in February 2006. After further amendments, Directive 2006/123 on services in the internal market, O.J. L 376/36 (Dec. 27, 2006), was adopted in extremely detailed form, with 15 pages of recitals and 18 of substantive text. Member State implementation was due by Dec. 28, 2009.

Obviously, only the highlights can be noted here. The directive clearly owes a great debt to Court of Justice case law—indeed, some critics contend that some directive provisions are less liberal than Court judgments. The directive covers most commercial service fields (see recital 33), but specifically excludes financial services, electronic communications, transport, healthcare, audiovisual services, gambling, social services and taxation (art.2). Furthermore, it is expressly stated that the directive will not affect labor law, criminal law, the protection of basic rights, or measures to promote cultural or linguistic diversity (art. 1).

One of the directive's purposes is to promote the providing of services across national borders. Accordingly, articles 5–8 require States to simplify and expedite any administrative procedures concerning service providers. Articles 9–15 require States to facilitate any establishment by a provider of services from another State. Article 9 notably forbids States to require an authorization for an establishment unless the authorization is justified by "an overriding reason relating to the public interest," a term defined in article 4(8) as any public interest recognized in the case law of the Court of Justice. Moreover, article 17 forbids States to require a trans-border service provider to have an establishment, or to obtain a national authorization or be registered with a professional body, unless provided for in this or another directive.

Two final provisions may well lead to changes in the rules governing lawyers, doctors and other professionals. Article 24 requires States to end any prohibitions on "commercial communications," which would principally mean restrictions on advertising, although States must ensure that professionals comply with rules that relate to "the independence, dignity and integrity of the profession, as well as to professional secrecy." In addition, article 25 prescribes that States shall eliminate restrictions on multidisciplinary practice, except insofar as justified by appropriate "rules governing professional ethics and conduct."

Although the general Services Directive does not achieve as much liberalization as the Commission had originally proposed, and the text is complicated and sometimes ambiguous, it still provides for valuable modifications in Member State rules in the direction of a more integrated market for services. The Court of Justice is bound to have occasion soon to interpret and apply some of its complex provisions. Professor Catherine Barnard provides a comprehensive and rather critical appraisal in C. Barnard, Unravelling the Services Directive, 45 Common Mkt. L. Rev. 323 (2008).

C. RIGHT TO RECEIVE SERVICES IN OTHER STATES

ECT Article 49 protects the "freedom to provide services" and Article 50 guarantees the right of a person providing a service to reside temporarily in the State where the service is provided. There is no express reference to any right of a person to travel to and stay in another State in order to receive services. (Note that TFEU Articles 56 and 57 replicate ECT Articles 49 and 50 without referring to a right to receive services.) Nonetheless, it was soon recognized that the recipients of services ought to have correlative rights.

Accordingly, both Council Directive 64/221 on public policy, public security and public health exceptions, and Council Directive 73/148 on rights of movement and residence, discussed in section A above, expressly covered recipients as well as providers of services. The Court of Justice first authoritatively interpreted ECT Articles 49 and 50 in that sense in *Luisi and Carbone,* a free movement of capital case discussed at page 1205, stating that a right to travel to other States to receive medical, educational and tourist services was implicit in Article 49.

COWAN v. TRÉSOR PUBLIC

Case 186/87, [1989] ECR 195.

[A French law provides that the state will pay compensation for serious injuries to French nationals who are victims of crimes. The law also grants such compensation to foreign nationals who hold a residence permit. Cowan, a UK national, was assaulted and seriously injured during a robbery at a metro station while on a visit to Paris. When Cowan applied for compensation, the French commission which makes such grants asked the Court of Justice whether the prohibition of discrimination on grounds of nationality contained in ECT Article 12 (now TFEU Article 18) required that compensation be paid to nationals of other Member States when injured during a visit to France.]

10   By prohibiting 'any discrimination on grounds of nationality' Article [12] of the Treaty requires that persons in a situation governed by Community law be placed on a completely equal footing with nationals of the Member State. In so far as this principle is applicable it therefore precludes a Member State from making the grant of a right to such a person subject to the condition that he reside on the territory of that State—that condition is not imposed on the State's own nationals.

                              * * *

15   [I]n its judgment *Luisi and Carbone*, the Court held that the freedom to provide services includes the freedom for the recipients of services to go to another Member State in order to receive a service there, without being obstructed by restrictions, and that tourists, among others, must be regarded as recipients of services.

16   [T]he French Government submitted that as Community law now stands a recipient of services may not rely on the prohibition of discrimination to the extent that the national law at issue does not create any barrier to freedom of movement. A provision such as that at issue in the main proceedings, it says, imposes no restrictions in that respect. Furthermore, it concerns a right which is a manifestation of the principle of national solidarity. Such a right presupposes a closer bond with the State than that of a recipient of services, and for that reason it may be restricted to persons who are either nationals of that State or foreign nationals resident on the territory of that State.

17   That reasoning cannot be accepted. When Community law guarantees a natural person the freedom to go to another Member State the protection of that person from harm in the Member State in question, on the same basis as that of nationals and persons residing there, is a corollary of that freedom of movement. It follows that the prohibition of discrimination is applicable to recipients of services within the meaning of the Treaty as regards protection against the risk of assault and the right to obtain financial compensation provided for by national law when that risk materializes. The fact that the compensation at issue is financed by the Public Treasury cannot alter the rules regarding the protection of the rights guaranteed by the Treaty.

                              * * *

20   [Accordingly,] the prohibition of discrimination laid down in particular in Article [12] of the EEC Treaty must be interpreted as meaning that in respect of persons whose freedom to travel to a Member State, in particular as recipients of services, is guaranteed by Community law that State may not make the award of State compensation for harm caused in that State to the victim of an assault resulting in physical injury subject to the condition that he hold a residence permit * * *.

NOTES AND QUESTIONS

1.   *Cowan* exemplifies the Court of Justice's philosophy that Treaty articles are to be interpreted expansively in order to further the basic goals of the Treaty. Do you agree with this teleological analysis of ECT Article 49 or do you feel it represents excessive judicial activism? In *Cowan*, the French law was clearly discriminatory, but is there a sufficient nexus to a Treaty-based right? In concluding that tourists have rights under ECT Articles 12 and 49, the Court has gone rather far, but the judgment has generally been approved. See the case notes by Professors Anthony Arnull in 14 Eur.L.Rev. 166 (1989) and Stephen Weatherill in 26 Common Mkt.L.Rev. 563 (1989). The Court has in effect created a right to travel, parallel in some respects to that recognized by the US Supreme Court in an equally broad reading of the US Constitution. There is no reason to doubt that the Court will recognize an implied right to receive services in interpreting TFEU Articles 56 and 57, which replicate ECT Articles 49 and 50.

2.   In *Cowan* the Court neither defined "tourist" nor specifically indicated what sort of services Cowan received that brought Article 49 into play. Advocate General Lenz's opinion provides a highly sophisticated analysis, suggesting that a tourist is anyone who crosses frontiers and receives economic services, such as those provided by hotels, restaurants, theaters or museums. He regarded even the metro, where Cowan was injured, as providing a service to tourists, because it constituted necessary local transportation. Do you agree with the Advocate General or would you limit the concept of tourist to persons who receive some significant minimum level of services specifically designed for travellers from other States?

3.   In Criminal Proceedings against Bickel and Franz, Case C–274/96, [1998] ECR I–7367, Bickel, an Austrian driver of a truck through Bolzano, and Franz, a German tourist in that region, both claimed the right to have criminal proceedings against them conducted in German, inasmuch as Bolzano is a German-speaking region and Italians resident there would have the right to the use of German in a criminal proceeding. Not surprisingly, the Court cited *Mutsch*, supra page 575, and concluded that Article 49's guarantee of no discrimination based on nationality provided each with that right as respectively a provider and a recipient of services. For the Court's more pioneering conclusion that each had such a right as a citizen of the Union, see page 622 supra.

4.   In Commission v. Italy (Museum fees), Case C–388/01, [2003] ECR I–721, the Commission contended that Italian regional authorities violated Articles 12 and 49 by charging fees for admission to museums and historic

sites to visitors from other States, while granting free admission to their residents. What should the Court decide? May Italy claim that it is not responsible because by law the museums are exclusively controlled by its regions?

5. In Criminal proceedings against Calfa, Case C–348/96, [1999] ECR I–11, Calfa, an Italian tourist in Crete, was convicted of the possession of prohibited drugs and sentenced to three months imprisonment. Under Greek law, the court was obliged to order her expulsion for life from Greece after conviction on a drug offense. Greek nationals can be forbidden to reside in a particular region, but only if convicted of drug dealing. The trial court asked the Court of Justice whether the expulsion for life was compatible with the Treaty. Recall the Court's views in *Rutili, Bouchereau* and *Adoui* in Chapter 15C. What do you think should be the reply to the Greek court?

In the next case, the Court had to consider again the question whether protection of a fundamental right can justify a limit upon a right of free movement.

OMEGA SPIELHALLEN v. BONN

Case C–36/02, [2004] ECR I–9609.

[Omega, a German company, operates a laserdome in the City of Bonn. Omega provides lasers that look like sub-machine-guns to players who shoot at sensory tags in firing corridors. When Omega began to allow players to shoot at tags worn by other players, Bonn forbid this type of game as an act of simulated homicide that violated fundamental values. The trial court sustained Bonn's order. On appeal, the Supreme Administrative Court held that Omega's killing simulation violated human dignity, a right stated in the German Constitution. However, that court asked the Court of Justice whether the ban on the game violated the freedom to provide services, inasmusch as Omega franchised the game from Pulsar, a UK company that operated it in the UK without hindrance from the authorities.]

25 [T]he contested order, by prohibiting Omega from operating its 'laser-drome' in accordance with the form of the game developed by Pulsar and lawfully marketed by it in the United Kingdom, particularly under the franchising system, affects the freedom to provide services which Article 49 EC guarantees both to providers and to the persons receiving those services established in another Member State. Moreover, in so far as use of the form of the game developed by Pulsar involves the use of specific equipment, which is also lawfully marketed in the United Kingdom, the prohibition imposed on Omega is likely to deter it from acquiring the equipment in question, thereby infringing the free movement of goods ensured by Article 28 EC.

28 Article 46 EC, which applies here by virtue of Article 55 EC, allows restrictions justified for reasons of public policy, public security or public health. In this case, the documents before the Court show that the grounds relied on by the Bonn police authority in adopting the

prohibition order expressly mention the fact that the activity concerned constitutes a danger to public policy. * * *

30   However, [a State's reliance on public policy] does not prevent judicial review of measures applying that derogation. In addition, the concept of 'public policy' in the Community context, particularly as justification for a derogation from the fundamental principle of the freedom to provide services, must be interpreted strictly, so that its scope cannot be determined unilaterally by each Member State without any control by the Community institutions * * *. Thus, public policy may be relied on only if there is a genuine and sufficiently serious threat to a fundamental interest of society.

31   The fact remains, however, that the specific circumstances which may justify recourse to the concept of public policy may vary from one country to another and from one era to another. The competent national authorities must therefore be allowed a margin of discretion within the limits imposed by the Treaty.

32   In this case, the competent authorities took the view that the activity concerned by the prohibition order was a threat to public policy by reason of the fact that, in accordance with the conception prevailing in public opinion, the commercial exploitation of games involving the simulated killing of human beings infringed a fundamental value enshrined in the national constitution, namely human dignity. * * *

33   [A]ccording to settled case-law, fundamental rights form an integral part of the general principles of law the observance of which the Court ensures, and * * * the Court draws inspiration from the constitutional traditions common to the Member States and from the guidelines supplied by international treaties for the protection of human rights on which the Member States have collaborated or to which they are signatories. The European Convention on Human Rights and Fundamental Freedoms has special significance in that respect [citing *Connolly*, supra page 201, and *Schmidberger*, supra page 491.]

34   As the Advocate General argues * * *, the Community legal order undeniably strives to ensure respect for human dignity as a general principle of law. There can therefore be no doubt that the objective of protecting human dignity is compatible with Community law, it being immaterial in that respect that, in Germany, the principle of respect for human dignity has a particular status as an independent fundamental right.

* * *

36   However, measures which restrict the freedom to provide services may be justified on public policy grounds only if they are necessary for the protection of the interests which they are intended to guarantee and only in so far as those objectives cannot be attained by less restrictive measures.

[39] In this case, it should be noted, that, * * * by prohibiting only the variant of the laser game the object of which is to fire on human targets and thus 'play at killing' people, the contested order did not go beyond what is necessary in order to attain the objective pursued by the competent national authorities.

NOTES AND QUESTIONS

1. *Omega* demonstrates that different States may have different conceptions of what constitutes a fundamental right and how rights should be protected. Pulsar, a UK franchisor, apparently can operate killing games legally in the UK. Do you find the German prohibition praiseworthy, or unduly sensitive? Could a US state or municipality prohibit laser killings simulations?

2. In a well-known judgment, Society for the Protection of Unborn Children Ireland v. Grogan, Case C–159/90, [1991] ECR I–4685, an Irish student group provided information on clinics in the UK where abortions were carried out. Article 40(3) of the Irish Constitution asserts "the right to life of the unborn" and requires its laws to "defend and vindicate that right." Dealing with a request to enjoin the students' activities, the High Court inquired whether the right to provide trans-border services was involved. The Court of Justice held that it was not, because ECT Article 50 covered only services "for remuneration," and the students provided the information free of charge. The Court did hold that providing abortions is a medical service which would fall under ECT Article 49 whenever legal in a Member States where the service is provided (¶ 18). However, the Court did not consider whether an individual has a right to travel to receive an abortion service in a State whose laws permit such services. For further discussion of other issues connected with *Grogan*, see Chapter 8F.

3. In Kohll v. Union des Caisses de Maladie, Case C–158/96, [1998] ECR I–1931, Kohll challenged a Luxembourg law which denied him the reimbursement of the cost of dental treatment provided by an orthodontist in another Member State because he had not obtained a prior authorization for such treatment. The issues and the Court's judgement paralleled those in *Decker*, supra page 460, where Luxembourg's rules requiring prior authorization for the purchase of eyeglasses outside Luxembourg were struck down. In *Kohll*, Luxembourg's alleged public health justification for the prior authorization obligation was not accepted. The Court observed that the quality of dental care throughout the Community must be considered "equivalent" in view of the professional harmonization directives described in the next chapter (¶¶ 47–48).

After *Kohll* it was predictable that the Court would have to confront a far more serious issue, namely, whether a State would have to reimburse the cost of medical care received by its nationals in other State's hospitals.

MULLER–FAURE v. ONDERLINGE WAARBORG–MAATSCHAPPIJ OZ

Case C–385/99, [2003] ECR I–4509.

[The Dutch Government's system of social security enables the reimbursement of most medical and dental costs, including hospital costs, to residents who subscribe to medical insurance funds. However, the reimbursement rules require prior authorisation for medical or dental services provided abroad (except for emergency care). Prior authorization is also required for non-emergency medical services provided in hospitals outside the Netherlands, except for a few authorized hospitals located in border areas close to the Netherlands. Without prior authorization, Muller–Faure received dental care principally for the fitting of six crowns, apparently because she had greater confidence in German than Dutch dentists. Van Riet obtained an arthroscopy and subsequent medical treatment in a Belgian hospital without prior authorisation, because she did not want to wait for the period necessary before similar care would become available in the Netherlands.

The Court first held that an obligation to obtain a prior authorization for out-of-state medical or hospital care constituted a deterrence to receipt of medical services elsewhere in the Union which in principle violates ECT Article 49, and hence had to be objectively justified.]

The risk that the protection of public health may be adversely affected.

67   It is apparent from the Court's case-law that the objective of maintaining a high-quality, balanced medical and hospital service open to all, may fall within one of the derogations provided for in Article [46] of the EC Treaty in so far as it contributes to the attainment of a high level of health protection. In particular, that Treaty provision permits Member States to restrict the freedom to provide medical and hospital services in so far as the maintenance of treatment capacity or medical competence on national territory is essential for public health, and even the survival of the population [citing *Kohll* and *Geraet–Smits*, infra note 1].

* * *

71   The objective of maintaining a balanced medical and hospital service open to all is inextricably linked to the way in which the social security system is financed and to the control of expenditure, which are dealt with below.

The risk of seriously undermining the financial balance of the social security system

72   It must be recalled, at the outset, that, according to the Court's case-law, aims of a purely economic nature cannot justify a barrier to the fundamental principle of freedom to provide services [citing *Kohll*].

73　However, in so far as, in particular, it could have consequences for the overall level of public-health protection, the risk of seriously undermining the financial balance of the social security system may also constitute *per se* an overriding general-interest reason capable of justifying a barrier of that kind [citing *Kohll* and *Geraet–Smits*].

74　It is self-evident that assuming the cost of one isolated case of treatment, carried out in a Member State other than that in which a particular person is insured with a sickness fund, can never make any significant impact on the financing of the social security system. Thus an overall approach must necessarily be adopted in relation to the consequences of freedom to provide health-related services.

Hospital Services

77　It is well known that the number of hospitals, their geographical distribution, the way in which they are organised and the facilities with which they are provided, and even the nature of the medical services which they are able to offer, are all matters for which planning must be possible.

* * *

80　[Such planning] assists in meeting a desire to control costs and to prevent, as far as possible, any wastage of financial, technical and human resources. Such wastage would be all the more damaging because it is generally recognised that the hospital care sector generates considerable costs and must satisfy increasing needs, while the financial resources which may be made available for health care are not unlimited * * *.

81　In those circumstances, a requirement that the assumption of costs, under a national social security system, of hospital treatment provided in a Member State other than that of affiliation must be subject to prior authorisation appears to be a measure which is both necessary and reasonable.

* * *

85　[However,]in order for a prior administrative authorisation scheme to be justified * * *, it must be based on objective, non-discriminatory criteria which are known in advance, in such a way as to circumscribe the exercise of the national authorities' discretion, so that it is not used arbitrarily. Such a prior administrative authorisation scheme must likewise be based on a procedural system which is easily accessible and capable of ensuring that a request for authorisation will be dealt with objectively and impartially within a reasonable time and refusals to grant authorisation must also be capable of being challenged in judicial or quasi-judicial proceedings.

86　In the main actions, the disputes do not concern the actual cover provided by the Netherlands sickness insurance scheme for the medical and hospital treatment with which Ms Müller–Fauré and Ms Van

Riet were provided. In those actions, what is disputed is whether it was a medical necessity for them to have the treatment at issue in Germany and Belgium respectively, rather than in the Netherlands.

* * *

89 The condition [for prior authorization] concerning the necessity of the treatment * * * can be justified under Article 49 of the Treaty, provided that the condition is construed to the effect that authorisation to receive treatment in another Member State may be refused on that ground only if treatment which is the same or equally effective for the patient can be obtained without undue delay from an establishment with which the insured person's sickness insurance fund has an agreement.

90 In order to [decide this] the national authorities are required to have regard to all the circumstances of each specific case and to take due account not only of the patient's medical condition at the time when authorisation is sought and, where appropriate, of the degree of pain or the nature of the patient's disability which might, for example, make it impossible or extremely difficult for him to carry out a professional activity, but also of his medical history.

91 [If] large numbers of insured persons [should] decide to be treated in other Member States even when the hospitals having agreements with their sickness insurance funds offer adequate identical or equivalent treatment, the consequent outflow of patients would be liable to put at risk the very principle of having agreements with hospitals and, consequently, undermine all the planning and rationalisation carried out in this vital sector in an effort to avoid the phenomena of hospital overcapacity, imbalance in the supply of hospital medical care and logistical and financial wastage.

92 However, a refusal to grant prior authorisation which is based not on fear of wastage resulting from hospital overcapacity but solely on the ground that there are waiting lists on national territory for the hospital treatment concerned, without account being taken of the specific circumstances attaching to the patient's medical condition, cannot amount to a properly justified restriction on freedom to provide services. It is not clear from the arguments submitted to the Court that such waiting times are necessary, apart from considerations of a purely economic nature which cannot as such justify a restriction on the fundamental principle of freedom to provide services, for the purpose of safeguarding the protection of public health. On the contrary, a waiting time which is too long or abnormal would be more likely to restrict access to balanced, high-quality hospital care.

Non-hospital Services

93 As regards non-hospital medical services * * *, no specific evidence has been produced to the Court * * * to support the assertion that, were insured persons at liberty to go without prior authorisation to

Member States other than those in which their sickness funds are established in order to obtain those services from a non-contracted provider, that would be likely seriously to undermine the financial balance of the Netherlands social security system.

* * *

95   [T]he documents before the Court do not indicate that removal of the requirement for prior authorisation for that type of care would give rise to patients travelling to other countries in such large numbers, despite linguistic barriers, geographic distance, the cost of staying abroad and lack of information about the kind of care provided there, that the financial balance of the Netherlands social security system would be seriously upset and that, as a result, the overall level of public-health protection would be jeopardised—which might constitute proper justification for a barrier to the fundamental principle of freedom to provide services.

96   Furthermore, care is generally provided near to the place where the patient resides, in a cultural environment which is familiar to him and which allows him to build up a relationship of trust with the doctor treating him. * * *

97   Those various factors seem likely to limit any financial impact on the Netherlands social security system of removal of the requirement for prior authorisation in respect of care provided in foreign practitioners' surgeries.

NOTES AND QUESTIONS

1.   In a time of ballooning medical costs, especially for hospital care, the sensitivity of the issue involved in requiring a State sponsored insurance fund to reimburse the cost of out-of-state treatment is patent. *Muller–Faure* is accordingly a major precedent. The Court accepted a prior authorization system for hospital treatment in other States in ¶ 81, but then stated important procedural limits in ¶ 85, and required a case-by-case examination in ¶ 90, with a warning in ¶ 92 that excessively long waiting time before treatment would not be justifiable. Do you think the Court strikes a reasonable balance between State medical and budgetary planning concerns, on the one hand, and some patients' desire to obtain out-of-state hospital care, on the other?

2.   Note the Court's conclusion in ¶¶ 93–97 that the insurance fund cannot require insured persons to obtain a prior authorization before seeking medical treatment outside of a hospital in other States. Why should the Netherlands have to reimburse a patient who believes that medical or dental treatment outside of a hospital is superior in quality, or may be obtained more rapidly in other States? The Court reasserts its holding in *Kohll* that the Treaty right to receive services should enable patients to choose at their option to travel to other States to receive medical or dental services outside of a hospital and still be reimbursed for the cost. Do you agree with the Court's view that the aggregate cost of such treatment would not be very substantial?

For a careful review of *Muller–Faure* and other cases, see P. Van Nuffel, Patients' Free Movement Rights and Cross–Border Access to Health Care, 12 Maastricht J. Eur. L. 3 (2005).

3. The Court repeated its analysis summarized above in note 1 in Watts v. Bedford Primary Care Trust, Case C–372/04, [2006] ECR I–4325, before providing guidance to the UK High Court concerning Watt's claim for reimbursement of the hospital costs in France for hip surgery to relieve severe arthritis, after Watts was informed that she must wait three months for surgery in the UK. The Court indicated that the High Court should determine whether the waiting time was justified or not "in the light of the patient's particular condition and clinical needs" (¶ 79), and the "degree of pain" and the nature of the patient's disability (¶ 119). Note that the UK has a National Health Service which provides all medical care, including hospital treatment, free of charge, directly or through agents like Bedford.

4. The Court frequently cited its prior judgment in Geraert–Smits v. Stichting Ziekenfonds, Case C–157/99, [2001] ECR I–5473. In that case, one patient received an unusual therapy in Germany for Parkinson's disease (presently incurable) and another patient, in a coma following an accident, received experimental neuro-stimulation treatment in an Austrian clinic (where, fortunately, he came out of his coma). In each case, the Dutch fund refused reimbursement because the treatment was not considered to be "normal" in Dutch medical circles. Van Nuffel's article, cited above, informs us that the Dutch fund maintained its refusal to reimburse the treatment costs even after the *Geraet–Smits* judgment. Do you think that the Dutch fund ought to reimburse, or not, the cost of these unusual or experimental treatments?

5. In Stamatelaki v. NPDD OAEE, Case C–444/05, [2007] ECR I–3185, a Greek national sought reimbursement of the substantial cost of his treatment in a private London hospital. The Greek law accorded an insured patient free treatment in private hospitals in Greece, but not elsewhere. The Court cited *Muller–Faure* concerning a State's legitimate public health concern in maintaining adequate hospital services (¶¶ 30–32), but held that Greece's absolute ban on the reimbursement of private hospital charges elsewhere violated the principle of proportionality, because a prior authorization scheme would serve the Greek public interest goal less restrictively (¶¶ 35–37).

D. CASE LAW ON THE RIGHT OF ESTAB-LISHMENT FOR INDIVIDUALS AND COMMERCIAL FIRMS

1. RULES CONCERNING THE RIGHT OF ESTABLISHMENT

Shortly before *van Binsbergen* was decided, the Court of Justice held that ECT Article 43 had direct effect insofar as it prohibited discrimination on the basis of nationality. The judgment, *Reyners v. Belgium,* involved professional establishment and is therefore excerpted in the next chapter. Subsequent judgments have invalidated other forms of discriminatory treatment, even in the absence of directives harmonizing rules in particular commercial or financial sectors. Moreover, the Court doctrine that rules limiting the right to provide services must be based on an important public interest has been carried over to the examination of rules limiting the right of establishment. Presumably the caselaw described hereinafter would likewise apply in Court judgments concerning TFEU Article 49, which replicates ECT Article 43.

COMMISSION v. ITALY

(Pharmacists' monopoly in retail pharmacies)
Case C–531/06 [2009] ECR I–4103.

[A 1991 Italian law restricted the operation of pharmacies to natural persons qualified as pharmacists, or to legal entities whose shareholders or members are qualified pharmacists. When the Commission brought a Treaty infringement proceeding to challenge the law, the Court accepted that the monopoly for pharmacists violated the right of establishment for non-pharmacists from other States, and turned to the issue of justification.]

50   [F]irst, the national legislation applies without discrimination on grounds of nationality.

51   Second, the protection of public health is one of the overriding reasons in the general interest which can justify restrictions on * * * the freedom of establishment and the free movement of capital.

52   More specifically, restrictions on those freedoms of movement may be justified by the objective of ensuring that the provision of medicinal products to the public is reliable and of good quality [citing *Doc Morris*, supra page 506].

53   Third, it must be examined whether the rule excluding non-pharmacists is appropriate for securing such an objective.

54   [W]here there is uncertainty as to the existence or extent of risks to human health, a Member State should be able to take protective measures without having to wait until the reality of those risks becomes fully apparent. Furthermore, a Member State may take the measures that reduce, as far as possible, a public-health risk [citing *Rosengren*, supra page 458], including, more specifically, a risk to the reliability and quality of the provision of medicinal products to the public.

55   In this context, attention is to be drawn to the very particular nature of medicinal products, whose therapeutic effects distinguish them substantially from other goods.

56   Those therapeutic effects have the consequence that, if medicinal products are consumed unnecessarily or incorrectly, they may cause serious harm to health, without the patient being in a position to realise that when they are administered.

57   Overconsumption or incorrect use of medicinal products leads, moreover, to a waste of financial resources which is all the more damaging because the pharmaceutical sector generates considerable costs and must satisfy increasing needs, while the financial resources which may be made available for healthcare are not unlimited, whatever the mode of funding applied (see by analogy, with regard to hospital treatment, *Muller–Faure*, supra). There is a direct link between those financial resources and the profits of businesses operating in the pharmaceutical sector because in most Member States the prescription of medicinal products is borne financially by the health insurance bodies concerned.

58   In the light of those risks to public health and to the financial balance of social security systems, the Member States may make persons entrusted with the retail supply of medicinal products subject to strict requirements, including as regards the way in which the products are marketed and the pursuit of profit. In particular, the Member States may restrict the retail sale of medicinal products * * * to pharmacists alone, because of the safeguards which pharmacists must provide and the information which they must be in a position to furnish to consumers.

* * *

61   It is undeniable that an operator having the status of pharmacist pursues, like other persons, the objective of making a profit. However, as a pharmacist by profession, he is presumed to operate the pharmacy not with a purely economic objective, but also from a professional viewpoint. His private interest connected with the making of a profit is thus tempered by his training, by his professional experience and by the responsibility which he owes, given that any breach of the rules of law or professional conduct undermines not only the value of his investment but also his own professional existence.

* * *

84   [In contrast,] a Member State may take the view that there is a risk that legislative rules designed to ensure the professional independence of pharmacists would not be observed in practice [by non-pharmacist owners of pharmacies] given that the interest of a non-pharmacist in making a profit would not be tempered in a manner equivalent to that of self-employed pharmacists and * * * that pharmacists, when employees, [might find] it difficult to oppose instructions given by [a non-pharmacist owner].

87   Accordingly, it has not been established that another measure that restricts the freedoms guaranteed by Articles 43 EC and 56 EC less than the rule excluding non-pharmacists would make it possible to ensure just as effectively the level of reliability and quality in the provision of medicinal products to the public that results from the application of that rule.

NOTES AND QUESTIONS

1. Do you agree with the Court's conclusion that the Italian law is justified by the public health concern for the sale of medicinal products only by qualified pharmacists? Note that while some Member States have a parallel law, others do not. Should that cast doubt on the Court's conclusion? Italy claimed that it was the subject of selective enforcement by the Commission because the Commission was only suing Italy, but the Court held in ¶ 23 that the Commission had discretion in deciding whether and when to bring an ECT Article 226 infringement proceeding. See Chapter 11A.

2. In Commission v. Greece (Optician branch shops), Case C–140/03, [2005] ECR I–3177, the Commission challenged a Greek law which forbid opticians to operate more than one shop, following a complaint by a company from another State that had been prevented from establishing several shops in Greece. The Court held that the protection of public health did not justify limiting opticians to one shop, but could proportionately be achieved by "requiring the presence of qualified, salaried opticians or associates in each optician's shop, rules governing civil liability . . . and rules requiring professional indemnity insurance" (¶ 35). Do you agree?

3. Sodemare is a Luxembourg holding company whose Italian subsidiary owns residential homes for elderly persons in the region of Lombardy. A Lombardy regional social welfare law provides subsidies for health-care services for elderly infirm people in authorized residence facilities. Only non-profit enterprises can receive long-term contracts from the Region to carry out the services and hence receive the subsidies. Although Sodemare was authorized by the region to operate an old people's home, its request for a health-care contract and subsidy was denied because it is a profit-making company. When Sodemare sued to obtain a contract, the administrative court inquired whether this constituted unjustified discrimination under ECT Article 43. The Court held that the Lombard Region was justified in limiting its health service contracts for the elderly and its subsidies to non-profit entities. Would you agree? See Sodemare SA v. Regione Lombardia, Case C–70/95, [1997] ECR I–3395.

COMMISSION v. ITALY

(Housing loans)
Case 63/86, [1988] ECR 29.

[Italy permitted only its own nationals to obtain preferential rate state loans to purchase residential housing and to buy inexpensive housing built or renovated with state funds. When sued in a Treaty infringement proceeding, Italy contended that "there is no direct link between the pursuit of occupations and the right of access to social housing or a reduced-rate mortgage loan [for] housing." While Italy accepted that migrant workers from other States should have access to the housing pursuant to ECT Article 39, it maintained that a requirement of national treatment for the self-employed in respect of housing could only be based on legislation adopted to implement ECT Article 43, much as Regulation

1612/68 (described in Chapter 14A) implemented the right of free movement of workers in ECT Article 39.]

13 [Articles 43 and 49] are thus intended to secure the benefit of national treatment for a national of a Member State who wishes to pursue an activity as a self-employed person in another Member State and they prohibit all discrimination on grounds of nationality resulting from national or regional legislation and preventing the taking up or pursuit of such an activity.

14 As is apparent from the general programmes which were adopted by the Council on 18 December 1961 * * * and which * * * provide useful guidance with a view to the implementation of the provisions of the Treaty relating to the right of establishment and the freedom to provide services, the aforesaid prohibition is concerned not solely with the specific rules on the pursuit of occupational activities but also with the rules relating to the various general facilities which are of assistance in the pursuit of those activities. Among the examples mentioned in the two programs are the right to purchase, exploit and transfer real and personal property and the right to obtain loans and in particular to have access to the various forms of credit.

15 For a natural person the pursuit of an occupation does not presuppose solely the possibility of access to premises from which the occupation can be pursued, if necessary by borrowing the amount needed to purchase them, but also the possibility of obtaining housing. It follows that restrictions contained in the housing legislation applicable to the place where the occupation is pursued are liable to constitute an obstacle to that pursuit.

16 If complete equality of competition is to be assured, the national of a Member State who wishes to pursue an activity as a self-employed person in another Member State must therefore be able to obtain housing in conditions equivalent to those enjoyed by those of his competitors who are nationals of the latter State. Accordingly, any restriction placed not only on the right of access to housing but also on the various facilities granted to those nationals in order to alleviate the financial burden must be regarded as an obstacle to the pursuit of the occupation itself.

17 That being so, housing legislation, even where it concerns social housing, must be regarded as part of the legislation that is subject to the principle of national treatment * * *.

NOTES AND QUESTIONS

1. If Italy had discriminated against other Community nationals in granting state loans to buy or rent business premises, the violation of ECT Article 43 would be evident. See Steinhauser v. City of Biarritz, Case 197/84, [1985] ECR 1819 (requiring national treatment for a German artist seeking access to the rental of city-owned shops to sell craft goods). The link between

Article 43 and residential housing is not so apparent. Do you agree with Italy that protection against discrimination in residential housing required Community legislation and could not be achieved through a Court gloss on Article 43? Or do you agree with the Court that such a right flows naturally from Article 43's goal of achieving "complete equality of competition"?

2. In *Schumacker*, supra page 579, we learned that a State's personal income tax rules cannot discriminate against non-resident migrant workers. In Jundt v. Finanzamt Offenburg, Case C–281/06, [2007] ECR I–12231, the Court held that Germany must permit a German resident who taught a course at the University of Strassbourg to deduct his related expenses from his fee for the course, inasmuch as the German tax rules would have permitted him to deduct expenses if he had taught at a German university. In the reverse situation, the Court held in Gerritse v. Finanzamt Neukolln, Case C–234/01, [2003] ECR I–5933, that a Dutch resident who received a fee for performing once as a drummer in Berlin was entitled to deduct his related travel expenses from the German income tax on his fee.

2. ESTABLISHMENT RIGHTS OF CORPORATIONS AND SHAREHOLDERS

REGINA v. SECRETARY OF STATE FOR TRANSPORT EX PARTE FACTORTAME

(Factortame II)
Case C–221/89, [1991] ECR I–3905.

[Among its efforts to prevent Spanish fishing interests from taking a part of the UK catch quota under the Common Fisheries Policy, the UK in 1988 amended its regulations for the registration of fishing vessels. The amendments required that: 1) a British fishing vessel be British-owned and be managed and controlled from within the UK; 2) if a British fishing vessel is owned by a company, the company must be a) incorporated and have its principal place of business in the UK; b) have 75% of its shares "legally and beneficially" owned by UK citizens; and c) have 75% of its directors be UK citizens. The plaintiffs, Spanish nationals who together owned 95 UK-registered fishing vessels, sued to enjoin the operation of these amendments as a violation of ECT Articles 12, 43 and 48. The trial court asked the Court of Justice to rule on the compatibility of the UK legislation with Community law. The power of the trial court to restrain enforcement of the 1988 UK law was the subject of the leading supremacy judgment, *Factortame I*, discussed at page 250.]

20 [T]he concept of establishment within the meaning of art. [43] of the Treaty involves the actual pursuit of an economic activity through a fixed establishment in another member state for an indefinite period.

21 Consequently, the registration of a vessel does not necessarily involve establishment within the meaning of the Treaty, in particular where the vessel is not used to pursue an economic activity or where the application for registration is made by or on behalf of a person who is

not established, and has no intention of becoming established, in the state concerned.

22   However, where the vessel constitutes an instrument for pursuing an economic activity which involves a fixed establishment in the member state concerned, the registration of that vessel cannot be dissociated from the exercise of the freedom of establishment.

23   It follows that the conditions laid down for the registration of vessels must not form an obstacle to freedom of establishment within the meaning of art. [43] of the Treaty.

* * *

26   The UK, Belgium, Denmark and Greece consider that the Treaty does not preclude a nationality requirement of the type at issue * * *. [They contend that] what is involved is not discriminatory treatment on grounds of nationality but a condition for the grant of nationality, and the member states are free to determine to whom they will grant or refuse their nationality, in the case of natural persons and ships alike.

27   In that connection, it must be observed that the concept of the "nationality" of ships, which are not persons, is different from that of the "nationality" of natural persons.

* * *

29   [I]n exercising its powers for the purposes of defining the conditions for the grant of its "nationality" to a ship, each member state must comply with the prohibition of discrimination against nationals of member states on grounds of their nationality.

30   It follows from the foregoing that a condition of the type at issue in the main proceedings, which stipulates that where a vessel is owned or chartered by natural persons they must be of a particular nationality and where it is owned or chartered by a company the shareholders and directors must be of that nationality, is contrary to art. [43] of the Treaty.

31   Such a condition is also contrary to art. [294] of the Treaty, under which member states must accord nationals of the other member states the same treatment as their own nationals as regards participation in the capital of companies or firms within the meaning of art. [43].

32   As for the requirement for the owners, charterers, managers and operators of the vessel and, in the case of a company, the shareholders and directors to be resident and domiciled in the member state in which the vessel is to be registered, it must be held that such a requirement, which is not justified by the rights and obligations created by the grant of a national flag to a vessel, results in discrimination on grounds of nationality. The great majority of nationals of the member state in question are resident and domiciled in that state

and therefore meet that requirement automatically, whereas nationals of other member states would, in most cases, have to move their residence and domicile to that state in order to comply with the requirements of its legislation. It follows that such a requirement is contrary to art. [43].

* * *

34   [However,] a requirement for the registration of a vessel to the effect that it must be managed and its operations directed and controlled from within the member state in which it is to be registered essentially coincides with the actual concept of establishment within the meaning of art. [43] et seq. of the Treaty, which implies a fixed establishment. It follows that those articles, which enshrine the very concept of freedom of establishment, cannot be interpreted as precluding such a requirement.

35   Such a requirement, however, would not be compatible with those provisions if it had to be interpreted as precluding registration in the event that a secondary establishment or the centre for directing the operations of the vessel in the member state in which the vessel was to be registered acted on instructions from a decision-taking centre located in the member state of the principal establishment.

36   Consequently, the reply to the national court must be that it is not contrary to Community law for a member state to stipulate as a condition for the registration of a fishing vessel in its national register that the vessel in question must be managed and its operations directed and controlled from within that member state.

Notes and Questions

1. *Factortame II* is part of a series of cases which have enriched Community law in several respects. The judgment in *Factortame II* confirmed the accuracy of the trial court's surmise in *Factortame I,* that the 1988 Merchant Shipping Act amendments violated Community law and should accordingly be enjoined. The basic principle that Member States may not discriminate against companies owned or managed by Community nationals follows naturally from the terms of ECT Articles 43 and 294. The difficult issue was whether this principle should apply to companies owning vessels, since States traditionally have discretion to determine the standards for granting vessels their "nationality." Do you agree with the Court's resolution of this issue? Remember that under ECT Article 46 States may limit establishment rights on grounds of public policy or public security. Presumably a State can invoke these considerations to prevent a company owned or managed by non-nationals from engaging in defense contracting. Why couldn't the UK rely on public policy to uphold its law?

2. The Court's language in ¶¶ 34–36 is worth noting. The Court allowed the UK to require that a vessel be "managed and its operations directed and controlled from within that member state." For all sorts of business reasons,

corporations create "paper subsidiaries," which have few or no employees and limited assets, in other States. Does the Court's language suggest that a parent's use of a "paper subsidiary" might be considered as an abuse of the right of establishment? See the Court's judgment in *Cadbury–Schweppes,* infra page 716.

3. In Commission v. Belgium (Registration of aircraft), Case C–203/98 [1999] ECR I–4899, a Belgian law permitted "foreigners" to register airplanes in Belgium and to operate such airplanes from Belgian airfields only if they had been resident or established in Belgium for one year. The Commission challenged the law as a violation of ECT Article 43. Should Article 43 apply to aircraft registration just as it does to the registration of ships?

LEWIS v. BT INVESTMENT MANAGERS

447 U.S. 27, 100 S.Ct. 2009, 64 L.Ed.2d 702 (1980).

[When Bankers Trust, a New York corporation, established a subsidiary in Florida to provide portfolio investment services and advice on industry conditions, the Florida legislature promptly adopted a statute prohibiting an out-of-state bank holding company from providing investment advisory services through a subsidiary or branch. There was evidence that the law was prompted by the local banking community. When Bankers Trust's challenge reached the Supreme Court, Justice Blackman's opinion for a unanimous Court held that the statute violated the dormant Commerce Clause.]

Over the years, the Court has used a variety of formulations for the Commerce Clause limitation upon the States, but it consistently has distinguished between outright protectionism and more indirect burdens on the free flow of trade. The Court initially observed that "where simple economic protectionism is effected by state legislation, a virtually per se rule of invalidity has been erected"].

> We readily accept the submission that, both as a matter of history and as a matter of present commercial reality, banking and related financial activities are of profound local concern. As appellees freely concede, sound financial institutions and honest financial practices are essential to the health of any State's economy and to the well-being of its people. * * *

> Nonetheless, it does not follow that these same activities lack important interstate attributes. An impressive array of federal statutes regulating not only the provision of banking services but also the formation of banking organizations, the rendering of investment advice, and the conduct of national investment markets, is substantial evidence to the contrary. * * * This Court has observed that the same interstate attributes that establish Congress' power to regulate commerce also support constitutional limitations on the powers of the States.

* * *

[The Florida statute] prevents competition in local markets by out-of-state firms with the kinds of resources and business interests that make them likely to attempt *de novo* entry. Appellant virtually concedes this effect * * *, and the circumstances of enactment suggest that it was the legislature's principal objective.

* * *

We are convinced that the disparate treatment of out-of-state bank holding companies cannot be justified as an incidental burden necessitated by legitimate local concerns.

* * *

Appellant has demonstrated no basis for an inference that all out-of-state bank holding companies are likely to possess the evils of monopoly power, that they are more likely to do so than their homegrown counterparts, or that they are any more inclined to engage in sharp practices than bank holding companies that are locally based. Nor is there any reason to conclude that outright prohibition of entry, rather than some intermediate form of regulation, is the only effective method of protecting against the presumed evils * * *.

* * *

In almost any Commerce Clause case it would be possible for a State to argue that it has an interest in bolstering local ownership, or wealth, or control of business enterprise. Yet these arguments are at odds with the general principle that the Commerce Clause prohibits a State from using its regulatory power to protect its own citizens from outside competition.

Notes and Questions

1. Only occasionally do dormant Commerce Clause considerations arise in the context of establishment of a subsidiary or branch. *Bankers Trust* demonstrates that clear discrimination against the subsidiaries of out-of-state corporate parents is virtually a per se violation of the dormant Commerce Clause.

CENTROS v. ERHVERVS–OG SELSKABSSTYRELSEN
Case C–212/97, [1999] ECR I–1459.

[Denmark requires 200,000 Danish Kroner (ca. $24,000) to be paid in as capital when a private limited company is formed, while the UK does not require any paid-in capital for such a company. (The Community company law directives do not require any initial paid-in capital for private limited companies—see section D.) Bryde and her husband created Centros, a UK company without paid-in capital, with its registered office at a friend's home, with no intention of doing business in the UK. Bryde,

Centros' sole director, applied to the Danish Companies Board to register a Centros branch in Denmark, in order to conduct a wine trading business. The Board rejected the application, deeming the creation of a branch to be an evasion of Danish company capital requirements. On appeal, the Danish court asked the Court of Justice whether the Board's rejection of the application violated the Brydes' right of establishment.]

15   [T]he Board does not in any way deny that a joint stock or private limited company with its registered office in another Member State may carry on business in Denmark through a branch.* * * In particular, it has added that, if Centros had conducted any business in England and Wales, the Board would have agreed to register its branch in Denmark.

* * *

17   [A] situation in which a company formed in accordance with the law of a Member State in which it has its registered office desires to set up a branch in another Member State falls within the scope of Community law. In that regard, it is immaterial that the company was formed in the first Member State only for the purpose of establishing itself in the second, where its main, or indeed entire, business is to be conducted.

19   [The freedom of establishment] conferred by Article [43] of the Treaty on Community nationals, includes the right for them to take up and pursue activities as self-employed persons and to set up and manage undertakings under the same conditions as are laid down by the law of the Member State of establishment for its own nationals.

20   The immediate consequence of this is that those companies are entitled to carry on their business in another Member State through an agency, branch or subsidiary. The location of their registered office, central administration or principal place of business serves as the connecting factor with the legal system of a particular State in the same way as does nationality in the case of natural person.

* * *

23   According to the Danish authorities, however, Mr. and Mrs. Bryde cannot rely on those provisions, since the sole purpose of the company formation which they have in mind is to circumvent the application of the national law governing formation of private limited companies and therefore constitutes abuse of the freedom of establishment.* * *

24   It is true that according to the case-law of the Court a Member State is entitled to take measures designed to prevent certain of its nationals from attempting, under cover of the rights created by the Treaty, improperly to circumvent their national legislation or to prevent individuals from improperly or fraudulently taking advantage of provisions of Community law [citing *Van Binsbergen* and *Veronica*, supra pages 663 and 665].

25   However, although the national courts may, case by case, take account—on the basis of objective evidence—of abuse or fraudulent conduct on the part of the persons concerned in order, where appropriate, to deny them the benefit of the provisions of Community law on which they seek to rely, they must nevertheless assess such conduct in the light of the objectives pursued by those provisions.

* * *

29   [T]he fact that a company does not conduct any business in the Member State in which it has its registered office and pursues its activities only in the Member State where its branch is established is not sufficient to prove the existence of abuse or fraudulent conduct which would entitle the latter Member State to deny that company the benefit of the provisions of Community law relating to the right of establishment.

* * *

32   [T]he Board argues that the requirement that private limited companies provide for and pay up a minimum share capital [protects] all creditors, whether public or private, by anticipating the risk of fraudulent bankruptcy due to the insolvency of companies whose initial capitalisation was inadequate.

34   [A]ccording to the court's case-law, national measures liable to hinder or make less attractive the exercise of fundamental freedoms guaranteed by the Treaty must fulfil four conditions: they must be applied in a non-discriminatory manner; they must be justified by imperative requirements in the general interest; they must be suitable for securing the attainment of the objective which they pursue; and they must not go beyond what is necessary in order to attain it [citing *Gebhard, infra* page 742].

35   Those conditions are not fulfilled in the case in the main proceedings. First, the practice in question is not such as to attain the objective of protecting creditors which it purports to pursue since, if the company concerned had conducted business in the United Kingdom, its branch would have been registered in Denmark, even though Danish creditors might have been equally exposed to risk.

37   Second, * * * it is possible to adopt measures which are less restrictive, or which interfere less with fundamental freedoms, by, for example, making it possible in law for public creditors to obtain the necessary guarantees.

38   Lastly, the fact that a Member State may not refuse to register a branch of a company formed in accordance with the law of another Member State in which it has its registered office does not preclude that first State from adopting any appropriate measure for preventing or penalizing fraud, * * * if need be in cooperation with the Member State in which it was formed, * * * where it has been established that

they are in fact attempting, by means of the formation of the company, to evade their obligations towards private or public creditors * * *. In any event, combating fraud cannot justify a practice of refusing to register a branch of a company which has its registered office in another Member State.

NOTES AND QUESTIONS

1. That a company incorporated in one Member State need not be doing business in its home State in order to create a branch that does business in another State is not a surprising conclusion, because it is a literal application of the text of ECT Article 43. The more debatable issue is whether the shareholders may use this device to avoid the host State paid-in capital requirements. Because the modern American corporate law view is that paid-in capital does not really protect creditors (see the discussion of the Second Company directive in section D infra), to American lawyers the Court's conclusion appears easily justifiable. Continental European corporate lawyers, accustomed to the view that capital somehow does protect creditors, may react critically to the judgement. The Court essentially repeated its holdings in *Centros* in Kamer van Koophandel v. Inspire Art Ltd., Case C–167/01, [2003] ECR I–10155, upholding the right of a Dutch national to establish an art gallery in Amsterdam as the sole operation of his solely-owned UK limited liability company. Does *Centros* suggest the desirability of harmonization of private limited company laws? Or is it preferable to let prospective shareholders opt among different corporate law systems, as is the case in the US?

2. In Uberseering BV v. Nordic Construction Company, Case C–208/00, [2002] ECR I–9919, two German shareholders acquired all the shares of a Dutch limited company, Uberseering, and moved its head office to Germany. Subsequently, a German court concluded that Uberseering had no legal capacity to sue a contractor for defective performance of a contract, because under German company law principles the Dutch company had been automatically liquidated when it moved its head office to Germany. In its reply to a reference from the German Supreme Court, the Court of Justice held that Uberseering's legal capacity continued under Dutch law and that the German refusal to treat the German head office as a branch of the Dutch company with the capacity to sue violated the company's right of establishment (¶ ¶ 80–82).

3. A Financial Times article in 2006 indicated that over 30,000 entities had incorporated in the UK, with their sole operations as branches in Germany, presumably in order to avoid paying in the fairly substantial capital, 25000 Euros, required for a German limited liability company (GmbH). UK authorities are concerned that many are failing to file their annual financial statements and record changes in management with the Company registry, as required by the First Company directive (see section D infra). The authorities may, of course, fine entities which fail to fulfil these obligations, but that does not provide protection to third party creditors who would like to examine the filings. Does this development call into question the Court's judgment in *Centros*, or not?

NOTE ON CORPORATE INCOME TAX ISSUES

We noted in Chapter 14A that when the Single European Act introduced ECT Article 95 (now replicated in TFEU Article 114) to enable harmonization to achieve the internal market, Article 95(2) specifically excluded the field of direct taxation, which accordingly can only be harmonized under ECT Article 94. Because Article 94 requires the Council to vote unanimously, every State has a veto on direct tax harmonization proposals. Not surprisingly, none have been adopted. A current effort by the Barosso Commission to harmonize certain substantive features of national tax systems without affecting rates of tax has not met with success. Because TFEU Articles 114(2) and 115 replicate ECT Articles 95(2) and 94, this state of affairs is unlikely to change.

Again, not surprisingly in the absence of legislation, since the 1990s the Court of Justice has dealt with numerous cases of direct or indirect discrimination in the national income tax treatment of corporations exercising the right of establishment in one way or another. Because income tax rules constitute a highly technical field, we note here only some Court judgments that are relatively easy to understand.

In Laboratoires Fournier v. Direction des Verifications, Case C–39/04, [2005] ECR I–2057, the Court held that France must provide a French pharmaceutical company with a tax deduction for the fees charged by research laboratories in other Member States for research projects it commissioned. The French claim that its public interest in promoting French research and development justified granting a tax deduction only if such research was carried out in its territory was rejected. The Court noted that ECT Article 163(1) on the promotion of Community research and development included the goal of removing "fiscal obstacles" to interstate cooperative research.

The Court upheld the right of an entity to use at its option either branches or subsidiaries in its exercise of the right of establishment in CLT–UFA v. Finanzamt Koln, Case C–253/03, [2006] ECR I–1831. The Court held that Germany could not tax the profits of a German branch of a Luxembourg company at a higher flat rate than it would the profits distributed by a German subsidiary of the company. Also in Lankhorst–Hohorst v. Finanzamt Steinfurt, Case C–324/00, [2002] ECR I–11779, the Court held that Germany could not deny a German subsidiary a deduction for interest paid on a large loan from its Dutch parent, treating the interest as though it were a disguised dividend, when Germany would allow the interest as an expense if paid by the subsidiary to a German parent.

Undoubtedly the two best known cases in this section both concerned UK rules. In Marks & Spencer v. Halsey, Case C–446/03, [2005] ECR I–10837, a large UK department store operator claimed as a deduction against its UK income taxes the losses of its operating subsidiaries in Belgium, France and Germany during a four-year period prior to the cessation of business of the subsidiaries. The UK tax law would have permitted Marks & Spencer to take the losses if incurred by UK subsidiaries. Although the Court recognized that denial of a deduction for losses of a foreign subsidiary might be justified in some instances, notably in a case where the subsidiary could claim the losses in its home State in future years, this was not the case where the subsidiary is ceasing operations (¶ 55). The UK rule accordingly violated Mark & Spencer's right to establish subsidiaries in other States (¶ 56).

In Cadbury Schweppes v. Commissioners of Inland Revenue, Case C–196/04, [2006] ECR I–7995, the well-known confectionary company, Cadbury Schweppes, used two wholly-owned Irish subsidiaries to borrow money for re-lending to finance other group subsidiaries. Because the Irish subsidiaries were taxed at a 10% rate in Ireland, far lower than the UK income tax, the UK authorities claimed that Cadbury–Schweppes should be taxed in the UK on the subsidiaries' profits under a tax law that provided that controlled foreign corporations (over 50% owned by the parent) are to be taxed together with the parent.

In a reference proceeding, the Court held that the fact that a parent establishes subsidiaries in a State with low taxation does not in itself constitute an abuse of the right of establishment (¶ 37, citing *Centros*). The Court further held that the UK could not apply "a general presumption of tax evasion" (¶ 50), but could restrict the establishment of subsidiaries in other States "to prevent conduct involving the creation of wholly artificial arrangements which do not reflect economic reality" (¶ 55). The Court of Justice finally instructed the referring court to determine whether Cadbury–Schweppes' use of its Irish subsidiaries reflected "economic reality" by examining whether they had physical existence "in terms of premises, staff and equipment" (¶ 67). Note that six Member States provided views in support of the UK, reflecting a concern that the Court's judgment could result in a wide-spread use of subsidiaries in low tax Member States in order to reduce the tax burden on their parents in higher tax States. Media reports indicate that the UK fears the loss of hundreds of millions of pounds in tax revenue as a consequence of the Court's judgments.

E. COMPANY LAW HARMONIZATION

The program to harmonize company laws, pursuant to ECT Article 44(2)(g), began in 1968. It has proved an arduous task, not only because of the great diversity in company law systems, but also because Member States strongly espouse the policies behind their own national provisions, so that a consensus is difficult to attain. Nonetheless, the program has produced many important directives.

Two quite different forms of companies exist in most continental states: 1) the public stock corporation (for example, the Societe Anonyme, or SA, in France, and Aktiengesellschaft, or AG, in Germany), which has a complex shareholding and management structure and is frequently quoted on stock exchanges; and 2) the private limited liability company (for example, the Societe a Responsibilite Limitee, or SARL, in France, and the Gesellschaft mit beschrankter Haftung, or GmbH, in Germany), which has a simple shareholding and management structure, is favored by small business entities, and is rarely quoted. The UK also has two types of companies, the public company and the private company, which imitate to some degree the two continental forms, but are not so clearly differentiated. Community harmonization efforts have concentrated on the public stock corporation form. On a comparative note, the US has traditionally used only a stock corporation form, sometimes quoted on stock exchanges, but in the last decade a relatively new Limited Liability Company form has become popular.

1. INITIAL DIRECTIVES

The three initial directives deal with aspects of company structure. The First Directive 68/151, O.J. L 85/1 (Mar. 14, 1968), Document 20 in the Selected Documents, covers both the public stock corporation and private limited liability company forms. Its principal effect is to require States to maintain a register, open to the public, which keeps of record a file for each company. The file at the register must include the instrument of constitution (articles of incorporation and by-laws), a list of the managers and members of the board of directors, a description of the capital, and the annual balance sheet and profit and loss statement. Directive 2003/58, O.J. L 221/13 (Sept. 4, 2003), enabled the filing of required documents by electronic means, commencing in 2005. In contrast, US state law usually requires only the articles of incorporation to be filed with a state office. A few states require the annual financial statements to be provided to all shareholders, but not to the public.

The Second Directive 77/91, O.J. L 26/1 (Jan. 31, 1977), which applies only to public stock corporations, requires the instrument of incorporation to describe the corporate purpose, the nature of share class rights and obligations, the composition and powers of management bodies, and the amount of capital. The directive requires a minimum of 25,000 Euros in capital, and sets out detailed rules on capital, capital increases and reductions, and procedures related to this subject. The directive also forbids companies to acquire their own shares, except on limited conditions (chiefly to facilitate employee stock option plans), and a 1992 amendment forbids a subsidiary from voting any shares it owns in its parent. Finally, the directive requires that all shareholders have preemptive rights, i.e., rights to subscribe to any capital increase in proportion to their existing shareholdings, unless the shareholders meeting withdraws the right when it authorizes the capital increase.

Ironically, shortly after this directive's adoption, article 6.21 of the US Model Business Corporation Act (MBCA) was amended to abolish the concept of capital as outmoded, serving no purpose, and potentially misleading to creditors. The MBCA reflects in this regard the views of most US corporate finance experts. Most US states have now abolished capital requirements, although Delaware has not. Moreover, most US state laws no longer require preemptive rights, but make them optional. See MBCA, article 6.30. In practice, corporations rarely opt to have preemptive rights, because they are perceived as an unnecessary complication and expense in issuing shares.

The Third Directive 78/855, O.J. L 295/36 (Oct. 20, 1978), creates a modern procedure for carrying out mergers, both between unrelated companies and between parents and subsidiaries. The Third Directive applies only to public stock corporations. Mergers may take place either through the transfer of all assets and liabilities from one company to another surviving entity (the acquisition mode), or through the formation of a new company to which two or more companies transfer all of their assets and liabilities. The directive sets out detailed procedures for the execution of mergers and for the protection of shareholders and bondholders. This directive is undoubtedly one of the most beneficial of all company law directives, because many States had totally outmoded rules on mergers prior to implementing the directive. The Third Directive presents more modern and better structured rules for mergers than those prevailing in the US. Although the MBCA has modern merger provisions, articles 11.01–.04, Delaware and many other US states have older and complicated merger rules.

Other important directives deal with accounting. The Fourth Directive 78/660, O.J. L 222/11 (Aug. 14, 1978), as amended, O.J. L 162/65 (June 26, 1999), set standards for annual financial statements and reports, while the Seventh Directive 83/349, O.J. L 193/1 (July 18, 1983) deals with those for consolidated accounts for groups of companies. The Fourth Directive on Accounting covers both public and private companies, whether quoted or not, so long as they attain a minimum level of assets, turnover and employees. The directive fixes in considerable detail the nature and layout of the annual balance sheet and profit and loss statement, and requires that both be audited. (Unfortunately, the directive does not cover the financial statement on cash flow, which in the US is considered to be of equal importance.) A crucial provision is article 2, which requires the financial reports to present a "true and fair view." Moreover, article 46 obliges companies to produce an annual report which presents a "fair review of the business, recent important events and likely future developments."

Regulation 1606/2002, O.J. L 243/1 (Sept. 11, 2002), on international accounting standards, supplemented by specific directives amending the accounting directives, essentially requires publicly quoted companies to use these standards as set by the International Accounting Standards Board, sited in London, subject to their acceptance by the Commission.

An essential accessory is Directive 84/253, O.J. L 126/20 (May 12, 1984), setting minimum standards for the training and certification of auditors. The accounting and auditors directives have radically improved the quality of accounting standards and auditors reports in many States. The directives have thus greatly aided business operations. For example, the ability to rely on the quality of financial statements for companies throughout the Community is indispensable to achieving securities law harmonization. In 2001 the Commission recommended that all company auditors be subject to regular quality reviews, either by peer reviews or periodic monitoring, to ensure more reliable audits, especially of quoted companies and financial institutions. Recommendation 2001/256, O.J. L 91/91 (Mar. 31, 2001).

In contrast, US state laws generally contain no direct requirements on the nature of financial statements, although case law on the fiduciary duty of management to shareholders requires that financial reports be reliable and not misleading. Federal securities regulations set precise requirements for the financial statements, auditors' reports and management operating reports of companies that issue shares to the public. It can fairly be said that the federal securities requirements are more detailed and more effectively policed in the US than are the accounting rules set by the Community directives, but the Community's accounting rules provide better standards for non-quoted companies than is the case in the U.S.

Notes and Questions

1. Although proposals for harmonization of state corporate laws through federal legislation have been advanced since the 1970s, the US continues to allow the states to set their own rules. Moreover, although the Model Business Corporation Act has influenced the corporate law in many states, Delaware, New York, California and other states follow their own policies. What factors have influenced the US and the EU to take different approaches in this sector?

2. Harmonization is most beneficial when a modern, carefully structured set of rules is substituted for older disparate regulation in the Member States. The merger directive is a good example. However, harmonization runs the risk of freezing in place rules which might otherwise evolve into better forms. For example, was it sensible to set complex and inflexible rules concerning capital in the Second Directive? The abolition of the concept of capital in article 6.21 of the MBCA provides a striking contrast. Does either the MBCA or the Second Directive represent an erroneous approach? Or do business differences between the EU and the US justify their opposite approaches?

In recent years, the Court has had several occasions to interpret provisions in the First, Second, and Fourth Directives.

COMMISSION v. GERMANY

(First Company Directive Penalties)
Case C–191/95, [1998] ECR I–5449.

[Contending that 93% of German companies failed to file their annual financial statements with the Register, the Commission brought a Treaty infringement proceeding against Germany for its failure to impose "appropriate penalties" under the First Company Directive. The Commission argued specifically that "appropriate penalties" were not possible when the court responsible for the Register had no power on its own motion to impose penalties for the company's non-compliance with the disclosure obligation.]

21   On 25 August 1993 the German Government declared itself ready to reinforce the penalties in cases where documents concerning annual accounts had not been disclosed * * * [and proposed] a draft concerning the introduction of reinforced penalties to enter into force, for all companies limited by shares, with progressive effect from 1 January 1999. In that connection, the German Government pointed out that if such provisions were introduced with immediate effect, the [German states], which had competence in such matters, would be unable to ensure immediate compliance, in view of the large number of proceedings that would have to be brought and the sizeable number of civil servants in the former [German states] who had been assigned to the reconstruction of the new [German states] following German reunification.

22   On 3 March 1994, the Commissioner responsible replied that penalties envisaged must be applicable immediately and without distinction to all companies of the types concerned which were not complying with their obligation of disclosure.

* * *

[After the Commission rejected the German proposal, Germany took no action on it, but maintained that its penalty system was not in violation of the directive. The Court summarily held otherwise.]

68   [I]t must be pointed out that the lack of appropriate penalties cannot be justified by the fact that, because of the large numbers involved, application of such penalties to all companies that do not publish their accounts would create considerable difficulties for the German administrative authorities which would be disproportionate to the aim pursued by the Community legislature. The Court has consistently held that a Member State may not plead internal circumstances in order to justify a failure to comply with obligations and time-limits resulting from rules of Community law.

DAIHATSU HANDLER v. DAIHATSU DEUTSCHLAND
Case C–97/96, [1997] ECR I–6843.

[Article 6 of the First Company Directive requires Member States to impose "appropriate penalties" for a company's failure to file its annual financial statements on the public Register. A German law provides for periodic penalties, but only shareholders, creditors and the works council (which represents the employees) may request a court to impose such penalties. The Daihatsu retail dealer association applied for the imposition of penalties to the court where Daihatsu Deutschland was entered on the Register, because the company had not filed its annual financial statements on the Register for several years. The trial court essentially asked the Court of Justice whether the German law had properly implemented the directive.]

17 [T]he German Government maintains that the Federal Republic of Germany has correctly transposed Article 6 of the First Directive. In accordance with Article [44(2)(g)] of the EC Treaty, the coordination of national systems of company law is designed to safeguard the interests of members 'and others'. The latter do not comprise all natural and legal persons but only those who have a legal relationship with the company. * * * German academic legal writing [considers] that the term 'others' * * * covers only creditors of the company.

[The Court then presented its conclusion.]

11 Article [44(2)(g)] of the Treaty refers to the need to protect the interests of others, generally, without distinguishing or excluding any categories falling within the ambit of that term.

20 Consequently, the term 'others' * * * cannot be limited merely to creditors of the company.

21 Moreover, the objective of abolishing restrictions on freedom of establishment [contained in Article 44(1)] cannot be circumscribed by the provisions of Article [44(2)which] merely sets out a non-exhaustive list of measures to be taken in order to attain that objective, as is borne out by the use in that provision of the words 'in particular'.

22 As regards Article 6 of the First Directive, the fourth recital in the preamble shows that disclosure of annual accounts is primarily designed to provide information for third parties who do not know or cannot obtain sufficient knowledge of the company's accounting and financial situation. Article 3 of the First Directive, which provides for the maintenance of a public register in which all documents and particulars to be disclosed must be entered, and pursuant to which copies of the annual accounts must be obtainable by any person upon application, confirms the concern to enable any interested persons to inform themselves of these matters. That concern also finds expression in the recitals in the preamble to the Fourth Directive, which refer to the need to establish in the Community minimum equivalent legal requirements as regards the extent of the financial information that should be made available to the public by companies that are in competition with one another.

23 In view of the foregoing considerations, the answer * * * must be that Article 6 of the First Directive is to be interpreted as precluding the legislation of a Member State from restricting to members or creditors of the company,* * *or the company's works council the right to apply for imposition of the penalty provided for by the law of that Member State in the event of failure by a company to fulfil the obligations

regarding disclosure of annual accounts laid down by the First Directive.

NOTES AND QUESTIONS

1. The First Company Directive's provision that Member States must impose "appropriate penalties" to enforce its obligations is paralleled by similar provisions in banking, securities, environmental protection and other harmonization directives. After the *Marshall II* judgment, supra page 359, held that State action to secure compliance with Community law must have a "real deterrent effect," the Commission has warned several States that their penalties to enforce some directives (e.g., on money laundering) were inadequate. The German First Company Directive penalties case is therefore an important precedent. Incidentally, the judgement is also of importance because of the Court's analysis of the "principle of collegiality" which requires the entire Commission to take the policy decision to send the reasoned opinion and to bring Germany before the Court, discussed supra, page 49.

2. Certainly, the reference in ECT Article 44(2) (g) to safeguards to protect "others" besides "members" is inherently ambiguous. In the context of the First Company Directive, "members" obviously means the shareholders, but who are the "others"? Germany's restriction of "others" to employees and creditors, who have a legal interest in knowing the company's financial health, has a certain plausibility. Do you agree with the Court's view in ¶ 22 of *Daihatsu*, which would permit anyone with any lawful interest (in *Daihatsu*, the company's retailers who were engaged in a dispute with the company) to force the filing of the annual financial statements?

Note the sharp contrast with US state corporate law—only California, New York, and a minority of states require that annual financial statements be provided automatically to shareholders. The laws on shareholder inspection rights require shareholders to have a proper purpose in order to obtain financial statements, which makes such statements often difficult to obtain, and generally unavailable to creditors and competitors. (Publicly quoted companies must, of course, disclose their annual financial statements in accordance with federal securities law.)

3. In Springer v. Zeitungsverlag Niederrhein, Cases C–435/02 & C–103/03, [2004] ECR I–8663, the Court went beyond *Daihatsu*. The Court held that even a competitor has the right to apply to the court register to compel a limited partnership to publish its annual financial statements. The Court reached this conclusion despite the fact that the entity concerned was in the press and publishing business, although the Court noted that "detailed information as to certain sensitive matters" need not be disclosed (¶ 55). Note that in Germany, as in many other States, the First and Fourth Directives apply to limited partnerships.

4. The Fourth Directive's guiding principle that annual financial statements must present a "true and fair view" was interpreted for the first time in Tomberger v. Gebruder von der Wettern, Case C–234/94, [1996] ECR I–3133, noted by W. Schon, 34 Common Mkt. L. Rev. 681 (1997), where a holding company's annual balance sheet was considered to properly include a

subsidiary's profit for the same financial year, provided the subsidiary had declared a dividend of the profit before the parent's results were audited and approved.

When an Italian trial court that was prosecuting Silvio Berlusconi, the Prime Minister of Italy, for preparing inaccurate financial statements referred questions concerning the First and Fourth Directives, the Court's judgment naturally attracted media attention.

CRIMINAL PROCEEDINGS AGAINST BERLUSCONI
Case C–387/02, [2005] ECR I–3565.

[Berlusconi, then chairman of the board of Fininvest, was accused of preparing false documents for Fininvest intended to increase reserves to be used for allegedly unlawful transactions in 1986–89. Before the referring magistrate concluded the proceedings, the Italian government amended the law to eliminate criminal penalties for false statements that do not misrepresent pre-tax profits by more than 5% or assets by more than 1%. The referring court inquired whether Article 6 of the First Directive which required States to impose penalties for failure to file financial statements implicitly covered filing false statements, and whether the Fourth Directive's Article 51, which requires sanctions for preparing false financial statements, precluded the Italian legislation.]

54   [P]enalties for offences resulting from false accounting, such as the penalties provided for in the new Articles 2621 and 2622 of the Italian Civil Code, are designed to punish serious infringements of the fundamental principle, compliance with which constitutes the core objective of the Fourth Companies Directive, which follows from the fourth recital in the preamble and from Article 2(3) and (5) of that directive, that annual accounts of companies coming within the scope of that directive must give a true and fair view of the company's assets and liabilities, financial position and profit or loss.

* * *

56   Concerning the system of penalties provided for under Article 6 of the First Companies Directive, the wording of that provision in itself indicates that that system is to be understood as covering not only the case of the absence of any disclosure of annual accounts but also the case of the disclosure of annual accounts which have not been drawn up in accordance with the rules prescribed by the Fourth Companies Directive in regard to the content of such accounts.

57   Article 6 of the First Companies Directive is not limited to imposing an obligation on Member States to provide for appropriate penalties in the case of failure to disclose the balance sheet and the profit and loss account, setting down as it does a similar obligation in respect of a failure to disclose those documents in the manner required by Article 2(1)(f) of the First Companies Directive.* * *.

58 It follows from the purpose of the Fourth Companies Directive, * * * in the absence in that directive of general rules on penalties, that, with the exception of the cases covered by the specific exemption contained in Article 51(3) of the Fourth Companies Directive, the Community legislature did intend to extend the system of penalties referred to in Article 6 of the First Companies Directive to cover infringements of the obligations contained in the Fourth Companies Directive and, in particular, the failure to publish annual accounts which, in respect of their content, satisfy the rules laid down in that regard.

* * *

61 An interpretation of Article 6 of the First Companies Directive to the effect that it also covers the failure to publish annual accounts drawn up in accordance with the rules laid down in regard to the content thereof is, moreover, confirmed by the context and objectives of the directives in question.

62 As the Advocate General has stressed * * * it is necessary in this regard to have particular consideration for the fundamental role played by publication of the annual accounts of companies having share capital and a fortiori of the annual accounts drawn up in accordance with the harmonised rules relating to their content, with a view to protecting the interests of third parties, an objective which is stressed in clear terms in the preambles to both the First and the Fourth Companies Directives.

63 It follows that the requirement that penalties, [for false accounting] be appropriate is laid down in Article 6 of the First Companies Directive.

64 [Moreover,] in order to clarify the scope of the requirement that the penalties set out in Article 6 of the First Companies Directive be appropriate, account may usefully be taken of the Court's established case-law on Article 5 of the Treaty, which sets out a similar requirement.

65 According to that case-law, while the choice of penalties remains within their discretion, Member States must ensure in particular that infringements of Community law are penalised under conditions, both procedural and substantive, which are analogous to those applicable to infringements of national law of a similar nature and importance and which, in any event, make the penalty effective, proportionate and dissuasive.

[However, the Court finally concluded that the Italian law eliminating criminal penalties had to be respected, because the Court respects fundamental rights, and "the retroactive application of the more lenient penalty forms part of the constitutional traditions of the Member States" (¶ 68).]

2. RECENT COMMUNITY COMPANY LAW INITIATIVES

In the last decade a new wave of legislation, Commission recommendations and studies have considerably advanced modern corporate law and especially corporate governance in the Community. However, as these are all complex and often highly technical, we will present only some highlights here.

The new wave began with efforts to adopt a directive regulating tender offers as a mechanism for corporate takeovers. The Commission's initial 1989 proposal gradually evolved through its review in the Council and Parliament, but ultimately was blocked when Parliament's efforts to adopt a conciliation committee compromise failed on a tie vote in July 2001. The Commission then turned to a committee of legal experts whose initial Report of the High Level Group of Company Law Experts on Nov. 4, 2002 made proposals for further legislative action in the field. A new Commission proposal culminated in Directive 2004/25 on takeover bids, O.J. L 142/12 (Apr. 30, 2004), which set out a procedure for tender offers, compulsory information in a tender bid for shares, the time frame, and protection for minority shareholders. However, a crucial compromise enables Member States to opt out of key directive provisions which essentially forbid a target board to use various devices to frustrate an unwanted bid. As many States have made use of the opt-out, the impact of the directive in facilitating tender offers and takeovers may prove to be rather limited in scope.

Meanwhile in May 2003 the Prodi Commission issued a White Paper on Modernizing Company Law and Enhancing Corporate Governance, COM (2003) 284, which announced its intention to concentrate on promoting voluntary national corporate governance codes (modeled largely on the Cadbury and subsequent codes in the UK). The Commission did indicate that it would propose several directives to enhance shareholder rights and corporate governance. The Commission adopted in October 2004 two Recommendations, one on achieving greater transparency and shareholder involvement in setting the remuneration of directors, and the second on the role of crucial board Audit, Compensation and Nomination committees and the standards for determining when directors can be considered to be independent for the purpose of serving those committees. The recommendations provide an interesting contrast to the compulsory rules set in the 2002 Sarbanes–Oxley Act.

Four important directives have recently been adopted. Directive 2005/56 on cross-border mergers, O.J. L 310/1 (Nov. 25, 2005), adopted after many years of legislative review, establishes a procedure for mergers of companies in two or more Member States. Directive 2006/43, O.J. L 157/87 (June 9, 2006), amends the 1984 directive on auditors to set higher standards for tests to determine an auditor's qualifications and to require three years of training, as well as to require an auditor's independence and objectivity. Directive 2006/46, O.J. L 224/1 (Aug. 16, 2006) obligates the managing and supervisory boards of corporations that must comply with the Fourth and Seventh company directives on accounting to have a collective duty to ensure that their financial statements are drawn up in accord with the rules, and further require the statements to include a corporate governance section indicating the corporate governance code applicable to the company. Finally, Directive 2007/36 on shareholder's voting rights, O.J. L 184/17 (July 14, 2007), enables shareholders of listed companies to vote by electronic means, facilitates their participation by proxy in meetings, and enables them to pose certain types of relevant questions at meetings.

We close by noting the adoption of Regulation 2157/2001 on the Statute for a European Company, O.J. L 249/1 (Nov. 10, 2001), a long detailed text that essentially replicates a national public company statute. The European Company, or SE, may have either a single or a two-tiered board structure and must have a minimum capital of 120,000 Euros. Intended largely to serve as a holding company for operating subsidiaries in several States, or as a means of achieving a trans-border merger, the SE is unlikely to achieve wide use. The issue of employee participation in the board was resolved by a compromise supplementary Directive 2001/86, O.J. L 294/22 (Nov. 10, 2001), which sets out different options, one of which must be selected after negotiation between management and employee representatives.

Further Reading

C. Barnard, The Substantive Law of the EU: the Four Freedoms (2d Oxford U.P. 2007)

P. Kapteyn et. al., eds., The Law of the European Union and the European Communities (4th ed. 2008)

J. Snell, Goods and Services in EU Law (Oxford U.P. 2002)

R. White, Workers, Establishment and Services in the European Union (Oxford U.P. 2004)

CHAPTER 18

RIGHTS OF PRACTICE FOR LAWYERS AND OTHER PROFESSIONALS

■ ■ ■

Achieving for professionals a right of establishment and freedom to provide transborder services represents a significant step toward attaining an integrated internal market. The operations of multinational enterprises are greatly facilitated by multinational professional firms offering accounting, legal, architectural, engineering, public relations and other services. In particular, the need for expert legal assistance provided on a Union-wide basis has steadily grown as the wave of harmonized Union legislation advances in such complex fields as banking, insurance, securities, intellectual property, telecommunications, public procurement, environmental protection and employee rights.

Although this chapter provides an overview of the rights of professionals generally, it concentrates on the right of lawyers to practice on a Union-wide basis. Several important Court judgments have dealt with lawyers' rights, providing a useful focus for our analysis. Building upon the Court's doctrines, two directives have substantially liberalized the rights of lawyers to practice throughout the Union, both in providing trans-border services and through a permanent establishment. We will contrast this liberal regime with the more restrictive state practice rules in the US. A final section of the chapter will describe the harmonized rules enabling Union-wide practice by doctors, dentists, engineers, accountants, pharmacists and other professionals.

A. TREATY PROVISIONS AND LEGISLATIVE MEASURES

1. INITIAL DEVELOPMENTS

Access to virtually all professions in the Member States requires a license or authorization, which is usually only granted upon the presentation of educational and/or professional training credentials. At the time the Community was created, persons seeking to obtain a professional license in a host Member State encountered great difficulty if they had been educated or professionally trained in another State. The initial 1957 European Economic Community Treaty contained an EECT Article 57, which sought to promote professional mobility by authorizing the mutual recognition of diplomas, which the Council could achieve by a qualified majority vote, and the harmonization of national rules governing professional activities, but the Council was generally required to act unanimously to do this.

Little progress was made until 1974. Commission proposals for directives harmonizing rules regulating specific professions under EECT Article 57 were blocked because the Council could not reach unanimous agreement on them. It was also generally believed that professionals from one Member State could not claim establishment rights in other States in the absence of a harmonization directive. The situation appeared quite bleak. Fortunately the Court of Justice ended this impasse.

REYNERS v. BELGIUM

Case 2/74, [1974] ECR 631.

[Reyners, a Dutch national, raised and educated in Belgium, had successfully obtained a Belgian law diploma and the other credentials necessary to acquire the status of an *avocat*. Because a Belgian law required Belgian citizenship as a condition for the status of *avocat,* his application was denied. On appeal, the Belgian Supreme Administrative Court asked the Court of Justice for a ruling on whether ECT Article 43 on the right of establishment had direct effect, and whether Belgium could restrict the profession of *avocats* to its nationals on the ground that these lawyers exercised "official authority" under ECT Article 45's exception to Article 43.]

21 [In] the Chapter on the right of establishment the "general programme" and the directives provided for by the Treaty are intended to accomplish two functions, the first being to eliminate obstacles in the way of attaining freedom of establishment during the transitional period, the second being to introduce into the law of Member States a set of provisions intended to facilitate the effective exercise of this freedom for the purpose of assisting economic and social interpenetration within the Community in the sphere of activities as self-employed persons.

* * *

23 The effect of the provisions of Article [43] must be decided within the framework of this system.

24 The rule on equal treatment with nationals is one of the fundamental legal provisions of the Community.

25 As a reference to a set of legislative provisions effectively applied by the country of establishment to its own nationals, this rule is, by its

essence, capable of being directly invoked by nationals of all the other Member States.

26   In laying down that freedom of establishment shall be attained at the end of the transitional period, [i.e., by Dec. 31, 1969], Article [43] thus imposes an obligation to attain a precise result, the fulfilment of which had to be made easier by, but not made dependent on, the implementation of a programme of progressive measures.

27   The fact that this progression has not been adhered to leaves the obligation itself intact* * *[after Dec. 31, 1969].

* * *

29   It is not possible to invoke against [the direct effect of Article 43] the fact that the Council has failed to issue the directives provided for by Articles [44] and [47] * * *.

30   After the expiry of the transitional period the directives provided for by the Chapter on the right of establishment have become superfluous with regard to implementing the rule on nationality, since this is henceforth sanctioned by the Treaty itself with direct effect.

31   These directives have however not lost all interest since they [may] make easier the effective exercise of the right of freedom of establishment.

[The Court then turned to the question concerning any exercise of "official authority" by lawyers.]

35   The Luxembourg Government and the [Belgian *avocat* association] consider that the whole profession of *avocat* is exonerated from the rules in the Treaty on the right of establishment by the fact that it is connected organically with the functioning of the public service of the administration of justice.

36   This situation (it is argued) results both from the legal organization of the Bar, involving a set of strict conditions for admission and discipline, and from the functions performed by the *avocat* in the context of judicial procedure where his participation is largely obligatory.

37   These activities, which make the advocate an indispensable auxiliary of the administration of justice, form a coherent whole, the parts of which cannot be separated.

38   The plaintiff in the main action, for his part, contends that at most only certain activities of the profession of *avocat* are connected with the exercise of official authority and that they alone therefore come within the exception created by Article [45] to the principle of free establishment.

* * *

43   Having regard to the fundamental character of freedom of establishment and the rule on equal treatment with nationals in the system of the Treaty, the exceptions allowed by the first paragraph of Article

[45] cannot be given a scope which would exceed the objective for which this exemption clause was inserted.

* * *

45 This need is fully satisfied when the exclusion of nationals is limited to those activities which, taken on their own, constitute a direct and specific connexion with the exercise of official authority.

* * *

48 In the absence of any directive issued under Article [47] for the purpose of harmonizing the national provisions relating * * * to professions such as that of *avocat,* the practice of such professions remains governed by the law of the various Member States.

* * *

50 This consideration must however take into account the Community character of the limits imposed by Article [45] on the exceptions permitted to the principle of freedom of establishment in order to avoid the effectiveness of the Treaty being defeated by unilateral provisions of Member States.

* * *

52 The most typical activities of the profession of *avocat,* in particular, such as consultation and legal assistance and also representation and the defence of parties in court, even when the intervention or assistance of the *avocat* is compulsory or is a legal monopoly, cannot be considered as connected with the exercise of official authority.

53 The exercise of these activities leaves the discretion of judicial authority and the free exercise of judicial power intact.

54 [Therefore,] the exception to freedom of establishment provided for by the first paragraph of Article [45] must be restricted to those of the activities referred to in Article [43] which in themselves involve a direct and specific connexion with the exercise of official authority.

NOTES AND QUESTIONS

1. The Court's holding that ECT Article 43's prohibition of discrimination based on nationality should have direct effect obviously has consequences for all professionals, not just lawyers. The Court's judgment came a few months before *van Binsbergen,* excerpted in the prior chapter, whose analysis closely follows *Reyners. Reyners* was decided only a few months after Application of Griffiths, 413 U.S. 717, 93 S.Ct. 2851, 37 L.Ed.2d 910 (1973), the US Supreme Court opinion which held that Connecticut could not make US citizenship a prerequisite for admission to the bar. Some observers have speculated that *Griffiths* influenced *Reyners.*

2. Although in retrospect the Court of Justice's conclusion in *Reyners* that lawyers do not exercise "official authority" seems fairly evident, it was

by no means an obvious result at the time. Incidentally, Advocate General Mayras, who urged that result, considered that judges, prosecutors, and lawyers employed by the state could be described as exercising "official authority." Would you agree? In Application of Griffiths, the US Supreme Court also rejected an argument that lawyers must be citizens because they serve as "officers of the court." Justice Powell's majority opinion held that "a lawyer is engaged in a private profession," and does not have a role similar to that of a judge, marshall or court clerk. Chief Justice Burger's dissent argued that the "concept of a lawyer as an officer of the court" is a traditional feature of the common law.

3.   In most continental States, a separate legal profession, the notaries, have a legal monopoly on the handling of estates, the transfer of titles to real estate, and some fundamental corporate formalities, all quite profitable types of legal affairs. Traditionally States have required notaries to have their nationality. Recently the Commission has challenged the nationality requirement, which the States justify by claiming that notaries exercise "official authority" under ECT Article 45. Pressure from the Commission induced five States to abandon the nationality requirement. In 2006, the Commission brought ECT Article 226 proceedings against seven other States that maintained the nationality requirement. The Court judgment in any of these proceedings is bound to attract considerable attention.

B.   LAWYERS' RIGHT TO PROVIDE SERVICES

An immediate consequence of the Court's landmark judgment in *Reyners* was the Council's willingness to adopt directives harmonizing the rules for the education and licensing of professionals, beginning with the medical profession (see section D infra). With regard to lawyers, the Council adopted Directive 77/249, O.J. L 78/17 (March 26, 1977), commonly called the Lawyers' Services Directive, which facilitated the effective exercise by lawyers of the freedom to provide trans-border services. The text is in Document 21 in the Selected Documents and should be read at this point. Although it does not resolve all the issues, the directive provides a framework permitting Member State lawyers to provide occasional cross-border services in other Community States.

NOTES AND QUESTIONS

1.   The list of national professions of lawyers in article 1(2) of the Lawyers' Services Directive did not include a number of organized legal professions, notably notaries and legal advisors (e.g., the *conseil juridique* in France and Belgium, and the *Rechtsbeistand* in Germany), who handle commercial and administrative law affairs. Is the omission of these types of legal professionals justified? Note that in *van Binsbergen,* excerpted in the previous chapter, the professional granted a right to provide cross-border services was a "legal representative," not a Dutch *advocaat.*

2.   Observe the limitations that article 5 places on cross-border practice in "legal proceedings" (not defined, but presumably meaning civil and criminal litigation). What might they be intended to achieve? Are they justified?

3.   Look at the method for determining applicable rules of professional conduct in article 4. Why is a distinction made between the services in 4(2) and 4(4)? Do you think that in the event of conflict between host State and home State rules, one should always prevail? If so, which one in article 4(2)? In article 4(4)?

COMMISSION v. GERMANY

(Lawyers' services)
Case 427/85, [1988] ECR 1123.

[Germany required a foreign lawyer providing services in litigation or in certain administrative proceedings to collaborate with a German lawyer (*Rechtsanwalt*), with the German lawyer assuming the primary role of "authorized representative or defending counsel." Moreover, the local German lawyer had to be present at all times during the court or administrative proceedings. The Commission brought a Treaty infringement action against Germany, which maintained that its approach was justified by article 5 of the 1977 directive, which gives Member States the option of requiring a foreign lawyer to work "in conjunction with" a host State lawyer.]

[12]   * * * [T]he freedom to provide services is one of the fundamental principles of the Treaty and may be restricted only by rules which are justified by the general good and are imposed on all persons pursuing activities in the host Member State, in so far as that interest is not safeguarded by the rules to which the provider of the service is subject in the Member State in which he is established.

* * *

[20]   According to the German Government, [its] rules are a direct consequence of Article 5 of the Directive, which provides that the German lawyer with whom the work in conjunction is to be carried out must practise before the judicial authority in question and is, "where necessary, answerable to that authority". [Accordingly,] the German lawyer must be constantly involved in the development of the case; such involvement in the case can be ensured only if * * * the German lawyer is present at the oral stage of the proceedings and if he can claim the status of authorized representative or defending counsel.

[21]   The German Government also claims that * * *[u]nlimited access by foreign lawyers to proceedings before German courts would be likely to create difficulties arising from insufficient knowledge of the rules of substantive and procedural law applied by those courts. Only the involvement of a local lawyer can ensure that cases are properly presented to the court.

* * *

[23]   [W]hilst the Directive allows national legislation to require a lawyer providing services to work in conjunction with a local lawyer, it is intended to make it possible for the former to carry out the tasks

entrusted to him by his client, whilst at the same time having due regard for the proper administration of justice. Seen from that viewpoint, the obligation imposed upon him to act in conjunction with a local lawyer is intended to provide him with the support necessary to enable him to act within a judicial system different from that to which he is accustomed and to assure the judicial authority concerned that the lawyer providing services actually has that support and is thus in a position fully to comply with the procedural and ethical rules that apply.

24   Accordingly, the lawyer providing services and the local lawyer, both being subject to the ethical rules applicable in the host Member State, must be regarded as being capable, in compliance with those ethical rules and in the exercise of their professional independence, of agreeing upon a form of cooperation appropriate to their client's instructions.

* * *

26   [T]he German Law of 1980 imposes upon the two lawyers who are required to work in conjunction obligations which go further than is necessary for the attainment of those objectives. Neither the presence of the German lawyer throughout the oral proceedings nor the requirement that the German lawyer must himself be the authorized representative or defending counsel nor the detailed provisions concerning proof of work in conjunction are in general necessary or even useful for the provision of the support required by the lawyer providing services.

27   * * * [T]he problem of possibly inadequate knowledge of German law referred to by the German Government to justify the requirements of the Law of 1980 forms part of the responsibility of the lawyer providing services vis-à-vis his client, who is free to entrust his interests to a lawyer of his choice.

NOTES AND QUESTIONS

1.   In the *German Lawyers' services* case, the Court's analysis in ¶¶ 23–26 applied the principle of *van Binsbergen* that restrictions on the right to provide services must be justified by the "general good." Do you think the Court has struck the proper balance between the right of cross-border legal practice and the protection of clients' interests? Should clients or a State fix the allocation of responsibility between host and home State lawyers in a legal proceeding?

1. DISTINGUISHING TEMPORARY PROVIDING OF SERVICES FROM ESTABLISHMENT

GEBHARD v. CONSIGLIO DELL'ORDINE DEGLI AVVOCATI DI MILANO

Case C–55/94, [1995] ECR I–4165.

[A German national, Gebhard, became a Rechtsanwalt in Stuttgart in 1977. During 1978–89, he practiced professionally in Milan as a "collaborator" with a firm of Italian lawyers. Since 1978, Gebhard has resided with his family in Milan, paying income tax only in Italy. In 1989, Gebhard opened his own office in Milan, chiefly representing German and Austrian clients in Italy, with the aid of Italian lawyers. However, around 35% of his practice consisted in the representation of Italian clients in Germany and Austria, and he remained a "collaborator" in a Stuttgart law firm.

In 1989, the Milan Bar Association began disciplinary proceedings against Gebhard because of his permanent practice in Italy using the title, "*Avvocato*," without being qualified as an Italian lawyer. When in 1992 the Milan Bar Council imposed upon him the sanction of a total prohibition of practice for six months, Gebhard appealed to the National Bar Council, claiming in particular that he had a right to practice in Italy under the Lawyers' Services Directive. In a preliminary reference, the National Bar Council inquired whether a 1982 Italian law had properly implemented the directive, and how to assess the criteria to be used in determining whether a lawyer's practice came under that directive. The Court provided guidelines on how to distinguish between a lawyer's right of establishment and a lawyer's right to provide services.]

22 The provisions of the chapter on services are subordinate to those of the chapter on the right of establishment in so far, first, as the wording of the first paragraph of Article [49] assumes that the provider and the recipient of the service concerned are "established" in two different Member States and, second, as the first paragraph of Article [50] specifies that the provisions relating to services apply only if those relating to the right of establishment do not apply. It is therefore necessary to consider the scope of the concept of "establishment".

23 The right of establishment, provided for in Articles [43 to 48] of the Treaty, is granted both to legal persons within the meaning of Article [48] and to natural persons who are nationals of a Member State of the Community. Subject to the exceptions and conditions laid down, it allows all types of self-employed activity to be taken up and pursued on the territory of any other Member State * * *.

24 It follows that a person may be established, within the meaning of the Treaty, in more than one Member State, in the case of members of the

professions, by establishing a second professional base [citing *Klopp, infra*].

25   The concept of establishment within the meaning of the Treaty is therefore a very broad one, allowing a Community national to participate, on a stable and continuous basis, in the economic life of a Member State other than his State of origin and to profit therefrom, so contributing to economic and social interpenetration within the Community in the sphere of activities as self-employed persons [citing *Reyners*].

26   In contrast, where the provider of services moves to another Member State, the provisions of the chapter on services, in particular the third paragraph of Article [50], envisage that he is to pursue his activity there on a temporary basis.

27   As the Advocate General has pointed out, the temporary nature of the activities in question has to be determined in the light, not only of the duration of the provision of the service, but also of its regularity, periodicity or continuity. The fact that the provision of services is temporary does not mean that the provider of services within the meaning of the Treaty may not equip himself with some form of infrastructure in the host Member State (including an office, chambers or consulting rooms) in so far as such infrastructure is necessary for the purposes of performing the services in question.

28   However, that situation is to be distinguished from that of Mr. Gebhard who, as a national of a Member State, pursues a professional activity on a stable and continuous basis in another Member State where he holds himself out from an established professional base to, amongst others, nationals of that State. Such a national comes under the provisions of the chapter relating to the right of establishment and not those of the chapter relating to services.

[In view of the Court's conclusion in ¶ 28 that Gebhard was established in Italy, the Court then gave guidance to the Italian bar on the extent to which he was subject to Italian bar rules—see page 742 infra.]

NOTES AND QUESTIONS

1.   In *Gebhard,* the Court's analysis of the distinction between the right of establishment and the right to provide services is its most precise and detailed one to date and clearly applies to commercial activities as well as to professional ones. Advocate General Leger's careful analysis undoubtedly helped the Court. What are the critical elements in drawing the distinction set forth in the judgment? How can a trans-border service provider have a permanent office or other infra-structure in a host State, and still be deemed to be only providing services rather than being established? In a financial services context, the Commission has stated its view that a bank may operate a group of automatic cash machines in a host State and still be considered only to be providing services. Do you agree with this basic approach?

2. When do you suppose a permanent office or infrastructure might prove useful for lawyers providing services in another State? Could administrative, secretarial or accounting personnel be employed permanently by such an office, provided they are not attempting to carry out any law practice? Under the test for temporary services set in ¶ 27 of the *Gebhard* judgment, could a German lawyer come to Paris or London ten times or more a year, totaling five or six months, to engage in international arbitration practice, without being deemed to be established?

3. In Sager v. Dennemeyer, Case C–76/90, [1991] ECR I–4221, the Court held that a German law restricting patent maintenance and the handling of routine patent renewals to lawyers only was disproportionate, thus permitting a UK patent agent company to provide these services in Germany. In sharp contrast, in Reiseburo Broede, Case C–3/95, [1996] ECR I–6511, the Court held that German rules restricting to lawyers the collection of debts in court proceedings satisfied the general good interest criterion because they "protect creditors or safeguard the sound administration of justice" (¶ 36). Accordingly, a French debt-collection enterprise was prevented from carrying out its activities in Germany. Most States do not restrict debt-collection to lawyers and the Commission considered the German rule to be disproportionate. On a comparative note, in National Revenue Corp. v. Violet, 807 F.2d 285 (1st Cir.1986), the First Circuit held that Rhode Island's statutory definition of debt collection as part of the practice of law violated the dormant Interstate Commerce Clause, noting that no other state restricted debt collection to attorneys.

BIRBROWER, MONTALBANO, CONDON & FRANK v. SUPERIOR COURT

17 Cal.4th 119, 70 Cal.Rptr.2d 304, 949 P.2d 1 (1998).

[In 1992–93, Birbrower, a New York law firm, performed legal services for a California corporation, ESQ Business Services. This corporation was owned by the Sandhu family who had been Birbrower clients since 1986, largely for New York matters. ESQ had a software development and marketing contract dispute with Tandem, another California corporation. The contract, which apparently had been drafted by Birbrower, was governed by California law. Two Birbrower attorneys traveled several times to California to perform legal services, notably negotiating with Tandem representatives and preparing and filing a complaint for arbitration in San Francisco. After the ESQ–Tandem dispute was settled, Birbrower requested fees in excess of one million dollars based on a fee agreement. ESQ sued to set aside the agreement, claiming that Birbrower had engaged in the unauthorized practice of law. The issue went to the California Supreme Court. Six justices concurred in Justice Chin's opinion.]

[After the State Bar Act comprehensively regulated the practice of law in 1927,] no one but an active member of the State Bar may practice law for another person in California. The prohibition against unauthorized law practice is within the state's police power and is designed to ensure that those performing legal services do so competently.

* * *

No one may recover compensation for services as an attorney at law in this state unless [the person] was at the time the services were performed a member of the State Bar.

* * *

In our view, the practice of law "in California" entails sufficient contact with the California client to render the nature of the legal service a clear legal representation. In addition to a quantitative analysis, we must consider the nature of the unlicensed lawyer's activities in the state. Mere fortuitous or attenuated contacts will not sustain a finding that the unlicensed lawyer practiced law "in California." The primary inquiry is whether the unlicensed lawyer engaged in sufficient activities in the state, or created a continuing relationship with the California client that included legal duties and obligations.

Our definition does not necessarily depend on or require the unlicensed lawyer's physical presence in the state. * * * [O]ne may practice law in the state in violation of [the State Bar Act] although not physically present here by advising a California client on California law in connection with a California legal dispute by telephone, fax, computer, or other modern technological means.

* * *

Birbrower argues that because out-of-state attorneys have been licensed to practice in other jurisdictions, they have already demonstrated sufficient competence to protect California clients. But Birbrower's argument overlooks the obvious fact that other states' laws may differ substantially from California law. Competence in one jurisdiction does not necessarily guarantee competence in another.

* * *

We conclude that Birbrower violated [the State Bar Act] by practicing law in California. To the extent the fee agreement allows payment for those illegal local services, it is void, and Birbrower is not entitled to recover fees under the agreement for those services. The fee agreement is enforceable, however, to the extent it is possible to sever the portions of the consideration attributable to Birbrower's services illegally rendered in California from those attributable to Birbrower's New York services.

[Justice Kennard's dissent argued that services connected with an arbitration should not be considered to be legal services that constituted the unauthorized practice of law. Shortly after *Birbrower* was decided, the California legislature amended its Rules of Court to permit out-of-state lawyers to appear in a private arbitration when authorized by the arbitration tribunal.]

NOTES AND QUESTIONS

1.   Because Birbrower involved a large New York law firm acting at its client's request in a significant transaction in California, and because the California Supreme Court's views are often influential, the judgment has attracted widespread attention in US law firms. Several other state and federal courts have reached similar conclusions. Thus, in Spivak v. Sachs, 16 N.Y.2d 163, 263 N.Y.S.2d 953, 211 N.E.2d 329 (N.Y. 1965), the New York Court of Appeals held that a California lawyer could not collect his fees for two weeks of work in New York, counseling a client on her divorce proceedings in Connecticut, even though the client expressly requested the lawyer to come to New York. Note that a lawyer's appearance in litigation in other states is regulated by *pro hac vice* rules of the host state, which the Supreme Court held to be within the total discretion of the host state in Leis v. Flynt, 439 U.S. 438, 99 S.Ct. 698, 58 L.Ed.2d 717 (1979).

2.   The American Law Institute's Restatement (Third) of the Law Governing Lawyers, § 3(3), Comment e (2000), criticizes *Birbrower* and *Spivak* as unduly restrictive, and urges that lawyers qualified in one state should be permitted to carry on temporary transborder legal practice in other states whenever the activities "arise out of or are otherwise reasonably relate[d] to the lawyer's practice" in his or her home state, especially when acting for a regular client of the lawyer, or when the issues mix home and host state law, or relate to federal law. R. Goebel, The Liberalization of Interstate Legal Practice in the European Union: Lessons For the United States? 34 Int'l Lawyer 307 (2000), criticized *Birbrower* and urged a change in US state policies to follow the liberal approach in the Community.

3.   In 2002, the American Bar Association issued a new Rule 5.5 in its Model Rules of Professional Conduct which significantly liberalized its prior attitude toward multi-jurisdictional practice. Most far-reaching is the endorsement of a lawyer's providing of "temporary" services in other States when they are "reasonably related to the lawyer's practice" where he or she is admitted. However, Rule 5.5 is still more restrictive than the Court's approach in *Gebhard*, because it forbids the lawyer to "establish an office or other systematic or continuous presence" unless this is otherwise permitted by the Model Rules, e.g., by partnership with a partner admitted to the host state bar.

C. LAWYERS' RIGHT OF ESTABLISHMENT

1. LIBERAL CASE LAW ON THE APPLICATION OF PRACTICE RIGHTS

THIEFFRY v. CONSEIL DE L'ORDRE DES AVOCATS À LA COUR DE PARIS

Case 71/76, [1977] ECR 765.

[Thieffry, a Belgian *avocat,* practiced in Brussels from 1956 to 1969, and then moved to Paris. In 1974, the University of Paris recognized Thieffry's Belgian law degree as the equivalent of a French law degree, apparently for the purpose of establishing his capacity to take the French bar examination, which he successfully passed in 1975. When Thieffry applied to the Paris bar council for admission as *avocat,* the council refused, on the ground that he had not received any French law degree, as required by the French law regulating the profession of *avocat.* On appeal, the Paris Court of Appeal asked the Court to rule on whether France could require applicants for the status of *avocat* to possess a French law degree.]

15   [F]reedom of establishment, subject to observance of professional rules justified by the general good, is one of the objectives of the Treaty.

16   In so far as Community law makes no special provision, these objectives may be attained by measures enacted by the Member States, which under Article [10] of the Treaty are bound to take "all appropriate measures, whether general or particular, to ensure fulfilment of the obligations arising out of this Treaty or resulting from action taken by the institutions of the Community", and to abstain "from any measure which could jeopardize the attainment of the objectives of this Treaty."

* * *

18   [Therefore,] it is incumbent upon the competent public authorities— including legally recognized professional bodies—to ensure that [any professional rule] or legislation is applied in accordance with the objective defined by the provisions of the Treaty relating to freedom of establishment.

19   In particular, there is an unjustified restriction on that freedom where * * * admission to a particular profession is refused to a person covered by the Treaty who holds a diploma which has been recognized as an equivalent qualification by the competent authority of the country of establishment and who furthermore has fulfilled the specific conditions regarding professional training in force in that country, solely by reason of the fact that the person concerned does not possess the national diploma * * *.

* * *

27   In these circumstances, * * * the act of demanding the national
     diploma prescribed by the legislation of the country of establishment
     constitutes, even in the absence of the directives provided for in
     Article [47], a restriction incompatible with the freedom of establish-
     ment guaranteed by Article [43] of the Treaty.

ORDRE DES AVOCATS AU BARREAU DE PARIS v. KLOPP

Case 107/83, [1984] ECR 2971.

[Klopp, a German *Rechtsanwalt* practicing in Düsseldorf, obtained a
doctorate from the University of Paris in 1969. He passed the French bar
examination in 1980 and sought to open a second law office in Paris,
intending to reside and practice in both Düsseldorf and Paris. Under Paris
bar rules established in accordance with French legislation, an *avocat* in
Paris may not have an office outside of the territorial jurisdiction of the
French court for the Paris region. The issue presented by the French
Supreme Court to the Court of Justice was whether this longstanding
French rule could prevail over the right of establishment.]

12   The Paris Bar Council and the French Government maintain that
     Article [43] of the Treaty makes access and exercise of freedom of
     establishment depend on the conditions laid down by the Member
     State of establishment. [The French rules] are applicable without
     distinction to French nationals and those of other Member States.
     Those provisions provide that an *avocat* may establish chambers in
     one place only.

* * *

16   The Paris Bar Council and the French Government [argue that the]
     rule that an *avocat* may have his chambers in one place only is based
     on the need for *avocats* to genuinely practice before a court in order to
     ensure their availability to both the court and their clients. It should
     be respected as being a rule pertaining to the administration of justice
     and to professional ethics, objectively necessary and consistent with
     the public interest.

     [The Court then stated its views.]

17   It should be emphasized that under the second paragraph of Article
     [43] freedom of establishment includes access to and the pursuit of the
     activities of self-employed persons "under the conditions laid down for
     its own nationals by the law of the country where such establishment
     is effected." It follows from that provision and its context that in the
     absence of specific Community rules in the matter each Member State
     is free to regulate the exercise of the legal profession in its territory.

18   Nevertheless that rule does not mean that the legislation of a Member
     State may require a lawyer to have only one establishment throughout
     the Community territory. Such a restrictive interpretation would

mean that a lawyer once established in a particular Member State would be able to enjoy the freedom of the Treaty to establish himself in another Member State only at the price of abandoning the establishment he already had.

19   That freedom of establishment is not confined to the right to create a single establishment within the Community is confirmed by the very words of Article [43] of the Treaty, according to which the progressive abolition of the restrictions on freedom of establishment applies to restrictions on the setting up of agencies, branches or subsidiaries by nationals of any Member State established in the territory of another Member State. That rule must be regarded as a specific statement of a general principle, applicable equally to the liberal professions, according to which the right of establishment includes freedom to set up and maintain, subject to observance of the professional rules of conduct, more than one place of work within the Community.

20   In view of the special nature of the legal profession, however, the second Member State must have the right, in the interests of the due administration of justice, to require that lawyers enrolled at a Bar in its territory should practise in such a way as to maintain sufficient contact with their clients and the judicial authorities and abide by the rules of the profession. Nevertheless such requirements must not prevent the nationals of other Member States from exercising properly the right of establishment guaranteed them by the Treaty.

21   In that respect * * * modern methods of transport and telecommunications facilitate proper contact with clients and the judicial authorities. Similarly, the existence of a second set of chambers in another Member State does not prevent the application of the rules of ethics in the host Member State.

22   [Therefore,]even in the absence of any directive coordinating national provisions governing access to the exercise of the legal profession, Article [43 prevents] a Member State from denying, on the basis of the national legislation and the rules of professional conduct which are in force in that State, to a national of another Member State the right to enter and to exercise the legal profession solely on the ground that he maintains chambers simultaneously in another Member State.

Notes and Questions

1.   Both in *Thieffry* and *Klopp*, the Court expanded the scope of the right of establishment by invalidating rules that were not discriminatory in any way. Do you think the Court's use of ECT Article 10 to achieve this result in *Thieffry* represents sound policy? *Klopp* also states an important principle: a Member State's professional rules will be allowed to limit an establishment right only if they are objectively justified by the "general good." This is the same principle that was applied to services in *van Binsbergen, Webb* and the *German insurance* case in the preceding chapter.

2. *Thieffry* was followed in Patrick v. Ministre des Affaires Culturelles, Case 11/77, [1977] ECR 1199, which required France to allow a British architect to qualify as an architect in France, because a French Culture Ministry decree treated his UK architect certificate as equivalent to one in France.

3. In Wouters v. Netherlands Bar Council, Case C–309/99, [2002] ECR I–1577, the principal issue referred to the Court was whether the Dutch bar association rule forbidding lawyers to be partners with professionals other than lawyers (commonly known as multi-disciplinary practice) violated ECT Article 81, which forbids anti-competitive agreements. The effort to strike down the Dutch bar prohibition was led by the large international accounting firms. The Dutch bar allowed lawyers to have partnerships with patent agents, tax advisors and notaries, but not other professionals.

The Court found that an important objective justification for the Dutch rule, namely that lawyers' professional ethics obligations, notably the duty "to avoid all risk of conflict of interest and the duty to observe strict professional secrecy" (¶ 100), would be jeopardized by partnership with non-lawyers (¶¶ 101–05). That some other States permitted such partnerships did not prevent the Netherlands bar from having stricter rules (¶ 108). The referring court had also inquired whether the Dutch bar rule violated the right of establishment. The Court's response was that any such violation was justified on the grounds previously mentioned (¶¶ 119–23). On a comparative note, the American Bar Association's annual meeting in 2000 rejected a proposal to amend its professional rules to permit multi-disciplinary partnerships in the U.S.

GEBHARD v. MILAN BAR COUNCIL

[For the description of facts, see page 734. The Court concluded its judgment by setting forth the rules governing the practice of law by a lawyer qualified in one Member State who has a permanent establishment in another Member State.]

33   Under the terms of the second paragraph of Article [43], freedom of establishment is to be exercised under the conditions laid down for its own nationals by the law of the country where establishment is effected.

34   In the event that the specific activities in question are not subject to any rules in the host State, so that a national of that Member State does not have to have any specific qualification in order to pursue them, a national of any other Member State is entitled to establish himself on the territory of the first State and pursue those activities there.

35   However, the taking-up and pursuit of certain self-employed activities may be conditional on complying with certain provisions laid down by law, regulation or administrative action justified by the general good, such as rules relating to organization, qualifications, professional ethics, supervision and liability [citing *Thieffry*]. Such provisions may stipulate in particular that pursuit of a particular activity is restricted

to holders of a diploma, certificate or other evidence of formal qualifications, to persons belonging to a professional body or to persons subject to particular rules or supervision, as the case may be. They may also lay down the conditions for the use of professional titles, such as *avvocato*.

36 Where the taking-up or pursuit of a specific activity is subject to such conditions in the host Member State, a national of another Member State intending to pursue that activity must in principle comply with them. It is for this reason that Article [47] provides that the Council is to issue directives, such as Directive 89/48 for the mutual recognition of diplomas, certificates and other evidence of formal qualifications [discussed in section D infra] * * *.

37 It follows, however, from the Court's case-law that national measures liable to hinder or make less attractive the exercise of fundamental freedoms guaranteed by the Treaty must fulfil four conditions: they must be applied in a non-discriminatory manner; they must be justified by imperative requirements in the general interest; they must be suitable for securing the attainment of the objective which they pursue; and they must not go beyond what is necessary in order to attain it.

38 Likewise, in applying their national provisions, Member States may not ignore the knowledge and qualifications already acquired by the person concerned in another Member State [citing *Vlassopoulou*, infra]. Consequently, they must take account of the equivalence of diplomas and, if necessary, proceed to a comparison of the knowledge and qualifications required by their national rules and those of the person concerned.

NOTES AND QUESTIONS

1. The principal importance of the *Gebhard* judgment lies in ¶ 37's express absorption of the *Cassis de Dijon* rule of reason doctrine into the establishment context. We noted that this doctrinal approach was taken with regard to services in the *German insurance* judgment in the preceding chapter, and with regard to establishment in *Centros*. Thus an important doctrine is now applied to the free movement of goods, the providing of transborder services, and the right of establishment.

2. Consider how the Italian National Bar Council should apply the Court's guidelines. May Gebhard be forbidden to use the title "avvocato"? (Could the Paris bar forbid a Belgian avocat established in Paris from using the title, "avocat"?) Does Gebhard have the right to practice law in some fashion permanently in Milan? For example, can he assist Italian clients in operations in Germany and Austria or provide general advice to any clients on German, Community or international law? Can he provide advice on Italian law or draft Italian commercial instruments? Can he, either regularly or occasionally, appear in an Italian court proceeding? After *Gebhard*, the answers were subject to considerable debate, with lawyers from different

countries tending to adopt radically different views. For a helpful appraisal, see the casenote by J. Lonbay, 33 Common Mkt. L. Rev. 1073 (1996).

2. THE DIRECTIVE ON THE ESTABLISHMENT OF LAWYERS

By the mid–1990's, many law firms in Member States (especially UK solicitor firms) had established branch offices in other States, usually staffed in part by lawyers using their home State titles and in part by host State lawyers. The UK itself has customarily permitted foreign lawyers and law firms (including US lawyers and law firms) to register with the solicitors' society and practice in their home State professional capacity, using their home State title. Germany's 1989 legal profession rules expressly permitted this, although lawyers from other Member States were only permitted to practice their home State law, Community law and international law; and several other Member States permitted or tolerated such practice to some extent. On the other hand, France's 1990 law merging the professions of *avocat* and *conseil juridique* (legal advisor) appeared to forbid lawyers from other Member States to practice unless they become French *avocats*.

Throughout the 1980's, the Council of Bars and Law Societies of the European Community (the CCBE), which had prepared the Code of Conduct discussed above, worked to agree upon a draft directive on the right of establishment for lawyers. The CCBE provided its final 1992 version to the Commission, which prompted the Commission to begin work on a directive to facilitate a lawyer's right of establishment. Although inspired in large measure by the CCBE's final version, the Commission proposal contained many significant differences.

In 1998, the Parliament and Council adopted by codecision Directive 98/5 on the establishment of lawyers, O.J. L 77/36 (Mar. 14, 1998) (see Document 22 in the Selected Documents). In its fifth recital the directive notes that a permanent right of establishment not only would benefit lawyers, but also their clients, in view of the increasing volume of transborder transactions engendered by the internal market.

Article 1 states that a lawyer (defined by the same list of professions as that figuring in the Lawyers' Services Directive) shall have the right of permanent practice, either self-employed or as an employee, in a host State. However, article 2 prescribes that the established lawyer must use his or her home State title, and article 4 notes that the host State may require that the home State title be clearly distinguished from the host State title if necessary for consumer protection. Further, article 3 requires that the established lawyer be inscribed on a special list in the host State.

Under article 5, the established lawyer will have broad practice rights, including the capacity to give opinions or provide services concerning the home State laws, Community or international law, and even the laws of the host State. Although the host State may limit any court appearance to the same degree as is the case in the Lawyers Services Directive, this is not usually a significant restriction. The only important restriction on practice is that the host State may forbid established lawyers from handling real estate title transfers or carrying out inheritance and estate law practice. Moreover, article 6 submits the established lawyer to the host State professional rules for practice on its territory, and article 7 provides for disciplinary proceedings under the host State rules, although with some cooperation with the home State authorities.

A somewhat complex article 10 enables the established lawyer to become integrated into the host State legal profession in an easier fashion than through the system of the Diploma Recognition Directive, described in section D infra, after an "effective and regular" practice of host State law for three years. However, the integrated lawyer may continue to use his or her home State title as well as that of the host State.

Finally, article 11 enables practice in association, by partnership or any other legal form, to the same degree that this is permitted to host State lawyers. Law firms may have branches in host States. Lawyers from any Community State may be associated with those from any other State or States.

The liberal provisions of the directive have enormously facilitated trans-border practice within the Community by individual lawyers and multinational law firms. Large firms in France, Germany, the UK and other States now usually have substantial branch offices in the leading commercial centers of the Community.

US and other non-Community lawyers and law firms have no claim to establishment rights in the Community under Article 43 (except in the case of dual nationals, provided that they obtain the status of lawyer in the Community State whose nationality they possess). Fortunately, at the present time most Member States permit non-Community lawyers to conduct most types of practice in their home State professional capacity, using the home State title, although sometimes only on a basis of reciprocity. Non–Community lawyers should obviously take care to ensure that they are permitted to take some form of legal action. In Foreign Trade Association v. Council, Case T 37/98, [2000] ECR II 373, the Court of First Instance held that the American partner of an American law office branch in Brussels did not have the status of a Community lawyer empowered to sign an appeal of a Council anti-dumping regulation on behalf of a client, and consequently dismissed the appeal.

On a comparative note, American lawyers who desire to practice on a permanent basis in a state other than that of their initial qualification must either pass the host state bar examination or be admitted on motion. However, only about half the states (including New York, but not California or Florida) permit admission on motion, and these states usually restrict it: a) to lawyers who have practiced for five years in their home state, and b) to lawyers from states that also admit on motion (i.e., they require reciprocal treatment). The restrictive state rules are usually justified by claims that they are necessary for consumer protection and to ensure that courts will have properly qualified litigating lawyers. Some leading commentators doubt the validity of these justifications. Professor Wolfram, a prominent expert on legal ethics, has trenchantly observed that there is a "distinct possibility that [local practice] rules are motivated by the local bar's desire to be protected against out-of-state competition." C. Wolfram, Modern Legal Ethics 865 (1986). Do you think that the Lawyers' Establishment Directive could, or should, serve as a model for liberalization of US state rules?

With regard to practice by foreign lawyers in the U.S., note that in August 1993, the American Bar Association approved Model Rules for Legal Consultants. The following November, the New York Court of Appeals made minor changes in its rules to follow this Model. Over twenty US states and the District of Columbia now have some form of legal consultant rule, permitting foreign lawyers with practice experience in their home State, usually five years, to provide legal advice on their home State law and carry out most forms of international business law practice. In point of fact, however, relatively few foreign lawyers qualify as Legal Consultants, because so many obtain LL.M. degrees in US law schools, which enable them to take the bar exam in New York and Washington, D.C., the primary cities of interest for international legal practice. For a useful review, see R. Goebel, Legal Practice Rights of Domestic and Foreign Lawyers in the United States, 49 Int'l & Comp. L.Q. 413 (2000).

LUXEMBOURG v. PARLIAMENT AND COUNCIL

(Lawyers' establishment directive)
Case C–168/98, [2000] ECR 9131.

[Luxembourg, which had voted against the Lawyers' Establishment Directive, challenged its validity, claiming that it violated Treaty rights, and harmed the interests of consumers and the sound administration of justice.]

[17]   The Grand Duchy of Luxembourg argues that * * * the right of establishment may not be granted in breach of overriding principles governing the self-employed professions, common to the laws of the various Member States.

[18]   [Luxembourg further] claims that, while harmonization may justify dispensing with any assessment of knowledge of international law, Community law and the law of the Member State of origin, no such dispensation can be contemplated as regards the law of the host Member State. The knowledge to be acquired in the field of national law, unlike the knowledge imparted in other training contexts, is not identical or even broadly the same from one Member State to another.

[20]   In [Luxembourg's view,] by abolishing all requirement of prior training in the law of the host Member State and by permitting migrant lawyers to practice that law, Directive 98/5 unjustifiably discriminates between nationals and migrants * * * contrary to Article [43] of the

Treaty, which does not authorize the Community legislature to abolish a requirement of prior training in a directive which does not purport to harmonize training conditions.

* * *

22 The Parliament and the Council, supported by [the Netherlands, Spain and the UK], deny the existence of any reverse discrimination. They submit that lawyers practicing under their home-country professional title and lawyers practicing under the professional title of the host Member State are in different situations, the first being subject to several restrictions on the pursuit of their activity. In any event, it is no part of the function of Article [43] of the Treaty to prescribe limits on the process of liberalizing access to self-employed activity.

[The Court then stated its conclusions.]

23 [T]he prohibition of discrimination laid down in Article [43] of the Treaty is only the specific expression of the general principle of equality which * * * requires that comparable situations should not be treated differently unless such difference in treatment is objectively justified.

24 In this case, the Community legislature has not infringed that principle, since the situation of a migrant lawyer practicing under his home-country title and the situation of a lawyer practicing under the professional title of the host Member State are not comparable.

25 Whereas the latter may undertake all the activities open or reserved to the profession of lawyer by the host Member State, the former may be forbidden to pursue certain activities and, with regard to the representation or defence of clients in legal proceedings, may be subject to certain obligations.

29 The complaint of discrimination against lawyers practicing under the professional title of the host Member State is therefore unfounded.

30 [Luxembourg further challenges] the validity of Directive 98/5 in the interests of consumers and in the interest of the proper administration of justice.

* * *

32 In that regard, the Court observes that * * * the Community legislature is to have regard to the public interest pursued by the various Member States and to adopt a level of protection for that interest which seems acceptable in the Community. It enjoys a measure of discretion for the purposes of its assessment of the acceptable level of protection.

33 In this instance it is clear that several of the provisions of Directive 98/5 lay down rules intended to protect consumers and to ensure the proper administration of justice.

34   Thus, Article 4 provides that a lawyer practicing under his home-country professional title is required to do so under that title, so that consumers are informed that the professional to whom they entrust the defense of their interests has not obtained his qualification in the host Member State and that his initial training did not necessarily cover the host Member State's national law.

35   [Moreover,] Article 5(2) and (3) authorize the host Member State, subject to certain conditions, to forbid migrant lawyers to undertake certain activities and to impose certain obligations on them in connection with the representation or defense of a client in legal proceedings.

36   Article 6(1) makes a lawyer practicing under his home-country professional title subject not only to the rules of professional conduct applicable in his home Member State but also to the same rules of professional conduct as lawyers practicing under the professional title of the host Member State in respect of all the activities which he pursues in its territory.

42   Furthermore, it should be noted that, quite apart from the applicable rules of professional liability, the rules of professional conduct applicable to lawyers generally entail, like Article 3.1.3 of the Code of Professional Conduct adopted by the Council of the Bars and Law Societies of the European Union (CCBE), an obligation, breach of which may incur disciplinary sanctions, not to handle matters which the professionals concerned know or ought to know they are not competent to handle.

43   It would therefore seem that the Community legislature, with a view to making it easier for a particular class of migrant lawyers to exercise the fundamental freedom of establishment, has chosen * * * a plan of action combining consumer information, restrictions on the extent to which or the detailed rules under which certain activities of the profession may be practiced, a number of applicable rules of professional conduct, compulsory insurance, as well as a system of discipline involving both the competent authorities of the home Member State and the host State. The legislature has not abolished the requirement that the lawyer concerned should know the national law applicable in the cases he handles, but has simply released him from the obligation to prove that knowledge in advance. It has thus allowed, in some circumstances, gradual assimilation of knowledge through practice, that assimilation being made easier by experience of other laws gained in the home Member State. It was also able to take account of the dissuasive effect of the system of discipline and the rules of professional liability.

NOTES AND QUESTIONS

1.   Luxembourg's principal argument was that the directive does not adequately protect clients against foreign lawyers who are insufficiently

trained in host State substantive and procedural law. What forms of protection for clients are contained in the directive? Do you consider them adequate? Overall, do you consider that the directive's goal of achieving a Community-wide integrated legal practice outweighs any risks to consumers? Certainly the branches of multinational law firms are apt to be serving only relatively sophisticated clients, but is that also true of individual practitioners?

2.   Luxembourg also argued reverse discrimination, i.e., that its lawyers had to prove their competence in its law, while lawyers from other Member States could, in effect, learn Luxembourg law in the course of their practice. What was the Court's response? What is your view on the issue?

3.   Continuing its efforts to exclude lawyers from other Member States, Luxembourg adopted a law in 2002 requiring lawyers to be proficient in French, the language used for its legislation, as well as German and Luxembourger, the languages also used in its administrative and court proceedings. In Commission v. Luxembourg (Language test for lawyers), Case C–193/05, [2006] ECR I–8673, the Court held that Directive 98/5 comprehensively preempted a State's power to set conditions for a lawyer's establishment other than those set in the directive (¶¶ 36–40). The Court noted that clients would be aware that an established lawyer coming from other States would not necessarily know the three specified languages (¶ 42), and that such a lawyer's obligation to comply with professional ethics would prevent him or her from handling a matter which required knowledge of one or more of the languages (¶ 44). Do you agree with the judgment? Do you think that Luxembourg should have been able to require a foreign lawyer to have an adequate knowledge of at least one of its languages? Note that most such foreign lawyers would probably be chiefly interested in practicing banking law, where English and French are the customary languages used in bank documents.

3.   PROFESSIONAL RULES GOVERNING LAWYER'S FEES

A 1993 Italian law regulating the profession of *avvocati* includes a provision enabling the National Council of the Bar to set fee scales for various litigation and general practice services on a bi-annual basis. After the Council sets the fee scales, they must be approved by the Minister of Justice, acting after obtaining an opinion from an Inter-ministerial Committee on prices.

In Criminal Proceedings against Arduino, Case C–35/99, [2002] ECR I–1529, the referring court inquired whether these compulsory fee scales violated the competition rules of ECT Article 81. The Court held that a State may use a professional organization to provide expert recommendations on fee scales which take into consideration the public interest (¶ 37), but concluded that the Italian system was deficient in failing to identify the public interest criteria and setting "procedural arrangements" to ensure that the National Council does act in the public interest (¶¶ 38–39). However, because the Minister of Justice has the ultimate power to set the fee scales and because the courts have the discretion to modify the fees in specific cases, the Court held that the Italian fee scales system did not violate Article 81 (¶¶ 41–44).

The Court soon had to examine the Italian fee scale system again, this time in the context of their impact on the right to provide trans-border services.

CIPOLLA v. FAZARI

Case C–94/04 and C–202/04, [2006] ECR I–11421.

[When a lawyer's clients contested his fees in a real estate proceeding, the lawyer sued to collect his fee, calculated on the basis of the fee scale. The trial court reduced his fee and on appeal, the appellate court inquired whether the Italian minimum fee scale violated ECT Article 81 or Article 49. In response, the Court reasserted its holding in *Arduino* that the Italian state-imposed fee scales did not violate Article 81. Although the Court could have invoked the internal affairs doctrine to decline to deal with the Article 49 question, it considered that a reply could be useful to the referring court (¶ 30). The Court initially observed that the Italian fee rules, though not discriminating against foreign service providers, would adversely affect them.]

59   [The compulsory fee scale] deprives lawyers established in a Member State other than the Italian Republic of the possibility, by requesting fees lower than those set by the scale, of competing more effectively with lawyers established on a stable basis in the Member State concerned and who therefore have greater opportunities for winning clients than lawyers established abroad.

60   Likewise, the prohibition [on fees that do not comply with the scale] limits the choice of service recipients in Italy, because they cannot resort to the services of lawyers established in other Member States who would offer their services in Italy at a lower rate than the minimum fees set by the scale.

61   However, such a prohibition may be justified where it serves overriding requirements relating to the public interest, is suitable for securing the attainment of the objective which it pursues and does not go beyond what is necessary in order to attain it.

62   In order to justify the restriction on freedom to provide services which stems from the prohibition at issue, the Italian Government submits that excessive competition between lawyers might lead to price competition which would result in a deterioration in the quality of the services provided to the detriment of consumers, in particular as individuals in need of quality advice in court proceedings.

63   According to the Commission, no causal link has been established between the setting of minimum levels of fees and a high qualitative standard of professional services provided by lawyers. In actual fact, quasi-legislative measures such as, inter alia, rules on access to the

legal profession, disciplinary rules serving to ensure compliance with professional ethics and rules on civil liability have, by maintaining a high qualitative standard for the services provided by such professionals which those measures guarantee, a direct relationship of cause and effect with the protection of lawyers' clients and the proper working of the administration of justice.

[The Court then stated its conclusions.]

64   In that respect, it must be pointed out that, first, the protection of consumers, in particular recipients of the legal services provided by persons concerned in the administration of justice and, secondly, the safeguarding of the proper administration of justice, are objectives to be included among those which may be regarded as overriding requirements relating to the public interest capable of justifying a restriction on freedom to provide services on condition, first, that the national measure at issue in the main proceedings is suitable for securing the attainment of the objective pursued and, secondly, it does not go beyond what is necessary in order to attain that objective.

65   It is a matter for the national court to decide whether, in the main proceedings, the restriction on freedom to provide services introduced by that national legislation fulfils those conditions. For that purpose, it is for that court to take account of the factors set out in the following paragraphs.

* * *

67   Although it is true that a scale imposing minimum fees cannot prevent members of the profession from offering services of mediocre quality, it is conceivable that such a scale does serve to prevent lawyers, in a context such as that of the Italian market which * * * is characterised by an extremely large number of lawyers who are enrolled and practising, from being encouraged to compete against each other by possibly offering services at a discount, with the risk of deterioration in the quality of the services provided.

68   Account must also be taken * * * of the fact that, in the field of lawyers' services, there is usually an asymmetry of information between 'client-consumers' and lawyers. Lawyers display a high level of technical knowledge which consumers may not have and the latter therefore find it difficult to judge the quality of the services provided to them.

69   However, the national court will have to determine whether professional rules in respect of lawyers, in particular rules relating to organisation, qualifications, professional ethics, supervision and liability, suffice in themselves to attain the objectives of the protection of consumers and the proper administration of justice.

NOTES AND QUESTIONS

1. Advocate General Poiares Maduro's opinion contended that Italy had not proved that legal services provided for a low fee would be inferior in quality, and cited economic literature to that effect. He concluded that Italy had not shown that it had a compelling public interest to justify minimum fee scales (while noting that the maximum fee scales were not at issue in the case). Overall, do you agree with the Advocate General, or with the Court? Does the Court's reference in ¶ 67 to the "extremely large number of lawyers" on the Italian market limit the holding? Note that Germany also has minimum fee scales which have not yet been examined by the Court.

2. On a comparative note, the Supreme Court in Goldfarb v. Virginia State Bar, 421 U.S. 773, 95 S.Ct. 2004, 44 L.Ed.2d 572 (1975), held that the minimum fee scales for lawyers set by the Virginia State Bar Association restrained competition between lawyers in violation of the Sherman Act and did not qualify for the state action exception to the anti-trust rules, even though the Virginia Supreme Court exercises general supervision over the bar association.

4. LAWYER'S RIGHT AND/OR DUTY OF SECRECY CONCERNING CLIENTS' AFFAIRS

Lawyers in all Member States have traditionally enjoyed a judicial respect for professional secrecy concerning their communications with clients and their legal representation of clients. Some States regard this as a right of lawyers, while others consider it to be a duty toward clients, but all national legal profession codes of conduct treat this right and/or duty as a particularly important one. In the well-known *AM & S* judgment (summarized at page 157), the Court of Justice held that the Commission power to investigate in anti-trust enforcement proceedings did not enable the Commission to examine legal advice provided by an independent lawyer.

Money-laundering to facilitate the movement of funds derived from criminal activities became a serious problem in the 1980s. When the Council adopted the first money-laundering directive in 1991 it required banks and other financial institutions to identify their customers and to notify public authorities of factual indications of money-laundering (see Chapter 32C infra). When Directive 2001/97, summarized at page 1232, amended the initial directive, it required lawyers and notaries similarly to identify their clients. However, in view of the special status of lawyers and notaries, article 6(3) permitted Member States to exempt them from notifying the authorities concerning "information they receive from or obtain on one of their clients, in the course of ascertaining the legal position for the client, or performing their task of defending, or representing their client, in or concerning judicial proceedings."

ORDRE DES BARREAUX v. CONSEIL

Case C–305/05, [2007] ECR I–5305.

[Several Belgian bar associations sued to annul the provision in the Belgian law implementing Directive 2001/97 which required lawyers to notify the authorities of possible money-laundering by the clients. They contended that even with the exception stated in article 6(3), the obligation violated their duty of professional secrecy and the fundamental right of every person to respect for the right of defense in a fair trial. The Belgian Constitutional Court asked the Court of Justice whether the Directive's relevant provision violated the fundamental right of a fair trial.]

29   [F]undamental rights form an integral part of the general principles of law whose observance the Court ensures. For that purpose, the Court draws inspiration from the constitutional traditions common to the Member States and from the guidelines supplied by international instruments for the protection of human rights on which the Member States have collaborated or to which they are signatories. In that regard, the ECHR has special significance. Thus the right to a fair trial, which derives inter alia from Article 6 of the ECHR, constitutes a fundamental right which the European Union respects as a general principle under Article 6(2) EU.

32   Lawyers would be unable to carry out satisfactorily their task of advising, defending and representing their clients, who would in consequence be deprived of the rights conferred on them by Article 6 of the ECHR, if lawyers were obliged, in the context of judicial proceedings or the preparation for such proceedings, to cooperate with the authorities by passing them information obtained in the course of related legal consultations.

33   [However,] it is clear from Article 2a(5) of Directive 91/308 that the obligations of information and cooperation apply to lawyers only in so far as they advise their client in the preparation or execution of certain transactions—essentially those of a financial nature or concerning real estate, as referred to in Article 2a(5)(a) of that directive— or when they act on behalf of and for their client in any financial or real estate transaction. As a rule, the nature of such activities is such that they take place in a context with no link to judicial proceedings and, consequently, those activities fall outside the scope of the right to a fair trial.

35   Given that the requirements implied by the right to a fair trial presuppose, by definition, a link with judicial proceedings, and in view of the fact that the second subparagraph of Article 6(3) of Directive 91/308 exempts lawyers, where their activities are characterised by such a link, from the obligations of information and cooperation laid down in Article 6(1) of the directive, those requirements are respected.

36 [T]he requirements relating to the right to a fair trial do not preclude the obligations of information and cooperation laid down in Article 6(1) of Directive 91/308 from being imposed on lawyers acting specifically in connection with the activities listed in Article 2a(5) of that directive, in cases where the second subparagraph of Article 6(3) of that directive does not apply, where those obligations are justified by the need—emphasised, in particular, in recital 3 of Directive 91/308— to combat money laundering effectively, in view of its evident influence on the rise of organised crime, which itself is a particular threat to society in the Member States.

37 [Accordingly,] the obligations of information and of cooperation with the authorities responsible for combating money laundering, laid down in Article 6(1) of Directive 91/308 and imposed on lawyers by Article 2a(5) of that directive, account being taken of the second subparagraph of Article 6(3) thereof, do not infringe the right to a fair trial as guaranteed by Article 6 of the ECHR and Article 6(2) EU.

Notes and Questions

1. Note that the Court did not recognize any specific form of professional secrecy or lawyer/client privilege as a fundamental right which must be respected. The Belgian court's question concerned only whether the lawyer's duty to inform authorities of evidence of money laundering could indirectly violate the right of a fair trial and the Court of Justice limited its response to that issue. Do you agree with the Court's conclusion in ¶¶ 35–37?

2. A thoughtful casenote by M. Luchtman & R. van der Hoeven, 46 Common Mkt. L. Rev. 301 (2009), queries whether the Court should not have further examined the nature of the lawyer's privilege of professional secrecy. In the US, court judgments and state ethics rules forbid lawyers to assist clients in committing crimes and require, or at least permit, lawyers to report to authorities a client's conduct that may lead to physical injury or death, but differ on whether lawyers may, or must, report evidence of a client's on going criminal conduct that has only financial consequences, e.g., securities fraud.

Note on the CCBE Code of Conduct for Lawyers

Some Member State professional rules for lawyers attempt to articulate ethical standards; some indicate a responsible mode of assisting courts and other instruments of justice; others attempt to protect client interests; others relate to the organization of the profession and protection of its reputation; and still other rules simply reflect traditional modes of practicing law in a Member State which need to be reexamined. Finally, some national rules, while perfectly appropriate for domestic legal practice, may not be sufficiently founded on "general good" considerations to represent justifiable limitations on cross-border legal practice.

Article 4 of the Lawyers' Services Directive does not conclusively determine the set of rules that should prevail in the event of conflict between host and home State rules of professional conduct. There is certainly a significant risk of such conflicts. For example, Member State professional rules for lawyers vary considerably on a wide variety of subjects: the permissibility of contingent fees; the application of fixed fee rates to various services; the right to sue for fees; the handling of client funds; the necessity for professional insurance and its scope; the permissibility of advertising or other public relations; the extent of the attorney-client privilege or professional secrecy; and the nature and extent of conflict of interest rules.

In an effort to reduce the risk of conflicts, the Council of Bars and Law Societies (CCBE) (comprised of all those in Member States and some neighboring ones) adopted on October 28, 1988, a Code of Conduct for Lawyers in the European Community. The Code was rapidly adopted by Member State authorities in all Community States.

The Code of Conduct is intended to set core principles for certain professional and ethical rules in a cross-border practice context, on matters such as confidential communications, conflicts of interest, respect for courts, protection of client funds, and malpractice insurance.In some cases, the Code does not try to harmonize concepts, but rather establishes a rule for the resolution of conflicts. Thus, it would require the service-providing lawyer to follow the host State rules on advertising, on contingent fees, and on the incompatibility of a lawyer's functioning in certain roles, such as membership on a corporation's board of directors. Home State rules are to be followed with respect to fee arrangements other than contingent fees.

Although many issues of potential conflict between home and host rules are only partially resolved, or not resolved at all, the Code of Conduct is quite valuable in promoting the resolution of some significant differences between national rules of professional conduct. For the text of the 1988 Code and an analysis by a CCBE expert, see J. Toulmin, A Worldwide Common Code of Professional Conduct?, 15 Ford. Int'l L.J. 673 (1991–1992). For a comparison of the CCBE Code of Conduct with US ethical rules, see L. Terry, Introduction to the EC's Legal Ethics Code, 7 Georgetown J. Legal Ethics 1 (1993).

D. COMMUNITY RULES CONCERNING ALL PROFESSIONS

1. THE MEDICAL PROFESSIONS

Reyners and *van Binsbergen* required host State authorities to treat professionals without discrimination on the basis of nationality. Still, this represented only partial progress. Before claiming either a right to perform services or to practice while residing in a host State, professionals had to prove that their other qualifications or credentials were substantially equal to those required for the comparable host State professionals. Obviously, this made the adoption of harmonization directives crucial.

The breakthrough for doctors came with Council Directive 75/363, O.J. L 167/14 (June 30, 1975), which established minimum standards for medical education and the diplomas granted on the completion of this education, and Council Directive 75/362, O.J. L 167/1 (June 30, 1975), which required mutual recognition of these diplomas. Because the Community had over 500,000 doctors at the time these directives were adopted, they had a major impact. The Council adopted similar directives with regard to nurses, dentists and veterinarians in the late 1970s and pharmacists in 1985.

These directives followed a common approach. First, they harmonized the professional education and training standards throughout the Community, effectively setting a basic floor of qualifications for all members of the profession in question. This made it relatively easy for these professionals to meet the requirements of practice in different Member States. Second, the medical professions directives required Member States to accept the diplomas of higher educational institutions in other Member States, thus enabling a foreign-trained professional to obtain fairly readily a host State license to practice. Incidentally, although consideration was given to allowing the host State to require proof of fluency in the host language, no provision to this effect was adopted. The directives tacitly assume that the foreign professional will attain sufficient knowledge of the host State language to be able to practice competently.

An issue beyond the coverage of the directives that occasionally arises is the scope of the monopoly on medical treatment States may accord to doctors.

CRIMINAL PROCEEDINGS AGAINST MAC QUEN

Case C–108/96, [2001] ECR I–837.

[A 1964 Belgian law governing the profession of opticians prescribes their activities to be the selling or repairing of optical articles designed to correct or improve vision and the filling of prescriptions from ophthalmologists for the purpose of correcting vision. A 1989 Belgian Supreme Court judgment held that opticians could not examine their client's vision other than by a method in which the client alone indicates any sight defects (e.g., by means of a chart viewed through lenses with different levels of strength). Mac Quen, manager of Grandvision, a Belgian subsidiary of a UK company, was prosecuted after the subsidiary offered a variety of eyesight examinations for vision defects through the use of modern technical equipment and computers, all permissible in the UK. The trial court asked the Court of Justice whether the Belgian limitations on opticians' services provided by the subsidiary violated the right of establishment of the UK parent. The Court initially noted that no EC directive harmonized national rules governing opticians.]

26 According to the Court's case-law, however, national measures liable to hinder or make less attractive the exercise of fundamental freedoms guaranteed by the Treaty can be justified only if they fulfil four

conditions: they must be applied in a non-discriminatory manner; they must be justified by overriding reasons based on the general interest; they must be suitable for securing the attainment of the objective which they pursue; and they must not go beyond what is necessary in order to attain that objective [citing *Gebhard*].

28   [T]he protection of public health is one of the reasons which may, under Article 46(1) EC), justify restrictions [on] foreign nationals. Protection of public health is therefore, in principle, also capable of justifying national measures which apply indiscriminately, such as those in this case.

* * *

30   The choice of a Member State to reserve to a category of professionals holding specific qualifications, such as ophthalmologists, the right to carry out objective eyesight examinations on their patients using sophisticated instruments that make it possible to assess internal eye pressure, determine the field of vision or analyse the condition of the retina, may be regarded as an appropriate means by which to ensure attainment of a high level of health protection.

31   That being so, it is necessary to consider whether the prohibition under challenge is necessary and proportionate to secure the objective of attaining a high level of health protection.

32   While it acknowledges the importance of public health, Grandvision denies that the mere fact that ophthalmologists have higher professional qualifications than opticians is such as to justify objective examinations of purely optical defects being reserved to them. It has not, Grandvision submits, been established that the use of those instruments by opticians involves a risk to public health, particularly bearing in mind the fact that the activities at issue in the main proceedings are lawful in other Member States even when carried out by opticians who are not qualified medical doctors.

33   [T]he fact that one Member State imposes less strict rules than another Member State does not mean that the latter's rules are disproportionate and hence incompatible with Community law.

34   The mere fact that a Member State has chosen a system of protection different from that adopted by another Member State cannot affect the appraisal as to the need for and proportionality of the provisions adopted.

35   [H]owever,* * *the prohibition under challenge, which is relied on in the main proceedings as the basis for criminal charges, is not expressly provided for by any legislative provision of national law but follows rather from the interpretation which the Belgian Supreme Court gave in 1989 to a number of relevant national provisions with a view to attaining a high level of protection of public health. It appears that that interpretation is based on an assessment of the risks to public health which might result if opticians were authorised to carry out certain eyesight examinations.

36 An assessment of this kind is liable to change with the passage of time, particularly as a result of technical and scientific progress. It is significant in this regard that the [Constitutional Court of Germany] concluded, in its decision of 7 August 2000, that the risks which might follow from authorising opticians to carry out certain examinations of their clients' eyesight, such as tonometry and computerised perimetry, are not such as to preclude them from conducting those examinations.

37 It is for the national court to assess, in the light of the Treaty requirements relating to freedom of establishment and the demands of legal certainty and the protection of public health, whether the interpretation of domestic law adopted by the competent national authorities in that regard remains a valid basis for the prosecutions brought in the case in the main proceedings.

NOTES AND QUESTIONS

1. Although the Court cites its doctrine that different States may protect public health interests in different ways, its reference to the evolution of technical progress and to a relevant German Constitutional Court judgement appears to be a hint that the trial court should permit opticians to carry out the examinations in question. If you were the trial court judge, how would you decide, knowing that your supreme court has not yet gone that far?

2. In Criminal proceedings against Bouchoucha, Case C–61/89, [1990] ECR I-3551, the Court held that France could include osteopathy within the sphere of medical practice, so that a French national could not rely on an osteopathy diploma obtained in the UK to practice osteopathy. The Court held that "the definition of acts restricted to the medical profession is, in principle, a matter for the Member States" (¶ 12).

3. In an early judgment interpreting the doctors' directives, Broekmeulen v. Huisarts Registratie Commissie, Case 246/80, [1981] ECR 2311, the Court established the principle that a national of one State may require his or her own State to recognize a diploma and related qualifications obtained in another State. The Court rejected Netherlands' attempt to use the internal affairs doctrine to argue that Broekmeulen had no treaty-based rights, and held that Broekmeulen's reliance on his medical degree from Belgium constituted an application of his right of free movement to study abroad.

4. Haim v. Kassenzahnarztliche Vereinigung Nordrhein, Case C–424/97, [2000] ECR 5123, involved the rules of Germany's social security system which required a dentist qualified in Belgium to speak German as a condition for practicing as a dentist in Germany. As noted above, the medical and dentist harmonization directives do not contain a requirement of competency in the host language. In agreement with the Advocate General, the Court nonetheless held:

59 [T]he reliability of a dental practitioner's communication with his patient and with administrative authorities and professional bodies constitutes an

overriding reason of general interest such as to justify making the appointment as a dental practitioner under a social security scheme subject to language requirements. Dialogue with patients, compliance with rules of professional conduct and law specific to dentistry in the Member State of establishment and performance of administrative tasks require an appropriate knowledge of the language of that State.

60 However, it is important that language requirements designed to ensure that the dental practitioner will be able to communicate effectively with his patients, whose mother tongue is that of the Member State concerned, * * * do not go beyond what is necessary to attain that objective. In this respect, it is in the interest of patients whose mother tongue is not the national language that there exist a certain number of dental practitioners who are also capable of communicating with such persons in their own language.

Do you consider the Court's approach to be the right one? To what degree does ¶ 60 affect the conclusion in ¶ 59?

5.   In the US, states require licenses for the practice of most professions, usually conditioned on the successful passage of an examination. In Dent v. West Virginia, 129 U.S. 114, 9 S.Ct. 231, 32 L.Ed. 623 (1889), the Supreme Court upheld a state license requirement for doctors against a Due Process Clause challenge as necessary "for the protection of society," but observed that the license must be based upon reasonable educational qualifications and an examination applied in a non-arbitrary manner.

2.   THE DIPLOMA RECOGNITION DIRECTIVE

The initial harmonization approach for professions suffered from two serious defects. First, it required considerable time and effort for the Commission to elaborate a commonly accepted course of studies and training for any particular profession, and then for the Council to reach agreement on the standards. (For pharmacists, this process took fifteen years from the initial Commission draft directive.) Second, for some professions the substantive materials covered in the education and training, as well as the scope of professional activities, vary so widely that it is difficult to develop a common course of studies. This is particularly the case for the legal profession, given the fundamental differences between the common law and the civil law systems, and profound differences in approach even within the civil law world.

Thus by the early 1980s, the pace of progress in attaining the rights of professionals to practice freely throughout the Community was clearly too slow, and a new approach was needed. Accordingly, in the June 1985 White Paper on Completing the Internal Market, the Commission proposed a general approach to cover all professions where the rules had not yet been harmonized. This approach, borrowed from the sphere of the free movement of goods, was to be one of mutual trust and mutual recognition: each Member State would trust the quality of higher education in every other State and recognize the other State's diplomas as being essentially equivalent to its own.

The ultimate result was Council Directive 89/48 of December 21, 1988 on a general system for the recognition of higher-education diplomas, O.J. L 19/16 (Jan. 24, 1989), commonly known as the Diploma Recognition Directive. The directive's importance can be seen from the long list of professionals covered, including accountants, lawyers, engineers, surveyors, patent agents, insurance agents, bankers, brokers, physicists, chemists, biologists, foresters, and librarians. The medical professions, pharmacists and architects continued to be covered by their specific directives.

The heart of the directive is the obligation placed on Member States to recognize any diploma or certificate awarded by a higher educational institution in any other Member State after a course of at least three years duration (art. 1(a)). Such a diploma must, generally speaking, be recognized as equivalent to a State's own higher-education diplomas when they are required for persons seeking access to a regulated profession (art. 3).

The directive applies to any Member State "national wishing to pursue a regulated profession in a host Member State in a self-employed capacity or as an employed person" (art. 2). Accordingly, a national of a non-Community state cannot benefit from the directive, even if he or she has obtained a diploma from an educational institution within the Community.

Once a foreign applicant fulfills all the conditions for admission to the host State's regulated profession, he or she will be fully integrated into that profession, using the host State professional title (art. 7). In effect, this protects the foreign professional, once admitted in the host State, from the risk of treatment as a "second-class citizen."

The principle of general recognition of diplomas has, however, important exceptions. These exceptions, described in article 4, essentially arise whenever there is a substantial difference in education and/or training between the host State and the home State of an applicant, and whenever there is a significant difference between the scope of practice between the two States involved. In the event that one of these exceptions applies, the host State may require the foreign applicant either to take an "aptitude test" to assess knowledge of certain subjects or to complete an "adaptation period" of practice of up to three years supervised by a host State professional. Accordingly, the directive's success will be determined to some degree by the leniency or rigor with which a host State decides to use aptitude tests and adaptation periods.

The Diploma Recognition Directive undoubtedly is of most value to young professionals. Increased opportunities for study in other countries, enhanced language capabilities, and social and marital ties with persons of other nationalities have all contributed to efforts by young professionals to reside and work in other States. The Community's Erasmus program, discussed in Chapter 16C, which facilitates studies in other States, also promotes professional mobility.

A useful supplement, Directive 92/51, O.J. L 209/25 (July 24, 1992), paralleled the Diploma Recognition Directive's provisions in requiring the mutual recognition of higher education certificates and diplomas awarded after less than three years. While principally of use for short term vocational training certificates, the directive may also be used to achieve the mutual recognition of masters' degrees (see *Kraus*, infra).

Both the Diploma Recognition Directive and Directive 92/51 have recently been replaced by Directive 2005/36, described below. The legislative process to adopt harmonization directives concerning professionals has been substantially modified since 1993. The Treaty of Maastricht amended EECT Article 57 to enable harmonizing directives concerning the regulation of professions to be adopted by codecision of the Council and Parliament, thus eliminating the need for Council unanimity. Subsequently EECT Article 57 was renumbered as ECT Article 47 by the Treaty of Amsterdam. Somewhat simplified, TFEU Article 53 essentially replaces ECT Article 47.

3. CREDENTIALS NOT COVERED BY DIRECTIVE 89/48 OR DIRECTIVE 92/51

KRAUS v. LAND BADEN–WÜRTTEMBERG

Case C–19/92, [1993] ECR I–1663.

[Kraus, a German national, obtained an LL.M. in 1988 from the University of Edinburgh after a year's study. A 1939 law permitted persons to use a German university degree title, but required a specific authorization from a German state in order to use the title of a degree given by a foreign university. Before granting such an authorization, the state of Baden–Württemberg required applicants to pay a 130 DM (ca. $65) fee. Kraus supplied a copy of his Edinburgh diploma, but refused to pay the fee, claiming that the German authorization procedure violated Community law. At this time, Kraus was engaged in the training period which leads to the attainment of the status of *Rechtsanwalt* (lawyer). However, Kraus had previously worked as a paid assistant to a German university professor, a post which sometimes leads toward the status of professor.

After refusal of the authorization, Kraus sued in an administrative court, which essentially asked the Court of Justice whether an authorization procedure only for foreign postgraduate degrees violated ECT Article 43, when the degree is not required for access to any profession, but could enhance the exercise of a profession.]

18   Although a postgraduate academic title is not usually a prerequisite for access to a profession, either as an employee or on a self-employed basis, the possession of such a title nevertheless constitutes * * * an

advantage for the purpose both of gaining entry to such a profession and of prospering in it.

19 Accordingly, in so far as it constitutes proof of possession of an additional professional qualification and thereby confirms its holder's fitness for a particular post, and * * * his command of the language of the country where it was awarded, a university diploma of the kind in point in the main proceedings is by its nature such as to improve its holder's chances of appointment as compared with those of other candidates who are unable to make use of any qualification supplementary to the basic education and training required for the post in question.

20 In some cases possession of a postgraduate academic title obtained in another State may even be a prerequisite for access to certain professions, where those professions require specific knowledge such as that evidenced by the diploma in question. That may be so in the case of a postgraduate diploma in law required, for example, for access to an academic career in the fields of international or comparative law.

21 Furthermore, the holder of [such] a diploma * * * may find himself in an advantageous position in the pursuit of his professional activity in so far, as through possession of that diploma, he can obtain higher remuneration or more rapid advancement or, in the course of his career, access to certain specific posts reserved to persons with particularly high qualifications.

* * *

23 It follows that the situation of a Community national who holds a postgraduate academic title which, obtained in another Member State, facilitates access to a profession or, at least, the pursuit of an economic activity, is governed by Community law, even as regards the relations between that national and the Member State whose nationality he possesses.

NOTES AND QUESTIONS

1. Although the preamble to Directive 92/51, which requires recognition of certificates obtained after less than three years' study, refers to mutual recognition of diplomas that lead to access to a profession, *Kraus* suggests that the directive might now be interpreted to encompass post-graduate degrees that only facilitate the exercise of a profession. Do you agree with the Court's conclusion that Article 43 implicitly provides rights to those who obtain Master's degrees in other Member States because they may enhance employment opportunities or professional income?

2. The Court has also given guidance on how Member States should treat persons who have acquired some qualifications in other States, but not a diploma that requires recognition. Prior to the effective date of the Diploma Recognition Directive, in Vlassopoulou v. Ministerium fur Justiz Baden–Wurttemberg, Case C–340/89, [1991] ECR I–2357, the Court held that Germa-

ny must examine the educational qualifications and professional experience of a Greek lawyer who applied to become a German lawyer, compare them with those of a German applicant, and give credit to the extent that the Greek lawyer's education and experience are comparable. Bobadilla v. Museo Nacional del Prado, Case C–234/97, [1999] ECR I–4773, followed *Vlassapoulou* in holding that Spain must consider Bobadilla's Bachelor's and Master's degrees in art history from Boston University and Newcastle Polytechnic in assessing her qualifications to become an art restorer.

4. DIRECTIVE 2005/36 ON THE RECOGNITION OF PROFESSIONAL QUALIFICATIONS

We previously noted in Chapter 14B that the Lisbon Agenda launched a legislative codification and modernization program. Accordingly, the Commission proposed a comprehensive directive to replace the Diploma Recognition Directive and the various sectoral directives. The Parliament and Council adopted Directive 2005/36 on the recognition of professional qualifications, O.J. L 255/22, (Sept. 9, 2005), which repealed the earlier directives and their amendments, but replicates most of their key substantive provisions. It does not, however, repeal either the Lawyers' Services or the Lawyers' Establishment Directive, which continue in force. Inasmuch as the 2005 directive contains long, complex provisions concerning the medical professions, accountants and pharmacists, one may wonder whether it might have been more effective to retain these sectional directives, merely updating them.

The 2005 directive contains provisions which replicate, but in greater detail, the substantive terms of the Diploma Recognition Directive, described previously. The 2005 directive continues the basic approach of mutual recognition of essentially equivalent professional qualifications (art. 13), with the use of adaptation periods and aptitude tests by the host State to compensate for any substantial differences in education or training.

The new directive makes several innovations. Articles 5–9 attempt to facilitate trans-border service-providing by professionals, although still reserving to the host State the power to apply appropriately its rules regulating the profession concerned. Article 15 authorizes two or more Member States to agree upon "common platforms" for the mode of compensating for differences in professional education or training between States for a given profession.

Like the comprehensive services directive described in Chapter 17B, the directive strives to simplify host State administrative formalities (arts. 50–52, with annexes), and encourages close cooperation between home and host State administrators (arts. 56–59). An interesting innovation, perhaps incited by the *Haim* judgment, is article 53, which requires that a professional established in a host State must possess "a knowledge of languages necessary."

Further Reading

C. Bernard, The Substantive Law of the EU: the Four Freedoms (Oxford U.P. 2004)

M. Daly & R. Goebel, eds., Rights, Liabilities and Ethics in International Legal Practice (Transnational Juris 1995)

M. Daly & R. Goebel, eds., Rights, Liabilities and Ethics in International Legal Practice (2d ed. 2005)

R. White, Workers, Establishment and Services in the European Union (Oxford U.P. 2004)

CHAPTER 19

INDUSTRIAL AND COMMERCIAL PROPERTY RIGHTS

■ ■ ■

The 1985 White Paper on Completing the Internal Market designated the field of industrial and commercial property rights as a prime area for Community legislative efforts. It was evident that the Community needed to achieve both harmonization of national rights and the creation of new types of rights in order to better achieve technological progress and commercial integration in the internal market. Moreover, as noted in Chapter 13A, EC Treaty Article 30 (renumbered as TFEU Article 36 by the Treaty of Lisbon) recognized industrial and commercial property rights as one of the exceptions permitting national rules to restrict the free movement of goods. Without harmonization, the national systems of such rights might lead to division of certain markets along national lines.

This chapter will first focus in section A on the Court of Justice's doctrines concerning the nature and scope of industrial and commercial property rights, including its acceptance of trade design rights and designations of origin as such rights. Section B describes the evolution of the Court doctrine that these rights can be "exhausted" when the products to which they apply are first placed on the market. Section C reviews the harmonization produced by the 1989 Trademark Directive and the Community-wide trademark system achieved by the 1994 Trademark Regulation. Section D concludes with a brief description of harmonization measures in the field of copyright, the unsuccessful effort to create a Community patent, and the adoption of the Biotechnological Patent Directive.

A. DETERMINATION OF RIGHTS QUALIFYING UNDER ECT ARTICLE 30 (NOW TFEU ARTICLE 36)

A natural first question is how to define the concept "industrial and commercial property rights." (Modern American authorities tend to prefer the generic title, intellectual property rights, but, for the sake of consistency, we shall use the Treaty terminology.)

The three traditional categories of such rights, recognized by all modern free-enterprise legal systems, are patents, trademarks and copyrights. Patent rights grant exclusive rights to inventors for the exploitation of their inventions for a period of years (usually 20). Trademark rights grant to the originators of marks exclusive rights for the exploitation of words or symbols in conjunction with specified products or services, either for a term, or in perpetuity. Copyright rights grant to authors or artists exclusive rights for the representation and reproduction of a written work, a theatrical or cinematographic production, a piece of music, an art object, and, more recently, software programs, for a long term of years (usually 50 or more). In each case, this legal monopoly exploitation right is granted as a reward for the benefit to society generally, and/or to industry and commerce, through the creation of the invention, mark, or written, musical or artistic work. Not surprisingly, Member States' legal systems initially had different approaches as to the precise definition of the rights, their acquisition, term, scope, administration, etc.

Inevitably, the Court of Justice was called upon to interpret and apply the Treaty rules in this sector. There are several major issues in the interplay between national industrial and commercial property rights and the Community principle of free movement of goods. The first is the determination of those national rights which qualify for recognition under Article 30. The second issue is the demarcation of the scope and level of protection of industrial and commercial property rights. Third is the issue of whether, and when, the exercise of these rights can be said to be "exhausted." A fourth issue is the level of the appropriate exploitation of these rights within the context of Community competition rules, a topic covered in Chapter 22, infra.

Note that the US has national legislation defining the nature and scope of patents, trademarks and copyrights, so that state rules do not, generally speaking, restrict the exploitation of these rights on the national marketplace. Hence there is no precise American analogue to many of the issues facing the Community.

The absence of a Treaty definition of industrial and commercial property rights makes it difficult to decide whether a national right should qualify for Article 30 protection, particularly when the right is protected in only one Member State, or a few States. Confronted with this issue, the Court of Justice might have emphasized the fundamental importance of the principle of free movement of goods and accordingly declined to recognize a particular type of right as one qualifying for Article 30 protection unless the right is one traditionally recognized in a substantial number of Member States. In fact, the Court did not take that approach, but rather has been quite deferential to each State's legal system in this regard.

That patents and trademarks, the quintessential industrial and commercial property rights, should qualify for the Article 30 exception was obvious. Copyright posed more of a problem, since some national systems classified it as an artistic or literary property right, rather than as an industrial or commercial property right. However, music copyright was implicitly recognized as qualifying under Article 30 in Deutsche Grammophon v. Metro, Case 78/70, [1971] ECR 487, and expressly recognized as so qualifying in Musik–Vertrieb v. GEMA, Cases 55 & 57/80, [1981] ECR 147.

1. TRADE DESIGN RIGHTS

Whether to classify trade design rights as industrial and commercial property rights posed greater difficulty. The Court first dealt with the issue in Keurkoop v. Nancy Kean Gifts, Case 144/81, [1982] ECR 2853. When Keurkoop imported handbags from Germany into the Netherlands, Nancy Kean Gifts obtained an injunction to prevent their sale on the basis of its registered design for a handbag which the imports allegedly infringed. In response to an appellate court's referral of questions, the Court of Justice held that trade design rights constituted a form of industrial and commercial property rights (¶ 14). Accordingly, the owner of a registered design could bar the marketing of imported products "identical in appearance to the protected design" (¶ 22).

A subsequent case raised more complex issues.

CONSORZIO ITALIANO v. REGIE NATIONALE DES USINES RENAULT

Case 53/87, [1988] ECR 6039.

[The French automobile manufacturer, Renault, obtained in Italy design rights for spare parts, allegedly ornamental in character. An Italian trade association of producers of automotive spare parts, the Consorzio Italiano, sued to have Renault's design rights declared void, so that the Italian competing producers could market spare parts for sale in Italy or export sale within the Community. The Italian court referred questions concerning Article 30.]

4   The national court considers that protective rights in respect of an ornamental design for the car bodywork parts are in conformity with Italian law. However, it considers that the exercise of the exclusive rights deriving therefrom appears, in this instance, to be contrary to the provisions of the Treaty.

5   It points out * * * that a return for the proprietor of the rights is already guaranteed by the exclusive rights in respect of the bodywork as a whole and that protection of separate bodywork components is therefore unjustified. It adds that Renault * * * enjoys a monopoly which enables it to eliminate competition from independent manufacturers of spare parts, and at the same time to continue to charge high prices.

6   [T]he national court [considers] that the protective rights vested in Renault may constitute a means of arbitrary discrimination or a

disguised restriction on trade between Member States within the meaning of Article [30] of the Treaty.

* * *

10 [First,] as the Court held in Keurkoop v. Nancy Kean Gifts, with respect to the protection of designs and models, in the present state of Community law and in the absence of Community standardization or harmonization of laws the determination of the conditions and procedures under which such protection is granted is a matter for national rules. It is for the national legislature to determine which products qualify for protection, even if they form part of a unit already protected as such.

11 [T]he authority of a proprietor of a protective right in respect of an ornamental model to oppose the manufacture by third parties, for the purposes of sale on the internal market or export, of products incorporating the design or to prevent the import of such products manufactured without its consent in other Member States constitutes the substance of his exclusive right. To prevent the application of the national legislation in such circumstances would therefore be tantamount to challenging the very existence of that right.

12 [R]estrictions on imports or exports justified on grounds of the protection of industrial and commercial property are permissible provided that they do not constitute a means of arbitrary discrimination or a disguised restriction on trade between the Member States. * * * [I]n the light of the documents before the Court * * * the exclusive right granted by the national legislation to the proprietors of protective rights in respect of ornamental models for car bodywork components may be enforced, without distinction, both against those persons who manufacture spare parts within national territory and against those who import them from other Member States, and such legislation is not intended to favour national products at the expense of products originating in other Member States.

13 Accordingly, * * * the rules on the free movement of goods do not preclude the application of national legislation under which a car manufacturer who holds protective rights in an ornamental design in respect of spare parts intended for cars of its manufacture is entitled to prohibit third parties from manufacturing parts covered by those rights for the purpose of sale on the domestic market or for exportation or to prevent the importation from other Member States of parts covered by those rights which have been manufactured there without his consent.

NOTES AND QUESTIONS

1. It is perhaps not surprising that the Court of Justice classified trade design rights as a type of industrial and commercial property, since most States protected trade designs, although some did so as a right analogous to

patents, and others as a right analogous to copyright. Do you think a State ought to have unfettered discretion to designate rights as industrial or commercial property rights, and to specify the persons entitled to acquire them, or that there should be some Community law minimum standard for this, just as there is in the Court's review of State health and safety rules that limit imports?

2.   A trade design for an automobile spare part may be very valuable indeed, given the large market not only for completed automobiles but also for spare parts for repairs. Consorzio Italiano argued that gross sales of spare parts in the Community in 1984 equaled $30 billion. Since an automobile manufacturer already receives an economic return for the sale of the automobile, the national court considered that the Italian law's creation of trade design protection for spare parts constituted a disproportionate use of Article 30. Are you satisfied with the Court of Justice's handling of this issue? Think about this question again after reading the exhaustion of rights cases in section D.

3.   After years of debate, Directive 98/71 on the legal protection of designs, O.J. L 289/28 (Oct. 28, 1998), harmonized national rules on the nature of design rights, their term of protection (from five to twenty-five years) and grounds for invalidity. Design rights are possible for jewelry, cars, furniture, consumer electronics, machinery, tools and many other products. The chief dispute during the drafting of the directive concerned the treatment of automotive spare parts. A Commission proposal to require car manufacturers to grant a compulsory license to spare parts producers for a "fair and reasonable remuneration" failed. The directive in recital 19 indicates that States will retain their present rules governing spare parts, which in many States permit car manufacturers to retain their design right monopoly over spare parts. Would you have supported the proposal for a compulsory license, which would have enabled competition in the spare parts market, while still granting the car producer a royalty on the parts?

Supplementing the Design Directive is Regulation 6/2002, O.J. L 3/1 (Jan. 5, 2002), on registered Community designs, which enables trade designs to be registered, if new and individual in character, with the Office for Harmonization in the Internal Market, which is already used for the registration of Community Trademarks (see infra). Registration grants exclusive rights to use or license the design anywhere in the Union for up to 25 years.

4.   Omitted from the excerpt of the *Consorzio* judgment is discussion of an important competition law issue. The monopoly granted by a national industrial or commercial property law to the owner of the right is a classic example of a potential dominant position on a competitive marketplace. Article 82 of the Treaty does not forbid a dominant position as such, but it does forbid its abuse. Accordingly, an industrial or commercial property owner's legal monopoly right does not violate Article 82, but the exercise of such a right may be deemed an abuse of the dominant position, especially when the exercise is considered to go beyond the essence of the right. See the discussion of the limits placed by Community competition law on the exercise of industrial and commercial property rights in Chapter 22.

2. DESIGNATIONS OF ORIGIN

Many European states have long protected references to the region in which certain products originate, commonly called designations or appellations of origin (e.g., Champagne or Cognac). These are not trademarks or trade names, because they do not identify a specific product, nor do they represent property rights as such. States protect designations of origin because they are deemed to serve a useful role in identifying to consumers products considered to possess special characteristics or higher quality.

Under Community law, the question immediately arises whether designations of origin may nonetheless be evaluated as sufficiently analogous to industrial and commercial product rights to warrant protection under Article 30. The favorable reference to appellations of origin in the Court of Justice's 1975 *Sekt and Weinbrand* judgement, *supra* page 445, suggested that they would so qualify. Only recently, however, has the question been unequivocally resolved.

Within the scope of the Common Agricultural Policy, the Council adopted Regulation 823/87 on quality wines produced in specified regions, O.J. L 84/59 (March 27, 1987), and later Regulation 2081/92 on designations of origin for agricultural products, O.J. L 208/1 (July 24, 1992). Both were intended to promote agricultural products and to provide clear and reliable information to consumers, while ensuring fair competition between producers. Article 2 of the 1992 Regulation limits designations of origin to the name of a region or place when the products concerned have characteristics "essentially or exclusively due to a particular geographical environment with its inherent natural and human factors" and the products are processed or manufactured in that geographic area. The Regulation sets up a system of Community registration (articles 5–7) and forbids the registration of generic names. The quality wine regulation's terms are essentially analogous, although setting more rigorous standards for verification of quality. Recently the quality wine regulation was repealed and its provisions absorbed into Regulation 491/2009, O.J. L 154/1 (June 17, 2009), on the common organisation of agricultural markets, and the designation of origin regulation codified in Regulation 510/2006, O.J. L 93/12 (Mar. 31, 2006).

The two regulations provide a substantial degree of legal certainty to a field of great practical importance in the European market place. Not surprisingly, the Court of Justice has had occasion to interpret the regulations and fit them into the context of free movement of goods.

BELGIUM v. SPAIN

(Rioja wine)

Case C–388/95, [2000] ECR I–3123.

[Since 1970, Spain has had rules permitting wine to be granted a "controlled designation of origin," which not only sets the conditions for qualifying wine from a specified region, but also requires that the wine be bottled in wine cellars within that region. Wine from the Rioja region was so qualified in 1991. Spain considers the regional bottling obligation to be justified under the wine quality regulation, which permits States to supplement the regulation's rules by others, "taking into account fair and traditional practices." Belgium used Article 227 to sue Spain, contending that the bottling obligation prevented the export of wine in bulk for bottling in Belgium, a violation of Article 29. The Court of Justice easily found that the regional bottling requirement represented a restriction on exports and then turned to the question of its justification.]

53   Community legislation displays a general tendency to enhance the quality of products within the framework of the common agricultural policy, in order to promote the reputation of those products, through *inter alia,* the use of designations of origin which enjoy special protection. That general tendency has become apparent in the quality wines sector * * *.

54   Designations of origin fall within the scope of industrial and commercial property rights. The applicable rules protect those entitled to use them against improper use of those designations by third parties seeking to profit from the reputation which they have acquired. They are intended to guarantee that the product bearing them comes from a specified geographical area and displays certain particular characteristics.

55   They may enjoy a high reputation amongst consumers and constitute for producers who fulfil the conditions for using them an essential means of attracting custom.

56   The reputation of designations of origin depends on their image in the minds of consumers. That image in turn depends essentially on particular characteristics and more generally on the quality of the product. It is on the latter, ultimately, that the product's reputation is based.

57   It must be observed that a quality wine is a very specific product, a fact not contested in relation to Rioja wine. Its particular qualities and characteristics, which result from a combination of natural and human factors, are linked to its geographical area of origin * * *.

58   The rules governing the Rioja [controlled designation of origin] are designed to uphold those qualities and characteristics. By ensuring that operators in the wine growing sector of the Rioja region * * * control bottling as well, they pursue the aim of better safeguarding the quality of the product and, consequently, the reputation of the designation * * *.

* * *

61   * * * [I]t is undisputed that the bottling of wine is an important operation which, if not carried out in accordance with strict requirements, may seriously impair the quality of the product. Bottling does not involve merely filling empty containers but normally entails,

before filling, a series of complex oenological operations (filtering, clarifying, cooling, and so on) which, if not carried out in accordance with the prescribed rules of the trade, may adversely affect the quality and alter the characteristics of the wine.

* * *

63   [Belgium contends nonetheless that] the bulk transport and bottling of wine outside the region may be carried out under conditions such as to safeguard its quality and reputation.

64   On the basis of the information produced to the Court in this case, it must be accepted that, in the best conditions, a wine's characteristics and quality may indeed be maintained when it has been transported in bulk and bottled outside the region of production.

65   However, in the case of bottling, the best conditions are more certain to be assured if bottling is done by undertakings established in the region of those entitled to use the designation and operating under their direct control, since they have specialised experience and thorough knowledge of the specific characteristics of the wine in question * * *.

* * *

74   [Accordingly,] the risk to which the quality of the product finally offered to consumers is exposed is greater where it has been transported and bottled outside the region of production than when those operations have taken place within the region.

NOTES AND QUESTIONS

1.   *Rioja wine* is a rare example of an ECT Article 227 proceeding, a direct dispute in the Court of Justice between Member States (see Chapter 11D), as well as a rare example of a measure equivalent to an export ban forbidden by ECT Article 29. It is also rare in that the Court effectively overruled a prior judgment, Etablissements Delhaize/Promalvin, Case C–47/90, [1992] ECR I–3669, which had held that regional bottling of Rioja wine was not essential to preserve its characteristics. In ¶ 52, the Court stated that "new information" warranted its change of view. The issue is manifestly a close one—with which side do you agree? The judgment's greatest importance is the unequivocal declaration in ¶ 54 that designations of origin constitute a type of industrial and commercial property rights. American intellectual property experts are unlikely to agree, because in the US unfair competition law principles constitute the legal basis for the protection of designations of origin.

2.   In Pike v. Bruce Church, 397 U.S. 137, 90 S.Ct. 844, 25 L.Ed.2d 174 (1970), the Arizona Fruit and Vegetable Standardization Act required cantaloupes grown in Arizona to be packed there as well in order to identified as of Arizona origin. Arizona contended the rule was needed to prevent deceptive packaging. Although recognizing the validity of the consumer interest, the Supreme Court applied its balancing test, and concluded that Arizona's

interest was minimal in comparison to the burden on interstate commerce. The Supreme Court declared that it "viewed with particular suspicion state statutes requiring business operations to be performed in the home State that could more efficiently be elsewhere." How do you think the Supreme Court would decide a case similar to *Rioja wine*, or the Court of Justice an analogue to *Pike*?

3.   The Court applied its reasoning in *Rioja Wine* in Consorzio del Prosciutto di Parma v. Asda Stores, Case C–108/01, [2003] ECR I–5121. A UK supermarket sold Parma ham that had been sliced and packaged outside Italy. A 1990 Italian law required that ham qualified as Parma ham (registered by the Commission as a designation of origin under Regulation 2081/92) only if it was sliced and packaged in the Parma region under supervision by Parma ham trade association inspectors. When the trade association sued in the UK to enjoin Asda from further sale of its Parma ham, the issue went to the House of Lords which referred questions under ECT Article 234. The Court concluded that slicing and packaging under supervision in the Parma region better safeguarded "the quality and authenticity of the product" (¶ 65), and therefore justified the Italian rule which otherwise constituted a restriction on exports under Article 29. Would you agree?

When the 1992 directive on designations of origin was amended in 2003 to make various technical improvements, the new Regulation 692/2003, O.J.L. 99/1 (Apr. 8, 2003), expressly permits a specification that a registered product must be packaged or bottled in the region of origin to safeguard quality.

4.   In Denmark v. Commission (Feta cheese), Case C–289/96, [1999] ECR I–1541, Denmark, France and Germany challenged a Commission decision that Feta cheese (soft white cheese soaked in brine) could be registered as a designation of origin by Greece under Regulation 2081/92. Supporting the Commission's decision were the facts that Feta cheese originated centuries ago in Greece and the southern Balkans, that Greece produced around three-quarters of all Feta cheese, and that 50% of those responding in a 1994 Eurobarometer survey identified it as originating in Greece. In reply, Denmark demonstrated that it has produced Feta cheese since 1963 under the name "Danish feta," and contended that Feta had become a generic name for cheese (like Edam or Emmenthal). The Court annulled the Commission decision and instructed it in further proceedings to consider "traditional fair practice and ... the likelihood of confusion," as well as the fact that non-Greek products had been legally marketed under the Feta cheese name throughout the Community for many years prior to the effective date of the Regulation.

Subsequently, in Germany v. Commission (Feta cheese), Cases C–465 and 466/02, [2005] ECR I–9115, the Court endorsed the Commission's final determination that Feta cheese qualified as a designation of origin for cheese produced in Greece on its mainland and the island of Lesbos, but not other Greek islands. Although "Feta" does not refer to a geographic region, it can still be registered under the regulation's article 2(3) as a traditional non-geographic name, in use since the seventeenth century. The Commission also found that Greece produced two thirds of all Feta cheese, and most of the cheese produced was consumed in Greece. That other States had produced smaller quantities of cheese marketed under the Feta name since the 1930s did not make the name generic.

5. Protecting designations of origin is an important Community concern in international trade. Settling a long-standing issue, on March 25, 1994 the EC and the US exchanged letters indicating their agreement that the US would protect "Scotch Whiskey," "Irish Whiskey," "Cognac," "Armangnac" and other names for well-known Community products, while the Community would protect "Tennessee Whiskey," "Bourbon Whiskey" and "Bourbon" for US products. O.J. L 157/36 (June 24, 1994). In the current Doha Round of WTO agricultural negotiations, the Community is requesting that 40 of its designations of origin should be protected in other nations, but its proposal appears unlikely to be accepted.

B. SCOPE AND PROTECTION OF INDUSTRIAL AND COMMERCIAL PROPERTY RIGHTS

1. PROPER PROTECTION OF NATIONAL RIGHTS

Once an industrial or commercial property right is recognized under ECT Article 30 (now TFEU Article 36), the next question concerns its proper scope and protection.

When a Member State law grants a monopoly of exploitation to the owner of such a right, it follows that the owner may forbid any unauthorized third party, or infringer, from any sale, use or other exploitation within that State. If an industrial or commercial property right has considerable economic significance, the owner in one State usually seeks to obtain parallel protection in all of the other States of the Union. This is not always possible, either because someone else has prior conflicting rights in another State, or because another State does not protect the right, or imposes differing requirements for recognition of the right.

In a leading early judgment, Parke, Davis v. Probel, Case 24/67, [1968] ECR 55, a major US pharmaceutical manufacturer held a Dutch patent for an antibiotic. Under Italian patent law at that time, patents were not available for pharmaceuticals. (Some developing countries even today contend that the social interest in having inexpensive drugs on the market outweighs the claim of a pharmaceutical inventor to a patent reward for its ingenuity and expense.) A Dutch drug wholesaler tried to sell the antibiotic, which had been lawfully produced in Italy by a company unrelated to Parke, Davis. The Court of Justice held that Parke, Davis could properly invoke Article 30 to bar any unauthorized sale of an infringing product in the Netherlands, even when the product was lawfully manufactured and marketed in another State.

Similarly, in EMI Electrola GmbH v. Patricia, Case 341/87, [1989] ECR 79, a British company, EMI Records, owned the reproduction and distribution rights to records made in 1958 by a popular British singer, Cliff Richard. The Danish copyright expired in 1983, after 25 years, but the German copyright continued until 1990. Because the records were in the public domain in Denmark, anyone could freely make and sell them there. A competitor of EMI made re-recordings of Richard's 1958 records in Denmark and tried to sell them in Germany. The Court of Justice held that EMI could rely on the longer German copyright term to bar the imports. Partly to prevent similar controversies, Directive 93/98 was adopted to harmonize the term of copyrights throughout the Community. See section D1.

Because *Parke, Davis* and *EMI Electrola* remain good law, they create the risk that the Union market can be effectively divided into national markets whenever unrelated parties have acquired identical or similar patent, trademark or copyright rights in different states. This happens not infrequently with regard to trademarks, when a mark owner in State A commences marketing in State B, where an unrelated party owns the same or a confusingly similar mark. An issue of great importance is how, under Community law, one should determine whether the two marks are indeed confusingly similar.

TERRAPIN (OVERSEAS) v. TERRANOVA INDUSTRIE
Case 119/75, [1976] ECR 1039.

[Terranova is a German company owning in Germany the registered trademarks "Terra" and "Terranova" for the category of construction materials. Terrapin is a UK company owning in the UK the registered trademark "Terrapin." Terrapin commenced selling prefabricated houses and components for the construction of such houses in Germany, using "Terrapin" as its mark and trade name. Terranova sued to enjoin the use of "Terrapin" either as a trademark or trade name. The German Supreme Court concluded that the two trademarks and trade names were confusingly similar under German law principles, but asked the Court of Justice whether Terrapin might have Treaty-based rights.]

7   [I]n the present state of Community law an industrial or commercial property right legally acquired in a Member State may legally be used to prevent under the first sentence of Article [30] of the Treaty the import of products marketed under a name giving rise to confusion where the rights in question have been acquired by different and independent proprietors under different national laws. If in such a case the principle of the free movement of goods were to prevail over the protection given by the respective national laws, the specific objective of industrial and commercial property rights would be undermined. In the particular situation the requirements of the free movement of goods and the safeguarding of industrial and commercial property rights must be so reconciled that protection is ensured for the legitimate use of the rights conferred by national laws, coming within the prohibitions on imports "justified" within the meaning of Article [30] of the Treaty, but denied on the other hand in respect of any improper

exercise of the same rights of such a nature as to maintain or effect artificial partitions within the common market.

NOTES AND QUESTIONS

1. The United Kingdom argued in support of Terrapin that there would have been no confusion of the two marks if UK trademark principles were applied, and that the German standards for confusion were too strict. The UK urged the Court to state that Community law required an examination to ensure that minimum standards for appraising confusion be applied. The Court obviously did not do this. As we shall see in Section C infra, the 1989 Trademark Directive did delineate circumstances in which the owner of a prior trademark can prevent confusion arising from the exploitation of an identical or similar subsequent mark, but the issue of confusion continues to arise frequently in Court judgments. An amusing point is that the German court's finding that "Terrapin" and "Terranova" are similar was in part based on a belief that both came from the Latin root "terra," meaning "earth." This is simply wrong, as in fact the word "terrapin" comes from the Algonquin Indian name for a turtle.

2. EXHAUSTION OF RIGHTS DOCTRINE

The most controversial aspect of Community law on industrial and commercial property rights is the exhaustion of rights doctrine. The essential idea is quite simple. An industrial or commercial property right owner has a monopoly over its economic exploitation. However, ECT Article 30, as an exception to the free movement of goods principle, should be read strictly, and the exercise of industrial or commercial property rights should be narrowly construed so as to be proportionate to the end served. Thus, once the owner has initially exploited its right by obtaining some form of economic reward as to a specific product, the economic monopoly ends: it has been "exhausted." This "exhaustion" concept is applied by many modern national legal systems (including the US) in their internal markets, but not in all, and is, of course, not even hinted at in the Treaty.

The exhaustion of rights doctrine made its first appearance in Deutsche Grammophon GmbH v. Metro, Case 78/70, [1971] ECR 487. The Court of Justice held that when Deutsche Grammophon, owner of a German music copyright, sold records through its French subsidiary in Alsace, it could not take advantage of Article 30 to bar the re-import and resale of the records in Germany. This doctrine sparked a controversy which erupted in full vigor in the next case, involving the pharmaceutical industry.

CENTRAFARM v. WINTHROP

Case 16/74, [1974] ECR 1183.

[Sterling Drug manufactured and sold in the UK a drug under the trademark, "Negram." Sterling's wholly-owned Dutch subsidiary Winthrop customarily marketed the drug, also under the trademark "Negram," in the Netherlands. A Dutch pharmaceutical wholesaler, Centrafarm, bought the drug in quantity in the UK and resold it in the Netherlands under the mark "Negram." The UK placed strict price controls on pharmaceuticals. Because the Netherlands did not have such price controls, Centrafarm could sell the drug at a substantial profit while still undercutting Winthrop's prices, which were nearly double those in the UK. Winthrop brought an action to enjoin the resale in the Netherlands as a trademark infringement. Centrafarm lost and appealed. The Dutch Supreme Court referred several questions to the Court of Justice.]

7   Inasmuch as it provides an exception to one of the fundamental principles of the Common Market, Article [30] in fact only admits of derogations from the free movement of goods where such derogations are justified for the purpose of safeguarding rights which constitute the specific subject-matter of this property.

8   In relation to trade marks, the specific subject-matter of the industrial property is the guarantee that the owner of the trade mark has the exclusive right to use that trade mark, for the purpose of putting products protected by the trade mark into circulation for the first time, and is therefore intended to protect him against competitors wishing to take advantage of the status and reputation of the trade mark by selling products illegally bearing that trade mark.

9   An obstacle to the free movement of goods may arise out of the existence, within a national legislation concerning industrial and commercial property, of provisions laying down that a trade mark owner's right is not exhausted when the product protected by the trade mark is marketed in another Member State, with the result that the trade mark owner can prevent importation of the product into his own Member State when it has been marketed in another Member State.

10   Such an obstacle is not justified when the product has been put onto the market in a legal manner in the Member State from which it has been imported, by the trade mark owner himself or with his consent, so that there can be no question of abuse or infringement of the trade mark.

11   In fact, if a trade mark owner could prevent the import of protected products marketed by him or with his consent in another Member State, he would be able to partition off national markets and thereby restrict trade between Member States, in a situation where no such restriction was necessary to guarantee the essence of the exclusive right flowing from the trade mark.

12 The question referred should therefore be answered to the effect that the exercise, by the owner of a trade mark, of the right which he enjoys under the legislation of a Member State to prohibit the sale, in that State, of a product which has been marketed under the trade mark in another Member State by the trade mark owner or with his consent is incompatible with the rules of the EEC Treaty concerning the free movement of goods within the Common Market.

* * *

15 [The next] question requires the Court to state, in substance, whether the trade mark owner can, notwithstanding the answer given to the first question, prevent importation of products marketed under the trade mark, given the existence of price differences resulting from governmental measures adopted in the exporting country with a view to controlling prices of those products.

16 It is part of the Community authorities' task to eliminate factors likely to distort competition between Member States, in particular by the harmonization of national measures for the control of prices and by the prohibition of aids which are incompatible with the Common Market, in addition to the exercise of their powers in the field of competition.

17 The existence of [price controls in one] Member State, however, cannot justify measures [in a second Member State] which are incompatible with the rules concerning the free movement of goods, in particular in the field of industrial and commercial property.

18 The question referred should therefore be answered in the negative.

NOTES AND QUESTIONS

1. In a parallel proceeding, Sterling Drug, which owned patents for the drug in both the UK and the Netherlands, brought an action against Centrafarm for patent infringement in the Netherlands. In replying to a preliminary reference, the Court of Justice held that Sterling Drug could not exercise its Dutch patent rights in such a case. The Court used language virtually identical to that of the *Winthrop* judgment. Centrafarm BV v. Sterling Drug Inc., Case 15/74, [1974] ECR 1147. Thus, the Community exhaustion of rights doctrine has been applied to patents, trademarks and copyright.

2. Centrafarm did not challenge the validity of Winthrop's trademark, so why isn't this a straightforward case of trademark infringement? Observe the Court's limitation of Article 30, as an exception to the fundamental principle of free movement of goods, to the narrowest exercise of a trademark right possible, an application of the principle of proportionality. The Court's approach in narrowly limiting the exercise of ECT Article 30 interests parallels that taken in limiting the protection of imperative state interests recognized under the *Cassis de Dijon* doctrine.

3. Consider paragraphs 8–11 of the judgment, analyzing the exercise of trademark rights in terms of the exhaustion doctrine. The Court of Justice is imposing an exhaustion of rights doctrine as to imported products legally

acquired under the same trademark elsewhere in the Community, on the policy ground that a broader protection of trademark exercise rights would represent a "disguised restriction on trade" forbidden by the final sentence of Article 30. The Court's conclusion reflects a concern that trademark owners might otherwise use the identical trademark in several Member States as a means to "partition off national markets." How does the exhaustion of rights doctrine prevent this from happening? Once again, Community market integration is the key policy motivation.

4. In this case, Winthrop was a wholly-owned subsidiary of Sterling. More often, a patent, trademark or copyright owner will grant licenses to independent third parties in different Community States. If the license is exclusive for an entire State, and the licensee by virtue of a clause in the license agreement attempts to bar imports of licensed products initially placed on the market in another State by the licensor or another licensee, then the license agreement will be deemed an agreement to restrict trade between Member States, and held to violate the competition law principles of Article 81(renumbered as TEFU Article 101 by the Treaty of Lisbon). This type of illegal license agreement clause (frequently called a "parallel export" or "parallel import" ban) is one of the most common violations of Article 81 and has been the subject of extensive case law ever since the landmark decision of *Consten and Grundig*, excerpted at page 825.

NOTE ON THE CONTROVERSY CONCERNING THE EXHAUSTION OF RIGHTS DOCTRINE

The Court of Justice's enunciation of the exhaustion of rights doctrine as to patents, trademarks and copyrights has great commercial significance. Substantial price differentials on various national markets, partly occasioned by the impact of government price controls in certain fields, existed in the 1970s and still exist today to a significant degree. Product fields marked by such differentials include automobiles, electronic consumer goods, pharmaceuticals, books and records.

This creates a temptation for owners of patent, trademark or copyright rights to try to use them to protect the price levels of their subsidiaries, licensees or distributors on national markets where high prices prevail. By the same token, wholesalers or retailers (such as Centrafarm) have a substantial incentive to seek to procure products in large quantities in Member States where prices are low, in order to resell them at good profits in States where prices are high.

Owners of industrial and commercial property rights complain—and not entirely without justification—that the Court's exhaustion of rights doctrine enables competing distributors to become "free riders," benefiting from the research and development, advertising, marketing, warranty protection and other costs which the owners of the rights incur. (See the discussion of distribution and "free riders" in Chapter 25, infra.) Those firms in product sectors where governmental price controls account for all or part of the price differentials complain that the Community should either eliminate these price controls or else create a Community-wide harmonized system of price controls.

A number of academic specialists in industrial and commercial property contend that the Court of Justice's exhaustion of rights doctrine fails to show proper respect for traditional concepts of these rights. (Note, however, that the Court has otherwise demonstrated great deference to idiosyncratic national law definition of industrial and commercial property rights, as manifested in *Nancy Kean* and *Consorzio*.) Commentators sympathetic to the Court's doctrine (as well as the Commission, which aggressively combats what it perceives to be abuses of industrial and commercial property rights, especially through competition law enforcement) respond that free movement of goods and Community market integration is an overriding goal. Concern for industrial and commercial property rights, just as concern for health, safety and consumer interests, must be tailored so as not excessively to hinder market integration.

Whatever view one may take on this controversy, the application of the exhaustion of rights doctrine has occasioned a complex body of case law.

CENTRAFARM v. AMERICAN HOME PRODUCTS
Case 3/78, [1978] ECR 1823.

[American Home Products (AHP) sold a drug with identical therapeutic qualities under the marks "Serenid D" in the UK and "Seresta" in the Netherlands. Because of the large price differential between the UK and the Netherlands, Centrafarm bought quantities of the drug in the UK and replaced "Serenid D" with "Seresta" before attempting to resell the drug in the Netherlands. In an injunction proceeding, the Dutch court made an Article 234 reference. The Court of Justice first discussed, in language nearly identical to that in *Winthrop*, the status of trademarks under ECT Article 30 as a limited derogation from the free movement of goods. After quoting paragraphs 7–8 of *Winthrop*, the Court then continued its analysis.]

12   [T]he precise scope of that exclusive right granted to the proprietor of the mark [is based upon] the essential function of the trade-mark, which is to guarantee the identity of the origin of the trade-marked product to the consumer or ultimate user.

13   This guarantee of origin means that only the proprietor may confer an identity upon the product by affixing the mark.

14   The guarantee of origin would in fact be jeopardized if it were permissible for a third party to affix the mark to the product, even to an original product.

15   [Therefore,] even where the manufacturer * * * is the proprietor of two different marks for the same product, [national legislation may prevent] an unauthorized third party from usurping the right to affix one or other mark to any part whatsoever of the production or to

change the marks affixed by the proprietor to different parts of the production.

* * *

17 The right granted to the proprietor to prohibit any unauthorized affixing of his mark to his product accordingly comes within the specific subject-matter of the trade-mark.

18 The proprietor of a trade-mark which is protected in one Member State is accordingly justified pursuant to the first sentence of Article [30] in preventing a product from being marketed by a third party in that Member State under the mark in question even if previously that product has been lawfully marketed in another Member State under another mark held in the latter State by the same proprietor.

19 Nevertheless it is still necessary to consider whether the exercise of that right may constitute a "disguised restriction on trade between Member States" within the meaning of the second sentence of Article [30].

20 [I]t may be lawful for the manufacturer of a product to use in different Member States different marks for the same product.

21 Nevertheless it is possible for such a practice to be followed by the proprietor of the marks as part of a system of marketing intended to partition the markets artificially.

22 In such a case the prohibition by the proprietor of the unauthorized affixing of the mark by a third party constitutes a disguised restriction on intra-Community trade for the purposes of the above-mentioned provision.

23 It is for the national court to settle in each particular case whether the proprietor has followed the practice of using different marks for the same product for the purpose of partitioning the markets.

Notes and Questions

1. Note that either party could win in the trial court, because that court has to determine whether AHP's motive in using two different marks for the same product was legitimate or improper. Exploiting the same mark for the entire Community (or indeed the entire world) is usually desirable, because it reduces advertising and marketing costs. That makes AHP's use of slightly different marks in the Netherlands and the UK look suspiciously like an effort to block parallel imports. However, sometimes, because of conflicting prior rights (as in *Terrapin*), a producer legitimately must use different marks for the same product in different countries. A producer may also legitimately use a different mark if the initial one has unfortunate connotations in another language (e.g., the inability to use the car brand "Nova" in a Spanish-speaking nation, because "no va" in Spanish means "doesn't go"). Accordingly, AHP might have had a justification for the use of different marks.

2. In the 1970s, Hoffmann–La Roche (HLR) sold its well-known drug "Valium" in different packages on different national markets. In Germany,

HLR marketed packages containing 20 to 50 tablets to consumers. In the UK, the HLR packages contained up to 500 tablets and sold at considerably lower prices. Centrafarm bought the drug in large quantities in the UK, then repackaged it into units with 1000 tablets for resale in Germany. Centrafarm put the "Valium" mark on the larger package, together with a notice that Centrafarm marketed the package. A German court found that the repackaging violated German trademark principles, but then asked the Court of Justice whether Community law would nonetheless permit Centrafarm to repackage the tablets and affix the "Valium" mark. What do you think? See Hoffmann–La Roche AG v. Centrafarm, Case 102/77, [1978] ECR 1139.

BRISTOL–MYERS SQUIBB & ORRS v. PARANOVA

[Paranova I]
Cases C–427/93, C–429/93 & C–436/93, [1996] ECR I–3457.

[Paranova, a parallel importer, developed a substantial business by buying pharmaceuticals cheaply in Greece, Portugal, Spain and the UK (all of which have price regulations), repackaging and relabeling them under the producers' trademarks, and reselling the products in Denmark. Paranova sometimes added information for users in Danish. Despite the costs involved, Paranova could sell more cheaply than the authorized distributors. Bristol–Myers and a German pharmaceutical producer sued for injunctions in Denmark. They relied heavily on the 1989 Trademark Directive's article 7 on exhaustion, which stipulated an exception to the usual exhaustion principle if the parallel importer "changed or impaired" the products. (The Trademark Directive is summarized in section C1 and reproduced in the Selected Documents.) The Court's lengthy judgment began by declaring in ¶ 36 that article 7 was not intended to change the Court's prior doctrine (and indeed could not, because Community legislation cannot deviate from free movement principles).]

40   Article 7 of the directive, like Article [30] of the Treaty, is intended to reconcile the fundamental interest in protecting trade mark rights with the fundamental interest in the free movement of goods within the common market, so that those two provisions, which pursue the same result, must be interpreted in the same way.

* * *

42   Article [30] allows derogations from the fundamental principle of the free movement of goods within the common market only in so far as such derogations are justified in order to safeguard the rights which constitute the specific subject-matter of the industrial and commercial property in question.

* * *

45   [T]he owner of a trade mark protected by the legislation of a Member State cannot rely on that legislation in order to oppose the importation or marketing of a product which was put on the market in another Member State by him or with his consent [citing Winthrop].

46   Trade mark rights are not intended to allow their owners to partition national markets and thus promote the retention of price differences which may exist between Member States. Whilst, in the pharmaceutical market especially, such price differences may result from factors over which trade mark owners have no control, such as divergent rules between the Member States on the fixing of maximum prices, * * *, or the maximum amount of medical expenses which may be reimbursed under sickness insurance schemes, distortions caused by divergent pricing rules in one Member State must be remedied by measures of the Community authorities and not by another Member State introducing measures which are incompatible with the rules on the free movement of goods [citing *Winthrop*].

47   In answering the question whether a trade mark owner's exclusive rights include the power to oppose the use of the trade mark by a third party after the product has been repackaged, account must be taken of the essential function of the trade mark, which is to guarantee to the consumer or end user the identity of the trade-marked product's origin by enabling him to distinguish it without any risk of confusion from products of different origin.

* * *

Artificial partitioning of the markets between Member States

52   Reliance on trade mark rights by their owner in order to oppose marketing under that trade mark of products repackaged by a third party would contribute to the partitioning of markets between Member States in particular where the owner has placed an identical pharmaceutical product on the market in several Member States in various forms of packaging * * *.

53   The trade mark owner cannot oppose the repackaging of the product in new external packaging when the size of packet used by the owner in the Member State where the importer purchased the product cannot be marketed in the Member State of importation by reason, in particular, of a rule authorizing packaging only of a certain size * * * or well-established medical prescription practices based, *inter alia*, on standard sizes recommended by professional groups and sickness insurance institutions.

* * *

55   The owner may, on the other hand, oppose the repackaging of the product in new external packaging where the importer is able to achieve packaging which may be marketed in the Member State of importation by, for example, affixing to the original external or inner packaging new labels * * * or by adding new user instructions or information in the language of the Member State of importation * * *.

* * *

Whether the original condition of the product is adversely affected

58 [I]t should be clarified at the outset that the concept of adverse effects on the original condition of the product refers to the condition of the product inside the packaging.

59 The trade mark owner may therefore oppose any repackaging involving a risk of the product inside the package being exposed to tampering or to influences affecting its original condition. * * *

60 As regards pharmaceutical products, * * * repackaging [is] not capable of affecting the original condition of the product where, for example, the trade mark owner has placed the product on the market in double packaging and the repackaging affects only the external layer, leaving the inner packaging intact * * *.

* * *

64 As for operations consisting in the fixing of self-stick labels to flasks, phials, ampoules or inhalers, the addition to the packaging of new user instructions or information in the language of the Member State of importation, or the insertion of an extra article, such as a spray, from a source other than the trade mark owner, there is nothing to suggest that the original condition of the product inside the packaging is directly affected thereby.

65 It should be recognized, however, that the original condition of the product inside the packaging might be indirectly affected where, for example:

    — the external or inner packaging of the repackaged product, or a new set of user instructions or information, omits certain important information or give inaccurate information concerning the nature, composition, effect, use or storage of the product, or

    — an extra article inserted into the packaging by the importer and designed for the ingestion and dosage of the product does not comply with the method of use and the doses envisaged by the manufacturer.

* * *

The other requirements to be met by the parallel importer

67 If the repackaging is carried out in conditions which cannot affect the original condition of the product inside the packaging, the essential function of the trade mark as a guarantee of origin is safeguarded. Thus, the consumer or end user is not misled as to the origin of the products, and does in fact receive products manufactured under the sole supervision of the trade mark owner.

* * *

70 Since it is in the trade mark owner's interest that the consumer or end user should not be led to believe that the owner is responsible for the repackaging, an indication must be given on the packaging of who repackaged the product.

* * *

75   Even if the person who carried out the repackaging is indicated on the packaging of the product, there remains the possibility that the reputation of the trade mark, and thus of its owner, may nevertheless suffer from an inappropriate presentation of the repackaged product.

76   In the case of pharmaceutical products, [for] which the public is particularly demanding as to the quality and integrity of the product, the presentation of the product may indeed be capable of inspiring public confidence in that regard. It follows that defective, poor quality or untidy packaging could damage the trade mark's reputation.

* * *

78   Finally, as the Court pointed out in *Hoffmann–La Roche*, the trade mark owner must be given advance notice of the repackaged product being put on sale. The owner may also require the importer to supply him with a specimen of the repackaged product before it goes on sale, to enable him to check that the repackaging is not carried out in such a way as directly or indirectly to affect the original condition of the product and that the presentation after repackaging is not likely to damage the reputation of the trade mark. Similarly, such a requirement affords the trade mark owner a better possibility of protecting himself against counterfeiting.

NOTES AND QUESTIONS

1.   During his long tenure on the Court (1988–2003), Advocate General Jacobs' expertise in the field of intellectual property rights greatly aided the Court through his analysis of complex fact patterns and his suggestions on new legal rules. This is manifest in *Paranova*, where the Court essentially followed his views. In ¶¶ 73–75 of his opinion, Advocate General Jacobs observed that the root of the problem is the wide disparity in pharmaceutical price levels due to the substantially different price restrictions and social security schemes in different States. In this state of affairs, do you think the Court has struck the proper balance between the interest of parallel importers, whose sales arguably promote an integrated European market, and the pharmaceutical producers' concern for the reputation of their trademarks, as well as for a fair return on their capital investment in research and development and on their production costs? Are the producers apt to be successful in lobbying for a Community-wide uniform system of price regulations in the pharmaceutical field?

2.   After *Paranova I*, is it fair to say that a parallel importer can usually relabel or repackage a product to meet the market needs in the State of sale, including applying the producer's trademark in that State? Note all the ways in which packages can be altered in ¶¶ 53–64. Do ¶¶ 65–68 represent signifi-

cant limitations upon the parallel importer? Do you agree with *Paranova I*, or do you think it goes too far?

3. Subsequently, in Pharmacia & Upjohn v. Paranova (Paranova II), Case C–379/97, [1999] ECR I–6927, the Court made clear that a trademark owner's use of different marks or packages in different States may constitute a partitioning of the market regardless of whether the trademark owner deliberately intended that result (¶ 36–40). This overrules *AHP's* requirement of such an intent in order to justify parallel imports.

BOEHRINGER INGELHEIM v. SWINGWARD

Case C–384/04, [2007] ECR I–3391.

[When Boehringer, a German pharmaceutical producer, sued to enjoin a parallel importer from selling its products in the UK, the High Court concluded that the parallel importers' repackaging violated the Court of Justice's standards, and enjoined their further sales. On appeal, the Court of Appeal referred a complicated set of questions concerning what sort of repackaging could be considered to be objectively necessary, who has the burden of proof concerning the necessity of repackaging, what rules govern relabelling without repackaging the imported product, and what remedies a trademark owner might obtain after a parallel importer violates his rights. The Court commenced with the relabelling issue.]

30   The change brought about by any new carton or relabelling of a trademarked medicinal product creates by its very nature real risks for the guarantee of origin which the mark seeks to protect. Such a change may thus be prohibited by the trade mark proprietor unless the new carton or relabelling is necessary in order to enable the marketing of the products imported in parallel and the legitimate interests of the proprietor are also safeguarded.

32   Accordingly, * * * Article 7(2) of Directive 89/104 must be construed as meaning that the proprietor may legitimately oppose further commercialisation of a pharmaceutical product imported from another Member State in its original internal and external packaging with an additional external label applied by the importer, unless

— it is established that reliance on trade mark rights by the proprietor in order to oppose the marketing of the overstickered product under that trade mark would contribute to the artificial partitioning of the markets between Member States;

— it is shown that the new label cannot affect the original condition of the product inside the packaging;

— the packaging clearly states who overstickered the product and the name of the manufacturer;

— the presentation of the overstickered product is not such as to be liable to damage the reputation of the trade mark and of its proprietor; thus, the label must not be defective, of poor quality, or untidy; and

— the importer gives notice to the trade mark proprietor before the overstickered product is put on sale, and, on demand, supplies him with a specimen of that product.'

[Next, the Court considered whether various types of repackaging violated the trademark owner's reputation.]

45   As the Commission correctly argues in its written observations, the fact that a parallel importer does not affix the trade mark to the new exterior carton ('de-branding') or applies either his own logo or a house-style or get-up or a get-up used for a number of different products ('co-branding'), or positions the additional label so as wholly or partially to obscure the proprietor's trade mark, or fails to state on the additional label that the trade mark in question belongs to the proprietor, or prints the name of the parallel importer in capital letters is, in principle, liable to damage the trade mark's reputation.

46   However, * * * the question whether the circumstances referred to * * * are liable to damage the trade mark's reputation is a question of fact for the national court to decide in the light of the circumstances of each case.

[Concerning the burden of proof, the Court held that the parallel importer must prove that it fulfilled the five conditions laid down in ¶ 32, supra (¶ 52). The Court finally held that the trademark owner may obtain damages when the parallel importer violated one of the five conditions. The national court should consider the extent of the damage caused to the trademark owner and decide upon a remedy that is "not only proportionate, but sufficiently effective and dissuasive" (¶ 59). This might be the remedy granted to a trademark owner against a seller of counterfeit products (¶ 63) (in practice, often an injunction plus substantial damages).]

NOTES AND QUESTIONS

1.   In her opinion, Advocate General Sharpston observed that after 30 years of caselaw, the Court's articulation of principles in this judgment should be sufficient for national courts in the future to avoid further references (¶ 3). One may certainly hope that this proves accurate. The Court largely followed her suggested response to the questions referred.

2.   Perhaps the most important part of the judgment is the Court's guidance on when types of relabelling and repackaging damage a mark's reputation. Certainly some types described in ¶ 45 appear to go too far. Do you agree with the balance struck here between market integration and the trademark owner's rights?

C. TRADEMARK HARMONIZATION AND COMMUNITY-WIDE TRADEMARK RIGHTS

When we examined the scope and protection of industrial and commercial property rights in section B, we observed that when unrelated parties have identical or similar rights in different States, the Community market can be fragmented into national markets. Two possible legislative solutions can be employed to reduce or eliminate this risk. One is to adopt a directive to harmonize the most important features of those laws, while still leaving the rights themselves a matter of national law. The second is to create a Community-wide system for a particular right. In the field of trademarks, both approaches are being used.

1. THE TRADEMARK DIRECTIVE

Legislation on trademarks represents the greatest success of the internal market program in this field. First came the adoption of Directive 89/104 to approximate laws relating to trademarks, O.J. L 140/1 (Feb. 11, 1989), effective since 1993. (See Document 23 in the Selected Documents.) A Whereas clause states that the directive is not intended to achieve "full-scale approximation," but only to harmonize those aspects of national law "which most directly affect the functioning of the internal market."

The directive covers all trademarks registered in any Member State, directly or by virtue of an international registration (art. 1). A trademark is defined as any sign, words, designs, letters, numbers, as well as the "shape of goods or their packaging" used to distinguish goods or services (art. 2). This definition is broader than the former law in some States, which did not recognize service marks, or marks based on the shape or form of packages or containers.

Article 3 harmonizes trademark registration requirements by forbidding registration of certain types of putative marks, including nondistinctive marks, deceptive marks, marks which are only descriptive of characteristics, quality, purpose or geographic origin of goods or services, marks which are contrary to public policy or morality, etc. Article 4(1) prohibits the registration of identical or similar marks in the same or a similar field of goods or services whenever "there exists a likelihood of confusion on the part of the public."

Article 5 grants the mark owner exclusive rights of exploitation within the national territory. It also entitles the owner to bring infringement actions against any sign which is identical with the mark in the field of registration, or against any sign which creates confusion as indicated in Article 4. Article 6 permits what is known as 'fair use' of the mark, e.g., when indicating "in accordance with honest practices" the purpose of a product intended as a spare part or accessory for a trademarked product.

Article 7 codifies the Court of Justice's exhaustion of rights doctrine as a limitation on infringement actions. (As noted above, the Court in *Paranova I* interpreted the directive's exhaustion of rights clause to have the same content as its prior doctrine.) Article 8 allows the mark owner to grant exclusive or non-exclusive licenses for all or only part of the field of goods or services, and for all or only part of the territory of the State concerned.

If a mark has not been put "to genuine use" within its registered field of goods or services within five years after registration, Article 10 permits the mark to be totally revoked (art. 12), or revoked as to some goods or services (art. 13), or partially invalidated (art. 11). For several States, these articles represent a significant change in law.

Directive 2008/95 on trade marks, O.J. L 299/25 (Nov. 8, 2005), slightly amends the original Trademark Directive. Virtually all the articles have retained the initial numbers and no change is substantial enough to merit reference.

Most of the questions referred to the Court of Justice concerning the Trademark Directive deal with the issue of confusion, covered in subsection 3 infra, but other directive provisions occasionally require interpretation. Thus in Matratzen Concord v. Hukla Germany, Case C–421/04, [2006] ECR I–2303, the issue was whether a Spanish entity could register "Matratzen," the German word for mattress, as a trademark for beds and related furniture in Spain. When a German competitor claimed that the word was merely descriptive and could not qualify as a trademark under article 3(1), the Court replied to the questions referred by a Spanish court by stating that "a term borrowed from the language of [another] Member State" could qualify for registration (¶ 22), but the referring court would have to decide whether "reasonably well-informed and reasonably observant and circumspect" customers would, or would not, find the word distinctive. Whatever the ultimate outcome in this case, the judgment establishes the principle that a descriptive word in one language can be a distinctive trademark in another.

In Celine Sarl v. Celine SA, Case C–17/06, [2007] ECR I–7041, the issue was whether a shop selling clothing under the name 'Celine' since 1950 was infringing the trademark, 'Celine', registered for clothes since 1948. The Court held that a company or shop name is not intended to describe goods or services, but rather the business itself, so that the name's use does not constitute an infringement of the rights of the trademark owner under article 5 of the directive (¶ 21). However, the shop owner would infringe the trademark if he put the shop name on clothing sold in the shop (¶ 22).

In Copad v. Christian Dior Couture, Case C–59/08, [2009] ECR I–3421, the Court upheld the right of Christian Dior to enforce a trademark license agreement clause which forbid the licensee to resell to discount stores. The Court held that article 8 of the directive, which authorized a licensor to enforce a clause protecting the quality of its goods, permitted protection of "the allure and prestigious image" of luxury goods, as well as their "material characteristics" (¶ 24). The national court was instructed to determine whether sale by the discount store in question would in fact detract from the products' image (¶ 32). The Court further held that the exhaustion doctrine did not bar enforcement, because resale in violation of a license clause could not be considered to be a sale with the trademark owner's consent (¶ 57).

2. THE TRADEMARK REGULATION

The Trademark Directive achieved a substantial degree of harmonization, clarifying trademark rights and eliminating some traditional peculiarities of national law. Nonetheless, the directive leaves trademark law still a matter of national law. Marks remain limited to the territory of each State, occasioning a risk of conflict between identical or similar marks recognized by different States as the marketing under the marks expands within the Community.

Obviously, a preferable approach is that of creating Community trademarks, registered only once, governed by a single set of rules, and valid throughout the entire Community (just as federally-registered trademarks are valid throughout the US). The legislative road to achieve this proved a rocky one. The Commission published a draft regulation in 1980, but only after the adoption of the Trademark Directive could serious progress be made on the regulation.

Council Regulation 40/94 on the Community trademark, O.J. L 11/1 (Jan. 14, 1994), permits persons to register a mark for the entire Community. Indeed, such a Community trademark cannot be revoked or prohibited except for the entire Community (art. 1), although it may be assigned for all or part of the Community (art. 17), or licensed, either exclusively or non-exclusively, for all or part of the Community (art. 22). The Community trademark is good for ten years, renewable for further ten year periods (art. 46). The substantive provisions of the Regulation relating to the trademark themselves essentially replicate the corresponding provisions of the Trademark Directive. The articles concerning the Trademark Office (OHIM) and its procedures are too long for summary here.

The initial Trademark Regulation was codified in Regulation 207/2009, O.J. L 78/1 (Mar. 24, 2009), but without major amendments. The Council adopted both Regulations pursuant to ECT Article 308, the implied legislative power provision, because the EC Treaty did not specifically include intellectual property rights among the Community's fields of action in Article 3. Note that the Treaty of Lisbon will avoid the use of the TFEU Article 352 that replaced EC Treaty 308, because a new TFEU Article 118 specifically grants the Parliament and Council the power to adopt "measures for the creation of European intellectual property rights," acting by codecision. However, the Council alone is to set the "language arrangement," acting unanimously after consulting the Parliament.

The Office for Harmonization in the Internal Market (Trademarks and Designs) (OHIM) opened for business on April 1, 1996, and was promptly flooded with applications for Community trademarks, almost one-third being filed by US owned enterprises. Every year thousands of applications are filed, most accepted, but some refused by the Trademark Office, or the subject of third party challenge. Because the OHIM has extensive powers in the registration process, including revocation proceedings, and a specialized trademark bar was expected to develop near the Office, several States wanted the Office site. The European Council allotted the Office to Spain, which chose Alicante, an attractive Mediterranean resort.

The OHIM has a Board of Appeal, with a further appeal possible to the Court of First Instance (art. 63), and a final appeal on the law to the Court of Justice. Since 1999, the Court of First Instance has reviewed a significant number of appeals from decisions of the Board of Appeal. Trademark appeals now represent about 25% of the CFI's caseload. The CFI has requested the Council to create a special tribunal to handle these appeals, just as staff cases are now reviewed by the Civil Service Tribunal, but thus far the Council has not acted.

Prior to its creation, there was considerable debate over how many languages the OHIM would use, because the use of each language would bring substantial translation costs. In a compromise solution, the Council decided that the OHIM would use English, French, German, Italian and Spanish as operational languages, one of which must be chosen by the applicant as a second language in addition to the applicant's own official language (art. 115).

The Trademark Regulation's provision that only five State languages would be used for operational purposes was challenged by a Dutch trademark lawyer in Kik v. OHIM, Case T–120/99, [2001] ECR II–2235. Kik filed a Community trademark application only in Dutch. When the application was rejected because it was not also filed in one of the five languages permitted, Kik appealed, claiming that the Trademark Regulation's failure to permit Dutch to be used constituted an indirect discrimination on nationality, prohibited by ECT Article 12. The Court of First Instance held that ECT Article 290 authorized the Council, acting unanimously, to set the "rules governing the languages of the institutions," which in turn enabled the Council to set the operational languages of the Trademark Office, and rejected the claim that this constituted indirect discrimination on nationality. The CFI judgment was appealed to the Court of Justice.

KIK v. OHIM

Case C–361/01, [2003] ECR I–8283.

82   As the appellant points out, the Treaty contains several references to the use of languages in the European Union. None the less, those references cannot be regarded as evidencing a general principle of

Community law that confers a right on every citizen to have a version of anything that might affect his interests drawn up in his language in all circumstances.

* * *

84   Moreover, Article [290] of the Treaty authorises the Council to determine the rules governing the languages of the institutions of the Community, acting unanimously. It was in application of that provision that it adopted Regulation No 1 * * * which lays down the official languages and working languages of the Community institutions.

* * *

88   Account must also be taken of the fact that the Community trade mark was created for the benefit not of all citizens, but of economic operators, and that economic operators are not under any obligation to make use of it.

* * *

91   Economic operators none the less have an interest in an instrument such as the Community trade mark, * * * which enables them to avoid filing multiple national trade mark applications, with all the translation costs that that entails. For persuasive evidence of that interest, it is sufficient to note the considerable number of Community trade mark applications which, surpassing initial predictions, have been filed since the Office was set up.

92   It follows from all of those facts that the language regime of a body such as the Office is the result of a difficult process which seeks to achieve the necessary balance between the interests of economic operators and the public interest in terms of the cost of proceedings, but also between the interests of applicants for Community trade marks and those of other economic operators in regard to access to translations of documents which confer rights, or proceedings involving more than one economic operator, such as opposition, revocation and invalidity proceedings.

93   The Court of First Instance was therefore right to find * * * that, in determining the official languages of the Community which may be used as languages of proceedings in opposition, revocation and invalidity proceedings, where the parties cannot agree on which language to use, the Council was pursuing the legitimate aim of seeking an appropriate linguistic solution to the difficulties arising from such a failure to agree.

NOTES AND QUESTIONS

1.   The Court's judgment is bound to be helpful in setting up language regimes for other Union bodies in the future, especially now that there are 27 official languages and 23 working languages. Note that the Civil Service Tribunal has opted to issue its judgments only in French.

2. As noted above, appeals from the OHIM constitute a substantial part of the CFI's annual caseload. The judgments usually involve technical interpretations of the Trademark Regulation. Space considerations prevent their coverage here. A significant number of the CFI's judgments are appealed on the law to the Court of Justice. The Court tends to give considerable deference to the CFI's interpretation of the regulation. See, e.g., DKV v. OHIM Case C–104/00, [2002] ECR I–7561, in which the Court affirmed the CFI's holding that 'Companyline' consisted merely of the linking of two generic words, and could not qualify as a mark in the field of insurance.

The Court of Justice did however reverse the CFI and modify the legal standard to be used in determining the distinctive character of trademarks in Procter and Gamble v. OHIM (Baby–Dry), Case C–383/99 P, [2001] ECR I–6251. The Court set the standard of "normal use from a consumer's point of view" (¶ 39) as the means of determining whether a combination of words sought to be used as a trademark were purely descriptive of the product, its purpose or characteristics, or were capable of distinguishing the product from those competitors (¶¶ 37–38). Applying this standard, the Court held that 'Baby–Dry', while certainly referring to the function of babies' diapers, nonetheless could not be said to represent "a familiar expression in the English language" and consequently did bestow a "distinctive power" to the mark (¶¶ 43–44).

In another noteworthy judgment, the Court affirmed a CFI holding that an applicant for a trademark for leather goods and clothing could not use a symbol identical to the stylized form of a maple leaf, the Canadian national emblem. The Trademark Regulation incorporates by reference a provision of the 1883 Paris Convention for the Protection of Industrial Property which prevents "flags, and other State emblems" from being used in trademarks. The Court then reversed the CFI to hold that service marks were implicitly barred as well. American Clothing Assoc. v. OHIM, Case C–202/08P, [2009] ECR I–___ (July 16, 2009). Could anyone obtain a Community trademark using a representation of Uncle Sam?

3. TRADEMARK CONFUSION AFTER THE TRADEMARK DIRECTIVE AND TRADEMARK REGULATION

Read carefully the Trademark Directive's article 4(1) on "the likelihood of confusion" with an earlier trademark as a bar to the registration of a new one, and article 5(1) on "the likelihood of confusion" with a registered trademark as the basis for an action to bar the use of an infringing mark. The Court has now set Community-wide standards for the rather elusive concept of confusion through its interpretation of the two parallel articles. The Trademark Regulation's articles 8 and 9 essentially replicate these provisions. Inasmuch as many questions relating to the issue of confusion are referred to the Court of Justice, we only present here several illustrative judgments.

SABEL v. PUMA

Case C–251/95, [1997] ECR I–6191.

[The German company, Puma, had registered a silhouette picture of a puma bounding towards the right as a trademark for leather products, handbags and clothing. When Sabel, a Dutch company, sought to register in Germany a mark composed of a silhouette picture of a cheetah bounding to the right above its name, Sabel, for the same product categories, Puma opposed the registration. On appeal, the Supreme Patent Court considered that there probably would be confusing similarity between the two marks based solely on customary German doctrine, but referred questions to the Court concerning the proper interpretation of article 4(1) of the Trademark Directive. The Court's reply not only provided guidance on the concept of confusion, but suggested that the risk of confusion in this case was minimal.]

22   Article 4(1)(b) of the Directive does not apply where there is no likelihood of confusion on the part of the public. * * * [T]he tenth recital in the preamble to the Directive [indicates] that the appreciation of the likelihood of confusion 'depends on numerous elements and, in particular, on the recognition of the trade mark on the market, of the association which can be made with the used or registered sign, of the degree of similarity between the trade mark and the sign and between the goods or services identified'. The likelihood of confusion must therefore be appreciated globally, taking into account all factors relevant to the circumstances of the case.

23   That global appreciation of the visual, aural or conceptual similarity of the marks in question, must be based on the overall impression given by the marks, bearing in mind, in particular, their distinctive and dominant components. The wording of Article 4(1)(b) of the Directive—" . . . there exists a likelihood of confusion on the part of the public" . . . —shows that the perception of marks in the mind of the average consumer of the type of goods or services in question plays a decisive role in the global appreciation of the likelihood of confusion. The average consumer normally perceives a mark as a whole and does not proceed to analyse its various details.

24   In that perspective, the more distinctive the earlier mark, the greater will be the likelihood of confusion. It is therefore not impossible that the conceptual similarity resulting from the fact that two marks use images with analogous semantic content may give rise to a likelihood of confusion where the earlier mark has a particularly distinctive character, either *per se* or because of the reputation it enjoys with the public.

25   However, in circumstances such as those in point in the main proceedings, where the earlier mark is not especially well known to the public and consists of an image with little imaginative content, the mere fact

that the two marks are conceptually similar is not sufficient to give rise to a likelihood of confusion.

LLOYD SCHUHFABRIK MEYER v. KLIJSEN HANDEL

Case C–342/97, [1999] ECR I–3819.

[Lloyd, a German manufacturer of shoes, has used the trade mark "Lloyd" since 1927. Klijsen, a Dutch manufacturer of shoes, obtained the mark "Loint's" for shoes in 1970 in the Netherlands and 1991 in Germany. When Lloyd sought to enjoin the use of "Loint's" as infringing on its German mark, the trial court referred questions concerning the application of article 5(1) of the Trademark Directive. The trial court noted that a survey indicated that 36% of those responding identified "Lloyd" as a brand of shoes. In its response, the Court provided more sophisticated and detailed criteria for determining whether confusion can occur.]

21   [F]or the purposes of art 5(1)(b) of the directive, there may be a likelihood of confusion, notwithstanding a lesser degree of similarity between the trade marks, where the goods or services covered by them are very similar and the earlier mark is highly distinctive.

22   In determining the distinctive character of a mark and, accordingly, in assessing whether it is highly distinctive, the national court must make an overall assessment of the greater or lesser capacity of the mark to identify the goods or services for which it has been registered as coming from a particular undertaking, and thus to distinguish those goods or services from those of other undertakings.

23   In making that assessment, account should be taken, in particular, of:

- the inherent characteristics of the mark, including the fact that it does or does not contain an element descriptive of the goods or services for which it has been registered;

- the market share held by the mark;

- how intensive, geographically widespread and long-standing use of the mark has been;

- the amount invested by the undertaking in promoting the mark;

- the proportion of the relevant section of the public which, because of the mark, identifies the goods or services as originating from a particular undertaking; and

- statements from chambers of commerce and industry or other trade and professional associations.

24   It follows that it is not possible to state in general terms, for example by referring to given percentages relating to the degree of recognition attained by the mark within the relevant section of the public, when a mark has a strong distinctive character.

25   In addition, the global appreciation of the likelihood of confusion must, as regards the visual, aural or conceptual similarity of the

marks in question, be based on the overall impression created by them, bearing in mind, in particular, their distinctive and dominant components. * * * [T]he perception of marks in the mind of the average consumer of the category of goods or services in question plays a decisive role in the global appreciation of the likelihood of confusion. The average consumer normally perceives a mark as a whole and does not proceed to analyse its various details [citing *Sabel*].

26 For the purposes of that global appreciation, the average consumer of the category of products concerned is deemed to be reasonably well-informed and reasonably observant and circumspect. However, account should be taken of the fact that the average consumer only rarely has the chance to make a direct comparison between the different marks but must place his trust in the imperfect picture of them that he has kept in his mind. It should also be borne in mind that the average consumer's level of attention is likely to vary according to the category of goods or services in question.

27 In order to assess the degree of similarity between the marks concerned, the national court must determine the degree of visual, aural or conceptual similarity between them and, where appropriate, evaluate the importance to be attached to those different elements, taking account of the category of goods or services in question and the circumstances in which they are marketed.

28 In the light of the foregoing, the answer to the questions referred to the court must be that it is possible that mere aural similarity between trade marks may create a likelihood of confusion within the meaning of art. 5(1)(b) of the directive. The more similar the goods or services covered and the more distinctive the earlier mark, the greater will be the likelihood of confusion.

NOTES AND QUESTIONS

1. Advocate General Jacobs, an acknowledged expert on trademarks, wrote the opinions in these and virtually all the other initial trademark cases. His careful reasoning has clearly influenced the Court's views. In ¶ 51 of his opinion in *Sabel*, he contends that in dealing with confusion in article 4(1), the directive is "laying down a common standard" which should not be set at too high a level because it is necessary to avoid "the effect of insulating the national markets". He further argued that "the directive should accordingly not be read as imposing the most restrictive standard found in the laws of member states." In ¶ 55, he contended that there must be "a genuine and properly substantiated likelihood of confusion" to justify any bar to a new mark. Does the Court's judgment follow this approach? Does it represent a better balance between the proper protection of trademarks and free movement of goods than the Court's early judgment in *Terrapin*, supra page 775?

2. The Court of Justice's more detailed guidance in *Lloyd* on how to interpret the concept of confusion still leaves considerable leeway to trial courts. Note the Court's emphasis on the "reasonably well informed and

reasonably observant" consumer standard, which we saw previously applied in the *Irish Hallmarking* judgment, supra page ___, and *Darbo*, supra page ___. Note that in ¶ 28 the Court states that aural similarity between marks may create confusion, even if there is no visual similarity. This is obviously important in comparing "Lloyd" and "Loint's." However, the trial court must make significant fact findings pursuant to ¶ 23 before reaching a final conclusion.

3.   In Ruiz–Picasso v. OHIM, Case C–361/04, [2006] ECR I–643, several of Picasso's heirs sought to prevent Daimler–Benz from registering "Picaro" as a Community trademark for cars and other vehicles on the ground that it would infringe their prior registered mark, "Picasso," in the same class. The OHIM rejected their request and the CFI affirmed. The CFI held that the pronunciation of "ss" was so different from an "r" that any visual or phonetic similarity was quite low. The CFI also held that there was no significant conceptual similarity, because "Picasso" is well-known as a reference to the renowned artist, while "Picaro" has no semantic meaning for the car-buying public. The Court of Justice affirmed both conclusions (¶¶ 22–25). The Court observed that the average consumer is apt to have a particularly high level of attention when purchasing cars, which would reduce any likelihood of confusion between the two marks (¶¶ 38–41). Note that the Court cited both *Sabel* and *Lloyd*, and essentially applied the same standard for determining confusion under the Trademark Regulation as under the Trademark Directive.

4.   Is 'Solvo' confusingly similar to 'Volvo'? The prior mark, Volvo, was registered, i.a., for computer software, while the applicant's, Solvo, was to be registered for computer programs for warehouse management systems. In Volvo v. OHIM, Case T–434/07, [2009] ECR II–___ (Dec. 2, 2009), the CFI reversed the OHIM, which found no risk of similarity, and held that the phonetic similarity of the two was so strong, with four identical letters, that they might be confusingly similar (¶ 42). The CFI then remanded the case to OHIM, in order to make an overall assessment of the likelihood of confusion by the "relevant public," which might be a relatively sophisticated "professional public" (¶¶ 48–50).

In contrast, the CFI held, affirming the OHIM, that 'Oli' was not sufficiently similar to Proctor & Gamble's well-know brand 'Olay,' because the two marks were neither visually nor aurally similar. Moreover, the applicant's mark, Oli, had a quite distinctive stylized appearance, whereas 'Olay' is composed of standard letters. Although the product categories for both marks were essentially the same or similar—soap, perfumery, cosmetic products, pharmaceutical products—the CFI agreed with OHIM's view that even average consumers would not find the two marks confusingly similar (¶ 49). See Procter & Gamble v. OHIM, Case T–240/08, [2009] ECR II–114 (July 8, 2009). Obviously, line-drawing is not easy.

5.   Arsenal Football Club v. Reed, Case C–206/01 [2002] ECR I–10273, attracted considerable attention in the UK. Arsenal, a well known football (soccer, in American usage) club in the UK, registered 'Arsenal' for a variety of clothing and footwear, produced and sold in substantial quantities. Reed sold football souvenirs from stalls near Arsenal's stadium. When Reed sold scarves marked with 'Arsenal' in large letters which had not been authorized

by Arsenal, Arsenal sued in tort for relief. Because Reed had placed a large notice disclaiming any authorization of the scarves, the trial court concluded that the scarves were perceived by consumers only as "badges of support, loyalty or affiliation." The trial court then asked the Court of Justice whether the use of a word identical with a trademark, placed on goods for which the trademark was issued, could be permitted when the seller expressly disclaimed any connection with the trademark owner. How do you think the Court should reply? Would not anyone who sees a buyer wearing the scarf (or who obtains a scarf as a gift from the buyer) think the scarf had been authorized by Arsenal?

A recent CFI judgment concerning the well-known Citibank financial group raised a different, though related issue: may the owner of marks with a high reputation in some fields prevent the registration of later marks in largely unrelated fields because they would take "unfair advantage" of the prior marks' reputation?

CITIGROUP v. OHIM

Case T–181/05, [2008] ECR II–669.

[Citigroup challenged an applicant's proposed registration of 'CITI' for services in the field of "custom agencies, property values, real estate agents, evaluation and administration of house contents." Citigroup had prior registrations of eleven Community marks in the fields of "financial services" and "real estate services," including CITIBANK, CITIBUSINESS, and THE CITI NEVER SLEEPS. The OHIM Board of Appeals held that Citigroup's only trademark with a reputation was CITIBANK, and then only for financial services. The Board then concluded that the applicant's CITI was confusingly similar in the field of real estate, but could be registered for customs services. Citigroup appealed and the CFI reversed OHIM on several grounds.]

60   Given that the services covered by the trade mark application are not similar to those for which the trade mark CITIBANK is registered, the application of Article 8(5) of Regulation No 40/94 presupposes that three conditions are satisfied, namely, first, that the marks at issue are identical or similar, second, that the earlier trade mark has a reputation, and third, that there is a risk that use without due cause of the trade mark applied for would take unfair advantage of, or be detrimental to, the distinctive character or the repute of the earlier trade mark.

61   Since those three conditions are cumulative, failure to satisfy one of them is sufficient to render inapplicable the provisions of Article 8(5) of Regulation No 40/94.

* * *

64   As regards the condition concerning whether the marks at issue are identical or similar, it is clear from the case-law of the Court of Justice in relation to the interpretation of Article 5(2) of [the Trademark

Directive] (the legislative content of which is, essentially, identical to that of Article 8(5) of Regulation No 40/94) that, to satisfy the condition concerning similarity, it is not necessary to prove that there exists, on the part of the relevant section of the public, a likelihood of confusion between the earlier mark with a reputation and the mark applied for. It is sufficient for the degree of similarity between those marks to have the effect that the relevant section of the public establishes a link between them.

65   The existence of such a link must be appreciated globally, taking into account all factors relevant to the circumstances of the case. In relation to the visual, aural and conceptual similarities, the comparison of the signs must be based on the overall impression produced by the marks, taking account, inter alia, of the distinctive and dominant elements of those marks.

66   At the visual level, the presence of the word element 'citi' in the two marks at issue results in their being somewhat similar. In addition, the fact that the trade mark applied for (CITI) is wholly included in the trade mark CITIBANK and that it is the first component of that mark reinforces that similarity at a visual level.

* * *

69   As regards the conceptual comparison of the marks at issue, it should be noted that the term 'citi', of itself, has no conceptual meaning other than being a contrived spelling of the English word 'city'. That component is common to both the marks at issue. The descriptive component 'bank' cannot be held to be the dominant element of the CITIBANK mark at a conceptual level. Since there are hundreds of banks whose names end in the 'bank' component (Comdirectbank, HypoVereinsbank, Commerzbank, etc.), it is the first part of their names that distinguishes them one from the other.

70   It is clear that the word element 'citi' suggests the English word 'city'. They are aurally identically and visually similar. The question thus arises as to whether or not 'citi' has a distinctive character and whether it calls to mind, above all, a city. In that regard, it should be stressed that the name of Citibank was originally City Bank of New York and that the applicants make frequent use of their trade mark THE CITI NEVER SLEEPS.

71   However, the spelling of 'citi' is different from that of the English word 'city' and a consumer of financial services does not choose such a service without having seen in writing the name of the financial institution in question. Furthermore, there are millions of non-English speakers included in the relevant public. In addition, as OHIM points out, there are no banks that offer their services solely in urban areas. Originally called the City Bank of New York, the bank was subsequently renamed Citibank, as a result of its evolution and its expansion.

72   It follows that the element 'citi' does have a distinctive character.

77   The proprietor of the earlier mark is not required to demonstrate actual and present harm to his mark. He must, however, adduce prima facie evidence of a future risk, which is not hypothetical, of unfair advantage or detriment.

78   Such a conclusion may be established, in particular, on the basis of logical deductions made from an analysis of the probabilities and by taking account of the normal practice in the relevant commercial sector as well as all the other circumstances of the case.

79   The concept of taking unfair advantage of the distinctive character or repute of the earlier mark is intended to encompass instances where there is clear exploitation and free-riding on the coattails of a famous mark or an attempt to trade upon its reputation.

80   Finally, the stronger the earlier mark's distinctive character and reputation, the easier it will be to accept that detriment has been caused to it for the purposes of Article 8(5) of Regulation No 40/94.

81   As has already been stated, the reputation of the trade mark CITI-BANK in the European Community in regard to banking services is not disputed. That reputation is associated with features of the banking sector, namely, solvency, probity and financial support to private and commercial clients in their professional and investment activities.

82   As OHIM recognises, there is a clear relationship—as well as an overlap in the applicants' and the intervener's groups of clients—between the services of customs agencies and the financial services offered by banks such as the applicants, in that clients who are involved in international trade and in the import and export of goods also use the financial and banking services which such transactions require. It follows that there is a probability that such clients will be familiar with the applicants' bank given its extensive reputation at international level.

83   In those circumstances, the Court holds that there is a high probability that the use of the trade mark applied for, CITI, by customs agencies, and therefore for financial agency activities in the management of money and real estate for clients, may lead to free-riding, that is to say, it would take unfair advantage of the well-established reputation of the trade mark CITIBANK and the considerable investments undertaken by the applicants to achieve that reputation. That use of the trade mark applied for, CITI, could also lead to the perception that the intervener is associated with or belongs to the applicants and, therefore, could facilitate the marketing of services covered by the trade mark applied for.

D. COPYRIGHTS AND PATENTS

1. COPYRIGHT AND RELATED RIGHTS

The initial impetus for harmonization of copyright law came from a major study project, the Commission's 1988 Green Paper on Copyright and the Challenge of Technology, COM (88) 172. After extensive commentary from both academic and business experts, the Commission's White Paper on Copyright and Neighboring Rights, COM (90) 584 final, set out a number of proposals for legislative action.

Perhaps the most important measure is Directive 93/98 harmonizing the term of protection of copyright and certain related fields, O.J. L 290/9 (Nov. 24, 1993). Although most Member States granted copyright protection for the life of the author(s) plus fifty years, several granted a longer term. Indeed, Germany's longer term enjoyed constitutional status.

The Copyright Term Directive chose to harmonize the term at life plus seventy years, the German model, explaining in recital 5 that this was in order to provide rights to two generations of author's descendants. The ironic result is that this harmonization directive creates a longer period in which a division of the market is possible, if different parties own copyrights in different States. Indeed, under article 10, the directive enables the revival of rights already expired in some States, if the term is still running in Germany or another longer term State. The new duration is accorded not only to authors of written material and music, but also to the principal director and other authors of cinematographic and audiovisual works (art. 2). The directive had a direct influence on the adoption by Congress in 1998 of a seventy year term after the death of the author for written works, music and cinematographic and audiovisual works, instead of the prior fifty year term. The directive was replaced, without substantial change, by a codified text, Directive 2006/116, O.J. L 372/17 (Dec. 27, 2006).

Directive 92/100 on rental and lending rights, O.J. L 346/61 (Nov. 27, 1992), is another innovative copyright directive, creating such rights in several States which had not previously recognized them. The directive established a common system for the recognition and protection of rights of authors, performing artists, and the producers of films, records and tapes when their works are the subject of commercial exploitation by rental or lending. A codified text, Directive 2006/116, O.J. L 376/28 (Dec. 27, 2006), has replaced the initial directive.

Another important initiative is Directive 93/83 coordinating copyright applicable to satellite broadcasting, O.J. L 248/15 (Oct. 6, 1993), which significantly facilitates transborder satellite and cable television transmission.

Directive 2001/84 on the resale right of authors of original art works, O.J. L 272/32 (Oct. 13, 2001), effective Jan. 1, 2006, is an important innovation that considerably benefits artists, harmonizing the rules in those States that recognized the right and creating it in others. Article 2 defines an "original work of art" to include painting, sculptures, drawings, engravings, tapestries, ceramics, glassware, photographs, etc.

Article 1 grants the author of such works "an inalienable right, which cannot be waived" to a resale right, a royalty on the sale price in any resale by art dealers, galleries and other art market professionals, although Article 3 permits States to eliminate royalties if the resale price is less than 300 Euros. Article 4 calculates the royalties on a sliding scale, starting at 4% for resale prices (net of taxes) up to 50,000 Euros, then 3% for amounts between that figure and 200,000 Euros, and so on down to 0.25% of a price exceeding 500,000 Euros. The total possible royalty is capped at 12,500 Euros. Articles 6 and 8 provide that an author's heirs should receive the royalty after his/her death, for a term of seventy years after death. Article 7 grants authors who are non-resident nationals of third states the resale right, but only on condition that the third state grants reciprocal rights. American artists can only be envious of their EU colleagues, unless the Congress or a state legislature should decide to create a parallel right.

In the neighboring rights field, the most significant breakthrough came with the adoption of Directive 91/250 on the legal protection of computer programs, O.J. L 122/42 (May 17, 1991). The proper mode and level of protection for computer software had long been uncertain. Five Member States had recognized a form of copyright for software, while others had relied on protection through contract and unfair competition principles.

Article 1 of the directive requires all States to give copyright protection to a computer program that is "original in the sense that it is the author's own intellectual creation." However, the ideas and principles which underlie a program, as well as the "interface" between the software and hardware, are not protected. Article 8 sets the term as the life of the author plus 50 years. Article 4 indicates the scope of protection: the reproduction of the program, its translation, adaptation or alteration, its sale, rental or other form of contractually authorized use. However, article 5 permits persons who have a right of use to make a back-up copy, as well as to study or test the program and to determine its underlying ideas and principles.

The computer software programs directive was adopted after lengthy review by the political institutions, aided by expert advisors from computer software producers and users, and attempted to strike a balance among the interests concerned. By ensuring a clear and definite form of copyright protection for computer programs throughout the Community, the directive has substantially improved the legal climate for the development and use of such programs. A codified text, Directive 2009/24, O.J. L 111/16 (May 5, 2009) replaced the initial text.

Another important neighboring rights measure is Directive 96/9/EC on the legal protection of databases, O.J. L 77/20 (Mar. 27, 1996). This creates a new *sui generis* exclusive economic right for the contents of a database (e.g., a telephone directory) if it cannot qualify for copyright protection, which is usually the case, thus protecting the investment costs of its maker.

2. PATENTS

The European Patent Convention (EPC) of Oct. 5, 1973, TS No. 20 (1978), 13 I.L.M. 270, which came into force in 1977, was not a Community endeavor as such, but strongly promotes the harmonization of patent rules. Most of the Member States and several non-EU nations have ratified it, so the EPC is effective throughout most of Europe.

The EPC provides that an inventor may apply for a European patent at the European Patent Office in Munich, or its branch in The Hague. After the Office has conducted a priority search and examined the application for the originality and capability of industrial use, it may grant a European patent. In that event, the inventor is deemed to have acquired a patent in each of the ratifying states for 20 years from the date of application. The EPC has also harmonized a number of key substantive patent law concepts in the ratifying states and provides for a central system to review challenges to the application or patent. However, many aspects of the European patent continue to be governed by different national laws.

Although nine Member States signed the Community Patent Convention (CPC), O.J. L 17/1 (Jan. 26, 1976), as modified, O.J. L 401/10 (Dec. 30, 1989), the CPC has never come into effect, because many States have not ratified it. On Feb. 5, 1999, the Commission adopted a communication proposing a regulation to create a Community patent system instead of the previous convention approach. The concept was endorsed by the Lisbon European Council in March 2000, and the Commission then issued its draft Community Patent Regulation on Aug. 1, 2000. Com (97) 314.

The draft regulation would enable the European Patent Office to issue a Community patent valid in all Member States, after the process of investigation and opportunity for challenge by third parties. Translation costs, presently quite substantial, would be reduced because the full text would be published only in either English, French, or German. (As a matter of fact, current practice makes English virtually the universal language for patents.) The draft foresees the creation of a specialized tribunal that would be competent for all issues of interpretation of the Regulation and the application of Community patents, subject to review by the Court of Justice, thus eliminating the risk of divergent interpretation by national courts. Unfortunately, progress on the draft is currently stalled because the Member States are unable to agree upon the appropriate language regime for the filing of patents. In March 2004 the Council proposed that patent claims be filed in all official languages, which would add considerable cost, provoking substantial opposition in the business community.

The Commission recently issued a Communication on Enhancing the Patent System in Europe, COM (2007) 165 (Apr. 3, 2007), which continued to urge the adoption of the Community Patent Convention. Perhaps more pragmatically important, the Commission proposed consideration of a Unified Patent Litigation System, whose crucial feature would be a new specialized patent court structure, creating regional patent courts with appellate review by a central court of appeal, that would replace the various current national courts with jurisdiction over European patents.

In order to compensate pharmaceutical producers for the lengthy delay in marketing drugs based upon patents due to the careful administrative review process before marketing authorization is granted, the Council adopted Regulation 1768/92 creating a supplementary protection certificate for medicinal products, O.J. L 182/1 (July 2, 1992). The regulation extends "the same rights as conferred by the basic patent" for a period of time that compensates partially for the review procedure delay, up to a maximum possible added period of five years.

The Council used Article 95 as the legal basis. Spain's challenge of the regulation occasioned an important judgment, Spain v. Council (Medicinal product certificates), excerpted at page 107 which is a prime example of the Court's acceptance of an implied Community power to legislate to achieve the internal market. The judgement removes any doubt that the Community has the legislative power to harmonize national intellectual property systems. Regulation 469/2009, O.J. L 152/1(June 16, 2009), recently codified the initial regulation, adding some amendments for clarification. As we previously noted, the Treaty of Lisbon's new TFEU Article 118 specifically authorizes the Parliament and the Council to adopt measures creating European intellectual property rights.

The most important recent achievement in the field of patents is Directive 98/44 on the legal protection of biotechnological inventions, O.J. L 213/13 (July 30, 1998). A prior draft version was rejected by Parliament in 1995, a rare instance where the Parliament would not accept a Conciliation Committee report in the codecision legislative process. The Commission began again in 1996, this time with success.

The biotechnological patent directive requires Member States to issue patents for products containing biological material or produced by genetic engineering, provided that they are susceptible of industrial application. At Parliament's insistence, a clause provides that the human body and its elements, including genes, cannot be patented, and another clause states that "processes for cloning human beings" and "uses of human embryos for industrial or commercial purposes" cannot be patented. The Commission's European Group on Ethics in Science and New Technologies shall evaluate "all ethical aspects of biotechnology."

NETHERLANDS v. PARLIAMENT

Case C–377/98, [2001] ECR I–7079.

[The Netherlands, supported by Italy, challenged the use of Article 95 to adopt the Biotechnological Inventions Directive. They also questioned whether the patentability of parts of the human body violated human dignity, a fundamental right.]

15   [R]ecourse to Article [95] as a legal basis is possible if the aim is to prevent the emergence of future obstacles to trade resulting from multifarious development of national laws provided that the emergence of such obstacles is likely and the measure in question is designed to prevent them.

* * *

18   By requiring the Member States to protect biotechnological inventions by means of their national patent law, the Directive in fact aims to prevent damage to the unity of the internal market which might result from the Member States' deciding unilaterally to grant or refuse such protection.

* * *

25   The patents to be issued under the Directive are national patents, issued in accordance with the procedures applicable in the Member States and deriving their protective force from national law. As the creation of a Community patent is neither the purpose nor the effect of the Directive, it does not introduce a new right which would require recourse to the legal basis afforded by Article [308] of the Treaty. That view is not affected by the fact that the inventions covered were not previously patentable in certain Member States—that, indeed, is precisely why harmonisation was warranted * * *.

* * *

69   The applicant submits that the patentability of isolated parts of the human body provided for by Article 5(2) of the Directive reduces living human matter to a means to an end, undermining human dignity. Moreover, the absence of a provision requiring verification of the consent of the donor or recipient of products obtained by biotechnological means undermines the right to self-determination.

70   It is for the Court of Justice, in its review of the compatibility of acts of the institutions with the general principles of Community law, to ensure that the fundamental right to human dignity and integrity is observed.

71   As regards respect for human dignity, this is guaranteed in principle by Article 5(1) of the Directive which provides that the human body at the various stages of its formation and development cannot constitute a patentable invention.

72 Nor are the elements of the human body patentable in themselves and their discovery cannot be the subject of protection. Only inventions which combine a natural element with a technical process enabling it to be isolated or produced for an industrial application can be the subject of an application for a patent.

73 Thus, as is stated in the 20th and 21st recitals of the preamble to the Directive, an element of the human body may be part of a product which is patentable but it may not, in its natural environment, be appropriated.

74 That distinction applies to work on the sequence or partial sequence of human genes. The result of such work can give rise to the grant of a patent only if the application is accompanied by both a description of the original method of sequencing which led to the invention and an explanation of the industrial application to which the work is to lead, as required by Article 5(3) of the Directive. In the absence of an application in that form, there would be no invention, but rather the discovery of a DNA sequence, which would not be patentable as such.

75 Thus, the protection envisaged by the Directive covers only the result of inventive, scientific or technical work, and extends to biological data existing in their natural state in human beings only where necessary for the achievement and exploitation of a particular industrial application.

76 Additional security is offered by Article 6 of the Directive, which cites as contrary to *ordre public* and morality, and therefore excluded from patentability, processes for cloning human beings, processes for modifying the germ line genetic identity of human beings and uses of human embryos for industrial or commercial purposes. The 38th recital of the preamble to the Directive states that this list is not exhaustive and that all processes the use of which offend against human dignity are also excluded from patentability.

77 It is clear from those provisions that, as regards living matter of human origin, the Directive frames the law on patents in a manner sufficiently rigorous to ensure that the human body effectively remains unavailable and inalienable and that human dignity is thus safeguarded.

Further Reading

The annual spring international intellectual property conference held at Fordham Law School results in a volume composed of all the papers presented at the conference. Fifteen volumes have been published under various titles by Juris Publishers. European Community legislation and case law is always featured in the conferences.

See also the books listed for further reading at the end of Chapter 13.

PART 4

COMPETITION POLICY

■ ■ ■

Western Europe was balkanized at the end of World War II. Each nation's borders were economic frontiers, and the frontiers were barriers to trade. Political and economic nationalism divided Europe.

The political economy of the nations varied. Some had statist regimes, with a plethora of state-owned enterprises. Most had significant degrees of government regulation. The nations were inhospitable to foreign investment, and high trade barriers in the form of quotas and tariffs kept out-of-state goods from flowing across the borders. The enterprises within each nation were plagued by inefficiencies and stagnation. Thus, European business lagged in a world on the brink of global trade and competition.

The Treaty establishing the European Economic Community of 1957 (subsequently the EC Treaty and now the Treaty on the Functioning of the European Union) was designed to foster peace among the nations and peoples of Europe by breaking down the economic barriers in the internal market and achieving one common market. The four freedoms of movement—goods, services, capital and people—would eliminate state barriers to trade, investment, and the establishment of business. Competition policy would ensure that business actors would not erect or re-erect barriers, exercise special privileges, or otherwise abuse their power.

With the traditional tariff and nontariff barriers removed, competition policy became the trade-and-competition policy for the internal market. National antidumping laws were forbidden. State aids were subjected to rules of transparency and were tightly restricted. Commercial actors, public as well as private, were forbidden to abuse a dominant position or enter agreements with the object or effect of restricting competition. State monopolies were prohibited from discriminating against non-nationals, particularly so as not to impair imports or exports.

From the outset the Treaty mandated, as one of the specified activities necessary to carry out the purposes of the Community, "the institution of a system insuring that competition in the common market is not distorted...." Article 3(f) ECT subsequently Article 3(1)(g); ultimately moved to a clause in Protocol 27 by the Treaty of Lisbon.

807

Under the Treaty, competition policy is carried out by five sets of principles. First, free movement—the four freedoms—provides a basic framework. Second, Article 101 TFEU (formerly Article 81 ECT) prohibits undertakings from making anticompetitive agreements, and Article 102 (ex 82 ECT) prohibits dominant undertakings from abusing their dominance. Third, public undertakings and undertakings to which Member States grant special or exclusive rights are, under Article 106 (ex 86 ECT), subject to the competition rules except to the extent that application of those rules would obstruct the performance of their public tasks. Fourth, since competition can be distorted not only by enterprises but also by state aids, Articles 107 to 109 (ex 87 to 89 ECT) provide for the identification of proposed state aids and justification or elimination of them.

Fifth, recognizing that *states* may unduly obstruct trade and competition, the Treaty imposes obligations on the Member States in addition to the state aid regime. The Treaty prohibits the Member States from adopting trade-restraining measures; for example, Article 34, ex 28 ECT, prohibits quantitative restrictions on imports and measures of equivalent effect. Also, the Treaty requires Member States to "progressively adjust any State monopolies of a commercial character" to assure no discrimination in procurement or marketing (Article 37, ex 31 ECT), and the TEU requires the Member States to "facilitate the achievement of the Union's tasks" and abstain from measures that could jeopardize achievement of the Union's objectives (Article 4 TEU, ex 10 ECT). Accordingly, Member States are restricted in adopting anticompetitive legislation, although this constraint is importantly qualified by states' rights to adopt nondiscriminatory regulation in pursuit of justifiable public ends.

The unitary quality of the European Union's competition policy is greater than that of the competition policy of the United States and of other nations and regions. In the United States, policy regarding public restraints is more sharply separated from policy regarding private restraints, states retain more sovereign power to enact laws that have anticompetitive impacts, and there is no system disciplining state-granted aids.

In Chapter 20 we introduce the Treaty provisions directed towards market actors ("undertakings"); namely, Articles 101 and 102 TFEU. At the outset we focus on the market-integrating aspects of the Community's competition policy. In Chapter 21 we consider a core anticompetitive restraint—agreements among competitors that have no purpose except to eliminate competition among the competitors; that is, cartels, which most commonly include market-division, price-fixing and bid rigging. In introducing the law against cartels we explain the economics of competition policy; and in connection with transnational cartels, we treat jurisdiction and jurisdictional conflicts.

While Article 101 governs anticompetitive agreements, Article 102 governs the conduct of firms in a dominant position. This major provision of EU competition law—abuse of dominance—is the subject of Chapter 22.

In Chapter 22 we ask: When does a firm have a dominant position, and when does conduct by that firm amount to a prohibited abuse?

We have mentioned cartels, which by definition eliminate competition. There are various other cooperations among competitors, many of which may improve production, distribution or economic or technological progress. Chapter 23 deals with these agreements, distinguishing permissible collaborations from forbidden ones.

Chapter 24 treats a related problem that arises under Article 101: agreements that impose vertical restraints. These are restraints in the course of distribution and licensing, including the licensing of technology. This chapter includes exclusionary and market-blocking restraints, and distribution of goods through selected outlets.

The law of mergers is covered in Chapter 25. This chapter presents the important Merger Regulation, including merger analysis and notification under the merger control system, and conflict and coordination in world merger review.

Chapter 26 concludes the study of competition law by addressing competition policy as it applies to action and measures by the state and to private action authorized or encouraged by the state. European competition law applies in a number of ways. Public enterprises and state granted monopolies are subject to competition principles. Member States are required to facilitate the achievement of the Union's tasks. All state aids must be reported and justified or eliminated. For private actors tasked by their state to take action that is anticompetitive, the umbrella of state protection is limited, especially when the action puts out-of-state Europeans on an unequal plane. Taken together with the positive freedoms of movement (the four freedoms), the European law as it constrains state acts and measures that harm trade and competition in the internal market rounds the circle of European competition policy.

Competition law and its enforcement form the fullest body of administrative law within the European Union. In most other areas the Member States are the principal agents for carrying out European law, which they are empowered and bound to do. In competition law, the Commission was the only significant administrator and enforcer of the law until May 2004, when powers of co-enforcement devolved to Member States. The Commission is still the policy-setter and the principal administrator and enforcer. Accordingly, many of the principal EU judgments on rights of defense and other issues of procedure and process are competition cases.

CHAPTER 20

THE TREATY, OBJECTIVES AND THE SINGLE MARKET

■ ■ ■

More than 100 jurisdictions—including the European Union—now have competition laws. Competition laws protect the dynamic process of competition. The process of competition rewards efficiency and inventiveness; it shakes out complacent and bad performers and induces the production and delivery of better goods and services and the provision of a range of goods and services at lower prices. It spurs innovation. It removes obstructions from the path of producers and it serves people in their capacity as consumers.

Every nation's competition law is a function of its context. Nowhere is this clearer than in Europe, where the competition provisions are embedded in a Treaty with larger goals. Consider the European context, as framed in the European competition policy reports and statements by Competition Commissioners, below.

A. THE OBJECTIVES OF EUROPEAN COMPETITION POLICY

Competition law is a vital part of European Union law. It is informed by many interrelated policies. Every year the Competition Directorate publishes a report on competition policy. From time to time it articulates the objectives of EU competition policy. Below are excerpts from Competition Policy reports. The 2008 Report does not contain a statement of objectives, but it prioritizes cartels, competition instruments in selected sectors, and competition policy in times of economic crisis. For the year 2010, we include a statement of Competition Commissioner and Commission Vice President Joaquín Almunia.

STATEMENT OF COMMISSIONER JOAQUÍN ALMUNIA ON LAUNCHING COMMISSION CONSULTATION ON RULES FOR HORIZONTAL COOPERATION AGREEMENTS

excerpt from press release IP/10/489, 4 May 2010.

Competition is one of the key tools for achieving a more competitive, connected, greener, knowledge based and inclusive society. Greater prosperity results from innovation and from using resources better, with knowledge as the key input. To make this transformation happen, Europe needs to use a number of tools, including competition, to drive companies to innovate and co-operate in efficiency enhancing projects.

EUROPEAN COMMISSION REPORT ON COMPETITION POLICY (2008)

Introduction

1. This year, for the first time, the Annual Report on Competition features a chapter focusing on a topic that is considered to be of particular importance in the field of competition policy. The topic chosen for this year is "Cartels and consumers".

* * *

FOCUS CHAPTER: CARTELS AND CONSUMERS

5. The fight against cartels is central to ensuring that the benefits of a properly functioning competition regime are offered to the final consumer in a given market for products or services. Cartels are amongst the most serious violation of competition law. They shield participants from competition, thus allowing them to raise prices, restrict output and divide markets. As a result, the money ends up in the wrong place, harming consumers through higher prices and leading to a narrower choice of products and services.

EUROPEAN COMMISSION REPORT ON COMPETITION POLICY (2006)

foreword by (then) Competition Commissioner Neelie Kroes.

The experience of the past fifty years of European integration shows that fair and undistorted competition in a single market works to the benefit of everyone in terms of prosperity, consumer choice, and sustainable employment.

'Free competition' is not an end in itself—it is a means to an end. When we strive to get markets working better, it is because competitive markets provide citizens with better goods and better services, at better prices. Competitive markets provide the right conditions for companies to innovate and prosper, and so to increase overall European wealth. More wealth means more money for governments to use to sustain the fabric of our societies and to guarantee social justice and a high-quality environment for generations to come.

When companies fix prices in markets like beer or elevators, customers pay higher prices and the economy at large picks up the bill. When companies abuse a dominant position, they not only exclude competitors but also dampen innovation since other companies know that however good their products are, they cannot compete on the merits. So our European anti-trust rules outlaw such behaviour throughout the Union, to the benefit of consumers.

European companies need to be able to take advantage of an open internal market, by creating efficiencies of scale and diversifying. Our merger control rules allow European champions to grow on their merits, developing into global players, provided that consumers are not harmed through reduced competition.

Our properly balanced state aids discipline prevents undue state intervention which would distort competition on the merits, but also increasingly helps Member States to target support where it is most effective in filling genuine gaps in the overall public interest, and so get real added value for tax-payers' money.

The spirit and objectives underlying the European competition rules, and the need to enforce them effectively, remain as pertinent today as ever before. But of course the environment in which competition policy functions changes and develops over time. European companies, employees and consumers are increasingly part of a global economy, and are having to adjust to reap the benefits globalisation has to offer.

European competition policy—the rules and their enforcement—must play its part in supporting this process:

- by continuing to uphold a level playing field in our internal market, since free and fair competition at home allows European companies to learn from experience how to stand up to global competitive pressure;

- by adapting to the realities of the day: in 2006 our ongoing state aid reform focused on the areas where limited amounts of aid can have most added value in terms of spurring on competitiveness and assisting change: training, regional cohesion, research, development and innovation. At the same time our reform is improving the business environment in Europe by increasing transparency and predictability and cutting red tape;

- by being better joined up: the mutual interaction of, for example, single market, consumer protection and trade policies with competition policy has never been more important. Sector inquiries and market monitoring are two tools we used in 2006 to identify remaining barriers to free competition—be they the result of business practices, regulation or other state action. They proved useful in several ways: paving the way for competition cases, shaping sector-specific legislation and embedding competition principles and market knowledge in wider European policymaking;

- by working more beyond our European borders: increasing globalization also means more multi-jurisdictional mergers, anti-competitive conduct and even state subsidisation across borders. International cooperation is vitally important for all modern competition authorities. Europe must continue to lead the way through day-to-day enforcement cooperation and bilateral and multilateral agreements. And we should use our common commercial policy to promote stronger multilateral state aid discipline elsewhere.

With these challenges in mind, the Report on Competition Policy 2006 shows how antitrust, merger control and state aid rules—the main instruments of European competition policy—were improved and effectively applied last year. The challenge of adapting to a new environment is certain to remain pertinent in 2007. The European Commission remains firm in its resolve to ensure that European competition policy meets the challenge and continues to guarantee open and better functioning markets, not as a goal in itself, but as a means to help ensure that Europe is a net winner of globalisation.

EUROPEAN COMMISSION REPORT ON COMPETITION POLICY (1999)

2   The first objective of competition policy is the maintenance of competitive markets. Competition policy serves as an instrument to encourage industrial efficiency, the optimal allocation of resources, technical progress and the flexibility to adjust to a changing environment. In order for the Community to be competitive on worldwide markets, it needs a competitive home market. Thus, the Community's competition policy has always taken a very strong line against price-fixing, market-sharing cartels, abuses of dominant positions, and anticompetitive mergers. It has also prohibited unjustified state-granted monopoly rights and state aid measures which do not ensure the long-term viability of firms but distort competition by keeping them artificially in business.

3   The second is the single market objective. An internal market is an essential condition for the development of an efficient and competitive industry. As the Community has progressively broken down government-erected trade barriers between Member States, companies operating in what they had regarded as "their" national markets were and

are for the first time exposed to competitors able to compete on a level playing field. There are two possible reactions to this: either to seek to compete on the merits, looking to expand into other territories and benefit from the opportunities offered by a single market, or to erect private barriers to trade—to retrench and act defensively—in the hope of preventing market penetration. The Commission has used its competition policy as an active tool to prevent this, prohibiting, and fining heavily the parties to, two main types of agreement: distribution and licensing agreements that prevent parallel trade between Member States, and agreements between competitors to keep out of one another's "territories". Moreover, the objectives of competition policy have been integrated into the Commission's new strategy for the European single market adopted on 24 November [1999]. The aim is to prevent anticompetitive practices from undermining the single market's achievements.

Three years earlier, the Report on Competition Policy put competition policy into this broader context:

EUROPEAN COMMISSION REPORT ON COMPETITION POLICY (1996)

2   Competition policy is both a Commission policy in its own right and an integral part of a large number of European Union policies and with them seeks to achieve the Community objectives set out in Article 2 of the [EC] Treaty, including the promotion of harmonious and balanced development of economic activities, sustainable and non-inflationary growth which respects the environment, a high level of employment and of social protection, the raising of the standard of living and quality of life, and economic and social cohesion.

3   In the final analysis, like all other Community policies, competition policy aims to enhance the economic prosperity of the European Union and the well-being of all its people.... [T]he Commission forcefully reaffirmed these ideas [in a communication,] stating that, "market forces produce a better allocation of resources and greater effectiveness in the supply of services, the principal beneficiary being the consumer, who gets better quality at a lower price". However, the Commission is also well aware that "these mechanisms sometimes have their limits; as a result the potential benefits might not extend to the entire population and the objective of promoting social and territorial cohesion may not be attained. The public authority must then ensure that the general interest is taken into account".

4   The positive interaction between competition policy and other Community policy areas was particularly evident on the employment front in

1996.... In line with the approach pursued through the Single European Act and the "White Paper on growth, competitiveness and employment", the [confidence] pact proposes four types of structural action: "to complete the internal market and implement it more effectively; to enhance the overall competitive environment in Europe; to help small and medium-sized enterprises; to open up wider access to the world market", the first three of which are closely linked to competition policy. The first two types of action involve essential competition policy objectives under Articles [101], [102] and [106] of the Treaty and the Merger Regulation. The third was pursued this year in the policy on state aid, with the adoption of a new, simpler and more broadly based *de minimis* rule, the introduction of new guidelines on aid for SMEs and a notice on the monitoring of state aid and reduction of labour costs.

5 If it is to perform its function fully, competition policy as a structural policy must work with and anticipate trends in the economy so as to ensure operation of markets without acting unduly as a brake on their performance. It must in particular:

—take account of globalisation;

—help to develop the full potential of the internal market;

—modernize its instruments. * * *

8 ... [T]he Commission's policy is to promote the competitiveness of European industry as a whole by strict enforcement of the competition rules applicable to Member States and those applicable to undertakings, looking at each market individually and taking account of its size.

Thus, in its policy on liberalization, through gradual and balanced liberalization of the network industries that are crucial to the competitiveness of European industry as a whole, such as telecommunications, energy and transport, the Commission's aim is to overcome the handicap created by the cost of such services for European firms.... Parallel to this, in the policy it pursues on state aid, the Commission may take a positive view of aid that allows the rationalization of production and the restructuring of a firm in order to enhance its competitiveness and in the long term safeguard employment. On the other hand, it takes a negative view of aid which merely bails out a firm without providing any guarantee of its future viability. In its antitrust and merger control policy, the Commission endeavours to prevent the foreclosure of European markets, and in particular of emerging or recently demonopolized markets, while at the same time fostering the development of a powerful European industry that can meet the challenges of world competition. * * *

Notes and Questions

1. Does the 1996 Report complement or complicate the statement of goals in the reports of 1999 and 2006?

2. Describe in your own words the goals of the competition policy of the European Union. Which of the following objectives do you think are most basic, and therefore should be preferred in the event of conflict or tension: consumer welfare, strength of European business, help for small and medium sized enterprises, market integration, market access, market liberalization, level playing field, fairness?

3. What is the relationship of competition policy to:

    a. the competitiveness of European businesses in world markets

    b. the environment

    c. employment

    d. cohesion (e.g. lifting up the poorest Member States)

    e. economic liberalization

    f. cartels

4. In the United States, competition law (antitrust) does not incorporate non-competition objectives, at least not in theory. Since the 1980s US antitrust law and policy has pursued the related goals of consumer welfare and efficiency. Antitrust officials often claim that antitrust policy should influence other policies such as trade, but that other policies such as trade should not influence antitrust.

5. What differences do you observe about the rhetoric of US and of EU competition policy? What are the advantages and disadvantages of couching competition law in a larger socio-political context?

It would be a mistake to infer from the foregoing excerpts that European competition law is amorphous. It is actually quite well anchored, as we shall see.

B. A NOTE ON INSTITUTIONS AND PROCEDURES

We have already studied the institutions of the European Union. The institutions form the background for competition legislation and enforcement.

Competition cases may be initiated in the Competition Directorate of the Commission (Directorate General for Competition). The Commission has powers to investigate and to obtain documents. The Commission may file a Statement of Objections (SO), which describes the conduct involved and contains an assessment. A compromise may be reached after the SO has been filed, and if it is, the Commission issues a preliminary assessment with commitments by the companies involved. Otherwise, the firms involved may file written objections, submit documents, and request a hearing, which is held before a hearing officer, who rules on procedural matters. The case handlers within the Competition Directorate draft a preliminary decision. The draft is vetted by the Legal Service (lawyers' lawyers to the various directorates of the Commission and to the other institutions) and by an advisory committee of Member State representatives. The resulting revised draft decision is submitted to and ordinarily adopted by the College of Commissioners. The firms involved and other persons with a special interest can seek annulment or modification of the decision in the General Court. Either party can appeal the court judgment to the Court of Justice. Competition law cases may be initiated also by national competition authorities and by private litigants in national courts.

With this brief description of institutions and some procedures, we turn to the major competition provisions of the Treaty on the Functioning of the European Union (TFEU).

C. INTRODUCTION TO ARTICLES 101 AND 102 AND THE IMPLEMENTING REGULATION

The Treaty specifies rules that regulate agreements and concerted practices, and rules that control dominant firm behavior. (Articles 101 and 102) Together with control of state aids (Articles 107 and 108), and with the Merger Regulation, first adopted in 1989, these provisions form the heart of European competition policy.

After the Treaty was adopted in 1957, it was necessary for the Council of the European Union to adopt legislation to implement the competition articles. The Council adopted the initial implementing measure in 1962. This was Regulation 17, which was replaced in 2004 with Regulation 1/2003.

Article 101(1) declares, in short, that agreements that distort competition are incompatible with the common market; Article 101(2) declares such agreements void; and Article 101(3) states that Article 101(1) may be declared inapplicable for agreements or practices that are economically progressive and benefit consumers. Article 102 prohibits abuse of a dominant position. We set forth below the text of Articles 101 and 102, and then describe the implementing regulation.

Article 101, ex 81 ECT

1. The following shall be prohibited as incompatible with the common market: all agreements between undertakings, decisions by associations of undertakings and concerted practices which may affect trade between Member States and which have as their object or effect the prevention, restriction or distortion of competition within the common market, and in particular those which:

   (a) directly or indirectly fix purchase or selling prices or any other trading conditions;

   (b) limit or control production, markets, technical development, or investment;

   (c) share markets or sources of supply;

(*d*) apply dissimilar conditions to equivalent transactions with other trading parties, thereby placing them at a competitive disadvantage;

(*e*) make the conclusion of contracts subject to acceptance by the other parties of supplementary obligations which, by their nature or according to commercial usage, have no connection with the subject of such contracts.

2. Any agreements or decisions prohibited pursuant to this Article shall be automatically void.

3. The provisions of paragraph 1 may, however, be declared inapplicable in the case of:

— any agreement or category of agreements between undertakings;

— any decision or category of decisions by associations of undertakings;

— any concerted practice or category of concerted practices;

which contributes to improving the production or distribution of goods or to promoting technical or economic progress, while allowing consumers a fair share of the resulting benefit, and which does not:

(*a*) impose on the undertakings concerned restrictions which are not indispensable to the attainment of these objectives;

(*b*) afford such undertakings the possibility of eliminating competition in respect of a substantial part of the products in question.

Article 102, ex 82 ECT

Any abuse by one or more undertakings of a dominant position within the common market or in a substantial part of it shall be prohibited as incompatible with the common market in so far as it may affect trade between Member States. Such abuse may, in particular, consist in:

(*a*) directly or indirectly imposing unfair purchase or selling prices or other unfair trading conditions;

(*b*) limiting production, markets or technical development to the prejudice of consumers;

(*c*) applying dissimilar conditions to equivalent transactions with other trading parties, thereby placing them at a competitive disadvantage;

(*d*) making the conclusion of contracts subject to acceptance by the other parties of supplementary obligations which, by their nature or according to commercial usage, have no connection with the subject of such contracts.

Note the examples of restrictive agreements or conduct in Article 101(1) and in Article 102. To what extent are they virtually identical? What is the major difference?

Why can restrictive agreements be justified but conduct that amounts to abuse of dominance cannot?

In 1962 the Council adopted Regulation 17 to give the Commission the necessary powers to administer and enforce the Treaty provisions, and to give procedural rights to individuals.

Regulation 17 provided that agreements, decisions and concerted practices within the scope of Article 101(1) had to be notified to the Commission; no exemption under Article 101(3) could be granted until notification had been filed. Parties to agreements and transactions that did not infringe Article 101(1) or Article 102 were entitled to a "negative clearance." That is, the Commission could certify that "on the basis of the facts in its possession, there are no grounds under Article [101(1)] or Article [102] of the Treaty for action."

Notified agreements that met the substantive criteria of Article 101(3) were entitled to exemption by the Commission, which alone had the power to exempt.

For agreements of a common and routine sort, such as exclusive distribution, the Commission adopted block exemptions. Block exemptions specified permissible and sometimes necessary clauses (white list), and impermissible clauses (black list). If agreements satisfied the white list and avoided the black list, the agreement was automatically exempt. In the relatively few cases in which a particular agreement might be anticompetitive even though it complied with the block exemption, the Commission could withdraw the benefits of the block exemption.

Regulation 17 authorized the Commission to terminate infringements and to impose large fines for violation of Articles 101 and 102. It could impose fines of 1000 to one million euros or 10% of the undertaking's past-year turnover, whichever is greater. But if an agreement within Article 101(1) had been notified and was later held not to be entitled to an exemption, no fines could be imposed for the period after notification and before the Commission's decision.

Regulation 17 also authorized the Commission to undertake investigations. When the Commission was on the trail of a violation and feared that, if it gave notice of its concerns, the evidence would disappear, the Commission could make surprise visits to search documents; i.e., "dawn raids."

Under Regulation 17 the Commission, and the Commission alone, could grant an exemption under Article 101(3).

Beginning in the late 1990s, the Competition officials worried that the notification and prior approval system was time-consuming, with little pay-off, and that it distracted the Competition Directorate from more important pursuits, such as cartels; and that the block exemptions had proliferated and their do's and don'ts were straight-jacketing business transactions. The Competition Directorate and the Commission undertook a program of modernisation. In 2003, it adopted Regulation 1/2003, which replaced Regulation 17.

The introduction of Regulation 1 was a dramatic event. It reflected significant procedural reform whereby powers would devolve to Member States but Member States would be obliged to carry out EU law and policy, and a new network of national authorities, combined with continuing sharing of information about all relevant national court judgments, would assure consistency and coherence.

The procedural modernisation was to have implications for substantive law principles and analysis, which were simultaneously being revised to incorporate a more economic approach.

Read Regulation 1/2003, which is Document 24 in the Selected Documents. Also, it is available at *http://ec.europa.eu/competition/antitrust/ legislation/regulations.html*.

Regulation 1 devolved enforcement powers to the Member States with respect to agreements that restrict competition. Regulation 1 abolished the requirement that agreements that fall within Article 101(1) must be notified. It made Article 101(3) directly effective, so that national competition authorities and national courts, as well as the Commission, could decide whether agreements fulfill the requirements of Article 101(3). This sharing of power lightened the Commission's workload, giving it more time to consider more serious restraints of Union-wide interest.

Regulation 1/2003 established the following procedures, among others:

1) Article 3 imposes two fundamental obligations on the courts and competition authorities of the Member States, to preserve the realm of EU law. First, where national competition law is applied to agreements and abusive practices that may affect trade between Member States, Article 3(1) imposes the obligation on national authorities and courts to apply Articles 101 and/or 102 concurrently with the national law. Second, Article 3(2) obliges the competition authorities and courts of the Member States not to invoke national law to prohibit agreements or concerted practices that may affect trade between Member States but that are not prohibited by Community competition law. Note that abuses of dominance are not in this category.

2) The Commission retained its ability to deal with any case affecting trade between Member States. When it does so, it relieves national authorities of their competence to apply EU law in the particular case. In addition, Article 10 equips the Commission with the sole power to adopt, on its own initiative and when the Community public interest so requires, ex ante decisions finding that a particular agreement or practice does not infringe Articles 101 or 102. An exercise of Article 10 power precludes national courts and competition authorities from adopting decisions in the same case that would run counter to the Commission's decision.

3) In order to ensure the consistent application of EU competition law throughout the Union, Regulation 1/2003 creates mechanisms for information sharing and consultation among national competition authorities and the center through the creation of the European Competition Network (ECN)—a robust network that has enhanced cooperation in handling cases, facilitated case allocation, and produced soft convergence of national laws and procedures. Also, national courts are entitled to ask the Commission for its support in the application of Articles 101 and 102, and both national competition authorities and the Commission are empowered to make amicus curiae submissions before national courts. The Commission is entitled to publish opinions on any particular novel or unresolved questions for the application of Article 101 or 102.

Regulation 1/2003 incorporates the preexisting fining power of the Commission and specifies that the Commission has power to impose any remedy of a behavioral or structural nature that is proportionate to the infringement and necessary to bring it effectively to an end, and enables the Commission to accept commitments offered by companies to solve the competition problem identified.

Regulation 1/2003 conferred additional investigative powers by empowering Commission officials to (i) seal premises for the period and to the extent necessary for their inspection, (ii) ask oral questions not linked to specific documents, and (iii) enter non-business premises when there is a reasonable suspicion that books and other records relevant for the inspection are being kept there.

Consider the virtues of Regulation 1/2003 in terms of devolution, empowerment, shared deliberation, cross-fertilization, coherence, and networking. What lessons might Regulation 1 hold for other communities of nations facing multiple and sometimes overlapping systems of law?

Regulation 1 governs the procedures and process for competition proceedings under EU law. Also relevant is a significant body of Court of Justice caselaw establishing rights of defense and articulating the bounds of legal privilege. A serious breach of rights of defense can have costly consequences, as seen in the case of *Schneider/Legrand*. Damages for failure to fully apprise the parties of the grounds for objection to the merger were at first assessed against the Commission by judgment of the General Court. However, the judgment was substantially annulled for lack of a direct causal link between the Commission's wrongful act and the loss suffered by the acquiring party. Case C–440/07 P, [2009] ECR I–06413.

Regulation 1/2003 governs public enforcement. The European system also contemplates private enforcement. In *Courage v. Crehan*, Case C–453/99, ECJ [2001] ECR I–6297, a tenant pub that had accepted a beer tying agreement sued the brewer for damages for alleged overcharges on beer. The suit was brought in a UK court. The brewer defended on grounds that a party to an illegal agreement cannot contest the agreement. On an Article 267 reference, the Court of Justice held: Not only is a party to an anticompetitive agreement not barred from suit (this may depend upon degree of complicity), but Articles 101 and 102 create rights for individuals that national courts must safeguard. "The full effectiveness of Article [101] ... would be put at risk if it were not open to any individual to claim damages for loss caused to him by a contract or by conduct liable to restrict or distort competition." "[A]ctions for damages before national courts can make a significant contribution to the maintenance of effective competition in the Community." paras. 26–27. Member States thus have an obligation to provide effective procedural vehicles for private action.

National courts, not EU institutions, have the competence to entertain damage actions by victims of infringements of Articles 101 and 102. Yet, many Member States' systems for private damage recovery are rudimentary. To facilitate the development of adequate Member State procedures, the Commission adopted a Green Paper (options paper) on private damages in December 2005, followed by a White Paper in April 2008. The Green Paper and supporting staff paper identified the obstacles to effective damage recovery in the Member States, such as lack of mechanisms for discovery of evidence, weakness of mechanisms for collective actions by victims, and rules that shift litigation costs to losing plaintiffs. The White Paper proposes minimum rules for compensatory damages and collective actions, including a form of opt-out collective action. It may be found at *http://ec.europa.eu/competition/antitrust/actions damages/files_white_paper/whitepaper_en.pdf*. The White Paper was intended to lead to a framework directive. The proposed legislation was much contested and the project has been delayed. Some detractors expressed fears of a litigious Europe. Some Member States such as Germany asserted the adequacy of their own systems and questioned the competence of the Union to intervene.

D. MARKET INTEGRATION AND THE BLOCKAGE OF IMPORTS

1. GENERAL

When business actors restrain the flow of trade over Member State lines, they may undermine market integration, harm competition, and violate Articles 101 and 102.

In this section we telescope three categories of such restraints, and concentrate on the third: vertical restraints blocking parallel imports.

First, competitors established in different Member States, feeling the heat of cross-border competition, might enter into a truce with their competitors, re-partitioning the common market. ("I take France, you take Germany.") In an economic as well as a Community sense, this is the worst kind of restraint. The competitors' agreement frustrates competition and its benefits for consumers and the economy, and it totally undermines the liberalizing effort to tear down barriers at Member State lines. Article 101 is applicable to such market-division cartels, which we treat in Chapter 21.

Second, a dominant firm that has the power to do so might block competitors from entering "its" Member State market. This is an equally harmful restraint. It keeps out competitors and makes it possible for the dominant firm to continue to exercise monopoly power, and in doing so it undermines market integration. Without the help of the state, however, a firm, acting alone, does not normally have such power; and when a state confers an exclusive right, often this is in response to a "public interest," as in the case of the Swedish alcohol monopoly (see Chapter 26). Market blockage by a dominant firm can be a serious abuse in violation of Article 102 in combination with Article 106. Abuse of dominance is treated in Chapter 22.

Third, a producer might prevent or restrict its product from being shipped from one Member State to another either to protect its designated distributor in a state from having to compete against the same-brand product shipped in from another distributor's territory, or to protect its profit margins where the product in the home state is price-controlled and shipment of the price-controlled product to a non-regulated state would undercut its profits and squeeze its investment in research. These restraints are vertical restraints; they are intra-brand restraints, and they are restraints against parallel imports.

We turn now to this latter form of restraint, first presenting the famous case of *Consten and Grundig*, which is followed by notes on related distributor cases, and second presenting the contemporary case of *GlaxoSmithKline*, suggesting a limited relaxation of the rule of *Consten and Grundig*.

2. PARALLEL IMPORTS

a. Consten and Grundig

Grundig, a manufacturer of radios, television sets, tape recorders, and dictating machines, appointed Consten to be its exclusive distributor in France. Consten and Grundig wanted Consten to be the only distributor of the Grundig products in France; thus, they wanted Consten to be able to exclude from France Grundig products put on the market in other Member States. To achieve this result they relied on the French trademark law as well as the distribution contract. Since French case law held that only the owner of a trademark was entitled to enforce the trademark, the parties agreed that Consten should apply for and own the trademark GINT (Grundig International). Consten and Grundig agreed that if Consten should cease to be the distributor for Grundig in France, Consten would assign the mark to Grundig. Grundig made similar exclusive distribution and trademark arrangements with each of its distributors in the other countries.

Recall that, before the Treaty was adopted, the Western European nations had high tariffs and low quotas. Quotas would prevent goods from moving across national borders. The Treaty required the Member States to remove the quotas and tariffs in the internal market. In the spring of 1961 when French quotas ended, the French discounter UNEF began purchasing GINT television sets, tape recorders, dictaphones and other electronic equipment from German wholesalers (who had also accepted export bans) and selling them in competition with Consten's dealers in France. Consten sued UNEF under French law for unfair competition and trademark infringement, alleging that UNEF knew that the sales to it were in breach of contract and that the sales by UNEF undermined Consten's contract. Thereupon, UNEF petitioned the Commission to declare the agreement between Consten and Grundig void under Article [101](2). Meanwhile, Regulation 17 came into effect, and Grundig filed a notification of its distribution agreement and sought an exemption under Article [101](3). In justification of the territorial division, Grundig argued that German buyers were familiar with its product and French buyers were not, and that the French market demanded a higher level of service and promotion than the German market. Moreover, it noted that Consten was responsible for guarantees, repair, customer service, accepting advance orders, maintaining stocks, and advertising in France. Grundig argued that cheap imports from Germany would undercut Consten's incentives to fulfill these duties, and that Consten's failure to fulfill its duties would undercut the brand's reputation and frustrate sales. Grundig depicted the market for electronics products as highly competitive, with prices dropping steadily even before UNEF's appearance on the French market.

The Commission refused to consider evidence of competition from competitors of Grundig, and denied Grundig's request for an exemption under Article [101](3). It observed that prices for Grundig products in France were substantially higher than prices for Grundig products in Germany. Consten and Grundig sued the Commission, seeking annulment of its decision.

The Advocate General, Karl Roemer, criticized the Commission for considering only competition among distributors of Grundig's products and not competition from competing brands. Advocate General Roemer said:

> [I]t is not proper if the Commission proceeds in such a manner that from the very outset it considers *exclusively* the last-mentioned internal competition [intrabrand competition] and completely neglects in its considerations the competition with similar products [interbrand competition]. In fact, it is conceivable that the competition between different products or, to be more precise, between different producers is so severe as not to leave any room worth mentioning for what was called internal competition in a product (possibly with regard to price and service).... Rightfully, it was ... therefore incumbent on the Commission to make a survey of the entire competition situation.... Such a survey of the effects on the market would possibly have led to a result favorable for the plaintiffs.... Such more favorable result

might have been possible in view of the relatively small share of Grundig in the French market for tape recorders and dictating machines (roughly 17 percent)—as far as we know, the Commission has not conducted any investigations concerning other products—or in view of the plaintiffs' allegation that the markets for television sets . . . and for transistor sets showed so severe a competition of various, and sometimes very strong producers of the Community and of third countries that it repeatedly became necessary to reduce the prices of Grundig sets considerably.

Because of the Commission's narrow concept of the term "restraint of competition," no such survey was made, and the Court of Justice in its proceeding cannot be obligated to make the survey itself belatedly. The only thing we can do in this situation is to find that the results which the Commission arrived at in the investigation of the criterion "restraint of competition" must be deemed to lack a sufficient foundation and must for that reason be rejected. * * *

The Court of Justice disagreed. Here are excerpts from its judgment.

CONSTEN AND GRUNDIG v. COMMISSION

Cases 56, 58/64, [1966] ECR 299, ECJ.

. . . [A]n agreement between producer and distributor which might tend to restore the national divisions in trade between Member States might be such as to frustrate the most fundamental objectives of the Community. The Treaty, whose preamble and content aim at abolishing the barriers between States, and which in several provisions gives evidence of a stern attitude with regard to their reappearance, could not allow undertakings to reconstruct such barriers. Article [101](1) is designed to pursue this aim, even in the case of agreements between undertakings placed at different levels in the economic process. . . .

The applicants and the German Government maintain that since the Commission restricted its examination solely to Grundig products the decision was based upon a false concept of competition and of the rules on prohibition contained in Article [101](1), since this concept applies particularly to competition between similar products of different makes. . . .

The principle of freedom of competition concerns the various stages and manifestations of competition. Although competition between producers is generally more noticeable than that between distributors of products of the same make, it does not thereby follow that an agreement tending to restrict the latter kind of competition should escape the prohibition of Article [101](1) merely because it might increase the former.

Besides, for the purpose of applying Article [101](1), there is no need to take account of the concrete effects of an agreement once it appears that it has as its object the prevention, restriction or distortion of competition.

Therefore the absence in the contested decision of any analysis of the effects of the agreement on competition between similar products of different makes does not, of itself, constitute a defect in the decision.

It thus remains to consider whether the contested decision was right in founding the prohibition of the disputed agreement under Article [101](1) on the restriction on competition created by the agreement in the sphere of the distribution of Grundig products alone. The infringement which was found to exist by the contested decision results from the absolute territorial protection created [by] the said contract in favour of Consten on the basis of French law. The applicants thus wished to eliminate any possibility of competition at the wholesale level in Grundig products in the territory specified in the contract essentially by two methods.

First, Grundig undertook not to deliver even indirectly to third parties products intended for the area covered by the contract. The restrictive nature of that undertaking is obvious if it is considered in the light of the prohibition on exporting which was imposed not only on Consten but also on all the other sole concessionnaires of Grundig, as well as the German wholesalers. Secondly, the registration in France by Consten of the GINT trade mark, which Grundig affixes to all its products, is intended to increase the protection inherent in the disputed agreement, against the risk of parallel imports into France of Grundig products, by adding the protection deriving from the law on industrial property rights. Thus no third party could import Grundig products from other Member States of the Community for resale in France without running serious risks. . . .

The situation as ascertained above results in the isolation of the French market and makes it possible to charge for the products in question prices which are sheltered from all effective competition. In addition, the more producers succeed in their efforts to render their own makes of product individually distinct in the eyes of the consumer, the more the effectiveness of competition between producers tends to diminish. Because of the considerable impact of distribution costs on the aggregate cost price, it seems important that competition between dealers should also be stimulated. The efforts of the dealer are stimulated by competition between distributors of products of the same make. Since the agreement thus aims at isolating the French market for Grundig products and maintaining artificially, for products of a very well-known brand, separate national markets within the Community, it is therefore such as to distort competition in the Common Market.

It was therefore proper for the contested decision to hold that the agreement constitutes an infringement of Article [101](1). No further considerations, whether of economic data (price differences between France and Germany, representative character of the type of appliance considered, level of overheads borne by Consten) or of the corrections of the criteria upon which the Commission relied in its comparisons between the situations of the French and German markets, and no possible favourable effects of the agreement in other respects, can in any way lead, in the face of abovementioned restrictions, to a different solution under Article [101](1) . . .

The applicants maintain more particularly that the criticized effect on competition is due not to the agreement but to the registration of the trade-mark in accordance with French law, which gives rise to an original inherent right of the holder of the trade-mark from which the absolute territorial protection derives under national law.

Consten's right under the contract to the exclusive use in France of the GINT trade-mark, which may be used in a similar manner in other countries, is intended to make it possible to keep under surveillance and to place an obstacle in the way of parallel imports. Thus, the agreement by which Grundig, as the holder of the trade-mark by virtue of an international registration, authorized Consten to register it in France in its own name tends to restrict competition. . . .

That agreement therefore is one which may be caught by the prohibition in Article [101](1). The prohibition would be ineffective if Consten could continue to use the trade-mark to achieve the same object as that pursued by the agreement which has been held to be unlawful.

[The Court did not interfere with the Commission's decision to deny an exemption under Article [101](3). It acknowledged that Consten, as Grundig's distributor in France, was required to perform various obligations such as to accept advance orders and to provide warranty and after-sales service. The Court stated that territorial protection would give the parties to the agreement an advantage in *their* production and distribution activities. But, it said, to qualify for exemption the "improvement must in particular show appreciable objective advantages of such a character as to compensate for the disadvantages which they cause in the field of competition," and must be indispensable. The argument that every "improvement as conceived by the parties to the agreement must be maintained intact" . . . "not only tends to weaken the requirement of indispensability but also among other consequences to confuse solicitude for the specific interests of the parties with the objective improvements contemplated by the Treaty."]

NOTES AND QUESTIONS

1. Is it true that the restraint results in isolation of the French market and means that GINT TVs are sheltered from all competition? How might it not be true, and why didn't the Court care?

2. How does the rule of *Consten and Grundig* increase market integration? Are you convinced?

3. Why do you suppose that German prices were lower than French prices? Why might you want to know? Is the answer relevant to (a) whether the restraint is caught by Article 101(1)? (b) whether the restraint is entitled to an exemption under Article 101(3)?

4. Grundig appointed an exclusive distributor for each territory; Grundig agreed that it, itself, would not distribute GINT-brand product in the assigned territory; and each distributor agreed with Grundig to "work" its territory. Thus far, these obligations are of the essence of an exclusive distribution agreement. The producer says to the distributor: I appoint you and you alone to distribute my product in this territory.

This simple agreement does not fall within Article 101(1). Why?

5. The additional obligations on both Consten and Grundig are the key obligations in the case. What were these additional obligations and why were they of particular concern? Did they lessen competition to the harm of consumers?

6. Note the relationship between French trademark law and EU competition law. Which has the upper hand? Is the Court's answer consistent with Article 345, preserving for the Member States the right to define property within their states? Did the Court properly resolve the tension between free movement/competition principles and the right to exclusive control over one's intellectual property?

7. In view of *Consten and Grundig,* can an agreement that absolutely eliminates parallel imports into a Member State ever be justified as essential for improvement of production or distribution? The rule of *Consten and Grundig* as limited to tight territorial protection still remains strong, but, as we will see below, allowances have been made at the margins.

8. The United States once had a legal rule very similar to the rule of *Consten and Grundig.* Under *United States v. Arnold, Schwinn & Co.,* 388 U.S. 365, 87 S.Ct. 1856, 18 L.Ed.2d 1249 (1967) (overruled in 1977), a manufacturer's imposition of absolute territorial restrictions on its distributors was held to be illegal on its face. A manufacturer could not lawfully assign an exclusive territory to a distributor, require the distributor to stay within the territory, and agree to keep parallel imports out of the territory. The existence of robust interbrand competition was irrelevant. The *Schwinn* decision protected the autonomy of distributors to sell where they wished. Ten years later the US Supreme Court overruled *Schwinn. Continental T.V., Inc. v. GTE Sylvania Inc.,* 433 U.S. 36, 97 S.Ct. 2549, 53 L.Ed.2d 568 (1977). In *Sylvania* the Supreme Court observed that non-price restraints imposed by a manufacturer on its own distributors can improve the efficiency and competitiveness of the manufacturer, and it held that improvements in interbrand competition (e.g., competition between Sylvania and Sony TVs) can outweigh any harm from the decrease in intrabrand competition (i.e., competition among Sylvania's own distributors). Thirty years later the Court went much further, viewing preservation of interbrand competition as the goal of the Sherman Act and ascribing no independent value to intrabrand competition. See *Leegin Creative Leather Products, Inc. v. PSKS,* Inc., 551 U.S. 877, 127 S.Ct. 2705, 168 L.Ed.2d 623 (2007).

US law presumes that competition among producers (interbrand competition) is likely to force manufacturers to behave competitively and to assure that vertical restraints on distributors are efficient and procompetitive. It presumes that interbrand competition is likely to pressure manufacturers to distribute their products as efficiently as possible. Can *Consten and Grundig* be reconciled with this line of reasoning? Is the difference justified by context?

b. Development of the Rule Against Market Partitioning

The rule of *Consten and Grundig* has remained a robust rule in the European Union. A tight territorial restraint at Member State boundaries is considered a "hard core" restraint. This does not rule out the possibility of an Article 101(3) justification, but for air-tight restraints, justification is unlikely to be successful. However, the sting of the *Consten* and *Grundig* rule has been removed by a body of law that allows sellers to restrain a dealer's *active* solicitation of sales outside of its territory—a concept we deal with in Chapter 24 along with the vertical block exemption and vertical guidelines.

The next leading Court of Justice case after *Consten and Grundig* was *Pioneer*.

MUSIQUE DIFFUSION FRANÇAISE v. COMMISSION
(*Pioneer*)

Cases 100–103/80, [1983] ECR 1825, ECJ.

[Pioneer Europe, a subsidiary of Pioneer Tokyo, had facilitated an agreement among the French, German and British distributors of its high fidelity sound equipment to stay out of one another's markets. Particularly, the agreement aimed to keep low-priced British and German product out of the high-priced French market. At the Court of Justice, Pioneer and its distributors lost all significant arguments, including the claims that there was no agreement, that their agreement, if any, did not affect Member State trade, and that the fines were set at an unprecedented level (2% to 4% of total turnover) and were disproportionate. The Court said, as to effect on trade and proportionality of the fines:]

Effect on trade

82   MDF and Pioneer GB ... consider that their market shares in 1976 were 3.38% in France and 3.18% in the United Kingdom. They maintain that such market shares are not sufficient for their conduct to be regarded as capable of affecting trade between Member States within the meaning of Article 85(1) of the Treaty. * * *

86   ... The studies produced by MDF and Pioneer GB show that the market in hi-fi products in France and the United Kingdom is very large but that it is markedly divided between a very great number of brands, so that the percentages stated by the applicants exceed those of most of their competitors. If regard is had solely to imported brands, it even seems that the two applicants were amongst the largest suppliers of the two markets. In those circumstances, regard being had to their absolute turnover figures, it cannot be denied that conduct by those undertakings seeking to restrain parallel imports and therefore to partition national markets was capable of exercising an

influence on the pattern of trade between Member States in a way capable of hindering the attainment of the objectives of a single market. * * *

Level of fines

104 According to the Commission, however, such a level is fully justified by the nature of the infringements. After 20 years of Community competition policy an appreciable increase in the level of fines is necessary, in its view, at least for types of infringement which have long been well defined and are known to those concerned, such as prohibitions on exports and imports. In fact those constitute the most serious infringements since they deprive consumers of all the benefits resulting from the elimination of customs duties and quantitative restrictions; they hinder the integration of the economies of the Member States and leave distributors and retailers in a position of subordination towards producers. Heavier fines are particularly necessary where, as in the present case, the principal aim of the infringement is to maintain a higher level of prices for consumers. The Commission states that many undertakings carry on conduct which they know to be contrary to Community law because the profit which they derive from their unlawful conduct exceeds the fines imposed hitherto. Conduct of that kind can only be deterred by fines which are heavier than in the past.

* * *

107 [T]he Commission was right to classify as very serious infringements prohibitions on exports and imports seeking artificially to maintain price differences between the markets of the various Member States. Such prohibitions jeopardize the freedom of intra-Community trade, which is a fundamental principle of the Treaty, and they prevent the attainment of one of its objectives, namely the creation of a single market.

* * *

In the 1990s, when the Italian lire was depressed, Volkswagen, maker of Volkswagens and Audis, tried to protect the German and Austrian dealers in its network from a shift of buyers to Italy. It entered into agreements with its subsidiaries and Italian dealers, imposing supply quotas and a bonus system designed to induce the Italian dealers to sell at least 85% of their available vehicles in Italy. The Commission severely fined Volkswagen for partitioning national markets. The Commission describes the case as follows, in the 1998 Competition Policy Report:

Opening-up of markets

68 The Commission has always kept a close eye on distribution agreements and their restrictive effects in so far as they hindered intra-

Community trade. Some exclusive distribution agreements lead to the setting-up of watertight national distribution networks. In particular, clauses which prohibit distributors from supplying customers based outside the contract territory. In this way, national markets are artificially isolated from one another. The Commission considers that measures should be taken to combat this situation, not just in order to reestablish effective competition between economic operators but also in order to promote market integration. In practice, the compartmentalization of national markets prevents price convergence within the Union and restricts access by consumers to the markets with the lowest prices. With the creation of the single currency, price differentials will be obvious because they will be expressed in euro. They will be increasingly viewed as unjustified by ordinary people, who will want to derive full benefit from economic and monetary union.

[69] In 1998 the Commission clearly demonstrated its determination to promote the opening-up of markets, a prime example of this being the *Volkswagen* case [O.J. L 124, 23/4/98]. Since 1995 the Commission had received numerous complaints from European consumers, particularly from Germany and Austria, who had been confronted with various difficulties when attempting to buy new Volkswagen and Audi cars in Italy. These consumers wanted to benefit from the price differentials between their Member State and Italy, where prices were particularly advantageous. Following a series of inspections at the offices of Volkswagen AG, Audi AG and Autogerma SpA, which is a subsidiary of Volkswagen and the official importer for both makes in Italy, and at the offices of a number of Italian dealers, the Commission concluded that Europe's largest motor-manufacturing group had been pursuing a market-partitioning policy in the Union for about 10 years. Volkswagen AG had systematically forced its dealers in Italy to refuse to sell Volkswagen and Audi cars to foreign buyers, especially from Germany and Austria. The Commission fined Volkswagen ECU 102 million, the largest fine ever imposed on a single company.

The General Court confirmed the existence and gravity of the infringements. It reduced the fine to 90 million euros since the Commission had overstated the time period of the infringement; still the fine set a record. *Volkswagen AG v. Commission*, Case T–62/98, [2000] ECR II–2707.

In what sense did the system of quotas and of bonuses based on sales in Italy "partition markets"? Should Volkswagen have been able to protect its German and Austrian dealers from the siphoning off of sales as a result of a bad exchange rate?

Volkswagen is one of several car brands that continued to be sold at widely varying prices in different Member States even after the introduction of the euro. Fines were imposed, also, on Opel and DaimlerChrysler for employing distribution systems that, in the view of the Commission, deprived consumers of their single-market right to buy a car wherever the price is lowest. In view of the persistence of the differentials, the Commission adopted a motor vehicle block exemption regulation, specifying restrictions permissible and not permissible under the law; see Chapter 24. Eventually, the market for the sale of cars approximated the single market goals. The sale of parts, servicing and warranties, however, remained restricted. A specialized sector regulation and block exemption were adopted and later revised. See *http://ec.europa.eu/competition/sectors/motor_vehicles/legislation/legislation.html*. Read the regulation. What restrictions are allowed, under the block exemption? What restrictions are not allowed? How important is the rule that qualified dealers with physical locations must be permitted to sell via the Internet?

In 2000, the Commission liberalized its policy on vertical restraints in general, but, it nonetheless preserved as a hard-core clause a restriction that absolutely prevents parallel imports from flowing over Member State lines. A somewhat revised block exemption regulation was adopted in 2010. See Chapter 24 infra, and Selected Document 26.

The policy against restraints on parallel imports and exports and the concern about partitioning markets has been reinforced in recent pharmaceutical cases, but with a nuance. In *GlaxoSmithKline v. Commission*, Case T–168/01, [2006] ECR II–02969, the General Court allowed a possible exception in the context of the pharmaceutical industry, where price is often capped by state regulation and pharmaceutical companies claim that dual pricing (freedom to export at a higher price) is necessary to obtain sufficient profits for investment in innovation. In *Glaxo*, the Commission flatly prohibited a clause in Glaxo's distribution agreements providing that Glaxo would charge the distributors a certain higher price for sales of its medicines that were not subject to the Spanish price cap; thus, effectively, for sales outside of Spain. The General Court held that the Commission improperly failed to consider whether advantages to competition of dual pricing for in-state and out-of-state destined sales outbalanced the disadvantages to competition of dual pricing. The Court of Justice agreed that the Commission was required to seriously consider Glaxo's evidence. Case C–501/06 P, [2009] ECR I–___ (6 Oct. 2009).

A second *Glaxo* case arose in a Greek court. GlaxoSmithKline AEVE, a dominant firm, cut back supply of medicines to its Greek wholesalers who bought the medicines not merely to distribute to the Greek (price-capped) market, as GSK desired, but to sell them into higher-priced states. The wholesalers sued GSK AEVE in the Greek court, which referred questions to the Court of Justice. The Court of Justice reaffirmed the strong principle against restraints on parallel imports. It held, nonetheless, that a dominant firm can limit orders to its wholesale customers to protect its commercial interests, but it can do so only to the extent that the limit is proportionate in view of the size of the national market and the firm's previous business relation with the wholesaler (e.g., the customary supply). *Sot. Lelos v. GlaxoSmithKline AEVE*, Cases C–468/06 to C–478/06, [2008] ECR I–7139. The Court of Justice expressed its continuing concern about parallel restraints as follows:

[65] [T]he Court has held that an agreement between producer and distributor which might tend to restore the national divisions in trade between Member States might be such as to frustrate the objective of the Treaty to achieve the integration of national markets through the establishment of a single market. Thus on a number of occasions the Court has held agreements aimed at partitioning national markets according to national borders or making the interpenetration of national markets more difficult, in particular those aimed at preventing or restricting parallel exports, to be agreements whose object is to restrict competition within the meaning of that Treaty article.

[66] In the light of the abovementioned Treaty objective as well as that of ensuring that competition in the internal market is not distorted, there can be no escape from the prohibition laid down in Article [102] for the practices of an undertaking in a dominant position which are aimed at avoiding all parallel exports from a Member State to other Member States, practices which, by partitioning the national markets, neutralize the benefits of effective competition in terms of the supply and the prices that those exports would obtain for final consumers in the other Member States.

Did GSK's restricted supply or differentially higher price of medicines to its Greek wholesalers partition markets? divert the natural flow of trade? undermine market integration? increase GSK's market power? hurt consumers? As to each, how? Did the Court weaken the rule of *Consten and Grundig*, or simply articulate a narrow exception? Do the Glaxo competition cases put a chink in the armor of the pharmaceutical intellectual property parallel import cases, Chapter 19, *supra*?

CONCLUSION

This chapter has stressed the market integration goal of EU competition law. The single-market objective focuses European competition policy on openness of markets as a combined pro-competition and pro-integration goal. Is the principle of freedom of parallel imports and exports in tension with the goal of efficiency, or does it normally reinforce the goal of efficiency? We explore this question further in Chapter 24, which addresses vertical restraints.

In the following chapter (Cartels), we see one point at which market integration and traditional competition goals incontestably converge: market-division cartels. Competitors divide markets at Member State boundaries, reinstating the economic borders that the Treaty removed. Even if you should question whether Grundig re-isolated France in an economic sense, you are not likely to question whether Nedchem and its quinine cartel co-conspirators tried to re-partition Europe; a matter to which we turn.

Chapter 21

Cartels

■ ■ ■

A. INTRODUCTION

Cartels are agreements among competitors to lessen the competition among them. They are the classic example of anticompetitive agreements. Cartels are a scourge on consumers. They rob consumers of hundreds of millions of euros a year, often for products that are necessities of life. Accordingly, the Competition Directorate of the European Commission allocates substantial resources to cartel enforcement.

Before embarking on the study of cartel law, re-read Article 101 of the Treaty. Note that Article 101(1) prohibits agreements that restrict competition by either object or effect. Cartels are prime examples of agreements that restrict competition by object.

In many of the Member States, cartels were an accepted business practice for years. Effective enforcement of the cartel prohibition that came into Europe with the EC Treaty of Rome required, and in some cases still requires, a change in culture.

The Commission frequently describes its aggressive stance against cartels. An example is found in its 1999 Report on Competition Policy, as follows:

44   Of all restrictions of competition, restrictive practices in the form of secret agreements are undoubtedly the most destructive. Very often, these practices involve a substantial number of economic operators in a given area of activity and, as such, they have a very marked impact on the relevant markets. Furthermore, they almost invariably concern prices and thus severely undermine competition. The Commission is committed to an extremely tough stance against cartels, particularly following the adoption of the euro as a common currency. The change-over to the euro in 11 Member States should increase price transparency within the Union and, as a result, intensify competition to the benefit of consumers. This must not be countered by restrictive agreements designed to sidestep market confrontation by artificially fixing prices or other trading conditions, which in the longer term

could push up inflation and undermine the foundations of economic and monetary union.

Cartels are usually secret, often carried out through trade associations, and often implemented by mechanisms that may give clues as to their existence. They usually take the form of agreements to fix prices or divide markets, i.e., to preserve domestic markets for domestic producers. Market division cartels seriously harm the market integration effort. Also, they remove producers' incentives to perform at the highest level possible, thus undermining the goal of producing robust and competitive businesses, and they keep prices higher and performance lower, thus harming buyers.

Cartels may be nation-wide, and therefore of special concern to an individual Member State; but in view of the tearing down of national barriers in Europe, they are more likely to be trans-European; and in view of the lowering of trade barriers in the world, they are more and more commonly world-wide. Lower trade and non-trade barriers tend to beget cartels, because firms that had enjoyed protection from competition by state barriers are suddenly confronted by competitive neighbors and often try to hold them back, and protect their own profit margins, by agreement. World cartels today are often challenged by the United States Justice Department, the European Commission, and authorities of many other countries. For example, in the 1990s, Asian and American producers of lysine, an amino acid used in animal foodstuffs for nutrition, fixed prices and sales quotas and carried on an extensive information exchange to support the price and quota fixing for sales worldwide including Europe. The cartel members were prosecuted criminally in the United States, resulting in high fines and jail terms. In Europe the Commission brought proceedings (no criminal prosecution is available under EU law) and levied fines against the US, Japanese and Korean conspirators totaling nearly 110 million euros.

Similarly a worldwide vitamins conspiracy—this time led by the Swiss firm Hoffmann–La Roche—produced US prison terms and US and EU fines.

Cartel fines are often severe. In 2007, the Commission took action against a cartel in the elevator market. It imposed a fine of € 479 million on ThyssenKrupp, and fines totaling € 992 million on all members of the elevator cartel combined. In 2008, the Commission proceeded against a cartel in the automobile glass market. It fined Saint–Gobain, a repeat offender, € 896 million, and assessed total fines against the members of the automobile glass cartel at more than € 1.3 billion. In 2009, the Commission imposed the second largest fine ever. This was in the gas cartel case. E.ON and GDF Suez were assessed € 553 million each, for a total of € 1.06 billion. These are the largest single-firm and industry-wide cartel fines imposed at this writing.

Detection of cartels is difficult. The task has been greatly aided by leniency or amnesty programs. Leniency programs not only help uncover specific cartels but also, in general, destabilize cartels, sowing seeds of mistrust among the cartel members. The leniency policy of the European Commission grants total immunity to cartel members who are the first to provide sufficient information to launch an inspection against an undetected cartel, and it grants a reduction of fines to others who provide sufficient information to prove the cartel. The informants must fully cooperate. The policy is described at *http://ec.europa.eu/competition/cartels/leniency/leniency.html*.

We begin this section with a short explanation of the economics of competition and of cartels. We then present cartel cases. The cases concern factual as well as legal analysis, particularly regarding proof of the existence of the cartel. We then reach the jurisdictional question: To what extent does the Treaty reach foreign firms that conspire abroad and harm the European market? Finally, we consider cartel defenses; in particular: Is there a crisis cartel defense?

B. CARTELS AND THE ECONOMICS OF COMPETITION

Certain basic economic principles undergird competition law. Moreover, economics can be applied to help a society achieve any of its goals more directly and at lower cost.

Many analysts assume that a system of free enterprise with competition law exists only to obtain a more efficient allocation of resources or only to prevent price rises to consumers, and that competition law has exactly and only this goal. This is not necessarily the case. Competition law may have other goals as well. In the European Union, these goals include market integration, openness, control of dominance, fairness, and competitiveness (the growth of efficient, dynamic and responsive firms for the sake of European economic strength in world markets). Pursuit of many of the goals tends to produce allocative efficiency or prevent consumer price-rises; thus the goals may share common ground. But sometimes goals other than efficiency (in its various forms) may be in tension with efficiency goals, and a society may choose them nonetheless. In either event, it is important to understand the basic principles of the economics of competition law in the service of efficiency.

Firms with sustained market power may have an incentive to act inefficiently, both in the sense of letting costs rise and in the sense of using their power to exploit buyers. Firms with monopoly power may have the incentive to preserve their monopolies by striking down competitors or blocking them from markets. Firms that have grown to monopoly or dominant size under conditions of free enterprise may have achieved their positions by competition on the merits. To preserve incentives to excel as well as to preserve a firm's organic efficiencies, we may wish to control a dominant firm's anticompetitive behavior and to work on other fronts to reduce barriers, rather than to strike down the structure itself. This is the approach of the European Union to dominant firms, as reflected in Article 102, as we will discuss in Chapter 22.

This section deals largely with the less ambiguous economic problem of cartels. In connection with cartels, the efficiency and non-efficiency goals of competition policy converge. A rule against cartels serves goals of efficiency, fairness, and market integration.

Here, then, is a brief introduction to market economics.

In a system of perfect competition, there would be a number of sellers, a number of buyers, and perfect market information available to all. The sellers, competing among themselves for business, would be induced to make and provide what their customers want. To do so they would aspire to be inventive and progressive and to minimize costs. The pressures of competition would keep prices near costs. The producers would make and provide as much product as the buyers wanted and were willing to buy at cost or more. Consumers would be sovereign.

The same responsiveness would be observed even in a market of few sellers if there were no significant barriers to entry into the market and if entry were very quick and easy. In that case, potential competitors would (in theory, for barriers are seldom so inconsequential) provide the same pressures as do actual competitors. Also, in theory, sophisticated and powerful buyers could provide the same pressures on sellers to behave competitively, especially if the buyers were in a position to enter the market themselves or to finance entry by others if they were not satisfied with the performance of the existing sellers. Further, in high technology markets marked by rapid changes in technology (new economy markets), the threat of break-through innovations by potential competitors may provide a pressure inducing responsiveness of even a dominant firm.

If all markets in the world were characterized by effective competition—with efficient and fully responsive sellers—competition itself would allocate resources to the production and distribution of all goods and services in the proportions buyers demand. The fullest possible production would then be squeezed out of the world's scarce resources. Demand would remain a function of the existing distribution of wealth, however, for the distribution of wealth influences what people choose to buy.

Real markets deviate substantially from the ideal. But nonetheless, competition tends to produce an efficient allocation of resources, push cost downwards, and help intermediate buyers and ultimately consumers get what they want, and at a price more or less near cost (including a reasonable return on investment). Competition is one of the most important mechanisms that society relies on to produce efficiency and serve consumers.

Competition also tends to keep markets free and open, and thereby to provide opportunities for entrepreneurs and small and medium-sized firms. Also, competition is a product of freedom of enterprise. It fosters diversity and pluralism, and it provides rewards based on merit. Therefore, competition both reflects and tends to support democratic institutions. Finally, forces of competition know no artificial divisions, such as national borders. If the French as well as the Germans demand sugar produced in Germany, the market will drive sugar across national lines. In that sense, competition is market integrating. Competition policy combined with the free movement principle is to the European Union what the free enterprise ethic combined with the interstate commerce clause of the Constitution is to the United States.

While competition and freedom to compete on the merits serve all of the above objectives, private firms can sometimes restrain competition and thereby undermine the objectives of competition policy. The most obvious way in which firms can restrain competition and harm consumers is by forming a cartel, which is a combination of competitors to eliminate the competition among them. The classic form of cartel is a price-fixing or market division agreement by all significant firms in the market. In theory, parties to a price-fixing agreement could agree to charge a high price and not to compete on price. If buyers have no good substitutes and barriers to entry are high, the conspirators would have the power to raise prices considerably above the competitive price (i.e., considerably higher than the cost of efficient firms including a reasonable return on investment). The cartel members would naturally be able to sell less product at this higher price. They would have to prevent the production and sale of more product, for extra production would drive the price back down. Accordingly, the cartel members would hold back output, and they would exploit the buyers who remain in the market. Essentially the same thing would happen if the parties agree to divide markets; each would become the monopolist in its market and would raise prices; buyers would demand less of the goods at the supracompetitive price, and the firms would reduce output.

This phenomenon may be depicted graphically as follows:

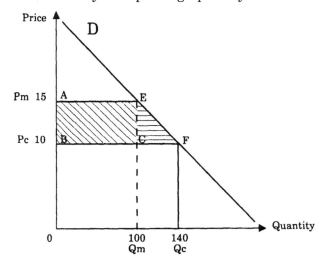

The demand curve (D) slopes downwards. The base line represents the quantity demanded at a given price. The vertical line at the left represents the price. Less is demanded as price rises. Therefore higher price yields lower quantity. If the firms' cost is 10 (the competitive price), and upon forming a cartel their profit-maximizing price is 15 (the monopoly price), given the depicted demand function, the cartel members would reduce production from 140 units to 100 units. They would make more money by producing less because of their ability to exploit the remaining customers. Society loses. Triangle CEF is called the dead weight or welfare loss. People wanted to buy the amount depicted by the triangle, and they were willing to buy it at cost or more, but this amount was never produced. Rectangle ABCE represents the product sold at the extra-high price, and it represents a wealth transfer. Under conditions of competition buyers would have kept the money represented by rectangle ABCE. The cartel empowered the sellers to extract this surplus from the buyers.

As noted, cartelists can use mechanisms other than price fixing to achieve the same ends. They can allocate territories so that each becomes a monopolist in its own territory. They can allocate customers, creating monopoly power over each customer. Or they can parcel out production quotas—one of the devices used by the OPEC (oil) cartel of the oil-producing nations. Setting quotas as a means of limiting output is the other side of the price-fixing coin. By setting a high price, the quantity demanded will fall. By setting quotas, the collaborators create scarcity and the price will rise. Several devices can be used in tandem. Cartelists often fix prices and then set quotas, to avoid squabbling about who gets to enjoy the high price. Moreover, if no member can sell more than a fixed quota, it will not be able to cheat on its co-conspirators (i.e., secretly violate its obligations) by selling more goods at a lower price.

We have spoken above of the static effect of cartels; that is, a cartel will normally cause the price of a known good, produced in known ways, to be higher and output to be lower than under conditions of independent decision-making. Cartels also have a negative dynamic effect. If firms have agreed not to compete and do not anticipate rivalry, they tend to let costs rise and their incentives to innovate to find new and better ways of pleasing their customers are muted. This effect is called x-inefficiency.

The objectives of the cartel can sometimes be achieved through means short of conspiracy. If a market is highly concentrated (i.e., there are few firms) and incumbents are insulated by barriers to entry—especially if the sellers are relatively similar to one another in cost structure and the product is homogeneous—the price and output moves of the incumbents may be relatively transparent to one another. The price that will maximize the profits of each is likely to be approximately the same. No firm would charge a price higher than the common price because it would be out-competed and it would lose its sales. None would venture to charge a lower price because competition would break out and all producers would be worse off: they would sell approximately the same quantity of goods but at a lower price. As a result, unless legal risks are sufficiently great, the firms may find it both possible and profitable to form a cartel, and they may be able to achieve cartel effects—higher price, lower output, lower dynamism—even without an explicit agreement.

In an oligopolistic market (one comprised of few firms), firms may coordinate their actions by price leadership. Also, they may coordinate by staying within their own traditional territories. A territorial strategy has often been employed by firms in Europe, where national markets were historically isolated by trade barriers. French firms feared that if they began to sell in Germany, German firms, in retaliation, would dump their product on the French market, and vice versa. Patterns of mutual deference or spheres of influence developed, reinforcing oligopoly behavior. The more concentrated the market, the less need there was for an explicit agreement, because the result could be achieved without one.

Since merging is one way to reduce the number of players in the market, and the fewness of players makes coordination easier, mergers that result in high concentration may produce cartel effects; i.e. the firms left in the market may adopt cooperative rather than competitive modes of behavior. Mergers, however, are integrative and may produce synergies and efficiencies, while cartels are virtually always inefficient and are by definition formed to suppress competition. Therefore the law treats cartels much more harshly than it treats mergers.

C. PROOF OF CARTELS

The most powerful and tempting way for firms to control the market is to join with one another, that is, to collaborate rather than to compete. Accordingly, all antitrust or competition laws prohibit certain combinations or concerted practices. In the Treaty, the prohibition is contained in Article 101. While it is not always clear whether a collaboration is one that harms competition, cartels are by definition agreements that harm competition. Thus, this section begins with the simple cartel.

The cases typically involve both basic and complex questions of fact and law. For example, as to the facts: Did the parties agree not to compete? Can an agreement be inferred from the firms' behavior and from facts about the market? As to the law: May the parties justify their agreement by showing that it did not harm competition; that it had no effect?

Cartel cases involving quinine, dyestuffs, cement and sugar were formative cases in the development of EU competition law. As you will see in the *Quinine* case below, much of the analysis concerns whether the Commission and court can infer from the facts that the firms had a cartel agreement. Consider also, as you read the *Quinine* case, what the firms did that would help to form a cartel, to make it work and to make it stable. What characteristics about the market and its structure made it more or less likely for a cartel to work?

Quinine is probably the earliest case of trans-Atlantic agency cooperation in prosecuting an international cartel.

Consider, as you read the case: What evidence was the give-away that the cartel continued to operate after 1962?

1. THE QUININE CASE

ACF CHEMIEFARMA v. COMMISSION
(*Quinine*)

Case 41/69, [1970] ECR 661, ECJ.

[Nedchem and five other Dutch firms, and Boehringer and Buchler, both German firms, produced quinine and quinidine, ingredients used to manufacture drugs to treat malaria and heart disease. In 1958 they entered into a series of agreements to reserve their home markets for themselves and to fix prices and quotas for exports to all other countries. After the German Federal Cartel Office discovered the cartel, Nedchem and Boehringer concluded a new agreement that excluded deliveries within the EC from the arrangement. In March 1960 Nedchem, the two German firms, and French and British producers of quinine and quinidine concluded a new export cartel agreement. The new agreement excluded sales into EC Member States, set quotas for exports to non-member nations, and reserved certain markets outside of the common market for specified cartel members. It also provided for equalization of quantities to be sold by members if quotas were exceeded or not reached and provided that no cartel member could cooperate in the production or sale of quinine or quinidine outside of the common market with firms not participating in the agreement. Each party agreed to supply the others with information about where, to whom, and how much they sold, on the basis of which Nedchem would equalize the quantities to be sold by each.

In April 1960, two gentlemen's agreements were drawn up among the parties—though never signed—which extended the provisions of the export agreements to sales within the common market and reserved home markets. The French parties agreed not to manufacture synthetic quinidine, and all parties agreed that noncompliance with the gentlemen's agreement would terminate the written export agreement and vice versa. The agreements were supplemented by a pool agreement for bark to make quinine. The parties would jointly purchase this critical raw material through Nedchem. Nedchem would buy stockpile surpluses of bark from the United States' General Services Administration, allocate the bark among the cartel members, and receive a two percent commission from the members.

In 1962, Regulation 17 went into effect, giving the Commission the powers necessary to enforce Article 101. Also in 1962, a dispute arose regarding the bark pool, and the parties claimed that they abandoned their gentlemen's agreement shortly thereafter.

In 1963–64 the United States, needing quinine to save the lives of sick American soldiers in Viet Nam, became suspicious of the existence of an international quinine cartel as a result of Nedchem's purchases of large quantities of the United States bark stockpile. The Department of Justice conducted extensive investigations (eventually resulting in civil and criminal cases under the US Sherman Act), and in 1967 it shared information with the European Commission. See 1 W. Fugate, Foreign Commerce and the Antitrust Laws § 4.2 (5th ed. 1996). The Commission and national authorities began investigations into whether and to what extent the gentlemen's agreements were being applied in the common market after 1962. The Commission found that violations continued until February 1965, and imposed fines.]

115   The defendant bases its view that the gentlemen's agreement was continued until February1965 on documents and declarations emanating from the parties to the agreement the tenor of which is indistinct and indeed contradictory so that it is impossible to conclude whether those undertakings intended to terminate the gentlemen's agreement at their meeting on 29 October 1962.

116   The conduct of the undertakings in the Common Market after 29 October 1962 must therefore be considered in relation to the following four points: sharing out of domestic markets, fixing of common prices, determination of sales quotas and prohibition against manufacturing synthetic quinidine.

Protection of the Producers' Domestic Markets

117   The gentlemen's agreement guaranteed protection of each domestic market for the producers in the various Member States.

118   After October 1962 when significant supplies were delivered on one of those markets by producers who were not nationals, as for example in the case of sales of quinine and quinidine in France, there was a substantial alignment of prices conforming to French domestic prices which were higher than the export prices to third countries.

119   It does not appear that there were alterations in the insignificant volume of trade between the other Member States referred to by the clause relating to domestic protection in spite of considerable differences in the prices prevailing in each of those States.

120   The divergences between the domestic legislation of those States cannot by itself explain those differences in price or the substantial absence of trade.

121   Obstacles which might arise in the trade in quinine and quinidine from differences between national legislation governing pharmaceutical products under trademark cannot relevantly be invoked to explain those facts.

122   The correspondence exchanged in October and November 1963 between the parties to the export agreement with regard to the protec-

tion of domestic markets merely confirmed the intention of those undertakings to allow this state of affairs to remain unchanged.

123   This intention was subsequently confirmed by Nedchem during the meeting of the undertakings concerned in Brussels on 14 March 1964.

124   From those circumstances it is clear that with regard to the restriction on competition arising from the protection of the producers' domestic markets the producers continued after the meeting on 29 October 1962 to abide by the gentlemen's agreement of 1960 and confirmed their common intention to do so.

125   The applicant maintains that owing in particular to the shortage of raw materials the sharing out of domestic markets, as emerges from the exchange of letters of October and November 1963, had no effect on competition in the Common Market.

126   Despite the scarcity of raw materials and an increase in the demand for the products in question, as the contested decision finds, a serious threat of shortage nevertheless emerged only in 1964 as a result of the interruption of Nedchem's supplies from the American General Service Administration.

127   On the other hand such a situation cannot render lawful an agreement the object of which is to restrict competition in the Common Market and which affects trade between the Member States.

128   The sharing out of domestic markets has as its object the restriction of competition and trade within the Common Market.

129   The fact that, if there were a threatened shortage of raw materials, such an agreement might in practice have had less influence on competition and on international trade than in a normal period in no way alters the fact that the parties did not terminate their activities.

130   Furthermore the applicant has furnished no conclusive evidence capable of proving that it had ceased to act in accordance with the agreement before the date of expiry of the export agreement.

131   Consequently, the submissions concerning that part of the decision relating to the continuation of the agreement on the protection of the producers' domestic markets until the beginning of February 1965 are unfounded.

Joint Fixing of Sales Prices

132   With regard to the joint fixing of sales prices for the markets which were not shared out, that is to say, the Belgo–Luxembourg Economic Union and Italy, the gentlemen's agreement provided for the application to such sales of the current prices for exports to third countries fixed by mutual agreement, in accordance with the export agreement.
     * * *

134   If, as the defendant maintains, the parties to the export agreement continued until February 1965 to apply their current export prices to

supplies to the above-mentioned Member States, it would follow that they continued to abide by that part of the gentlemen's agreement relating to the joint fixing of sales prices.

135   With regard to the period from November 1962 to April 1964, the figures supplied by the defendant show a substantial and constant identity between the current prices fixed for export within the framework of the agreement and the prices maintained by the undertakings concerned, including the applicant, for their sales in unprotected domestic markets in the Community.

136   Where such prices deviate from the scale of export prices they do so in terms of rebates or increases corresponding generally to those agreed on under the gentlemen's agreement.

137   The applicant had supplied no evidence capable of proving that this argument is unfounded.

138   Moreover the increase in prices of 15%, which was jointly decided upon on 12 March 1964 under the export agreement which led Nedchem to withdraw its opposition, was uniformly applied—although that undertaking would have preferred to continue to fix lower prices—with regard to supplies to Italy, Belgium and Luxembourg also.

139   These circumstances show that with regard to sales prices the parties to the export agreement continued after October 1962 to act in the Common Market as if the gentlemen's agreement of 1960 were still in force. * * *

2. THE DYESTUFFS CASE

Enterprises in all six of the original Member States, and ICI in the UK (before it joined the Community), were charged with fixing the prices of dyestuffs and dividing markets. The Commission brought proceedings in 1972, the year before the United Kingdom joined the European Community. ICI sought dismissal on jurisdictional grounds; but ICI had subsidiaries in the European Community, and the Court of Justice held the parent and subsidiaries to be one economic entity with sufficient presence in Europe. See, for jurisdictional aspects, section E infra.

Ten large producers supplied 80% of the dyestuffs market. There were more than a thousand different dyestuffs, and specialty markets tended to be oligopolistic. The prices on the various national markets differed from country to country.

The basic pattern of behavior was one of price leadership, with one firm announcing its intention to increase prices by a stated percentage, often to take effect at a specified later date. The competitors usually followed suit, often announcing within two or three days their intention to raise prices by the same percentage.

The dyestuff companies argued that the Commission had proved no agreement or concertation; merely, it had shown oligopoly behavior (the tendency of oligopolists to act interdependently because of the structure of the market). The Commission disagreed, and the Court of Justice upheld the Commission's decision. Here is an excerpt. We caution, however, that demands of the law for proof of agreement have become greater over time. Hold your judgment until after you have read *Wood pulp* at point 4 below, and then ask yourself how will the rulings in the early cases—*Quinine*, *Dyestuffs* and *Sugar*—stand up after *Wood pulp*.

IMPERIAL CHEMICAL INDUSTRIES LTD. v. COMMISSION (DYESTUFFS)

Cases 48, 49, 51–57/69, [1972] ECR 619, ECJ.

66   Although parallel behaviour may not by itself be identified with a concerted practice, it may however amount to strong evidence of such a practice if it leads to conditions of competition which do not correspond to the normal conditions of the market, having regard to the nature of the products, the size and number of the undertakings, and the volume of the said market. * * *

109   ... [A]lthough parallel conduct in respect of prices may well have been an attractive and risk-free objective for the undertakings concerned, it is hardly conceivable that the same action could be taken spontaneously at the same time, on the same national markets and for the same range of products.

110   Nor is it any more plausible that the increases of January 1964, introduced on the Italian market and copied on the Netherlands and Belgo–Luxembourg markets, which have little in common with each other either as regards the level of prices or the pattern of competition, could have been brought into effect within a period of two to three days without prior concertation. * * *

118   Although every producer is free to change his prices, taking into account in so doing the present or foreseeable conduct of his competitors, nevertheless it is contrary to the rules on competition contained in the Treaty for a producer to cooperate with his competitors, in any way whatsoever, in order to determine a coordinated course of action relating to a price increase and to ensure its success by prior elimination of all uncertainty as to each other's conduct regarding the essential elements of that action, such as the amount, subject-matter, date and place of the increases.

119   In these circumstances and taking into account the nature of the market in the products in question, the conduct of the applicant, in conjunction with other undertakings against which proceedings have been taken, was designed to replace the risks of competition and the hazards of competitors' spontaneous reactions by cooperation constituting a concerted practice prohibited by Article [101](1) of the Treaty. * * *

3. THE SUGAR CARTEL CASE

The *Sugar cartel* case was the last of the formative cartel judgments. Suiker Unie v. Commission (Sugar cartel), Cases 40–48, 50, 54–56, 111, 113–114/73, [1975] ECR 1663, Court of Justice. Among other things, various sugar producers from the Netherlands, Belgium and Germany allegedly entered into understandings and practices to coordinate their behavior in order to moderate the impact of overproduction of sugar in Belgium and to restrain the Belgian dealers from exporting large amounts of Belgian sugar to the Netherlands. The firms denied that they had a cartel. Further, they argued that the sugar market was so highly regulated by national quotas and a community-wide intervention purchase price that it was impossible for private parties to distort trade. The Court disagreed on both counts, noting that the government regulation left "a residual field of competition." It found a multitude of serious infringements. The case is well known for its definition of the word "concert":

172　SU and CSM submit that since the concept of "concerted practices" presupposes a plan and the aim of removing in advance any doubt as to the future conduct of competitors, the reciprocal knowledge which the parties concerned could have of the parallel or complementary nature of their respective decisions cannot in itself be sufficient to establish a concerted practice; otherwise every attempt by an undertaking to react as intelligently as possible to the acts of its competitors would be an offence.

173　The criteria of coordination and cooperation laid down by the caselaw of the Court, which in no way require the working out of an actual plan, must be understood in the light of the concept inherent in the provisions of the Treaty relating to competition that each economic operator must determine independently the policy which he intends to adopt on the common market including the choice of the persons and undertakings to which he makes offers or sells.

174　Although it is correct to say that this requirement of independence does not deprive economic operators of the right to adapt themselves intelligently to the existing and anticipated conduct of their competitors, it does however strictly preclude any direct or indirect contact between such operators, the object or effect whereof is either to influence the conduct on the market of an actual or potential competitor or to disclose to such a competitor the course of conduct which they themselves have decided to adopt or contemplate adopting on the market.

NOTES AND QUESTIONS

1. In *Quinine*, consider the evidence (esp. paras. 118–124)—which was only circumstantial—from which the Court concluded that the gentlemen's agreements continued after 1962. Did the facts raise an inference that the agreements continued in force? How strong was the alternative inference

that, after 1962, the parties had no agreement with respect to sales in the Community; that each one simply chose to follow past patterns of behavior and hoped that its export partners would do so too? Does the latter scenario constitute concerted action under *Quinine*? *Dyestuffs*? *Sugar*? In the 1970s and 1980s the law was still evolving; the issue of proof of concerted action was to come before the Court once again in *Wood pulp*, point 4 below.

2. In an important American case, motion picture distributors changed their pattern of behavior in a sudden, dramatic, uniform, and exploitative way. Moreover, the change in behavior was profitable if all firms did the same thing; but if only one of them had raised its prices, it would have priced itself out of the market. As the Supreme Court concluded, it would strain credulity to believe that each firm acted independently. The Supreme Court upheld the lower court's finding of conspiracy under Section 1 of the Sherman Antitrust Act.* *Interstate Circuit, Inc. v. United States*, 306 U.S. 208, 59 S.Ct. 467, 83 L.Ed. 610 (1939). But the Supreme Court has also held that mere conscious parallelism is not equivalent to a combination or conspiracy and therefore does not constitute a violation of the Sherman Act. *Theatre Enterprises, Inc. v. Paramount Film Distributing Corp.*, 346 U.S. 537, 74 S.Ct. 257, 98 L.Ed. 273 (1954). The Court has dismissed cases of parallel action that can be explained just as plausibly by independent or interdependent action. See *Twombly v. Bell Atlantic Corp.*, 550 U.S. 544, 127 S.Ct. 1955, 167 L.Ed.2d 929 (2007); *Matsushita Electrical Industrial Co., Ltd. v. Zenith Radio Corp.*, 475 U.S. 574, 106 S.Ct. 1348, 89 L.Ed.2d 538 (1986).

3. Note how the quinine export cartel tended to facilitate a domestic (European) cartel. Note also how the parties used various devices that helped to make the cartel work. For example, by pooling raw material purchases in the early years of the agreement and by designating one of their members—Nedchem—to be their purchasing agent and to allocate the raw material in accordance with assigned quotas, the firms could police their own cartel agreement and be sure that no one cheated by producing too much. Likewise, as a result of sharing extensive information with one another, cheating from their agreement would become obvious, and cheating was explicitly punishable by expulsion from both cartels. Finally, the agreement not to produce synthetic quinine by the French, who were selling at a particularly high price in France, tended to keep off the market a substitute product that could have undermined the cartel by driving down the cartel price.

4. After the *Quinine* case, can firms defend their conduct on grounds that their agreement had no effect because market forces overwhelmed their attempt to raise prices (i.e., they tried to run a cartel, but they failed)? Can they successfully argue that an aborted cartel had no effect on trade between Member States? Should "no effect" be a defense? Why? See *United States v. Socony-Vacuum Oil Co., Inc.*, 310 U.S. 150, 60 S.Ct. 811, 84 L.Ed. 1129 (1940) (lack of effect is not a defense to a cartel violation under US law).

5. Why was the quinine export agreement as such of no interest to the Court? What is the scope of EU law with respect to export cartels selling to

---

* Section 1 of the Sherman Act (15 U.S.C. § 1) provides in relevant part:

Every contract, combination in the form of trust or otherwise, or conspiracy, in restraint of trade or commerce among the several states, or with foreign nations, is declared to be illegal.

destinations outside of the European Union? Consult the language of the TFEU Article 101.

Like European Union law, United States antitrust law excludes from its scope export cartels that hurt foreigners only. See the Foreign Trade Antitrust Improvements Act of 1982, codified in the Sherman Antitrust Act as Section 7A (15 U.S.C. § 6a). Is this good policy? Comment from the point of view of world-wide free movement and efficiency, and then from the point of view of sovereignty of nations.

4. WOOD PULP

United States, Canadian, Finnish, Swedish and Norwegian firms shipped wood pulp to the European Community. The Commission alleged and found that the US, Canadian and Finnish firms concerted on prices, and it imposed large fines. The companies sought annulment of the Commission decision before the Court of Justice. They asserted lack of jurisdiction by reason of extraterritoriality. Also, they claimed that there was not sufficient evidence from which the Commission could find concert of action. The *Sugar* judgment, quoted above, was the common referent for the definition of concertation.

ÅHLŠTRÖM OSAKEYHTIÖ v. COMMISSION
(*Wood Pulp*)
(proof of agreement)
Cases C–89, 104, 114, 116–117, 125–129/85, [1993] ECR I–1307, ECJ.

[The Commission brought proceedings against 40 wood pulp producers from the United States, Canada and Finland and three of their trade associations for concerting on price announcements and on price. The producers made quarterly price announcements sometimes simultaneously and sometimes nearly so. Prices were almost always quoted in dollars, a practice that both increased the transparency of the producers' intentions to one another and assured that shifts in exchange rates in the various Member States would have no impact. Prices and price changes tended to be uniform. The Commission found, for example:

> that the prices announced by the Canadian and US producers were the same from the first quarter of 1975 to the third quarter of 1977 and from the first quarter of 1978 to the third quarter of 1981, that the prices announced by the Swedish and Finnish producers were the same from the first quarter of 1975 to the second quarter of 1977 and from the third quarter of 1978 to the third quarter of 1981 and, finally, that the prices of all the producers were the same from the first quarter of 1976 to the second quarter of 1977 and from the third quarter of 1979 to the third quarter of 1981.

The Commission determined that the pulp producers had engaged in concerted conduct in violation of Article 101.

The Court annulled most of the Commission's decision.]

A.   *Quarterly price announcements as the infringement*

59   According to the Commission's first hypothesis, it is the system of quarterly price announcements in itself which constitutes the infringement of art. [101] of the Treaty.

60   First, the Commission considers that that system was deliberately introduced by the pulp producers in order to enable them to ascertain the prices that would be charged by their competitors in the following quarters. The disclosure of prices to third parties, especially to the press and agents working for several producers, well before their application at the beginning of a new quarter, gave the other producers sufficient time to announce their own, corresponding, new prices before that quarter and to apply them from the commencement of that quarter.

61   Secondly, the Commission considers that the implementation of that mechanism had the effect of making the market artificially transparent by enabling producers to obtain a rapid and accurate picture of the prices quoted by their competitors. * * *

63   According to the court's judgment in *Suiker Unie* ..., a concerted practice refers to a form of co-ordination between undertakings which, without having been taken to the stage where an agreement properly so-called has been concluded, knowingly substitutes for the risks of competition practical co-operation between them. In the same judgment, the court added that the criteria of co-ordination and co-operation must be understood in the light of the concept inherent in the provisions of the Treaty relating to competition that each economic operator must determine independently the policy which he intends to adopt on the common market.

64   In this case, the communications arise from the price announcements made to users. They constitute in themselves market behaviour which does not lessen each undertaking's uncertainty as to the future attitude of its competitors. At the time when each undertaking engages in such behaviour, it cannot be sure of the future conduct of the others.

65   Accordingly, the system of quarterly price announcements on the pulp market is not to be regarded as constituting in itself an infringement of art. [101](1) of the Treaty.

B.   *Concertation on announced prices as the infringement*

66   In the second hypothesis, the Commission considers that the system of price announcements constitutes evidence of concertation at an earlier stage.... [T]he Commission states that, as proof of such concertation, it relied on the parallel conduct of the pulp producers in the period from 1975 to 1981 and on different kinds of direct or indirect exchange of information. * * *

70   Since the Commission has no documents which directly establish the existence of concertation between the producers concerned, it is necessary to ascertain whether the system of quarterly price announcements, the simultaneity or near-simultaneity of the price announcements and the parallelism of price announcements as found during the period from 1975 to 1981 constitute a firm, precise and consistent body of evidence of prior concertation.

71   In determining the probative value of those different factors, it must be noted that parallel conduct cannot be regarded as furnishing proof of concertation unless concertation constitutes the only plausible explanation for such conduct. It is necessary to bear in mind that, although art. [101] of the Treaty prohibits any form of collusion which distorts competition, it does not deprive economic operators of the right to adapt themselves intelligently to the existing and anticipated conduct of their competitors. * * *

*(a) System of price announcements * * ***

74   In their pleadings, on the other hand, the applicants maintain that the system is ascribable to the particular commercial requirements of the pulp market. * * *

76   The experts [appointed by the Court] observe first that the system of announcements at issue must be viewed in the context of the long-term relationships which existed between producers and their customers and which were a result both of the method of manufacturing the pulp and of the cyclical nature of the market. In view of the fact that each type of paper was the result of a particular mixture of pulps having their own characteristics and that the mixture was difficult to change, a relationship based on close co-operation was established between the pulp producers and the paper manufacturers. Such relations were all the closer since they also had the advantage of protecting both sides against the uncertainties inherent in the cyclical nature of the market: they guaranteed security of supply to buyers and at the same time security of demand to producers.

77   The experts point out that it is in the context of those long-term relationships that, after the Second World War, purchasers demanded the introduction of that system of announcements. Since pulp accounts for between 50–75 per cent of the cost of paper, those purchasers wished to ascertain as soon as possible the prices which they might be charged in order to estimate their costs and to fix the prices of their own products. However, as those purchasers did not wish to be bound by a high fixed price in the event of the market weakening, the announced price was regarded as a ceiling price below which the transaction price could always be renegotiated.

78   The explanation given for the use of a quarterly cycle is that it is the result of a compromise between the paper manufacturers' desire for a degree of foreseeability as regards the price of pulp and the producers'

desire not to miss any opportunities to make a profit in the event of a strengthening of the market.

79   The US dollar was, according to the experts, introduced on the market by the North American producers during the 1960s. That development was generally welcomed by purchasers who regarded it as a means of ensuring that they did not pay a higher price than their competitors.

(b) Simultaneity or near-simultaneity of announcements

81   According to the applicants, the simultaneity or near-simultaneity of the announcements—even if it were established—must instead be regarded as a direct result of the very high degree of transparency of the market. Such transparency, far from being artificial, can be explained by the extremely well-developed network of relations which, in view of the nature and the structure of the market, have been established between the various traders. * * *

83   First, ... a buyer was always in contact with several pulp producers. One reason for that was connected with the paper-making process, but another was that, in order to avoid becoming overdependent on one producer, pulp buyers took the precaution of diversifying their sources of supply. With a view to obtaining the lowest possible prices, they were in the habit, especially in times of falling prices, of disclosing to their suppliers the prices announced by their competitors.

84   Secondly, it should be noted that most of the pulp was sold to a relatively small number of large paper manufacturers. Those few buyers maintained very close links with each other and exchanged information on changes in prices of which they were aware.

85   Thirdly, several producers who made paper themselves purchased pulp from other producers and were thus informed, in times of both rising prices and falling prices, of the prices charged by their competitors. That information was also accessible to producers who did not themselves manufacture paper but were linked to groups that did.

86   Fourthly, that high degree of transparency in the pulp market resulting from the links between traders or groups of traders was further reinforced by the existence of agents established in the Community who worked for several producers and by the existence of a very dynamic trade press. * * *

88   Finally, it is necessary to add that the use of rapid means of communications, such as the telephone and telex, and the very frequent recourse by the paper manufacturers to very well-informed trade buyers meant that, notwithstanding the number of stages involved—producer, agent, buyer, agent, producer—information on the level of the announced prices spreads within a matter of days, if not within a matter of hours on the pulp market. * * *

Conclusions

126 Following that analysis, it must be stated that, in this case, concertation is not the only plausible explanation for the parallel conduct. To begin with, the system of price announcements may be regarded as constituting a rational response to the fact that the pulp market constituted a long-term market and to the need felt by both buyers and sellers to limit commercial risks. Further, the similarity in the dates of price announcements may be regarded as a direct result of the high degree of market transparency, which does not have to be described as artificial. Finally, the parallelism of prices and the price trends may be satisfactorily explained by the oligopolistic tendencies of the market and by the specific circumstances prevailing in certain periods. Accordingly, the parallel conduct established by the Commission does not constitute evidence of concertation.

NOTES AND QUESTIONS

1. In para. 64 the Court says that the system of quarterly price announcements "does not lessen each undertaking's uncertainty as to the future attitude of its competitors." Why not? Argue for the Commission that the system lessens uncertainty. Would this interpretation change the outcome?

2. In para. 71 the Court declares that parallel conduct cannot furnish proof of concertation "unless concertation constitutes the only plausible explanation for such conduct." Why such a heavy burden? If agreement was the most probable explanation of the parallel price moves, should the Court have drawn an inference of a concerted practice?

3. The buyers desired advance price information. Does that explain the quarterly price announcements? Does it explain the virtual simultaneity of the price announcements? Does it explain the uniform price rises?

4. Consider, once again, the definition of "concertation." When you read the excerpts from the *Sugar* case, did you infer that oligopolistic interdependence was to be treated as concertation? What do you now believe is the relationship between oligopolistic interdependence and concertation under EU law?

In the United States, the Supreme Court has similarly moved from a soft test for proof of "combination" or "concert" to a demanding standard that puts a significant burden on the plaintiff. Compare *Interstate Circuit* with *Matsushita,* page 847 supra. What are the policy reasons for a rigorous standard of proof?

5. Observe the conundrum of oligopoly behavior. A few firms in a high barrier market may be able to mimic the effects of a cartel without an explicit agreement or even an understanding. Should this phenomenon be relevant to a judicial construction of the word "concert"?

D. MAY CARTELS BE JUSTIFIED?— CRISIS CARTELS

Whole industries may fall into crises of overcapacity. Should the competitors be allowed to combine, in order to lift themselves out of the crisis?

The Irish beef industry faced such a crisis. The Irish government requested the industry to agree to a plan of rationalization, and, in response, all of the principal Irish beef processors, accounting for 93% of the Irish industry, formed an association and entered into a rationalization agreement. The Irish Competition Authority challenged the agreement. The Irish court sided with the Irish government and the industry, finding that the industry was in survival mode and it needed to be rationalized; the rationalization would save costs and help to restore the industry to efficiency and competitiveness; and that no credible evidence had been adduced to show that the agreement would restrict or distort competition or hurt consumers.

The Irish court made a reference to the Court of Justice of the European Union for a ruling on the interpretation of the Treaty.

COMPETITION AUTHORITY OF IRELAND v. BEEF INDUSTRY DEVELOPMENT SOCIETY LTD. (*BIDS*)

Case C–209/07, [2008] ECR I–8637, ECJ.

11 Having informed BIDS . . . that it considered the BIDS arrangements [to reduce crisis overcapacity in the Irish beef industry] contrary to Article [101(1) TFEU], the Competition Authority applied to the High Court, for an order restraining BIDS and Barry Brothers from giving effect to them.

12 . . . [T]he High Court dismissed that application. It held that the agreement between BIDS and Barry Brothers did not fall under the prohibition laid down in Article [101(1) TFEU] but nor did it satisfy the requirements for exemption laid down in Article [101(3) TFEU].

13 The Competition Authority appealed against that decision to the Supreme Court, which decided to stay the proceedings and to refer the following question to the Court of Justice for a preliminary ruling:

'Where it is established to the satisfaction of the court that:

(a) there is overcapacity in the industry for the processing of beef which, calculated at peak throughput, would be approximately 32%;

(b) the effect of this excess capacity will have very serious consequences for the profitability of the industry as a whole over the medium term;

(c) while ... the effects of surplus requirements have not been felt to any significant degree as yet, independent consultants have advised that, in the near term, the overcapacity is unlikely to be eliminated by normal market measures, but over time the overcapacity will lead to very significant losses and ultimately to processors and plants leaving the industry;

(d) processors of beef representing approximately 93% of the market for the supply of beef of that industry have agreed to take steps to eliminate the overcapacity and are willing to pay a levy in order to fund payments to processors willing to cease production, and

the said processors, comprising 10 companies, form a corporate body ("the society") for the purpose of implementing an arrangement with the following features:

— [goers] killing and processing 420 000 animals per annum, representing approximately 25% of active capacity would enter into an agreement with [stayers] to leave the industry and to abide by the following terms;

— goers would sign a two year non-compete clause in relation to the processing of cattle on the entire island of Ireland;

— the plants of goers would be decommissioned;

— land associated with the decommissioned plants would not be used for the purposes of beef processing for a period of five years;

— compensation would be paid to goers in staged payments by means of loans made by the stayers to the society;

— a voluntary levy would be paid to the society by all stayers at the rate of EUR 2 per head of the traditional percentage kill and EUR 11 per head on cattle kill above that figure;

— the levy would be used to repay the stayers' loans; levies would cease on repayment of the loans;

— the equipment of goers used for primary beef processing would be sold only to stayers for use as back-up equipment or spare parts or sold outside the island of Ireland;

— the freedom of the stayers in matters of production, pricing, conditions of sale, imports and exports, increase in capacity and otherwise would not be affected,

and that it is agreed that such an agreement is liable, for the purpose of application of Article [101(1) TFEU], to have an appreciable effect on trade between Member States, is such arrangement to be regarded as having as its object, as distinct from effect, the prevention, restriction or distortion of competition within the common market and therefore, incompatible with Article [101](1) of the Treaty [on the Functioning of the European Union]?'

The question referred for a preliminary ruling

14 By its question, the national court asks, in essence, whether agreements with features such as those of the BIDS arrangements are to be regarded, by reason of their object alone, as being anti-competitive and prohibited by Article [101(1) TFEU] or whether, on the other hand, it is necessary, in order to reach such a conclusion, first to demonstrate that such agreements have had anti-competitive effects.

15 It must be recalled that, to come within the prohibition laid down in Article [101(1) TFEU], an agreement must have 'as [its] object or effect the prevention, restriction or distortion of competition within the common market'. . . .

16 In deciding whether an agreement is prohibited by Article [101(1) TFEU], there is therefore no need to take account of its actual effects once it appears that its object is to prevent, restrict or distort competition within the common market. . . .

17 The distinction between 'infringements by object' and 'infringements by effect' arises from the fact that certain forms of collusion between undertakings can be regarded, by their very nature, as being injurious to the proper functioning of normal competition. * * *

19 . . . BIDS submits that [its] arrangements do not come within the category of infringements by object, but should, on the contrary, be analysed in the light of their actual effects on the market. It argues that the BIDS arrangements, first, are not anti-competitive in purpose and, second, do not entail injurious consequences for consumers or, more generally, for competition. It states that the purpose of those arrangements is not adversely to affect competition or the welfare of consumers, but to rationalise the beef industry in order to make it more competitive by reducing, but not eliminating, production overcapacity.

20 That argument cannot be accepted.

21 In fact, to determine whether an agreement comes within the prohibition laid down in Article [101(1) TFEU], close regard must be paid to the wording of its provisions and to the objectives which it is intended to attain. In that regard, even supposing it to be established that the parties to an agreement acted without any subjective intention of restricting competition, but with the object of remedying the effects of a crisis in their sector, such considerations are irrelevant for the purposes of applying that provision. Indeed, an agreement may be regarded as having a restrictive object even if it does not have the restriction of competition as its sole aim but also pursues other legitimate objectives. It is only in connection with Article [101(3) TFEU] that matters such as those relied upon by BIDS may, if appropriate, be taken into consideration for the purposes of obtaining an exemption from the prohibition laid down in Article [101(1) TFEU].

22 BIDS argues, in addition, that the concept of infringement by object should be interpreted narrowly. Only agreements as to horizontal price-fixing, or to limit output or share markets, agreements whose anti-competitive effects are so obvious as not to require an economic analysis come within that category.... * * *

32 The matters brought to the Court's attention show that the BIDS arrangements are intended to improve the overall profitability of undertakings supplying more than 90% of the beef and veal processing services on the Irish market by enabling them to approach, or even attain, their minimum efficient scale. In order to do so, those arrangements pursue two main objectives: first, to increase the degree of concentration in the sector concerned by reducing significantly the number of undertakings supplying processing services and, second, to eliminate almost 75% of excess production capacity.

33 The BIDS arrangements are intended therefore, essentially, to enable several undertakings to implement a common policy which has as its object the encouragement of some of them to withdraw from the market and the reduction, as a consequence, of the overcapacity which affects their profitability by preventing them from achieving economies of scale.

34 That type of arrangement conflicts patently with the concept inherent in the ... Treaty provisions relating to competition, according to which each economic operator must determine independently the policy which it intends to adopt on the common market. Article [101(1) TFEU] is intended to prohibit any form of coordination which deliberately substitutes practical cooperation between undertakings for the risks of competition.

35 In the context of competition, the undertakings which signed the BIDS arrangements would have, without such arrangements, no means of improving their profitability other than by intensifying their commercial rivalry or resorting to concentrations. With the BIDS arrangements it would be possible for them to avoid such a process and to share a large part of the costs involved in increasing the degree of market concentration as a result, in particular, of the levy of EUR 2 per head processed by each of the stayers.

36 In addition, the means put in place to attain the objective of the BIDS arrangements include restrictions whose object is anti-competitive.

37 As regards, in the first place, the levy of EUR 11 per head of cattle slaughtered beyond the usual volume of production of each of the stayers, it is, as BIDS submits, the price to be paid by the stayers to acquire the goers' clientele. However, it must be observed, as did the Advocate General ..., that such a measure also constitutes an obstacle to the natural development of market shares as regards some of the stayers who, because of the dissuasive nature of that levy, are deterred from exceeding their usual volume of production. That meas-

ure is likely therefore to lead to certain operators freezing their production.

38 As regards, secondly, restrictions imposed on the goers as regards the disposal and use of their processing plants, the BIDS arrangements also contain, by their very object, restrictions on competition since they seek to avoid the possible use of those plants by new operators entering the market in order to compete with the stayers. As the Competition Authority pointed out in its written observations, since the investment necessary for the construction of a new processing plant is much greater than the costs of taking over an existing plant, those restrictions are obviously intended to dissuade any new entry of competitors throughout the island of Ireland.

39 Finally, the fact that those restrictions, as well as the non-competition clause imposed on the goers, are limited in time is not such as to put in doubt the finding as to the anti-competitive nature of the object of the BIDS arrangements.... [S]uch matters may, at the most, be relevant for the purposes of the examination of the four requirements which have to be met under Article [101(3) TFEU] in order to escape the prohibition laid down in Article [101(1) TFEU].

40 In the light of the foregoing considerations, the reply to the question referred must be that an agreement with features such as those of the standard form of contract concluded between the 10 principal beef and veal processors in Ireland, who are members of BIDS, and requiring, among other things, a reduction of the order of 25% in processing capacity, has as its object the prevention, restriction or distortion of competition within the meaning of Article [101(1) TFEU].... * * *

NOTES AND QUESTIONS

1. What was the purpose of the agreement? Was BIDS' purpose to address the crisis of overproduction of beef in Ireland by reducing overcapacity, thereby resuscitating the industry and making it more competitive? Assume that BIDS and the Irish government thought there was a good chance that the plan would succeed. Is such an agreement caught by Article 101(1) as a restraint by object? Should it be?

2. BIDS maintained in the Irish court that, if caught by Article 101(1), the agreement should be exempted under Article 101(3). This issue was not before the European Court, but assume that it was and that you were the Advocate General—the jurist who advises the judges. Write your opinion. (The Advocate General's opinion is scholarly advice for the use of the judges.)

3. In *Dutch brickmakers*, the European Commission exempted, under Article 101(3), a rationalization agreement by brickmakers who were plagued by overcapacity. The brickmakers agreed to reduce surplus capacity over a limited period of time while not making any agreement on prices. *Stichting Baksteen*, Case IV/34.456, O.J. L 131/15 (May 26, 1994). This case is exceptional, and may be the last crisis cartel ever to be approved by the Commission.

The wisdom of allowing judicial or administrative authorization of crisis or restructuring cartels is much debated. United States law makes no allowance for crises, on the theory that market solutions are better than private solutions, and a crisis justification for cartels would weaken the clear rule of law. Germany and the UK once allowed authorization of crisis cartels in the public interest. They have revised their laws to mirror Article 101. Until 1999, Japanese law allowed authorization of depression and rationalization cartels. This authorization was repealed. Anti–Monopoly Law of Japan, § 24(3), Law No. 54, 1947 (amended).

4. See Chapter 26 for an account of the European Competition Commissioner's and the Competition Directorate's role in responding to the urgent public needs in the financial crisis of 2008–09, presenting competition as part of the solution, not part of the problem.

E. WORLD CARTELS AND OFFSHORE CARTELS—JURISDICTION, COMITY, AND COOPERATION

1. EFFECTS, SOVEREIGNTY, AND RESTRAINT

A conspiracy in one country may harm consumers in another country, or in the world.

The United States was the pioneer of the "effects" doctrine, under which US law catches offshore anticompetitive conduct targeted at Americans. This is the holding of *United States v. Aluminum Co. of America* (*Alcoa*), 148 F.2d 416 (2d Cir.1945). (See *Notes and Questions* below.) For many years America's trading partners, and particularly the UK, adamantly opposed application of the effects doctrine to their nationals, labeling the doctrine an affront to their sovereignty.

But as years went by, other nations began to feel the threat of offshore anticompetitive acts targeted at their nation, and some form of the effects doctrine became necessary self-protection.

The first major European Court case on point was the dyestuffs cartel, *Imperial Chemical Industries Ltd. v. Commission*, Cases 48, 49, 51–57/69, [1972] ECR 619, supra. ICI, a UK company, was part of the dyestuffs cartel. The UK had not yet joined the European Community. ICI sought dismissal for lack of jurisdiction. The Commission rejected ICI's argument, and applied the effects test. On appeal, the Court of Justice sidestepped the controversy surrounding the effects doctrine. ICI had subsidiaries in the Community, and, the Court said, ICI exercised "decisive influence" over them. Therefore the parent and its subsidiaries were one economic unit. The Court said, in para. 130:

> By making use of its power to control its subsidiaries established in the Community, the applicant was able to ensure that its decision was implemented on that market.

The question of jurisdiction over off-shore actors arose in a starker form in *Wood pulp*. Not all of the alleged conspirators had subsidiaries in Europe. Sixteen years had passed since *Dyestuffs*. Globalization had increased nations' vulnerability to offshore cartels.

United States, Finnish, Swedish and Canadian firms exported wood pulp into the common market, themselves or through export associations. Many years before, to facilitate exports, the United States had enacted the Webb–Pomerene Act. The US wood pulp firms were members of a Webb–Pomerene Association, and the Webb–Pomerene Act exempted the exporters and their association from the United States antitrust laws except to the extent that their conduct harmed competition in the United States.

The European Commission charged the wood pulp firms and two of their export associations with fixing the price of wood pulp that was being sold to buyers in the Community. The Commission found infringements and imposed fines. The firms sued for annulment, on grounds that included lack of jurisdiction. The jurisdictional issue reached the Court of Justice before the question of proof of the cartel, treated above. Assume for purposes of the jurisdictional matter that there was in fact a cartel agreement.

ÅHLŠTRÖM OSAKEYHTIÖ v. COMMISSION
(*Wood Pulp*)

(jurisdiction)

Cases C–89, 104, 114, 116–117, 125–129/85, [1988] ECR 5193, ECJ.

3   [T]he Commission set out the grounds which in its view justify the Community's jurisdiction to apply Article [101] of the Treaty to the concertation in question. It stated first that all the addressees of the decision were either exporting directly to purchasers within the Community or were doing business within the Community through branches, subsidiaries, agencies or other establishments in the Community. It further pointed out that the concertation applied to the vast majority of the sales of those undertakings to and in the Community. Finally it stated that two-thirds of total shipments and 60% of consumption of the product in question in the Community had been affected by such concertation. The Commission concluded that: "The effect of the agreements and practices on prices announced and/or charged to customers and on resale of pulp within the EEC was therefore not only substantial but intended, and was the primary and direct result of the agreements and practices." * * *

6   All the applicants which have made submissions regarding jurisdiction maintain first of all that by applying the competition rules of the Treaty to them the Commission has misconstrued the territorial scope of Article [101]. They note that in its judgment of 14 July 1972 in Case 48/69 (*ICI v. Commission* [1972] ECR 619) the Court did not adopt the "effects doctrine" but emphasized that the case involved conduct restricting competition within the common market because of the

activities of subsidiaries which could be imputed to the parent companies. The applicants add that even if there is a basis in Community law for applying Article [101] to them, the action of applying the rule interpreted in that way would be contrary to public international law which precludes any claim by the Community to regulate conduct restricting competition adopted outside the territory of the Community merely by reason of the economic repercussions which that conduct produces within the Community.

7   The applicants which are members of the KEA [Kraft Export Association] further submit that the application of Community competition rules to them is contrary to public international law in so far as it is in breach of the principle of non-interference. They maintain that in this case the application of Article [101] harmed the interest of the United States in promoting exports by United States undertakings as recognized in the Webb Pomerene Act of 1918 under which export associations, like the KEA, are exempt from United States anti-trust laws.

8   Certain Canadian applicants also maintain that by imposing fines on them and making reduction of those fines conditional on the producers giving undertakings as to their future conduct the Commission has infringed Canada's sovereignty and thus breached the principle of international comity. * * *

Territorial Scope of Article [101] and Public International Law

(a) The Individual Undertakings

11   In so far as the submission concerning the infringement of Article [101] of the Treaty itself is concerned, it should be recalled that that provision prohibits all agreements between undertakings and concerted practices which may affect trade between Member States and which have as their object or effect the restriction of competition within the common market.

12   It should be noted that the main sources of supply of wood pulp are outside the Community, in Canada, the United States, Sweden and Finland and that the market therefore has global dimensions. Where wood pulp producers established in those countries sell directly to purchasers established in the Community and engage in price competition in order to win orders from those customers, that constitutes competition within the common market.

13   It follows that where those producers concert on the prices to be charged to their customers in the Community and put that concertation into effect by selling at prices which are actually coordinated, they are taking part in concertation which has the object and effect of restricting competition within the common market within the meaning of Article [101] of the Treaty.

14   Accordingly, it must be concluded that by applying the competition rules in the Treaty in the circumstances of this case to undertakings whose registered offices are situated outside the Community, the

Commission has not made an incorrect assessment of the territorial scope of Article [101].

15 The applicants have submitted that the decision is incompatible with public international law on the grounds that the application of the competition rules in this case was founded exclusively on the economic repercussions within the common market of conduct restricting competition which was adopted outside the Community.

16 It should be observed that an infringement of Article [101], such as the conclusion of an agreement which has had the effect of restricting competition within the common market, consists of conduct made up of two elements, the formation of the agreement, decision or concerted practice and the implementation thereof. If the applicability of prohibitions laid down under competition law were made to depend on the place where the agreement, decision or concerted practice was formed, the result would obviously be to give undertakings an easy means of evading those prohibitions. The decisive factor is therefore the place where it is implemented.

17 The producers in this case implemented their pricing agreement within the common market. It is immaterial in that respect whether or not they had recourse to subsidiaries, agents, sub-agents, or branches within the Community in order to make their contacts with purchasers within the Community.

18 Accordingly the Community's jurisdiction to apply its competition rules to such conduct is covered by the territoriality principle as universally recognized in public international law.

19 As regards the argument based on the infringement of the principle of non-interference, it should be pointed out that the applicants who are members of KEA have referred to a rule according to which where two States have jurisdiction to lay down and enforce rules and the effect of those rules is that a person finds himself subject to contradictory orders as to the conduct he must adopt, each State is obliged to exercise its jurisdiction with moderation. The applicants have concluded that by disregarding that rule in applying its competition rules the Community has infringed the principle of non-interference.

20 There is no need to enquire into the existence in international law of such a rule since it suffices to observe that the conditions for its application are in any event not satisfied. There is not, in this case, any contradiction between the conduct required by the United States and that required by the Community since the Webb Pomerene Act merely exempts the conclusion of export cartels from the application of United States anti-trust laws but does not require such cartels to be concluded. * * *

22 As regards the argument relating to disregard of international comity, it suffices to observe that it amounts to calling in question the Community's jurisdiction to apply its competition rules to conduct

such as that found to exist in this case and that, as such, that argument has already been rejected.

23   Accordingly it must be concluded that the Commission's decision is not contrary to Article [101] of the Treaty or to the rules of public international law relied on by the applicants.

(b) KEA

24   According to its Articles of Association, KEA is a non-profit-making association whose purpose is the promotion of the commercial interests of its members in the exportation of their products and it serves primarily as a clearing-house for its members for information regarding their export markets. KEA does not itself engage in manufacture, selling or distribution.

25   It should further be pointed out that within KEA a number of groups have been formed, including the Pulp Group, to cover the different sectors of the pulp and paper industry. Under Article 1 of the by-laws of KEA, undertakings may only join KEA by becoming a member of one of those groups. Article 2 of the by-laws provides that the groups enjoy full independence in the management of their affairs. * * *

27   It is apparent from the foregoing that KEA's price recommendations cannot be distinguished from the pricing agreements concluded by undertakings which are members of the Pulp Group and that KEA has not played a separate role in the implementation of those agreements.

28   In those circumstances the decision should be declared void in so far as it concerns KEA.

NOTES AND QUESTIONS

1.   Since the 1940s, US courts have had "effects" jurisdiction; that is, if foreigners act, even abroad, with the intent to affect US commerce and they cause a direct effect on US commerce, the United States courts have subject matter jurisdiction and the Sherman Act applies. *United States v. Aluminum Co. of America*, 148 F.2d 416 (2d Cir.1945). US courts may not, however, require foreign firms acting in their home territory to do what their home government forbids, or to abstain from doing what their home government requires, for such an order would interfere impermissibly with the sovereignty of the foreign state. See *United States v. Watchmakers of Switzerland Info. Center*, 1963 (CCH) Trade Cas. ¶ 70,600 (S.D.N.Y.1962); 1965 (CCH) Trade Cas. ¶ 71,352 (S.D.N.Y.1965) (judgment revised to apply only to conduct that operated outside of Switzerland).

In the 1960s and 1970s, applications of the *Alcoa* doctrine were criticized by various nations, especially Great Britain, whose nationals were sued for treble damages in US courts as members of world cartels that had targeted American buyers.

In response to the criticism and to threats of retaliation by trading partners, some United States courts developed balancing principles. They stated that courts either lack jurisdiction or should refrain from exercising jurisdiction if foreign nations' and foreign nationals' interests in nonapplication of US law outbalance the United States' interest in enforcement. *Timberlane Lumber Co. v. Bank of America*, 549 F.2d 597 (9th Cir.1976); *Mannington Mills, Inc. v. Congoleum Corp.*, 595 F.2d 1287 (3rd Cir.1979).

In 1993 the United States Supreme Court decided its first antitrust extraterritoriality case in a quarter of a century. Lloyds of London reinsurers had agreed in London with Americans, and some had agreed in London only among themselves, to reduce the coverage of reinsurance policies that they would offer on the US market. When sued, these British defendants moved to dismiss, asserting that the US court lacked jurisdiction or that comity considerations required dismissal. They claimed that their conduct was lawful where performed (in the UK), and that in view of the UK regulatory policy, which conferred the right of self-regulation on Lloyds of London, a conflict existed that required dismissal of the case against them by the US court. The Supreme Court disagreed. It noted that there was no direct conflict, for the UK law did not require (much less encourage) the London firms to boycott the American insurers. In this context, the Court stated:

> [I]t is well established by now that the Sherman Act applies to foreign conduct that was meant to produce and did in fact produce some substantial effect in the United States.

Hartford Fire Ins. Co. v. California, 509 U.S. 764, 796, 113 S.Ct. 2891, 125 L.Ed.2d 612 (1993).

Is there any difference between the holding of *Hartford* and the holding of *Wood pulp*? Has the European Union essentially adopted the effects test?

2. Would the outcome of *Wood pulp* have been the same if the producers sold FOB New York without knowledge that the wood pulp was being shipped directly into the European Union? Should the rules of jurisdiction be the same regardless whether the sale and transfer of title took place in New York or the Netherlands? Is the harm to competition within the European Union the same in either case? Are the sovereignty interests of the affected countries the same? See, for a theory of jurisdiction, E. Fox, National Law, Global Markets, and *Hartford*: Eyes Wide Shut, 68 Antitrust L.J. 73 (2000).

3. In *Wood pulp,* why did the Court declare void the Commission's decision against KEA? What would the result have been if there were no sector groups within KEA and if KEA's price recommendations were autonomous and distinct from joint actions of its members? Was the jurisdictional decision regarding KEA harder than the jurisdictional decision regarding the individual producers?

4. In 1982 the United States Congress, responding especially to concerns of American business that US antitrust law was following them into foreign markets and imposing extra costs, adopted the Foreign Trade Antitrust Improvements Act (FTAIA). The FTAIA cut back the reach of the Sherman Act in matters involving foreign commerce, principally to protect US sellers from Sherman Act challenges for their activity abroad. The statute carves out import commerce, which remains subject to preexisting rules supporting

effects jurisdiction. As to all other commerce with foreign nations, the statute provides that the Sherman Act shall not apply unless:

"(1) such conduct has a direct, substantial and reasonably foreseeable effect—

(A) on [domestic] trade or commerce ... or (B) on export trade or commerce ... [and]

(2) such effect gives rise to a claim under [the Sherman Act], other than this section...."

For actions based on (1)(B) the statute expressly applies only to injury to export business in the United States.

Paragraph (2) might have meant only that the FTAIA itself did not create a substantive cause of action. But the US Supreme Court construed the paragraph to mean: Foreign victims who bought their price-fixed goods abroad cannot recover damages under the Sherman Act unless the US effect of the cartel ("such effect") "gives rise to" the particular plaintiff's Sherman Act claim. *F. Hoffmann–La Roche v. Empagran S.A.*, 542 U.S. 155, 124 S.Ct. 2359, 159 L.Ed.2d 226 (2004). Since buyers abroad are normally injured by the price fixing, not its US effect, *Empagran* significantly limits foreign victims' access to Sherman Act treble damage remedies. In its *Empagran* ruling, the US Supreme Court invoked a principle of statutory interpretation: A nation should not interfere unduly with the sovereign authority (including here, the competition law enforcement schemes) of other nations.

UK courts have been somewhat more generous in hosting out-of-state claimants suing out-of-state cartelists—at least when the out-of-staters are European. A German company that bought price-fixed vitamins in Germany from Roche Germany was allowed to sue the cartelists (British, German, Swiss and French) in the UK. *Provimi Ltd. v. Roche Products Ltd.*, [2003] Queens Bench Division.

2. COOPERATION, AND SEEDS OF A GLOBAL REGIME

The European Union, the United States, and other trading partners recognize the need for cooperation and coordination. Europe and the United States intensely and productively cooperate informally on many matters. They have a working group on mergers, and their staffs cooperate in vetting mergers of common interest to the extent they can do so consistent with confidentiality obligations. Often the merger partners waive confidentiality so that the merger can be approved more expeditiously. Confidentiality obligations are, however, a significant obstruction to cooperation in cartel investigations.

The European Union has entered into a number of bilateral agreements for cooperation on competition policy. The European Union entered into a cooperation agreement with the United States effective in 1991, wherein the parties promised to notify and confer regarding intended antitrust action that may adversely affect the important interests of the other (negative comity). In 1998 the US and the EU strengthened a commitment to inform the other when anticompetitive activities harming their citizens were occurring on the soil of the other. In specified circumstances, each undertook to consider withholding its own enforcement while the notified jurisdiction was taking action to cure the violation (positive comity). The numerous EU bilateral antitrust agreements are linked to the Competition Directorate's web site at *http://ec.europa.eu/competition/international/legislation/legislation.html.*

The EU has advocated a world competition agreement within the framework of the World Trade Organization (WTO), starting with building blocks of cooperation; commitments of transparency, due process, and technical assistance to developing countries; and a substantive commitment of nations to enact and maintain an anti-cartel law. See Commission, Communication to the Council: Towards an International Framework of Competition Rules, COM(96) 284 final. The proposal faced preliminary opposition from the United States and from developing countries. After revisions, it appeared on the Ministerial Declaration of the Doha trade round of the World Trade Organization. Caught in the crossfire of the dispute on agricultural subsidies, the competition item of the Doha agenda became side-tracked and then withdrawn, and it is unlikely to reappear on a WTO agenda for some years.

The Competition Directorate of the European Commission is a founding member of the International Competition Network (ICN), a virtual network of the antitrust authorities of the world formed in 2001 to discuss a range of practical and policy competition issues, formulate and spread best practices, and promote convergence. The Competition Directorate is active in most working groups, including one on cartels. In the absence of international law, the ICN has become the major world forum for international cooperation and convergence on competition issues, and the European Commission is a major player.

CHAPTER 22

ABUSE OF A DOMINANT POSITION

■ ■ ■

A. THE TREATY

Article 102 (formerly Article 82 of the EC Treaty) forbids the abuse of a dominant position. It provides:

Article 102

Any abuse by one or more undertakings of a dominant position within the internal market or in a substantial part of it shall be prohibited as incompatible with the internal market in so far as it may affect trade between Member States.

Such abuse may in particular consist in:

(a) directly or indirectly imposing unfair purchase or selling prices or other unfair trading conditions;

(b) limiting production, markets or technical development to the prejudice of consumers;

(c) applying dissimilar conditions to equivalent transactions with other trading parties, thereby placing them at a competitive disadvantage;

(d) making the conclusion of contracts subject to acceptance by the other parties of supplementary obligations which, by their nature or according to commercial usage, have no connection to the subject of such contracts.

The drafters of Article 86 (the original Treaty number) drew upon the law of West Germany and also the law of the United States. German law prohibits market-dominant enterprises from abusing their single-firm or group dominance by hindering competitors or exploiting or discriminating against buyers or sellers. Act Against Restraints of Competition § 19. Section 2 of the United States Sherman Antitrust Act provides that no person shall "monopolize, or attempt to monopolize, or combine or conspire with any other person or persons, to monopolize...." 15 U.S.C. § 2.

United States antitrust law was adopted at the time of the industrial revolution in response to a distrust of bigness and a fear of excessive concentration of private power. See E. Fox, The Modernization of Anti-trust: A New Equilibrium, 66 Cornell L.Rev. 1140 (1981). German cartel law was adopted at the end of World War II in connection with American aid under the Marshall Plan. By safeguarding freedom of trade, the German law was designed to diffuse power and to prevent the ascendancy of another Hitler. The law was welcomed by the Freiburg School, which espoused a "social market economy." A. Peacock and H. Willgerodt, eds., German Neo–Liberals and the Social Market Economy (1989); J. Maxeiner, Policy and Methods in German and American Antitrust Law (1986); V. Berghahn, The Americanization of West German Industry, 1945–1973 (1986); D. Gerber, Law and Competition in Twentieth Century Europe: Protecting Prometheus (1998).

Among the Western European nations, however, fear of big business was not the problem. Europe was a continent of many small nations, each isolated by high trade barriers. Private business firms were normally operating below efficient scale. Consolidations, particularly cross-border consolidations, were welcomed in order to increase efficiency and integrate the Common Market. When adopted in 1957, Article 86 [now 102] was seen not as a means to check the size of business but as a vehicle for regulating the conduct of firms that had economic power. See R. Joliet, Monopolisation and Abuse of Dominant Position: A Comparative Study of American and European Approaches to the Control of Economic Power 8–13, 131–33 (1970).

Review the four examples of abuses set forth in Article 102. What generalizations can you make about the type of conduct or transactions that the signers of the Treaty wished to prevent? Does Article 102 appear to deal only with conduct, or also with business structure (e.g., mergers)? Does it seem designed to help buyers and consumers? sellers? also competitors? Does it seem designed to achieve only efficiency or also fairness?

Compare the substance, form and structure of Article 102 with that of Article 101. What is similar and what is different about the examples of offenses? Why does Article 101 authorize exemptions while Article 102 does not? Would you expect the Article 101(3) justifications to be applicable in some way to the conduct of a dominant firm?

For 40 years, application of Article (now) 102 proceeded in a rather formalistic mode. Beginning in the late 1990s and proceeding especially in the early 2000s, the Competition Directorate and the European Commission embarked on a program to modernize European competition law, which entailed moving from formalistic analysis to effects-based analysis and employing "sound economics." Article 102 and its applications to various types of conduct were reviewed, resulting in issuance of Guidance on the Commission's Enforcement Priorities in Applying Article 82 EC Treaty [now 102 TFEU] to Abusive Exclusionary Conduct by Dominant Undertakings. The Guidance document is Document 25 of the Selected Documents. Also, it is available at *http://ec.europa.eu/competition/antitrust/ art82/index.html.*

Abuse of dominance issues are among the most controversial issues of competition law in the world today. While this chapter proceeds methodically and sometimes technically through issues of market definition, dominance, exploitative conduct, and various forms of exclusionary conduct from price predation to refusals to deal, bear in mind that there is a strong undercurrent of policy and philosophical controversy. Why does and should Europe have an abuse of dominance prohibition? Is it to protect small and powerless market actors from abuse, or only to protect consumers? Is it to assure a level playing field or only to enhance efficiencies? Is there a danger, as many Americans assert, that Europe is protecting competitors from efficient and innovative competitors (sometimes American firms), or is there a danger that lax enforcement will protect dominant firms from the challenges of competition?

Should abuse of dominance law (for US, monopolization law) be only reluctantly applied, on the theory that single-firm (non-cartel) action is usually aligned with consumers' interests, or should enforcers be vigilant to break the power of dominant firms and assure better access to markets for all market players? Which tilt in competition policy is likely to make Europe—or any nation—more competitive, and which is likely to make firms better able to adjust and respond to the changing markets of the world? Perspectives on these questions inform virtually every issue covered in this chapter, from whether dominance can be inferred from high market shares and high barriers, to whether dominant firms should have special responsibilities to firms without power, to what is a foreclosure that shifts the burden of justification to the dominant firm.

B. DOMINANCE

Article 102 prohibits abuse of a "dominant position." The Court of Justice defined dominant position in *Hoffmann–La Roche v. Commission*, Case 85/76, [1979] ECR 461:

38 The dominant position ... referred to [in Article 102] relates to a position of economic strength enjoyed by an undertaking which enables it to prevent effective competition being maintained on the relevant market by affording it the power to behave to an appreciable extent independently of its competitors, its customers and ultimately of the consumers.

39 Such a position does not preclude some competition, which it does where there is a monopoly or a quasi-monopoly, but enables the undertaking which profits by it, if not to determine, at least to have an appreciable influence on the conditions under which that competition will develop, and in any case to act largely in disregard of it so long as such conduct does not operate to its detriment.

A dominant position must also be distinguished from parallel courses of conduct which are peculiar to oligopolies in that in an oligopoly the courses of conduct interact, while in the case of an undertaking occupying a dominant position the conduct of the undertaking which derives profits from that position is to a great extent determined unilaterally.

The existence of a dominant position may derive from several factors which, taken separately, are not necessarily determinative but among these factors a highly important one is the existence of very large market shares.

40 A substantial market share as evidence of the existence of a dominant position is not a constant factor and its importance varies from market to market according to the structure of these markets, especially as far as production, supply and demand are concerned. * * *

41 Furthermore although the importance of the market shares may vary from one market to another the view may legitimately be taken that very large shares are in themselves, and save in exceptional circumstances, evidence of the existence of a dominant position.

An undertaking which has a very large market share and holds it for some time, by means of the volume of production and the scale of the supply which it stands for—without those having much smaller market shares being able to meet rapidly the demand from those who would like to break away from the undertaking which has the largest market share—is by virtue of that share in a position of strength which makes it an unavoidable trading partner and which, already because of this secures for it, at the very least during relatively long periods, that freedom of action which is the special feature of a dominant position. * * *

48 On the other hand the relationship between the market shares of the undertaking concerned and of its competitors, especially those of the next largest, the technological lead of an undertaking over its competitors, the existence of a highly developed sales network and the absence of potential competition are relevant factors, the first because it enables the competitive strength of the undertaking in question to be assessed, the second and third because they represent in themselves technical and commercial advantages and the fourth because it is the consequence of the existence of obstacles preventing new competitors from having access to the market.

A dominant position connotes economic power in a market, power to impose market terms on consumers, or more generally power to hinder the maintenance of effective competition. The Court of Justice has stated that market shares of 40% and upwards, combined with entry barriers and a size gap with the next largest firm, presumptively confer dominance. In *Hoffmann–La Roche*, a 47% share of one market (Vitamin A) was held to be enough to confer dominance in view of the structure of the market (the next largest competitors had 27% and 18%), Roche's technological lead over its competitors, the absence of potential competition, and Roche's overcapacity.

The Court in *AKZO* said, quoting from *Hoffmann–La Roche:* "very large market shares are in themselves, and save in exceptional circumstances, evidence of the existence of a dominant position." The Court in *AKZO* added: "That is the situation where there is a market share of 50% such as that found to exist in this case." *AKZO* Chemie BV v. Commission, Case 62/86, [1991] ECR I–3359, para. 60.

Can a firm be dominant if it does not have the power to raise its prices significantly above its costs (and thus charge supracompetitive prices)? Can a firm be dominant because exogenous factors have produced a temporary shortage of the goods it produces, or because distributors or customers have locked themselves into a position of dependence on the firm?

In its Guidance document, Selected Document 25, the Commission defines market power and identifies factors necessary to assess it. See Guidance, IIIA, paras. 9–18:

> Dominance entails that the ... competitive constraints are not sufficiently effective and hence that the firm in question enjoys substantial market power over a period of time. (para. 10)

An undertaking "capable of profitably increasing prices above the competitive level for a significant period of time does not face sufficiently effective constraints and can thus generally be regarded as dominant." Assessment will take account of the competitive structure of the market, including constraints by suppliers/competitors, by the credible threat of entry or expansion, and by buyer power. Market shares are "a useful first indication" but their meaningfulness will be interpreted in light of market dynamics and trends over time. (paras. 11–13)

Read paragraphs 9 to 18 of the Guidance document. To what extent does the Commission's guidance change or deepen the law or rules of *Hoffmann–La Roche* and *AKZO*? Might the Commission's guidance eventually cause a change in the law as formulated by the Court? How might this happen?

Collective Dominance

Article 102 prohibits abuse of a dominant position by "one or more undertakings." What is collective dominance within the meaning of this clause?

Collective dominance is not simply cartel behavior, which is caught, if at all, by Article 101. *Società Italiano Vetro SpA v. Commission (Italian flat glass)*, Case T–68, 77 & 78/89, [1992] ECR II–1403. In *Italian flat glass* the General Court declared that to establish an infringement of Article 102 "it is not sufficient ... to 'recycle' the facts constituting an infringement of Article [101]...." Id., para. 360. But, the Court has said, independent entities can be "united by such economic links that ...

together they hold a dominant position vis-à-vis the other operators on the same market." *Deutsche Grammophon Gesellschaft GmbH v. Metro–SB–Grossmärkte GmbH & Co. KG*, Case 78/70, [1971] ECR 487.

In *Compagnie Maritime Belge*, members of a shipping conference in the liner market between northern Europe and western Africa joined together as "fighting ships" to destroy an independent competitor. Shipping conferences are authorized by regulation to cooperate on rates and allocation of cargo, and they enjoy a limited block exemption from Articles 101 and 102. The liners defended Article 102 charges by denying, among other things, that they held a collective dominant position. They asserted that there were no economic links between them apart from the conference agreement, and that the Commission was merely transposing an Article 101 complaint. Rejecting these arguments, the Court of Justice declared that links are relevant but not necessary for the existence of a collective dominant position. "[I]t must be ascertained whether economic links exist between the undertakings concerned which enable them to act together independently of their competitors, their customers and consumers." But the critical question is whether "from an economic point of view [the undertakings] present themselves or act together on a particular market as a collective entity." "[A] liner conference [as defined in the block exemption] can be characterised as a collective entity which presents itself as such on the market vis-à-vis both users and competitors." *Compagnie Maritime Belge Transports SA v. Commission*, Cases C–395/96P and C–396/96P, [2000] ECR I–1365, paras. 42, 36, 48.

Must the collectively dominant firms act as if they were one?

US law does not have an identical concept. But compare *E.I. du Pont de Nemours & Co. v. FTC*, 729 F.2d 128 (2d Cir.1984), which states in dictum that oligopolists' non-collusive adoption of the same oppressive, unjustified anticompetitive business practices could constitute an unfair method of competition within the meaning of Section 5 of the Federal Trade Commission Act. Section 5 of the FTC Act, unlike the Sherman Act, requires neither joint action nor monopolistic power.

C. MARKET DEFINITION

If a firm is dominant, it is dominant within a defined market. Market definition—determination of both the product market and the geographic market—must precede a determination of dominance.

Most competition decisions and judgments involve market definition. In 1997 the Commission issued a Notice on the Definition of the Relevant Market. The Notice may be found at *http://ec.europa.eu/competition/antitrust/legislation/market.html*. Excerpts follow.

> The main purpose of market definition is to identify in a systematic way the competitive constraints that the undertakings involved face. The objective of defining a market in both its product and geographic dimension is to identify those actual competitors of the undertakings

involved that are capable of constraining their behaviour and of preventing them from behaving independently of an effective competitive pressure. It is from this perspective, that the market definition makes it possible, inter alia, to calculate market shares that would convey meaningful information regarding market power for the purposes of assessing dominance or for the purposes of applying Article [101]. * * *

Relevant product markets are defined as follows:

"A relevant product market comprises all those products and/or services which are regarded as interchangeable or substitutable by the consumer, by reason of the products' characteristics, their prices and their intended use."

Relevant geographic markets are defined as follows:

"The relevant geographic market comprises the area in which the undertakings concerned are involved in the supply and demand of products or services, in which the conditions of competition are sufficiently homogeneous and which can be distinguished from neighbouring areas because the conditions of competition are appreciably different in those areas". * * *

Competitive constraints

Firms are subject to three main sources of competitive constraints: demand substitutability, supply substitutability and potential competition. From an economic point of view, for the definition of the relevant market, demand substitution constitutes the most immediate and effective disciplinary force on the suppliers of a given product, in particular in relation to their pricing decisions. A firm or a group of firms cannot have a significant impact on the prevailing conditions of sale, such as prices, if its customers are in a position to switch easily to available substitute products or to suppliers located elsewhere. Basically, the exercise of market definition consists in identifying the effective alternative sources of supply for the customers of the undertakings involved, both in terms of products/services and geographic location of suppliers. * * *

The assessment of demand substitution entails a determination of the range of products which are viewed as substitutes by the consumer. One way of making this determination can be viewed, as a thought experiment, postulating a hypothetical small, non-transitory change in relative prices and evaluating the likely reactions of customers to that increase. The exercise of market definition focuses on prices for operational and practical purposes, and more precisely on demand substitution arising from small, permanent changes in relative prices. This concept can provide clear indications as to the evidence that is relevant to define markets.

Conceptually, this approach implies that starting from the type of products that the undertakings involved sell and the area in which they sell them, additional products and areas will be included into or excluded from the market definition depending on whether competition from these other products and areas affect or restrain sufficiently the pricing of the parties' products in the short term.

The question to be answered is whether the parties' customers would switch to readily available substitutes or to suppliers located elsewhere in response to an hypothetical small (in the range 5%–10%), permanent relative price increase in the products and areas being considered. If substitution would be enough to make the price increase unprofitable because of the resulting loss of sales, additional substitutes and areas are included in the relevant market. This would be done until the set of products and geographic areas is such that small, permanent increases in relative prices would be profitable.

* * *

Generally, and in particular for the analysis of merger cases, the price to take into account will be the prevailing market price. This might not be the case where the prevailing price has been determined in the absence of sufficient competition. In particular for investigation of abuses of dominant positions, the fact that the prevailing price might already have been substantially increased will be taken into account.

* * *

NOTES AND QUESTIONS

1. To define a market, one must start with a hypothesis. We seek to define an area wherein, if there were only one firm, this firm—the hypothetical monopolist—could exploit its customers, raising price and lowering output, without fear that other suppliers would simply fill the slack. We normally start with the smallest plausible market hypothesis. Thus, if the putative dominant firm is United Brands (see Section D.2. infra), we may start with bananas; we would not start with all fruit. Bananas are a distinctive fruit, and we do not know how many people readily substitute other fruit for bananas. If in all significant geographic areas people switch readily or would do so if the banana czar raised its prices, a banana producer would not have market power.

2. In the *Italian banana tax* case, a major question was whether untaxed imported bananas would push down the price of Italian table fruit. If so, the Italian tax on bananas was protectionist; it would have removed an important procompetitive force and thus protected Italian fruit growers from the competition of non-Italian fruit growers. *See Commission v. Italy (Banana tax)*, Case 184/85, [1987] ECR 2013. Is it possible for both of the following propositions to be true at the same time: 1) bananas imported into Italy without a tax would cause the price of Italian table fruit to be lower than it otherwise would have been, and 2) a banana monopolist in the EU would have power to sell bananas at a supracompetitive price in one or more Member States despite competition from other table fruit? If so, both markets—Italian table fruit in the tax case, and bananas in the competition case—may properly be identified as relevant product markets. That is, bananas could play a procompetitive role

in keeping down the price (and keeping up the quality) of non-banana table fruit, even while Dole-brand bananas could play a more powerful role than apples in keeping down the price (and keeping up the quality) of Chiquita bananas.

3. As we proceed to examine the offense of abuse we will consider many cases that have a relevant market component. We do not always concentrate on market definition. As you read the cases that follow, apply the principles of this section to the market definitions accepted by the Court, and ask yourself whether you agree with the Court's market definition or whether a different one would have been more plausible.

D. ABUSIVE CONDUCT

1. INTRODUCTION

Article 102 lists four particular practices that may be abusive. The list includes some conduct that is directly associated with the existence of market power and is often referred to as exploitative in that it represents the use of power over price to extract more than "fair" or "competitive" prices from customers. Imposing unfair prices and limiting production fall within this category. Other conduct on the list is coercive, such as requiring a contracting party to accept an obligation that has no relationship to the subject of the contract, or conduct that is otherwise unfair, such as discriminating among customers and thereby placing the disfavored customer at a competitive disadvantage.

In this section we deal with a variety of possible abuses of dominance, including excessive pricing, discriminatory pricing, refusals to deal, requirements and exclusive dealing contracts, tying, loyalty rebates, and price predation.

We deal first with excessive and discriminatory prices. Excessive prices are an exploitative abuse. Discriminatory pricing has two prongs—one of which might be excessive (exploitative) and one might be predatory (exclusionary en route to exploitation). Second, we deal with exclusionary practices. Exclusionary practices are the subject of the Commission's Guidance document.

2. EXCESSIVE AND DISCRIMINATORY PRICES AND UNFAIR TERMS

BRITISH LEYLAND PLC v. COMMISSION

Case 226/84, [1986] ECR 3263, ECJ.

[The United Kingdom gave British Leyland the exclusive right to determine whether imported British Leyland cars conformed to UK national standards, and to issue certificates of conformity. British Leyland arbitrarily refused to grant certain certificates to applicants and it set much higher fees for left-hand-drive than for right-hand-drive cars.]

27　As the Court held in its judgment in *General Motors*, an undertaking abuses its dominant position where it has an administrative monopoly and charges for its services fees which are disproportionate to the economic value of the service provided.

28　It appears from the documents before the Court and the information provided by the parties that, in the case of both right-hand-drive and left-hand-drive vehicles, in order to issue a certificate of conformity it is necessary to determine from the chassis number the date of manufacture of the vehicle. It is then possible to identify the number of the corresponding NTA certificate. It is, therefore, a simple administrative check which cannot entail significant costs. For left-hand-drive vehicles the certificate is in principle issued before conversion, if they are converted to right-hand-drive. The only difference in relation to the issue of a certificate for a right-hand-drive vehicle lies in the need to verify that the four alterations essential for a left-hand-drive vehicle have been made, namely the adjustment of headlights, full beam and dipped, the calibration of the speedometer in miles per hour, the adaptation of the rear fog lamp and the addition of a wing-mirror on the right front door. That verification does not require an inspection of the vehicle. It is effected on the basis of a certificate furnished by a garage and, on the basis of the cost incurred, cannot therefore justify the charging of different fees for the issue of certificates of conformity according to whether the vehicles are right-hand-drive or left-hand-drive. Initially the fee for left-hand-drive vehicles was six times greater than that for right-hand-drive vehicles.

29　Moreover, BL itself admitted at the hearing that the difference which existed at one time according to whether the certificate was requested by a dealer, who was charged UK £150, or by a private individual, who was charged only UK £100, was not based on the cost but on the consideration that the trader who was carrying out a transaction for gain could be required to pay a higher fee. The fact that the fee was first reduced to UK £100 and then UK £50, whilst for right-hand-drive vehicles it remained at UK £25, also suggests that it was fixed solely with a view to making the re-importation of left-hand-drive vehicles less attractive.

30　In those circumstances, the Commission was entitled to conclude that the fee was fixed at a level which was clearly disproportionate to the economic value of the service provided and that that practice constituted an abuse by BL of the monopoly it held by virtue of the British rules.* * *

33　Finally, BL's argument that the amount of the fee had no detrimental effect on the volume of the re-importations is, as the Court has already stated above, irrelevant.

34　In conclusion, it must be held that the complaints made by the Commission in the contested decision are established.

British Leyland was a toll-taker, enabled by government license. Moreover, while the fact of excessiveness is usually extremely difficult to determine, in *British Leyland* it was obvious. Further, in this case, the exploitation was a means of market segmentation—a core offense.

Some years earlier, the Commission pressed a more ambiguous case of unfair pricing, and also a case of discriminatory pricing, against United Brands.

UNITED BRANDS CO. v. COMMISSION

(pricing practices)
Case 27/76, [1978] ECR 207, ECJ.

[United Brands was the biggest banana producer in the world and in the Community. It was a vertically integrated company that grew bananas in South America, bought from other growers half of the bananas it sold, and accounted for some 40% of the sales of bananas in the Community, which was more than twice that of its nearest rival. It owned and promoted the Chiquita brand, the best known and the most heavily advertised brand in the world. Its system of distribution involved sales to ripeners/distributors, who would buy the green bananas, ripen them in special sheds and in specified gases, and resell them. The Commission alleged a series of abuses, including the cut-off of a Danish ripener/distributor, excessive pricing and discriminatory pricing.

United Brands sold all bananas to its distributors free on rail Rotterdam or Bremerhaven. There was a 100% difference between the prices charged to the distributor for Ireland, where Chiquita was an unknown brand and demand was low, and the prices charged to the distributor for Denmark, where the brand was well known and demand was strong. There were also disparities between the price charged to the Danish distributors and to the distributors for the other Member States. United Brands' prices were approximately 7% higher than the prices of its nearest rivals, and they were 30% to 40% higher than unbranded bananas. The Commission found discriminatory and excessive pricing violations and ordered United Brands to reduce its prices to distributors other than the distributors for Ireland by at least 15%.]

*1. Discriminatory prices * * **

208   The Commission blames the applicant for charging each week for the sale of its branded bananas—without objective justification—a selling price which differs appreciably according to the Member State where its customers are established. * * *

212   The price customers in Belgium are asked to pay is on average 80% higher than that paid by customers in Ireland.

213   The greatest difference in price is 138% between the delivered Rotterdam price charged by UBC to its customers in Ireland and the f.o.r. Bremerhaven price charged by UBC to its customers in Denmark,

that is to say the price paid by Danish customers is 2.38 times the price paid by Irish customers. * * *

225   In fact the bananas sold by UBC are all freighted in the same ships, are unloaded at the same cost in Rotterdam or Bremerhaven and the price differences relate to substantially similar quantities of bananas of the same variety, which have been brought to the same degree of ripening, are of similar quality and sold under the same "Chiquita" brand name under the same conditions of sale and payment for loading on to the purchaser's own means of transport and the latter have to pay customs duties, taxes and transport costs from these ports. * * *

232   These discriminatory prices, which varied according to the circumstances of the Member States, were just so many obstacles to the free movement of goods and their effect was intensified by the clause forbidding the resale of bananas while still green and by reducing the deliveries of the quantities ordered.

233   A rigid partitioning of national markets was thus created at price levels, which were artificially different, placing certain distributor/ripeners at a competitive disadvantage, since compared with what it should have been competition had thereby been distorted.

234   Consequently the policy of differing prices enabling UBC to apply dissimilar conditions to equivalent transactions with other trading parties, thereby placing them at a competitive disadvantage, was an abuse of a dominant position.

2.   *Unfair prices* * * *

252   The questions ... to be determined are whether the difference between the costs actually incurred and the price actually charged is excessive, and, if the answer to this question is in the affirmative, whether a price has been imposed which is either unfair in itself or when compared to competing products.

253   Other ways may be devised—and economic theorists have not failed to think up several—of selecting the rules for determining whether the price of a product is unfair. * * *

258   The Commission bases its view that prices are excessive on an analysis of the differences—in its view excessive—between the prices charged in the different Member States and on the policy of discriminatory prices which has been considered above.

259   The foundation of its argument has been the applicant's letter of 10 December 1974 which acknowledged that the margin allowed by the sale of bananas to Irish ripeners was much smaller than in some other Member States and it concluded from this that the amount by which the actual prices f.o.r. Bremerhaven and Rotterdam exceed the delivered Rotterdam prices for bananas to be sold to Irish customers c.i.f. Dublin must represent a profit of the same order of magnitude.

260   Having found that the prices charged to ripeners of the other Member States were considerably higher, sometimes by as much as 100%, than the prices charged to customers in Ireland it concluded that UBC was making a very substantial profit.

261   Nevertheless the Commission has not taken into account in its reasoning ... a confidential document ... pointing out that the prices charged in Ireland had produced a loss.

262   The applicant also states that the prices charged on the relevant market did not allow it to make any profits during the last five years, except in 1975. * * *

264   However unreliable the particulars supplied by UBC may be (and in particular the document mentioned previously which works out the "losses" on the Irish market in 1974 without any supporting evidence), the fact remains that it is for the Commission to prove that the applicant charged unfair prices.

265   UBC's retraction, which the Commission has not effectively refuted, establishes beyond doubt that the basis for the calculation adopted by the latter to prove that UBC's prices are excessive is open to criticism and on this particular point there is doubt which must benefit the applicant, especially as for nearly 20 years banana prices, in real terms, have not risen on the relevant market. * * *

267   In these circumstances it appears that the Commission has not adduced adequate legal proof of the facts and evaluations which formed the foundation of its finding that UBC had infringed Article [102] of the Treaty by directly and indirectly imposing unfair selling prices for bananas.

NOTES AND QUESTIONS

1. Excessive pricing is an exploitative violation. It signifies that a dominant firm uses its market power to overcharge consumers. Many antitrust regimes prohibit excessive pricing, which may be seen as the principal, most direct economic evil of monopoly. The challenges of detection, surveillance, and appropriate relief, however, are great and counsel caution in applying the law.

2. What is the relationship between excessive and discriminatory pricing in *United Brands?* Is one offense more central than the other to Community objectives?

3. The Court called the discriminatory prices "just so many obstacles to the free movement of goods." (para. 232) Is price discrimination a barrier to free movement? What were the real barriers to free movement? Why did the Court blame lack of mobility of the bananas on the price discrimination rather than on the green banana clause?

4. Price discrimination can be a way to exploit (to get more money from those who are willing to pay more), and it can be a way to compete (to lower prices and make more sales). United Brands was apparently charging high

prices where consumers had a strong preference for bananas, and low prices to break into markets where Chiquita was not well known and other fruits were in strong demand. In areas in which demand for Chiquita bananas was strong, was the real question who would get the extra profits, United Brands or its distributor? Would prohibition of price discrimination mean everyone would get the Irish price?

5. United States antitrust law does not prohibit excessive pricing. It prohibits price discrimination only if the discriminatory pricing is likely to produce monopoly (invoking the Sherman Act) or hurt disfavored buyers in their competition with favored ones (invoking the Robinson–Patman Act). The US antitrust agencies seldom enforce the Robinson–Patman Act because they fear that most applications of this law are anticompetitive. (Why?) As a result, most Robinson–Patman actions are private actions. Competitors of the price discriminator have been greatly restricted in their ability to sue, however (imagine Standard Fruit suing United Brands for price discrimination among UB's dealers), because they must prove antitrust injury and antitrust damages, and this requires proof that consumers are harmed. This is hard to prove. See, e.g., Brooke Group Ltd. v. Brown & Williamson Tobacco Corp., 509 U.S. 209, 113 S.Ct. 2578, 125 L.Ed.2d 168 (1993), page 919 infra.

As for excessive pricing, the Court of Appeals for the US Second Circuit said in Berkey Photo, Inc. v. Eastman Kodak Co.:

> Excessive prices, maintained through exercise of a monopolist's control of the market, constituted one of the primary evils that the Sherman Act was intended to correct. . . .

> But unless the monopoly has bolstered its power by wrongful actions, it will not be required to pay damages merely because its prices may later be found excessive. Setting a high price may be a use of monopoly power, but it is not in itself anticompetitive. Indeed, although a monopolist may be expected to charge a somewhat higher price than would prevail in a competitive market, there is probably no better way to guarantee that its dominance will be challenged than by greedily extracting the highest price it can. . . . Judicial oversight of pricing policies would place the courts in a role akin to that of a public regulatory commission. . . . We would be wise to decline that function unless Congress clearly bestows it upon us.

Berkey Photo, Inc. v. Eastman Kodak Co., 603 F.2d 263, 294 (2d Cir.1979), cert. denied, 444 U.S. 1093 (1980).

The Supreme Court of the United States confirmed this limit of the Sherman Act in *Trinko*, see page 885 below, where it went much further, stating that monopoly prices should be welcomed; high prices invite competition. Do *Kodak* and *Trinko* reflect a major difference between US and EU competition law? What should happen when high prices do not attract entry?

3.   EXCLUSIONARY CONDUCT

a.   Introduction

We turn to exclusionary or foreclosing violations. Examine the scheme of the Commission's guidance on exclusionary practices. See, again, Selected Document 25. The Commission begins its discussion of harm from foreclosure as follows:

> The aim of the Commission's enforcement activity in relation to exclusionary conduct is to ensure that dominant undertakings do not impair effective competition by foreclosing their rivals in an anticompetitive way and thus having an adverse impact on consumer welfare, whether in the form of higher price levels than would have otherwise prevailed or in some other form such as limiting quality or reducing consumer choice. In this document the term "anticompetitive foreclosure" is used to describe a situation where effective access of actual or potential competitors to supplies or markets is hampered or eliminated as a result of the conduct of the dominant undertaking whereby the dominant undertaking is likely to be in a position to profitably increase prices to the detriment of consumers.... (Guidance, para. 19)

Even where it finds anticompetitive foreclosure, the Commission will examine claims by the dominant undertaking that its conduct is justified by objective necessity or efficiency.

As you begin your study of Refusal to deal, below, read the Commission guidance, in the Guidance Document, on refusal to supply, paras. 74–89. The Commission's guidance is intended to incorporate the more economic approach. For all of the cases below, consider whether the Commission's analysis does or does not align with the courts' analysis. If not, identify divergences.

b. Refusal to Deal

ESSENTIAL FACILITY AND DUTY TO GIVE ACCESS

Ownership of or control over an essential facility presents a special case of duty to deal, duty not to exclude, and duty to treat competitors and customers fairly and non-discriminatorily.

The Commission first invoked the essential facility concept in the case of *Sealink*. Sealink owned Holyhead Harbour, which was the only port in the UK serving Ireland for the transport of passengers and cars on the central corridor route. Sealink also operated a car ferry. B&I Line was a rival car ferry operator. Its berth was in the mouth of the narrow Holyhead Harbor. When a Sealink vessel passed a B&I vessel, it so agitated the water that B&I had to lift the ramp that connected the boat to the dock and stop loading or unloading. Sealink then scheduled more frequent sailings of its own vessels, making the disturbances intolerable to B&I. B&I sought interim measures, which the Commission granted. It said:

> A dominant undertaking which both owns or controls and itself uses an essential facility, i.e., a facility or infrastructure without access to which competitors cannot provide services to their customers, and which refuses its competitors access to that facility or grants access to

competitors only on terms less favourable than those which it gives its own services, thereby placing the competitors at a competitive disadvantage, infringes Article [102] if the other conditions of that Article are met. A company in a dominant position may not discriminate in favour of its own activities in a related market (Case C–260/89, Elliniki Radiophonia, ¶¶ [36–38]). The owner of an essential facility which uses its power in one market in order to strengthen its position in another related market, in particular, by granting its competitor access to that related market on less favourable terms than those of its own services, infringes Article [102] when a competitive disadvantage is imposed upon its competitor without objective justification.

This was accepted by Sealink through its subsidiary, SHL, when it stated that no agreement would be given to vary schedules if this compromised its ability to provide an acceptable level of service to all port users. . . . This is particularly so where the physical configuration of the port has obliged operators to accept differences in the services they are offered by the operator of the essential facility, in order to maximize its efficient utilization.

The owner of the essential facility, which uses the essential facility, may not impose a competitive disadvantage on its competitor, also a user of the essential facility, by altering its own schedule to the detriment of the competitor's service, where, as in this case, the construction or the features of the facility are such that it is not possible to alter one competitor's service in the way chosen without harming the other's. Specifically, where, as in this case, the competitor is already subject to a certain level of disruption from the dominant undertaking's activities, there is a duty on the dominant undertaking not to take any action which will result in further disruption. That is so even if the latter's actions make, or are primarily intended to make, its operations more efficient. Subject to any objective elements outside its control, such an undertaking is under a duty not to impose a competitive disadvantage upon its competitor in the use of the shared facility without objective justification.

B&I Line plc v. Sealink Harbours Ltd. and Sealink Stena Ltd., Case IV/34.174, [1992] not officially reported, as quoted in John Temple Lang, Defining Legitimate Competition: Companies' Duties to Supply Competitors, And Access to Essential Facilities, 1994 Fordham Corporate Law Institute (B. Hawk ed. 1995), pp. 245, 362–63.

Subsequent port cases, particularly where the state owned the port, confirmed the principle. See Chapter 26, infra, Part B.

Did Sealink have a legitimate reason to expand its schedule? Should this have been an objective justification? Should a firm that has made the investment in the essential infrastructure be allowed to prefer itself over its rivals in uses of the infrastructure?

For many years US cases also applied an essential facility doctrine where the duty to grant access would not impair the defendant's own performance. Examples are the telecommunications cases before the break-up of AT&T, when AT&T held the nation's long distance telephone service monopoly, the local service monopolies, and the local loop bottleneck gateway to the local markets. See *MCI Communications Corp. v. American Telephone & Telegraph Co.*, 708 F.2d 1081 (7th Cir.1983); *United States v. American Telephone & Telegraph Co.*, 524 F.Supp. 1336, 1352 (D.D.C.1981). Some time after the *AT&T* cases, US authorities and jurists began to fear that an overbroad essential facilities doctrine undermined incentives to invest, to innovate, and to compete. For change in the US approach, see *Verizon Communications Inc. v. Law Offices of Curtis V. Trinko*, infra at page ___. Consider the effect of duties to deal on incentives to invest, innovate and compete as you read the following cases. Is the concern well-taken or not?

OTHER DUTIES TO DEAL THAT MAY OR MAY NOT INVOLVE AN ESSENTIAL FACILITY

ISTITUTO CHEMIOTERAPICO ITALIANO SPA v. COMMISSION
(*Commercial Solvents*)

Cases 6, 7/73, [1974] ECR 223, ECJ.

[Commercial Solvents Corporation was a manufacturer of raw materials—nitropropane and aminobutanol—which were used to manufacture ethambutol, an antituberculosis drug. Aminobutanol was also used as an emulsifier for paint. Commercial Solvents Corporation acquired 51 percent of the shares of an Italian company, Istituto, which bought the raw materials from its parent, Commercial Solvents, and sold them to another Italian company, Zoja, which used them to manufacture ethambutol-based specialties.

Istituto sought to acquire Zoja, but the negotiations aborted. Istituto then increased the price at which it sold aminobutanol to Zoja. Zoja, however, discovered a cheaper source for aminobutanol—firms that bought the raw material from Commercial Solvents for use in paint. Zoja persuaded Istituto to cancel a large part of Zoja's order. Soon thereafter, Zoja's supply of cheaper aminobutanol dried up, largely because Commercial Solvents forbade its paint-making customers to resell aminobutanol for pharmaceutical use. Commercial Solvents then announced that it was withdrawing from the market for sales of the raw material, and it integrated vertically, using the raw material for its own production. When Zoja tried to reorder aminobutanol from Commercial Solvents, Commercial Solvents refused to accept the order.

The Commission held that Commercial Solvents had a dominant position in the market for the raw material and ordered Commercial Solvents to resume supplying Zoja and to pay a fine for the refusal to sell.]

23   The applicants state that they ought not to be held responsible for stopping supplies of aminobutanol to Zoja for this was due to the fact that in the spring of 1970 Zoja itself informed Istituto that it was cancelling the purchase of large quantities of aminobutanol which had been provided for in a contract then in force between Istituto and Zoja. When at the end of 1970 Zoja again contacted Istituto to obtain this product, the latter was obliged to reply, after consulting CSC, that in the meantime CSC had changed its commercial policy and that the product was no longer available. The change of policy by CSC was, they claim, inspired by a legitimate consideration of the advantage that would accrue to it of expanding its production to include the manufacture of finished products and not limiting itself to that of raw material or intermediate products. In pursuance of this policy it decided to improve its product and no longer to supply aminobutanol save in respect of commitments already entered into by its distributors. * * *

25   However, an undertaking being in a dominant position as regards the production of raw material and therefore able to control the supply to manufacturers of derivatives, cannot, just because it decides to start manufacturing these derivatives (in competition with its former customers) act in such a way as to eliminate their competition which in the case in question would amount to eliminating one of the principal manufacturers of ethambutol in the Common Market. Since such conduct is contrary to the objectives expressed in Article 3[(1)(g)] [now in a protocol] of the Treaty and set out in greater detail in Articles [101] and [102], it follows that an undertaking which has a dominant position in the market in raw materials and which, with the object of reserving such raw material for manufacturing its own derivatives, refuses to supply a customer, which is itself a manufacturer of these derivatives, and therefore risks eliminating all competition on the part of this customer, is abusing its dominant position within the meaning of Article [102]. In this context it does not matter that the undertaking ceased to supply in the spring of 1970 because of the cancellation of the purchases by Zoja, because it appears from the applicants' own statement that, when the supplies provided for in the contract had been completed, the sale of aminobutanol would have stopped in any case. * * *

28   ... [T]he applicants do not seriously dispute the statement in the Decision in question to the effect that "in view of the production capacity of the CSC plant it can be confirmed that CSC can satisfy Zoja's needs, since Zoja represents a very small percentage (approximately 5–6%) of CSC's global production of nitropropane." It must be concluded that the Commission was justified in considering that such statements could not be taken into account.

UNITED BRANDS CO. v. COMMISSION

(refusal to deal)
Case 27/76, [1978] ECR 207, ECJ.

[In another aspect of the *United Brands* case, supra page 876, United Brands cut off the supply of Chiquita bananas to Olesen, one of its ripener/distributors in Denmark, after Olesen became the exclusive distributor for its chief competitor, producer of the Dole banana, and Olesen allegedly was pushing Dole at the expense of Chiquita.]

182　... [I]t is advisable to assert positively from the outset that an undertaking in a dominant position for the purpose of marketing a product—which cashes in on the reputation of a brand name known to and valued by the consumers—cannot stop supplying a long standing customer who abides by regular commercial practice, if the orders placed by that customer are in no way out of the ordinary.
　　* * *

189　Although it is true, as the applicant points out, that the fact that an undertaking is in a dominant position cannot disentitle it from protecting its own commercial interests if they are attacked, and that such an undertaking must be conceded the right to take such reasonable steps as it deems appropriate to protect its said interests, such behaviour cannot be countenanced if its actual purpose is to strengthen this dominant position and abuse it.

190　Even if the possibility of a counter-attack is acceptable that attack must still be proportionate to the threat taking into account the economic strength of the undertakings confronting each other.

191　The sanction consisting of a refusal to supply by an undertaking in a dominant position was in excess of what might, if such a situation were to arise, reasonably be contemplated as a sanction for conduct similar to that for which UBC blamed Olesen.

192　In fact UBC could not be unaware of that fact that by acting in this way it would discourage its other ripener/distributors from supporting the advertising of other brand names and that the deterrent effect of the sanction imposed upon one of them would make its position of strength on the relevant market that much more effective.

193　Such a course of conduct amounts therefore to a serious interference with the independence of small and medium sized firms in their commercial relations with the undertaking in a dominant position and this independence implies the right to give preference to competitors' goods.

194　In this case the adoption of such a course of conduct is designed to have a serious adverse effect on competition on the relevant banana market by only allowing firms dependant upon the dominant undertaking to stay in business. * * *

NOTES AND QUESTIONS

1. What main principle of law governs these two cases? Cite the key paragraph in each judgment. Is this principle based on: efficiency and consumer interests? fairness and rights of competitors?

2. Is there a possible set of facts that would have justified United Brands' conduct? Commercial Solvents' conduct?

3. In *Oscar Bronner*, the Court of Justice rejected the claim of Bronner, owner of a small daily newspaper, that the distribution system of Mediaprint, the near-monopolist publisher and owner of the only nation-wide newspaper distribution system in Austria, was an essential facility to which he had a right of access. The Court said that Mediaprint's refusal to distribute Bronner's newspaper would not amount to an abuse of dominance unless it was "likely to eliminate all competition in the daily newspaper market on the part of the person requesting the service and that such refusal be incapable of being objectively justified, [and] also that the service in itself be indispensable to carrying on that person's business, inasmuch as there is no actual or potential substitute in existence for that home-delivery scheme." para. 41. Bronner had not made this case. Among other things, there were no technical or legal obstacles preventing Bronner, alone or in combination with other small papers, from setting up an alternative distribution system. *Oscar Bronner GmbH & Co. KG v. Mediaprint Zeitungs-und Zeitschriftenverlag GmbH & Co.*, Case C–7/97, [1998] ECR I–7791. Can *Oscar Bronner* be distinguished from *Commercial Solvents* and *United Brands*?

4. Is withdrawal of supply treated the same or differently from de novo refusal to supply? Should it be treated differently? How does the Commission's guidance answer this question?

5. US law applies a strong presumption of freedom of firms to choose to deal or not, as exemplified in the *Trinko* case below.

VERIZON COMMUNICATIONS INC. v. LAW OFFICES OF CURTIS V. TRINKO

Supreme Court of the United States
540 U.S. 398, 124 S.Ct. 872, 157 L.Ed.2d 823 (2004).

JUSTICE SCALIA:

[Verizon was the incumbent local exchange carrier (ILEC) serving New York State. This meant that Verizon owned the elements of the local loop—facilities necessary to connect long distance lines with the local market. When competition in the local telephone service markets became technologically feasible, Congress passed the 1996 Telecommunications Act to facilitate entry into the local markets. Among other things, the statute required the ILECs to give the new local exchange carriers (competitive LECs or CLECs) access to the elements of the local loop on reasonable non-discriminatory terms. Verizon, in order to keep its customers from defecting to new entrants and to limit entry, discriminated against the CLECs, disrupting their service and making it unreliable.

Complaints to this effect were investigated and verified by the Federal Communications Commission, which fined Verizon and enjoined its discriminatory and exclusionary practices.

Plaintiffs were customers of the discriminated against CLECs. They sued for damages for their loses. (There was a serious standing problem, but this was not the basis of the decision.) Verizon moved to dismiss on the pleadings, meaning that, accepting all of the facts pleaded as true, Verizon claimed that plaintiffs had no basis for suit. Verizon maintained that it had no antitrust duty to the CLECs not to discriminate.

The Court first noted that the Telecommunications Act contained a savings clause preserving applicability of the antitrust laws; therefore the antitrust laws were not preempted by the Telecoms Act. The Court then turned to the question whether a telecom monopoly's denial of full interconnection services to rivals in order to limit their entry constituted a violation of Section 2 of the Sherman Act, which states: No person shall "monopolize".]

III

... The mere possession of monopoly power, and the concomitant charging of monopoly prices, is not only not unlawful; it is an important element of the free-market system. The opportunity to charge monopoly prices—at least for a short period—is what attracts "business acumen" in the first place; it induces risk taking that produces innovation and economic growth. To safeguard the incentive to innovate, the possession of monopoly power will not be found unlawful unless it is accompanied by an element of anticompetitive *conduct.*

Firms may acquire monopoly power by establishing an infrastructure that renders them uniquely suited to serve their customers. Compelling such firms to share the source of their advantage is in some tension with the underlying purpose of antitrust law, since it may lessen the incentive for the monopolist, the rival, or both to invest in those economically beneficial facilities. Enforced sharing also requires antitrust courts to act as central planners, identifying the proper price, quantity, and other terms of dealing—a role for which they are ill-suited. Moreover, compelling negotiation between competitors may facilitate the supreme evil of antitrust: collusion. Thus, as a general matter, the Sherman Act "does not restrict the long recognized right of [a] trader or manufacturer engaged in an entirely private business, freely to exercise his own independent discretion as to parties with whom he will deal." *United States* v. *Colgate & Co.,* 250 U.S. 300, 307 (1919).

However, "[t]he high value that we have placed on the right to refuse to deal with other firms does not mean that the right is unqualified." *Aspen Skiing Co.* v. *Aspen Highlands Skiing Corp.,* 472 U.S. 585, 601 (1985). Under certain circumstances, a refusal to cooperate with rivals can constitute anticompetitive conduct and violate § 2. We have been very cautious in recognizing such exceptions, because of the uncertain virtue of forced sharing and the difficulty of identifying and remedying anticompetitive conduct by a single firm. The question before us today is whether the allegations of respondent's complaint fit within existing exceptions or provide a basis, under traditional antitrust principles, for recognizing a new one. * * *

[The Court answered in the negative. Verizon did not engage in a voluntary course of dealing with its rivals; it supplied them because of statutory compulsion. Moreover, the unbundled elements to which rivals sought fair access did not even exist as a marketed product apart from the 1996 Act. Further, if there is an essential facilities doctrine, it was not available here.] The 1996 Act's extensive provision for access makes it unnecessary to impose a judicial doctrine of forced access. To the extent respondent's "essential facilities" argument is distinct from its general § 2 argument, we reject it.

IV

Finally, we do not believe that traditional antitrust principles justify adding the present case to the few existing exceptions from the proposition that there is no duty to aid competitors.... * * *

... [Here, the regulatory] regime was an effective steward of the antitrust function.

Against the slight benefits of antitrust intervention here, we must weigh a realistic assessment of its costs. Under the best of circumstances, applying the requirements of § 2 "can be difficult" because "the means of illicit exclusion, like the means of legitimate competition, are myriad." *United States* v. *Microsoft Corp.*, 253 F.3d 34, 58 (CADC 2001) (en banc) *(per curiam)*. Mistaken inferences and the resulting false condemnations "are especially costly, because they chill the very conduct the antitrust laws are designed to protect." *Matsushita Elec. Industrial Co.* v. *Zenith Radio Corp.*, 475 U.S. 574, 594 (1986). The cost of false positives counsels against an undue expansion of § 2 liability....

Even if the problem of false positives did not exist, conduct consisting of anticompetitive violations of § 251 [Telecoms Act duty to give access] may be, as we have concluded with respect to above-cost predatory pricing schemes, "beyond the practical ability of a judicial tribunal to control." *Brooke Group Ltd.* v. *Brown & Williamson Tobacco Corp.*, 509 U.S. 209, 223 (1993). Effective remediation of violations of regulatory sharing requirements will ordinarily require continuing supervision of a highly detailed decree. We think that Professor Areeda got it exactly right: "No court should impose a duty to deal that it cannot explain or adequately and reasonably supervise.... An antitrust court is unlikely to be an effective day-to-day enforcer of these detailed sharing obligations.[4]

---

4. The Court of Appeals also thought that respondent's complaint might state a claim under a "monopoly leveraging" theory.... We disagree. To the extent the Court of Appeals dispensed with a requirement that there be a "dangerous probability of success" in monopolizing a second market, it erred. In any event, leveraging presupposes anticompetitive conduct, which in this case could only be the refusal-to-deal claim we have rejected.

The 1996 Act is in an important respect much more ambitious than the antitrust laws. It attempts *"to eliminate the monopolies* enjoyed by the inheritors of AT&T's local franchises." *Verizon Communications Inc.* v. *FCC,* 535 U.S., at 476 (emphasis added). Section 2 of the Sherman Act, by contrast, seeks merely to prevent *unlawful monopolization.* It would be a serious mistake to conflate the two goals. The Sherman Act ... does not give judges *carte blanche* to insist that a monopolist alter its way of doing business whenever some other approach might yield greater competition. We conclude that respondent's complaint fails to state a claim under the Sherman Act. * * *

NOTES AND QUESTIONS

1. *Trinko* is a regulated industries case, but it is also, more broadly, a refusal to deal and exclusionary strategy case. What are the main elements that form the Court's perspective on the role of antitrust in the case of unilateral (monopoly/abuse of dominance) conduct? Is the Court more concerned about exclusion of rivals? freedom (for whom)? property rights? innovation and economic growth? Elaborate on the Court's concern about false positives. Is the Court predominantly concerned with consumer interests? Does it have a distinct idea of how to protect consumer interests? Does it give courts wide berth to intervene to make markets more responsive to consumers?

2. How would the *Commercial Solvents* and *United Brands* cases be resolved under US law? What, if any, additional facts would you need to know? In *United Brands,* how would the following alternative assumptions affect your analysis under US law: (1) Because of the great demand for Chiquita bananas and the large firm size needed to enjoy economies of scale, all distributor/ripeners needed to carry some Chiquita brand bananas to be efficient. (2) Contrariwise, small distributor/ripeners were able to capture all economies of scale. Why were the answers to these questions not important in the *United Brands* case?

IS INTELLECTUAL PROPERTY A SPECIAL CASE?

A firm may own intellectual property rights, which typically grant the exclusive right to practice, use or license a patent, trademark, copyright or design. If the owner of intellectual property has a dominant position and declines to license it, is the duty to deal relaxed further on grounds that the intellectual property owner has state-granted exclusive rights? Or is the duty to deal stronger on grounds that the intellectual property right reflects exclusive privileges and the state-granted rights may be used to obstruct free movement of goods and to partition the common market?

Intellectual property rights are a subject of Article 36 (ex 30 ECT) of the Treaty, which provides that Articles 34 and 35, guaranteeing free movement of goods, shall not preclude "restrictions on imports, exports or goods in transit justified on grounds of ... the protection of industrial and commercial property" as long as such restrictions are not "a means of arbitrary discrimination or a disguised restriction on trade between Member States." Does this language imply a hospitable stance towards intellectual property rights? Does it imply that intellectual property rights normally trump free movement rights? The Court of Justice held, in Deutsche Grammophon Gesellschaft GmbH v. Metro–SB–Grossmärkte GmbH, Case 78/70, [1971] ECR 487, para. 11:

> Article [36] only admits derogations from [free movement principles] to the extent to which they are justified for the purpose of safeguarding rights which constitute the specific subject-matter of such property.

What does "the specific subject matter of such property" mean? Remember that in *Consten and Grundig,* page 825 supra, with the blessing of Grundig, Consten had tried to use its exclusive rights to the trademark GINT (Grundig International) to keep imported GINT products out of France, because it, Consten, had been appointed the exclusive distributor in France. The Court held that Consten and Grundig's agreement to restrain parallel imports could not be justified as a "mere" exercise of trademark rights.

In 1988 the Court of Justice considered questions posed to it by national courts regarding exclusive design rights in automobile parts of Volvo and Renault. In the *Volvo* judgment the Court said:

> [T]he rights of the proprietor of a protected design to prevent third parties from manufacturing and selling or importing, without its consent, products incorporating the design constitutes the very subject-matter of his exclusive right. It follows ... that a refusal to grant such a license cannot in itself constitute an abuse of a dominant position.

> [T]he exercise of an exclusive right by the proprietor of a registered design in respect of car body panels may be prohibited by Article [102] if it involves, on the part of an undertaking holding a dominant position, certain abusive conduct such as the arbitrary refusal to supply spare parts to independent repairers, the fixing of prices for spare parts at an unfair level or a decision no longer to produce spare parts for a particular model even though many cars of that model are still in circulation, provided that such conduct is liable to affect trade between Member States.

Volvo AB v. Erik Veng (UK) Ltd., Case 238/87, [1988] ECR 6211, paras. 8–9.

When is such a refusal to supply "arbitrary," and when, on the other hand, does it go to the heart of the industrial property owner's right of exclusivity?

The principle of deference to IP holders' essential rights was tested in a case in which the copyright holders' right not to license conflicted directly with the public's right to competition. (But doesn't it always?) The question arose whether each of the three significant TV broadcasters in Ireland was required to license its TV schedules to a third party who proposed to publish a consolidated TV guide.

RADIO TELEFIS EIREANN v. COMMISSION
(*Magill*)

Cases C–241/91P and C–242/91P, [1995] ECR I–743, ECJ.

[Radio Telefis Eireann ("RTE"), BBC, and Independent Television Publications ("ITP") operated TV stations. Each published weekly listings of its programs in Ireland and Northern Ireland, gave newspapers its schedule free on a daily basis, and claimed copyright protection over its program listings. At that, time, no composite TV guide existed. Magill conceived the idea to publish a weekly magazine, the Magill TV Guide, listing all available TV programs in Ireland and Northern Ireland. It sought licenses from RTE, BBC and ITP, but the licenses were denied. Magill nonetheless proceeded with the publication. In a suit by the three copyright owners, the Irish High Court enjoined Magill from using the copyrighted listings of RTE, BBC and ITP. Magill complained to the Commission. The Commission found that each of the three broadcasters had and abused a dominant position. Two of the stations challenged the decision, claiming that they had done nothing more than exercise their rights under the Irish copyright law. The Irish copyright law protected a TV station's schedule of its programs. Although this was a protection not extended by laws of other nations, the law itself was valid under Articles 34/36, for it conferred intellectual property rights and was not an arbitrary discrimination or disguised restriction on trade between Member States. [Reread Articles 34, 36 and 345.] The TV stations claimed that they had done nothing more than exercise their copyright right to refuse to license. Moreover, each station argued that it was not dominant; it supplied less than a third of the market. The General Court upheld the Commission, and the stations appealed.]

(a) Existence of a dominant position

46   So far as dominant position is concerned, it is to be remembered at the outset that mere ownership of an intellectual property right cannot confer such a position.

47   However, the basic information as to the channel, day, time and title of programmes is the necessary result of programming by television stations, which are thus the only source of such information for an undertaking, like Magill, which wishes to publish it together with commentaries or pictures. By force of circumstance, RTE and ITP, as the agent of ITV, enjoy, along with the BBC, a *de facto* monopoly over the information used to compile listings for the television programmes received in most households in Ireland and 30% to 40% of households in Northern Ireland. The appellants are thus in a position to prevent effective competition on the market in weekly television magazines. [They therefore] occupied a dominant position. . . .

(b) Existence of abuse

48   With regard to the issue of abuse, the arguments of the appellants and IPO wrongly presuppose that where the conduct of an undertaking in

a dominant position consists of the exercise of a right classified by national law as "copyright", such conduct can never be reviewed in relation to Article [102] of the Treaty.

49   Admittedly, in the absence of Community standardization or harmonization of laws, determination of the conditions and procedures for granting protection of an intellectual property right is a matter for national rules. Further, the exclusive right of reproduction forms part of the author's rights, so that refusal to grant a licence, even if it is the act of an undertaking holding a dominant position, cannot in itself constitute abuse of a dominant position.

50   However, it is also clear from that judgment ... that the exercise of an exclusive right by the proprietor may, in exceptional circumstances, involve abusive conduct.

51   In the present case, the conduct objected to is the appellants' reliance on copyright conferred by national legislation so as to prevent Magill—or any other undertaking having the same intention—from publishing on a weekly basis information (channel, day, time and title of programmes) together with commentaries and pictures obtained independently of the appellants.

52   Among the circumstances taken into account by the [General Court] in concluding that such conduct was abusive was, first, the fact that there was, according to the findings of the [General Court], no actual or potential substitute for a weekly television guide offering information on the programmes for the week ahead. On this point, the [General Court] confirmed the Commission's finding that the complete lists of programmes for a 24–hour period—and for a 48–hour period at weekends and before public holidays—published in certain daily and Sunday newspapers, and the television sections of certain magazines covering, in addition, "highlights" of the week's programmes, were only to a limited extent substitutable for advance information to viewers on all the week's programmes. Only weekly television guides containing comprehensive listings for the week ahead would enable users to decide in advance which programmes they wished to follow and arrange their leisure activities for the week accordingly. The [General Court] also established that there was a specific, constant and regular potential demand on the part of consumers....

53   Thus the appellants—who were, by force of circumstance, the only source of the basic information on programme scheduling which is the indispensable raw material for compiling a weekly television guide—gave viewers wishing to obtain information on the choice of programmes for the week ahead no choice but to buy the weekly guides for each station and draw from each of them the information they needed to make comparisons.

54   The appellants' refusal to provide basic information by relying on national copyright provisions thus prevented the appearance of a new product, a comprehensive weekly guide to television programmes,

which the appellants did not offer and for which there was a potential consumer demand. Such refusal constitutes an abuse under heading (b) of the second paragraph of Article [102] of the Treaty.

55 Second, there was no justification for such refusal either in the activity of television broadcasting or in that of publishing television magazines. . . .

56 Third, and finally, as the [General Court] also held, the appellants, by their conduct, reserved to themselves the secondary market of weekly television guides by excluding all competition on that market since they denied access to the basic information which is the raw material indispensable for the compilation of such a guide.

57 In the light of all those circumstances, the [General Court] did not err in law in holding that the appellants' conduct was an abuse of a dominant position within the meaning of Article [102] of the Treaty.
* * *

NOTES AND QUESTIONS

1. From what facts did the Court find dominance? Was each of the three broadcasters dominant?

2. What is the holding of *Magill*? When does a dominant firm's refusal to license intellectual property constitute an abuse? Does *Magill* erode the rule in *Volvo*? What is the significance of the fact that the TV stations "prevented the appearance of a new product"? If the stations had formed a joint venture to produce a TV guide, could they have lawfully refused to grant a license to Magill?

3. Examine the Court's reasoning. Intellectual property embodies the right to refuse to grant a license. The right of exclusivity is the essence of intellectual property rights, even if a holder of the right is dominant. *Magill*, para. 49. How and when does the right of exclusivity cease to become an essential ingredient of the intellectual property right? Does it lose this character whenever competition and consumer interests would be better served by the grant of a license? If so, doesn't Article 102 eclipse Article 36? How does the Court prevent this eclipse? Is the limiting rule arbitrary, or principled?

4. There is an unexplored question in *Magill*: Was the Irish copyright law excessive in protecting the mere listing of a TV schedule? Is copyright protection of the schedule even arguably necessary or important to preserve incentives to invent and to be creative? Few other countries protect a mere schedule. For the United States, *see Feist Publications, Inc. v. Rural Telephone Service Co., Inc.*, 499 U.S. 340, 111 S.Ct. 1282, 113 L.Ed.2d 358 (1991), which holds that alphabetical listings of names and numbers in telephone book white pages are not protectable by copyright because they are merely lists of non-copyrightable facts. The Court could not have solved the *Magill* problem by declaring that Ireland stepped out of bounds by trying to give copyright protection to TV listings, for, under the Treaty, Ireland alone had the right to declare the scope of Irish property interests. (Article 345). Could

it have solved the problem by declaring that, on the particular facts, the Article 102 interests outweighed the Article 36 interests? Is part of the solution to consider the effect of antitrust enforcement on incentives to create? What impact was the antitrust enforcement in *Magill* likely to have on incentives to create or broadcast innovative programming?

IMS HEALTH GmbH & CO. AND NDC HEALTH GmbH & CO.

Case C–418/01, [2004] ECR I–5039, ECJ.

[IMS Health Inc. was a market research company that provided services to the pharmaceutical industry. It devised a "brick structure" in which it divided Germany into geographic areas that were used to measure and report sales of individual pharmaceutical products. Its efforts culminated in the development of the 1860 brick structure—a format for categorizing and reporting data that was the central feature of its regional and wholesaler data-information services. The format was protected by German copyright law.

National Data Corporation entered the German market to provide marketing data to the pharmaceutical industry, in competition with IMS. The pharmaceutical companies wanted the data only in the 1860 format. NDC asked IMS for a license for the 1860 format, but IMS refused. It thereupon began selling marketing data to the pharmaceutical industry based on copies of the 1860 brick structure.

IMS brought proceedings in a German court to prohibit NDC from using the IMS brick structure, on grounds that the brick structure was a data base protected by copyright and IMS had the right to refuse to license it. The German court granted the injunction but then stayed the proceedings, observing that IMS could not refuse to license NDC if the refusal constituted an abuse of dominance under Article 102. The national court referred to the Court of Justice questions concerning the circumstances under which such a refusal constitutes an abuse. The Court of Justice answered: Only in exceptional circumstances may the exercise of an exclusive (IP) right constitute an abuse of dominance. First, access to the product, service or IP must be indispensable to enable the undertaking to carry on business in a market.]

28   [To determine indispensability,] it must be determined whether there are products or services which constitute alternative solutions, even if they are less advantageous, and whether there are technical, legal or economic obstacles capable of making it impossible or at least unreasonably difficult for any undertaking seeking to operate in the market to create, possibly in cooperation with other operators, the alternative products or services.... [I]n order to accept the existence of economic obstacles, it must be established, at the very least, that the creation of those products or services is not economically viable for production on a scale comparable to that of the undertaking which controls the existing product or service. * * *

38   [Where access is indispensable,] it is sufficient that three cumulative conditions be satisfied, namely, that that refusal is preventing the emergence of a new product for which there is a potential consumers demand, that it is unjustified and such as to exclude any competition on a secondary market. * * *

44   ... [I]t is sufficient that a potential market or even hypothetical market can be identified. Such is the case where the products or services are indispensable in order to carry on a particular business and where there is an actual demand for them on the part of undertakings which seek to carry on the business for which they are indispensable.

45   Accordingly, it is determinative that two different stages of production may be identified and that they are interconnected, the upstream product is indispensable in as much as for supply of the downstream product.

46   Transposed to the facts of the case in the main proceedings, that approach prompts consideration as to whether the 1860 brick structure constitutes, upstream, an indispensable factor in the downstream supply of German regional sales data for pharmaceutical products.

47   It is for the national court to establish whether that is in fact the position, and, if so be the case, to examine whether the refusal by IMS to grant a licence to use the structure at issue is capable of excluding all competition on the market for the supply of German regional sales data on pharmaceutical products. * * *

NOTES AND QUESTIONS

1.   If all four of the above elements are proved (indispensability and the three "sufficient" conditions), is IMS's copyrighted brick structure an essential facility?

2.   With *Magill* as the base line, did the Court expand the category of duty to license IP rights?

3.   Who won on the question whether there must be two markets?

4.   How likely is NDC to prevail on each necessary element of its case? Which will be the hardest hurdle to overcome?

5.   The next important refusal-to-deal case is *Microsoft*. The US Department of Justice had already brought a monopolization case against Microsoft and had won a large part of it, as we note below. The European case involved practices later in time from those challenged in the US; and they were practices of a different sort. By the time the European Commission brought proceedings, blatantly predatory and coercive acts of the sort condemned in the US case were not so apparent.

MICROSOFT CORP. v. COMMISSION

(interoperability)
Case T–201/04, [2007] ECR II–1491, General Court, Grand Chamber.

[The European Commission brought proceedings against Microsoft, a "super-dominant" firm with more than 90% of the PC operating systems market, for abusing its dominant position in violation of Article 102. The Commission found two sets of Microsoft's practices to be illegal: 1) Bundling its media player with its operating system (Windows), which had become the standard in the market. RealNetworks had pioneered the media player and RealNetworks' player was popularly used with Windows. Thereafter Microsoft made its own media player and bundled it with Windows, foreclosing media player rivals from the most efficient channels to the market. 2) Refusal to deal, in the form of refusing to provide workgroup server software rivals with full interoperability information to connect with Windows and with Microsoft's workgroup server software. Workgroup servers are servers used by small enterprises to interconnect file, printing, document-sharing and management functions of all PCs within the enterprise. Novell and others had pioneered workgroup server software. Before Microsoft developed such software of its own, it gave full interoperability information to the workgroup server software providers. Then Microsoft made its own workgroup server software and withheld from its rivals the full information they needed for seamless interoperability. Microsoft noted that it provided a good deal of interoperability information and claimed that it had no legal duty to help its rivals. Belatedly, it also claimed that its interface protocols containing the withheld interoperability information contained intellectual property and that it had a right of absolute exclusivity of its intellectual property.

For remedies, the Commission ordered Microsoft to supply the full interoperability protocols, offer an unbundled version of Windows without the media player, and pay a fine of € 497 million for the two violations.

Microsoft appealed to the General Court. At this point, we cover only the interoperability (duty to deal) issue.

Microsoft contended that disclosure of the interface protocols would entail disclosure of intellectual property. The Commission disputed this claim but nonetheless argued that the circumstances satisfied the criteria of *Magill/IMS*: (1) access [here, to the complete interoperability information] must be indispensable, (2) the refusal must exclude any effective competition on a neighboring market, and (3) the refusal must prevent the appearance of a new product for which there is a potential consumer demand. 4) If the criteria are satisfied, it then falls to the dominant firm to prove an objective justification.

The Court first held that the Commission did not err in finding that seamless interoperability was indispensable to efficient operation of rivals, and that the refusal gave rise to a risk of elimination of competition. The Court then summarized the evidence showing the sharp rise of Microsoft's share of workgroup server software, to more than 60%, and the decline of the competitors' shares, as soon as Microsoft stopped providing full interoperability information. It gave examples of how Microsoft killed off two of competitors' products, NDS for NT developed by Novell, and PC NetLink developed by Sun Microsystems, by withholding interoperability information. See facts at para. 654 below]. * * *

593   The above factors confirm that Microsoft's refusal has the consequence that its competitors' products are confined to marginal positions or even made unprofitable. The fact that there may be marginal competition between operators on the market cannot therefore invalidate the Commission's argument that all effective competition was at risk of being eliminated on that market. * * *

(3) The new product * * *

647   The circumstance relating to the appearance of a new product, as envisaged in *Magill* and *IMS Health*, cannot be the only parameter which determines whether a refusal to license an intellectual property right is capable of causing prejudice to consumers within the meaning of Article [102(b)]. As that provision states, such prejudice may arise where there is a limitation not only of production or markets, but also of technical development. * * *

650   . . . [T]he Commission was correct to observe that '[owing] to the lack of interoperability that competing work group server operating system products can achieve with the Windows domain architecture, an increasing number of consumers are locked into a homogeneous Windows solution at the level of work group server operating systems'.

651   . . . Microsoft's refusal prevented its competitors from developing work group server operating systems capable of attaining a sufficient degree of interoperability with the Windows domain architecture, with the consequence that consumers' purchasing decisions in respect of work group server operating systems were channelled towards Microsoft's products. The Court has also already observed that it was apparent from a number of documents in the file that the technologies of the Windows 2000 range, in particular Active Directory, were increasingly being taken up by organisations. As interoperability problems arise more acutely with work group server operating systems in that range of products than with those of the preceding generation, the increasing uptake of those systems merely reinforces the 'lock-in' effect referred to in the preceding paragraph.

652   The limitation thus placed on consumer choice is all the more damaging to consumers because, as already observed, they consider that non-Microsoft work group server operating systems are better than Windows work group server operating systems with respect to a series of features to which they attach great importance, such as 'reliability/availability of the ... system' and 'security included with the server operating system'.

653   In the second place, the Commission was correct to consider that the artificial advantage in terms of interoperability that Microsoft retained by its refusal discouraged its competitors from developing and marketing work group server operating systems with innovative features, to the prejudice, notably, of consumers. That refusal has the consequence that those competitors are placed at a disadvantage by comparison with Microsoft so far as the merits of their products are concerned, particularly with regard to parameters such as security, reliability, ease of use or operating performance speed.

654   The Commission's finding that '[i]f Microsoft's competitors had access to the interoperability information that Microsoft refuses to supply, they could use the disclosures to make the advanced features of their own products available in the framework of the web of interoperability relationships that underpin the Windows domain architecture' is corroborated by the conduct which those competitors had adopted in the past, when they had access to certain information concerning Microsoft's products. The two examples which the Commission gives ..., 'PC NetLink' and 'NDS for NT', speak volumes in that regard. PC NetLink is software developed by Sun on the basis of AS/U, which had been developed by AT&T using source code which Microsoft had licensed to it in the 1990s. A document submitted by Microsoft during the administrative procedure shows that the innovative features and added value that PC NetLink brought to Windows work group networks was used as a selling point for that product. Likewise, in its marketing material, Novell highlighted the new features which NDS for NT—software which it had developed using reverse engineering—brought to the Windows domain architecture (in this instance Windows NT).

655   The Commission was careful to emphasise, in that context, that there was 'ample scope for differentiation and innovation beyond the design of interface specifications'. In other words, the same specification can be implemented in numerous different and innovative ways by software designers. * * *

659   Last, Microsoft's argument that it will have less incentive to develop a given technology if it is required to make that technology available to its competitors is of no relevance to the examination of the circumstance relating to the new product, where the issue to be decided is the impact of the refusal to supply on the incentive for Microsoft's competitors to innovate and not on Microsoft's incentives to innovate. That is an issue which will be decided when the Court examines the circumstance relating to the absence of objective justification.

660   In the third place, the Commission is also correct to reject as unfounded Microsoft's assertion during the administrative procedure

that it was not demonstrated that its refusal caused prejudice to consumers.

661 First of all, as has already been observed, the results of the third Mercer survey show that, contrary to Microsoft's contention, consumers consider non-Microsoft work group server operating systems to be better than Windows work group server operating systems on a number of features to which they attach great importance. * * *

664 Last, it must be borne in mind that it is settled case-law that Article [102] covers not only practices which may prejudice consumers directly but also those which indirectly prejudice them by impairing an effective competitive structure. In this case, Microsoft impaired the effective competitive structure on the work group server operating systems market by acquiring a significant market share on that market. * * *

(4) The absence of objective justification

666 In the first place, Microsoft claims that the refusal to supply the information was objectively justified by the intellectual property rights which it holds over the 'technology' concerned. It has made significant investment in designing its communication protocols and the commercial success which its products have achieved represents the just reward. It is generally accepted, moreover, that an undertaking's refusal to communicate a specific technology to its competitors may be justified by the fact that it does not wish them to use that technology to compete with it.

667 In the reply, Microsoft relies on the fact that the technology which it is required to disclose to its competitors is secret, that it is of great value for licensees and that it contains significant innovation.

668 In its answer to one of the written questions put by the Court, the applicant adds that it had an objective justification for not licensing the technology 'given the prejudice to incentives to innovate that would have resulted if Sun (or others) had used that technology to build a "functional equivalent" that would compete against Microsoft's products on the same market'. * * *

697 The Court finds that, as the Commission correctly submits, Microsoft, which bore the initial burden of proof, did not sufficiently establish that if it were required to disclose the interoperability information that would have a significant negative impact on its incentives to innovate.

698 Microsoft merely put forward vague, general and theoretical arguments on that point.... Microsoft merely stated that '[d]isclosure would ... eliminate future incentives to invest in the creation of more intellectual property', without specifying the technologies or products to which it thus referred. * * *

701   It follows that it has not been demonstrated that the disclosure of the information to which that remedy relates will significantly reduce—still less eliminate—Microsoft's incentives to innovate.

702   In that context, the Court observes that it is normal practice for operators in the industry to disclose to third parties the information which will facilitate interoperability with their products and Microsoft itself had followed that practice until it was sufficiently established on the work group server operating systems market. Such disclosure allows the operators concerned to make their own products more attractive and therefore more valuable. In fact, none of the parties has claimed in the present case that such disclosure had had any negative impact on those operators' incentives to innovate. * * *

710   The Commission came to a negative conclusion [that Microsoft had failed to prove an objective justification] but not by balancing the negative impact which the imposition of a requirement to supply the information at issue might have on Microsoft's incentives to innovate against the positive impact of that obligation on innovation in the industry as a whole, but after refuting Microsoft's arguments relating to the fear that its products might be cloned, establishing that the disclosure of interoperability was widespread in the industry concerned and showing that IBM's commitment to the Commission in 1984 was not substantially different from what Microsoft was ordered to do in the contested decision and that its approach was consistent with Directive 91/250 [on the legal protection of computer programs, which considers disclosure of interoperability information beneficial to innovation].

711   It follows from all of the foregoing considerations that Microsoft has not demonstrated the existence of any objective justification for its refusal to disclose the interoperability at issue. * * *

Notes and Questions

1. Were the *IMS/Magill* criteria faithfully applied to determine whether the refusal excluded "any effective competition"? Were the *IMS/Magill* criteria faithfully applied to determine whether the refusal prevented the appearance of a new product for which there is a potential consumer demand? Should the *IMS/Magill* criteria be necessary conditions for determining whether Microsoft's withholding interoperability information harmed competition and constituted abuse of dominance? If not, what would have been an appropriate framework for analysis?

2. What does paragraph 664 mean? Will it affect your counseling of dominant firms?

3. How crucial to the case are incentives to innovate? How crucial is the question whether Microsoft's incentives or the rivals' incentives would be more seriously impaired? What role was played by burdens of proof in this regard? Do you agree with the Court's treatment, or would you propose a different treatment?

4. How would the US *Trinko* Court have framed the question about incentives? Might it have asked: Did Microsoft have a duty to increase the incentives of rivals? What presumptions and burdens of proof flow from the way in which the question is asked?

5. US cases have held that an intellectual property owner has an absolute right to merely refuse to license its intellectual property. See *Independent Serv. Organizations Antitrust Litigation (CSU v. Xerox)*, 203 F.3d 1322 (Fed. Cir. 2000), cert. denied, 531 U.S. 1143 (2001). How would the US courts decide *Magill*, assuming the copyright protection was valid? How would they decide *IMS*?

c. Exclusive Dealing and Loyalty Rebates

Refusals to deal are the tip of the iceberg of the abuse-of-dominance offense. From the outset of its application of Article 102, the Court of Justice cautioned dominant firms not to foreclose markets to the detriment of other market actors. In early years the Court was particularly concerned with dominant firms' advantages over their smaller rivals. In later years, the Commission and the Courts—especially the General Court—prioritized consumers' interests.

Ask yourself as you read the cases: who and what are the Commission and the Courts trying to protect? competition? competition process? efficiency? innovation? By what means are they trying to do so—protecting the process? protecting competitors' access? protecting the competitive structure of markets? protecting freedom? Do the answers change as the Commission and Courts mature? For the Commission's guidance, see Guidance Document, Selected Document 25, paras. 31–45. You may note that the Court of Justice judgments, even the modern ones, may not yet have absorbed or accepted the more economic approach of the Commission or the General Court. But the cases are normally initiated by the Commission, which is committed to bringing only cases that meet its standard of "sound economics." Consider whether any of the Court of Justice cases below are cases that the Commission would not bring today, perhaps because harm to consumers and the market is not clear.

HOFFMANN–LA ROCHE & CO. AG v. COMMISSION
(*Vitamins*)

Case 85/76, [1979] ECR 461, ECJ.

[Hoffmann–La Roche had a dominant position in each of several vitamins. These included vitamin A, of which it held 47%, and vitamin B$_6$, of which it held more than 80%. Roche had contracted with 22 large purchasers, including Merck and Unilever, for the sale of vitamins to them.

Some purchasers agreed to buy several kinds of vitamins exclusively from Roche. Some contracts were requirements contracts, entered into at the request of purchasers who wanted assurance that their requirements would be filled.

In other cases, buyers agreed to buy most of their needs from Roche, and Roche agreed to give the buyer "fidelity rebates." These discounts became effective as to all past purchases when the buyer passed certain thresholds representing portions of the requirements of the buyer. The rebates applied cumulatively to the purchase of more than one kind of vitamin.

Many of the fidelity rebate contracts contained "English clauses." Under these clauses, if a customer received a better offer from a competitor and Roche refused to lower its price to meet the better offer, the customer was free to obtain supplies from the competitor without losing the benefit of the rebate. To meet the conditions of the escape clause, the better terms had to be offered by another competitor operating in Europe and on the same scale as Roche, and the offer had to be comparable.

Roche also entered into several contracts with large purchasers tailored to the parties' needs. For example, it had a contract with Merck for the sale of vitamin B_6. In the Merck contract, Roche recited that it planned to double its production capacity and would like to cover part of Merck's requirements. Merck agreed to buy from Roche its requirements above its own manufacturing capacity. Roche agreed to give Merck a 20% discount, Merck agreed not to resell the vitamins purchased at this discount, and Roche agreed to buy its requirements of phosphoric ester from Merck under the same conditions.

The Court of Justice held that the exclusive supply and requirements contracts were an abuse of a dominant position, even when entered into at the request of the purchaser. As for the Merck contract, the Court concluded that the purpose was to secure a stable market for Roche's increased production and to protect Roche from "the risks of competition," and that it, too, offended Article 102.

The fidelity rebates were also singled out for condemnation. The rebates constituted price discrimination based on loyalty, not quantity discounts based on lower costs. Once a purchaser began to buy from Roche, the Court said, the customer had a "powerful incentive" not to buy elsewhere.]

The Court

[89] An undertaking which is in a dominant position on a market and ties purchasers—even if it does so at their request—by an obligation or promise on their part to obtain all or most of their requirements exclusively from the said undertaking abuses its dominant position within the meaning of Article [102] of the Treaty, whether the obligation in question is stipulated without further qualification or whether it is undertaken in consideration of the grant of a rebate.

The same applies if the said undertaking, without tying the purchasers by a formal obligation, applies, either under the terms of agreements concluded with these purchasers or unilaterally, a system of fidelity rebates, that is to say discounts conditional on the customer's obtaining all or most of its requirements—whether the quantity of its purchases be large or small—from the undertaking in a dominant position.

90   Obligations of this kind to obtain supplies exclusively from a particular undertaking, whether or not they are in consideration of rebates or of the granting of fidelity rebates intended to give the purchaser an incentive to obtain his supplies exclusively from the undertaking in a dominant position, are incompatible with the objective of undistorted competition within the Common Market, because—unless there are exceptional circumstances which may make an agreement between undertakings in the context of Article [101] and in particular of paragraph (3) of that article, permissible—they are not based on an economic transaction which justifies this burden or benefit but are designed to deprive the purchaser of or restrict his possible choices of sources of supply and to deny other producers access to the market.

The fidelity rebate, unlike quantity rebates exclusively linked with the volume of purchases from the producer concerned, is designed through the grant of a financial advantage to prevent customers from obtaining their supplies from competing producers. Furthermore the effect of fidelity rebates is to apply dissimilar conditions to equivalent transactions with other trading parties in that two purchasers pay a different price for the same quantity of the same product depending on whether they obtain their supplies exclusively from the undertaking in a dominant position or have several sources of supply.

Finally these practices by an undertaking in a dominant position and especially on an expanding market tend to consolidate this position by means of a form of competition which is not based on the transactions effected and is therefore distorted.

91   ... The concept of abuse is an objective concept relating to the behaviour of an undertaking in a dominant position which is such as to influence the structure of a market where, as a result of the very presence of the undertaking in question, the degree of competition is weakened and which, through recourse to methods different from those which condition normal competition in products or services on the basis of the transactions of commercial operators, has the effect of hindering the maintenance of the degree of competition still existing in the market or the growth of that competition. * * *

A few years later, the Court summarized the concept of abuse in another major exclusive dealing case, *Michelin I*:

70   Article [102] covers practices which are likely to affect the structure of a market where, as a direct result of the presence of the undertaking in question, competition has already been weakened and which, through recourse to methods different from those

governing normal competition in products or services based on traders' performance, have the effect of hindering the maintenance or development of the level of competition still existing on the market.

NV Nederlandsche Banden–Industrie Michelin v. Commission, Case 322/81, [1983] ECR 3461.

Michelin II came before the General Court 20 years later. The Court continued to reflect the concern that fidelity rebates harm competition.

MANUFACTURE FRANÇAISE DES PNEUMATIQUES MICHELIN v. COMMISSION
(*Michelin II*)

Case T–203/01, [2003] ECR II–4071, General Court.

[*Michelin*, the dominant French supplier of replacement tires, fashioned a complex system of loyalty rebates and discounts to its dealers. Discounts were based both on the quantity of tires purchased over time and the quality of service by the dealers to their customers. They were applied in the year following the reference period; they were non-transparent and in part subjective. The Court found that the dealers were placed in a position of uncertainty and therefore they minimized their risks by buying from Michelin and not its competitors. Moreover, Michelin gave preferential prices to members of the Michelin Friends Club, who were required to promise that they would maintain a certain market share, to stock a certain number of Michelin tires, and to promote Michelin tires (for which they also got training and financial support).

The General Court held that the discounts were unfair and abusive. It declared that loyalty discounts are not necessarily illegal, but, to be valid, must be based on a countervailing advantage that is economically justifiable, such as economies of scale passed on to the customer.]

97   However, an undertaking in a dominant position has a special responsibility not to allow its conduct to impair genuine undistorted competition on the common market (*Michelin* v *Commission*, paragraph 57). Not all competition on price can be regarded as legitimate. An undertaking in a dominant position cannot have recourse to means other than those within the scope of competition on the merits.

98   In those circumstances, it is necessary to consider whether, in spite of appearances, the quantity rebate system applied by the applicant is based on a countervailing advantage which may be economically justified or, in other words, if it rewards an economy of scale made by the applicant because of orders for large quantities. If increasing the quantity supplied results in lower costs for the supplier, the latter is entitled to pass on that reduction to the customer in the form of a more favourable tariff. * * *

100   It must be borne in mind that, according to settled case-law, discounts granted by an undertaking in a dominant position must be based on a

countervailing advantage which may be economically justified. A quantity rebate system is therefore compatible with Article [102] if the advantage conferred on dealers is justified by the volume of business they bring or by any economies of scale they allow the supplier to make.

101 It must be stated first of all that, in the contested decision, the Commission makes express reference to that case-law, stating that a rebate can only correspond to the economies of scale achieved by the firm as a result of the additional purchases which consumers are induced to make. After examining the arrangements, the Commission, paraphrasing the judgment in *Michelin* v *Commission*, concludes that the quantity rebate system [was] not based on any economic service justifying [it].

102 It follows that the Commission did not alter the scope of the contested decision by claiming, in its defence, that the quantity rebates were not justified by economies of scale. * * *

To whom were the rebates unfair? Why wasn't the lower price to the customers an economic justification?

By the time the next major fidelity rebate case came to the Court of Justice, the Court spoke in terms of harm to consumers as well as harm to excluded competitors. Consider whether consumers were indeed the beneficiaries of the judgment.

BRITISH AIRWAYS PLC v. COMMISSION

Case C–95/04 P, [2007] ECR I–2331, ECJ.

* * *

3 BA, which is the largest United Kingdom airline, concluded agreements with travel agents established in the United Kingdom and accredited by the International Air Transport Association (IATA), which included not only a basic commission system for sales by those agents of tickets on BA flights ('BA tickets') but also three distinct systems of financial incentives: 'marketing agreements', 'global agreements', and, subsequently, a 'performance reward scheme', applicable from 1 January 1998.

4 The marketing agreements enabled certain travel agents, namely those with at least GBP 500 000 in annual sales of BA tickets, to receive payments in addition to their basic commission, in particular a performance reward calculated on a sliding scale, based on the extent to which a travel agent increased the value of its sales of BA tickets, and subject to the agent's increasing its sales of such tickets from one year to the next. * * *

7   The second type of incentive agreements, known as global agreements, was concluded with three travel agents, entitling them to receive additional commissions calculated by reference to the growth of BA's share in their worldwide sales.

8   On 17 November 1997, BA sent all travel agents established in the United Kingdom a letter in which it explained the detailed operation of a third type of incentive agreements, namely the new performance reward scheme.

9   Under that system, the basic commission rate was reduced to 7% for all BA tickets (as opposed to the previous rates of 9% for international tickets and 7.5% for domestic tickets), but each agent could earn an additional commission of up to 3% for international tickets and up to 1% for domestic tickets. The size of the additional variable element depended on the travel agents' performance in selling BA tickets. The agents' performance was measured by comparing the total revenue arising from the sales of BA tickets issued by an agent in a particular calendar month with that achieved during the corresponding month in the previous year. The benchmark above which the additional variable element became payable was 95% and its maximum level was achieved if an agent's performance level was 125%. * * *

11 On 14 July 1999 the Commission adopted the contested decision, holding, that, by applying the marketing agreements and the new performance reward scheme (jointly, 'the bonus schemes at issue') to travel agents established in the United Kingdom, BA abused its dominant position on the United Kingdom market for air travel agency services. That abusive conduct, by rewarding loyalty from the travel agents and by discriminating between travel agents, had the object and effect of excluding BA's competitors from the United Kingdom markets for air transport. * * *

[The General Court dismissed the appeal.]

The first plea, alleging errors in law in assessment of exclusionary effect

68   ... [I]n determining whether, on the part of an undertaking in a dominant position, a system of discounts or bonuses which constitute neither quantity discounts or bonuses nor fidelity discounts or bonuses within the meaning of the judgment in *Hoffmann–La Roche* constitutes an abuse, it first has to be determined whether those discounts or bonuses can produce an exclusionary effect, that is to say whether they are capable, first, of making market entry very difficult or impossible for competitors of the undertaking in a dominant position and, secondly, of making it more difficult or impossible for its co-contractors to choose between various sources of supply or commercial partners.

69   It then needs to be examined whether there is an objective economic justification for the discounts and bonuses granted. . . .

70   With regard to the first aspect, the case-law gives indications as to the cases in which discount or bonus schemes of an undertaking in a dominant position are not merely the expression of a particularly favourable offer on the market, but give rise to an exclusionary effect.

71   First, an exclusionary effect may arise from goal-related discounts or bonuses, that is to say those the granting of which is linked to the attainment of sales objectives defined individually.

72   It is clear ... that the bonus schemes at issue were drawn up by reference to individual sales objectives, since the rate of the bonuses depended on the evolution of the turnover arising from BA ticket sales by each travel agent during a given period.

73   It is also apparent from the case-law that the commitment of cocontractors towards the undertaking in a dominant position and the pressure exerted upon them may be particularly strong where a discount or bonus does not relate solely to the growth in turnover in relation to purchases or sales of products of that undertaking made by those co-contractors during the period under consideration, but extends also to the whole of the turnover relating to those purchases or sales. In that way, relatively modest variations—whether upwards or downwards—in the turnover figures relating to the products of the dominant undertaking have disproportionate effects on co-contractors (see, to that effect, *Michelin*, paragraph 81).

74   The [General Court] found that the bonus schemes at issue gave rise to a similar situation. Attainment of the sales progression objectives gave rise to an increase in the commission paid on all BA tickets sold by the travel agent concerned, and not just on those sold after those objectives had been attained. It could therefore be of decisive importance for the commission income of a travel agent as a whole whether or not he sold a few extra BA tickets after achieving a certain turnover. The [General Court] Instance ... states that the progressive nature of the increased commission rates had a 'very noticeable effect at the margin' and emphasises the radical effects which a small reduction in sales of BA tickets could have on the rates of performance-related bonus.

75   Finally, the Court took the view that the pressure exerted on resellers by an undertaking in a dominant position which granted bonuses with those characteristics is further strengthened where that undertaking holds a very much larger market share than its competitors.... It held that, in those circumstances, it is particularly difficult for competitors of that undertaking to outbid it in the face of discounts or bonuses based on overall sales volume. By reason of its significantly higher market share, the undertaking in a dominant position generally constitutes an unavoidable business partner in the market. Most often, discounts or bonuses granted by such an undertaking on the basis of overall turnover largely take precedence in absolute terms, even over more generous offers of its competitors. In order to attract the co-contractors of the undertaking in a dominant position, or to receive a sufficient volume of orders from them, those competitors would have to offer them significantly higher rates of discount or bonus.

76   In the present case, ... BA's market share was significantly higher than that of its five main competitors in the United Kingdom.... [T]he rival airlines were not in a position to grant travel agents the same advantages as BA, since they were not capable of attaining in the United Kingdom a level of revenue capable of constituting a sufficiently broad financial base to allow them effectively to establish a reward scheme similar to BA's.

77   Therefore, the [General Court] was right to examine ... whether the bonus schemes at issue had a fidelity-building effect capable of producing an exclusionary effect. * * *

[regarding objective economic justification:]

86   ... It has to be determined whether the exclusionary effect arising from such a system, which is disadvantageous for competition, may be counterbalanced, or outweighed, by advantages in terms of efficiency which also benefit the consumer. If the exclusionary effect of that system bears no relation to advantages for the market and consumers, or if it goes beyond what is necessary in order to attain those advantages, that system must be regarded as an abuse.

87   [The General Court made no error in concluding] that those systems were not based on any objective economic justification. * * *

The second plea, alleging error in not examining the probable effects of the conduct or taking account of evidence that they had no material effect on competing airlines [also held to be unfounded] * * *

The third plea, alleging that the [General Court] erred in not examining whether BA's conduct involved a "prejudice [to] consumers" within the meaning of [TFEU Article 102(b)]

106   Moreover, ... Article [102] is aimed not only at practices which may cause prejudice to consumers directly, but also at those which are detrimental to them through their impact on an effective competition structure, such as is mentioned in Article 3(1)(g) EC [now moved to a protocol].

107   The [General Court] was therefore entitled, without committing any error of law, not to examine whether BA's conduct had caused prejudice to consumers within the meaning of subparagraph (b) of the second paragraph of Article [102], but to examine ... whether the bonus schemes at issue had a restrictive effect on competition and to conclude that the existence of such an effect had been demonstrated by the Commission in the contested decision.

* * *

NOTES AND QUESTIONS

1. Why was the market UK travel agent services rather than UK air travel? Did this choice of market definition affect the result?

2. Who were the victims of BA's conduct? What market effect was necessary to condemn BA's practice? What effect on consumers was necessary? Were consumers probably hurt?

3. What additional facts would you like to know in assessing the market effects of the conduct?

4. A case similar to the European *British Airways* case was brought by rival Virgin Atlantic Airways against BA in US courts. Virgin alleged that BA's incentive agreements with travel agencies and corporate customers, with incentive discounts based on target thresholds, shifted so much business away from Virgin that it frustrated Virgin's efforts to expand service from London Heathrow to five US markets. Virgin claimed that BA's agreements resulted in below-cost pricing, and that BA offset its loss by supra-competitive pricing on its monopoly routes. The court gave summary judgment to BA, stating that Virgin's evidence did not support its below-cost claim or its recoupment claim, that the discounts were competition itself, and that Virgin failed to show how consumers were harmed. *Virgin Atlantic Airways Ltd. v. British Airways PLC*, 257 F.3d 256 (2d Cir. 2001). Identify the differences in concern, emphasis, and appreciation of consumer harm in the two cases against British Airways.

5. Are fidelity rebate cases (or should they be) predatory pricing cases? That is, should the plaintiff lose unless it can prove that the undertaking charged a below cost price that was likely to wipe out the competition and ultimately result in a monopoly price, exploiting consumers? Rebates mean lower prices. Aren't low prices good for consumers—at least absent a predatory pricing scenario? Or are the fidelity rebate cases about competitors' rights not to be foreclosed, rather than consumers' rights to lower prices? We treat predatory pricing below.

6. Intel is the largest producer of computer microprocessors in the world. When its only significant competitor, AMD, made a strongly-competitive chip, Intel adopted a strategy of rebates to computer manufacturers conditional on their loyalty, it made direct payments to customers to postpone the launch of new AMD product, and it engaged in other exclusionary acts often concealing from the public the exclusionary conditions. The Commission found that the practices undermined competitors' ability to compete on the merits, reduced consumer choice, hindered innovation, and harmed consumers. It found a violation of Article 102 and ordered a fine of 1.06 billion euros. Read the decision. It may be found at *http://ec.europa.eu/competition/sectors/ ict/intel.html*. If there is not time to read the decision, read the Commission's press release at *http://europa.eu/rapid/pressReleasesAction.do?reference=IP/ 09/745*. Intel strongly contests the decision and the fine and has appealed. Read Intel CEO's immediate response to the decision. *http://news.cnet.com/ 8301-13924_3-10239824-64.html*. In subsequent responses, Intel contests the application of the law as well as the findings of fact, calling all of its acts procompetitive and beneficial to consumers, and noting that no competitor

has been excluded from the market and prices have been constantly falling. Construct Intel's argument on appeal. Is it convincing?

d. Tying and Bundling

Tying, in the context of an abuse violation, involves a dominant firm's use of its power in one market to require buyers to accept another product. Bundling is a similar practice; it involves offering several products together. Pure bundling implies that the firm offers the products only in a package and not separately. Mixed bundling involves offering the products both as a bundle and separately, with the bundled price being a discounted price. For a violation, must competition be harmed in one of the markets? Must the tie or bundling practice increase or maintain the dominant firm's market power or create market power in the second market? Or is it enough that the practice fences out competitors from significant opportunities otherwise open to them, and the dominant firm has no good defense, such as: the practice is procompetitive or efficient and consumers get a fair share of the benefits?

Read the Commission guidance, Selected Document 25, paras. 46–61.

TETRA PAK INTERNATIONAL SA v. COMMISSION

(tying)

C–333/94P, [1996] ECR I–5951, ECJ.

[Tetra Pak was a Swiss-based group that made packaging machines and packaging for liquid and semi-liquid food, especially for milk. It operated in the aseptic sector, especially for UHT milk, and also in the non-aseptic sector. It accounted for 78% of both sectors combined, which was seven times more than its leading competitor. The structure of the market for aseptic packaging systems was quasi-monopolistic, with Tetra Pak having 90% to 95% of EU sales.

In the non-aseptic sector the market was oligopolistic. Tetra–Pak held 50% to 55%, and the Norwegian group Elopak held 27%, followed by PKL with 11%. Non-aseptic packaging, principally of fresh pasteurized milk, requires less sterility and less sophisticated equipment than aseptic packaging. Tetra Pak's principal non-aseptic carton was the Tetra Rex, which was in direct competition with Elopak's Pure–Pak.

The Commission charged Tetra Pak with tying and predatory pricing. It asserted four separate markets: aseptic cartons, aseptic filling machines, non-aseptic cartons, and non-aseptic filling machines, and it introduced evidence showing Tetra Pak's dominance in the aseptic sector. The Commission found that Tetra Pak had a dominant position on the aseptic markets and abused its dominance by its commercial practices on the non-aseptic markets; namely, requiring buyers of its non-aseptic machines to use Tetra Pak cartons for those machines, and predatorily pricing the non-aseptic cartons in Italy and the non-aseptic machines in the UK.

The General Court upheld the decision. It found that the numerous exclusionary provisions in its sales and lease contracts were part of "an overall strategy aiming to make the customer totally dependent on Tetra Pak for the entire life of the machine once purchased or leased, thereby excluding in particular any possibility of competition at the level both of cartons and of associated products." Moreover, the tied sales and other exclusivity provisions could not be justified.]

137   [E]ven if [normal commercial] usage were shown to exist, it would not be sufficient to justify recourse to a system of tied sales by an undertaking in a dominant position. Even a usage which is acceptable in a normal situation, on a competitive market, cannot be accepted in the case of a market where competition is already restricted. The Court of Justice has in particular ruled that, where an undertaking in a dominant position directly or indirectly ties its customers by an exclusive supply obligation, that constitutes an abuse since it deprives the customer of the ability to choose his sources of supply and denies other producers access to the market....

138   As for the fundamental justification pleaded by Tetra Pak, concerning the integrated and indivisible nature of its packaging systems as a matter of economics, the court has already also found ... that it does not stand up to examination. The technical considerations and those relating to product liability, protection of public health and protection of its reputation put forward by Tetra Pak must be assessed in the light of the principles enshrined in the judgment in *Hilti v EC Commission*, ... in which the [General Court] held that it was: "... clearly not the task of an undertaking in a dominant position to take steps on its own initiative to eliminate products which, rightly or wrongly, it regards as dangerous or at least as inferior in quality to its own products."

139   In this case, reliability of the packaging equipment for dairies and other users and compliance with standards of hygiene in relation to the final consumer could be ensured by disclosing to users of Tetra Pak machines all the technical specifications concerning the cartons to be used on those systems, without the applicant's intellectual property rights being thereby prejudiced. Moreover, the measures imposed on Tetra Pak inform any customers purchasing or leasing a machine of the specifications which packing cartons must meet in order to be used on its machines. Furthermore and in any event, even if using another brand of cartons on Tetra Pak machines involved a risk it was for the applicant to use the possibilities afforded it by the relevant national legislation in the various member states.

140   In those circumstances, it is clear that the tied-sale clauses and the other clauses referred to in the decision went beyond their ostensible purpose and were intended to strengthen Tetra Pak's dominant position by reinforcing its customers' economic dependence on it. Those clauses were therefore wholly unreasonable in the context of protecting public health, and also went beyond the recognised right of an undertaking in a dominant position to protect its commercial

interests. . . . Whether considered in isolation or together, they were unfair.

[Tetra Pak argued on appeal that the tie-in neither strengthened its dominant position in the tying market nor threatened to create a new dominant position in the market of the tied product. In other words, it argued, as a result of the tie, it got more sales but did not get market power on the non-aseptic market; it could not charge consumers more. In such a case, it argued, there could be no violation of Article 102. The Court of Justice rejected this argument as a matter of law. It referred extensively to the judgment of the General Court, and said:]

27   It is true that application of art. [102] presupposes a link between the dominant position and the alleged abusive conduct, which is normally not present where conduct on a market distinct from the dominated market produces effects on that distinct market. In the case of distinct, but associated, markets, as in the present case, application of art. [102] to conduct found on the associated, non-dominated, market and having effects on that associated market can only be justified by special circumstances.

28   In that regard, the [General Court] first considered . . . that it was relevant that Tetra Pak held 78 per cent of the overall market in packaging in both aseptic and non-aseptic cartons, that is to say seven times more than its closest competitor. . . . [I]t stressed Tetra Pak's leading position in the non-aseptic sector. Then . . . it found that Tetra Pak's position on the aseptic markets, of which it held nearly a 90 per cent share, was quasi-monopolistic. It noted that that position also made Tetra Pak a favoured supplier of non-aseptic systems. Finally, . . . it concluded that, in the circumstances of the case, application of art. [102] was justified by the situation on the different markets and the close associative links between them.

29   The relevance of the associative links which the [General Court] thus took into account cannot be denied. The fact that the various materials involved are used for packaging the same basic liquid products shows that Tetra Pak's customers in one sector are also potential customers in the other. That possibility is borne out by statistics showing that in 1987 approximately 35 per cent of Tetra Pak's customers bought both aseptic and non-aseptic systems. It is also relevant to note that Tetra Pak and its most important competitor, PKL, were present on all four markets. Given its almost complete domination of the aseptic markets, Tetra Pak could also count on a favoured status on the non-aseptic markets. Thanks to its position on the former markets, it could concentrate its efforts on the latter by acting independently of the other economic operators.

30   The circumstances thus described, taken together and not separately, justified the [General Court], without any need to show that the undertaking was dominant on the non-aseptic markets, in finding that

Tetra Pak enjoyed freedom of conduct compared with the other economic operators on those markets.

31 Accordingly, the [General Court] was right to accept the application of art. [102] of the treaty in this case, given that the quasi-monopoly enjoyed by Tetra Pak on the aseptic markets and its leading position on the distinct, though closely associated, non-aseptic markets placed it in a situation comparable to that of holding a dominant position on the markets in question as a whole.

NOTES AND QUESTIONS

1. What was the relationship between Tetra Pak's dominance in the aseptic market and the effect of its conduct on competition in the non-aseptic market? (Does para. 29 help you answer these questions?) In what market was Tetra Pak's dominance abused?

2. If the non-aseptic market had been atomistic and competitive, would the outcome have been the same?

3. For more than half a century, the United States has had a per se rule against forced tying by a firm with market power. E.g., *International Salt Co. v. United States*, 332 U.S. 392, 68 S.Ct. 12, 92 L.Ed. 20 (1947); *Eastman Kodak Co. v. Image Technical Services*, 504 U.S. 451, 112 S.Ct. 2072, 119 L.Ed.2d 265 (1992); *Jefferson Parish Hospital District No. 2 v. Hyde*, 466 U.S. 2, 32, 104 S.Ct. 1551, 80 L.Ed.2d 2 (1984). Justifications such as good will, safety and reputation may possibly be admissible, but they are seldom proved. *E.g., International Salt Co. v. United States*, 332 U.S. 392, 68 S.Ct. 12, 92 L.Ed. 20 (1947).

This qualified per se rule evolved at a time when US antitrust law embraced open-market and diversity values. US law subsequently shifted its focus to consumer welfare and placed faith in firms—even dominant firms—to behave competitively. The Supreme Court retreated from per se concepts and has questioned the continued validity of the rule against tying. *Illinois Tool Works Inc. v. Independent Ink, Inc.*, 547 U.S. 28, 126 S.Ct. 1281, 164 L.Ed.2d 26 (2006). Indeed, tying is a form of leveraging, and the Supreme Court said in *Trinko* that there is no leveraging violation in the absence of a dangerous probability of monopolizing a second market. See footnote 4 in *Trinko*, supra at page 885.

Judge Thomas Penfield Jackson rejected a leveraging claim at the outset of the US *Microsoft* case (thus, before the *Trinko* decision). He dismissed the claim alleging that Microsoft's use of its power in the operating system market to get market share in the browser market at the expense of Netscape amounted, in itself, to a violation of the Sherman Act. *United States v. Microsoft Corp.*, 1998–2 CCH Trade Cas. ¶ 72,261. Dismissal of this claim was not appealed. Almost every other holding of Judge Jackson was appealed. On the appeal, the Court held Microsoft's tying illegal where it was combined with a clear predatory act (Microsoft tied its browser with its operating system and commingled code so that removal of Netscape's browser from Windows would disable other functions of Windows). But the court reversed Judge Jackson's holding that Microsoft's mere bundling of its browser with its operating system was illegal per se. *United States v. Microsoft Corp.*, 253 F.3d 34 (D.C. Cir.), cert. denied, 534 U.S. 952 (2001).

The European *Microsoft* case was decided several years later. We have already summarized the facts and studied the interoperability portion of the judgment. See page 895 supra, and re-read the facts. Following are excerpts from the portion of the case on bundling the media player with the operating system.

MICROSOFT CORP. v. COMMISSION

(bundling)

Case T–201/04, [2007] ECR II–1491, General Court, Grand Chamber.

See background facts at page 895 supra.

The tying restricts competition on the media player market

The foreclosure of competition

1038   ... [I]n the first place, it is clear that owing to the bundling, Windows Media Player enjoyed an unparalleled presence on client PCs throughout the world, because it thereby automatically achieved a level of market penetration corresponding to that of the Windows client PC operating system and did so without having to compete on the merits with competing products. It must be borne in mind that it is common ground that Microsoft's market share on the client PC operating systems market is more than 90% and that the great majority of sales of Windows client PC operating systems (approximately 75%) are made through OEMs [original equipment manufacturers], who pre-install Windows on the client PCs which they assemble and distribute. Thus, the figures ... show that in 2002 Microsoft had a market share of 93.8% by units shipped on the client PC operating systems market and that Windows—and, as a result, Windows Media Player—was pre-installed on 196 million of the 207 million client PCs shipped in the world between October 2001 and March 2003.

* * *

1088   It follows from the foregoing considerations that the final conclusion which the Commission sets out concerning the anti-competitive effects of the bundling is well founded. The Commission is correct to make the following findings:

— Microsoft uses Windows as a distribution channel to ensure for itself a significant competitive advantage on the media players market;

— because of the bundling, Microsoft's competitors are a priori at a disadvantage even if their products are inherently better than Windows Media Player;

— Microsoft interferes with the normal competitive process which would benefit users by ensuring quicker cycles of innovation as a consequence of unfettered competition on the merits;

— the bundling increases the content and applications barriers to entry, which protect Windows, and facilitates the erection of such barriers for Windows Media Player;

— Microsoft shields itself from effective competition from vendors of potentially more efficient media players who could challenge its position, and thus reduces the talent and capital invested in innovation of media players;

— by means of the bundling, Microsoft may expand its position in adjacent media-related software markets and weaken effective competition, to the detriment of consumers;

— by means of the bundling, Microsoft sends signals which deter innovation in any technologies in which it might conceivably take an interest and which it might tie with Windows in the future.

1089   The Commission therefore had ground to state that there was a reasonable likelihood that tying Windows and Windows Media Player would lead to a lessening of competition so that the maintenance of an effective competition structure would not be ensured in the foreseeable future.... * * *

Absence of objective justification

[Microsoft claimed that efficiency gains outweighed any anticompetitive effects; that consumers want one product, preinstalled; that the tying produces efficiencies and enhances technical performance; that adding components piecemeal can create conflicts and cause malfunction; and that removing components degrades the system. The Court held that the Commission appropriately rejected the factual assertions or found that the benefits could be attained in the less restrictive ways.] * * *

1159   Last, the Court notes that ... Microsoft does not show that the integration of Windows Media Player in Windows creates technical efficiencies or, in other words, that it 'lead[s] to superior technical product performance'. * * *

1165   The Court further considers that Microsoft cannot contend that the removal of Windows Media Player from the system consisting of Windows Media Player and Windows will entail a degrading of the operating system. Thus, Windows XP Embedded can be configured in such a way as not to include Windows Media Player without having any effect on the integrity of the other functionality of the operating system. Furthermore, throughout the period between June 1998 and May 1999, when Microsoft first integrated WMP 6 in its Windows client PC operating system without allowing OEMs or users to remove it from that system, Microsoft offered its streaming media player as separate application software, without any effect on the functioning of the Windows operating system.... * * *

NOTES AND QUESTIONS

1. Microsoft owned a "ubiquitous" network, which could and did carry its media player. How important is ubiquitous distribution to a user's choice of media player? If you were the BBC and had to decide how to distribute your content over the Internet, might you choose ubiquitous software over software with some better qualities? Does this mean that the owner of the ubiquitous network must share it with its competitors?

2. Would you predict that Microsoft's bundling would cause the total output of media player software to go down and the price to go up? that Microsoft would eventually get a monopoly in media players for PCs?

3. Did the bundling affect competition in the PC operating system market?

4. Can harm to competition be assessed without considering the effect of the finding of a violation on Microsoft's incentives to innovate and its efficiencies? Was it assessed without considering these elements?

5. Did the Court give short shrift to any aspect of Microsoft's objective justifications?

6. Do you use more than one media player? Do you use WMP? Consider the market changes since 2002/03. What implications does the fast-changing technology have for the application of competition law to new economy markets?

7. How would the US *Microsoft* court (D.C. Circuit) have analyzed the same problem?

8. Would the Commission guidance indicate any different analysis or result in *Tetra Pak* or *Microsoft*?

e. Price Predation and Price Squeezes

Antitrust proceedings are frequently triggered by complaints of rivals, and rivals, when they complain, often complain about prices that are too low. They complain that the dominant firm is pricing strategically low to price the rivals out of the market, after which (they allege) the dominant firm will charge a yet higher monopoly price. For many years, many jurisdictions, including the United States, listened sympathetically to such complaints, and sometimes found violations and enjoined the "predatory" pricing. (Might this approach be problematic for competition and consumers? Why?)

In more recent times, jurisdictions have toughened up their standards for a predatory pricing violation. Moreover, courts have identified more and more "exclusionary" conduct as merely low price competition that should be encouraged and thus conduct that, if it is illegal at all, must fit the tough criteria for illegal predatory pricing.

We start here with predatory pricing; then add a note on predatory buying, and then turn to price squeezes imposed by vertically integrated dominant firms.

For Commission guidance, see Selected Document 25 paras. 22–26 (cost benchmarks, and "as efficient competitor concept"), paras. 62–73 (predation), and paras. 79–89 (margin squeeze). Note that the Commission values "[v]igorous price competition [as] generally beneficial to consumers.... [T]he Commission will normally only intervene where the conduct concerned has already been or is capable of hampering competition from competitors which are considered to be as efficient as the dominant undertaking." However "in certain circumstances a less efficient competitor may also exert a constraint which should be taken into account...." For example, an abusive practice excluding the competitor from network and learning effects may prevent the competitor from achieving efficiencies. (paras. 22, 23)

AKZO CHEMIE BV v. COMMISSION

Case C–62/86, [1991] ECR I–3359, ECJ.

[AKZO, a large Dutch multinational firm, and ECS (Engineering and Chemical Supplies Ltd.), a small UK firm, both manufactured organic peroxides. AKZO had a market share of 50%. Benzoyl peroxide is the most important organic peroxide. Benzoyl peroxide is a bleaching agent for flour and is also used in plastics as an initiator of the polymer production process. ECS was engaged in the flour segment of the market. For a decade, ECS was content with its sales for the flour business, but in 1979 it developed excess capacity and started to sell to plastics makers, soliciting and selling to some of AKZO's customers. An AKZO official told ECS's manager Sullivan "that AKZO would take aggressive commercial action on the milling products unless [Sullivan] refrained from supplying his products to the plastics industry." The AKZO official told Sullivan AKZO would pry away ECS's flour customers at prices far below prevailing prices. When ECS ignored AKZO's threats, AKZO implemented selective, low prices, with the intent to damage the business of ECS.

From the end of 1980 for about four years, AKZO targeted ECS's customers in the flour segment, selling to them at prices that were below its average total cost and that were much lower than the previously prevailing rates. Meanwhile, AKZO charged its own loyal customers (whose business was not at risk) about sixty percent more than the targeted customers of ECS. As part of its strategy, AKZO sold these customers flour milling complements they needed at prices below AKZO's average variable cost, and it sold them some vitamin mixes (which it bought specifically for resale to these customers) below its own purchase price. ECS's business declined by about seventy percent in four years, and its profit margins fell.

The Commission initiated proceedings and obtained an interim order enjoining AKZO's conduct. In its decision on the merits, the Commission noted AKZO's "clear predatory intent" as well as its scheme of price discrimination. However, perhaps because of the interim order, the predatory campaign had little affect on ECS. ECS's share in the flour additive sector went from 35% to 30%, and AKZO's share went from 52% to 55%.

Placing much weight on AKZO's intent to eliminate its competitor, the Commission found an infringement and levied a fine of 10 million ECUs on AKZO.]

A. *Dominant position*

60   With regard to market shares the Court has held that very large shares are in themselves, and save in exceptional circumstances, evidence of the existence of a dominant position (judgment in Case 85/76 *Hoffmann–La Roche v Commission* [1979] ECR 461, paragraph 41). That is the situation where there is a market share of 50% such as that found to exist in this case.

61   Moreover, the Commission rightly pointed out that other factors confirmed AKZO's predominance in the market. In addition to the fact that AKZO regards itself as the world leader in the peroxides market, it should be observed that, as AKZO itself admits, it has the most highly developed marketing organization, both commercially and technically, and wider knowledge than that of their competitors with regard to safety and toxicology...

62   The pleas put forward by AKZO in order to deny that it had a dominant position within the organic peroxides market as a whole must therefore be rejected.

B. *Abuse of a dominant position*

63   According to the contested decision (point 75) AKZO had abusively exploited its dominant position by endeavouring to eliminate ECS from the organic peroxides market mainly by massive and prolonged pricecutting in the flour additives sector. * * *

69   It should be observed that ... the concept of abuse is an objective concept relating to the behaviour of an undertaking in a dominant position which is such as to influence the structure of a market where, as a result of the very presence of the undertaking in question, the degree of competition is weakened and through recourse to methods which, different from those which condition normal competition in products or services on the basis of the transactions of commercial operators, has the effect of hindering the maintenance of the degree of competition still existing in the market or the growth of that competition.

70   It follows that Article [102] prohibits a dominant undertaking from eliminating a competitor and thereby strengthening its position by using methods other than those which come within the scope of competition on the basis of quality. From that point of view, however, not all competition by means of price can be regarded as legitimate.

71   Prices below average variable costs (that is to say, those which vary depending on the quantities produced) by means of which a dominant undertaking seeks to eliminate a competitor must be regarded as abusive. A dominant undertaking has no interest in applying such prices except that of eliminating competitors so as to enable it subsequently to raise its prices by taking advantage of its monopolistic position, since each sale generates a loss, namely the total amount of the fixed costs (that is to say, those which remain constant regardless of the quantities produced) and, at least, part of the variable costs relating to the unit produced.

72   Moreover, prices below average total costs, that is to say, fixed costs plus variable costs, but above average variable costs, must be regarded as abusive if they are determined as part of a plan for eliminating a competitor. Such prices can drive from the market undertakings which are perhaps as efficient as the dominant undertaking but which, because of their smaller financial resources, are incapable of withstanding the competition waged against them.

73   These are the criteria that must be applied to the situation in the present case. * * *

114   The prices charged by AKZO to its own customers were above its average total costs, whereas those offered to customers of ECS were below its average total costs.

115   AKZO is thus able, at least partly, to set off losses resulting from the sales to customers of ECS against profits made on the sales to the 'large independents' which were among its customers. This behaviour shows that AKZO's intention was not to pursue a general policy of favourable prices, but to adopt a strategy that could damage ECS. The complaint is therefore substantiated. * * *

140   By maintaining prices below its average total costs over a prolonged period, without any objective justification, AKZO was thus able to damage ECS by dissuading it from making inroads into its customers. * * *

[The Court concluded that AKZO, at various times, offered customers of ECS prices lower than AKZO's total or average variable costs, and did so as part of its threat to obtain ECS's withdrawal from the plastics sector.]

162   . . . [I]t must be observed that the infringement committed by AKZO is particularly serious, since the behaviour complained of was intended to prevent a competitor from extending its activity into a market in which AKZO held a dominant position.

[The Court reduced the fine to 7.5 million ECUs—predecessor to the euro—on grounds that the controlling law had not previously been specified and the infraction did not have a significant effect on market shares.]

NOTES AND QUESTIONS

1. Why does the Court require below-cost pricing as a necessary element of the violation? Why should it not be sufficient that the dominant firm lowered its prices strategically to eliminate or wound its rivals?

2. Was AKZO's below-cost pricing a strategy to: 1) drive out the competitors and raise price? 2) compete? 3) divide markets? What is the significance of these different hypotheses?

3. In what respect does the Commission guidance differ from the Court's analysis?

4. In the United States, a pioneer in low-priced, no-frills, non-branded cigarettes sued a major tobacco company for embarking on a predatory pricing campaign to destroy or marginalize the new product. This case, *Brooke Group,* was later cited to the European Court of Justice by a low-pricing firm that was accused of predatory pricing by the European Commission and tried to defend its conduct as procompetitive. (See *Tetra Pak* at page 921 infra.)

BROOKE GROUP LTD. v. BROWN & WILLIAMSON TOBACCO CORP.

Supreme Court of the United States
509 U.S. 209, 113 S.Ct. 2578, 125 L.Ed.2d 168 (1993).

JUSTICE KENNEDY: [Cigarette manufacturing is a concentrated industry dominated by only six firms, including the two parties here. In 1980, petitioner (hereinafter Liggett) pioneered the economy segment of the market by developing a line of generic cigarettes offered at a list price roughly 30% lower than that of branded cigarettes. By 1984, generics had captured 4% of the market at the expense of branded cigarettes, and respondent Brown & Williamson entered the economy segment, beating Liggett's net price. Liggett responded in kind, precipitating a price war, which ended, according to Liggett, with Brown & Williamson selling its generics at a loss. Liggett filed this suit, alleging, inter alia, that volume rebates by Brown & Williamson to wholesalers amounted to price discrimination that had a reasonable possibility of injuring competition in violation of § 2(a) of the Clayton Act, as amended by the Robinson–Patman Act. Liggett claimed that the rebates were integral to a predatory pricing scheme, in which Brown & Williamson set below-cost prices to pressure Liggett to raise list prices on its generics, thus restraining the economy segment's growth and preserving Brown & Williamson's supracompetitive profits on branded cigarettes. After a jury returned a verdict in favor of Liggett, the District Court held that Brown & Williamson was entitled to judgment as a matter of law. The Court of Appeals affirmed.] * * *

Liggett contends that Brown & Williamson's discriminatory volume rebates to wholesalers threatened substantial competitive injury by furthering a predatory pricing scheme designed to purge competition from the economy segment of the cigarette market.... [W]hether the claim alleges predatory pricing under § 2 of the Sherman Act or primary-line price discrimination under the Robinson–Patman Act, two prerequisites to recovery remain the same. First, a plaintiff seeking to establish competitive injury resulting from a rival's low price must prove that the prices complained of are below an appropriate measure of its rival's costs.... Although [we have] reserved as a formal matter the question " 'whether recovery should ever be available ... when the pricing in question is above some measure of incremental cost,' " ... the reasoning in [our] opinions suggests that only below-cost prices should suffice, and we have rejected elsewhere the notion that above-cost prices that are below general market levels or the costs of a firm's competitors inflict injury to competition cognizable under the antitrust laws.... As a general rule, the exclusionary effect of prices above a relevant measure of cost either reflects the lower cost structure of the alleged predator, and so represents competition on the merits, or is beyond the practical ability of a judicial tribunal to control without courting intolerable risks of chilling legitimate price-cutting....

Even in an oligopolistic market, when a firm drops its prices to a competitive level to demonstrate to a maverick the unprofitability of straying from the group, it would be illogical to condemn the price cut: The antitrust laws then would be an obstacle to the chain of events most conducive to a breakdown of oligopoly pricing and the onset of competition. Even if the ultimate effect of the cut is to induce or reestablish supracompetitive pricing, discouraging a price cut and forcing firms to maintain supracompetitive prices, thus depriving consumers of the benefits of lower prices in the interim, does not constitute sound antitrust Policy....

The second prerequisite to holding a competitor liable under the antitrust laws for charging low prices is a demonstration that the competitor had a reasonable prospect, or, under § 2 of the Sherman Act, a dangerous probability, of recouping its investment in below-cost prices.... "For the investment to be rational, the [predator] must have a reasonable expectation of recovering, in the form of later monopoly profits, more than the losses suffered." ... Recoupment is the ultimate object of an unlawful predatory pricing scheme; it is the means by which a predator profits from predation. Without it, predatory pricing produces lower aggregate prices in the market, and consumer welfare is enhanced. Although unsuccessful predatory pricing may encourage some inefficient substitution toward the product being sold at less than its cost, unsuccessful predation is in general a boon to consumers.

That below-cost pricing may impose painful losses on its target is of no moment to the antitrust laws if competition is not injured: ...

Even an act of pure malice by one business competitor against another does not, without more, state a claim under the federal antitrust laws; those laws do not create a federal law of unfair competition....

For recoupment to occur, below-cost pricing must be capable, as a threshold matter, of producing the intended effects on the firm's rivals, whether driving them from the market, or, as was alleged to be the goal here, causing them to raise their prices to supracompetitive levels within a disciplined oligopoly. This requires an understanding of the extent and duration of the alleged predation, the relative financial strength of the predator and its intended victim, and their respective incentives and will.... The inquiry is whether, given the aggregate losses caused by the below-cost pricing, the intended target would likely succumb.

If circumstances indicate that below-cost pricing could likely produce its intended effect on the target, there is still the further question whether it would likely injure competition in the relevant market. The plaintiff must demonstrate that there is a likelihood that the predatory scheme alleged would cause a rise in prices above a competitive level that would be sufficient to compensate for the amounts expended on the predation, including the time value of the money invested in it. As we have observed on a prior occasion, "[i]n order to recoup their losses, [predators] must obtain enough market power to set higher than competitive prices, and then must sustain those prices long enough to earn in excess profits what they earlier gave up in below-cost prices." *Matsushita*, 475 U.S., at 590–591.

Evidence of below-cost pricing is not alone sufficient to permit an inference of probable recoupment and injury to competition. Determining whether recoupment of predatory losses is likely requires an estimate of the cost of the alleged predation and a close analysis of both the scheme alleged by the plaintiff and the structure and conditions of the relevant market.... If market circumstances or deficiencies in proof would bar a reasonable jury from finding that the scheme alleged would likely result in sustained supracompetitive pricing, the plaintiff's case has failed....

These prerequisites to recovery are not easy to establish, but they are not artificial obstacles to recovery; rather, they are essential components of real market injury. As we have said in the Sherman Act context, "predatory pricing schemes are rarely tried, and even more rarely successful," *Matsushita*, and the costs of an erroneous finding of liability are high.... * * *

... While a reasonable jury could conclude that Brown & Williamson's intent was anticompetitive and that the price of its generics was below its costs for 18 months, the evidence was inadequate to show a reasonable prospect of cost recoupment. * * *

Affirmed.

The *Brooke Group* assumptions and standards have been questioned in scholarly literature. The legal rule, however, remains a strong one in the United States.

Tetra Pak International SA v. Commission, Case C–333/94P, [1996] ECR I–5951, involved a predatory pricing claim as well as a tying claim.

(See tying part of case supra.) Tetra Pak noted that the sales below cost took place only on the non-dominated market (non-aseptic cartons) and argued that Tetra Pak had no realistic chance of recouping its losses since competition would prevent it from raising its prices; it urged the Court of Justice to adopt the rule in *Brooke Group*. The Court declined. It confirmed that recoupment is not a constituent element of a price predation case under European law. Thus:

41   In *AKZO* this court did indeed sanction the existence of two different methods of analysis for determining whether an undertaking has practised predatory pricing. First, prices below average variable costs must always be considered abusive. In such a case, there is no conceivable economic purpose other than the elimination of a competitor, since each item produced and sold entails a loss for the undertaking. Secondly, prices below average total costs but above average variable costs are only to be considered abusive if an intention to eliminate can be shown.

42   ... For sales of non-aseptic cartons in Italy between 1976 and 1981, ... prices were considerably lower than average variable costs. Proof of intention to eliminate competitors was therefore not necessary. In 1982, prices for those cartons lay between average variable costs and average total costs. For that reason ... the [General Court] was at pains to establish—and the appellant has not criticised it in that regard—that Tetra Pak intended to eliminate a competitor. * * *

44   Furthermore, it would not be appropriate, in the circumstances of the present case, to require in addition proof that Tetra Pak had a realistic chance of recouping its losses. It must be possible to penalise predatory pricing whenever there is a risk that competitors will be eliminated. The [General Court] found ... that there was such a risk in this case. The aim pursued, which is to maintain undistorted competition, rules out waiting until such a strategy leads to the actual elimination of competitors.

NOTE ON FRANCE TELECOM SA v. COMMISSION (*WANADOO*)

The Commission charged Wanadoo, later acquired by France Télécom, with charging residential customers a price below average variable cost for high speed Internet access, and later a price below average total cost, as part of a plan to preempt the market in high-speed Internet access during a key phase in its development. It found a violation of Article 102. The Court affirmed.

The Court rejected the following claims of error:

(1) The claim that Wandadoo's (WIN's) high market share did not prove its dominant position, because its share fell (from 72% to about 63%) and the market was fast-growing. The Court said: WIN "had a very high market share which, save in exceptional circumstances, proves that it

had a dominant position within the meaning of the case-law...." ¶ 103. The Court confirmed that WIN had a dominant position, noting that WIN itself forecast that it would hold at least 60% of the market. The Court stated that WIN's link-up with the network of France Télécom gave it competitive advantages that contributed to its dominance.

(2) The claim that WIN had the right to align its prices to those of its competitors, even if those prices were below costs. The Court said: "Even a dominant firm must generally be allowed to take reasonable steps to protect its own interests, but this right is not absolute.... [S]uch behaviour cannot be countenanced if its actual purpose is to strengthen this dominant position and abuse it." ¶ 185.

(3) The claim that competition was robust, there was no possibility of ousting existing competitors, and barriers were low; there could be no anticompetitive effect. The Court said, citing *AKZO*, where prices are below average variable costs, an anticompetitive effect is presumed, because the only interest the undertaking may have is eliminating competitors. Where prices are merely below average total costs, the Commission must prove predatory intent, and it did so—showing an express plan "to pre-empt" the market. Moreover "it is clear" that WIN's conduct "had the effect of discouraging rival undertakings." ¶ 214. Moreover, it was no defense that the low pricing would result in economies of scale and learning effects, promising profitability later [presumably at the same low price]. ¶ 215–217.

(4) The claim that the Commission should have been required to prove a realistic chance of recoupment of losses. Citing *Tetra Pak*, the Court reaffirmed that proof of recoupment is not necessary.

The Court of Justice affirmed on all counts. Case T–340/03, [2007] ECR II–00107, *aff'd*, Case C–202/07 P, [2009] ECR I–02369.

NOTES AND QUESTIONS

1. Why might Tetra Pak have charged a price below its marginal cost if it could not later expect to make up the losses in higher than competitive prices for non-aseptic cartons? Would Brown & Williamson have charged a price below its marginal cost if it did not expect to protect its branded cigarette sales from erosion?

2. Regarding *Wanadoo*, comment on each of the four rejected claims. Was the Court right to reject the claims?

3. Explain the differences between US and EU law regarding the importance (or not) of eliminatory intent.

4. Why do the European predatory pricing cases focus on the dominant firm's elimination of a competitor and the US cases do not?

5. In *Weyerhaeuser Co. v. Ross–Simmons Hardwood Lumber Co.*, 549 U.S. 312, 127 S.Ct. 1069, 166 L.Ed.2d 911 (2007), Weyerhaeuser, one of the largest hardwood lumber manufacturers in the world, accounted for 65% of purchases of alder sawlogs in the Pacific Northwest of the United States (which was held to be the product and geographic market). It pursued a

strategy to overpay for alder sawlogs, buying and stockpiling more than it needed, to deprive its smaller competitors of the logs that they needed, squeeze out its competitors, and thereby get monopsony power over its suppliers. Its strategy caused the closure of the plant of Ross–Simmons, which sued for damages. Ross–Simmons got a jury verdict in its favor. The Supreme Court reversed the lower courts. It held that predatory buying is the mirror image of predatory selling and noted that Ross–Simmons had not proved that Weyerhaeuser paid so much for the logs that it could not cover revenues from them nor that, if it did lose money to buy the logs, it could recoup that investment in predation (the *Brooke Group* test, as applied to predatory buying). Should Ross–Simmons have to prove the *Brooke Group* elements? Would it have to satisfy the price predation test if the case arose in Europe?

6.   Pacific Bell was the incumbent telephone service provider in an area on the West Coast of the United States. It provided local telephone service and, as the historical incumbent (and former lawful monopolist before technology made competition feasible), owned the elements of the local loop in the area. It also supplied digital subscriber line (DSL) service—for fast computer access through phone lines—to Internet service providers (ISPs) at wholesale, and sold DSL service to its own customers at retail. During some periods it charged its retail customers for DSL less than it charged the ISPs at wholesale. The price of wholesale service was regulated. That is, Pacific Bell proposed the rate; the Federal Communications Commission approved it, which it must do for all filed rates unless they are "unjust and unreasonable."

The ISPs sued for an unlawful price squeeze under Section 2 of the Sherman Act. Pacific Bell moved for judgment on the pleadings, arguing that, after *Trinko* (see page 885 supra), a monopolist in a regulated industry has no antitrust duty to deal and no duty to avoid a price squeeze; if there is a problem, it should be resolved by the regulatory agency. The lower courts declined to dismiss the price squeeze case, holding that price squeeze claims survive *Trinko*. The Supreme Court reversed. Since there was no antitrust duty to supply the DSL transport service to the rivals, there was no antitrust duty to refrain from squeezing them out of business. Plaintiffs would have a cause of action only if they could meet the tough requirements for proving that defendant's low retail price was predatory. *Pacific Bell Telephone Co. v. linkLine Communications, Inc.*, 555 U.S. ___, 129 S.Ct. 1109, 172 L.Ed.2d 836 (2009).

7.   Deutsche Telekom was the dominant provider of telecom services in Germany and had sole access to the local loop. DT was regulated by the German Regulatory Authority, which imposed price ceilings. DT charged new entrants into the local telecom service market higher fees for wholesale access to the local loop than it charged its customers for services including DSL for fast-speed Internet connection. The competing providers of DSL service complained to the European Commission. The Commission found a margin squeeze in violation of Article 102. The General Court affirmed. DT, it said, had a duty to provide competitors access to the local loop. It therefore had a duty not to create a margin squeeze. DT had sufficient scope to eliminate the margin squeeze either on terms consistent with the regulation or, if not, by applying to the German regulatory body for price adjustments. The General Court said:

234   According to the Commission, the applicant's pricing practices restricted competition in the market for retail access services. It reaches that conclusion in the contested decision ... on the basis of the very existence of the margin squeeze. It maintains that it is not necessary to demonstrate an anti-competitive effect, although, in the alternative, it examines that effect....

235   Given that, until the entry of a first competitor on the market for retail access services, in 1998, the applicant had a monopoly on that retail market, the anti-competitive effect which the Commission is required to demonstrate relates to the possible barriers which the applicant's pricing practices could have created for the growth of competition in that market.

236   In that respect it must be borne in mind that the applicant owns the fixed telephone network in Germany and, moreover, that it is not disputed that, as the Commission notes ... there was no other infrastructure in Germany at the time of the adoption of the decision that would have enabled competitors of the applicant to make a viable entry onto the market in retail access services.

237   Having regard to the fact that the applicant's wholesale services are thus indispensible to enabling a competitor to enter into competition with the applicant on the downstream market in retail access services, a margin squeeze between the applicant's wholesale and retail charges will in principle hinder the growth of competition in the downstream markets. If the applicant's retail prices are lower than its wholesale charges, or if the spread between the applicant's wholesale and retail charges is insufficient to enable an equally efficient operator to cover its product-specific costs of supplying retail access services, a potential competitor who is just as efficient as the applicant would not be able to enter the retail access services market without suffering losses.

238   Admittedly, as the applicant maintains, its competitors will normally resort to cross-subsidisation, in that they will offset the losses suffered on the retail access market with the profits made on other markets, such as the telephone calls markets. However, in view of the fact that, as the owner of the fixed network, the applicant does not need to rely on wholesale services in order to be able to offer retail access services and therefore, unlike its competitors, does not have to try to offset losses suffered on the retail access market on account of the pricing practices of a dominant undertaking, the margin squeeze identified in the contested decision distorts competition not only on the retail access market but also on the telephone calls market....

239   Furthermore, the small market shares acquired by the applicant's competitors in the retail access market since the market was liberalised by the entry into force of the TKG on 1 August 1996 are evidence of the restrictions which the applicant's pricing practices have imposed on the growth of competition in those markets.... * * *

261   [T]he applicant submits that RegTP [the German regulator] alone is responsible for the margin squeeze alleged by the Commission. The alleged margin squeeze is the direct consequence of regulatory decisions

of RegTP ... and of the regulatory approach underpinning them. The Commission is wrong to find that the applicant has infringed Article [102], because the applicant was simply complying with the binding decisions of RegTP, which gave rise to a legitimate expectation by the applicant. Through the medium of the contested decision, the Commission is subjecting the applicant's pricing practices to double regulation, thereby infringing the principle of proportionality and the legal certainty guaranteed by the division of powers under Community law in relation to charges in the telecommunications sector. Furthermore, by adopting the contested decision, the Commission is trying to correct the German authorities' exercise of their own regulatory powers, whereas it should to that end have initiated proceedings for failure to fulfil obligations. By proceeding in this way, the Commission has misused its powers. * * *

263   In the first place, as regards the applicant's complaint that the Commission has subjected the applicant's pricing practices to double regulation and thereby infringed the principles of proportionality and of legal certainty, it must be held that the legal framework to which the applicant refers above does not affect the powers which the Commission derives directly from Article 7(1) of Council Regulation (EC) No 1/2003 to find infringements of Articles [101 and 102].

264   It has already been held that, between 1 January 1998 and 31 December 2001, the applicant had sufficient scope to end the margin squeeze identified in the contested decision and, from 1 January 2002, sufficient scope to reduce that margin squeeze. [The applicant could have increased its retail prices; it could have applied for increases in the retail price cap; moreover, through its applications it influences the level of the prices set by the regulators; paras. 97–151]; para. 104.] Its conduct therefore falls within the scope of Article [102].

265   While it is not inconceivable that the German authorities also infringed Community law ... by opting for a gradual rebalancing of connection and call charges, such a failure to act, if it were to be established, would not remove the scope which the applicant had to reduce the margin squeeze. * * *

267   In the second place, as regards the complaint relating to the protection of legitimate expectations, it must be borne in mind that, in a number of decisions taken in the period covered by the contested decision, RegTP did in fact consider whether a margin squeeze resulted from the applicant's charges. However, in its decisions, after finding the negative spread between the applicant's wholesale and retail prices, RegTP took the view in each case that other operators should be able to offer their end-users competitive prices by resorting to cross-subsidisation of access services and call services.

268   The fact remains that RegTP's decisions do not include any reference to Article [102]. In addition, RegTP's statement that '[c]ompetitors are not so prejudiced with regard to their competitive opportunities in the local network by the slight difference between retail and wholesale prices as to make it economically impossible for them to enter the market successfully or even to remain in the market' does not imply that the applicant's

pricing practices do not distort competition within the meaning of Article [102]. On the contrary, it follows implicitly but necessarily from RegTP's decisions that the applicant's pricing practices have an anti-competitive effect, since the applicant's competitors have to resort to cross-subsidisation in order to be able to remain competitive on the market in access services. * * *

271 In the contested decision, the Commission refers only to the applicant's pricing practices and not to the decisions of the German authorities. Even if RegTP had infringed a Community rule and even if the Commission could have initiated proceedings against the Federal Republic of Germany for failure to fulfil obligations, such possibilities cannot affect the lawfulness of the contested decision. In that decision, the Commission merely found that the applicant had committed an infringement of Article [102], a provision which concerns only economic operators, not the Member States. The Commission did not therefore misuse its powers by making that finding on the basis of Article [102].

Deutsche Telekom AG v. Commission, Case T–271/03, 2006 ECR II–01747, General Court.

Then Competition Commissioner Kroes said, in a press release welcoming the judgment, "This [the margin squeeze] was clearly harmful to consumers, because competition between operators is the best means to bring overall prices down." MEMO/08/232 of 10/04/2008

Does it matter whether Deutsche Telekom must lower its wholesale price or raise its retail price? Does it matter whether the low retail price is a predatory price?

How would the European Commission and Courts decide the US *linkLine* case? What resolution is best for consumers? Note that the cases involve the relationship between a regulatory regime and antitrust rules.

CONCLUSION

Take stock, now, of the EU principles and rules that govern abuse of a dominant position. What is the overall perspective of the European Union on how to identify whether practices of dominant firms that tend to exclude or make life hard for rivals constitute abuse of dominance? What is the overall perspective in the United States?

To what extent are the following observations true, and to what extent do they explain the differences?

- The US Supreme Court cases presume that dominant firm conduct, unconstrained by antitrust intervention, is generally good for consumers. They reflect a concern that antitrust authorities and courts will err, prohibiting procompetitive and innovative conduct and chilling invention.

- European Union competition law, influenced by its market integration and thus "openness" tradition, privileges openness and access, is suspicious of dominant firm conduct that tends to fence out rivals who would otherwise have greater incentives to invent, and reflects confidence that prudent intervention will facilitate the functioning of the market.

CHAPTER 23

HORIZONTAL RESTRAINTS UNDER ARTICLE 101

■ ■ ■

A. AGREEMENTS AMONG COMPETITORS— GENERAL

In Chapter 21 we dealt with hard core cartels: agreements among competitors specifically designed to lessen the competition among them. There are many other kinds of collaborations among competitors, often designed for legitimate purposes, such as sharing risks and creating synergies, getting market information, setting standards to facilitate trade, and protecting the environment.

Read Article 101 again. Consider the structure of 101(1), (2) and (3). Note that Article 101(1) prohibits agreements that may affect trade between Member States that "have as their object or effect" the "prevention, restriction or distortion of competition." Article 101(2) declares such agreements void. Article 101(3) declares that 101(1) may be declared inapplicable if the agreement 1) contributes to improving production or distribution or promoting technical or economic progress, 2) allows consumers a fair share of the benefits, 3) does not impose unnecessary restrictions (any restrictions must be "indispensable to the attainment of [the above] objectives"), and 4) does not give the firms concerned the possibility to eliminate competition in a substantial part of the market.

When we studied cartels, in cases in which a cartel (e.g. competitors' price-fixing or market division) agreement was proved, few of the nuances of Article 101 came into play. Cartels by their nature have the object to distort competition. Moreover, they always have this effect unless the cartel members' predictions and expectations go awry; and they virtually never can be justified because by their nature they suppress competition, hold back efficiency and progress, and harm consumers.

The only important open question at the outset was whether crisis or depression cartels could be justified under Article 101(3) on the theory that suppressing competition in the short run could produce healthy competition in the longer run. But this theory did not fit well with the language of Article 101(3); it was substantially rejected, although the Commission preserved a very small and rarely available gateway. See *Dutch brickmakers* (note 3 at page 857 supra). Most other antitrust jurisdictions have entertained the same problem, and most have similarly rejected a crisis or depression cartel defense; although in some jurisdictions the law provides the possibility of a public interest defense that might allow the authority to approve such a cartel. See Anti–Monopoly Law of the People's Republic of China (2008), Article 15.

When we turn to agreements among competitors other than hard-core cartels, and later, vertical agreements (agreements between buyers and suppliers, see Chapter 24), we meet the following issues:

1) When is the restraint so insignificant that it is below the threshold of Article 101?

2) What does "prevent, restrict or distort" competition mean, such that a restraint is caught by Article 101(1) and needs examination under 101(3)?

3) When may or must Article 101(1) be declared inapplicable by reason of Article 101(3)? This concept is often translated into: When is an agreement entitled to an "exemption"? But note: This use of the word "exemption" is very particular. It does not or does not usually mean that anticompetitive agreements can be exempted because of some higher public interest. It means that agreements caught by the wide net of Article 101(1) can be shown to be procompetitive, efficient, or technically progressive; if they fulfill the four conditions of Article 101(3) they are not proscribed.

The answer to the first question is the most objective. It is governed by the Commission Notice on Agreements of Minor Importance which do not Appreciably Restrict Competition under Article 81(1) [now 101(1)], which may be found at *http://ec.europa.eu/competition/antitrust/legislation/legislation.html*. The Notice provides, in part:

COMMISSION NOTICE ON AGREEMENTS OF MINOR IMPORTANCE WHICH DO NOT APPRECIABLY RESTRICT COMPETITION UNDER ARTICLE 81(1) (NOW 101(1)) (de minimis notice)

O.J. C 368 of 22 Dec. 2001.

* * *

2.   In this notice the Commission quantifies, with the help of market share thresholds, what is not an appreciable restriction of competition under Article [101]. This negative definition of appreciability does not imply that agreements between undertakings which exceed the thresholds set out in this notice appreciably restrict competition. Such agreements may still have only a negligible effect on competition and may therefore not be prohibited by Article [101](1)(2).

3. Agreements may in addition not fall under Article [101](1) because they are not capable of appreciably affecting trade between Member States. This notice does not deal with this issue. It does not quantify what does not constitute an appreciable effect on trade. It is however acknowledged that agreements between small and medium-sized undertakings, as defined in the Annex to Commission Recommendation 96/280/EC(3), are rarely capable of appreciably affecting trade between Member States. Small and medium-sized undertakings are currently defined in that recommendation as undertakings which have fewer than 250 employees and have either an annual turnover not exceeding EUR 40 million or an annual balance-sheet total not exceeding EUR 27 million. * * *

7. The Commission holds the view that agreements between undertakings which affect trade between Member States do not appreciably restrict competition within the meaning of Article [101](1):

(a) if the aggregate market share held by the parties to the agreement does not exceed 10% on any of the relevant markets affected by the agreement, where the agreement is made between undertakings which are actual or potential competitors on any of these markets (agreements between competitors); or

(b) if the market share held by each of the parties to the agreement does not exceed 15% on any of the relevant markets affected by the agreement, where the agreement is made between undertakings which are not actual or potential competitors on any of these markets (agreements between non-competitors).

In cases where it is difficult to classify the agreement as either an agreement between competitors or an agreement between non-competitors the 10% threshold is applicable. * * *

11. Points 7, 8 and 9 do not apply to agreements containing any of the following hardcore restrictions:

(1) as regards agreements between competitors as defined in point 7, restrictions which, directly or indirectly, in isolation or in combination with other factors under the control of the parties, have as their object:

    (a) the fixing of prices when selling the products to third parties;

    (b) the limitation of output or sales;

    (c) the allocation of markets or customers; * * *

We are left with the principal questions under Article 101: 1) What is the scope of Article 101(1)? How wide a net is spread by 101(1)? 2) What agreements within the net are valid because they fulfill the requirements of 101(3)? And: Who must prove what, under Article 101(3)?

Before we turn to these questions, we describe certain procedures and practices that sidestep the need to answer the questions.

Under prior practice, and under the now superseded Implementing Regulation 17/62, as noted earlier, parties whose agreements were caught by Article 101(1) were obliged to file them with the Commission. The Commission could grant a negative clearance; i.e., an opinion that the agreement was not caught by Article 101(1); or could grant an exemption—usually for a term of years and with conditions; or it could deny an exemption. From the time the agreement was notified until such a time as the Commission denied an exemption, the agreement was considered not to be void under Article 101(2) and the Commission could impose no fines for that period. The Commission became overwhelmed with notifications of agreements, most of which were routine and posed no antitrust problem. To alleviate the literally mounting burden, the Commission began to issue block exemption regulations in areas of frequent contracting, declaring the subject agreements exempt from notification and automatically entitled to an Article 101(3) exemption if they contained certain mandatory or allowed clauses (white list) and contained no prohibited clauses (black list). Most of the block exemptions that issued covered vertical agreements of specified sorts. A few—notably specialization agreements and research and development agreements—covered agreements between competitors.

Although firms could seek individual exemptions, the process took time and effort, and if the agreement was in an area subject to a block exemption, it was convenient for the firms to get the benefit of the ready-made exemption. Therefore they usually tailored their agreement to fit the requirements of the block exemption. Eventually, the Competition Directorate and the Commission came to recognize the straight-jacket effect of the block exemptions, which were formalistic and overly-detailed. At the same time, the Competition Directorate and the Commission were moving towards effects-based analysis rather than formalistic rules, and also they were recognizing the extent to which the notification and clearance procedure, in a context in which exemption authority lay solely within the Commission, was overwhelming it and distorting priorities. Accordingly, the Commission proposed and the Council legislated dramatic changes. Council Regulation 1/2003 (Selected Document 24) superseded Regulation 17 in May 2004. Article 101 in its entirety was declared directly effective, meaning that Article 101(1)–(3) is effectively part of national law and national authorities and national courts, as well as the Commission, can declare agreements compatible with Article 101. The notification and clearance procedure was abolished. The Commission withdrew some block exemptions and liberalized others, retaining some in order to give guidance and greater certainty.

Analysis moved away from a formalistic approach. The question became, for the most part, not whether certain clauses were present or absent, but whether the agreement was likely to promote competition and benefit consumers, or to harm competition and consumers. Still, the structure of Article 101—first spreading a wide net to catch all agreements that may distort, prevent or restrict competition, and then requiring their justification—would continue to play a role in analysis, including the assignment of burdens of proof or burdens of producing evidence.

In the sections following, we examine materials that demonstrate the analysis used to determine whether a cooperation or collaboration falls within Article 101(1), and if so whether it is entitled to an exemption because of net positive effects on competition (including efficiency and innovation). We then consider whether and when non-competition/efficiency/innovation objectives may be admissible. Finally we turn to the horizontal block exemptions.

B. THE REACH OF ARTICLE 101(1)

Modernisation, including the devolution of powers to Member State courts and authorities, might have provided grounds for removing the line between Article 101(1) and (3) in favor of an integrated analysis: Does this agreement create or is it a use of market power likely to harm consumers and the functioning of the market? If the agreement has some anticompetitive aspects, does it have outbalancing procompetitive aspects? Can the anticompetitive aspects be eliminated without destroying the procompetitive ones? However, the structure of the Treaty is unchanged. Under the Treaty one still must ask: Does this agreement fall within Article 101(1)?

Until the late 1990s, the European Commission and courts treated agreements between or among significant competitors as almost perfunctorily falling within Article 101(1). That approach has been modified.

In December 2000 the Commission issued guidelines on the applicability of Article 101. Those guidelines are now under review, with the expectation that revised guidelines will issue in December 2010. Read the draft horizontal guidelines. See the link at *http://ec.europa.eu/competition/consultations/2010_horizontals/index.html*.

Below are excerpts from court judgments. We reserve for the end of the discussion on application of Article 101(3) special cases on labor and the professions that place certain subject matters beyond the reach of Article 101(1), for policy reasons and despite some harm to competition. The initial discussion concerns whether an agreement entails a threshold case of object or effect of harm to competition.

In very brief summary, to fall within Article 101(1), the agreement must either have the object of distorting or restricting competition or be likely to affect negatively the parameters of competition such as price, output, innovation, and the variety and quality of goods or services. Cartels have the object to harm competition, and thus are caught automatically. Competitors' sharing of confidential information on terms of price to consumers or intermediaries may also have the prohibited object. (See *T–Mobile*, page 943 infra.) The two cases directly below concern effect.

EUROPEAN NIGHT SERVICES v. COMMISSION

Cases T–374–375, 384 & 388/94, [1998] ECR II–3141, General Court.

[Four railway firms—the railway companies of Britain (BR), Germany (DB), the Netherlands (NS), and France (SNCF)—agreed to form a joint venture, European Night Services (ENS), to provide overnight passenger rail services between the UK and the continent by way of the Channel Tunnel. They filed their agreements with the Commission, seeking a negative clearance or an exemption under the regulation applying competition rules to rail transport. The Commission found, as the relevant markets, the market for the transport of business travelers (for whom air travel, among other things, is a substitute) and the market for the transport of leisure travelers (for whom car travel, among other things, is a substitute). It made no reference in its decision to market shares of ENS or any competing operators, but later referred to data in the parties' notification to contend that a conservative estimate of ENS' market share was 7% to 8%. The Commission denied a negative clearance and granted an exemption for a period of eight years on condition that the parent companies supply equivalent services on the same terms to any international grouping of railways and any transport operator wishing to compete with ENS in the Channel Tunnel. The railways appealed, contending that the Commission had not shown grounds for application of Article [101] (1), that ENS' market share was less than 5% on most routes and in any case was insignificant, and that in any event the conditions imposed by the Commission were disproportionate and improper and the term of exemption was too short. The General Court said:]

As to the appreciable effect of the agreement

102   ... [E]ven if, as noted above, ENS's share of the tourist travel market was in fact likely to exceed 5 per cent on certain routes, attaining 7 per cent on the London–Amsterdam route and 6 per cent on the London–Frankfurt/Dortmund route, it must be borne in mind that, according to the case law, an agreement may fall outside the prohibition in Article [101](1) of the Treaty if it has only an insignificant effect on the market, taking into account the weak position which the parties concerned have on the product or service market in question.... With regard to the quantitative effect on the market, the Commission has argued that, in accordance with its notice on agreements of minor importance, Article [101](1) applies to an agreement when the market share of the parties to the agreement amounts to 5 per cent.[*] However, the mere fact that that threshold may be reached and even exceeded does not make it possible to conclude with certainty that an agreement is caught by Article [101] (1) of the Treaty. Point 3 of that notice itself states that "the quantitative definition of 'appreciable' given by the Commission is, however, no

---

* Eds.: The then-applicable Notice on Agreements of Minor Importance set a 5% threshold. This was later raised to 10% for competitors, 15% for non-competitors.

absolute yardstick" and that in "individual cases . . . agreements between undertakings which exceed these limits may . . . have only a negligible effect on trade between Member States or on competition, and are therefore not caught by Article [101](1)" . . . . It is noteworthy, moreover, if only as an indication, that that analysis is corroborated by the Commission's 1997 notice on agreements of minor importance . . . according to which even agreements which are not of minor importance can escape the prohibition on agreements on account of their exclusively favourable impact on competition.

103   That being so, where, as in the present case, horizontal agreements between undertakings reach or only very slightly exceed the 5 per cent threshold regarded by the Commission itself as critical and such as to justify application of Article [101](1) of the Treaty, the Commission must provide an adequate statement of its reasons for considering such agreements to be caught by the prohibition in Article [101](1) of the Treaty. Its obligation to do so is all the more imperative here, where, as the applicants stated in their notification, ENS has to operate on markets largely dominated by other modes of transport, such as air transport, and where, on the assumption of an increase in demand on the relevant markets and having regard to the limited possibilities for ENS to increase its capacity, its market shares will either fall or remain stable. . . . * * *

105   It must be concluded from the foregoing that the contested decision does not contain a sufficient statement of reasons to enable the Court to make a ruling on the shares held by ENS on the various relevant markets and, consequently, on whether the ENS agreements have an appreciable effect on trade between Member States, and the decision must therefore be annulled on that ground. * * *

O2 (GERMANY) GmbH & CO. OHG v. COMMISSION

Case T–328/03, [2006] ECR II–1231, General Court.

[O2 and T–Mobile were both operators of digital mobile telecommunications networks and services in Germany. They agreed to share infrastructure and national roaming capability for third generation GSM mobile telecommunications (3G) on the German market. T–Mobile had 100% of the market for wholesale access to national roaming for 2G. There were three other licensees for national roaming for 3G, of which O2 was the smallest and weakest. The agreement gave O2 the right to roam on T–Mobile's network in highest density areas (50% population coverage) and reciprocal roaming outside of that area. The roaming rights were to be phased out, with roaming in urban areas to last for a shorter period.

The Commission found that the infrastructure sharing did not fall within Article 101(1); but it found that the roaming agreement came within Article 101(1), and it gave an Article 101(3) exemption. O2 sought an annulment, arguing that the roaming agreement did not fall within Article 101(1). The General Court agreed with O2.]

68   Moreover, in a case such as this, where it is accepted that the agreement does not have as its object a restriction of competition, the effects of the agreement should be considered and for it to be caught by the prohibition it is necessary to find that those factors are present which show that competition has in fact been prevented or restricted or distorted to an appreciable extent. The competition in question must be understood within the actual context in which it would occur in the absence of the agreement in dispute; the interference with competition may in particular be doubted if the agreement seems really necessary for the penetration of a new area by an undertaking (*Société minière et technique* at 249–250).

69   Such a method of analysis, as regards in particular the taking into account of the competition situation that would exist in the absence of the agreement, does not amount to carrying out an assessment of the pro—and anti-competitive effects of the agreement and thus to applying a rule of reason, which the Community judicature has not deemed to have its place under Article [101(1)]. * * *

72   The examination of competition in the absence of an agreement appears to be particularly necessary as regards markets undergoing liberalisation or emerging markets, as in the case of the 3G mobile communications market here at issue, where effective competition may be problematic owing, for example, to the presence of a dominant operator, the concentrated nature of the market structure or the existence of significant barriers to entry—factors referred to, in the present case, in the Decision. * * *

81   It is apparent from the Decision that, as regards the effects of national roaming on competition on wholesale markets, the Commission states that '[n]ational roaming between network operators ... by definition restricts competition between these operators in all related network markets on key parameters such as coverage, quality and transmission rates'.

82   Next, the Commission states that national roaming 'restricts competition on scope and on speed of coverage because instead of rolling out its own network to obtain the maximum degree of coverage of territory and population within the shortest period of time, a roaming operator will rely for its roamed traffic on the degree of coverage achieved by the network of the visited operator'. It adds that '[n]ational roaming also restricts competition on network quality and on transmission rates, because the roaming operator will be restricted by the network quality and the transmission rates available to it on the visited network that are a function of the technical and commercial choices made by the operator of the visited network' and that 'the wholesale rates that [O2] will be able to charge to purchasers of its own wholesale network and access services will be constrained by the wholesale rates it has to pay to T–Mobile'. * * *

108 The dependence criticised by the Commission thus stems from de facto inequality that the agreement specifically seeks to rebalance by placing O2 in a more favourable competitive position while its actual situation appears to be the least competitive compared with the other operators, which are actual or potential competitors, identified by the Decision. O2's dependence on T–Mobile's network is moreover designed to be temporary since it is intended to diminish over the duration of the agreement at the pace of the timetable for phasing out roaming access rights provided for in the amended provisions of the notified agreement, which were submitted to the Commission for examination as part of the administrative procedure. On that point, the Decision, which, as previously stated, contains no concrete evidence, fails to establish the restrictive effects of the agreement on the roll-out of O2's networks. A fortiori, the Commission has failed to show that the agreement seeks to slow down, if not to limit, the roll-out of the applicant's network, as it submits in its pleadings. The letters submitted during the proceedings by the defendant, notably those of 4 March 2003 and 9 April 2003, show on the contrary that the agreement seeks to enable the applicant to roll out its 3G network in a profitable way in accordance with the requirements imposed by its licence in terms of the timetable and coverage.

109 In the present case, it cannot therefore be ruled out that a roaming agreement of the type concluded between T–Mobile and O2, instead of restricting competition between network operators, is, on the contrary, capable of enabling, in certain circumstances, the smallest operator to compete with the major players, such as in this case T–Mobile but also D2 Vodafone on the retail market, or even dominant operators, as T–Mobile is on the wholesale market.

110 That particular context, resulting from the specific characteristics of the relevant emerging market, was not taken into account in the assessment of whether the agreement was compatible with the common market under Article [101(1) TFEU] and Article 53(1) of the EEA Agreement.

111 By contrast, when, under the provisions of Article [101(3) TFEU] and Article 53(3) of the EEA Agreement, the Commission, considering that the agreement was necessary and that, without it, O2 would not have been able to gain access to the market efficiently, decided to grant an exemption, it took account of that particular context.

112 Thus, the Decision finds that as a result of the agreement O2 will be in a better competitive position in the area subject to an obligation of providing 50% population coverage by 31 December 2005 and that, outside that area, it is unlikely that it would have been able to fulfil its obligations under its licence. It is also stated that since O2 is 'the smallest operator in the German mobile market with a small share of the 2G market (about 8%) it is unlikely to be in a position to quickly build out a high-quality network covering a sufficient area to enable

the company to compete effectively from the outset against other established licensed operators of 3G networks and services in Germany'.

113 In a more general and conclusive assessment, the Decision adds that 'O2 ... ['s] roaming on T–Mobile's 3G network even in the main urban areas for a limited period of time is considered proportionate and indispensable, where this might not necessarily be the case for operators with more established market positions'. It states in conclusion that '[w]ithout access to national roaming for 3G services on T–Mobile's network, O2 ... would be a less effective competitor during its roll-out phase and would be unlikely to enter 3G wholesale and retail markets as a nationwide competitor (or in any event as a competitor offering the broadest geographical scope that is likely to be available at that time)'.

114 It is therefore apparent from the examination carried out under Article [101(3) TFEU] and Article 53(3) of the EEA Agreement that, in the light of the specific characteristics of the relevant emerging market, O2's competitive situation on the 3G market would probably not have been secure without the agreement, and it might even have been jeopardised. Those assessments confirm that the Commission's presuppositions in its examination under Article [101(1) TFEU] and Article 53(1) of the EEA Agreement have not been established. * * *

116 It follows from the foregoing that the Decision, in so far as it concerns the application of Article [101(1) TFEU] and Article 53(1) of the EEA Agreement, suffers from insufficient analysis, first, in that it contains no objective discussion of what the competition situation would have been in the absence of the agreement, which distorts the assessment of the actual and potential effects of the agreement on competition and, second, in that it does not demonstrate, in concrete terms, in the context of the relevant emerging market, that the provisions of the agreement on roaming have restrictive effects on competition, but is confined, in this respect, to a petitio principii and to broad and general statements. * * *

NOTES AND QUESTIONS

1.   The Court in *ENS* proceeded to analyze the case on the assumption that the agreement fell within Article 101(1). See page 949 infra.

2.   After *ENS*, how is the Commission to determine whether an agreement has no more than a negligible effect on competition and therefore is not even caught by Article 101(1)? Is a combined market share below 10% presumptively negligible? But isn't the ENS project apparently one of major importance? How does market definition affect the decision? Could the Commission have avoided the problem by finding a rail transport market between UK and the continent? in 1998?

3.   If there is a competitive harm regarding the formation of the venture, what is it? What would be the railroads' response?

4. Is the Commission required, or even authorized, to weigh competitive benefits against competitive harms in determining whether an agreement is caught by Article 101(1)?

Note the railroads' and the Commission's different approaches to whether an agreement is caught by Article 101(1):

130   [According to the railroads,] the case law ... establishes that [the Commission] is bound [under 101(1)] to apply a "rule of reason" and to balance the competitive benefits and harms of the agreement. [The Commission disagrees. It says that] such an approach is required in the context of Article [101] (3) of the Treaty but not in respect of the appraisal of restrictions of competition under Article [101](1).

Who is right?

In *Métropole TV,* six major firms in the French TV sector formed a satellite TV joint venture, TPS, which entered the market dominated by Canal+. The applicants argued that they were entitled to negative clearance [declaration of not being caught by Article 101(1)], rather than exemption, of a clause providing that certain channels were to be broadcast exclusively on TPS. Their argument depended upon the availability of rule-of-reason analysis under Article 101(1). The General Court rejected this approach, holding that the clause was caught by Article 101(1) because it restricted competition; the competitors of TPS were denied access to programs considered attractive to numerous French viewers. The positive effects had to be weighed under Article 101(3). *Métropole Télévision (M6) v. Commission,* Case T–112/99, [2001] ECR II–2459.

5. In *Asnef–Equifax,* Case C–238/05, [2006] ECR I–11125, Spain made a reference to the Court of Justice under Article 267 to determine the applicability of Article 101(1) to agreements for the exchange of information among financial institutions regarding the solvency of customers. The Court responded that whether there was a restriction of competition within the meaning of Article 101(1) depended on the economic context as well as the terms of agreement; for example whether the market was concentrated and whether, under all the market circumstances, the exchange was likely to lead to collective anticompetitive action. This was an inquiry for the national court to undertake. From the mere existence of the exchange, the likelihood of anticompetitive action could not be inferred. (See further treatment of the case under *Information Exchanges* at page 944 infra.)

The proper application of Article 101 is of particular interest to the Member States, for Article 3(2) of Regulation 1/2003 provides that if an agreement, decision or concerted practice capable of affecting trade between Member States is not prohibited by Article 101, it cannot be prohibited by national competition law.

6. The Court in O2 cited *Métropole* with approval. The judgment emphasizes the Commission's burden to prove that the agreement restricted competition compared with what the situation would have been in the absence of the agreement.

7. In the United States, the structure of analysis takes a somewhat different form. If the agreement is clearly anticompetitive (usually meaning price-raising) and clearly without pro-competitive virtue, it may be condemned on its face. If the agreement does not meet this threshold but still, from economic learning and experience, the anticompetitive impact seems obvious, the burden shifts to the defendant to explain why the restraint is unlikely to harm consumers *or* is likely to offer offsetting competitive benefits. In both categories, the plaintiff need not offer a market analysis. But if the competitive harm is more ambiguous, the plaintiff must offer a market analysis and demonstrate how the agreement is likely to create or enhance market power, to the detriment of consumers. *Polygram Holding, Inc. v. FTC*, 416 F.3d 29 (D.C. Cir. 2005), offers a helpful statement and analysis.

As we proceed to examine the requirements of Article 101(3), consider how the question—what is caught by Article 101(1)—may still have significance despite modernisation and the direct effectiveness of Article 101 in its entirety. Once an agreement is caught by Article 101(1), the undertakings have the burden to justify under Article 101(3). Note the four necessary conditions for the justification. If the agreement is caught by Article 101(1), can the undertakings prevail by showing that the agreement did not in fact restrict competition? Or is restriction of competition conclusively presumed, and does the undertaking thus need to prove offsetting pro-competitive or pro-efficiency effects?

C. ARTICLE 101(3): EFFECTS OF THE AGREEMENT ON COMPETITION, EFFICIENCY, INNOVATION

1. INTRODUCTION AND GUIDELINES

If an agreement falls within Article 101(1), it must, to be valid, satisfy the four conditions of Article 101(3); namely: 1) contribute to improving production or distribution of goods or promoting technical or economic progress (identified in Commission guidelines as "efficiency gains"), 2) while allowing consumers a fair share of benefits; 3) the agreement must not impose restrictions indispensable to the attainment of the above objectives, and 4) it must not afford the undertakings the possibility to eliminate competition in respect of a substantial part of the products concerned.

In 2004 the Commission issued guidelines on the application of Article 101(3) of the Treaty. These are available at *http://ec.europa.eu/competition/ antitrust/legislation/art81_3.html*. (Remember to watch for guidelines expected to be issued in December 2010.) The Guidelines were motivated by the need to give guidance to the Member States' authorities and courts, which would be applying Article 101(3) for the first time. The Guidelines state:

> [13]   The objective ... of Article 101 is to protect competition on the market as a means of enhancing consumer welfare and of ensuring an efficient allocation of resources. Competition and market integration serve these ends since the creation and preservation of an open single market promotes an efficient allocation of resources throughout the Community for the benefit of consumers.

The 2004 Guidelines go on to state that they present an analytical framework and methodology based on "the economic approach." "[R]eflected in Article [101(3)] ... is the assessment of the positive economic effects of restrictive agreements." paras. 5, 32.

The 2004 Guidelines identify certain principles as follows:

3.1   General principles

> [40]   Article [101](3) of the Treaty only becomes relevant when an agreement between undertakings restricts competition within the meaning of Article [101](1). In the case of non-restrictive agreements there is no need to examine any benefits generated by the agreement.

> [41]   Where in an individual case a restriction of competition within the meaning of Article [101](1) has been proven, Article [101](3) can be invoked as a defence. According to Article 2 of Regulation 1/2003 the burden of proof under Article [101](3) rests on the undertaking(s) invoking the benefit of the exception rule. Where the conditions of Article [101](3) are not satisfied the agreement is null and void, cf. Article [101](2). However, such automatic nullity only applies to those parts of the agreement that are incompatible with Article [101], provided that such parts are severable from the agreement as a whole. If only part of the agreement is null and void, it is for the applicable national law to determine the consequences thereof for the remaining part of the agreement.

> [42]   According to settled case law the four conditions of Article [101](3) are cumulative, i.e. they must all be fulfilled for the exception rule to be applicable. If they are not, the application of the exception rule of Article [101](3) must be refused. The four conditions of Article [101](3) are also exhaustive. When they are met the exception is applicable and may not be made dependent on any other condition. Goals pursued by other Treaty provisions can be taken into account to the extent that they can be subsumed under the four conditions of Article [101](3). * * *

> [47]   Any claim that restrictive agreements are justified because they aim at ensuring fair conditions of competition on the market is by nature unfounded and must be discarded. The purpose of Article [101] is to protect effective competition by ensuring that markets remain open and competitive. The protection of fair conditions of competition is a task for the legislator in compliance with Com-

munity law obligations and not for undertakings to regulate themselves. * * *

According to the 2004 Guidelines, are non-competition justifications admissible? What do you learn from para. 42?

What does the Commission mean by agreements "aim[ing to] ensur[e] fair competition" (para. 47)? Give an example. Why is such an agreement the antithesis of a procompetitive agreement?

––––––––––

Agreements, or decisions of undertakings—which may be by-laws of associations, tend to fall into two categories: 1) Loose agreements, which contemplate no integration of the entities, and 2) tighter agreements, which contemplate integration. An agreement to exchange information is typical of the first category. A joint venture or alliance is typical of the second category. The tightest joint ventures are concentrations covered by the Merger Regulation, which we deal with in Chapter 25.

2. LOOSE AGREEMENTS

a. Agreements to Exchange Information

Economics teaches that information (knowledge of the market) is good. It helps sellers understand supply and demand; it helps them determine the efficient amount for them to produce, and where, to whom, and how much to sell. Similarly it helps buyers understand the efficient amount of goods or services to buy and the lowest price at which they can buy. Information helps make markets work.

But in highly concentrated, high-barrier markets where firms have incentives to behave cooperatively, the sharing of market information can have outbalancing negative qualities. Oligopolists' knowledge of the sensitive business details of one another can help them coordinate and stabilize prices upwards. When firms are few, aggregated data can usually be disaggregated. Moreover when the information is obtained as the result of agreement among the firms, the danger signals are compounded: firms are not likely to give their sensitive information (e.g. cost, output, forecasts) to a competitor if they expect the data to be used against them. They are more likely to share the information if they can expect cooperation in lessening competition.

Often, when market conditions point to a negative (price-raising) effect, one suspects that the data sharing agreement is meant to facilitate a cartel; for, as we saw in the cartel chapter, cartelists need to know the most sensitive information about one another to find a joint profit-maximizing price, and they need to police their cartel agreement to prevent defection. Information sharing supports both tasks.

NOTE ON JOHN DEERE LTD. V. COMMISSION

The Agricultural Engineers Association was a trade association of producers and importers of agricultural tractors in the UK. It had some 200 members, and was open to membership by all other agricultural tractor companies. The market was oligopolistic; the four largest firms accounted for almost 80% of sales. The firms' market shares were stable and entry barriers were high. The product was homogeneous. The association organized an exchange of information among its members (who accounted for 88% of sales) based on the information contained in registration forms that were required to be filed by the UK. The data revealed great detail of sales and market shares, broken down by year, quarter, month and week, and by country, region, county, and dealer territory, and made it possible to identify not only the sales of each producer but also the imports and exports between dealer territories.

The information exchanged did not directly concern prices, and there was no evidence that the information exchange was designed in support of a cartel. Indeed, there was no claim that the *object* of the agreement was to harm trade or competition; and the Commission was unable to establish that the agreement, which was in force for 20 years, produced an actual anticompetitive effect (higher prices).

The Commission found that the information exchange agreement was caught by Article 101(1) and was not entitled to an exemption. The General Court agreed. It upheld Commission findings that the data exchange (1) disadvantaged non-members, who would not have the benefit of the information exchanged; (2) produced *potential* anticompetitive effects among members, by providing a forum for facilitating a high price policy; and (3) made it possible for each participating manufacturer to monitor *its* dealers' sales and thus made "it possible for [manufacturers] to confer absolute territorial protection on each of their dealers." para. 96. Further, the association did not show that the restrictions on competition resulting from the agreement were indispensable, "particularly with regard to the objectives of contributing to economic progress and equitable distribution of the benefits." para. 105. Case T–35/92, [1994] ECR II–957. The Court of Justice affirmed. Case C–7/95 P, [1998] ECR I–3111. It rejected John Deere's arguments, among others, that Article 101(1) does not prohibit purely potential effects on competition, and that the General Court improperly inferred harm to competition from high concentration without any evidence of higher prices or changes in the pattern of trade.

John Deere was the first prohibition by the Commission and Court of a pure information exchange of non-price information; that is, an information exchange not as part of a cartel.

Notes and Questions

1. Were the Court and Commission correct? How is such an agreement "exclusionary" to non-members? How does the exchange of sales information harm competition among members? Do you suspect that the members shared sales data to compete or to lessen competition? Do you believe that this exchange of information chilled parallel imports; i.e., kept each producer's product within each of its dealer's territories and thus kept the producer's product from competing with itself? Could this have been a device to help the producers cartelize? Which of the possible effects would most concern you if you were a competition authority?

2. In *T–Mobile Netherlands*, Case C–8/08, 2009 ECR I–04529, ECJ, representatives of the five big mobile telephone operators "held a meeting . . . [on 13 June 2001 at which] they discussed . . . the reduction of standard dealer renumerations for postpaid subscriptions [commissions to their agents for distributing their product to consumers], which was to take effect on or about 1 September 2001." They shared confidential information in their discussions. para. 12. When challenged, the firms argued that they had not made an agreement (the Dutch court found to the contrary) and that their conversations had no effect on consumer prices. The Dutch court made a preliminary reference. The Court of Justice held that, for a concerted practice to have an anticompetitive object, "it is sufficient that it has the potential to have a negative impact on competition." In the case of an anticompetitive object, it is not necessary that there be an anticompetitive effect, which "can only be of relevance for determining the amount of any fine and assessing any claim for damages." paras. 30, 31. "Article [101] . . . is designed to protect not only the immediate interests of individual competitors or consumers but also to protect the structure of the market and thus competition as such." para. 38

Does this mean that the information exchange agreement was automatically caught by Article 101(1)? Do you think that it was merely a benign or procompetitive agreement to exchange information and thus get knowledge? Or was it a thinly veiled attempt to ratchet down commissions payable to the agents?

Note on *Wirtschaftsvereinigung Stahl*

Excerpt from 1997 Report on Competition Policy, p. 127

On 26 November the Commission adopted a decision under Article 65 of the ECSC Treaty [the counterpart to Article 101 in the now-expired Coal and Steel Treaty] prohibiting an information exchange system notified by Wirtschaftsvereinigung Stahl, the German steel industry association. The system, which had not been implemented, provided for the exchange between association members of sensitive, recent and individualised data on supplies of more than 40 steel products in the various Member States, broken down by steel quality. The exchange would also have concerned the breakdown by consumer sector and the market shares of member companies on the German market. The leading German steel producers were to have participated in the system.

After analysing these homogeneous product markets in detail, the Commission drew a distinction between two types of market. It raised no objection to the exchange of sensitive information on dispersed markets. On the other hand, it did prohibit the exchange of data on all markets for flat products and on the markets for beams, sheet piling, permanent way material and wire rod of stainless steel. These are concentrated markets characterized by low import penetration, stable trade flows between Member States and chronic overcapacity.

The notified information exchange agreement would have restricted competition between the parties by increasing market transparency to such a degree that any independent competitive action on the part of one company would have been noticed immediately by its competitor, which would have been able to take suitable retaliatory measures such as systematically canvassing customers or offering temporary or local selective discounts. This increased transparency would thus have been liable to deter companies from trying to increase their market shares, a fundamental competitive activity. In addition, the frequency of the exchange, i.e. monthly, and the freshness of the data exchanged (one month old) would have reduced considerably the time during which a company could have derived any benefit from behaving competitively.

The decision is consistent with the Commission's practice, which has been upheld by the General Court [citing *John Deere*], of viewing as anti-competitive any systems involving the exchange of sensitive, recent and individualised data on a concentrated market in homogeneous products.

What was the principal harm feared from the steel industry's information exchange? In which case—tractors or steel—is the concern of cartel-like or cooperative pricing behavior stronger?

ASNEF–EQUIFAX v. ASOCIACIÓN DE USUARIOS DE SERVICIOS BANCARIOS (AUSBANC)
Case C–238/05, [2006] ECR I–11125, ECJ.

[Financial institutions in Spain agreed to exchange information about solvency of customers and lateness of payment. They planned to establish a register for such information. The Spanish competition authority authorized the register for five years on condition that the register be available to all financial institutions on a non-discriminatory basis and that it not disclose the information it contained on lenders. Ausbanc, an association of bank users, sought an annulment in a Spanish court. It alleged that the register would facilitate a boycott against poor credit risks. The Spanish court made an Article 267 reference to the Court of Justice regarding applicability and treatment under Article 101. The CJEU identified the various questions of fact regarding economic and legal context that the national court would have to decide, and it gave considerable guidance both as to when Article 101(1) would apply and when the Article 101(3) criteria would be satisfied.]

55   ... [R]egisters such as the one at issue in the main proceedings, by reducing the rate of borrower default, are in principle capable of improving the functioning of the supply of credit. As the Advocate General observed, ... if, owing to a lack of information on the risk of borrower default, financial institutions are unable to distinguish those borrowers who are more likely to default, the risk thereby borne by such institutions will necessarily be increased and they will tend to factor it in when calculating the cost of credit for all borrowers, including those less likely to default, who will then have to bear a higher cost than they would if the institutions were in a position to evaluate the probability of repayment more precisely. In principle, registers such as that mentioned above are capable of reducing such a tendency.

56   Furthermore, by reducing the significance of the information held by financial institutions regarding their own customers, such registers appear, in principle, to be capable of increasing the mobility of consumers of credit. In addition, those registers are apt to make it easier for new competitors to enter the market.

57   None the less, whether or not there is in the main proceedings a restriction of competition within the meaning of Article [101(1) TFEU] depends on the economic and legal context in which the register exists, and in particular on the economic conditions of the market as well as the particular characteristics of the register.

58   In that regard, first of all, if supply on a market is highly concentrated, the exchange of certain information may, according in particular to the type of information exchanged, be liable to enable undertakings to be aware of the market position and commercial strategy of their competitors, thus distorting rivalry on the market and increasing the probability of collusion, or even facilitating it. On the other hand, if supply is fragmented, the dissemination and exchange of information between competitors may be neutral, or even positive, for the competitive nature of the market. In the present case, it is common ground, ... that the referring court premised its reference for a preliminary ruling on the existence of 'a fragmented market', which it is for that court to verify.

59   Secondly, in order that registers such as that at issue in the main proceedings are not capable of revealing the market position or the commercial strategy of competitors, it is important that the identity of lenders is not revealed, directly or indirectly. In the present case, it is apparent from the decision for referral that the Tribunal de Defensa de la Competencia imposed on Asnef–Equifax, which accepted it, a condition that the information relating to lenders contained in the register not be disclosed.

60   Thirdly, it is also important that such registers be accessible in a nondiscriminatory manner, in law and in fact, to all operators active in the relevant sphere. If such accessibility were not guaranteed, some of those operators would be placed at a disadvantage, since they would have less information for the purpose of risk assessment, which would also not facilitate the entry of new operators on to the market.

61   It follows that, provided that the relevant market or markets are not highly concentrated, that the system does not permit lenders to be identified and that the conditions of access and use by financial institutions are not discriminatory, an information exchange system such as the register is not, in principle, liable to have the effect of restricting competition within the meaning of Article [101(1)].

62   While in those conditions such systems are capable of reducing uncertainty as to the risk that applicants for credit will default, they are not, however, liable to reduce uncertainty as to the risks of competition. Thus, each operator could be expected to act independently and autonomously when adopting a given course of conduct, regard being had to the risks presented by applicants. Contrary to Ausbanc's contention, it cannot be inferred solely from the existence of such a credit information exchange that it might lead to collective anti-competitive conduct, such as a boycott of certain potential borrowers.

63   Furthermore, since, as the Advocate General observed, . . . any possible issues relating to the sensitivity of personal data are not, as such, a matter for competition law, they may be resolved on the basis of the relevant provisions governing data protection. In the main proceedings, it is apparent from the documents before the Court that, under the rules applicable to the register, affected consumers may, in accordance with the Spanish legislation, check the information concerning them and, where necessary, have it corrected, or indeed deleted.

The applicability of Article [101(3)]

64   Only if the referring court finds, in the light of the considerations set out at paragraphs 58 to 62 of this judgment, that there is indeed in the dispute before it a restriction of competition within the meaning of Article [101(1)] will it be necessary for that court to carry out an analysis by reference to Article [101(3)] in order to resolve that dispute.

65   The applicability of the exemption provided for in Article [101(3)] is subject to the four cumulative conditions laid down in that provision. First, the arrangement concerned must contribute to improving the production or distribution of the goods or services in question, or to promoting technical or economic progress; secondly, consumers must be allowed a fair share of the resulting benefit; thirdly, it must not impose any non-essential restrictions on the participating undertakings; and, fourthly, it must not afford them the possibility of eliminating competition in respect of a substantial part of the products or services in question.

66   It is clear from the documents before the Court, and in particular from the second question referred by the national court, that that court

seeks an answer from the Court in respect of, in particular, the second of those conditions, which provides that consumers are to be allowed a fair share of the profit resulting from the agreement, decision or practice in question. The national court asks, in essence, whether, where all consumers do not derive a benefit from the register, the register might none the less benefit from the exemption provided for in Article [101(1)].

67   Apart from the potential effects described at paragraphs 55 and 56 of this judgment, registers such as the one at issue in the main proceedings are capable of helping to prevent situations of overindebtedness for consumers of credit as well as, in principle, of leading to a greater overall availability of credit. In the event that the register restricted competition within the meaning of Article [101(1)], those objective economic advantages might be such as to offset the disadvantages of such a possible restriction. It would be for the national court, if necessary, to verify that.

68   Admittedly, in principle it is not inconceivable that, as Ausbanc suggests, certain applicants for credit will, owing to the existence of such registers, be faced with increased interest rates, or even be refused credit.

69   However, without its being necessary to decide whether such applicants would none the less benefit from a possible credit discipline effect or from protection against overindebtedness, that circumstance cannot in itself prevent the condition that consumers be allowed a fair share of the benefit from being satisfied.

70   Under Article [101(3)], it is the beneficial nature of the effect on all consumers in the relevant markets that must be taken into consideration, not the effect on each member of that category of consumers.

71   Moreover, as follows from paragraphs 55 and 67 of this judgment, registers such as the one at issue in the main proceedings are, under favourable conditions, capable of leading to a greater overall availability of credit, including for applicants for whom interest rates might be excessive if lenders did not have appropriate knowledge of their personal situation. * * *

————

Read the paragraphs of the proposed horizontal guidelines that apply to exchange of information. *http://ec.europa.eu/competition/consultations/2010_horizontals/index.html*. Apply them to *John Deere*, *T–Mobile*, the German steel exchange, and *Asnef–Equifax*.

b. Standard Setting

Standard-setting organizations are regarded as increasingly important in facilitating innovation, particularly in information technologies such as for computer chips. It has become common for holders of intellectual property rights to commit to disclose their intellectual property while standards are being created, and, if the standard incorporates their intellectual property, to commit to license it on fair, reasonable, and non-discriminatory terms (FRAND terms). In high profile cases involving Rambus and Qualcomm, the Commission suspected the undertaking of staging a patent ambush: advocating a standard incorporating the firm's IP, failing to disclose the IP, and charging high royalties after the standard is adopted. The *Rambus* case resulted in a settlement without fines, and the *Qualcomm* case was dropped for failure of proof of wrongdoing. Obviously drawing from these experiences, the Commission has included standard-setting in its proposed draft guidelines on horizontal co-operation agreements that are expected to become effective in December 2010. The guidelines specify conditions under which standard-setting agreements will not give rise to competition concerns. See link at *http://ec. europa.eu/competition/consultations/2010_horizontals/index.html.*

c. Decisions of Associations

Article 101 applies also to decisions, including by-laws, of associations. Associations of competitors are often breeding grounds for illegal conspiracies. For example, agreements to exchange information may be the tip of the iceberg of a price-fixing cartel.

However, associations and societies often play useful functions that, rather than suppressing the market, help it work. They may undertake tasks that need to be done. The question is often whether some of the clauses and restrictions have gone too far; whether they have crossed the line from facilitating competition to suppressing it. This is often the nature of the inquiry in connection with collecting societies.

In the matter of *CISAC* (International Confederation of Societies of Authors and Composers), music authors—lyricists and composers—gave collecting societies the right to license their works, and the collecting societies agreed to license the work and to police copyright infringements.

Collecting societies exist in most Member States and their members are the authors in that state. The *CISAC* case concerns 24 collecting societies located in the European Economic Area. The membership agreements of most collecting societies contained a membership clause that forbids an author to choose or switch to another (e.g., out-of-state) membership society, and territorial restrictions that 1) prohibit a collecting society from offering licenses to commercial users outside of their domestic territory, and 2) contain exclusivity agreements that authorize another collecting society to be the exclusive administrator of its portfolio on another territory. The collecting societies had bi-lateral reciprocal representation agreements that gave each other the right to grant licenses for the works of their respective members in the territory of the collecting society. As a result, music providers could not get a pan-European license but had to negotiate separately with each national society.

The Commission issued a decision prohibiting the membership clauses and prohibiting the societies from agreeing among themselves to limit territories. It determined that the agreements were a significant impediment to a single market, and that the membership agreements anticompetitively limited the choice of authors.

Then Competition Commissioner Neelie Kroes said: "This decision will benefit cultural diversity by encouraging collecting societies to offer composers and lyricists a better deal in terms of collecting the money to which they are entitled. It will also facilitate the development of satellite, cable and internet broadcasting, giving listeners more choice and giving authors more potential revenue. However, the Commission has been careful to ensure that the benefits of the collective rights management system are not put into question in terms of levels of royalties for authors and available music repertoire." Press Release, Commission prohibits practices which prevent European collecting societies from offering choice to music authors and users, 16 July 2008, IP/08/1165. CISAC has appealed to the General Court. Case T–442/08.

3. TIGHTER AGREEMENTS

Firms may form joint ventures and alliances to share risks and areas of expertise and thus to create synergies. These are procompetitive properties. The combination can, however, also have some anticompetitive aspects. For example, it might combine important competitors in a concentrated market, and the partners might otherwise be in a position to continue their competition against one another. Also, the partners might incorporate unnecessary or unreasonably restrictive ancillary restrictions, such as certain exclusive dealing that lessens outsiders' access. In the rare case, a joint venture might be an essential facility that outsiders cannot duplicate and that outsiders must be able to access to compete effectively.

The principal judgment on procompetitive and anticompetitive effects of joint ventures is *European Night Services,* which we studied above in connection with applicability of Article 101(1). Here are excerpts from the judgment regarding Article 101(3).

EUROPEAN NIGHT SERVICES LTD. v. COMMISSION

Cases T–374–375, 384 & 388/94, [1998] ECR II–3141, General Court.
(read facts at page 933 supra)

As to the Commission's requirement that the parent railroads supply to competitors of ENS the same necessary services that they supply to ENS

205   According to paragraph 79 of the contested decision, the aim of [requiring ENS to supply services to competitors] is that of "preventing the restrictions of competition from going beyond what is indispensable". * * *

207   ... [E]ven if the Commission had made an adequate and correct assessment of the restrictions of competition in question, it would be necessary to consider whether it was a proper application of Article

[101] (3) to impose on the notifying parties the condition that train paths, locomotives and crews must be supplied to third parties on the same terms as to ENS, on the ground that they are necessary or that they constitute essential facilities, as discussed by the parties in their pleadings and at the hearing. * * *

209   ... [W]ith regard to an agreement such as that in the present case, setting up a joint venture, which falls within Article [101](1) of the Treaty, the Court considers that neither the parent undertakings nor the joint venture thus set up may be regarded as being in possession of infrastructure, products or services which are "necessary" or "essential" for entry to the relevant market unless such infrastructure, products or services are not "interchangeable" and unless, by reason of their special characteristics—in particular the prohibitive cost of and/or time reasonably required for reproducing them—there are no viable alternatives available to potential competitors of the joint venture, which are thereby excluded from the market.

210   The question whether the Commission could validly regard the supply of (a) train paths, (b) locomotives and (c) crews to ENS by its parent undertakings as necessary or essential services which had to be made available to third parties on the same terms as to ENS and whether, in so doing, it provided a valid statement of reasons for its decision must be examined in the light of the above considerations and by analogy with the case law.... Finally, that examination will also serve as the

basis for determining whether the Commission made a correct analysis of the alleged restrictions of competition with regard to third parties arising out of the special relationship between the parent undertakings and ENS.

211   With regard, first, to train paths, [the Commission's decision is based on a false premise because it erroneously treated ENS as a transport operator].

212   With regard, second, to the supply of locomotives, as pointed out above, locomotives cannot be regarded as necessary or essential facilities unless they are essential for ENS's competitors, in the sense that without them they would be unable either to penetrate the relevant market or to continue operating on it. However, since the decision defined the relevant market as the market for the transport of business travellers and the market for the transport of leisure travellers, both of which are intermodal, and since ENS's market share does not exceed 7 per cent to 8 per cent according to the Commission, or 5 per cent according to the notification of the parties, on either of those intermodal markets, it cannot be accepted that a possible refusal by the notifying undertakings to supply ENS's competitors with special locomotives for the Channel Tunnel could have the effect of excluding such competitors from the relevant market as thus defined. It has not been demonstrated that an undertaking

having such a small market share can be in a position to exert any influence whatever on the functioning or structure of the market in question.

213   Only if the market under consideration were the completely different, intramodal, market for business and leisure travel by rail, on which the railway undertakings currently hold a dominant position, could a refusal to supply locomotives possibly have an effect on competition. However, it was not that intramodal market which was finally considered relevant by the Commission, but the intermodal market.... * * *

215   As the applicants have argued, the contested decision does not contain any analysis demonstrating that the locomotives in question are necessary or essential. More specifically, it is not possible to conclude from reading the contested decision that third parties cannot obtain them either directly from manufacturers or indirectly by renting them from other undertakings. Nor has any correspondence between the Commission and third parties, demonstrating that the locomotives in question cannot be obtained on the market, been produced before the Court. As the applicants have stated, any undertaking wishing to operate the same rail services as ENS through the Channel Tunnel may freely purchase or rent the locomotives in question on the market....

216   ... [T]he Commission has ... merely asserted that ... only the notifying undertakings actually possess such locomotives. That argument cannot, however, be accepted. The fact that the notifying undertakings have been the first to acquire the locomotives in question on the market does not mean that they are alone in being able to do so.

217   Consequently, the Commission's assessment of the necessary or essential nature of the special locomotives designed for the Channel Tunnel and, thus, the obligation imposed on the parent undertakings to supply such locomotives to third parties are vitiated by an absence or, at the very least, an insufficiency of reasoning.

218   For the same reasons, the obligation imposed on the parent undertakings also to supply train crews for special locomotives for the Channel Tunnel to third parties is similarly vitiated by an absence or an insufficiency of reasoning.

219   Consequently, the contested decision is vitiated by an absence or, at the very least, an insufficiency of reasoning in so far as it requires the applicants to supply to third parties in competition with ENS the same "necessary services" as it supplies to ENS. * * *

221   As regards, first, access to infrastructure (train paths), it is true that access for third parties may in principle be hindered when it is controlled by competitors; nevertheless, the obligation of railway undertakings which are also infrastructure managers to grant such

access on fair and non-discriminatory terms to international groupings competing with ENS is explicitly provided for and guaranteed by
Directive 91/440. The ENS agreements therefore cannot, by definition, impede access to infrastructure by third parties. As regards the
supply to ENS of special locomotives and crew for the Channel
Tunnel, the mere fact of its benefitting from such a service could
impede access by third parties to the downstream market only if such
locomotives and crew were to be regarded as essential facilities. Since
. . . they cannot be categorised as such, the fact that they are to be
supplied to ENS under the operating agreements for night rail
services cannot be regarded as restricting competition *vis-à-vis* third
parties. That aspect of the Commission's analysis of restrictions of
competition *vis-à-vis* third parties is therefore also unfounded.

As to duration of the exemption granted

222 The applicants emphasise that the ENS agreements relate to a major
long-term investment and that the return on the project is dependent
on the securing of advantageous 20–year financing for the purchase of
the specialised rolling stock, so that the limitation of the exemption to
eight years is inadequate. . . . * * *

230 . . . [E]ven if it is assumed that the Commission's assessment of the
restrictions on competition in the contested decision was adequate
and correct, the Court considers that the duration of an exemption
granted under Article [101] (3) of the Treaty—or, as here, Article 5 of
Regulation 1017/68—and Article 53(3) EEA must be sufficient to
enable the beneficiaries to achieve the benefits justifying such exemption, namely, in the present case, the contribution to economic
progress and the benefits to consumers provided by the introduction
of new high-quality transport services. . . . Since, moreover, such
progress and benefits cannot be achieved without considerable investment, the length of time required to ensure a proper return on that
investment is necessarily an essential factor to be taken into account
when determining the duration of an exemption, particularly in a
case such as the present, where it is undisputed that the services in
question are completely new, involve major investments and substantial financial risks and require the pooling of know-how by the
participating undertakings.

231 The consideration set out in . . . the decision, that "the duration of
the exemption will therefore depend inter alia on the period for which
it can reasonably be supposed that market conditions will remain
substantially the same," cannot, therefore, be regarded as decisive, on
its own, for determining the duration of the exemption, without also
taking account of the length of time necessary to enable the parties to
achieve a satisfactory return on their investment.

232 However, the contested decision does not contain any detailed assessment of the length of time required to achieve a return on the
investments in question under conditions of legal certainty, in the

light, in particular, of the fact that the parties have entered into financial commitments covering a period of 20 years for the purchase of the special rolling stock.... * * *

234   Consequently, the Commission's decision to limit the duration of the exemption granted for the ENS agreements is in any event vitiated by an absence of reasoning. * * *

[T]he contested decision must be annulled.

NOTES AND QUESTIONS

1. Would you describe ENS as a procompetitive joint venture? Why? Should the joint venture have an Article 101 obligation to give competitors access to the tunnel (had it not been provided by agreement)? What was the Court's concern with imposing conditions on the joint venture? Was it well taken?

2. If, in *ENS*, the market were rail travel and the joint venturers were the only firms that possessed locomotives fit to travel through the Channel Tunnel, would the Commission's requirement that the joint venturers supply locomotives to third parties on the same terms as they supply ENS withstand scrutiny?

3. Today, after modernisation, *ENS* would not seek a negative clearance or exemption. It would simply, after consulting its lawyers, proceed with the venture. If the Commission, a national authority in an affected Member State, or a private party that considered itself harmed, brought proceedings, would the analysis differ? Would the outcome differ? Note that, under the old Regulation 17, if an agreement fell within Article 101(1) but was justified under Article 101(3), the Commission was likely to impose conditions and would limit any exemption to a term of years. Is the system under Regulation 1/2003 superior?

INNOVATION AND COMPETITIVENESS

Consider the following two matters, as summarized by the Commission in its 1996 Competition Policy Report, both of which involve strategic alliances—i.e., synergistic joint ventures that enable the partners to enter new markets and expand their capabilities.

Excerpt from 1996 Report on Competition Policy, p. 121 Atlas/GlobalOne

On 17 July [1996] the Commission authorized the Atlas project, a joint venture between Deutsche Telekom AG (DT) and France Télécom (FT) aimed at providing telecommunications services to large users in Europe. The services provided by Atlas include network services, outsourcing and very small aperture satellite (VSAT) services. The Commission also authorized the proposed GlobalOne joint venture, an alliance between Atlas and Sprint Corporation (Sprint) for the supply of the above services worldwide. Within GlobalOne, the parties will provide the same services as within Atlas, together with traveller services and telecommunications services to other telecommunications organizations (TOs).

In the relevant markets, the services provided to corporate users raise important issues to do with competition in the EEA. This is the case, for example, with the market for the transmission of data via terrestrial networks. DT and FT have market shares there well in excess of 70% in Germany and France respectively, buttressed by a legal monopoly over the supply of infrastructure. In addition, the Atlas project provided for the elimination of a competitor of DT in Germany, namely FT's local subsidiary, Info AG.

In the course of the proceeding, France and Germany first of all undertook to liberalize the alternative infrastructures by introducing a system under which licences would be granted to any operator meeting certain technical requirements, thereby making competitors less dependent on the networks of FT and DT. The Commission made the Atlas/GlobalOne authorization conditional on the granting of the first two infrastructure licences in France and Germany.

DT and FT have postponed the transfer of their domestic data transmission networks to the joint venture pending full liberalization of infrastructure services in France and Germany. FT has undertaken to sell Info AG. This modified contractual framework, coupled as it is with strict conditions and obligations, will help to ensure that the two projects satisfy an increasingly urgent demand and compete with the few telecommunications services providers existing at world level without, however, resulting in any elimination of competition. * * *

Iridium

The Commission, by formal decision, gave the green light to the creation of Iridium, a company led by the US corporation Motorola, which intends to provide from the last quarter of 1998 global digital wireless communications services using a constellation of 66 low earth orbit (LEO) satellites, to be launched and placed in orbit during the next 24 months. Services will include mobile voice telephony, paging and basic data services (such as facsimile) and will be provided via portable hand-held (dual mode or single mode) telephones, vehicle-mounted telephones, pagers and other subscriber equipment.

Apart from Motorola, Iridium is owned by 16 strategic investors including a number of telecommunication services providers and equipment manufacturers from around the world. Two European companies figure among those strategic investors: Stet (Italy; 3.8%) and Vebacom (Germany; 10%). Each of the two has its own gateway service territory covering different parts of Europe and the associated exclusive right to construct and operate a gateway within its respective territory.

In the decision, the creation of Iridium has been concluded to fall outside the scope of both Article [101(1) of the TFEU] and Article 53(1) of the EEA [European Economic Area] Agreement. In this respect, it was concluded that none of the strategic investors could be reasonably expected to separately assume the very high level of investments required (nearly

USD 5 billion) and the very high risk of technical and commercial failure associated with such a new system. In addition, no investor has all the necessary licences to operate such a system.

Satellite systems like Iridium (commonly referred to as S–PCS systems) are expected to complement wireless terrestrial mobile technologies (such as GSM) in areas where those terrestrial technologies have failed to penetrate (i.e. rural parts of the developed world and both urban and rural parts of lower income countries) or where terrestrial roaming is not available because of incompatible technologies. In addition, S–PCS systems are expected to act as a complement and even a substitute for the public switched fixed telephone network, enhancing service coverage in remote areas of low population density and/or where the terrestrial infrastructure is very poor.

The same conclusion as to the inapplicability of the competition rules of both the [TFEU] and the EEA Agreement was reached in respect of several ancillary restraints; namely as regards the distribution of the Iridium services and the pricing policies which Iridium may suggest as guidelines to gateways investor operators.

NOTES AND QUESTIONS

1. Did Iridium restrict or distort competition? Were its members competitors? potential competitors?

2. How did the agreement of Atlas and GlobalOne restrict competition? How did the Commission counteract the problems? How did the Commission use the occasion to impose conditions that would increase competition?

3. Describe the Commission's approach towards innovation and competitiveness.

D. ARTICLE 101(1) AND (3)—PUBLIC POLICY; NON–COMPETITION GOALS

1. INTRODUCTION

We have seen from the Commission's guidelines on the application of Article 101(3) that an agreement falls within Article 101(1) if it restricts competition, and that an Article 101(3) exemption is available only if it has offsetting procompetitive (including efficiency and innovation) effects. What if the agreement is intended to pursue an important public policy objective? Are there any exceptions from the formulation above?

2. LABOR

ALBANY INTERNATIONAL BV AND TEXTILE INDUSTRY PENSION FUNDS

Case C–67/96, [1999] ECR I–5751, ECJ.

[The Netherlands maintains a pension system. A compulsory statutory scheme entitles the whole population to receive a basic pension, calculated by reference to the statutory minimum wage. This amount, however, is quite limited.

Industry sectors are covered by supplementary pensions managed by collective schemes negotiated in the context of collective worker-employer agreements. The law requires employers in the sector to be affiliated with the sectoral fund, subject to satisfying conditions for exemption.

Albany International BV was a textile company. It was not party to the collective agreement. It provided its own supplementary coverage through an insurer of its choice; it sought and was denied an exemption from the statutory scheme, and it refused to pay its mandatory contributions to the statutorily designated fund, the Textile Industry Trade Fund. When sued for arrears, it challenged the Dutch law's requirement of compulsory affiliation, and the collective agreement providing for the designated fund, as contrary to Articles 3(1)(g) [now in Protocol 27], TEU 4(3), and TFEU, 101, 102 and 106.[*] Questions were referred to the Court of Justice.]

47   Albany contends that the request by management and labour to make affiliation to a sectoral pension fund compulsory constitutes an agreement between the undertakings operating in the sector concerned, contrary to Article [101] (1) of the Treaty.

48   Such an agreement, in its view, restricts competition in two ways. First, by entrusting the operation of a compulsory scheme to a single manager, it deprives the undertakings operating in the sector concerned of the possibility of affiliation to another pension scheme managed by other insurers. Second, that agreement excludes the latter insurers from a substantial part of the pension insurance market.

49   The effects of such an agreement on competition are 'appreciable' because it affects the entire Netherlands textile sector. They are aggravated by the cumulative effect of making affiliation to pension schemes compulsory in numerous sectors of the economy and for all undertakings in those sectors.

---

* Eds.: Article 3(1)(g) ECT required "a system ensuring that competition in the internal market is not distorted"; TEU Article 4(3) requires the Member States to "facilitate the achievement of the Union's tasks"; Article 106 requires public and state-privileged undertakings to abstain from measures inconsistent with the non-discrimination mandate and the competition rules and to comply with the competition rules as long as compliance does not obstruct their performance of public tasks. The interaction of these provisions is further treated in the chapter on the state, Chapter 26.

50   Moreover, such an agreement affects trade between Member States in so far as it concerns undertakings which engage in cross-frontier business and deprives insurers established in other Member States of the opportunity to offer a full pension scheme in the Netherlands either by virtue of cross-frontier services or through branches or subsidiaries.

51   Therefore, according to Albany, by creating a legal framework for, and acceding to a request from, the two sides of industry to make affiliation to the sectoral pension fund compulsory, the public authorities favoured or furthered the implementation and operation of agreements between undertakings operating in the sectors concerned which are contrary to Article [101](1) of the Treaty, thereby infringing Articles [ECT 3(1)(g), TEU 4(3) and TFEU 101].

52   It is necessary to consider first whether a decision taken by the organisations representing employers and workers in a given sector, in the context of a collective agreement, to set up in that sector a single pension fund responsible for managing a supplementary pension scheme and to request the public authorities to make affiliation to that fund compulsory for all workers in that sector is contrary to Article [101] of the Treaty. * * *

54   ... [I]t is important to bear in mind that, under Article [3(1)(g) and (j)] of the EC Treaty, the activities of the Community are to include not only a 'system ensuring that competition in the internal market is not distorted' but also 'a policy in the social sphere'. Article 2 of the EC Treaty provides that a particular task of the Community is 'to promote throughout the Community a harmonious and balanced development of economic activities' and 'a high level of employment and of social protection'.[*]

55   In that connection, Article 118 of the EC Treaty[**] ... provides that the Commission is to promote close cooperation between Member States in the social field, particularly in matters relating to the right of association and collective bargaining between employers and workers.

56   Article 118b of the EC Treaty adds that the Commission is to endeavour to develop the dialogue between management and labour at European level which could, if the two sides consider it desirable, lead to relations based on agreement.

57   Moreover, Article 1 of the Agreement on social policy (OJ 1992 C 191, p. 91) states that the objectives to be pursued by the Community and the Member States include improved living and working conditions, proper social protection, dialogue between management and labour, the development of human resources with a view to lasting high employment and the combatting of exclusion.

---

* Eds.: Now substantially incorporated into TEU Article 3(3).

** Eds.: Article 118 ECT has been repealed. Social rights are protected in the TEU Article 3(3) and in the Charter of Fundamental Rights of the European Union, annexed to and part of the Treaties.

58   Under Article 4(1) and (2) of the Agreement, the dialogue between
      management and labour at Community level may lead, if they so
      desire, to contractual relations, including agreements, which will be
      implemented either in accordance with the procedures and practices
      specific to management and labour and the Member States, or, at the
      joint request of the signatory parties, by a Council decision on a
      proposal from the Commission.

59   It is beyond question that certain restrictions of competition are
      inherent in collective agreements between organisations representing
      employers and workers. However, the social policy objectives pursued
      by such agreements would be seriously undermined if management
      and labour were subject to Article [101] (1) of the Treaty when seeking
      jointly to adopt measures to improve conditions of work and employ-
      ment.

60   It therefore follows from an interpretation of the provisions of the
      Treaty as a whole which is both effective and consistent that agree-
      ments concluded in the context of collective negotiations between
      management and labour in pursuit of such objectives must, by virtue
      of their nature and purpose, be regarded as falling outside the scope of
      Article [101](1) of the Treaty.

61   The next question is therefore whether the nature and purpose of the
      agreement at issue in the main proceedings justify its exclusion from
      the scope of Article [101](1) of the Treaty.

62   First, like the category of agreements referred to above which derive
      from social dialogue, the agreement at issue in the main proceedings
      was concluded in the form of a collective agreement and is the
      outcome of collective negotiations between organisations representing
      employers and workers.

63   Second, as far as its purpose is concerned, that agreement establishes,
      in a given sector, a supplementary pension scheme managed by a
      pension fund to which affiliation may be made compulsory. Such a
      scheme seeks generally to guarantee a certain level of pension for all
      workers in that sector and therefore contributes directly to improving
      one of their working conditions, namely their remuneration.

64   Consequently, the agreement at issue in the main proceedings does
      not, by reason of its nature and purpose, fall within the scope of
      Article [101](1) of the Treaty.

NOTES AND QUESTIONS

1. Albany articulated a number of ways in which the requirement of
compulsory affiliation harmed competition: it could not choose its own insurer; it could get a better rate from its own insurer, which was likely to be more
efficient than a monopolist fund; insurers—including non-Dutch insurers—
would be deprived of access to the market. Indeed the Court, finding the
sectoral pension fund to be an undertaking, observed that the fund was

engaged in economic activity in competition with insurance companies, and that its pursuit of a social objective through cross-subsidization of risks ("manifestations of solidarity") could render its services less competitive than comparable services. paras 84–86. See also paras 97–98: competition was restricted; firms might otherwise provide their workers with a superior scheme. Why wouldn't these effects bring the agreement within Article 101(1), leaving the question of overriding social benefits for analysis under 101(3), if social benefits were an admissible justification?

2.   Did the Court simply, in effect, grant an exemption to bona fide labor agreements? Was this a good idea?

In the United States, Section 6 of the Clayton Act grants an antitrust exemption to agreements among workers (e.g., collaboration under the auspices of labor unions). "The labor of a human being is not a commodity or article of commerce." The courts have expanded the exemption to cover bona fide labor negotiations, including by employers, and the resulting collective bargaining agreements. This is called the non-statutory labor exemption.

3.   After *Albany,* and in view of the Court's invocation of the social aspects of the Treaty, how would you expect the Commission and Court to treat agreements other than collective bargaining agreements that promise benefits to jobs and workers? Can benefits to workers and the economy be balanced against harms to competition as aspects of economic progress under Article 101(3)?

3.   THE LIBERAL PROFESSIONS

The Court of Justice has decided important cases on the regulation of the liberal professions and its effect on competition. See *Wouters* (immediately below), *Arduino,* Case C–35/99, [2002] ECR I–1529, and *Cipolla* and *Macrino,* Cases C–94/04 and 202/04, [2006] ECR I–11421. *Arduino* and *Cipolla* concern mandatory fee schedules for Italian lawyers. The Court has ruled that the state can authorize self-regulation by a professional body setting mandatory minimum fees as long as the state retains the decision-making powers and establishes sufficient control mechanisms.

Commission Reports of 2004 and 2005 observe a trend of Member States to deregulate, and they find that countries with little regulation of the liberal professions serve consumers no less well than countries with significant regulation of the professions. The reports are available at *http://ec.europa.eu/competition/sectors/professional_services/reports/reports. html.*

WOUTERS ET CIE
Case C–309/99, [2002] ECR I–1577, ECJ.

[This judgment arises out of the request for a preliminary ruling referred to the Court by the Netherlands Council of State in the framework of proceedings initiated by Wouters and other members of the Bar seeking to set aside the decisions of the Amsterdam and Rotterdam Bar prohibiting them from practicing law in full partnership with accountants. Those decisions were adopted pursuant to the Regulation on Joint Professional Activity adopted by the Bar of the Nederland in 1993 ("the 1993 Regulation"). The 1993 Regulation prohibits members of the Bar to "assume or maintain any obligations which might jeopardize the free and independent exercise of their profession, including ... the relationship of trust between lawyer and client" and to "enter into or maintain any professional partnership unless the primary purpose of each partner's respective profession is the practice of the law." Wouters and his colleagues claimed that the decisions of the Amsterdam and Rotterdam Bar, as well as the 1993 Regulation, were incompatible with the Treaty provisions on competition, right of establishment and freedom to provide services.]

Question 1(a)

56 The question to be determined is whether, when it adopts a regulation such as the 1993 Regulation, a professional body is to be treated as an association of undertakings or, on the contrary, as a public authority.

[The Court answered that the bar is to be treated as an association of undertakings.] * * *

Question 2

73 By its second question the national court seeks, essentially, to ascertain whether a regulation such as the 1993 Regulation which, in order to guarantee the independence and loyalty to the client of members of the Bar who provide legal assistance in conjunction with members of other liberal professions, adopts universally binding rules governing the formation of multi-disciplinary partnerships, has the object or effect of restricting competition within the common market and is likely to affect trade between Member States. * * *

84 The prohibition at issue in the main proceedings prohibits all contractual arrangements between members of the Bar and accountants which provide in any way for shared decision-making, profit-sharing or for the use of a common name, and this makes any form of effective partnership difficult. * * *

86 It appears to the Court that the national legislation in issue in the main proceedings has an adverse effect on competition and may affect trade between Member States.

87 As regards the adverse effect on competition, the areas of expertise of members of the Bar and of accountants may be complementary. Since legal services, especially in business law, more and more frequently require recourse to an accountant, a multi-disciplinary partnership of members of the Bar and accountants would make it possible to offer a wider range of services, and

indeed to propose new ones. Clients would thus be able to turn to a single structure for a large part of the services necessary for the organisation, management and operation of their business (the 'one-stop shop' advantage).

88   Furthermore, a multi-disciplinary partnership of members of the Bar and accountants would be capable of satisfying the needs created by the increasing interpenetration of national markets and the consequent necessity for continuous adaptation to national and international legislation.

89   Nor, finally, is it inconceivable that the economies of scale resulting from such multi-disciplinary partnerships might have positive effects on the cost of services.

90   A prohibition of multi-disciplinary partnerships of members of the Bar and accountants, such as that laid down in the 1993 Regulation, is therefore liable to limit production and technical development within the meaning of Article [101](1)(b) of the Treaty. * * *

97   However, not every agreement between undertakings or every decision of an association of undertakings which restricts the freedom of action of the parties or of one of them necessarily falls within the prohibition laid down in Article [101](1) of the Treaty. For the purposes of application of that provision to a particular case, account must first of all be taken of the overall context in which the decision of the association of undertakings was taken or produces its effects. More particularly, account must be taken of its objectives, which are here connected with the need to make rules relating to organisation, qualifications, professional ethics, supervision and liability, in order to ensure that the ultimate consumers of legal services and the sound administration of justice are provided with the necessary guarantees in relation to integrity and experience.... It has then to be considered whether the consequential effects restrictive of competition are inherent in the pursuit of those objectives.

98   Account must be taken of the legal framework applicable in the Netherlands, on the one hand, to members of the Bar and to the Bar of the Netherlands, which comprises all the registered members of the Bar in that Member State, and on the other hand, to accountants. * * *

102   [The members of the Bar] should be in a situation of independence vis-à-vis the public authorities, other operators and third parties, by whom they must never be influenced. They must furnish, in that respect, guarantees that all steps taken in a case are taken in the sole interest of the client.

103   By contrast, the profession of accountant is not subject, in general, and more particularly, in the Netherlands, to comparable requirements of professional conduct. * * *

[105] ... The Bar of the Netherlands was entitled to consider that members of the Bar might no longer be in a position to advise and represent their clients independently and in the observance of strict professional secrecy if they belonged to an organisation which is also responsible for producing an account of the financial results of the transactions in respect of which their services were called upon and for certifying those accounts. * * *

[107] A regulation such as the 1993 Regulation could therefore reasonably be considered to be necessary in order to ensure the proper practice of the legal profession, as it is organised in the Member State concerned. * * *

NOTES AND QUESTIONS

1. Describe the harm to competition likely to result from the bar's regulatory rule.

2. Would a similar self-regulatory restraint be caught by Article 101(1) if imposed by non-professionals? by non-lawyers? May accountants agree that accounting firms may not combine with economists' firms? May plumbing firms agree not to allow their members to be electricians or contractors?

3. Why is the lawyers' restraint not subject to examination under Article 101(3)? Analyze the bar rule under Article 101(3). Does it satisfy the conditions?

4. In *Cipolla* and *Macrino,* cases C–94/04 and 202/04, [2006] ECR I–11421, Italy set a mandatory minimum fee schedule for lawyers based on a schedule prepared by a lawyers' association. The minimum fee requirement disadvantaged out-of-state lawyers (among others) in their attempts to compete by discounting. The Court of Justice acknowledged that the measure restrained cross-border services, but held that the restraint could be justified if it met overriding requirements relating to the public interest such as protection of consumers and administration of justice, and if the restraint was proportional to the objective. What is the measure's probable effect on consumers (clients)? What is the public interest in setting a minimum fee? Do you think a public interest concern can outweigh the harm to consumers? Is *Cipolla* consistent with the principles of Article 61 (Member States may not impair free movement of services based on nationality or residence)? With the combination of Articles TEU 4(3) (Member State duty of loyalty to facilitate the tasks of the Union), and TFEU 61, 101, and 102? See Chapter 26 as to the permissibility of the state restraint.

5. In the United States, lawyers may not lawfully agree among themselves that no law firm will integrate with an accountants' or economists' firm. But lawyers (bar associations) may and do propose that state courts adopt such a rule; and state courts typically mandate the separation as a "rule of ethics." State court rules are state action and are not subject to antitrust. Is mandated separation of lawyer/economist/accountant firms wise? efficient? good for clients?

4. THE ENVIRONMENT AND COMPETITIVENESS

European Union policy supports environmental measures and the integration of environmental concerns into the various Community policies. In its 1998 Competition Policy Report, the Commission summarized as follows its activity regarding competition and the environment:

129 At the Cardiff European Summit, the Member States recalled the provisions of the Treaty of Amsterdam [Article 6] stipulating that Community policies should take account of environmental protection with a view to achieving sustainable development, an approach which was endorsed at the Vienna Summit. In its XXVth the Report on Competition Policy, the Commission spelt out its position regarding implementation of the Community competition rules in the environmental field. In particular, it stated: 'When the Commission examines individual cases, it weighs up the restrictions of competition arising out of an agreement against the environmental objectives of the agreement, and applies the principle of proportionality in accordance with Article [101](3). In particular, improving the environment is regarded as a factor which contributes to improving production or distribution or to promoting economic or technical progress.' In that connection, 1998 was marked by four cases reflecting the Commission's commitment to take a positive approach to environmental issues in its competition analyses.

130 The Commission approved the agreement signed by the European Association of Consumer Electronics Manufacturers (EACEM) and 16 of its members, all major manufacturers of television sets and video cassette recorders. This agreement is a voluntary commitment to reduce the electricity consumption of this equipment when it is in stand-by mode. The Commission exempted the agreement under Article [101](3) on the ground that the energy-saving and environmental benefits of the scheme clearly represented technical and economic progress and, by their nature, would be passed on to consumers. The energy saving could amount to 3.2 TWh a year from 2005. This reduction in energy consumption will have a significant impact in terms of the management of energy resources, reductions in CO_2 emissions and, accordingly, measures to counter global warming. The Commission also ascertained that the scheme would not eliminate competition in the affected markets and that its restrictive effect was essential to achieving its full benefits.

131 The Association of European Automobile Manufacturers (ACEA) has undertaken, on behalf of its members, to reduce CO_2 emissions from passenger cars. This effort is in line with the Community policy of reducing CO_2 emissions into the atmosphere. ACEA has set a reduction target of 25% by 2008. The Commission and the Member States will monitor the efforts made to achieve that target. The Commission also took the view that this agreement between European automobile

manufacturers did not infringe the competition rules. ACEA determines an average reduction target for all its members, but each of them is free to set its own level, which will encourage them to develop and introduce new CO_2-efficient technologies independently and in competition with one another. Accordingly, ACEA's voluntary agreement does not constitute a restriction of competition and is not caught by Article [101](1).

132   [EUCAR is the European Council for Automotive Research and Development. It consists of Opel, BMW (including Rover), Mercedes, Fiat, Ford PSA, Porsche, Renault, VW and Volvo.] In the *EUCAR* case, the Commission adopted a favourable stance on a cooperation agreement between Europe's leading motor manufacturers which is designed to boost research in the [European] motor industry, particularly on environmental issues. Most of the projects that will be developed involve experimental research on, for example, limiting noise or emission pollution caused by motor vehicles. The products obtained from this research may not be directly usable in a specific type of vehicle. The Commission therefore took the view that the research was at the pre-competitive stage and that the agreements did not infringe Community law.

133   Finally, the Commission approved the membership agreements of Valpak, a non-profit-making, industry-led compliance scheme operating in the United Kingdom which has been set up to discharge the packaging waste recovery and recycling obligations of its members. The legal framework set up in the United Kingdom to implement the [EU] directive [on packaging waste] provides scope for competition in the market for compliance-scheme services which seek to fulfil recovery and recycling obligations on behalf of a business. While Valpak is currently the largest compliance scheme operating in the United Kingdom, other competing schemes exist and have notified their arrangements to the Commission.

134   Following its examination of Valpak's membership agreements, the Commission concluded that the agreements restricted competition within the meaning of Article [101](1) because they obliged businesses wishing to join the scheme to transfer the totality of their obligations in all packaging materials. This 'all or nothing' approach, which transposes a regulatory provision, restricts the extent to which Valpak and other schemes will be able to compete against one another on a material-specific basis. The Commission went on to consider whether the notified arrangements could benefit from exemption under Article [101](3). In view of the emerging nature of the market and the likelihood that Valpak and other schemes would be obliged to invest in the United Kingdom's collection and/or reprocessing infrastructure in order to meet their members' obligations in the future, the Commission concluded that an 'all or nothing' approach was necessary, at least in the short term, if schemes such as Valpak were to succeed in securing sufficient funding to allow the necessary

investment to take place. The Commission informed Valpak at the same time that it reserved the right to reexamine the case after three years.

NOTES AND QUESTIONS

1. Consider, with respect to each agreement described above, the possible harm to competition. Is each agreement caught by Article 101(1)? Do you agree with the Commission's analysis regarding when an exemption is necessary?

2. A Danish recycling law limited bottle types for beer and soft drinks sold in Denmark, creating an obstacle to out-of-state beer and soft drink sellers. The limitation of bottle types—to those most commonly used in Denmark—facilitated recycling and helped protect the environment. See *Commission v. Denmark*, Case 302/86, [1988] ECR 4607. Suppose the restraint was imposed by agreement among the Danish beverage makers and their retailers, rather than by the legislature of Denmark. Analyze the agreement. Does it fall within Article 101(1)? Does it satisfy the conditions of Article 101(3)? Suppose the Danish beverage makers make a convincing case that the proliferation of non-recyclable bottles will impose serious costs on the environment. How should the Commission make the trade-off between free movement, competition and the environment?

3. May the European beef processors agree not to supply beef to wholesalers or retailers that sell beef injected with hormones?

4. Under US antitrust law, an agreement that has anticompetitive aspects can be justified only by outbalancing procompetitive aspects. *National Society of Professional Engineers v. United States,* 435 U.S. 679, 98 S.Ct. 1355, 55 L.Ed.2d 637 (1978). Even if competitive price-bidding by professional engineers would cause engineers to cut corners and design unsafe buildings, the engineers may not decide to ban price-bidding. Regulation should specify minimum safety standards for building designs. How would each of the above agreements described in the Competition Policy Report fare under US law? Which is the better approach—that of the US or of the EU? Or are they effectively the same?

CECED

Commission Decision, Case IV F 1/36.718 O.J. L 187/47 (26 July 2000).

[Almost all producers and importers of washing machines in Europe entered into an agreement designed to reduce energy consumption and thereby to reduce polluting emissions from washing machines. The agreement was notified to the Commission by their trade association, the European Council of Domestic Appliance Manufacturers (CECED). Under the agreement, the producers and importers agreed to stop producing for, and importing into, the EU the least energy efficient washing machines, designated as categories D to G by a Commission Directive. Categories D to G represented 10%–11% of all washing machines sold in the EU, and comprised a significant proportion of the sales of some of the agreeing manufacturers. Energy efficiency was an import focus of advertising and sales. The market was fragmented. The agreeing manufacturers accounted for more than 95% of the market.

The Commission granted a short (less than one-year) exemption, stating, as to the four conditions of Article 101(3):]

— The agreement objectively contributes to technical and economic progress, by focusing production on more efficient machines. Such benefits would be unlikely or would occur less quickly without the agreement.

— Consumers derive benefits at the same time individually and for society as a whole: likely higher purchase costs of more efficient washing machines are quickly compensated by savings in electricity bills; the agreement contributes to [EU] environmental objectives and the benefits very largely exceed potential cost increases triggered as a result of the agreement. Even if individual purchasers were not to derive the financial benefits that they actually attain, the magnitude of environmental benefits is such that the net contribution to society's economic welfare would still be positive.

— The restrictions of competition are indispensable to attaining those benefits. Consumers do not sufficiently take external costs into account in their purchase decisions. The application of a minimum efficiency ratio mitigates this market failure. Alternatives such as public awareness campaigns or application of ecolables would be complementary, rather than substitutable to the agreement.

— The agreement does not eliminate competition. Various technical means to improve energy efficiency of washing machines are economically available to all manufacturers; competition remains also on important purchase criteria such as prices, technical effectiveness, brand image etc.; finally, 90% of sales of washing machines are not directly concerned.

NOTES AND QUESTIONS

1. Are you confident that consumer benefits of the washing machine agreement outweigh costs? What about the consumers who prefer the low price, or other features of machines that happen to fall within categories D to G, and who prefer not to be altruistic?

2. What is the significance of the fact that some of the collaborating manufacturers made D-to-G machines? Would the agreement be more suspect if none of them did? Even so, can we trust these producers to set the standard in the public interest?

3. Suppose you represent a Canadian manufacturer whose washing machines are low priced, offer features householders love, and fall within category D. Your client's machines are relatively new, and its European fortunes—and market share—are fast rising. It is suddenly faced with a private European boycott. Your client and its loyal European consuming public consider a suit to annul the Commission decision granting exemption.

Frame your analysis of the anticompetitive effects of the CECED agreement. Review each of the four requirements for exemption. Which are most vulnerable? What are your odds of winning in court?

4. If the European Union wanted energy standards that excluded machines in categories D to G, why did it not adopt legislation setting an energy efficiency floor that excluded those categories?

5. Might the Commission exemption constitute a blockage of market access to exporters from other nations in violation of the General Agreement on Tariffs and Trade (GATT)? Article XI of the GATT prohibits states from imposing quantitative restrictions on imports. Article XX provides a derogation for a state measure necessary for health and safety; this must be backed up by scientific evidence.

6. Having in mind the cases involving labor, the liberal professions, the environment, and competitiveness, comment on how the Community seeks to blend its competition enforcement with other public policy goals. Has it achieved a wise balance? Is it wise to try to achieve a balance? Are non-competition justifications admissible? Why do you think the Commission did not want the Member States to apply non-competition offsets to competition harms?

E. BLOCK EXEMPTIONS

We noted at the outset of the chapter the two important block exemptions on horizontal cooperation: research and development, and specialisation. In year 2000, the Commission revised most block exemptions in an attempt to move from a formalistic regulatory approach to a more open economic approach, and it is in the process of revising then again, to be effective December 2010. The Commission recognizes that most R&D cooperation and most specialisation agreements are efficient.

1. RESEARCH AND DEVELOPMENT

Research and development lies at the core of innovation, competition, and competitiveness. The R&D block exemption singles out cooperative research and development for protection. The block exemption is contained in Commission Regulation 2659/2000, O.J. L 304/7 (Dec. 5, 2000), and is available at *http://ec.europa.eu/competition/antitrust/legislation/horizontal.html*.

Of course not all R&D agreements fall within Article 101(1). Collaboration of small enterprises are normally not caught. Moreover, collaboration on pure R&D even by large firms generally does not fall within Article 101(1) unless the parties agree not to carry out R&D in the same field.

Article 1 of the regulation declares exempt joint R&D and joint exploitation of its results, and necessary ancillary restraints including agreement not to carry out independently or with third parties R&D in the same or a closely related field, as long as the parties' market share does not exceed 25% and the agreement does not include black-listed clauses. Moreover, to qualify for block exemption: 1) each party must have access to the results in order to further its research, 2) the supplying partner, in the event of specialisation not entailing joint distribution, must fulfill orders for supplies from other partners, and 3) in the event of joint exploitation, the results must be IP-protected and must be sufficiently important; they must "substantially contribute to technical or economic progress and ... be decisive for the manufacture of the contract products or the application of the contract processes." Art. 3(4). The regulation contains a blacklist of clauses that disqualify agreements from exemption.

Parties to agreements that fall outside of the block exemption (e.g., because their market share exceeds 25%), may seek an individual exemption.

The proposed revised block exemption (see link at *http://ec.europa.eu/competition/consultations/2010_horizontals/index.html*) would make only minor changes. One change would require the parties to disclose all relevant pending and existing intellectual property rights.

In the same year that the EU adopted its first block exemption for joint research and development, the United States Congress enacted the National Cooperative Research Act (NCRA) of 1984, which was amended in 1993. 15 U.S.C.A. § 4301. The US Congress feared that the antitrust laws were chilling research and development, especially in view of the fact that successful private plaintiffs in US antitrust lawsuits are entitled to three times the damages they suffer. The NCRA states that research joint ventures shall be judged under a rule of reason in view of all relevant market facts and shall not be condemned per se. Also, the Act provides a notification procedure. If a transaction is notified and is later found to lessen competition, the parties can be assessed compensatory damages but not treble damages. This protection applies to the production phase of a research joint venture but only if the principal production facilities are in the United States and the controlling persons are American or from a country with equally favorable antitrust treatment. (Is this consistent with GATT obligations of non-discrimination?) A notified transaction may be enjoined if it is found to be anticompetitive. The NCRA applies equally to large and small firms.

Would you expect the US statute to encourage research and development? Would you expect the European block exemption to encourage research and development?

2. SPECIALISATION

The specialisation block exemption is provided by Commission Regulation 2658/2000, and may be found at O.J. L 304/3 (Dec. 5, 2000). It is available at *http://ec.europa.eu/competition/antitrust/legislation/horizontal.html*.

At the outset, the Commission contemplated reciprocal specialisation: one firm made product *A,* the other made complementary product *B;* they would each agree to supply their specialty product to the other, and they would each agree not to manufacture the product that was the specialty of the other. More recently, firms began to adopt unilateral specialisation: *A* outsources from *B; B* agrees to manufacture and supply to *A* all of its needs of an input. *A* agrees to cease its production of that input. The block exemption covers reciprocal specialisation and unilateral specialisation between competitors. The regulation recites that specialisation agreements generally contribute to improving production or distribution because they enable firms to concentrate on the manufacture of certain products and thus to operate more efficiently and supply goods more cheaply.

Article 1 of the specialisation regulation declares exempt agreements for specialisation, including ancillary restraints necessary for their implementation, where the combined market shares do not exceed 20%, except for agreements containing black-listed provisions. The exemption also applies where the parties agree to exclusive purchase or supply in the context of specialisation or joint production, or the parties do not separately distribute the objects of specialisation but provide for joint distribution or distribution by a non-competitor. (Arts. 3, 4)

Black list. The exemption does not apply to agreements that have as their object price fixing to third parties, limiting output or sales, or allocating markets or customers.

Parties whose agreement falls outside the block exemption may seek individual exemption.

The proposed revision would make only minor changes.

Why is it necessary for competitors, seeking to achieve the efficiency benefits of specialisation, to promise to stay out of the manufacturing market of the other? In the United States, this aspect of specialisation agreements would normally be regarded as a cartel-like violation of the law unless the parties could show that the commitment was necessary to make the joint venture work.

CONCLUSION

In the late 1990s and early 2000s, the European Commission began to shift from formalistic rules to effects-based analysis. How well is it doing? Are the European courts synchronized with the Commission? Are Member State authorities and courts well positioned to handle economic analysis? Are they likely to do so in harmony with the European Commission and courts?

CHAPTER 24

VERTICAL RESTRAINTS UNDER ARTICLE 101

■ ■ ■

A. VERTICAL RESTRAINTS AND THEIR EFFECTS

Vertical restraints are restraints in the course of distributing a product or service, or in the course of bringing technology and its commercial applications to market.

In distribution agreements, a producer might instruct its distributor where or to whom to sell the product, and at what price. Since a producer offers a particular kind or brand of product, the restraints that a producer imposes on its distributors are called intrabrand restraints.

Intrabrand restraints may help a producer get to market more efficiently, e.g., by giving the distributor a stronger incentive to work its territory and by preventing "free riders" (who do not invest in the territory) from "skimming the cream" off the top of the demand primed by the designated distributor's investment. If the restraints are cost-effective and if the brands in the market compete robustly against one another, the interbrand competition may ensure that consumers receive the benefits of the restraints.

However, intrabrand restraints may also help the producer *exploit* the consumer. For example, in a concentrated, high barrier market, the restraints may help the few producers coordinate their prices; or they may help an individual producer that has market power extract more money from consumers. They may also suppress innovation in the methods and systems of distribution, such as the Internet. Moreover, vertical restraints may be procured by powerful distributors to help form a distributor cartel. For these reasons, resale price fixing agreements that set minimum prices (RPM) are regarded as a hard core restraint in the EU (although justification is possible) and in many other jurisdictions. Economists, however, point out that RPM can be an efficient business strategy to induce distributors to provide more service. In view of efficient uses of RPM that may increase interbrand competition, the United States recently abandoned its nearly century-old per se rule against RPM agreements.

Other vertical restraints include exclusive selling ("I will sell to you alone and not to your competitors"), exclusive buying (single branding or requirements contracts), selective distribution, franchising, tying contracts, and export restrictions. Technology licensing restrictions are also a form of vertical restraint.

We have seen that a principal goal of EU competition law is to integrate the common market. Can intrabrand restraints that prevent parallel imports calcify price differentials among Member States and undermine the market integration goal? But can prohibition of those restraints undermine the efficiency goal? Is there a tension between integration and efficiency?

B. A NOTE ON THE EFFECT OF MODERNISATION

Before the final years of the 1990s, vertical restraints were regarded in the EU with great suspicion. This was especially true of restraints that could tend to keep a seller's product from crossing Member State borders, for the restraint then had a market integration dimension as well.

Several block exemptions were adopted, in particular on exclusive distribution, exclusive purchasing and franchising, designed not only to give more certainty to business but also to regulate and generally suppress vertical restraints. The area became rule-bound with a heavy hand, rather than concept or theory-driven. The effect was not unlike the effect and treatment in the United States through the 1960s and early 1970s, where, too, vertical restraints were treated with much suspicion; for example, they were regarded as schemes by powerful producers to rein in the autonomy of their distributors, thereby also depriving consumers of the benefits that more autonomous distributors would bring; or as schemes to fence out rivals.

In the United States a sea-change came in the late 1970s and continued to evolve through the 2006 Term of the US Supreme Court when, in *Leegin*, it overturned the per se rule against agreements that fix resale prices. *Leegin Creative Products, Inc. v. PSKS, Inc.*, 551 U.S. 877, 127 S.Ct. 2705, 168 L.Ed.2d 623 (2007). As we see below when we study *Leegin*, the contemporary US perspective is hospitable towards vertical restraints, regarding them as normally efficient means to get to market and seldom capable of aggrandizing market power.

In the European Union the inhospitality perspective lasted until the late 1990s when the Competition Directorate rethought the appropriate analysis of vertical restraints and, in 1997, published a green paper which proposed a more economic, more sympathetic, and less restrictive approach. Block exemptions were liberalized. Less restrictive block exemptions were regarded as a wise methodology to give guidance and more certainty.

Block exemptions were liberalized in 2000 and again in 2010. The 2010 block exemption regulation is Selected Document 26. It and accompanying guidelines can be found at *http://ec.europa.eu/competition/antitrust/legislation/vertical.html.*

We have thus far looked at administrative practice. The case law of the courts is higher authority. For most of the rest of this chapter we deal with the case law.

We turn to parallel imports and exports, exclusive purchasing, tying and other foreclosures, selective distribution, franchising, and finally more detail on the existing block exemptions.

As you read the cases, be aware of their dates of decision; particularly whether they were decided before June 1999, when the notification process was abolished for vertical restraints. Consider how the earlier cases might be decided under modern economic concepts, influenced as always by the market integration goals.

Remember that the process of notification and individual exemption is a mode of the past; but still, agreements must be analyzed under the Treaty provisions, Article 101(1) and (3).

C. IS THERE AN AGREEMENT WITHIN ARTICLE 101(1)?

Normally a vertical agreement will fall within Article 101(1) if the restraint is not de minimis and the restraint has an impact on intrabrand competition (see *Consten and Grundig,* which we discuss again below) or interbrand competition. This will be especially so where the supplier imposes obligations on its distributor not to buy from its competitors, or imposes customer, territory or price restraints or requires a tie-in, unless the restraints are objectively necessary, for example, to penetrate a market or to guard against a health or safety hazard.

Would proof that robust interbrand competition would protect consumer welfare take the agreement out of Article 101(1)? Why might this point still matter despite elimination of the notification requirement?

An important battleground is whether an agreement is present at all, for unilateral conduct does not fall within Article 101.

In *Bayer v. Commission* (Adalat), Case T–41/96, [2000] ECR II–3383, Bayer, producer of the cardio-vascular-treating drug Adalat, faced several Member States with widely varying price ceilings. The controlled price in France and Spain was 40% lower than in the UK. Certain wholesale customers of Bayer France and Bayer Spain increased their orders disproportionately, clearly to take advantage of the higher profits in the UK. In response, Bayer France and Bayer Spain limited fulfillment of orders to the quantities expected to be demanded in the territory. Allegedly, the wholesalers acquiesced in the de facto export ban in order to continue receiving supplies. The Commission found that the conduct was concerted and violated Article 101(1). It imposed a fine of 3 million euros. The General Court annulled the decision, however, concluding that there was no "common intention" between Bayer and the wholesalers. It said:

71   Th[e] case law shows that a distinction should be drawn between cases in which an undertaking has adopted a genuinely unilateral measure, and thus without the express or implied participation of another undertaking, and those in which the unilateral character of the measure is merely apparent. Whilst the former do not fall within Article [101] (1) of the Treaty, the latter must be regarded as revealing an agreement between undertakings and may therefore fall within the scope of that article. That is the case, in particular, with practices and measures in restraint of competition which, though apparently adopted unilaterally by the manufacturer in the context of its contractual relations with its dealers, nevertheless receive at least the tacit acquiescence of those dealers.

COMMISSION v. VOLKSWAGEN AG

(vertical agreement)

Case C–74/04P, [2006] ECR I–06585, CJEU.

[Volkswagen and its dealers signed dealership agreements, giving each dealer a contract territory for a range of vehicles and stating that "Volkswagen AG will issue non-binding recommendations concerning retail prices and discounts."

Volkswagen became concerned that its German dealers were discounting the VW Passat and representatives made calls to the German dealers asking them to stop discounting. The Commission brought proceedings alleging that Volkswagen and the German dealers agreed to a strict price discipline for sales of the VW Passat, in violation of Article 101(1). The General Court annulled, on grounds that the Commission had not proved an agreement. The Commission appealed to the Court of Justice.]

34   The Commission maintains essentially that the [General Court] could not, without committing an error of law, be unaware that, in signing a dealership agreement, dealers give their prior consent to all measures adopted by the motor vehicle manufacturer in the context of that contractual relationship.

35   In support of its argument, the Commission refers to settled case-law according to which a call by a motor vehicle manufacturer to its authorised dealers does not constitute a unilateral act but an agreement within the meaning of Article [101(1)] if it forms part of a set of continuous business relations governed by a general agreement drawn up in advance.

36   However, the case-law to which the Commission refers does not imply that any call by a motor vehicle manufacturer to dealers constitutes an

agreement within the meaning of Article [101(1)] and does not relieve the Commission of its obligation to prove that there was a concurrence of wills on the part of the parties to the dealership agreement in each specific case. * * *

38   As stated by Volkswagen ..., to find otherwise would have the effect of reversing the burden of proof of the existence of a breach of the competition rules and contravening the principle of presumption of innocence.

39   The will of the parties may result from both the clauses of the dealership agreement in question and from the conduct of the parties, and in particular from the possibility of there being tacit acquiescence by the dealers in a call from the manufacturer....

40   In the present case, with respect to the first possibility, the Commission inferred that there was a concurrence of wills between the parties solely on the basis of the clauses of the dealership agreement in question. The [General Court] then had to proceed, as it did, to consider whether those calls were explicitly contained in the dealership agreement or, at the very least, whether the clauses of that agreement authorised motor vehicle manufacturers to make such calls.

41   It should be borne in mind that, in ... *Ford* v *Commission,* the Court rejected an argument based on the allegedly unilateral nature of certain measures of selective distribution of motor vehicles, stating that dealership agreements must necessarily leave certain aspects for subsequent decision by manufacturers and that such decisions were expressly provided for in Annex 1 to the dealership agreement in question.

42   Likewise, in ... Case C–338/00 P *Volkswagen* v *Commission,* this Court held that the Court of First Instance had found correctly that measures taken by Volkswagen to limit the deliveries of motor vehicles to Italian dealers, implemented with the express aim of blocking re-exports from Italy, was part of the ongoing commercial relationship between the parties to the dealership agreement; the Court of First Instance relied, inter alia, on the fact that the dealership agreement in question provided for the possibility of limiting such deliveries. * * *

46   With respect to the second possibility, that is, in the absence of relevant contractual provisions, the existence of an agreement within the meaning of Article [101(1)] presupposes the dealers' explicit or tacit acquiescence to the measure adopted by the motor vehicle manufacturer.

47   In the present case, since the Commission did not rely on there being explicit or tacit acquiescence by the dealers, this second possibility is not relevant for the present dispute. * * *

52   ... [T]he [General Court], in the specific assessment of the dealership agreement, found that those clauses could not be regarded as having authorised Volkswagen to issue binding recommendations to the deal-

ers concerning prices of new vehicles and that the calls at issue did not constitute an agreement within the meaning of Article [101(1)]. * * *

56   It follows that the appeal should be dismissed as unfounded.

D. PARALLEL IMPORTS AND EXPORTS AND DUAL PRICING

The first vertical restraint case to reach the Court was *Consten and Grundig,* which we studied in Chapter 20 and revisit here.

CONSTEN AND GRUNDIG v. COMMISSION

Cases 56, 58/64, [1966] ECR 299, ECJ. Reread case, at pp. 823, 825 *supra.*

Also reread the *Pioneer* and *Volkswagen* cases, at pages 829–32 supra.

Note on *Distillers Company Ltd. v. Commission*

Distillers Company Ltd. (DCL), the world's largest seller of Scotch whiskey, established 38 subsidiaries producing spirits in the United Kingdom. It accounted for approximately 70% of all gin sales in the UK, 30% to 50% of Scotch whiskey in the UK, and lower percentages on the Continent.

DCL imposed the following conditions of sale:

(a) "[T]he various allowances, rebates and discounts are designed to meet the particular requirements of the home trade and customers are only entitled to them when the goods are in fact consumed within the UK."

(b) "Accordingly, if you wish to buy for export to other Common Market countries you must indicate this on your order and purchase must be made at the gross price."

(c) "... If ... a customer obtains or claims any home trade allowances, rebates or discounts in respect of goods which he has bought and any of those goods turn up in any country outside the UK, the right is reserved for all companies in the DCL group to sell thereafter to such customer only at the gross price."

The punitive measures were to be applicable in the following circumstances:

"When a DCL subsidiary has a reasonable belief that any quantity of goods bought by the purchaser from any DCL subsidiary has been or will be consumed outside the United Kingdom;

even when the exports are made by a subsequent purchaser;

regardless of the quantity ordered, until and to the extent that the purchaser produces evidence satisfactory to the selling DCL subsidiary company that the goods will be consumed in the United Kingdom."

When investigated by the Commission, Distillers claimed that its dual pricing was justified by the following facts: In the UK its brands were very well known, prices were depressed by price controls, and Distillers sold directly to very large and powerful brewery groups that had retail outlets and that demanded very low prices. Outside of the UK, the brands were unknown. Moreover, France banned advertisements, and some countries imposed discriminatory taxes. Distillers had to invest significant additional amounts of money for promotion on the Continent if it was to sell there at all.

The Commission declared that Distillers price agreements would not be granted an exemption under Article 101(3) because the dual pricing system interfered with parallel imports and isolated the UK market. Distillers then withdrew Johnnie Walker Red Label and Dimple Haig whiskeys from sale in the UK, stating that it could not make sales at the higher price in the UK and it could not cover promotion costs if it sold at the lower price on the Continent. It announced a new brand to replace Johnnie Walker. Distillers sued for annulment of the Commission's decision. The Court of Justice held, simply, that the legal effect of Distillers' failure to notify the price terms was that the price terms could not be exempted. Case 30/78, [1980] ECR 2229.

NOTES AND QUESTIONS

1. Could Consten and Grundig meet the requirements of Article 101(3) today? Would the evidence of interbrand competition be excluded today?

Consten and Grundig is generally understood as a market integration case. Imposing tight territorial restrictions at Member State lines is anathema to the market integration principle of the EU. (Should it be? Might such territorial assignments and allocations increase the efficiency of distribution?) Note that the block exemption, applicable for under 30% market share, recognizes the efficiency of territorial assignments and generally allows them as long as distributors may accept unsolicited bids from outside of the territory. Thus, distributors can be subject to active restraints (not to solicit actively outside of the territory), but not also passive restraints.

2. Did Distillers' price agreements "isolate" the UK market? How? Would Distillers be likely to satisfy Article 101(3) today?

3. *GlaxoSmithKline* put a dent in the unwavering EU rule against restraints of parallel imports.

GLAXOSMITHKLINE SERVICES UNLIMITED v. COMMISSION

(Spanish price ceiling)
Case T–168/01, [2006] ECR II–02969, General Court.

[Spanish legislation capped the price of pharmaceuticals sold to pharmacies and hospitals and covered by Spanish reimbursement rules. GlaxoSmithKline, a major pharmaceutical producer, made agreements with its wholesalers that for all other products (i.e. pharmaceuticals not for the domestic market), GSK would charge a price set by objective economic factors, and that this would be the price that GSK had initially proposed to the Spanish government as the reimbursement price plus a cost-of-living adjustment. (Clause 4 of the General Sales Conditions) The Commission found that the clause violated Article 101. In so holding, the Commission discounted GSK's arguments and evidence as to the virtues and advantages of Clause 4. GSK asked the General Court to annul the Commission's decision.]

295 In the light of the structure of GSK's arguments and also of the discussion of that point during the administrative procedure, the Decision could not avoid examining, first of all, whether parallel trade led to a loss in efficiency for the pharmaceutical industry in general, and for GSK in particular. . . .

296 However, a comparison of the evidence provided by GSK with the other evidence invoked by the Commission in the Decision clearly reveals that in the medicines sector the effect of parallel trade on competition is ambiguous, since the gain in efficiency to which it is likely to give rise for intrabrand competition, the role of which is limited by the applicable regulatory framework, must be compared with the loss in efficiency to which it is likely to give rise for interbrand competition, the role of which is central.

297 In those circumstances, the Commission could not refrain from examining, second, whether Clause 4 of the General Sales Conditions could enable GSK's capacity for innovation to be reinstated and thus could give rise to a gain in efficiency for interbrand competition.

298 That, moreover, formed the very core of the prospective analysis which the Commission was under a duty to carry out in order to respond to GSK's request for an exemption. According to the consistent case-law cited . . ., it is necessary to determine whether the agreement prohibited on account of the disadvantage which it represents for competition (Article [101(1)]) presents an advantage of such a kind as to offset that disadvantage (Article [101(3)]).

299 The Commission was therefore still required to examine GSK's arguments relating to the advantages expected of Clause 4 of the General Sales Conditions. In that regard, recital 156 to the Decision, the only recital susceptible of attesting to an examination on that point, indicates essentially:

'[I]t is a matter of discretion for pharmaceutical companies to decide how much they wish to invest in R&D. Any savings they might hypothetically make by preventing parallel trade would therefore not automatically lead to higher R&D investments. It is conceivable that these savings might merely be added to the companies' profits. Obviously, the generation of extra profits alone cannot justify an exemption. In this regard, GSK's argument would mean that the first condition for [the application of Article [101(3)] would be fulfilled for every agreement that could be said to contribute to an increase in the revenues of a firm engaged in R&D. The condition would in any case be meaningless, since it is in the nature of any agreement restricting competition to be likely to increase a firm's earnings.'

300 However, GSK did not claim that the creation of additional profits would in itself justify an exemption. On the contrary, it maintained that parallel trade prevented it from making the profits necessary for the optimum financing of its R&D, that Clause 4 of the General Sales Conditions would enable it to increase its revenues and that it would have every interest, in the light of the fierce interbrand competition, of the central role played by innovation in that competition and of the methods of financing R&D, in investing a part of this surplus in R&D in order to overtake its competitors or to ensure that it would not be overtaken by them. In other words, it claimed that its General Sales Conditions should be exempted because they would have not merely the immediate effect of increasing its revenues, but above all the secondary effect of increasing its capacity for innovation. Furthermore, it maintained that that advantage must be compared with the fact that, when it was obtained by parallel traders, that surplus did not constitute an advantage, because, not being obliged to engage in genuine competition among themselves, the parallel traders reduced prices only to the extent necessary to attract retailers and therefore kept most of that surplus for themselves, as GSK again submitted at the hearing.

301 The Commission could not merely reject those arguments outright on the ground that the advantage described by GSK would not necessarily be achieved, as it did at recital 156 to the Decision, but was required, in accordance with the case-law, also to examine, as specifically as possible, in the context of a prospective analysis, whether, in the particular circumstances of the case and in the light of the evidence submitted to it, it seemed more likely that the advantages described by GSK would be achieved or, on the contrary, that they would not. It was not entitled to consider, in a peremptory manner and without providing proper arguments, that the factual arguments and the evidence submitted by GSK must be regarded as hypothetical, as it maintained most recently at the hearing. * * *

303 It follows from the foregoing that the Decision is vitiated by a failure to carry out a proper examination, as the Commission did not validly take into account all the factual arguments and the evidence pertinently submitted by GSK, did not refute certain of those arguments even though they were sufficiently relevant and substantiated to require a response, and did not substantiate to the requisite legal standard its conclusion that it was not proved, first, that parallel trade was apt to lead to a loss in efficiency by appreciably altering GSK's capacity for innovation and, second, that Clause 4 of the General Sales Conditions was apt to enable a gain in efficiency to be achieved by improving innovation.

*The balancing exercise * * **

306   ... [T]he Commission's finding that Clause 4 of the General Sales Conditions restricts competition is well founded only in so far as it finds that Clause 4 has the effect of depriving final consumers of medicines reimbursed by a national sickness insurance scheme of the advantage which they would have derived, in regard to prices and costs, from the participation of the Spanish wholesalers in intrabrand competition on the markets of destination of the parallel trade from Spain.

307   Consequently, the Commission's conclusion that there is no need to carry out a balancing exercise, which would show in any event that the advantage associated with Clause 4 does not offset the disadvantage which it represents for competition, cannot be upheld. The Commission was required, first, to conduct an appropriate examination of GSK's factual arguments and evidence, in order to be in a position to carry out, second, the complex assessment necessary in order to weigh up the disadvantage and the advantage associated with Clause 4 of the General Sales Conditions.

Conclusion

308   It follows from the foregoing that the Commission could not lawfully conclude that, as regards the existence of a contribution to the promotion of technical progress, GSK had not demonstrated that the first condition for the application of Article [101(3)] was satisfied. In those circumstances, there is no need to examine GSK's arguments relating to a contribution to the improvement of the distribution of medicines.

c) Evidence of the advantage being passed on to the consumer, of the indispensability of Clause 4 of the General Sales Conditions and of the absence of the elimination of competition

309   As stated previously, it follows from the Decision and from the oral argument presented at the hearing that the summary conclusions which the Commission reached concerning the existence of a passing-on to consumers, the indispensability of Clause 4 of the General Sales Conditions and the absence of elimination of competition rest on the conclusion relating to the existence of a gain in efficiency.

310   In so far as that conclusion is vitiated by illegality, in that it concerns the existence of a contribution towards the promotion of technical progress, those conclusions are themselves invalid.

311   In so far as, when it examined whether Clause 4 of the General Sales Conditions would or would not eliminate competition for a substantial part of the products, the Commission further stated ... that, in any event, for several of the leading products affected by the General Sales Conditions, GSK held substantial market shares (for example, for Zofran, Flixonase, Zovirax and Imigran) in one or more Member States, it remains necessary to review that assessment.

312 In that regard, it must be observed that the Commission acknowledged at the hearing that it had not really resolved the question of GSK's market power and further stated that it would have had to continue with the analysis in order to determine that point.

313 In fact, owing to the particular legal and economic context of the sector under consideration, the fact of holding substantial market shares, which, moreover, is limited to certain of the relevant products, of which the Commission provided only four examples, clearly does not in itself make it possible to conclude, in a convincing manner, that competition would be eliminated for a substantial part of the relevant products.

314 In effect, irrespective of the question of the definition of the relevant products market, which has been debated by the parties, a number of elements relied on by GSK during the administrative procedure, and then in its written submissions, prevent such a conclusion from being reached automatically.

315 In particular, GSK's argument to which reference is made at recital 188 to the Decision ... was not so irrelevant that the Commission could refrain from making it the subject of a specific assessment under the fourth condition for the application of Article [101(3)]. In effect, the fact that Clause 4 of the General Sales Conditions prevents the limited pressure which might exist, owing to parallel trade from Spain, on the price and the cost of medicines in the geographic markets of destination must be related to the facts, put forward by GSK and not disputed by the Commission, that competition by innovation is very fierce in the sector and that competition on price exists in another form, although by law it emerges only when, upon expiry of the patent, manufacturers of generic medicines are able to enter the market. In those circumstances, it was still necessary ... to assess what form of competition must be given priority with a view to ensuring the maintenance of effective competition sought by Article 3(1)(g) EC [now in a protocol] and Article [101].

4. *Conclusion* * * *

317 Accordingly, the Decision must be annulled in so far as, in Article 2, it rejects GSK's request for an exemption.

NOTES AND QUESTIONS

1. On reconsideration, what must the Commission establish, or decide on the basis of sufficient evidence, to deny the exemption? What must GSK establish to entitle it to an exemption? Is the Commission well placed to conduct the balancing exercise?

2. Is *GSK* a small or large wedge in the door of allowing restraints on parallel imports if justified by (imperative?) considerations of efficiency and innovation? Is the holding likely to be limited to pharmaceuticals?

A related case arose in Greece, wherein GlaxoSmithKline's Greek subsidiary, GSK AEVE, cut back the supply of medicines to wholesalers who sold into higher-priced export markets. The wholesalers sued. GSK AEVE justified on grounds of the Greek price-capping legislation; the claim that the trans-shipping wholesalers, not the consumer, profit from parallel imports/exports; and the claim that GSK AEVE had to stem the tide of low-priced exports for the sake of its investments in R&D. The Greek court referred questions to the Court of Justice. The Court, applying Article 102, confirmed the strong principle against restraints on parallel trade but allowed an exception.

SOT. LELOS KAI SIA EE v. GLAXOSMITHKLINE AEVE

Cases C–468/06–C–478/06, [2008] ECR I–07139, ECJ.

52   The first thing to consider is GSK AEVE's argument that parallel trade in any event brings only few financial benefits to the ultimate consumers.

53   In that connection, it should be noted that parallel exports of medicinal products from a Member State where the prices are low to other Member States in which the prices are higher open up in principle an alternative source of supply to buyers of the medicinal products in those latter States, which necessarily brings some benefits to the final consumer of those products.

54   It is true, as GSK AEVE has pointed out, that, for medicines subject to parallel exports, the existence of price differences between the export-ing and the importing Member States does not necessarily imply that the final consumer in the importing Member State will benefit from a price corresponding to the one prevailing in the exporting Member State, inasmuch as the wholesalers carrying out the exports will themselves make a profit from that parallel trade.

55   Nevertheless, the attraction of the other source of supply which arises from parallel trade in the importing Member State lies precisely in the fact that that trade is capable of offering the same products on the market of that Member State at lower prices than those applied on the same market by the pharmaceuticals companies.

56   As a result, even in the Member States where the prices of medicines are subject to State regulation, parallel trade is liable to exert pressure on prices and, consequently, to create financial benefits not only for the social health insurance funds, but equally for the patients con-cerned, for whom the proportion of the price of medicines for which they are responsible will be lower. At the same time, as the Commis-sion notes, parallel trade in medicines from one Member State to another is likely to increase the choice available to entities in the latter Member State which obtain supplies of medicines by means of a public procurement procedure, in which the parallel importers can offer medicines at lower prices.

57   Accordingly, without it being necessary for the Court to rule on the question whether it is for an undertaking in a dominant position to assess whether its conduct vis-à-vis a trading party constitutes abuse

in the light of the degree to which that party's activities offer advantages to the final consumers, it is clear that, in the circumstances of the main proceedings, such an undertaking cannot base its arguments on the premiss that the parallel exports which it seeks to limit are of only minimal benefit to the final consumers. * * *

65   In relation to the application of Article [101] of the ... Treaty, the Court has held that an agreement between producer and distributor which might tend to restore the national divisions in trade between Member States might be such as to frustrate the objective of the Treaty to achieve the integration of national markets through the establishment of a single market. Thus on a number of occasions the Court has held agreements aimed at partitioning national markets according to national borders or making the interpenetration of national markets more difficult, in particular those aimed at preventing or restricting parallel exports, to be agreements whose object is to restrict competition within the meaning of that Treaty article. * * *

67   Although the degree of price regulation in the pharmaceuticals sector cannot therefore preclude the Community rules on competition from applying, the fact none the less remains that, when assessing, in the case of Member States with a system of price regulation, whether the refusal of a pharmaceuticals company to supply medicines to wholesalers involved in parallel exports constitutes abuse, it cannot be ignored that such State intervention is one of the factors liable to create opportunities for parallel trade.

68   Furthermore, in the light of the Treaty objectives to protect consumers by means of undistorted competition and the integration of national markets, the Community rules on competition are also incapable of being interpreted in such a way that, in order to defend its own commercial interests, the only choice left for a pharmaceuticals company in a dominant position is not to place its medicines on the market at all in a Member State where the prices of those products are set at a relatively low level. * * *

70   In that respect, and without it being necessary to examine the argument raised by GSK AEVE that it is necessary for pharmaceuticals companies to limit parallel exports in order to avoid the risk of a reduction in their investments in the research and development of medicines, it is sufficient to state that, in order to appraise whether the refusal by a pharmaceuticals company to supply wholesalers involved in parallel exports constitutes a reasonable and proportionate measure in relation to the threat that those exports represent to its legitimate commercial interests, it must be ascertained whether the orders of the wholesalers are out of the ordinary.

71   Thus, although a pharmaceuticals company in a dominant position, in a Member State where prices are relatively low, cannot be allowed to cease to honour the ordinary orders of an existing customer for the sole reason that that customer, in addition to supplying the market in

that Member State, exports part of the quantities ordered to other Member States with higher prices, it is none the less permissible for that company to counter in a reasonable and proportionate way the threat to its own commercial interests potentially posed by the activities of an undertaking which wishes to be supplied in the first Member State with significant quantities of products that are essentially destined for parallel export.

72   In the present cases, the orders for reference show that, in the disputes which gave rise to those orders, the appellants in the main proceedings have demanded not that GSK AEVE should fulfil the orders sent to it in their entirety, but that it should deliver them quantities of medicines corresponding to the monthly average sold during the first 10 months of 2000. In 6 of the 11 actions in the main proceedings, the appellants asked for those quantities to be increased by a certain percentage, which was fixed by some of them at 20%.

73   In those circumstances, it is for the referring court to ascertain whether the abovementioned orders are ordinary in the light of both the previous business relations between the pharmaceuticals company holding a dominant position and the wholesalers concerned and the size of the orders in relation to the requirements of the market in the Member State concerned. * * *

76   ... [A] producer of pharmaceutical products must be in a position to protect its own commercial interests if it is confronted with orders that are out of the ordinary in terms of quantity. Such could be the case, in a given Member State, if certain wholesalers order from that producer medicines in quantities which are out of all proportion to those previously sold by the same wholesalers to meet the needs of the market in that Member State.

77   In view of the foregoing, the answer to the questions referred should be that Article 102 must be interpreted as meaning that an undertaking occupying a dominant position on the relevant market for medicinal products which, in order to put a stop to parallel exports carried out by certain wholesalers from one Member State to other Member States, refuses to meet ordinary orders from those wholesalers is abusing its dominant position. It is for the national court to ascertain whether the orders are ordinary in the light of both the size of those orders in relation to the requirements of the market in the first Member State and the previous business relations between that undertaking and the wholesalers concerned.

* * *

NOTES AND QUESTIONS

1.   Did GSK AEVE's constraint on supply to the wholesaler/exporters harm market integration? How? Did it have positive as well as negative effects for consumers (people needing medications)? Does the rule of the case tend to

limit the negative effects (higher prices in a neighboring state) while freeing up procompetitive aspects (more innovation, made possible by sales at market price or above)? Or is the rule calibrated to something else entirely, such as fairness to traditional customers? How will the rule of the case make a difference—to the conduct of GSK AEVE, to consumers, to likelihood of innovation?

2. Why did the Court reserve the question whether a dominant firm can justify its conduct vis-à-vis a trading party by showing benefit to consumers? (para. 57)

E. RESALE PRICE MAINTENANCE: EUROPE, AND A VIEW FROM THE US

Like Europe, the United States took a skeptical stance towards vertical restraints for many years, believing that they impaired the give-and-take dynamic of the competition process and thus harmed powerless market actors and consumers. US antitrust law condemned, per se, agreements between a manufacturer and a distributor as to the price, customers or territories at which, to whom, or where the distributor must sell.

The Chicago School revolution began to take root in the late 1970s and found particularly fertile ground after the election of Ronald Reagan in 1980. One centerpiece claim of Chicago was the perversity of inhospitality towards vertical restraints. Chicago School theorists saw vertical restraints as a way to realize efficiencies and compete in interbrand markets. If a number of producers occupied a market and there was no conspiracy among them, each one would have the incentive to design its distribution system in a way most likely to get to market efficiently and to sell the most it could of its product. No one could get market power by a vertical restraint. Indeed, even if there were few producers (but no cartel) or a monopoly producer with the power to charge a supra-competitive price, each would take its profit from its first sale (e.g., to wholesalers) and still would have the incentive to design its distribution system in order to serve consumers efficiently. After the Chicago School revolution began, the Supreme Court overturned the vertical per se rules, one by one. By 2007, there was only one remaining per se rule against a vertical distribution restraint—the nearly century-old rule against minimum re-sale price maintenance agreements. *Dr. Miles Medical Co. v. John D. Park & Sons*, 220 U.S. 373, 31 S.Ct. 376, 55 L.Ed. 502 (1911). This rule was challenged in *Leegin,* a case to which we turn in a moment.

Meanwhile, Europe and many other jurisdictions, as well as states of the United States, likewise condemned RPM agreements. In Europe they were held to fall categorically into Article 101(1) because they have the object to restrict competition (albeit intrabrand competition). They are recognized as a hard core violation in the vertical block exemption regulation and vertical guidelines. They may be entitled to an Article 101(3) exemption in particular instances, as in the case of newspaper and periodical distribution where RPM constitutes "the sole means of supporting the financial burden resulting from the taking back of unsold copies ... if the latter practice constitutes the sole method by which a wide selection of newspapers and periodicals can be made available to readers...." The decision-maker "must take account of those factors...." *SA Binon & Cie v. SA Agence et Messageries de la Presse*, Case 243/83, [1985] ECR 2015, paras. 44–46.

In the United States, the eyes turned to *Leegin*.

LEEGIN CREATIVE LEATHER PRODUCTS, INC. v. PSKS, INC.

Supreme Court of the United States
551 U.S. 877, 127 S.Ct. 2705, 168 L.Ed.2d 623 (2007).

[Leegin was a small designer, producer and distributor of leather accessories, including belts it sold under the brand name "Brighton." It sold its products across the United States in more than 5000 retail stores.

PSKS, which operates Kay's Kloset, was a women's apparel store in Lewisville, Texas. It bought Brighton brand from Leegin since 1995. While it bought from many other manufacturers as well, Brighton was its most important brand.

In 1997 Leegin established a policy of not selling to retailers who sold Brighton goods below its suggested prices. It explained that it thought consumers were "perplexed by promises of product quality and support of product which we believe is lacking in ... larger stores. Consumers are further confused by the ever popular sale, sale, sale, etc." Leegin wanted to "break away from the pack by selling [at] specialty stores" that offer consistently great quality merchandise and support.

PSKS pledged to adhere to the suggested prices, but later marked down its Brighton line by 20% to compete with nearby retailers. Leegin demanded that PSKS stop discounting, and when PSKS refused, Leegin stopped supplying its belts to PSKS. PSKS sued. At trial, in view of *Dr. Miles*, the district court excluded Leegin's proffer of testimony regarding the procompetitive effect of its pricing policy. The jury found that Leegin had entered into vertical resale price agreements, and returned a verdict for PSKS, amounting as trebled to a judgment of nearly $4 million.

The Court granted certiorari to determine whether resale price maintenance should continue to be per se illegal.]

JUSTICE KENNEDY * * *

Resort to *per se* rules is confined to restraints, like those mentioned [competitor price-fixing or market division], "that would always or almost always tend to restrict competition and decrease output." *Business Electronics*, [485 U.S.] at 723. To justify a *per se* prohibition a restraint must have "manifestly anticompetitive" effects, and "lack ... any redeeming virtue,".... * * *

The reasons upon which *Dr. Miles* relied do not justify a *per se* rule. As a consequence, it is necessary to examine, in the first instance, the economic effects of vertical agreements to fix minimum resale prices, and to determine whether the *per se* rule is nonetheless appropriate.

A

* * *

The justifications for vertical price restraints are similar to those for other vertical restraints. Minimum resale price maintenance can stimulate interbrand competition—the competition among manufacturers selling different brands of the same type of product—by reducing intrabrand competition—the competition among retailers selling the same brand. The promotion of interbrand competition is important because "the primary purpose of the antitrust laws is to protect [this type of] competition." Khan, 522 U.S., at 15. A single manufacturer's use of vertical price restraints tends to eliminate intrabrand price competition; this in turn encourages retailers to invest in tangible or intangible services or promotional efforts that aid the manufacturer's position as against rival manufacturers. Resale price maintenance also has the potential to give consumers more options so that they can choose among low-price, low-service brands; high-price, high-service brands; and brands that fall in between.

Absent vertical price restraints, the retail services that enhance interbrand competition might be underprovided. This is because discounting retailers can free ride on retailers who furnish services and then capture some of the increased demand those services generate. Consumers might learn, for example, about the benefits of a manufacturer's product from a retailer that invests in fine showrooms, offers product demonstrations, or hires and trains knowledgeable employees. Or consumers might decide to buy the product because they see it in a retail establishment that has a reputation for selling high-quality merchandise. If the consumer can then buy the product from a retailer that discounts because it has not spent capital providing services or developing a quality reputation, the high-service retailer will lose sales to the discounter, forcing it to cut back its services to a level lower than consumers would otherwise prefer. Minimum resale price maintenance alleviates the problem because it prevents the discounter from undercutting the service provider. With price competition decreased, the manufacturer's retailers compete among themselves over services.

Resale price maintenance, in addition, can increase interbrand competition by facilitating market entry for new firms and brands. "[N]ew manufacturers and manufacturers entering new markets can use the restrictions in order to induce competent and aggressive retailers to make the kind of investment of capital and labor that is often required in the distribution of products unknown to the consumer." GTE Sylvania, [433 U.S.] at 55.... New products and new brands are essential to a dynamic economy, and if markets can be penetrated by using resale price maintenance there is a procompetitive effect.

Resale price maintenance can also increase interbrand competition by encouraging retailer services that would not be provided even absent free riding. It may be difficult and inefficient for a manufacturer to make and enforce a contract with a retailer specifying the different services the retailer must perform. Offering the retailer a guaranteed margin and threatening termination if it does not live up to expectations may be the most efficient way to expand the manufacturer's market share by inducing the retailer's performance and allowing it to use its own initiative and experience in providing valuable services. . . .

B

While vertical agreements setting minimum resale prices can have procompetitive justifications, they may have anticompetitive effects in other cases; and unlawful price fixing, designed solely to obtain monopoly profits, is an ever present temptation. Resale price maintenance may, for example, facilitate a manufacturer cartel. An unlawful cartel will seek to discover if some manufacturers are undercutting the cartel's fixed prices. Resale price maintenance could assist the cartel in identifying price-cutting manufacturers who benefit from the lower prices they offer. Resale price maintenance, furthermore, could discourage a manufacturer from cutting prices to retailers with the concomitant benefit of cheaper prices to consumers.

Vertical price restraints also "might be used to organize cartels at the retailer level." A group of retailers might collude to fix prices to consumers and then compel a manufacturer to aid the unlawful arrangement with resale price maintenance. In that instance the manufacturer does not establish the practice to stimulate services or to promote its brand but to give inefficient retailers higher profits. Retailers with better distribution systems and lower cost structures would be prevented from charging lower prices by the agreement. . . .

A horizontal cartel among competing manufacturers or competing retailers that decreases output or reduces competition in order to increase price is, and ought to be, *per se* unlawful. To the extent a vertical agreement setting minimum resale prices is entered upon to facilitate either type of cartel, it, too, would need to be held unlawful under the rule of reason. This type of agreement may also be useful evidence for a plaintiff attempting to prove the existence of a horizontal cartel.

Resale price maintenance, furthermore, can be abused by a powerful manufacturer or retailer. A dominant retailer, for example, might request resale price maintenance to forestall innovation in distribution that decreases costs. A manufacturer might consider it has little choice but to accommodate the retailer's demands for vertical price restraints if the manufacturer believes it needs access to the retailer's distribution network. A manufacturer with market power, by comparison, might use resale price maintenance to give retailers an incentive not to sell the products of smaller rivals or new entrants. As should be evident, the potential anticompetitive consequences of vertical price restraints must not be ignored or underestimated.

C

Notwithstanding the risks of unlawful conduct, it cannot be stated with any degree of confidence that resale price maintenance "always or almost always tend[s] to restrict competition and decrease output." *Business Electronics.* . . . As the [*per se*] rule would proscribe a significant amount of procompetitive conduct, these agreements appear ill suited for *per se* condemnation. * * *

Respondent also argues the *per se* rule is justified because a vertical price restraint can lead to higher prices for the manufacturer's goods. . . . Respondent is mistaken in relying on pricing effects absent a further showing of anticompetitive conduct. . . . For, as has been indicated already, the antitrust laws are designed primarily to protect interbrand competition, from which lower prices can later result. The Court, moreover, has evaluated other vertical restraints under the rule of reason even though prices can be increased in the course of promoting procompetitive effects. And resale price maintenance may reduce prices if manufacturers have resorted to costlier alternatives of controlling resale prices that are not *per se* unlawful.

Respondent's argument, furthermore, overlooks that, in general, the interests of manufacturers and consumers are aligned with respect to retailer profit margins. . . .

* * *

Resale price maintenance, it is true, does have economic dangers. If the rule of reason were to apply to vertical price restraints, courts would have to be diligent in eliminating their anticompetitive uses from the market. This is a realistic objective, and certain factors are relevant to the inquiry. For example, the number of manufacturers that make use of the practice in a given industry can provide important instruction. When only a few manufacturers lacking market power adopt the practice, there is little likelihood it is facilitating a manufacturer cartel, for a cartel then can be undercut by rival manufacturers. Likewise, a retailer cartel is unlikely when only a single manufacturer in a competitive market uses resale price maintenance. Interbrand competition would divert consumers to lower priced substitutes and eliminate any gains to retailers from their price-fixing agreement over a single brand. Resale price maintenance should be subject to more careful scrutiny, by contrast, if many competing manufacturers adopt the practice. . . .

The source of the restraint may also be an important consideration. If there is evidence retailers were the impetus for a vertical price restraint, there is a greater likelihood that the restraint facilitates a retailer cartel or supports a dominant, inefficient retailer. If, by contrast, a manufacturer adopted the policy independent of retailer pressure, the restraint is less likely to promote anticompetitive conduct. . . .

As a final matter, that a dominant manufacturer or retailer can abuse resale price maintenance for anticompetitive purposes may not be a serious concern unless the relevant entity has market power. If a retailer lacks market power, manufacturers likely can sell their goods through rival retailers. . . .

The rule of reason is designed and used to eliminate anticompetitive transactions from the market. This standard principle applies to vertical price restraints. A party alleging injury from a vertical agreement setting minimum resale prices will have, as a general matter, the information and resources available to show the existence of the agreement and its scope of operation. As courts gain experience considering the effects of these restraints by applying the rule of reason over the course of decisions, they can establish the litigation structure to ensure the rule operates to eliminate anticompetitive restraints from the market and to provide more guidance to businesses. . . . * * *

Justice Breyer, joined by Justices Stevens, Souter and Ginsburg, dissenting: [After noting information that prices go up when minimum resale pricing is allowed, citing a study showing a 19% to 27% price rise during the period of fair trading laws, and cataloging possible harms and benefits of resale price maintenance:] * * *

The Sherman Act seeks to maintain a marketplace free of anticompetitive practices, in particular those enforced by agreement among private firms. The law assumes that such a marketplace, free of private restrictions, will tend to bring about the lower prices, better products, and more efficient production processes that consumers typically desire. . . . * * *

The case before us asks which kind of approach the courts should follow where minimum resale price maintenance is at issue. Should they apply a per se rule (or a variation) that would make minimum resale price maintenance always (or almost always) unlawful? Should they apply a "rule of reason"? Were the Court writing on a blank slate, I would find these questions difficult. But, of course, the Court is not writing on a blank slate, and that fact makes a considerable legal difference. * * *

The upshot is, as many economists suggest, sometimes resale price maintenance can prove harmful; sometimes it can bring benefits. . . . But before concluding that courts should consequently apply a rule of reason, I would ask such questions as, how often are harms or benefits likely to occur? How easy is it to separate the beneficial sheep from the antitrust goats?

Economic discussion, such as the studies the Court relies upon, can *help* provide answers to these questions, and in doing so, economics can, and should, inform antitrust law. But antitrust law cannot, and should not, precisely replicate economists' (sometimes conflicting) views. That is because law, unlike economics, is an administrative system the effects of which depend upon the content of rules and precedents only as they are applied by judges and juries in courts and by lawyers advising their clients. And that fact means that courts will often bring their own administrative judgment to bear, sometimes applying rules of *per se* unlawfulness to business practices even when those practices sometimes produce benefits. . . .

I have already described studies and analyses that suggest (though they cannot prove) that resale price maintenance can cause harms with some regularity—and certainly when dealers are the driving force. But what about benefits? How often, for example, will the benefits to which the Court points occur in practice? I can find no economic consensus on this point. There is a consensus in the literature that "free riding" takes place. But "free riding" often takes place in the economy without any legal effort to stop it. Many visitors to California take free rides on the Pacific Coast Highway. We all benefit freely from ideas, such as that of creating the first supermarket. Dealers often take a "free ride" on investments that others have made in building a product's name and reputation. The question is how often the "free riding" problem is serious enough significantly to deter dealer investment.

To be more specific, one can easily *imagine* a dealer who refuses to provide important presale services, say a detailed explanation of how a product works (or who fails to provide a proper atmosphere in which to sell expensive perfume or alligator billfolds), lest customers use that "free" service (or enjoy the psychological benefit arising when a high-priced retailer stocks a particular brand of billfold or handbag) and then buy from another dealer at a lower price. Sometimes this must happen in reality. But does it happen often? We do, after all, live in an economy where firms, despite *Dr. Miles'* *per se* rule, still sell complex technical equipment (as well as expensive perfume and alligator billfolds) to consumers.

All this is to say that the ultimate question is not whether, but *how much,* "free riding" of this sort takes place. And, after reading the briefs, I must answer that question with an uncertain "sometimes." . . .

How easily can courts identify instances in which the benefits are likely to outweigh potential harms? My own answer is, *not very easily.* For one thing, it is often difficult to identify *who*—producer or dealer—is the moving force behind any given resale price maintenance agreement. . . . For another thing, as I just said, it is difficult to determine just when, and where, the "free riding" problem is serious enough to warrant legal protection.

I recognize that scholars have sought to develop check lists and sets of questions that will help courts separate instances where anticompetitive harms are more likely from instances where only benefits are likely to be found. But applying these criteria in court is often easier said than done. The Court's invitation to consider the existence of "market power," for example, invites lengthy time-consuming argument among competing experts, as they seek to apply abstract, highly technical, criteria to often ill-defined markets. And resale price maintenance cases, unlike a major merger or monopoly case, are likely to prove numerous and involve only private parties. One cannot fairly expect judges and juries in such cases to apply complex economic criteria without making a considerable number of mistakes, which themselves may impose serious costs. . . .

Are there special advantages to a bright-line rule? Without such a rule, it is often unfair, and consequently impractical, for enforcement officials to bring criminal proceedings. And since enforcement resources are limited, that loss may tempt some producers or dealers to enter into agreements that are, on balance, anticompetitive.

. . . The question before us is not what should be the rule, starting from scratch. We here must decide whether to change a clear and simple price-related antitrust rule that the courts have applied for nearly a century. * * *

Meanwhile, while the US Supreme Court considered and reversed the US ban on resale price maintenance agreements, the European Commission was reexamining its treatment of vertical restraints including RPM. In 2010, it issued a revised block exemption and vertical guidelines. *http:// ec.europa.eu/competition/antitrust/legislation/vertical.html*. Read the regulation containing the block exemption. (Selected Document 26) You will note that the regulation exempts vertical agreements where the seller occupies less than 30% of the market and the buyer accounts for less than 30% of purchases, unless the agreement contains a hard core restriction. Minimum RPM is a hard core restriction. It could theoretically get an individual exemption under Article 101(3), but this would be rare. Become familiar with the block exemption and the vertical guidelines that relate to RPM. The section of the guidelines on RPM is printed below.

GUIDELINES ON VERTICAL RESTRAINTS (2010)

European Commission Notice
available at *http://ec.europa.eu/competition/antitrust/legislation/vertical.html*
(resale price maintenance)

2.10. *Resale price restrictions*

(223) As explained in section III.3, resale price maintenance (RPM), that is agreements or concerted practices having as their direct or indirect object the establishment of a fixed or minimum resale price or a fixed or minimum price level to be observed by the buyer, are treated as a hardcore restriction. Including RPM in an agreement gives rise to the presumption that the agreement restricts competition and thus falls within Article 101(1). It also gives rise to the presumption that the agreement is unlikely to fulfil the conditions of Article 101(3), for which

reason the block exemption does not apply. However, undertakings have the possibility to plead an efficiency defence under Article 101(3) in an individual case. It is incumbent on the parties to substantiate that likely efficiencies result from including RPM in their agreement and demonstrate that all the conditions of Article 101(3) are fulfilled. It then falls to the Commission to effectively assess the likely negative effects on competition and consumers before deciding whether the conditions of Article 101(3) are fulfilled.

(224) RPM may restrict competition in a number of ways. Firstly, RPM may facilitate collusion between suppliers by enhancing price transparency in the market, thereby making it easier to detect whether a supplier deviates from the collusive equilibrium by cutting its price. RPM also undermines the incentive for the supplier to cut its price to its distributors, as the fixed resale price will prevent it from benefiting from expanded sales. This negative effect is in particular plausible if the market is prone to collusive outcomes, for instance if the manufacturers form a tight oligopoly, and a significant part of the market is covered by RPM agreements. Secondly, by eliminating intra-brand price competition, RPM may also facilitate collusion between the buyers, i.e. at the distribution level. Strong or well organised distributors may be able to force/convince one or more suppliers to fix their resale price above the competitive level and thereby help them to reach or stabilise a collusive equilibrium. This loss of price competition seems especially problematic when the RPM is inspired by the buyers, whose collective horizontal interests can be expected to work out negatively for consumers. Thirdly, RPM may more in general soften competition between manufacturers and/or between retailers, in particular when manufacturers use the same distributors to distribute their products and RPM is applied by all or many of them. Fourthly, the immediate effect of RPM will be that all or certain distributors are prevented from lowering their sales price for that particular brand. In other words, the direct effect of RPM is a price increase. Fifthly, RPM may lower the pressure on the margin of the manufacturer, in particular where the manufacturer has a commitment problem, i.e. where he has an interest in lowering the price charged to subsequent distributors. In such a situation, the manufacturer may prefer to agree to RPM, so as to help it to commit not to lower the price for subsequent distributors and to reduce the pressure on its own margin. Sixthly, RPM may be implemented by a manufacturer with market power to foreclose smaller rivals. The increased margin that RPM may offer distributors, may entice the latter to favour the particular brand over rival brands when advising customers, even where such advice is not in the interest of these customers, or not to sell these rival brands at all. Lastly, RPM may reduce dynamism and innovation at the distribution level. By preventing price competition between different distributors, RPM may prevent more efficient retailers from entering the market and/or acquiring sufficient scale with low prices. It also may prevent or hinder the entry and expansion of distribution formats based on low prices, such as price discounters.

(225) However, RPM may not only restrict competition but may also, in particular where it is supplier driven, lead to efficiencies, which will be assessed under Article 101(3). Most notably, where a manufacturer introduces a new product, RPM may be helpful during the introductory period of expanding demand to induce distributors to better take into account the manufacturer's interest to promote the product. RPM may provide the distributors with the means to increase sales efforts and if the distributors in this market are under competitive pressure this may induce them to expand overall demand for the product and make the launch of the product a success, also for the benefit of consumers.* Similarly, fixed resale prices, and not just maximum resale prices, may be necessary to organise in a franchise system or similar distribution system applying a uniform distribution format a coordinated short term low price campaign (2 to 6 weeks in most cases) which will also benefit the consumers. In some situations, the extra margin provided by RPM may allow retailers to provide (additional) pre-sales services, in particular in case of experience or complex products. If enough customers take advantage from such services to make their choice but then purchase at a lower price with retailers that do not provide such services (and hence do not incur these costs), high-service retailers may reduce or eliminate these services that enhance the demand for the supplier's product. RPM may help to prevent such free-riding at the distribution level. The parties will have to convincingly demonstrate that the RPM agreement can be expected to not only provide the means but also the incentive to overcome possible free riding between retailers on these services and that the pre-sales services overall benefit consumers as part of the demonstration that all the conditions of Article 101(3) are fulfilled.

(226) The practice of recommending a resale price to a reseller or requiring the reseller to respect a maximum resale price is covered by the Block Exemption Regulation when the market share of each of the parties to the agreement does not exceed the 30 % threshold, provided it does not amount to a minimum or fixed sale price as a result of pressure from, or incentives offered by, any of the parties. For cases above the market share threshold and for cases of withdrawal of the block exemption the following guidance is provided.

(227) The possible competition risk of maximum and recommended prices is that they will work as a focal point for the resellers and might be followed by most or all of them and/or that maximum or recommended prices may soften competition or facilitate collusion between suppliers.

(228) An important factor for assessing possible anti-competitive effects of maximum or recommended resale prices is the market position of the supplier. The stronger the market position of the supplier, the higher the risk that a maximum resale price or a recommended resale price leads to a more or less uniform application of that price level by the resellers,

---

* This assumes that it is not practical for the supplier to impose on all buyers by contract effective promotion requirements. . . .

because they may use it as a focal point. They may find it difficult to deviate from what they perceive to be the preferred resale price proposed by such an important supplier on the market.

(229) Where appreciable anti-competitive effects are established for maximum or recommended resale prices, the question of a possible exemption under Article 101(3) arises. For maximum resale prices, the efficiency described in paragraph 107, point 6 (avoiding double marginalisation), may be particularly relevant. A maximum resale price may also help to ensure that the brand in question competes more forcefully with other brands, including own label products, distributed by the same distributor.

NOTES AND QUESTIONS

1. In the US *Leegin* case, who has the stronger argument, Justice Kennedy or Justice Breyer?

2. Under US law, "rule of reason" entails analysis of the market facts to determine whether the undertaking is likely to get or increase market power, harming consumers, as a result of the challenged conduct or practice. The Court, by Justice Kennedy, said: "just" raising price is not equivalent to harm to consumers. The higher price might mean more service or more demand. (Is this perspective accepted in Europe?) In some cases, rule of reason analysis can involve short cuts; e.g., if the challenged conduct is usually harmful a presumption might be applied, and the conduct might be declared illegal unless the undertaking comes forward with an efficiency justification. This is called a structured rule of reason. If you were to suggest a structured rule of reason for RPM, what would that rule be? Is your proposed rule likely to be acceptable to Justice Kennedy?

3. Consider the US Court's assertions: Protecting interbrand competition is "the primary purpose of the antitrust laws"; higher prices are irrelevant "absent a further showing of anticompetitive conduct."

4. Compare the European block exemption and guidelines with the US *Leegin* case. What different perceptions do you observe about the possible harms and possible benefits of RPM? Is the structure of analysis, including burdens of proof, likely to lead to different results? What would be the outcome of the *Leegin* case (agreement not to discount a minor brand of fine belts) in each jurisdiction—US after trial, and EU?

———————

We have just looked at distribution restraints of the sort that constrain the choices of chosen distributors as to the price at which they must sell or the customers to whom or territories in which they may sell. Other vertical restraints require exclusive buying or selling, force the distributor to buy unwanted items or to buy only from designated sellers, foreclose outsiders from entering the distribution network, or, as in franchising, combine several of the above restraints to foster uniformity. As you read cases decided before approximately year 2000, and especially cases denying or conditioning exemptions, consider whether those cases accord with the new economic approach, which would protect consumers and the market from uses of market power. Note that cases of exclusionary conduct entail many of the same concepts as do abuse of dominance cases under Article 102. Indeed, if the undertaking is dominant, an anticompetitive exclusionary agreement can be condemned under both Articles 101 and 102.

F. SINGLE BRANDING (EXCLUSIVE PURCHASING), TYING AND RELATED FORECLOSURES

A producer or other seller of a product may wish to obligate its distributor or other buyers to buy the product, or a portion of its needs, only from the seller, or to buy a second product from the seller. For example, in *Hoffmann–La Roche,* page 868 supra, vitamin producer Merck contracted with the dominant vitamin producer Hoffmann–La Roche to buy from Roche its needs of vitamin B_6 in excess of its own manufacturing capacity. And in *Tetra Pak,* page 909 supra, the dominant supplier of aseptic cartons for milk and juice required buyers to buy, also, their needs of non-aseptic cartons. In both cases the Court condemned the restraints as abuses of dominance in violation of Article 102 on grounds that they "deprive[d] the purchaser of or restrict[ed] his possible choices of sources of supply and . . . den[ied] other producers access to the market." [quoting from *Hoffmann–La Roche*].

Exclusive, single-branding, requirements or tie-in contracts may also be caught by Article 101(1). Under what conditions? How and when can they be justified under Article 101(3)?

STERGIOS DELIMITIS v. HENNINGER BRÄU AG
Case C–234/89, [1991] ECR I–935, ECJ.

[Stergios Delimitis rented a pub from Henninger Bräu, agreeing to sell only Henninger Bräu beer in the pub. Asserting that the contract violated Article 101 and was void, Delimitis failed to pay rent, and Henninger deducted the rent from Delimitis' rental deposit. Delimitis sued for return of the rent. Henninger relied on the contract, which presumably was not intended to harm competition but reflected the brewery's desire for an assured outlet for its beer and Delimitis' desire for the premises and an assured supply.

The national court sought a preliminary ruling on whether the contract was caught by Article 101(1) and if so whether it fell within the then block exemption on exclusive purchasing. The Court of Justice set forth the following framework for determining whether exclusive contracts that are part of a network of similar contracts have the effect, if not the object, of "preventing, restricting or distorting competition":]

15　　. . . [I]t is necessary to analyse the effects of a beer supply agreement, taken together with other contracts of the same type, on the opportunities of national competitors or those from other Member States, to gain access to the market for beer consumption or to increase their market share and, accordingly, the effects on the range of products offered to consumers. * * *

18 [The relevant market is] the national market for beer distribution in premises for the sale and consumption of drinks.

19 In order to assess whether the existence of several beer supply agreements impedes access to the market as so defined, it is further necessary to examine the nature and extent of those agreements in their totality, comprising all similar contracts tying a large number of points of sale to several national producers. The effect of those networks of contracts on access to the market depends specifically on the number of outlets thus tied to national producers in relation to the number of public houses which are not so tied, the duration of the commitments entered into, the quantities of beer to which those commitments relate, and on the proportion between those quantities and the quantities sold by free distributors.

20 The existence of a bundle of similar contracts, even if it has a considerable effect on the opportunities for gaining access to the market, is not, however, sufficient in itself to support a finding that the relevant market is inaccessible, inasmuch as it is only one factor, amongst others, pertaining to the economic and legal context in which an agreement must be appraised. The other factors to be taken into account are, in the first instance, those also relating to opportunities for access.

21 In that connection it is necessary to examine whether there are real concrete possibilities for a new competitor to penetrate the bundle of contracts by acquiring a brewery already established on the market together with its network of sales outlets, or to circumvent the bundle of contracts by opening new public houses. For that purpose it is necessary to have regard to the legal rules and agreements on the acquisition of companies and the establishment of outlets, and to the minimum number of outlets necessary for the economic operation of a distribution system. The presence of beer wholesalers not tied to producers who are active on the market is also a factor capable of facilitating a new producer's access to that market since he can make use of those wholesaler's sales networks to distribute his own beer.

22 Secondly, account must be taken of the conditions under which competitive forces operate on the relevant market. In that connection it is necessary to know not only the number and the size of producers present on the market, but also the degree of saturation of that market and customer fidelity to existing brands, for it is generally more difficult to penetrate a saturated market in which customers are loyal to a small number of large producers than a market in full expansion in which a large number of small producers are operating without any strong brand names....

23   If an examination of all similar contracts entered into on the relevant market and the other factors relevant to the economic and legal context in which the contract must be examined shows that those agreements do not have the cumulative effect of denying access to that market to new national and foreign competitors, the individual agreements comprising the bundle of agreements cannot be held to restrict competition within the meaning of Article [101](1) of the Treaty. They do not, therefore, fall under the prohibition laid down in that provision.

24   If, on the other hand, such examination reveals that it is difficult to gain access to the relevant market, it is necessary to assess the extent to which the agreements entered into by the brewery in question contribute to the cumulative effect produced in that respect by the totality of the similar contracts found on that market. Under the Community rules on competition, responsibility for such an effect of closing off the market must be attributed to the breweries which make an appreciable contribution thereto. Beer supply agreements entered into by breweries whose contribution to the cumulative effect is insignificant do not therefore fall under the prohibition under Article [101](1). * * *

27   The reply to be given to the first three questions is therefore that a beer supply agreement is prohibited by Article [101](1) of the Treaty, if two cumulative conditions are met. The first is that, having regard to the economic and legal context of the agreement at issue, it is difficult for competitors who could enter the market or increase their market share to gain access to the national market for the distribution of beer in premises for the sale and consumption of drinks. The fact that, in that market, the agreement in issue is one of a number of similar agreements having a cumulative effect on competition constitutes only one factor amongst others in assessing whether access to that market is indeed difficult. The second condition is that the agreement in question must make a significant contribution to the sealing-off effect brought about by the totality of those agreements in their economic and legal context. The extent of the contribution made by the individual agreement depends on the position of the contracting parties in the relevant market and on the duration of the agreement.

NOTES AND QUESTIONS

1. *Delimitis* was considered a break-through judgment, prior to which single-branding contracts with significant producers were deemed almost automatically caught by Article 101(1) and thus were in need of justification.

2. What do you suppose was Delimitis' theory of the case—and its theory of antitrust harm?

SCHÖLLER LEBENSMITTEL v. COMMISSION

Case T–9/93, [1995] ECR II–1611, General Court.

[Langnese–Iglo, a subsidiary of Unilever, and Schöller Lebensmittel were the leading firms in Germany in the sale of ice cream; particularly impulse-buying ice cream. Each, separately, had a network of agreements with the sellers requiring that the retailers purchase ice cream only from it, or supplying freezers "free" and requiring that the retailer use the freezer only for the supplier's ice cream and not for the ice cream of competitors.

Mars, a French manufacturer of ice cream bars, was trying to pierce the German impulse ice cream market. Finding the two firms' supply contracts to be road blocks to market access, Mars complained to the Commission. The Commission brought proceedings against each. The Commission withdrew a comfort letter that it had previously given to Schöller and decided both the question of applicability of Article 101(1) and the question of entitlement of the applicants to an individual exemption.

In *Schöller,* the court first examined whether the contested supply agreements had an appreciable effect on competition. It found "that the applicant holds a strong position in the relevant market"; it held "more than 25 per cent" in the traditional trade, and, by its agreements, tied more than 10% of the sales outlets. Combined with Langnese's contracts, the tied portion of the market exceeded 30%.]

83   With respect to [other] factors, the Commission has drawn attention to the existence of additional substantial barriers to access to the market, both in the grocery trade and in the traditional trade.... [A]ccess to the market for new competitors is made more difficult by the existence of a system under which a large number of freezer cabinets are lent by the applicant to retailers both in the grocery trade and in the traditional trade ..., the retailers being obliged to use them exclusively for the applicant's products.

84   The Court considers that the Commission was right to treat that factor as contributing to making access to the market more difficult. The necessary consequence of that situation is that any new competitor entering the market must either persuade the retailer to exchange the freezer cabinet installed by the applicant for another, which involves giving up the turnover in the products from the previous supplier, or to persuade the retailer to install an additional freezer cabinet, which may prove impossible, particularly because of lack of space in small sales outlets. Moreover, if the new competitor is able to offer only a limited range of products, as in the case of the intervener, it may prove difficult for it to persuade the retailer to terminate its agreement with the previous supplier.

85   It is also apparent from the documents before the Court that, in the traditional trade, there are numerous individual retailers whose aver-

age turnover is rather low. The establishment of a profitable distribution system therefore presupposes that a new competitor must have a large number of retailers concentrated within a specified geographical area which can be supplied through regional or central warehouses. The fact that there are no independent intermediaries means that this fragmentation of demand constitutes an additional barrier to access to the market. Finally, the Commission rightly took into account the fact that the applicant's product brands are very well known.

86 In those circumstances, the Court considers that examination of all the similar agreements concluded on the market and of other aspects of the economic and legal context in which they operate ... shows that the exclusive purchasing agreements concluded by the applicant are liable appreciably to affect competition within the meaning of Article [101] (1) of the Treaty.

87 In view of the strong position occupied by the applicant in the relevant market and, in particular, its market share, the Court considers that the agreements contribute significantly to the closing-off of the market.

88 In view of all the foregoing, the Court considers that the Commission was right to conclude that the contested agreements give rise to an appreciable restriction of competition in the relevant market. * * *

139 In considering whether the Commission was right to refuse to grant an individual exemption, it must first be borne in mind that an individual exemption decision may be granted only if, in particular, the four conditions laid down by Article [101](3) of the Treaty are all met by the agreement in question, with the result that an exemption must be refused if any of the four conditions is not met. * * *

142 As regards the first of the four conditions laid down by Article [101](3) of the Treaty, the Court points out that, according to that provision, the agreements capable of being exempted are those which contribute "to improving the production or distribution of goods or to promoting technical or economic progress". It is settled law that the improvement cannot be identified with all the advantages which the parties obtain from the agreement in their production or distribution activities. The improvement must in particular display appreciable objective advantages of such a character as to compensate for the disadvantages which they cause in the field of competition.

143 ... Although it is apparent ... that exclusive purchasing agreements lead in general to an improvement in distribution, in that they enable the supplier to plan the sale of his goods with greater precision and for a longer period and ensure that the reseller's requirements will be met on a regular basis for the duration of the agreement, and even if it is assumed that it would be necessary for the applicant, for reasons of cost, to terminate supplies to certain small sales outlets if it were obliged to give up supplies to them on an exclusive basis, the Commission considers nevertheless that the contested agreements do not give

rise to objective and specific advantages for the public interest such as to compensate for the disadvantages which they cause in the field of competition.

144 In support of that argument, the Commission states, first, that, in view of the strong position on the market held by the applicant, the contested agreements do not . . . have the effect of intensifying competition between different brands of products. The Commission rightly took the view that the network of agreements at issue constitutes a major barrier to access to the market, with the result that competition is restricted.

145 . . . [It is clear] that the Commission considered that supplies to any small sales outlets abandoned by the applicant, for reasons of costs, would be taken over either by other suppliers, for example small local producers, or by independent dealers selling several ranges of products. Moreover, the Commission points out that the applicant itself recognised that it continues to supply even very small sales outlets, whose annual turnover hovers around 300 German marks, in those cases where their geographical situation is favourable.

146 Against that background, it must be borne in mind that the intervener, Mars, stated that it is wholly exceptional for impulse products to be distributed using a transport system owned by the producers. The parties agree that it is only in Germany, Denmark and Italy that undertakings in the Unilever group, including Langnese, have concluded exclusive agreements covering sales outlets.

147 Although the applicant claims that it would be obliged, for reasons of cost, to cease supplying a number of small sales outlets if it had to give up its exclusive purchasing agreements, the Court considers that it has not provided any evidence to show that such a situation would be liable to jeopardise regular supplies of impulse ice-cream to the territory as a whole and, in particular, that the small sales outlets concerned would not subsequently be supplied by other suppliers or wholesalers, simply as a consequence of the unrestricted competition which would then prevail. Nor has the applicant produced any convincing evidence of the special conditions in Germany which made it necessary to create an ice-cream distribution system belonging to the producers. The Court therefore considers that the applicant has not shown that the Commission committed a manifest error of assessment in considering that the contested agreements did not fulfil the first condition laid down by Article [101](3) of the Treaty. . . . * * *

NOTES AND QUESTIONS

1. Is an impulse ice cream market in Germany plausible? If Schöller supplied the entire market, could it probably raise its prices to a supracompetitive level without loosing so many customers (to packaged ice cream or something else) that the price rise would not be worth it? (Assume that the answer is affirmative as you proceed to analyze the problem.)

2. Did Schöller have market power? Is market power important to the decision? Should it be?

3. What were the effects of the exclusivity and freezer clauses on competitors? on potential competitors? on consumers? Which effects are most important?

4. What were the efficiencies of the exclusive supply contracts? of the "free" freezer arrangements? How, in your view, do the efficiencies balance against the anticompetitive aspects of the agreements? What was the court's view?

5. What was the strongest case for granting the exemption? Was the Commission right to deny it?

6. If you were Mars and if you could not expect the European Commission to grant you relief from your competitors' exclusivity and freezer clauses, what strategies would you adopt?

7. If Schöller and Langnese withdrew the exclusivity obligation and offered retailers the choice of a) freezers for sale at market price, b) freezers for rent at market price, or c) freezers "free" with an obligation to use only the supplier's ice cream in the freezer, would the new arrangement be permissible? What if virtually all of the retailers chose option (c)? See *Van den Bergh Foods Ltd.* (subsidiary of Unilever), Cases IV/34.073, 34.395, 35.436, Commission Decision 98/531, O.J. L 246/1 (Sept. 4, 1998). *Langnese–Iglo GmbH v. Commission, Case T–7/93*, the companion case to *Schöller,* is reported at [1995] ECR II–1533, aff'd, [1998] ECR I–5609.

8. The Irish court took an entirely different view of the freezer arrangement and its effects. Masterfoods (Mars) had been enlisting numerous retailers in Ireland to stock and display Mars bars in their freezers. HB Ice-cream (of the Unilever family), the dominant impulse ice cream seller in Ireland, sought to enforce its exclusive contracts with the retailers. In 1992 it persuaded an Irish court to permanently restrain Masterfoods from inducing breach of HB's contracts. The Irish court, by Judge Lynch, analyzed the contracts as follows:

> I think that a breach of paragraph (e) [distorting competition by imposing unrelated obligations] does not arise at all in this case. The contracts in question are bailments of freezers whether they be on loan or hire. The terms objected to relate to the very basis of the contract of bailment, namely, the purpose for which the goods (the freezers) are bailed to the bailee (the retailer). The freezers are bailed to the bailees for the purpose of storing, selling and advertising HB ice cream products only. Those terms are not supplementary obligations nor by their nature or according to commercial usage do they not have an essential connection with the contracts of bailment. They do. It would seem that none of the particular breaches set out in paragraphs (a) to (e) of Article [101] (1) apply: certainly, none clearly apply to the facts of Article [101] if it was reasonably clear that there was a contravention of the general intention of the article. Is it reasonably likely that these contracts of bailment of freezers may affect trade between member states of the European Community and may prevent, restrict or distort competition within the

common market? I am not satisfied that Mars has made out a sufficient prima facie or serious case to that effect.

H.B. Ice-cream Ltd. v. Masterfoods Ltd. (trading as Mars Ireland), [1990] 2 IR 463.

Masterfoods complained to the European Commission about the exclusivity clauses and the Irish court injunction. The Commission, after finding that 40% of sales outlets in Ireland were tied up by the exclusivity clause, held:

> [T]he exclusivity provision in the freezer-cabinet agreement concluded between HB and retailers in Ireland, for the placement of cabinets in retail outlets which have only one or more freezer cabinets supplied by HB for the stocking of single-wrapped items of impulse ice cream, and not having a freezer cabinet either procured by themselves or provided by another ice-cream manufacturer constitutes an infringement of Article [101](1) of the Treaty. * * *

> HB's inducement to retailers in Ireland to enter into freezer-cabinet agreements subject to a condition of exclusivity by offering to supply them with one or more freezer cabinets for the stocking of single-wrapped items of impulse ice cream and to maintain the cabinets, free of any direct charge, constitutes an infringement of Article [102] of the Treaty.

Van den Bergh Foods Ltd., Cases IV/34.073, IV/34.395 and IV/35.436, Commission Decision 98/531 of 11 March 1998, O.J. L 246/1 (Sept. 4, 1998), Arts. 1, 3.

Meanwhile, the Irish Supreme Court stayed the Irish appeal and asked the European Court of Justice whether its obligation of sincere cooperation (TEU Art. 4(3)) required it to stay the Irish case pending the disposition of Van den Bergh's appeal. The Court of Justice responded in the affirmative, holding that Ireland could not maintain a judgment inconsistent with the Community disposition of the same issue. Masterfoods Ltd. (Mars Ireland), Case C–344/98, [2000] ECR I–11369.

On its appeal from the Commission decision, Van den Bergh stressed that the retailers were free to terminate their contract with HB or to install freezers not belonging to HB; and it argued that their freedom to do so meant that there was no foreclosure. The General Court responded that the retailers had little incentive to exercise this freedom, and seldom did. It noted also the unique circumstances of the market, including the limited space in the retail stores and the popularity of HB's ice cream, and concluded that the Commission did not err in finding that the clause produced a sufficiently high degree of foreclosure to constitute an infringement. *Van den Bergh Foods v. Commission*, Case T–65/98 R, [2003] ECR II–4653.

9. The 2010 Guidelines on Vertical Restraints cover the range of exclusionary agreements. Read again the block exemption (Selected Document 26), and read the framework for analysis of individual cases (Vertical Guidelines paras. 96–127) and the analysis of single-branding (129–150), exclusive distribution (151–167), exclusive supply (192–202), and tying (214–222). *http://ec. europa.eu/competition/antitrust/legislation/vertical.html*. Applying the guidelines, would you come to any different conclusions in the cases above? If you need more facts, specify what facts you would need.

10. Look at the guidelines' treatment of Internet freedoms and restrictions. See Vertical Guidelines paragraphs 51–54 and 64. Are the lines drawn in the appropriate place? Consider, for example, that sending unsolicited promotional e-mails to specified customers outside of an assigned territory is an "active" sale. An agreement may prohibit such a practice and still qualify for the block exemption. Requiring exclusive distributors to reroute web customers to the distributor in their territory would involve a lost opportunity for a "passive" sale, and would be prohibited. But, without losing eligibility for the exemption, sellers can restrict sales to distributors with brick-and-mortar outlets, who then can sell on the Internet, and the sellers can block on-line sales of their goods by distributors without brick-and-mortar outlets. Are the Internet provisions appropriately protective of brand owners' needs to guard against free riders? or too restrictive of the freedom of eBay and its ilk to give good deals to consumers?

11. US law tends to examine more skeptically, first, the market power of the seller, and second, the feared inability of outsiders to reach the market efficiently notwithstanding exclusivity clauses. Also, US courts would tend to perceive the freezer clause more sympathetically, as a good deal for the retailer. But if the undertaking had significant market power and if its exclusive contract requirements excluded efficient outsiders such that the price of the product (impulse ice cream) was artificially increased, the clause would be likely to offend US law also. See, e.g., *United States v. Dentsply Int'l Inc.*, 399 F.3d 181 (3d Cir. 2005), cert. denied, 546 U.S. 1089.

G. BLOCK EXEMPTIONS: HISTORY AND REFORM

As soon as the first implementing regulation, Regulation 17, became effective in 1962, thousands of notifications of distribution agreements began flooding the Competition Directorate, which was obliged to examine each to determine whether an exemption should issue. The Commission responded to the unmanageable work load, as well as the opportunity to give guidance, by issuing its first block exemption regulation (BER), Commission Regulation 67/67, regarding agreements for the exclusive distribution of goods and agreements for the licensing of intellectual property. The Commission issued superseding BERs as well as new specialized ones for patents, knowhow, and motor vehicle distribution. The BERs provided detailed roadmaps of what parties must, could, and must not do in order to have the benefit of exemption without filing a notification and seeking an individual exemption.

Business firms organized entire distribution systems to conform with the block exemptions, since analysis of restraints outside of the block exemptions was uncertain. Eventually, the system of detailed block exemptions came under severe criticism. They were formalistic. They straight-jacketed business transactions. They were not united by any economic or other theory.

The Commission launched an intensive reexamination of its treatment of vertical restraints and in particular the block exemptions. In 1997 it issued an influential green paper, which included economic analysis recognizing the efficiency properties of most vertical restraints. At the conclusion of the long process of reexamination and in the years thereafter, important changes were made. First, the Council amended Regulation 17 (later replaced by Regulation 1/2003) to exempt all vertical agreements from the requirement that they be notified in order to secure an exemption effective from the date of the agreement. Council Regulation 1216/99, O.J. L 148/5 (June 15, 1999).

Second, the Commission and Council liberalized the block exemptions, eliminating much detail. They issued a general vertical block exemption and guidelines for analysis of agreements that fall outside of the block exemption, culminating in the revised general vertical block exemption and guidelines of 2010, referenced above.

Two specific vertical BERs that still remain concern technology transfer and motor vehicles.

A revised motor vehicle block exemption regulation and guidelines were issued in May 2010. The block exemption applies to agreements between motor vehicle manufacturers and their authorized dealers, repairers and spare part distributors. The legislation acknowledges that strong competition now exists in the sale of new vehicles, while impediments continue in the repair, maintenance and spare parts markets. To come within the block exemption, an agreement must not have as its object, among other things: i) the restriction of sales of spare parts to independent repairers; ii) the restriction on the supplier to sell spare parts, repair tools, diagnostic or other equipment to authorized or independent distributors or repairers or end users; or iii) the restriction of the supplier's ability to put its trademark visibly on components used for initial assembly of motor vehicles or spare parts. To get advantage of the block exemption, manufacturers must not have more than 30% of the market, and they must not limit warranties to authorized garages for oil changes or any other car services. The BER provides flexibility in the organization of distribution networks in which multi-brand dealers co-exist. For new car sales, the sector-specific BER is to be phased out; after 2013, the general vertical BER will apply. The regulation and guidelines are available at *http://ec.europa.eu/competition/sectors/motor_vehicles/legislation/legislation.html*.

The technology transfer block exemption, effective in May 2004, covers patents, know-how, design rights, and software copyrights. The regulation contains a list of hardcore prohibitions. For obtaining the benefit of the block exemption, it imposes a cap of 20% for licensing between competitors and 30% for licensing between non-competitors. Analysis outside of the block exemption is explained in accompanying guidelines. The regulation and guidelines are available at *http://ec.europa.eu/competition/antitrust/legislation/transfer.html*.

Notes and Questions

1.   Do you agree with the Commission's characterizations and analysis? Would you have formulated any categories or analysis differently? In what respect?

2.   Applying the modernized analysis to the facts of the following cases, consider whether the restraints fall clear of Article 101(1), if not whether they come within the vertical block exemption, and if not whether they probably would be justified under the framework of the vertical guidelines:

Consten and Grundig

Pioneer

Delimitis

Schöller

Masterfoods

Leegin, if it occurred in Europe.

CHAPTER 25

MERGERS

■ ■ ■

A. INTRODUCTION

The Treaty of Rome establishing the European Economic Communities (1957) was not directed against mergers. Facing trade barriers at every frontier, many business enterprises were too small to be efficient. Mergers—especially mergers between firms from different Member States—held the promise of promoting market integration. Moreover, the Member States were not prepared to yield to Community sovereignty over the structure of their economies, and Community competence over mergers was regarded by many as unreasonably intrusive. Accordingly, the competition provisions of the Treaty did not mention mergers. Article 85 EEC, now 101 TFEU, was designed to regulate agreements and ongoing collaborations. Article 86 EEC, now 102 TFEU, was designed to regulate the behavior of dominant firms.

By contrast to the EEC Treaty, the European Coal and Steel Treaty—which had been adopted six years earlier and has now expired—specifically prohibited mergers that created power "to determine prices, to control or restrict production or distribution or to hinder effective competition in a substantial part of the market ...." (Art. 66 para. 2) Thus, from the start, the Member States expressly conceded control over coal and steel mergers, underscoring the deliberateness of the omission of merger control in the EEC Treaty.

Finally, in 1989, the Council promulgated the Merger Regulation, officially providing a merger control system for the Union.

The adoption of European merger control coincided with important economic and political changes in the world. In November 1989 the Berlin Wall fell. Members of the former Soviet block and many others adopted merger control. More than 75 nations now have merger control/notification regimes. Since many of the possibly anticompetitive mergers are between firms that operate in transnational markets, problems of jurisdiction, conflict, and cooperation emerge. We return to these challenges below, after discussing the concept and detail of the Merger Regulation.

B. THE MERGER REGULATION

1. COVERAGE AND PROCEDURES

After 16 years of debate, on December 21, 1989 the Council adopted the Merger Control Regulation, with an effective date of September 21, 1990.* It was amended in 2004. The Merger Regulation (Selected Document 27) has three major purposes: (1) to provide specific authority for the Commission to challenge mergers and acquisitions that would harm competition, and thus to put an end to the debate whether the Treaty conferred such authority; (2) to provide a structure for merger control, giving the Commission necessary market information before mergers are consummated and the power to stop anticompetitive mergers before their consummation; and (3) to centralize merger enforcement in the hands of the Community authorities so that enterprises would not be subject to multiple and potentially inconsistent substantive standards, notice requirements and waiting periods.

Specifically, subject to exceptions that we note below, the parties to a concentration with a Community dimension must file premerger notification forms and wait until final decision. The Commission has exclusive power, vis-à-vis Member State authorities, to allow or disallow these transactions. The Member States have ceded authority to prevent or authorize such transactions, except when legitimate national interests such as security, plurality of media, and prudential concerns are at stake, and except in certain circumstances when a distinct State market is affected.

A concentration has a Community dimension when:

(a) the combined aggregate worldwide turnover of all the undertakings concerned is more than 5 billion euros; and

(b) the aggregate Community-wide turnover of each of at least two of the undertakings concerned is more than 250 million euros, unless each of the undertakings concerned achieves more than two-thirds of its aggregate Community-wide turnover within one and the same Member State.

Concentrations also have a Community dimension and thus come within the Merger Regulation if:

(1) The undertakings have combined aggregate world-wide turnover of at least 2.5 billion euros,

(2) The undertakings have combined aggregate turnover of at least 100 million euros in at least three Member States,

(3) At least two of the undertakings have at least 25 million euros turnover in the same three Member States, and

---

* Council Regulation 4064/89, O.J. L 395/1 (Dec. 30, 1989). The Merger Regulation as amended, Council Regulation 139/2004, O.J. L 24/1 (Jan. 29, 2004), and merger guidelines, may be found at *http://ec.europa.eu/competition/mergers/legislation/legislation.html.*

(4) At least two undertakings have at least 100 million euros turnover in the Community,

unless each of the undertakings achieves more than two-thirds of its aggregate Community-wide turnover in the same Member State.

Concentrations below the thresholds remain subject to the laws of the Member States.

In some cases a concentration even with a Community dimension threatens competition in a distinct market within one Member State. In such cases the Member State authority may ask the Commission to refer the concentration to it, and the Commission *may* grant the reference; but if the affected territory is not a substantial part of the common market, the Commission *must* grant the reference. The applicable clause—Article 9—was called the German clause, since it was proposed by Germany in response to its concerns that Germany would be stripped of its power to prohibit concentrations that uniquely harmed Germany. Another clause, Article 22, known as the Dutch clause, allows the Commission to investigate mergers not of Community dimension at the request of one or more Member States. Article 4 introduces a pre-notification referral system which allows allocation of the review of a merger to the best-placed authority before a formal filing.

Joint ventures are "concentrations" if they are created to "perform[] on a lasting basis all the functions of an autonomous economic entity." These joint ventures are called "full-function" joint ventures. Full-function joint ventures get the benefit of the one-stop Merger Regulation if they meet the thresholds. If the joint venture may give rise to coordination of the competitive behavior of firms that remain independent, or if it entails ancillary agreements that are not obviously directly related and necessary to the concentration, the Commission must appraise its potentially cooperative or exclusionary aspects under Article 101 or 102.

Concentrative transactions with a Community dimension must be notified to the Commission. The Commission must then evaluate the concentration to determine whether it is compatible with the common market. A concentration covered by the regulation may not be put into effect before a final decision. If the Commission advances to the stage of opening proceedings, it must do so within one month of the notification, and it must render its decision within four months thereafter.

The Merger Regulation provides that the implementing legislation that empowers Commission enforcement of Articles 101 and 102 does not apply to concentrations, whether they fall above or below the thresholds. Moreover, the Commission has represented that it will not normally apply Articles 101 or 102 to concentrations. Therefore the Merger Regulation has effectively become the only European Community measure for controlling concentrations.

2. THE SUBSTANTIVE STANDARD

Initially the Merger Regulation proscribed only such mergers that created or strengthened a *dominant position* that would significantly impede competition in the common market. This wording proved to be too narrow, because it seemed to ignore oligopoly effects. The 2004 revision accordingly expanded the coverage.

The substantive standard is set forth in Article 2 of the revised Merger Regulation, which provides:

1. Concentrations within the scope of this Regulation shall be appraised in accordance with the following provisions with a view to establishing whether or not they are compatible with the common market.

In making this appraisal, the Commission shall take into account:

(a) the need to maintain and develop effective competition within the common market in view of, among other things, the structure of all the markets concerned and the actual or potential competition from undertakings located either within or without the Community;

(b) the market positions of the undertakings concerned and their economic and financial power, the alternatives available to suppliers and users, their access to supplies or markets, any legal or other barriers to entry, supply and demand trends for relevant goods and services, the interests of the intermediate and ultimate consumers, and the development of technical and economic progress provided that it is to consumers' advantage and does not form an obstacle to competition.

2. A concentration which would not significantly impede effective competition in the common market or in a substantial part of it, in particular as a result of the creation or strengthening of a dominant position, shall be declared compatible with the common market.

3. *A concentration which would significantly impede effective competition, in the common market or in a substantial part of it, in particular as a result of the creation or strengthening of a dominant position, shall be declared incompatible with the common market.* [Italics added.]

This standard is called the SIEC standard; the question is whether the merger would "significantly impede effective competition."

The body of the Merger Regulation is preceded by a number of recitals. Recital 23 states that the Community must place its competition appraisal within the framework of the fundamental objectives of the Community referred to in the Treaty. Recital 15 states:

(32) Concentrations which, by reason of the limited market share of the undertakings concerned, are not liable to impede effective compe-

tition may be presumed to be compatible with the common market. Without prejudice to Articles [101] and [102] of the Treaty, an indication to this effect exists, in particular, where the market share of the undertakings concerned does not exceed 25% either in the common market or in a substantial part of it.

NOTES AND QUESTIONS

1. Review the substantive standard for proscribing concentrations under the Merger Regulation. In considering whether the merger is compatible with the internal market, is the Commission limited to weighing procompetitive and anticompetitive aspects of the concentration? If the acquisition impedes effective competition, is it relevant that the acquisition also saves jobs? that it produces productive efficiencies that help the firm compete in world markets? that it creates a European champion that by some measure might make Europe better off? If the acquisition is not likely to harm consumers, is it relevant that it will destroy small and middle-sized firms?

2. US law prohibits mergers "the effect [of which] may be substantially to lessen competition." Clayton Act, § 7. In Europe, this is sometimes called the SLC test. (The UK also has an SLC test.) For the United States, there is nothing magic in the words "substantially to lessen competition." The inquiry is whether the merger is anticompetitive.

US analysis of mergers of competitors is largely congruent with EU analysis, although US analysts are more likely to use a robust-market assumption; namely, the assumption that actual or near competitive forces will constrain the merging parties from getting or using market power.

The United States does not have one-stop shopping. The United States federal merger law may be enforced by the Justice Department or the Federal Trade Commission, by the attorney general of any affected states, and by private parties. See *California v. American Stores Co.*, 495 U.S. 271, 110 S.Ct. 1853, 109 L.Ed.2d 240 (1990). In addition, the states that have antimerger laws may seek to enforce them against mergers with local effects even though interstate commerce is also affected. Aware of the costs of multiple overlapping merger laws, the state attorneys general collaborate on the substantive standard for prohibition, and they invite merging parties to make joint filings with all interested states. Moreover, the state enforcers collaborate with the federal enforcers.

State enforcement played a noticeable role in the United States in the 1980s when the federal government's market philosophy resulted in an unusually low level of merger challenges.

Should the United States adopt the European Union approach of centralized enforcement? Is there a need for multinational cooperation in merger control, as more and more mega-mergers have impacts around the world?

C. THE ECONOMICS OF MERGER ANALYSIS

1. INTRODUCTION

In this section we review some basic economics that may guide analysis of competitive harms, principally from a consumer or efficiency point of view. First, we analyze the effects of mergers on competition, assuming the relevant market. Second, we return to the question of market definition, which is guided by the Commission's December 1997 Notice on Definition of Relevant Market.

2. COMPETITION–LESSENING EFFECTS

Mergers may harm competition, causing output to fall and prices to rise or suppressing incentives to innovate, by creating or entrenching market power or facilitating its exercise. It can do this by one of two routes: creating or entrenching single firm power (dominance or other unilateral power), or creating or entrenching a tight oligopoly wherein the few remaining firms in a market are likely to behave like collaborators rather than rivals. Oligopoly behavior is sometimes called cartel-like or cooperative behavior.

The negative effects (principally higher price and lower output, and chilled incentives to invent)* cannot be expected if barriers to entry are low, strong potential competitors are waiting in the wings, smaller firms can easily and quickly expand without rising costs, or big buyers credibly threaten to integrate backwards if their suppliers do not perform competitively. In such cases the market may regulate itself. The economic forces put pressure on the existing market actors, causing them to be responsive to buyers' needs.

Of all mergers, mergers of competitors are most likely to harm competition. Also, mergers between a leading firm and a most important potential competitor can have the same cartel or dominance-creating effect. Potential competitors can exert competitive pressure on prices. Incumbents may hold their prices down so as not to attract their entry. If a dominant firm acquires the most or only important potential competitor, the acquisition removes this competitive check. Also, if the potential entrant would have entered the market on its own and added a dynamic force to an oligopolistic or monopolistic market, the merger would prevent this force from materializing.

Mergers between buyers and suppliers ("vertical mergers") can also lessen competition, although in many cases they simply reshuffle buyer and supplier alliances. Vertical mergers may make it more likely that the firms will deal with each other to the exclusion of or in preference to dealing with others. Favoring one's own is especially likely in times of short supply or contracted demand.

---

* Also, at high levels of concentration, loss of choice.

Most often, a vertical merger is efficient and does not foreclose unintegrated rivals from access to needed supplies or outlets, raising their costs and pushing up price. The rivals may be able to buy from other suppliers or to supply other buyers, or to integrate vertically by contract or acquisition. But if leading firms in their respective fields merge, if barriers to entry are high, if concentration at the relevant market level is high, and if foreclosure of unintegrated rivals from necessary inputs or outlets threatens to squeeze rivals out of the market or incapacitate them, a vertical merger may increase dominance or facilitate oligopoly behavior in the relevant market, raising consumer prices. EU competition law has been concerned also with competitors' access to markets, key assets and infrastructure (gateways), and with competitors' rights to compete on the merits free from blockage by a dominant firms' bundling and other strategies; but these factors must be linked with consumer harm.

Mergers that are neither horizontal, potential-horizontal nor vertical are called conglomerate mergers. The label merely signifies an "all other" category. Conglomerate mergers are much less likely than horizontal, potential-horizontal or vertical mergers to lessen competition and harm consumers. In some cases however, merging partners may be able to use leverage to create competition-lessening foreclosures (see vertical effects, above). In the United States today, the law treats anticompetitive effects of conglomerate mergers as negligible and speculative, and conglomerate mergers are substantially discounted as a source of competitive concern. In the EU, enforcers and policymakers are more likely to entertain arguments that the merger is likely to lead to a deterioration of the competitive structure of the market, and arguments that the merged firm will control the gateway to important inputs or outlets.

3. OTHER EFFECTS

Mergers may produce efficiencies; they may increase competition; and mergers between firms from different Member States may increase market integration. A merger may create synergies, as vertical mergers are especially likely to do. Also, they may yield economies of scope, as is often the case for mergers between firms that produce complementary products distributed through the same distribution channels. If the market is already competitive, market forces are likely to cause cost savings to be passed on to consumers. If the market is monopolistic or oligopolistic, the merging partners are more likely to retain most of the savings and possibly raise prices as well.

4. COMPETITIVENESS

It is possible for a merger to yield efficiencies and increase the merged firm's competitiveness in world markets and at the same time to lessen competition in the domestic market. Despite world competition, competition may be lessened in the domestic market if that market is concentrated and the merged firm has (for example) locational or cultural advantages or the home market maintains barriers to foreign competition. To address the situation in which these two effects (efficiency in global competition and power at home) coexist, the regulating nation must make a policy judgment as to which costs it wishes to avoid and which benefits it wishes to attain. US law holds that a merger that lessens competition in the United States is illegal regardless of the claim that the merger helps the firm compete in global markets. The claim that a merger that increases market power in the United States may enhance global competitiveness is regarded with skepticism and in fact is rarely substantiated. In contemplating this trade-off for the European Union, policymakers might (if the law allows them) want to consider the welfare of European consumers versus gains from greater economic strength abroad. Also of relevance is the speed with which remaining internal and European barriers may be dismantled, for without barriers to entry into the Union, European consumers are not likely to be subject to exploitation by producers of traded and non-perishable goods.

5. MARKETS, CONCENTRATION, BARRIERS, AND EFFICIENCIES

In the paragraphs above we assumed well-defined markets, high concentration therein, and significant barriers to entry. All three of these concepts require detailed, fact-specific evaluation. Market definition is the crucial first step in merger analysis, particularly where the concern is that merging competitors will coordinate their behavior and thus act like a cartel. Earlier we described the methodologies used to define markets, treating a market as an area in which, if there were a single seller, that firm would have market power; it would be able to raise the price of its product substantially and profitably for a significant period of time without fear that too many of its customers would shift to another product. All good substitutes are included in the market. Study the Notice on market definition, summarized in Chapter 22.

Volvo wished to acquire control of Scania. Both firms were important Swedish truck makers. Neither made light trucks, and Scania had only a small position in medium trucks. Both were active in Europe and the world in sales of heavy trucks. In heavy trucks, they were particularly strong in Sweden, and also in Norway, Finland and Ireland. The merged firm would have held 31% of all heavy trucks in the European Economic Area (EEA). DaimlerChrysler was the number two firm with about 20%. The merged firm would have held 90% of Swedish sales and 50% of Irish sales. The two merging firms were the closest competitors to one another. Servicing contracts generally were valid only in the area within which the vehicle was sold.

Was there a product market of heavy trucks (more than 16 tons)? Was the geographic market national? European? worldwide?

The Commission found a heavy truck market. Heavy trucks had a distinctive technical configuration. Engines and axels on heavy trucks were more sophisticated and more durable, which are qualities necessary for transporting heavy loads long distances. Heavy trucks are produced from different production lines than lighter trucks, and they appeal to different groups of customers. Therefore, competition from other (non-heavy) trucks was not a sufficiently good constraint to hold prices down and to incentivize responsive performance.

Moreover, the Commission found that the geographic markets were national. The Commission observed differences among nations in purchasing habits, technical requirements, price levels, and market shares. For example, prices were 10% to 20% higher in Sweden than in Denmark or Norway, and the price differentials did not lead to significant cross-border trade. Sales normally included a local service package that tended to attract local buyers to local sellers, and purchasing was normally done on a national basis.

Do you agree with the Commission's geographic market definition? Do you need more information? What would you like to know? See Volvo/Scania, Comp/M. 1672 (March 15, 2000) (prohibiting the merger).

After defining the relevant market, the analyst normally counts sales or capacity of each firm in the market and assigns a market share to each. There are two accepted frameworks for counting what is in the market. One is the snapshot method—to count what is actually there; i.e., to record who sells how much of the relevant product. The other is the method employed both by the 1997 Commission Notice and by the 2010 United States Federal Agency Merger Guidelines: to incorporate, as if already in the market, the goods that would quickly flow into the market if a hypothetical monopolist should try to raise price. The latter method incorporates the near potential competition. Whether or not near potential competition is incorporated directly into the market, it is a positive force that should be taken into account.

Next one must measure concentration. There are two recognized ways of stating the measurement of concentration. One is the use of n-firm concentration ratios;* e.g., the top two firms account for $x\%$ of the market; the top four firms account for $y\%$ of the market. The second is the use of the Herfindahl–Hirschman Index (HHI). To calculate the HHI, one lists each firm in the market and its market share, squares each market share, and then adds the squares of the shares. The sum of the squares is the HHI index number. Under each methodology, the key figures are those that represent the increase in concentration and the post-merger concentration. As a rule of thumb a market is likely to be considered not concentrated unless at least the three leading firms have 75% or more of the market, or the market has an HHI of 2000 or 2500 or more. The bare figures greatly overgeneralize facts, and the analysis should remain fact-specific.

---

* "N" represents an unspecified number.

Barriers and other hurdles to entry and expansion are then assessed. Even if a market is highly concentrated, the threat of entry may keep behavior competitive if entry at an efficient scale can be easily achieved in a year or two.

Efficiencies may be relevant in two quite different ways. First, if the merger produces cost savings and the market is competitive (the firms behave rivalrously), the cost savings may be passed on to consumers and the cost-saving strategies may be mimicked by competitors. These effects are directly relevant to whether competition is helped or hurt by the merger. Second, in some cases even where a merger lessens competitive rivalry, cost savings may neutralize the price effect facing consumers, or in any event the producer's gain may be greater than the consumers' loss. This latter aspect is an efficiency *defense*. Community law has not adopted an efficiency defense in this sense. Few jurisdictions have done so where the merger lessens competition and raises prices to consumers.

D. SUBSTANTIVE LAW UNDER THE MERGER REGULATION

1. MERGERS OF COMPETITORS THAT INCREASE DOMINANCE

In the first year of the Merger Regulation, the Commission cleared all notified mergers. Then, in the thirteenth month, the Commission examined the acquisition of de Havilland, the second largest commuter aircraft manufacturer in the world, by a joint venture owned by France and Italy that was the largest commuter aircraft manufacturer in the world. This is an early case. Bear in mind that in cases prior to 2000 the Commission took short-cuts and perhaps sometimes too quickly presumed that merging firms' advantages that would hurt their rivals were also anticompetitive.

We will explore in this chapter when advantages from mergers reflect efficiencies and are likely to benefit consumers, and when they are simply advantages of power likely to hurt consumers.

a. Note on *Aerospatiale–Alenia/De Havilland*

The United States aircraft manufacturer, Boeing, agreed to sell its Canadian aircraft subsidiary de Havilland to a joint venture of two European firms, Aerospatiale of France and Alenia e Selenia of Italy. The joint venture, ATR, was the world's leading producer of turboprop or commuter aircraft; de Havilland was the number two producer. British Aerospace and Fokker were the only other significant European competitors. Japanese firms were not in the market and not likely to enter "such a low-technology non-strategic market." Other possible potential competitors, notably firms from Indonesia and Eastern Europe, were either in financial difficulties or not capable of producing a product of sufficient quality for the world market.

The acquisition would lead to an increase in market shares for ATR in the world market for commuters between 40 to 59 seats from 46% to 63%. The nearest competitor (Fokker) would have 22%. ATR would increase its share of the overall worldwide commuter market of 20 to 70 seats from 30% to 50%. Saab, the nearest competitor, would have 19%. The new entity would account for half the world market and more than two and a half times the share of its nearest competitor. The Commission was concerned that the merger would confer advantages on ATR/de Havilland that would seriously jeopardize the survival of the remaining small competitors and would thus lead to a monopoly and prohibited the merger. Commission Decision 91/619, O.J. L 334/42 (1991). This was the Commission's first merger prohibition.

The Governments of France and Italy, owners of the would-be acquirer ATR, were highly critical of the Commission's decision. So, too, was Commissioner Bangemann, Commissioner for the Internal Market, who argued that the acquisition was good for Europe and that the Competition Directorate and the Commission had improperly failed to take account of the interests of Europe—as opposed to merely the interests of competition. They threatened to press for an amendment to the Merger Regulation to assure that the Commission could weigh industrial policy.

Look again at the Merger Regulation. (No relevant language has been changed since its adoption.) Can the Commission legally take industrial policy into account? On what basis, and if so how and to what extent? Is it good or bad policy to allow an industrial policy counterweight to a dominance-creating merger?

Meanwhile, Canada, home to de Havilland, had cleared the merger. Canada had strongly supported the merger because de Havilland was in financial difficulties and constantly needed subsidies—which Canada paid—to protect Canadian jobs. The acquisition by ATR had seemed a promising route to turn around the fortunes of de Havilland. When the acquisition was declared illegal, Canada sought another suitor for de Havilland. It identified Bombardier, which acquired de Havilland but required a continuing and even greater subsidy.

After *de Havilland,* potential for international controversy increased. The EU, the US, and numerous other jurisdictions have pre-merger notification and reporting systems that are triggered by a significant but relatively modest level of sales in the jurisdiction. By the early 1990s, the EU, the US, and other jurisdictions freely applied their laws to mergers of firms located abroad that had effects within their territories. Conflict was sure to follow.

b.   Boeing/McDonnell Douglas

In the same year that *de Havilland* was decided, the EU and the US anticipated the need for greater cooperation, and entered into the Cooperation Agreement of 1991. In this agreement, each party agreed to notify the other upon becoming aware "that their enforcement activities may affect important interests of the other party." "[W]ithin the framework of its own laws and to the extent compatible with its important interests," each agreed "to take into account the important interests of the other Party," and to seek "an appropriate accommodation of the competing interests." The agreement was invoked six years later, in connection with Boeing's plan to acquire McDonnell Douglas.

Boeing was the largest manufacturer of commercial jet aircraft in the world, accounting for about 64% of world market sales. Its only competitors were McDonnell Douglas, with about 5%, and Airbus Industrie, with about 30%. Airbus was a consortium of manufacturers in Britain, France, Germany and Spain. Those countries had helped to finance Airbus.

Boeing and McDonnell Douglas were US companies and had no production assets in Europe, although they regularly made sales there. McDonnell Douglas also produced military jets, and its technology portfolio included patents from research and development undertaken with US government financing. In the commercial jet market, McDonnell Douglas had failed to invest in important new-generation developments and was facing financial and competitive difficulties. Its market share was withering. Boeing, meanwhile, had recently concluded 20–year exclusive supply agreements with the three big American airlines that were the most important launch customers for new generation aircraft—Delta, American, and Continental. The exclusive supply agreements represented about 11% of all world purchases of big commercial jets.

Commercial jet airplanes are very complex and sell in the range of $32 million to $171 million each. An order from an airline is typically worth billions of dollars. In view of the fact that each sale to an airline is so significant, Airbus and Boeing were fierce competitors for sales around the world.

Boeing and McDonnell Douglas filed premerger notifications in the United States and in the European Union. European Competition Commissioner Karel Van Miert immediately expressed concerns about the merger and the exclusive agreements. On the US side, the Federal Trade Commission opened an investigation. The European Commission and the FTC made notifications to one another under the 1991 agreement, and the European and American officials shared their perspectives. They sharply disagreed on the analysis of anticompetitive effects.

Early on, politicians entered the fray, with Europeans declaring that the merger was blatantly anticompetitive and seriously harmful to competition and to Airbus, and Americans declaring that the merger was good for the American economy. Laura D'Andrea Tyson, former head of the Council of Economic Advisors, was quoted in the Washington Post (May 4, 1997, p. H6) as saying that this merger was good for America "even if consumers of airplane seats are somewhat worse off." European Competition Commissioner Van Miert threatened that, if the merger should be consummated without European approval, the European Commission would impose prohibitive fines on Boeing and might seize Boeing planes flying into the European Union.

On July 1, 1997, the US FTC issued a statement announcing the closing of its investigation.

MATTER OF BOEING COMPANY/McDONNELL DOUGLAS CORPORATION

US Federal Trade Commission, Statement
CCH Trade Reg. Rep. [1997–2001 Transfer Binder] ¶ 24,295 (July 1, 1997).

After an extensive and exhaustive investigation, the Federal Trade Commission has decided to close the investigation of The Boeing Company's proposed acquisition of McDonnell Douglas Corporation. For reasons discussed below, we have concluded that the acquisition would not substantially lessen competition or tend to create a monopoly in either defense or commercial aircraft markets.

[First, the Commission disclaims any attempt to support a national champion, which, it states, it has no power to do.]

On its face, the proposed merger appears to raise serious antitrust concerns. The transaction involves the acquisition by Boeing, a company that accounts for roughly 60% of the sales of large commercial aircraft, of a non-failing direct competitor in a market in which there is only one other significant rival, Airbus Industrie, and extremely high barriers to entry. The merger would also combine two firms in the U.S. defense industry that develop fighter aircraft and other defense products. Nevertheless, for reasons we will now discuss, we do not find that this merger will substantially lessen competition in any relevant market. * * *

The evidence collected during the staff investigation, including the virtually unanimous testimony of forty airlines that staff interviewed, revealed that McDonnell Douglas's commercial aircraft division, Douglas Aircraft Company, can no longer exert a competitive influence in the worldwide market for commercial aircraft. Over the past several decades, McDonnell Douglas has not invested at nearly the rate of its competitors in new product lines, production facilities, company infrastructure, or research and development. As a result, Douglas Aircraft's product line is not only very limited, but lacks the state of the art technology and performance characteristics that Boeing and Airbus have developed. Moreover, Douglas Aircraft's line of aircraft do not have common features such as cockpit design or engine type, and thus cannot generate valuable efficiencies in interchangeable spare parts and pilot training that an airline may obtain from a family of aircraft, such as Boeing's 737 family or Airbus's A–320 family.

In short, the staff investigation revealed that the failure to improve the technology and efficiency of its commercial aircraft products has lead to a deterioration of Douglas Aircraft's product line to the point that the vast majority of airlines will no longer consider purchasing Douglas aircraft and that the company is no longer in a position to influence significantly the competitive dynamics of the commercial aircraft market.

* * *

Procedurally, the closing of the investigation was not a judicial finding that the merger was lawful under US law. Unlike a decision in Europe, an initial US decision not to challenge a merger does not preclude subsequent challenge. It remained theoretically possible for the merger to be tested in the US courts; e.g. in a private action by Airbus or in a suit by a state attorney general, if not by the Federal Government. Nonetheless, immediately after the FTC closed its investigation, the US Government (the Clinton Administration) began to take an active political role in defending the merger to Europe. Key White House officials, including the President of the United States, argued to key European officials, including the President of the European Commission, that the merger was not anticompetitive, that it was important to the defense interests of the United States (because the military assets of McDonnell Douglas would be best preserved in the hands of Boeing), and to employment in the United States, and that the United States was "considering how to retaliate against Europe if it makes good on its threat to try and undermine the merger of [the] U.S. aerospace giants...." The Washington Post, July 17, 1997, p. C1. Reportedly, the administration officials were considering imposing tariffs on European planes, limiting flights between the United States and France (the most adamant objector to the merger), and filing a protest with the World Trade Organization in view of European subsidies to Airbus.

Meanwhile, Boeing was negotiating with the European Commission, and at the eleventh hour it agreed to conditions acceptable to the Commission. The conditions were not acceptable to France, however, which maintained that only a prohibition would cure the essential problems. On July 30, 1997, the European Commission issued its decision in *Boeing/McDonnell Douglas,* Case IV/M877, O.J. L 336/16 (Dec. 8, 1997).

The Commission concluded that Boeing held a dominant position and that the acquisition would strengthen its dominant position. It was expected to do so by, among other things, increasing Boeing's market share of large commercial aircraft from 64% to 70%, taking one of Boeing's only two remaining competitors off the market, further foreclosing the market, increasing Boeing's ability to entice airlines into exclusivity deals with it since it would be able to offer the advantages of a larger family of planes, and giving Boeing access to US government-funded R&D and intellectual property acquired from military and space functions of McDonnell Douglas. On the basis of significant commitments by Boeing, the Commission cleared the merger.

Boeing undertook, among other things: not to enforce its exclusivity rights under the agreements with American, Delta and Continental; not to enter into exclusive agreements until 2007; not to "use its privileged access to the existing fleet in service of DAC [Douglas Aircraft Corporation] aircraft in order to leverage its opportunities for persuading current DAC operators to purchase Boeing aircraft"; to license to competitors upon request all US-funded patents usable in the manufacture or sale of commercial jet aircraft; and not to leverage its relationship with suppliers to refuse to deal with Boeing's competitors or to grant preferential treatment to Boeing.

NOTES AND QUESTIONS

1. How did the merger create or strengthen a dominant position if Airbus would remain a good competitive check on Boeing, which the Commission assumed?

What is the significance of the fact that Boeing would gain a fuller line of jet planes, and that buyers (the airlines) saved money and time—including pilot training costs and replacement and maintenance costs—by dealing with one producer? What is the significance of the fact that Boeing would have access to technology that was funded by the US Government?

What is the significance of the facts that: McDonnell Douglas was "no longer a real force in the market for the sale of new aircraft on a stand-alone basis" (para. 58); no one but Boeing wanted to acquire McDonnell Douglas; and, if the merger was prohibited Boeing would probably absorb McDonnell Douglas' share anyway (all acknowledged in the decision)?

Did the Commission confuse unfairness to Airbus (or a competitive advantage over Airbus) with harm to competition and consumers? Did it want to protect Airbus from efficient competition from Boeing?

2. If the merger did strengthen Boeing's dominance, was France correct that a prohibition was the best remedy?

3. Comment on the statement by the US Federal Trade Commission. Was the national aspect argument irrelevant? Should it be?

Was *Boeing–McDonnell Douglas* purely a competition case? Who had the stronger side of the argument: the Europeans, most of whom seemed to believe that the US green light was industrial policy to promote Boeing as the US national champion? or the Americans, most of whom seemed to believe that the EU opposition was industrial policy to protect Airbus as the European champion? See E. Fox, Antitrust Regulation Across National Borders: The United States of Boeing versus the European Union of Airbus, 16 Brookings Review 30 (Winter 1998).

4. Many mergers today are new economy mergers, involving high technology and fast-changing markets. In the face of fast-changing markets, where the market leader today may be eclipsed tomorrow, enforcers are more reluctant to intervene. Where, however, the merged firm may become the "gatekeeper" to the market (control access), enforcement may occur.

In 2000, then Competition Commissioner Mario Monti described the Commission's approach to new economy mergers. He gave examples of two recent cases; one concerning a European market and the other a world-wide market:

> "First, the *Vodafone/Mannesmann* transaction raised competition concerns on the emerging market for pan-European seamless mobile telephony services. The merged company, with its extensive network, would be in a unique position vis-à-vis its competitors to roll out such services. In order to remedy these concerns, *Vodafone* accepted to give competitors non-discriminatory access to its integrated network. However, in order to ensure that competitors would not exclusively rely on the merged company, neglecting the development of their own infrastructure, the Commission limited the undertaking to three years. The Commission considered, inter alia, that in this period, UMTS licenses would be awarded in sufficient number to allow competitors to replicate the Vodafone network.

> Second, in June this year [2000], the Commission prohibited the merger between the two US communications companies *MCI World-Com* and *Sprint*. It found that the combination of the parties' extensive Internet networks and large customer bases would have allowed the merged entity to dictate terms and conditions for access to its Internet networks in a manner that could have had significant anticompetitive effects and hindered innovation. The Commission's investigation, which was carried out in close co-operation with the American antitrust authorities, showed that despite liberalisation, regional and local providers are still dependent on the largest top-level providers to gain full and effective access to the Internet."

Mario Monti, European Competition Policy for the 21st Century, Chapter 15 in 2000 Fordham Corp. L. Inst. (B. Hawk ed. 2001).

NOTES AND QUESTIONS

1. In the above examples, was the Commission wisely proactive or overly aggressive in intervening in new economy mergers?

2. Consider the parallel with Article 102 concerns when a single firm becomes a gatekeeper—but by internal growth and (perhaps) anticompetitive strategies? Look again at the *Microsoft* case in Chapter 22, the interoperability problem.

c. The Failing Firm Defense

FRANCE v. COMMISSION (KALI + SALZ)
Cases C–68/94, C–30/95, [1998] ECR I–1375, ECJ.

[After the fall of the Berlin wall and in view of the plan and then the reality of German unification, Germany established the Treuhandanstalt ("Treuhand"), a public institution entrusted with the task of restructuring the firms of the former German Democratic Republic. The Treuhand had title to, among others, Mitteldeutsche Kali AG ("MdK"), which held all of the GDR's operations in potash and rock salt. The business had escalating losses and was likely to close down if not taken over by a private firm. The only available, willing purchaser was Kali und Salz AG ("K+S"), a subsidiary of BASF chemicals group. It was proposed that K+S buy 51% of the stock of MdK, leaving 49% with the Truehand. This would result in K+S's achieving 98% of the German market for potash-salt-based products for agricultural use.

With respect to the German market:]

11   ... [A]pplying the theory of the 'failing company defence', [the Commission] reached the conclusion that the proposed concentration was not the cause of the strengthening of the dominant position of K+S on the German market.... [T]he conditions for the 'failing company defence' were met, namely that K+S's dominant position would be reinforced even in the absence of the merger, because MdK would withdraw from the market in the foreseeable future if it was not acquired by another undertaking and its market share would then accrue to K+S; it can be practically ruled out that an undertaking other than K+S would acquire all or a substantial part of MdK'.... The Commission further observed in point 95 that, given the severe structural weakness of the regions in East Germany which were affected by the proposed concentration, and the likelihood of serious consequences for them of the closure of MdK, the conclusion it had reached was also in line with the fundamental objective of strengthening the Community's economic and social cohesion, referred to in the 13th recital in the preamble to the Regulation.

[France sought annulment of the Commission's decision to allow the acquisition with respect to the German market without imposing any conditions. The Court of Justice rejected this claim.] * * *

111   It appears from point 71 of the contested decision that, in the Commission's opinion, a concentration which would normally be considered as leading to the creation or reinforcement of a dominant position on the part of the acquiring undertaking may be regarded as not being the cause of it if, even in the event of the concentration being prohibited, that undertaking would inevitably achieve or reinforce a dominant position. Point 71 goes on to state that, as a general matter, a concentration is not the cause of the deterioration of the competitive structure if it is clear that:

   — the acquired undertaking would in the near future be forced out of the market if not taken over by another undertaking,

   — the acquiring undertaking would gain the market share of the acquired undertaking if it were forced out of the market,

   — there is no less anticompetitive alternative purchase. * * *

[The Commission was entitled to conclude that there was an "absence of a causal link between the concentration and the deterioration of the competitive structure of the German market...." In this case "it is not possible ... to attach any condition whatever to [the] declaration of the concentration's compatibility." para. 124.]

NOTES AND QUESTIONS

1. US caselaw, to which the Court referred, also contains a failing firm defense. See *Citizen Publishing Co. v. United States*, 394 U.S. 131, 89 S.Ct. 927, 22 L.Ed.2d 148 (1969).

2. Note the Commission's industrial policy argument, in paragraph 11: Saving MdK will save jobs in the former East Germany and strengthen economic and social cohesion. Is this argument admissible under the Merger Regulation? Would it have saved the merger if there were a causal link between the concentration and the entrenchment of monopoly power? Should it have? Look again at the statement referenced. Was it a part of the ratio decidendi of the judgment, or just an observation of a welcome by-product?

In the United States, saving jobs and community formed a major part of the reason for creating the failing firm defense. See International Shoe Co. v. FTC, 280 U.S. 291, 302, 50 S.Ct. 89, 74 L.Ed. 431 (1930). However, the defense, when recognized by the US agencies, is treated on economic grounds much like the causal link analysis.

3. Why wasn't the causal link between the concentration and the harm to competition similarly lacking in *Boeing,* given the Commission's concessions that: "[I]t has to be concluded that DAC is today no longer a real force in the market on a stand-alone basis." (para. 59) "[D]ue to the deterioration of the situation of DAC ..., only Boeing is prepared to take over MDC's commercial aircraft business." (para. 60).

2. MERGERS OF COMPETITORS THAT FACILITATE COORDINATED BEHAVIOR (COLLECTIVE DOMINANCE)

As we have noted, the original text of the Merger Regulation prohibited *dominance* that may impede effective competition. The Commission soon had to confront the limits of the word "dominance." Could the word be stretched to cover duopoly and oligopoly?

The Court of Justice responded to the dilemma. In *Kali und Salz* the court held that the 1989 Merger Regulation caught mergers that create or strengthen a "collective dominant position" likely to have a significant effect on competition. It stated that collective dominance might be established if the firms remaining on the market have "close commercial links" such as participation in export cartels to third countries, joint ventures, and buyer/supplier relationships. Cases C–68194, 30195, [1998] ECR I–1375.

Gencor/Lonrho was decided under the 1989 Merger Regulation in the wake of the caselaw language of "links" that justified finding dominance in an oligopolistic market. We present it here not for the semantic challenge but for the substantive question: By what theory was this merger anticompetitive in view of the fact that other players remained on the market? We look at *Gencor/Lonrho* and then *Airtours,* a case that ushered in modern analysis of how a merger of firms in an oligopoly may harm competition by cooperative effects.

GENCOR LTD. v. COMMISSION

Case T–102/96, [1999] ECR II–753, General Court.

[Two South African platinum and rhodium mining companies merged, combining Implats, a subsidiary of Gencor, having about 17% of world market sales, and LPD (a subsidiary of the UK firm, Lonrho), having about 15% of sales. The combined firm would have had 32% of sales. The leading firm, Anglo American ("Amplats"), had about 43% of sales. Together the two resulting South African firms would have held about 89% of world reserves. Russia, through its firm Almaz, had a 22% share of sales and 10% of reserves. North American producers accounted for 5% of sales and had 1% reserves; and recycling firms accounted for 6% of sales. Russia was expected to dispose of its stocks in two years.

The Commission found that the concentration would create a dominant duopoly and was therefore incompatible with the common market, and it prohibited the concentration. Gencor contested the decision. The General Court analyzed as follows the evidence regarding whether the merger did indeed create a market structure in which the resulting two leading firms would gain collective dominance.]

222   ... [G]iven the similarity in the market shares, shares of world reserves and cost structures of the undertakings at issue, the Commission was entitled to conclude that, following the concentration, the interests of Amplats and Implats/LPD with regard to the development of the market would have coincided to a higher degree and that this alignment of interests would have increased the likelihood of anticompetitive parallel behaviour, for example restrictions of output.
* * *

Characteristics of the market

[The Commission was entitled to find high transparency of price, production, sales, reserves, and new investment; and that given slow growth in demand, new competitors would not be encouraged to enter the market and existing competitors would not be encouraged to adopt aggressive strategies to capture additional demand.]

248   The applicant points out in that regard that the South African Government's letter of 19 April 1996 indicates that world reserves outside South Africa and Zimbabwe could theoretically satisfy world demand for 20 years. * * *

252   As regards the applicant's argument that the 37% of the market accounted for by the marginal sources of supply and other influences would have curbed price increases, the Commission points out that the South African producers alone accounted for 63% of the market in 1995, a figure that was to increase significantly (to a level approaching 80%) when, from 1997, Russia would no longer be selling from its stocks. Furthermore, a significant proportion of the marginal competition was hypothetical and could not in any event have exerted any pressure on the market for some years. * * *

254   The applicant's view has no factual basis. . . . * * *

264   The applicant claims that the Commission did not take account of the case-law of the General Court ('*Flat Glass*' case) which, in the context of Article [102] of the Treaty, requires for findings of collective dominance that there be structural links between the two undertakings, for example through a technological lead by agreements or licences, which give them the power to behave independently of their competitors, of their customers and, ultimately, of consumers. In the instant case, the Commission has failed to demonstrate the existence of structural links or to prove that the merged entity and Amplats intended to behave as if they constituted a single dominant entity. . . .
       * * *

The Court

273   In its judgment in the *Flat Glass* case, the Court referred to links of a structural nature only by way of example and did not lay down that such links must exist in order for a finding of collective dominance to be made. * * *

276   Furthermore, there is no reason whatsoever in legal or economic terms to exclude from the notion of economic links the relationship of interdependence existing between the parties to a tight oligopoly within which, in a market with the appropriate characteristics, in particular in terms of market concentration, transparency and product homogeneity, those parties are in a position to anticipate one another's behaviour and are therefore strongly encouraged to align their conduct in the market, in particular in such a way as to maximise their joint profits by restricting production with a view to increasing prices. In such a context, each trader is aware that highly competitive action on its part designed to increase its market share (for example a price cut) would provoke identical action by the others, so that it would derive no benefit from its initiative. All the traders would thus be affected by the reduction in price levels.

277   That conclusion is all the more pertinent with regard to the control of concentrations, whose objective is to prevent anti-competitive market structures from arising or being strengthened. Those structures may result from the existence of economic links in the strict sense argued by the applicant or from market structures of an oligopolistic kind

where each undertaking may become aware of common interests and, in particular, cause prices to increase without having to enter into an agreement or resort to a concerted practice. * * *

279 The Commission was entitled to conclude, relying on the envisaged alteration in the structure of the market and on the similarity of the costs of Amplats and Implats/LPD, that the proposed transaction would create a collective dominant position and lead in actual fact to a duopoly constituted by those two undertakings. * * *

NOTES AND QUESTIONS

1. Gencor argued (and the South African authorities maintained) that the combination of Implats and LPD would create a more efficient number two firm that could and would better compete against the dominant firm, Amplats. Who was probably correct—Gencor and South Africa, or the European Commission? What are the most important points on each side?

2. Did the Commission have to prove that Amplats and the merged firm would collude, at least tacitly, and thereby behave like *one* dominant firm? Or was it enough for the Commission to prove that the firms would behave interdependently, taking into account the probable strategies of one another and estimating if and when they would be jointly served by higher prices?

3. What is the significance of the Russian stocks? Why wouldn't Implats/LPD raise prices immediately and expect Amplats and Almaz to follow or at least not increase their output?

4. South Africa argued that it was not necessary to stop the merger; that if the merger did create conditions that made collaborative behavior more likely, and if the merger did eventually produce such behavior, it would (and authorities should) intervene at that point to stop the behavior. Was this a plausible tack?

The theory of collective dominance was tested further in *Airtours/First Choice,* involving a merger from four to three firms in the short haul holiday (air and hotel) package market. The post-merger shares were 32% for Airtours/First Choice, 27% for Thomson, and 20% for Thomas Cook. The Commission found that the market was characterized by stagnant demand, a low level of innovation, low price sensitivity, and similar cost structures of the three market leaders, with commercial links, transparency, and interdependence among them. It found that the merger would have significantly reduced fringe firms' ability to provide charter airline seats, thereby reducing the competitive threat of mavericks. Stating that collective dominance is "not just about tacit collusion," the Commission found that the resulting three leading firms would hold a collective dominant position after the merger, and it prohibited the merger.

AIRTOURS v. COMMISSION

Case T–342/99, [2002] ECR II–2585, General Court.

[Airtours, a British firm operating in the UK, sold package holidays for short-haul destinations such as Spain, Greece and Turkey. Four significant firms occupied the UK market for short-haul foreign package holidays; namely: Thomson—27%, Thomas Cook—20%, Airtours—21%, and First Choice—11%. Thus, the four firms occupied 79% of the market. All four operated charter airlines and travel agencies as well as tour operations. Airtours sought to take over First Choice. The takeover would have made Airtours number one with 32% of the market.

Many small tour operators occupied the market. In general they did not own charter airlines or travel agencies. The three largest of these held between 1.7% and 2.9% of the market. Several hundred accounted for less than 1% each.

Agreeing with a 1997 UK Monopolies and Mergers Commission Report, the Commission observed that the market had been competitive. It determined, however, that increased concentration and vertical integration had occurred since the MMC Report; that Airtours' takeover of First Choice would further increase the transparency of the market and the interdependence of the big firms; and that the remaining three big players would mutually restrict capacity, knowing that, by doing so, they would all be better off and that if any one of the three decided not to go along there would be oversupply and serious financial consequences for all. The Commission determined further that the smaller operators, already marginalized, would be further marginalized, since they would lose First Choice as a supplier of airline seats and as a potential distribution channel; and in any event the small operators would not have the ability to offset capacity reductions by the big three. As a result, capacity would be tightened and prices would rise, thus creating a collective dominant position impeding competition in violation of the Merger Regulation.

Airtours brought suit in the General Court for annulment of the Commission's decision.]

58   Where, for the purposes of applying Regulation No 4064/89, the Commission examines a possible collective dominant position, it must ascertain whether the concentration would have the direct and immediate effect of creating or strengthening a position of that kind, which is such as significantly and lastingly to impede competition in the relevant market. If there is no substantial alteration to competition as it stands, the merger must be approved.

59   It is apparent from the case law that 'in the case of an alleged collective dominant position, the Commission is ... obliged to assess, using a prospective analysis of the reference market, whether the concentration which has been referred to it leads to a situation in which effective competition in the relevant market is significantly impeded by the undertakings involved in the concentration and one or more other undertakings which together, in particular because of factors giving rise to a connection between them, are able to adopt a common policy on the market and act to a considerable extent independently of their competitors, their customers, and also of consumers.' (citing Kali & Salz and Gencor). * * *

61 A collective dominant position significantly impeding effective competition in the common market or a substantial part of it may thus arise as the result of a concentration where, in view of the actual characteristics of the relevant market and of the alteration in its structure that the transaction would entail, the latter would make each member of the dominant oligopoly, as it becomes aware of common interests, consider it possible, economically rational, and hence preferable, to adopt on a lasting basis a common policy on the market with the aim of selling at above competitive prices, without having to enter into an agreement or resort to a concerted practice within the meaning of Article [101] and without any actual or potential competitors, let alone customers or consumers, being able to react effectively.

62 As the applicant has argued and as the Commission has accepted in its pleadings, three conditions are necessary for a finding of collective dominance as defined:

— first, each member of the dominant oligopoly must have the ability to know how the other members are behaving in order to monitor whether or not they are adopting the common policy. As the Commission specifically acknowledges, it is not enough for each member of the dominant oligopoly to be aware that interdependent market conduct is profitable for all of them but each member must also have a means of knowing whether the other operators are adopting the same strategy and whether they are maintaining it. There must, therefore, be sufficient market transparency for all members of the dominant oligopoly to be aware, sufficiently precisely and quickly, of the way in which the other members' market conduct is evolving;

— second, the situation of tacit coordination must be sustainable over time, that is to say, there must be an incentive not to depart from the common policy on the market. As the Commission observes, it is only if all the members of the dominant oligopoly maintain the parallel conduct that all can benefit. The notion of retaliation in respect of conduct deviating from the common policy is thus inherent in this condition. In this instance, the parties concur that, for a situation of collective dominance to be viable, there must be adequate deterrents to ensure that there is a long-term incentive in not departing from the common policy, which means that each member of the dominant oligopoly must be aware that highly competitive action on its part designed to increase its market share would provoke identical action by the others, so that it would derive no benefit from its initiative;

— third, to prove the existence of a collective dominant position to the requisite legal standard, the Commission must also establish that the foreseeable reaction of current and future competitors, as well as of consumers, would not jeopardise the results expected from the common policy.

63   ... [W]here the Commission takes the view that a merger should be prohibited because it will create a situation of collective dominance, it is incumbent upon it to produce convincing evidence thereof. The evidence must concern, in particular, factors playing a significant role in the assessment of whether a situation of collective dominance exists, such as, for example, the lack of effective competition between the operators alleged to be members of the dominant oligopoly and the weakness of any competitive pressure that might be exerted by other operators.

64   Furthermore, the basic provisions of Regulation No 4064/89, in particular Article 2 thereof, confer on the Commission a certain discretion, especially with respect to assessments of an economic nature, and, consequently, when the exercise of that discretion, which is essential for defining the rules on concentrations, is under review, the Community judicature must take account of the discretionary margin implicit in the provisions of an economic nature which form part of the rules on concentrations. * * *

[Airtours claimed that the Commission 1) had failed to prove that the market had become noncompetitive, and 2) that it had failed to prove that the three remaining large tour operators would have an incentive to cease competing with each other. 3) In any event, cooperating industry members would have no means to discipline a cheating (competitive) member; and 4) in any event, smaller operators, new entrants, and consumers could and would react to any capacity restrictions by, in the case of suppliers, adding capacity, and in the case of consumers, shifting their business to the smaller operators.

The Court accepted each of Airtours' claims. For example (after determining that the premerger market was competitive and that an increased level of vertical integration after the MMC Report was procompetitive because it increased efficiency and limited interdependence of the large tour operators):]

120   It follows from the foregoing that the Commission made errors of assessment in its analysis of competition obtaining in the relevant market prior to the notification. First, it did not provide adequate evidence in support of its finding that there was already a tendency in the industry to collective dominance and, hence, to restriction of competition, particularly as regards capacity setting. Second, it did not take into account, as it should have done, the fact that the main tour operators' market shares have been volatile in the past and that such volatility is evidence that the market was competitive. * * *

[The market was not transparent.]

165   ... [I]t is necessary to mention the practical difficulties, to which the applicant has drawn attention, which make it very difficult to find out what capacity is projected by each of the other large tour operators during the planning period, inasmuch as their decisions on total capacity for a given season consolidate a whole range of individual decisions, taken on a resort-by-resort and flight-by-flight basis and varying from one season to the next.

166 The applicant maintains, without challenge from the Commission, that it serves around 50 destinations from 21 United Kingdom airports, which represents more than 1000 permutations, and that it varies those permutations appreciably from one season to the next. Thus, for the summer of 1999, Airtours increased its capacity to Fuerteventura by 19%, although it reduced its departures to that destination from Manchester by 13%, while departures from Cardiff were increased by 42%. Similarly, Airtours' capacity to Minorca was reduced by 9%, with departures to that destination from Manchester being reduced by 33% and departures from Scottish airports being increased by 25%. By way of example, within the '3–star/self-catering category,' which according to the Decision accounts for the large majority of short-haul package holidays, there are differences as to the airport and the departure date, the length of the stay and the resort. It should be observed in this respect that the argument that little differentiation is made for the air component does not alter the fact that decisions relating to airline capacity are taken airport by airport and flight by flight.

167 So, contrary to the Commission's contention, capacity decisions do not involve merely increasing or reducing overall capacity, without taking account of the differences between the various categories of package holidays, which are differentiated by destination, departure date, departure airport, aircraft model, type and quality of accommodation, length of stay and, finally, price. To be able to develop their package holidays, tour operators must take into account a series of variables, such as the availability of accommodation at the various destinations and the availability of airline seats on various dates and at different times of the year. As the applicant has argued, capacity decisions are necessarily taken on a 'micro' level. * * *

169 It follows that, on the face of it, the complexity of the capacity planning procedure, the development of the product and its marketing is a major obstacle to any attempt at tacit coordination. In a market in which demand is on the whole increasing, but is volatile from one year to the next, an integrated tour operator will have difficulty in interpreting accurately capacity decisions taken by the other operators concerning holidays to be taken a year and a half later.

170 However, despite the fact that each tour operator takes capacity decisions on the basis of a miscellaneous set of factors, it is nevertheless necessary to consider whether, in practice, at the time when total capacity is set, each member of the oligopoly can know 'the overall level of capacity' (number of holidays) offered by the individual integrated tour operators.

171   The Commission alleges ... that 'each of the four integrated operators is thus well able to monitor the total amount of holidays offered by each of the others [during the planning period] and that changes made by each individual operator at that stage may be identified by the other major tour operators as a result of their dealings with hotels or their discussions about seat requirements and availability, the purpose of which is to obtain or supply capacity or to negotiate swaps of seats and slots.'

172   However, the Commission fails to prove those allegations. * * *

181   It follows from the foregoing that the Commission's examination of competition obtaining between the main tour operators at the time of the notification was inadequate, and that the Commission made errors of assessment concerning the development and predictability of demand, demand volatility and the degree of market transparency, and that it wrongly concluded that those factors were, in this instance, conducive to the creation of a collective dominant position. * * *

[The Court found also that the firms had no effective retaliatory strategies that they could apply in the event of cheating, and, moreover, that the hundreds of small operators could respond effectively to a reduction of capacity by the larger ones. It annulled the decision.]

NOTES AND QUESTIONS

1. In view of *Airtours,* what must the Commission prove to establish a case of collective dominance?

2. What level of scrutiny did the Court give to the Commission's findings of mixed basic and economic facts—such as whether the market was competitive, and whether the smaller firms would be marginalized? Why were the Commissions' findings not within the margin of appreciation to which the Commission is normally entitled?

3. In *Sony/BMG (Impala)* v. Commission, Case T–464/04, [2006] ECR II–2289, the General Court annulled a Commission decision *authorizing* a joint venture between Sony and Bertlesmann that combined their recorded music activities. In its Statement of Objections, the Commission had concluded that the joint venture would probably produce collective dominance effects, in view of high concentration and the high degree of transparency in the market. On further investigation, the Commission concluded that the market was not transparent and that collective dominance effects were not likely to result.

Annulling the clearance, the General Court stated that the Commission had not sufficiently explained the reversal of its position since it issued the Statement of Objections. It thought that collective dominance effects were plausible. It disagreed that promotional discounting of music undermined the transparency necessary for coordinated effects, and it stated that retaliatory measures against cheaters appeared to be available. Thus, the General Court ruled, the Commission had committed manifest errors of assessment. On appeal, however, the Court of Justice set aside the judgment. The Court of

Justice noted that nothing in the Merger Regulation "imposes different standards of proof in relation to decisions approving a concentration, on the one hand, and decisions prohibiting a concentration, on the other" (para. 46), thus rejecting the Commission's argument that its burden was lighter in clearing than in prohibiting a merger. On the substance, the Court of Justice held that the General Court had misconstrued the principles for analysis concerning market transparency in the context of collective dominance. (para. 133)

The Court summarized and clarified the elements of proof of collective dominance effects (now "coordinated effects") as follows.

BERTELSMANN AG v. COMMISSION
(*Impala*)

Case C–413/06 P, [2008] ECR I–4951, ECJ.

* * *

120   In the case of an alleged creation or strengthening of a collective dominant position, the Commission is obliged to assess, using a prospective analysis of the reference market, whether the concentration which has been referred to it will lead to a situation in which effective competition in the relevant market is significantly impeded by the undertakings which are parties to the concentration and one or more other undertakings which together, in particular because of correlative factors which exist between them, are able to adopt a common policy on the market (see *Kali & Salz)* in order to profit from a situation of collective economic strength, without actual or potential competitors, let alone customers or consumers, being able to react effectively.

121   Such correlative factors include, in particular, the relationship of interdependence existing between the parties to a tight oligopoly within which, on a market with the appropriate characteristics, in particular in terms of market concentration, transparency and product homogeneity, those parties are in a position to anticipate one another's behaviour and are therefore strongly encouraged to align their conduct on the market in such a way as to maximise their joint profits by increasing prices, reducing output, the choice or quality of goods and services, diminishing innovation or otherwise influencing parameters of competition. In such a context, each operator is aware that highly competitive action on its part would provoke a reaction on the part of the others, so that it would derive no benefit from its initiative.

122   A collective dominant position significantly impeding effective competition in the common market or a substantial part of it may thus arise as the result of a concentration where, in view of the actual characteristics of the relevant market and of the alteration to those characteristics that the concentration would entail, the latter would make each member of the oligopoly in question, as it becomes aware

of common interests, consider it possible, economically rational, and hence preferable, to adopt on a lasting basis a common policy on the market with the aim of selling at above competitive prices, without having to enter into an agreement or resort to a concerted practice within the meaning of Article 101 and without any actual or potential competitors, let alone customers or consumers, being able to react effectively.

123   Such tacit coordination is more likely to emerge if competitors can easily arrive at a common perception as to how the coordination should work, and, in particular, of the parameters that lend themselves to being a focal point of the proposed coordination. Unless they can form a shared tacit understanding of the terms of the coordination, competitors might resort to practices that are prohibited by Article [101] in order to be able to adopt a common policy on the market. Moreover, having regard to the temptation which may exist for each participant in a tacit coordination to depart from it in order to increase its short-term profit, it is necessary to determine whether such coordination is sustainable. In that regard, the coordinating undertakings must be able to monitor to a sufficient degree whether the terms of the coordination are being adhered to. There must therefore be sufficient market transparency for each undertaking concerned to be aware, sufficiently precisely and quickly, of the way in which the market conduct of each of the other participants in the coordination is evolving. Furthermore, discipline requires that there be some form of credible deterrent mechanism that can come into play if deviation is detected. In addition, the reactions of outsiders, such as current or future competitors, and also the reactions of customers, should not be such as to jeopardise the results expected from the coordination. * * *

131   It is true that the [General Court] referred to the possibility of a 'known set of rules' governing the grant of discounts by the majors. However—as the appellants rightly submit in the context of the second specific criticism mentioned in paragraph 113 of this judgment, which relates to the question whether certain discount variations established by the Commission in the contested decision were liable to call into question the possibility of adequate monitoring of mutual compliance with the terms of any tacit coordination there may have been—the [General Court] was content to rely on unsupported assertions relating to a hypothetical industry professional. [T]he [General Court] itself acknowledged that Impala, the applicant before that court, 'admittedly did not explain precisely what those various rules governing the grant of campaign discounts are'.

132   It must be pointed out in that regard that Impala represents undertakings which, even if they are not members of the oligopoly formed by the majors, are active on the same markets. In those circumstances, it is clear that the [General Court] disregarded the fact that

the burden of proof was on Impala in relation to the purported qualities of such a hypothetical 'industry professional'.

3. MERGERS THAT CREATE NON–COORDINATED EFFECTS

On revising the Merger Regulation in 2004, the Commission was aware of a class of anticompetitive mergers of competitors that would not fall into the language of dominance or collective dominance. There was a gap. This was a major reason for the revision.

For example, if two firms merge that are major competitors to one another, and each is the second choice of consumers who prefer the other, their combination may allow the merged firm to raise prices profitably even if other competitors on the market do not follow suit. The United States calls this phenomenon "unilateral effects," because the merged firm can get power acting on its own. The EU calls the phenomenon "non-coordinated effects," recognizing that the effect may be not only unilateral. The price rise might trigger a price adjustment upwards of the remaining firms on the market. Thus, recital 25 says:

(25) In view of the consequences that concentrations in oligopolistic market structures may have, it is all the more necessary to maintain effective competition in such markets. Many oligopolistic markets exhibit a healthy degree of competition. However, under certain circumstances, concentrations involving the elimination of important competitive constraints that the merging parties had exerted upon each other, as well as a reduction of competitive pressure on the remaining competitors, may, even in the absence of a likelihood of coordination between the members of the oligopoly, result in a significant impediment to effective competition. The Community courts have, however, not to date expressly interpreted Regulation (EEC) No 4064/89 as requiring concentrations giving rise to such non-coordinated effects to be declared incompatible with the common market. Therefore, in the interests of legal certainty, it should be made clear that this Regulation permits effective control of all such concentrations by providing that any concentration which would significantly impede effective competition, in the common market or in a substantial part of it, should be declared incompatible with the common market. The notion of 'significant impediment to effective competition' in Article 2(2) and (3) should be interpreted as extending, beyond the concept of dominance, only to the anti-competitive effects of a concentration resulting from the non-coordinated behaviour of undertakings which would not have a dominant position on the market concerned.

4.　MERGERS OTHER THAN MERGERS OF COMPETITORS

a.　Leverage and Foreclosure Effects

Mergers of firms that are not competitors (non-horizontal mergers) may be divided into two categories: vertical mergers and conglomerate mergers. Vertical mergers are mergers of firms in the buyer-supplier line. Conglomerate mergers are all mergers other than horizontal or conglomerate. For vertical mergers, we may worry that, by reason of the merger, unintegrated rivals will be foreclosed from an important source of supply or outlet, barriers to entry may rise, upping the stakes and thus likelihood of entry, and perhaps so insulating the market that the risk of oligopolistic coordination or of dominance is increased. Conglomerate mergers may entail the same foreclosure concerns when buyers of one partner's product also need the other partner's product, leading to a tying or bundling effect and steering business away from unintegrated rivals because of leverage, not merits.

In early days of enforcement of the Merger Regulation, the Commission was worried about foreclosure; it was concerned that large firms, especially multi-product firms, would get unfair advantages over their rivals and distort the playing field. *Boeing/McDonnell Douglas* is an example. When consumers, not competitors, later became the focus of inquiry, the Commission—under prodding by the General Court, took seriously two important points: 1) a vertical or conglomerate merger may bring benefits to consumers, 2) it takes more than a loose foreclosure story (e.g., that life is more difficult for rivals) to harm competitors in a way that will harm market competition. Indeed, a merger that integrates complementary products or functions may benefit consumers in ways that rivals are incentivized to emulate, and the competitive pressure may cause rivals to find ways to outcompete the integrating firm, and 3) vertical and conglomerate mergers do not by their *nature* harm competition, as offending horizontal mergers do. They do not take a competitor off the market. They do not create a structure that may predictably produce a price rise even in the absence of an agreement. It takes *action* to foreclose rivals, such as forcing customers to accept a product they would not otherwise buy from that firm. If that conduct is itself illegal, is the law likely to deter the conduct, so that the whole merger need not be prohibited simply because the conduct might occur?

These aspects lurked in *Tetra Laval/Sidel*, and later in *GE/Honeywell*.

TETRA LAVAL BV v. COMMISSION
(*Tetra/Sidel*)

Cases C–12/03 P and C–13/03 P, [2005] ECR I–1113, ECJ.

[Tetra Laval, a French firm and the world leader in the market for packaging milk, juice and other liquids in cartons, acquired the stock of its French rival Sidel, a leading producer of plastic containers for liquids by polyethylene terephthalate equipment (PET). The Commission declared the acquisition incompatible with the common market principally on grounds that Tetra Laval would use its dominance in the asceptic carton market to leverage itself into dominance in the PET packaging equipment market and that removing Sidel as a potential competitor to Tetra would strengthen Tetra's dominant position on the carton packaging markets.

The Commission ordered the parties to undo the merger. The parties sought an annulment. The General Court annulled the prohibition for lack of sufficient evidence and the Court of Justice upheld the General Court].

39 Whilst the Court recognises that the Commission has a margin of discretion with regard to economic matters, that does not mean that the Community Courts must refrain from reviewing the Commission's interpretation of information of an economic nature. Not only must the Community Courts, inter alia, establish whether the evidence relied on is factually accurate, reliable and consistent but also whether that evidence contains all the information which must be taken into account in order to assess a complex situation and whether it is capable of substantiating the conclusions drawn from it. Such a review is all the more necessary in the case of a prospective analysis required when examining a planned merger with conglomerate effect. * * *

44 The analysis of a 'conglomerate-type' concentration is a prospective analysis in which, first, the consideration of a lengthy period of time in the future and, secondly, the leveraging necessary to give rise to a significant impediment to effective competition mean that the chains of cause and effect are dimly discernible, uncertain and difficult to establish. That being so, the quality of the evidence produced by the Commission in order to establish that it is necessary to adopt a decision declaring the concentration incompatible with the common market is particularly important, since that evidence must support the Commission's conclusion that, if such a decision were not adopted, the economic development envisaged by it would be plausible.

45 It follows from those various factors that the [General Court] did not err in law when it set out the tests to be applied in the exercise of its power of judicial review or when it specified the quality of the evidence which the Commission is required to produce in order to demonstrate that the requirements of Article 2(3) of the Regulation are satisfied. * * *

75 However, it would run counter to the Regulation's purpose of prevention to require the Commission, as [the General Court held], to examine, for each proposed merger, the extent to which the incentives to adopt anticompetitive conduct would be reduced, or even eliminated, as a result of the unlawfulness of the conduct in question, the likelihood of its detection, the action taken by the competent authorities, both at Community and national level, and the financial penalties which could ensue. * * *

[78] Consequently, the [General Court] erred in law in rejecting the Commission's conclusions as to the adoption by the merged entity of anti-competitive conduct capable of resulting in leveraging on the sole ground that the Commission had, when assessing the likelihood that such conduct might be adopted, failed to take account of the unlawfulness of that conduct and, consequently, of the likelihood of its detection, of action by the competent authorities, both at Community and national level, and of the financial penalties which might ensue.... *　*　*

Nᴏᴛᴇs ᴀɴᴅ Qᴜᴇsᴛɪᴏɴs

1. Why are "the chains of cause and effect" so "dimly discernible, uncertain and difficult to establish" in conglomerate mergers as opposed to mergers of competitors? Consider the charge: Tetra, dominant in packaging liquids in aseptic cartons, a declining segment, will increase its dominance by acquiring Sidel, dominant in packaging liquids in stretch blown plastic bottles, a growing segment, and vice versa. How would the acquisition increase dominance? Would it happen naturally or would Tetra/Sidel have to *do* something to leverage power from one market (assuming it is a market) to the other? What would it have to do? On what would the likelihood of its strategy and the success of its strategy depend? How is Article 102 relevant?

2. A few years before the Court judgment in *Tetra,* General Electric Company, the world's largest producer of jet engines, announced that it planned to acquire Honeywell International, a leading firm in the production of navigating equipment and other jet aircraft components, as well as a producer of jet engines. Both firms were US companies, with assets also in Europe and elsewhere, doing business world-wide. GE first notified the planned merger to the US authorities. The Antitrust Division vetted the merger, found anticompetitive horizontal overlaps in engine production, and cleared the merger after requiring a spin off of the offending assets. After the spin off, it regarded the merger as almost entirely conglomerate. The United States generally has no antitrust concerns with conglomerate mergers.

3. GE then sought clearance by the European Commission. The Commission identified a number of vertical and conglomerate (leveraging and foreclosure) concerns and a horizontal concern regarding jet engine overlap that was not worrisome to the US authority. It analyzed the problems, found anticompetitive effects (e.g., that GE would prevail upon its engine customers to use Honeywell avionics in their aircraft, lowering prices for the bundle, marginalizing Honeywell's rivals, and later raising prices), and prohibited the merger. The prohibition evoked the ire of many Americans, including antitrust officials, the Secretary of the Treasury, and Senators.

GE sought an annulment of the Commission decision, and its case came to the General Court after the judgment in *Tetra Laval,* which had set the standard of review and the standard of proof for vertical and conglomerate effects. The General Court upheld the Commission decision prohibiting the GE/Honeywell merger, but only on grounds of a horizontal overlap of engines.

As for the conglomerate grounds, the Court engaged in an extensive analysis of the facts and held that the Commission could not conclude from the facts that a merged GE/Honeywell was likely to engage in bundling. Its customers could not be pressured to accept a bundle they did not want. *General Electric v. Commission (GE/Honeywell)*, Case T–210/01, [2005] ECR II–5575, General Court.

4. For the backstory of the star-crossed GE/Honeywell merger, see Eleanor Fox, *GE/Honeywell:* The U.S. Merger that Europe Stopped—A Story of the Politics of Convergence, Chapter 12 in ANTITRUST STORIES (Eleanor Fox and Daniel Crane, eds., Foundation 2007).

5. Regarding jet engine starters: GE was dominant in jet engines, Honeywell held more than 50% of the market for engine starters, and barriers to entry into engine starters were high. The Commission thought the merger would harm competition by giving GE incentives to manipulate the starter supply. The Court reversed this holding because the Commission had failed to consider the possible deterrent effect of Article 102.

Should it have been enough, for proof of a violation, that the merged firm controlled an input essential to its rivals? Would you expect the merged firm to deny engine starters to its competitors? Would you expect the merged firm to manipulate the supply of this necessary ingredient in subtle and not always detectable ways?

6. Suppose the Commission had proved that the merged firm would probably have engaged in bundling. Would the Court have agreed that this was an anticompetitive practice? See *British Airways* and other Article 102 case law, *supra*. Would US authorities and courts have so agreed? The US authorities that cleared the GE/Honeywell merger argued that if the merged firm bundled Honeywell's avionics products with GE's engines, it would save costs of double marginalization and the bundle would be efficient.

7. Energias de Portugal (EDP) and Gas de Portugal (GDP) proposed to merge. EDP was dominant on all electricity markets in Portugal. GDP was dominant on most gas markets in Portugal, and was the monopoly supplier of gas to electricity producers, which used gas to power their new plants. GDP was the most likely important potential competitor in electricity. EDP was a major customer of GDP. Portugal owned significant shareholdings in both firms and "appear[ed] to be the real architect" of the merger.

The Commission prohibited the merger. It found anticompetitive horizontal effects in the electricity market through the elimination of GDP as the most likely important potential competitor, and anticompetitive non-horizontal effects on wholesale electricity markets in view of EDP's preferred access to confidential information of its competitors, preferred access to the available gas resources in Portugal, and the possibility and intention to increase the production costs of its competitors.

Although the merging parties had offered commitments that held near-term benefits in the gas sector, the Commission determined that the advantages would not offer a better situation than GDP's potential entry into electricity markets. The General Court upheld the prohibition. EDP–Energias de Portugal SA v. Commission, Case T–87/05, [2005] ECR II–3745.

8. The Commission's experience with vertical and conglomerate mergers ultimately led to guidelines on non-horizontal mergers, which are available at the link at *http://ec.europa.eu/competition/mergers/legislation/notices_on_substance.html*.

E.　THE INTERNATIONAL DIMENSION

In 1988 the Court of Justice decided, in *Wood pulp* (see page 859 supra), that European competition law reprehends off-shore cartels "implemented" in the Community. In 1997, the European Commission vetted Boeing's acquisition of McDonnell Douglas (two US firms with no assets in Europe but which did business in a world market). The Commission nearly enjoined the acquisition, which had been cleared by US authorities, but in the end allowed it subject to important conditions. See page 1016 supra. (The United States authorities, too, freely challenge off-shore mergers that hurt their interests.)

In 1999, the European Commission enjoined the merger of Gencor and LPD (Lonrho), two South African firms, one of which had a presence in Europe. The General Court affirmed. See page 1024. This was the first merger prohibited and aborted on grounds of collective dominance. In 2001, the Commission prohibited the GE/Honeywell merger, which had been approved by the US authorities. The General Court affirmed the prohibition. We deal here with the jurisdictional issues raised in *Gencor/Lonrho*.

NOTE ON *GENCOR LTD. V. COMMISSION*

See facts at page 1024 supra.

After the South African platinum mining companies, Gencor and LPD, agreed to merge, the South African Competition Board vetted the merger and found no competition problem. The European Commission vetted the merger and was concerned that, when the Russian stocks were depleted in a couple of years, Gencor/LPD (Lonrho) and Anglo American, the world market leader, would jointly exercise dominant market power (collective dominance). Recall that LPD's parent, Lonrho, was a British firm, and Lonrho maintained its principal sales office in Belgium.

Examining the proposed merger, the Competition Directorate of the European Commission invited comment from the South African authorities. The South African Deputy Minister of Foreign Affairs officially submitted his government's observations to the Commission. He stated in a letter to the European Commission that the South African Government favored the consolidation. As to competitive effects, the Minister noted that the two remaining platinum firms in South Africa were now more equally matched, and he conveyed the South African view that the market would work better with two equally matched competitors than under market domination by Anglo American. The Minister did not contest the intervention of the European Community. However, he wrote: "Having regard to the importance of mineral resources to the South African economy," South Africa favored allowing the consolidation and attacking any collusion between Anglo American and Gencor/LPD if and when it arose. (judgment, para. 3)

The European Commission prohibited the merger. Gencor sought annulment in the General Court on both jurisdictional and substantive grounds. Gencor argued that the Community had no jurisdiction over this concentration since it involved economic activities conducted within the territory of a non-member country and had been approved by authorities of that country. Gencor contended that the Merger Regulation applies only to concentrations carried out within the Community. It based its construction on the language of the Merger Regulation (especially recitals), the Treaty articles on which the Regulation was based, and the international law principle of territoriality. Gencor distinguished the *Wood pulp* case, wherein the Court of Justice had asserted jurisdiction over an offshore cartel designedly raising prices in Europe, on grounds that the cartel was implemented in Europe. Gencor said, of *Wood pulp:* While the high prices were agreed to offshore, the conspiracy to raise prices was implemented by selling at the conspiratorial prices into the Community. By contrast, the platinum merger was implemented in South Africa and "is thus primarily relevant to the industrial and competition policy of that non-member country." (para. 56)

The General Court rejected Gencor's construction of the Regulation. Case T–102/96, [1999] ECR II–753. The Court said:

> According to *Wood pulp,* the criterion as to the implementation of an agreement is satisfied by mere sale within the Community, irrespective of the location of the sources of supply and the production plant. It is not disputed that Gencor and Lonrho carried out sales in the Community before the concentration and would have continued to do so thereafter. (para. 87)

The court proceeded to assess the legitimacy of jurisdiction under international law. Noting that the transaction entailed merger of the firms' marketing operations throughout the world, including the Community, it said:

> Application of the Regulation is justified under public international law when it is foreseeable that a proposed concentration will have an immediate and substantial effect in the Community. (para. 90)

The court concluded that the merger's effect in the Community would be immediate, substantial and foreseeable. It construed "immediate" to include "medium term"—after Russian platinum stocks were exhausted and thus after a force that could be disruptive of Anglo and Gencor's duopoly behavior would have been removed. It concluded that an *abuse* (a price rise resulting from collective behavior) need not be immediate; it is enough that a transaction causes a lasting structural alteration, making abusive behavior economically rational.

As to substantiality of the effect, Gencor claimed that the merging parties' sales and market shares in Europe were too small to cause a substantial effect and that the merging parties' greater sales elsewhere—Japan and the United States—undermined "substantiality." The court rejected this claim. It said:

> The fact that, in a world market, other parts of the world are affected by the concentration cannot prevent the Community from exercising its control over a concentration which substantially affects competition within the common market by creating a dominant position.

Likewise, the court rejected the claim that the exercise of jurisdiction violated an international principle of non-interference, if there is such a principle, or the principle of proportionality. The court said that there was no conflict between the laws of the two jurisdictions and therefore no interference because South Africa did not require the firms to do what the European Community required them not to do. Nor was it shown how the completion of the merger would enhance South Africa's vital economic or commercial interests.

Moreover, as the European Commission had argued, the merger was like an export cartel. Only a small amount of platinum was sold in South Africa. South Africa stood to gain more by exploiting the world than it stood to lose by exploiting its own consumers.

Thus, the Court held, it had jurisdiction.

South Africa did not further resist the result of *Gencor/Lonrho*. But when, two years later, the European Commission signaled its serious problems with the GE/Honeywell merger, US senators, cabinet members, and the President declared the European "intrusion" into the "American" merger inappropriate. After the European prohibition, US Assistant Attorney General in charge of Antitrust Charles James issued a statement taking issue with the European analysis, not with the assertion of jurisdiction. "Antitrust laws protect competition, not competitors," he said. The merger "would have been procompetitive and beneficial to consumers.... [The European Commission] apparently concluded that a more diversified, and thus more competitive GE, could somehow disadvantage other market participants.... This matter points to the continuing need ... to move toward a greater policy convergence."[3]

NOTES AND QUESTIONS

1. In *Gencor/Lonrho*, was the Court's concept of conflict the same as or different from that of the US Supreme Court in *Hartford* (see page 863 supra)? Was there really no conflict?

2. Does the European Commission have subject matter jurisdiction over off-shore mergers? Does *Wood pulp* help you answer the question? The US

---

3. 81 BNA Antitrust & Trade Reg. Rep. 15 (July 6, 2001).

federal antitrust agencies' 1995 International Guidelines declare that the US agencies have jurisdiction to challenge an anticompetitive merger of foreign firms that hurts US consumers; and that they even have jurisdiction to challenge an off-shore merger that hurts US exporters as long as it also hurts foreign consumers (but query whether subsequent caselaw may have put such mergers beyond reach). Antitrust Enforcement Guidelines for International Operations (April 1995), 4 CCH Trade Reg. Rep. ¶ 13,107, Illustrative Example H.

Is there anything to be said for a rule of law that would give only the United States the right to enjoin a merger of US firms with substantial sales (and thus consumers) in the United States, and only the EU the right to prohibit a merger of European firms with substantial sales in the European Economic Area? What if the merger harms consumers beyond the borders of the home country? (*Gencor/Lonrho*) What if the merger harms only producer interests (e.g., rights of access to markets) and the foreign law protects these interests? (Compare *Boeing/McDonnell Douglas*.)

3. Do these cases—mergers in global markets having impacts around the world—suggest a need for international law or principles? Philip Condit, then Chairman of Boeing, told the Washington Post [July 24, 1997, E1] at the conclusion of Boeing's negotiations with the EU to settle the merger challenge: "In a global economy, a single set of rules is, in fact, preferable[.] Over time, we have to keep working in that direction."

Comment on Mr. Condit's statement. Is it realistic? How might we reach a single set of merger rules for the world? How—and by whom—might the single set be applied, objectively and without nationalistic bias?

The competition-law nations of the world (more than 100) have moved far in the direction of convergence of procedure and process in premerger notification requirements. They are moving towards convergence of some substantive standards, albeit with a margin of difference. The major forum for convergence is the International Competition Network—a virtual network of the antitrust authorities of the world. A description of their initiatives, and the documents that comprise their growing work product, are available at *www.internationalcompetitionnetwork.org*. (Click on "By Working Group"; select "Mergers.") A common approach, however, does not always mean common outcomes when several jurisdictions rule upon the same transnational merger. Market conditions sometimes differ from nation to nation. Moreover, as in *GE/Honeywell*, different analysts may apply different presumptions, often affecting market definition and assessment of competitive effects.

CHAPTER 26

THE STATE AND COMPETITION

■ ■ ■

A. INTRODUCTION

From the outset, state monopoly, state-granted benefits and privileges, and state power co-opted by private interests posed serious problems. For some Member States, the state was *the* problem. In some states, business—especially in basic goods and services—was run by state or state-privileged monopolies. These enterprises were dominant by reason of privilege, not by reason of skill, foresight or inventiveness. By the nature of their operations, these enterprises were a major obstacle to achieving a common market. They tended to procure goods only from their nationals (and procurement by state enterprises represented a sizeable percentage of GDP). In offering goods or services, they were often nationalistic and discriminatory. They often had leverage to exclude competitors, and their large presence and connections, themselves, chilled entry. It was predictable that several articles of the Treaty would be addressed to the problem of the state in the market and that from the outset the Commission would have a sharp eye on state monopolies of a commercial character and firms that held privileges bestowed by the state.

Ports, and discriminatory access to them, presented a good example of state monopoly abuses. The ports cases are also a good example of application, jointly, of two or more Treaty articles, such as Articles 102 and 106—abuse of dominance, and limits on the conduct of public undertakings and those granted special or exclusive rights. Other combinations of Treaty articles that came into common use are Article 3(1)(g) (the Community must ensure that competition is not distorted) (now in Protocol 27) and TEU Article 4(3) (states have a duty to cooperate in carrying out the tasks of the Community), along with Articles TFEU 101 and 102 and the various articles facilitating free movement and prohibiting discrimination, such as Articles 18, 34, 35 and 56.

State-granted aids and other subsidies to domestic businesses were likewise a major problem. Each of the states had subsidized "its" firms as and when it chose, often responding to powerful private interests or trying to puff-up domestic champions to give them a competitive edge over their neighbors, undermining competitive opportunities of out-of-state firms;

thus, the importance of Articles 107–108—prohibiting state aid unless authorized.

When the financial crisis hit Europe in 2008, the Competition Commissioner, Neelie Kroes, gave a speech: "EU competition rules—part of the solution for Europe's economy." Speech/08/625, 18 Nov. 2008. She decried state aids that would simply dump one nation's crisis onto the others. She said:

> Were it not for the State aid rules, there was a real risk that national governments would have been forced into a costly and damaging subsidy race, wasting billions upon billions of taxpayers' money competing with each other's largesse rather than focussing the money where it was most needed. Were it not for the state aid rules, we could have been faced with beggar thy neighbour policies that could have undermined the solutions that governments were putting in place....
> * * *
> The European Single Market's role is all the more vital during periods of economic difficulties—together we stand, divided we fall. The Single Market will attenuate any economic downturn and accelerate recovery. Which is why, despite siren calls to the contrary, we need to ensure that the Single Market functions as well as possible at this crucial moment, which means enforcing the antitrust and state aid rules as diligently as ever.

Commissioner Kroes immediately gave guidance on circumstances in which state aid would be approved (in general, approval would be possible when the aid was focused on growth and the future), and when it would be disapproved. The intensifying financial crisis, however, put her principles under pressure.

We start with ports cases as an example of abuse of power of state-owned or recently privatized firms, depriving rivals of access to infrastructure facilities. These cases are a fortiori examples of violation of Article 102. We then treat the compatibility of state monopoly and monopoly privileges with the Treaty. We proceed to ask when anticompetitive state measures violate the competition provisions in combination with other articles, such as Article TEU 4(3) and TFEU 101, and when state measures shield anticompetitive private action that they facilitate. Finally, we turn to the Treaty provisions that control state distortions of competition by grants of aid.

B. PORTS CASES, AND A NOTE ON LIBERALIZATION

Ports and ports authorities were principally owned by states. They were literally and figuratively gateways to markets. Typically, states adopted measures to bolster ports' powers to exclude; and exclusion, discrimination and exploitation were common. The ports cases are, therefore, helpful illustrations of 1) factually, problems of state ownership and exclusive privilege, and 2) legally, the interrelationship of Treaty articles applied to address the problems of abuse, promote liberalization, and assure non-discriminatory access.

We note here cases and measures revolving around two ports—the Port of Rødby, Denmark, and the Port of Genoa, Italy.

PORT OF RØDBY

94/119/EC, Commission decision of 21 Dec. 1993, O.J. L 055 26 January 1994 at 0052.

[DSB was a Danish public undertaking which operated as a department of the transport ministry. It held the exclusive right to organize railroad traffic in Denmark, owned the Port of Rødby, and operated ferry services between Denmark and neighboring countries. Stena was a Swedish shipping group which specialized in ferry services and wished to operate between Denmark and Germany (Puttgarden), which essentially links eastern Denmark with Germany and the rest of western Europe.

Stena requested permission from the Danish government to use the existing port facilities at Rødby or to build a port in the vicinity. The Danish government refused. Stena complained to the Commission.]

Abuse of dominant position

12   The refusal to allow 'Euro–Port A/S', a subsidiary of the Swedish group [Stena] to operate from Rødby has the effect of eliminating a potential competitor on the Rødby–Puttgarden route and hence of strengthening the joint dominant position of DSB and DB on that route.

According to the case law of the Court, an abuse within the meaning of Article [102] is committed in cases where, without any objective necessity, an undertaking holding a dominant position on a particular market reserves to itself an ancillary activity which might be carried out by another undertaking as part of its activities on a neighbouring but separate market, with the possibility of eliminating all competition from such undertaking.

Thus an undertaking that owns or manages and uses itself an essential facility, i.e. a facility or infrastructure without which its competitors are unable to offer their services to customers, and refuses to grant them access to such facility is abusing its dominant position.

Consequently, an undertaking that owns or manages an essential port facility from which it provides a maritime transport service may not, without objective justification, refuse to grant a shipowner wishing to operate on the same maritime route access to that facility without infringing Article [102].

13   According to the case-law of the Court, Article [106] (1) prohibits Member States from placing, by law, regulation or administrative provision, public undertakings and undertakings to which they grant exclusive rights in a position in which those undertakings could not

place themselves by their own conduct without infringing Article [102]. The Court added that, where the extension of the dominant position of a public undertaking or an undertaking to which the State has granted exclusive rights resulted from a State measure, such a measure constituted an infringement of Article [106], read in conjunction with Article [102] of the Treaty. . . .

Thus, for the reasons given above, any firm in the same position as DSB which refused to grant another shipping operator access to the port it controlled would be abusing a dominant position. Where, as in the present case, a Member State has refused such access and has strengthened the effects of the refusal by also refusing to authorize the construction of a new port, it constitutes a State measure in breach of Article [106], read in conjunction with Article [102].

14 The reasons given by the Danish Transport Ministry for rejecting both requests of 'Euro–Port A/S' . . . are the following:

— the plan of 'Euro–Port A/S' . . . (Stena), to build a new terminal is not acceptable as that undertaking has allegedly 'not established that there is an unsatisfied demand for a ferry service' and it is 'most unlikely that such a demand would arise' . . .

— 'Euro–Port A/S' (Stena) could not operate from the existing port facilities as this would have the effect of preventing the companies already operating in the port from expanding their activities. * * *

The Commission concludes . . . that:

— there was indeed an unsatisfied demand for ferry services in May 1990 since one year later DSB and DB had expanded their services,

— the increase in the activities of DB and DSB in 1991 confirms that the port of Rødby was not saturated.

15 The Commission also considers that there is no evidence that the existing facilities at Rødby would today be saturated or that, subject to alterations which Stena has informed the Commission it is prepared to finance, existing port capacity is unable to cope with an increase in trade. The Commission also notes that the Swedish group (Stena) has acquired land adjacent to the port facilities of Rødby which is perfectly suitable for development as a terminal by Stena.

It therefore concludes that there are no technical constraints preventing the Stena group from sailing between Rødby and Puttgarden.

16 In their letter of 22 February 1993 which constitutes the reply to the letter of formal notice sent by the Commission on 24 November 1992, the Danish authorities rejected the latter's request, stressing that their refusals were justified under Community law. They stated that it would be impossible to allow Stena access to the existing facilities,

giving technical reasons and referring for the first time, without any further details, to obligations incumbent upon DB and DSB in the general interest.

This would appear to indicate that, in the view of the Danish authorities, the technical feasibility of access to the port is not a problem or is not the only problem and that they also have a duty to protect the public undertaking DSB from a competitor on the market for ferry services.

Nor can the Commission share the view of the Danish authorities that the alleged saturation of the existing port facilities would make pointless any attempt to introduce competition since this could not in any event lead to an increase in the number of sailings between Rødby and Puttgarden.

Even on a saturated market, an improvement in the quality of products or services offered or a reduction in prices as a result of competition is a definite advantage for consumers; this could also lead to an increase in demand which, in the present case, could be met by expanding the port. * * *

Article [106] (2)

18   The Commission considers that the application of the competition rules in the present case does not impede the particular task entrusted to the public undertaking DSB namely to organize rail services and manage the port facilities at Rødby. Therefore the exception provided for in Article [106] (2) does not apply. * * *

CONCLUSION

19   In view of the foregoing, the Commission considers that the measures referred to in paragraphs 1 and 2 constitute infringements of Article [106] (1) of the Treaty, read in conjunction with Article [102].

––––––––––––

The Commission subsequently refined the remedy. It "became apparent that establishing competing facilities, especially in the case of nationwide networks, requires a great deal of investment and is usually inefficient. So the European Commission developed the concept of legally separating the provision of the network from the commercial services using the network." *http://ec.europa.eu/competition/liberalisation/overview_ en.html.* What are the merits of this structural remedy?

MERCI CONVENZIONALI PORTO DI GENOVA v. SIDERURGICA GABRIELLI SPA
Case C–179/90, [1991] ECR 5889, ECJ.

[The Italian Navigation Code established an exclusive right to organize dock work for third parties, and required retention of dock work companies that employed only registered workers of Italian nationality. Carriers coming to port were not permitted to use their crew to load and unload. The organizer of dock work was generally controlled by the port authority.

Merci enjoyed the exclusive right to organize dock work. Siderurgica Gabrielli SpA arrived in the Port of Genoa with goods, but Merci delayed in providing unloading services and Siderurgica Gabrielli suffered damages, for which it sought compensation. The Italian court asked the Court of Justice whether the Italian rules violated TEU Article 4(3) and TFEU Articles 34 (free movement of goods), 45 (free movement of workers), 102 and 106 and whether Siderurgica Gabrielli had a remedy.

Advocate General Van Gerven pinpointed the anticompetitive and discriminatory effects inherent in the Italian law:

22 [W]e must now consider whether these abuses of a dominant position within the meaning of Article [102]—in so far as the national court regards them as established—are imposed, or facilitated, or made inevitable by the relevant national legislation. I think there can be little doubt about this. In fact, the scale of charges and other, presumably unfair, contractual conditions applied by Merci and Compagnia are made possible, if not inevitable, by the national legislation applicable and are facilitated, if not made compulsory, by the port authorities under the powers conferred on them by national legislation. The other abuses too are made possible by that legislation. But for the monopoly for the performance of dock work conferred on it by the Italian legislation, Compagnia could certainly not have afforded to abstain from using modern technology, and it is clear also that the dissimilar treatment of trading parties was possible only as a result of the monopoly granted to Merci and the complexity and lack of transparency of the scale of charges devised by the authority.

The Court ruled]:

19 [I]t appears from the circumstances described by the national court and discussed before the Court of Justice that the undertakings enjoying exclusive rights in accordance with the procedures laid down by the national rules in question are, as a result, induced either to demand payment for services which have not been requested, to charge disproportionate prices, to refuse to have recourse to modern technology, which involves an increase in the cost of the operations and a prolongation of the time required for their performance, or to grant price reductions to certain consumers and at the same time to offset such reductions by an increase in the charges to other consumers.

20 In these circumstances it must be held that a Member State creates a situation contrary to Article [102] of the Treaty where it adopts rules of such a kind as those at issue before the national court, which are capable of affecting trade between Member States as in the case of the main proceedings, regard being had to the factors mentioned in ...

this judgment relating to the importance of traffic in the Port of Genoa.

21 As regards the interpretation of Article [34] of the Treaty requested by the national court, it is sufficient to recall that a national measure which has the effect of facilitating the abuse of a dominant position capable of affecting trade between Member States will generally be incompatible with that article, which prohibits quantitative restrictions on imports and all measures having equivalent effect (see Case 13/77 GB–INNO–BM v ATAB [1977] ECR 2115, paragraph 35) in so far as such a measure has the effect of making more difficult and hence of impeding imports of goods from other Member States.

22 In the main proceedings it may be seen from the national court's findings that the unloading of the goods could have been effected at a lesser cost by the ship's crew, so that compulsory recourse to the services of the two undertakings enjoying exclusive rights involved extra expense and was therefore capable, by reason of its effect on the prices of the goods, of affecting imports.

23 It should be emphasized in the third place that even within the framework of Article [106], the provisions of Articles [34], [45] and [102] of the Treaty have direct effect and give rise for interested parties to rights which the national courts must protect (see in particular, as regards Article [102] of the Treaty.

24 The answer to the first question, as reformulated, should therefore be that:

Article [106](1)] of the ... Treaty, in conjunction with Articles [34], [45] and [102] of the ... Treaty, precludes rules of a Member State which confer on an undertaking established in that State the exclusive right to organize dock work and require it for that purpose to have recourse to a dock-work company formed exclusively of national workers; Articles [34], [45] and [102] of the Treaty, in conjunction with Article [106], give rise to rights for individuals which the national courts must protect.

———

Following the judgment, Italy revised its law to open up competition for port-handling. The Commission, however, was not satisfied. It found that local authorities systematically refused to grant operating licenses to potential competitors of long-established dock services companies. Italy, in response, issued a license. XXVth Report on Competition Policy (1995), pp. 58–59. The Commission again found that the Italian reform was insufficient and indeed that it created new problems. It found additional infringements by decision of 97/744, 21 October 1997.

The port cases reflect principles and problems common to a range of infrastructure industries and regulated sectors, including transport, post, telecommunications and energy. The law that applies to restrictive state measures and to abusive action by undertakings is intertwined. In some sectors, notably energy and telecommunications, major liberalization projects, aided by framework directives, are under way. The objective is to improve conditions of competition, not just to prevent its restriction. See Neelie Kroes, Improving Competition in European Energy Markets through Effective Unbundling, Chapter 9 in 2007 Fordham Competition Law Institute, International Antitrust Law & Policy, p. 247 (B. Hawk ed. 2008).

C. STATE MONOPOLIES OF A COMMERCIAL CHARACTER—APPLICATION OF ARTICLES 34 AND 37

While the ports cases clarify duties of state monopolies not to discriminate, exclude and thereby harm competition, a yet more conceptual, more basic question about the essence of the political economy of the Community was to arise: Did the Treaty adopt a rule of free enterprise? Did it tolerate state-owned monopoly? And even if so, were new nationalizations inconsistent with the Treaty?

In 1962, Italy nationalized its electricity industry, transferring all of the assets of the nationalized firms to ENEL. Mr. Costa, a lawyer, refused to pay three euros of his electric bill and sued for a declaration that the nationalization act was void as inconsistent with the Treaty and that his debt was void. He came before an ideologically sympathetic magistrate in Milan, who agreed with him that nationalization violated Community law. He later came before a hostile Italian Supreme Court, and was derided by an indignant Italian government. He ultimately suffered dismissal of his case for lack of standing, without having received an answer from the Court of Justice whether nationalization was or was not permissible under the Treaty. See *Costa v. ENEL*, Case 6/64, [1964] ECR 585, page 235 supra, ruling that Article 37, prohibiting any new commercial monopoly giving rise to national discrimination in procuring or marketing goods, is directly effective.

We begin with the unanswered question in *Costa:* Is the creation of a new state monopoly by nationalization consistent with the Treaty?

The principal relevant provision of the Treaty is Article 37, which must be read together with Article 34, which prohibits Member States from imposing quotas or tariffs or measures of equivalent effect; that is, from unduly restricting trade.

Article 37, ex 31 ECT

1. Member States shall adjust any State monopolies of a commercial character so as to ensure that no discrimination regarding the conditions under which goods are procured and marketed exists between nationals of Member States.

The provisions of this Article shall apply to any body through which a Member State, in law or in fact, either directly or indirectly supervises, determines or appreciably influences imports or exports between Member States. These provisions shall likewise apply to monopolies delegated by the State to others.

2. Member States shall refrain from introducing any new measure which is contrary to the principles laid down in paragraph 1 or which restricts the scope of the Articles dealing with the prohibition of customs duties and quantitative restrictions between Member States.
* * *

To address a serious problem of alcohol abuse, Sweden brought the liquor business under state control. It formed a state-owned company, V&S, with exclusive rights to produce and export spirits and to import beer, wine and spirits. It formed another state-owned company, Systembolaget, and gave it the exclusive right to sell alcoholic beverages at wholesale to restaurants and the exclusive right to sell alcoholic beverages at retail.

To facilitate its accession to the European Union, Sweden abolished the privileges of V&S and the wholesale privileges of Systembolaget and replaced them with a system of licenses, while retaining for Systembolaget its retail monopoly. Licenses for import, export, production, and wholesaling were to be issued at the discretion of the Alcohol Inspectorate upon the making of an application, which required documentation and the payment of a high, non-reimbursable fee. The fees, including annual renewal fees, were much higher per litre for low sales volume than for high sales volume, and thus the fee structure favored the large incumbent supplier, V&S.

Advocate General Elmer, on a reference involving the criminal prosecution of an unauthorized wine importer, summarized the basis and workings of the Swedish system as follows:

> The fundamental aim of Swedish alcohol policy throughout the twentieth century has been to limit the effect of market forces, namely competition and private profits. The reason for this was the conviction that competition and private profits encourage active marketing and active selling, which lead to increased consumption. The greater the number of undertakings having an interest in increased alcohol sales, the better alcoholic beverages will fare in the competition for consumers' money. In the case of a sector which society does not wish to see expand, market mechanisms such as competition and profit are not particularly suitable as means of control.
>
> In the Government's view, the principle of limiting private profits in the alcohol trade remains valid ... (*Franzen*; see additional excerpts from his opinion infra.)

FRANZEN
(*Swedish Alcohol Monopoly*)

Case C–189/95, [1997] ECR I–5909, ECJ.

[Harry Franzen, without a license, imported wine from Denmark and sold it in Sweden. Prosecuted for a criminal violation, he pled that the Swedish law was invalid for violating Articles 34 and 37. The national court referred questions to the Court of Justice.

Advocate General Elmer agreed with Mr. Franzen that the Swedish alcohol monopoly violated Community law. The advocate general said that Article 34 "is intended to ensure access to the market of products from other Member States" (para. 59) and "to prevent lacunae in the protection of free movement" (para. 65). As to Article 37:]

Advocate General Elmer

68   ... Article [37] of the Treaty refers to the traders who supply the market in products. That provision therefore differs from Article [34] of the Treaty, first by being limited to discrimination and secondly by not protecting the free movement of goods as such but by protecting the traders of the other Member States who participate in the free movement of goods.

69   That was confirmed in ... Commission v. Greece [[1990] ECR I–4747], where the Court held that to maintain in force the State's rights with regard to the importation and marketing of petroleum products gave rise to discrimination within the meaning of Article [37](1) against exporters established in other Member States. Presumably, the determining factor in that case was that the State's monopoly was of such a kind as to prevent certain traders, in particular those with whom the Greek State's monopoly did not have commercial relations, from exporting to the Greek market. There was therefore discrimination between nationals of the Member States, as mentioned in Article [37] (1).

70   I could also refer to the Manghera judgment [1976 ECR 91]. In that judgment the Court, after stating that the exclusive right to import manufactured tobacco products enjoyed by the monopoly of the Italian State constituted, in respect of Community exports, discrimination prohibited by Article [37](1) of the Treaty, held that that provision must be interpreted "as meaning that ... every national monopoly of a commercial character must be adjusted so as to eliminate the exclusive right to import from other Member States". That finding is quite general and must be interpreted as meaning that the Court accepted that national import monopolies in themselves constitute discrimination between nationals of the Member States and that it is therefore unnecessary to ascertain on a case-by-case basis whether such import monopolies actually lead to discrimination between nationals of the Member States. * * *

72   Furthermore, in its decisions the Court has sometimes applied Articles [34] and [37] concurrently to a national monopoly of a commercial character and sometimes applied only Article [34] to exclusive rights conferred on a national monopolistic undertaking. Thus in ... Commission v. Greece, the Court held that the exclusive right to import and market finished petroleum products was contrary to both Article [34] and Article [37](1). In the telecommunications terminals judgment [France v. Commission, [1991] ECR I–1223] the Court held that exclusive rights to import and market terminal equipment constituted a measure having equivalent effect to a quantitative restriction on imports within the meaning of Article [34] of the Treaty.

> The advocate general concluded that the Swedish monopoly and regulation necessarily hindered trade in violation of Article 34; that it had the same effect as an import monopoly and therefore a discriminatory effect in violation of Article 37; and that the system was not justified under Article 36 since health and life could be protected by less restrictive means. The Court did not entirely agree.]

The Court

The rules relating to the existence and operation of the monopoly

[The Retail Monopoly]

39   The purpose of Article [37] of the Treaty is to reconcile the possibility for Member States to maintain certain monopolies of a commercial character as instruments for the pursuit of public interest aims with the requirements of the establishment and functioning of the common market. It aims at the elimination of obstacles to the free movement of goods, save, however, for restrictions on trade which are inherent in the existence of the monopolies in question.

40   Thus, Article [37] requires that the organization and operation of the monopoly be arranged so as to exclude any discrimination between nationals of Member States as regards conditions of supply and outlets, so that trade in goods from other Member States is not put at a disadvantage, in law or in fact, in relation to that in domestic goods and that competition between the economies of the Member States is not distorted.

41   In the present case, it is not contested that, in aiming to protect public health against the harm caused by alcohol, a domestic monopoly on the retail of alcoholic beverages, such as that conferred on Systembolaget, pursues a public interest aim.

42   It is therefore necessary to determine whether a monopoly of this kind is arranged in a way which meets the conditions referred to in paragraphs 39 and 40 above. * * *

The monopoly's sales network

53 Mr Franzen contends that the sales network maintained by Systembolaget is restricted and does not offer the full range of beverages available, which restricts even more the possibilities of sale.

54 It is true that a monopoly such as Systembolaget has only a limited number of 'shops'. However, it does not appear from the information provided to the Court that the number of sales outlets are limited to the point of compromising consumers' procurement of supplies of domestic or imported alcoholic beverages.

55 First of all, under the agreement which it has made with the State, Systembolaget must establish or close sales outlets on the basis of management constraints, consumer demand and the necessities of alcohol policy and ensure that each commune which so wishes has a sales outlet and that all points of the territory are served at least by dispatch deliveries.

56 Second, according to the information provided to the Court, alcoholic beverages may be ordered and supplied in the monopoly's 384 'shops', through around 550 sales outlets as well as along 56 bus routes and on 45 rural post rounds. Furthermore, there is at least one 'shop' in 259 of the 288 Swedish communes and Systembolaget is planning for every commune to have at least one 'shop' in 1998.

57 Finally, even if the retail network of Systembolaget is still imperfect, this circumstance does not adversely affect the sale of alcoholic beverages from other Member States more than the sale of alcoholic beverages produced in Sweden.

The promotion of alcoholic beverages

58 Mr Franzen also contends that the system for promoting alcoholic beverages favours the marketing of beverages produced in Sweden. He points out that the promotion of alcoholic beverages is confined to mere provision of information about the products, varying in form depending on whether the products are in the 'basic' assortment or in the 'by order' assortment, that the information is provided by the monopoly alone, without any control by suppliers and, furthermore, that suppliers may not canvas persons in charge of the monopoly's 'shops'.

59 As far as these points are concerned, it must be observed first of all that the restriction of the possibilities for promoting alcoholic beverages to the public is inherent in the situation where there is only one operator on the market for their retail.

60 Second, the monopoly rules do not prohibit producers or importers from promoting their products to the monopoly. . . .

61 It must also be pointed out that the promotion of alcoholic beverages to the public is subject, in the Member State in question, to a general restriction, the validity of which has not been called in question by the national court nor challenged by Mr Franzen. That restriction consists, in particular, of a ban on advertising on radio and television and

in all newspapers or other periodicals, that is to say the means traditionally used by producers to promote their products to the public. However, alcoholic beverages selected by Systembolaget may be advertised in written material available at sales outlets. Furthermore, any alcoholic beverage may be mentioned in press articles. * * *

64 Finally, it must be noted that the method of promotion used by the monopoly applies independently of products' origin and is not in itself apt to put at a disadvantage, in fact or in law, beverages imported from other Member States in relation to those produced on national territory. * * *

66 So, having regard to the evidence before the Court, it appears that a retail monopoly such as that in question in the main proceedings meets the conditions for being compatible with Article [37] of the Treaty. . . .

Article 34 [The Production and Wholesaling Restrictions]

68 . . . Mr Franzen observes that the monopoly may obtain supplies only from holders of production licences or wholesale licences whose grant is subject to restrictive conditions and that such an obligation necessarily impedes imports of products from other Member States. * * *

70 In a national system such as that in question in the main proceedings, only holders of production licences or wholesale licences are allowed to import alcoholic beverages, that is to say traders who fulfil the restrictive conditions to which issue of those licences is subject. According to the information provided to the Court during the proceedings, the traders in question must provide sufficient personal and financial guarantees to carry on the activities in question, concerning in particular their professional knowledge, their financial capacity and possession of storage capacity sufficient to meet the needs of their activities. Furthermore, the submission of an application is subject to payment of a high fixed charge . . . , which is not reimbursed if the application is rejected. Finally, in order to keep his licence, a trader must pay an annual supervision fee, which is also high. . . .

71 The licensing system constitutes an obstacle to the importation of alcoholic beverages from other Member States in that it imposes additional costs on such beverages, such as intermediary costs, payment of charges and fees for the grant of a licence, and costs arising from the obligation to maintain storage capacity in Sweden.

72 According to the Swedish Government's own evidence, the number of licences issued is low (223 in October 1996) and almost all of these licences have been issued to traders established in Sweden.

73 Domestic legislation such as that in question in the main proceedings is therefore contrary to Article [34] of the Treaty.

74 The Swedish Government has, however, invoked Article [36] of the . . . Treaty. It maintains that its legislation was justified on grounds relating to the protection of human health.

75 It is indeed so that measures contrary to Article [34] may be justified on the basis of Article [36] of the Treaty. All the same, according to established case-law (Cassis de Dijon . . .), the domestic provisions in question must be proportionate to the aim pursued and not attainable by measures less restrictive of intra-Community trade.

76 Although the protection of human health against the harmful effects of alcohol, on which the Swedish Government relies, is indisputably one of the grounds which may justify derogation from Article [34] of the Treaty, the Swedish Government has not established that the licensing system set up by the Law on Alcohol, in particular as regards the conditions relating to storage capacity and the high fees and charges which licence-holders are required to pay, was proportionate to the public health aim pursued or that this aim could not have been attained by measures less restrictive of intra-Community trade.

77 It must therefore be held that Articles [34] and [36] of the Treaty preclude domestic provisions allowing only traders holding a production licence or a wholesale licence to import alcoholic beverages on conditions such as those laid down by Swedish legislation.

NOTES AND QUESTIONS

1. What is the practical effect of the judgment? Why can Sweden keep its retail monopoly? Must it abandon its import and wholesale monopoly?

2. The New York Times assessed the impact of the judgment on Sweden in an article, Europe Making Sweden Ease Alcohol Rules, Mar. 28, 2001, Int'l ed., p. A1:

> . . . [P]iece by piece, Sweden is being forced to take apart its anti-alcohol policies because most violate the European Union's rules of fair competition. Some liquor stores are open late and on Saturdays. A few have been remade into cheerfully decorated self-service stores. And wine lovers can delight in a wide selection. * * *
>
> Experts say that what is happening in Sweden over alcohol policy is in many ways a prime example of the difficulties the European Union faces as it tries to extend its reach and harmonize policies. Stretching from freezing climates to desert regions and incorporating vastly different cultures, the union is seeing that what may be a market commodity in one country is a health issue in another.
>
> "On this issue, we can't even really understand each other," said Dr. Gunar Agren, the executive manager of Sweden's National Institute of Health. "We just see things very differently and in fact we have different problems with alcohol."

Is this criticism fair? Is the *Franzen* judgment a triumph of free movement and free competition over monopoly? or a triumph of European regulation over national cultural choices?

3. How did the Swedish alcohol system harm competition? Who was hurt? Consider all of Mr. Franzen's arguments. Were the harms Mr. Franzen

identified essentially costs the nation was willing to pay for a national social policy? Or were they harms also to the whole Union? When effects of national, market-restricting policies spill over to other nations, who should decide whether the costs are worth the benefits?

The Court of Justice has dealt with related problems in the free movement cases; especially cases under Article 34, which prohibits Member States from imposing "quantitative restrictions on imports and all measures having equivalent effect." The case law strongly disfavors restraints on free movement but admits an exception where the restriction (such as health and safety standards that may impede trade) is necessary to satisfy important public interest objectives that take precedence over free movement. *Rewe–Zentral v. Bundesmonopolverwaltung Fur Branntwein (Cassis de Dijon)*, Case 120/78, [1979] ECR 649. Moreover, if the allegedly offending measures are merely "selling arrangements"—time, place and manner of sale, with no discriminatory effect in law or in fact—the state prerogative is recognized; the measure does not fall within Article 28, and no justification is necessary. *Keck and Mithouard*, Cases C–267 & 268/91, [1993] ECR I–6097 (holding not within Article 34 a French law prohibiting retail prices of less than acquisition cost, even though the law had the effect of keeping out of France low-priced, non-monopolistic cross-border trade). *Keck* overturned precedent that would have required France to justify the below-cost ban because of its effect on trade. Under the older precedent, France would have been required to show that the restraint was not only warranted by an important public interest but was proportional to it.

Is the Court's approach in *Franzen* consistent with its approach in *Keck?*

4. In view of *Franzen*, was Mr. Costa right or wrong?

5. A decade later, Klas Rosengren and 10 other Swedes ordered Spanish wine through a Danish web site, which offered wine at lower prices than Systembolaget, the Swedish retail alcohol monopoly. Systembolaget confiscated Rosengren's wine on grounds that Swedish law prohibited its citizens from importing wine from other EU countries. Rosengren sued in a Swedish court. Systembolaget defended that its law was justified as a means of preventing alcohol abuse. The Swedish Court referred the question of the legality of the Swedish ban to the Court of Justice, which ruled for Rosengren. The Court held that the ban restricted trade in violation of Article 34 and was a disproportionate means to protect the health of Swedish citizens. *Klas Rosengren et al.*, Case 170/04, [2007] ECR I–04071.

D. EXCLUSIVE PRIVILEGES—ARTICLE 106

Article 106 prohibits public undertakings and undertakings to which Member States grant special or exclusive rights from violating the competition provisions insofar as application of those rules does not obstruct the performance of the tasks assigned. Specifically:

Article 106, ex 86 ECT

1. In the case of public undertakings and undertakings to which Member States grant special or exclusive rights, Member States shall

neither enact nor maintain in force any measure contrary to the rules contained in this Treaty, in particular to those rules provided for in Article 18 [non-discrimination] and Articles 101 to 109 [restrictive agreements, abuse of dominance, state aids].

2. Undertakings entrusted with the operation of services of general economic interest or having the character of a revenue-producing monopoly shall be subject to the rules contained in this Treaty, in particular to the rules on competition, insofar as the application of such rules does not obstruct the performance, in law or in fact, of the particular tasks assigned to them. The development of trade must not be affected to such an extent as would be contrary to the interests of the Community. * * *

The next case asks when enjoyment of a state-granted monopoly right, which is the right to keep out the competition, violates Article 106.

HOFNER v. MACROTRON GmbH

Case C–41/90, [1991] ECR I–1979, ECJ.

[German law, intended to achieve a high level of employment and to improve the distribution of jobs, conferred on the Bundesanstalt für Arbeit (Federal Employment Office) the exclusive right of placement; i.e. exclusivity as employment agent. The law required the Office to provide the service free of charge. Placement activities by others were punishable by fine. Messrs. Höfner and Elser contracted with Macrotron to present to Macrotron a suitable candidate for the post of sales manager, for a fee. They presented such a candidate, but Macrotron decided not to employ him and refused to pay the fee stipulated, alleging, inter alia, that the contract was void by reason of the German law. Höfner and Elser rejoined that the German law was void because it unnecessarily restrained their competition in violation of Article 106, and exclusion of their competition amounted to abuse of dominance under Article 102. The national court referred questions to the Court of Justice.]

16   In its fourth question, the national court asks more specifically whether the monopoly of employment procurement in respect of business executives granted to a public employment agency constitutes an abuse of a dominant position within the meaning of Article [102], having regard to Article [106](2)....

17   According to the appellants in the main proceedings, an agency such as the Bundesanstalt is both a public undertaking within the meaning of Article [106](1) and an undertaking entrusted with the operation of services of general economic interest within the meaning of Article [106] (2) of the Treaty. The Bundesanstalt is therefore, they maintain, subject to the competition rules to the extent to which the application thereof does not obstruct the performance of the particular task assigned to it, and it does not in the present case. The appellants also claim that the action taken by the Bundesanstalt, which extended its

statutory monopoly over employment procurement to activities for which the establishment of a monopoly is not in the public interest, constitutes an abuse within the meaning of Article [102] of the Treaty. They also consider that any Member State which makes such an abuse possible is in breach of Article [106](1) and of the general principle whereby the Member States must refrain from taking any measure which could destroy the effectiveness of the Community competition rules.

18   The Commission takes a somewhat different view. The maintenance of a monopoly on executive recruitment constitutes, in its view, an infringement of Article [106](1) read in conjunction with Article [102] of the Treaty where the grantee of the monopoly is not willing or able to carry out that task fully, according to the demand existing on the market, and provided that such conduct is liable to affect trade between Member States. * * *

21   It must be observed, in the context of competition law, first that the concept of an undertaking encompasses every entity engaged in an economic activity, regardless of the legal status of the entity and the way in which it is financed and, secondly, that employment procurement is an economic activity.

22   The fact that employment procurement activities are normally entrusted to public agencies cannot affect the economic nature of such activities. Employment procurement has not always been, and is not necessarily, carried out by public entities. That finding applies in particular to executive recruitment.

23   It follows that an entity such as a public employment agency engaged in the business of employment procurement may be classified as an undertaking for the purpose of applying the Community competition rules.

24   It must be pointed out that a public employment agency which is entrusted, under the legislation of a Member State, with the operation of services of general economic interest ... remains subject to the competition rules pursuant to Article [106] (2) of the Treaty unless and to the extent to which it is shown that their application is incompatible with the discharge of its duties.

25   As regards the manner in which a public employment agency enjoying an exclusive right of employment procurement conducts itself in relation to executive recruitment undertaken by private recruitment consultancy companies, it must be stated that the application of Article [102] of the Treaty cannot obstruct the performance of the particular task assigned to that agency in so far as the latter is manifestly not in a position to satisfy demand in that area of the market and in fact allows its exclusive rights to be encroached on by those companies.

26   Whilst it is true that Article [102] concerns undertakings and may be applied within the limits laid down by Article [106](2) to public undertakings or undertakings vested with exclusive rights or specific rights, the fact nevertheless remains that the Treaty requires the Member States not to take or maintain in force measures which could destroy the effectiveness of that provision.... * * *

29   ... [T]he simple fact of creating a dominant position of that kind by granting an exclusive right within the meaning of Article [106](1) is not as such incompatible with Article [102] of the Treaty. A Member State is in breach of the prohibition contained in those two provisions only if the undertaking in question, merely by exercising the exclusive right granted to it, cannot avoid abusing its dominant position.

30   Pursuant to Article [102](b), such an abuse may in particular consist in limiting the provision of a service, to the prejudice of those seeking to avail themselves of it.

31   A Member State creates a situation in which the provision of a service is limited when the undertaking to which it grants an exclusive right extending to executive recruitment activities is manifestly not in a position to satisfy the demand prevailing on the market for activities of that kind and when the effective pursuit of such activities, by private companies is rendered impossible by the maintenance in force of a statutory provision under which such activities are prohibited and nonobservance of that prohibition renders the contracts concerned void. * * *

34   In view of the foregoing considerations, it must be stated in reply to the fourth question that a public employment agency engaged in employment procurement activities is subject to the prohibition contained in Article [102] of the Treaty, so long as the application of that provision does not obstruct the performance of the particular task assigned to it. A Member State which has conferred an exclusive right to carry on that activity upon the public employment agency is in breach of Article [106] (1) of the Treaty where it creates a situation in which that agency cannot avoid infringing Article [102] of the Treaty. That is the case, in particular, where the following conditions are satisfied:

— the exclusive right extends to executive recruitment activities

— the public employment agency is manifestly incapable of satisfying demand prevailing on the market for such activities

— the actual pursuit of those activities by private recruitment consultants is rendered impossible by the maintenance in force of a statutory provision under which such activities are prohibited and non-observance of that prohibition renders the contracts concerned void

— the activities in question may extend to the nationals or to the territory of other Member States.

NOTES AND QUESTIONS

1.　What is the standard for running afoul of Article 106? How difficult will it be for Messrs. Höfner and Elser to win their argument before the national court?

2.　Note the difference between plaintiffs' proposed formulation and the Commission's. Which did the Court accept? Which is the more workable? Which is the better standard, given the Community's dual interests in respecting Member State regulation in the public interest and supporting freedom of competition?

3.　Does the Court in effect require an efficiency audit of the Federal Employment Office to determine whether it can satisfy demand? Isn't the Office's ability to satisfy demand a function of the resources the German government makes available to it? Why does the Community care whether Germany sufficiently funds its free employment service? Do all dominant firms abuse their dominance by simply not providing enough goods or service (at what price level?), or is it critical that the government-granted exclusive privilege prevents anyone else from serving the market?

4.　Messrs. Höfner and Elser also claimed a violation of Article 56 (Member States may not restrict freedom to provide services in respect of nationals of Member States) in conjunction with Article 18 (no discrimination on grounds of nationality); but since all parties, including the employment candidate, were German, the Court found Article 56 inapplicable. If the candidate or the private employment agency were Belgian, would Article 56 protect the private agency's right to its fee?

5.　In *Régie des Postes v. Corbeau*, Case C–320/91, [1993] ECR I–2533, a Belgian law—enacted before the development of courier service—gave exclusive mail delivery rights to the Belgian Post Office and prohibited private mail delivery. Mr. Corbeau set up a private mail delivery service in Liège. Corbeau collected mail from his clients and guaranteed delivery before noon the following day to all addressees within town limits. He delivered in-town mail and dispatched the out-of-town mail by post. When prosecuted, Corbeau asserted a violation of Article 106.

In an Article 267 reference, the Court of Justice advised the Belgian court that an undertaking charged with the provision of universal service may not restrict competition more than necessary to achieve its public mission in view of contemporary market conditions, leaving it to the national court to determine what was more than necessary.

Was Corbeau skimming the cream from the Belgian Post's business? At some point, would cream-skimming compromise the economic stability of the post office and disable it from fulfilling its obligation to provide universal service? How can the national court determine how much competition is too much competition for the Belgian Post to fulfill its public mission?

6.　There is, however, a gap in the coverage of Articles 101, 102 and 106. State bodies are subject to those Treaty obligations only if they carry out economic activities. Bodies that regulate the market but do not participate in it are not covered. In *FENIN v. Commission,* Case C–205/03 P, [2006] ECR I–6295, the Court of Justice acknowledged that the public bodies that ran the Spanish national healthcare system and provided free services funded by social security contributions and other state funding were not "undertakings," and it held that a state body that is not an undertaking does not become so in its role as purchaser of goods—here, medical goods and equipment. The purchasing activity is not "dissociable from the service subsequently provided." The holding of *FENIN* means that suppliers to state bodies carrying out public functions are not protected by Article 102 from the state body's exploitative and discriminatory purchasing conduct. Does this holding shield too much activity from the antitrust provisions? Is it sufficient protection that the state is subject to Treaty Article 18, prohibiting discrimination based on nationality?

ALBANY INTERNATIONAL BV AND TEXTILE INDUSTRY PENSION FUNDS

Case C–67/96, [1999] ECR I–5751, ECJ
(see additional facts at 956 supra, excerpt regarding Art. 101).

[Albany International, a textile firm that wished to provide pensions for its workers through an insurer of its choice, contended that the Dutch law granting to a specified fund an exclusive right to manage supplementary textile industry pensions violated Articles 102 and 106. Citing Höfner, the Court repeated that mere creation of a dominant position (which the Netherlands conferred on the pension fund) is not incompatible with Article 102. Rather, to run afoul of the law, the Member State must create a situation in which the undertaking cannot avoid abusing its dominance.]

98 It is therefore necessary to consider whether, as contended by the Fund, the Netherlands Government and the Commission, the exclusive right of the sectoral pension fund to manage supplementary pensions in a given sector and the resultant restriction of competition may be justified under Article [106](2) of the Treaty as a measure necessary for the performance of a particular social task of general interest with which that fund has been charged. * * *

102 It is important to bear in mind first of all that, under Article [106](2) of the Treaty, undertakings entrusted with the operation of services of general economic interest are subject to the rules on competition in so far as the application of such rules does not obstruct the performance, in law or in fact, of the particular tasks assigned to them.

103 In allowing, in certain circumstances, derogations from the general rules of the Treaty, Article [106](2) of the Treaty seeks to reconcile the Member States' interest in using certain undertakings, in particular in the public sector, as an instrument of economic or fiscal policy with the Community's interest in ensuring compliance with the rules on competition and preservation of the unity of the common market.

104 In view of the interest of the Member States thus defined they cannot be precluded, when determining what services of general economic

interest they entrust to certain undertakings, from taking account of objectives pertaining to their national policy or from endeavouring to attain them by means of obligations and constraints which they impose on such undertakings.

105 The supplementary pension scheme at issue in the main proceedings fulfils an essential social function within the Netherlands pensions system by reason of the limited amount of the statutory pension, which is calculated on the basis of the minimum statutory wage.

106 Moreover, the importance of the social function attributed to supplementary pensions has recently been recognised by the Community legislature's adoption of Council Directive 98/49/EC of 29 June 1998 on safeguarding the supplementary pension rights of employed and self-employed persons moving within the Community.

107 Next, it is not necessary, in order for the conditions for the application of Article [106] (2) of the Treaty to be fulfilled, that the financial balance or economic viability of the undertaking entrusted with the operation of a service of general economic interest should be threatened. It is sufficient that, in the absence of the rights at issue, it would not be possible for the undertaking to perform the particular tasks entrusted to it, defined by reference to the obligations and constraints to which it is subject or that maintenance of those rights is necessary to enable the holder of them to perform tasks of general economic interest which have been assigned to it under economically acceptable conditions.

108 If the exclusive right of the fund to manage the supplementary pension scheme for all workers in a given sector were removed, undertakings with young employees in good health engaged in non-dangerous activities would seek more advantageous insurance terms from private insurers. The progressive departure of 'good' risks would leave the sectoral pension fund with responsibility for an increasing share of 'bad' risks, thereby increasing the cost of pensions for workers, particularly those in small and medium-sized undertakings with older employees engaged in dangerous activities, to which the fund could no longer offer pensions at an acceptable cost.

109 Such a situation would arise particularly in a case where, as in the main proceedings, the supplementary pension scheme managed exclusively by the Fund displays a high level of solidarity resulting, in particular, from the fact that contributions do not reflect the risk, from the obligation to accept all workers without a prior medical examination, the continuing accrual of pension rights despite exemption from the payment of contributions in the event of incapacity for work, the discharge by the Fund of arrears of contributions due from an employer in the event of insolvency and the indexing of the amount of pensions in order to maintain their value.

110 Such constraints, which render the service provided by the Fund less competitive than a comparable service provided by insurance compa-

nies, go towards justifying the exclusive right of the Fund to manage the supplementary pension scheme.

111 It follows that the removal of the exclusive right conferred on the Fund might make it impossible for it to perform the tasks of general economic interest entrusted to it under economically acceptable conditions and threaten its financial equilibrium. * * *

[The Fund has the power to grant exemptions from its own exclusivity. It has the duty to grant such exemptions if specific criteria are met, thus providing a check against discriminatory or arbitrary denials.]

122 Finally, as regards Albany's argument that an adequate level of pension for workers could be assured by laying down minimum requirements to be met by pensions offered by insurance companies, it must be emphasised that, in view of the social function of supplementary pension schemes and the margin of appreciation enjoyed, according to settled case-law, by the Member States in organising their social security systems, it is incumbent on each Member State to consider whether, in view of the particular features of its national pension system, laying down minimum requirements would still enable it to ensure the level of pension which it seeks to guarantee in a sector by compulsory affiliation to a pension fund.

123 The answer to the third question must therefore be that Articles [102] and [106] of the Treaty do not preclude the public authorities from conferring on a pension fund the exclusive right to manage a supplementary pension scheme in a given sector.

NOTES AND QUESTIONS

1. Does the Court grant wide berth to the state to carry out its social purpose of solidarity, despite the fact that its chosen solution might block competition and not be efficient? Or does the Court imply some level of serious scrutiny? If the Netherlands can assure an adequate level of pensions by laying down minimum requirements, must it abandon its system of granting an exclusive right to a chosen fund? See para. 122. Who determines whether adequate pensions can be assured by less restrictive means? Does para. 122 mean that a grant of exclusive rights can, in itself, violate the Treaty simply because it restricts competition and the restriction was unnecessary to achieve the public goal?

2. Since the late 1970s, the Commission and Courts have taken a number of actions to limit the power of state-owned monopolies and undertakings enjoying exclusive rights. In 1980 the Commission issued a directive under Article [106](3) requiring Member States to reveal financial information about their state-owned enterprises. Commission Directive 80/723, O.J. L 195/35 (29 July 1980), amended by Commission Directive 85/413, O.J. L 229/20 (28 Aug. 1985).

In a number of situations the case is a straightforward Article 102 case, and the fact of state ownership or state-granted privilege does not provide a shield. In *British Telecom* (Italy v. Commission), the Court held that a state telecommunications monopoly abused its dominance by preventing private message-forwarding agencies from receiving and forwarding international telephone calls. Case 41/83, [1985] ECR 873. In *Telemarketing,* the Court stated that a broadcasting monopoly enterprise would abuse its dominant position by refusing to sell broadcasting time to a telemarketing firm that competed with the monopoly firm's subsidiary. *Centre Belge d'Études de Marché–Télémarketing SA v. Compagnie Luxembourgeoise de Télédiffusion SA*, Case 311/84, [1985] ECR 3261.

E. STATE MEASURES THAT RESTRICT COMPETITION OR FACILITATE PRIVATE RESTRICTIONS

1. STATE RESPONSIBILITY

State legislation is a frequent source of distortion of competition. Distortions may result from national laws on price control, sector regulation (e.g., oil, tobacco, transport), taxation, and various social and national industrial policies.

To what extent does TEU Article 4, the competition articles, and the freedoms of movement suggest a broad preemption by Community competition policy of anticompetitive state legislation? The Court bowed in the direction of a broad preemption in *NV GB–INNO–BM v. Vereniging van de Kleinhandelaars in Tabak* (*INNO/ATAB*), Case 13/77, [1977] ECR 2115. There the Court said, regarding a Belgian law requiring, for tax collection purposes, that tobacco products be sold at a price affixed to the label by the manufacturer or importer:

> [W]hile it is true that Article [now 102] is directed at undertakings, nonetheless it is also true that the Treaty [now TEU 4] imposes a duty on Member States not to adopt or maintain in force any measure which could deprive that provision of its effectiveness. Id., para. 31.

But in the years after *INNO/ATAB,* the Court backed away from a strong view of Member State duties not to restrain competition unnecessarily. Especially since the *Keck* "revolution" in 1993 (see Part III page 496 supra), the Court has been reluctant to condemn Member States' regulatory laws for undermining Articles 101 and 102. Three competition cases decided at the time of *Keck* reflect the new deference in adopting measures that have anticompetitive effects; namely, *Ohra, Meng* and *Reiff.*

Ohra, a Dutch insurance firm that dealt directly with customers rather than through intermediaries, tried to become more competitive by giving credit cards to its customers. Ohra was prosecuted for violating a Dutch law that prohibited insurance companies and their agents from granting rebates or other things of value. Ohra responded that the law was anticompetitive and constituted a violation of Member States' obligations under Articles 3(1)(g) [now in a protocol] and TEU 4(3), as linked with TFEU 101 and 102.

In *Meng,* in the face of a similar German law, insurance agent Meng rebated his commissions to his clients. When prosecuted, he presented the same defense as Ohra: he was competing; the prohibition was illegal.

Reiff involved a German law that delegated truck tariff-setting to tariff boards whose members were appointed by the Federal Minister upon the recommendation of the truckers themselves. In setting the tariffs, the board members were obliged to take account of the public interest criteria laid down by the public authority, and the Minister of Transport was entitled to participate in the meetings, to reject tariffs that were not in the public interest, and to set tariffs himself. A trucking company charged Reiff, a shipper, a price less than the mandated tariff. The federal office proceeded against Reiff for the difference, and Reiff defended on grounds that the the law was anticompetitive and void. *Ohra Schadeverzekeringen NV v. Netherlands (Ohra)*, Case C–245/91, [1993] ECR I–5851; *W. Meng v. Germany (Meng)*, Case C–2/91, [1993] ECR I–5751; *Gebrüder Reiff GmbH & Co. KG v. Bundesanstalt für den Güterfernverkehr (Reiff)*, Case C–185/91, [1993] ECR I–5801.

The three cases came to the Court of Justice on Article 267 references. The Court held: A Member State would infringe Articles 3(1)(g) [now in a protocol] and TEU 4(3) if it "requires or favors the adoption of agreements, decisions or concerted practices contrary to Article [TFEU 101], or reinforces such effects, or deprives its own legislation of its official character by delegating economic responsibility to private traders" (quoting from *INNO/ATAB)*. It held that none of the three laws fit the prohibited category.

Do you agree? What are the anticompetitive effects in each case? In which of the cases can you make the best argument that the national measure would tend to reinforce a private cartel or that it delegated economic responsibility for an anticompetitive act to private traders?

The question remained: How broadly or narrowly would the Court construe its mandate that the State must not undermine the effectiveness of Articles 101 and 102?

CONSORZIO INDUSTRIE FIAMMIFERI
(*Italian matches*)

(responsibility of state)
Case C–198/01, [2003] ECR I–8055, ECJ.

[In *Consorzio Industrie Fiammiferi (Italian matches)*, Case C–198/01, [2003] ECR I–8055, Italy, by an 80 year-old Royal Decree, organized a match cartel. Italy required the Italian match producers to join a consortium. The minister was required to set the price for matches, and the consortium of competitors was required to allocate quotas. Government officials had the duty to oversee the quotas. A German match producer complained to the Italian Antitrust Authority that it was having difficulty entering the Italian market. Swedish producers later complained that they were denied a fair quota and could sell only to the Italian match consortium. The Italian Antitrust Authority opened proceedings. It found Treaty violations both by Italy and by the Italian producers. An Italian Tribunal referred questions to the Court of Justice. Here is the response of the Court regarding Italy's responsibility.]

45 ... [A]lthough Articles [101 and 102 TFEU] are, in themselves, concerned solely with the conduct of undertakings and not with laws or regulations emanating from Member States, those articles, read in conjunction with Article [4 TEU], which lays down a duty to cooperate, none the less require the Member States not to introduce or maintain in force measures, even of a legislative or regulatory nature, which may render ineffective the competition rules applicable to undertakings.

46 The Court has held in particular that Articles [4 TEU and 101 TFEU] are infringed where a Member State requires or favours the adoption of agreements, decisions or concerted practices contrary to Article [101 TFEU] or reinforces their effects, or where it divests its own rules of the character of legislation by delegating to private economic operators responsibility for taking decisions affecting the economic sphere.

47 Moreover, since the Treaty of Maastricht entered into force, the ... Treaty has expressly provided that in the context of their economic policy the activities of the Member States must observe the principle of an open market economy with free competition....

48 It is appropriate to bear in mind, second, that in accordance with settled case-law the primacy of Community law requires any provision of national law which contravenes a Community rule to be disapplied, regardless of whether it was adopted before or after that rule.

49 The duty to disapply national legislation which contravenes Community law applies not only to national courts but also to all organs of the State, including administrative authorities, which entails, if the circumstances so require, the obligation to take all appropriate measures to enable Community law to be fully applied.

50 Since a national competition authority such as the Authority is responsible for ensuring, *inter alia*, that Article [101 TFEU] is observed and that provision, in conjunction with Article [4 TEU], imposes a duty on Member States to refrain from introducing measures contrary to the Community competition rules, those rules would be rendered less effective if, in the course of an investigation under [101 TFEU] into the conduct of undertakings, the authority were not able to declare a national measure contrary to the combined provisions of Articles [4 TEU] and [101 TFEU] and if, consequently, it failed to disapply it.

51 In that regard, it is of little significance that, where undertakings are required by national legislation to engage in anti-competitive conduct, they cannot also be held accountable for infringement of Articles [101 and 102 TFEU]. Member States' obligations under Articles 3(1)(g) EC (now in a protocol), [4 TEU, 101 TFEU and 102 TFEU], which are distinct from those to which undertakings are subject under Articles [101 and 102 TFEU], none the less continue to exist and therefore the national competition authority remains duty-bound to disapply the national measure at issue.

CIPOLLA v. FAZARI AND MACRINO v. MELONI

Joined cases C–94/04 and C–202/04, [2006] ECR I–11421, ECJ.

[Pursuant to a 73–year old Italian law, Italy adopted maximum and minimum fee schedules for lawyers, from which there could be no derogation except in narrow circumstances. The schedules were based on a draft prepared by the National Lawyers' Council—a professional body of lawyers. In connection with three fee disputes, an Italian court referred to the Court of Justice questions regarding the validity of the Italian law.]

46 According to settled case-law, although it is true that Articles [101 and 102] are, in themselves, concerned solely with the conduct of undertakings and not with laws or regulations emanating from Member States, those articles, read in conjunction with Article [TEU 4(3)], which lays down a duty to cooperate, none the less require Member States not to introduce or maintain in force measures, even of a legislative or regulatory nature, which may render ineffective the competition rules applicable to undertakings.

47 The Court has held, in particular, that Articles [TEU 4(3) and TFEU 101] are infringed where a Member State requires or encourages the adoption of agreements, decisions or concerted practices contrary to Article [101] or reinforces their effects, or where it divests its own rules of the character of legislation by delegating to private economic operators responsibility for taking decisions affecting the economic sphere.

48 In that respect, the fact that a Member State requires a professional organisation composed of lawyers, such as the CNF, to produce a draft scale of fees does not, in the circumstances specific to the cases in the main proceedings, appear to establish that that State has divested the scale finally adopted of its character of legislation by delegating to lawyers responsibility for taking decisions concerning them.

49 Although the national legislation at issue in the main proceedings does not contain either procedural arrangements or substantive requirements capable of ensuring with reasonable probability that, when producing the draft scale, the CNF conducts itself like an arm of the

State working in the public interest, it does not appear that the Italian State has waived its power to make decisions of last resort or to review implementation of that scale.

50   First, the CNF is responsible only for producing a draft scale which, as such, is not binding. Without the Minister of Justice's approval, the draft scale does not enter into force and the earlier approved scale remains applicable. Accordingly, that Minister has the power to have the draft amended by the CNF. Furthermore, the Minister is assisted by two public bodies, the Consiglio di Stato and the CIP, whose opinions he must obtain before the scale can be approved.

51   Secondly, Article 60 of the Royal Decree–Law provides that fees are to be settled by the courts on the basis of the criteria referred to in Article 57 of that decree-law, having regard to the seriousness and number of the issues dealt with. Moreover, in certain exceptional circumstances and by duly reasoned decision, the court may depart from the maximum and minimum limits fixed pursuant to Article 58 of the Royal Decree–Law.

52   In those circumstances, the view cannot be taken that the Italian State has waived its power by delegating to private economic operators responsibility for taking decisions affecting the economic sphere, which would have the effect of depriving the provisions at issue in the main proceedings of the character of legislation.

53   Nor ... is the Italian State open to the criticism that it requires or encourages the adoption by the CNF of agreements, decisions or concerted practices contrary to Article [101] or reinforces their effects, or requires or encourages abuses of a dominant position contrary to Article [102] or reinforces the effects of such abuses. * * *

Free movement of services

58   The prohibition of derogation, by agreement, from the minimum fees set by a scale such as that laid down by the Italian legislation is liable to render access to the Italian legal services market more difficult for lawyers established in a Member State other than the Italian Republic and therefore is likely to restrict the exercise of their activities providing services in that Member State. That prohibition therefore amounts to a restriction within the meaning of Article [56].

59   That prohibition deprives lawyers established in a Member State other than the Italian Republic of the possibility, by requesting fees lower than those set by the scale, of competing more effectively with lawyers established on a stable basis in the Member State concerned and who therefore have greater opportunities for winning clients than lawyers established abroad.

60   Likewise, the prohibition thus laid down limits the choice of service recipients in Italy, because they cannot resort to the services of lawyers established in other Member States who would offer their

services in Italy at a lower rate than the minimum fees set by the scale.

61 However, such a prohibition may be justified where it serves over-riding requirements relating to the public interest, is suitable for securing the attainment of the objective which it pursues and does not go beyond what is necessary in order to attain it.

62 In order to justify the restriction on freedom to provide services which stems from the prohibition at issue, the Italian Government submits that excessive competition between lawyers might lead to price compe-tition which would result in a deterioration in the quality of the services provided to the detriment of consumers, in particular as individuals in need of quality advice in court proceedings.

63 According to the Commission, no causal link has been established between the setting of minimum levels of fees and a high qualitative standard of professional services provided by lawyers. In actual fact, quasi-legislative measures such as, inter alia, rules on access to the legal profession, disciplinary rules serving to ensure compliance with professional ethics and rules on civil liability have, by maintaining a high qualitative standard for the services provided by such profession-als which those measures guarantee, a direct relationship of cause and effect with the protection of lawyers' clients and the proper working of the administration of justice.

64 In that respect, it must be pointed out that, first, the protection of consumers, in particular recipients of the legal services provided by persons concerned in the administration of justice and, secondly, the safeguarding of the proper administration of justice, are objectives to be included among those which may be regarded as overriding require-ments relating to the public interest capable of justifying a restriction on freedom to provide services ..., on condition, first, that the national measure at issue in the main proceedings is suitable for securing the attainment of the objective pursued and, secondly, it does not go beyond what is necessary in order to attain that objective.

65 It is a matter for the national court to decide whether, in the main proceedings, the restriction on freedom to provide services introduced by that national legislation fulfils those conditions. For that purpose, it is for that court to take account of the factors set out in the following paragraphs.

66 Thus, it must be determined, in particular, whether there is a correla-tion between the level of fees and the quality of the services provided by lawyers and whether, in particular, the setting of such minimum fees constitutes an appropriate measure for attaining the objectives pursued, namely the protection of consumers and the proper adminis-tration of justice.

67 Although it is true that a scale imposing minimum fees cannot prevent members of the profession from offering services of mediocre quality,

it is conceivable that such a scale does serve to prevent lawyers, in a context such as that of the Italian market which, as indicated in the decision making the reference, is characterised by an extremely large number of lawyers who are enrolled and practising, from being encouraged to compete against each other by possibly offering services at a discount, with the risk of deterioration in the quality of the services provided.

68   Account must also be taken of the specific features both of the market in question, as noted in the preceding paragraph, and the services in question and, in particular, of the fact that, in the field of lawyers' services, there is usually an asymmetry of information between 'client-consumers' and lawyers. Lawyers display a high level of technical knowledge which consumers may not have and the latter therefore find it difficult to judge the quality of the services provided to them.

69   However, the national court will have to determine whether professional rules in respect of lawyers, in particular rules relating to organisation, qualifications, professional ethics, supervision and liability, suffice in themselves to attain the objectives of the protection of consumers and the proper administration of justice.

70   Having regard to the foregoing, the answer to the fourth and fifth questions ... must be that legislation containing an absolute prohibition of derogation, by agreement, from the minimum fees set by a scale of lawyer's fees such as that at issue in the main proceedings for services which are (a) court services and (b) reserved to lawyers constitutes a restriction on freedom to provide services laid down in Article [56]. It is for the national court to determine whether such legislation, in the light of the detailed rules for its application, actually serves the objectives of protection of consumers and the proper administration of justice which might justify it and whether the restrictions it imposes do not appear disproportionate in the light of those objectives.

* * *

NOTES AND QUESTIONS

1.   Do paragraphs 48 to 53 surprise you, after *Italian matches*?

2.   What is the argument, contrariwise, that setting minimum lawyer fees harms free movement *and* consumers and is not justified on its face? What is the argument that the Italian law requires or facilitates an illegal agreement among lawyers? Note the Commission's argument that enforced price floors do not correlate with higher quality services. Note also that, in most jurisdictions, competitors have a right to combine to procure government action—a point relevant to Private Responsibility, below.

3.   How will the national court determine whether the law "actually serves the objectives of the protection of consumers and the proper administration of justice" and whether the restrictions are "disproportionate in light

of those objectives"? Would a bright line (e.g., no minimum fees) have been superior? Italy, in fact, proceeded to abolish minimum lawyer fees.

4. See, for the Court's treatment of lawyers' agreements that restrict competition, *Wouters,* in Chapter 23. Is the Court especially deferential to agreements among professionals that may restrict competition, or has it struck the right balance?

In the United States, professionals, when carrying on their commercial activities, are fully subject to the antitrust laws. But states may regulate lawyers and other professionals in the public interest. For example, the state may limit the number of lawyers in the state through state bar examinations. See *Hoover v. Ronwin*, 466 U.S. 558, 104 S.Ct. 1989, 80 L.Ed.2d 590 (1984).

2. PRIVATE RESPONSIBILITY

Private actors may avoid responsibility on grounds that the anticompetitive act was not theirs; it was the act of the state.

COMMISSION AND FRANCE v. LADBROKE RACING LTD.

Cases C–359/95 P and C–379/95 P, [1997] ECR I–6265, ECJ.

[French law created Pari Mutuel Urbain (PMU) as a joint service of the authorized racing companies to manage their rights in off-track betting, and it granted PMU exclusive rights to run off-track betting on horse races held in France and horse race betting organized in France. French law prohibited anyone other than PMU to place or accept bets on horse races.

Ladbroke Racing Ltd., an operator of off-track betting, lodged with the Commission a complaint against France under Article 106, and a complaint against the ten main racing companies in France and PMU under Articles 101 and 102.

Before taking a position on the Article 106 claim, which included allegations of illegal state aid, the Commission rejected the allegations of violation of Articles 101 and 102 on grounds that those articles did not apply.

The General Court annulled the Commission's decision to reject the complaint, on grounds that a definitive determination could not be made by the Commission before completing its investigation regarding the compatibility of the French law with the competition rules. The Commission and France appealed to the Court of Justice.]

[20]   ... [T]he Commission submits that it is necessary to distinguish between State measures requiring undertakings to engage in conduct contrary to Articles [101] and [102] and measures that do not require any conduct contrary to those rules but simply create a legal framework that itself restricts competition. In the first case, the Commission considers that Article [101] remains applicable to undertakings'

conduct despite the existence of national statutory obligations and irrespective of the possible application of Articles 3[(1)](g)[now in protocol], [TEU 4] and [TFEU 101] of the Treaty with regard to those State measures. In fact, the Commission argues that an undertaking can and, by virtue of the primacy of Community law and the direct effect of Articles [101](1) and [102] of the Treaty, must refuse to comply with a State measure that requires conduct contrary to those provisions.

21   In the second case, by contrast, Article [101] may in certain circumstances not apply. That is the case here, since the 1974 legislation does not require the conclusion of an agreement between the main racing companies but itself grants the PMU the exclusive right to organize off-course totalizator betting. The restriction of competition thus flowed directly from the national legislation, without any action on the part of undertakings being necessary. * * *

33   Articles [101] and [102] of the Treaty apply only to anti-competitive conduct engaged in by undertakings on their own initiative. If anti-competitive conduct is required of undertakings by national legislation or if the latter creates a legal framework which itself eliminates any possibility of competitive activity on their part, Articles [101] and [102] do not apply. In such a situation, the restriction of competition is not attributable, as those provisions implicitly require, to the autonomous conduct of the undertakings.

34   Articles [101] and [102] may apply, however, if it is found that the national legislation does not preclude undertakings from engaging in autonomous conduct which prevents, restricts or distorts competition.

35   When the Commission is considering the applicability of Articles [101] and [102] of the Treaty to the conduct of undertakings, a prior evaluation of national legislation affecting such conduct should therefore be directed solely to ascertaining whether that legislation prevents undertakings from engaging in autonomous conduct which prevents, restricts or distorts competition.

[The Commission was therefore entitled to find Articles 101 and 102 inapplicable without completing its investigation into the compatibility of the French legislation with the competition law. The Court set aside the judgment of the General Court.]

NOTES AND QUESTIONS

1. Describe the anticompetitive aspects of the French off-track betting system. Why might France desire such a system nonetheless?

2. The Commission held that there was no *private* anticompetitive action. Defend the result, including the distinction made by the Commission in paragraphs 20–21.

3. What do paragraphs 33 and 34 mean?

4. Were the state measures (apart from state aid) likely to be compatible with Article 106? What if the PMU establishments shut their doors at 5:00 p.m. and gamblers claimed they were shut out of betting? (Consider *Höfner.*) Would the outcome of the case have been different if the PMU were an undertaking in the sole control of the ten racing companies?

COMMISSION v. ITALY (*CNSD*)

C–35/96, [1998] ECR I–3851, ECJ.

[Customs agents are professionals who offer services to carry out customs formalities relating to the import, export and transit of goods, and related monetary, fiscal and commercial services. In Italy the Departmental Councils of Customs Agents, whose members are elected by the customs agents, are constituted by Italian law to supervise the activity of the customs agents. Also constituted by Italian law, the Consiglio Nazionale degli Spedizionieri Doganali (National Council of Customs Agents, or CNSD) governs the Departmental Councils. It is legally responsible for setting the tariff for the services provided by customs agents on the basis of proposals from the Departmental Councils. Its members are customs agents elected by the Departmental Councils. Customs agents who deviate from the tariff are subject to discipline, which can include suspension or removal from the register of customs agents.

The Commission brought an action against Italy under Article 258 for a declaration that Italy failed to fulfill its obligations TEU 4 and TFEU 101 by requiring the CNSD to adopt a decision by an association of undertakings (a minimum compulsory tariff; i.e. to price fix) contrary to Article 101.

A related action by the Commission for a declaration that Italy's law infringed Articles 28 and 30 (no duties or measures of equivalent effect) failed on grounds that importers did not need to use the services of professional customs agents in all circumstances.

In connection with Articles TEU 4 and TFEU 101, Italy argued that the customs agents were professionals exercising a liberal profession; that their activity was intellectual, and that they and their association CNSD were not "undertakings" subject to Article 101.

The Court held first that CNSD engaged in economic activity on the market and therefore was an association of undertakings.]

43   ... [T]he CNSD is responsible for setting the tariff for the professional services of customs agents on the basis of proposals from the Departmental Councils (Article 14(d) of Law No 1612/1960)....

44   It follows that the members of the CNSD cannot be characterised as independent experts and that they are not required, under the law, to set tariffs taking into account not only the interests of the undertakings or associations of undertakings in the sector which has appointed them but also the general interest and the interests of undertakings in other sectors or users of the services in question.

45 Secondly, it must be held that the decisions by which the CNSD set a uniform, compulsory tariff for all customs agents restrict competition within the meaning of Article [101] of the Treaty and are capable of affecting intra-Community trade.

46 The tariff directly sets the prices for customs agents' services. It provides, for each separate type of operation, the maximum and minimum prices which can be charged to customers. Furthermore, the tariff lays down various scales on the basis of the value or the weight of the goods to be cleared through customs or of the specific type of goods, or type of professional service.

47 Lastly, the tariff is mandatory (Article 5), so that a customs agent may not depart from it on his own initiative. Only the CNSD is empowered to provide for derogations.... * * *

51 From the foregoing considerations, it follows that, in adopting the tariff, the CNSD infringed Article [101] (1) of the Treaty.

52 Thirdly, the question of the extent to which that infringement can be attributed to the Italian Republic must be considered.

53 Although Article [101] of the Treaty is, in itself, concerned solely with the conduct of undertakings and not with measures adopted by Member States by law or regulation, the fact nevertheless remains that Article [101] of the Treaty, in conjunction with Article [TFEU 4], requires the Member States not to introduce or maintain in force measures, even of a legislative nature, which may render ineffective the competition rules applicable to undertakings (for Article [101] of the Treaty, see *Van Eycke, Reiff*).

54 Such would be the case if a Member State were to require or favour the adoption of agreements, decisions or concerted practices contrary to Article [101] or to reinforce their effects, or to deprive its own rules of the character of legislation by delegating to private economic operators responsibility for taking decisions affecting the economic sphere (see *Van Eycke, Reiff*).

55 By adopting the national legislation in question, the Italian Republic clearly not only required the conclusion of an agreement contrary to Article [101] of the Treaty and declined to influence its terms, but also assists in ensuring compliance with that agreement.

56 First, Article 14(d) of Law No 1612/1960 requires the CNSD to compile a compulsory, uniform tariff for the services of customs agents.

57 Secondly, ... the national legislation in question wholly relinquished to private economic operators the powers of the public authorities as regards the setting of tariffs.

58 Thirdly, the Italian legislation expressly prohibits registered customs agents from derogating from the tariff on pain of exclusion, suspension or removal from the register.

59   Fourthly, ... the Decree of the Minister for Finance of 6 July 1988 bestowed upon [the tariff] the appearance of a public regulation. First, publication in the 'General Series' of the *Gazzetta Ufficiale della Repubblica Italiana* gave rise to a presumption of knowledge of the tariff on the part of third parties, to which the CNSD's decision could never have laid claim. Second, the official character thus conferred on the tariff facilitates the application by customs agents of the prices that it sets. Lastly, its nature is such as to deter customers who might wish to contest the prices demanded by customs agents.

60   In the light of the foregoing considerations, it must be held that, by adopting and maintaining in force a law which, in granting the relative decision-making power, requires the CNSD to adopt a decision by an association of undertakings contrary to Article [101], consisting of setting a compulsory tariff for all customs agents, the Italian Republic has failed to fulfil its obligations under Articles [TEU 4] and [TFEU 101] of the Treaty.

* * *

In *Consorzio Industrie Fiammiferi (Italian matches)*, Case C–198/01, [2003] ECR I–8055, see facts at p. 1066 supra (state responsibility), the Italian Antitrust Authority also held that the Italian match producers violated the competition law to the extent that they took autonomous action in fixing quotas. Although the match producers were required by law to set quotas and government officials had the duty to oversee the quotas, the producers had the power to divvy up the quotas in the most anticompetitive way.

The Court of Justice substantially agreed with the Italian Authority. Not only did the national competition authority have the *duty* to disapply the national law, which required an agreement of competitors and legitimized and reinforced its anticompetitive effects. The private quota-setting could be sufficiently autonomous to merit antitrust condemnation even though the state fixed the price. See Eleanor Fox, State Action in Comparative Context: What if *Parker v. Brown* were Italian, Chap. 19 in 2003 Fordham Corp. L. Inst., International Antitrust Law & Policy (B. Hawk ed. 2004).

NOTES AND QUESTIONS

1. In the aftermath of *CNSD,* can the Italian government take back its decision-making prerogative and set the tariff itself? If so, is the probable effect of the Court's judgment merely to cause the government to take on this tariff-setting task? Or is the government likely to rethink whether the public interest requires price-setting?

2. Is the judgment unfair to CNSD, which was held to have acted pursuant to the command of its government? Note the Court's choices. It could have regarded CNSD as protected from an Article 101 violation by state command. But if it had recognized CNSD's state action defense, could it have

held Italy to be in violation of Articles TEU 4 read together with TFEU 101? Reread paragraphs 53–55.

3. Is *CNSD* consistent with *Ladbroke?* Where is the private autonomous action in *CNSD?*

4. In *Italian matches,* did the producers have sufficient autonomy to be held responsible? Is the problem only that the Italian producers were nationalistic quota-assigners? Will the ministry now set the quotas as well as the prices? Would it have any interest in doing so if it cannot divvy up the market among the Italians? Would a discriminatory allocation by the state violate Articles 18 and 34?

5. What is added by *Cipolla* to consideration of the validity of the Italian law?

6. US law is nearly identical in result. A person or firm that merely follows an anticompetitive command of the state (e.g. not to advertise) is protected from antitrust liability by the state action defense; but a state of the United States may not delegate to private parties the power (and duty) to fix prices and shield them from federal liability for price fixing. *California Retail Liquor Dealers Ass'n v. Midcal Aluminum, Inc.,* 445 U.S. 97, 100 S.Ct. 937, 63 L.Ed.2d 233 (1980); *Schwegmann Bros. v. Calvert Distillers Corp.,* 341 U.S. 384, 71 S.Ct. 745, 95 L.Ed. 1035 (1951).

7. In other respects, also, United States law is somewhat similar to European Community law on state action, supremacy and preemption, but the Community institutions have far broader power than United States courts to override anticompetitive state legislation by virtue of the free movement principles. When Congress passed the US antitrust laws, it could have chosen to preempt anticompetitive state law that affected interstate commerce, but it did not. Accordingly, subject to the constraint of the commerce clause in the US Constitution, states of the United States may adopt and enforce regulatory statutes that have significant anticompetitive effects. See, e.g., *Exxon Corp. v. Governor of Maryland,* 437 U.S. 117, 98 S.Ct. 2207, 57 L.Ed.2d 91 (1978) (prohibiting oil producers/refiners from operating retail service stations in the state for fear that they would favor their own stations). Moreover, antitrust laws of the US states—even law that is more prohibitory than federal antitrust law—is normally valid, and it functions in tandem with federal law. *California v. ARC America Corp.,* 490 U.S. 93, 109 S.Ct. 1661, 104 L.Ed.2d 86 (1989) (allowing California to authorize indirect purchaser lawsuits even though federal law disallows them). Private parties acting under a lawful but anticompetitive state regime are protected from federal antitrust enforcement as long as the state has clearly articulated its policy that displaces competition with regulation and supervises the private action. *Southern Motor Carriers Rate Conference, Inc. v. United States,* 471 U.S. 48, 105 S.Ct. 1721, 85 L.Ed.2d 36 (1985).

A state may not impose an unreasonable burden on interstate commerce (e.g., discrimination against imports); but seldom is such a burden found when the law applies equally to residents and outsiders. Compare *Exxon Corp. v. Governor of Maryland,* supra, with *West Lynn Creamery v. Healy,* 512 U.S. 186, 114 S.Ct. 2205, 129 L.Ed.2d 157 (1994). Even a law that gives preference to in-state facilities might be justified where, for example, it is part of an environmental program that internalizes costs. *United Haulers v. Oneida–Herkimer Solid Waste Mgmt. Authority*, 550 U.S. 330, 127 S.Ct. 1786, 167 L.Ed.2d 655 (2007).

F. STATE AID

1. INTRODUCTION

States are tempted to give money and other benefits to support local firms and to attract other business. Frequently they are asked to favor one competitor, sector or region over another, often to save a failing business and to save jobs. At mid-twentieth century, extensive state support of industry was the norm in Europe. If trade barriers were removed but state aids flourished, Europe would never be one common market.

Thus, in order to contain state aids and provide transparency for permissible aid, the Treaty includes Articles 107–109.

State aid is "any aid granted by a Member State or through state resources in any form whatsoever...." Direct subsidy is the most common form of aid, but state aid also includes exemptions from fiscal or social charges, credit guarantees, credit at low interest, credit or equity investments that would not be available in the market, payment by the state of a higher price to domestic suppliers, sale by the state below the market price to domestic buyers, assumption by the state of part of an undertaking's risk, tax concessions (e.g., to encourage the takeover of an ailing firm), and virtually any other benefit conferred by the state on terms that would not be acceptable to a private investor.

Article 107(1) declares that any state aid that "distorts or threatens to distort competition by favouring certain undertakings or the production of certain goods shall, insofar as it affects trade between Member States, be incompatible with the common market." Paragraphs (2) and (3) are derogations from this general prohibition.

Paragraph (2) lists forms of aid that "shall be compatible" with the common market. Aid that shall be compatible under paragraph (2) is:

(a) aid of a social character granted to individual consumers without discrimination as to origin of products,

(b) damage relief in natural disasters or exceptional occurrences, and

(c) aid to the economy of certain areas of the Federal Republic of Germany affected by the division of Germany insofar as it is required to compensate for economic disadvantages caused by that division.

Paragraph (3) specifies aid that the Commission *may* declare compatible with the common market. Frequently invoked by Member States, this section empowers the Commission to declare compatible aid in the following five categories:

(a) "aid to promote the economic development of areas where the standard of living is abnormally low or where there is serious underemployment";

(b) "aid to promote the execution of an important project of common European interest or to remedy a serious disturbance in the economy of a Member State";

(c) "aid to facilitate the development of certain economic activities or of certain economic areas, where such aid does not adversely affect trading conditions to an extent contrary to the common interest";

(d) "aid to promote cultural and heritage conservation where such aid does not affect trading conditions and competition in the Community to an extent that is contrary to the common interest"; and

(e) other categories added by decision of the Council.

Article 108 sets forth a notification, waiting and adjudication procedure for state aids. Member States must notify to the Commission all proposed measures of state aid that may affect Member State commerce. The proposed measures must not be put into effect until clearance. The Commission may authorize the aid without conditions, authorize the aid after agreed modifications, or open formal proceedings. The Commission must give notice to concerned parties to submit their comments. If the Commission finds that the proposed aid is not compatible with the common market or that aid is being misused, it must direct the state to abolish or alter the aid within a specified time period. If the Member State fails to comply, the Commission or an interested Member State may refer the matter to the Court of Justice. If a Member State grants illegal aid, it must recover it from the recipient.

Regulations provide exemptions for aid to small and medium-sized enterprises, for job training, and for *de minimis* aid. Guidelines clarify limits of aid for environmental protection, research and development, employment and training, rescue and restructuring, and regional aid.

There is considerable case law on what is a state aid. Does a privatized transport enterprise receive state aid when the state continues to cover the costs of public service obligations? Altmark Trans sought to organize public transport in a new East German länder. In *Altmark Trans GmbH, Regierungspräsidium Magdeburg,* Case C–280/00, [2003] ECR I–7747, the Court of Justice held that public subsidies for transportation services are not state aids, and therefore do not require notification and justification, where they constitute compensation for the discharge of public service obligations. Such subsidies fall outside of Article 107 if the following conditions are satisfied: 1) the recipient must be required to discharge clearly defined public service obligations, 2) the formula for calculating the compensation must be established beforehand in an objective and transparent matter, 3) the compensation must not exceed what is necessary to discharge the public service, and 4) either the undertaking must be chosen in a public procurement procedure or the level of compensation needed to fulfill the public service obligation must have been determined on the basis of the costs of a typical, well-run undertaking.

Similarly and earlier, Germany decided to promote windmill energy. German law obliged all regional public electricity suppliers to buy windmill power as a portion of their energy and to pay for the wind-generated electricity at a price higher than the price of other energy; and it obliged upstream electricity suppliers to pay to the regional suppliers a part of the extra costs. PreussenElektra, an upstream supplier, tried to avoid paying part of the extra costs of windmill energy on grounds that its supplementary payment to the regional supplier (Schleswag, which happened to be Preussen's own subsidiary) would constitute an illegal subsidy of wind energy. The Court rejected the argument. It ruled that PreussenElektra's supplementary payment, although commanded by the state, was merely a private payment and did not take the mantle of German aid. *Preussen-Elektra,* C–379/98, [2001] ECR I–2099. Why wasn't the supplementary payment in fact a subsidy? Did this interpretation bless an end run around Article 107? Could Preussen and Schleswag sue Germany for maintaining a state measure that restrained trade by putting them at a competitive disadvantage vis-à-vis Electricité de France and others in violation of Article 34 or 35?

2. STATE AID POLICY

State aid control is a major facet of Community policy. It accounts for half of the enforcement activity of the Competition Directorate. It has particular importance in the wake of the financial crisis commencing in 2008, as nations are tempted to pour subsidies into "their own" firms at the expense of cross-border competition. The following remarks of Competition Commissioner Joaquín Almunia highlights the place of state aid policy in the European Union and in the world.

COMPETITION, STATE AID AND SUBSIDIES IN THE EUROPEAN UNION

Joaquín Almunia, Vice President and Commissioner for Competition
9th Global Forum on Competition, Paris, 18 February 2010.

Ladies and gentlemen,

I'm very pleased to be here today in only the second week as Competition Commissioner . . . .

My key priority for the next five years is the same as it was under my previous responsibility as Commissioner for Economic and Financial Affairs: to help overcome the current financial and economic crisis and ensure that Europe emerges better equipped for balanced and sustainable growth and more jobs. This is an ambition which we all share for our respective countries—and the reason why we are meeting here at the OECD, to work together to achieve this ambition.

This is also the aim of the proposals the new European Commission is preparing for what we call "The EU 2020 Strategy": to lay the foundations for a more dynamic, knowledge-based, socially inclusive and greener economy that is both sustainable and fair.

I believe that competition policy has a vital role to play in this regard, by making markets work better, for the benefit of business and consumers. . . .

Competition policy is sometimes thought of as only addressing the behaviour of companies and businesses: cartels or abuses of market power, or mergers whose impact on competition needs to be assessed. But state subsidies to business ("state aid" in EU Treaty language) can also distort competition. A review of the impact of subsidies is, I believe, an important aspect of competition policy.

Subsidies are of course an essential tool for policy makers and governments. Government measures to support the financial system and other sectors of the economy over the past 18 months are a case in point. It is widely acknowledged that the money governments poured or committed in support of financial institutions prevented a catastrophic collapse of the global banking system.

On top of the immediate reactions needed to avoid a meltdown of the economy, in normal times subsidies can help remedy a market failure, promote investment in environmentally friendly technologies, or foster economic and social development in a particularly depressed region. These are important public policy objectives—and it is crucial to ensure that governments have the best-designed tools available to achieve these objectives.

Our aim in recent years, before the crisis emerged, has been to ensure that subsidies are targeted towards horizontal objectives such as these, and to prevent subsidies that merely keep inefficient firms on life-support. In the mid–1990s, around 50 per cent of government subsidies to industry and services in the EU were earmarked for horizontal objectives as opposed to individual bailouts. By 2008 this figure had risen to nearly 90 per cent.

Overall, government subsidies in the EU amounted to just over 0.5 per cent of EU GDP in the period 2004–2008, excluding measures to address the financial and economic crisis. Over the longer term subsidies are on a downward trend, since they are down from nearly 1 per cent of EU GDP in the 1990s.

The EU system for reviewing State subsidies

What we have in the EU is a system that requires the European Commission to review state subsidies to business and to assess their impact on competition. The fundamental principles were laid down in 1957, as a necessary condition to achieving a common market in goods and services in the EU, and remain unchanged today in the new Lisbon Treaty. A single market across the EU requires a level playing field between businesses in different Member States, so that our review of subsidies looks not only at the impact on competition between businesses in a given country, but also at the impact on cross-border competition.

What we do is essentially carry out a balancing exercise, weighing up the efficiency and equity benefits that are expected to result from a subsidy, against the negative effects the subsidy might have on competition in the EU and on trade between EU Member States.

Specifically we consider whether the government's objective in providing the subsidy does not run counter to the common interest of EU Member States—including growth, employment, regional development, the environment, or research and development.

One element we take into account is whether the subsidy addresses a market failure. For instance, we recognise that small businesses find it difficult to access risk capital because of high transaction costs to assess small projects compared to the expected gains from investment. So subsidies to facilitate access to risk capital may be acceptable. Similarly, we are happy to encourage subsidies for the extension of broadband to remote regions, which is not profitable under normal market circumstances. Likewise, we allow subsidies to cover part of the costs of a research project knowing that markets are not always ready to take on the full risk of research especially when profitability horizon is very long.

We check that, in practice, the subsidy will help achieve that objective, that it creates the right incentives for companies to adjust their behaviour. We also check that the subsidy is proportionate, i.e. that the same adjustments to company behaviour could not be obtained with lower subsidy.

This balancing exercise, based on an economic assessment of the impact of the measure, is carried out before the subsidy is implemented. It can lead to the Commission imposing conditions to minimise the distortion of competition, for instance, a reduction in the amount of the subsidy. This helps ensure that subsidy measures do not have an unduly distortive effect on competition in the EU. It also gives Member States an insight into the effectiveness of a planned subsidy and whether it will give value for money to the taxpayer.

Of course, what we don't do—thankfully—is review every single subsidy measure adopted by EU Member States. Following recent reforms, far fewer measures require notification to the Commission. Some of them do not distort competition or trade between Member States, others benefit from a general exemption laid down by regulation, or a general scheme (for instance for aid to research and development, development of small businesses, training and the creation of new jobs, etc). The Commission only carries out an in-depth, individual, review of those large subsidies which have the potential to be really harmful to competition. And what I want to do is to make sure our procedures for notification and review are as simple and streamlined as possible, so as to keep the bureaucratic burden to a minimum.

However, where we find that a State subsidy is unlawful—that is it violates our rules for its acceptance—it must be recovered in full. That is the only effective way of remedying the distortion of competition created by the subsidy.

Why it works

I've mentioned before the role of state subsidies in the global financial crisis. Let me come back to this issue.

Early action by the European Commission helped ensure a common approach by Member States to financial sector bail-outs. Member States may have adopted different measures—those which they felt were best suited to their respective market situation—whether guarantee schemes, recapitalisation measures, or impaired asset relief measures, or a mixture of these. But the European Commission required that all of these measures complied with certain fundamental principles—non-discriminatory access to national schemes, subsidies limited to what was necessary, mechanisms to prevent abuse of state support, restructuring measures for certain financial institutions that received large amounts of aid.

This helped keep to a minimum any distortions of competition between banks within and across national borders, and helped preserve the integrity of the EU internal market. It prevented costly and damaging subsidy races between Member States, with each trying to outdo the other in an attempt to prevent business moving away.

Going forward, EU policy on reviewing State subsidies—notably through the restructuring measures being agreed as a condition of approving bank subsidies—is helping rebuild viable financial institutions which are able to carry out the essential function of providing finance to the real economy.

Reviewing subsidies at national, supranational and international level?

Naturally, the EU perspective on the control of subsidies is closely associated with its powers and role as a supranational body, pursuing common EU objectives such as a level playing field for business and the internal market.

But the underlying principle—that subsidies should not unfairly distort competition between businesses so that companies can compete on merit to the benefit of consumers—is equally important at national level and on national markets for goods or services. Creating or supporting a national champion creates domestic casualties too—those companies that are not chosen for government support. Measures to support inward investment may result in obvious rewards—but it may be worth assessing for just how long those measures continue to produce net benefits, in particular if such support is open-ended.

National regimes for reviewing state subsidies do exist—for instance in Spain, my own country, the national competition authority has the power to issue opinions on subsidies granted by the regions or the central government. On the other hand, countries that are candidates to join the

EU are required to set up systems for reviewing State subsidies. One of them, Croatia, has a system that mirrors the EU system—with the national competition authority entrusted with the relevant powers. Looking further afield, Russia also has a system of subsidy control and the Mexican competition authority has powers to deliver opinions on the impact of subsidies on inter-State trade.

I believe that there is scope for individual countries outside the EU to consider adopting a system of controlling State subsidies, for the benefit of business environment and quality of public policies.

What about the international level?

All of us here today recognise the benefits of open markets and t he downsides of protectionism. Subsidies can be an instrument of protectionism, countering the benefits of trade liberalisation. The WTO rules on subsidies for goods can play a role in removing the most harmful subsidies—but no rule can be applied properly without transparency. So I fully endorse the OECD ministerial conclusions of last June which state that government measures to support industry must be transparent and WTO consistent. Transparency helps contain protectionist measures by opening them up to public scrutiny—and helps ensure a level playing field for business in markets across the world.

With this in mind, I welcome the initiative by WTO Director General Pascal Lamy to report quarterly on measures adopted by G20 countries to counter the crisis. This is particularly important since the G20 is leading the drive towards a coordinated route out of the crisis for the world economy. In a move which underlines the importance we attach to transparency, the EU has already introduced this principle and reports regularly on all Member State actions, regardless of their G20 status. The next report will be published in early March. I look forward for other countries to follow that lead.

Conclusion * * *

The EU rules on government subsidies are a key element of EU competition policy in that they help maintain a level playing field for business within Member States and across Europe. They have proved their worth in the context of the financial and economic crisis, helping avoid damaging subsidy races between EU Member States and minimising the distortions of competition resulting from large-scale government bail-outs for financial institutions.

But rules on government subsidies are not an exclusive EU issue. They have a place in all competition regimes—whether national, federal, supranational or international. They help maintain the level playing field between businesses implanted within a country, across regions, and across national borders. They help open up markets to international trade. Ultimately, they help governments assess the effectiveness of proposed subsidy measures, and help channel funds to where they are the most necessary and can deliver the most benefit to taxpayers.

3. LEGISLATIVE FRAMEWORK

State aid policy has passed through several phases of legislation. The current General Block Exemption Regulation was adopted in July 2008. The GBER incorporates into a single text block exemptions on investment aid for SMEs, research and development aid in favor of SMEs, and aid for employment, training, and regional development. Also included are an exemption for aid for environmental protection, risk capital, R&D for large firms, innovation, newly created small enterprises, and enterprises newly created by female entrepreneurs. The GBER raises the notification ceiling for investment and employment aid for SMEs to 7.5 million euros.

The state aid legislation can be found at the links at *http://ec.europa. eu/competition/state_aid/legislation/legislation.html*. The financial crisis of 2008–09 prompted the establishment of an Economic Crisis Team and the adoption of a temporary framework, which can be found at *http://ec. europa.eu/competition/state_aid/legislation/temporary.html*.

NOTES AND QUESTIONS

1. Article 107(1) prohibits state aid that "distorts or threatens to distort competition by favouring certain [firms or goods]...." What does "distort[ing] competition" mean? Does the phrase mean the same thing in Article 107(1) as in Article 101(1)?

2. Do you agree that state aid normally "distorts competition"? In what sense? Does it harm competition from the viewpoint of consumers? from the viewpoint of competitors? from the vantage of protecting the competition process and the right to compete on the merits? Can state aid intensify competition? How can or should the Commission and Court deal with procompetitive effects (lower prices, more business formation) of state aids?

3. The United States, in contrast with the EU, has no national subsidy control, except as required by the GATT/WTO, and except for prohibition of discriminatory subsidies that impose a burden on interstate commerce. See *West Lynn Creamery v. Healy*, 512 U.S. 186, 114 S.Ct. 2205, 129 L.Ed.2d 157 (1994). US law reflects the belief that freedom of state and local governments to grant subsidies or other benefits, whether to compete for business establishment or to prop up business in financial difficulty, is a healthy form of state autonomy and competition. See *Camps Newfound/Owatonna, Inc. v. Town of Harrison*, 520 U.S. 564, 589, 117 S.Ct. 1590, 137 L.Ed.2d 852 (1997); and see Justice Scalia, dissenting, at 605–08. Are there good reasons why Europe has state aid control and the United States does not?

4. Firms in Europe frequently challenge a grant of state aid to their rivals, and typically they are accorded standing to do so. Thus, when Ford and Volkswagen set up a joint venture in Portugal to make multi-purpose vehicles—a new endeavor for both joint venture partners—Matra, the dominant

maker of MPVs, complained that Portugal's grant of infrastructure aid to the new entrant violated Article 107, and that the joint venture agreement itself violated Articles 101 and 102 in part because the aid distorted competition. (How would Matra argue this point?) Matra lost on the merits; both the aid and the joint venture were allowed. See *Matra Hachette SA v. Commission*, Case T–17/93, [1994] ECR II–595.

Why would a firm challenge a grant of aid to its rival? Why, in particular, would a dominant firm challenge a grant of aid to a new entrant? Is the complainant likely to be complaining about harm to competition, about unfair advantages, or about competition itself? Would buyers of the products produced by a subsidized firm ever have an interest in challenging a state aid? Would it be accurate to view rivals' complaints about grants of state aid as complaints about *unfair* competition?

5. Explain the relationship between the state aid body of law and the antitrust (Articles 101 and 102) and merger control bodies of law. While there are many differences, Europe took advantage of the synergies of its laws in the financial crisis of 2008, using its combined powers of subsidy control, merger control and restructuring, and doing so on an emergency basis. See Neelie Kroes, Competition Law in an Economic Crisis, Fiesole, *http://ec.europa.eu/competition/speeches/index_speeches_by_the_commissioner.html*, click on 11 September 2009.

CONCLUSION

In this chapter we have examined state interventions, considered how state actions may harm trade and competition, and observed how the Treaty limits anticompetitive state actions. It is often said that, for harms to competition, the state is the biggest culprit because it can erect impenetrable barriers and privilege itself, its businesses and its friends as no private actor can do without the help of the state. But of course the state is also a guardian of the public good. Through Articles TEU 4 and TFEU 34, 35, 37, 56 and 106 in tandem with 101 and 102, and 107–109, the Treaty attempts to do the job of limiting the anticompetitive, trade-restraining excesses of the state, particularly when they undermine the coherence of the internal market. Thus, in matters of constraining excessive and unjustified state action, competition and internal-market policy converge.

AFTERWORD

■ ■ ■

The competition policy of the EU has been an ambitious, evolving, and largely successful enterprise, despite some false starts entailing over-regulation and rigid rules. The genius of the enterprise is hard to dispute. Europe has proved that undue public anticompetitive restraints and undue private anticompetitive restrains are often integral, and that a common market cannot be created without coherent, community-wide, competition law. Even while US antitrust looks inward in the sense of dissociating antitrust from political economy and from links with adjacent disciplines such as trade, European competition policy acknowledges the links and seeks a coherent conception that takes account of neighboring values and objectives. The EU model, still evolving as it incorporates more economics and less formalism, appears to have become the model or referent of choice for the newer antitrust jurisdictions of the world. Thus, this study of the competition law of the European Union has relevance and application well beyond Europe.

PART 5

EXTERNAL RELATIONS AND
COMMERCIAL POLICY

∎ ∎ ∎

From the very outset, the nature of the EU has required it to have extensive dealings with nonmember countries. It started out as a customs union, which required one of its principal activities to be the operation of a common commercial policy. In today's world, tariffs and other international trade policies are negotiated bilaterally and multilaterally. Consequently, the EU has extensive dealings with the rest of the world, through a vast network of multilateral and bilateral agreements.

The EU's relationships with third countries are not limited to implementation of the common customs tariff and the common commercial policy. The creation of internal market has led to EU involvement in almost all areas of economic activity, many of which also have an external aspect. For example, to establish a common transport policy, the EU must deal with transportation into and out of the EU, and that requires dealing with third countries. To take another example, the EU has a common fisheries policy, which has inevitably led to a series of fisheries agreements with third countries.

Over time, as the EU has taken steps toward closer political union, the Member States have cooperated in foreign affairs, first under European Political Cooperation and now as part of the EU's Common Foreign and Security Policy.

This Part of the casebook examines the external relations power and the common commercial policy of the EU. Chapter 27 commences with an examination of the scope of the EU's external relations policy under the TFEU, focusing on the applicable provisions of the Treaty and several important decisions by the Court of Justice. In particular, we consider the breadth of the term "common commercial policy" and the extent to which the Court of Justice has implied external powers in Treaty provisions that make no explicit reference to such powers. The precise scope of the EU's powers is important because the Member States will be prohibited from acting where the EU's powers are deemed exclusive. We also consider in Chapter 27 the extent to which the EU's international agreements can be invoked by private parties in Member State courts and the development of the EU's Common Foreign and Security Policy.

The remainder of Part 5 deals with the common commercial policy and the EU's relations generally with the rest of the world. We start in Chapter 28 with an overview of the EU's preferential trading relationships with third countries. These relationships are most developed with the nonmember countries in Europe and with the former colonies of Member States. In Chapter 29, we examine the current scope of the common commercial policy. In particular, we look in some depth at the EU's participation in the World Trade Organization, which is the basis for its commercial relationships with its most important trading partners, including the United States. We then examine the EU customs rules and its rules against unfairly traded goods, such as those that are dumped, subsidized or traded in violation of WTO rules. A significant amount of the work of lawyers specializing in EU law involves these trade rules.

CHAPTER 27

THE EXTERNAL RELATIONS POWERS
OF THE EUROPEAN UNION

■ ■ ■

A number of difficult legal issues arise in respect of the EU's external relations powers. First, there is a question of authority. On what basis does the EU exercise its external relations activities? Second, there is the question of exclusivity. To what extent can the Member States act independently of, or participate jointly with, the EU in an area where the EU has competence under the treaties? Third, it is necessary to consider how the EU's external relations powers are divided among the EU's institutions. May the Commission act independently of the Council? What is the European Parliament's role? We examine these questions in this chapter, and also consider the extent to which litigants may invoke the EU's international agreements in EU and Member State courts. We conclude with a brief look at the EU's Common Foreign and Security Policy and two important cases involving EU-imposed economic sanctions.

A. THE TREATY PROVISIONS ON EXTERNAL RELATIONS

The EEC and the EC treaties did not provide general external relations powers for the European Community. Initially, the Community was given the power to enter into international agreements in respect of a few specific subjects, most notably the common commercial policy, and to enter into association agreements. However, because some EC rules had international ramifications or needed international agreements in order to make them effective, the Court of Justice inevitably had to play a critical role in defining the scope of the EU's foreign affairs powers. It has done so through several sweeping opinions. With the coming into effect of the Treaty of Lisbon, the EU treaties now contain general provisions on the EU's powers in external relations. We shall first review those express grants of power and then consider how the EU negotiates treaties and what role the European Parliament has in external relations.

1. EXPRESS GRANTS OF EXTERNAL RELATIONS POWERS

Part Five of the TFEU provides for external action by the EU and has specific provisions on the common commercial policy, cooperation with third countries, relations with third countries and international organizations, and the conclusion of international agreements. More generally, Article 216 TFEU, which is new with the Lisbon Treaty, provides:

> (1) The Union may conclude an agreement with one or more third countries or international organizations where the Treaties so provide or where the conclusion of an agreement is necessary in order to achieve, within the framework of the Union's policies, one of the objectives referred to in the Treaties, or is provided for in a legally binding Union act or is likely to affect common rules or alter their scope.

> (2) Agreements concluded by the Union are binding upon the institutions of the Union and its Member States.

Article 3(2) TFEU, which is also new, specifies that the Union has exclusive competence for the conclusion of an international agreement when that is provided for in Union legislation, is necessary to exercise its internal competence or may affect common rules or alter their scope. As we will see, the terms in these provisions are attempts to summarize the rich Court of Justice jurisprudence in this area and can be understood only in light of that jurisprudence, which we examine later.

As noted, the TFEU contains a number of provisions regarding specific subject-matters that also empower the Union to enter into international agreements. For example, in the case of the common commercial policy, Article 207(3) so provides, while Article 217 allows for association agreements, which are "agreements establishing an association involving reciprocal rights and obligations, common action and special procedure". These two provisions were in the Treaty of Rome and have been used extensively in the past. Over time, additional express powers were added, including, for example, provisions for international agreements on development cooperation (Article 209(2)), economic and technical cooperation with developed countries (Article 212(3)), humanitarian aid (Article 214(4)), research and development cooperation (Article 186), environmental matters (Article 191(4)), monetary union (Article 219), neighboring countries (Lisbon TEU Article 8) and the common foreign and security policy (Lisbon TEU Article 27). A number of these specific grants of power provide that Member States retain authority to negotiation on the subject matters in question. See, e.g., Articles 191(4), 209(2), 212(3), 219(5).

The TFEU also provides that the Union shall cooperate as appropriate and maintain relations with the United Nations and other international organizations (Article 220). There are numerous Union diplomatic delegations to third countries and international organizations, which the

Treaty places under the authority of the High Representative for Foreign Affairs and Security Policy (Article 221). Delegations from many third countries and international organizations are accredited to the EU in Brussels as well.

2. THE NEGOTIATION AND APPROVAL OF INTERNATIONAL AGREEMENTS AND THE ROLE OF THE EUROPEAN PARLIAMENT

The process of negotiating and approving Union agreements has changed over the years. Typically, the rules have required agreements to be negotiated by the Commission (subject to receiving a mandate from the Council) and to be formally concluded on the approval of the Council. The vote required in the Council has varied depending on the circumstances. The extent to which the European Parliament has had to consent or be consulted in respect of international agreements has expanded over time. Originally, it only had to be consulted in respect of association agreements. In the case of commercial policy agreements, no parliamentary consultation was required. However, under the Luns–Westerterp procedures, the Council voluntarily committed itself to inform Parliament prior to commencing negotiations and prior to signing and formally concluding association agreements (1964) and commercial agreements (1973).[1] In addition, the Stuttgart European Council concluded in 1983 that, as a matter of policy, Parliament should be consulted prior to the conclusion of all significant international agreements.[2]

As a result of the Lisbon Treaty, Article 218 TFEU now specifies the following procedures for negotiating and concluding international agreements for the Union, without prejudice to the specific provisions of Article 207 governing common commercial policy agreements, which we examine in Chapter 29. Article 218 specifies that on recommendation of the Commission (or, where appropriate, the High Representative), the Council authorizes negotiations and specifies the negotiators (normally the Commission or, where appropriate, the High Representative). The Council may address directives to the negotiator and appoint an oversight committee. Before formally concluding an agreement on the recommendation of the negotiator, the Council must obtain the consent of the European Parliament for (i) association agreements, (ii) accession to the ECHR (see Chapter 6(A) supra), (iii) agreements establishing a specific institutional framework by organizing cooperation procedures, (iv) agreements having important budgetary implications for the Community and (v) agreements covering fields to which either the ordinary legislative procedure applies or the special legislative procedure where consent by Parliament is required.

---

1. Bull. EC 1973–10, p. 90. See generally J.–V. Louis & P. Brückner, Relations Extérieures 42–44, in 12 J. Megret et al., eds., Le Droit de la Communauté Économique Européenne (Editions de l'Université de Bruxelles 1980).

2. Solemn Declaration on European Union, para. 2.3.7., in Bull. EC 1983–6, pp. 26–27.

In other cases, Parliament must be consulted. In any event, Parliament has no power to amend agreements.

Article 218(8) specifies that the Council shall act by qualified majority, except that unanimity is required for (i) association agreements, (ii) accession to the ECHR, (iii) agreements with accession candidates under Article 212 TFEU, and (iv) an agreement covers a field for which unanimity is required for adoption of Union acts.

Article 218(11) has one other important feature, originating in the Treaty of Rome. It establishes a reference procedure that allows the Parliament, the Commission, the Council or a Member State to obtain an opinion of the Court of Justice as to whether an envisaged agreement is compatible with the Treaties. If it is not, then it must be revised or the Treaties amended before the Union may enter into the agreement. This provision has allowed the Court to play a critical role in defining the external relations powers of the Union and its institutions.

One interesting question presented by Article 218's rules on Parliamentary consent is how to determine precisely when parliamentary consent is required. In particular, what exactly is "an agreement establishing a specific institutional framework by organizing cooperation procedures"? What would constitute "important budgetary implications"? The Court of Justice considered the latter question in the following case.

PARLIAMENT v. COUNCIL

(EC/Mauritania fisheries agreement)
Case C–189/97, [1999] ECR I–4741.

[In 1996, the EC and Mauritania entered into a fisheries agreement that provided for five annual payments to Mauritania of approximately 50 million ECU. The Commission proposed a regulation to conclude the agreement that provided for the assent of Parliament to be obtained. The Council, however, decided to adopt a regulation on the conclusion of the agreement based on treaty provisions dealing with the common agricultural policy, in conjunction with the equivalent of what is now Article 218(6)(b). In its regulation, the Council simply referred to Parliament's "opinion". In its consideration of the agreement, Parliament had substituted what is now Article 218(6)(a) for the legal basis cited by the Council and assented to the adoption of the regulation. Parliament then sued the Council, claiming that its prerogatives had been infringed because its assent was required for an agreement with important budgetary implications.

Parliament argued that "in determining whether an agreement has important budgetary implications, the criteria to be taken into account should include the fact that expenditure under the agreement is spread over several years, the relative share of such expenditure in relation to the expenditures of the same kind under the budget heading concerned, and the rate of increase in expenditure under the agreement in question in relation to the financial section of the previous agreement" (para. 20). In that regard, it noted that the payments represented "more than 20% of the appropriations entered under the budget heading concerned (heading B7–8000, international fisheries agreements) [and that] the outlay in favor of [Mauritania had] increased more than fivefold in relation to the previous agreement" (para. 21).

The Council maintained that "in order to assess whether an agreement has important budgetary implications, it is necessary to refer to the overall budget of the Community, and that it did not act in a manifestly erroneous and arbitrary manner in seeking merely an opinion of the Parliament for a fisheries agreement under which the annual expenditure amounted to 0.07% of that budget" (para. 24).

The Court rejected the Council's argument, noting "that appropriations allocated to the external operations of the Community traditionally account for a marginal fraction of the Community budget. Thus, in 1996 and 1997, those appropriations, grouped under subsection B7, external operations, barely exceeded 5% of the overall budget. In those circumstances, a comparison between the annual financial cost of an agreement and the overall Community budget scarcely appears significant, and to apply such a criteria might render the relevant wording of [what is now Article 218(6)(a)(iv)] of the Treaty wholly ineffective" (para. 26). As to Parliament's criteria, the Court ruled:]

29   As regards the three criteria proposed by Parliament, the Court finds that the first of them may indeed contribute towards characterizing an agreement as having important budgetary implications. Relatively modest annual expenditures may, over a number of years, represent a significant budgetary outlay.

30   The second and third criteria put forward by Parliament do not, however, appear to be relevant. In the first place, budget headings, which can be moreover be altered, vary substantially in importance, so that the relative share of the expenditure under the agreement may be large in relation to the appropriations of the same kind entered under the budget heading concerned, even though the expenditure in question is small. Moreover, the rate of increase in expenditure under the agreement may be high in comparison with that arising from the previous agreement, whilst the amounts involved may still be small.

31   As has been pointed out in paragraph 26 of this judgment, a comparison between the annual financial cost of an international agreement and the overall budget scarcely appears significant. However, comparison of the expenditure under an agreement with the amount of the appropriations designed to finance the Community's external operations * * * enables that agreement to be set in context of the budgetary outlay approved by the Community for its external policy. That comparison thus offers a more appropriate means of assessing the financial importance which the agreement actually has for the Community.

32   Where, as in this case, a sectoral agreement is involved, the above analysis may, in appropriate cases, and without excluding the possibility of taking other factors into account, be complemented by a comparison between the expenditures entailed by the agreement and the whole of the budgetary appropriations for the sector in question, taking the internal and external aspects together. Such a comparison makes it possible to determine, from another angle and in an equally consistent context, the financial outlay approved by the Community in entering into that agreement. However, since the sectors vary substantially in terms of their budgetary importance, that examination cannot result in the financial implications of an agreement being found to be important where they do not represent a significant share of the appropriations designed to finance the Community's external operations.

33   In this case, the fisheries agreement with Mauritania was concluded for five years, which is not a particularly lengthy period. Moreover, the financial compensation for which it makes provision is split into annual tranches the amounts of which vary between ECU 51,560,000 and ECU 55,160,000. In respect of the previous budgetary years, those amounts, whilst exceeding 5% of expenditures on fisheries, represent barely more than 1% of the whole of the payment appropriations allocated for external operations of the Community, a proportion which, whilst far from negligible, can scarcely be described as important. In those circumstances, if the Council had taken that comparison into account, it would also have been entitled to take the view that the fisheries agreement with Mauritania did not have important budgetary implications for Community within the meaning of the second subparagraph of [what is now] Article [218(6)(a)(iv) TFEU].

NOTES AND QUESTIONS

1. Do you agree with the Court's analysis? Does it potentially allow too many agreements to escape the scrutiny of the parliamentary consent requirement?

2. As to the level of spending that would have important budgetary implications, it is especially noteworthy that the Council conceded that the budgetary implications of the fisheries agreement with Morocco, which apparently involved a little more than twice the outlay of the Mauritania agreement, were important (Judgment, para. 27).

3. In France v. Commission (Antitrust agreement with US), Case C-327/91, [1994] ECR I-3641, the Court of Justice held that the Commission did not have the power to conclude an agreement on application of competition laws with the US. The agreement provided for various forms of cooperation in the field of competition law (e.g., notifications, exchange of information, consultations). While the parties recognized certain Commission powers with respect to concluding administrative or working agreements with other international organizations, the Court relied on the explicit grant of the power to

the Council to conclude agreements under what is now Article 218 TFEU as the basis for its decision.

B. THE COURT OF JUSTICE AND THE COMMUNITY'S POWERS IN EXTERNAL RELATIONS

As noted above, the Lisbon Treaty for the first time added a provision dealing in general with the Union's external relations powers. The language of that provision, Article 216, is in essence an attempt to summarize the state of the Court of Justice's jurisprudence on that question and can be understood only in light of some of the cases that we will now examine.

1. IMPLIED POWERS: THE ERTA CASE

The first major case in which the Court of Justice discussed the external relations power was the so-called *ERTA* case, which involved a dispute between the Commission and the Council over whether the Commission or the Member States had the right to negotiate the European Road Transport Agreement (ERTA, or AETR in French) with non Member States.

COMMISSION v. COUNCIL
(ERTA)
Case 22/70, [1971] ECR 263.

1. The Initial Question

6   The Commission takes the view that Article 75 of the Treaty [now 91 TFEU], which conferred on the Community powers defined in wide terms with a view to implementing the common transport policy, must apply to external relations just as much as to domestic measures in the sphere envisaged.

7   It believes that the full effect of this provision would be jeopardized if the powers which it confers, particularly that of laying down "any appropriate provisions", within the meaning of subparagraph (1)(c) of the article cited, did not extend to the conclusion of agreements with third countries.

8   Even if, it is argued, this power did not originally embrace the whole sphere of transport, it would tend to become general and exclusive as and where the common policy in this field came to be implemented.

9   The Council, on the other hand, contends that since the Community only has such powers as have been conferred on it, authority to enter into agreements with third countries cannot be assumed in the absence of an express provision in the Treaty.

10 More particularly, Article 75 [now 91 TFEU] relates only to measures internal to the Community, and cannot be interpreted as authorizing the conclusion of international agreements.

¹¹ Even if it were otherwise, such authority could not be general and exclusive, but at the most concurrent with that of the Member States.

¹² In the absence of specific provisions of the Treaty relating to the negotiation and conclusion of international agreements in the sphere of transport policy—a category into which, essentially, the AETR falls—one must turn to the general system of Community law in the sphere of relations with third countries.

¹³ Article 210 [now Lisbon TEU Article 47] provides that "The Community shall have legal personality".

¹⁴ This provision, placed at the head of Part Six of the Treaty, devoted to "General and Final Provisions", means that in its external relations the Community enjoys the capacity to establish contractual links with third countries over the whole field of objectives defined in Part One of the Treaty, which Part Six supplements.

¹⁵ To determine in a particular case the Community's authority to enter into international agreements, regard must be had to the whole scheme of the Treaty no less than to its substantive provisions.

¹⁶ Such authority arises not only from an express conferment by the Treaty—as is the case with Articles 113 [now 207 TFEU] and 114 [now deleted] for tariff and trade agreements and with Article 238 [now 217 TFEU] for association agreements—but may equally flow from other provisions of the Treaty and from measures adopted, within the framework of those provisions, by the Community institutions.

¹⁷ In particular, each time the Community, with a view to implementing a common policy envisaged by the Treaty, adopts provisions laying down common rules, whatever form these may take, the Member States no longer have the right, acting individually or even collectively, to undertake obligations with third countries which affect those rules.

¹⁸ As and when such common rules come into being, the Community alone is in a position to assume and carry out contractual obligations towards third countries affecting the whole sphere of application of the Community legal system.

¹⁹ With regard to the implementation of the provisions of the Treaty the system of internal Community measures may not therefore be separated from that of external relations.

²⁰ Under Article 3(e) [now repealed], the adoption of a common policy in the sphere of transport is specially mentioned amongst the objectives of the Community.

²¹ Under Article 5 [now Lisbon TEU Article 4], the Member States are required on the one hand to take all appropriate measures to ensure fulfillment of the obligations arising out of the Treaty or resulting from action taken by the institutions and, on the other, hand, to abstain from any measure which might jeopardize the attainment of the objectives of the Treaty.

22 If these two provisions are read in conjunction, it follows that to the extent to which Community rules are promulgated for the attainment of the objectives of the Treaty, the Member States cannot, outside the framework of the Community institutions, assume obligations which might affect those rules or alter their scope.

23 According to Article 74 [now 90 TFEU], the objectives of the Treaty in matters of transport are to be pursued within the framework of a common policy.

24 With this in view, Article 75(1) directs the Council to lay down common rules and, in addition, "any other appropriate provisions".

25 By the terms of subparagraph (a) of the same provision, those common rules are applicable "to international transport to or from the territory of a Member State or passing across the territory of one or more Member States".

26 This provision is equally concerned with transport from or to third countries, as regards that part of the journey which takes place on Community territory.

27 It thus assumes that the powers of the Community extend to relationships arising from international law, and hence involve the need in the sphere in question for agreements with the third countries concerned.

28 Although it is true that Articles 74 and 75 do not expressly confer on the Community authority to enter into international agreements, nevertheless the bringing into force, on 25 March 1969, of Regulation No 543/69 of the Council on the harmonization of certain social legislation relating to road transport necessarily vested in the Community power to enter into any agreements with third countries relating to the subject-matter governed by that regulation.

29 This grant of power is moreover expressly recognized by Article 3 of the said regulation which prescribes that: "The Community shall enter into any negotiations with third countries which may prove necessary for the purpose of implementing this regulation".

30 Since the subject-matter of the AETR falls within the scope of Regulation No 543/69, the Community has been empowered to negotiate and conclude the agreement in question since the entry into force of the said regulation.

31 These Community powers exclude the possibility of concurrent powers on the part of Member States, since any steps taken outside the framework of the Community institutions would be incompatible with the unity of the Common Market and the uniform application of Community law.

32 This is the legal position in the light of which the question of admissibility has to be resolved.

[The Court found the Commission's application to be admissible.]

3.   Substance

68   Essentially, the Commission disputes the validity of the proceedings of 20 March 1970 on the ground that they involved infringements of provisions of the Treaty, more particularly of Articles 75, 228 and 235 [now 91, 218 and 352 TFEU] concerning the distribution of powers between the Council and the Commission, and consequently the rights which it was the Commission's duty to exercise in the negotiations on the AETR.

* * *

77   If these various provisions are read in conjunction, it is clear that wherever a matter forms the subject of a common policy, the Member States are bound in every case to act jointly in defence of the interests of the Community.

78   This requirement of joint action was in fact respected by the proceedings of 20 March 1970, which cannot give rise to any criticism in this respect.

79   Moreover, it follows from these provisions taken as a whole, and particularly from Article 228(1), that the right to conclude the agreement was vested in the Council.

80   The Commission for its part was required to act in two ways, first by exercising its right to make proposals, which arises from Article 75(1) and the first paragraph of Article 116 [now deleted], and, secondly, in its capacity as negotiator by the terms of the first subparagraph of Article 228(1).

[The Court then noted that an earlier version of the AETR had been drawn up in 1962, at a time when power to conclude the agreement was still vested in the Member States. The negotiations involved in the case were not aimed at working out a new agreement, but simply at introducing into the version drawn up in 1962 such modifications as were necessary to enable all the contracting parties to ratify it.]

85   It appears therefore that on 20 March 1970 the Council acted in a situation where it no longer enjoyed complete freedom of action in its relations with the third countries taking part in the same negotiations.

86   At that stage of the negotiations, to have suggested to the third countries concerned that there was now a new distribution of powers within the Community might well have jeopardized the successful outcome of the negotiations, as was indeed recognized by the Commission's representative in the course of the Council's deliberations.

87   In such a situation it was for the two institutions whose powers were directly concerned, namely, the Council and the Commission, to reach agreement, in accordance with Article 15 of the Treaty of April 1965 establishing a Single Council and a Single Commission of the European Communities, on the appropriate methods of cooperation with a view to ensuring most effectively the defence of the interests of the Community.

88　It is clear from the minutes of the meeting of 20 March 1970 that the Commission made no formal use of the right to submit proposals open to it under Articles 75 and 116.

89　Nor did it demand the simple application of Article 228(1) in regard to its right of negotiation.

90　It may therefore be accepted that, in carrying on the negotiations and concluding the agreement simultaneously in the manner decided on by the Council, the Member States acted, and continue to act, in the interest and on behalf of the Community in accordance with their obligations under Article 5 of the Treaty.

91　Hence, in deciding in these circumstances on joint action by the Member States, the Council has not failed in its obligations arising from Articles 75 and 228.

92　For these reasons, the submission must be rejected.

* * *

Opinion of Advocate–General Dutheillet De Lamothe Delivered on 10 March 1971

* * *

It should be emphasized from the outset that * * * the only title devoted to transport [in the Treaty], has no express provision relating to the Community's "treaty-making power", to use an expression employed by Anglo–Saxon lawyers.

To vest authority or power in the Community to negotiate and conclude agreements with third countries relating to transport, it is thus necessary:

— either to declare applicable to this matter the provisions appearing in the parts of the Treaty devoted to matters other than transport;

— or to interpret certain of the general provisions of the Treaty as also applying to transport.

For my part I consider that both these solutions would involve the Court in a discretionary construction of the law, or, in other words, a judicial interpretation far exceeding the bounds which the Court has hitherto set regarding its power to interpret the Treaty.

* * *

No matter what legal basis the Court finds for it, recognition of the Community's authority in external matters for negotiating and concluding the AETR concedes by implication that the Community authorities exercise, in addition to the powers expressly conferred upon them by the Treaty, those implied powers whereby the Supreme Court of the United

States supplements the powers of the federal bodies in relation to those of the confederated States.

I for my part consider that Community powers should be regarded as those termed in European law "conferred powers" (in French, "compétences d'attribution").

Such conferred powers may indeed be very widely construed when they are only the direct and necessary extension of powers relating to *intra-Community* questions, as the Court has already ruled with regard to the ECSC.

But can the Community's authority to conclude agreements with third countries in the sphere of transport be so widely construed?

This is not in fact as necessary as has recently been asserted before the Court. Even without according it "implied powers", with regard to transport the Community is not in a state of "permanent weakness", to borrow the expression recently employed by the Commission's agent. Article 235 [now 352 TFEU] exists precisely to vest in the Community whatever powers it may need.

On the other hand, this is extremely difficult from the legal point of view, on the basis of the provisions at present in force.

It appears clear from the general scheme of the Treaty of Rome that its authors intended strictly to limit the Community's authority in external matters to the cases which they expressly laid down.

In this connexion a comparison between the ECSC Treaty and the Treaty of Rome is instructive. Whereas in the ECSC Treaty the negotiators of 1951 laid down that (Article 6): "In international relations, the Community shall enjoy the legal capacity it requires to perform its functions and attain its objectives", the negotiators of the Treaty of Rome in 1957 merely provided that the Community shall have legal personality (Article 210 [now Lisbon TEU Article 47]), although, with regard to external relations, they expressly laid down in Article 228 [now 218 TFEU] that the Community's authority in external matters may only be exercised "where this Treaty [*so*] provides".

Is it not the case that to recognize that the Community has implied powers with regard to negotiations with third countries would far exceed the intentions of the authors of the Treaty and of the States which signed and accepted it?

This is my view, and it is the principle reason which brings me to propose to the Court a relatively strict interpretation of the Treaty in this sphere.

NOTES AND QUESTIONS

1. Do you find the reasoning of the Court or of the Advocate–General to be more persuasive? Why? Suppose the Court had adopted the position espoused by the Advocate–General. What sort of problems would such a decision have created for the Community?

2.   The Court of Justice elaborated on the scope of the *ERTA* case in its 1994 opinion on EU adherence to the Agreement Establishing the World Trade Organization. We will postpone consideration of that case until Chapter 29, where that agreement is described in some detail.

3.   The Advocate–General notes his opposition to the US Supreme Court cases that give "implied" powers to the federal government. As you read the rest of the cases in this section, you might consider how much the US federal government and in particular the President have relied on implied powers in the field of foreign affairs. For example, in Missouri v. Holland, 252 U.S. 416, 40 S.Ct. 382, 64 L.Ed. 641 (1920), the Supreme Court held that a valid treaty (with Canada relating to migratory birds) must prevail over state law, even if a United States federal statute on the subject might be considered an unconstitutional interference with state power in the absence of a treaty. Justice Holmes said in this case (252 U.S. at 433):

> * * * Acts of Congress are the supreme law of the land only when made in pursuance of the Constitution, while treaties are declared to be so when made under the authority of the United States. It is open to question whether the authority of the United States means more than the formal acts prescribed to make the convention. We do not mean to imply that there are no qualifications to the treaty-making power; but they must be ascertained in a different way. It is obvious that there may be matters of the sharpest exigency for the national well-being that an act of Congress could not deal with but that a treaty followed by such an act could, and it is not lightly to be assumed that, in matters requiring national action, "a power which must belong to and somewhere reside in every civilized government" is not to be found.

Subsequent cases suggest some limitations on the treaty-making power, such as constitutional civil liberties limitations (see Reid v. Covert, 354 U.S. 1, 77 S.Ct. 1222, 1 L.Ed.2d 1148 (1957), holding that United States civilian dependents of armed forces members overseas could not constitutionally be tried by a court martial, even though an executive agreement or treaty would so provide).

The Supreme Court has found that the US President has certain powers in foreign affairs. Consider United States v. Curtiss–Wright Export Corp., 299 U.S. 304, 57 S.Ct. 216, 81 L.Ed. 255 (1936) (expansive view of President's "inherent" foreign affairs powers); Dames & Moore v. Regan, 453 U.S. 654, 101 S.Ct. 2972, 69 L.Ed.2d 918 (1981) (President held to have authority to terminate claims against Iran in US courts as part of hostage settlement). Does the Commission have such powers? Recall France v. Commission (Antitrust agreement with US), noted in prior section.

4.   As to the question of the Community's legal capacity to enter into international agreements, where in the Treaty does the *ERTA* Court find that capacity?

5.   If the Union enters into an international agreement in respect of a particular subject, does its action preempt action by the Member States? In other words, is the EU's power to make international agreements an exclusive one? Examine Article 3(2), which is new with the Lisbon Treaty. Many years ago, in Local Cost Standard, Opinion 1/75, [1975] ECR 1355, when the Court

of Justice was asked whether the EU had exclusive power to enter into an understanding with the other parties to the Organization for Economic Cooperation and Development (OECD) concerning conditions for granting export credits, the Court responded ([1975] ECR at 1363–64):

> * * * [T]he subject-matter of the standard, and therefore of the Understanding, is one of those measures belonging to the common commercial policy prescribed by Article 113 [now 207 TFEU; the revisions over time of Article 113 EEC and the current text of Article 207 TFEU are examined in Chapter 29(B) infra].
>
> Such a policy is conceived in that article in the context of the operation of the Common Market, for the defence of the common interests of the Community, within which the particular interests of the Member States must endeavour to adapt to each other.
>
> Quite clearly, however, this conception is incompatible with the freedom to which the Member States could lay claim by invoking a concurrent power, so as to ensure that their own interests were separately satisfied in external relations, at the risk of compromising the effective defence of the common interests of the Community.
>
> In fact any unilateral action on the part of the Member States would lead to disparities in the conditions for the grant of export credits, calculated to distort competition between undertakings of the various Member States in external markets. Such distortion can be eliminated only by means of a strict uniformity of credit conditions granted to undertakings in the Community, whatever their nationality.
>
> It cannot therefore be accepted that, in a field such as that governed by the Understanding in question, which is covered by export policy and more generally by the common commercial policy, the Member States should exercise a power concurrent to that of the Community, in the Community sphere and in the international sphere. The provisions of Articles 113 and 114 [now deleted] concerning the conditions under which, according to the Treaty, agreements on commercial policy must be concluded show clearly that the exercise of concurrent powers by the Member States and the Community in this matter is impossible.
>
> To accept that the contrary were true would amount to recognizing that, in relations with third countries, Member States may adopt positions which differ from those which the Community intends to adopt, and would thereby distort the institutional framework, call into question the mutual trust within the Community and prevent the latter from fulfilling its task in the defence of the common interest.
>
> It is of little importance that the obligations and financial burdens inherent in the execution of the agreement envisaged are borne directly by the Member States. The "internal" and "external" measures adopted by the Community within the framework of the common commercial policy do not necessarily involve, in order to ensure their compatibility with the Treaty, a transfer to the institutions of the Community of the obligations and financial burdens which they may involve: such measures are solely concerned to substitute for the unilateral action of the Member

States, in the field under consideration, a common action based upon uniform principles on behalf of the whole of the Community.

For a more recent discussion of related issues, see Opinion 1/03 (Lugano Convention), [2006] ECR I–1145.

6. Somewhat in contrast, in an opinion on the power of the EU to conclude an International Labor Organization (ILO) convention on safety in the use of chemicals at work, Opinion 2/91, [1993] ECR I–1061, the Court ruled that the EU's competence in this field was not exclusive. It noted that Member States were also free to act in certain respects in this field since Article 118a(3) [now 153(4) TFEU] allowed them to impose stricter rules than specified by the Union in respect of worker safety and that rules stricter than those mandated by the ILO convention were permitted by that convention. The Court noted that there were some areas covered by the convention where the EU harmonization rules were widespread and related to the removal of trade barriers and that as to those areas Member States could not undertake commitments outside the framework of Union institutions. Thus, it ruled that there was joint competence to conclude the ILO convention. How does this opinion relate generally to the issue of subsidiarity (discussed in Chapter 4(D) supra)? We consider more generally the issue of so-called mixed agreements below.

7. *ERTA* and *Local Cost Standard* involved subject areas where the Treaty calls for common policies. Do you think that the Court would view the Union's powers as broadly in other subject areas? How do Articles 3(2) and 216 TFEU, which are new with the Lisbon Treaty, affect your answer? In fashioning your answer, it may be useful to consider the Court's standard summary of its jurisprudence in this area:

103　The Court has already held in the *ERTA* judgment, that the Community's competence to conclude international agreements arises not only from an express conferment by the Treaty but may equally flow from other provisions of the Treaty and from measures adopted, within the framework of those provisions, by the Community institutions; that, in particular, each time the Community, with a view to implementing a common policy envisaged by the Treaty, adopts provisions laying down common rules, whatever form these may take, the Member States no longer have the right, acting individually or even collectively, to undertake obligations towards non-member countries which affect those rules or distort their scope; and that, as and when such common rules come into being, the Community alone is in a position to assume and carry out contractual obligations towards non-member countries affecting the whole sphere of application of the Community legal system.

* * *

105　If the Member States were free to enter into international commitments affecting the common rules adopted on the basis of the Treaty, that would jeopardize the attainment of the objective pursued by those rules and would thus prevent the Community from fulfilling its task in the defense of the common interest.

* * *

108   According to the Court's case-law, [the Community acquires an external competence by reason of the exercise of its internal competence] where the international commitments fall within the scope of the common rules (*ERTA* judgment, paragraph 30), or in any event within an area which is already largely covered by such rules (Opinion 2/91, paragraph 25). In the latter case, the Court has held that Member States may not enter into international commitments outside the framework of the Community institutions, even if there is no contradiction between those commitments and the common rules.

109   Thus it is that, whenever the Community has included in its internal legislative acts provisions relating to the treatment of nationals of non-member countries or expressly conferred on its institutions powers to negotiate with non-member countries, it acquires an exclusive external competence in the spheres covered by those acts.

110   The same applies, even in the absence of any express provision authorizing its institutions to negotiate with non-member countries, where the Community has achieved complete harmonization in a given area, because the common rules thus adopted could be affected within the meaning of the *ERTA* judgment if the Member States retained freedom to negotiate with non-member countries.

Commission v. Germany (air transport), Case C–476/98, [2002] ECR I–9855.

8.   Review what is now Article 352 TFEU. Would it have been appropriate for the *ERTA* Court to suggest the use of this article if there was no explicit authority in the Treaty to enter into an international agreement? How would such a decision, as compared to the Court's actual decision, affect the powers of the EU institutions in the international arena? In particular, what are the voting rules in the Council and the powers of Parliament in respect of an agreement negotiated under what are now Articles 207 (commercial policy), Article 217 (association agreements) and Article 352 TFEU? See Commission v. Council (Generalized tariff preferences I), Case 45/86, [1987] ECR 1493.

9.   In 2008, the Court of Justice had occasion to consider the role of Article 352 (as renumbered by the Lisbon Treaty) in an important fundamental rights case. Kadi v. Council, Case C–402/05, [2008] ECR I–6351. The case concerned the EU's implementation of UN Security Council resolutions calling for the freezing of assets of certain individuals and entities associated with certain terrorist organizations. The regulation was challenged on the ground that the stated basis for action—what are now TFEU Articles 75 (relating to restriction on capital movements with third countries), 215 (relating to restrictions imposed on third countries pursuant to the common foreign and security policy (and since 2010, on individuals also) and 352—was not a proper legal basis. The Court agreed that Articles 75 and 215 could not in themselves serve as a basis for restrictions on individuals since they author-

ized actions taken against third countries only (and, by implication, the rulers of a third country and those associated with them). Likewise, the Court was of the view that Article 352 by itself could not serve as a legal basis since it was concerned with objectives of the Community, which at the time was legally distinct from the Union, while the matter at hand related to one of the objectives of the Union (i.e. one related to the common foreign and security policy). Nonetheless, the Court found that the regulations could be upheld:

213   The contested regulation, inasmuch as it imposes restrictive measures of an economic and financial nature, plainly falls within the ambit *ratione materiae* of Articles [75 and 215].

214   To that extent, the inclusion of those articles in the legal basis of the contested regulation was therefore justified.

215   Furthermore, those provisions are part of the extension of a practice based, before the introduction of Articles [75 and 215] by the Maastricht Treaty, on Article [207], which consisted of entrusting to the Community the implementation of actions decided on in the context of European political cooperation and involving the imposition of restrictive measures of an economic nature in respect of third countries.

216   Since Articles [75 and 215] do not, however, provide for any express or implied powers of action to impose such measures on addressees in no way linked to the governing regime of a third country such as those to whom the contested regulation applies, that lack of power, attributable to the limited ambit *ratione materiae* of those provisions, could be made good by having recourse to Article [352] as a legal basis for that regulation in addition to the first two provisions providing a foundation for that measure from the point of view of its material scope, provided, however, that the other conditions to which the applicability of Article [352] is subject had been satisfied.

* * *

222   The objective pursued by the contested regulation is immediately to prevent persons associated with Usama bin Laden, the Al–Qaeda network or the Taliban from having at their disposal any financial or economic resources, in order to impede the financing of terrorist activities.

223   [T]hat objective can be made to refer to one of the objects which the EC Treaty entrusts to the Community. * * *

224   In this regard it may be recalled that Article [352], being an integral part of an institutional system based on the principle of conferred powers, cannot serve as a basis for widening the scope of Community powers beyond the general framework created by the provisions of the EC Treaty as a whole.

225   The objective pursued by the contested regulation may be made to refer to one of the objectives of the Community for the purpose of Article [352], with the result that the adoption of that regulation did

not amount to disregard of the scope of Community powers stemming from the provisions of the EC Treaty as a whole.

226   Inasmuch as they provide for Community powers to impose restrictive measures of an economic nature in order to implement actions decided on under the CFSP, Articles [75 and 215] are the expression of an implicit underlying objective, namely, that of making it possible to adopt such measures through the efficient use of a Community instrument.

227   That objective may be regarded as constituting an objective of the Community for the purpose of Article [352].

* * *

229   Implementing restrictive measures of an economic nature through the use of a Community instrument does not go beyond the general framework created by the provisions of the EC Treaty as a whole, because such measures by their very nature offer a link to the operation of the common market, that link constituting another condition for the application of Article [352].

230   If economic and financial measures such as those imposed by the contested regulation, consisting of the, in principle generalised, freezing of all the funds and other economic resources of the persons and entities concerned, were imposed unilaterally by every Member State, the multiplication of those national measures might well affect the operation of the common market. Such measures could have a particular effect on trade between Member States, especially with regard to the movement of capital and payments, and on the exercise by economic operators of their right of establishment. In addition, they could create distortions of competition, because any differences between the measures unilaterally taken by the Member States could operate to the advantage or disadvantage of the competitive position of certain economic operators although there were no economic reasons for that advantage or disadvantage.

Accordingly, the Court found that the regulations had a proper legal basis. Are you persuaded by the Court's intricate reasoning? How did the Court use Articles 75 and 215 to buttress its reliance on Article 352? How did the Court fit the measure into the framework of Community policy? As noted above, Article 215 now allows measures to be taken against individuals.

2. MIXED AGREEMENTS

International agreements are often complex and deal with more than one narrow subject. As a consequence, it is to be expected that the Court of Justice's approach to the issues of competence and exclusivity may often lead to the result that the Union has the exclusive competence to deal with certain parts of a proposed international agreement, but not others. What is to be done in such a case?

This issue first prominently featured in the so-called *Rubber Agreement* opinion, which involved an agreement negotiated as part of an

Integrated Program for Commodities developed by UNCTAD, the United Nations Conference on Trade and Development. UNCTAD was created in part to give developing countries a greater say in international trade negotiations than they felt that they had in GATT. It did not supplant GATT (nor the WTO) as the principal forum for international trade negotiations, however, except in the case of some commodities.

Under its commodities program, UNCTAD hoped to promote agreements between the producers and users of specific commodities: bananas, cocoa, coffee, sugar, meat, tea, vegetable oils, cotton, hard fibers, jute, natural rubber, timber, bauxite, copper, iron ore, manganese, phosphate and tin. In the case of natural rubber, the agreement established an organization to hold a "buffer stock" of rubber, which would be increased through market purchases of rubber when the price of rubber was low and reduced when the price of rubber was high. The basic aim of the program was to smooth out fluctuations in the price of rubber, so as to provide increased and stable export earnings for the developing countries exporting rubber. In addition, the agreement provided for development aid to those countries.

INTERNATIONAL AGREEMENT ON NATURAL RUBBER

Opinion 1/78, [1979] ECR 2871.

[The Commission asked the Court to give its opinion under Article 300 [now 218(11) TFEU] on whether the Community was competent to conclude the International Agreement on Natural Rubber.]

IV.   The Subject–Matter and Objectives of the Agreement Envisaged

* * *

37   The central question raised by the Commission's request is whether the international agreement on rubber comes as a whole or at least in essentials within the sphere of the "common commercial policy" referred to in Article 113 EEC [now 207 TFEU].[3] It is common ground that the agreement envisaged is closely connected with commercial policy. The difference of views relates to the extent of the sphere of application of Article 113 so that it remains uncertain whether that provision entirely covers the subject-matter of the agreement in question.

* * *

---

3. At the time of the case, the relevant text of Article 113 EEC read as follows: "The common commercial policy shall be based on uniform principles, particularly in regard to changes in tariff rates, the conclusion of tariff and trade agreements, the achievement of uniformity in measures of liberalization, export policy and measures to protect trade such as those to be taken in the event of dumping or subsidies." The revisions over time of Article 113 and the current text of Article 207 TFEU are examined in Chapter 29(B) infra.

(a) Consideration of the Agreement's Links With Commercial Policy and Development Problems

41   By its special machinery as much as by certain aspects of its legal structure, the International Agreement on Natural Rubber which it is proposed to conclude stands apart from ordinary commercial and tariff agreements which are based primarily on the operation of customs duties and quantitative restrictions. The agreement in question is a more structured instrument in the form of an organization of the market on a world scale and in this way it is distinguished from classical commercial agreements. * * *

42   [UNCTAD's] Nairobi Resolution, which is the basis of the negotiations in progress on natural rubber, shows that commodity agreements have complex objectives. * * * As regards, more particularly, the interests of the developing countries, it is true that commodity agreements may involve the granting of advantages which are characteristic of development aid; it must however be acknowledged also that for those countries such agreements respond more fundamentally to the preoccupation of bringing about an improvement in the "terms of trade" and thus of increasing their export earnings. This characteristic is particularly brought out in the agreement in question, which seeks to establish a fair balance between the interests of the producer countries and those of the consumer countries. * * *

43   The link between the various agreements on commodities which were emphasized by the Nairobi Resolution must also be taken into account. As an increasing number of products which are particularly important from the economic point of view are concerned, it is clear that a coherent commercial policy would no longer be practicable if the Community were not in a position to exercise its powers also in connexion with a category of agreements which are becoming, alongside traditional commercial agreements, one of the major factors in the regulation of international trade.

44   * * * It is therefore not possible to lay down, for Article 113 of the EEC Treaty, an interpretation the effect of which would be to restrict the common commercial policy to the use of instruments intended to have an effect only on the traditional aspects of external trade to the exclusion of more highly developed mechanisms such as appear in the agreement envisaged. A "commercial policy" understood in that sense would be destined to become nugatory in the course of time. Although it may be thought that at the time when the Treaty was drafted liberalization of trade was the dominant idea, the Treaty nevertheless does not form a barrier to the possibility of the Community's developing a commercial policy aiming at a regulation of the world market for certain products rather than at a mere liberalization of trade.

45   Article 113 empowers the Community to formulate a commercial "policy", based on "uniform principles" thus showing that the question of external trade must be governed from a wide point of view and

not only having regard to the administration of precise systems such as customs and quantitative restrictions. The same conclusion may be deduced from the fact that the enumeration in Article 113 of the subjects covered by commercial policy (changes in tariff rates, the conclusion of tariff and trade agreements, the achievement of uniformity in measures of liberalization, export policy and measures to protect trade) is conceived as a non-exhaustive enumeration which must not, as such, close the door to the application in a Community context of any other process intended to regulate external trade. A restrictive interpretation of the concept of common commercial policy would risk causing disturbances in intra-Community trade by reason of the disparities which would then exist in certain sectors of economic relations with non-member countries.

46   Moreover, when the whole canvas of existing and planned agreements is considered it appears that as far as the Community is concerned a wide range of interests is involved in the negotiation of those agreements and that there are connexions with the most varied spheres in which the Community has undertaken responsibilities. Thus, * * * there are other agreements, for example those concerning products such as wheat, oils and fats and sugar, in which the Community is interested also as a producer and by which its export policy, expressly mentioned in Article 113 as being amongst the objectives of the common commercial policy, is affected. * * * Several of the agreements belonging to this category are furthermore directly related to the execution of the common agricultural policy.

(b) The Agreement's Links With General Economic Policy

47   In its arguments the Council has raised the problem of the interrelation within the structure of the Treaty of the concepts of "economic policy" and "commercial policy". In certain provisions economic policy is indeed considered primarily as a question of national interest; such is the meaning of that concept in Articles 6 [now deleted] and 145 [now deleted] which, for that reason, prescribe for the Member States nothing more than a duty to ensure co-ordination. In other provisions economic policy is envisaged as being a matter of common interest * * *

48   The considerations set out above already form to some extent an answer to the arguments relating to the distinction to be drawn between the spheres of general economic policy and those of the common commercial policy since international co-operation, inasmuch as it does not belong to commercial policy, would be confused with the domain of general economic policy. If it appears that it comes, at least in part, under the common commercial policy, as has been indicated above, it follows clearly that it could not, under the name of general economic policy, be withdrawn from the competence of the Community.

49   * * * [W]here the organization of the Community's economic links with non-member countries may have repercussions on certain sectors of economic policy such as the supply of raw materials to the Community or price policy, as is precisely the case with the regulation of international trade in commodities, that consideration does not constitute a reason for excluding such objectives from the field of application of the rules relating to the common commercial policy. Similarly, the fact that a product may have a political importance by reason of the building up of security stocks is not a reason for excluding that product from the domain of the common commercial policy.

* * *

V.   Problems Raised by the Financing of the Agreement and by Other Specific Provisions

52   Consideration must still be given, having regard to what has been stated above as regards correspondence between the objective and purposes of the agreement envisaged and the concept of common commercial policy, whether the detailed arrangements for financing the buffer stock, or certain specific clauses of the agreement, concerning technological assistance, research programmes, the maintenance of fair conditions of labour in the rubber industry and consultations relating to national tax policies which may have an effect on the price of rubber lead to a negation of the Community's exclusive competence.

* * *

56   The Court takes the view that the fact that the agreement may cover subjects such as technological assistance, research programmes, labour conditions in the industry concerned or consultations relating to national tax policies which may have an effect on the price of rubber cannot modify the description of the agreement which must be assessed having regard to its essential objective rather than in terms of individual clauses of an altogether subsidiary or ancillary nature. * * * The negotiation and execution of these clauses must therefore follow the system applicable to the agreement considered as a whole.

* * *

58   [With regard to the system of financing,] the Court feels bound to have regard to two possible situations: one in which the financial burdens envisaged by the agreement would be entered in the Community budget and one in which the burdens would be directly charged to the budgets of the Member States. * * *

59   In the first case no problem would arise as regards the exclusive powers of the Community to conclude the agreement in question. * * *

60   * * * If on the other hand the financing is to be by the Member States that will imply the participation of those States in the decision-making

machinery or, at least, their agreement with regard to the arrangements for financing envisaged and consequently their participation in the agreement together with the Community. The exclusive competence of the Community could not be envisaged in such a case, [which was in fact the situation in the *Rubber Agreement* case.]

NOTES AND QUESTIONS

1. Who really won the *Rubber Agreement* case—the Commission or the Council and the Member States? What difference does it make if the Member States are or are not involved in the negotiations? How might their individual interests diverge from the Union's interests? How might their participation affect the results of the negotiations?

2. The Court affirmed its broad reading of "common commercial policy" in Commission v. Council (Generalized tariff preferences I), Case 45/86, [1987] ECR 1493. The Court elaborated on the scope of Article 113 in its 1994 opinion on EC adherence to the Agreement Establishing the World Trade Organization. We will postpone consideration of that case until Chapter 29, where that agreement is described in some detail. The scope of the common commercial policy has been expanded by recent treaty amendments. The new text, which is found in Article 207 TFEU, is described in notes to Chapter 29(B)(1) infra.

3. Is the basis of the *Rubber Agreement* decision different from that of the *ERTA* decision? Is the Court concerned with implied or explicit powers in the *Rubber Agreement* case? Do you agree with the Court's expansive reading of "common commercial policy"?

4. The opinion in the *Rubber Agreement* case deals with the problems of so-called mixed agreements, international agreements in which both the EU and the Member States participate because neither has exclusive competence over the matters dealt with in the agreements. For example, many trade and association agreements require direct financial help from Member States and therefore must be signed by them in addition to the EU. Examples of mixed multilateral agreements would include commodities agreements, the Ozone Layer Convention and the Law of the Sea Convention. The latter involves fishing, an exclusive concern of the EU, but also deep sea mining and the peaceful passage of warships, concerns of the Member States (see Note 6 below).

5. If both the EU and the Member States have some competence in respect of the subject matter of an international agreement, what sort of obligations do they have to cooperate with each other in the negotiations? This issue is addressed in the *WTO* opinion excerpted in Chapter 29(B)(1) infra.

6. If the subject matter of an international agreement is exclusively within the competence of the Union, is a mixed agreement appropriate? How does uncertainty about the respective roles of the Union and its Member States in external affairs affect third parties? If you were representing the United States in negotiations with the EU, what might you do to reduce such uncertainty?

In this regard, the Law of the Sea Convention, which the EU ratified in 1998, requires that "[a]t the time of signature an international organization [defined to include the EU] shall make a declaration specifying the matters governed by this Convention in respect of which competence has been transferred to that organization by its member states which are signatories, and the nature and extent of that competence." (Annex IX, art. 2) In its declaration the EU noted that the division of competence between it and its Member States was subject to change over time ("continuous development") and it stated that it would amend its declaration as necessary.[4]

C. INTERNATIONAL AGREEMENTS IN UNION LAW

One interesting issue that arises in respect of international agreements entered into by the EU is their position in EU law. Article 216(2) TFEU provides that "[a]greements concluded by the Union are binding upon the institutions of the Union and on its Member States." The EEC and EC Treaties had similar provisions. This raises the question of whether such agreements can be invoked by litigants in EU and Member State courts.

OPEL AUSTRIA GMBH v. COUNCIL
Case T–115/94, [1997] ECR II–39.

[On December 20, 1993, the Council adopted a regulation imposing a duty of 4.9% on F–15 car gearboxes produced by General Motors Austria and originating in Austria. It did so to offset certain state aids extended by Austria to General Motors. The regulation was adopted on the basis of the common commercial policy power and a 1972 Council regulation on imposition of safeguards provided for in the Austria–EC Free Trade Agreement ("FTA"). That agreement was superseded by the European Economic Area ("EEA") Agreement, which entered into force on January 1, 1994 and which is described in Chapter 28. The following decision of the Court of First Instance was not appealed.]

89   The applicant * * * claims that the EEA Agreement was part of the factual and legal situation existing at the time when the contested regulation was adopted on 20 December 1993 and that, by adopting that regulation a few days before the EEA Agreement entered into force, the Council infringed the principle of public international law ("the principle of good faith") according to which, pending the entry into force of an international agreement, the signatories to an international agreement may not adopt measures which would defeat its object and purpose.

90   The Court holds in this connection, first, that the principle of good faith is a rule of customary international law whose existence is

---

4. United Nations, Multilateral Treaties Deposited with the Secretary General, Status as of 31 December 1989, XXI.6, 785–786 (1990); Council Decision of March 23, 1998, Annex II, O.J. L179/129–130 (June 23, 1998).

recognized by the International Court of Justice and is therefore binding on the Community.

91　That principle has been codified by Article 18 of the first Vienna Convention, which provides as follows:

"A State is obliged to refrain from acts which would defeat the object and purpose of a treaty when:

(a) it has signed the treaty or has exchanged instruments constituting the treaty subject to ratification, acceptance or approval, until it shall have made its intention clear not to become a party to the treaty or

(b) it has expressed its consent to be bound by the treaty, pending the entry into force of the treaty and provided that such entry into force is not unduly delayed."

92　In this case, the Council adopted the contested regulation on 20 December 1993, that is to say, seven days after the Communities, as the last Contracting Parties, had approved the EEA Agreement * * *. Accordingly, as from 13 December 1993 the Communities were aware [that the EEA Agreement was to enter into force on January 1, 1994].

93　Secondly, the principle of good faith is the corollary in public international law of the principle of protection of legitimate expectations which, according to the case-law, forms part of the Community legal order. Any economic operator to whom an institution has given justified hopes may rely on the principle of protection of legitimate expectations.

94　In a situation where the Communities have deposited their instruments of approval of an international agreement and the date of entry into force of that agreement is known, traders may rely on the principle of protection of legitimate expectations in order to challenge the adoption by the institutions, during the period preceding the entry into force of that agreement, of any measure contrary to the provisions of that agreement which will have direct effect on them after it has entered into force.

[The Court first determined that the relevant provisions of the EEA Agreement took the place of the provisions of the FTA and that the EEA Agreement was applicable to the products at issue in this case.]

100　Secondly, it is necessary to consider whether Article 10 of the EEA Agreement is capable of having direct effect following the entry into force of that agreement.

101　As appears from Article 228(7) of the EC Treaty [now 216(2) TFEU], international agreements concluded by the Community in conformity with the Treaty are binding on the institutions and the Member States. It is settled case-law that the provisions of such an agreement form an integral part of the Community legal order once the agreement has entered into force. It is also settled case-law that the provisions of such an agreement may have direct effect if they are unconditional and sufficiently precise.

102   In that regard, the Court observes that nothing in the case-file suggests that the EEA Agreement, which was concluded by the Community on the basis of Article 238 of the EC Treaty [now 217 TFEU], was not concluded in conformity with the Treaty. It follows that since the Agreement entered into force on 1 January 1994 the provisions of the Agreement form an integral part of the Community legal order. It should also be borne in mind that the first sentence of Article 10 of the EEA Agreement provides that customs duties on imports and exports and any charges having equivalent effect are prohibited between the Contracting Parties. The second sentence of that article provides that, without prejudice to the arrangements set out in Protocol 5, customs duties of a fiscal nature are likewise prohibited. Article 10 thus lays down an unconditional and precise rule, subject to a single exception which is itself unconditional and precise. It follows that ever since the EEA Agreement entered into force Article 10 has had direct effect.

103   Thirdly, it is necessary to decide whether, by reintroducing a duty of 4.9%, the contested regulation infringed Article 10 of the EEA Agreement.

104   Article 6 of the EEA Agreement provides:

"Without prejudice to future developments of case-law, the provisions of this Agreement, in so far as they are identical in substance to corresponding rules of the Treaty establishing the European Economic Community and the Treaty establishing the European Coal and Steel Community and to acts adopted in application of these two Treaties, shall, in their implementation and application, be interpreted in conformity with the relevant rulings of the Court of Justice of the European Communities given prior to the date of signature of this Agreement."

105   The Council contends that, notwithstanding that provision, Article 10 of the EEA Agreement should not be interpreted in the same way as the corresponding provisions of the EC Treaty, because there are major differences between the EC Treaty and the EEA Agreement.

106   That argument cannot be accepted. It is clear from the case-law that in order to determine whether the interpretation of a provision contained in the EC Treaty must be extended to an identical provision contained in an agreement such as the EEA Agreement, that provision should be analysed in the light of both the purpose and the objective of the Agreement and in its context. According to Article 1(1) of the EEA Agreement, the aim of that agreement is to promote a continuous and balanced strengthening of trade and economic relations between the Contracting Parties with equal conditions of competition, and the respect of the same rules, with a view to creating a homogeneous European Economic Area. To that end, the

Contracting Parties decided to eliminate virtually all trade barriers, in conformity with the provisions of the GATT on the establishment of free-trade areas.

107   In that context, the EEA Agreement involves a high degree of integration, with objectives which exceed those of a mere free-trade agreement. Thus, as is clear from Article 1(2), the EEA involves, inter alia, the free movement of goods, persons, services and capital and the setting up of a system ensuring that competition is not distorted and that the rules relating thereto are equally respected. The rules applicable to relations between the Contracting Parties in the fields covered by the Agreement essentially correspond to the parallel provisions of the EC and ECSC Treaties and the measures adopted in pursuance of those treaties. * * *

* * *

110   It follows from those findings that Article 6 of the EEA Agreement must be interpreted as meaning that where a provision of the EEA Agreement is identical in substance to corresponding rules of the EC and ECSC Treaties and to the acts adopted in application of those two treaties it must be interpreted in conformity with the relevant rulings of the Court of Justice and of the Court of First Instance given prior to the date of signature of the EEA Agreement.

111   The Court further finds that Article 10 of the EEA Agreement is identical in substance to Articles 12, 13, 16 and 17 of the EC Treaty [Article 12 is now Article 38 TFEU; the rest have been deleted] which, with effect from the end of the transitional period, prohibit customs duties on imports or exports and any charges having equivalent effect between the Member States. Consequently, by virtue of Article 6 of the EEA Agreement, Article 10 must be interpreted in conformity with the relevant rulings of the Court of Justice and the Court of First Instance prior to the date of signature of the Agreement.

* * *

119   In view of all these factors, it is accordingly necessary to consider whether, following the entry into force of the EEA Agreement, the contested regulation is contrary to Article 10 of that agreement when interpreted, pursuant to Article 6, in conformity with the relevant rulings of the Court of Justice and the Court of First Instance prior to the date of signature of the EEA Agreement.

* * *

121   [I]t is settled case-law that "any pecuniary charge, however small and whatever its designation and mode of application, which is imposed unilaterally on domestic or foreign goods by reason of the fact that they cross a frontier, and which is not a customs duty in the strict sense, constitutes a charge having equivalent effect within the mean-

ing of Articles 9 and 12 of the Treaty [now Articles 31 and 38 TFEU], even if it is not imposed for the benefit of the State, is not discriminatory or protective in effect or if the product on which the charge is imposed is not in competition with any domestic product'' (Sociaal Fonds voor de Diamantarbeiders v. Brachfeld, paragraph 15/18, [excerpted in Chapter 12(A)]).

122   The measure introduced by the contested regulation constitutes a pecuniary charge imposed unilaterally by the Community on F–15 gearboxes by reason of the fact that they cross a frontier. Consequently, it must be held that the measure constitutes, at the very least, a charge having equivalent effect within the meaning of Article 10 of the EEA Agreement and it is unnecessary to determine whether it must be regarded as a customs duty on imports in the strict sense. It is therefore clear that, following the entry into force of the EEA Agreement, the contested regulation was contrary to that article.

123   It follows that, by adopting the contested regulation in the period preceding the entry into force of the EEA Agreement after the Communities had deposited their instruments of approval, the Council infringed the applicant's legitimate expectations.

NOTES AND QUESTIONS

1. The position of international law in the Union was underscored in Commission v. Germany (International Dairy Arrangement), Case C–61/94, [1996] ECR I–3989, where the Court permitted the Commission to initiate what is now an Article 258 action against Germany for failing to comply with an international agreement that had been ratified by the Community in a Council decision. The Court noted that under then Article 211 (now Lisbon TEU Article 17(1)), "the Commission is responsible for ensuring application of the Treaty, and, accordingly, compliance with international agreements concluded by the Community which, pursuant to Article 228 [now 216 TFEU], are binding both on the Community institutions and the Member States'' (para. 15).

2. In Hauptzollamt Mainz v. C.A. Kupferberg & Cie., Case 104/81, [1982] ECR 3641, the Court of Justice examined the EC–Portuguese Free Trade Agreement, which was in force prior to Portugal's accession to the Union. The case involved Article 21 of the Agreement, which provided that the parties would not implement tax measures that resulted, directly or indirectly, in discrimination between the domestic and imported products. The company involved claimed that Germany had engaged in such discrimination and that Article 21 was directly applicable. The Court concluded (at 3665):

23   * * * In order to reply to the question on the direct effect of the first paragraph of Article 21 of the Agreement between the Community and Portugal it is necessary to analyse the provision in the light of both the object and purpose of the Agreement and of its context.

24   The purpose of the Agreement is to create a system of free trade in which rules restricting commerce are eliminated in respect of virtually all trade in products originating in the territory of the parties, in particular by abolishing customs duties and charges having equivalent effect and eliminating quantitative restrictions and measures having equivalent effect.

25   Seen in that context the first paragraph of Article 21 of the Agreement seeks to prevent the liberalization of the trade in goods through the abolition of customs duties and charges having equivalent effect and quantitative restrictions and measures having equivalent effect from being rendered nugatory by fiscal practices of the Contracting Parties. That would be so if the product imported of one party were taxed more heavily than the similar domestic products which it encounters on the market of the other party.

26   It appears from the foregoing that the first paragraph of Article 21 of the Agreement imposes on the Contracting Parties an unconditional rule against discrimination in matters of taxation, which is dependent only on a finding that the products affected by a particular system of taxation are of like nature, and the limits of which are the direct consequence of the purpose of the Agreement. As such this provision may be applied by a court and thus produce direct effects throughout the Community.

The Court in *Kupferberg* ultimately concluded that the German law did not violate the EC–Portuguese Agreement.

    3.   Should the fact that the other party to an international agreement might not allow litigants to invoke the agreement in its domestic courts cause the Court of Justice to adopt a similar policy for itself and Member State courts? In *Kupferberg* the Court rejected such an argument.

    4.   In Polydor Ltd. v. Harlequin Record Shops Ltd., Case 270/80, [1982] ECR 329, which also involved the interpretation of the EC–Portuguese Free Trade Agreement, the Court was faced with a case involving records lawfully made and marketed in Portugal by the Portuguese copyright holder and then exported to the United Kingdom, where another party held the copyright. As explained in Chapter 19(B)(2) supra, under the Court's interpretation of Articles 34 and 36 TFEU, a product marketed by the copyright holder in Member State A can often be lawfully exported to Member State B, even if another party holds the copyright in Member State B. The question in this case was whether Articles 14(2) and 23 of the Agreement, which were almost identical to Articles 34 and 36 TFEU, should be interpreted in the same way. The Court concluded at 348–349:

14   The provisions of the Agreement on the elimination of restrictions on trade between the Community and Portugal are expressed in terms which in several respects are similar to those of the EEC Treaty on the abolition of restrictions on intra-Community trade. Harlequin and Simons pointed out in particular the similarity between the terms of Articles 14(2) and 23 of the Agreement on the one hand and those of Articles 30 and 36 of the EEC Treaty [now 34 and 36 TFEU] on the other.

15   However, such similarity of terms is not a sufficient reason for transposing to the provisions of the Agreement the above-mentioned case-law,

which determines in the context of the Community the relationship between the protection of industrial and commercial property rights and the rules on the free movement of goods.

16   The scope of that case-law must indeed be determined in the light of the Community's objectives and activities as defined by * * * the EEC Treaty. As the Court has had occasion to emphasize in various contexts, the Treaty, by establishing a common market and progressively approximating the economic policies of the Member States, seeks to unite national markets into a single market having the characteristics of a domestic market.

17   Having regard to those objectives, the Court, *inter alia,* in Terrapin (Overseas) Ltd. v. Terranova Industrie [see Chapter 19(B)(1) supra], interpreted Articles 30 and 36 of the [EEC] Treaty as meaning that the territorial protection afforded by national laws to industrial and commercial property may not have the effect of legitimizing the insulation of national markets and of leading to an artificial partitioning of the markets and that consequently the proprietor of an industrial or commercial property right protected by the law of a Member State cannot rely on that law to prevent the importation of a product which has lawfully been marketed in another Member State by the proprietor himself or with his consent.

18   The considerations which led to that interpretation of Articles 30 and 36 of the [EEC] Treaty do not apply in the context of the relations between the Community and Portugal as defined by the Agreement. It is apparent from an examination of the Agreement that although it makes provision for the unconditional abolition of certain restrictions on trade between the Community and Portugal, such as quantitative restrictions and measures having equivalent effect, it does not have the same purpose as the EEC Treaty, inasmuch as the latter, as has been stated above, seeks to create a single market reproducing as closely as possible the conditions of a domestic market.

19   It follows that in the context of the Agreement restrictions on trade in goods may be considered to be justified on the ground of the protection of industrial and commercial property in a situation in which their justification would not be possible within the Community.

20   In the present case such a distinction is all the more necessary inasmuch as the instruments which the Community has at its disposal in order to achieve the uniform application of Community law and the progressive abolition of legislative disparities within the common market have no equivalent in the context of the relations between the Community and Portugal.

21   It follows from the foregoing that a prohibition on the importation into the Community of a product originating in Portugal based on the protection of copyright is justified in the framework of the free-trade arrangements established by the Agreement by virtue of the first sentence of Article 23. The findings of the national court do not disclose any factor which would permit the conclusion that the enforcement of copyright in a case such as the present constitutes a means of arbitrary discrimination

or a disguised restriction on trade within the meaning of the second sentence of that article.

Do you agree with the Court's distinction in para. 18? Isn't the goal of both the EU and the Agreement liberalization of trade and market integration?

5. The Court on several occasions has ruled that workers (or their families) may rely on the provisions of EU-third country association/cooperation agreements to challenge discrimination against them in respect of certain unemployment or disability benefits. See, e.g., Yousfi v. Belgium, Case C–58/93, [1994] ECR I–1353; Office National de l'Emploi v. Kziber, Case C–18/90, [1991] ECR I–199. The two cited cases involved Articles 40 and 41 of the EC–Morocco Cooperation Agreement, which require Member States to treat Moroccan workers employed in their territory non-discriminatorily in terms of working conditions and remuneration and to treat family members living with them non-discriminatorily in respect of social security. See also Eroglu v. Land Baden–Württemberg, Case C–355/93, [1994] ECR I–5113 (Association Agreement with Turkey).

Article 6(1) of Decision 1/80 of the EC–Turkey Association Council (established under the EC–Turkey Association Agreement) provides that the EU and Turkey will be "guided by Articles [45–47 TFEU] for the purposes of progressively securing freedom of movement for workers between them." In Recep Tetik v. Land Berlin, Case C–171/95, [1997] ECR I–329, the Court ruled that since Article 6 of Decision 1/80 has direct effect and may be relied upon by Turkish nationals in Member State courts, a Turkish worker who had been legally employed for more than four years in a Member State, who had voluntarily left his employment in order to seek new work in the same Member State and who was unable immediately to enter into a new employment relation, had a right of residence for a reasonable period of time for the purpose of seeking new employment. The Court noted that it was for the Member State concerned (or in the absence of legislation, the Member State's courts) to fix such reasonable period. See also Eyüp v. Landesgeshäftsstelle des Arbeitsmarktservice Vorarlberg, Case C–65/98, [2000] ECR I–4747 ("family member" for purposes of five-year lawful residence requirement for employment rights under Decision 1/80 includes person who was married to worker for two years, divorced but cohabited with worker for ten years and then remarried to worker for four years).

6. Jany v. Staatssecretaris van Justitie, Case C–268/99, [2001] ECR I–8615, involved several Czech and Polish women who claimed to work as self-employed prostitutes, but were denied Dutch residence permits. In replying to a preliminary reference by a Dutch court, the Court of Justice ruled that the provisions on the right of establishment in the EC–Czech and EC–Poland Association Agreements had direct effect and could be relied upon by individuals. Moreover, their provisions on self-employed individuals should have the same meaning and scope as those in the EC Treaty. Accordingly, the Court was of the view that prostitution pursued in a self-employed capacity was a service provided for remuneration and thereby covered under the provisions at issue. While the Court recognized that the right of establishment gave, as a corollary, a right of residence, it found that the right was not unqualified. In particular, it noted that a Member State could require that a person had

sufficient financial resources to carry out the activity in question in a self-employed capacity and could require that the person was truly self-employed and not in a relationship of subordination.

7. The Court of Justice has not been receptive to arguments that GATT or WTO provisions should be given direct effect. See Chapter 29(B)(2) infra. After reading that material, do you think the cases discussed here and the *Portuguese Republic* case in Chapter 29 are consistent? The Court has also declined to give direct effect to the UN Convention on the Law of the Sea. Intertanko v. Secretary of State for Transport, Case C–308/06, [2008] ECR I–4057, criticized by Wouters and de Man in 103 AJIL 555 (2009). According to the Court, this result was dictated by "the nature and broad logic of [the Convention]".

8. If an international agreement concluded by the EU is found to be directly applicable, would such an agreement prevail over (a) the EU treaties? (b) EU acts adopted subsequently to its conclusion? (c) EU acts adopted prior to conclusion of the agreement? (d) the constitution of a Member State? (e) Member State legislation adopted after its conclusion? (f) such legislation adopted prior to conclusion of the agreement?

9. Under US law, an international agreement is not self-executing "(a) if the agreement manifests an intention that it shall not become effective as domestic law without the enactment of implementing legislation, (b) if the Senate in giving consent to a treaty, or Congress by resolution, requires implementing legislation, or (c) if implementing legislation is constitutionally required." Restatement of the Law: The Foreign Relations Law of the United States (Third) sec. 111(4) (1987).

D. THE COMMON FOREIGN AND SECURITY POLICY

Ever since the early days of the EEC there have been proposals that the Member States coordinate their foreign policies, from both those who wanted to see Europe progress beyond economic union toward political union and those who viewed common efforts in foreign relations as a practical means to increase the influence of the Member States in world affairs.

The basis for Member State cooperation in foreign policy, which initially was known as European Political Cooperation (EPC), grew out of a decision at the 1969 Hague summit of the heads of state and government to have the Member State foreign ministers study ways of achieving progress toward political unification. Successive summit meetings at Copenhagen in 1973, London in 1981 and Stuttgart in 1983 substantially reinforced EPC, but EPC was not given a treaty basis until its inclusion in title III of the Single European Act, which came into effect in 1987. This foundation was significantly expanded by title V of the Treaty on European Union, which provides for a Common Foreign and Security Policy (CFSP). The TEU's provisions on the CFSP were modified in the Amsterdam, Nice and Lisbon Treaties and are now contained in TEU Articles 21–46.

One striking innovation in the Lisbon Treaty is the expansion of the position of High Representative of the Union for Foreign Affairs and Security Policy, who is charged with conducting the Union's common foreign and security policy and who is authorized to make proposals in connection therewith (Article 22(2) TEU). The High Representative is to be appointed by the European Council, with the agreement of the President of the Commission and subject to the consent of Parliament to the overall Commission (Articles 17(7), 18(1) TEU). The High Representative is to take part in the work of the European Council and will chair the Council of Ministers when it is acting in its new Foreign Affairs Council formation, in which it is charged with fleshing out the Union's external policies on the basis of strategic guidelines laid down by the European Council (Article 16(6) TEU). The High Representative would also be a Vice–President of the Commission, where he or she would be responsible for handling external relations and for coordinating other aspects of the Union's external action (Article 18(4) TEU). Thus, both the common foreign and security policy, on the one hand, and the external relations and actions of the Union now handled by the Commission, on the other, would be unified in one person. The President of the Council—also a new position created by the Lisbon Treaty—is also given a foreign affairs role. Article 15(6) TEU specifies that the President is to ensure the external representation of the Union on issues concerning its common foreign and security policy, but that role is said to be without prejudice to the role of the High Representative. How that will work in practice is not completely clear, nor is it clear how much of a foreign affairs role the President of the Commission will have.

As of December 2009, Herman van Rompuy, a former Belgian prime minister, was President of the Council and Catherine Ashton of the UK was the High Representative. She had previously been Commissioner for Trade.

The Court of Justice has only very limited jurisdiction in respect of the CFSP (art. 24(1) TEU), see Chapter 5(B)(4) supra, although actions taken under the TFEU to implement foreign policy decisions may be reviewed by the Court. In this section, we will outline briefly the operation of the Common Foreign Policy and the Common Security Policy and then consider cases where trade and other sanctions imposed pursuant to the Common Foreign Policy were challenged in the Court of Justice.

1. THE COMMON FOREIGN POLICY

The Lisbon Treaty on European Union provides that "[t]he Union shall define and pursue common policies and actions * * * in all fields of international relations" (art. 21(2) TEU). Its actions shall be guided by the principles that inspired its creation (art. 21(1) TEU) and shall have the specific objectives listed in Article 21(2) TEU. As to the Member

States, they "shall support the Union's external and security policy actively and unreservedly in a spirit of loyalty and mutual solidarity and shall comply with the Union's action in this area. * * * They shall refrain from any action which is contrary to the interests of the Union or likely to impair its effectiveness as a cohesive force in international relations." Art. 24(3) TEU.

Under Article 26 TEU the European Council is responsible for identifying the Union's strategic interests, determining the objectives of and defining the general guidelines of the CFSP. The decision-making procedures are set out in Article 31 TEU. As a general principle, decisions under the CFSP are taken by the Council acting unanimously, although abstentions do not prevent the adoption of decisions. When abstaining, a Member State may qualify its abstention by making a formal declaration. In that case, it is not obligated to apply the decision, but must accept that the decision commits the Union. The Member State concerned, in the spirit of mutual solidarity, is expected to refrain from any action likely to conflict with or impede Union action based on that decision. If the Member States qualifying their abstentions in this way represent more than one-third of the Member States comprising more than one-third of the EU population, the decision would not be adopted.

In a significant derogation from the foregoing general unanimity principle, certain implementation decisions and proposals made by the High Representative (excluding those having military or defense implications) may be adopted by the Council acting by a qualified majority. However, if a Member State declares formally that, for vital and stated reasons of national policy, it intends to oppose the adoption of a decision by qualified majority, a vote on the decision is not be taken. In such a case, if a compromise cannot be reached, the Council, acting by a qualified majority, may refer the matter to the European Council, for decision by unanimity.

Prior to 2010, the CFSP was implemented by the European Council, the General Affairs Council (which meets at least monthly and decided on external relations issues), Coreper (which meets regularly to prepare Council meetings), the Political and Security Committee (consisting of Member State representatives of ambassadorial rank, which meets twice a week), as well as staff structures that monitor international political developments on a round-the-clock basis. All of this activity produces numerous EU statements on foreign policy issues. The Council section of the EU website is an excellent, up-to-date source of Union pronouncements on foreign affairs. With the ratification of the Lisbon Treaty, the new President and a new Foreign Affairs Council will also be involved in implementation.

The High Representative is obligated to consult regularly the European Parliament on the main aspects of the CFSP and "shall ensure that the views of the European Parliament are duly taken into consideration" (Article 36 TEU).

It is too early to evaluate the effectiveness of the most recent changes in the operation of the CFSP. However, for materials evaluating the EPC and CFSP over the years, see John Peterson & Helen Sjursen, eds., A Common Foreign Policy for Europe: Competing Visions of the CFSP (1998); Jan Zielonka, ed., Paradoxes of European Foreign Policy (1998); Alan Cafruny & Patrick Peters, eds., The Union and the World (1998); A. Pijpers, E. Regelsberger & W. Wessels, eds., European Political Cooperation in the 1980s: A Common Foreign Policy for Western Europe? (1988).

2. THE COMMON SECURITY POLICY

The Lisbon TEU provides that the common security and defense policy shall be an integral part of the CFSP. Article 42(1) TEU. It is intended to provide the Union with civil and military assets provided by the Member States that can be used outside the Union for peace-keeping, conflict prevention and strengthening international security. It is specifically provided that this "shall include the progressive framing of a common Union defense policy," which will lead to a common defense, should the European Council so decide. Article 42(2) TEU. The TEU specifies that the EU Security Policy shall not prejudice the specific character of the security and defense policy of certain Member States and shall respect the obligations of certain Member States, which see their common defense realized in the North Atlantic Treaty Organization (NATO) and shall be compatible with the common security and defense policy established within that framework. Article 42(2) TEU. Decisions relating to the security policy are to be adopted by the Council acting unanimously on a proposal by the High Representative or a Member State. Article 42(4) TEU.

The Council website lists the peace-keeping and other operations undertaken by the EU, which have mainly been mounted in the Balkans and Africa. The website also details the progress towards the creation of the common defense policy and the expansion and improvement of EU military force capabilities.

Two of the more interesting issues in respect of the common security policy are how its relationship with NATO evolves and whether the policy leads to tensions with the US.

3. SANCTIONS FOR POLITICAL PURPOSES

Article 215 TFEU provides that if a decision adopted pursuant to the CFSP calls for the Union to interrupt or reduce economic relations with a third country, the Council shall take measures, by qualified majority, acting on a proposal from the High Representative and the Commission. This provision was added by the 1993 Maastricht Treaty and clarified the legal basis for imposing trade sanctions for political purposes. The Lisbon Treaty further clarified that the procedures could be used to impose restrictive measures on individuals (an issue raised in the *Kadi* case, which was considered in the notes to the *ERTA* case and is further examined below). Two other TFEU provisions are also relevant to sanctions. Article 75 authorizes restrictions on movements of capital and payments in order to combat terrorism. More generally, Article 347 requires Member States to consult on the need to take actions together so as to prevent the functioning of the common market being affected by measures that an individual Member State may be called upon to take in the event of serious internal disturbances, war or serious international tension constituting a threat of war.

While actions taken under the TEU in connection with the CFSP are not reviewable in the Court of Justice, the legislative measures imposing sanctions are reviewable and such measures have led to a number of cases in the Court of Justice. We excerpt two of the more important sanction cases.

BOSPHORUS HAVA YOLLARI TURIZM VE TICARET AS v. MINISTER FOR TRANSPORT, ENERGY & COMMUNICATIONS

Case C–84/95, [1996] ECR I–3953.

[Bosphorus Hava Yollari Turizm ve Ticaret AS ("Bosphorus Airways") is a Turkish company which operated principally as an air charterer and travel organizer. In April 1992, it leased two aircraft owned by the Yugoslav national airline JAT. The lease covered only the aircraft. Bosphorus Airways provided its own crews and had complete control of the day-to-day management of the aircraft. JAT remained the owner of the aircraft. It appeared that the lease was entered into in complete good faith and was not intended to circumvent the sanctions against the Yugoslavia which had been decided by United Nations resolutions and implemented in the Community by Regulation 990/93. Under the sanctions, the rent due under the lease was paid into blocked accounts, not to JAT. The aircraft were used exclusively by Bosphorus Airways for flights between Turkey on the one hand and several Member States and Switzerland on the other.

One of the aircraft was later seized by Irish authorities under Article 8 of Regulation 990/93, which provided that all aircraft "in which a majority or controlling interest is held by a person or undertaking in or operating from the Federal Republic of Yugoslavia (Serbia and Montenegro) shall be impounded by the competent authorities of the Member States". The Supreme Court of Ireland stayed the proceedings and asked for a preliminary ruling from the Court of Justice on whether Article 8 applied to an aircraft leased under the above-described conditions.]

9   In support of its argument, Bosphorus Airways submits that the aim of the regulation in question is to penalize the Federal Republic of Yugoslavia and its nationals as well as to apply sanctions against them, but is certainly not to extend those sanctions unnecessarily to wholly

innocent parties pursuing their activities from a neighboring State, with which, moreover, the Community has friendly relations.

10   That argument cannot be accepted.

11   As the Court has stated in its case-law, in interpreting a provision of Community law it is necessary to consider its wording, its context and its aims.

12   Nothing in the wording of [Article 8] suggests that it is based on a distinction between ownership of an aircraft on the one hand and its day-to-day operation and control on the other. Nor is it anywhere stated in that provision that it is not applicable to an aircraft owned by a person or undertaking based in or operating from the Federal Republic of Yugoslavia if that person or undertaking does not have day-to-day operation and control of the aircraft.

13   As to context and aims, it should be noted that by Regulation No 990/93 the Council gave effect to the decision of the Community and its Member States, meeting within the framework of political cooperation, to have recourse to a Community instrument to implement in the Community certain aspects of the sanctions taken against the Federal Republic of Yugoslavia by the Security Council of the United Nations * * *.

14   To determine the scope of the first paragraph of Article 8 of Regulation No 990/93, account must therefore also be taken of the text and the aim of those [UN] resolutions, [one of] which provides that "all States shall impound all vessels, freight vehicles, rolling stock and aircraft in their territories in which a majority or controlling interest is held by a person or undertaking in or operating from the Federal Republic of Yugoslavia (Serbia and Montenegro)".

15   Thus the wording of [the UN Resolution] confirms that [Article 8] is to apply to any aircraft which is the property of a person or undertaking based in or operating from the Federal Republic of Yugoslavia, and that it is not necessary for that person or undertaking also to have actual control of the aircraft. The word "interest" in [the UN resolution] cannot, on any view, exclude ownership as a determining criterion for impounding. Moreover, that word is used in that paragraph in conjunction with the word "majority", which clearly implies the concept of ownership.

16   That conclusion is borne out by the fact that most of the language versions of [Article 8] use terms with explicit connotations of ownership. * * *

17   Furthermore, the impounding of any aircraft owned by a person or undertaking based in or operating from the Federal Republic of Yugoslavia, even if an undertaking such as Bosphorus Airways has taken over its day-to-day operation and control, contributes to restricting the exercise by the Federal Republic of Yugoslavia and its nationals of their

property rights and is thus consistent with the aim of the sanctions, namely to put pressure on that republic.

18 By contrast, the use of day-to-day operation and control, rather than ownership, as the decisive criterion for applying the measures prescribed by [Article 8] would jeopardize the effectiveness of the strengthening of the sanctions, which consist in impounding all means of transport of the Federal Republic of Yugoslavia and its nationals, including aircraft, in order further to increase the pressure on that republic. The mere transfer of day-to-day operation and control of means of transport, by a lease or other method, without transferring ownership would allow that republic or its nationals to evade application of those sanctions.

Fundamental rights and the principle of proportionality

19 Bosphorus Airways submits, in the second place, that to interpret [Article 8] as meaning that an aircraft whose day-to-day operation and control are carried out under a lease by a person or undertaking not based in or operating from the Federal Republic of Yugoslavia must nevertheless be impounded because it belongs to an undertaking based in that republic, would infringe Bosphorus's fundamental rights, in particular its right to peaceful enjoyment of its property and its freedom to pursue a commercial activity, in that it would have the effect of destroying and obliterating its air charter and travel organization business.

20 That interpretation, according to Bosphorus Airways, would also infringe the principle of proportionality, since the owner of the aircraft in question has already been penalized by the rent being held in blocked accounts and the impounding of the aircraft was therefore a manifestly unnecessary penalty, disproportionate with respect to a wholly innocent party.

21 It is settled case-law that the fundamental rights invoked by Bosphorus Airways are not absolute and their exercise may be subject to restrictions justified by objectives of general interest pursued by the Community.

22 Any measure imposing sanctions has, by definition, consequences which affect the right to property and the freedom to pursue a trade or business, thereby causing harm to persons who are in no way responsible for the situation which led to the adoption of the sanctions.

23 Moreover, the importance of the aims pursued by the regulation at issue is such as to justify negative consequences, even of a substantial nature, for some operators.

24 The provisions of Regulation No 990/93 contribute in particular to the implementation at Community level of the sanctions against the Federal Republic of Yugoslavia adopted, and later strengthened, by several resolutions of the Security Council of the United Nations. The third recital in the preamble to Regulation No 990/93 states that "the

prolonged direct and indirect activities of the Federal Republic of Yugoslavia (Serbia and Montenegro) in, and with regard to, the Republic of Bosnia–Herzegovina are the main cause for the dramatic developments in the Republic of Bosnia–Herzegovina"; the fourth recital states that "a continuation of these activities will lead to further unacceptable loss of human life and material damage and to a further breach of international peace and security in the region"; and the seventh recital states that "the Bosnian Serb party has hitherto not accepted, in full, the peace plan of the International Conference on the Former Yugoslavia in spite of appeals thereto by the Security Council".

25 It is in the light of those circumstances that the aim pursued by the sanctions assumes especial importance, which is, in particular, in terms of Regulation No 990/93 and more especially the eighth recital in the preamble thereto, to dissuade the Federal Republic of Yugoslavia from "further violating the integrity and security of the Republic of Bosnia–Herzegovina and to induce the Bosnian Serb party to cooperate in the restoration of peace in this Republic".

26 As compared with an objective of general interest so fundamental for the international community, which consists in putting an end to the state of war in the region and to the massive violations of human rights and humanitarian international law in the Republic of Bosnia–Herzegovina, the impounding of the aircraft in question, which is owned by an undertaking based in or operating from the Federal Republic of Yugoslavia, cannot be regarded as inappropriate or disproportionate.

NOTES AND QUESTIONS

1. For many years, the Community only occasionally imposed trade sanctions for political reasons. For example, it imposed sanctions on Rhodesia (now Zimbabwe) in the 1960s and 1970s, in accordance with a UN Security Council resolution, in an effort to pressure the white minority government in that country to permit black majority rule. In 1980, the Member States in consultation with the Community took certain measures against Iran in an effort to get Iran to release the hostages taken at the US embassy in Teheran. Community measures were taken against Soviet Union to protest its invasion of Afghanistan and its intervention in Poland in 1981–1982, and imports from Argentina were suspended during the Falklands Islands crisis of 1982. In 1990, in accordance with UN Security Council resolutions, the Community prohibited all trade between the Community and Iraq, except for certain foodstuffs and medicines, in an effort to get Iraq to withdraw from Kuwait. Subsequently, as exemplified by the instant case, it has applied trade sanctions in an attempt to force negotiated settlements to the various conflicts in the former Yugoslavia. Some of these actions have been controversial politically. For example, despite the adoption of binding Community measures suspending imports from Argentina, Italy and Ireland refused to implement the suspension in part. At times, there was considerable disagreement over the legal basis for implementing trade sanctions. As noted above, this legal basis issue has now been clarified. In recent years, the EU has become much more

active in imposing sanctions. As of March 2010, 25 countries and several terrorist groups were listed as being subject to EU sanctions on the Council website.

2. While the decision of the Court is not surprising, do you think that Bosphorus Airways was treated fairly? Even if justified, was the decision proportional? Could some use be found for the payments due, such as redirection to programs for the benefit of refugees?

KADI v. COUNCIL

Case C–402/05, [2008] ECR I–6351.

[This case concerned the EU's implementation of UN Security Council resolutions calling for the freezing of assets of certain individuals and entities associated with certain terrorist organizations.]

280   The Court will now consider the heads of claim in which the appellants complain that the Court of First Instance, in essence, held that it followed from the principles governing the relationship between the international legal order under the United Nations and the Community legal order that the contested regulation, since it is designed to give effect to a resolution adopted by the Security Council under Chapter VII of the Charter of the United Nations affording no latitude in that respect, could not be subject to judicial review of its internal lawfulness, save with regard to its compatibility with the norms of *jus cogens*, and therefore to that extent enjoyed immunity from jurisdiction.

281   In this connection it is to be borne in mind that the Community is based on the rule of law, inasmuch as neither its Member States nor its institutions can avoid review of the conformity of their acts with the basic constitutional charter, the EC Treaty, which established a complete system of legal remedies and procedures designed to enable the Court of Justice to review the legality of acts of the institutions.

282   It is also to be recalled that an international agreement cannot affect the allocation of powers fixed by the Treaties or, consequently, the autonomy of the Community legal system, observance of which is ensured by the Court by virtue of the exclusive jurisdiction conferred on it by Article 220 EC [replaced in substance by Lisbon TEU Article 19], jurisdiction that the Court has, moreover, already held to form part of the very foundations of the Community (see, to that effect, Opinion 1/91 [1991] ECR I–6079) [excerpted in Chapter 28(A)(1) infra].

283   In addition, according to settled case-law, fundamental rights form an integral part of the general principles of law whose observance the Court ensures. For that purpose, the Court draws inspiration from the constitutional traditions common to the Member States and from the guidelines supplied by international instruments for the protection of human rights on which the Member States have collaborated

or to which they are signatories. In that regard, the ECHR has special significance.

284   It is also clear from the case-law that respect for human rights is a condition of the lawfulness of Community acts and that measures incompatible with respect for human rights are not acceptable in the Community.

285   It follows from all those considerations that the obligations imposed by an international agreement cannot have the effect of prejudicing the constitutional principles of the EC Treaty, which include the principle that all Community acts must respect fundamental rights, that respect constituting a condition of their lawfulness which it is for the Court to review in the framework of the complete system of legal remedies established by the Treaty.

286   In this regard it must be emphasised that, in circumstances such as those of these cases, the review of lawfulness thus to be ensured by the Community judicature applies to the Community act intended to give effect to the international agreement at issue, and not to the latter as such.

* * *

288   [A]ny judgment given by the Community judicature deciding that a Community measure intended to give effect to such a resolution is contrary to a higher rule of law in the Community legal order would not entail any challenge to the primacy of that resolution in international law.

* * *

290   It must therefore be considered whether, as the Court of First Instance held, as a result of the principles governing the relationship between the international legal order under the United Nations and the Community legal order, any judicial review of the internal lawfulness of the contested regulation in the light of fundamental freedoms is in principle excluded, notwithstanding the fact that, as is clear from the decisions referred to in paragraphs 281 to 284 above, such review is a constitutional guarantee forming part of the very foundations of the Community.

291   In this respect it is first to be borne in mind that the European Community must respect international law in the exercise of its powers. * * *

294   [T]he Community [must] attach special importance to the fact that, in accordance with Article 24 of the Charter of the United Nations, the adoption by the Security Council of resolutions under Chapter VII of the Charter constitutes the exercise of the primary responsibility with which that international body is invested for the maintenance of peace and security at the global level, a responsibility which, under Chapter VII, includes the power to determine what and who poses a

threat to international peace and security and to take the measures necessary to maintain or restore them.

* * *

296 [W]hen the object is to implement a resolution of the Security Council adopted under Chapter VII of the Charter of the United Nations, * * * the Community is to take due account of the terms and objectives of the resolution concerned and of the relevant obligations under the Charter of the United Nations relating to such implementation.

* * *

298 It must however be noted that the Charter of the United Nations does not impose the choice of a particular model for the implementation of resolutions adopted by the Security Council under Chapter VII of the Charter, since they are to be given effect in accordance with the procedure applicable in that respect in the domestic legal order of each Member of the United Nations. The Charter of the United Nations leaves the Members of the United Nations a free choice among the various possible models for transposition of those resolutions into their domestic legal order.

299 It follows from all those considerations that it is not a consequence of the principles governing the international legal order under the United Nations that any judicial review of the internal lawfulness of the contested regulation in the light of fundamental freedoms is excluded by virtue of the fact that that measure is intended to give effect to a resolution of the Security Council adopted under Chapter VII of the Charter of the United Nations.

300 What is more, such immunity from jurisdiction for a Community measure like the contested regulation, as a corollary of the principle of the primacy at the level of international law of obligations under the Charter of the United Nations, especially those relating to the implementation of resolutions of the Security Council adopted under Chapter VII of the Charter, cannot find a basis in the EC Treaty.

* * *

306 Article 300(7) EC [now 216(2) TFEU] provides that agreements concluded under the conditions set out in that article are to be binding on the institutions of the Community and on Member States.

307 Thus, by virtue of that provision, supposing it to be applicable to the Charter of the United Nations, the latter would have primacy over acts of secondary Community law (see, to that effect, Case C–308/06 *Intertanko and Others* [2008] ECR I–0000, paragraph 42 and case-law cited).

308 That primacy at the level of Community law would not, however, extend to primary law, in particular to the general principles of which fundamental rights form part.

309   That interpretation is supported by Article 300(6) EC [now 218(11) TFEU], which provides that an international agreement may not enter into force if the Court has delivered an adverse opinion on its compatibility with the EC Treaty, unless the latter has previously been amended.

* * *

316   As noted above in paragraphs 281 to 284, the review by the Court of the validity of any Community measure in the light of fundamental rights must be considered to be the expression, in a community based on the rule of law, of a constitutional guarantee stemming from the EC Treaty as an autonomous legal system which is not to be prejudiced by an international agreement.

317   The question of the Court's jurisdiction arises in the context of the internal and autonomous legal order of the Community, within whose ambit the contested regulation falls and in which the Court has jurisdiction to review the validity of Community measures in the light of fundamental rights.

318   It has in addition been maintained that, having regard to the deference required of the Community institutions vis-à-vis the institutions of the United Nations, the Court must forgo the exercise of any review of the lawfulness of the contested regulation in the light of fundamental rights, even if such review were possible, given that, under the system of sanctions set up by the United Nations, having particular regard to the re-examination procedure which has recently been significantly improved by various resolutions of the Security Council, fundamental rights are adequately protected.

* * *

321   [T]he existence, within that United Nations system, of the re-examination procedure before the Sanctions Committee, even having regard to the amendments recently made to it, cannot give rise to generalised immunity from jurisdiction within the internal legal order of the Community.

322   Indeed, such immunity, constituting a significant derogation from the scheme of judicial protection of fundamental rights laid down by the EC Treaty, appears unjustified, for clearly that re-examination procedure does not offer the guarantees of judicial protection.

* * *

326   It follows from the foregoing that the Community judicature must, in accordance with the powers conferred on it by the EC Treaty, ensure the review, in principle the full review, of the lawfulness of all Community acts in the light of the fundamental rights forming an integral part of the general principles of Community law, including review of Community measures which, like the contested regulation,

are designed to give effect to the resolutions adopted by the Security Council under Chapter VII of the Charter of the United Nations.

* * *

[The Court then turned to the substantive claims.]

334   [I]n the light of the actual circumstances surrounding the inclusion of the appellants' names in the list of persons and entities covered by the restrictive measures contained in Annex I to the contested regulation, it must be held that the rights of the defence, in particular the right to be heard, and the right to effective judicial review of those rights, were patently not respected.

335   According to settled case-law, the principle of effective judicial protection is a general principle of Community law stemming from the constitutional traditions common to the Member States, which has been enshrined in Articles 6 and 13 of the ECHR, this principle having furthermore been reaffirmed by Article 47 of the Charter of fundamental rights of the European Union, proclaimed on 7 December 2000 in Nice.

336   In addition, having regard to the Court's case-law in other fields, it must be held in this instance that the effectiveness of judicial review, which it must be possible to apply to the lawfulness of the grounds on which, in these cases, the name of a person or entity is included in the list forming Annex I to the contested regulation and leading to the imposition on those persons or entities of a body of restrictive measures, means that the Community authority in question is bound to communicate those grounds to the person or entity concerned, so far as possible, either when that inclusion is decided on or, at the very least, as swiftly as possible after that decision in order to enable those persons or entities to exercise, within the periods prescribed, their right to bring an action.

337   Observance of that obligation to communicate the grounds is necessary both to enable the persons to whom restrictive measures are addressed to defend their rights in the best possible conditions and to decide, with full knowledge of the relevant facts, whether there is any point in their applying to the Community judicature, and to put the latter fully in a position in which it may carry out the review of the lawfulness of the Community measure in question which is its duty under the EC Treaty.

338   So far as concerns the rights of the defence, in particular the right to be heard, with regard to restrictive measures such as those imposed by the contested regulation, the Community authorities cannot be required to communicate those grounds before the name of a person or entity is entered in that list for the first time.

339   As the Court of First Instance stated in paragraph 308 of *Yusuf and Al Barakaat*, such prior communication would be liable to jeopardise

the effectiveness of the freezing of funds and resources imposed by that regulation.

* * *

344 [While there may be concerns over what can be disclosed to sanction targets in a case such as this,] it is none the less the task of the Community judicature to apply, in the course of the judicial review it carries out, techniques which accommodate, on the one hand, legitimate security concerns about the nature and sources of information taken into account in the adoption of the act concerned and, on the other, the need to accord the individual a sufficient measure of procedural justice.

* * *

348 Because the Council neither communicated to the appellants the evidence used against them to justify the restrictive measures imposed on them nor afforded them the right to be informed of that evidence within a reasonable period after those measures were enacted, the appellants were not in a position to make their point of view in that respect known to advantage. Therefore, the appellants' rights of defence, in particular the right to be heard, were not respected.

349 In addition, given the failure to inform them of the evidence adduced against them and having regard to the relationship, referred to in paragraphs 336 and 337 above, between the rights of the defence and the right to an effective legal remedy, the appellants were also unable to defend their rights with regard to that evidence in satisfactory conditions before the Community judicature, with the result that it must be held that their right to an effective legal remedy has also been infringed.

350 Last, it must be stated that that infringement has not been remedied in the course of these actions. Indeed, given that, according to the fundamental position adopted by the Council, no evidence of that kind may be the subject of investigation by the Community judicature, the Council has adduced no evidence to that effect.

351 The Court cannot, therefore, do other than find that it is not able to undertake the review of the lawfulness of the contested regulation in so far as it concerns the appellants, with the result that it must be held that, for that reason too, the fundamental right to an effective legal remedy which they enjoy has not, in the circumstances, been observed.

352 It must, therefore, be held that the contested regulation, in so far as it concerns the appellants, was adopted without any guarantee being given as to the communication of the inculpatory evidence against them or as to their being heard in that connection, so that it must be found that that regulation was adopted according to a procedure in which the appellants' rights of defence were not observed, which has

had the further consequence that the principle of effective judicial protection has been infringed.

353   It follows from all the foregoing considerations that the pleas in law raised by Mr Kadi and Al Barakaat in support of their actions for annulment of the contested regulation and alleging breach of their rights of defence, especially the right to be heard, and of the principle of effective judicial protection, are well founded.

[Kadi also claimed a breach of his property rights, which the Court upheld given the facts of the case and especially Kadi's inability to challenge his listing. However, in its general analysis the Court suggested that the challenged measures "cannot *per se* be regarded as inappropriate or disproportionate" (citing *Bosphorus*) (para. 363) and, after noting certain applicable derogations and exemptions, stated that the measures "might, in principle, be justified" (para. 366). The property rights issues raised in *Kadi* are examined in more detail in Chapter 6(A)(2) supra.]

NOTES AND QUESTIONS

1.   Did the Court give adequate consideration to the Union's obligations under international law in the *Kadi* case? Is that case consistent with *Bosphorus*? One could argue that the cases excerpted and noted in this chapter and in Chapter 29 demonstrate the Court's willingness to give priority to international law or agreements varies in difference settings. Are there principles that can be adduced from the Court's decisions that make it various approaches to international law consistent and coherent?

2.   Note that the Court in *Kadi* gave effect to its judgment only after a three month delay. What could be done in that period to ensure that the sanctions applied to Kadi continued in effect? In fact, the Commission supplied Kadi and the foundation with the "narrative summaries of reasons" of the UN Committee for including them in the list of individuals and entities subject to sanctions and asked for any comments they might have. Kadi and the foundation supplied comments, but the Commission concluded that they should nevertheless be subject to the sanctions "given the preventive nature of the freezing of funds and economic resources". Accordingly, their listing as being subject to sanctions was continued. Commission Regulation 1190/2008, O.J. L 322/25. Kadi has challenged that continuation in a case pending as of this writing. Since the *Kadi* decision, the Commission has offered those newly subjected to sanctions an opportunity to find out the basis for their inclusion and to comment thereon. It also informs them of the possibility of a court challenge under Article 263. Is this sufficient to address the problems found by the Court in *Kadi*?

CHAPTER 28

PREFERENTIAL ARRANGEMENTS AND
ACCESSION NEGOTIATIONS

■ ■ ■

Companies based in the EU trade all over the world and the EU imports a significant amount of goods and services from the rest of the world. Indeed, in 2009 the EU reported that its Member States account for 19% of world imports and exports. While individual transactions in international trade are largely conducted pursuant to private contracts, the general framework in which such trade occurs is usually established by international agreements, such as the WTO Agreement and any number of multilateral, regional and bilateral agreements.

As we saw in Chapter 27, the Union is responsible for negotiating and applying such agreements since they are part of its common commercial policy. Before we examine the key components of that policy, it is useful to consider in overview the general framework of the Union's commercial relations with the rest of the world. In this chapter, we examine the Union's relations with other countries in Europe and the Mediterranean region, as well as its relations with the third world, much of which was governed by Europe in the past. In Chapter 29, we examine the World Trade Organization and the EU's position therein, paying particular attention to its trading relationship with the United States, which is largely WTO-based. As we will see, many of the Union's agreements regulating trade with third countries deal with other issues as well, particularly development assistance and cooperative arrangements in a wide range of fields. The EU's commercial relations with Europe can be divided usefully into three parts: first, its relations with the other industrialized countries of Western Europe, notably the EFTA countries; second, its relations with the countries of Central Europe; and finally, its relations with its neighbors in Eastern Europe and the Mediterranean.

A. THE EU AND THE EFTA COUNTRIES

1. THE HISTORY OF EU–WESTERN EUROPEAN RELATIONS

After the European Economic Community was founded in 1957, seven European countries, led by the United Kingdom, negotiated a free trade agreement in 1960, known as the European Free Trade Association (EFTA) or the Stockholm Convention.[1] Generally speaking, the EFTA countries wanted to liberalize trade among themselves but also wanted a looser form of confederation than the EEC Treaty established. The current members of EFTA are Iceland, Liechtenstein, Norway and Switzerland. Austria, Denmark, Finland, Portugal, Sweden and the United Kingdom were once members of EFTA but subsequently joined the EC.

EFTA is a free trade area, rather than a customs union like the EC. The basic feature of a free trade area is the elimination of trade barriers between its members. In the case of EFTA, customs duties and import quotas on trade in industrial products between EFTA members were eliminated by 1966. Agricultural and fisheries products are excluded from EFTA's free trade provisions, although EFTA does promote trade within EFTA of those products. EFTA differs from a customs union in that it does not have a common commercial policy toward third countries. Such a policy is required for customs unions under WTO rules. EFTA does, however, enter into free trade agreements with third countries. Indeed, it had signed 18 FTAs as of September 2009. Among its FTA partners are Canada, Chile, Korea, Mexico and Singapore.

EFTA contains provisions designed to ensure that fair competition prevails in trade between EFTA countries. It thus bans certain state aids and restrictive business practices, such as agreements between companies that prevent, restrict or distort competition and actions that take unfair advantage of a dominant position. EFTA also attempts to reduce technical barriers to trade among its member states. A major revision of the EFTA Convention, the Vaduz Convention of June 21, 2001, covers free movement of persons, intellectual property rights, investment, services and government procurement.

From the foregoing, it is clear that EFTA bears some similarity to the EU in terms of its trade-related provisions. Nonetheless, it is a fundamentally different organization. The EFTA secretariat does not resemble the EU Commission at all; it has relatively few permanent employees. There is no court with jurisdiction comparable to the Court of Justice, nor is there an independent parliament. EFTA affairs are overseen by the EFTA Council, which normally consists of the heads of the member state delegations to EFTA, but which twice a year meets at the ministerial level.

---

1. Additional information on EFTA, including legal texts, is available at www.efta.int. An updated EFTA convention (the Vaduz Convention) was signed on June 21, 2001.

The Council has the power to take certain decisions that are binding on the member states, but generally the Council acts only by unanimous vote. Thus, EFTA does not have the lawmaking and law administering bodies found in the EU. As noted by the Court of Justice in its *EEA* opinion (set out below), the EU involves the significant transfer of sovereign powers from the Member States to Union institutions, but EFTA does not.

It was inevitable that the EU and EFTA would have close economic ties. In connection with the 1973 accession to the EEC of Denmark and the United Kingdom (both EFTA members), the EEC negotiated virtually identical free trade agreements with each of the EFTA members. As a result, trade in industrial products between the EU and the EFTA countries has been free of duties and quotas since 1984. Many barriers to trade in agricultural products remain, however. The agreements provided that certain state aids and restrictions on competition were incompatible with the proper functioning of the agreements. They also contained provisions designed to prevent discrimination in internal taxation. As we saw in Chapter 27(C) supra, in the *Polydor* and *Kupferberg* cases, these agreements may be invoked by individuals in some circumstances in EU and Member State courts.

The achievement in 1984 of the elimination of duties and quotas on EU–EFTA trade in industrial products raised the question of how the EU–EFTA relationship would evolve thereafter. This issue was addressed at the first formal ministerial level meeting between the EU, its Member States and the members of EFTA, which occurred in Luxembourg in 1984. That meeting produced the so-called Luxembourg Declaration, which called for increased cooperation in many fields between the EU and EFTA, "with the aim of creating a dynamic European economic space."[2]

2. THE EUROPEAN ECONOMIC AREA

The implementation by the EU of its single market program raised the question of how completion of the internal market would affect the EFTA countries. The continuation of the existing free trade arrangements was never in question. What was uncertain was the degree to which a closer relationship between the EU and the EFTA countries would develop. Generally, the EFTA countries pressed for a closer relationship, in part to obtain the benefits of participating in a larger market, in part out of fear of EU protectionism—the possibility that a "Fortress Europe" would result from the 1992 single market program. The EU was receptive to expanding its relationship with the EFTA countries, and the result was an agreement, signed in May 1992, on a European Economic Area (EEA). The agreement came into force on January 1, 1994, as noted in the *Opel Austria* case in Chapter 27(C) supra.

The EEA agreement provides for very close economic ties between the Union and the EFTA countries (save for Switzerland, which has not joined

---

2. Declaration issued following Ministerial meeting between the European Community and its Member States and the States of the European Free Trade Association (Luxembourg, April 9, 1984), reproduced in Bull. EC 1984–4, p. 9.

the EEA). For the three EFTA countries that joined the EU in 1995 (Austria, Finland and Sweden), the agreement eased their accession since they were required under the EEA to adopt many EU measures. For the remaining EFTA countries in the EEA (Iceland, Liechtenstein and Norway), the agreement ensures that they will have a privileged position among the Union's trading partners.

The EEA agreement is divided into six substantive parts, dealing with free movement of goods, free movement of persons, services and capital, competition and other common rules, miscellaneous provisions relevant to the four freedoms, cooperation outside the four freedoms and institutional provisions. Although it is very broad, the agreement does not create a customs union, the EFTA states remain free to follow their own commercial policies toward the rest of the world.

In respect of free movement of goods, the agreement prohibits customs duties and charges having equivalent effect, internal taxation that discriminates against imports, as well as import and export quotas, subject to exceptions of the sort permitted by Article 36 of the TFEU. In addition, the agreement provides that antidumping measures, countervailing duties and measures against illicit commercial practices shall not be applied to trade between the parties. There are, however, special rules for agricultural and maritime products, coal, steel and energy. Indeed, fishing rights were one of the most controversial issues at the conclusion of the negotiations.

The agreement provides for free movement of workers among the EU Member States and the other EEA countries. It specifically requires the abolition of any discrimination based on nationality as regards employment, remuneration and other conditions of work and employment. The agreement also contains provisions on coordination of social security rules and for the mutual recognition of diplomas.

Freedom of establishment is instituted under terms similar to the EU, as is the freedom to provide services. There are special provisions applicable to transport services, where the issue of transalpine trucking rights proved to be very controversial. The agreement also provides for the free movement of capital, subject to various derogations and safeguard measures.

The agreement's rules on competition are similar to those in the EU. Application of the rules is complicated, however, by a division of enforcement responsibility between the Commission and the so-called EFTA Surveillance Authority, a body established by the EFTA states. The Surveillance Authority essentially has jurisdiction of TFEU Article 101–type cases (i) when only trade between EFTA states is involved, (ii) when only trade between one EU member state and EFTA states is involved and 33% or more of the turnover in the EEA of the involved undertakings is in the EFTA states, and (iii) when the effects on trade between EU Member States are negligible. TFEU Article 102–type cases are handled depending on where the dominant position exists. Where it exists in both the EU and an EFTA jurisdiction(s), the rules for Article 101–type cases are applied. Mergers subject to control under the EU merger regulation are to be handled in accordance with that regulation, with the EFTA Surveillance Authority handling other mergers subject to the agreement (without prejudice to the rights of EU Member States to deal with such mergers). The Authority is based in Brussels, is headed by a three-person body appointed for four-year terms and is assisted by a staff, which numbered about 60 in 2009.

In the case of state aids, the agreement contains a provision similar to TFEU Article 107. It also provides for the review of all existing systems of aid, by the EU in the case of EU Member States and by the EFTA Surveillance Authority in case of the EFTA countries.

The EEA agreement contains provisions on social policy, consumer protection, environment and company law. The approach taken in this part of the EEA agreement is to set out a general statement in which the parties recognize the importance of the subject and then to provide that the EU measures listed in various annexes will be adopted by the other EEA countries. The chapter on the environment specifically provides that parties may maintain or introduce more stringent protective measures so long as they are compatible with the EEA agreement.

Finally, the EEA agreement provides for cooperation between the EU and the other EEA states in a number of subject areas, including research and technical development; information services; the environment; education, training and youth; social policy; consumer protection; small and medium-sized enterprises; tourism; the audiovisual sector; and civil protection. The EEA countries also agreed to contribute to a "cohesion fund" for the benefit of the EU's poorer Member States.

From this outline of the substantive provisions of the EEA agreement, it should be clear that the obligations of the EEA states are similar in many respects to the obligations of EU Member States. This is underscored by the fact that the many annexes to the agreement listed approximately 1500 EU legislative measures that EEA states agreed to observe. By 2008, the annexes listed over 5000 measures.

The institutional provisions of the EEA are complex. While the EEA states do not have the right to participate directly in EU decision-making, when the EU decides to adopt or amend legislation covered by the agreement, it informs them and consults with them. When such new EU legislation is adopted, the EEA Joint Committee (composed of representatives of the EU and the other EEA states, with each side having one vote) normally includes the legislation in the coverage of the EEA agreement. If the Joint Committee is unable to agree to apply the new measure, it considers whether there are acceptable alternatives. If none can be found, the EEA states are not bound by the new measure.

In addition, the Joint Committee is charged with promoting the uniform interpretation of the provisions of the EEA agreement and Union law and is empowered to settle any dispute over interpretation of the EEA agreement. Its activities in this regard do not affect the case law of the Court of Justice. However, as part of this function, it is authorized to ask the Court of Justice to give a ruling on the interpretation of the relevant provisions. The Court of Justice is of the opinion that its rulings in such cases would be binding on all parties. European Economic Area, Opinion 1/92, [1992] ECR I–2821.

The agreement also establishes an EEA Council, to which problems under the agreement may be referred. It consists of representatives of the EU Council and Commission and of the other EEA states. Council decisions are to be made by agreement between the EU and EEA representatives.

Also, an EFTA Court has been created to hear appeals from the EFTA Surveillance Authority and disputes between EFTA states. It also gives advisory opinions to courts in EFTA states on interpretation of EEA rules. The EFTA Court has jurisdiction only within the framework of EFTA and has no personnel or functional links to the Court of Justice. The EFTA Court is based in Luxembourg and consists of three judges (one from each EEA State) assisted by a dozen staff members. It hears only a handful of cases per year.

Finally, the EEA agreement provides that courts in an EEA state can request the Court of Justice to decide on the interpretation of a provision of the EEA agreement which is identical in substance to a provision of EU law. The Court of Justice views that its decision in such a case would be binding.

Notes and Questions

1. The EEA structure is quite elaborate given that only Iceland, Liechtenstein and Norway participate. Initially, some thought that the EEA could be used more broadly as a stage in the accession process (e.g., for Eastern Europe), but that has not happened. For the moment, it does not seem likely that Norway will soon join the EU. Norwegian voters have twice rejected accession after the Norwegian government had negotiated it (1972 and 1994), although as the EU expands to the East, Norway may conclude that accession is needed to avoid marginalization in European affairs.

2. For many years it was thought unlikely that Iceland would subject its prized fishing industry to the common fisheries policy. However, the 2008–2009 financial crisis hit Iceland particularly hard and as a consequence EU membership seemed more attractive to it. Consequently, Iceland applied for membership in July 2009. In February 2010, the Commission recommended that negotiations for Iceland's accession to the EU be opened after evaluating Iceland's situation with respect to the so-called Copenhagen criteria for accession, which are described in more detail in Section B infra. In respect of the political criteria, the Commission noted that, although Iceland met that criteria, it needed to strengthen judicial independence and mechanisms to prevent conflicts of interest. As to the economic criteria, the Commission noted the serious affects that the financial crisis had had on Iceland and the

resultant need for certain reform measures and policy adjustments. Overall, Iceland was viewed as a functioning market economy. As to the *acquis*, in the Commission's view, Iceland is well prepared to take on EU membership obligations. Beyond the fields covered by the EEA, the Commission noted that Iceland would have to undertake serious efforts to ensure implementation of the *acquis* in the areas of fisheries, agriculture and rural development, environment, free movement of capital and financial services in order to meet the accession criteria. In addition, as a practical matter, Iceland will also have to resolve its differences with the UK and the Netherlands over compensation for losses suffered by their nationals as a result of the failures of certain Icelandic banks. Negotiations started on July 27, 2010.

3. Despite the rejection by Swiss voters of EEA membership (and the resultant cessation of EU accession negotiations), the EU and Switzerland continue to work toward closer economic integration. In 1999, the EU and Switzerland reached agreements dealing with free movement of persons, air and land transport, agriculture, public procurement, research and mutual recognition. Switzerland ratified the agreements in October 2000, following a 67% approval vote in a referendum. While the Swiss government continues to plan for eventual accession despite voter turndown of the EEA, it is not clear that Switzerland will soon apply for membership.

4. One of the difficult issues in the EEA negotiations was the question of precisely how EFTA or the EFTA countries could be given some role in EU decisions that affect the EEA and what effect such a role would have on the EU decision-making process. For example, would it make the process more cumbersome and slower? How would votes be weighted? How was this issue resolved? How much influence will the EFTA countries have in your view? Do you think that countries that do not undertake the full burdens of EU membership should have any special input into EU decision-making?

5. The EEA agreement gave rise to the following important Court of Justice opinion on the institutional structure of the EU and the position of the Court of Justice in that structure.

EUROPEAN ECONOMIC AREA
Opinion 1/91, [1991] ECR I–6079.

[As initially agreed upon, the EEA agreement established an EEA Court, to consist of five judges from the Court of Justice and three chosen by the EFTA states. The EEA Court would have heard, inter alia, disputes concerning the application of the EEA agreement referred to it by the Joint Committee or a party to the EEA. In considering the agreement's consistency with the EC Treaty, the Court of Justice first noted the fundamental differences between the European Community and the EEA.]

13 Before considering the questions raised by the Commission's request for an opinion, it is appropriate to compare the aims and context of the agreement, on the one hand, with those of the Community, on the other.

14 The fact that the provisions of the agreement and the corresponding Community provisions are identically worded does not mean that they

must be interpreted identically. An international agreement is to be interpreted not only on the basis of its wording, but also in light of its objectives.

[The Court then contrasted the objectives of the EEA, which it noted "concerned * * * free trade and competition * * * between the Contracting Parties" (para. 15) with the objectives of the Community, where the EEC Treaty "aims to achieve economic integration" and the Single European Act made it clear that "the objective of all of the Community treaties is to contribute together to making concrete progress towards European unity" (para. 17). In then examined the context in which the EEA and the Community agreements were situated.]

20   The EEA is to be established on the basis of an international treaty which, essentially, merely creates rights and obligations as between the Contracting Parties and provides for no transfer of sovereign rights to the inter-governmental institutions which it sets up.

21   In contrast, the EEC Treaty, albeit concluded in the form of an international agreement, none the less constitutes the constitutional charter of a Community based on the rule of law. As the Court of Justice has consistently held, the Community treaties established a new legal order for the benefit of which the States have limited their sovereign rights, in ever wider fields, and the subjects of which comprise not only Member States but also their nationals (citing *Van Gend & Loos*). The essential characteristics of the Community legal order which has thus been established are in particular its primacy over the law of the Member States and the direct effect of a whole series of provisions which are applicable to their nationals and to the Member States themselves.

[The Court accordingly concluded that these divergences stood in the way of achieving the objective of homogeneity in the interpretation and application of the two treaties. It then switched to an examination of whether the proposed system of courts might undermine the autonomy of the Community legal order in pursuing its own particular objectives.]

33   The expression "Contracting Parties" is defined in Article 2(c) of the agreement. As far as the Community and its Member States are concerned, it covers the Community and the Member States, or the Community, or the Member States, depending on the case. Which of the three possibilities is to be chosen is to be deduced in each case from the relevant provisions of the agreement and from the respective competences of the Community and the Member States as they follow from the EEC Treaty and the ECSC Treaty.

34   This means that, when a dispute relating to the interpretation or application of one or more provisions of the agreement is brought before it, the EEA Court may be called upon to interpret the expression "Contracting Party", within the meaning of Article 2(c) of the agreement, in order to determine whether, for the purposes of the provision at issue, the expression "Contracting Party" means the

Community, the Community and the Member States, or simply the Member States. Consequently, the EEA Court will have to rule on the respective competences of the Community and the Member States as regards the matters governed by the provisions of the agreement.

35 It follows that the jurisdiction conferred on the EEA Court under Article 2(c), Article 96(1)(a) and Article 117(1) of the agreement is likely adversely to affect the allocation of responsibilities defined in the Treaties and, hence, the autonomy of the Community legal order, respect for which must be assured by the Court of Justice pursuant to Article 164 of the EEC Treaty [now 19 Lisbon TEU]. This exclusive jurisdiction of the Court of Justice is confirmed by Article 219 of the EEC Treaty [now 344 TFEU], under which Member States undertake not to submit a dispute concerning the interpretation or application of that treaty to any method of settlement other than those provided for in the Treaty. Article 87 of the ECSC Treaty [now expired] embodies a provision to the same effect.

* * *

40 An international agreement providing for [its own] system of courts is in principle compatible with Community law. The Community's competence in the field of international relations and its capacity to conclude international agreements necessarily entails the power to submit to the decisions of a court which is created or designated by such an agreement as regards the interpretation and application of its provisions. [The Court then noted the difference here, where there was overlap between the agreements and their provisions.]

* * *

47 The threat posed by the court system set up by the agreement to the autonomy of the Community legal order is not reduced by the fact that Articles 95 and 101 of the agreement seek to create organic links between the EEA Court and the Court of Justice by providing that judges from the Court of Justice are to sit on the EEA Court and in its chambers. * * *

48 On the contrary, it is to be feared that the application of those provisions will accentuate the general problems arising from the court system to be set up by the agreement.

49 In this connection, it should be borne in mind that the EEA Court is to ensure the sound operation of rules on free trade and competition under an international treaty which creates obligations only between the Contracting Parties.

50 In contrast, the Court of Justice has to secure observance of a particular legal order and to foster its development with a view to achieving the objectives set out in particular in Articles 2, 8a and 102a of the EEC Treaty [now 3–6 Lisbon TEU and 21 & 120 TFEU] and to attaining a European Union among the Member States, as is stated in

the Solemn Declaration of Stuttgart of 19 June 1983 (section 2.5) referred to in the first recital in the preamble to the Single European Act. In that context, free trade and competition are merely means of achieving those objectives.

51 Consequently, depending on whether they are sitting on the Court of Justice or on the EEA Court, the judges of the Court of Justice who are members of the EEA Court will have to apply and interpret the same provisions but using different approaches, methods and concepts in order to take account of the nature of each treaty and of its particular objectives.

52 In those circumstances, it will be very difficult, if not impossible, for those judges, when sitting in the Court of Justice, to tackle questions with completely open minds where they have taken part in determining those questions as members of the EEA Court.

53 However, since the judicial system set up by the agreement is in any event incompatible with the EEC Treaty it is unnecessary to give fuller consideration to this question or to the question whether the system is not liable to raise serious doubts as to the confidence which individuals are entitled to have in the ability of the Court of Justice to carry out its functions in complete independence.

* * *

69 In its last question, the Commission asks whether Article 238 of the EEC Treaty [now 217 TFEU], which deals with the conclusion by the Community of association agreements with a third State, a union of States or an international organization, authorizes the establishment of a system of courts as provided for in this agreement. The Commission stated in this connection that, in the event that the Court were to answer this question in the negative, Article 238 could be amended so as to permit such a system to be set up.

70 As already pointed out in paragraph 40, an international agreement providing for a system of courts, including a court with jurisdiction to interpret its provisions, is not in principle incompatible with Community law and may therefore have Article 238 of the EEC Treaty as its legal basis.

71 However, Article 238 of the EEC Treaty does not provide any basis for setting up a system of courts which conflicts with Article 164 of the EEC Treaty [now 19 Lisbon TEU] and, more generally, with the very foundations of the Community.

72 For the same reasons, an amendment of Article 238 in the way indicated by the Commission could not cure the incompatibility with Community law of the system of courts to be set up by the agreement.

NOTES AND QUESTIONS

1. This is an important "constitutional" case that expresses important principles in respect of the organization of the Union and the role and powers of its institutions. Recall that the case was cited in *Kadi,* para. 282, in Chapter 27(D) supra, in respect of the exclusivity of the Court of Justice's jurisdiction, something the Court sees as "part of the very foundations of the Community."

2. The Commission had suggested that what is now Article 217 TFEU could be amended to permit association agreements to contain the sort of judicial arrangements proposed for the EEA. In paragraphs 71 and 72 of its opinion, is the Court suggesting that certain basic EU principles (such as the court system) cannot be altered, even by amendment; or only that an amendment of Article 217 cannot alter the basic principles of the EU's judicial system? What is the authority for either position? Is the transfer of former Article 164 of the EEC Treaty to the TEU relevant to considering this issue today?

B. CENTRAL AND EASTERN EUROPE

1. HISTORY OF EC–EASTERN EUROPEAN RELATIONS

Prior to the Second World War there was extensive trade between the countries of Eastern and Western Europe, but those trade flows dried up during the Cold War. However, as the Cold War ended at the outset of the 1990s, and the East European countries became more democratic and market-oriented, commercial relations between the EU and the countries of Eastern Europe grew much closer. Indeed, the great economic success of the EU compared to Eastern Europe was an important factor in spurring the political and economic changes in that region. In the course of the 1990s, the Union entered into association agreements, known as "Europe Agreements," with the countries of Eastern Europe. These agreements were much more comprehensive than past EU association agreements. Most significantly, the agreements explicitly provided for the possibility that the countries could accede to the EU in the future and all of them did.

2. THE ACCESSION OF THE COUNTRIES OF CENTRAL AND EASTERN EUROPE

After the establishment of democratic governments in Central and Eastern Europe in the 1989–1991 period, the countries of that region sought to join the European Union. As noted above, the Europe Agreements explicitly foresaw the possibility of accession for Bulgaria, the Czech Republic, Estonia, Hungary, Latvia, Lithuania, Poland, Romania, Slovakia and Slovenia. In addition, Cyprus, Malta, Turkey and the Western Balkan countries have also aspired to EU membership.

Article 49 of the Lisbon Treaty on European Union provides that any European State that respects the values of Article 2 of the Treaty (respect for human dignity, freedom, democracy, equality, the rule of law and respect for human rights) may apply to the Council for membership. Ultimately, the Council must act unanimously on applications, after consulting the Commission and receiving the assent of the Parliament. The conditions of accession and any adjustments to the existing treaties are set out in an agreement between the applicant and the other Member States. That agreement is subject to ratification in accordance with their respective constitutional requirements.

The basic criteria that countries must meet to join the EU were elaborated at the 1993 Copenhagen European Council as follows:

— the stability of institutions guaranteeing democracy, the rule of law, human rights and respect for and protections of minorities (the so-called political criterion);

— the existence of a functioning market economy as well as the capacity to cope with competitive pressure and market forces within the EU (the economic criterion); and

— the ability to take on the obligations of membership including adherence to the aims of political, economic and monetary union (the *acquis communitaire* criterion).

The 1995 Madrid European Council added the further requirement that candidates must have created conditions for integration by adopting appropriate administrative structures.

Following the applications of the 13 countries mentioned above, the Commission evaluated the political, economic and administrative conditions of the applicants and issued opinions in respect thereof. As a result of those evaluations, in 1998, the EU opened negotiations with six candidate countries: Cyprus, the Czech Republic, Estonia, Hungary, Poland and Slovenia. Subsequently, in 2000, negotiations were opened with Bulgaria, Latvia, Lithuania, Malta, Romania and the Slovak Republic. As described in the notes following this section, negotiations with Turkey have proceeded separately.

In considering the actual process of accession negotiations for the various applicants, it is useful to examine each of the above-mentioned three criteria.

First, in respect of the political criterion, there were some concerns raised simply because the ten former Communist countries had only a decade's worth of experience as democracies, with modern judicial systems based upon the rule of law. Moreover, there were specific concerns regarding human rights (e.g., the rights of Russian residents in the Baltic states; the rights of gypsies in central Europe) and the rule of law (e.g., existence of organized crime and government corruption). In the accession process, the EU put considerable pressure on candidate countries to demonstrate that they were effectively dealing with issues such as these.

It also funded programs designed to promote respect for human rights and the rule of law, including through education programs for national judges in EU legal principles.

Second, in respect of the economic criterion, the focus was on whether the candidates had viable market economies. In particular, the issue was whether their economic institutions and firms could cope with the competitive and market forces that would ensue when they entered the Union. This was a serious concern since most of the applicant countries had state-controlled economies until shortly before the accession negotiations began. The experience of integrating the economies of the two parts of Germany following reunification had demonstrated that even with very substantial government assistance for infrastructure projects and other reforms, the task is a formidable one. It was feared that similar problems would arise in integrating the candidate countries into the EU. In this regard, it should be mentioned that part of the accession process involved substantial EU financial assistance to help address potential problem areas.

Third, and of fundamental importance, was the *acquis communitaire* criterion.[3] New members must take on all obligations contained in the treaties, as well as subscribe to the broad statements of objectives for the future such as are contained in Article 3 of the TEU. In that sense, the negotiations on the *acquis* would seem to be straightforward. The candidate countries must accept the *acquis*. Thus, the end-point of the negotiating process was clear; and the only issues were in respect of transitions— both for the candidates and the Member States. In practical terms, the negotiations were organized around 31 chapters covering all aspects of the *acquis*. In the negotiations on each chapter, the EU indicated what was required to implement the acquis, the parties evaluated what had been (and was planned to be) done in respect of such implementation, considered whether transitional provisions would be needed and discussed ways in which the EU could facilitate implementation.

The Commission reported regularly and in detail on the state of the negotiations, discussing the extent to which the three basic criteria had been met. In the case of the *acquis*, the Commission reports contained a very detailed discussion of the state of implementation.

The accession negotiations between the EU and Cyprus, the Czech Republic, Estonia, Hungary, Latvia, Lithuania, Malta, Poland, the Slovak Republic and Slovenia were completed in December 2002 and the accession treaty was signed in Athens on April 16, 2003. During 2003, nine of the ten candidate countries held referenda to consider the question of whether to accede to the EU and in each country the voters approved accession. Except for Malta, where the referendum vote was close (53.6% approval), the referenda easily endorsed EU membership. The new members formally joined the EU on May 1, 2004. Negotiations with Bulgaria

---

3. The meaning of this term has been elaborated upon by Professor Goebel in Roger J. Goebel, The European Union Grows: The Constitutional Impact of the Accession of Austria, Finland and Sweden, 18 Fordham J. Intl. L. 1092, 1140–1157 (1995).

and Romania took longer, but they ultimately joined the EU on January 1, 2007.

The formal treaties and acts of accession, which are most conveniently available on the Commission website, are quite long because they contain the specific exceptions and transition periods applicable to each new Member State. With their accession, the new Member States became subject to the full range of Union obligations, except as provided in the treaties or acts. The task of bringing their laws and regulations into compliance with those obligations was a massive one. It was, of course, well underway prior to their formal accession since the Union views progress on implementing the *acquis* as a prime indicator of whether a candidate is ready for membership. In addition to recasting their laws and regulations, the new Member States had to improve substantially their administrative and judicial capacity to make the new laws and rules operationally effective. To assist in this, the Commission initiated an action plan to strengthen the administrative and judicial capabilities of each applicant in 2002, with special attention given to educating judges about the fundamental principles of Union law.

Among the principal transition periods and special arrangements for the first ten acceding countries were the following:

- Free movement of workers—each existing Member State was allowed to retain its existing restrictions on free movement of workers from the new Member States (other than Cyprus and Malta) for an initial two-year period, renewable for up to seven years. This was a particular concern of Germany and Austria.

- Environmental protection—substantial periods of time were provided for the new Member States to phase in particular rules or remove certain hazards (such as dismantling nuclear facilities in Lithuania and the Slovak Republic).

- Land purchases by non-nationals—Malta was allowed to prohibit foreign ownership of secondary residences (no time limit), while Cyprus, the Czech Republic, Hungary and Poland were permitted to restrict such ownership for five years. All of the Central European states except Slovenia received a derogation to protect ownership of agricultural and forest land for seven years, with a possible three-year extension by the Commission (12 years for Poland). As regards its real estate market, Slovenia was allowed to resort to a general economic safeguard clause for up to seven years.

- Common Agricultural Policy—the new Member States, many of which have very significant farm sectors, were to be phased into the CAP over 10 years, initially receiving only 25% of the normal subsidies. Considerable attention to reforms in the agriculture sectors of the new members was thought to be needed.

For a compact summary of the various derogations, see EC Commission, Report on the Results of the Negotiations on the Accession of Cyprus,

Malta, Hungary, Poland, the Slovak Republic, Latvia, Estonia, Lithuania, the Czech Republic and Slovenia to the EU (January 2003), available on the Commission Enlargement website. Many of the transition periods have expired or soon will.

The new Member States will likely receive a significant amount of Union structural and infrastructure aid funds in the future. None of the new Member States met the criteria for membership in the monetary union and adoption of the Euro as its currency, although several subsequently became part of the Euro area (Slovenia in 2007, Cyprus and Malta in 2008, Slovakia in 2009 and Estonia in 2011 (expected)).

NOTES AND QUESTIONS

1. The accession of Cyprus raised the question of whether the EU should admit only the Greek half of the island or whether a settlement of the long-running dispute between the Greek and Turkish halves should be required. The Helsinki European Council (December 1999) stressed that a settlement would facilitate accession, but was not a prerequisite. Shortly before accession, the Greek Cypriots in a referendum soundly rejected a UN plan for uniting the island. The plan easily passed on the Turkish side. Consequently, only the Greek part of Cyprus acceded to the EU.

2. The situation of Turkey has presented delicate problems for the EU. Turkey is a long-standing member of NATO and an important strategic ally of the EU. At the same time, Greece (a Member State since 1981) and Turkey have had stormy relations at times, including in the recent past. Moreover, while part of Turkey is in Europe, the vast majority of the country is in Asia and it is overwhelming Muslim, unlike Europe. However, the 1963 association agreement with Turkey foresaw possible accession (as did the 1961 agreement with Greece) and that association agreement has led to the formation of the EU–Turkey customs union. Formal accession negotiations with Turkey were opened in October 2005. It was generally expected that the negotiations would proceed slowly, with membership not occurring before 2015. Indeed, it is perceived that there is a bit of enlargement fatigue in the EU at the moment. That, controversy over Turkish treatment of Cyprus and the apparent lack of enthusiasm for Turkish membership among some existing members may mean that the negotiations will drag on for some time. In the Commission's most recent report on "Enlargement Strategy and Main Challenges 2009–2010", COM (2009)533 (final), it concluded that Turkey needed to make significant further progress in the areas, inter alia, of public administration reform, women's rights, human rights and protection of minorities.

3. As to the Western Balkans, the EU commenced accession negotiations with Croatia in 2005 and the Commission described the negotiations as entering the "decisive phase" in 2008. Since the start of the negotiations, 33 chapters have been opened, of which 22 had been provisionally closed as of July 2010. In February 2010, Enlargement Commissioner Füle called on Croatia to pursue economic and political reforms with an emphasis on the judiciary and the public administration, on the fight against organized crime and corruption and ensure continued progress on the minority rights and

refugee return. Macedonia was accepted as a candidate for accession in 2005, but negotiations have not yet started as it is not yet viewed as ready. The EU has entered into stabilization and association agreements with the other West Balkan states: Albania (2008); Bosnia & Herzegovina (2008); Montenegro (2007); Serbia, including Kosovo (2008). These agreements aim at preparing the countries for future accession as the Europe Agreements did earlier for the Eastern and Central European Member States.

4.   After the 2004–2007 enlargements, some argued that the EU should slow down its expansion and take time to integrate more fully its new Member States. As noted above, the EU has in fact continued to prepare for the future membership of the countries of the Western Balkans and Turkey. The experience of the recent enlargements has led, however, to some changes in approach. For example, in an attempt to improve the quality of the enlargement process, the EU is now placing more focus on improving at the outset the adherence of candidate countries to the rule of law and principles of good governance, in particular to combat organized crime and corruption. The need for this can be seen in the situation in Bulgaria where in 2009 the EU felt forced to withhold temporarily funds budgeted for Bulgaria pending improvements in governance structures. While the enlargement process is moving forward, it is quite likely that the new candidate countries will find themselves subject to more scrutiny than was applied in the past as to whether they have met the Copenhagen criteria. This may prolong the current enlargement phase.

C.   THE EUROPEAN NEIGHBORHOOD POLICY

The Lisbon Treaty introduced a new undefined concept—neighboring countries—in Article 8 TEU. It provides that the Union shall develop a special relationship with neighboring countries and authorizes the Union to conclude agreements with such states containing reciprocal rights and obligations as well as the possibility of undertaking activities jointly. The aim is to establish an area of prosperity founded on Union values and characterized by peaceful cooperation.

This provision seems to ratify the EU's 2004 European Neighborhood Policy, which is designed to improve its relations with countries on the periphery of the EU that are not soon expected to accede to the EU. The policy is built on (i) the Partnership and Cooperation Agreements (PCAs) that the EU has with Armenia, Azerbaijan, Georgia, Moldova and Ukraine and (ii) its so-called Euro–Med agreements with Algeria, Egypt, Israel, Jordan, Lebanon, Morocco, the Palestinian Territory and Tunisia. Although Russia is within the neighborhood, the EU's relations with it are pursued separately through a so-called strategic partnership. There are three other countries in the neighborhood—Belarus, Libya and Syria— that are not parties to a PCA or Euro–Med agreement and for which the policy has not yet been activated.

The policy builds on the PCAs, which cover trade, political cooperation, environmental protection and collaboration in scientific and cultural matters, and the Euro–Med agreements. The latter agreements have been entered into under the 1995 Barcelona Declaration, which called for the creation of a free trade zone in the area, and contain provisions on trade, on harmonization of rules and on political aspects, such as respect for democratic principles and human rights. As summarized in brief by the Commission, the policy calls for the EU to extend to these countries many of the benefits of its internal market and to offer them additional trade concessions and financial assistance. In exchange, the EU's neighbors would make greater commitments to democratic reform and market economy structures, and pay greater respect to human rights.

D. THE EU AND THE DEVELOPING WORLD

The original members of the European Economic Community had extensive colonial holdings in 1957, and the United Kingdom, which joined the Community in 1973, headed a commonwealth organization made up of former British colonies. Thus, from the outset, the EU has had to deal with trade relations between the Member States and their colonies, most of which soon became independent countries. In addition, it had to develop a commercial policy toward developing countries that had no special ties with the various Member States. In this section, we examine briefly how it has dealt with these countries.

1. THE LOMÉ CONVENTIONS AND THE COTONOU AGREEMENT

The first association agreement involving the EU and the developing world was the Yaoundé Convention of 1963 with 18 former French and Belgian African colonies. Six years later the second Yaoundé Convention was concluded for the period 1969–1975 and the EU entered into the Arusha Agreement with Kenya, Tanzania and Uganda. These agreements dealt with trade issues and also provided for financial and technical aid. With the accession of the United Kingdom in 1973, it became necessary to consider how to establish analogous relations with Commonwealth countries. The result was the first Lomé Convention, signed in 1975 between the EU and its Member States and 46 countries in Africa, the Caribbean and the Pacific (often called the "ACP countries"). Lomé I was followed by Lomé II (signed in 1979), Lomé III (signed in 1984) and Lomé IV (signed in 1989). The first three Lomé agreements had terms of 5 years; Lomé IV was concluded for a ten year period ending March 1, 2000.

Lomé IV was replaced by the Cotonou Agreement, which was signed by 77 ACP countries in June 2000 and will last for 20 years. From the EU perspective, there are five pillars of the Cotonou Agreement. First, it has a comprehensive political dimension in which respect for human rights, democratic principles and the rules of law is stressed. Second, the agreement promotes a participatory approach that promotes the involvement of civil society. Third, as for development, the key objective is poverty reduction. As to trade, the agreement continued the provisions of Lomé IV through 2008, by which time it was expected that there would be new economic partnerships agreements (EPAs, which are expanded free-trade areas) in place, to be implemented by 2020. Finally, the agreement provides for expanded EU financial contributions (€20 billion over 5–7 years).

Negotiations on EPAs are being conducted on a regional basis. As of August 2009, a comprehensive EPA had been reached with the countries of the Caribbean region. As to the other regions, EPA negotiations continue, with some regions and individual countries having reached interim agreements (especially in respect of trade issues) pending completion of comprehensive EPAs.

2. ASIAN AND LATIN AMERICAN COUNTRIES

Most of the developing countries of Latin America and Asia are not in ACP group. The EU has, however, been pursuing increasingly closer relations with many of these countries. For example, since 1971 it has extended preferential tariff treatment to them as part of its generalized system of preferences (GSP). This system provides duty free treatment for industrial products and reduced duties on agricultural products. The basic benefits provided under the EU's GSP scheme are not as favorable as those provided under the Cotonou Agreement, in particular because for some sensitive products there are quantitative limits on the preferences granted. The GSP program provides expanded benefits to 16 vulnerable developing countries as a special incentive arrangement to promote sustainable development, human rights, labor standards and good governance and assist them in the ratification and implementation of international agreements on those topics. In addition, the GSP program provides quota-free, tariff free access to 50 least developed countries under the so-called Everything But Arms scheme.

In the 1980s, the EU embarked on a program of negotiating cooperation agreements with individual countries (such as Argentina, Brazil, Mexico and Uruguay in Latin America and Bangladesh, India, Pakistan and Sri Lanka in Asia) and regional groupings (such as the Andean Pact, the Association of South–East Asian Nations (ASEAN) and the Gulf Cooperation Council). Generally these agreements are framework agreements that cover trade, economic cooperation and development cooperation.

More recently, the EU has signed free-trade agreements with Chile, Mexico and South Africa and is negotiating free-trade agreements with ASEAN, Colombia, the Gulf States, India, Korea, Mercosur and Peru. In some cases, these agreements have been sought to counter the affect of US FTAs. For example, the FTA with Mexico was inspired in large part to counter the effects of the North American Free Trade Agreement (NAF-TA)—a free trade agreement among Canada, Mexico and the United States.

NOTES AND QUESTIONS

1. From the perspective of developing countries, the value of preferential tariff treatment has been declining as tariff rates generally decline. The difference between a 30% tariff and tariff free treatment is significant; the difference between a 4% tariff (which is about the average tariff in the EC, Japan and the US) and a 0% tariff may not be. Should anything be done about this? What?

2. In recent years, the developing countries have pressed in GATT, the WTO and elsewhere for differential and more favorable treatment in many contexts. There is controversy over whether it has benefited from this approach. Some believe that developing countries would have been better off if they had not asked for special treatment, but rather had opened their economies to imports and promoted foreign investment, which would probably have resulted in expanded exports. Some of these issues are treated in R. Hudec, Developing Countries in the GATT Legal System (Gower 1987).

CHAPTER 29

THE COMMON COMMERCIAL POLICY: THE EU IN THE WTO

■ ■ ■

An introduction to the World Trade Organization (WTO)[1] is essential to an understanding of the EU's common commercial policy. The most important Court of Justice case on the scope of the EU's external powers concerns the EU's accession to the WTO. The WTO dispute settlement system is now the arena in which major trade disputes between the EU and other industrialized countries are resolved. The WTO is also the forum where the EU negotiates generally on international trade issues. In the GATT Uruguay Round negotiations (1986–1994), which led to the creation of the WTO, agricultural trade and subsidies were a major issue, directly impacting the EU common agricultural policy (CAP), which accounts for a majority of the EU's budgetary outlays. Indeed, much of the impetus in recent years to reform the CAP has come from the need for the EU to be in a position to negotiate in the WTO.

The Commission has a particularly important role in respect of international trade negotiations in light of the Treaty's provisions on the common commercial policy in Article 207. Since the 1960's, it has been accepted as the EU spokesperson, first in GATT and now in the WTO. Indeed, except on budgetary and personnel issues, the Member State representatives typically do not utter a word at formal WTO meetings.

In this chapter, we describe the WTO, its basic principles and rules, and its dispute settlement system, highlighting those aspects of particular concern to the EU. We then examine two important Court of Justice decisions relating to the WTO. A description of the common commercial policy follows, focusing on how its scope has been expanded in response to the Court of Justice decision on EU adherence to the WTO and on the respective roles of the Commission, Council and Parliament. We briefly examine a number of the EU's major commercial policy instruments— anti-dumping, anti-subsidy and safeguard rules. We conclude with an examination of EU–US relations.

---

1. Extensive information on the WTO is available at www.wto.org.

A. THE WORLD TRADE ORGANIZATION

The Marrakesh Agreement Establishing the World Trade Organization assigns three important functions to the WTO. First, the WTO oversees the operation of the WTO agreements on international trade. These include (i) the General Agreement on Tariffs and Trade (GATT) and 12 related agreements on trade in goods dealing with agriculture, sanitary measures, textiles, technical barriers to trade, dumping, subsidies, safeguards, trade-related investment measures, customs valuation, import licensing, pre-shipment inspection and rules of origin; (ii) the General Agreement on Trade in Services (GATS); and (iii) the Agreement on Trade–Related Aspects of Intellectual Property (TRIPS Agreement). Second, the WTO serves as a forum for trade negotiations. Third, the WTO administers a dispute settlement system, described below, which has come to play a very significant role in EU–US relations.

The WTO Agreement does not contain a specific list of basic principles, but there are four that can be gleaned from its preamble and the rules of the various agreements: trade liberalization; nondiscrimination in international trade; fair trade; and transparency.

1. TRADE LIBERALIZATION

The preamble to the WTO Agreement calls for expansion of trade in goods and services so as to raise standards of living. This is to be accomplished through reciprocal arrangements to reduce substantially tariffs and other barriers to trade. The preamble also provides that this should be accomplished while allowing optimal use of the world's resources in accordance with the objective of sustainable development, so as to protect and preserve the environment. In addition, it recognizes the need for positive efforts to ensure that developing countries secure a share in the growth of international trade.

The WTO agreements implement the preamble's direction to reduce barriers to international trade by defining the types of barriers that are generally permitted and by limiting their use through negotiations. For example, in the area of trade in goods, the two principal instruments used by nations to keep out imports are tariffs and quotas. Under WTO rules, the use of quotas and other non-tariff barriers is severely restricted, and while tariffs are permitted, members are encouraged over time to reduce them. The WTO's ambitions in this are similar to those of Articles 28–37 TFEU, albeit more limited in scope and effect.

GATT Article II obligates WTO members not to charge tariffs in excess of maximum levels that they have negotiated for specific products. In GATT jargon, countries "bind" their tariffs on specific products. Beginning in 1947, GATT sponsored eight "rounds" of tariff negotiations, and as a result average tariff rates for the major industrialized countries have fallen from around 40% to less than 5%. Tariff negotiations are based upon the idea of reciprocity: each member offers tariff reductions so as to achieve a mutually acceptable balance. However, it is for each member to assess for itself whether it is satisfied with the outcome of a negotiation. Since different members make tariff concessions on different products, there is no GATT-wide rate for a specific product. Rather, the applicable bound tariff rates on a specific product vary from country to country.

The trade-increasing effects of an agreement to lower tariffs can be offset indirectly by any number of actions by the importing country. To counter this possibility, GATT contains provisions designed to protect the integrity of tariff bindings. For example, there is a separate agreement to standardize the valuation of goods for tariff assessment purposes and there are rules limiting the use of fees for customs inspections or other services.

GATT Article XI prohibits the use of quotas and other restrictions on imports besides duties. While it has not been interpreted as expansively as Article 34 TFEU, Article XI has been interpreted broadly. However, for most of GATT's history, trade in agricultural and textile products was largely conducted outside of GATT rules, and quotas and similar restrictions were common. With the advent of the WTO, these two sectors have been brought back under GATT disciplines.

In the case of agriculture, in the Agreement on Agriculture, WTO members agreed to convert their non-tariff import restrictions on agricultural products to tariffs and generally not to use such restrictions in the future. The initial tariffs were set at very high levels, but it is expected that they will be reduced over time. In addition, certain minimum market access is to be provided. As to domestic farm subsidies, developed WTO members agreed to cut specified domestic subsidies. The aim is to encourage the use of subsidies, such as direct income supports, that do not promote production or distort trade flows. In respect of export subsidies, the agreement requires that they be reduced over time.

The negotiation of the Agreement on Agriculture was quite difficult for the EU. The common agricultural policy (CAP), which came into existence in the 1960's was based on a number of basic principles, including a preference for EU production and a desire to attain self-sufficiency in basic agricultural products. The implementation of that policy resulted in high target prices being set for basic commodities produced in the EU, with the EU being the buyer of last resort. Over time, the CAP resulted in significant surpluses in some products where the EU had been a net importer (e.g., cereals and sugar). Since the EU was often the buyer of last resort, the CAP was a very expensive program but reform seemed almost impossible. The EU's use of export subsidies to reduce its costs by enabling EU surpluses to be marketed overseas caused tensions both with the United States, which countered with its own export promotion schemes, and with other agricultural exporters, who were unable to counter-subsidize and thus felt victimized by both the EU and the US.

To implement the EU preference, the EU kept out certain foreign agricultural products through the use of variable levies, which were charges on imports adjusted as frequently as necessary to make exporting to the EU unprofitable whatever the level of prevailing world prices. While never the subject of GATT dispute settlement, some argued that the levies were GATT-inconsistent. As the foregoing description of the WTO Agriculture Agreement indicates, the EU has had to change the CAP so as to convert its levies to tariffs and to allow some, albeit limited, access to EU markets. It has also had to limit its use of agricultural export subsidies.

In the case of textiles, starting in 1974, international trade between the developed and developing countries was conducted under the so-called Multi–Fibre Arrangement (MFA). Under the MFA, the EU and other developed countries negotiated specific quotas for the textile and apparel products. To meet concerns of developing countries, the WTO Agreement on Textiles and Clothing required that MFA quotas be phased out in four stages, ending in 2005.

Unlike GATT which dealt with services trade only incidentally, the WTO Agreement includes a General Agreement on Trade in Services (GATS). GATS defines trade in services as the supply of a service (i) from the territory of one member to another, (ii) in the territory of one member to a consumer of another member, and (iii) by a service supplier of one member through commercial presence or (iv) the presence of natural persons in the territory of another. This categorization resembles in part the way in which the EU has treated services (see Chapter 17 supra).

The basic obligation of GATS is to provide most-favored-nation treatment in respect of services and service suppliers, with the possibility of members listing specific exceptions, which are in principle for at most 10 years and subject to negotiation in future liberalizing rounds. Insofar as market access is concerned, WTO members have made market opening commitments in specific service sectors. It is up to each member, in negotiations with others, to determine sectors in which its market access commitments are made. Those commitments may be made subject to qualifications. GATS contains a national treatment obligation, but it only applies in service sectors where market access commitments have been made and, moreover, may be made subject to qualifications. A new round of negotiations in the services area started in 2000. A major issue for the EU has been to avoid making commitments in the audio-visual sector. The sensitivity of this sector, particularly to the French, has led to special treatment of the sector (along with cultural, educational, social and health services) in Article 207 (discussed in section C below).

2. NONDISCRIMINATION

The second general principle and rule by which the WTO attempts to achieve its objective of increasing international trade and economic well being is to eliminate discrimination in international trade. GATT does this through two provisions: Article I—the most-favored-nation clause—which prohibits discrimination among foreign countries in certain trade matters and Article III—the national treatment clause—which prohibits discrimination between national and foreign products in certain trade matters.

GATT Article I—the so-called MFN clause—essentially bans discrimination based on the source of goods with respect to customs matters, internal taxes and internal sales regulations. If an advantage of any kind in respect of those subjects is extended to the products of one country it must immediately and unconditionally be extended to the like products coming from all WTO members. Thus, if a tariff of 5% is assessed on goods of one country, a higher tariff must not be assessed on like goods coming from WTO members. The most-favored-nation concept is very basic to GATT and many other GATT provisions contain MFN or similar nondiscrimination rules.

There are two major exceptions to the MFN obligation. First, it does not apply in the case of free trade areas and customs unions qualifying under GATT Article XXIV. The EU is, of course, the prime example of a customs union, and as noted in the preceding chapter, it has a network of free trade agreements with other countries. The second exception to the MFN requirement is that it does not preclude granting differential and more favorable treatment to developing countries, which the EU does in a number of ways, as discussed in the Chapter 28.

The national treatment clause of GATT Article III establishes the general principle that WTO members should not distinguish between products of domestic origin and those of foreign origin with respect to (i) internal taxes and charges, (ii) laws, regulations and requirements affecting the internal sale, offering for sale, purchase, transportation, distribution or use of products or (iii) internal quantitative regulations requiring the mixture, processing or use of products in specific amounts or proportions. The basic idea underlying Article III and the national treatment clause is that once goods have cleared border controls (tariffs paid, other entry conditions satisfied), they should be treated no differently than domestically produced goods. In the words of Article III:1, tax and regulatory measures "should not be applied to imported or domestic products so as to afford protection to domestic production." This has been interpreted to mean that a regulation must not adversely modify the conditions of competition between domestic and imported products. In the words of one panel report, Article III:4 requires effective equality of opportunities for imported products in so far as the application of internal sales regulations is concerned.

There have been several WTO/GATT cases in the sector of alcoholic beverages involving Article III:2's ban on discriminatory internal taxes. Although the cases have generally dealt only with distilled liquors and thus do not go as far as the EU cases under Article 110 TFEU (recall the cases in Chapter 12(B)), they obviously raise similar issues.

There are two important exceptions in the national treatment clause. These exceptions permit discrimination against imported goods in the case of government procurement policies and permit the payment of subsidies exclusively to domestic producers. As to government procurement, it should be noted that most industrialized WTO members, including the EU, are parties to an agreement on government procurement that requires national treatment in respect of procurement contracts entered into by certain government agencies where the contracts exceed certain threshold amounts. In the case of domestic subsidies, there are rules relating to their use in the WTO agreements on subsidies and agriculture.

3. PROMOTING FAIR INTERNATIONAL TRADE

The WTO agreements contain several provisions that can be characterized as fair trade provisions. Indeed, the whole of the TRIPS Agreement may be viewed in that light. In addition, GATT contains provisions dealing with the practice of dumping and the export of subsidized products, which are elaborated upon in separate agreements on dumping and subsidies.

GATT Article VI condemns, but does not prohibit, dumping, which is effectively defined as the sale of a product for export at a price below that charged in the home market or below that necessary to recover the cost of producing the product. It authorizes antidumping duties to be imposed to offset dumping if a country's domestic industry is materially injured. The EU's rules on imposition of antidumping duties, which are based on the WTO rules, are described briefly in Section C below.

Under the WTO Agreement on Subsidies and Countervailing Measures, a subsidy is defined as a financial contribution by a government or public body that confers a benefit. Under the agreement, export subsidies and subsidies contingent upon the use of domestic over imported goods are prohibited (except as allowed by the Agreement on Agriculture). The agreement contains an illustrative list of export subsidies. In addition, the agreement provides that no member should cause, through the use of any specific (i.e., not generally available), nonagricultural subsidy, adverse effects to the interests of other members. Three types of adverse interests are listed: injury to the domestic industry of another member; nullification or impairment of benefits accruing to other members under GATT rules (e.g., tariff bindings); and serious prejudice to the interests of another member. Finally, the agreement authorizes the use of countervailing duties if a specific subsidy causes material injury to a member's domestic industry. The EU rules on countervailing duties are briefly described in Section C below.

The Agreement on Trade–Related Aspects of Intellectual Property Rights (TRIPS Agreement) is quite broad in scope. In general terms, it is designed to provide minimum levels of intellectual property protection, without creating new barriers to trade, and to provide a framework for dealing with international trade in counterfeit goods. The latter issue is of particular interest of the EU because of its production of luxury goods. The TRIPS agreement's substantive obligations can be divided into three types. First, there is a series of basic principles, such as general MFN and national treatment obligations. Second, there are specified minimum standards of protection for copyrights, trademarks, geographical indications, industrial designs, patents, integrated circuits and trade secrets. This has resulted in some harmonization of intellectual property rights legislation in the EU, a subject of Chapter 19. Third, there are minimum standards required for the enforcement of intellectual property rights. For example, national judicial authorities must have the power to order provisional measures and to enjoin violations and award damages in appropriate cases.

4. TRANSPARENCY OF INTERNATIONAL TRADE REGULATIONS

One of the most useful underlying principles of the WTO Agreement promotes the transparency of international trade regulations. One major hindrance to international trade is the difficulty of finding out the rules that are applicable in faraway markets. The WTO's rules on transparency are designed to address this issue. There are three kinds of transparency provisions. First, GATT Article X requires the publication of laws, regulations, judicial decisions and administrative rulings pertaining to a wide range of trade matters. It also requires mechanisms to review decisions of lower level officials. Second, most WTO agreements require notification to the WTO of various laws and regulations affecting trade, in some cases in advance so that affected parties may comment. In addition, they often require WTO members to establish enquiry points where further information can be obtained about such laws and regulations. The WTO maintains these notifications in a central registry. Third, there are regular procedures for reviews of members' trade policies. The most far-reaching review is through the Trade Policy Review Mechanism, pursuant to which the trade policies of WTO members are reviewed by the WTO Secretariat and other members on a regular basis.

5. THE MAJOR EXCEPTIONS TO THE BASIC RULES

There are four major exceptions to WTO rules. They deal with quite different issues—national security, balance of payments, safeguards and public policy, but they are usefully treated together to facilitate comparisons of the different extent to which they may be invoked and to which they are subject to multilateral control.

GATT Article XXI—the so-called national security exception—provides that GATT does not prevent any member from taking any action which it considers necessary for the protection of its essential security interests (i) relating to fissionable materials, (ii) relating to arms traffic and traffic in goods carried on for the purpose of military supply and (iii) taken in time of war or other emergency in international relations. GATS and the TRIPS Agreement have similar provisions.

A WTO member experiencing balance-of-payments problems may impose trade restrictive measures under GATT Articles XII and XVIII:B (applicable to developing countries) and GATS Article XII. There is a WTO Committee on Balance-of-Payments Restrictions that monitors the use of trade measures taken because of such problems.

The most important exception to the bound tariff levels and the ban on quotas is the so-called Escape Clause of GATT Article XIX. It is a basic GATT tenet that expanded international trade is desirable. It has long been recognized, however, that international trade, even if beneficial overall, produces winners and losers within a national economy. As lower-priced or higher-quality imports gain market share, consumers obviously benefit, but the domestic producer of competing products loses market share and may have to lay off workers or even close down. Recognizing this reality, GATT Article XIX provides that if a product is being imported in such increased quantities as to cause or threaten serious injury to domestic producers of like or directly competing products, a WTO member may impose import restrictions temporarily.

The use of the Article XIX exception is governed by the WTO Agreement on Safeguards. The agreement requires that investigations be held to determine whether the conditions of Article XIX have been met. Safeguard measures are not to be imposed for more than four years (subject to extension for up to four more years) and are to be progressively liberalized over their effective period. They may be imposed selectively (i.e. on a non-MFN basis) only in limited circumstances. In some circumstances the member imposing a safeguard measure may have to provide compensation to adversely affected WTO members, but normally not during the first three years of a safeguard measure. The EU rules on safeguards are described briefly in Section C below. The EU seldom imposes safeguards under WTO rules, although it had challenged successfully in WTO dispute settlement proceedings safeguards imposed by Argentina, Korea and the United States.

GATT Article XX provides a general exception to GATT provisions for measures that are (i) not applied in an arbitrary or unjustifiably discriminatory manner between members, (ii) not a disguised restriction on international trade and (iii), inter alia, necessary to protect public morals or health or to secure compliance with GATT consistent regulations or related to the conservation of exhaustible natural resources. GATS Article XIV is similar. In WTO dispute settlement, the meaning of Article XX has been evolving. There are two important WTO agreements related to Article XX—the Agreement on Sanitary and Phytosanitary Measures (the SPS Agreement) and the Agreement on Technical Barriers to Trade (the TBT Agreement).

GATT Article XX(b) allows for measures necessary to protect health. This provision is effectively interpreted in the SPS Agreement, which covers measures applied to protect humans, animals and plants from the diseases and pests. Under the SPS Agreement, SPS measures must be necessary and based on science. In particular, they are to be based on a risk assessment, which evaluates the likelihood of the occurrence of the negative consequences aimed at by the SPS measure. Any measure must be rationally related to the risk assessment. Second, measures are not to discriminate arbitrarily or unjustifiably between members where identical or similar conditions prevail, nor in a manner that would constitute a disguised restriction on trade, nor be unnecessarily trade restrictive. Third, the agreement promotes the use of international standards, although it clearly gives each WTO member the right to set its own level of protection. In addition, the agreement has a number of transparency provisions. One of the more controversial recent trade disputes between the EU and the US concerns the EU ban on beef from cattle treated with growth hormones. This dispute is described Section D below.

The WTO Agreement on Technical Barriers to Trade (the TBT Agreement) applies to technical regulations (excluding SPS measures) and standards. Its basic obligation is a commitment to provide MFN and national treatment and to ensure that technical regulations on products are not applied with a view to or with the effect of creating unnecessary obstacles to international trade. The agreement accordingly provides that such regulations shall not be more trade restrictive than necessary to fulfill a legitimate objective, such as the protection of human health or safety. The agreement also establishes similar rules with respect to standards and conformity assessment procedures. One of the principles of the agreement is transparency, and it has detailed rules calling for publication of proposed technical regulations for comment prior to their implementation. The agreement promotes the use of international instead of national standards, the use of performance rather than design criteria and the recognition of testing in foreign laboratories. The approach of the agreement is not so dissimilar to EU activities in the technical harmonization area described in Chapter 14.

6. THE WTO DISPUTE SETTLEMENT MECHANISM

The WTO agreements provide extensive rights and impose many duties on WTO members and their conduct of international trade. Obviously, a mechanism is needed to resolve disputes over what these rules mean and whether they have been broken in a specific case. Without such a mechanism, the elaborate structure of rights and duties would mean little. In the WTO, the rules for dispute resolution are contained in the WTO Dispute Settlement Understanding (DSU). The DSU grew out of GATT practice dating back to the 1950s, whereby disputes were referred to panels of individuals for resolution, with the panel reports being subject to adoption by the GATT parties, who acted by consensus.

Although the GATT system was quite successful, the requirement that a panel report be adopted by a consensus (which included the losing party) sometimes resulted in stalemate. As explained below, a major innovation of the DSU is that reports are adopted unless there is a consensus *not to adopt the report.* This fundamental change in approach was accepted by the EU and Japan, who generally had preferred a less adjudicative approach to GATT dispute settlement, in exchange for (i) the creation of an appeals process and (ii) a commitment by the US to bring all WTO disputes to the WTO and not to act unilaterally under Section 301 of its 1974 Trade Act.

Among the general provisions of the DSU are (i) a commitment on the part of WTO Members to submit all WTO-related disputes to the WTO system and not to take unilateral action; (ii) a statement that the aim of dispute settlement is to secure a positive solution to a dispute and that a solution that is acceptable to the parties and consistent with the WTO agreements is preferred; and (iii) a statement that the dispute settlement system serves to preserve the rights and obligations of members and to clarify the existing provisions of WTO agreements in accordance with the customary rules of interpretation of public international law, but must not add to or diminish the rights and obligations provided in the agreements. The DSU attempts to ensure prompt resolution of disputes by establishing rather tight timeframes for each phase of the four phases of the process: consultations, panel proceedings, appellate review and surveillance of implementation.

A WTO member may ask for consultations with another member if the complaining member believes that the other member has violated a WTO agreement or otherwise nullified or impaired benefits accruing to it. The goal of the consultation stage is to enable the disputing parties to understand better the factual situation and the legal claims in respect of the dispute and to resolve the matter without further proceedings.

If consultations fail to resolve the dispute within 60 days of the request for consultations, the complaining WTO member may demand the establishment of a panel of three independent experts to rule on the dispute. Most panelists are current or former government officials and come from a wide range of WTO members. The DSU provides that panelists serve in their individual capacities and there are rules of conduct to ensure their impartiality. DSU article 11 provides that a panel shall make an objective assessment of the matter before it, including an objective assessment of the facts of the case and the applicability of and conformity with the relevant WTO agreements.

There are normally two meetings between the panel and the parties to discuss the substantive issues in the case. Each meeting is preceded by the filing of written submissions. After the hearings with the parties are concluded, the panel submits an interim report to the parties for comment. Thereafter, a final report is issued. After its circulation to WTO members, the final report is referred for formal adoption to the WTO Dispute Settlement Body, which oversees the operation of the dispute settlement system. Adoption is automatic unless there is a consensus not to adopt the report or an appeal of the report to the WTO Appellate Body. The panel process is supposed to be completed in nine months, although many cases take somewhat longer to complete, particularly where a panel feels the need to consult experts.

The possibility of an appeal is a new feature of the WTO dispute settlement system. The Appellate Body consists of seven individuals, appointed by the DSB for four-year terms, renewable once. The Appellate Body hears appeals of panel reports in divisions of three, although its rules provide for the division hearing a case to exchange views with the other four Appellate Body members before the division finalizes its report. The members of the division that hears a particular appeal are selected by a secret procedure that is based on randomness, unpredictability and the opportunity for all members to serve without regard to national origin. The Appellate Body's report is to be issued within 90 days of the appeal and is adopted automatically by the DSB, absent consensus to the contrary.

The final phase of the WTO dispute settlement process is the surveillance stage. This is designed to ensure that the results contained in adopted panel/Appellate Body reports are implemented. If a violation is found, the report typically recommends that the member concerned bring the offending measure into conformity with its WTO obligations. While the report may suggest ways of implementation, it is ultimately left to the member to determine how it will implement the report. Under the surveillance function, the offending member is required to state its intentions with respect to implementation within 30 days of the adoption of the applicable report by the DSB. If immediate implementation is impractical, it is to be afforded a reasonable period of time for implementation. Absent agreement, that period of time may be set by arbitration. The DSU provides that, as a guideline for the arbitrator, the period should not exceed 15 months. If a party fails to implement the report within the reasonable period of time, the prevailing party may request compensation. If that is not forthcoming, it may request the DSB to authorize it to suspend concessions owed to the non-implementing party (i.e., take retaliatory action). DSB authorization is automatic, absent consensus to the contrary, subject to arbitration of the level of suspension if requested by the non-implementing member. If there is a dispute over whether implementation has taken place, the matter is referred back to the original panel for an expedited decision.

The WTO dispute settlement system has been quite active since the founding of the WTO on January 1, 1995. As of September 2009, there had been 400 consultation requests. According to the WTO website, as of September 2009, the EU had been a complainant in 81 cases, a respondent in 65 cases and a third party in 82 cases. It has most frequently brought cases against the US (31), India (10), Argentina (7) and Japan (7). The US (19), Canada (8), Brazil (6) and India (6) have been the most frequent complainants against the EU. These statistics demonstrate the very important role that WTO dispute settlement plays in the EU's relations with its major trading partners. This is particularly true of its relationship with the US, which is discussed in Section D below. In fact, the statistics do not tell the whole story because the EU has been involved in many other cases that have settled or where it was an interested third party. Moreover, because of its role as a forum for negotiations, many other aspects of the EU's common commercial policy are dealt with in the WTO.

7. FUTURE WTO NEGOTIATIONS

An attempt to launch a new round of WTO negotiations at a WTO ministerial meeting in Seattle in 1999 was unsuccessful and occasioned violent protests against such negotiations. For the most part, the same issues were considered in November 2001 at a WTO ministerial meeting in Doha, Qatar, where it was agreed to launch negotiations on a broad range of topics. Those topics include (i) the trade and environment interface; (ii) competition and (iii) investment, which were strongly pushed by the EU (for the latter two subjects, it was agreed that the negotiations would only start in 2004 following an agreement on modalities of negotiation in 2003). The EU was unsuccessful in avoiding the adoption of a negotiating goal calling for the phasing out of agricultural export subsidies, but succeeded in avoiding any target date for such phase-out. There are also negotiations on services, specific intellectual property issues (e.g., geographical indications), tariff levels, trade facilitation and WTO rules on dumping and subsidies. At the 2003 ministerial meeting in Cancun, the EU abandoned its attempt to include competition and investment in the negotiations when no agreement could be reached on modalities. Since the 2001 launch of the negotiations, there have been many meetings at different levels, but an overall agreement has proved to be elusive (although breakthroughs have sometime been reported as being imminent).

B. THE COURT OF JUSTICE AND THE WTO AGREEMENT

The Court of Justice has considered the WTO Agreement in two major contexts—in defining the scope of the EU's implied and explicit powers in respect of the common commercial policy and in decisions on its possible direct effect. We consider both issues in this section.

1. THE SCOPE OF ARTICLE 113 EC: THE COMMON COMMERCIAL POLICY

The negotiations that led to the creation of the WTO dealt with trade in services and certain aspects of intellectual property. During the negotiations, the Commission had acted as the sole negotiator on behalf of the EU and the Member States, but it had been agreed that its role was without prejudice to the issue of competence under the Treaty. When the negotiations were successfully completed and the agreement signed in April 1994, the question was thus presented: Who had the power to conclude the WTO agreements and, in particular, the General Agreement on Trade in Services (GATS) and the Agreement on Trade–Related Aspects of Intellectual Property Rights (TRIPs)? Were they within the exclusive purview of the EU? Only within the competence of the Member States? Within the joint competence of the EU and the Member States? In addition, there was the issue of representation of the EU in the WTO. The EU had exclusively represented the Member States in GATT, but did the addition of these new subject matters—services and intellectual property—mean that the Member States would now have an independent role in the WTO? In an opinion of major importance the Court of Justice addressed these issues in November 1994. The Court acted quickly—only seven months elapsed between the request and the opinion—and it heard all six Advocates-General (although their opinions were not published).

At the time of the case, the relevant text of Article 113 EC read as follows:

> The common commercial policy shall be based on uniform principles, particularly in regard to changes in tariff rates, the conclusion of tariff and trade agreements, the achievement of uniformity in measures of liberalization, export policy and measures to protect trade such as those to be taken in the event of dumping or subsidies.

OPINION 1/94

[1994] ECR I–5267.
(World Trade Organization—WTO).

VII. Article 113 of the EC Treaty, GATS and TRIPs

35 The Commission's main contention is that the conclusion of both GATS and TRIPs falls within the exclusive competence conferred on the Community in commercial policy matters by Article 113 of the EC Treaty. That point of view has been vigorously disputed * * * by the Council, by the Member States * * * and by the European Parliament. * * *

A. GATS

* * *

38 As regards [services other than transport], it should be recalled at the outset that in Opinion 1/75 [*Local Cost Standard*, see Chapter 27(B)(1), Note 5] the Court, which had been asked to rule on the scope of Community competence as to the arrangements relating to a local cost standard, held that "the field of common commercial policy, and more particularly that of export policy, necessarily covers systems of aid for exports and more particularly measures concerning credits for the financing of local costs linked to export operations." The local costs in question concerned expenses incurred for the supply of both goods and services. Nevertheless, the Court recognized the exclusive

competence of the Community, without drawing a distinction between goods and services.

39 In its Opinion 1/78 [*Rubber Agreement*, see Chapter 27(B)(2)], the Court rejected an interpretation of Article 113 "the effect of which would be to restrict the common commercial policy to the use of instruments intended to have an effect only on the traditional aspects of external trade." On the contrary, it considered that "the question of external trade must be governed from a wide point of view," as is confirmed by "the fact that the enumeration in Article 113 of the subjects covered by commercial policy ... is conceived as a non-exhaustive enumeration."

40 The Commission points out in its request for an opinion that in certain developed countries the services sector has become the dominant sector of the economy and that the global economy has been undergoing fundamental structural changes. The trend is for basic industry to be transferred to developing countries, whilst the developed economies have tended to become, in the main, exporters of services and of goods with a high value-added content. The Court notes that this trend is borne out by the WTO Agreement and its annexes, which were the subject of a single process of negotiation covering both goods and services.

41 Having regard to this trend in international trade, it follows from the open nature of the common commercial policy, within the meaning of the Treaty, that trade in services cannot immediately, and as a matter of principle, be excluded from the scope of Article 113, as some of the Governments which have submitted observations contend.

42 In order to make that conclusion more specific, however, one must take into account the definition of trade in services given in GATS in order to see whether the overall scheme of the Treaty is not such as to limit the extent to which trade in services can be included within Article 113.

43 Under Article I(2) of GATS trade in services is defined, for the purposes of that agreement, as comprising four modes of supply of services: (1) cross-frontier supplies not involving any movement of persons; (2) consumption abroad, which entails the movement of the consumer into the territory of the WTO member country in which the supplier is established; (3) commercial presence, i.e. the presence of a subsidiary or branch in the territory of the WTO member country in which the service is to be rendered; (4) the presence of natural persons from a WTO member country, enabling a supplier from one member country to supply services within the territory of any other member country.

44 As regards cross-frontier supplies, the service is rendered by a supplier established in one country to a consumer residing in another. The supplier does not move to the consumer's country; nor, conversely, does the consumer move to the supplier's country. That situation is,

therefore, not unlike trade in goods, which is unquestionably covered by the common commercial policy within the meaning of the Treaty. There is thus no particular reason why such a supply should not fall within the concept of the common commercial policy.

45 The same cannot be said of the other three modes of supply of services covered by GATS, namely, consumption abroad, commercial presence and the presence of natural persons.

46 As regards natural persons, it is clear from Article 3 of the Treaty, which distinguishes between "a common commercial policy" in paragraph (b) and "measures concerning the entry and movement of persons" in paragraph (d), that the treatment of nationals of non-member countries on crossing the external frontiers of Member States cannot be regarded as falling within the common commercial policy. More generally, the existence in the Treaty of specific chapters on the free movement of natural and legal persons shows that those matters do not fall within the common commercial policy.

47 It follows that the modes of supply of services referred to by GATS as "consumption abroad," "commercial presence" and the "presence of natural persons" are not covered by the common commercial policy.

* * *

B. TRIPs

54 The Commission's argument in support of its contention that the Community has exclusive competence under Article 113 is essentially that the rules concerning intellectual property rights are closely linked to trade in the products and services to which they apply.

55 It should be noted, first that Section 4 of Part III of TRIPs, which concerns the means of enforcement of intellectual property rights, contains specific rules as to measures to be applied at border crossing points. As the United Kingdom has pointed out, that section has its counterpart in the provisions of Council Regulation 3842/86 of 1 December 1986 laying down measures to prohibit the release for free circulation of counterfeit goods. Inasmuch as that regulation concerns the prohibition of the release into free circulation of counterfeit goods, it was rightly based on Article 113 of the Treaty: it relates to measures to be taken by the customs authorities at the external frontiers of the Community. Since measures of that type can be adopted autonomously by the Community institutions on the basis of Article 113 of the EC Treaty, it is for the Community alone to conclude international agreements on such matters.

56 However, as regards matters other than the provisions of TRIPs on the release into free circulation of counterfeit goods, the Commission's arguments cannot be accepted.

[Although the Court conceded that there is a connection between intellectual property rights and trade in goods, it noted that is not enough to bring such rights them within the scope of Article 113 EC, especially since they affect internal trade just as much as, if not more than, international trade. Moreover, the Court noted that while what are now Articles 114, 115 and 352 TFEU provide a basis for harmonizing national laws on intellectual property, the decision-making rules under those articles differed from those applicable under Article 113 EC.]

60 If the Community were to be recognized as having exclusive competence to enter into agreements with non-member countries to harmonize the protection of intellectual property and, at the same time, to achieve harmonization at Community level, the Community institutions would be able to escape the internal constraints to which they are subject in relation to procedures and to rules as to voting.

* * *

71 In the light of the foregoing, it must be held that, apart from those of its provisions which concern the prohibition of the release into free circulation of counterfeit goods, TRIPs does not fall within the scope of the common commercial policy.

VIII.   The Community's Implied External Powers, GATS and TRIPs

72 In the event of the Court rejecting its main contention that the Community has exclusive competence pursuant to Article 113, the Commission maintains in the alternative that the Community's exclusive competence to conclude GATS and TRIPs flows implicitly from the provisions of the Treaty establishing its internal competence, or from the existence of legislative acts of the institutions giving effect to that internal competence, or else from the need to enter into international commitments with a view to achieving an internal Community objective. The Commission also argues that, even if the Community does not have adequate powers on the basis of specific provisions of the Treaty or legislative acts of the institutions, it has exclusive competence by virtue of Articles 100a and 235 of the Treaty [now Articles 114 and 352 TFEU]. The Council and the Member States which have submitted observations acknowledge that the Community has certain powers, but deny that they are exclusive.

A.   GATS

73 With particular regard to GATS, the Commission cites three possible sources for exclusive external competence on the part of the Community: the powers conferred on the Community institutions by the Treaty at internal level, the need to conclude the agreement in order to achieve a Community objective, and, lastly, Articles 100a and 235 [114 and 352 TFEU].

74 The Commission argues, first, that there is no area or specific provision in GATS in respect of which the Community does not have corresponding powers to adopt measures at internal level. According to the Commission, those powers are set out in the chapters on the right of establishment, freedom to provide services and transport. Exclusive external competence flows from those internal powers.

75   That argument must be rejected.

76   It was on the basis of Article 75(1)(a) [now 91(1)(a) TFEU] which, as regards that part of a journey which takes place on Community territory, also concerns transport from or to non-member countries, that the Court held in *ERTA* that the "powers of the Community extend to relationships arising from international law, and hence involve the need in the sphere in question for agreements with the third countries concerned."

77   However, even in the field of transport, the Community's exclusive external competence does not automatically flow from its power to lay down rules at internal level. As the Court pointed out in *ERTA*, the Member States, whether acting individually or collectively, only lose their right to assume obligations with non-member countries as and when common rules which could be affected by those obligations come into being. Only in so far as common rules have been established at internal level does the external competence of the Community become exclusive. However, not all transport matters are already covered by common rules.

78   The Commission asserted at the hearing that the Member States' continuing freedom to conduct an external policy based on bilateral agreements with nonmember countries will inevitably lead to distortions in the flow of services and will progressively undermine the internal market. * * *

79   In reply to that argument, suffice it to say that there is nothing in the Treaty which prevents the institutions from arranging, in the common rules laid down by them, concerted action in relation to non-member countries or from prescribing the approach to be taken by the Member States in their external dealings. * * *

* * *

81   Unlike the chapter on transport, the chapters on the right of establishment and on freedom to provide services do not contain any provision expressly extending the competence of the Community to "relationships arising from international law." As has rightly been observed by the Council and most of the Member States which have submitted observations, the sole objective of those chapters is to secure the right of establishment and freedom to provide services for nationals of Member States. They contain no provisions on the problem of the first establishment of nationals of non-member countries and the rules governing their access to self-employed activities. One cannot therefore infer from those chapters that the Community has exclusive competence to conclude an agreement with non-member countries to liberalize first establishment and access to service markets, other than those which are the subject of cross-border supplies within the mean-

ing of GATS, which are covered by Article 113 (see paragraph 42 above).

* * *

87   Third, the Commission refers to Articles 100a and 235 of the Treaty [now Articles 114 and 352 TFEU] as the basis of exclusive external competence.

88   As regards Article 100a, it is undeniable that, where harmonizing powers have been exercised, the harmonization measures thus adopted may limit, or even remove, the freedom of the Member States to negotiate with non-member countries. However, an internal power to harmonize which has not been exercised in a specific field cannot confer exclusive external competence in that field on the Community.

89   Article 235, which enables the Community to cope with any insufficiency in the powers conferred on it, expressly or by implication, for the achievement of its objectives, cannot in itself vest exclusive competence in the Community at international level. Save where internal powers can only be effectively exercised at the same time as external powers (see paragraph 85 above), internal competence can give rise to exclusive external competence only if it is exercised. This applies a fortiori to Article 235.

90   Although the only objective expressly mentioned in the chapters on the right of establishment and on freedom to provide services is the attainment of those freedoms for nationals of the Member States of the Community, it does not follow that the Community institutions are prohibited from using the powers conferred on them in that field in order to specify the treatment which is to be accorded to nationals of non-member countries. Numerous acts adopted by the Council on the basis of Articles 54 and 57(2) of the Treaty [now 50 and 53 TFEU]—but not mentioned by it—contain provisions in that regard. The Commission has listed them in response to a question from the Court.

91   It is evident from an examination of those acts that very different objectives may be pursued by incorporation of external provisions.

92   The directives on coordination of disclosure requirements and company accounts applied only to companies as such and not to their branches. That gave rise to some disparity, as regards the protection of members and third parties, between companies operating in other Member States by setting up branches and companies operating there by setting up subsidiaries. Consequently, Council Directive 89/666/ EEC, which is based on Article 54 of the Treaty [now 50 TFEU], was introduced to regulate the disclosure requirements applying to such branches. In order to avoid any discrimination based on a company's country of origin, that directive also had to cover branches established by companies governed by the laws of non-member countries.

93   Moreover, the Second [Banking] Directive, which is based on Article 57(2) of the Treaty [now 53 TFEU], contains a Title III "on relations with third countries." That directive established a system of uniform authorization and requires the mutual recognition of controls.

94   Once it is authorized in one Member State, a credit institution may pursue its activities in another Member State (for example, by setting up a branch there) without having to seek fresh authorization from that State. In those circumstances, it was enough for a credit institution having its seat in a nonmember country to establish a subsidiary in a Member State or to acquire control of an establishment having its seat there to enable it to set up branches in all the Member States of the Community without having to seek further authorizations. For that reason, Title III of that directive provides for a series of measures, including negotiation procedures, with a view to obtaining comparable competitive opportunities for Community credit institutions in nonmember countries. Similar provisions have been adopted in the field of insurance and in the field of finance.

95   Whenever the Community has included in its internal legislative acts provisions relating to the treatment of nationals of non-member countries or expressly conferred on its institutions powers to negotiate with non-member countries, it acquires exclusive external competence in the spheres covered by those acts.

96   The same applies in any event, even in the absence of any express provision authorizing its institutions to negotiate with non-member countries, where the Community has achieved complete harmonization of the rules governing access to a self-employed activity, because the common rules thus adopted could be affected within the meaning of *ERTA* if the Member States retained freedom to negotiate with non-member countries.

97   That is not the case in all service sectors, however, as the Commission has itself acknowledged.

98   It follows that competence to conclude GATS is shared between the Community and the Member States.

B. *TRIPs*

[The Commission raised arguments similar to the foregoing in respect of the TRIPS Agreement. The Court rejected them for the same reasons set out above in respect of GATS. Although the Court rejected Member State arguments that suggested that the Community lacked powers in respect of some matters covered by the TRIPS Agreement (e.g., the requirement for effective protection of intellectual property rights through judicial remedies), the lack of harmonization in many of the areas covered by the TRIPS Agreement led it to conclude that the Community and the Member States were jointly competent to conclude the TRIPS Agreement.]

IX. The Duty of Cooperation Between the Member
States and the Community Institutions

106 At the hearing, the Commission drew the Court's attention to the problems which would arise, as regards the administration of the agreements, if the Community and the Member States were recognized as sharing competence to participate in the conclusion of the GATS and TRIPs agreements. While it is true that, in the negotiation of the agreements, the procedure under Article 113 of the Treaty prevailed subject to certain very minor adjustments, the Member States will, in the context of the WTO, undoubtedly seek to express their views individually on matters falling within their competence whenever no consensus has been found. Furthermore, interminable discussions will ensue to determine whether a given matter falls within the competence of the Community, so that the Community mechanisms laid down by the relevant provisions of the Treaty will apply, or whether it is within the competence of the Member States, in which case the consensus rule will operate. The Community's unity of action *vis-à-vis* the rest of the world will thus be undermined and its negotiating power greatly weakened.

107 In response to that concern, which is quite legitimate, it must be stressed, first, that any problems which may arise in implementation of the WTO Agreement and its annexes as regards the coordination necessary to ensure unity of action where the Community and the Member States participate jointly cannot modify the answer to the question of competence, that being a prior issue. As the Council has pointed out, resolution of the issue of the allocation of competence cannot depend on problems which may possibly arise in administration of the agreements.

108 Next, where it is apparent that the subject-matter of an agreement or convention falls in part within the competence of the Community and in part within that of the Member States, it is essential to ensure close cooperation between the Member States and the Community institutions, both in the process of negotiation and conclusion and in the fulfilment of the commitments entered into. That obligation to cooperate flows from the requirement of unity in the international representation of the Community.

109 The duty to cooperate is all the more imperative in the case of agreements such as those annexed to the WTO Agreement, which are inextricably interlinked, and in view of the cross-retaliation measures established by the [WTO] Dispute Settlement Understanding. Thus, in the absence of close cooperation, where a Member State, duly authorized within its sphere of competence to take cross-retaliation measures, considered that they would be ineffective if taken in the fields covered by GATS or TRIPs, it would not, under Community law, be empowered to retaliate in the area of trade in goods, since that is an area which on any view falls within the exclusive competence of the Community under Article 113 of the Treaty. Conversely, if the Community were given the right to retaliate in the sector of goods but found itself incapable of exercising that right, it would, in the absence of close cooperation, find itself unable, in law, to retaliate in the areas covered by GATS or TRIPs, those being within the competence of the Member States.

NOTES AND QUESTIONS

1. The Court also ruled that the EU had the exclusive power to conclude the GATT-related agreements on trade in goods, including products subject to the ECSC and Euratom Treaties, and that Article 113 EC was a sufficient basis for such action, even in respect of the agreements on agriculture and sanitary and phytosanitary measures. In this regard, the Court stated:

29   * * * "The objective of the [WTO] Agreement on Agriculture is to establish, on a worldwide basis, a fair and market-oriented agricultural trading system" (see the preamble to that Agreement). The fact that commitments entered into under that Agreement require internal measures to be adopted on the basis of [another] Article of the Treaty does not prevent the international commitments themselves from being entered into pursuant to Article 113 alone.

The Court also rejected the argument that because the Member States would contribute to the operating budget of the WTO, there was joint competence (*cf. Rubber Agreement*). The Court drew a distinction between an operating budget and a "financial policy instrument," such as was involved in the *Rubber Agreement* case.

2. Would you say that the Court's opinion on the WTO Agreements represents an advance on, retreat from, or a simple application of, the principles adopted in the *ERTA* and the *Rubber Agreement* cases discussed in Chapter 27? Why?

3. The Court took the position that since title V covers international agreements on transport, Article 113 EC does not. See Opinion, para. 48. What implications could this have for the scope of Article 113 EC? Is it consistent with the Court's position that the WTO Agreement on Agriculture falls under Article 113 EC? See Note 1 above. What difference does it make in a procedural sense (approvals, etc.)? The separateness of transport is confirmed in Article 207(5) TFEU.

4. In its argument, the Commission cited various Community instruments and agreements that in the past had been adopted solely under Article 113 EC and that contained provisions on services or intellectual property rights in general. The Court dismissed the examples without much discussion. Does that mean that those instruments and agreements were invalid? Is such past practice relevant in EU Treaty interpretation?

5. In respect of areas of joint competence in the WTO, do you think that the duty of cooperation discussed by the Court at the end of its opinion will adequately solve the problems raised by the Commission? At the WTO, the Commission normally speaks for the EU and its Member States (except on

budgetary matters, since the Member States pay their own dues). The WTO Agreement provides that the EU and its Member States cannot cast more than 27 votes, even though the EU itself and all 27 Member States are WTO members. Since WTO decisions are virtually always taken by consensus, this has not been an issue.

6. The current treaty provisions on the common commercial policy are dealt with in Section C below.

2. DIRECT EFFECT OF THE WTO AGREEMENT

The Court of Justice held on several occasions that the General Agreement on Tariffs and Trade did not have direct effect. See, e.g., International Fruit Co. v. Produktschap, Cases 21–24/72, [1972] ECR 1219; Germany v. Council (Bananas), Case C–280/93, [1994] ECR I–4973. In *International Fruit*, the Court described GATT as "characterized by the great flexibility of its provisions," in particular those related to safeguards and dispute settlement (para. 21). Given the changes introduced by the WTO Agreement, particularly in respect of more detailed rules and the strengthened dispute settlement system, the question naturally arose whether the Court would find that the WTO Agreement could have such effect.

PORTUGUESE REPUBLIC v. COUNCIL

Case C–149/96
[1998] ECR I–7379.

[In 1994, the Community negotiated agreements related to textile products with India and Pakistan. The agreements were approved in a decision adopted by qualified majority, over the objections of Greece, Spain and Portugal. Portugal subsequently challenged the decision on grounds that it violated WTO rules, as well as certain rules and principles of Community law. The Court addressed the WTO issue as follows:]

35 It should also be remembered that according to the general rules of international law there must be *bona fide* performance of every agreement. Although each contracting party is responsible for executing fully the commitments which it has undertaken it is nevertheless free to determine the legal means appropriate for attaining that end in its legal system, unless the agreement, interpreted in the light of its subject-matter and purpose, itself specifies those means.

36 While it is true that the WTO agreements, as the Portuguese Government observes, differ significantly from the provisions of GATT 1947, in particular by reason of the strengthening of the system of safeguards and the mechanism for resolving disputes, the system resulting from those agreements nevertheless accords considerable importance to negotiation between the parties.

37 Although the main purpose of the mechanism for resolving disputes is in principle, according to Article 3(7) of the Understanding on Rules

and Procedures Governing the Settlement of Disputes (Annex 2 to the WTO), to secure the withdrawal of the measures in question if they are found to be inconsistent with the WTO rules, that understanding provides that where the immediate withdrawal of the measures is impracticable compensation may be granted on an interim basis pending the withdrawal of the inconsistent measure.

38   According to Article 22(1) of that Understanding, compensation is a temporary measure available in the event that the recommendations and rulings of the dispute settlement body provided for in Article 2(1) of that Understanding are not implemented within a reasonable period of time, and Article 22(1) shows a preference for full implementation of a recommendation to bring a measure into conformity with the WTO agreements in question.

39   However, Article 22(2) provides that if the member concerned fails to fulfil its obligation to implement the said recommendations and rulings within a reasonable period of time, it is, if so requested, and on the expiry of a reasonable period at the latest, to enter into negotiations with any party having invoked the dispute settlement procedures, with a view to finding mutually acceptable compensation.

40   Consequently, to require the judicial organs to refrain from applying the rules of domestic law which are inconsistent with the WTO agreements would have the consequence of depriving the legislative or executive organs of the contracting parties of the possibility afforded by Article 22 of that memorandum of entering into negotiated arrangements even on a temporary basis.

41   It follows that the WTO agreements, interpreted in the light of their subject-matter and purpose, do not determine the appropriate legal means of ensuring that they are applied in good faith in the legal order of the contracting parties.

42   As regards, more particularly, the application of the WTO agreements in the Community legal order, it must be noted that, according to its preamble, the agreement establishing the WTO, including the annexes, is still founded, like GATT 1947, on the principle of negotiations with a view to "entering into reciprocal and mutually advantageous arrangements" and is thus distinguished, from the viewpoint of the Community, from the agreements concluded between the Community and non-member countries which introduce a certain asymmetry of obligations, or create special relations of integration with the Community, such as the agreement which the Court was required to interpret in *Kupferberg*.

43   It is common ground, moreover, that some of the contracting parties, which are among the most important commercial partners of the Community, have concluded from the subject-matter and purpose of the WTO agreements that they are not among the rules applicable by their judicial organs when reviewing the legality of their rules of domestic law.

44 Admittedly, the fact that the courts of one of the parties consider that some of the provisions of the agreement concluded by the Community are of direct application whereas the courts of the other party do not recognize such direct application is not in itself such as to constitute a lack of reciprocity in the implementation of the agreement.

45 However, the lack of reciprocity in that regard on the part of the Community's trading partners, in relation to the WTO agreements which are based on reciprocal and mutually advantageous arrangements and which must *ipso facto* be distinguished from agreements concluded by the Community, referred to in paragraph 42 of the present judgment, may lead to disuniform application of the WTO rules.

46 To accept that the role of ensuring that those rules comply with Community law devolves directly on the Community judicature would deprive the legislative or executive organs of the Community of the scope for maneuver enjoyed by their counterparts in the Community's trading partners.

47 It follows from all those considerations that, having regard to their nature and structure, the WTO agreements are not in principle among the rules in the light of which the Court is to review the legality of measures adopted by the Community institutions.

48 That interpretation corresponds, moreover, to what is stated in the final recital in the preamble to Decision 94/800 [approving the WTO Agreement], according to which "by its nature, the Agreement establishing the World Trade Organization, including the Annexes thereto, is not susceptible to being directly invoked in Community or Member State courts".

49 It is only where the Community intended to implement a particular obligation assumed in the context of the WTO, or where the Community measure refers expressly to the precise provisions of the WTO agreements, that it is for the Court to review the legality of the Community measure in question in the light of the WTO rules.

50 It is therefore necessary to examine whether, as the Portuguese Government claims, that is so in the present case.

51 The answer must be in the negative. The contested decision is not designed to ensure the implementation in the Community legal order of a particular obligation assumed in the context of the WTO, nor does it make express reference to any specific provisions of the WTO agreements. Its purpose is merely to approve the Memoranda of Understanding negotiated by the Community with Pakistan and India.

52 It follows from all the foregoing that the claim of the Portuguese Republic that the contested decision was adopted in breach of certain rules and fundamental principles of the WTO is unfounded.

NOTES AND QUESTIONS

1.   Is the Court's reasoning in this case consistent with its reasoning in the cases we examined in Chapter 27(C) supra? Are you persuaded by the Court's argument that direct effect should not be recognized because it would take away the Community's "right" to delay implementation? Is that a "right" or simply a provision of a detailed dispute settlement system that has provisions dealing with non-compliance? Does the existence of the reasoned opinion procedure of Article 258 and the possibility of fines under Article 260 suggest that Member States also have a right to delay implementation of Union legislation and choose those alternatives?

2.   The Court refers to a Council Decision in paragraph 48. Should this sort of statement by the Council affect the Court's analysis of the issue in this case? In cases involving other Union legislation?

3.   For examples of para. 49, see Nakajima v. Council, [1991] ECR I–2069 and the following:

PETROTUB SA v. COUNCIL & COMMISSION
Case C–76/00, [2003] ECR I–79.

53   [I]t is settled case-law of the Court of Justice that, having regard to their nature and structure, the WTO Agreement and the agreements and understandings annexed to it are not in principle among the rules in the light of which the Court is to review the legality of measures adopted by the Community institutions, pursuant to the first paragraph of Article 230 EC [now 263 TFEU].

54   However, where the Community intended to implement a particular obligation assumed in the context of the WTO, or where the Community measure refers expressly to precise provisions of the agreements and understandings contained in the annexes to the WTO Agreement, it is for the Court to review the legality of the Community measure in question in the light of the WTO rules (see, in particular, *Portugal* v. *Council*, paragraph 49).

55   The preamble to the basic [anti-dumping] regulation, and more specifically the fifth recital therein, shows that the purpose of that regulation is, *inter alia*, to transpose into Community law as far as possible the new and detailed rules contained in the [WTO's] 1994 Anti-dumping Code, which include, in particular, those relating to the calculation of dumping, so as to ensure a proper and transparent application of those rules.

56   It is therefore established that the Community adopted the basic regulation in order to satisfy its obligations arising from the 1994 Anti-dumping Code and that, by means of Article 2(11) of that regulation, it intended to implement the particular obligations laid down by Article 2.4.2 of that code. To that extent, as is clear from the case-law cited in paragraph 54 of the present judgment, it is for the

Court to review the legality of the Community measure in question in the light of the last-mentioned provision.

* * *

58 [I]t was not expressly specified in Article 2(11) of the basic regulation that the explanation required by Article 2.4.2 of the 1994 Anti-dumping Code had to be given by the Community institution in the event of recourse to the asymmetrical method. [However, that] may be explained by the existence of Article [288] of the Treaty. Once Article 2.4.2 is transposed by the Community, the specific requirement to state reasons laid down by that provision can be considered to be subsumed under the general requirement imposed by the Treaty for acts adopted by the institutions to state the reasons on which they are based.

* * *

60 [I]t must be held that a Council regulation imposing definitive anti-dumping duties and having recourse to the asymmetrical method for the purposes of calculating the dumping margin must in particular contain, as part of the statement of reasons required by Article [288] of the Treaty, the specific explanation provided for in Article 2.4.2 of the 1994 Anti-dumping Code.

C. THE COMMON COMMERCIAL POLICY TODAY

1. THE TREATY PROVISIONS ON THE COMMON COMMERCIAL POLICY

Initially, the most comprehensive treatment in the EEC Treaty of the external relations powers of the EEC was found in Article 113's provisions on the common commercial policy. The *Rubber Agreement* case gave a broad reading to its scope, but the *WTO Opinion* was not so expansive. Consequently, both the Nice and Lisbon Treaties expanded the scope of the common commercial policy CCP. They also modified the process by which CCP-related agreements are approved and the CCP is implemented.

The CCP is now defined to include agreements relating to trade in goods and services, the commercial aspects of intellectual property and foreign direct investment. Formerly, the CCP was implemented through Commission proposals approved by a qualified majority of the Council. Now Article 207(2) TFEU provides:

> The European Parliament and the Council, acting by means of regulations in accordance with the ordinary legislative procedure, shall adopt measures defining the framework for implementing the common commercial policy.

In the case of agreements negotiated under the CCP, the Commission conducts the negotiations in consultation with a special committee appointed by the Council. In practice, this committee is also involved the day-to-day operation of the CCP. The Commission is required to report regularly to Parliament on the progress of negotiations.

The Council continues to be authorized to approve CCP agreements by a qualified majority, but unanimity is needed in respect of agreements dealing with services, intellectual property or investment if the agreements include provisions for which unanimity is required for the adoption of internal rules. Unanimity is also required in certain circumstances in respect of agreements dealing with trade in cultural and audio-visual services and trade in social, education and health services. The precise interpretation of these limitations is not completely clear, although they are arguably much less convoluted than they were in the Nice Treaty. The scope of those provisions is the subject of Commission v. Council, Case C–13/07, which was pending at the time this Chapter was written.

NOTES AND QUESTIONS

1. Why the special rules for audio-visual and education services? Exactly when do they apply?

2. What are "measures defining the framework for implementing the [CCP]"? Does the phrase include the measures themselves—such an anti-dumping regulation?

3. Recall from Chapter 27 that Parliamentary consent is required for agreements covering fields to which the ordinary legislative process applies (Article 218(6)(a)(v) TFEU). Does this provision combined with Article 207(2) TFEU mean that Parliamentary consent is needed for CCP agreements?

2. THE CUSTOMS UNION

The European Union is a customs union (Article 28 TFEU), an area that is within its exclusive competence (Article 3(a) TFEU). Under the GATT rule permitting customs unions, the constituent members must eliminate duties and commercial restrictions on trade amongst themselves and establish substantially the same duties and commercial restrictions toward nonmembers (GATT art. XXIV). Thus, the TFEU provides for the creation of a common customs tariff applicable to goods imported from abroad (Arts. 31–32) and a common commercial policy for dealing with third countries (Articles 206–207). Initially, the ECC tariff was set at the arithmetical average of the duties charged by the four relevant Member State jurisdictions (West Germany, France, Italy and the Benelux countries, who had already formed a customs union among themselves). There were, of course, many exceptions, but by July 1, 1968, there was a single external tariff. The tariff rates have been reduced over time as a result of the Union's participation in GATT and WTO tariff-cutting negotiations.

When a new state accedes to the EU, its tariffs are aligned with EU tariffs. If the new Member State has previously agreed to limit its tariffs in the WTO and the alignment process leads to an increase in its tariffs for a particular product, the Union may have to compensate other WTO members for such increase by lowering the EU tariff on other products.

The operation of a comprehensive customs system is very complex. Since different goods are subject to different tariff rates, every good that might be traded must be categorized in order to determine the applicable tariff rate. The classification system used by the EU and others is based on the so-called Harmonized System of the World Customs Organization. It categorizes products into 99 main chapters, with thousands of headings and subheadings. It is, of course, inevitable that there will be products that arguably fit in more than one place in the list. For example, in Bienengraber & Co. v. Hauptzollamt Hamburg–Jonas, Case 38/85, [1986] ECR 811, the Court of Justice was faced with the question of how to classify "Kikis," which were "half human in appearance, in so far as their hands, feet, the shape of their eyes, cheeks and mouth are concerned, and half animal, with regard in particular to their nose and tail and to the fur which covers their torso and limbs." (para. 3). The importer claimed that the Kikis were dolls. However, the notes to the CCT provided that "only * * * such articles as are representations of human beings (including those of a caricature type)" were to be regarded as dolls. (para. 11). The German customs authorities rejected the importer's claim on the basis of (i) an opinion poll in which 71% of the mothers interviewed thought that the Kikis represented an animal rather than a human being and (ii) an expert opinion from a customs training college that they represented animals. The Court concluded (paras. 12–13):

> Inasmuch as the representation of a human being may, according to the wording of those Explanatory Notes, be deformed or even stylized, it may also include certain characteristics borrowed from the animal kingdom. Such animal characteristics must, however, remain minor and secondary and must not put in question the general appearance of the figure which must essentially correspond to that of a human being.

> The answer to the questions referred by the Bundesfinanzhof must therefore be that Note 3 to Chapter 97 of the Common Customs Tariff is to be interpreted as meaning that a figure may be regarded as a doll within the meaning of subheading 97.02 A of the Common Customs Tariff only if any animal features which it may have are minor and secondary and the figure's general appearance is essentially that of a human being.

Who won? The case highlights an important aspect of customs law. There is always an attempt made, in light of the relevant notes, to give the normal meaning to words used in a classification description.

The second issue that arises is valuation. Since most tariffs are ad valorem, it is necessary to determine the value on which the percentage rate will be applied. The EU rules on valuation are based on the WTO Customs Valuation Agreement. The essential feature of the WTO agreement is the requirement that normally the "transaction value," i.e. the price actually paid by the buyer of the good, should be the basis for valuing a good for customs purposes. Prior to the adoption of the code, the major trading nations used many different methods to value goods for customs purposes. There are exceptions to the general rule. For example, transactions between related companies may be treated differently if there is reason to think the transaction value is not an arm's-length price.

Even if an import has been properly classified and valued, it still may not be possible to assess the duty because different duty rates may be applicable to the same product depending on the product's origin. For example, many goods from many countries may enter the EU duty free, either because they originate in countries with whom the EU has a free trade area (such as the EFTA countries) or in developing countries to which the EU grants tariff preferences. Rules to determine the origin of goods are obviously necessary and may be quite complex. Indeed, origin determinations have become much more difficult as globalization has led to many more products being composed of parts from different jurisdictions.

Obviously, customs rules have to be very detailed, but clear and simple enough so that they can be readily and consistently applied by thousands of customs inspectors in the multitude of transactions that occur each day. Needless to say, despite the best efforts of customs officials, ambiguities inevitably arise, and many customs questions ultimately end up in the courts.

Although the EU establishes the tariff rates and detailed customs rules, it does not have a customs service. Thus, it is left to the Member States and their respective customs services to apply the rules. The EU does, however, keep the revenues collected (minus an administrative charge) as part of its own resources. This arrangement explains why EU customs law cases usually come to the Court of Justice as Article 267 references from national courts. The involvement of so many national customs services means that the EU's application of its tariff is not completely uniform—a matter of some annoyance to its trading partners, which has resulted in complaints being brought in the WTO. The TFEU has a specific provision—Article 33—on customs cooperation that aims at reducing disparities in the application of the rules.

3. SAFEGUARD MEASURES

As described earlier in this chapter, WTO rules generally prohibit the imposition of quantitative and other nontariff restrictions on imports. Article XIX of GATT 1994 and the WTO Agreement on Safeguards, however, allow a WTO Member to impose such restrictions if its domestic injury has been "seriously injured" or is threatened with serious injury by imports. The EU recognizes these WTO rules in its common rules for imports, established by Regulation 3285/94.[2] The EU has made only very limited use of safeguards.

---

2. Council Regulation 3285/94 of Dec. 22, 1994, O.J. L 349/53 (Dec. 31, 1994) (as amended).

4. EXPORT ARRANGEMENTS

The common commercial policy extends to exports as well as imports. The common rules for exports, which are contained in Regulation 2603/69,[3] establish the basic principle that the export of products from the EU to third countries shall be free of quantitative restrictions. Regulation 2603/69, art. 1. A number of products are exempted from this free export principle, particularly oil products and products subject to restriction pursuant to a decision under the common foreign and security policy (see Chapter 27). The rules provide for the possibility of EU protective measures limiting exports of specific products in order to prevent a critical situation arising from shortages of essential products or to allow fulfillment of international undertakings. Regulation 2603/69, arts. 6–9. Protective measures have generally not been imposed under the common rules. In addition, the EU has limited certain exports for environmental or security reasons outside of the framework of the common rules.

5. EU REMEDIES FOR UNFAIR INTERNATIONAL TRADE PRACTICES

In this subsection, we describe briefly the remedies that are available under EU rules for EU industries that have been injured by unfair international trade practices. The first such practice that we examine is dumping—the export of goods to the EU at a price below the exporter's home market price or below their cost of production. We then consider a second unfair trade practice—direct and indirect government subsidization of exports. Finally, we turn to the EU's Trade Barriers Regulation, which establishes a procedure under which the EU may initiate challenges to trade barriers of other countries in the World Trade Organization.

At the outset you will properly ask: What does "unfair" mean? Why and to whom is the practice unfair? Having studied the competition chapters, you know that less efficient competitors virtually always see competition as unfair, yet competition is normally treated as being in the public interest because it promotes a progressive, vibrant economy, and it benefits consumers. Indeed, as we saw in Part IV, the Treaty generally fosters competition by regulating anticompetitive behavior. When you examine the EU rules against unfair international trade practices, you should consider whether they are designed to promote competition or simply to protect EU-based competitors. For example, how do the rules on dumping compare to those on predatory pricing discussed in Chapter 22(D)(5) supra? How different is the treatment of foreign subsidies and EU domestic subsidies (see Chapter 26 supra)? Should similar foreign and domestic activities be treated the same? If not, why not?

a. Regulation of Dumped Imports

The EU adopted its first antidumping regulation in 1968. The current

---

3. Council Regulation 2603/69 of Dec. 20, 1969, O.J. L 324/25 (Dec. 12, 1969) (as amended).

version is contained in Regulation 384/96.[4] The Commission reports annually on its administration of the EU's antidumping rules, as well as on the other regulations governing unfair trade practices discussed in this chapter and provides comprehensive statistics of its activities on the External Trade website.

The process by which dumped imports may be made subject to antidumping duties under EU law is quite complex and provides much work for a small group of specialized lawyers in Brussels. In this subsection, we will first lay out the basic terms of the antidumping regulation and the procedures followed by the Commission in antidumping investigations.

The EU antidumping regulation establishes three prerequisites for imposing antidumping duties: the product must have been dumped, an EU industry must have been materially injured as a result and the imposition of an antidumping duty must be in the EU's interest.

Dumping

The regulation provides that "[a] product shall be considered to have been dumped if its export price to the Community is less than the normal value of the like product" (art. 2(2)). The essential questions raised by that test are: What is normal value? What is the export price? How are they compared?

Normal Value. "[N]ormal value shall normally be based on the prices paid or payable, in the ordinary course of trade, by independent customers in the exporting country." Art. 2(1). On the basis of this definition, dumping is often described as international price discrimination, i.e., exporting at a price below one's home market price, and, in fact, higher average sales prices in the home country are often the basis on which the existence of dumping is established. In many cases, however, normal value is established by other methods. In particular, there are special rules for cases (i) where there have been few or no sales in the home market, (ii) where home-market sales have been made at a loss, (iii) where the goods have originated in a non-market economy and (iv) where the home-market sales have otherwise not been made in the ordinary course of trade (e.g., between related companies).

Export Price. The export price, against which the normal value is to be compared, is defined as "the price actually paid or payable for the product sold from the exporting country to the Community" (art. 2(8)). In certain cases, and in particular when the exporter and importer are related (which is often the case), the export price may be constructed on the basis of the price at which the exported product is first sold to an independent buyer. If there is no resale to an independent buyer or when the product is not sold in the condition imported, the export price may be constructed on any reasonable basis.

---

4.   Council Regulation 384/96 of Dec. 22, 1995, O.J. L 56/1 (Mar. 6, 1996) (as amended).

Comparison of Export Price With Normal Value. The normal value and export price of a product usually need to be adjusted so that they can be fairly compared. Article 2(10) provides that a "fair comparison * * * shall be made at the same level of trade and in respect of sales made at as nearly as possible the same time." It provides for adjustments to account for factors that affect price comparability such as differences in respect of physical characteristics; import charges and indirect taxes; discounts and rebates (including for quantities); level of trade (where shown by consistent and distinct differences in functions and prices of the seller for the different levels of trade, adjustment to be based on the market value of the difference); transport, insurance, handling, loading and ancillary costs; packing; credit; after-sales cost (e.g., warranties); commissions and currency conversions. Adjustments are always necessary and many of the contested issues in a case involve the appropriateness and amount of the adjustments. The goal of the adjustment process is to arrive at a comparable "ex-factory" normal value and export price.

Once normal value and export prices have been adjusted so that they are comparable, they are compared and a dumping margin is calculated.

Material Injury

An antidumping duty may not be imposed unless it is determined that an EU industry has been injured by the dumping. Injury is defined as "material injury to the Community industry, threat of material injury to the Community industry or material retardation of the establishment of such an industry" (art. 3(1)). Dumped imports from several countries may be cumulated in assessing injury.

The regulation treats at length the criteria pursuant to which injury is to be determined (art. 3(2)–(8)). The specific factors that must be examined in the injury investigation are: (a) the volume of dumped imports (and, in particular, whether there has been a significant increase in absolute or percentage terms relative to Community production or consumption); (b) the effect of dumped imports on prices in the Community market (and, in particular, whether there has been significant price undercutting); and (c) the "consequent" impact on Community industry, as indicated by whether it is still recovering from the effects of past dumping or subsidization; the magnitude of the dumping margin; actual or potential declines in sales, profits, output, market share, productivity, return on investments, capacity utilization; and actual and potential negative effects on cash flow, inventories, employment, wages, growth, and ability to raise capital. The list is not exhaustive and no one factor is decisive. Art. 3(5).

The causal connection that must be found is stated as follows: "It must be demonstrated * * * that dumped imports are causing injury * * *. Specifically, this shall entail a demonstration that the volume and/or price levels identified [in Article 3(3)] are responsible for an impact on the Community industry as provided for in [Article 3(5)], and that this

impact exists to a degree which enables it to be classified as material."
Art. 3(6).

If dumping is found, injury is likely to be found as well. The existence
of dumping implies that imports are selling at a price below that at which
they otherwise should have been sold. These lower prices may well result
in the EU industry losing some sales, which will have a negative impact on
its production, capacity utilization, market share and profits. But that is
not always the case, and noninjury findings do occur. EU industry may be
able to undersell the dumped imports at a reasonable profit, or its injury
may be due to factors other than dumping, such as low-priced, undumped
goods from other sources within or without the EU.

EU Interest

In addition to findings of dumping and material injury caused thereby, the regulation requires that imposition of a duty be in the EU's
interest (arts. 7(1), 9(4)). EU interest is defined in detail in Article 21. It
provides that the interests of users and consumers shall be considered,
although "the need to eliminate the trade distorting effects of injurious
dumping and to restore effective competition shall be given special consideration." Art. 21(1). Representative users and consumer organizations, as
well as EU industry and importers, are authorized to provide and receive
information and are entitled to a hearing (if they set out particular
reasons why they should be heard). Art. 21(2)–(3). Since the imposition of
an antidumping duty will normally raise the cost of a product to its
purchasers, the argument is often raised by such purchasers or the
exporters that it is not in the EU's interest to impose such a duty. That
argument is usually rejected on the grounds that it is in the EU's interest
to afford relief to EU industry, particularly where that industry is technologically important or represents significant capital investment and employment.

Procedural Aspects of the EC Antidumping Regulation

An antidumping investigation is normally commenced in response to
the filing of a complaint by an industry trade association alleging that the
EU industry has been injured or is threatened with injury by dumped
products. The Commission makes an effort to verify the principal allegations in the complaint before actually opening an investigation. The
Commission is required to decide whether or not to initiate an investigation within 45 days of receiving a complaint. Art. 5(9). Provisional measures, if any, are to be imposed within nine months of initiation (but not
within 60 days thereof). Art. 7(1). Finally, investigations are normally to
be concluded within one year, or at most, 15 months. Art. 6(9).

If, following consultation with its Advisory Committee of Member
State representatives, the Commission decides to initiate an investigation,
the Commission publishes a notice in the Official Journal. This notice
specifies the product subject to investigation, the time period covered, the
exporting countries and the known producers, exporters and importers.

The Commission sends a copy of the notice and a questionnaire to those importers, exporters and producers known to be involved. The questionnaire requests data on all export sales to the Community and in the home market during the investigation period, which is normally the six to twelve months immediately preceding the opening of the investigation. The exporter may be asked to complete a section of the questionnaire on its production costs. The questionnaire also inquires into the existence of factors typically justifying adjustments to the normal value or export price. The Commission simultaneously secures information from all EU producers in order to determine whether an EU industry has been materially injured by dumping.

After the Commission has received responses to its questionnaires, it typically proceeds to verify the accuracy of the responses. This normally means that the Commission officials assigned to the case will travel to visit the parties responding to the questionnaire to check their original invoices and other records to see that the answers in the questionnaire are accurate. For companies located outside the EU, there is no obligation to cooperate with a Commission investigation. However, in the case of noncooperation, the Commission is authorized to base its findings on available facts, which may be the allegations of the complaining industry or information supplied by competitors (art. 7(7)(b)). Thus, while cooperation is not required, it may be the only practical response to an investigation.

Once an investigation is initiated, essentially three results are possible: termination, "settlement" or imposition of antidumping duties.

First, after consulting with its advisory committee of Member State representatives, the Commission may conclude that the investigation should be terminated, either because there is no evidence of dumping or no evidence of injury (art. 9).

Second, the Commission, after consulting with the advisory committee, may "settle" the investigation by adopting a formal decision to accept an undertaking from the exporters concerned to raise their prices or take other action so that the dumping margin or the injurious effects thereof are eliminated (art. 8). The terms of an undertaking are the subject of negotiation and vary from case to case. Typically, the Commission aims to require the exporters to agree to procedures to ensure that no dumping will occur in the future (e.g., reporting requirements). An exporter generally prefers an undertaking to a duty because it would rather keep the extra profit from the required price increase than pay a tax to the EU in the form of higher duties. In addition, the exporter has the possibility at any time to ask the Commission to modify the undertaking in light of changed circumstances, a request to which the Commission can respond promptly, whereas an exporter that is subject to a duty may find it much more difficult to have the duty modified in light of changed circumstances since the investigation will normally have to be reopened, which can be a lengthy process.

Third, the Commission may impose provisional duties, normally after consulting with the advisory committee. Its decision may be overruled by a qualified majority of the Council. Art. 7(4), (6). Provisional duties may be imposed for six months without consent of the exporters, and for a total of nine months with their consent. Art. 7(7). It is not necessary to pay the provisional duty, but security for payment thereof must be posted when goods under investigation are imported. Thereafter (assuming no undertaking is accepted), on the basis of a Commission proposal in light of the facts as finally established, the Council may adopt a definitive antidumping duty by a simple majority. The simple majority requirement (introduced in the mid–1990s) makes it more difficult than in the past for the less protectionist Member States to block imposition of antidumping duties or to moderate their levels.

Duties are usually ad valorem and are set at different rates for different companies, depending on the margins of dumping established for each company. The EU imposes a duty in an amount less than the full margin of dumping if it determines that the lesser duty will eliminate the injury to EU industry (art. 9(4)). Antidumping duties expire after five years unless they are extended following a review that examines whether their expiration would result in renewed injury to EU industry (art. 11(2)).

Court Review

Decisions by the Court of Justice and the Court of the First Instance in antidumping cases have played a significant role in expanding the opportunities for judicial review and protecting procedural rights under EU law. See Chapter 5 supra. It is less clear that the courts have had much impact on the development of the substantive aspects of EU antidumping law, however, because they tend to accord considerable deference to decisions of the Commission and the Council in what are viewed as matters of economic assessment.

The EU makes extensive use of its antidumping procedures. As of August 31, 2009, the EU had 131 antidumping duties in the force and 50 investigations were pending, with China being the principal target.

b. Regulation of Subsidized Imports

WTO rules permit a WTO member to impose countervailing duties to offset the effect of subsidized imports if those imports cause material injury to its domestic industry. As in the case of dumping, there is a WTO agreement—the Agreement on Subsidies and Countervailing Measures (the SCM Agreement)—that governs the use of countervailing duties. It establishes procedural requirements similar to those established for dumping investigations.

The SCM Agreement defines a subsidy as a financial contribution by a government or a public body that confers a benefit. It prohibits the use of nonagricultural export subsidies and subsidies contingent on the use of domestic instead of imported products. (A separate agreement deals with agricultural subsidies.) The SCM Agreement also provides that WTO members should not cause adverse effects to the interests of other members through the use of specific, nonagricultural subsidies. A specific subsidy is one that is limited to an enterprise or industry or group of enterprises or industries. A nonspecific subsidy would be one that is available automatically to any entity that meets general eligibility criteria. The agreement's limitations only apply to specific subsidies.

In light of the detailed provisions of the SCM Agreement, the EU adopted Council Regulation 2026/97 on protection against subsidized imports.[5] The regulation restates the SCM Agreement's definition of subsidy and its specificity requirement. Arts. 2–3. It contains specific rules for calculating the amount of the countervailing duties, which are based on a calculation of the benefit of the subsidy to the recipient (as opposed to the cost to the government, which was formerly the EU standard and which is considered to be narrower). Art. 5. The regulation's provisions on injury and procedures are generally similar to those in the antidumping regulation, although the details of the two regulations differ in some respects (provisional duties are limited to four months; the de minimis thresholds are different; there is more involvement of the subsidizing government in a subsidies/countervailing duty investigation).

When the EU initiates countervailing duty investigations, there are three issues that must be resolved: to what extent have imports been subsidized? has an EU industry suffered or is it threatened with material injury? and would imposition of countervailing duties be in the interest of the EU? The last two issues are essentially treated in the same manner as if they arose in an antidumping case. The first issue involves determinations of whether a government benefit is a subsidy, as defined by the Regulation, and whether it is "specific" in nature, so as to be countervailable. If a subsidy is countervailable, then it must be valued overall and on a unit basis so that duties may be imposed.

The EU does not make extensive use of countervailing duty actions. As of August 31, 2009, the EU had 8 countervailing duties in force.

c. The Trade Barriers Regulation

The Trade Barriers Regulation (TBR)[6] provides a mechanism by which (i) an EU industry may complain to the Commission that it has suffered injury as a result of obstacles to trade that have an effect on the EU market and (ii) EU enterprises may complain to the Commission that they have suffered adverse effects as a result of obstacles to trade that have an effect on a third-country market. TBR, arts. 3–4. An "obstacle to trade" is defined principally as a trade practice of a third country that

---

5. Council Regulation 2026/97 of Oct. 6, 1997, O.J. L 288/1 (Oct. 21, 1997) (as amended).

6. Regulation 3286/94, O.J. L 349/71 (Dec. 22, 1994) (as amended).

international trade rules prohibit. TBR, art. 2(1). Thus, the TBR can be invoked with the aim of obtaining access to third-country markets when such access is being denied contrary to the WTO agreements. In essence, the conditions for invoking the TBR are that (i) a trade barrier exists in a third country that violates an international agreement; (ii) the barrier adversely affects the trade of the EU petitioner and (iii) it is in the EU's interest to take action against the third country. The TBR, which was adopted in 1994, replaced the so-called new commercial policy instrument of 1984.

When a complaint against a trade barrier is filed with the Commission, it normally decides within 45 days whether to open an investigation. If it does so, it gathers information from the EU complainant and the country involved, as well as from other interested parties. The Commission's investigation is to be completed within five to seven months, at the end of which the Commission is to report to an Advisory Committee. If the Commission concludes that a trade barrier exists, the Commission will attempt to arrange for the removal of barrier. If the third country involved declines to take appropriate action, then the Commission may pursue international dispute settlement possibilities (most likely at the WTO). If the EU prevails in dispute settlement and the third country fails to bring its measure into compliance with its international obligations, the Council may adopt "retaliatory" measures within 30 days on the basis of a Commission proposal. Through August 2009, the Commission had initiated 24 TBR investigations.

The TBR (and its predecessor) were in large part designed to counter a similar procedure that exists under US law: Section 301 of the Trade Act of 1974. This provision allows US entities to as the US Trade Representative to take action against a foreign country on the grounds that it has violated an agreement with the US or has engaged in unjustifiable, unfair or discriminatory practices that burden US commerce. The EU unsuccessfully challenged the WTO-consistency of Section 301 in WTO dispute settlement. For more materials on Section 301, see J. Jackson, W. Davey & A. Sykes, International Economic Relations, ch. 7 (West 5th ed. 2008).

D. THE EU AND THE US

In this section we consider the EU's view of its trading relationship with the US and then in the notes consider the US view, as well as some of the main disputes pending between them as of 2009. While this section highlights disputes, it is important to keep in mind that there are huge trade and investment flows between the EU and the US and almost all proceed without any problems. Moreover, the US and the EU have a number of mechanisms involving consultations on a myriad issues that aim to facilitate trade. Nonetheless, some issues are difficult to resolve.

EUROPEAN COMMISSION, 2008 REPORT ON UNITED STATES BARRIERS TO TRADE AND INVESTMENT (JULY 2009)

The European Union and the United States are each other's main trading partners and enjoy the largest bilateral trade relationship in the world. In 2007 their combined economies accounted for nearly 60% of global GDP, approximately 33% of world trade in goods and 44% of world trade in services. The total flow of Foreign Direct Investment (FDI) between the EU and the US was approximately €147 billion. The EU FDI stock held in the US amounts to roughly €926 billion. Total FDI stocks held in each other's countries reach approximately €1.89 trillion.

* * * The size and importance of the bilateral trade relationship makes the EU and the US the key players on the global scene. EU–US economic cooperation defines the priorities to be addressed in different fora and sets the pace in the WTO. Europe and the US support a "rules-based" trading system and are working towards a successful conclusion of the Doha Development Agenda (DDA) round of trade talks.

In 2007, the EU and the US launched a new effort, the Transatlantic Economic Council (TEC), to integrate our economies even more fully by identifying key areas where greater convergence between economies and systems could reap rewards on both sides of the Atlantic. Bringing together governments, the business community and consumers, the TEC holds the promise of an ever deeper and more mutually productive transatlantic relationship. * * *

[T]here still exist trade barriers and differences that hinder trade and investment. This annual report on US trade barriers from the European Commission highlights some of the impediments that the European Union encounters when doing business with the US * * * While the overall economic impact of outstanding EU–US trade disputes constitutes only a small proportion of the total EU–US trade volume, our differences should be carefully managed to prevent unnecessary conflict, including costly and time-consuming litigation, and damage to the economies on both sides of the Atlantic. * * *

* * *

3.1. _Extraterritoriality._ US provisions having extraterritorial effect are a frequently used tool to implement US policies across their own border. Today, the US has a number of such provisions in place which hamper international trade and investment and may not as such conform to international trade law. These include for example the Cuban Liberty and Democratic Solidarity Act, known as the Helms Burton Act [and] the Iran–Libya Sanctions Act (ILSA). * * * These extraterritorial provisions continue to cause problems for EU companies. Subsequently the EU has expressed its opposition to this kind of legislation, or any secondary boycott or legislation having extraterritorial effects, through a number of representations and steps, such as the Council Regulation 2271/96 (the so-called "Blocking Statute") of 22 November 1996. Other trading partners of the US, such as Canada and Mexico, have strengthened or adopted similar blocking legislation. * * *

3.2. Unilateralism. 'Unilateralism' may take the form of either unilateral sanctions or unilateral retaliatory measures against allegedly 'offending' countries or companies. Both types of measures are based on an exclusive US assessment of the actions of a foreign country or its legislation and administrative practice irrespective of multilaterally agreed rules. This approach has in the past cast doubt on US support for a multilateral rules-based system to address trade problems. Whilst the US has in practice made extensive use of the WTO fora, including its dispute settlement system, it has not renounced the possibility of taking actions unilaterally. * * *

4. Tariff Barriers. Despite the substantial tariff reduction and elimination agreed in the Uruguay Round, the US retains a number of significant duties and tariff peaks in various sectors including food products, textiles, footwear, leather goods, ceramics, glass and railway cars. The EU hopes to achieve further reductions of US tariffs within the context of the ongoing Doha Development Round. * * *

5.1. Regulatory Divergences. In a global economy international standards are an indispensable tool to eliminate technical barriers to trade, to facilitate and increase market access, to improve the quality and safety of products and services, and to promote and disseminate know-how and technologies. For governments, the use of international standards in the context of their regulatory policy is also an important element for the implementation of the WTO–TBT Agreement. All parties to the Technical Barriers to Trade (TBT) Committee are committed to the wider use of international standards as the basis for their regulation. However, regulatory barriers have also long been recognised as significant impediments to trade and investment between the EU and the US. A particular problem in the US is the relatively low level of implementation and use of international standards set by the international standardisation bodies. The EC and the US are examining how international standards are used in their respective bodies of legislation. A report on the use of standardisation in legislation will be produced in mid–2009 for the Transatlantic Economic Council (TEC), which will provide a basis for identifying possible new areas for convergence. Furthermore, EU exporters to the US market face steep regulatory barriers. In the US, products are increasingly being required to conform to multiple technical regulations regarding consumer protection (including health and safety) and environmental protection. Although, in general, not *de jure* discriminatory, the complexity of US regulatory systems can represent an important structural impediment to market access. [Examples cited include a burdensome pharmaceutical approval system, various labeling requirements, product safety requirements based in part on factors other than safety, differences in food safety standards and requirements.]

5.5. *Sanitary and Phytosanitary Measures.* In the agricultural area, a number of sanitary and phytosanitary (SPS) issues remain a significant source of difficulty for EU producers. Most problematic in this respect is the trading of animal products. For example, since 1997 the US has had special rules in place on the import of ruminant animals (beef, sheep, goats) and products thereof from all European countries based on concerns about Bovine Spongiform Encephalopathy, commonly termed BSE. Although the EU and US collaborated closely towards the adoption of a global BSE standard in the Global Animal Health Organisation (OIE), and although the US insist that their trading partners, notably in Asia, use this standard to assess the risk of US beef, the US remains unwilling to use these agreed rules for EU products. * * *

5.6. *Public Procurement.* In the field of public procurement, the main US trade barriers are contained in a wide array of clauses in federal, state and local legislation and regulation giving preference to domestic suppliers or products, or excluding foreign bidders or products altogether. In addition, there are federal restrictions on the use of federal grant money by State and local government. These restrictions are called 'Buy America' (Buy America Act or BAA) and were reinforced in February 2009 by the American Recovery and Reinvestment Act (ARRA) which foresees additional "Buy American" provisions. Taken together, these restrictions, which include also the "Buy America" provisions of the Department of Transportation (DoT), cover a significant proportion of public purchasing in the US. Furthermore, as the U.S. International Trade Commission noted in its 2004 report: "The Economic Effects of Significant U.S. Import Restraints", the complexity and partially overlapping nature of existing restrictions makes it nearly impossible to determine the total value of government-purchased imports subject to these restrictions. * * *

5.7. *Trade Defence Instruments.* Several US trade defence measures have been brought by the European Union to the WTO Dispute Settlement system. Many aspects of US trade defence legislation and practices have already been ruled as inconsistent with WTO Agreements. Implementation by the US of these WTO findings has, at best, also been slow. The methodology and application of US trade defence instruments has been challenged frequently and successfully—and not only by the EU—in the WTO Dispute Settlement system, such as the laws, regulations and methodology for calculating dumping margins (*zeroing*). * * * For many years the US kept in place antidumping and countervailing duty measures on firms dating back as far as 1985, often with no justification. However, the U.S. International Trade Commission has decided in recent years to revoke most of those measures. Together with a successful outcome of the ongoing WTO disputes on zeroing this has significantly reduced the number and scope of EU products subject to US TDI. There is however, no indication that the US approach will change for measures more recently imposed. * * *

5.8. *Subsidies.* The EU continues to be concerned about the significant direct and indirect government support given to US farmers and industry by means of direct subsidies, protective legislation and tax policies. In June 2008 the US passed the 2008 Farm Act (Food Conservation and Energy Act (FCEA) of 2008). Despite a consensus among WTO Members that farm policies should be reformed in the direction of less trade-distorting forms of support, the 2008 Farm Act went in the opposite direction, just like the 2002 Farm Bill and again reinforced the trade distorting nature of US farm subsidies. * * *

On 6 October 2004, the EU initiated a WTO dispute settlement procedure against a number of US federal, state and local subsidies to Boeing. This action followed the US purported unilateral withdrawal from the 1992 EC–US Agreement on Trade in Large Civil Aircraft on the same day and the initiation of WTO dispute settlement procedures against alleged European support for Airbus. US subsidies challenged by the EU in the WTO include a $4 billion package in the State of Washington (combining tax breaks, tax exemptions or tax credits), infrastructure projects for the exclusive benefit of Boeing, $16.6 billion funding from NASA and DoD for aeronautics R & D and a $900 million package in the State of Kansas in the form of tax breaks and subsidised bonds. WTO panel proceedings in both cases are ongoing, and are expected to last well into 2009. The EU also remains concerned about the significant level of subsidies to the US shipbuilding, aircraft engine manufacturers and steel industries. [The report also cited subsidies to the airline industry and biodiesel.]

6.1. *Foreign Direct Investment Limitations.* The Foreign Investment and National Security Act of 2007 ("FINSA") amends the so-called Exon–Florio amendment of the Defense Production Act of 1950, which authorises the US President to investigate foreign acquisitions, mergers, and takeovers of, or investments in, US companies from a national security perspective. * * * [T]he EU remains concerned about the legal and economic costs for investors and investments that undergo CFIUS review, as well as about uncertainties inherent to this review and its ultimate outcome (such as the circumstances under which the President or CFIUS could reopen a transaction). Finally, the EU is concerned by the absence of any judicial review of CFIUS decisions by US Courts.

US restrictions on foreign investment are particularly evident in the shipping, energy and communications sectors. Apart from this matter, the EU would like the US to resolve outstanding foreign ownership issues to allow the EU–US agreement on aviation services to be brought to a rapid conclusion. * * *

7.1. *Copyright and Related Areas.* Despite a number of positive changes in US legislation following the Uruguay Round, copyright issues are still problematic [citing the "Irish Music" case]. Despite losing a WTO case on the issue, the US has not yet brought its Copyright Act into compliance with [WTO rules]. Furthermore, European industry complains that producers and performers do not enjoy broadcasting rights or public performance rights in the US. * * *

7.2. *Appellations of Origin and Geographical Indications.* Difficulties to protect their rights and the continuing misuse of EU geographical indications on food and drinks produced or sold in the US, especially in the wine sector, as well as other food products, like cheese or meat products, is a source of considerable frustration for EU producers. Particularly problematic is the fact that the US still considers a number of European wine names as 'semi-generics'. US producers making use of 'semi-generics' can take advantage of, or could damage, the reputation of the Community geographical indications in question. Since June 2006 negotiations have been taking place in order to reach an agreement to diminish the material impact on the legal status of the semi-generics in the US market. * * *

[The report also dealt with various services issues, cargo security concerns, patent differences and other regulatory divergences.]

NOTES AND QUESTIONS

1. The Commission's report on US trade barriers appears annually and is a response to an annual US report that lists trade barriers of US trading partners. As usual, the US 2009 National Trade Estimate Report on Foreign Trade Barriers contains a long list of EU barriers (pp. 177–210). In a separate report on its activities in 2008, the US Trade Representative listed negotiations on the following major trade and investment issues involving the EU: technical standards, chemicals registration, Airbus subsidies, the EU banana regime, hormone-treated beef, EU approval and treatment of biotech products, SPS standards, classification of information technology products, wine trade and tariff adjustment issues arising from enlargement.

2. In many respects, the controversial issues between the EU and the US remain largely the same over time. In particular, the EU has long been particularly critical of what it views as extra-territorial US legislation (e.g., the Helms–Burton Act) and US unilateralism (Section 301 of the 1974 Trade Act). In agriculture, the US has long criticized EU subsidies, while the EU has been reluctant to accept imports of hormone treated beef and, more recently, biotech products generally. In aircraft, the US claims that EU Member States subsidize Airbus, while the EU argues that Boeing is subsidized indirectly through military and space contracts.

3. In addition to the Airbus–Boeing subsidy matter, where WTO proceedings will not be completed for some years, six particularly controversial disputes between the EU and the US have come to the WTO dispute settlement system: Bananas, Hormones, GMOs, Helms–Burton, Section 301 and Foreign Sales Corporations. The underlying facts of each are detailed below.

Bananas. In 1993, the Council created a common market organization for bananas. The regulation provided for subsidies to EU banana production up to certain levels (mainly in the Canary Islands and the French West Indies), tariff-free treatment for bananas from ACP countries within certain limits (see Chapter 28) and a tariff quota for bananas from other third countries. Additional imports were possible only after payment of very high duties. Licenses to use the third-country tariff quota, which were quite valuable, were split between those who had traditionally dealt in third-country bananas and those who had traditionally dealt in ACP bananas.

Several GATT parties in the third-country category successfully challenged the rules in a GATT panel proceeding in 1994. Although the EU did not permit the panel report to be adopted, it reached a settlement with some of the parties that gave them specific shares of the third-country quota. After formation of the WTO, a new challenge was brought by one of the GATT complainants that had not settled (Guatemala), two new members (Ecuador and Honduras), Mexico and the US. The result was that the banana regime was found to be discriminatory under both GATT and GATS because of discrimination in allocating licenses for third-country bananas to EU and ACP operators, as well as in respect of quota shares given to the countries that had settled.

The EU adopted a new banana import regime as of the beginning of 1999, which was immediately challenged in the WTO, and again a violation of WTO rules was found, and the US and later Ecuador were authorized to take retaliatory action. In the case of the US, it imposed 100% tariffs on $191 million of EU products. As of April 2001, the EU and the US announced a settlement of the matter, but the settlement was ultimately not successfully implemented. In 2008 the US and Ecuador prevailed in new WTO claims that the latest EU banana regime was still in violation of WTO nondiscrimination rules. As of 2010, it appears that this case has been settled, with the EU agreeing to tariff levels acceptable to the US and Latin American exporters.

Hormones. In a challenge by the US and Canada to the EU's ban on imports of meat and meat products from cattle treated with growth promoting hormones, the WTO dispute settlement system ruled that the EU ban was not based on a risk assessment, as required by the WTO's SPS Agreement. Although given 15 months to implement the result, the EU admitted that the various studies it had commissioned of the safety of the six hormones at issue had not been completed, and the US and Canada were authorized to take retaliatory action in mid–1999. On the basis of the completed studies, the EU took the position that one of the hormones at issue is carcinogenic and should be banned, while there is insufficient evidence to conclude that the other five are safe, such that they should be provisionally banned. It enacted legislation to that effect and brought a WTO challenge to the continued application of retaliatory measures by the US and Canada. In 2009, following a somewhat inconclusive result in the EU's WTO proceeding, the EU and the US reached a settlement pursuant to which the US sanctions would be removed in return for increased access to the EU market for non-hormone treated beef.

GMOs. Although not related to the *Hormones* case, another similar dispute between the EU and the US involves the EU hesitancy to approve the use of genetically modified organisms (GMOs). A high percentage of certain US crops (e.g., corn, cotton and soybeans) are grown from genetically modified seeds. The US successfully challenged an EU moratorium on such approvals in the WTO, but even with the lifting of the moratorium, approvals have been slow to materialize and the matter is still very contentious.

In addition, in September 2003, the EU adopted new rules in respect of authorizing, labeling and tracing of GMO products. Under the rules, a system of authorizing GMO food is established. As to labeling, retailers will be required to label food consisting of or containing GMOs, including food produced from or containing ingredients produced from GMOs. Food produced from GMOs is defined as food derived in whole or part from GMOs but not consisting of or containing GMOs. The contents of the labels are specified (e.g., "This product contains genetically modified organisms" or "This product produced from genetically modified [name of organism]"). Since it is impossible to be sure that products do not contain minute traces of GMOs, the presence of GMO material in conventional food does not have to be labeled if it is below 0.9% of the food ingredients considered individually, provided that this presence is adventitious or technically unavoidable. Regulation 1829/2003 of September 22, 2003 on genetically modified food and feed, O.J. L 268/1 (October 18, 2003). New rules were also adopted to require that the movement of GMO products be tracked and labeled through production and distribution. Regulation 1830/2003 of September 22, 2003, O.J. L 268/24 (October 18, 2003). The US has expressed concern about the cost and practicality of the tracing requirement and sees no reason for labeling products that it views as safe. It seems possible that this issue will become a more serious dispute in the future.

Helms–Burton. A major controversy in EU–US relations in 1996 concerned the so-called Helms–Burton Act, the popular name of the "Cuban Liberty and Democratic Solidarity Act of 1996". Among other things, this Act reaffirms the long-standing US economic embargo of Cuba. It also provides for the establishment of a civil cause of action against persons who "traffic" in (e.g., own, lease, use, manage or derive commercial benefit from) property confiscated by the Cuban government after Fidel Castro came to power in 1959. A successful plaintiff would be entitled to recover treble the value of the property, plus attorneys' fees and costs. The US President has the power to postpone indefinitely (but only for six months at a time) the creation of this civil cause of action, and US Presidents have so far acted to do so. In addition, the Act provides for the exclusion from entry into the United States of persons involved with trafficking in such property, such as officials (and their families) of companies who traffic in such property. These exclusion rules remain in effect and in the mid 1990's several European business persons were denied entry into the US.

The EU strongly protested this legislation as extraterritorial and brought a complaint against the US in the WTO. It also enacted legislation designed to counteract the effects of the Helms–Burton Act. Council Regulation 2271/96, O.J. L 309/1 (Nov. 29, 1996). The Regulation specifically forbids compliance with the Helms Burton Act (and the Iran/Libya Sanctions Act) by any EU natural or legal person; declares invalid and unenforceable any US judgment or order issued pursuant to the legislation; and, through a so-called "clawback" provision, permits EU persons to sue in the EU to recover any damages paid to a successful US plaintiff under the legislation. In addition, the Regulation provides for (i) the possible imposition of visa and immigration restrictions on US interests, (ii) a requirement that all EU nationals notify the Commission of any adverse economic effects suffered as a result of the legislation and (iii) the compilation of a "watch list" of US companies invoking the legislation.

As a result of an indication by President Clinton that he would continue to postpone the effectiveness of the civil liability provisions of the Act and apparent non-enforcement of the visa provisions, the WTO proceeding was abandoned. Since the law remains on the books, however, the dispute may re-ignite.

Section 301. Section 301 of the US Trade Act of 1974 establishes a procedure under which the US government may initiate investigations of other countries' trade practices, at the request of a private party or on its own initiative, and take action against them if they are found to be in violation of an international agreement or if they are unjustifiable, unreasonable or discriminatory in a way that burdens US commerce. This provision is quite controversial in the world at large because of its invocation by the US government to take various unilateral actions to protest other countries' trade, intellectual property or investment policies. In 1999, the EU challenged Section 301 in the WTO. According to the EU, Section 301 violated the WTO Dispute Settlement Understanding (DSU) because it required the US Trade Representative to make determinations of WTO-inconsistency prior to the completion of the relevant WTO dispute settlement proceedings. The WTO panel found that while the US statute appeared on its face to violate the DSU, it was not inconsistent with the DSU given certain formal US undertakings to act under Section 301 consistently with the rules of the DSU. Both the EU and the US claimed victory and neither appealed. From the standpoint of the EU, it would be difficult in the future for the US to act inconsistently with the undertakings relied upon by the panel and thus difficult for the US to act unilaterally.

US Foreign Sales Corporations. In February 2000, the EU successfully established in WTO dispute settlement that the tax treatment given by the US to so-called foreign sales corporations was a prohibited export subsidy. The US subsequently changed the law in question in November 2000, but the EU maintained that the new legislation still provided an export subsidy and the matter was referred back to WTO dispute settlement where a decision in favor of the EU was adopted early in 2002. The EU was subsequently authorized to take retaliatory measures in an amount of $4 billion, which far exceeds the amount of the retaliatory measures taken against the EU by the US in *Bananas* and *Hormones*. The EU chose to phase in the retaliation gradually and Congress ultimately changed the US rules (twice) in order to meet EU objections.

PART 6

FREE MOVEMENT OF CAPITAL AND ECONOMIC AND MONETARY UNION

■ ■ ■

Free movement of capital is an essential prerequisite for achieving the internal market and a necessary precondition for Economic and Monetary Union (EMU). Although free movement of capital was one of the four freedoms in the initial EEC Treaty, progress towards its attainment was limited until 1988. Chapter 30 describes the initial developments, the 1988 liberalization directive, the Maastricht Treaty provisions that firmly established free movement of capital, and recent Court case law.

Linked to free movement of capital is the goal of an integrated financial market. Chapter 30 also describes the essential legal principles of EU law in this sector, together with a survey of the legislation and case law intended to achieve banking and securities law harmonization.

In recent years, no political and legal development in the European Union has been more important than the creation of the Economic and Monetary Union. Building upon proposals made by Commission President Jacques Delors and national central bank governors, the Treaty of Maastricht introduced Monetary Union as a primary treaty goal in 1993. By 1998, twelve Member States achieved the economic and monetary criteria set to enable the creation of the European Central Bank (ECB).

Chapter 31 reviews the planning for Monetary Union and the economic criteria necessary for States to join in it, and then describes the structure, role and policy goals of the ECB. The chapter next reviews the launch of the Euro as a single currency for the Euro-zone States, now numbering sixteen. The final section indicates the current status of Monetary Union and the changes brought by the Lisbon Treaty.

CHAPTER 30

FREE MOVEMENT OF CAPITAL AND THE INTEGRATED FINANCIAL MARKET

■ ■ ■

Free movement of capital is a vital accessory to the other three basic freedoms. Free movement of goods is impeded if payment for the goods is restricted. Free movement of workers is limited if workers cannot bring funds from the home State or if their income and savings cannot be freely transferred back to the home State. The right of establishment for commercial and financial enterprises and the right to provide cross-border services are substantially frustrated by significant restrictions on capital movements. Moreover, free movement of capital is essential to achieve an integrated financial market in which banking, securities, insurance, and other financial enterprises can operate without hindrance throughout the Community. Likewise, free movement of capital is an indispensable precondition for Monetary Union, because centralized monetary control by the European Central Bank would be ineffectual if Member States could regulate capital movements.

This chapter will first indicate in section A the limited progress toward free movement of capital until the end of the 1980's. Section B then describes the Maastricht Treaty provisions mandating free movement, with limited exceptions for important public interests, together with the Court case law reviewing State rules that are indirect limitations on free movement of capital or limit capital movements based upon alleged important interests. We will present in section C the Union goal of an integrated financial market, describing the key legislation and Court judgements in the sector of banking law, and a brief survey of securities law. The next chapter, devoted to Economic and Monetary Union, will cover the link between free movement of capital and EMU.

A. INITIAL DEVELOPMENTS

1. EEC TREATY PROVISIONS AND LEGISLATION

In post-World War II Europe, nations followed radically different policies on the restriction of capital movements. Germany, the Netherlands and the Scandinavian states generally followed a philosophy of monetary liberalism, allowing capital to flow freely across their frontiers. France, Greece, Italy, Portugal and Spain imposed restrictive regulations on many types of capital movements. Other states, like the UK, used regulations to restrict capital movements only in times of monetary crisis.

Restrictions on capital movements are commonly called exchange and investment controls. They serve several distinct functions, among them, restriction on capital outflows (especially in a monetary crisis), limitation on the import or export of certain goods or services in accordance with foreign trade policy, and restriction on all or certain types of foreign investment in pursuit of national economic, security, or industrial development policies. Depending on the policy goal, exchange and investment controls restrict a variety of transactions, for example, the transfer of currency (especially in large amounts), payment for certain types of imports or exports, foreign-source borrowing or lending, the purchase or sale of realty, the purchase or sale of securities, the transfer abroad of royalties on intellectual property rights, and the inward or outward flow of investment capital and repatriation of the proceeds of investment.

The initial 1957 European Economic Community Treaty devoted a chapter to the progressive liberalization of capital movements. The core provision was Article 67(1) (now deleted):

> During the transitional period [i.e., before Dec. 31, 1969] and to the extent necessary to ensure the proper functioning of the common market, Member States shall progressively abolish between themselves all restrictions on the movement of capital belonging to persons resident in Member States and any discrimination based on the nationality or on the place of residence of the parties or on the place where such capital is invested.

The initial EECT Article 69 (now deleted) authorized the Council to issue directives to implement Article 67 by a qualified majority vote. Article 73 (now deleted), permitted "protective measures in the field of capital movements." The Commission was given the power to authorize a State to take protective measures at a time of "disturbances in the functioning of the capital market." In case of urgency, a Member State could act itself, subject to review by the Commission.

An initial EECT Article 106 (now deleted) required Member States to authorize payments for the trans-border movements of goods and services. Such "current payments" represent a form of capital movement, but are less apt to be restricted than long-term capital movements. The obligation to allow such current payments was designed to proceed in tandem with the liberalization of the movement of goods, services and persons as each would be achieved pursuant to the Treaty.

The EEC made substantial progress toward free movement of capital in its initial years. Indeed, this was one of the most significant achievements of the early common market. To implement Article 67, the Council adopted the First Directive 921/60, O.J. English Spec.Ed.1960, at 49, which was amended to achieve a greater degree of liberalization by the Second Directive 63/21, O.J. English Spec.Ed. 1963–64, at 5.

The First and Second Directives freed most common commercial and private movements of capital from any form of exchange control. Among the movements thus freed were most direct investments or disinvestments of a commercial character; investments in real estate; personal capital movements, such as gifts, transfers on inheritance or transfers when a person changes residence from one Member State to another; the transfer of insurance premiums and payments; short and medium term loans related to commercial transactions or services; and the purchase or sale of securities on stock exchanges anywhere in the Community. However, States were not required to liberalize many important types of capital movements, notably most common banking or finance transactions, such as the placing of funds in current or long-term deposit accounts, and non-commercial loans and credits.

Unfortunately, the initial progress was not maintained. Many Member States entered a period of monetary instability in the 1970s, which was exacerbated by the energy recession. In addition, Greece, Portugal and Spain had exchange control regulations which the respective treaties of accession allowed them to maintain. France, Italy and other States took advantage of the safeguard measures allowed by EECT Article 73 and the Commission almost routinely authorized the measures until the late 1980s. Thus, national exchange control systems represented a far more serious barrier to the free movement of capital in the 1970s and 80s than they did in the 1960s.

NOTES AND QUESTIONS

1. Why do some nations rely upon exchange controls as a means to protect monetary stability while others do not? Is the difference chiefly a reflection of varying levels of economic strength? Or is it primarily based on different policy views as to the degree to which governments should intervene in monetary affairs? Do you think exchange controls are ever economically justified?

2. Many states use direct investment controls as a means to prevent or restrict foreign investment in agriculture or industry. Do you think that investment controls represent sound policy when applied to sensitive industries, such as defense procurement, utilities and transport? When applied to high technology industries? When applied to any other form of industry or agriculture? Or do you regard investment controls as merely a protectionist device? Note that since 1988, pursuant to the Exon–Florio amendment to the omnibus trade act, 50 U.S.C.A. § 2170, the US also restricts foreign investment in sensitive industries. Thus, in the mid–1990s, Thomson–Brandt, majority owned by the French government, protested the US government's refusal to let it buy a US aerospace defense contractor.

2. EARLY CASE LAW OF THE COURT OF JUSTICE

After the Court had held that so many other Treaty articles had direct effect, it was inevitable that this issue would be raised concerning EECT Article 67. In Criminal proceedings against Casati, Case 203/80, [1981] ECR 2595, Casati, an Italian national resident in Germany, was prosecuted for violation of Italian exchange controls when he attempted to take out of Italy large sums of Lira, the Italian currency. Casati claimed that the then Article 67 should have direct effect, negating the Italian exchange controls.

In its judgement, the Court declined to give Article 67 direct effect, concluding that the clause, "to the extent necessary to ensure the proper functioning of the Common Market," conditioned the goal of free movement of capital, and necessarily implied that Council legislation was necessary in order to achieve free movement. The Court emphasized the economic sensitivity of regulations of capital movements.

Subsequently, in Luisi and Carbone v. Ministero del Tresoro, Cases 286/82 & 26/83, [1984] ECR 377, the Court did strike down one feature of Italian exchange control regulations. An Italian decree forbid Italian residents to take out of Italy more than small stated amounts of Lira. When prosecuted for violating the decree, Luisi claimed that he intended to pay for medical treatment in Germany, and Carbone contended that he wanted to cover his expenses during three months of tourism in Germany. The Court observed that the export of currency to pay for medical or touristic services represented a current payment, covered by the then EECT Article 106. The Court concluded that free movement of currency for current payments for services had to be permitted, because free movement of services was guaranteed with direct effect after December 31, 1969. However, the Court noted that Italy retained a right to verify whether its currency was taken out of its borders genuinely for use to pay for services, or constituted a disguised transfer of capital.

Although *Luisi and Carbone* had only a limited impact, the judgement was certainly popular with business travelers, students and tourists who had previously been restricted in the duration and nature of their travel due to the limits set by Italian, French, and other exchange controls on the maximum amount of the currency they were permitted to take abroad. As we observed in Chapter 17D, the Court's holding that Community nationals have a right to receive services in other States, as well as to perform them there, has proved to be a seminal judgment.

B. SUCCESS IN ACHIEVING FREE MOVEMENT OF CAPITAL

1. THE 1988 DIRECTIVE: LEGISLATIVE LIBERALIZATION

The Commission's 1985 White Paper on Completing the Internal Market, urged greater liberalization of capital movements, but did not call for the removal of all exchange controls. As the internal market program moved forward, however, the Commission concluded that the time was ripe to propose an end to exchange controls. The adoption of Directive 88/361 to implement EECT Article 67 testifies to the strength of the Member States' commitment to the internal market goal. The adoption of such a far-reaching measure became possible only because the States viewed it as indispensable to an integrated financial market.

The 1988 directive mandated the abolition of virtually all restrictions on capital movements by July 1, 1990. Under article 4, Member States were allowed to verify the nature of capital movements for statistical purposes and to adopt measures to prevent violations of their taxation laws or rules applicable in the supervision of financial institutions. Although some consideration had been given to eliminating any possibility of safeguard measures, article 3 continued to permit the States to adopt them, but under more stringent conditions than in the past.

France, Italy and Spain rapidly implemented the directive and ended their exchange control systems. This was a dramatic development, since their systems dated to the 1950s. Greece, Ireland and Portugal ended their restrictions on capital movements in the early 1990s. Finland and Sweden accepted free movement of capital immediately upon accession in 1995. However, Austria received a derogation to retain its regulation limiting foreign ownership of secondary residences for five years after accession and several Central European and Mediterranean States received similar derogations for their restrictions on foreign ownership of land for agricultural use or secondary residences for up to seven years after accession.

The 1988 directive was crucial to the success of an integrated financial market because it permitted the free transfer of capital for any purpose. In particular, it permitted cross-border banking and other credit operations, which were not liberalized by the First and Second Directives. Also, the 1988 directive contributed strongly to the sense of Community citizenship, because individuals and enterprises could transfer their funds freely throughout the Community.

2. THE MAASTRICHT TREATY MANDATES FREE MOVEMENT OF CAPITAL

The Maastricht Treaty deleted the entire initial Treaty chapter on capital and replaced it with an express ban on restrictions upon capital movements, effective on Jan. 1, 1994, with very limited exceptions. The new text was intended to provide a Treaty-based assurance that free movement of capital would be ensured in the progressive evolution of EMU.

ECT Article 56 (initially EECT Article 73b, and now TFEU Article 63) prohibits "all restrictions on the movement of capital," as well as all restrictions on current payments, not only between Member States, but also between States and third countries. However, ECT Article 57 grants an exception for pre–1994 restrictions, under either national or Community law, upon capital coming from third states for use in direct investment and in the sectors of real estate, financial services, and securities markets.

More important is ECT Article 58 (now TFEU Article 65), which permits Member States to take measures that restrict capital or payment movements for the purpose of preventing "infringements of national law," especially in the sensitive sectors of taxation and supervision of financial institutions. The article also permits measures based upon public policy or public security (presumably to control terrorism, drug traffic or other serious crimes).

NOTES AND QUESTIONS

1. Recall that article 3 of the 1988 directive permitted Member States to adopt emergency safeguard restrictions on capital movements. Was this directive provision still valid after 1994, when ECT Article 56 became effective? On November 24, 1992, the Commission informed the Council of its view that the safeguard provisions of article 3 of the 1988 directive would become redundant after Article 56 became effective, but that no amendment need be undertaken.

2. ECT Article 57 (now TFEU Article 64) permitted Member States to retain pre–1994 measures restricting direct investment from third countries. Such restrictions are common for certain sensitive industries, such as defense contracting or the media. Some States have also occasionally restricted direct investment from abroad in high technology industries. The article is the sort of Treaty provision which raises concern about "fortress Europe." Do you think such concerns are justified? Remember that the US has analogous restrictions on foreign investment. Moreover, an OECD study in 2003 concluded that the EU Member States had far lower barriers to foreign investment than the US, Canada and other industrialized nations.

3. COURT JUDGMENTS CONCERNING FREE MOVEMENT OF CAPITAL

Should ECT Articles 56 and 58 have direct effect? How broad or narrow are the Article 58 exceptions for Member State measures to prevent infringements of national law? When do State measures indirectly restrict capital movements? The Court has had to address each of these issues. Note that there is no reason to believe that the Court's case law in the following judgments has been affected by the replacement of ECT Articles 56–58 by TFEU Articles 63–65.

SVENSSON v. MINISTRE DU LOGEMENT

Case C–484/93, [1995] ECR I–3955.

[A married Swedish couple, residing in Luxembourg, borrowed from a Belgian bank in order to finance the construction of their house in Luxembourg. When they applied in 1991 for an interest rate subsidy from the Luxembourg authorities, they were turned down, because the subsidy was only provided for housing loans made by Luxembourg credit institutions. When they sued to demand the subsidy, the Luxembourg court asked whether the Luxembourg rule violated the Treaty rules on free movement of capital. At the time of the refusal of the subsidy, Directive 88/361 had become effective. The Court noted that Directive 88/361 clearly prohibited State restrictions on inter-state financial loans and credits.]

10   Provisions implying that a bank must be established in a Member State in order for recipients of loans residing in its territory to obtain an interest rate subsidy from the State out of public funds are liable to dissuade those concerned from approaching banks established in another Member State and therefore constitute an obstacle to movements of capital such as bank loans.

11   It should also be noted that by virtue of Article [51(2)] of the Treaty "the liberalization of banking and insurance services connected with movements of capital shall be effected in step with the progressive liberalization of movement of capital". Since transactions such as building loans provided by banks constitute services within the meaning of Article [49] of the Treaty, it is also necessary to ascertain whether the rule referred to by the national court is compatible with the Treaty provisions on freedom to provide services.

12   [A] rule which makes the grant of interest rate subsidies subject to the requirement that the loans have been obtained from an establishment approved in the Member State in question constitutes discrimination against credit institutions established in other Member States, which is prohibited by the first paragraph of Article [49] of the Treaty.

[The Court rejected Luxembourg's contention that the housing subsidies constitute nearly 1% of its annual budget, so that paying the subsidy to persons who financed their housing purchases from institutions that did not pay taxes to Luxembourg would represent a serious cost. The Court held that a State's purely economic considerations did not qualify for a public policy exception.]

CRIMINAL PROCEEDINGS AGAINST SANZ DE LERA

Cases C–163/94, 165/94 and 250/94, [1995] ECR I–4821.

[Several Spanish and Turkish defendants were prosecuted for attempting to take over 5 million Pesetas each (ca. 35,000 dollars) to Switzerland and Turkey, respectively, without the prior authorization required for the export of banknotes under a 1991 Spanish decree. The Spanish court sought guidance from the Court of Justice on whether either a prior authorization or a prior declaration before the export of banknotes to a non-Community state was consonant with the new Maastricht Treaty capital provisions.]

22   [T]he measures which are necessary to prevent the commission of certain infringements and are permitted by Article 4(1) of [Directive 88/361], in particular those designed to ensure effective fiscal supervision and to prevent illegal activities such as tax evasion, money laundering, drug trafficking or terrorism, are also covered by Article [58(1)].

23   It is therefore necessary to consider whether the requirement of an authorization or a prior declaration for the export of coins, banknotes or bearer cheques is necessary in order to uphold the objectives pursued and whether those objectives might be attained by measures less restrictive of the free movement of capital.

24   [A]uthorization has the effect of suspending currency exports and makes them conditional in each case upon the consent of the administrative authorities, which must be sought by means of a special application.

25   The effect of such a requirement is to cause the exercise of the free movement of capital to be subject to the discretion of the administrative authorities and thus be such as to render that freedom illusory [citing *Luisi and Carbone, supra*].

26   However, the restriction on the free movement of capital resulting from that requirement could be eliminated without thereby detracting from the effective pursuit of the aims of those rules.

27   As the Commission has rightly pointed out, it would be sufficient to set up an adequate system of declarations indicating the nature of the planned operation and the identity of the declarant, which would require the competent authorities to proceed with a rapid examination of the declaration and enable them, if necessary, to carry out in due time the investigations found to be necessary to determine whether capital was being unlawfully transferred and to impose the requisite penalties if national legislation was being contravened.

28   Thus, unlike prior authorization, such a system of declarations would not suspend the operation concerned but would nevertheless enable the national authorities to carry out, in order to uphold public policy, effective supervision to prevent infringements of national law and regulations.

29   As regards the Spanish Government's argument that only a system of authorization makes it possible to establish that a criminal offence has been committed and impose penalties under criminal law, such considerations cannot justify the maintenance of measures which are incompatible with Community law.

30   It follows that Articles [56(1) and 58(1)] of the Treaty preclude rules which make the export of coins, banknotes or bearer cheques condi-

tional on prior authorization but do not by contrast preclude a transaction of that nature being made conditional on a prior declaration.

[The Court then held, not surprisingly, that Articles 56(1) and 58(1)(b) had direct effect.]

NOTES AND QUESTIONS

1. *In Svensson* the Court had no difficulty in concluding in ¶ 10 that denial of an interest rate subsidy to persons securing mortgage loans outside of Luxembourg constituted an indirect restriction upon free movement of capital. In the remainder of the judgement, the Court's analyzed Luxembourg's attempt to justify its violation of the plaintiff's rights to receive trans-border financial services. *Svensson* is an important precedent with regard to the conduct of any type of trans-border financial services, not just banking. *Svensson* makes obvious that trans-border financial services can no longer be limited by any form of capital restriction, except to prevent violations of national tax and prudential supervision rules, or to achieve a public interest exception. For a useful discussion of *Svensson*'s implications, see the casenote by V. Hatzopoulos, 33 Common Mkt. L. Rev. 569 (1996).

2. What is the significance of the Court's conclusion in *Sanz de Lera* that the principal substantive provisions of ECT Articles 56 and 58 have direct effect? Does Directive 88/361 serve any useful purpose after the Court's ruling? Undoubtedly, the substantive provisions of TFEU Articles 63 and 65 likewise have direct effect, because they replicate ECT Articles 56 and 58.

3. The principal importance of *Sanz de Lera* lies in the Court's broad reading of Article 56 and its unwillingness to allow Spain to require any form of prior authorization system before the export of banknotes. Obviously, this is a sensitive sector, since unregulated export of banknotes can exacerbate the already serious problem of money-laundering for terrorism, drug traffic, etc. Do you agree with the Court that a prior declaration system will serve just as well? For a useful review, see the casenote by F. Castillo de la Torre, 33 Common Mkt. L. Rev. 1065 (1996).

ASSOCIATION EGLISE DE SCIENTOLOGIE DE PARIS v. THE PRIME MINISTER

Case C–54/99, [2000] ECR I–1335.

[A 1989 French decree forbids all foreigners from making certain direct investments unless the Minister for the Economy has granted a prior authorization. A 1996 law stipulates that foreign investments which "represent a threat to public policy, public health or public security," or which are made in the research, production or trade in arms or munitions, require such a prior authorization. The Paris Church of Scientology sued to set aside these rules as violations of the free movement of capital. In an ECT Article 234 proceeding, the French Supreme Administrative Court inquired whether the French rules were permitted by the exceptions in ECT Article 58.]

17   [W]hile Member States are still, in principle, free to determine the requirements of public policy and public security in the light of their national needs, those grounds must, in the Community context and as derogations from the fundamental principle of free movement of capital, be interpreted strictly, so that their scope cannot be determined unilaterally by each Member State without any control by the Community institutions. Thus, public policy and public security may be relied on only if there is a genuine and sufficiently serious threat to a fundamental interest of society [citing *Rutili* ¶ 28, supra page 591]. Moreover, those derogations must not be misapplied so as, in fact, to serve purely economic ends (to this effect, see *Rutili*, ¶ 30). Further, any person affected by a restrictive measure based on such a derogation must have access to legal redress.

18   Second, measures which restrict the free movement of capital may be justified on public-policy and public-security grounds only if they are necessary for the protection of the interests which they are intended to guarantee and only in so far as those objectives cannot be attained by less restrictive measures (see, to this effect *Sanz de Lera*).

19   However, although the Court has held * * * that systems of prior authorisation were not, in the circumstances particular to [the export of currency in *Sanz de Lera*, supra], necessary in order to enable the national authorities to carry out checks designed to prevent infringements of their laws and regulations * * *, it has not held that a system of prior authorisation can never be justified, particularly where such authorisation is in fact necessary for the protection of public policy or public security.

20   In the case of direct foreign investments, the difficulty in identifying and blocking capital once it has entered a Member State may make it necessary to prevent, at the outset, transactions which would adversely affect public policy or public security. It follows that, in the case of direct foreign investments which constitute a genuine and sufficiently serious threat to public policy and public security, a system of prior declaration may prove to be inadequate to counter such a threat.

21   In the present case, however, * * * prior authorisation is required for every direct foreign investment which is 'such as to represent a threat to public policy [and] public security,' without any more detailed definition. Thus, the investors concerned are given no indication whatever as to the specific circumstances in which prior authorisation is required.

22   Such lack of precision does not enable individuals to be appraised of the extent of their rights and obligations deriving from Article [56] of the Treaty. That being so, the system established is contrary to the principle of legal certainty.

23   [Accordingly,] Article [58(1)(b)] of the Treaty must be interpreted as precluding a system of prior authorisation for direct foreign investments which confines itself to defining in general terms the affected

investments as being investments that are such as to represent a threat to public policy and public security, with the result that the persons concerned are unable to ascertain the specific circumstances in which prior authorisation is required.

IN RE ALBORE

Case C–423/98, [2000] ECR I–5965.

[Albore, an Italian notary, sued to compel the Naples Property Registry to record the sale to a German national of real property situated on the island of Ischia. A 1976 Italian law forbids the sale of real property to non-nationals when located in zones "designated as being of military importance by decree of the Minister for Defence." Ischia is such a zone. The Naples Court of Appeal asked the Court of Justice whether the Italian law qualified as an Article 58 exception.]

18   Although no justification is mentioned in the order for reference * * *, it is clear from the objective of the legislation at issue that the contested measure may be regarded as having been adopted in relation to public security, a concept which, within the meaning of the Treaty, includes the external security of a Member State.

19   However, the requirements of public security cannot justify derogations from the Treaty rules such as the freedom of capital movements unless the principle of proportionality is observed, which means that any derogation must remain within the limits of what is appropriate and necessary for achieving the aim in view.

20   Furthermore, under [Article 58(3)], such requirements may not be relied on to justify measures constituting a means of arbitrary discrimination or a disguised restriction on the free movement of capital.

21   In that regard, a mere reference to the requirements of defense of the national territory * * * cannot suffice to justify discrimination on grounds of nationality against nationals of other Member States regarding access to immovable property on all or part of the national territory of the first State.

22   The position would be different only if it were demonstrated, for each area to which the restriction applies, that non-discriminatory treatment of the nationals of all the Member States would expose the military interests of the Member State concerned to real, specific and serious risks which could not be countered by less restrictive procedures.

23   In the absence of any evidence enabling the Court to examine whether the existence of such circumstances might be demonstrated in relation to the island of Ischia, it is for the national court to decide, in the case before it, whether or not there is sufficient justification within the meaning of the foregoing paragraph.

NOTES AND QUESTIONS

1. As noted previously, many (perhaps all) Member States continue to restrict or totally forbid foreign capital investments in sectors considered to affect public security, especially defense, as well as other sensitive sectors which are deemed vital for public policy reasons, such as the media or energy. In *Paris Church of Scientology*, the French rules were obviously intended to give the government a wide power of discretion in identifying and restricting sensitive foreign investments. (Note that the US Department of Commerce regulations on foreign direct investment are equally vague in specifying the sectors involved.) Do you agree with the Court conclusion that the French restrictions are simply too indefinite? How easy will it be for the government to be more precise and detailed, and what risks would that involve? Do you think the French requirement of authorization before investment in the arms and munition field is definite enough to qualify for the Article 58 exception? Note finally how the Court has brought to its interpretation of Article 58 the doctrine limiting the concepts of public policy and public security first enunciated in *Rutili* with regard to the same exceptions to free movement of workers. Is that sensible?

2. Although Ischia, like its more famous neighbor, Capri, is renowned as a holiday resort, Italy presumably felt that its coastal islands have a strategic national defense importance. In view of the Court's "real, specific and serious risks" standard in evaluating whether public security rules may appropriately limit capital investment in real estate, do you think the Naples court in *Albore* will now register, or not, the sale of realty to a German buyer? Could the Italian law be properly invoked to forbid the sale of realty immediately adjacent to a military airfield? A civil airfield? Realty located 30 miles from an airfield?

3. In Minister voor Wonen v. Woningstichting Sint Servatius, Case C–567/07, [2009] ECR I–__ (Oct. 1, 2009), the issue referred to the Court was whether the free movement of capital was violated when the Dutch public housing authorities forbid a Dutch foundation, created to fund public housing, to finance a housing project in Belgium. The Court held that a State may legitimately require institutions created to finance "the accommodation needs" in the Netherlands to obtain a prior authorization before financing projects elsewhere (¶¶ 33–34). However, the Court added that the authorization system must be "based on objective, non-discriminatory criteria known in advance," so as to properly limit the authorities' discretion and permit judicial review (¶¶ 35–39).

4. An 1871 Austrian law governing real estate mortgages required that the Land Register could only record mortgages denominated in Austrian schillings, but did not forbid mortgage loans denominated in foreign currencies as such. In an Article 234 reference proceeding, the Court of Justice held that the ban on recording a mortgage in a foreign currency would reduce the effectiveness of a foreign currency mortgage and hence constituted an indirect restriction on the free movement of capital (¶¶ 26–28). In re Trummer and Mayer, Case C–222/97, [1999] ECR I–1661.

NOTE ON RESTRICTIONS ON LAND OWNERSHIP

Several European countries seek to limit or prohibit the ownership of secondary residences (e.g., holiday or part time retirement homes) by non-resident foreign nationals. Denmark obtained a Protocol to the Treaty of Maastricht enabling it to retain its restrictions of that sort. We noted previously that several Central European and Mediterranean States obtained derogations enabling them to keep restrictions on foreign ownership of agricultural land and secondary residences for up to seven years after accession. Austria obtained an accession treaty derogation for five years for its restrictions on foreign ownership of land for secondary residences. Several court judgments have not only interpreted the scope of the derogation, but indicate the nature of public interests that may justify land use regulation.

In Konle v. Austria, Case C–302/97, [1999] ECR I–3099, the Court of Justice held that Austria's 1996 law on secondary residences was significantly different from the law in effect at the time of its accession in 1995, and therefore was not protected by the derogation stipulated in the accession treaty. The 1996 law required a prior authorization before the purchase of land in Tyrol and generally forbid a purchase for use as a secondary residence. Although the Court accepted that regulation requiring prior authorization before a purchase of land could be justified on public interest grounds, in order to preserve "a permanent population and an economic activity independent of the tourist sector in certain regions," the Court then held that a prior authorization regulation can be accepted "only if it is not applied in a discriminatory manner and if the same result cannot be achieved by other less restrictive procedures" (¶ 40). The Court ultimately concluded that the Austrian authorization procedure gave too great a discretionary latitude to the officials, which in practice had a discriminatory impact on non-nationals, and hence constituted an indirect limit on free movement of capital in violation of Article 56.

Subsequently, in Salzmann v. Austria, Case C–300/01, [2003] ECR I–4899, the issue presented was whether the local authorities could require prior authorization under land use planning rules before a house was constructed as a permanent residence, not a part-time holiday dwelling. In that context the Court held that a prior authorization regulation would be disproportionate to the protection of the public interest, because a regulation requiring only a prior declaration to the authorities which could be verified during construction, supplemented by adequate "pecuniary sanctions" and the possibility that the contract of sale could be annulled, would adequately serve to enforce the land use rules (¶¶ 51–52).

A later judgment considered whether land use regulation could be used to protect agricultural land.

OSPELT v. AUSTRIA

Case C–452/01, [2003] ECR I–9743.

[A Liechtenstein national who owned a castle in Austria, together with land leased to farmers, sought to transfer the land to a foundation, which intended to continue the policy of leasing the land to farmers. Austrian authorities refused to permit the sale, applying a regional law intended to "preserve agricultural and forestry plots of family farming." When the trial court referred questions concerning the compatibility of the rules with free movement of capital, the Court of Justice first held that the capital provisions of the EEA Treaty, to which Liechtenstein is a party, replicated those of ECT Articles 56–58.

The Court then reached the important conclusion that national or regional rules protecting the ownership of agricultural land, if applied without discrimination based on nationality, pursued a public interest objective sufficient to limit the free movement of capital (¶ 38).]

39 [P]reserving agricultural communities, maintaining a distribution of land ownership which allows the development of viable farms and sympathetic management of green spaces and the countryside as well as encouraging a reasonable use of the available land by resisting pressure on land, and preventing natural disasters are social objectives.

* * *

43 Indeed, the objective of sustaining and developing viable agriculture on the basis of social and land planning considerations entails keeping land intended for agriculture in such use and continuing to make use of it under appropriate conditions. In that context, prior supervision by the competent authorities does not merely reflect a need for information but is intended to ensure that the transfer of agricultural land will not lead to their ceasing to be used as intended or to a use which might be incompatible with their long-term agricultural use.

[The Court, however, finally concluded that the Austrian rule intended to protect agricultural land violated the principle of proportionality when used to forbid the land transfer to the foundation, because the foundation's express intent to retain the system of leased farms would not reduce land used for agricultural purposes, and actually benefitted farmers who did not "have the resources to own the land" (¶ 51).]

NOTES AND QUESTIONS

1. Regional and local land use rules intended to retain the agricultural or forestry character of land are common in many States. The Court's holding in *Ospelt* that such rules serve a legitimate public interest that can limit the free movement of capital accordingly has considerable consequence. After the various accession treaty derogations expire, the Member States that currently enjoy them can rely on *Ospelt* to maintain non-discriminatory and proportionate land use rules.

2. In Criminal Proceedings against Festersen, Case C–370/05, [2007] ECR I–1129, a Danish law sought to protect agricultural land by requiring any new owner of a farm to reside there for eight years. When Festersen, a German buyer of a farm, was convicted for violating the residence requirement, the appellate court inquired whether the residence obligation violated Article 56. Citing *Ospelt*, the Court held that protection of agricultural land did constitute a public interest that might limit free movement of capital (¶ 28), and accepted that a residence obligation was likely to preserve "an agricultural community" (¶ 31). However, the Court noted that a residence requirement did not guarantee that a resident owner would in fact choose to farm the land (¶ 30). Moreover, the Court observed that a person's right to choose freely his place of residence constituted a fundamental human right (¶ 35). Accordingly, the Danish restriction had to be proportionately applied. The Court concluded that Denmark had failed to prove that more appropriate and less restrictive measures could not be found to protect agricultural land (¶¶ 39–41).

4. LIMITS ON PRIVATIZED ENTITIES THROUGH GOLDEN SHARES

When Member States began to privatize many state-owned companies during the 1980s, in many cases they adopted special rules intended to enable the government to continue to wield veto powers either against any transfer of control of the privatized companies to new owners, or against sales of substantial assets, or against changes in managerial operational policies. Sometimes these rules were embodied in administrative regulations, such as an obligation for the company to obtain prior authorization from a cabinet minister, but they were often also embodied in provisions of the company's articles of incorporation, which frequently gave the government a share with extraordinary voting or veto rights. This latter device gave use to the popular term, 'golden shares.'

In 1997, the Commission issued a communication concerning intra-EU investments, O.J. L C–220/15 (July 19, 1997), that surveyed a variety of these governmental devices to retain some measure of control, concluded that many were not justified by public interest objectives, and indicated that it would bring actions for infringement against States for unjustified rules. The Commission began a series of such Treaty infringement proceedings in 1998, culminating in three landmark judgments on June 4, 2002.

In Commission v. Portugal (Golden shares), Case C–367/98, [2002] ECR I–4731, the Court easily concluded that a 1990 Portuguese law governing privatization of banks violated Article 56 because it required a government authorization before foreign ownership could exceed 25% of the capital of the privatized companies, a manifest example of discrimination based on nationality (¶ 40). The Court also held that Portugal's requirement of prior authorization for any acquisition of shares in excess of 10% likewise violated Article 56, even though not discriminating on the basis of nationality, because this was not justified by any public interest (other than an alleged financial interest of Portugal—an economic interest never permitted by the Court) (¶¶ 49–53).

When France privatized the large oil company, Elf–Aquitaine, it retained a 'golden share' with the right to approve any shareholding by a person or company that exceeds 10%, 20%, or one-third of all shares, as well as any proposed sale or mortgage of major corporate assets. These government rights were challenged in Commission v. France (Golden shares), Case C–483/99, [2002] ECR I–4781.

Although the Court recognized that "overriding requirements of the general interest" could justify limits on the free movement of capital (¶ 45,) and that "the safeguarding of supplies of petroleum products in the event of a crisis" could be classified as a "legitimate public interest" (¶ 47, citing *Campus Oil*, page ___ supra), the Court concluded that the French rules lacked any "indication whatever as to the specific objective circumstances in which prior authorization will be granted or refused" and accordingly violated "the principle of legal certainty" (¶ 50) and were disproportionate to their aim (¶ 51).

In the Commission's third proceeding, against Belgium, the Court set standards for State post-privatization controls that were permissible.

COMMISSION v. BELGIUM

(Golden shares)
Case C–503/99, [2002] ECR I–4809.

[By 1994 decrees, Belgium retained certain 'golden share' control rights concerning privatized gas distribution and pipeline companies. Notably, the Minister for Energy could appoint two non-voting members of the boards of directors, who could propose to the Minister the annulment of board decisions considered to be contrary to Belgium's stated energy policies. The companies also had to give advance notice of any sale or mortgage of their "strategic assets" to the Minister, who could exercise a veto power. The 1994 decrees required the Minister to act within short time periods and permitted the companies to appeal to the Minister's decision to the Belgium supreme administrative court. The Court of Justice commenced its analysis by repeating the conclusion that securing supplies of natural gas and other energy sources constituted a public security interest.]

47   However, the Court has also held that the requirements of public security, as a derogation from the fundamental principle of free movement of capital, must be interpreted strictly, so that their scope cannot be determined unilaterally by each Member State without any control by the Community institutions. Thus, public security may be relied on only if there is a genuine and sufficiently serious threat to a fundamental interest of society.

48   It is necessary, therefore, to ascertain whether the legislation in issue enables the Member State concerned to ensure a minimum level of

energy supplies in the event of a genuine and serious threat, and whether or not it goes beyond what is necessary for that purpose.

49   First of all, it should be noted that the regime in issue is one of opposition. It is predicated on the principle of respect for the decision-making autonomy of the undertaking concerned, inasmuch as, in each individual case, the exercise of control by the minister responsible requires an initiative on the part of the Government authorities. No prior approval is required. Moreover, in order for that power of opposition to be exercised, the public authorities are obliged to adhere to strict time-limits.

50   Next, the regime is limited to certain decisions concerning the strategic assets of the companies in question, including in particular the energy supply networks, and to such specific management decisions relating to those assets as may be called in question in any given case.

51   Lastly, the Minister may intervene * * * only where there is a threat that the objectives of the energy policy may be compromised. Furthermore, * * * any such intervention must be supported by a formal statement of reasons and may be the subject of an effective review by the courts.

52   The scheme therefore makes it possible to guarantee, on the basis of objective criteria which are subject to judicial review, the effective availability of the lines and conduits providing the main infrastructures for the domestic conveyance of energy products, as well as other infrastructures for the domestic conveyance and storage of gas, including unloading and cross-border facilities. Thus, it enables the Member State concerned to intervene with a view to ensuring, in a given situation, compliance with the public service obligations incumbent on SNTC and Distrigaz, whilst at the same time observing the requirements of legal certainty.

1.   The Portuguese, French and Belgian golden share cases provide a useful operating primer for assessing the validity of the numerous types of government control devices for recently privatized companies. What were the features of the Belgian rules that enabled the Court to hold that they were proportionate to the protection of its public security interest? The Court's conclusions are not surprising, following its judgments in *Campus Oil* and *Scientologie*. Consider how to apply them in Commission v. Spain (Golden Shares), Case C–463/00, [2003] ECR I–4581. A 1995 Spanish law governing privatized companies requires prior authorization for a transfer of shares amounting to a certain percentage (usually 10%), or for a merger, sale of substantial assets or voluntary liquidation. The companies involved were in the petroleum, telecommunications, banking, tobacco and electricity sectors. Should any of these qualify for a public interest exception? What other conditions must the Spanish rules satisfy in order to meet the proportionality standards set by the Court in the *Belgian Golden share* judgment?

2. Should the Court recognize a concern for a functional national postal service as a public interest justifying a golden share in a privatized national postal entity? This was the issue in Commission v. The Netherlands (Golden share in postal company), Case C–282/04, [2006] ECR I–9141. Although the Court accepted that providing universal postal service throughout the State constituted a public interest, it held that the Netherland did not make its exercise of various limitations on management decisions subject to any "precise criterion," making any "effective judicial control" ineffective (¶ 40). The Netherlands had also kept a golden share in the privatized telecommunications entity, but did not try to prove it had a public interest justifying the share.

In 2007 the Volkswagen case attracted considered media attention and posed somewhat more difficult issues. In Germany, provisions in a public stock corporation's articles of incorporation may limit a shareholder's vote to a specified percent of the total share votes, usually 20%. The articles may increase the majority for extraordinary shareholder decisions (e.g., to approve mergers, dissolution) above the corporate code level of 75%. The articles may also stipulate that certain shareholders may designate up to one-third of the directors on the Supervisory Board.

COMMISSION v. GERMANY

(Volkswagen golden share structure)
Case C–112/05, [2007] ECR I–8995.

[Since 1960, a German law has governed specific aspects of Volkswagen AG's corporate structure. Currently the law provides that no shareholder may vote more than 20% of the total share vote, regardless of the shares owned, and that extraordinary shareholder decisions require an 80% majority. The law further provides that the state of Lower Saxony has the right to appoint two members of the Supervisory Board, so long as it is a shareholder, and Lower Saxony currently exercises its right. Germany has the same right, but no longer appoints directors because it has ceased to own shares. Volkswagen has a Supervisory Board of twenty directors, ten elected by shareholders and ten elected by the employees, pursuant to Germany's worker co-determination rules. The Commission brought an Article 226 proceeding to challenge the Volkswagen law as a violation of Article 56. The Court first considered the cap on share votes at 20% and the extraordinary shareholder majority level of 80%.]

39   [Although a provision of] the Law on public limited companies lays down the principle that voting rights must be proportionate to the share of capital, the second sentence thereof allows a limitation on the voting rights in certain cases.

40   However, as the Commission has correctly noted, there is a difference between a power made available to shareholders, who are free to decide whether or not they wish to use it, and a specific obligation imposed on shareholders by way of legislation, without giving them the possibility to derogate from it.

41   [Moreover, another provision] of the Law on public limited companies, as amended by the Law on the control and transparency of companies, removed the possibility of inserting a limitation on voting rights in the articles of association of listed companies. As the Commission has submitted, * * * since Volkswagen is a listed company, a ceiling on the voting rights cannot for that reason normally be inserted into its articles of association.

45   As the Federal Republic of Germany has observed, the percentage of 75% of the share capital provided for in the Law on public limited companies may be increased and fixed at a higher level by the particular company's articles of association. However, as the Commission has correctly noted, it is open to shareholders to decide whether or not to make use of that power. Conversely, the fact that the threshold of the required majority has been fixed by Paragraph 4(3) of the VW Law at more than 80% of the capital results, not from the will of the shareholders, but * * * from a national measure.

46   This requirement, derogating from general law, and imposed by way of specific legislation, thus affords any shareholder holding 20% of the share capital a blocking minority.

* * *

49   According to the information provided to the Court, while the Federal State has chosen to part with its interest in the capital of Volkswagen, the Land of Lower Saxony still retains an interest in the region of 20%.

50   Paragraph 4(3) of the VW Law thus creates an instrument enabling the Federal and State authorities to procure for themselves a blocking minority allowing them to oppose important resolutions, on the basis of a lower level of investment than would be required under general company law.

51   By capping voting rights at the same level of 20%, Paragraph 2(1) of the VW Law supplements a legal framework which enables the Federal and State authorities to exercise considerable influence on the basis of such a reduced investment.

52   By limiting the possibility for other shareholders to participate in the company with a view to establishing or maintaining lasting and direct economic links with it which would make possible effective participation in the management of that company or in its control, this situation is liable to deter direct investors from other Member States.

53   This finding cannot be undermined by the argument advanced by the Federal Republic of Germany to the effect that Volkswagen's shares are among the most highly-traded in Europe and that a large number of them are in the hands of investors from other Member States.

54   As the Commission has argued, the restrictions on the free movement of capital which form the subject-matter of these proceedings relate to

direct investments in the capital of Volkswagen, rather than portfolio investments made solely with the intention of making a financial investment and which are not relevant to the present action. As regards direct investors, it must be pointed out that, by creating an instrument liable to limit the ability of such investors to [engage in] effective participation in the management of that company or in its control, Paragraphs 2(1) and 4(3) of the VW Law diminish the interest in acquiring a stake in the capital of Volkswagen.

56   It must therefore be held that the combination of Paragraphs 2(1) and 4(3) of the VW Law constitutes a restriction on the movement of capital within the meaning of Article 56(1) EC.

[The Court then considered the power of Lower Saxony and Germany each to designate two members of the Supervisory Board.]

60   Such an entitlement constitutes a derogation from general company law, which restricts the rights of representation conferred on certain shareholders to one third of the number of the shareholders' representatives on the supervisory board. As the Commission has argued * * *, in the case of Volkswagen, the number of [directors on the Supervisory Board] who may be appointed by the Federal State and the Land of Lower Saxony may not exceed a maximum of three [out of the 10 elected by shareholders] according to general company law.

61   This right of appointment is therefore a specific right, which derogates from general company law and is laid down by a national legislative measure for the sole benefit of the Federal and State authorities.

62   The right of appointment conferred on the Federal State and the Land of Lower Saxony thus enables them to participate in a more significant manner in the activity of the supervisory board than their status as shareholders would normally allow.

65   The fact that the supervisory board, as the Federal Republic of Germany submits, is not a decision-making body, but a simple monitoring body, is not such as to undermine the position and influence of the Federal and State authorities concerned. While German company law assigns to the supervisory board the task of monitoring the company's management and of providing reports on that management to the shareholders, it confers significant powers on that body, such as the appointment and dismissal of the members of the executive board, for the purpose of performing that task. Furthermore, as the Commission has pointed out, approval by the supervisory board is necessary for a number of transactions, including, in addition to the setting-up and transfer of production facilities, the establishment of branches, the sale and purchase of land, investments and the acquisition of other undertakings.

66   By restricting the possibility for other shareholders to participate in the company with a view to establishing or maintaining lasting and direct economic links with it such as to enable them to participate

effectively in the management of that company or in its control, Paragraph 4(1) of the VW Law is liable to deter direct investors from other Member States from investing in the company's capital.

[The Court finally held that Germany had not shown why the provisions in question protected any public interest, e.g., the interests of employees or minority shareholders.]

NOTES AND QUESTIONS

1. Note that not only Germany, but many other States have corporate laws that permit similar caps on shareholder votes, extraordinary vote majorities, and designation of directors which can enable certain shareholders to control a public corporation. The Court's judgment in no way questions the validity of such corporate law devices, it only invalidates Germany's creation of a specific regime for one corporation. A company law harmonization directive could limit or eliminate these devices, but no one envisions such a directive. For a useful review of the judgment, see the casenote by W.–G. Ringe, 45 Common Mkt. L. Rev. 537 (2008). Note that most American states permit similar corporate control devices to be used to maintain control in family groups (e.g., the Ford family's ownership of shares with 50% of all votes), or as 'poison pill' arrangements to deter hostile takeovers.

2. By threatening or commencing Treaty infringement actions, the Commission has been able to induce several States to revise or abandon golden share devices in privatizing companies. Thus in 2006, Spain abandoned a number of restrictions concerning the utility Endesa during a takeover bid by Eon, a German group, after Commission protests, and France modified its proposed limits on Gaz de France to retain only a veto on the disposition of strategic assets.

C. THE INTEGRATED FINANCIAL MARKET

One of the key aspects of the internal market is the integrated financial services market. The Commission stressed this in the 1985 White Paper on Completing the Internal Market (see Chapter 14B), urging the use of the *Cassis de Dijon* approach of mutual trust and mutual recognition to facilitate cross-border provision of financial services. The Commission further urged that future harmonization be carried out on the basis of "home country control," i.e., "attributing the primary task of supervising the financial institution to the competent authorities of its Member State of origin." This would be facilitated by a "minimum harmonisation of surveillance standards," so that all State authorities would be following a comparable approach in supervision.

One of the great achievements of the White Paper program was the adoption of key harmonization directives in the banking, securities and insurance industries. Space considerations prevent coverage of insurance, but we will describe below harmonization directives in the banking and securities fields. Having largely harmonized and liberalized the rules governing its own financial sector, the Community has become the most vigorous advocate for international liberalization of financial services in the GATS negotiations within the WTO. See Chapter 29A.

Building upon the basic legislative harmonization program, in October 1998 the Commission proposed a Framework for Action in the financial services sector, followed by an action plan of May 11, 1999 containing specific proposals for policies and measures, both refinements in existing directives and totally new initiatives. A Commission White Paper on Financial Services (Dec. 5, 2006) concluded that the desired legislation had been largely attained, with policy attention now to be directed to better implementation and enforcement.

Naturally, the doctrines of the Court of Justice have contributed substantially to efforts to achieve an integrated financial marketplace. In Chapter 17B, we observed how the 1986 *German insurance* judgement set out the general good or public interest principle as the standard for evaluating whether national rules in the insurance sector (and, analogously, for all the financial fields) could be permitted even though they limit the free providing of services. That judgement also recognized consumer protection as an important public interest justifying such State regulation.

1. BASIC BANKING LAW HARMONIZATION

Efforts to harmonize national banking laws initially lagged behind harmonization in the insurance and securities sectors. However, the White Paper on Completing the Internal Market gave banking law harmonization a strong impetus, producing a series of important directives starting in 1989.

The First Directive 77/780 on credit institutions, O.J. L 322/30 (Dec. 17, 1977), represented the first step in harmonization efforts. In article 1, the directive defined a "credit institution" as an entity which receives deposits from the public and grants "credits for its own account." (Such an entity is usually called a bank.) The directive then required Member States to set up a system for the authorization and regulation of all credit institutions. Such institutions could be authorized only if they satisfied certain minimum criteria concerning their funds and management (art. 3), a provision now superseded by the Second Directive.

Interstate banking by means of branches was covered in article 4, which required host States to authorize all branches on the same basis as domestic banks. This had the effect of obliging branches to maintain minimum funds in the host State and of confining them to the financial activities permitted for host State banks. Finally, the First Directive required cooperation between home and host State authorities and created an Advisory Committee, representing the appropriate authorities in all Member States, that would assist the Commission in the banking sector.

As noted above, the White Paper called for a new approach in the financial services industry: home State control and mutual recognition.

The momentum of the White Paper program enabled the adoption of the Second Directive 89/646 on credit institutions, O.J. L 386/1 (Dec. 30, 1989), commonly called the Second Banking Directive, considered by many to be the greatest achievement in the financial services field. The Second Banking Directive, Document 28 in the Documents Supplement, is long and complicated. We present here only a brief sketch.

The Second Directive covers only credit institutions as defined in the First Directive. The Commission had proposed covering also financial lending institutions, such as those engaged in financing home mortgages or car purchases, or providing consumer credit, but the Council declined to go that far. Trans-border operations of such financial institutions continues to be governed by the Treaty rules on free movement of services and the right of establishment as applied in Court case-law.

Following the approach of the White Paper, the Second Directive enunciates three key policies: home State control of branches in other states, minimum harmonization of essential standards, and universal banking activities.

The shift from host State supervision of branches to the supervision of branches by the authorities of the State of the head office, or home State, commonly called the "single license" approach, reflects the acceptance of the mutual trust principle. Each State trusts the quality of banking supervision by the others. Article 19 details the review of a branch that home State authorities are supposed to carry out, including examinations of the adequacy of the branch's administrative structure and its financial situation. Article 19(4) does permit a host State to impose rules that serve to protect an "interest of the general good." However, article 6 bars the host State from obliging a branch of a Union-based bank to obtain an authorization and from requiring any local "endowment capital." The host State may monitor a branch's compliance with that State's own monetary policy measures (art. 14).

The Second Banking Directive harmonizes several substantive requirements for credit institutions. Each must have a minimum capital of 5 million Euro (arts. 4 and 10) and must be managed by shareholders whose identity and background is disclosed to the authorities (arts. 5 and 11). The home State authorities must carry out "prudential supervision" and ensure that credit institutions possess "sound administrative and accounting procedures and adequate internal control mechanisms" (art. 13).

The Second Banking Directive's third important feature is its authorization of "universal banking." Article 18 states that a branch may carry on in a host State any of the activities that the head office may engage in under the home State's regulations, so long as the activities are listed in the Annex to the directive. This Annex lists some activities generally recognized as appropriate for banks, such as the acceptance of deposits, making of loans, and issuance of letters of credit, travellers' checks and credit cards. However, the Annex also lists finance leasing and dealing in securities, including the handling of customers' securities accounts, trading as a broker or for the bank's own account, and participation in the issuance of shares. Previously, banks in Germany and the Netherlands were permitted to engage in the securities business, but banks in most Member States were not. Although Article 18 does not oblige host States to modify their rules to permit domestic banks to engage in underwriting or trading in securities, or any other activities that they are at present forbidden to perform, it is generally believed that competitive market pressures are apt to lead to this result.

Finally, although the principal focus of the Second Banking Directive is upon operations conducted through branches, article 18 provides that a bank may carry out any trans-border services in other States that it is authorized to perform pursuant to the Annex in its home State. As banks frequently conduct some types of trans-border service operations without the use of branches (e.g., making large commercial loans to enterprises in other States), this provision has considerable importance.

If a bank from a third country, as the US, should establish or acquire a credit institution as a subsidiary in a Member State, that entity would have to comply with all the rules of the State of establishment, but could then operate through branches anywhere in the Union on the same basis as a Member State bank. The initial Commission proposal for the Second Banking Directive would have granted rights to banks from third states only on the basis of reciprocity. US banks and the US Government vigorously protested the reciprocity provision and the text was modified to read in its present more moderate form. Article 9 only requires that Union credit institutions receive in a third state "national treatment" and "effective market access," both terms having a recognized meaning within GATT.

Although credit institutions tend to carry on business in other Member States through branches, they may also do so through subsidiaries. The Second Banking Directive does not cover subsidiaries. The consolidated supervision of a parent and its subsidiaries is achieved by Directive 83/350, O.J. L 193/18 (July 18, 1983), which makes the authorities of a parent institution's State responsible for supervising all subsidiaries (defined as entities majority-owned or controlled)—again, home State rather than host State control. If a credit institution has a shareholding of 50% or less in an entity in another State, then the home and host State authorities together decide which is to supervise the subsidiary. In 1992, the Council substantially revised the consolidated supervision directive, O.J. L 110/52 (Apr. 28, 1992), in order to prescribe more precisely the responsibilities of the supervisory authority.

In Chapter 14B, we noted that the SLIM program endeavored to codify legislation in particular fields. In March 2000, the First and Second Banking Directives, together with the consolidated supervision and several supplementary directives, were all codified in Directive 2000/12, O.J. L 126/1 (May 26, 2000). This was subsequently updated in Directive 2006/48, O.J. L 177/1 (June 30, 2006).

NOTES AND QUESTIONS

1. What is the policy promoted by the Second Banking Directive's designation of the home State authorities as responsible for supervision of branches throughout the Union? In the *German insurance* case, supra page 671, the Court of Justice stated that consumer interests might limit the right to provide financial services. Do you think that home State supervision protects sufficiently host State consumers (e.g., depositors, borrowers, clients of securities brokerage operations)? Can the home State authorities easily investigate and penalize possible misconduct by a branch? In general, do you agree with the policy decision to give the home State authorities the responsibility for supervising host State branches?

2. Some banks in Germany and the Netherlands act as insurance agents and brokers. May they do so through branches in other States? Why do you think insurance brokerage is not included on the Annex, even though the Annex lists aspects of the securities business? Do you think that the decision to allow host State branches to engage in the securities business if their home office can do so represents sound policy?

3. The *German insurance* judgment influenced the language in article 19(4) of the Second Banking Directive. What sort of limits might a host State impose on a branch to serve an "interest of the general good"? Presumably the host State may require the branch to respect its usury law limiting interest on loans, or any other rules protecting consumer interests in a proportionate manner. Might a host State successfully invoke article 19(4) to prevent a branch from dealing in securities? Might a host State require the manager of a branch to speak the host State language, or one of them?

2. COURT JUDGMENTS CONCERNING INTERSTATE BANKING

SOCIETE CIVILE IMMOBILIERE PARODI v. BANQUE H. ALBERT DE BARY

Case C–222/95, [1997] ECR I–3899.

[In 1984, Banque de Bary, a Dutch bank, lent Parodi, a French real estate company, a mortgage loan of 930,000 German Marks. De Bary never obtained an authorization from the French authorities to conduct business as a bank in France. The 1984 French law on the supervision of credit institutions was intended to implement the First Banking Directive. In 1990, Parodi sued to contest the validity of the interest upon de Bary's loan. (Apparently Parodi did not challenge its obligation to repay the loan principal.) Parodi appealed an adverse judgment to the French Supreme Court, which asked the Court of Justice whether Banque De Bary had a right to provide a mortgage loan in France under the First Banking Directive and ECT Article 49 on the right to provide services.]

[19] Even if a national rule such as the 1984 Law is not discriminatory and applies without distinction to national providers of services and to

those of other Member States, it none the less makes it more difficult for a credit institution established in another Member State and authorized by the supervisory authority of that Member State to grant a mortgage loan in France in so far as it requires that institution to obtain a fresh authorization from the supervisory authority of the State of destination. Such a national rule thus creates a restriction on the freedom to provide services.

* * *

21 [A]s a fundamental principle of the Treaty, the freedom to provide services may be limited only by rules which are justified by imperative reasons relating to the public interest and which apply to all persons or undertakings pursuing an activity in the State of destination, in so far as that interest is not protected by the rules which the person providing the services is subject in the Member State in which he is established. In particular, those requirements must be objectively necessary in order to ensure compliance with professional rules and to guarantee the protection of the recipient of services and they must not exceed what is necessary to attain those objectives [citing *Webb* and *German insurance*, supra].

* * *

26 [A]s Community law stood at the time of the facts in the main proceedings, there were within the banking sector imperative reasons relating to the public interest capable of justifying the imposition by the [host] Member State of conditions regarding access to the activity of credit institutions and their supervision which could go beyond the minimum conditions required by the first banking directive * * *.

27 It is for the national court to determine whether the French legislation contains conditions of this kind * * * and whether such conditions are in accordance with the criteria established by the case-law cited in paragraph 21 of this judgement.

28 As the Advocate General rightly notes * * *, the Court does not have information as to the exact purpose served by the authorization required by the national legislation * * *. However, the national provisions applicable in the main proceedings do not appear to be specifically designed to protect borrowers but rather to give effect to prudential rules intended to guarantee that the banks are solvent in regard to savers.

29 Furthermore, a distinction must be drawn according to the nature of the banking activity in question and of the risk incurred by the person for whom the service is intended. Thus, the conclusion of a contract for a mortgage loan presents the consumer with risks that differ from those associated with the lodging of funds with a credit institution. In this regard, the need to protect the borrower will vary according to the

nature of the mortgage loans, and there may be cases where, precisely because of the nature of the loan granted and the status of the borrower, there is no need to protect the latter by the application of the mandatory rules of his national law.

* * *

32   The reply to the question submitted must therefore be that, with regard to the period preceding the entry into force of the second banking directive, Article [49] of the Treaty must be construed as precluding a Member State from requiring a credit institution already authorized in another Member State to obtain an authorization in order to be able to grant a mortgage loan to a person resident within its territory, unless that authorization is required of every person or company pursuing such an activity within the territory of the Member State of destination; is justified on grounds of public interest, such as consumer protection; and is objectively necessary to ensure compliance with the rules applicable in the sector under consideration and to protect the interests which those rules are intended to safeguard, and the same result cannot be achieved by less restrictive rules.

NOTES AND QUESTIONS

1.   States often treat the sector of real estate housing mortgage loans as one involving serious consumer and bank solvency interests and regulate it carefully. In *Parodi*, what principles applicable to mortgage loan regulation did the Court derive from its prior case law on the freedom to provide financial services? Should an entity taking a mortgage on commercial property be considered to require consumer protection? What about housing mortgages? Article 19(4) of the Second Banking Directive permits the host State to limit branch operations on the basis of its rules protecting a "general good interest." After France implemented the Second Directive, could it rely on Article 19(4) to bar a French branch of a Dutch bank from providing either commercial or residential mortgages if the Dutch bank is authorized to do so in the Netherlands?

2.   A French law requires a group tour operator to obtain a financial guarantee from a French bank or insurance company to cover the cost of repatriation of the travelers to their homes in the event that the tour operator becomes insolvent, or otherwise incapable of covering the cost. When Ambry was prosecuted for handling a group tour arrangement with a guarantee supplied by an Italian tour company, the trial court inquired whether the French law was compatible with the Second Banking Directive and ECT Article 49. The Court held that the French law violated both (¶¶ 28–30), and could not be justified by the claim that the funds for repatriation can be obtained immediately only from a French institution, when Ambry was not given the opportunity to prove otherwise (¶¶ 32–38). See Criminal Prosecution of Ambry, Case C–410/96, [1998] ECR I–7875.

CAIXA–BANK FRANCE v. MINISTERE DE L'ECONOMIE

Case C–442/02, [2004] ECR I–8961.

[A French law forbids banks to pay interest on 'sight' accounts (usually checking or bank card accounts). When Caixa–Bank, a French subsidiary of a Spanish bank, proposed to pay 2% interest on 'sight' accounts with balances of 1500 Euros, the French authorities prohibited this. On appeal, the Supreme Administrative Court inquired whether the prohibition violated the right of establishment. The Court initially observed that the Second Banking Directive had no application, because Caixa–France was a subsidiary.]

12   A prohibition on the remuneration of sight accounts such as that laid down by the French legislation constitutes, for companies from Member States other than the French Republic, a serious obstacle to the pursuit of their activities via a subsidiary in the latter Member State, affecting their access to the market. That prohibition is therefore to be regarded as a restriction within the meaning of Article 43 EC.

13   That prohibition hinders credit institutions which are subsidiaries of foreign companies in raising capital from the public, by depriving them of the possibility of competing more effectively, by paying remuneration on sight accounts,[as compared] with the credit institutions traditionally established in the Member State of establishment, which have an extensive network of branches and therefore greater opportunities than those subsidiaries for raising capital from the public.

14   Where credit institutions which are subsidiaries of foreign companies seek to enter the market of a Member State, competing by means of the rate of remuneration paid on sight accounts constitutes one of the most effective methods to that end. Access to the market by those establishments is thus made more difficult by such a prohibition.

* * *

16   The restriction on the pursuit and development of the activities of those subsidiaries resulting from the prohibition at issue is all the greater in that it is common ground that the taking of deposits from the public and the granting of credits represent the basic activities of credit institutions.

17   It is clear from settled case-law that where * * * such a measure applies to any person or undertaking carrying on an activity in the territory of the host Member State, it may be justified where it serves overriding requirements relating to the public interest, is suitable for securing the attainment of the objective it pursues and does not go beyond what is necessary in order to attain it.

* * *

20 [The French government submits] that the prohibition at issue in the main proceedings is necessary for maintaining the provision of basic banking services without charge. Introducing remuneration for sight accounts would substantially increase the operating costs of banks, which, to recover those costs, would increase charges and introduce charges for the various banking services currently provided free, in particular the issuing of cheques.

22 Even supposing that removing the prohibition of paying remuneration on sight accounts necessarily entails for consumers an increase in the cost of basic banking services or a charge for cheques, the possibility might be envisaged inter alia of allowing consumers to choose between an unremunerated sight account with certain basic banking services remaining free of charge and a remunerated sight account with the credit institution being able to make charges for banking services previously provided free, such as the issuing of cheques.

23 As regards, next, the French authorities' concern to encourage long-term saving, it must be observed that, while the prohibition of remuneration on sight accounts is indeed suitable for encouraging medium and long-term saving, it nevertheless remains a measure which goes beyond what is necessary to attain that objective.

24 In the light of the above considerations, the answer to the questions referred for a preliminary ruling must be that Article 43 EC precludes legislation of a Member State which prohibits a credit institution which is a subsidiary of a company from another Member State from remunerating sight accounts in euros opened by residents of the former Member State.

NOTES AND QUESTIONS

1. ECT Article 43 (now TFEU Article 49) grants the right of establishment without discrimination on the basis of nationality. The French prohibition of interest on sight accounts applies to all banks. How, then, can it violate Article 43? Note the Court's answer in ¶ 14: the law makes market access by a subsidiary of another Member State bank more difficult. Advocate General Tizzano advocated this approach in ¶¶ 66–76. The approach distinctly resembles the market access exception to the *Keck* doctrine in *Gourmet*, supra page 504. However, should the market access theory always apply in an establishment context? If a large Spanish bank buys a large French bank which has many branches and depositors, and operates it as a subsidiary, could the subsidiary rely on Article 43 to offer interest-bearing sight accounts?

2. Suppose Caixa–Bank were a branch of a Spanish bank, instead of a subsidiary, and accordingly the Second Banking Directive applied. The French branch would then be able to offer the interest-bearing sight account if the Spanish authorities permitted it in Spain, pursuant to the Annex, unless the French authorities could prove a general good interest justified the prohibition. Obviously, the Court analysis in ¶¶ 20–24 would then apply to reject the general good claim.

3.　SUPPLEMENTAL BANKING LEGISLATION

The minimum harmonization of the Second Banking Directive is supplemented by several other technical directives of considerable importance. Directive 89/299, O.J. L 124/16 (May 5, 1989), which sets the rules for a credit institution's capital and other "own funds," Directive 89/647, O.J. L 386/14 (Dec. 30, 1989), which indicates the requisite solvency ratio for banks, and Directive 93/6 on capital adequacy for banks and for investment service institutions, O.J. L 141/1 (June 11, 1993), were all rapidly adopted. The three directives were all included in the codified bank directive text mentioned above. Following new guidelines issued in 2004 by the Basel international committee on banking supervision, Directive 2006/48, O.J. L 177/201 (June 30, 2006), revised the capital adequacy rules.

Directive 94/19 on deposit-guarantee schemes, O.J. L 135/5 (May 31, 1994), is noteworthy because it was the first directive adopted under the codecision procedure after the Council and Parliament accepted a conciliation committee report. The directive requires all States to have some form of guarantee ensuring that each depositor will receive up to 20,000 Euros if the deposits are unavailable for 21 days. A State may set a higher guarantee level for its banks and branches of banks from other States. However, a branch in a host State cannot offer its depositors a higher guarantee level than that set in the host State, even if its home office must provide a higher level to home State depositors because of the home State rules.

Germany, which voted against the directive, unsuccessfully challenged it in an Article 230 proceeding, based in part on the directive's alleged violation of the principle of subsidiarity. This aspect of the judgment is excerpted at page 118, supra. Germany also argued that the directive did not adequately protect consumer interests, an aspect dealt with at page 1317 infra.

In an unusual case, the Court of Justice was asked by the German Supreme Court whether either the deposit-guarantee directive or the second banking directive implicitly created a duty upon the German bank supervisory authorities to protect depositors who lost funds in excess of the Euro 20,000 guarantee in a bank insolvency. In Paul v. Germany, Case C–222/02, [2004] ECR I–9425, the Court held that the provisions of both directives represented only the essential harmonization necessary to achieve their goals, and neither created a specific duty upon supervisory authorities to protect individuals, as opposed to protecting the public interest in general. The Court accepted the validity of the German law that obliged the supervisory authority to exercise its powers "only in the public interest". Note that the trial court held that Germany was liable to pay the plaintiffs the 20,000 Euro guarantee, because Germany had failed to implement the deposit guarantee directive within the time period stated in the directive, but they lost much larger amounts on deposit.

Directive 91/308, O.J. L 166/77 (June 28, 1991), on the prevention of money laundering, was inspired by the UN's 1988 Vienna Convention on illicit traffic in narcotic substances, and accordingly only forbids money laundering of the proceeds of drug dealing. Banks and financial institutions are obligated to verify the identity of their customers and to examine any transaction likely to constitute money laundering, reporting on their own initiative any suspicious transactions to the authorities. They are specifically required in article 11 to set up "adequate procedures of internal control" and to carry out training programs for employees to combat money laundering. The directive did not expressly require States to make money laundering a criminal offense because of doubts that the EC Treaty grants any implicit legislative power to do that, but article 14 obligates States to "take appropriate measures to ensure full application" of the directive. A 1998 Commission report indicated that all States had made money laundering of the proceeds from illicit drug traffic a criminal offense.

Directive 2001/97, O.J. L 344/76 (Dec. 28, 2001), substantially amended the 1991 money laundering directive. Money laundering is defined in Article 1 as any dealing in property intended to conceal its source in any form of serious criminal activity, including fraud and corruption. Articles 2 and 3 oblige auditors, accountants, tax advisors, notaries and lawyers, art dealers and casinos to identify their clients, and article 6 requires them to report any factual evidence of money laundering to the authorities. However, by article 6(3) notaries and lawyers are exempt from reporting to the authorities information they obtained "in the course of ascertaining the legal position for their client or performing their task of defending or representing their client in, or concerning judicial proceedings." The Court's judgment in *Ordre de Barraux*, supra page 753, concluded that protection of a client's right to legal representation in order to receive a fair trial did not prevent a lawyer's fulfillment of obligations under articles 2, 3 and 6 of the directive, in view of the exception in article 6(3).

Directive 2005/60, O.J. L 309/15 (Nov. 25, 2005), the third money laundering directive, codified the first two, adding the financing of terrorism to the definition of conduct that constitutes money laundering. Article 2 also imposes the directive's verification and reporting duties on all "natural or legal persons dealing in goods" when cash payments of 15000 Euros or more are involved. All the other earlier directive provisions are made more precise and detailed. Article 23(2) replicates the second Directive's article 6(3).

After three years of studies showed that customers faced high fees, delays and inadequate information in cross-border funds transfers, the Commission proposed in 1994 a directive to regulate such transfers. Directive 97/5 on cross-border credit transfers, O.J. L 43/25 (Feb. 14, 1997), sets out minimum standards for the information to be provided on credit transfer conditions, the maximum permissible time period for the execution of the transfer, and the identification of the person (sender and/or beneficiary) who bears the administrative charges for the transfer.

The initial directive was replaced by Directive 2007/64 on payment services in the internal market, O.J. L 319/1 (Dec. 5, 2007), which covers in extremely detailed fashion all forms of cross-border payments, requires banks, post offices, and other money transfer institutions to obtain an authorization, and sets out obligations intended to protect the payer and payee from excessive charges or delays.

The above summary of the harmonization of Member State banking rules makes it quite clear that in a remarkably short period of time— approximately ten years—the structure was set in place to enable Community-wide banking operations. Not only did this greatly advance the attainment of the internal market, it also promoted greater competition among banks and more efficient and less costly banking services, all without sacrificing consumer protection of depositors and borrowers. In recent years, bank mergers and acquisitions, both within States and across their borders, have increased in number and size. The largest European banks are now active competitors with the largest US, Japanese and Hong–Kong banks on the international financial marketplace.

4.　SECURITIES LAW HARMONIZATION

The process of harmonization of securities law began in the late 1970s as an outgrowth of company law harmonization. Space considerations permit only the summary of the most important directives. The First Directive 79/279, O.J. L 66/21 (Mar. 16, 1979), lays down the conditions for quotation of securities on a stock exchange. These conditions cover in great detail the share and capital structure and the management of the issuing company, as well as the nature and rights of the quoted securities. The 1979 directive establishes the principle that a company that satisfies these conditions may be quoted on any official stock exchange in the Union.

The Second Directive 80/390, O.J. L 100/1 (Apr. 17, 1980), standardizes the "listing particulars" or the public information required for quoted shares (equivalent to a registration statement in the US), describing the essential financial information for the listed company and the rights of the quoted securities. This promotes investor confidence in dealing with stock or other securities quoted on exchanges outside of the country of residence of the investor. Moreover, this 1980 directive was significantly amended in 1987, O.J. L 185/81 (July 4, 1987), to establish the principle of reciprocal recognition, which means that if a security is listed on an exchange in its home country and is simultaneously or very soon thereafter to be quoted on a stock exchange in another Member State, then the second stock exchange must accept as fully adequate the listing particulars that were accepted by the first exchange. This obviously facilitates the quotation of securities on two or more exchanges in different parts of the Union.

Directive 94/18, O.J. L 135/1 (May 31, 1994), amending the Second Directive 80/390 on listing particulars, is also intended to promote cross-border securities dealing. The amendment authorizes States to permit "companies of high quality and international standing," which have been listed for over three years on another State's regulated exchange, to become listed on their exchange(s) by publishing certain minimum information and providing the latest annual financial statements.

The Third Directive 82/121, O.J. L 48/26 (Feb. 20, 1982), requires the regular publication of information by quoted companies in annual and semi-annual reports. The reports must describe the financial statements and operating information in considerable detail, and include the auditor's certification. Both annual and semi-annual reports must be published and made available to the public, which again promotes investor confidence in companies quoted on different exchanges within the Union.

Directive 88/627, O.J. L 348/62 (Dec. 17, 1988), requires the disclosure of major shareholdings in a quoted company. Shareholders who acquire amounts of voting stock which reach certain thresholds (10%, 20%, one-third, 50%, two-thirds, or 90%), or dispose of voting stock to go below these thresholds, are obliged to disclose this to the company involved within seven calendar days. The quoted company must in turn disclose to the general public the identity of the shareholder and the stock amount involved within nine calendar days. The directive's provisions parallel to some degree the requirements of § 13D of the 1934 Securities Exchange Act, but, unlike § 13D, the directive does not require the shareholder to disclose its intent vis-à-vis the quoted company (e.g., to attempt to take control of the company involved, or modify its structure or management, or to remain a passive investor).

In 2001, the Parliament and Council codified, without further change, the First, Second and Third Directives, together with Directive 88/627, in Directive 2001/34, O.J. L 184/1 (July 6, 2001). Directive 2003/71, O.J. L 345/64 (Dec. 31, 2003) on the prospectus when securities are offered to the public, amends the codification in order to set common standards for prospectuses with the intent of facilitating stock offerings simultaneously on several exchanges. Also, Directive 2004/109, O.J. L 390/38 (Dec. 31, 2004), amends the codification to update the rules requiring periodic reports to shareholders, notably to require interim management statements from issuers that do not provide quarterly reports.

Until the mid–1980s, only France and the United Kingdom prohibited insider trading. Prompted to some degree by the international insider trading scandals of the late 1980s, the Council adopted Directive 89/592 on insider dealing, O.J. L 334/30 (Nov. 18, 1989). The directive defines inside information and insider dealing, and forbids persons who have acquired inside information from trading in quoted securities, or providing tips to others who trade in such securities. The directive's definitions and prohibitions are more precise and detailed than the famous US securities Rule 10b 5.

In 2003, the Directive was significantly amended by Directive 2003/6 on insider dealing and market manipulation, O.J. L 96/16 (Apr. 12, 2003). Far more detailed than the initial 1989 insider trading directive, Directive 2003/6 broadens the scope of forbidden securities conduct by specifying forms of abusive market manipulation, some representing innovations that have developed in the last few years. Each Member State must have a single administrative authority with jurisdiction over all aspects of securities and derivatives trading. Article 14 requires the States to ensure that administrative sanctions to enforce the law are "effective, proportionate and dissuasive" and mentions the possibility that States will employ criminal sanctions. The duty of inter-state cooperation among the authorities is set forth in more detailed provisions.

After four years of difficult debate, in 1993 the Council adopted Directive 93/22 on investment services in the securities field, O.J. L 141/27 (June 11, 1993), regulating the status and activities of stockbrokers and financial advisors in the securities sector. Although initially modeled on the Second Banking Directive, Directive 93/22 has some quite distinctive provisions. To some extent, these represent compromises between the view of the more liberal northern States and that of the Mediterranean States which preferred stricter regulation. The basic principle remains that of a 'single license' enabling brokerage firms, underwriters and financial advisors established in any State to operate throughout the Community, with the home State responsible for authorization and ongoing prudential supervision. However, under article 11, the host State may adopt compulsory "rules of conduct" for the protection of "clients and the integrity of the market," and under article 21 the host State must require daily and hourly disclosure of minimum information on financial market transactions.

Viewed as an ensemble, the securities directives represent a remarkable body of sophisticated regulation of stock exchanges and companies issuing shares, both in terms of investor protection and adoption of modern forms of raising capital. While they may have only moderately improved the regulation of issuers of securities and of trading on the London Exchange, the directives have transformed and modernized the regulation of the securities markets in many States. The stock exchanges in London, Frankfurt, and Paris have flourished, adding many new quoted companies and expanding enormously in market volume and technical trading sophistication, while smaller exchanges in Amsterdam, Brussels, Madrid, Milan and elsewhere now also offer modern securities trading with investor safety.

This development is situated in a wider context, that of an evolving international securities market. The US Securities and Exchange Commission and the Commission's Directorate–General on Financial Institutions have regular contacts to exchange information and ideas.

We conclude by examining a prominent judgment concerning rules regulating the marketing of securities.

ALPINE INVESTMENTS v. MINISTER VAN FINANCIEN
Case C–384/93, [1995] ECR I–1141.

[As part of its overall securities regulations, the Netherlands adopted in 1991 a rule totally forbidding the solicitation by telephone of brokerage transactions for commodities futures, or the actual sales by telephone of commodities futures, when the customers have not previously authorized the telephone contact. This form of telephone marketing is commonly referred to as "cold calling." The Ministry of Finance acted after numerous complaints from investors. The ban applied both to telephone marketing within and outside the Netherlands.

Alpine Investments, a commodities broker which had engaged in "cold calling"(allegedly with no customer complaints), challenged the ban under ECT Articles 49 and 50. The Court readily found that restrictions on trans-border marketing by telephone could violate Article 49 even though the service provider does not physically move from its State of establishment (¶¶ 20–22), and even though the marketing restrictions are imposed by the State where the telephone calls originated, rather than by the State of residence of the consumer. (¶ 30.) The Court turned then to the more difficult issues.]

40   The national court's third question asks whether imperative reasons of public interest justify the prohibition of cold calling and whether that prohibition must be considered to be objectively necessary and proportionate to the objective pursued.

41   The Netherlands Government argues that the prohibition of cold calling in off-market commodities futures trading seeks both to safeguard the reputation of the Netherlands financial markets and to protect the investing public.

42   Financial markets play an important role in the financing of economic operators and, given the speculative nature and the complexity of commodities futures contracts, the smooth operation of financial markets is largely contingent on the confidence they inspire in investors. That confidence depends in particular on the existence of professional regulations serving to ensure the competence and trustworthiness of the financial intermediaries on whom investors are particularly reliant.

43   Although the protection of consumers in the other Member States is not, as such, a matter for the Netherlands authorities, the nature and extent of that protection does none the less have a direct effect on the good reputation of Netherlands financial services.

44   Maintaining the good reputation of the national financial sector may therefore constitute an imperative reason of public interest capable of justifying restrictions on the freedom to provide financial services.

45   As for the proportionality of the restriction at issue, it is settled case-law that requirements imposed on the providers of services must be

appropriate to ensure achievement of the intended aim and must not go beyond that which is necessary in order to achieve that objective.

46   As the Netherlands Government has justifiably submitted, in the case of cold calling the individual, generally caught unawares, is in a position neither to ascertain the risks inherent in the type of transactions offered to him nor to compare the quality and price of the caller's services with competitors' offers. Since the commodities futures market is highly speculative and barely comprehensible for non-expert investors, it was necessary to protect them from the most aggressive selling techniques.

47   Alpine Investments argues however that the Netherlands Government's prohibition of cold calling is not necessary because the Member State of the provider of services should rely on the controls imposed by the Member State of the recipient.

48   That argument must be rejected. The Member State from which the telephone call is made is best placed to regulate cold calling. Even if the receiving State wishes to prohibit cold calling or to make it subject to certain conditions, it is not in a position to prevent or control telephone calls from another Member State without the cooperation of the competent authorities of that State.

49   Consequently, the prohibition of cold calling by the Member State from which the telephone call is made, with a view to protecting investor confidence in the financial markets of that State, cannot be considered to be inappropriate to achieve the objective of securing the integrity of those markets.

NOTES AND QUESTIONS

1.   The Court has accepted a new "imperative reason of public interest," namely the protection of a financial market's reputation for integrity. Do you agree that this represents a sufficiently important interest to limit financial service-providing, or do you think the trans-border financial market should largely be self-regulating? The Court's view can be read as an endorsement of the general policy approach in the recent Community legislation in banking, securities and insurance which reserves the chief supervisory role to the home State authorities (the State where the financial enterprise's center is located), rather than those of the host State (the State where the consumers of the trans-border transaction are located). For valuable appraisals of the judgment, see the casenotes by V. Hatzopoulos, 32 Common Mkt. L. Rev. 1427 (1995), and P. Knobl, 2 Maastricht J. Eur. & Comp. L. 306 (1995).

2.   Perhaps Alpine Investment's best argument was that a total ban was too severe and disproportionate. The UK, which has a far more important financial market than that in the Netherlands, permitted 'cold calling,' subject to verification of tape-recordings of actual calls. Why should the Dutch have to impose a total ban? The Court's acceptance of the Dutch ban is reminiscent of its acceptance of the total French marketing ban on language instruction courses in *Buet,* supra page 546, in both instances respecting the

regulatory authority's discretion in responding to numerous consumer complaints.

3. Directive 2002/65 on the distance marketing of financial services, O.J. L 271/16 (Oct. 9, 2002), regulates the sale of contracts for credits cards, bank services, securities, investment funds, pension plans, etc., by telephone, fax or the internet, requiring clear and comprehensive information to be presented before a contract is concluded. It requires States either to forbid 'cold calling' unless the customer expressly consents to it, or to enable potential recipients of calls to forbid them by entering his or her name on a register for this purpose.

4. A Greek company, Ntionik, provided to the Athens stock exchange an inaccurate statement of its profits for the fiscal year 2000 as part of the listing information given to investors in executing a capital increase. When the Capital Markets Commission discovered this, it imposed a fine of 90,000 Euros on Ntionik and 60,000 Euros on each member of Ntionik's board of directors. On appeal, the Council of State asked the Court whether the Commission's fines on all board members properly applied Directive 2001/342 article 21, which requires Member States to ensure that a listed company provides accurate listing information. The Court held that in the absence of harmonized standards for penalties, Greece could apply proportionate penalties (¶ 54), which could include penalties imposed on the entire board of directors, and not just the chairman of the board and the managing director who had certified the listing particulars to the Amsterdam exchange (¶ 55). Would you agree? Is this policy of collective responsibility of the board for a securities listing violation a desirable one? See Ntionik AE v. Epitropi Kefalaiagoras, Case C–430/05, [2007] ECR I–5835.

Further Reading

Books

C. Bernard, The Substantive Law of the EU: the Four Freedoms (2d. ed. Oxford U.P. 2007)

P. Kapteyn & P. Verloren Van Themaat, The Law of the European Union and the European Communities (4th ed. Kluwer 2008)

CHAPTER 31

ECONOMIC AND MONETARY UNION

■ ■ ■

No more important political or economic development occurred in the European Union in the 1990s than the creation of the Economic and Monetary Union (EMU). The European Council and the Commission, during the successive presidencies of Jacques Delors, viewed EMU as providing four substantial benefits: a centralized and stable monetary system, a single European currency, a significant reduction in cross-border financial and commercial transaction costs, and a better integrated competitive marketplace for producers and consumers.

Certainly the Monetary Union radically changed the economic landscape of the Community. The constitutional and political implications of EMU are also dramatic: a further substantial transfer of sovereignty to a central structure, the European Central Bank (ECB), together with the creation of the Euro as a powerful symbol of European integration.

This Chapter will first set out the goals, benefits and drawbacks of EMU, the early stages of economic and monetary cooperation, and the preparations for the final stage of EMU. The structure of the European Central Bank (ECB) is then analyzed, with special emphasis upon the principle of independence, the treaty-mandated goal of price stability, and issues concerning its democratic accountability and transparency. Next we will describe the regulatory framework and the practical preparation for the launch of the Euro as a single currency. We will then review the ECB's operations in the control of monetary policy, and the role of the Economic and Finance (Ecofin) Council in the coordination of national economic policy, particularly the application of the Stability and Growth Pact. Finally, we will examine the relatively minor changes brought by the Lisbon Treaty.

The role of the European Council in deciding upon the key aspects of the proposed structure of EMU, and in promoting its steady evolution toward reality, was an unusually marked one. As we shall see, successive meetings of the European Council resulted in crucial policy decisions in shaping the progress toward EMU. Moreover, the EC Treaty itself specified that the decision upon the designation of the Member States that qualified to join in its final stage had to be taken by the Council meeting in the unusual composition of the Heads of State and Government, effectively the European Council, instead of its more customary composition of finance ministers or foreign affairs ministers.

In the creation of a Monetary Union, not only should tribute be paid to the vision of Commission President Jacques Delors, but also to the political will of Chancellor Kohl of Germany and President Mitterand of France, who together provided the principal leadership in the key policy decisions. Also playing important roles in the political process were Prime Ministers Dehaene of Belgium, Lubbers of the Netherlands and Gonzalez of Spain. We should also note the less prominent but quite crucial role of the central bank governors, such as Pohl of the the German Central Bank, and Duisenberg of the Dutch Central Bank, who, together with their staffs, provided much of the expertise necessary in the drafting of the various treaty provisions.

R. Lastra, Legal Foundations of International Monetary Stability (Oxford U.P. 2006), provides a recent comprehensive review of ECB structure and operations. R. Smits, The European Central Bank (Kluwer 1997), is an authoritative review of the EMU Treaty provisions and the developments before 1997. R. Goebel, European Economic and Monetary Union: Will the EMU Ever Fly?, 4 Colum. J. Eur. L. 249 (1998), provides a detailed review prior to the final third stage of EMU.

A. THE GOALS, BENEFITS AND DRAWBACKS OF ECONOMIC AND MONETARY UNION

The Economic and Monetary Union has transformed the European Union in a more fundamental manner than any other development the substantial achievement of the internal market program. Indeed, the 1995 Green Paper on the Introduction of the Single Currency depicted EMU as the "logical and essential complement" to the internal market. The rapid preparation and attainment of the Monetary Union undoubtedly stemmed in large measure from the generally satisfactory progress in attaining the internal market.

EMU's principal components are: (1) an institutional structure, with the European Central Bank at its center; (2) ECB control of monetary policy for those States that have joined in the final stage of EMU (which we will hereinafter call the 'Euro-zone States'); (3) a single currency, the Euro, replacing prior national currencies in the Euro-zone States. Each will be described in greater detail later, but some preliminary notes should be made.

An integrated Community monetary system with a European Central Bank at its core has long been seen as essential to achieve greater monetary stability. The necessity to meet rather high economic and monetary standards in order to participate in the Monetary Union compelled virtually all the Member States to adopt stricter monetary policies during the 1990s. Because the European Central Bank has the power to adopt stable monetary policy programs and the power to implement them, with a minimum of political interference from Member State governments and Community institutions, EMU has produced a more solid monetary structure for the Euro-zone States.

With regard to the adoption of the single currency, the Euro, the Commission has estimated that use of a single currency saves the Euro-zone States annually around 20 billion Euros, or approximately 0.3–0.4% of GDP, through the elimination of currency-related transaction costs (i.e., the expense of changes in currency when transacting commercial and personal affairs across frontiers within the Euro-zone). After the elimination of different national currencies, financial and commercial enterprises need no longer use currency options, futures or insurance to hedge against shifts in national currency value when transacting trans-border financial and commercial affairs within the Euro-zone States.

But there is a further economic benefit flowing from a single currency, namely, the achievement of far greater price and cost transparency in all trans-border financial, commercial and private transactions. Thus, purchasers of raw materials and supplies, intermediate distributors of products, persons providing services, and consumers of goods, services or credit are all able easily and quickly to compare prices or expenses when dealing with domestic and foreign parties.

On the global monetary stage, EMU now plays a leading role. Use of the Euro for international trade and investment has become more substantial than the use of individual national currencies, even the German mark. Moreover, the existence of a European Central Bank with a mandate for price stability and a strong currency has promoted the use of the Euro in international trade and investment. The Euro has become second only to the US dollar in global transactions, especially in trans-border credit and financial operations.

Finally, EMU has had a great impact on the political aspect of the European Union. One of the most essential types of sovereign power, namely the control over monetary policy, has been transferred by the Euro-zone States to a Union institution. It is true that, as we shall see later, the institution, the European Central Bank, is independent of the traditional Union political institutions, namely the Commission, Council and Parliament. Nevertheless, power over monetary policy in these States rests with a *Union* entity. Such a transfer of vital power necessarily diminishes the role of national governments to a significant degree.

The transfer of monetary power to the European Central Bank and the creation of a single common currency also produce significant psychological consequences. Citizens of the Euro-zone Member States perceive more readily the extent, importance and hopefully the value of European integration. Replacement of national currency and coins by the Euro constitutes a far more meaningful symbol of Union integration than the European passport or the Union flag can ever be. Migrant workers and professionals in particular see tangible benefits from the use of the Euro, since they are able to compare income levels and the cost of living in different Member States, as well as to transfer funds without currency exchange costs to a new place of residence or back to their home State.

The Monetary Union has, however, several major drawbacks. The most obvious is that the European Union has become 'two tiered' in monetary affairs: although currently sixteen Member States have joined in the Euro-zone, eleven remain outside, some voluntarily, others because they are unable to meet the conditions for joining. Moreover, it is quite likely that this division between the 'ins' and the 'outs' will prove permanent. This has obvious adverse consequences for the integrated economic market and may provoke important policy differences in other sectors as well.

Secondly, the ECB decides on a common monetary policy for all the Euro-zone States, although it may not be the most desirable for each one, and even adverse to the economic circumstances of some. This is often called the 'one size fits all' problem. The ECB necessarily shapes its policy to benefit the largest economies (notably Germany and France). Occasionally, this policy can be counter-productive for other States.

Third, the Euro-zone States have a natural tendency to coordinate their economic policies more closely, excluding the 'outs.' Because the 'Euro Group' finance ministers meet periodically, a certain degree of friction has arisen with the other finance ministers. (The Lisbon Treaty formalizes the status of the Euro Group, but limits its functions, as we shall see in section G below).

Finally, in late 2009 a severe crisis developed when in Greece the newly-elected Socialist government of Prime Minister Papandreou disclosed that faulty statistics had concealed the dimensions of its annual public deficit and over-all accumulated debt. The on-going crisis in 2010, described in section G2 infra, demonstrates the dangerous absence of any political structure to ensure that States within the Euro-zone follow appropriate fiscal policies.

B. THE EVOLUTION TOWARD MONETARY UNION

1. THE EEC TREATY: ECONOMIC COORDINATION

At the time the European Economic Community began in 1958, the global monetary system governed by the Bretton Woods accords and supervised by the International Monetary Fund (IMF) provided a substantial degree of international monetary stability. In the halcyon days of the 1950s and 1960s, the currency exchange rates of different countries were fixed in relation to one another, and the US dollar, backed by substantial gold reserves, provided substantial stability to the fixed exchange rate system. Accordingly, the authors of the EEC Treaty presumably saw no need for far-reaching initiatives in the monetary sector. The initial EECT Articles 103–105 on Economic Policy merely required Member States to pursue stable economic policies, and to coordinate economic and monetary policies.

The Community first felt a need to create its own monetary structure at the end of the 1960s, when the world monetary system currency governing exchange rates under the 1946 Bretton Woods accords started to break down. As world trade and investment expanded enormously in the 1960s, nations became much more interdependent, both in economic and monetary terms. Then, as the economies of some countries developed far more rapidly than others, and as certain states suffered serious bouts of inflation, balance of payments difficulties became inevitable. France, Italy, and the UK were compelled to devalue their currencies in successive monetary crises, while Germany, the Netherlands and Switzerland were obliged to revalue them.

The most serious international monetary crisis arose when the dollar came under severe pressure in 1971. President Nixon decided to end the gold standard on August 15, 1971, allowing the dollar to float against other currencies. The Smithsonian Accord of December 18, 1971 institutionalized the system of such floating rates. However, because floating exchange rates create uncertainty and instability in both medium and long-term financial and commercial transactions, ever since 1971 governments have sought to find a way to return to some form of fixed, or at least relatively stable, rates.

Making use of then EEC Treaty Article 105, the Commission and Council began a series of attempts to alleviate monetary crises in particular Member States and to coordinate economic and monetary policy in order to achieve greater stability within the Community. Unfortunately, the energy recession of the mid–1970s and further monetary crises in certain Member States prevented these Community measures from becoming truly effective. Coordination efforts were reduced, rather than enhanced, in the late 1970s. The goal of a union receded farther into the distance.

2. THE EUROPEAN MONETARY SYSTEM

In the late 1970s, the leadership of President Giscard d'Estaing of France, Chancellor Helmut Schmidt of Germany, both former finance ministers, and Commission President Roy Jenkins, previously the UK Chancellor of the Exchequer, caused new attention to be focused on monetary coordination and stabilization. The European Council Meeting at Bremen in August 1978 officially endorsed the concept of a European Monetary System (EMS), which came into force in March 1979. Bull. EC 1978–6, at 5.

The EMS created an artificial European monetary unit, the European Currency Unit, or ECU. The value of the ECU was fixed as a composite of a "basket" of Member State currencies with weighted values one to another, based upon a macroeconomic calculation of the proportionate strength of the national economy underlying each State's currency.

The European Community calculated all its revenues and expenditures in the form of ECUs. This enabled a standard base to be used in the calculation of budget items from year to year. The ECU was quoted on monetary exchanges and floated against the dollar and other currencies. For example, in June 1992, one ECU equaled $1.35. The ECU was, of course, not an actual currency: there were no bills or coins denominated in ECU, nor was the ECU used as legal tender for everyday private commercial transactions. Nonetheless, the Community's use of ECU facilitated the creation of the Euro.

The second component of the European Monetary System was the stabilization of the exchange rates of the currencies of the Member States participating in the EMS. This was called the Exchange Rate Mechanism (ERM). The exchange rates were fixed in 1979 and were changed during the 1980s only at relatively infrequent intervals. A very moderate degree of floating was allowed between currencies, within a band with a maximum range of 2.25% above or below the exchange rate. The functional merit of this limited rate of fluctuation around pegged rates set for long periods of time was that it served as a reasonably close approximation of the fixed rates of the Bretton Woods system. This meant that financial institutions, commercial enterprises, and private investors could enter into medium and long-term transactions with a reasonable assurance that neither an unexpectedly large exchange rate gain nor loss would occur at the end of the transaction.

The third component of the European Monetary System was a credit mechanism by which short and medium support could be given to Member States encountering serious monetary troubles. A reserve fund of 25 billion ECU was created, composed of the equivalent of 20% of the gold and 20% of the dollars held by each participating central bank.

The operational success of EMS in the 1980s created a climate of confidence. The Commission under President Delors and the political leadership in most Member States believed that the monetary stability provided by the EMS enabled the Community to commence plans for a Monetary Union. These plans reached fruition in the EMU provisions of the Treaty of Maastricht at the end of 1991.

Unfortunately, successive crises on the international money markets in September 1992 and August 1993 severely shook confidence in the EMS. Each time enormous speculation in the currency markets attacked the French franc, the UK pound and other national currencies in favor of the German mark, always seen as the safest long term currency. The Community was compelled to enlarge radically the fluctuation bands of the ERM from 2.25% to 15% above or below the central standard rate. Although the exchange markets then quieted without a devaluation of the franc, the ERM never formally returned to a narrower band. Indeed, at the end of 1993, some media commentators questioned whether it was still possible to proceed with the plans for EMU.

Fortunately, after 1995 the currency markets in the Community calmed down and exchange rate shifts were minor. By the end of 1996, the currencies of almost all the States operating within the Exchange Rate Mechanism were well within the 2.25% fluctuation band that had prevailed in the 1980s.

3. PLANNING FOR ECONOMIC AND MONETARY UNION

In January 1985, when a new Commission took office under the Presidency of Jacques Delors, its initial agenda included efforts to attain EMU as well as to complete the internal market. Accordingly, in the late 1980s as the Community progressed toward achievement of the internal market program, proposals for EMU moved to center stage. At its June 1988 Hanover meeting, the European Council "confirmed the objective of progressive realization of economic and monetary union." Bull. EC 1988–6, at 20. It created a special committee, chaired by Delors, to study and propose "concrete stages" toward this goal. The committee consisted of all the central bank governors and several economic and banking experts. Delors himself was sophisticated in monetary affairs, having served as France's Minister of the Economy and worked for the French Central Bank early in his career.

The Delors Committee Report of April 17, 1989 provided a thorough review of the essential character of an Economic and Monetary Union. Bull. EC 1989–4, at 8. Due partly to the practical nature of the committee's proposals, and partly to respect for the high qualifications of the committee itself, this report not only formed the basis for all subsequent discussions, but largely shaped the agenda of the 1990–91 Intergovernmental Conference which produced the Treaty of Maastricht.

The Delors Report defined the EMU's goal as the common management of monetary and economic policies by a central bank (modeled on the German Central Bank and the US Federal Reserve) to attain common macroeconomic goals. The Delors Report was quite pragmatic in setting out three stages in the progress toward Monetary Union. The final stage would give the ECB responsibility for monetary policy, and lead to the creation of a common Community currency. Because so many of the report's proposals were adopted in the Treaty of Maastricht, we need not go into detail at this point.

The Delors Report initiated a widespread debate on the necessity for, and the goals of, an EMU, both at the Community level and in the private sector, and the topic received great attention in the media. It quickly became the most fascinating single idea for the further political and economic development of the European Community since the June 1985 White Paper on Completing the Internal Market. Although most commentary on the Delors Report was favorable, John Major, then UK Chancellor of the Exchequer, issued on November 2, 1989 a policy statement advocating national control over monetary policy and criticizing any transfer of power to a centralized bureaucracy, specifically repudiating the idea of a single European currency.

At this point, the reaction of the European Council to the Delors Report became critical. At its December 1989 meeting in Strasbourg, the European Council approved the main themes of the Delors Report, and decided, despite the opposition of the United Kingdom, to call an intergovernmental conference for the purpose of adopting an Economic and Monetary Union.

The Intergovernmental Conference worked earnestly for nearly a year on the EMU proposal. Most of the text was prepared by technical experts representing Germany and the Netherlands, both States with powerful central banks and a tradition of strict monetary policy and hard currencies. Reaching a consensus proved extremely difficult, due not only to UK opposition, but also to hesitations on the part of other States. Ultimately, several issues were left to the European Council meeting at Maastricht in December 1991, which, after intensive debate, arrived at essential compromises. The most decisive compromise was to adopt Protocols allowing the UK and Denmark to opt out of EMU.

4.   THE EMU PROVISIONS OF THE TREATY OF MAASTRICHT

No aspect of the Maastricht Treaty is of greater importance than the provisions on EMU. Article 2 of the TEU lists an economic and monetary union and a single currency as among the principal objectives of European Union. A new ECT Article 4 declares that Community activities shall include, i.a. "the close coordination of Member States' economic policies," "the definition and conduct of a single monetary policy," and "the introduction of a single currency."

The EC Treaty provisions on EMU are extremely complicated. At the outset, it should be emphasized that the Monetary Union was considered to be an integral part of the European Community, and not a separate intergovernmental "pillar," as the Common Foreign and Security Policy and Cooperation in Justice and Home Affairs. Although it has many distinctive features, Monetary Union was woven into the institutional framework of the Community.

Pursuant to a decision of the 1989 Strassbourg European Council, on June 1, 1990, the Community began the first stage of progress toward the EMU. The first stage had three different components: 1) free movement of capital, already achieved by the 1988 directive described in Chapter 30A; 2) adherence of all Member States to the Exchange Rate Mechanism of the EMS; and 3) an increased level of monetary coordination, both by governmental action and through coordination among the central banks. Somewhat curiously, the Maastricht Treaty never refers to the first stage.

ECT Article 116 set Jan. 1, 1994 as the starting date for the second stage. During the second stage, Member States were obligated to conduct strict economic and monetary policies in order to achieve several convergence criteria set out in the Treaty. Only upon satisfactory attainment of these criteria could States become eligible to join in the third stage of Monetary Union.

The Treaty set Jan. 1, 1999 as the latest possible date for the commencement of the third and final stage for those States which had satisfied the convergence criteria. The States joining in the third stage would yield control of their monetary policy to the European System of Central Banks. Subsequently, the States in the final stage would have their national currencies replaced by a single currency.

Not surprisingly, the Maastricht Treaty's provisions on EMU proved to be highly controversial during the debates over its ratification in many States. Some political parties, prominent politicians and media leaders opposed a Community-wide centralized monetary structure and feared the loss of sovereignty necessarily involved. Not only did many citizens of some States share these concerns, but they particularly opposed the loss of their currencies, which always are a strong symbol of nationality. This was undoubtedly a factor in the rejection of the Treaty in the first Danish referendum in 1992, and the Danish government's exercise of its opt-out presumably contributed to the ultimate vote in favor of ratification in the second Danish referendum in May 1993. Opposition to EMU within the Conservative Party was one of the factors occasioning Prime Minister Major's extremely narrow one-vote margin in favor of ratification in the UK Parliament's vote in July 1993. Eventually, however, all the Member States ratified the Treaty of Maastricht, which entered into effect on Nov. 1, 1993, enabling the formal start of the second stage on Jan. 1, 1994.

5. ECONOMIC COORDINATION: 1994–98

On Jan. 1, 1994, the European Monetary Institute (EMI), composed of a President named by the Council, initially Alexandre Lamfalussy and later Wim Duisenberg, and one governor from each national central bank, began operations. The EMI was sited in Frankfurt in accord with a European Council decision reached with some difficulty (the UK sought the seat for London, and the Netherlands for Amsterdam). The European Central Bank, as the successor to the EMI, likewise has its seat in Frankfurt.

In 1994, the EMI started the task of advising Member States on their monetary policies. Together with the Commission, the EMI provided the recommendations for legislation and policy in preparing the transition to the third stage of monetary union. In particular, the EMI commenced the technical preparation for the bank notes that would be used as the single currency—an essential step because of the substantial lead-time necessary before billions of notes could be printed and issued.

The Maastricht Treaty introduced ECT Article 99, which bound Member States to "regard their economic policies as a matter of common concern" and to coordinate them in accordance with guidelines set by the Council, acting by qualified majority. An unusual feature of this coordination is that the Ecofin Council must submit its draft guidelines to the European Council for its "conclusion" on them. This is one of the rare instances in which the EC Treaty recognized a specific role for the European Council, presumably both because setting these guidelines constitutes a politically sensitive matter and because the European Council's "conclusion" adds political weight to the Ecofin Council's guidelines. As is typical in EMU decision-making, the Parliament is only to be kept informed and has no role in the shaping of the guidelines.

Promptly in 1994, the Community began the coordination of national economic policies. Over time, the Commission guidelines for economic coordination have become more detailed and precise. The procedure begins each spring, when all Member States prepare draft budgets and economic forecasts for the following year and present them to the Commission for review. The Commission carefully reviews each draft budget and forecast, both in the light of each State's economy and those of the Broad Economic Policy Guidelines (BEPG) established for the Community as a whole, and makes recommendations for each State. Making use of the Commission analysis, the Ecofin Council in June establishes draft guidelines for each State, often suggesting significant budget modifications or other economic actions. The June European Council meeting then states its "conclusions," and the Ecofin Council formally provides its guidelines to each Member State. In the summer and early fall, each State reacts to the guidelines, usually in accord with them, although occasionally disagreeing with them. In late fall, the Commission reviews again each State's final budget and economic forecasts. The process ends with a final Ecofin Council review of the status of each State's budget and forecast, sometimes with further recommendations.

Commentators have stressed that the economic coordination established by the Maastricht Treaty is purely inter-governmental in character, in contrast to the Community's centralized monetary control by the ECB for States in the third stage. Although this is certainly true, there are valid reasons for the difference in approach. It is obvious that a monetary union cannot function well without coordination of economic policies, because of the substantial spill-over effect of governmental economic policy decisions upon monetary conditions. However, centralized Community economic policy-making would require an enormous cession of national sovereignty, because of the close link between economic policy and fiscal policy, tax collection, social security and social welfare systems, and so on.

In any event, in recent years the economic coordination process has exerted a strong influence on the economic policy of the States and a more Community-wide approach to economic policies.

NOTES AND QUESTIONS

1. Note that no Member State may opt out of the economic coordination process. Because of its role in this process, the Council composed of Economic and Finance Ministers, usually called the Ecofin Council, has grown greatly in importance. How significant do you think are the respective roles of the Commission and the European Council in the coordination process? The Parliament plays no role—do you consider this exclusion justified, or is it another example of a "democratic deficit"?

2. Although the drafters of the Maastricht Treaty decided that centralized monetary control was possible and essential,they did not believe that centralized economic control was either feasible or desirable. Would you agree? It is likely that any of the sensitive fields of national economic policy could ever be transferred to centralized EU control?

6. THE CONVERGENCE CRITERIA

A key feature of the plan for EMU was the idea that Member States must prove their economic and monetary capability to comply with the obligations of central monetary control. Germany and the Netherlands in particular were concerned that their steady economic growth and monetary stability should not be jeopardized by the inclusion of States in the final stage of EMU if they might thereafter promote inflation or loose money policies. High standards for economic and monetary performance were accordingly inserted into the Treaty.

ECT Articles 104 and 121, supplemented by the Treaty Protocols on the Excessive Deficit Procedure and on the Convergence Criteria, set in specific terms the economic and monetary conditions Member States must meet for eligibility to participate in the third and final stage of monetary union. Three of these conditions proved surprisingly attainable. The first is "a high degree of price stability," measured by the attainment of an inflation rate close to that of the three best performing Member States in terms of price stability.

Regulation 2494/95 on harmonized indices of consumer prices, O.J. L 257/1 (Oct. 27, 1995), established for the first time Community-wide standards for this vitally important index, essential to ensure the accuracy of inflation statistics. More accurate Member State and Community-wide consumer inflation statistics, based upon the directive's standards, accordingly became available in 1996 and 1997 for use in assessing satisfaction of the inflation convergence criterion.

In the period 1994–1997, the Member States made highly satisfactory progress in lowering their inflation rates, in some cases to one half or one third of their prior level. This taming of prior high inflation rates certainly represents one of the most obvious benefits achieved in the process of achieving the Monetary Union. By the end of 1997, the Commission estimated the average inflation rate of all Member States to be at around

2.1%. The average inflation rate for the three best performing member States was around 1.5%.

Closely connected to the inflation rate criterion is the second one, requiring Member States' long term interest rates to attain a level not exceeding by more than 2% the level of the three best performing States. Long term interest rates tend to move in tandem with inflation rates (although not invariably), and these rates fell throughout the Union in 1994–1997.

The third criterion is that a Member State's currency must remain within "the normal fluctuation margins provided for by the exchange rate mechanism of the European Monetary System without severe tensions for at least the last two years before the examination". As noted above, fortunately the foreign exchange markets entered a period of relative calm in late 1995 that continued during 1996 and 1997.

The fourth and by far the most difficult criterion is that Member States must not have an excessive deficit. Under ECT Article 104 and the Protocol on the Excessive Deficit Procedure, this criterion has two aspects: (1) the current annual government deficit should not exceed 3% of the national gross domestic product (GDP) at market prices; and (2) the accumulated total government debt should not exceed 60% of the annual GDP.

The target figures of 3% and 60% of annual national GDP respectively were set late in the Intergovernmental Conference, based upon a study made by the Monetary Committee. In view of the traditional use of deficit financing by many Member States to meet current social and economic needs, and the enormous accumulated government debt loads of several States, satisfying the excessive deficit criterion was always recognized as the "make or break" factor in qualification for the final stage.

Although almost all Member States made remarkable progress in 1995–1997 toward reducing their annual deficit and lowering their accumulated total debt, nonetheless, many would have been unable to meet the Protocol criteria if these were to be applied strictly. This is especially true for the total government debt criterion, because at the end of 1997, Belgium, Greece and Italy had total accumulated governmental debt levels well in excess of 100% of their annual GDP, and the Netherlands and Sweden had debt levels in excess of 70% of their annual GDP.

Foreseeing this possibility, the drafters of the relevant Treaty provisions decided that the Council must be able to exercise a certain degree of flexibility. Although Article 121 stipulates that Member States must not have an excessive deficit, it cross-references to Article 104(6), which gives the Council the responsibility for deciding "after an overall assessment whether an excessive deficit exists." The Council in turn works on the basis of a Commission report which need only find that the current annual deficit "has declined substantially and continuously" and is "close to the reference level," and that the total accumulated government debt "is sufficiently diminishing and approaching the reference value at a satisfactory pace."

In addition to the convergence criteria, the Maastricht Treaty stated one political condition for entry into the third stage. Article 116(5) required that all States must make their central banks independent during the second stage. Traditionally only the German and Dutch central banks had enjoyed virtual independence from the political authorities. In 1994, France and Spain enacted legislation making their central banks independent of their governments. In a somewhat surprising decision, immediately after Prime Minister Blair took office in the UK in June 1997, his Labor government made the Bank of England independent. However, successive Swedish governments have always refused to grant independence to its central bank.

7. THE DECISION TO LAUNCH THE THIRD AND FINAL STAGE OF EMU

In the spring of 1998, the time came to assess the efforts of the Member States that wanted to join in the third and final stage of EMU. The Mediterranean States in particular made remarkable progress in 1996–97, due in large measure to the determination of their governments (notably Prime Minister Prodi, who pledged to resign if Italy did not make it), and strong support by the media and business leaders. On the other hand, France and Germany encountered severe last minute difficulties in 1997—France, because of the expensive measures taken by the newly-elected Socialist Government of Prime Minister Jospin to combat high unemployment, and Germany due to the continued high cost of integrating an economically-weak East Germany.

On March 24–25, 1998, the European Monetary Institute and the Commission issued reports which concluded that every State but Greece had met the convergence criteria described. This was a decidedly liberal decision, since Belgium and Italy continued to have a total government debt level of around 120% of GDP, and France, Germany and Italy narrowly managed to hit the current deficit target of 3% of GDP only by extraordinary and somewhat controversial revenue and tax measures.

For a critical review of the convergence criteria and the degree to which some Member States had only marginally satisfied them, see P. Beaumont & N. Walker, The Euro and European Legal Order 169, in P. Beaumont & N. Walker, Legal Framework of the Single European Currency (Hart 1999). For an appraisal of the convergence criteria by a leading Princeton economist, see P. Kenen, The Transition to EMU: Issues and Implications, 4 Colum. J. Eur. L. 359 (1998).

Accordingly, on May 3, 1998, the Council, in its extraordinary composition of Heads of State or Government, decided that eleven Member States (Austria, Belgium, Finland, France, Germany, Ireland, Italy, Luxembourg, the Netherlands, Portugal and Spain) qualified for entry into the third stage on January 1, 1999. Subsequently, in June 2000 the Council, in its extraordinary composition of Heads of State or Government, endorsed Greece's entry into the third stage on Jan. 1, 2001. This group of Member States that have entered the third stage are often said to comprise the Euro-zone, or the Euro-area. Denmark and the United Kingdom remained outside the third stage, in virtue of their Maastricht Treaty Protocols.

Sweden is a somewhat curious case, because it did not negotiate for an opt-out Protocol at the time of its accession to the EU in 1995, but nonetheless failed to meet the EC Treaty condition that it make its central bank independent. Despite this failure, no one expects the Commission to bring an infringement action against Sweden to compel it to make its central bank independent—essentially, Sweden is being permitted to opt out of the third stage without a Treaty Protocol to that effect.

Immediately after deciding upon the States which would enter the third stage on January 1, 1999, the Heads of State and Government designated Wim Duisenberg, the former head of the Dutch Central Bank, well-known as an advocate of strict monetary policy, as the first European Central Bank President. They also named the other five Executive Board members, choosing prominent economists and national central bank members, for staggered terms of four to eight years. The European Central Bank commenced operations on July 1, 1998, working intensively to take basic policy decisions, recruit and structure its staff, set its internal procedures and otherwise prepare to undertake its responsibilities. Its actual control of monetary policy started on January 1, 1999.

8. THE 'INS' AND THE 'OUTS'

Although the political leadership of the Community could take great satisfaction in the decision that twelve Member States joined in the third and final stage of EMU—a higher figure than even optimists had hoped for when the Maastricht Treaty was drafted—nonetheless there was a fly in the ointment. The Union is now divided into a 'two-tier' structure, perhaps permanently.

The UK, Denmark and Sweden continue to have complete autonomy in the control of their monetary policy, which is set by their central banks independently of the ECB. The three countries likewise retain their own currencies, a crucial factor for the UK in view of the traditional importance of the pound as an international currency.

Both Denmark and Sweden have tried unsuccessfully to secure the approval of their people for entering the Euro-zone. Denmark held a referendum on Sept. 28, 2000, but a narrow 53% majority opposed the move. A Swedish referendum on Sept. 23, 2003 produced a decisive 56% negative vote. Neither State is likely to hold another referendum in the near future.

As for the UK, the successive Labor governments of Prime Minister Blair and Brown took the policy position that the UK should ultimately join the Euro-zone, but only when several crucial economic criteria are met. The most important condition is that both the UK and the Euro-zone should be enjoying a comparable period of GNP growth, low inflation and moderate unemployment—a condition unlikely to be satisfied soon. Moreover, the Conservative party has opposed the UK's entry into EMU ever since Prime Minister Thatcher, a position currently taken by Prime Minister Cameron.

As for the twelve Central European and Mediterranean States, all indicated before their accession their desire to join the Euro-zone. Until the global recession began in 2009, all had satisfactory rates of GNP growth, but many had high inflation and annual deficits in excess of 3%. Nonetheless, Cyprus, Malta, Slovenia and the Slovak Republic were able to satisfy the convergence criteria described previously, and joined the Euro-zone in 2007 and 2008, making a total of sixteen States in the final stage of Monetary Union. In June 2010, the Council endorsed Estonia's adoption of the Euro in January 2011. Unfortunately, the current recession makes it quite difficult for any other Central European State to be able to satisfy the convergence criteria in the near future.

ECT Article 122(1) regulates the status of the States that remain outside the Euro-zone, which are called "Member States with a derogation." Not surprisingly, these States do not share in the decision-making procedures within the Euro-zone. They are not involved in the selection of the members of the Executive Board of the ECB nor in the adoption of measures taken to introduce or regulate the Euro. Naturally, their central bank governors are not members of the ECB's Governing Council.

On the other hand, so long as any States remain outside the Euro-zone, the Protocol on the Statute of the ECB provides that there shall be a General Council, composed of the President and Vice–President of the ECB together with the governors of all Member State national central banks. This General Council coordinates monetary policy between the Euro-zone and the States with a derogation. Moreover, the economic coordination procedures described in section C1 above continue to fully apply to them.

The Luxembourg European Council in December 1997 dealt with relations between the 'ins' and the 'outs', deciding that the finance minister of the Euro-zone States may meet informally as the Euro Group within the Ecofin Council to discuss policy issues concerning the Euro and monetary matters, but that the entire Ecofin Council must vote to take legally binding measures in accordance with the Maastricht Treaty's provisions in this regard. This policy decision is of considerable importance, because some States participating in the third stage had wanted a Council consisting only of the participating States to meet and vote separately—an approach that the UK vehemently opposed. As we shall see in section G, the Lisbon Treaty now formally regulates the status of the Euro Group.

C. THE EUROPEAN CENTRAL BANK

The heart of the Delors Plan was the creation of a powerful body for the control of monetary policy throughout the Monetary Union. This is the European Central Bank, functioning at the core of the European System of Central Banks, which is composed of all 27 national central banks. The essential role of the ECB, working through the ESCB, is to set the monetary policy of the Euro-zone States, determining the goals of that policy in accord with the objectives set in the Treaty (see sub-section 3), and adopting the rules and regulations to execute it. This power of the ECB makes its structure and its relations with the political institutions of great political and practical importance. The ECB's decisions and operations are closely watched by business and financial institutions and the media. Indeed, its current President, Jean–Claude Trichet, is probably second in popular recognition only to Commission President Barroso.

1. STRUCTURE, POWERS AND JUDICIAL REVIEW

ECT Article 107 (now TFEU Article 129) declares that the ESCB is composed of the ECB and the participating national central banks (NCBs). The "decision-making bodies" of the ECB are its Executive Board and the Governing Council. The Protocol on the Statute of the ESCB and the ECB specifies that the Executive Board is composed of the President, the Vice–President and four members, all named for eight years by common accord of the Euro-zone States, without any possibility of reappointment.

The Protocol further provides that the ECB's Governing Council is composed of the Executive Board and the Governors of the participating NCBs (currently the Governing Council has a total of twenty-two members). The Governing Council has the primary power to set policy guidelines and take decisions on "monetary objectives, key interest rates and the supply of reserves," while the Executive Board implements these policies and decisions in conjunction with the NCBs (Protocol art. 12). The Governing Council meets at least ten times a year and can act by simple majority vote (but press releases indicate that the Governing Council strives for a consensus, if possible).

Apart from its control of monetary policy (discussed below), the ECB has control of the emission and supply of the Euro as legal currency. ECT Article 106 (now TFEU Article 128) gives the ECB the exclusive power to issue banknotes, operating through the NCBs. Although the same article authorizes the Council to determine the denomination and design of coins, and the Euro-zone States to issue them, the ECB must approve the volume of coins issued, as part of its control of the supply of money.

The European Central Bank has been granted a substantial degree of regulatory power. Pursuant to ECT Article 110 (now TFEU Article 132), the ECB may issue regulations to implement its monetary policy, to govern the minimum reserves which it requires banking institutions to keep on deposit with the ECB and national central banks, and to regulate bank clearing and payment systems. The Council could also authorize the ECB to carry out prudential supervision of financial institutions, but this presently seems quite unlikely. The ECB may also take binding decisions or issue recommendations or opinions.

In view of the scope of the European Central Bank's role and tasks, and the dimension of its regulatory powers, it is important that the EC Treaty clearly delineates the principle of judicial review. The Maastricht Treaty amended ECT Article 230 (now TFEU Article 263) to grant the Court of Justice jurisdiction over actions brought by Member States, the Council, the Commission or private parties against the ECB to review the legality of its acts, and for actions brought by the ECB against the Community political institutions in order to protect its "prerogatives." ECT Article 234 (now TFEU Article 267) was amended to include the acts of the ECB among those which may be the subject of questions referred to the Court of Justice by national courts.

It is likely that recourse to a legal challenge of an ECB decision would rarely occur, and the Court is certain to give a broad field of discretion to the ECB's monetary measures. Nonetheless, the possibility of review by the Court of Justice should serve as a restraint against arbitrary, poorly reasoned or inadequately justified rules or decisions, in line with well-established Court precedents on the need for a reasoned basis for Council, Commission and Parliamentary acts. For an appraisal of judicial review, see the excellent study by Prof. Paul Craig, EMU, the ECB and Judicial Review, in P. Beaumont & N. Walker, The Legal Framework of the Single European Currency (Hart 1999).

2. THE PRINCIPLE OF INDEPENDENCE

ECT Article 108 (now TFEU Article 130) states the important principle that the ECB and the ESCB shall have total independence in their decision making. They are categorically forbidden to take instructions either from Community institutions or from Member States. This provision represents a major policy decision, because most central banks were not independent of their governments prior to the 1990's, and because some Member States were reluctant to allow the ECB and ESCB to enjoy total independence from the Council. Indeed, France even proposed that the European Council should be able to give guidelines to the ECB just as it did to the Community's political institutions, but Germany vetoed the suggestion.

The principle of independence was strongly advocated by Germany, whose Central Bank enjoys such independence from its government, as critical in order to ensure that the ECB and the ESCB would have the freedom to follow strict, and hence often unpopular, monetary policies. Accessory to the principle of independence of the ECB is that of the independence of the national central banks and their members, because the national central banks represent the usual operational arm of the ESCB. Giving the ECB Executive Board members a relatively long eight year term, but excluding any possibility of a second term, was intended to reinforce their independence.

A legitimate question may be raised as to the wisdom of incorporating the principle of independence into the EC Treaty as a constitutional principle. As some commentators have observed, this gives the ECB greater independence than the US Federal Reserve Board and virtually all central banks prior to EMU. On a comparative note, the US Federal Reserve Board does not enjoy constitutional status and, although it enjoys great independence by custom, nothing prevents the Congress from adopting legislation mandating certain goals or policies, a power that the Congress has on rare occasion exercised.

Perhaps the best academic commentaries on the subject of the strict independence accorded by the Treaty to the ECB, the ESCB and the national central banks are by Prof. Rosa Lastra, EMU and Central Bank Independence (arguing that a high level of independence promotes price stability, but that independence must be balanced by democratic accountability), and by Professors Jakob de Haan and Laurence Gormley, Independence and Accountability of the ECB (arguing for functional autonomy rather than strict independence and urging greater accountability for the ECB), both contained in M. Andenas, ed., European Economic and Monetary Union (Kluwer 1997).

Although there is no evidence that the independence of the ECB or the ESCB in their monetary operations has been disregarded since 1999, a disquieting note was struck at the time of the European Council's choice of Wim Duisenberg in May 1998 as the first President of the ECB. President Chirac of France proposed instead Jean–Claude Trichet, the Governor of the Bank of France, and attempted to block the otherwise unanimous preference for Duisenberg. A compromise was struck: Duisenberg declared that he "would not want to serve the full term" of eight years at some point after he reached 68, i.e. around 2003. The European Council then informally agreed that Trichet would ultimately serve the remainder of the term. The general reaction of the media and subsequent academic commentators was that this sort of compromise was not only unseemly, but jeopardized the independence of the ECB. In fact, President Duisenberg did retire in 2003, and the European Council then designated Jean–Claude Trichet as President for a full eight-year term.

Somewhat surprisingly, the extent of the ECB's independence became a crucial issue in a significant Court judgment in 2003. When discussing efforts to combat fraud in Community expenditures in Chapter 3E, we noted that the Commission created in 1999 the European Anti–Fraud Office (commonly called OLAF), to combat "fraud, corruption and any other illegal activity." The Parliament and Council then adopted Regulation 1073/1999, O.J. L 136/1 (May 25, 1999), authorizing OLAF to carry out investigations within all Community institutions, agencies and bodies, with a right of immediate access to all accounts and documents.

Although the ECB was undoubtedly fully aware of the Regulation, it adopted its own procedures, creating an Anti–Fraud Committee composed of three independent outsiders with impeccable credentials, with full power to carry out internal investigations with in the ECB. Presumably the ECB believed in good faith that Regulation 1073/1999 did not apply to it because of its Treaty guarantee of independence.

COMMISSION v. EUROPEAN CENTRAL BANK

(ECB independence)

Case C–11/00, [2003] ECR I–7147.

[In 2000 the Commission, supported by the Council, sued the ECB to annul its decision creating the Anti–Fraud Committee and compel it to accept OLAF's jurisdiction to investigate ECB accounts and documents. The ECB contended that its Treaty grant of independence insulated it from any outside investigation by OLAF. The Court of Justice decided in favor of the Commission.]

92 [U]nder Article 4(2) EC and Article 105(1) EC, the primary objective of the ESCB, at the heart of which is the ECB, is to maintain price stability and, without prejudice to this objective, to lend support to the general economic policies in the European Community, with a view to contributing to the achievement of the objectives of the Community as laid down in Article 2 EC, which include an economic and monetary union and also the promotion of sustainable and non-inflationary growth. It follows that the ECB, pursuant to the EC Treaty, falls squarely within the Community framework.

* * *

114 In the ECB's submission, the guarantee of independence covers not only the performance of the ESCB's basic tasks as set out in Article 105(2) EC but, more generally, the exercise of all the ECB's other powers under the EC Treaty, that is to say, particularly the powers which are conferred on it by Articles 12.3 and 36.1 of the ESCB Statute concerning its internal organisation and the conditions of employment of its staff, and which include the adoption of anti-fraud measures.

* * *

118 [T]he ECB submits that conferring on OLAF power to conduct internal investigations within the ECB undermines its independence, since both the exercise of such a power and the mere threat of its being exercised are capable of bringing pressure to bear on the members of the Governing Council or the Executive Board of the ECB and of jeopardising their independence when taking decisions.

119 Although it concedes that the likelihood that such pressure might ever be exerted in practice or that it might have any impact on decision-making within the ECB is 'extremely small', the ECB maintains that the need to maintain the complete confidence of unstable financial markets makes it essential to avoid any situation potentially capable, even from the aspect of form or mere appearances, of giving rise to fear that OLAF's powers might be such as to put the Commission in a position to influence the ECB.

* * *

130 [T]he draftsmen of the EC Treaty clearly intended to ensure that the ECB should be in a position to carry out independently the tasks conferred upon it by the Treaty.

* * *

134 As is clear from the wording of Article 108 EC, the outside influences from which that provision seeks to shield the ECB and its decision-making bodies are those likely to interfere with the performance of the 'tasks' which the EC Treaty and the ESCB Statute assign to the ECB. As the Advocate General has pointed out * * *, Article 108 EC seeks, in essence, to shield the ECB from all political pressure in order to enable it effectively to pursue the objectives attributed to its tasks, through the independent exercise of the specific powers conferred on it for that purpose by the EC Treaty and the ESCB Statute.

135 By contrast, as the Commission and the interveners have rightly pointed out, recognition that the ECB has such independence does not have the consequence of separating it entirely from the European Community and exempting it from every rule of Community law. First, it is evident from Article 105(1) EC that the ECB is to contribute to the achievement of the objectives of the European Community, whilst Article 8 EC states that the ECB is to act within the limits of the powers conferred upon it by the EC Treaty and the ESCB Statute. Second, as the Commission has observed, the ECB is, on the conditions laid down by the EC Treaty and the ESCB Statute, subject to various kinds of Community controls, notably review by the Court of Justice and control by the Court of Auditors.* * *

136 It follows from the foregoing that there are no grounds which prima facie preclude the Community legislature from adopting * * * legislative measures capable of applying to the ECB.

137 Furthermore, as pointed out by the Commission and by the Advocate General * * *, the ECB has not established how the fact that it is subject to measures adopted by the Community legislature in the area of fraud prevention and the prevention of any other unlawful activities detrimental to the European Community's financial interests, such as the measures provided for in Regulation No 1073/1999, is such as to undermine its ability to perform independently the specific tasks conferred on it by the EC Treaty.

138 First, neither the fact that OLAF was established by the Commission and is incorporated within the Commission's administrative and budgetary structures * * *, nor the fact that the Community legislature has conferred on such a body external to the ECB powers of investigation on the conditions laid down in Regulation No 1073/1999, is *per se* capable of undermining the ECB's independence.

139 [T]he rules put in place by the regulation reflect the settled intention of the Community legislature to subject the powers conferred on OLAF, first, to guarantees intended to ensure OLAF's complete independence, in particular from the Commission, and, second, to strict observance of the rules of Community law * * *.

* * *

162 [Finally,] although it is indisputable that certain kinds of sensitive information relating to the activities of the ECB must be subject to confidentiality so that the tasks conferred on it by the EC Treaty are not jeopardised, it should be observed in that regard that Regulation No 1073/1999 specifically provided that OLAF's internal investigations must be carried out under the conditions and in accordance with the procedures provided for in the regulation and in the decisions adopted by each institution, body, office and agency.* * * [I]t is therefore not inconceivable that certain matters specific to the performance of the ECB's tasks will, where appropriate, be taken into account by the ECB when it adopts [its internal decision to implement the procedures] of Regulation No 1073/1999. * * *.

NOTES AND QUESTIONS

1. The Court essentially followed the careful analysis provided by Advocate General Francis Jacobs. Do you think the Court is right in concluding that the ECB's independence is essentially limited to its functional monetary policy operations? Could there be any risk of abuse in subjecting the ECB and its officials to OLAF's power to conduct investigations into claims of fraud and financial misconduct? If OLAF were not itself declared to be to be independent by the Commission decision creating it, would your view change?

2. One of the ECB's arguments was that its internal anti-fraud procedures could co-exist with those of OLAF. The Court concluded otherwise. Nothing in the ECB's procedures directly interfered with those of the OLAF. The recitals in the ECB's decision creating its internal procedures certainly indicate that the ECB believed that it was not subject to OLAF's review, but is that a sufficient reason to strike down the ECB's procedures? What harm, if any, would OLAF suffer by permitting the ECB to have its own anti-fraud procedures? Would not the independent experts in the proposed ECB Anti-Fraud Committee be more apt to be expert in dealing with financial misconduct at the ECB than the personnel of OLAF?

3. PRICE STABILITY AND SECONDARY OBJECTIVES OF THE ECB AND THE ESCB

ECT Article 105(1) (now TFEU Article 127(1)) set "price stability" as the "primary objective" of the ESCB, thus accepting the German argument that the success of the Bundesbank's monetary policy was due in large measure to its principal emphasis on price stability. Price stability is equated with a low inflation rate for consumer products and services. The Treaty fixed no specific target for price stability. This left the ECB with considerable discretion in fixing some appropriate target rate for low inflation for the Euro-zone.

Even before the ECB assumed its control of monetary policy on Jan. 1, 1999, it set the most important elements of its "monetary policy strategy" on Oct. 13, 1998. The ECB then adopted the following standard: "Price stability shall be defined as a year-on-year increase in the Harmonized Index of Consumer Prices (HICP) for the Euro area of below 2%."

Since 1996 a regulation has set common standards for each State's calculation of its consumer price increases, so that the HICP can be considered a reliable measuring indicator for the entire Community. Also, the EMI had previously considered a 2% annual increase in inflation as the appropriate ceiling for price stability, so that the ECB's decision to use 2% as the maximum acceptable level for consumer price inflation was not surprising.

In a press release, the ECB noted several implications that can be drawn from its standard for price stability. The reference to the Euro area as a whole meant that the ECB would "not react to specific regional or national developments." Price stability would be measured "over the medium term" (presumably meaning annually, as a rule), so that the ECB would not seek to control "short term volatility in prices." Also implicit in the definition is that the ECB would act against any deflation in consumer prices that might occur in a serious recession. Indeed, subsequently the ECB has indicated that it regards inflation that is close to, but less than 2% per year, to be not of concern, because most economist consider that a low level of inflation necessarily accompanies economic growth.

As a secondary duty, the ESCB is required by ECT Article 105 (now TFEU Article 127) to "support the general economic policies in the Community." The ESCB is also to "act in accordance with the principle of an open market economy with free competition," a major innovation in the Maastricht Treaty urged by Germany as a "ground rule" for ESCB action. But although the ESCB will certainly often develop rules and shape decisions to achieve some secondary objective, ECT Article 105(1)declares this to be "without prejudice to the objective of price stability," which is thus categorically given the primary emphasis.

This Treaty emphasis upon price stability was demanded by Germany, whose fear of inflation is understandable, given its catastrophic inflation during the 1920s. Germany's enviable post World War II record of low inflation was due in large measure to its Central Bank's strict monetary policies. A low inflation rate encourages long-term investment and promotes confidence in long-term supply contracts, market stability, greater certainty in budgetary planning and tax collection, stable securities markets, insurance for long-term savings, social protection for pensioners, and so on.

But giving primary policy emphasis upon achieving and keeping a low inflation rate may handicap Member State action to combat economic and monetary crises and, in particular, efforts to reduce high unemployment and concomitant social distress. European and American economists are, not surprisingly, divided upon their assessment of the degree of social and economic harm produced by high inflation versus that produced by high unemployment, and upon the precise nature of the link between inflation rates and unemployment rates.

On a comparative note, in the United States the Federal Reserve places a high premium on maintaining price stability, but that is not its only concern. The statutory goal set for the Board of Governors of the Federal Reserve system is to "promote effectively the goals of maximum employment, stable prices, and moderate long-term interest rates." It is noteworthy that for the Federal Reserve price stability is not given special priority and that "maximum employment" is a specific goal, indeed the first mentioned. The Full Employment and Balanced Growth Act of 1978 required the Federal Reserve to provide detailed bi-annual economic reports to Congress, including specifically "past and prospective developments in employment, unemployment, production, investment, real income, productivity, international trade and payments, and prices."

In view of this more balanced presentation of the Federal Reserve's various goals in developing monetary policy, some commentators have questioned whether "price stability" ought to have been stated to be the primary goal of the ECB in the Maastricht Treaty. This is particularly true in view of the grave problem of persistently high unemployment levels in many Member States. Thus, during the severe 1991–1994 recession in the Community some Member States were especially hard hit— Finland, Portugal and Spain had unemployment at or approaching 20%. Indeed, unemployment averaged over 10% at the end of 1996.

The Treaty of Amsterdam, effective May 1, 1999, highlighted the importance of Community activity to promote employment by amending TEU Article 2 to insert "a high level of employment" as a Treaty goal. Similarly, Article 2 of the EC Treaty was amended to include among the Community's tasks "a high level of employment and social protection," immediately before "sustainable and non-inflationary growth." The Amsterdam Treaty's emphasis on the promotion of high employment naturally lent vigor to the arguments of those political leaders and media and academic commentators who urge the ECB to give greater weight to this goal in developing its monetary policies.

Nonetheless, the ECB view, articulated by President Duisenberg and currently by President Trichet, is that the ECB only has the capacity to work for price stability and would be ineffective in trying to achieve other goals. The ECB considers that unemployment levels can only be reduced by structural measures, such as governmental action to reduce labor rigidity and the level of social welfare benefits and to encourage capital investment.

On a comparative note, as previously observed, the Federal Reserve does take employment levels into consideration in determining its monetary policies. This was strikingly the case in the 1996–99 period when the Federal Reserve, under the leadership of Chairman Greenspan, declined to raise interest rates to cut off incipient inflation that was widely predicted to develop inevitably when unemployment dropped below 6% (in application of an economic theory, the well-known Phillips curve). During those years, the national unemployment rate declined steadily past 5% and down to around 4%, without a sharp increase in inflation. The Federal Reserve also rejects the idea of a specific inflation target level. In October 2001, Chairman Greenspan declared that "a specific numerical inflation target would represent an unhelpful and false precision."

For a legal and political critique of the Treaty emphasis on price stability, see the views of Prof. Matthias Herdegen of Bonn, Price Stability and Budgetary Restraints in the EMU: The Law as Guardian of Economic Wisdom, 35 Common Mkt. L. Rev. 9 (1998). Ottmar Issing, an ECB Executive Board member, defended the ECB position in The ECB's Monetary Policy Experience After the First Year, 22 J. Policy Modeling 325 (2000). A critical view is presented by the well-known US economist Martin Feldstein, The ECB and The Euro: The First Year, 22 J. Policy Modeling 325 (2000).

NOTES AND QUESTIONS

1. Apart from Germany, no other Member State had price stability as the primary objective of its central bank. Do you agree that price stability should be the sole objective of the ECB? Do you think that the Treaty should state the ECB's primary objective, or that this should be left to secondary legislation, which could conceivably be amended from time to time?

2. If the Federal Reserve can take into account the level of unemployment in setting target interest rates, do you think the ECB could likewise do so? Or do you believe that the European high unemployment levels are due to structural factors beyond the influence of the ECB?

4. DEMOCRATIC ACCOUNTABILITY AND TRANSPARENCY

As we have already briefly indicated, the European Parliament was given only a modest role in the developmental stages of EMU, and in its operational structure in the final stage. Parliament need only be consulted in the Council's crucial decision on which Member States qualify for entry into the final stage of Monetary Union, and in the designation of the members of the ECB's Executive Board.

In several resolutions during and after the 1990–91 IGC, Parliament requested at least some share in the decision-making process in the creation of the Monetary Union and in operations thereafter. Both the Parliament and a significant number of academic commentators regard its absence from this process as one of the most important and regrettable illustrations of the "democratic deficit." In particular, one may wonder why the Parliament does not have the right to assent to the determination of the States that qualify for the final stage of EMU, considering that a decision of such capital political importance ought to have the strongest democratic support.

Parliament has also complained that it lacked any formal voice in the designation of Executive Board members, despite its request to be involved in this process. On a comparative note, in the US the President's nominees for the Federal Reserve Board are subject to confirmation hearings and must be approved by the Senate. Some commentators support the Parliament's position, considering that not only is democratic legitimacy better respected by a system of formal hearings and approval by the Parliament, but the process enables a careful and public review of a nominee's credentials and policy views.

Fortunately, in 1998 President Duisenberg and the other Executive Board nominees did appear voluntarily before Parliament in what were popularly called confirmation hearings, and Parliament endorsed all the nominees. In an April 1998 resolution, Parliament called upon the Member States not to designate any nominee whom it did not endorse. As the initial Executive Board members have ended their terms, the nominees to succeed them have continued the practice of undergoing such confirmation hearings.

The Parliament's role with regard to ECB operations is decidedly modest. Parliament must give its assent to any Council legislation granting the ECB powers of prudential supervision over credit institutions and other financial institutions, or in any change in significant provisions of the Statute of the ESCB, but such legislation is not very likely. Otherwise the drafters of the EMU Treaty articles considered that the principle of independence dictated that Parliament should be given no role of legislative supervision over the ECB's monetary policy decisions and regulations.

Some commentators argue that this total insulation of monetary decision making from democratic control is a highly debatable proposition. Making it hard for Parliament to interfere with the ECB's control of monetary policy is one thing, making it impossible (by the Treaty itself) is quite another. The strongest critique has been offered by Professors L. Gormley & J.de Haan in their article, "The Democratic Deficit of the European Central Bank," 21 European L. Rev. 95, (1996), which concludes that "monetary policy ultimately must be controlled by democratically elected politicians." Id. at 112.

Obviously, the drafters of the Treaty believed that Parliament should have no direct role in the shaping of monetary policy, which should be left exclusively to the technical expertise of the ECB and the national central banks. Although the ECB thus has an extraordinary level of autonomy in its control of monetary policy, it is by no means exempt from democratic accountability—the obligation to explain and perhaps defend its actions and views to the political institutions, namely the Commission, the Ecofin Council and particularly the Parliament. ECT Article 113 requires the ECB to provide an annual report to the Parliament, the Council, the Commission and the European Council. The same article permits Parliament committees to hold sessions to hear the views of the ECB President and other Executive Board members.

On April 2, 1998, Parliament adopted a prominent resolution on the democratic accountability of the ECB. Parliament stressed that such accountability was essential to balance the independence of the ECB, which goes further than that of any prior central bank. Parliament requested that the ECB President or other Executive Board members meet quarterly with its economic committee to assess monetary and economic developments.

Fortunately, the ECB's reaction was favorable. President Duisenberg and other initial ECB members stressed the ECB's desire to be highly transparent, equal to or better than any other central bank in that regard. Although the ECB's meetings and deliberations are strictly secret and its internal votes confidential (unlike the Federal Reserve and the Bank of England, which each provide minutes of their meetings and a summary of votes several weeks after each meeting),the ECB provides a report after each monthly or special meeting and the ECB President customarily holds a news conference at that time. The ECB President or another representative also attends quarterly meetings with the Parliament to explain current ECB policy and its views on economic developments, and to answer questions in quite lively sessions.

Moreover, in addition to its annual report, which provides each spring an extensive survey of economic and monetary conditions in the preceding year, the ECB publishes a monthly bulletin, which provides interim economic information and an analysis of ECB monetary decisions. The ECB also publishes a plethora of studies and reports on monetary and economic topics, most of them posted on its active website.

For an assessment of the democratic accountability of the ECB and the transparency of its operations, see a trio of contrasting articles: Professor William Buiter's initial strong critique, Alice in Euroland, 37 J. Common Mkt Studies 181 (1999); ECB Executive Board member Ottmar Issing's vigorous defense, The Eurosystem: Transparent and Accountable, or 'Willem in Euroland,' 37 J. Common Mkt. Studies 503 (1999), and a more neutral appraisal by Professors Jakob de Haan & Sylvester Eijffinger, The Democratic Accountability of the ECB: A Comment on Two Fairy Tales, 38 J. Common Mkt. Studies 393 (2000). F. Amtenbrink & K. Van Duin provide a current appraisal in The ECB before the European Parliament: Theory and Practice after 10 Years of Monetary Dialogue, 34 Eur. L. Rev. 561 (2009).

NOTES AND QUESTIONS

1. Do you think that there exists a "democratic deficit" in the creation and operation of EMU, or do you think that the decision-making process should be essentially left to monetary experts and insulated from parliamentary intervention? Specifically, should the Parliament be empowered to approve the nominations to the ECB Executive Board, just as it approves the proposed candidates for a new Commission? Should the Parliament have a right of assent, or veto, when new States (whether Denmark, the UK or Sweden, or the Member States in Central Europe) seek to join the Euro-zone?

2. How important is the principle of the democratic accountability of the ECB? Should any political body—the European Council, the Ecofin Council, or Parliament—have the power to provide general or long-term policy guidelines to the ECB (as the Congress can to the Federal Reserve)?

3. What importance does the ECB seem to be giving to the transparency of its decision-making and policies? How useful do its reports to Parliament seem to be? Do you think that increased transparency is still necessary, e.g., in the form of minutes of its meetings made public several weeks after the meeting, as the Federal Reserve does?

D. THE INTRODUCTION AND USE OF THE EURO

From the outset of planning for EMU, the introduction of a new single currency for the Euro-zone States was seen as not only integral to the success of EMU, but providing perhaps its greatest benefits. At the very least, the adoption of a simple currency eliminates transaction costs accompanying the transfer of products and services across frontiers.

The greatest economic benefits provided by a single currency are the creation of immediate price transparency for consumers in the choice of products and services throughout the Euro-zone (notably for tourists and persons residing in frontier zones, or for those purchasing cars, computers or other higher-priced items), and the promotion of greater market integration and inter-state competition, especially in the financial sector, but also for many commercial and professional products and services. These two benefits should in theory lead to two others—a reduction in the inflation rate for widely-distributed consumer products and an increase in competitiveness for Euro-zone enterprises, especially in the financial sector.

Finally, and of great importance to the Community political leadership, is the symbolic value represented by the adoption of a single currency. The use of the Euro by all residents in the Euro-zone inevitably brings home to them on a daily basis a realization of their status as citizens of the European Union.

1. POLICY DECISIONS AND LEGISLATION

The Madrid European Council in December 1995 took the most important policy decisions concerning the Euro as a currency. This meeting endorsed the "scenario for the changeover to the single currency," largely as proposed by the Commission and the EMI. The European Council also adopted the name, "Euro," for the banknotes and largest denomination coins for the new single currency, considering the name to be "simple" and to "symbolize Europe" while being easy to use in all languages.

The scenario, or timetable, called for the preparation and approval of all essential legislation concerning the introduction of the Euro in 1997–1998. During 1999–2001, the Euro would be used for Community and participating Member State accounts, loans and inter-state financial transactions. Banks, financial institutions and commercial enterprises might use the Euro in their transactions starting in 1999, but would not be required to do so (the principle commonly known as "no prohibition, no compulsion"). Euro banknotes and coins should be introduced and become legal tender on January 1, 2002, and national currency should cease to be legal tender no later than June 30, 2002.

Two key regulations set out the legal terms upon which the Euro should be introduced and operate as the sole currency for the Euro-zone States. The first was Council Regulation 974/98 on the introduction of the Euro, O.J. L 139/1 (May 11, 1998), which essentially gave legal force to the policy decisions reached by the Madrid European Council in December 1995. Articles 10–11 mandated the ECB to put Euro banknotes into circulation on Jan. 1, 2002 and the Member States to issue Euro and cent coins at the same date, both assuming the status of legal tender. Article 12 required participating states to "ensure adequate sanctions against counterfeiting" of Euros.

Of equal importance was Council Regulation EC 1103/97 on certain provisions relating to the introduction of the Euro, O.J. L 162/1 (June 19, 1997). Article 2 of the regulation specified that any reference in a legal instrument to an ECU should be replaced by one to a Euro, on a one ECU to one Euro basis. The regulation was commonly known as the "continuity of contracts regulation," because that was its principal subject. Although a recital to the regulation notes that "it is a generally accepted principle of law" that the continuity of contracts and other legal instruments is not affected by the "introduction of a new currency," nonetheless the regulation was adopted "in order to reinforce legal certainty and clarity." The key provision is Article 3, which stated:

"The introduction of the Euro shall not have the effect of altering any term of a legal instrument or of discharging or excusing performance under any legal instrument, nor give a party the right unilaterally to alter or terminate such an instrument. This provision is subject to anything which parties may have agreed."

This legally binding rule of continuity of contracts was meant to bar completely any claim for recission, cancellation or non-performance under national law based on statutory or case law rules on frustration, impossibility, material alteration of terms, inequity, and so forth. Thus, the regulation provided clear guidance to business operators and avoided unnecessary litigation.

The final crucial decision enabling the use of the Euro as a "virtual currency" during the 1999–2001 transition period was the adoption of irrevocable conversion rates between the Euro and each participating State's national currency. This was achieved by a Council Regulation fixing the rates in accord with the market rates prevailing on Dec. 31, 1998. Thus, during the transition period, one Euro equalled approximately 1.96 German Marks, 6.6 French Francs, 166.4 Spanish Pesetas, 1940 Italian Lira, etc.

2. PRACTICAL PREPARATIONS FOR THE INTRODUCTION OF THE EURO

The Commission's 1995 Green Paper on the Introduction of the Single Currency described the principal technical problems that had to be faced and some of the practical measures necessary in moving toward the introduction of the Euro. The Commission indicated that the banking industry and the financial sector would require massive revision of denominations of loans, deposits, security instruments and operating procedures, and that automatic teller machines had to be modified, computer software programs revised, and so on. Public administrators, especially the tax, social security and budgetary authorities, would likewise have to restructure their accounts and their receipts and payment systems, while in the private sector the retail industry would need to revise its accounting and payment system.

Because it took several years to print and safely store the enormous number of new Euro banknotes to issue as legal tender on January 1, 2002, the EMI moved rapidly in 1995 to set the technical specifications for the banknotes, with denominations of 5, 10, 20, 50, 100, 200 and 500. The EMI decided to use non-existent monuments and bridges with a European cultural flair on the banknote faces, together with the European flag and a map depicting Western Europe. Each denomination has a different size and a different color and possesses tactile qualities intended to help the visually impaired to differentiate them. At the start of 1997, the Commission introduced the symbol of the Euro, inspired by the Greek letter epsilon—a written capital E with a small second bar through the middle.

ECT Article 106 (now TFEU Article 128) gives the Council the power to determine the nature of Euro coins. Council Regulation 975/98 on the denominations and technical specifications of Euro coins, O.J. L 139/6 (May 11, 1998), set the standards for the coins. The Council decided to issue one and two Euro coins, and 1, 2, 5, 10, 20 and 50 cent coins. The regulation set their shape, size, color and edges, and observed that the vending machine association representatives and the European Blind Union were duly consulted to ensure that the coins would be as suitable as possible for convenient and safe use.

The Commission and the ECB estimated that around 15 billion bank notes and 55 billion coins had to be printed and minted before Jan. 1, 2002. This herculean task required not only intensive speed, but also careful security precautions, especially in the storage and transport of the currency and coins.

A Commission Recommendation concerning dual display of prices, O.J. L 130/26 (May 1, 1998), urged retailers and others to employ such dual displays of prices in order to familiarize consumers with the exchange rates. The dual displays were to be "unambiguous, easily identifiable and clearly legible." The Commission also urged banks and utilities to issue statements and bills on a dual basis.

By all media reports, the initial launch of the Euro as legal tender in January 2002 proved highly successful. In the main the changeover went smoothly. The ECB estimated that 95% of all cash transactions were in Euros within the Euro-zone by the end of the third week in January. A 1998 Commission Recommendation to banks had urged that they should not charge customers for the exchange of national currencies into Euros in "household amounts" and banks respected this recommendation. The media reported that the public was enthusiastic in its acceptance of the Euro. The concern that merchants would seize the conversion period as an occasion to round up prices sharply does not seem to have been justified. According to a Eurobarometer poll in November 2002, a majority of people reported that they had no difficulty in converting to Euros, and less than 10% reported that they had experienced serious difficulties.

A Commission report on the introduction of the Euro, issued on Dec. 19, 2002, COM (2002) 747, indicated the massive nature of the change-over. The Commission stated that by October, there were 7.4 billion banknotes in circulation with a total of 321 billion Euros, augmented by 38 billion coins worth almost 12 billion Euros. The report concluded that banking and retail sectors had successfully adapted to the Euro, although in some States the complicated conversion calculation prompted retailers to continue using dual price displays. The Commission contended that the Euro's introduction had not significantly increased inflation, despite the belief of many consumers that it had done so, especially in cafes, restaurants, hotels and transport.

The Commission has long been concerned by the substantial charges banks levy on cross-border currency transfers, disproportionate both to the banks' internal costs and to their charges on intra-state transfers. Accordingly the Commission proposed, and the Council and Parliament adopted Regulation 2560/2001 on cross-border payments in Euros, O.J. L 344/13 (Dec. 12, 2001), which required banks to disclose precisely their specific charges for cross-border transfers, both to the senders and the recipients of the funds. Charges to customers for any form of electronic payment transaction throughout the Euro-zone (including withdrawals of cash from an ATM machine) up to the amount of 50,000 Euros must be identical to charges made for such transactions within the home State of the bank or other financial institution.

3. THE EURO AS A GLOBAL CURRENCY

On international currency markets, the Euro floats vis-a-vis the US dollar, the pound, the yen, etc. On Jan. 1, 1999, the initial exchange rate was 1 Euro to $1.17. Over the years since then, the Euro first dropped sharply and then rose until 2009, partly due to different economic cycles in the US and the Euro-zone, and partly due to the dollar's standing as the principal international currency used in trade for commodities and as the primary international reserve currency for nations and large investors. The Euro's low came in October 2000 at 82 cents to the dollar, and it remained at less than one dollar until 2003. During that year, the Euro rose to one Euro to $1.25, and tended to rise during 2004–09. The exchange rate was one Euro to $1.43 at the end of 2009, but has steadily declined in 2010 to around $1.20–1.25 in mid-year.

The general view among economists is that the Euro's rise has not been due to greater economic growth in the Euro-zone as compared to the US, because the Euro-zone experienced a recession in 2003, anemic to moderate growth in 2004–07, and a severe recession since 2008. Rather the rise is largely due to the huge annual trade deficit between exports and imports (especially oil) in the US, as well as several large annual budgetary deficits partly caused by the war in Iraq. The Euro's strength versus the dollar obviously is adverse to Euro-zone exports to the US, but it has on the other hand drawn financial investment to the Euro-zone and augmented the role of the Euro as a global currency.

International economists have long observed that certain currencies are dominant global currencies, a role filled by the UK pound before World War II and the dollar since then. A global currency is considered to be one because of its use as a unit of account to calculate the value of goods, especially commodities; as a medium of trade and investment, for the pricing of products and services and the denomination of large-scale loans and securities; and as a store of value, principally as a reserve currency held by central banks in addition to gold. In recent years the Euro has become second only to the dollar, easily surpassing the pound and the yen. Thus, trade in products to and from the Euro-zone is usually denominated in Euros; Russia, Japan, China and other nations hold large reserves in Euros; and the oil-producing countries price some of their exports in Euros.

A substantial volume of Euro banknotes circulate outside the Euro-zone. Montenegro uses the Euro instead of printing its own currency. Many people in Central Europe, in Russia and elsewhere keep Euro banknotes as their personal reserves.

E. RECENT DEVELOPMENTS

1. THE STABILITY AND GROWTH PACT

A major debate in 1996 concerned the Commission's proposed "stability and growth pact," intended to ensure that Member States would continue strict monetary policies and budgetary discipline after they entered the final stage of EMU. Obviously, European Central Bank standards for centralized monetary policy could be undermined if some States could "backpedal" to their former easy money and excessive deficit policies without any effective sanction. Germany fought vigorously for strict standards, while most other States wanted more lenient ones. The December 1996 Dublin European Council adopted a compromise position, which was implemented in 1997.

The initial Stability and Growth Pact was embodied in two Council Regulations. Regulation 1466/97, O.J. L 209/1 (August 2, 1997), sets out the system for on-going surveillance by the Commission and the Council of each State's annual budget and its overall economic performance. Each State participating in the third stage is obligated each spring to prepare an annual "stability program," showing a budget in surplus or close to balance, indicating key economic developments in GDP, employment and inflation, and outlining economic policy measures. These are to be made public, which ensures that opposition party leaders, financial and business experts and the media can all review and debate the reliability of the government's program.

Both the Commission and the Ecofin Council then provide evaluations of the economic realism of the State's program, and can issue recommendations, which can represent an "early warning" to a State that its budget may produce an excessive deficit. The Regulation's prescribed system of surveillance of Euro-zone States' stability programs is grafted upon the economic coordination described in section C1.

Regulation 1467/97, O.J. L 209/6 (August 2, 1997), prescribed the mode by which the Council can determine that a State has developed an excessive annual deficit and sets penalties for a State's failure to take adequate corrective action when it has an excessive annual deficit. The basic penalty imposed is the obligation on the deficient State to provide to the Community a non-interest bearing deposit equal at least to 0.2% of its GDP—obviously a very large amount. Failure of a State to correct its deficit status within two years could lead to a Council decision to convert the deposit into a fine. This potential fine is so large as to make it unlikely that a State will not take the necessary corrective action. Indeed, the excessive deficit regulation was probably intended never to be applied in practice, but to serve as a deterrent threat.

In 2003, Germany experienced a recession with falling tax revenues and unemployment nearing 10%. The annual budget of Socialist government under Chancellor Schroeder exceeded the 3% deficit ceiling in 2002 and 2003, and was likely to do so in 2004. France also went into recession in 2003, and its annual budget exceeded 3% in 2003, and was expected to do so in 2004. In the summer of 2003, the Ecofin Council warned both States that they might face the penalties set in the Excessive Deficit Regulation unless they reduced the deficit below 3%. President Chirac and Chancellor Schroeder both refused, citing the need to stimulate an economic recovery. Many economists supported their view—indeed, even Commission President Prodi characterized the SGP as "stupid" in November 2002.

At a crucial Ecofin Council on Nov. 25, 2003, the Commission proposed the start of the process to impose penalties on France and Germany, but only a few small States were willing to vote in favor. (France voted against proposed sanctions on Germany, and Germany against those proposed for France.) In January 2004, the Commission sued the Council under ECT Article 232 for its failure to act. The Council maintained that ECT Article 104(11) gave it discretion to decide whether or not to launch the sanction process.

The Court's judgment, Commission v. Council (SGP sanctions) Case C–27/04, [2004] ECR I–6649, was praised as 'solomonic' in the media, because both the Commission and the Council could point to some Court conclusions in their favor. The Court's most significant holding was that the Council had discretion to decide whether or not to commence the sanction procedure even after a Commission conclusion that a State was failing to correct an excessive deficit. On the other hand, the Court emphasized that the Council did have a duty to act at some point, because the EC Treaty Article 104 placed on the Council the responsibility for making States observe the requisite budgetary discipline.

In view of the judgment, and the fact that several other States breached the 3% excessive deficit ceiling in 2003, the EU's political leaders realized that the SGP regulations needed to be amended. After difficult negotiations skillfully led by Luxembourg's Prime Minister Juncker in March 2005, the Council reached agreement on amendments. The revised Excessive Deficit Regulation 1056/2005, O.J. L 174/5 (June 27, 2005), enables the Council to excuse an excessive deficit whenever a State experiences "a negative growth rate" or even "a protracted period of very low growth." Moreover, both the Commission and the Council are authorized to review many additional economic factors in evaluating whether an excessive deficit needs to be corrected.

For a review of the initial and revised SGP regulations and the Court judgment, see R. Goebel, Economic Governance in the European Union:

Should Fiscal Stability Outweigh Economic Growth in the Stability and Growth Pact? 31 Fordham Int'l J. 1266 (2008). The amended Excessive Deficit Regulation has enabled the Commission and the Council to be more lenient in accepting State deficits in excess of 3% incurred to stimulate growth and provide social benefits during the unusually severe recession that started in late 2008.

2. RECENT ECB POLICY AND OPERATIONS

Before examining ECB monetary policy intended to achieve price stability, we should note some of the other important operational functions of the ECB. Article 18 of the Protocol on the Statute of the ESCB and the ECB authorizes the ECB and national central banks to conduct open market operations in the financial markets by buying and selling, borrowing and lending Euros, other important national currencies and precious metals, and may conduct credit operations with banks and other financial market participants. Lending funds to banks during periods of monetary crisis in order to provide them with the necessary liquidity to continue their own inter-bank and lending operations, is an important part of the ECB's control of monetary policy.

The Statute's article 22 authorizes the ECB to set regulations "to secure efficient and sound clearing and payment systems." Pursuant to this provision, the ECB regulates the Target payment settlement system, initially launched by the EMI and now in use by over 30,000 banks throughout the Union, processing annually over four million domestic and cross-border payments.

As previously noted, Jean–Claude Trichet, the French central bank governor, replaced Wim Duisenberg as ECB President in October 2003 for a full eight year term. By 2006, all of the other initial Executive Board members had completed their terms, staggered to replace one member each year. The change in membership of the Executive Board has had no impact on EB monetary policy which continues to be very strict.

The Euro-zone States all enjoyed a modest economic recovery in 2004, averaging a GDP growth rate around 2–2.5%, but inflation also remained around 2%. ECB policy remained constant, focusing on keeping inflation in check rather than stimulating growth. That picture remained essentially unchanged in 2005–07, although growth and inflation increased slightly. A sharp conflict arose between the ECB and the Euro Group of Euro-zone finance ministers, led by its President, the Luxembourg Prime Minister Juncker, which contended that the ECB should reduce its target interest rate and follow monetary policies intended to stimulate economic growth. The ECB firmly rejected this advice. ECB President Trichet famously said, "I'm Mr. Euro," indicating that the ECB alone should exercise monetary policy control. For a thoughtful review, see Rene Smits, The ECB's Independence and its Relations with Economic Policymakers, 31 Fordham Int'l L. J. 1614 (2008).

By the start of 2008, however the global recession had begun in several EU States and soon spread to virtually all the others. Hardest hit by a dramatic drop in housing prices and bank failures were Ireland, Spain, and the UK, while Germany, Italy and most of the Central European States suffered from severe declines in export sales and hence GDP. Unemployment rose dramatically in Spain, nearing 20%, and in Ireland, Germany, the UK and the Baltic States. During 2009 the ECB acted energetically to help preserve bank liquidity and prevent bank insolvencies by providing extraordinarily large credit support of over 400 billion Euros at a 1% interest rate to banks, and reduced its target interest rate level to 1% in order to stimulate lending and growth. At the start of 2010, the ECB estimated the recession to have reduced EU GDP by around 4%. Economic statistics in early 2010 indicate that France, Germany, Italy and the UK have emerged from recession, although they continue to have high unemployment.

Toward the end of 2009, the Euro-zone nations learned of a new problem. The newly-elected Greek Socialist government of Prime Minister Papandreou announced that financial mis-management of the prior Conservative government, together with its deliberate concealment of certain state pension and other expenses, meant that Greece would have an unprecedented 12% annual deficit. Because Greece already had global debt amounting to nearly 110% of its annual GDP, the financial markets immediately severely downgraded Greece's sovereign debt. Despite the new government's adoption of strict restraints on government spending, Greece faced the risk of default when large issues of sovereign debt issues came to maturity in mid–2010.

Initially, the other Euro-zone States were extremely reluctant to provide any financial support for Greece. Notably, Chancellor Merkel of Germany declined to lend any funds to prevent Greece's default. Public opinion in Germany and elsewhere strongly opposed financial assistance to Greece, considering that its social welfare system was too generous and its tax collection inadequate. However, Commission President Barroso, the new European Council President Van Rompuy, Luxembourg Prime Minister Juncker, Prime Minister Sarkozy of France, and ECB President Trichet gradually elaborated proposals to support Greece. Meanwhile the Papandreou government moved ahead on austerity spending cuts despite popular demonstrations and strikes, notably increasing the value added tax from 19 to 23%, cutting public sector wages by 20%, and raising the retirement age for public sector employees to 65 from 61.

Ultimately in May 2010, the European political leaders agreed upon an enormous financial support package, assisted by the IMF, which is providing a 250 million Euro credit line. The Commission will create a Special Purpose Vehicle to borrow up to 440 million Euros on bond markets to relend as needed to Greece, which can then pay-off its current sovereign debt issues when due. Meanwhile the ECB will continue to provide 1% interest rate loans to banks for six months and to buy Member State and corporate debt on the open market to support prices.

This unprecedented financial rescue operation was intended not only to provide crucial support to Greece, but also to prevent a ripple effect, inasmuch as the financial markets had also downgraded the sovereign debt of Ireland, Portugal and Spain, struggling to reduce deficits due to their severe recessions. The crisis demonstrated that neither the ECB nor the Euro Group leadership had the capacity alone to cope with the financial plight of the Greek government. Indeed, the Commission was probably the most helpful, both in supporting the Papandreou government's austerity measures, and in facilitating the IMF assistance.

3. THE TREATY OF LISBON

The Lisbon Treaty's TEU Article 13 has formally added the European Central Bank to the list of the seven Union institutions, and the TFEU provisions concerning EMU and the role and powers of the ECB essentially replicate the ECT articles described previously. Thus, TFEU Article 282(1) provides that the ECB shall "conduct the monetary policy of the Union" in conjunction with the national central banks of the Euro-zone States. TFEU Article 282(2) sets "price stability" as the primary objective of the ECB, which shall secondarily "support the general economic policies in the Union." Articles 283–84 replicate ECT Articles 112–13 in describing the Executive Board and the Governing Council of the ECB and the relations between the ECB and the Commission, Council and Parliament.

Note that the TFEU does not grant Parliament any general supervisory power over the ECB and its policies. The Parliament has gained some additional powers. Thus under TFEU Article 121(6) the Parliament will join with the Council in the ordinary legislative procedure in adopting regulations for the multilateral surveillance of national economic policies, under TFEU Article 129(3) in amending most provisions of the Statute of the ESCB and ECB, and under TFEU Article 113 in adopting measures concerning the use of the Euro.

The TFEU largely replicates all of the economic and monetary provisions of the EC Treaty except, of course, deleting those concerning the EMI and the second stage. TFEU Article 139 retains the ECT's description of the convergence criteria that must be satisfied before a State qualifies to join the Euro-zone and TFEU Article 140 prescribes that the Council, acting on the basis of a Commission proposal, and "after consulting the European Parliament and after discussion in the European Council," shall decide by qualified vote whether a State has satisfied the criteria. These provisions accordingly now govern the process of deciding whether any further Central European States might qualify to join the Euro-zone in the future. The Lisbon Treaty also retained the prior Protocols on the Excessive Deficit Procedure and on the Convergence Criteria, and the two Protocols enabling Denmark and the UK to opt out of the final stage of Monetary Union.

The Lisbon Treaty's principal innovation is its treatment of the Euro Group of the finance ministers of the States within the Euro-zone. TFEU

Article 136 authorizes the finance ministers of the States within the Euro-zone, acting by a special qualified majority vote, to adopt measures concerning multi-lateral surveillance and economic policy guidelines that concern only these States. A new Protocol on the Euro Group authorizes these ministers to meet informally "to discuss questions related to the specific responsibilities they share with regard to the single currency." The Euro Group has in fact been doing this since 1999. The Protocol also authorizes these ministers to elect a President for a two and a half year term. Again, they have already been doing this informally. Luxembourg's Prime Minister Jean–Claude Juncker, who also serves as finance minister, has been serving as President, chairing the Euro Group meetings and serving as spokesman to the ECB and the political institutions.

Further Reading

M. Andemas, ed., European Economic and Monetary Union (Kluwer 1997)

P. Beaumont & N. Walker, ed., The Legal Framework of The Single European Currency (Hart 1999)

L. Bini Smaghi & D. Gros, Open Issues in European Central Banking (St. Martin's, 2000)

C. Crouch, ed., After the Euro (Oxford, 2000)

P. DeGrauwe, Economics of Monetary Union (6th ed. Oxford U.P. 2005)

R. Lastra, Legal Foundations of International Monetary Stability (Oxford U.P. 2006)

R. Smits, The European Central Bank (Kluwer 1997)

PART 7

SPECIFIC COMMUNITY POLICIES

■ ■ ■

This part covers five important topics. We first turn to environmental protection, a field in which the EU has long been active. Chapter 32 describes in general terms the scope of the EU's harmonization efforts and examines the difficult problem of ensuring enforcement of EU norms. We also consider the extent to which independent Member State regulation of the environment is permitted.

Chapter 33 deals with the subject of consumer protection. After a review of the evolution of EU policies in this field, we examine three specific areas where the EU has been active in adopting harmonization directives—misleading advertising, unfair contract terms and products liability.

Since the 1970s, social policy, and particularly the protection of employee rights, has been an important field of EU action. In Chapter 34, we describe the major employee protection directives and their interpretation by the Court of Justice, and examine EU social policy generally.

Because equal treatment of women and men has become such an active aspect of EU social policy, Chapter 35 principally covers this topic. Our initial focus is the equal pay mandate of the Treaty and its interpretation by the Court of Justice. We also analyze the directives intended to achieve equal treatment between women and men in the workplace, including the topic of positive action or reverse discrimination. The chapter concludes with a review of the recent Council directives prohibiting discrimination based, i.a., on race and ethnic origin, age, disability, and sexual orientation, and the Court caselaw applying the directives.

Finally, Chapter 36 examines the EU's recent legislative activities in the area of civil justice, including principally jurisdiction and the recognition and enforcement of judgments (the subject of the Brussels I Regulation of 2000 and its predecessor 1968 Brussels Convention), and related ECJ case law interpretations. Treated more briefly are the EU's other recent civil justice regulations on, among other things, choice of law in contract and tort (the so-called Rome I and II Regulations) and on judicial cooperation in service of process and evidence. The chapter concludes with a glance at certain highly tentative steps toward harmonization of private law.

CHAPTER 32

ENVIRONMENTAL PROTECTION

■ ■ ■

In this chapter, we examine an issue that has become much more important over time than it was at the time the EEC Treaty was signed in 1957—the protection of the environment. In 1987, its importance to the EU was explicitly recognized in the Single European Act, which added provisions on the environment and required that Commission proposals to complete the internal market that concerned environmental protection take as a base a high level of protection. Modifications or elaborations of these provisions have been included in subsequent treaties. As a result, today one of the EU's aims is "a high level of protection and improvement of the quality of the environment" (Article 3 Lisbon TEU). Moreover, Article 11 TFEU specifies "Environmental protection requirements must be integrated into the definition and implementation of the Union's policies and activities, in particular with a view toward sustainable development." The following materials explore the legal basis for EU action on the environment, trace the development of EU legislation and activity in these fields and consider two particular problems: the failure of Member States to implement EU environmental rules and the extent to which Member States may legislate independently on the environment.

A. THE ENVIRONMENT IN THE TREATY

1. THE LEGAL BASIS FOR EU ACTIVITIES

Even in the absence of express treaty provisions dealing directly with the environment, the EU has had an active environmental policy since the 1970s. Indeed, the EU's active role in environmental matters is an excellent example of how the EU has grown to encompass areas not originally contemplated and how that growth has been supported by the Court of Justice.

In 1972, a summit of EU leaders in Paris laid down a series of basic environmental principles. This was followed by the adoption of the EU's first environmental action program, covering the five-year period 1972–1976. Subsequent multi-year programs followed, and the sixth program (covering the period through 2010) is described below. Also as a result of the Paris summit, a separate service was created in the Commission to deal with environmental and consumer issues. Today, there is a separate Environment Directorate–General.

The motivation behind EU activity in the environmental area is multiple. First, the economic recovery of the Member States after World War II and the resulting dramatic rise in living standards made many Europeans sensitive to new aspects of the quality of their lives. Development and growth at any cost were no longer acceptable. Thus, a significant political constituency to protect and improve the environment appeared. Second, pollution does not respect borders and therefore by its very nature is a transnational problem. This is particularly true in the EU where a single river may flow through several countries and where airborne pollution quickly moves from its source to neighboring countries.

In addition, uncoordinated efforts by the Member States to deal with environmental issues plainly could cause a fragmentation of the internal market. An EU policy accordingly seemed imperative, though there was bound to be a lingering question over the precise extent to which a Member State may take action that goes beyond standards set by the EU.

Through 1986, the EU's specific environmental initiatives were based on general treaty provisions, such as that on the harmonization of Member State laws that "directly affect the establishment or functioning of the common market." Because these provisions required unanimity, the pace of environmental regulation at the EU level was slowed. The unanimity requirement also raised the risk that the EU standard adopted would be that of the Member State having or supporting the lowest standard, thereby weakening any EU legislation.

The Single European Act added a new title on the environment to the Treaty in 1987. This title, which is Title XX in the TEFU, has since been amended in respect of some details. It contains three articles. The first—Article 191 TFEU—lays down the objectives of Union environmental policy, identifies basic principles in this area and lists particular factors to be taken into account in preparing Union environmental initiatives.

Article 191(1) provides that the Union policy on the environment shall contribute to the pursuit of the following objectives:

— preserving, protecting and improving the quality of the environment

— protecting human health

— prudent and rational utilization of natural resources

— promoting measures at the international level to deal with regional or worldwide environmental problems, and, in particular, climate change.

Article 191(2) specifies that in achieving these objectives Union policy on the environment shall aim at a high level of protection and shall be based on the precautionary principle and on the principles that preventive action should be taken, environmental damage should be rectified at the source of the problem and the polluter should pay.

Since the Maastricht Treaty, qualified majority voting in Council combined with appropriate parliamentary input has sufficed for the adoption of most environmental measures. Under the Lisbon Treaty, the ordinary legislative procedure applies (Article 192 TFEU). However, unanimity in the Council and parliamentary consultation is required for environmental (i) provisions primarily of a fiscal nature, (ii) measures concerning town and country planning, land use and management of water resources and (iii) measures significantly affecting a Member State's choice between different energy sources and the general structure of its energy supply.

Article 193 TFEU provides that Union measures adopted under Article 192 shall not prevent any Member State from maintaining or introducing more stringent protective measures compatible with the Treaty.

NOTES AND QUESTIONS

1. Article 191(3) TFEU lists a number of factors of which "the Union shall take account" in preparing EU environmental actions. Included are (i) available scientific and technical data, (ii) environmental conditions in the various regions of the Union, (iii) the potential costs and benefits of an action or lack of action and (iv) the economic and social development of the Union as a whole and the balanced development of its regions. May a failure to meet these requirements be invoked in the Court of Justice as a basis for overturning Union environmental activities? See generally D. Vandermeersch, The Single European Act and the Environmental Policy of the European Economic Community, 12 Eur.L.Rev. 407 (1987).

For example, suppose there is little or no scientific basis for a Union environmental directive? May the directive be voided on that ground? The Court rejected an analogous attack in The Queen v. Minister of Agriculture, Fisheries & Food: ex parte FEDESA, Case C–331/88, [1990] ECR I–4023, which involved a ban on the use of certain growth hormones in beef production adopted under the common agricultural policy. Is that case distinguishable on the ground that the agricultural provisions do not contain a "scientific basis" requirement? The Maastricht Treaty added the requirement that Union policy be based on the precautionary principle. How would that affect a challenge to Union environmental legislation on the grounds that it lacked an adequate scientific basis?

The requirement in Article 191(3) that costs and benefits be considered is similar to the general Union legal requirement that measures be proportional. Do you think that the inclusion of this specific provision might cause the Court of Justice to examine Union environmental legislation more carefully than it otherwise would when such legislation is attacked on proportionality grounds?

Article 191(3) further requires that consideration be given to the levels of development in various regions of the Union. A similar requirement is found in Article 27 TFEU on the internal market in general. May a less developed Member State insist legally on less strict controls or demand a derogation for less developed regions? In this respect, it should be noted that the Maastricht Treaty added a fifth paragraph to Article 191, to the effect that if a measure involves costs deemed disproportionate for the public authorities of a Member State, the Council shall lay down appropriate provisions in the form of temporary derogations and/or financial support from the cohesion fund.

Although the Court of Justice might conceivably invoke these factors as a reason for invalidating Union legislation, the Court's tendency to defer to the judgment of the Commission and Council would seem to make that unlikely. If that is the case, did the listing of these factors serve any useful purpose? Does a more detailed specification of the Union's role in environmental regulation help legitimate Union action in this arena? Does it increase the likelihood of Union action? Does it make stricter rules more likely?

2. Union action in the environmental area usually takes the form of directives. Would Article 192 permit the use of other legislative forms?

3. The use of directives in the environmental area leaves some discretion to the Member States on how to implement EU rules and considerable discretion in respect of their enforcement. Do you think that it would be desirable to reduce that discretion, for example through the use of regulations or an EU enforcement agency? Assuming that the result was more effective enforcement of EU rules, would such an approach be consistent with the principle of subsidiarity? Would such an approach have any impact on the strictness of EU rules? On subsidiarity, see Chapter 13(C) supra.

4. To the extent that environmental policy is implemented by directive, how can an affected individual challenge EU environmental rules in the Court of Justice? Review the materials in Chapters 5 and 7 supra.

5. One of the principles of EU environmental policy is that the polluter should pay. See Article 191(2). May a Member State, consistent with this principle, subsidize some or all of the cost of installing pollution control equipment? The Union has rather strict rules limiting state aids for environmental purposes. See Community Guidelines on States Aid for Environmental Protection, O.J. C 82/1 (Apr. 1, 2008).

6. To what extent may a taxpayer challenge a waste tax assessed without specific consideration of the amount of waste produced by the taxpayer? Would such a tax violate the polluter-pays principle? See Futura Immobiliare srl Hotel Futura v. Comune di Casoria, Case C–254/08, [2009] ECR I–___ (July 16, 2009) (waste tax can be based on estimate of waste production, but local court should check to see if disproportionate).

2. THE COURT OF JUSTICE AND EC ENVIRONMENTAL LEGISLATION

Early on, the Court of Justice had to consider the extent to which the EEC had the power to carry out an environmental program at all and the relationship between environmental rules and such fundamental Treaty principles as the free movement of goods. More recently, the Court has had to decide how narrowly or expansively to interpret EU environmental directives. The following cases consider these issues.

COMMISSION v. ITALY

(Sulphur Content of Fuels)
Case 92/79, [1980] ECR 1115.

[The Commission brought a treaty infringement action against Italy for its failure to implement Directive 75/716 relating to the sulphur content of certain liquid fuels.]

4   [The Italian Government argues] that the subject-matter of the directive lies "at the fringe" of Community powers and that it is actually a convention drawn up in the form of a directive.

* * *

7   As regards the Italian Government's argument that the directive is actually a convention drawn up in this special form, it need only be recalled that the Court has already said in Case 38/79, *Commission v. Italy* [1970] ECR 47, that a measure which has the features of a decision when viewed in the light of its objective and the institutional framework within which it has been drawn up, cannot be described as an "international agreement". The same considerations apply where a Council directive is concerned.

8   As regards the observations of the Italian Government concerning the powers of the Community in the matter, it should be observed that the directive has been adopted not only within the Programme of Action of the Communities on the Environment; it also comes under the General Programme for the elimination of technical barriers to trade which result from disparities between the provisions laid down by law, regulation or administrative action in Member States, adopted by the Council on 28 May 1969. In this sense it is validly founded upon Article 100 EEC [now 115 TFEU]. Furthermore it is by no means ruled out that provisions on the environment may be based upon Article 100 of the Treaty. Provisions which are made necessary by considerations relating to the environment and health may be a burden upon the undertakings to which they apply and if there is no harmonization of national provisions on the matter, competition may be appreciably distorted.

* * *

PROCUREUR DE LA RÉPUBLIQUE v. ASSOCIATION DE DÉFENSE DES BRÛLEURS D'HUILES USAGÉES (ADBHU)

Case 240/83, [1985] ECR 531.

[Articles 2–4 of Directive 75/439 on the disposal of waste oils required Member States to take the measures necessary to ensure the safe collection and disposal of waste oils, preferably by recycling. Article 5 provided that if the aims of those articles could not be met, then "Member States shall take the necessary measures to ensure that one or more undertakings carry out the collection and/or disposal of the products offered to them by the holders, where appropriate in the zone assigned to them by the appropriate authorities." Article 6 provided that "any undertaking which disposes of waste oils must obtain a permit." The French decree that implemented Directive 75/439 divided France into zones and authorized waste oil collectors and disposers to operate on a zone-by-zone basis.]

9   The national court asks whether the system of permits is compatible with the principles of free trade, free movement of goods and freedom of competition, but does not elaborate further. In that connection it should be borne in mind that the principles of free movement of goods and freedom of competition, together with freedom of trade as a fundamental right, are general principles of Community law of which the Court ensures observance. The above-mentioned provisions of the directive should therefore be reviewed in the light of those principles.

* * *

12   In the first place it should be observed that the principle of freedom of trade is not to be viewed in absolute terms but is subject to certain limits justified by the objectives of general interest pursued by the Community provided that the rights in question are not substantively impaired.

13   There is no reason to conclude that the directive has exceeded those limits. The directive must be seen in the perspective of environmental protection, which is one of the Community's essential objectives. It is evident, particularly from the third and seventh recitals in the preamble to the directive, that any legislation dealing with the disposal of waste oils must be designed to protect the environment from the harmful effects caused by the discharge, deposit or treatment of such products. It is also evident from the provisions of the directive as a whole that care has been taken to ensure that the principles of proportionality and non-discrimination will be observed if certain restrictions should prove necessary. In particular, Article 5 of the directive permits the creation of a system of zoning "where the aims defined in Articles 2, 3 and 4 cannot otherwise be achieved".

14   In the second place, as far as the free movement of goods is concerned, it should be stressed that the directive must be construed in the light of

the seventh recital in the preamble thereto, which states that the treatment of waste oils must not create barriers to intra-Community trade. As the Court has already ruled * * *, an exclusive right of that kind does not automatically authorize the Governments of the Member States to establish barriers to exports. Indeed, such a partitioning of the markets is not provided for in the Council Directive and would be contrary to the objectives laid down therein.

15 It follows from the foregoing that the measures prescribed by the directive do not create barriers to intra-Community trade, and that in so far as such measures, in particular the requirement that permits must be obtained in advance, have a restrictive effect on the freedom of trade and of competition, they must nevertheless neither be discriminatory nor go beyond the inevitable restrictions which are justified by the pursuit of the objective of environmental protection, which is in the general interest. That being so, Articles 5 and 6 cannot be regarded as incompatible with the fundamental principles of Community law mentioned above.

NOTES AND QUESTIONS

1. In *Commission v. Italy,* Italy questioned the EU's powers in the area of the environment. How did the Court respond? How did the Court respond to a similar challenge in the *ADBHU* case? What was the basis of the *ADBHU* Court's characterization in paragraph 13 in 1985 of environmental protection as one of the EU's "essential objectives"?

2. In light of the Court's decisions in *Commission v. Italy* and *ADBHU,* was the new section on the environment in the Single European Act necessary? How much did it add to the EU's powers? In considering your answer, recall the issues raised in the notes at the end of section (A)(1) of this chapter.

3. After *ADBHU,* to what extent will environmental considerations justify EU imposed limitations on the free movement of goods?

B. COMMUNITY ENVIRONMENTAL LEGISLATION AND ACTIVITIES

The EU's environmental activities range over a wide field. To give the student a sense of their scope, we include a short excerpt from the sixth action program (covering the years 2001–2010) and the 2008 Commission review of EU environmental policies.

ENVIRONMENT 2010: OUR FUTURE, OUR CHOICE: THE SIXTH ENVIRONMENTAL ACTION PROGRAM OF THE EUROPEAN COMMUNITY 2001–2010

Commission Website, August 2001.[1]

[The Commissioner for the Environment, Margot Wallstrom, presented the Commission's proposed program for 2001–2010 in the following terms:]

The new Environment Action Program entitled *Environment 2010: Our Future, Our Choice* takes a wide-ranging approach to these challenges and gives a strategic direction to the Commission's environmental policy over the next decades, as the Community prepares to expand its boundaries.

The new program identifies four priority areas: climate change, nature and biodiversity, environment and health, and natural resources and waste.

To achieve improvements in these areas, the new Program sets out five approaches. These emphasize the need for more effective implementation and more innovative solutions. The Commission recognizes that a wider constituency must be addressed, including business who can only gain from a successful environmental policy. The Program seeks new and innovative instruments for meeting complex environmental challenges. Legislation is not abandoned, but a more effective use of legislation is sought together with a more participatory approach to policy making.

The five key approaches are to ensure the implementation of existing environmental legislation; integrate environmental concerns into all relevant policy areas; work closely with business and consumers to identify solutions; ensure better and more accessible information on the environment for citizens; and develop a more environmentally conscious attitude toward land use.

The new Program provides the environmental component of the Community's forthcoming strategy for sustainable development. It continues to pursue some of the targets from the Fifth Environment Action Program, which came to an end in 2000. But the new Sixth Environment Action Program * * * goes further, adopting a more strategic approach. It calls for the active involvement and accountability of all sections of society in the search for innovative, workable and sustainable solutions to the environmental problems we face.

2008 ENVIRONMENT POLICY REVIEW

Communication from the Commission to the Council and the European Parliament
COM(2009) 304.

Environment policy has left the sidelines and is now one of the most important policy issues. 96% of Europeans say protecting the environment

---

1. http://www.europa.eu.int/comm/environment/newprg/index.htm, visited August 27, 2001.

is important to them and they are very concerned about issues such as climate change and pollution. Environment policy considerations increasingly spill over into transport, energy, agricultural, cohesion, industrial and research and development policies. Energy policy aims, among others, to move us to a low-carbon economy. Issues of sustainable development underpin decisions on the use of structural funds. Agriculture policy increasingly promotes sustainable land and resource management. The "Health Check" of the Common Agricultural Policy in November 2008 proposed a further shift of EU funding towards rural development, away from direct payments. Member States are required to spend these Community funds to address among others the challenges of biodiversity and nature protection, renewable energy, waste and water management, clean transport and climate change. Yet many environmental degradation trends are not being reversed. The effort and investment needed to move to a low-carbon resource-efficient economy will be significant.

* * *

Climate Change. The consequences of climate change are already being felt, with rising sea levels and more frequent extreme weather. The Fourth Assessment Report of the Intergovernmental Panel on Climate Change projected that global average surface temperatures could rise by 1.8–4.0° this century, and if unchecked, would reach the threshold at which catastrophic change becomes far more likely. * * * In October 2008 the annual progress report on implementing the Kyoto Protocol showed that the EU and most Member States are on track to meet their commitments. The projections indicate that the EU–15 will achieve its –8% target through existing measures, the purchase of emission credits from third countries and forestry activities that absorb carbon. Measures under discussion could bring more reductions. Still, the EU accounts for about 10.5% of global emissions and its efforts will not be enough to mitigate climate change unless further action is taken globally. * * *

Commission proposals for integrated climate change and energy policy were endorsed by the Council in March 2007. The EU committed to cut its greenhouse gas (GHG) emissions by 30% of 1990 levels by 2020 if other developed countries agreed comparable reductions or by at least 20% if they did not. In January 2008 the Commission translated these commitments into concrete action by adopting a Climate and Energy package, with proposals to improve the EU Emissions Trading System (ETS) by covering more GHGs and more sectors, and by setting a tighter EU-wide emissions cap and emission reduction targets for sectors not in the ETS, such as road transport, buildings, services and agriculture. During 2008 the European Council and Parliament reached an agreement on the inclusion of aviation in the EU ETS. GHG emissions from flights to, from and within the EU will be included in the ETS from 2012. The package included also a proposal for a Directive with legally binding targets for increasing renewable energy to a 20% share by 2020, with a 10% share of renewable energy in the transport sector; and a regulatory framework for safe, reliable deployment of carbon capture and geological storage technologies. It was adopted by Parliament and Council in December 2008.

* * *

Biodiversity. The loss of biological diversity both within Europe and globally, exacerbated by climate change, poses a grave threat to our quality of life, our natural environment and our economy. Nature has an intrinsic value but humans also depend on the goods and services provided by ecosystems for their material survival. If we continue with "business-as-usual" there will be severe economic losses. The first results of 'The Economics of Ecosystems & Biodiversity' study, released at the 9th Conference of the Convention on Biological Diversity in May 2008, estimated that the annual value of the global loss of ecosystem services is €50 billion. Rising temperatures and the acidification of the oceans mean that 60% of coral reefs will be lost by 2030. Some 11% of natural areas will be lost globally by 2050, mainly from conversion to agriculture, expansion of infrastructure and climate change. The cumulated welfare losses could reach 7% of GDP. In 2001 governments agreed to halt the loss of EU biodiversity by 2010 and to restore habitats. They also committed to help significantly reduce global biodiversity loss by 2010. Since then EU governments have put in place policies and laws to safeguard biodiversity. The Birds and Habitats Directives provide a solid legislative basis for protecting important species and habitats, especially through Natura 2000. This EU-wide network of protected areas covers 17% of EU land and is being extended to our seas. * * * However, EU biodiversity continues to be degraded. A 2008 mid-term review of the Biodiversity Action Plan found that, despite progress, it is highly unlikely that we will achieve the goal to halt biodiversity loss by 2010 with current efforts.

At global level, biodiversity loss is even more worrying. Protection of the world's remaining forests is the most pressing challenge. 13 million hectares of tropical forests—an area approximately the size of Greece—disappear every year. This threatens the livelihood of an estimated 1.6 billion poor people who rely heavily on forests for their livelihoods and has major impacts on species loss and climate change. Deforestation is responsible for approximately 20% of global GHG emissions, more than all EU emissions put together. In 2008 the Commission presented two initiatives to protect global forests: a Regulation obliging timber and timber product traders to seek guarantees that the timber was cut legally in the country of origin; and a Communication proposing to halve gross tropical deforestation by 2020 and halt global forest loss by 2030. Beyond spending on targeted actions in 2008, this will require further EU funding; some could come from auctioning allowances in the EU ETS. In addition, the Commission is assessing the possibility of establishing sustainability criteria for biomass, which could also have a positive effect on discouraging deforestation. In the framework of the EU Forest Law Enforcement Governance and Trade (FLEGT) initiative, which aims at stopping illegal logging, an agreement was reached with Ghana. This will only allow EU sales of Ghanaian timber products with a license attesting their legality. Talks continue with other African and Asian tropical timber exporting states. * * *

Chemical Regulation. After years of preparation, REACH—Registration, Evaluation, Authorization and Restriction of Chemicals—became operational in June. Before December companies submitted over 2 million preliminary information dossiers for over 100 000 chemical substances to the Chemicals Agency—about 15 times more than expected. REACH is replacing 40 legislative texts and creating one EU-wide system to manage chemicals produced in or imported into the EU. Under the new regulation, industry has to prove that chemicals are safe. The new system encourages or sometimes requires some substances to be replaced by less dangerous alternatives. New chemicals must be registered before they are manufactured or marketed. For existing ones, companies can benefit from phased registration deadlines, if pre-registered in 2008. Other measures for chemicals have been adopted or are under preparation. One regulation introduces a new system for classifying, labeling and packaging hazardous substances. Another regulation will ban all mercury exports from 2011. In December final agreement was reached on the Framework Directive on the sustainable use of pesticides. Member States must enforce regular inspection of pesticide application equipment and ban aerial spraying. In 2009, the Commission will revise the Biocides Directive, partly to adapt it to REACH.

Air. Air quality is important for European citizens, and the EU has been very active. In June the Directive on ambient air quality and cleaner air came into force, a key measure under the 2005 Thematic Strategy. It demonstrates the EU's commitment to improving air quality by obliging Member States to reduce exposure to fine particles (PM2.5) in urban areas by an average of 20% by 2020 compared to 2010. New vehicle emission standards (Euro 5 and 6) were also formally adopted in 2007, setting tighter limits on emissions of particles from 2009 and of NOx from 2014. Euro 5 will lead to the introduction of particle filters for diesel cars. In July 2008, the Commission put forward "Greening Transport" initiatives to make transport more sustainable. It includes, for example, a strategy on pricing transport modes to better reflect their real cost to society and a proposal to allow Member States to better internalize these in road tolls for lorries. * * *

Water. In 2008 the Council approved a Directive on environmental quality standards for surface water. It specifies concentration limits for over 30 polluting substances, such as pesticides, heavy metals and biocides and is the final major piece of legislation to support the Water Framework Directive (WFD). The legal framework for water management is based on river basin districts instead of administrative boundaries and aims to achieve good water quality for all EU water bodies as a rule by 2015. The next stage is to develop river basin management plans in 2009. Member States must have introduced water prices that reflect true costs by 2010. Water pricing will stimulate cost-efficient investment in water efficiency, increasingly needed in regions short of water. A study has demonstrated that water efficiency in the EU could improve by nearly 40% through technology alone. The Marine Strategy Framework Directive completes the legislative coverage of the entire water cycle. Like the WFD it is built on an "ecosystem-based approach". The Directive requires Member States to develop "marine strategies" with the measures needed to achieve or maintain good environmental status of the EU's marine waters by 2020. The Marine Strategy Framework Directive is the environmental pillar of EU Integrated Maritime Policy and when properly implemented, will help to better integrate environmental needs into sectors such as fisheries, shipping or tourism.

Sustainable consumption and production. Preventing pollution and repairing damage is not enough. Sustainable economic growth means we need to change our patterns of consumption and production. We must improve the environmental performance of products over their life cycle, boost demand for greener products and help consumers make informed choices. In July 2008 the Commission presented an Action Plan on Sustainable Consumption and Production and Sustainable Industrial Policy. At its core is the creation of a dynamic legislative structure to continuously improve the environmental performance of products and foster their uptake by consumers. Minimum requirements and voluntary advanced benchmarks can be set for the environmental performance of 'energy-related' products under the proposal of a revised Ecodesign Directive. The revised Energy Labeling Directive proposed in November will set mandatory labeling and harmonized minimum performance product characteristics for public procurement and incentives. A Directive on the Promotion of Clean and Energy Efficient Road Transport Vehicles was adopted by the Council in March 2009. It requires lifetime energy and environmental aspects to be taken into account when purchasing public transport road vehicles. Products and services with the best environmental performance can be identified by a revised Ecolabel, while initiatives on Green Public Procurement and lead markets will foster market take-up of green products and services creating conditions to stimulate innovation. Cooperation with the European retail sector will also be stepped up. The voluntary eco-management and audit scheme 'EMAS', which helps companies optimize their production processes, has been revised and a voluntary environmental technology verification scheme planned for 2009 aims to boost the confidence of buyers in the performance of new environmental technologies. Beyond that, the Commission will propose more action on incentives for green products and services, notably building upon the lead market initiatives.

Waste and Recycling. EU waste management policy aims at reducing the environmental and health impacts of waste and improving Europe's resource efficiency. It applies a "waste hierarchy": waste prevention is best, followed by re-use, recycling and other recovery, with disposal the last resort. Long-term objectives are laid down in the 2005 Thematic Strategy on waste, which calls for a resource-efficient recycling society:

avoiding waste but using unavoidable waste as a resource where possible. It also guides new policy initiatives such as modernising laws, reducing administrative burden and boosting recycling. The revised Waste Framework Directive, adopted in November, anchors the five-step waste hierarchy in law. It focuses on waste prevention, committing Member States to preparing national waste prevention programmes, and sets targets to recycle waste from households and similar waste streams (50% by 2020) and construction and demolition waste (70% by 2020).

The Commission proposed in November an EU Strategy for better ship dismantling as part of its Action Plan for an Integrated Maritime Policy. Many ships from Europe end up on beaches in South Asia for their valuable scrap metal, where a lack of environmental protection and safety measures results in accidents, health risks and pollution. The strategy includes measures to implement the future international Convention on safe ship recycling and to better enforce EU waste shipment law. In December the Commission proposed revised Directives on Waste Electrical and Electronic Equipment and on Restricting the use of certain Hazardous Substances in such equipment. They aim to increase the environmental benefit and cost-effectiveness of the policies and overcome enforcement problems. They provide new national collection targets, more ambitious recovery and recycling targets and reinforce producer responsibility. * * *

Implementation. * * * In November, the Commission set out plans to improve implementation of EU environmental laws. Close cooperation with Member States is crucial as it ensures national implementing rules are adopted on time and correctly applied. To improve its enforcement work, the Commission will focus on fundamental or systematic breaches, including major defects in national implementing rules, tolerance of illegal landfills, serious gaps in permits for industries and failure to designate key natural sites. Permanent implementation networks involving Commission and Member State staff will be created. The transitional periods for some new Member States to apply some key pieces of environmental laws will come to an end, demanding further attention. The aim of this new approach to implementation and enforcement is to use a broad set of tools to prevent breaches of the law, such as targeted use of EU funds and enhanced pre-accession support for enlargement countries.

NOTES AND QUESTIONS

1. How would you compare EU activities in the environmental area with those of the US? While such a comparison is obviously difficult, in 1990 some differences were highlighted in D. Hackett & E. Lewis, European Economic Community Environmental Requirements, in P. Thieffry & G. Whitehead, eds., The European Economic Community: Products Liability Rules and Environmental Policy 253–283 (Practicing L.Inst.1990). At the time, the authors noted that the EU has tended to follow US regulatory patterns, although as a general rule it appeared that there is less effective enforcement of environmental regulations in the EU than in the United States. This

problem, which is due in part to the failure of Member States to implement directives in a timely manner and to lax enforcement activity by some Member States after implementation occurs, is well recognized in the EU and is discussed in the next section.

As to specific subjects, Hackett and Lewis concluded that the EU had regulated air pollution less comprehensively than the US Clean Air Act. On the other hand, they found that the EC's regulation of water generally paralleled the US Clean Water Act. With respect to hazardous waste, they found that the EU placed a much greater emphasis on waste prevention and reduction than did the United States. They also found that the control of waste disposal varied considerably by Member State, with Denmark, Germany and the Netherlands having the most comprehensive regulatory schemes.

It is interesting to speculate on causes of the differences in approach between the EU and the United States. For example, the emphasis on waste prevention may reflect the relative lack of disposal sites in Europe. What might explain other differences?

A comparison as of 2010 would probably conclude that the EU has done more in respect of environmental protection than the US, although Member State implementation problems remain a concern. This is particularly true in respect of waste control and product recycling. It is certainly the case that in recent years, the EU has presented itself as much more environmentally concerned than the US, particularly in respect of control of genetically modified organisms and the international efforts to reduce greenhouse gas emissions pursuant to the Kyoto Protocol to the UN Framework Convention on Climate Change. As to the latter, after the US effectively declared the Kyoto Protocol to be unacceptable, the EU was instrumental at the Bonn Conference, July 16–27, 2001, in brokering a compromise among other participants that enabled the protocol to come into force, although follow-up work in this area has been difficult.

2.   As noted above, one area in which the EU has been much more active than the US is in the area of waste management, particularly in requiring that packaging materials be recovered and recycled to a significant degree (European Parliament and Council Directive 94/62 of Dec. 20, 1994, on packaging and packaging waste, O.J. L 365/10 (Dec. 31, 1994)) (amended in 2004 and 2005) and in requiring recycling of products at the end of their useful lives. The prime example of the latter is European Parliament and Council Directive 2000/53 of 18 September 2000 on end-of-life vehicles, O.J. L 269 (Oct. 21, 2000) (amended in 2003, 2005 and 2008), which requires vehicle manufacturers to reduce the use of hazardous substances when designing vehicles; design and produce vehicles which facilitate recovery and recycling at the end of their lives; and increase the use of recycled materials in vehicle manufacture. Member States must set up collection systems for end-of-life vehicles and the last holder of an end-of-life vehicle will be able to dispose of it free of charge.

Another area of activity not common to the US is the EU's promotion of eco-labeling. The EU Ecolabel is a voluntary scheme aimed at encouraging businesses to market environmentally sound products and services. It permits a business to mark its product or service with a label that consumers will recognize as signifying that the product or service is environmental friendly. The criteria for being able to affix the Ecolabel are based on studies which analyze the impact of the product or service on the environment throughout its life-cycle, starting from raw material extraction in the pre-production stage, through to production, distribution and disposal. The current legislation is European Parliament and Council Regulation 66/2010 of 25 November 2009, O.J. L 27/1 (Jan. 30, 2010).

C.　THE ENVIRONMENTAL IMPACT ASSESSMENT DIRECTIVE

While it is impossible to examine the many EU environmental directives in any detail, in this section we will focus on one of the more important directives: the environmental impact assessment (EIA) directive, Council Directive 85/337/EEC, O.J. L 175/40 (July 5, 1985) (as amended in 1997 and 2003), which is found in the Documents Supplement (Document No. 29). As described by the Commission in a 2009 review of its application and effectiveness, "The Directive aims to protect the environment and the quality of life, while ensuring approximation of national laws with regard to the assessment of the environmental effects of public and private projects. It is a key instrument of environmental integration, covering a wide range of projects and making them environmentally sustainable. The means of achieving this objective are laid down in Article 2(1) of the Directive, which states that, before development consent is given, certain public and private projects likely to have significant environmental effects by virtue, *inter alia*, of their nature, size or location are made subject to a requirement for development consent and an EIA. The Directive harmonises the principles of the EIA by introducing minimum requirements, in particular with regard to the type of projects that should be subject to assessment, the main obligations of the developers, the content of the assessment and the participation of the competent authorities and the public." Commission Report . . . on the application and effectiveness of the EIA Directive, COM(2009) 378 final. There is also a directive on strategic environmental assessment, European Parliament and Council Directive 2001/42/EC, O.J. L197/30 (July 21, 2001), which requires certain public plans and programs (as opposed to projects) to undergo an environmental assessment before they are adopted.

WORLD WILDLIFE FUND v. AUTONOME PROVINZ BOZEN

Case C–435/97, [1999] ECR I–5613.

[The Administrative Court, Province of Bolzano requested a preliminary ruling on the interpretation of Council Directive 85/337 on the assessment of the effects of certain public and private projects on the environment ("the Directive", which is set out in the Selected Documents). The questions arose in proceedings seeking to overturn certain governmental decisions concerning the expansion of Bolzano–St Jacob

Airport. In connection with the expansion, the runway was to be extended to 1400 meters, which meant that the project fell within Annex II of the Directive. See Annex I(7)(a); Annex II(10)(d). As such, the project was subject to Article 4(2) of the Directive. It appeared that the purpose of the project was to transform an airfield, which had formerly been used largely for non-commercial purposes into an airport with regular scheduled flights, as well as charter and cargo flights. The expansion was provided for in the regional development plan, adopted by law, which required that an environmental impact study be carried out. Such a study was undertaken, although it was accepted that it did not meet the requirements of the Directive. The proceedings were brought by persons living near the airport and two environmental associations.]

34   By its first and second questions, which should be considered together, the national court essentially raises two issues.

35   The first is whether Articles 4(2) and 2(1) of the Directive are to be interpreted as conferring on a Member State the power to exclude, from the outset and in their entirety, from the environmental impact assessment procedure established by the Directive certain classes of projects falling within Annex II to the Directive, including modifications to those projects, * * * even if they have significant effects on the environment.

36   In that regard, the second subparagraph of Article 4(2) of the Directive confers on Member States a measure of discretion to specify certain types of projects which will be subject to an assessment or to establish the criteria or thresholds applicable. However, the limits of that discretion are to be found in the obligation set out in Article 2(1) that projects likely, by virtue inter alia of their nature, size or location, to have significant effects on the environment are to be subject to an impact assessment.

* * *

38   The Court [has] held that a Member State which established criteria or thresholds at a level such that, in practice, an entire class of projects would be exempted in advance from the requirement of an impact assessment would exceed the limits of its discretion under Articles 2(1) and 4(2) of the Directive unless all projects excluded could, when viewed as a whole, be regarded as not being likely to have significant effects on the environment.

39   As regards modifications to such projects, the Court [has] found that the mere fact that the Directive did not expressly refer to modifications to projects included in Annex II, as opposed to modifications to projects included in Annex I, did not justify the conclusion that they were not covered by the Directive.

40   Thus, observing that the scope of the Directive was wide and its purpose very broad, the Court [has] held that the Directive covered "modifications to development projects" even in relation to projects

falling within Annex II, on the ground that its purpose would be undermined if "modifications to development projects" were so construed as to enable certain works to escape the requirement of an impact assessment when, by reason of their nature, size or location, they were likely to have significant effects on the environment.

41 The second issue raised * * * is whether * * * Articles 4(2) and 2(1) of the Directive * * * confer on a Member State the power to exclude from the assessment procedure established by the Directive a specific project * * * as not being likely to have significant effects on the environment, either under national legislation * * * or on the basis of an individual examination of the project.

* * *

43 [The second subparagraph of Article 4(2) of] the Directive confers a measure of discretion on the Member States and does not therefore prevent them from using other methods to specify the projects requiring an environmental impact assessment under the Directive. So the Directive in no way excludes the method consisting in the designation, on the basis of an individual examination of each project concerned or pursuant to national legislation, of a particular project falling within Annex II to the Directive as not being subject to the procedure for assessing its environmental effects.

44 However, the fact that the Member State has the discretion referred to in the previous paragraph is not in itself sufficient to exclude a given project from the assessment procedure under the Directive. If that were not the case, the discretion accorded to the Member States by Article 4(2) of the Directive could be used by them to take a particular project outside the assessment obligation when, by virtue of its nature, size or location, it could have significant environmental effects.

45 Consequently, whatever the method adopted by a Member State to determine whether or not a specific project needs to be assessed, be it by legislative designation or following an individual examination of the project, the method adopted must not undermine the objective of the Directive, which is that no project likely to have significant effects on the environment, within the meaning of the Directive, should be exempt from assessment, unless the specific project excluded could, on the basis of a comprehensive assessment, be regarded as not being likely to have such effects.

46 It should be added, with regard to the exclusion of the project at issue * * * from the assessment procedure * * *, that, even if that project concerns the only airport in the province which can be restructured and it has actually been specified by the legislature, the latter cannot in any event exempt the project from the assessment obligation unless, on the date [on which it adopted the relevant legislation, the legislature] was able to assess precisely the overall environmental impact which all the works entailed by the project were likely to have.

47 As for the exclusion of the project on the basis of an individual examination carried out by the national authorities, the file shows that the contested measures were preceded by an environmental impact study carried out by a team of experts, that information was communicated to the municipalities concerned and that the public was informed by press notices. In addition, the environmental agency [was] consulted.

48 It is for the national court to review whether, on the basis of the individual examination carried out by the competent authorities which resulted in the exclusion of the specific project at issue in the main proceedings from the assessment procedure established by the Directive, those authorities correctly assessed, in accordance with the Directive, the significance of the effects of that project on the environment.

49 In view of the foregoing considerations, the answer to the first and second questions must be that Articles 4(2) and 2(1) of the Directive are to be interpreted as not conferring on a Member State the power either to exclude, from the outset and in their entirety, from the environmental impact assessment procedure established by the Directive certain classes of projects falling within Annex II to the Directive, including modifications to those projects, or to exempt from such a procedure a specific project, * * * either under national legislation or on the basis of an individual examination of that project, unless those classes of projects in their entirety or the specific project could be regarded, on the basis of a comprehensive assessment, as not being likely to have significant effects on the environment. It is for the national court to review whether, on the basis of the individual examination carried out by the national authorities which resulted in the exclusion of the specific project at issue from the assessment procedure established by the Directive, those authorities correctly assessed, in accordance with the Directive, the significance of the effects of that project on the environment.

50 [The third question relates to Article 2(1) and (2) and asks whether alternative procedures] established within the meaning of Article 2(2), * * * must satisfy the requirements of Articles 3 and 5 to 10 of the Directive, including public participation as provided for in Article 6.

51 In its order for reference the national court explains that it has doubts as to whether the [alternative] procedure laid down in [the local law] is appropriate for fully identifying the effects of the project on the environment. It states that neither noise nor the effects on the atmosphere were investigated, as Article 3 of the Directive requires, and that the public did not participate in that procedure, contrary to Article 6 of the Directive.

52 In that regard, Article 2(2) of the Directive provides: "The environmental impact assessment may be integrated into the existing procedures for consent to projects in the Member States, or, failing this,

into other procedures or into procedures to be established to comply with the aims of [the] Directive." It is therefore clear from that provision that the Directive does not prevent the assessment procedure which it introduces from being incorporated in a national procedure which exists or is to be established, provided that the aims of the Directive are met.

53　However, where a project requires assessment within the meaning of the Directive, a Member State cannot, without undermining the Directive's objective, use an alternative procedure, even one incorporated in a national procedure which exists or is to be established, to exempt that project from the requirements laid down in Articles 3 and 5 to 10 of the Directive.

* * *

56　[The fourth question relates to Article 1(5). It] provides that the Directive is not to apply "to projects the details of which are adopted by a specific act of national legislation, since the objectives of [the] Directive, including that of supplying information, are achieved through the legislative process".

57　That provision accordingly exempts projects envisaged by the Directive from the assessment procedure subject to two conditions. The first requires the details of the project to be adopted by a specific legislative act; under the second, the objectives of the Directive, including that of supplying information, must be achieved through the legislative process.

* * *

60　* * * If the specific legislative act by which a particular project is adopted, and therefore authorised, does not include the elements of the specific project which may be relevant to the assessment of its impact on the environment, the objectives of the Directive would be undermined, because a project could be granted consent without prior assessment of its environmental effects even though they might be significant.

61　That interpretation is borne out by the sixth recital in the preamble to the Directive, which states that development consent for public and private projects which are likely to have significant effects on the environment should be granted only after prior assessment of the likely significant environmental effects of those projects, and that this assessment must be conducted on the basis of the appropriate information supplied by the developer, which may be supplemented by the authorities and by the people who may be concerned by the project.

62　It follows that the details of a project cannot be considered to be adopted by a Law, for the purposes of Article 1(5) of the Directive, if the Law does not include the elements necessary to assess the environmental impact of the project but, on the contrary, requires a study to be carried out for that purpose, which must be drawn up subsequently, and if the adoption of other measures are needed in order for the developer to be entitled to proceed with the project.

* * *

68   By its sixth question, the national court is essentially asking whether Articles 4(2) and 2(1) of the Directive are to be interpreted as meaning that, where the discretion conferred by those provisions has been exceeded by the legislative or administrative authorities of a Member State, individuals may rely on those provisions before a court of that Member State against the national authorities and thus obtain from the latter the setting aside of the national rules or measures incompatible with those provisions. In such a case, the national court is asking whether it is for the authorities of the Member State to take, according to their relevant powers, all the general or particular measures necessary to ensure that projects are examined in order to determine whether they are likely to have significant effects on the environment and, if so, to ensure that they are subject to an impact assessment.

69   As regards the right of individuals to rely on a directive and of the national court to take it into consideration, the Court has already held that it would be incompatible with the binding effect conferred on directives by [the Treaty] for the possibility for those concerned to rely on the obligation which directives impose to be excluded in principle. Particularly where the Community authorities have, by directive, imposed on Member States the obligation to pursue a particular course of conduct, the effectiveness of such an act would be diminished if individuals were prevented from relying on it in legal proceedings and if national courts were prevented from taking it into consideration as a matter of Community law in determining whether the national legislature, in exercising its choice as to the form and methods for implementing the directive, had kept within the limits of its discretion set out in the directive.

70   Consequently, if that discretion has been exceeded and the national provisions must therefore be set aside on that account, it is for the authorities of the Member State, according to their relevant powers, to take all the general or particular measures necessary to ensure that projects are examined in order to determine whether they are likely to have significant effects on the environment and, if so, to ensure that they are subject to an impact.

NOTES AND QUESTIONS

1.   Do you agree with the Court's interpretation of the Directive? Has it effectively removed discretion that the Member States probably thought they had retained for themselves on adoption of the Directive? In particular, consider the two conditions imposed by the Court for the application of article 1(5)?

2. Does the Court give the Directive direct effect? What precise rights are given to individuals to invoke the Directive?

WELLS v. SECRETARY OF STATE FOR TRANSPORT, LOCAL GOVERNMENT AND THE REGIONS

Case C–201/02, [2004] ECR I–723.

[In this case, the Court found that an environmental assessment under Directive 85/337 should have been carried out before the issuance of a mining permit. The following sections of the Court's analysis deal with the right of individuals to invoke the directive and the question of appropriate remedies when the directive has not been followed.]

54   By its fourth and fifth questions, which it is appropriate to consider together, the referring court essentially asks whether, in circumstances such as those of the main proceedings, an individual may, where appropriate, rely on Article 2(1) of Directive 85/337, read in conjunction with Articles 1(2) and 4(2) thereof, or whether the principle of legal certainty precludes such an interpretation.

55   According to the United Kingdom Government, acceptance that an individual is entitled to invoke Article 2(1) of Directive 85/337, read in conjunction with Articles 1(2) and 4(2) thereof, would amount to inverse direct effect directly obliging the Member State concerned, at the request of an individual, such as Mrs Wells, to deprive another individual or individuals, such as the owners of Conygar Quarry, of their rights.

56   As to that submission, the principle of legal certainty prevents directives from creating obligations for individuals. For them, the provisions of a directive can only create rights. Consequently, an individual may not rely on a directive against a Member State where it is a matter of a State obligation directly linked to the performance of another obligation falling, pursuant to that directive, on a third party.

57   On the other hand, mere adverse repercussions on the rights of third parties, even if the repercussions are certain, do not justify preventing an individual from invoking the provisions of a directive against the Member State concerned.

58   In the main proceedings, the obligation on the Member State concerned to ensure that the competent authorities carry out an assessment of the environmental effects of the working of the quarry is not directly linked to the performance of any obligation which would fall, pursuant to Directive 85/337, on the quarry owners. The fact that mining operations must be halted to await the results of the assessment is admittedly the consequence of the belated performance of that State's obligations. Such a consequence cannot, however, as the United Kingdom claims, be described as inverse direct effect of the provisions of that directive in relation to the quarry owners.

* * *

62   By its third question, the referring court essentially seeks to ascertain the scope of the obligation to remedy the failure to carry out an assessment of the environmental effects of the project in question.

63   The United Kingdom Government contends that, in the circumstances of the main proceedings, there is no obligation on the competent authority to revoke or modify the permission issued for the working of Conygar Quarry or to order discontinuance of the working.

64   As to that submission, it is clear from settled case-law that under the principle of cooperation in good faith laid down in Article 10 EC [now Article 4(3) Lisbon TEU] the Member States are required to nullify the unlawful consequences of a breach of Community law. Such an obligation is owed, within the sphere of its competence, by every organ of the Member State concerned.

65   Thus, it is for the competent authorities of a Member State to take, within the sphere of their competence, all the general or particular measures necessary to ensure that projects are examined in order to determine whether they are likely to have significant effects on the environment and, if so, to ensure that they are subject to an impact assessment. Such particular measures include, subject to the limits laid down by the principle of procedural autonomy of the Member States, the revocation or suspension of a consent already granted, in order to carry out an assessment of the environmental effects of the project in question as provided for by Directive 85/337.

66   The Member State is likewise required to make good any harm caused by the failure to carry out an environmental impact assessment.

67   The detailed procedural rules applicable are a matter for the domestic legal order of each Member State, under the principle of procedural autonomy of the Member States, provided that they are not less favorable than those governing similar domestic situations (principle of equivalence) and that they do not render impossible in practice or excessively difficult the exercise of rights conferred by the Community legal order (principle of effectiveness).

68   So far as the main proceedings are concerned, if the working of Conygar Quarry should have been subject to an assessment of its environmental effects in accordance with the requirements of Directive 85/337, the competent authorities are obliged to take all general or particular measures for remedying the failure to carry out such an assessment.

69   In that regard, it is for the national court to determine whether it is possible under domestic law for a consent already granted to be revoked or suspended in order to subject the project in question to an assessment of its environmental effects, in accordance with the requirements of Directive 85/337, or alternatively, if the individual so agrees, whether it is possible for the latter to claim compensation for the harm suffered.

NOTES AND QUESTIONS

1. What, if anything, does the *Wells* case add to the *WWF* case insofar as allowing challenges by individuals to Member State action or inaction in the environmental field?

2. Does the Court give the English court much guidance on the appropriate remedy? What does the last clause of the last sentence of paragraph 69 mean?

3. *Wells* is examined in Chapter 7(D) supra as an example of so-called "triangular" situations of direct effect.

COMMISSION v. IRELAND

(Environmental impact assessment)
C–215/06, [2008] ECR I–4911.

54 As the Irish legislation stands, it is undisputed that environmental impact assessments and planning permissions must, as a general rule, be respectively carried out and obtained, when required, prior to the execution of works. Failure to comply with those obligations constitutes under Irish law a contravention of the planning rules.

55 However, it is also undisputed that the Irish legislation establishes retention permission and equates its effects to those of the ordinary planning permission which precedes the carrying out of works and development. The former can be granted even though the project to which it relates and for which an environmental impact assessment is required pursuant to Articles 2 and 4 of Directive 85/337 as amended has been executed.

56 In addition, the grant of such a retention permission, use of which Ireland recognises to be common in planning matters lacking any exceptional circumstances, has the result, under Irish law, that the obligations imposed by Directive 85/337 as amended are considered to have in fact been satisfied.

57 While Community law cannot preclude the applicable national rules from allowing, in certain cases, the regularisation of operations or measures which are unlawful in the light of Community law, such a possibility should be subject to the conditions that it does not offer the persons concerned the opportunity to circumvent the Community rules or to dispense with applying them, and that it should remain the exception.

58 A system of regularisation, such as that in force in Ireland, may have the effect of encouraging developers to forgo ascertaining whether intended projects satisfy the criteria of Article 2(1) of Directive 85/337 as amended, and consequently, not to undertake the action required for identification of the effects of those projects on the environment and for their prior assessment. The first recital of the preamble to

Directive 85/337 however states that it is necessary for the competent authority to take effects on the environment into account at the earliest possible stage in all the technical planning and decision-making processes, the objective being to prevent the creation of pollution or nuisances at source rather than subsequently trying to counteract their effects.

59 Lastly, Ireland cannot usefully rely on *Wells*. Paragraphs 64 and 65 of that judgment point out that, under the principle of cooperation in good faith laid down in Article 10 EC [now Article 4(3) Lisbon TEU), Member States are required to nullify the unlawful consequences of a breach of Community law. The competent authorities are therefore obliged to take the measures necessary to remedy failure to carry out an environmental impact assessment, for example the revocation or suspension of a consent already granted in order to carry out such an assessment, subject to the limits resulting from the procedural autonomy of the Member States.

60 This cannot be taken to mean that a remedial environmental impact assessment, undertaken to remedy the failure to carry out an assessment as provided for and arranged by Directive 85/337 as amended, since the project has already been carried out, is equivalent to an environmental impact assessment preceding issue of the development consent, as required by and governed by that directive.

61 It follows from the foregoing that, by giving to retention permission, which can be issued even where no exceptional circumstances are proved, the same effects as those attached to a planning permission preceding the carrying out of works and development, when, pursuant to Articles 2(1) and 4(1) and (2) of Directive 85/337 as amended, projects for which an environmental impact assessment is required must be identified and then—before the grant of development consent and, therefore, necessarily before they are carried out—must be subject to an application for development consent and to such an assessment, Ireland has failed to comply with the requirements of that directive.

NOTES AND QUESTIONS

1. What does this case add to *WWF* and *Wells*?

2. What would Ireland have to do to bring its procedures into conformity with EU rules?

D. MEMBER STATE REGULATION OF THE ENVIRONMENT

A diversity of opinion among the Member States as to whether particular environmental measures are necessary is probably inevitable. This presents two problems. First, those that think the measures are too strict may fail to implement them in a timely matter. Second, those that believe that they are not strict enough may want to take action on their own in the environmental area.

1. MEMBER STATE IMPLEMENTATION OF EU LEGISLATION

The problem of non-implementation of EU legislation by Member States is not unique to the environmental area. However, it has been a particular problem in that area. Many Member States do not have good records in faithfully implementing EU environmental legislation. This problem has led the Commission to consider how implementation might better be achieved. This was highlighted in a Commission communication to the Council and Parliament of October 22, 1996:

IMPLEMENTING COMMUNITY ENVIRONMENTAL LAW

PART I: INTRODUCTION

3. Achieving the goal of a high level of environmental protection is only possible if our legal framework is being properly implemented. If the strong *acquis communautaire* on the environment is not properly complied with and equally enforced in all Member States, the Community's future environmental policies cannot be effective and its Treaty objectives cannot be fully and constantly met. The environment will either remain unprotected or the level of protection in different Member States and regions of the Community will be uneven and might, *inter alia*, lead to distortions of competition.

* * *

5. Within this context, there are weaknesses in the current state of implementation of Community environmental law in most parts of the Community, and more action is needed in order to improve the situation. The Commission's own statistics on implementation show the following: In 1995, Member States had notified implementing measures for only 91% of the Community's environmental directives, leaving as many as 20 or 22 directives not transposed in some Member States. In the same year the Commission registered a total of 265 suspected breaches of Community environmental law, based on complaints from the public, Parliamentary questions and petitions and cases detected by the Commission: this is over 20% of all the infringements registered by the Commission in that year. In October 1996 over 600 environmental complaints and infringement cases were outstanding against Member States, with eighty five of the latter awaiting determination by the Court of Justice.

6. The Commission's infringement procedures demonstrate the ways in which problems of implementation arise within the Community. Some legislation causes similar difficulties in most Member States: the Commission has had to begin "horizontal" actions against most Member States in relation to the notification of habitat sites under Directive 92/43/EEC and

in relation to Directive 91/676/EEC on agricultural nitrates in water. Other infraction procedures show the variety of environmental problems within the Community: although waste disposal is a major concern to European Union citizens and leads to many complaints to the Commission, in some Member States the main concern is illegal waste dumps while in others it is emissions from waste incinerators. Infraction proceedings also show the intractable nature of some environmental problems: many current cases relate to directives adopted in the 1970s: Directive 76/160/EEC on bathing water and Directive 76/464/EEC on dangerous substances in surface water are two examples where there are continuing problems of compliance in some Member States. * * *

* * *

10. The Commission, as guardian of the European Community Treaty, has the responsibility of ensuring that Community legislation is applied. It exercises this responsibility mainly through exercising the power to bring infringement proceedings against Member States under Article 169 EEC [now 258 TFEU]. This power is a very important and necessary tool for the Commission with respect to enforcement, as shown by the statistics on infringements given above. The Commission intends to continue to make full use of its enforcement powers based on Article 169.

* * *

12. However, it must be recognized that the procedure under Article 169 may be both lengthy and formal, and was not particularly designed with environmental law cases in mind. Because it operates on decisions and actions after they have been taken, even if Community law is applied as a result, it is not always the best way to prevent degradation or damage to the environment from taking place.

13. There are further fundamental problems with the use of Article 169 EEC [now 258 TFEU] and Article 171 EEC [now 260 TFEU] as the sole means of enforcing Community environmental law apart from the limitations mentioned above. Many environmental regulations and directives have to be applied on a daily basis by large numbers of people throughout the Member States. It would be neither possible nor practical for all the legal actions which could arise from these cases to be channeled through one enforcing authority, the Commission, and one court of law, the Court of Justice. In addition, Article 169 creates a Community "enforcement mechanism" which is directed only against the central governments of the Member States: the Commission is unable to oversee, on the ground, the application of individual decisions (either voluntary or binding) necessary to comply with Community legislation.

14. Nor is it possible for a single, Community wide, judicial enforcement system to take into account the legal and administrative structures at national, regional and local levels within the Member States through which Community environmental measures are applied. The use of such structures is essential to the incorporation of Community environmental

law into national systems and to their practical application. Consequently, alternative methods of enforcement which can give full effect to these national and local conditions, which are vital to the proper protection of the environment, are required. * * *

15. Finally, there is a wide disparity in environmental inspection mechanisms among the Member States. Although the Commission, as the guardian of the Treaty, has the role of ensuring that Member States comply with Community environmental laws, there are no generally applicable Community level mechanisms for the monitoring of the practical application of those laws within the Member States. Thus the Commission has only limited powers to monitor the correct application of Community environmental law. It is almost entirely dependent on information supplied to it on an ad hoc basis by complaints, by petitions to and written and oral questions from the European Parliament, by non-governmental organizations, by the media and by the Member States themselves. Although this information is very valuable to the Commission at the current stage, sole reliance on such ad hoc and unverifiable reporting systems and sources of information could have severely detrimental consequences for the environment in the longer term.

* * *

PART II: NEW AREAS FOR ACTION

* * *

25. The Commission under Article 155 EEC [now Article 17(1) Lisbon TEU] has the duty to ensure timely and correct transposition by the Member States, by using political pressures and, if necessary, court action under Articles 169 and 171 EEC [now 258 and 260 TFEU]. It may also need to generally keep under review the practical application of the legislation and its enforcement in order to ensure that they are carried out in a satisfactory manner. However, this is a Community enforcement mechanism directed only towards Member State central governments. The Commission simply cannot monitor the thousands of individual decisions taken each year in accordance with the transposed or directly applicable environmental legislation, in the different parts and levels of authority within the Member States. The daily application and enforcement of those laws in specific cases must be fully ensured by the authorities in the Member States through mechanisms which will strengthen enforcement and, at the same time, ease the control of Member States by the Commission.

Member State inspection tasks

26. Article 5 EEC [now Article 4(3) Lisbon TEU], as interpreted by the Court of Justice * * *, binds Member States to make whatever provision for enforcement is effective, proportionate, and equivalent to that for Member State's national laws. This general principle of Community law, although fundamental, has resulted in a wide disparity in

enforcement agencies or mechanisms among the Member States, with some putting considerable resources into well-supported inspectorates or other agencies which monitor the practical application of Community environmental law and other making lesser provision or none at all. Moreover, where provision is made, it is varied: inspection competencies are not always exercised by a single national body, but are often decentralized or shared among several layers of authority (local, regional, national, etc.). In a number of cases, environmental inspections form only a part of the responsibilities of the relevant competent authorities. In some Member States, such as Denmark or the UK, the competent authority, in addition to inspecting for compliance, also makes decisions on the grant of permits or bringing of court actions for enforcement, while in other Member States (such as the Netherlands) these tasks are separated.

27.   This wide disparity cannot be considered as satisfactory with reference to the objective of correct and level enforcement at the Community level. The need exists to ensure that minimum inspections tasks are carried out, such as the process of monitoring whether the requirements of Community environmental laws, in particular those relating to industrial emissions and environmental quality standards, are in practice being applied. The need exists also to ensure that this is the case in all Member States.

* * *

Member State environmental complaints and investigation procedure

31.   Court action to enforce Community environmental law within the Member States also has a number of disadvantages which prevent its being used effectively to protect the environment in such cases. Some of these problems arise in relation to issues of access to justice which are discussed in the next section. However, even apart from questions of access, there are inherent problems within legal systems, including e.g. costs and delays, which can make it unhelpful as a means for individuals to enforce Community environmental law: litigation should be the solution of last resort. A non-judicial complaint investigation procedure could have the advantage of avoiding these inherent problems: it could contribute to a quick and low cost settlement of an issue more accessible to the citizen without any need for legal assistance.

32.   The advantages of considering environmental concerns at a local rather than Community level, coupled with the characteristics of speed, low cost and ease of use by citizens and environmental organizations, if applied across the Community, could lead to significant improvements in ensuring the proper implementation of Community environmental law. The Commission will therefore consider whether there is a need to establish minimum criteria for a procedural mechanism for handling environmental complaints and carrying out of investigations (a function which could also be similar to the functions of an ombudsman) in cases where problems arise in relation to the practical application and enforce-

ment of Community environmental legislation by public authorities. These tasks could be carried out either within Member State's existing structures, or by the setting up of ad-hoc bodies.

* * *

Access to Justice

36. Judicial litigation is a last resort to solve problems. However, a Community based on the rule of law has to ensure that laws are respected and if necessary enforced. The role of the courts is crucial in that respect, especially for environmental matters where the source of a problem or damage is geographically confined but the effects may be widespread. Access to justice is, in general, sufficiently ensured if economic interests are at stake. Enforcement of legislation designed to create the framework for prosperous business, for instance in the industrial, commercial or agricultural sector, is likely to be encouraged by economic operators with sufficient resources to fight for enforcement. This is not necessarily the case for ecological interests. Economic operators do not perceive their role as being one of supervising other business' compliance with environmental legislation.

37. Enforcement of environmental law, in contrast to other areas of Community law such as the internal market and competition, therefore mainly rests with public authorities, and is dependent on their powers, resources and goodwill. Their ability to take into account the need to protect the environment may be limited by any of these factors. It is therefore important that supplementary avenues for improving enforcement of Community environmental law are available. In particular, actions by non-governmental organizations and/or citizens in relation to the application and enforcement of environmental laws (in administrative, civil or criminal courts, as appropriate to the structures of the Member State concerned) would assist in the protection of the environment.

* * *

40. Better access to courts for non-governmental organizations and individuals would have a number of helpful effects in relation to the implementation of Community environmental law. First, it will make it more likely that, where necessary, individual cases concerning problems of implementation of Community law are resolved in accordance with the requirements of Community law. Second, and probably more important, it will have a general effect of improving practical application and enforcement of Community environmental law, since potentially liable actors will tend to comply with its requirements in order to avoid the greater likelihood of litigation.

41. Finally, access to Member States' courts would have the desirable effect of channeling litigation on the enforcement of Community environmental law to the most appropriate level, i.e. regional and national. * * *

42.   Restrictions on access to the courts arise in two main ways. Firstly, because legal procedures in the Member States create obstacles to the bringing of enforcement actions in relation to environmental law. For example, a special interest may have to be proven in order to bring a case. For reasons of legal history, such special interests are usually of a type which is easy for a property owner or economic operator to satisfy but less easy for environmental interest groups to satisfy. A further example is that appropriate court procedures may not exist to enable environmental interests to be protected: court procedures which are mainly designed to protect economic interests may not provide appropriate forms of action and remedies for environmental problems. Secondly, the cost of bringing enforcement actions in relation to environmental interests may be prohibitive.

* * *

NOTES AND QUESTIONS

1.   The non-implementation of environmental directives remains a problem. In its June 2009 EU website presentation on its work, the Commission's Legal Service reported that as of December 31, 2007, it was dealing with 742 cases involving alleged infringements of environmental directives—more cases than arose from any other subject matter.[2]

2.   The problem of non-implementation is a particularly serious one in the environmental area, but it obviously arises in other areas as well. As a result, the Commission's thinking on this issue in the context of the environment may have broader general implications as well. We have studied a number of Court of Justice decisions that address in one way or another the problem of non-implementation and attempt to provide rules that mitigate the effects on citizens of non-implementation. The decisions include those on direct effect, damages for non-implementation (*Frankovich*), and judicial interpretation (*Marleasing*) that were examined in Part II. How would you assess the effectiveness of those decisions in promoting implementation of environmental directives? What about imposing fines pursuant to Article 260 TFEU on non-implementing Member States? The Court has occasionally done so. See Chapter 11 supra.

3.   How would you evaluate the effectiveness of the Commission's specific proposals in the foregoing excerpt? What other alternatives might be tried? In particular, would it be possible to include provisions in directives for pollution control that could effectively allow the Court to find private rights of action as it did in the *WWF* and *Wells* cases?

4.   In the excerpt, the Commission proposed minimum inspection standards, and a recommendation on inspection criteria was adopted in 2001. Recommendation 2001/331of the European Parliament and of the Council of April 4, 2001 providing for minimum criteria for environmental inspections in

---

2.   Presentation of the Legal Services and Its Activities 12 (June 2009), http://ec.europa.eu/dgs/legal_service/pdf/sj_en.pdf (visited October 29, 2009).

the Member States, O.J. L 118 (April 27, 2001). In 2007, the Commission reported that all Member States had submitted information on their implementation of the recommendation. In the Commission's view, the information provided indicated that few Member States had fully implemented the recommendation. Communication from the Commission of November 14, 2007 on the review of Recommendation 2001/331/EC providing for minimum criteria for environmental inspections in the Member States. COM(2007) 707 final. The Commission did not, however, consider it appropriate to make the recommendation binding.

5.　In the excerpt, the Commission also proposed increased public access to court enforcement proceedings in the environmental area. This followed on its 1998 proposal (COM(98) 344 final) that the EU sign, along with the Member States, the so-called Aarhus Convention on Access to Information, Public Participation in Decision-making and Access to Justice in Environmental Matters. The Convention addresses some of the issues raised by the Commission in its report on implementation. In essence, it would require measures that would promote public participation in the making and enforcement of environmental laws. The text of the Convention is available at http://www.unece.org/env/pp/treatytext.htm.

The EU has taken a number of steps that are aimed at improving environmental law enforcement along the lines promoted by the Convention, including (i) Directive 2004/35 of the European Parliament and of the Council of 21 April 2004 on environmental liability with regard to the prevention and remedying of environmental damage, O.J. L 143/56 (April 30, 2004) (amended in 2006). The Directive establishes a framework for environmental liability based on the "polluter pays" principle, with a view to preventing and remedying environmental damage. It provides that persons adversely affected by environmental damage should be entitled to ask the competent authority to take action and should have access to procedures for the review of the competent authority's decisions, acts or failure to act; (ii) Directive 2003/4 of the European Parliament and of the Council of June 28, 2003 on public access to environmental information, O.J. L 41/26 (February 14, 2003); and (iii) Directive 2003/35 of the European Parliament and of the Council of May 26, 2003 providing for public participation in respect of certain plans or programs relating to the environment, O.J. L 156/17 (June 25, 2003). A 2003 proposal on access to justice in this area has not been adopted.

Overall, the EU and its Member States get mixed reviews on their implementation of the judicial access provisions of the Convention. A 2009 report for the Institute for European Environmental Policy concluded that the EU's implementation was unsatisfactory because of the limitations on plaintiffs' standing in Article 263 TFEU and that five Member States could be rated as having unsatisfactory implementation, 10 as "could be better", nine as satisfactory and one as good. Pallemaerts, Compliance by the European Community with its Obligations on Access to Justice as a Party to the Aarhus Convention (June 2009).

2. MEMBER STATE ENVIRONMENTAL MEASURES

A second issue that arises in respect of Member States and the environment is the extent to which Member States may adopt their own environmental rules. As noted earlier, Article 193 TFEU allows Member States in certain circumstances to adopt stricter rules than contained in an EU environmental directive. Beyond that, there is the question of how Member State legislation in the environmental area should be analyzed under general EU rules. In that regard the following two well-known cases are of particular importance.

COMMISSION v. DENMARK
(Beverage containers)
Case 302/86, [1988] ECR 4607.

1 [T]he Commission of the European Communities brought an action under Article 169 of the EEC Treaty [now Article 258 TFEU] for a declaration that by introducing and applying by Order No. 397 of 2 July 1981 a system under which all containers for beer and soft drinks must be returnable, the Kingdom of Denmark had failed to fulfil its obligations under Article 30 of the EEC Treaty [now Article 34 TFEU].

2 The main feature of the system which the Commission challenges as incompatible with Community law is that manufacturers must market beer and soft drinks only in re-usable containers. The containers must be approved by the National Agency for the Protection of the Environment, which may refuse approval of new kinds of container, especially if it considers that a container is not technically suitable for a system for returning containers or that the return system envisaged does not ensure that a sufficient proportion of containers are actually re-used or if a container of equal capacity, which is both available and suitable for the same use, has already been approved.

3 Order No. 95 of 16 March 1984 amended the aforementioned rules in such a way that, provided that a deposit-and-return system is established, non-approved containers, except for any form of metal container, may be used for quantities not exceeding 3000 hectolitres a year per producer and for drinks which are sold by foreign producers in order to test the market.

* * *

6 The first point which must be made in resolving this dispute is that, according to an established body of case-law of the Court, in the absence of common rules relating to the marketing of the products in question, obstacles to free movement within the Community resulting from disparities between the national laws must be accepted in so far as such rules, applicable to domestic and imported products without

distinction, may be recognized as being necessary in order to satisfy mandatory requirements recognized by Community law. Such rules must also be proportionate to the aim in view. If a Member State has a choice between various measures for achieving the same aim, it should choose the means which least restricts the free movement of goods.

7   In the present case the Danish Government contends that the mandatory collection system for containers of beer and soft drinks applied in Denmark is justified by a mandatory requirement related to the protection of the environment.

8   The Court has already held in the *ADBHU* case that the protection of the environment is "one of the Community's essential objectives", which may as such justify certain limitations of the principle of the free movement of goods. That view is moreover confirmed by the Single European Act.

9   In view of the foregoing, it must therefore be stated that the protection of the environment is a mandatory requirement which may limit the application of Article 30 of the Treaty.

10   The Commission submits that the Danish rules are contrary to the principle of proportionality in so far as the aim of the protection of the environment may be achieved by means less restrictive of intra-Community trade.

11   In that regard, it must be pointed out that in [*ADBHU*] the Court stated that measures adopted to protect the environment must not "go beyond the inevitable restrictions which are justified by the pursuit of the objective of environmental protection".

12   It is therefore necessary to examine whether all the restrictions which the contested rules impose on the free movement of goods are necessary to achieve the objectives pursued by those rules.

13   First of all, as regards the obligation to establish a deposit-and-return system for empty containers, it must be observed that this requirement is an indispensable element of a system intended to ensure the re-use of containers and therefore appears necessary to achieve the aims pursued by the contested rules. That being so, the restrictions which it imposes on the free movement of goods cannot be regarded as disproportionate.

14   Next, it is necessary to consider the requirement that producers and importers must use only containers approved by the National Agency for the Protection of the Environment.

15   The Danish Government stated in the proceedings before the Court that the present deposit-and-return system would not work if the number of approved containers were to exceed 30 or so, since the retailers taking part in the system would not be prepared to accept too many types of bottles owing to the higher handling costs and the need for more storage space. For that reason the Agency has hitherto followed the practice of ensuring that fresh approvals are normally accompanied by the withdrawal of existing approvals.

[16] Even though there is some force in that argument, it must nevertheless be observed that under the system at present in force in Denmark the Danish authorities may refuse approval to a foreign producer even if he is prepared to ensure that returned containers are re-used.

[17] In those circumstances, a foreign producer who still wished to sell his products in Denmark would be obliged to manufacture or purchase containers of a type already approved, which would involve substantial additional costs for that producer and therefore make the importation of his products into Denmark very difficult.

[18] To overcome that obstacle the Danish Government altered its rules by the aforementioned Order No. 95 of 16 March 1984, which allows a producer to market up to 3000 hectolitres of beer and soft drinks a year in non-approved containers, provided that a deposit-and-return system is established.

[19] The provision in Order No. 95 restricting the quantity of beer and soft drinks which may be marketed by a producer in non-approved containers to 3000 hectolitres a year is challenged by the Commission on the ground that it is unnecessary to achieve the objectives pursued by the system.

[20] It is undoubtedly true that the existing system for returning approved containers ensures a maximum rate of re-use and therefore a very considerable degree of protection of the environment since empty containers can be returned to any retailer of beverages. Non-approved containers, on the other hand, can be returned only to the retailer who sold the beverages, since it is impossible to set up such a comprehensive system for those containers as well.

[21] Nevertheless, the system for returning non-approved containers is capable of protecting the environment and, as far as imports are concerned, affects only limited quantities of beverages compared with the quantity of beverages consumed in Denmark owing to the restrictive effect which the requirement that containers should be returnable has on imports. In those circumstances, a restriction of the quantity of products which may be marketed by importers is disproportionate to the objective pursued.

[22] It must therefore be held that by restricting, by Order No. 95 of 16 March 1984, the quantity of beer and soft drinks which may be marketed by a single producer in non-approved containers to 3000 hectolitres a year, the Kingdom of Denmark has failed, as regards imports of those products from other Member States, to fulfil its obligations under Article 30 [now 34 TFEU] of the EEC Treaty.

NOTES AND QUESTIONS

1. The extent to which Member States may justify measures restricting the free movement of goods on grounds of so-called "mandatory requirements" is dealt with more generally in Chapter 13 (B) and (C).

2. As noted earlier, the Treaty contains a number of provisions recognizing the right of a Member State to take unilateral action. Does the Court's decision in *Beverage containers* suggest limits on the Member States' right to invoke these provisions? To what extent does Article 34 TFEU, in particular, limit that right?

3. Are you satisfied with thoroughness of the Court's analysis of the facts? How does it compare in your view to the approach that a US court would take? As to the substance, how would a law similar to the Danish bottle law be analyzed in the United States? In particular, could an argument be made that it violated the commerce clause? In Minnesota v. Clover Leaf Creamery Co., 449 U.S. 456, 101 S.Ct. 715, 66 L.Ed.2d 659 (1981), the US Supreme Court was faced with a Minnesota statute banning the retail sale of milk in plastic nonreturnable, nonrefillable containers, but permitting such sale in other nonreturnable, nonrefillable containers, such as paperboard milk cartons. The Court upheld the statute against challenges on equal protection and commerce clause grounds. In doing so it noted (449 U.S. at 471, 101 S.Ct. at 727):

> When legislating in areas of legitimate local concern, such as environmental protection and resource conservation, States are nonetheless limited by the Commerce Clause. If a state law purporting to promote environmental purposes is in reality "simple economic protectionism," we have applied a "virtually *per se* rule of invalidity." Philadelphia v. New Jersey, 437 U.S. 617, 624, 98 S.Ct. 2531, 2535, 57 L.Ed.2d 475 (1978). Even if a statute regulates "evenhandedly," and imposes only "incidental" burdens on interstate commerce, the courts must nevertheless strike it down if "the burden imposed on such commerce is clearly excessive in relation to the putative local benefits." Pike v. Bruce Church, Inc., 397 U.S. 137, 142, 90 S.Ct. 844, 847, 25 L.Ed.2d 174 (1970).

The Court concluded that the Minnesota statute was evenhanded and did not effect simple protectionism, even though the trial court had found that the "actual basis [for the statute] was to promote the economic interests of certain segments of the local dairy and pulpwood industries at the expense of the economic interest of other segments of the dairy industry and the plastics industry." 449 U.S. at 475, 101 S.Ct. at 729. In the Court's view, the burden on interstate commerce was "relatively minor" (449 U.S. at 472, 101 S.Ct. at 728) and the relatively greater burden on the out-of-state plastics industry compared to the Minnesota pulpwood industry was not "clearly excessive" (449 U.S. at 473, 101 S.Ct. at 729). How does this result compare with that in the *Beverage containers* case?

COMMISSION v. BELGIUM

(Walloon waste)

Case C–2/90, [1992] ECR I–4431.

[At issue in the case was a Walloon Region regulation that prohibited the deposit in Wallonia of waste produced elsewhere. As to hazardous waste, the Court found that the regulation was inconsistent with a Community directive applicable to hazardous waste. As to nonhazardous waste, which was not subject to comprehensive Community regulation, the Court concluded that a ban on importation of such waste would violate what is now Article 34 TFEU, since it viewed waste as a product the movement of which could not be impeded under that Article. The Court noted, however, that since the accumulation of waste threatens the environment, measures that control it typically can be justified by public-interest objectives (referred to as "mandatory" or "imperative" requirements prior to *Keck*), such as environmental protection. While normally the excuse of a public-interest objective can be relied upon only where there is not discrimination between national and imported products, the Court viewed waste as a special case:]

30   With respect to the environment, it is important to note that waste is matter of a special kind. Accumulation of waste, even before it becomes a health hazard, constitutes a danger to the environment, regard being had in particular to the limited capacity of each region or locality for waste reception.

31   In the instant case the Belgian Government argued, without being contradicted by the Commission, that in view of the abnormal large-scale inflow of waste from other regions for tipping in Wallonia, there was a real danger to the environment, having regard to the limited capacity of that region.

32   It follows that the argument that the contested measures were justified by imperative requirements of environmental protection must be considered to be well founded.

33   The Commission argues, however, that those imperative requirements cannot be relied upon in the present case, given that the measures in question discriminate against waste originating in other Member States, which is no more harmful than waste produced in Wallonia.

34   Imperative requirements can indeed be taken into account only in the case of measures which apply without distinction to both domestic and imported products. However, in assessing whether or not the barrier in question is discriminatory, account must be taken of the particular nature of waste. The principle that environmental damage should as a matter of priority be remedied at source, laid down by Article 130r(2) of the Treaty [now Article 191(2) TFEU] as a basis for action by the Community relating to the environment, entails that it is for each region, municipality or other local authority to take appropriate steps to ensure that its own waste is collected, treated and disposed of; it must accordingly be disposed of as close as possible to the place where it is produced, in order to limit as far as possible the transport of waste.

35   Moreover, that principle is consistent with the principles of self-sufficiency and proximity set out in the Basel Convention of 22 March 1989 on the control of transboundary movements of hazardous wastes and their disposal, to which the Community is a signatory.

[36] It follows that having regard to the differences between waste produced in different places and to the connection of the waste with its place of production, the contested measures cannot be regarded as discriminatory.

Notes and Questions

1.   Do you accept the Court's conclusion that waste can be categorized by place of origin and that a ban on non-local waste is not discriminatory because such waste is a different good than local waste? Could such reasoning be expanded to find other differences in what appear to be like products in a way that would undermine Article 34 TFEU?

2.   It is interesting to compare this result with US cases. In Fort Gratiot Sanitary Landfill, Inc. v. Michigan Dept. of Natural Resources, 504 U.S. 353, 112 S.Ct. 2019, 119 L.Ed.2d 139 (1992); Chemical Waste Mgt., Inc. v. Hunt, 504 U.S. 334, 112 S.Ct. 2009, 119 L.Ed.2d 121 (1992) the US Supreme Court concluded that a ban or discrimination against out-of-state waste violated the Commerce Clause of the US Constitution. What fundamental difference is there between the EU Treaties and the US Constitution that helps explain why the US Supreme Court has reached a different result in these similar cases? Does the US Constitution need an environmental clause?

CHAPTER 33

CONSUMER PROTECTION

■ ■ ■

The impetus for an EU consumer protection policy, like that for the environment, came from the Paris leadership summit in 1972. In 1975, the Council adopted a preliminary program for consumer protection. Since that time multi-year programs have been regularly adopted. In this chapter, we first review the evolution of the legal basis for EU action on consumer protection and then overview the EU's activities in this field. Thereafter, we examine three important areas of EU activity: consumer advertising, unfair contract terms and products liability.

A. THE LEGAL BASIS FOR EU CONSUMER PROTECTION ACTIVITIES

The EEC Treaty directed the Community to take the interests of consumers into account in certain aspects of the common agricultural policy (see what is now Article 39(1)(e) TFEU) and competition rules (see what is now Article 101(3) TFEU). It did not initially contain any general provisions on consumers, with the result that consumer protection legislation was based on harmonization or general powers. Unlike the case of the environment, the Single European Act did not add a title on consumer protection. However, it added a provision on completing the internal market, which required the Commission to take as a base "a high level of protection" in formulating proposals for completion of the internal market that dealt with consumer protection.

The Maastricht Treaty formally made "the strengthening of consumer protection" an EU activity. Moreover, it inserted a new provision, which is now found in Article 169 TFEU. Article 169(1) TFEU sets as a goal "a high level of consumer protection" and provides that the Union "shall contribute to protecting the health, safety and economic interests of consumers, as well as promoting their right to information, education and to organize themselves in order to safeguard their interests." The ordinary legislative procedures apply to the adoption of consumer protection measures. As in the case of the environment, Member States are allowed to take more stringent actions in the consumer protection field than taken by the Union (Article 169(4) TFEU). Thus, although many consumer interest measures had been adopted since the recognition of the importance of consumer protection in the early 1970s, the Maastricht Treaty amendments formally authorized legislative action and highlighted its importance.

The 1998 Amsterdam Treaty added a new provision—now Article 12 TFEU—that provides: "Consumer protection requirements shall be taken into account in defining and implementing other Union policies and activities." Thus, consumer protection, like environmental protection, is increasingly being given a privileged position in Union legislative and administrative action.

However, consumer protection does not necessarily always triumph over internal market considerations. In Germany v. Parliament and Council, Case C–233/94, [1997] ECR I–2405, one of the grounds for Germany's challenge to the Bank Deposit Guarantee Directive was that the directive's provisions constituted a compromise average level of consumer protection, rather than the high level sought by what is now Article 169 TFEU. In para. 48, the Court rejected this, declaring that:

> "although consumer protection is one of the objectives of the Community, it is clearly not the sole objective.* * * [T]he Directive aims to promote the right of establishment and the freedom to provide services in the banking sector. Admittedly, there must be a high level of consumer protection concomitantly with those freedoms; however, no provision of the Treaty obliges the Community legislature to adopt the highest level of protection which can be found in a particular Member State. The reduction in the level of protection which may thereby result in certain cases * * * does not call into question the general result which the Directive seeks to achieve, namely a considerable improvement in the protection of depositors within the Community."

In another case, the Court held that what is now Article 169 TFEU did not justify changing the Court's general view that directives do not have the horizontal direct effect. El Corte Ingles, Case C–192/94, [1996] ECR I–1281.

B. OVERVIEW OF COMMUNITY CONSUMER PROTECTION ACTIVITIES

Against this background detailing the legal basis on which the Union is authorized to act to protect consumers, we now take a brief overview of its activities in this field. We begin with an excerpt from the first basic statement of policy in this area, and then consider excerpts from the EU Consumer Policy Strategy for 2007–2013.

PRELIMINARY PROGRAM OF THE EUROPEAN ECONOMIC COMMUNITY FOR A CONSUMER PROTECTION AND INFORMATION POLICY

O.J. C 92/2 (Apr. 25, 1975).

II.　Objectives of Community Policy Towards Consumers

14.　Given the tasks assigned to the Community, it follows that all action taken has repercussions on the consumer. One of the Community's prime objectives, in general terms, is therefore to take full account of consumer interests in the various sectors of Community activity, and to satisfy their collective and individual needs. Thus there would seem to be a need to formulate a specific Community consumer information and protection policy. In relation to the other common policies, such a policy would take the form of a general guideline aimed at improving the position of consumers whatever the production, distribution or service sector in question. The aims of such a policy are to secure:

A.　effective protection against hazards to consumer health and safety,

B.　effective protection against damage to consumers' economic interests,

C.　adequate facilities for advice, help and redress,

D.　consumer information and education,

E.　consultation with and representation of consumers in the framing of decisions affecting their interests.

A.　*Protection of Consumer Health and Safety*

15.　Measures for achieving this objective should be based on the following principles:

(a)(i) Goods and services offered to consumers must be such that, under normal or foreseeable conditions of use, they present no risk to the health or safety of consumers. There should be quick and simple procedures for withdrawing them from the market in the event of their presenting such risks.

In general, consumers should be informed in an appropriate manner of any risk liable to result from a foreseeable use of goods and services, taking account of the nature of the goods and services and of the persons for whom they are intended.

(ii) The consumer must be protected against the consequences of physical injury caused by defective products and services supplied by manufacturers of goods and providers of services.

(iii) Substances or preparations which may form part of or be added to foodstuffs should be defined and their use regulated, for example by endeavoring to draw up in Community rules, clear and precise positive lists. Any processing which foodstuffs may undergo should also be defined and their use regulated where this is required to protect the consumer.

Foodstuffs should not be adulterated or contaminated by packaging or other materials with which they come into contact, by their environment, by the conditions in which they are transported or stored or by persons coming into contact with them, in such a way that they affect the health or safety of consumers or otherwise become unfit for consumption.

(iv) Machines, appliances and electrical and electronic equipment and any other category of goods which may prejudicially affect the health and safety of consumers either in themselves or by their use, should be covered by special rules and be subject to a procedure recognized or approved by the public authorities (such as type approval or declaration of conformity with harmonized standards or rules) to ensure that they are safe for use.

(v) Certain categories of new products which may prejudicially affect the health or safety of consumers should be made subject to special authorization procedures harmonized throughout the Community.

* * *

B.   Protection of the Economic Interests of the Consumers

18.   This kind of protection should be ensured by laws and regulations which are either harmonized at Community level or adopted directly at that level and are based on the principles set out below.

19.   (a)(i) Purchasers of goods or services should be protected against the abuse of power by the seller, in particular against one-sided standard contracts, the unfair exclusion of essential rights in contracts, harsh conditions of credit, demands for payment for unsolicited goods and against high-pressure selling methods.

(ii) The consumer should be protected against damage to his economic interests caused by defective products or unsatisfactory services.

(iii) The presentation and promotion of goods and services, including financial services, should not be designed to mislead, either directly or indirectly, the person to whom they are offered or by whom they have been requested.

(iv) No form of advertising—visual or aural—should mislead the potential buyer of the product or service. An advertiser in any medium should be able to justify, by appropriate means, the validity of any claims he makes.

(v) All information provided on labels at the point of sale or in advertisements must be accurate.

(vi) The consumer is entitled to reliable after-sales service for consumer durables including the provision of spare parts required to carry out repairs.

(vii) The range of goods available to consumers should be such that as far as possible consumers are offered an adequate choice.

EU CONSUMER POLICY STRATEGY 2007–2013: EMPOWERING CONSUMERS, ENHANCING THEIR WELFARE, EFFECTIVELY PROTECTING THEM

Communication From the Commission to the Council, the European
Parliament and the European Economic and Social Committee
COM(2007) 99 final, 5–8.

In the period 2007–2013, consumer policy is uniquely well placed to help the EU rise to the twin challenges of growth and jobs and reconnecting with its citizens. The Commission will have three main objectives over this period:

1. To empower the consumer. Putting consumers in the driving seat benefits citizens but also boosts competition significantly. Empowered consumers need real choices, accurate information, market transparency and the confidence that comes from effective protection and solid rights.

2. To enhance EU consumer's welfare in terms of price choice, quality, diversity, affordability and safety. Consumer welfare is at the heart of well-functioning markets.

3. To protect consumers effectively from the serious risks and threats that they cannot tackle as individuals. A high level of protection against these threats is essential to consumer confidence.

The Commission's aim is to achieve in this way by 2013 a more integrated and more effective internal market, in particular the retail dimension. Consumers will have an equally high level of confidence in products, traders, technologies and selling methods in retail markets throughout the EU based on an equally high level of protection. Consumer markets will be competitive, open, transparent and fair. Products and services will be safe. Consumers will have access to essential services at affordable prices. Traders, but especially SMEs, will be able to market and sell simply to consumers throughout the EU.

In achieving these three objectives the Commission will be guided by the relevant articles of the Treaty which are also reflected in the operational objectives of the new consumer financial programme 2007–2013 which sets out the legal framework for EU consumer policy expenditure in the period covered by the strategy:

(a) To ensure a high level of consumer protection through a simple legal framework, improved evidence, better consultation and better representation of consumers' interests.

(b) To ensure the effective application of the rules notably through enforcement cooperation, information, education and redress.

Although the financial resources for consumer policy are limited, the program provides a number of different instruments to support the priorities set out below, notably on consumer enforcement, information and education.

These objectives reflect a high degree of continuity with previous EU consumer policy goals. 2007–2013 will however see a change in gear from the past and different priorities for action. In particular EU consumer policy will interact more closely with other policies both at EU level. Much closer cooperation with the Member States will also be pursued, reflecting the growing interdependence between EU and national consumer policies. There have been suggestions that the circumstances of consumers in the 12 new Member States call for a completely separate strategy. In its consultations on the present document the Commission found little support for this view. To attain the objectives set out above, EU consumer policy will focus on the following priority areas:

Better monitoring of consumer markets and national consumer policies

Better Regulation and the need to re-connect with EU citizens call for the greater development of monitoring tools and indicators to assess market function in consumer terms. Policymakers also need to develop a more sophisticated understanding of consumer behavior to devise better regulation. Tools are needed to monitor markets in terms of core outcomes such as safety, satisfaction, price and complaints but also to monitor better the integration of the retail internal market and the effectiveness of national consumer policy regimes. To reflect the significant contribution of national consumer policy to competitiveness, consumer policy should be recognised in the implementation of the Lisbon Strategy at EU and national level. Consumer and competition policymakers and enforcers at EU and national level should cooperate more closely to further their common goal of consumer welfare.

Better consumer protection regulation

The existing consumer protection rules at EU level guarantee core consumer protection in all Member States. In many, they are the cornerstone of national consumer protection regimes. However, the EU contribution is not widely known by consumers, although, it is a reality in their daily lives. For example, as many as 15% of consumers have returned a defective product in the previous twelve months, a right which is guaranteed by EU rules. The EU rules are also increasingly ill adapted to the digital economy revolution in products, services and retail channels. * * *

Most of the existing EU consumer rules are based on the principle of 'minimum harmonization'. Legislation explicitly recognizes the right of Member States to add stricter rules to the EU rules which set a floor. This approach was entirely valid at a time when consumer rights were very different between the Member States and e-commerce was nonexistent. The previous strategy set out a new approach based on "full harmonization". This simply means that, in order both to improve the internal market and to protect consumers, legislation should not, within its given scope, leave room for further rules at national level.

The Commission's recent Green Paper set out the three main options: full harmonization, possibly complemented on a case-by-case basis by mutual recognition for certain non essential aspects not fully harmonized; minimum harmonization with mutual recognition; minimum harmonization with the country of origin approach.

In future, each regulatory problem and the need for any proposals will continue to be judged on its own merits and the full range of regulatory instruments considered. If legislative proposals are identified as the appropriate response, targeted full harmonization of consumer protection rules at an appropriately high level will tend to be the Commission's approach. The Commission will also carry out a robust Impact Assessment of any legislative proposals and work closely with stakeholders to understand fully the impact of the different options and to build consensus on the way forward so that consumer policy is a model of Better Regulation.

The choice the EU faces is a clear one: if it is serious about the growth and jobs agenda, it needs a well-functioning Internal Market. A well-functioning Internal Market requires harmonization on certain issues. Harmonization is not possible without Member States' willingness to adjust certain practices and rules. At the same time, the Commission will not instigate a race to the bottom. It will always strive for a high level of protection.

Better enforcement and redress

The previous strategy placed a strong emphasis on enforcement and this will continue. The application of consumer law calls for action from many actors: consumers; traders, the media, consumer NGO's, self-regulatory bodies and public authorities. Action will focus on implementing the initiatives that have been started, filling the gaps that remain and ensuring coordination and coherence. The Commission will also monitor the effectiveness of national enforcement regimes through surveys and other tools.

Better informed and educated consumers

The EU can add significant value to national, regional and local efforts to inform and educate consumers, through close cooperation with the Member States. In particular the European Consumer Centre network should develop further as the EU's interface with consumers.

Putting consumers at the heart of other EU policies and regulation

Consumers are directly affected by many EU policies such as the internal market, enterprise, environment, financial services, transport, competition, energy and trade. Progress has been made in the integration of consumer interests notably in product safety, transport, telecommunications, energy, and competition. The aim for the future is to build on these achievements in order to make integration of consumer interests more systematic.

There are two main issues to be addressed. First, while liberalization of essential services has delivered considerable benefits for most consumers, safeguards will continue to be needed for the few for who markets do not work. Affordable access to essential services for all is both essential for a modern and flexible economy but also for social inclusion. Showing that no consumer is left behind will also help to sustain political support for measures on essential services. Second, measures at EU level also require a greater emphasis on the monitoring of key consumer markets to ensure positive outcomes for consumers. Finally, essential services also need stronger guarantees of market transparency and better complaint and redress mechanisms.

NOTES AND QUESTIONS

1. In light of the foregoing description of EU activities, how successful would you say the EU has been in achieving its objectives in respect of consumer protection, as excerpted above? How have the foci of its policies changed in recent years? See generally Stephen Weatherill, EC Consumer Law and Policy (2005).

2. How can the EU be sure that its consumer protection program achieves the optimal level of protection? Suppose, for example, that you are a producer whose business is restricted by a directive, the scientific basis of which you believe is questionable, or a consumer who wants access to risky but useful products that are banned, or a consumer who would prefer to pay a lower price and accept an obligation (such as taking responsibility for use of a lost credit card). How can you challenge the EU action to which you object? Are you likely to succeed?

C. EU CONSUMER ADVERTISING RULES

Regulation of advertising to protect a variety of consumer interests is manifestly one of the EU's major concerns. The initial 1984 Directive 84/450 on misleading advertising, which was amended in 1997 to cover comparative advertising as well, was codified in 2006.[1] The directive is found in the Selected Documents as Document No. 30. Article 2(a) of the directive defines "misleading advertising" as "any advertising which in any way, including its presentation, deceives or is likely to deceive the persons to whom it is addressed or whom it reaches and which, by reason of its deceptive nature, is likely to affect their economic behavior or which, for those reasons, injures or is likely to injure a competitor." The directive

---

1. Directive 2006/114/EC of the European Parliament and of the Council of 12 December 2006 concerning misleading and comparative advertising, O.J. L 376/21 (Dec. 27, 2006).

requires Member States to ensure that adequate and effective means exist for the control of misleading advertising, such as by empowering courts to order the cessation of misleading advertising. Courts must also be authorized to require in appropriate cases that an advertiser furnish evidence as to the accuracy of factual claims in its advertising.

"Comparative advertising" is defined in Article 2(c) as "any advertising which explicitly or by implication identifies a competitor or goods or services offered by a competitor." The directive requires that comparative advertising be permitted if, inter alia, it is not misleading, objectively compares one or more material, relevant, verifiable and representative features of those goods or services (including price), does not create confusion between the advertiser and a competitor and does not discredit or denigrate the trademarks, trade names or other distinguishing signs of a competitor.

COMPLAINT AGAINST X

Case C–373/90, [1992] ECR I–131.

[Richard–Nissan, the exclusive French distributor for Nissan vehicles, sued to enjoin press advertisements placed by X, a local car dealer in Bergerac, offering to sell Nissan cars originally bought in Belgium. The advertisements stated: "Buy your new vehicle cheaper" and indicated that the cars had a "One year manufacturer's guarantee." Richard–Nissan claimed that the advertisements were false and misleading, in violation of the French law intended to implement Directive 84/450.

Richard–Nissan argued that the imported cars had been registered in Belgium, so that, although never driven, they were not "new," that they could be sold below Nissan dealer prices only because the Belgian models had fewer accessories than those sold in France, and that X had no authorization to provide a manufacturer's warranty. The Court began by noting the importance of parallel importers:]

12 [T]hese aspects of the advertising are of great practical importance for the business of parallel car importers, and, as the Advocate General has pointed out, parallel imports enjoy a certain amount of protection in Community law because they encourage trade and help reinforce competition.

13 On the first point, concerning the claim that the cars in question are new, it should be noted that such advertising cannot be considered misleading within the meaning of Article 2 just because the cars were registered before importation.

14 It is when a car is first driven on the public highway, and not when it is registered, that it loses its character as a new car. Moreover, as the Commission has pointed out, registration before importation makes parallel import operations considerably easier.

15 It is for the national court, however, to ascertain in the circumstances of the particular case and bearing in mind the consumers to which the

advertising is addressed, whether the latter could be misleading in so far as, on the one hand, it seeks to conceal the fact that the cars advertised as new were registered before importation and, on the other hand, that fact would have deterred a significant number of consumers from making a purchase, had they known it.

16 On the second point, concerning the claim that the cars are cheaper, such a claim can only be held misleading if it is established that the decision to buy on the part of a significant number of consumers to whom the advertising in question is addressed was made in ignorance of the fact that the lower price of the vehicles was matched by a smaller number of accessories on the cars sold by the parallel importer.

17 Thirdly and finally, regarding the claim about the manufacturer's guarantee, it should be pointed out that such information cannot be regarded as misleading advertising if it is true.

18 It should be remembered in this respect that in Case 31/85 *ETA v DK Investment* [1985] ECR 3933 the Court held that a guarantee scheme under which a supplier of goods restricts the guarantee to customers of his exclusive distributor places the latter and the retailers to whom he sells in a privileged position as against parallel importers and distributors and must therefore be regarded as having the object or effect of restricting competition within the meaning of Article 85(1) of the Treaty (paragraph 14).

19 [T]herefore * * * Council Directive 84/450 of 10 September 1984 must be interpreted as meaning that it does not preclude vehicles from being advertised as new, less expensive and guaranteed by the manufacturer when the vehicles concerned are registered solely for the purpose of importation, have never been on the road, and are sold in a Member State at a price lower than that charged by dealers established in that Member State because they are equipped with fewer accessories.

NOTES AND QUESTIONS

1. Which two groups are intended to be protected by Directive 2006/114? Do you agree that they both need protection? What sort of relief is required to be provided by Directive 2006/114? Is it of more interest to consumers or competitors or both?

2. In *X*, the trial court must still determine whether "a significant number of consumers" might be deceived by the advertisements in paras. 15–16. Do you think in fact that some consumers might consider it deceptive to call the imports cheaper if the lower price is due only to the absence of customary accessories? The thrust of the Court's judgment in *X* is certainly to apply leniently the directive to the advertisements of a parallel importer. Do you recall why parallel importers are favorably regarded from the prior coverage of the exhaustion doctrine in intellectual property rights and the

application of Article 101 TFEU to vertical distribution? Do you agree with the application of this policy in *X*?

3. We have already examined a number of advertising cases. How would you compare the result in the Swedish *Consumer Ombudsman* case (Chapter 17(B)(3)) that permitted Sweden to apply Directive 84/450's misleading advertising rules to television advertising rebroadcast from the UK, with the results finding advertising not to be misleading in *Clinique* and *Mars*, Chapter 13(D)(2) supra and in *Adolf Darbo*, Chapter 14(C)(2) supra? Should the Court in the Swedish case have noted a *caveat* that what is deemed "misleading" should not be too strictly defined under purely local rules, but must have a Union content to prevent undue interference with the internal market goal? For other judgments attempting to balance the internal market goal underlying harmonization directives on the labeling of foodstuffs and crystal glass with that of the legitimate protection of consumer interests, see *Meyhui* and *Piageme II*, Chapter 14(C)(3) supra.

4. Some laws, ostensibly for consumer protection, may not be in the consumer's economic interest. Certain advertising restrictions may prevent deception, but they may also make it difficult for new suppliers to break into a market, thereby stifling potential competition that might lead to lower prices. This side effect raises the question of whether Member State advertising rules might violate Article 34 TFEU.

For example, at one time Luxembourg prohibited advertisements of temporary price reductions that (i) cited the difference between the old and temporary new prices or (ii) indicated that the new prices would be in effect for only a limited time. How could these rules be justified as consumer protection measures? Could they be challenged under Article 34? In GB–INNO–BM v. Confederation du Commerce Luxembourgeois, Case C–362/88, [1990] ECR I–683, the Court of Justice ruled that they were incompatible with what is now Article 34 TFEU:

18   [U]nder Community law concerning consumer protection the provision of information to the consumer is considered one of the principal requirements. Thus Article [34] cannot be interpreted as meaning that national legislation which denies the consumer access to certain kinds of information may be justified by mandatory requirements concerning consumer protection.

19   In consequence, obstacles to intra-Community trade resulting from national rules of the type at issue in the main proceedings may not be justified by reasons relating to consumer protection. They thus fall under the prohibition laid down in Article [34] of the Treaty.

For further materials on the relationship of Article 34 and Member State consumer protection laws, see Chapter 13(C)(2) and the *Buet* case in Chapter 14(C)(5) supra.

5. Prior to a 1997 amendment to Directive 84/450, a number of Member States prohibited comparative advertising (advertising which explicitly or by implication identifies a competitor or goods or services offered by a competitor). To what extent does Directive 2006/114 now require that comparative

advertising be permitted? What are the limits on its use? Do those limits strike a fair balance between the interests of consumers and competitors?

6. In De Landtsheer Emmanuel SA v. Comité Interprofessionnel du Vin de Champagne, C–381/05, [2007] ECR I–3115, paras. 17–19, the Court of Justice had occasion to note:

> The test for determining whether an advertisement is comparative in nature is thus whether it identifies, explicitly or by implication, a competitor of the advertiser or goods or services which the competitor offers. The mere fact that an undertaking solely refers in its advertisement to a type of product does not mean that the advertisement in principle falls outside the scope of the directive. Such an advertisement is capable of being comparative advertising provided a competitor or the goods or services which it offers may be identified as actually referred to by the advertisement, even if only by implication.

If no competitor can be identified, then the rules on comparative advertising do not apply. Such advertising would be assessed under other applicable national or EU rules (para. 56).

PIPPIG AUGENOPTIK v. HARTLAUER HANDELSGESELLSCHAFT
Case C–44/01, 2003 ECR I–3095.

[This case concerned questions referred to the Court of Justice by the Austrian Supreme Court in respect of Directive 84/450 [References to the article equivalents in the codified version—Directive 2006/114—are given in brackets.] Pippig operated three opticians' shops in Linz, Austria. It obtained its supplies from a variety of manufacturers. Hartlauer was a commercial company operating throughout Austria. It mainly sold spectacles of little-known brands at low prices. It also sold better known brands obtained outside normal distribution channels, particularly parallel imports. In 1997, Hartlauer circulated an advertising leaflet stating that 52 price comparisons for spectacles carried out over six years had shown a total price differential of [Austrian Shillings—"ATS"] 204,777, or ATS 3,900 on average per pair of spectacles, between the prices charged by Hartlauer and those of traditional opticians. The leaflet claimed in particular that, for a clear Zeiss lens, opticians made a profit of 717%. It also contained a direct comparison between the price of ATS 5,785 charged by Pippig for Titanflex Eschenbach spectacles with Zeiss lenses and the price of ATS 2,000 charged by Hartlauer for spectacles of the same model but with lenses of the Optimed brand. That price comparison was also made in advertisements on various radio and TV channels, but those ads did not state that the spectacles compared had lenses of different brands. The TV ads showed the shop front of 'Pippig'. Pippig brought legal proceedings against Hartlauer, demanding that Hartlauer refrain from all such comparative advertising on price on the grounds that it was misleading and discrediting. Pippig also sought damages.]

34 [C]oncerning the application of Article 7(2) of Directive 84/450 [now Article 8(1), first subparagraph] to all the elements of comparison, the

Court notes that, according to Article 2(2)(a) of Directive 84/450 [now Article 2(c)], comparative advertising means any advertising which explicitly or by implication identifies a competitor or goods or services offered by a competitor.

35   As the Court has already held, that is a broad definition covering all forms of comparative advertising, so that, in order for there to be comparative advertising, it is sufficient for there to be a statement referring even by implication to a competitor or to the goods or services which he offers (Case C–112/99 *Toshiba Europe* [2001] ECR I–7945, paragraphs 30 and 31).

36   All comparative advertising is designed to highlight the advantages of the goods or services offered by the advertiser in comparison with those of a competitor. In order to achieve that, the message must necessarily underline the differences between the goods or services compared by describing their main characteristics. The comparison made by the advertiser will necessarily flow from such a description.

37   Therefore, in the context of Directive 84/450, it is not necessary to establish distinctions in the legislation between the various elements of comparison, that is to say the statements concerning the advertiser's offer, the statements concerning the competitor's offer, and the relationship between those two offers.

38   [C]oncerning the application to comparative advertising of stricter national provisions on protection against misleading advertising, the Court takes the view that the objective of Directive 84/450 is the establishment of conditions in which comparative advertising must be regarded as lawful in the context of the internal market.

39   To that end, Article 3a of Directive 84/450 [now Article 4] enumerates the conditions to be satisfied, including the requirement that comparative advertising must not be misleading * * * (see Article 3a(1)(a) of Directive 84/450 [now Article 4(a)]).

40   The Community legislature having carried out only a minimal harmonization of national rules on misleading advertising, Article 7(1) of Directive 84/450 [now Article 8(1) first subparagraph] allows Member States to apply stricter national provisions in that area, to ensure greater protection of consumers in particular.

41   However, Article 7(2) of Directive 84/450 expressly provides that Article 7(1) does not apply to comparative advertising so far as the comparison is concerned.

42   Thus, the provisions of Directive 84/450 on the conditions for comparative advertising to be lawful on the one hand refer to Article 7(1), as regards the definition of misleading advertising (Article 3a(1)(a)) and, on the other hand, exclude the application of that same provision (Article 7(2)). Faced with that apparent textual contradiction, those provisions must be interpreted in such a way as to take account of the objectives of Directive 84/450 and in the light of the case-law of the

Court according to which the conditions required of comparative advertising must be interpreted in the sense most favorable to it (*Toshiba Europe*, paragraph 37).

43   According to the second recital in the preamble to Directive 97/55, the basic provisions governing the form and content of comparative advertising should be uniform and the conditions of the use of comparative advertising in the Member States should be harmonized. According to the third recital, the acceptance or non-acceptance of comparative advertising according to the various national laws may constitute an obstacle to the free movement of goods and services and create distortions of competition. The 18th recital excludes stricter national provisions on misleading advertising being applied to comparative advertising, given that the aim of the Community legislature in adopting Directive 97/55 was to establish conditions under which comparative advertising is to be permitted throughout the Community.

44   It follows that Directive 84/450 carried out an exhaustive harmonization of the conditions under which comparative advertising in Member States might be lawful. Such a harmonization implies by its nature that the lawfulness of comparative advertising throughout the Community is to be assessed solely in the light of the criteria laid down by the Community legislature. Therefore, stricter national provisions on protection against misleading advertising cannot be applied to comparative advertising as regards the form and content of the comparison.

* * *

48   [A]ccording to the 14th recital in the preamble to Directive 97/55,] it may be indispensable, in order to make comparative advertising effective, to identify the goods or services of a competitor, making reference to a trade mark or trade name of which the latter is the proprietor.

* * *

51   In the context of comparative advertising, therefore, it is open to an advertiser to state the trade mark of a competitor.

52   It is possible that, in particular circumstances, the omission of such a statement in an advertising message involving a comparison might mislead, or at least be capable of misleading, the persons to whom it is addressed, thereby making it misleading within the meaning of Article 2(2) of Directive 84/450.

53   In cases where the brand name of the products may significantly affect the buyer's choice and the comparison concerns rival products whose respective brand names differ considerably in the extent to which they are known, omission of the better-known brand name goes against Article 3a(1)(a) of Directive 84/450 [now 4(a)], which lays down one of the conditions for comparative advertising to be lawful.

54   Given the cumulative nature of the requirements set out in Article 3a(1) of Directive 84/450, such comparative advertising is prohibited by Community law.

55   It is, however, for the national court to verify in each case, having regard to all the relevant factors of the case which is brought before it, whether the conditions set out in paragraph 53 of this judgment are met, taking into account the presumed expectations of an average consumer who is reasonably well informed and reasonably observant and circumspect (Case C–220/98 *Estee Lauder* [2000] ECR I–117, paragraphs 27 and 30).

* * *

57   In its second question, the referring court asks essentially whether differences in the method of obtaining supplies of the products whose qualities are compared may have an impact on the lawfulness of the comparative advertising.

* * *

61   As has been pointed out in paragraph 44 of this judgment, Directive 84/450 carried out an exhaustive harmonization of the conditions under which comparative advertising may be lawful in Member States. Those conditions, which are set out in Article 3a(1) of that directive, do not include a requirement that the compared products be obtained through the same distribution channels.

62   Moreover, such a condition would be contrary both to the objectives of the internal market and to those of Directive 84/450.

63   In the first place, in completing the internal market as an area without internal frontiers in which free competition is to be ensured, parallel imports play an important role in preventing the compartmentalization of national markets.

64   Secondly, it is clear from the second recital in the preamble to Directive 97/55 that comparative advertising is designed to enable consumers to make the best possible use of the internal market, given that advertising is a very important means of creating genuine outlets for all goods and services throughout the Community.

* * *

72   By its fourth question, the national court first asks whether a price comparison entails discrediting the competitor and is therefore unlawful for the purposes of Article 3a(1)(e) of Directive 84/450 [now 4(e)] when the products are chosen in such a way as to obtain a price difference greater than the average price difference and/or the comparisons are repeated continuously, creating the impression that the competitor's prices are excessive. Secondly, it asks whether, on a proper interpretation of that provision, comparative advertising is

unlawful where, in addition to citing the name of the competitor, it reproduces the competitor's logo and a picture of its shop.

* * *

80 Concerning the first part of the question, the Court takes the view that comparing rival offers, particularly as regards price, is of the very nature of comparative advertising. Therefore, comparing prices cannot in itself entail the discrediting or denigration of a competitor who charges higher prices, within the meaning of Article 3a(1)(e) of Directive 84/450.

81 The choice as to the number of comparisons which the advertiser wishes to make between the products which he is offering and those offered by his competitors falls within the exercise of his economic freedom. Any obligation to restrict each price comparison to the average prices of the products offered by the advertiser and those of rival products would be contrary to the objectives of the Community legislature.

82 In the words of the second recital in the preamble to Directive 97/55, comparative advertising must help demonstrate objectively the merits of the various comparable products. Such objectivity implies that the persons to whom the advertising is addressed are capable of knowing the actual price differences between the products compared and not merely the average difference between the advertiser's prices and those of its competitors.

83 As for the second part of the question, concerning the reproduction in the advertising message of the competitor's logo and a picture of its shop front, it is important to note that, according to the 15th recital in the preamble to Directive 97/55, use of another's trade mark, trade name or other distinguishing marks does not breach that exclusive right in cases where it complies with the conditions laid down by the directive.

84 Having regard to the above considerations, the answer to the fourth question must be, first, that a price comparison does not entail the discrediting of a competitor, within the meaning of Article 3a(1)(e) of Directive 84/450 either on the grounds that the difference in price between the products compared is greater than the average price difference or by reason of the number of comparisons made. Secondly, Article 3a(1)(e) of Directive 84/450 does not prevent comparative advertising, in addition to citing the competitor's name, from reproducing its logo and a picture of its shop front, if that advertising complies with the conditions for lawfulness laid down by Community law.

NOTES AND QUESTIONS

1. The *Toshiba* case referred to in the *Pippig* involved a suit brought by Toshiba against Katun, a company that sold spare parts and supplies that

could be used in Toshiba photocopiers. In Katun's catalogs, each list of spare parts and supplies was made up of four columns—the first containing Toshiba's product/order number for the product, the second containing Katun's product/order number, the third containing a description of the product and the fourth containing an indication of the models for which the product could be used. Toshiba objected to the use of its product numbers, which it alleged was unnecessary and misled the customers by suggesting that the products were of equivalent quality, thereby exploiting Toshiba's reputation. Katun replied, inter alia, that its customers were specialized traders that were well aware that Katun was not selling products of the original manufacturer. The Court concluded:

> **59**   In the present case, it appears that Katun would have difficulty in comparing its products with those of Toshiba Europe if it did not refer to the latter's order numbers. It also seems clear from the examples of Katun's lists of spare parts and consumable items set out in the order for reference that a clear distinction is made between Katun and Toshiba Europe, so that they do not appear to give a false impression concerning the origin of Katun's products.

Toshiba Europe GmbH v. Katun Germany GmbH, Case C–112/99, 2001 ECR I–7945.

2. Note the different perspectives of the Austrian lower courts, which upheld much of Pippig's claim, as opposed to that of the Court of Justice, which has a much more accepting view of comparative advertising.

3. The basic US federal law on misleading advertising is Section 43(a) of the Lanham Act, codified at 15 U.S.C.A. sec. 1125, which provides in relevant part:

> Any person who * * * in commercial advertising or promotion, misrepresents the nature, characteristics, quality, or geographic origin of his or another person's goods, services, or commercial activities, shall be liable in a civil action by any person who believes that he or she is likely to be damaged by such act.

In Pizza Hut, Inc. v. Papa John's Intern., Inc., 227 F.3d 489 (5th Cir. 2000), the court noted that a prima facie case of false advertising under section 43(a) requires the plaintiff to establish: A false or misleading statement of fact about a product; such statement either deceived, or had the capacity to deceive a substantial segment of potential consumers; the deception is material, in that it is likely to influence the consumer's purchasing decision; and the plaintiff has been or is likely to be injured as a result of the statement at issue.

The Papa John's case involved (i) Papa John's four-word slogan "Better Ingredients. Better Pizza;" a series of ads touting taste test results comparing Papa John's and Pizza Hut's pizzas, based on which Papa John's claimed that it "won big time;" and a series of ads comparing specific ingredients used in its pizzas with those used by its "competitors" in which Papa John's touted the superiority of its sauce and its dough. Pizza Hut did not contest the truthfulness of the underlying factual assertions made by Papa John's, but argued that differences cited made no difference in pizza dough.

A jury found that the slogan and the "sauce and dough" claims were false or misleading and deceptive or likely to deceive consumers. The jury also determined that Papa John's "taste test" ads were not deceptive or likely to deceive consumers, and that Papa John's "ingredients claims" were not false or misleading. The District Court thereupon concluded:

> When the "Better Ingredients. Better Pizza." slogan is considered in light of the entirety of Papa John's post-May 1997 advertising which violated provisions of the Lanham Act and in the context in which it was juxtaposed with the false and misleading statements contained in Papa John's print and broadcast media advertising, the slogan itself became tainted to the extent that its continued use should be enjoined.

The Court of Appeals reversed on the grounds that

> (1) the slogan, standing alone, is not an objectifiable statement of fact upon which consumers would be justified in relying, and thus not actionable under section 43(a); and (2) while the slogan, when utilized in connection with some of the post-May 1997 comparative advertising—specifically, the sauce and dough campaigns—conveyed objectifiable and misleading facts, Pizza Hut has failed to adduce any evidence demonstrating that the facts conveyed by the slogan were material to the purchasing decisions of the consumers to which the slogan was directed.

Among the points made by the Court of Appeals were the following:

> Under section 43(a) a plaintiff must demonstrate that the commercial advertisement or promotion is either literally false, or that [if the advertisement is not literally false,] it is likely to mislead and confuse consumers. If the statement is shown to be misleading, the plaintiff must also introduce evidence of the statement's impact on consumers, referred to as materiality.

> Essential to any claim under section 43(a) is a determination of whether the challenged statement is one of fact—actionable under section 43(a)—or one of general opinion—not actionable under section 43(a). Bald assertions of superiority or general statements of opinion cannot form the basis of Lanham Act liability. Rather the statements at issue must be a specific and measurable claim, capable of being proved false or of being reasonably interpreted as a statement of objective fact.

> One form of non-actionable statements of general opinion under section 43(a) has been referred to as "puffery." * * * A leading authority on unfair competition has defined "puffery" as an "exaggerated advertising, blustering, and boasting upon which no reasonable buyer would rely," or "a general claim of superiority over a comparative product that is so vague, it would be understood as a mere expression of opinion." 4 J. Thomas McCarthy, McCarthy on Trademark and Unfair Competition § 27.38 (4th ed.1996).

As noted, in the view of the Court of Appeals the slogan standing alone was a statement of non-actionable opinion. Nonetheless, when the slogan was viewed in the context of the misleading comparative "sauce and dough" ads, the court found:

A reasonable consumer would understand the slogan, *when considered in the context of the comparison ads,* as conveying the following message: Papa John's uses "better ingredients," which produces a "better pizza" because Papa John's uses "fresh-pack" tomatoes, fresh dough, and filtered water. In short, Papa John's has given definition to the word "better." Thus, when the slogan is used in this context, it is no longer mere opinion, but rather takes on the characteristics of a statement of fact. When used in the context of the sauce and dough ads, the slogan is misleading for the same reasons we have earlier discussed in connection with the sauce and dough ads.

However, in the court's view, Pizza Hut had failed to adduce evidence establishing that the misleading statement of fact conveyed by the ads and the slogan was material to the consumers to which the slogan was directed. Since evidence of materiality is necessary to establish liability under the Lanham Act, the court found for Papa John's and reversed the district court.

Same result under the EU Directive?

D. PROTECTION OF ECONOMIC INTERESTS

1. UNFAIR CONTRACT TERMS

One of the more important EU measures intended to protect the legal and economic interests of consumers is Directive 93/13, O.J. L 95/29 (Apr. 21, 1993), on Unfair Terms in Consumer Contracts, which is contained in the Selected Documents as Document No. 31. This type of legislation began in Scandinavia in the 1960s and spread to most Member States, but varied considerably in scope. The directive covers only contracts between sellers or suppliers and consumers, not contracts between businessmen or professionals *inter se.*

The following recent case sheds light on the Court of Justice's approach to the interpretation of this directive and of consumer protection rules in general. We consider the specific provisions of the directive in the notes following the case.

OCEANO GRUPO EDITORIAL SA v. MURCIANO QUINTERO

Case C–240/98, [2000] ECR I–4941.

[The defendants contracted with plaintiffs for the purchase by installments of an encyclopedia for personal use. The contracts conferred jurisdiction on the courts in Barcelona (Spain), a city in which none of the defendants is domiciled but where the plaintiffs have their principal place of business. Defendants did not pay the sums due and the plaintiffs brought summary procedures to obtain an order that the defendants should pay those sums. Notice of the claims was not served on the defendants since the national court had doubts as to whether it had jurisdiction over the actions in question.]

19   * * * It decided to stay the proceedings and to refer to the Court of Justice for a preliminary ruling the following question * * *:

"Is the scope of the consumer protection provided by [the 'unfair contracts' directive] such that the national court may determine of its own motion whether a term of a contract is unfair when making its preliminary assessment as to whether a claim should be allowed to proceed before the ordinary courts?"

* * *

21   First, it should be noted that, where a term of the kind at issue in the main proceedings has been included in a contract concluded between a consumer and a seller or supplier within the meaning of the Directive without being individually negotiated, it satisfies all the criteria enabling it to be classed as unfair for the purposes of the Directive.

22   A term of this kind, the purpose of which is to confer jurisdiction in respect of all disputes arising under the contract on the court in the territorial jurisdiction of which the seller or supplier has his principal place of business, obliges the consumer to submit to the exclusive jurisdiction of a court which may be a long way from his domicile. This may make it difficult for him to enter an appearance. In the case of disputes concerning limited amounts of money, the costs relating to the consumer's entering an appearance could be a deterrent and cause him to forgo any legal remedy or defense. Such a term thus falls within the category of terms which have the object or effect of excluding or hindering the consumer's right to take legal action, a category referred to in subparagraph (q) of paragraph 1 of the Annex to the Directive.

23   By contrast, the term enables the seller or supplier to deal with all the litigation relating to his trade, business or profession in the court in the jurisdiction of which he has his principal place of business. This makes it easier for the seller or supplier to arrange to enter an appearance and makes it less onerous for him to do so.

24   It follows that where a jurisdiction clause is included, without being individually negotiated, in a contract between a consumer and a seller or supplier within the meaning of the Directive and where it confers exclusive jurisdiction on a court in the territorial jurisdiction of which the seller or supplier has his principal place of business, it must be regarded as unfair within the meaning of Article 3 of the Directive in so far as it causes, contrary to the requirement of good faith, a significant imbalance in the parties' rights and obligations arising under the contract, to the detriment of the consumer.

25   As to the question of whether a court seised of a dispute concerning a contract between a seller or supplier and a consumer may determine of its own motion whether a term of the contract is unfair, it should be noted that the system of protection introduced by the Directive is based on the idea that the consumer is in a weak position vis-a-vis the

seller or supplier, as regards both his bargaining power and his level of knowledge. This leads to the consumer agreeing to terms drawn up in advance by the seller or supplier without being able to influence the content of the terms.

26   The aim of Article 6 of the Directive, which requires Member States to lay down that unfair terms are not binding on the consumer, would not be achieved if the consumer were himself obliged to raise the unfair nature of such terms. In disputes where the amounts involved are often limited, the lawyers' fees may be higher than the amount at stake, which may deter the consumer from contesting the application of an unfair term. While it is the case that, in a number of Member States, procedural rules enable individuals to defend themselves in such proceedings, there is a real risk that the consumer, particularly because of ignorance of the law, will not challenge the term pleaded against him on the grounds that it is unfair. It follows that effective protection of the consumer may be attained only if the national court acknowledges that it has power to evaluate terms of this kind of its own motion.

27   Moreover, as the Advocate General pointed out in paragraph 24 of his Opinion, the system of protection laid down by the Directive is based on the notion that the imbalance between the consumer and the seller or supplier may only be corrected by positive action unconnected with the actual parties to the contract. That is why Article 7 of the Directive, paragraph 1 of which requires Member States to implement adequate and effective means to prevent the continued use of unfair terms, specifies in paragraph 2 that those means are to include allowing authorized consumer associations to take action in order to obtain a decision as to whether contractual terms drawn up for general use are unfair and, if need be, to have them prohibited, even if they have not been used in specific contracts.

28   As the French Government has pointed out, it is hardly conceivable that, in a system requiring the implementation of specific group actions of a preventive nature intended to put a stop to unfair terms detrimental to consumers' interests, a court hearing a dispute on a specific contract containing an unfair term should not be able to set aside application of the relevant term solely because the consumer has not raised the fact that it is unfair. On the contrary, the court's power to determine of its own motion whether a term is unfair must be regarded as constituting a proper means both of achieving the result sought by Article 6 of the Directive, namely, preventing an individual consumer from being bound by an unfair term, and of contributing to achieving the aim of Article 7, since if the court undertakes such an examination, that may act as a deterrent and contribute to preventing unfair terms in contracts concluded between consumers and sellers or suppliers.

29   It follows from the above that the protection provided for consumers by the Directive entails the national court being able to determine of its own motion whether a term of a contract before it is unfair when making its preliminary assessment as to whether a claim should be allowed to proceed before the national courts.

30   As regards the position where a directive has not been transposed, it must be noted that it is settled case-law [citing *Marleasing* and *Faccini Dori*, see Chapter 7 supra] that, when applying national law, whether adopted before or after the directive, the national court called upon to interpret that law must do so, as far as possible, in the light of the wording and purpose of the directive so as to achieve the result pursued by the directive and thereby comply with the third paragraph of Article 189 of the EC Treaty [now 288 TFEU].

31   Since the court making the reference is seised of a case falling within the scope of the Directive and the facts giving rise to the case postdate the expiry of the period allowed for transposing the Directive, it therefore falls to that court, when it applies the provisions of national law * * *, to interpret them, as far as possible, in accordance with the Directive and in such a way that they are applied of the court's own motion.

32   It is apparent from the above considerations that the national court is obliged, when it applies national law provisions predating or postdating the said Directive, to interpret those provisions, so far as possible, in the light of the wording and purpose of the Directive. The requirement for an interpretation in conformity with the Directive requires the national court, in particular, to favor the interpretation that would allow it to decline of its own motion the jurisdiction conferred on it by virtue of an unfair term.

NOTES AND QUESTIONS

1. More recent cases demonstrate that the Court remains committed to a broad interpretation of Directive 93/13. In Claro v. Centro Movil Milenium SL, Case C–168/05, 2006 ECR I–10421, it ruled that in a suit to enforce an arbitral award, a consumer may challenge the fairness of an arbitration clause even if no such challenge was made in the arbitration itself. In Cofidis SA v. Fredout, Case 473/00, 2002 ECR I–10875, the Court ruled that Directive 93/13 precludes a national provision which, in a proceeding brought by a seller against a consumer on the basis of a contract between them, prohibits the national court, on expiry of a limitation period, from finding of its own motion or following a plea raised by the consumer that a contract term is unfair. In Commission v. Italy, Case C–372/99, 2002 ECR I–819, the Court ruled that Article 7(3) of Directive 93/13 requires the setting up of procedures that may be directed against conduct limited to recommending the use (as opposed to the actual use) of unfair contract clauses.

2. In US law, probably the most important provision on unfair consumer terms is section 2–302 of the Uniform Commercial Code, which provides:

"If the court as a matter of law finds the contract or any clause of the contract to have been unconscionable at the time it was made the court may refuse to enforce the contract, or it may enforce the remainder of the contract without the unconscionable clause, or it may limit the application of any unconscionable clause as to avoid any unconscionable result."

The Code does not define "unconscionable", rather it is left to the court (not a jury). The comments to Section 2–302 state that "the basic test is whether, in light of the general commercial background and the commercial needs of the particular trade or case, the clauses involved are so one-sided as to be unconscionable under the circumstances existing at the time of the making of the contract."

A leading treatise on contracts notes that courts have tended to focus on the absence of meaningful choice (procedural unconscionability, which may include questionable bargaining practices and difficult-to-understand or -read language) and unreasonably favorable terms (substantive unconscionability). E. Allan Farnsworth, Contracts 311 (3rd ed.1999). According to Farnsworth, judges have been "cautious" in finding unconscionability. Id. at 312.

3. Directive 93/13 is contained in the Selected Documents and merits close reading. How is it similar in approach to Section 2–302? How does it differ? Which is the better approach? Which is more likely to lead to a voiding of a contract term?

4. To the extent that the provisions of Directive 93/13 go beyond the usual consumer protection afforded by the UCC and case law interpreting "contracts of adhesion" in the US, can a US internet merchant avoid the directive's terms by subjecting a contract with an EU consumer to the law of a US state? See Jane K. Winn & Mark Webber, The Impact of EU Unfair Contract Terms Law on US Business-to-Consumer Internet Merchants, 62 Business Lawyer 209 (November 2006).

5. Article 3 defines an unfair contract term as one creating "a significant imbalance in the parties' rights and obligations ... to the detriment of the consumer," if contained in a "pre-formulated standard contract" or one otherwise not "individually negotiated." Is that definition sufficiently precise? Consider the Annex's "non-exhaustive" list of unfair terms. Are some fairly common in US standard form contracts? What about (e), (f), (n) and (q)? Do you think the directive represents a policy approach that is desirable, or does it interfere too much with the marketplace? Article 5 also requires that consumer contracts be "drafted in plain, intelligible language," with any ambiguity construed in favor of the consumer.

6. Under article 6, unfair contract terms are not binding, but the contract itself may survive, if appropriate after the severance of the illegal terms. How would that decision be made?

7. Could a corporation rely on Directive 93/13? In Cape Snc v. Idealservice Srl, Case C–541/99, [2001] ECR I–9049, the Court concluded that "consumer" as used in the directive refers solely to natural persons.

2.　OTHER DIRECTIVES PROTECTING CONSUMER INTERESTS

Another important directive protecting consumer economic interests is that on distance sales, Directive 97/7, O.J. L 144/19 (June 4, 1997), which governs all product or service sales by mail, telephone, television, computer, fax, etc., with the exception of financial services. The directive requires precise indication of the contract terms and a right of withdrawal without penalty within seven working days after the contract is entered into. (Note that the Dutch rules protecting purchasers of commodities in "cold calling" telephone sales are analyzed in *Alpine Investments*, Chapter 30(C)(4) supra.

Directive 94/47 on rights to use immovable properties on a time-share basis, O.J. L 280/83 (Oct. 29, 1994), protects persons who buy long-term interests enabling the use of realty for stated periods each year, an arrangement particularly popular in the resorts in the Mediterranean States. After the Commission pledged itself in 1992 to a review of draft directives in order to apply the principle of subsidiarity, the Commission proposed to withdraw this draft. However, objections from Parliament saved the time-share proposal, and the draft received rather expeditious treatment in the Council, where the UK strongly supported it.

Directive 99/44 on sale of consumer goods and associated guarantees, O.J. L 171/12 (July 7, 1999), would harmonize Member State rules on those subjects. The basic obligation to be imposed is that the seller must deliver goods conforming to the contract of sale. In the event of nonconformity being discovered within two years, the consumer would be entitled, subject to certain limits, to have the goods brought into conformity free-of-charge through repair or replacement, or to have an appropriate price adjustment, or to have the contract rescinded.

Dillenkofer v. Germany, Cases 178/94 et seq., [1996] ECR I–4845, involved the interpretation of Directive 90/314 on package travel, package holiday and package tours, O.J. L 158/59 (June 23, 1990). Article 7 of the directive requires the organizer of such package holiday arrangements to "provide sufficient evidence of security for the refund of money paid over and for the repatriation of the consumer in the event of insolvency." Germany, the Netherlands and the UK argued that this article's purpose was to create a level competitive playing field for package holiday providers, in view of the directive's use of what is now Article 114 TFEU as its legal basis. The Court rejected this view, concluding that recitals to the directive demonstrated that it was also intended to protect consumer interests, while article 7 was clearly intended to provide a financial security to consumers in the event of the insolvency of the organizer. This conclusion was essential in order to enable the trial court to find Germany liable in damages to the consumers injured by Germany's failure to implement Directive 90/314 in time. The Commission is studying the possibility of updating this Directive.

Directive 98/27 on injunctions to protect consumers' interests, O.J. L 166/51 (June 11, 1998), as amended, requires Member States to ensure that injunctive relief is available expeditiously in the enforcement of rules implementing eleven named consumer rights directives. Public and private bodies organized to protect consumer interests, when authorized by States, would have the power to seek such injunctions. The eleven directives include those mentioned earlier in this chapter dealing with unfair commercial practices, medicinal products advertising, unfair contract terms, timeshares, distance sales, package travel, guarantees and off-premises contracts.

In 2005, Directive 2005/29 on unfair business-to-consumer commercial practices, O.J. L 149/22 (June 11, 2005) was adopted. It prohibits unfair commercial practices. A practice is unfair if it is contrary to requirements of professional diligence or it materially distorts (or is likely to distort) the economic behavior of the average consumer (or, the average member of the group when a practice is directed at a particular group of consumers (e.g., consumers of a certain age)). The directive specifies certain misleading and aggressive practices as unfair. Almost all Member States have notified the Commission that they have implemented the Directive. The Commission has published an informative booklet giving guidance on what the Directive covers.

On October 8, 2008, the Commission issued a proposal for a Directive on Consumer Rights, which would replace existing directives on unfair contract terms, sales of consumer goods and guarantees, distance selling and doorstep selling. It is aimed at achieving full harmonization in these areas and it is noted that the current approach allows too much Member State discretion which has resulted in market fragmentation and in considerable expense for businesses that have to comply with varying rules. COM(2008) 614 final.

E. THE PRODUCTS LIABILITY DIRECTIVE

The EU first considered the need for a directive on products liability in the 1970s, but because of the disagreement over what it should provide, final agreement on a text could not be reached until 1985.[2] The directive is reproduced in the Selected Documents as Document No. 32 and should be read at this point.

The directive's basic provision is article 1, which states: "the producer [which is defined to include an importer] shall be liable for damage caused by a defect in his product." However, "the injured person shall be required to prove the damage, the defect and the causal relationship between the defect and the damage" (art. 4).

The directive provides in article 6 that a product is defective when it does not provide the safety that a person is entitled to expect, taking all

---

2. Council Directive 85/374 of July 25, 1985 on the approximation of the laws, regulations and administrative provisions of the Member States concerning liability for defective products, O.J. L 210/29 (Aug. 7, 1985).

circumstances into account, including the use to which the product could reasonably be expected to be put. The producer's defenses are listed in article 7. The main defenses are that the defect did not exist when the product was put into circulation or that the state of scientific and technical knowledge at the time when the product was put into circulation was not such as to enable the existence of the defect to be discovered (the "state of the art" or "developmental risk" defense). Whether or not to grant this last defense was one of the most controversial issues in the formulation of the directive. Article 15 provides that a Member State can choose to eliminate this defense and requires the Commission to report in 1995 on the effect of the defense and the Council to consider whether to repeal it.

The directive also allows a Member State to put a cap on damages of not less than 70 million Euro for a producer's liability caused by identical items with the same defect (art. 16).

The scope of the directive was expanded in 1999 to primary agricultural products and game products.

According to a 1999 Commission Green Paper on Liability for defective products (COM (1999) 396 final, July 28, 1999), all of the then Member States except Finland and Luxembourg retained the developmental risk defense option (with an exception for food and medicinal products in Spain and products derived from the human body in France). Damage caps have been set only by Germany, Portugal and Spain.

COMMISSION v. UNITED KINGDOM

(Product liability directive)
Case C–300/95, [1997] ECR I–2649.

[The UK Consumer Protection Act 1987 provides in section 4 that a producer can avoid liability if he establishes

> that the state of scientific and technical knowledge at the relevant time was not such that a producer of products of the same description as the product in question might be expected to have discovered the defect if it had existed in his products while they were under his control.

The Commission contended that this provision deviated significantly from article 7(e) of the Product Liability Directive by substituting "a subjective assessment based on the behavior of a reasonable producer" for the "objective" test of article 7(e). The UK replied that its version was intended also to be objective, and that in any event section 1 of the 1987 Act required it to be construed in accord with the directive.]

24   In order for a producer to incur liability for defective products under Article 4 of the Directive, the victim must prove the damage, the defect and the causal relationship between defect and damage, but not that the producer was at fault. However, in accordance with the principle of fair apportionment of risk between the injured person and

the producer set forth in the seventh recital in the preamble to the Directive, Article 7 provides that the producer has a defense if he can prove certain facts exonerating him from liability, including "that the state of scientific and technical knowledge at the time when he put the product into circulation was not such as to enable the existence of the defect to be discovered" (Article 7(e)).

25 Certain general observations can be made as to the wording of Article 7(e) of the Directive.

26 First, as the Advocate General rightly observes in paragraph 20 of his Opinion, since that provision refers to "scientific and technical knowledge at the time when [the producer] put the product into circulation", Article 7(e) is not specifically directed at the practices and safety standards in use in the industrial sector in which the producer is operating, but, unreservedly, at the state of scientific and technical knowledge, including the most advanced level of such knowledge, at the time when the product in question was put into circulation.

27 Second, the clause providing for the defense in question does not contemplate the state of knowledge of which the producer in question actually or subjectively was or could have been apprised, but the objective state of scientific and technical knowledge of which the producer is presumed to have been informed.

28 However, it is implicit in the wording of Article 7(e) that the relevant scientific and technical knowledge must have been accessible at the time when the product in question was put into circulation.

29 It follows that, in order to have a defense under Article 7(e) of the Directive, the producer of a defective product must prove that the objective state of scientific and technical knowledge, including the most advanced level of such knowledge, at the time when the product in question was put into circulation was not such as to enable the existence of the defect to be discovered. Further, in order for the relevant scientific and technical knowledge to be successfully pleaded against the producer, that knowledge must have been accessible at the time when the product in question was put into circulation. On this last point, contrary to what the Commission seems to consider, Article 7(e) of the Directive raises difficulties of interpretation which, in the event of litigation, the national courts will have to resolve having recourse, if necessary, to Article 177 [now 267 TFEU] of the EC Treaty.

* * *

37 [Finally,] the Court has consistently held that the scope of national laws, regulations or administrative provisions must be assessed in the light of the interpretation given to them by national courts (see, in particular, Case C–382/92 *Commission v. United Kingdom* [1994] ECR I–2435, paragraph 36). Yet in this case the Commission has not referred in support of its application to any national judicial decision

which, in its view, interprets the domestic provision at issue inconsistently with the Directive.

38   Lastly, there is nothing in the material produced to the Court to suggest that the courts in the United Kingdom, if called upon to interpret section 4(1)(e), would not do so in the light of the wording and the purpose of the Directive so as to achieve the result which it has in view and thereby comply with the third paragraph of Article 189 [now 288 TFEU] of the Treaty (see, in particular, Case C–91/92 *Faccini Dori v. Recreb* [1994] ECR I–3325, paragraph 26). Moreover, section 1(1) of the Act expressly imposes such an obligation on the national courts.

39   It follows that the Commission has failed to make out its allegation that, having regard to its general legal context and especially section 1(1) of the Act, section 4(1)(e) clearly conflicts with Article 7(e) of the Directive. As a result, the application must be dismissed.

COMMISSION v. FRANCE

(Product liability directive)
Case C–52/00, [2002] ECR I–3827.

[The Commission brought an action against France for failure to implement Directive 85/374 by (i) providing in its implementation law for the possibility of recovering property damage of less than €500; (ii) by providing that the supplier of a defective product is to be liable in all cases and on the same basis as the producer; and (iii) by providing that the manufacturer must prove that it has taken appropriate steps to avert the consequences of a defective product in order to be able to rely on the grounds of exemption from liability provided for in Article 7(d) and (e) of the Directive. The Court first discussed in general the extent of Member State discretion in implementing the Directive.]

13   In the French Government's view, the Directive must be interpreted in the light of the growing importance of consumer protection within the Community, as reflected in the latest version of Article 153 EC [now 169]. The wording of Article 13 of the Directive, which uses the term 'rights', shows that it does not seek to prevent achievement of a higher national level of protection. That analysis is also borne out by the fact that the Directive itself enables the Member States to depart in certain respects from the rules which it lays down.

14   In that connection it should be pointed out that the Directive was adopted by the Council by unanimity under Article [115]. Unlike Article [114], which was inserted into the Treaty after the adoption of the Directive and allows for certain derogations, that legal basis provides no possibility for the Member States to maintain or establish provisions departing from Community harmonizing measures.

15   Nor can Article 153 [now 169 TFEU], likewise inserted into the Treaty after the adoption of the Directive, be relied on in order to justify

interpreting the directive as seeking a minimum harmonization of the laws of the Member States which could not preclude one of them from retaining or adopting protective measures stricter than the Community measures. In fact, the competence conferred in that respect on the Member States by Article 153(5) concerns only the measures mentioned at paragraph 3(b) of that article, that is to say measures supporting, supplementing and monitoring the policy pursued by the Member States. That competence does not extend to the measures referred to in paragraph 3(a) of Article 153, that is to say the measures adopted pursuant to Article 95 [now 114 TFEU] in the context of attainment of the internal market * * *. Furthermore, as the Advocate General noted, Article 153 is worded in the form of an instruction addressed to the Community concerning its future policy and cannot permit the Member States, owing to the direct risk that would pose for the *acquis communautaire*, autonomously to adopt measures contrary to the Community law contained in the directives already adopted at the time of entry into force of that law.

16 Accordingly, the margin of discretion available to the Member States in order to make provision for product liability is entirely determined by the Directive itself and must be inferred from its wording, purpose and structure.

17 In that connection it should be pointed out first that, as is clear from the first recital thereto, the purpose of the Directive in establishing a harmonized system of civil liability on the part of producers in respect of damage caused by defective products is to ensure undistorted competition between traders, to facilitate the free movement of goods and to avoid differences in levels of consumer protection.

18 Secondly, it is important to note that unlike, for example, Directive 93/13 on unfair terms in consumer contracts, the Directive contains no provision expressly authorizing the Member States to adopt or to maintain more stringent provisions in matters in respect of which it makes provision, in order to secure a higher level of consumer protection.

19 Thirdly, the fact that the Directive provides for certain derogations or refers in certain cases to national law does not mean that in regard to the matters which it regulates harmonization is not complete.

20 Although Articles 15(1)(a) and (b) and 16 of the Directive permit the Member States to depart from the rules laid down therein, the possibility of derogation applies only in regard to the matters exhaustively specified and it is narrowly defined. Moreover, it is subject *inter alia* to conditions as to assessment with a view to further harmonization, to which the penultimate recital in the preamble expressly refers. * * *

21 In those circumstances Article 13 of the Directive cannot be interpreted as giving the Member States the possibility of maintaining a

general system of product liability different from that provided for in the Directive.

22 The reference in Article 13 of the Directive to the rights which an injured person may rely on under the rules of the law of contractual or non-contractual liability must be interpreted as meaning that the system of rules put in place by the Directive, which in Article 4 enables the victim to seek compensation where he proves damage, the defect in the product and the causal link between that defect and the damage, does not preclude the application of other systems of contractual or non-contractual liability based on other grounds, such as fault or a warranty in respect of latent defects.

23 Likewise the reference in Article 13 to the rights which an injured person may rely on under a special liability system existing at the time when the Directive was notified must be construed, as is clear from the third clause of the 13th recital thereto, as referring to a specific scheme limited to a given sector of production.

24 It follows that, contrary to the arguments put forward by the French Republic, the Directive seeks to achieve, in the matters regulated by it, complete harmonization of the laws, regulations and administrative provisions of the Member States.

25 The Commission's pleas must be examined in the light of those considerations.

First plea: incorrect transposition of Article 9(b) of the Directive

26 The Commission points out that, unlike Article 9(b) of the Directive, Article 1386–2 of the Civil Code covers all damage to private and public property, with no lower threshold of €500.

27 The French Government does not deny that discrepancy but relies on four arguments in order to justify it. First, by depriving the victim of a right of action, the lower threshold infringes the fundamental right of access to the courts guaranteed by Article 6 of the European Convention for the Protection of Human Rights and Fundamental Freedoms of 4 November 1950. Secondly, the threshold is also contrary to the principle of equal treatment inasmuch as it creates unfair inequalities between both producers and consumers. Thirdly, it has the same effect as a rule granting total exemption from tortious liability, which under French law is contrary to public policy. Fourthly, those criticisms are borne out by the fact that in its Green Paper of 28 July 1999 on liability for defective products (COM (1999) 396 final) the Commission proposes that the threshold be abolished.

28 As regards the first two arguments, which question the legality of the threshold provided for in the Directive, it should be borne in mind in the first place that the system of remedies set up by the Treaty distinguishes between the remedies provided for in Articles 226 and 227 [now 258 and 259 TFEU], whereby a declaration that a Member State has failed to fulfill its obligations may be sought, and those

provided for in Articles 230 and 232 [now 263 and 265 TFEU], which seek judicial review of the lawfulness of measures adopted by the Community institutions or of the institutions' failure to adopt measures. Those remedies serve different purposes and are subject to different rules. In the absence of a provision of the Treaty expressly permitting it to do so, a Member State cannot, therefore, properly plead the unlawfulness of a decision addressed to it as a defense in an action for a declaration that it has failed to fulfill its obligations arising out of its failure to implement that decision. Nor can it plead the unlawfulness of a directive which the Commission alleges it to have infringed.

29   Moreover, as the Advocate General noted, the limits set by the Community legislature to the scope of the Directive are the result of a complex balancing of different interests. As is apparent from the first and ninth recitals in the preamble to the Directive, those interests include guaranteeing that competition will not be distorted, facilitating trade within the common market, consumer protection and ensuring the sound administration of justice.

30   The consequence of the choice made by the Community legislature is that, in order to avoid an excessive number of disputes, in the event of minor material damage the victims of defective products cannot rely on the rules of liability laid down in the Directive but must bring an action under the ordinary law of contractual or non-contractual liability.

31   In those circumstances the threshold provided for in Article 9(b) of the Directive cannot be regarded as affecting victims' rights of access to the courts.

32   Similarly, the fact that different systems of liability apply to the producers and victims of defective products does not constitute an infringement of the principle of equal treatment where the differentiation dependent on the nature and amount of the damage suffered is objectively justified.

33   As regards the third argument raised by the French Government, alleging that the threshold provided for in Article 9(b) of the Directive is incompatible with French public policy, suffice it to state that under the Court's settled case-law recourse to provisions of domestic law to restrict the scope of the provisions of Community law would have the effect of undermining the unity and efficacy of that law and cannot consequently be accepted.

34   With regard to the reference by the French Government to the Commission's Green Paper, suffice it also to recall that the fact that the Commission, with a view to a possible amendment to the Directive, decided to consult the interested parties as to the expediency of abolishing the threshold provided for in Article 9(b) of the Directive cannot dispense the Member States from the obligation to comply with the provision of Community law currently in force.

35　It follows that the Commission's first plea is well founded.

[The Court also upheld the Commission's other two claims.]

Notes and Questions

1. In Sanchez v. Medicina Asturiana SA, Case C–183/00, [2002] ECR I–3901, the issue concerned a 1984 Spanish law that provided, according to the referring Spanish court, more extensive rights for consumers than those provided for in the 1996 Spanish law that implemented Directive 85/374. At issue was whether Article 13 of the Directive permitted the broader Spanish law. Article 13 provides:

> This Directive shall not affect any rights which an injured person may have according to the rules of the law of contractual or non-contractual liability or a special liability system existing at the moment when this Directive is notified.

What should the Court's response be? According to the Court:

31　The reference in Article 13 of the Directive to the rights which an injured person may rely on under the rules of the law of contractual or non-contractual liability must be interpreted as meaning that the system of rules put in place by the Directive, which in Article 4 enables the victim to seek compensation where he proves damage, the defect in the product and the causal link between that defect and the damage, does not preclude the application of other systems of contractual or non-contractual liability based on other grounds, such as fault or a warranty in respect of latent defects.

32　Likewise the reference in Article 13 to the rights which an injured person may rely on under a special liability system existing at the time when the Directive was notified must be construed, as is clear from the third clause of the 13th recital thereto, as referring to a specific scheme limited to a given sector of production.

33　Conversely, a system of producer liability founded on the same basis as that put in place by the Directive and not limited to a given sector of production does not come within any of the systems of liability referred to in Article 13 of the Directive. That provision cannot therefore be relied on in such a case in order to justify the maintenance in force of national provisions affording greater protection than those of the Directive.

2. Would it be permissible to require a consumer to pay for the use of a non-conforming product until a conforming replacement was supplied? Quelle AG v. BVV, Case–404/06, 2008 ECR I–2685 (no).

3. To what extent might differences among the Member States' implementing legislation (e.g., different defenses, different damage caps, different rules on recoverable damages) impair the directive's harmonizing effect? To what extent might they create a problem of forum shopping?

4. Can the prospect of liability for defective products justify behavior that would otherwise violate EU law? For example, could a maker of nail guns

justify certain anticompetitive actions on the grounds that its competitors' nails were not compatible with its nail guns and inferior to its own nails, such that it had to discourage their use to avoid potential liability for defective products? See Hilti AG v. Commission, Case T–30/89, [1991] ECR II–1439.

5. Despite the adoption and implementation of the products liability directive by the Member States, products liability litigation remained relatively uncommon in Europe as of the beginning of the 1990s. Among the reasons cited for the directive's limited effect were "[t]he absence in Europe of an entrepreneurial plaintiff's bar, the presence of substantial court user fees and cost-shifting rules, the unavailability of juries and general limits on damages." R. Weber, E.C. Directive Follows U.S. No–Fault Approach, But Litigation is Rare, Nat'l L.J., Dec. 23, 1991, at 30–31. The Commission noted in its third report on the Directive in 2006 that there had been some experience with use of the Directive in all of the EC–15 Member States. It did not specify how much use had occurred. In any event, it concluded that no changes were needed. COM(2006) 496 final.

6. In 1992, the Council adopted a directive on product safety that covers products not covered by specific directives. It was replaced in 2001.[3] The general rule is that suppliers may place only safe products on the market (art. 3(1)), a safe product being defined as one that during its normal or reasonably foreseeable conditions of use does not present any risk, or only minimal risks compatible with the product's use considered to be acceptable and consistent with a high standard of protection for the safety and health of persons. In assessing the acceptability of risk, consideration is to be given, inter alia, to the product's labeling and the warnings and instructions provided (art. 2(b)).

Under the directive, which applies when there is no specific Community rules governing the safety of a product, suppliers are deemed to meet the general safety requirement if they meet specific Member State safety requirements (art. 3(2)). In the absence of a more specific rule, safety is to be assessed by reference to voluntary standards and good practice codes, the state of the art and technology, as well as to the safety that users or consumers may reasonably expect (art. 3(3)).

The directive requires Member States to establish authorities to monitor compliance with safety standards. These authorities would also be responsible for collecting information and investigating complaints about the safety of products. The directive also requires that they have the power to impose sanctions for violations, including the power to ban products from the market, but it does not require that consumers be given a damage remedy for unsafe products. It also provides for information exchange between the Commission and the Member States.

How does the product safety directive, as described here, compare with the products liability directive? Is the coverage of the two directives—unsafe products vs. defective products—the same? How does it differ? How do the remedies for an injured consumer compare? How would you expect laws based on the two directives to be coordinated?

---

3. Directive 2001/95/EC of the European Parliament and of the Council of 3 December 2001 on general product safety, O.J. L 11/4 (January 15, 2002).

7. Article 13 of the product safety directive authorizes the Commission in certain circumstances to require Member States to take temporary action in respect of a product if the product raises a serious risk to health and safety. A German challenge to the legal basis of this provision in the 1992 version of the directive is noted and briefly excerpted at Chapters 3(B) and 5(D)(3)(a) supra. Germany v. Council, Case C–359/92, [1994] ECR I–3681.

8. A number of questions can be raised about the directive. In answering them, the student should consider how the same question would be answered in the United States?

(a) Does the plaintiff have to prove the producer was at fault?

(b) How does the plaintiff establish that a product was defective? Is the test objective or subjective?

(c) What if the plaintiff has used a product in an unexpected way?

(d) What kind of damages may be recovered? May the plaintiff recover for pain and suffering?

(e) May a producer avoid liability by including an exculpatory clause in its sales contract?

(f) What is the statute of limitations under the directive?

For reference, in 1997, the Restatement of the Law Third: Torts–Products Liability was adopted by the American Law Institute. Among its key provisions are

Sec. 1—One engaged in the business of selling or otherwise distributing products who sells or distributes a defective product is subject to liability for harm to persons or property caused by the defect.

Sec. 2—A product is defective when, at the time of sale or distribution, it contains a manufacturing defect, is defective in design, or is defective because of inadequate instructions or warnings. A product:

(a) contains a manufacturing defect when the product departs from its intended design even though all possible care was exercised in the preparation and marketing of the product;

(b) is defective by design when the foreseeable risks of harm posed by the product could have been reduced or avoided by the adoption of a reasonable alternative design by the seller or other distributor, or a predecessor in the commercial chain of distribution, and the omission of the alternative design renders the product not reasonably safe;

(c) is defective because of inadequate instructions or warnings when the foreseeable risks of harm posed by the product could have been reduced or avoided by the provision of reasonable instructions by the seller or other distributor, or a predecessor in the commercial chain of distribution, and the omission of the instructions or warnings renders the product not reasonably safe.

Sec. 15—Whether a product defect caused harm to persons or property is determined by the prevailing rules and principles governing causation in tort.

Sec. 21—For purposes of this Restatement, harm to persons or property includes economic loss if caused by harm to:

(a) the plaintiff's person; or

(b) the person of another when harm to the other interferes with an interest of the plaintiff person protected by tort law; or

(c) the plaintiff's property other than the defective product.

CHAPTER 34

SOCIAL POLICY

▪ ▪ ▪

Social policy ranks among the most important fields of action of the Community. Ever since the European Council endorsed the Social Action Program of 1974, the political institutions of the Community have adopted numerous and far-reaching legislative measures, which have in many instances been broadened in impact by liberal interpretation by the Court of Justice. Most of this legislation is intended to secure for employees various rights and benefits, but some of the provisions have an impact on other aspects of society. Although much of the legislation and case law merely follows prevailing national views on the continent, some of it represents dramatic innovations in employee rights protection. There is no doubt that social policy is, as the Court of Justice has said, one of the fundamental aspects of the Community.

The over-all picture is one of sharp contrast with prevailing legislation and practices in the US. Although the US adopted legislation in the 1940s to protect the collective interests of workers organized in unions, with regard to individual employees both the US and its states follow the traditional view that employees are agents and may be dismissed at will by their employers. The US has virtually no legislation protecting individual employees apart from the prohibition of discrimination based on race or sex contained in the civil rights act. This chapter accordingly yields two benefits: it surveys a major field of regulation of concern to lawyers representing clients in the Community, and it provides the basis for a valuable exercise in comparative law and policy.

This chapter first presents a review of the evolution in Treaty provisions and social action, including policies intended to promote employment. Section B describes two important measures providing economic rights to employees, the Collective Redundancy Directive and the Transfer of Undertakings Directive, both the subject of numerous Court judgments. Next, the chapter describes Community action to achieve worker health and safety in section C, concentrating upon the directives on working time and the protection of pregnant workers. The final section surveys other recent legislation, notably the directives on parental leave and worker information and consultation.

A. TREATY PROVISIONS, THE SOCIAL CHARTER AND SOCIAL ACTION PROGRAMS

1. THE EEC TREATY AND THE 1974 SOCIAL ACTION PROGRAM

The initial Treaty of Rome devoted two chapters to social policy. The key provision, the initial EECT Article 117, stated:

> Member States agree upon the need to promote improved working conditions and an improved standard of living for workers....
>
> They believe that such a development will ensue not only from the functioning of the common market, which will favour the harmonization of social systems, but also from ... the approximation of provisions laid down by law, regulation or administrative action.

The text reflects a certain ambivalence. Apparently some Member States thought that the achievement of the common market would inevitably improve the conditions of workers, while others felt that the Community would have to harmonize national laws for this purpose. In any event, EECT Article 117 did not expressly grant any legislative power, so that social policy measures had to be adopted under EECT Article 100 (now TFEU Article 115), the initial provision authorizing harmonization of rules to achieve the common market. (See Chapter 14A.) That in turn meant that the Council of Ministers had to act by a unanimous vote and the Parliament only had to be consulted.

Another important social policy provision was the initial EECT Article 118, which assigned the Commission the "task of promoting close cooperation between Member States in the social field" through studies and consultations with regard, for example, to employment, labor law and working conditions, social security, the right of association and collective bargaining. Article 118 did not, however, grant the Commission any legislative power. In Germany v. Commission (Immigration of non-Community workers), Case 281/85, [1987] ECR 3203, the Court held that Article 118 could not be construed to give the Commission implied power to take decisions binding the Member States.

EECT Article 119, establishing the principle of equal pay for men and women, rapidly acquired such importance that we will cover it in depth in the next chapter.

The early social policy chapters did provide for substantial Community social assistance programs, notably the European Social Fund, a vehicle for making substantial funds available for "the task of rendering the employment of workers easier and of increasing their geographical and occupational mobility within the Community" (EECT Article 123, now TFEU Article 162). The Fund's resources have been used principally for vocational training and resettlement allowances for workers in depressed industries.

Although in 1987 the Single European Act introduced EECT Article 100a (now, as revised, TFEU Article 114), which authorized the Council to adopt most harmonization measures by qualified majority voting, Article 100a(2) continued to require unanimous Council action to adopt measures "relating to the rights and interests of employed persons". (See Chapter 14B.) The then UK government of Prime Minister Thatcher insisted on this in order to ensure that the UK would retain an effective veto on any such legislation.

The Single European Act also added EECT Article 118a (later absorbed into ECT Article 137). This set the specific goal of improving "the health and safety of workers." Equally important, it authorized the Council to adopt directives by qualified majority vote, acting "in cooperation" with the Parliament. As we shall see in section C, Article 118a was used to adopt a considerable body of legislation.

Social policy first became an important field of Community legislation in the 1970s. At their Paris meeting in October 1972, the Heads of State and Government urged that action be undertaken in the social field, which incited the Council of Ministers to adopt a Social Action Program, O.J. C 13/1 (Feb. 12, 1974). An initial wave of social harmonization legislation followed in the late 1970s, due largely to the keen interest manifested by the Socialist governments in Germany under Chancellors Brandt and Schmidt, Labor governments in the UK under Prime Ministers Wilson and Callaghan, and the progressive government in France under President Giscard d'Estaing.

2. THE SOCIAL CHARTER AND THE 1989 SOCIAL ACTION PROGRAM

The climate for social policy legislation changed significantly in the early 1980s. In large measure, this was the result of political change: Margaret Thatcher, an implacable foe of new social legislation, had become the UK Prime Minister and the Christian Democrats under Chancellor Kohl replaced the Socialist government in Germany. Accordingly, no new measures for the protection of any economic interests of employees were passed. When the Commission issued the White Paper of June 1985 on Completing the Internal Market, its legislative program did not include social policy measures.

This state of affairs pleased neither the Parliament nor the organized labor movement and both urged that further social legislation be made a component of the internal market program. With impetus from Jacques Delors, President of the Commission and himself a leading French Socialist, the Commission proposed a Community Charter of the Fundamental Social Rights of Workers, which was reviewed and debated throughout 1989. At the Strasbourg European Council Meeting in December 1989, all the Member States but the UK endorsed the Social Charter of 1989, as it is popularly known.

The Preamble to the Social Charter adopts as its basic premise that "in the context of the establishment of the single European market, the same importance must be attached to the social aspects as to the economic aspects." However, the Preamble contains a very important reservation in the form of the "principle of subsidiarity," which places responsibility for action in some fields of social policy with "Member States or their constituent parts," rather than Community-wide legislation. The idea behind subsidiarity is that action should not be taken at the Community level when the States can more appropriately act. It is worth noting that the Social Charter's inclusion of the principle of subsidiarity preceded the Maastricht Treaty's enunciation of the principle generally in EECT Article 3b (now stated in the Lisbon TEU Article 5(3)). See Chapter 4D.

Although the Social Charter is a highly important statement of policy, much of the text does not represent any new or revolutionary thinking. Many of the sections state employee rights and interests which had already largely been attained, for example, the sections proclaiming the right to free movement of workers, safer work site conditions, access to vocational training and equal rights for women. In contrast, several sections of the Social Charter were more novel. Thus, a section entitled "Improvement of Living and Working Conditions" referred to a "right to a weekly rest period and to annual paid leave, the duration of which must be harmonized;" and another section dealt with "Information, Consultation and Participation for Workers." Both have influenced subsequent legislation.

There is also a section called "Freedom of Association and Collective Bargaining" which refers to a "dialogue between the two sides of industry at the European level." In this connection, the Commission has sponsored, since 1985, annual meetings of the Union of Industries of the EC (UNICE) and the European Trade Union Confederation (ETUC) in order to forward social dialogue at the European level.

For a detailed analysis of the terms of the Social Charter, see R. Goebel, Employee Rights in the European Community: A Panorama from the 1974 Social Action Program to the Social Charter of 1989, 17 Hastings Int'l & Comp. L. Rev. 1 (1993).

At the end of 1989, the Commission issued a new social action program intended to implement many of the provisions of the Social Charter. In the early 1990s, the Commission proposed over 20 draft directives, almost all of which have now been adopted and are described in sections C and D below. The Commission did not, however, propose any measures concerning minimum wages, rights of association in unions, or retirement benefits, because these are subjects considered to be appropriate only for Member State action in accordance with the principle of subsidiarity.

After the Labor party took over the UK government following the May 1997 election, Prime Minister Blair naturally permitted the Social Charter to become a unanimous Member State declaration of the rights of workers. Not surprisingly, the Treaty of Amsterdam then amended the Preamble to the TEU to state the Union's "attachment to fundamental social rights" as defined in the 1989 Social Charter. Since then the Court of Justice has cited the Charter as a source of fundamental rights. The social chapter of the Nice Charter of Fundamental Rights replicates some Social Charter provisions.

3. THE MAASTRICHT TREATY'S SOCIAL PROTOCOL

The Intergovernmental Conference in 1990–91 proposed a new Treaty social chapter, but the UK, then led by Prime Minister Major, adamantly opposed it. One of the key compromises of the December 1991 European Council meeting at Maastricht was the decision to place this proposed chapter in a Social Agreement annexed to a Social Protocol.

The Social Protocol, effective on November 1, 1993 with the Maastricht Treaty itself, lasted until the Treaty of Amsterdam came into effect on May 1, 1999. The Social Protocol effectively created a "two-tier" Community in the sphere of employee rights. An Agreement on Social Policy, annexed to the Social Protocol, enabled all the Member States but the UK to adopt most social policy measures by a qualified majority vote, instead of unanimity. Any legislative or other measures adopted in this manner would be binding on the entire EU, except for the UK. When Austria, Finland and Sweden entered the Union in 1995, they adhered to the Social Protocol.

Several legislative measures, including the well-known parental leave and European works council consultation directives described in section D, were adopted in 1994–96 through the procedures authorized by the Social Protocol. Not surprisingly, the UK Labor government under Prime Minister Blair agreed in December 1997 to have these directives made applicable to the UK as well.

4. THE SOCIAL CHAPTER OF THE TREATY OF AMSTERDAM

Because the UK elected the Labor government of Prime Minister Blair a few weeks before the conclusion of the 1996–97 Intergovernmental Conference, that IGC was able to provide a new social chapter in the Treaty of Amsterdam, largely incorporating the provisions of the Social Agreement. This new social chapter is one of the most important substantive changes made by the Amsterdam Treaty to the EC Treaty.

The social goals of the Community were set out in ECT Article 136 (replacing EECT Article 117), which refers to the 1989 Social Charter, and then lists "the promotion of employment, improved living and working conditions, . . . proper social protection, dialogue between management and labour, the development of human resources with a view to lasting high employment and the combating of exclusion" as the social action goals.

Unlike the initial EEC Treaty, ECT Article 137 (now TFEU Article 153) contained an express grant of legislative power which authorizes measures concerning worker health and safety, work conditions, information and consultation of workers, and equality between men and women. Legislation could usually be adopted by qualified majority vote in the Council and the parliamentary codecision procedure. However, the text specifically excluded any legislative power concerning "pay, the right of association, the right to strike or the right to impose lock-outs" (presumably in application of the principle of subsidiarity). Also, another provision required a unanimous vote in the Council, after consulting the Parliament, for measures in several fields, notably social security, and employee co-determination (i.e., the system for authorizing employees to elect members of the board of directors in companies employing large numbers of workers in Germany and some other States—see Chapter 17D.)

The social chapter also included ECT Articles 138 and 139 (now TFEU Articles 154 and 155), largely taken over from the Social Agreement, which enabled another mode of creating Community rules. The Commission could propose measures to be examined in a dialogue between representative bodies for management and labor at the Community level. These bodies might then reach framework agreements, which the Council could give binding effect by a qualified majority vote. Somewhat curiously, Parliament is not involved.

The Lisbon Treaty's TFEU Articles 151–64 on social policy largely replicate ECT Articles 136–48, only substituting the Union for the Community and the ordinary legislative process for codecision.

5. EMPLOYMENT POLICY ACTION AND THE TREATY OF AMSTERDAM

In the mid–1990s, Member State leaders and the Commission became extremely concerned over the persistent high rate of unemployment, which rose to an average of over ten percent in the 1991–93 recession. At the request of the European Council, the Commission produced in late 1993 the White Paper on Growth, Competitiveness and Employment, COM (93) 700. The White Paper analyzed the serious problems caused by permanent structural and technological unemployment, together with the challenges posed by international competition from high technology nations on the one hand, and mass-production low-labor cost nations on the other. The Commission urged a greater emphasis on education and skills training, aid to new technology and trans-European infra-structure, and greater labor flexibility and mobility.

In successive meetings in Brussels, Corfu, Madrid, Florence, Essen and Dublin in the 1990s, the European Council urged Commission and Council action to implement some of the key proposals of the White Paper. In view of this ongoing concern, it is not surprising that the Treaty of Amsterdam contains a new Title VIII on Employment. Indeed, the importance of Community activity to promote employment is highlighted through the amendment of TEU Article 2 and ECT Article 2 to insert "a high level of employment" as a Treaty goal.

ECT Article 125 required the Community to develop "a coordinated strategy for employment and particularly for promoting a skilled, trained and adaptable workforce." To this Article 127(2) notably adds: "the objective of a high level of employment shall be taken into consideration in the formulation and implementation of Community policies and activities." ECT Article 128 required the Council and Commission to make a joint annual report on employment to the European Council, which shall then adopt conclusions on the basis of which the Council, by qualified majority vote, shall draw up guidelines for Member States. The approach is analogous to that used in the economic coordination provisions of the EMU, discussed in Chapter 33C.

The Lisbon Treaty's TFEU Title IX on Employment, Articles 145–50, replicates the former ECT Articles 125–30.

Building upon the Treaty of Amsterdam's new emphasis on employment policies, when the European Council at Lisbon in March 2000 adopted the Lisbon Strategy for making the Union internationally competitive by 2010 (see Chapter 14B), the policy program included an emphasis on improving the quality of the workforce, especially through information technology. The December 2000 Nice European Council approved a new European Social Agenda, emphasizing the development of a cutting-edge information-based economy, greater labor mobility, improvement job education and training, and protection against social exclusion.

Unfortunately, the European recession in 2001–03 raised unemployment again, with some improvement in 2004–07, although high unemployment in several new Central European States raised concern. We noted in Chapter 1 that most western States maintained restrictions on migrant labor from the new States for several years. The recent extremely severe global recession in 2008–10 has brought unemployment to the unusually high levels of nearly 18% in Spain and an average of over 8% elsewhere. At least in early 2010, France, Germany, the UK and the Benelux ended their recessions and are reducing unemployment.

B.　THE 1974 SOCIAL ACTION PROGRAM: LEGISLATION AND CASE LAW

The initial 1974 Social Action Program yielded three important directives intended to achieve economic protection for employees in the context of lay-offs, acquisitions and corporate restructuring and bankruptcies. Not only has this legislation had a substantial impact, but it has given rise to a constant stream of Court judgments which have, in general, broadened the scope of the legislation and enhanced the employee rights stated therein. This provides the basis for a valuable comparison with American law.

1. THE 1975 DIRECTIVE ON COLLECTIVE REDUNDANCIES

Protection from mass lay-offs (or what the British would call collective redundancies) was a natural candidate for Community action, both because many States had some form of protection and because unions strongly supported a Community measure. Accordingly, Directive 75/129 on collective redundancies, O.J. L 48/29 (Feb. 22, 1975), was the first major social policy measure of the 1970s. (Read carefully Document 33 in the Selected Documents.)

This directive protects employees in any business entity employing more than 20 workers, when a given number are dismissed or laid off within a 30–day period for general business or economic reasons, rather than any work-related deficiencies of the workers. The usual "trigger" number of dismissals is 10 when the business employs less than 100 workers, 10% or more when 100 to 300 workers are employed, and 30 or more if 300 or more workers are employed (art. 1). The protective rules of the directive expressly do not apply to employees of public authorities or to employees hired for limited periods of time.

The Collective Redundancy Directive protects employees in several ways. The first element of protection is that the employer must give advance notice, 30 days minimum, to the employee representatives in the business entity and also to the public labor authorities (arts. 3, 4). The employer must provide both the employee representatives and the authorities with "all relevant information" as to the dismissals, especially the number of workers to be dismissed, the period of time involved, the criteria used in selecting redundant workers, and the nature of any redundancy benefits, if provided (arts. 2, 3).

The directive also obligates the employer to carry out "consultations" with the employee representatives on the proposed dismissals in order to try to reach agreement on ways of "avoiding collective redundancies or reducing the number of workers affected, and of mitigating the consequences" (art. 2(2)). Further, the public authorities may "seek solutions to the problems raised by the projected collective redundancies" (art. 4(2)). In some States, as a matter of practice the employer has little choice but to accept such government-proposed "solutions," even though the directive makes no reference to their legal effect.

Moreover, the directive allows the Member States to adopt rules even more favorable to workers (art. 5), and some States do that. German law, for example, requires binding arbitration when the employer and the employee representatives cannot reach agreement, and French and Dutch rules give the labor inspectors effective veto power over proposed dismissals.

Directive 92/56, O.J. L 245/3 (Aug. 26, 1992), amended the initial text in order to create consultation rights when the decision to dismiss is not taken by the employer, but rather by the management of a parent which controls the employer, but is located in a different Member State. Further, a new article 6 requires Member States to ensure that the employees or their representatives will have administrative and/or judicial recourse to enforce the directive's obligations. Later, Directive 98/59, O.J. L 225/16 (Aug. 12, 1998), added some minor amendments to improve the procedure, and Directive 2002/14, O.J. L (Mar. 23, 2002) codified the prior directives.

In several noteworthy judgments, the Court has liberally interpreted the scope of the information and consultation rights enunciated in the directive.

COMMISSION v. UNITED KINGDOM

(Collective redundancies)
Case C–383/92, [1994] ECR I–2479.

[The Commission sued the United Kingdom for defective implementation of the collective redundancies directive. The UK law only obliged employers who had voluntarily accepted trade unions (a minority of all employers) to deal with union representatives in the event of a collective redundancy. Whether the UK ought to have imposed this obligation upon all employers was the principal question. Other issues concerned the meaning of "consultation," and whether the UK had provided adequate sanctions to enforce the rules.]

14 The United Kingdom acknowledges that representation of workers in [UK] undertakings * * * has traditionally been based on voluntary recognition of trade unions by employers and for that reason an employer who does not recognize a trade union is not subject to the obligations laid down in the directive. However, it contends that the directive was not intended to amend national rules or practices concerning the designation of workers' representatives. * * * It also argues that the directive is limited to a partial harmonization of the rules for the protection of workers in the event of collective redundancies and that it does not require Member States to provide for specific representation of workers in order to comply with the obligations which it lays down.

15 The United Kingdom's point of view cannot be accepted.

16 By harmonizing the rules applicable to collective redundancies, the Community legislature intended both to ensure comparable protection for workers' rights in the different Member States and to harmonize the costs which such protective rules entail for Community undertakings.

* * *

17 Contrary to the United Kingdom's contention, * * * [the directive] leaves to Member States only the task of determining the arrangements for designating the workers' representatives who, depending on the circumstances, must or may intervene in the collective redundancy procedure under Articles 2 and 3(2).

20 The interpretation proposed by the United Kingdom would allow Member States to [limit the directive's application only to] undertakings where national law provides for the designation of workers' representatives. Such an interpretation would thus permit Member States to deprive Articles 2 and 3(2) of the directive of their full effect.

* * *

27 In those circumstances, United Kingdom law, which allows an employer to frustrate the protection provided for workers by Articles 2 and 3 of the directive, must be regarded as contrary to those articles.

[The Commission found a further deficiency in the UK wording which only obliged employers to "consider" the views of the workers' representatives, rather than to engage in the consultations specified by the directive.]

36 [Moreover, the UK rules] do not require an employer to consult workers' representatives "with a view to reaching an agreement", as required by Article 2(1) of the directive, nor do they specify that such consultations must, at least, "cover ways and means of avoiding collective redundancies or reducing the number of workers affected, and mitigating the consequences", as required by Article 2(2).

37 The Commission's third complaint must therefore be upheld.

[Finally, the Commission claimed that the UK had not created adequate sanctions.]

40 Where a Community directive does not specifically provide any penalty for an infringement or refers for that purpose to national laws, regulations and administrative provisions, Article [10] of the Treaty requires the Member States to take all measures necessary to guarantee the application and effectiveness of Community law. For that purpose, while the choice of penalties remains within their discretion, they must ensure in particular that infringements of Community law are penalized under conditions, both procedural and substantive, which are analogous to those applicable to infringements of national law of a similar nature and importance and which, in any event make the penalty effective, proportionate and dissuasive.

41 [Under the UK law,] a "protective award" which an employer may be ordered to make to a dismissed employee if he has failed to comply with the obligation to consult and inform the workers' representatives * * * may be set off against any amounts which he may otherwise be required to pay to that employee under the latter's contract of employment or in respect of breach of that contract * * *.

[42]   [Consequently,] the United Kingdom legislation largely deprives [the "protective award"] sanction of its practical effect and its deterrent value.

[43]   The Commission's fourth complaint must therefore be upheld.

Nᴏᴛᴇs ᴀɴᴅ Qᴜᴇsᴛɪᴏɴs

1.   Under the Conservative governments of Prime Ministers Thatcher and Major, the United Kingdom adamantly opposed Community legislation creating a mandatory system of worker consultation, such as exists in one form or another on the continent. See section D4, *infra*. At ¶ 9 in his opinion, Advocate General van Gerven refers to the "politically sensitive nature" of the issue, and agrees with the UK that the directive was never intended to create a general system of workers' representatives. Nonetheless he concludes that the directive's objective would be frustrated if a State does not oblige employers to deal with worker representatives before a collective redundancy, at least on an *ad hoc* basis. However, the UK partial harmonization argument is certainly plausible. Do you agree with the UK, or with the Court and the Advocate General? Does the outcome of this case put the camel's nose under the tent?

2.   Note that the UK conceded the other defects in its legislation, and had indeed partly remedied them in 1993. The Commission asked the Court not to treat the issues as moot and the Court agreed. How important is the Court's interpretation of the directive in ¶ ¶ 36–37? Is consultation now tantamount to good faith bargaining?

3.   Some internal market directives (e.g., those regulating insider trading or money laundering) expressly require States to impose adequate sanctions. Not only does the Collective Redundancy Directive not expressly require sanctions, but it was the 1992 amendment discussed above that introduced article 6, which requires States to "ensure that judicial and/or administrative procedures for the enforcement of obligations under this directive are available to the workers' representatives and/or workers." In ¶ 40, the Court nonetheless concluded that ECT Article 10 (now TEU Article 4(3)) imposed a duty upon States to create "effective, proportionate and dissuasive" sanctions. Do you agree, or do you think sanctions should be obligatory only if expressly required by the directive? Would UK employers be apt to obey this directive if only trivial penalties were imposed for violations? For further discussion of appropriate sanctions to enforce Community rules, see Chapter 10A supra.

CONFEDERATION GENERALE DU TRAVAIL (CGT) v. PREMIER MINISTRE

Case C–385/05, [2007] ECR I–611.

[The French government, concerned about the high levels of unemployment of young people, adopted in June 2005 a law that permitted employers to hire persons under 26 but not count them until Dec. 31, 2007 in calculations of the total workforce for labor law purposes. A French labor union challenged the law as a violation of the Collective Redundancy Directive.]

28 [I]t is clear from the Court's case-law that the encouragement of recruitment constitutes a legitimate aim of social policy and that, in choosing the measures capable of achieving the aims of their social and employment policy, the Member States have a broad margin of discretion.

29 However, the margin of discretion which the Member States enjoy in matters of social policy cannot have the effect of frustrating the implementation of a fundamental principle of Community law or of a provision of that law.

31 [P]ursuant to Article 2(d) of Directive 2002/14, 'employee' means any person who, in the Member State concerned, is protected as an employee under national employment law and in accordance with national practice.

32 It follows that, since it is not disputed that the workers aged less than 26 referred to in the national provision at issue in the main proceedings are protected by national employment legislation, they are employees within the meaning of Directive 2002/14.

* * *

41 In the light of the foregoing, * * * Article 3(1) of Directive 2002/14 is to be interpreted as precluding national legislation which excludes, even temporarily, a specific category of workers from the calculation of staff numbers within the meaning of that provision.

NOTES AND QUESTIONS

1. The Court's strict construction of the obligation to count all employees for the purpose of calculating the threshold numbers in the 2002 version of the Collective Redundancy Directive does not permit France to apply its own policy to combat unemployment among young people. Do you agree with the Court's conclusion? Note that France could adopt other incentives to employers to hire younger people, e.g., subsidy payments or lower taxes.

2. In Rodriguez Mayor v. Herencia yacente de las Heras Davila, Case C–323/08, [2009] ECR ___ (Dec. 10, 2009), the employees of an unincorporated enterprise owned by de las Heras Davila claimed compensation for the failure to carry out the consultation procedure when their employment ended upon the death of the owner. His heirs abandoned the inheritance, so the business terminated with his death. Not surprisingly, the Court held that the directive did not cover termination of employment due to the employer's death. Suppose the heirs had accepted the inheritance generally, but decided to close the business employing the plaintiff s. Should the consultation obligation then apply?

MONO CAR STYLING v. DERVIS ODEMIS

Case C–12/08. [2009] ECR I–___ (July 16, 2009).

[When Mono Car risked insolvency, it notified its employee representatives and consulted them in accordance with the provisions of the Belgian law implementing the 1998 version of the Collective Redundancy Directive. Following this consultation, and in agreement with the employee representatives and the competent administrative authority, Mono Car dismissed 30 employees. Some of those dismissed sued to challenge alleged defects in the consultation procedure, requesting damages. The trial court granted them partial relief, and an appellate court referred questions to the Court of Justice.]

38   [I]t is clear, first of all, from the text and scheme of Directive 98/59 that the right to information and consultation which it lays down is intended for workers' representatives and not for workers individually.

39   Thus, * * *, Article 1(1) of the directive, which contains definitions for the purposes thereof, defines the expression 'workers' representatives' but not 'workers'. Similarly, Article 2 of the directive sets out the employer's obligations and the right to information and consultation but refers only to workers' representatives. In the same manner, Article 3 of the directive requires that notice be given to the competent public authority of any projected collective redundancies with all relevant information concerning those redundancies and the consultations with workers' representatives, to whom the employer is to forward a copy of the notification and who may send any comments they may have to the public authority concerned, but such possibilities are not open to workers.

40   Secondly, the collective nature of the right to information and consultation also flows from a teleological interpretation of Directive 98/59. In so far as the information and consultation provided for in the directive are intended * * * to permit, first, the formulation of constructive proposals covering * * * ways and means of avoiding collective redundancies or reducing the number of workers affected, and of mitigating the consequences of such redundancies and, secondly, the possible submission of comments to the competent public authority, workers' representatives are best placed to achieve the objective which the directive seeks to attain.

41   Finally, the Court has already had occasion to rule that the right to information and consultation, previously provided for in an identical manner by Directive 75/129, is exercised through workers' representatives.

42   It must therefore be held that the right to information and consultation provided for in Directive 98/59, in particular by Article 2 thereof,

is intended to benefit workers as a collective group and is therefore collective in nature.

NOTES AND QUESTIONS

1. Do you agree with the Court's conclusion? Does not the very name of the Collective Redundancy Directive and the specific references to the employee representatives in the substantive provisions justify the exclusion of individual worker complaints? Note that most continental labor law systems do protect individual workers by referring that they may only be dismissed for good cause, but such protection is quite distinct from the economic motives for dismissal on which this directive is focused.

We noted above that a 1992 amendment made the directive applicable when the decision to dismiss is taken by a parent company located in a different Member State. A recent noteworthy judgment interpreted the amendment.

AKAVAN ERITYISALOJEN KESKUSLIITTO v. FUJITSU SIEMENS COMPUTERS

Case C–44/08, [2009] ECR I–___ (Sept. 10, 2009).

[After Fujitsu and Siemens merged certain computer operations into FSC (Holding), a Dutch company, the new group parent began operations in 1999. At a meeting on Dec. 14, 1990, the FSC (Holding) board considered a management proposal to eliminate a factory in Finland operated by a subsidiary, FSC, but without taking a specific decision. On Feb. 1, 2000, FSC closed the factory, dismissing 450 out of 490 employees, after consultation with the employee representatives from Dec. 20, 1999—Jan. 31, 2000. A union acting on behalf of the dismissed employees sued FSC, claiming that FSC (Holding), the parent, had taken the decision to close the factory before any consultations, thus violating the directive. The trial court decided in favor of FSC. The Finnish supreme court referred several questions, notably on when the employer's obligation to consult should begin, and what are the employing subsidiary's obligations.]

36 By its first question, the referring court seeks clarification of the meaning of the expression 'is contemplating collective redundancies', in Article 2(1) of Directive 98/59 * * *. The court asks * * * whether [the obligation to consult with employees] arises when it is established that strategic decisions or changes in the business of the undertaking will make collective redundancies of employees necessary, or when the adoption of such decisions or changes, as a result of which it is to be expected that such redundancies will become necessary, are contemplated.

* * *

38 [A]s is clear from the wording of Articles 2(1) and 3(1) of Directive 98/59, the obligations of consultation and notification imposed on the employer come into being prior to the employer's decision to terminate

employment contracts. In such a case, there is still a possibility of avoiding or at least reducing collective redundancies, or of mitigating the consequences.

39   Under Article 2(1) of Directive 98/59, the employer has the obligation to start consultations with the workers' representatives in good time if he 'is contemplating collective redundancies'. As stated by the Advocate General * * *, it is clear from comparison of various language versions of that provision that the Community legislature envisaged that the obligation at issue to hold consultations would arise in connection with the existence of an intention on the part of the employer to make collective redundancies.

40   The references in Articles 3 and 4 of Directive 98/59 to 'projected' collective redundancies confirm that the existence of such an intention is the factor which triggers the obligations laid down by that directive, in particular by Article 2.

* * *

42   [Moreover,] the obligation to hold consultations laid down in Article 2, [is] also triggered in situations where the prospect of collective redundancies is not directly the choice of the employer.

43   Under Article 2(4) of that directive, the employer is responsible for compliance with the information and consultation requirements stemming from that directive, even if the decision on collective redundancies is made not by the employer, but by the undertaking controlling the employer, and even though the employer may not have been immediately and properly informed of that decision.

44   Against an economic background marked by the increasing presence of groups of undertakings, that provision serves to ensure, where one undertaking is controlled by another, that the purpose of Directive 98/59 * * * to promote greater protection for workers in the event of collective redundancies, is actually achieved.

* * *

47   * * * As is clear from the first subparagraph of that Article 2(2), the consultations must cover, inter alia, the possibility of avoiding or reducing the collective redundancies contemplated. A consultation which began when a decision making such collective redundancies necessary had already been taken could not usefully involve any examination of conceivable alternatives with the aim of avoiding them.

* * *

49   [Accordingly,] the answer to be given to the first question referred is that Article 2(1) of Directive 98/59 must be interpreted to mean that the adoption, within a group of undertakings, of strategic decisions or of changes in activities which compel the employer to contemplate or to plan for collective redundancies gives rise to an obligation on that employer to consult with workers' representatives.

[The Court then turned to the obligations of FSC, the employing subsidiary.]

57 [U]nder Article 2(1) and (3) and Article 3(1) and (2) of Directive 98/59, the only party on whom the obligations to inform, consult and notify are imposed is the employer, in other words a natural or legal person who stands in an employment relationship with the workers who may be made redundant.

58 An undertaking which controls the employer, even if it can take decisions which are binding on the latter, does not have the status of employer.

* * *

63 As regards the time at which that obligation arises, it is evident, as observed by the Finnish Government, that consultations with the workers' representatives can be started only if it is known in which undertaking collective redundancies may be made. Where the parent company of a group of undertakings adopts decisions likely to have repercussions on the jobs of workers within that group, it is for the subsidiary whose employees may be affected by redundancies, in its capacity as their employer, to start consultations with the workers' representatives. It is therefore not possible to start such consultations until such time as that subsidiary has been identified.

* * *

69 [I]t is always for the subsidiary, as the employer, to undertake consultations * * * and, if necessary, itself to bear the consequences of failure to fulfil the obligation to hold consultations if it has not been immediately and properly informed of a decision by its parent company making such redundancies necessary.

70 [Moreover,] the Court has previously ruled that, where Directive 98/59 is applicable, * * * the consultation procedure must be completed before any decision on the termination of employees' contracts is taken.

71 [Consequently,] a decision by the parent company which has the direct effect of compelling one of its subsidiaries to terminate the contracts of employees affected by the collective redundancies can be taken only on the conclusion of the consultation procedure within that subsidiary, failing which the subsidiary, as the employer, is liable for the consequences of failure to comply with that procedure.

NOTES AND QUESTIONS

1. The Court's guidance may not benefit the Finnish employees in this case, because ¶ 27 indicates that the trial court had made a factual determination that the parent company had not taken a final decision to close the factory on Dec. 14, 1999, and that FSC dismissed the employees on Feb. 1, 2000 only after "genuine and appropriate" consultation failed to provide an

alternative. Nonetheless, the guidance will be useful, because parent or group companies often take a definitive decision to close a subsidiary operation, entailing dismissal of employees, prior to any consultation between the subsidiary and its employees. In that case, the subsidiary may become liable to the employees for damages, or for fines imposed by the State, if it is unable to discuss in good faith modes of migrating the consequences.

2. In Rockfon A/S v. Specialarbejderforbundet i Danmark, Case C–449/93, [1995] ECR I–4291, a group of four production companies employed altogether 1085 workers in a Danish town. A parent management decision required all four companies to have a joint personnel department. In 1989, Rockfon, one of the four companies, followed the instructions of the personnel department and dismissed 24 of its 162 employees without respecting the notification and consultation procedures of the Collective Redundancy Directive. In a suit by dismissed employees, the Danish Labour Council found the directive inapplicable, because it treated the dismissal as one executed by the larger group, in which the "trigger" number of 30 dismissed workers was not attained. An appellate court asked the Court of Justice whether this conclusion was right, or whether Rockfon should be considered the dismissing "establishment" within the terms of article 1(1)a of the directive, in which case the dismissal of 24 employees exceeded the 10% trigger based on 162 employees, requiring notification and consultation. The Court held that Rockfon, as a separate legal entity with a distinct production purpose and workforce, should be bound by the directive's obligations. Would you agree?

3. In Athinaiki Chartopoiia v. Panagiotidis, Case C–270/05, [2007] ECR I–1499, the Court went further, holding that "a distinct entity, having a certain degree of performance and stability * * * which has a workforce, technical means and a certain organizational structure" (§ 27) was bound to comply with the directive, even though the production unit in question was not a separate legal entity, but rather one of three operational units of a company in three different locations. The Court considered that the fact that all management decisions (including the closing of the production unit, which employed 420 workers) were taken by the company's headquarters, was irrelevant.

NOTE ON **WARN**

The Collective Redundancies Directive has an American analogue, the Worker Adjustment and Retraining Notification Act of 1988, 29 U.S.C.A. §§ 2101–2109, popularly called WARN, which was adopted after some 15 years of legislative debate. The EC directive apparently influenced the earliest bills. For a review of WARN's background and scope, see C. Yost, The Worker Adjustment and Retraining Notification Act of 1988, 38 Cath.U.L.Rev. 675 (1989).

WARN covers not only the usual form of collective dismissal, a "mass layoff", but also the special case of a dismissal caused by a "plant closing." Every enterprise employing more than 100 employees is subject to WARN. A layoff of 50 or more employees at one job site within 30 days triggers the protective rules for a "plant closing." The dismissal of at least 50 workers, provided that constitutes at least one-third of the work-force, or the dismissal of 500 or more workers, even if that is less than one-third of the work-force, triggers the rules governing a "mass layoff."

If WARN applies, the employer must give 60 days advance notice to union or other employee representatives, to the appropriate state labor authority and to the chief elected official of the local government. Failure to give notice gives rise to economic sanctions: payment of usual salary or other remuneration to each dismissed worker for the missed notice period, and damages of $500 per day of missed notice payable to the local government. In United Food and Commercial Workers Union Local 751 v. Brown Group, Inc., 517 U.S. 544, 116 S.Ct. 1529, 134 L.Ed.2d 758 (1996), the Supreme Court held that unions had the right to sue to enforce WARN'S procedures, notably to recover damages on behalf of individual employees. WARN does not, however, mandate any form of consultation with either the employee representatives or the local government, and is therefore not as far-reaching as the Collective Redundancy Directive.

NOTES AND QUESTIONS

1. What is your impression of the value of the consultation provisions of the Collective Redundancy Directive? For example, what steps might the employee representatives suggest in order to reduce the size of proposed lay-offs or to mitigate their effect? Do you think employers would be apt to accept such suggestions or ignore them? Is it desirable or generally a waste of time to involve public authorities? Do you think that the employer's obligation to consult with the employees and the public authorities will have beneficial social and perhaps even economic effects? Was it sensible or unfortunate that WARN does not contain such a provision?

2. Do you think laws like the Collective Redundancies Directive and WARN are helpful because they contribute to social dialogue and help alleviate genuine social distress in a lay-off, or that they are harmful because they slow the process of making businesses more efficient and competitive? If both these views are correct to some extent, where should the balance be struck? Would it be helpful to have empirical studies on the effect of the directive and of WARN? Can empirical studies measure social benefits or only economic factors?

3. Does the passage of WARN suggest that our employee rights rules are apt to be influenced in other ways by the more far-reaching ones in the Community, or are the US and the EC just too different?

2. THE 1977 TRANSFER OF UNDERTAKINGS DIRECTIVE

When all or part of an enterprise is transferred from one owner to another in an acquisition, merger or restructuring, it frequently occurs that some employees are dismissed either before the transfer or shortly after it occurs. The new owner usually views such dismissals as essential to efficient restructuring, but the employees naturally would like some form of protection. The desire to achieve such protection in a reasonable form inspired the second major employee rights measure, Directive 77/187 on the safeguarding of employees' rights in the event of transfers of undertakings, businesses, or parts of businesses, O.J. L 61/26 (Mar. 5, 1977), often called the "acquired rights" directive. Incidentally, the words "entity" or "enterprise" are useful synonyms for the somewhat awkward word, "undertaking," a poor translation of the French "entreprise."

The Transfer of Undertakings Directive basically aims to protect certain so-called "acquired rights" of employees when all or part of the entity by which they are employed is transferred to a new owner. The directive declares that the employees are entitled to keep the employee relationship, as well as any specific contractual rights (art. 3(1)). Moreover, any collective bargaining agreement which bound the old employer continues to bind the new employer (art. 3(2)). The concept of a transfer of a business is a broad one, covering not only an acquisition or merger, but, as we shall see from the case law, other legal transactions as well.

The directive also significantly limits a new employer's ability to use the transfer of the business as an occasion for reducing or dismissing the entire work force (art. 4). (For that matter, if the former employer, at the request of the new one, were to reduce the work force prior to the transfer, the dismissal of a sufficiently large number would trigger the procedures required by the Collective Redundancy Directive.) A new employer can reduce the work force only if justified for "economic, technical, or organizational reasons" (art. 4(1)). Moreover, any "substantial change in working conditions to the detriment of the employee" is considered as a constructive dismissal (art. 4(2)).

The directive guarantees employees certain information and consultation rights which largely parallel those provided by the Collective Redundancy Directive. Both the old and new employer must inform employee representatives of "the legal, economic and social implications" of the transfer and any "measures envisaged in relation to the employees" (art. 6(1)). The new employer must consult with the employees' representatives on any measures affecting employees (such as dismissals or reallocation of employees) "with a view to seeking agreement" on the application of the measures (art. 6(2)).

As in the case of the Collective Redundancies Directive, this directive does not totally preempt Member State law, but rather allows States to have supplementary rules more favorable to employees (art. 7).

The directive was amended by Directive 98/50, O.J. L 201/88 (June 29, 1998), notably to add an article enabling judicial appeals, but also to insert language intended to conform to interpretation by the Court of Justice. A consolidated text appears in Directive 2001/23, O.J. L 82/16 (Mar. 22, 2001).

Overall, the "acquired rights" directive makes it more difficult to carry through an acquisition or a merger in the Community, because besides negotiating the acquisition or merger itself, prospective buyers must also consult with employee representatives if they contemplate reducing the work force or rationalizing the operations in any manner that would affect employees.

The US does not have any comparable federal legislation, but a rather complex case law governs the subject of corporate successor liability. If a corporation disappears in a merger, the surviving entity constitutes a legal successor bound by the collective bargaining agreements and the employee relations of the former entity, because there exists a "substantial continuity of identity in the business enterprise." John Wiley & Sons, Inc. v. Livingston, 376 U.S. 543, 551, 84 S.Ct. 909, 915, 11 L.Ed.2d 898, 905 (1964).

An asset acquisition sometimes also creates successorship rights, even though the former entity's employee relations and collective bargaining agreement are not automatically transferred. In Fall River Dyeing & Finishing Corp. v. NLRB, 482 U.S. 27, 107 S.Ct. 2225, 96 L.Ed.2d 22 (1987), defendant purchased the realty and operating assets of a liquidated entity. Defendant then used the assets to carry on the same business in the same premises with about half the liquidated entity's customers. Since over half of defendant's workforce had been employed by the liquidated entity, and these workers had essentially the same job classifications, the defendant was held to be a corporate successor bound to bargain with the liquidated entity's union. In contrast is Howard Johnson Co. v. Detroit Local Joint Executive Bd., 417 U.S. 249, 94 S.Ct. 2236, 41 L.Ed.2d 46 (1974), where defendant leased motel premises, bought from the landlord most operating assets, and continued the motel business. However, defendant hired only a few of the landlord's employees, and these were only a minority of defendant's employees. The Supreme Court did not consider that this amounted to a corporate succession and collective bargaining rights were not continued. See D. Oesterle, The Law of Mergers and Acquisitions (West 1999); see also Silver, Reflections on the Obligations of a Successor Employer, 2 Cardozo L.Rev. 545 (1981).

Since the mid–1980s, the Court has frequently had occasion to interpret the scope of application of the directive and the nature of the rights that it grants. This body of case law is now quite complex, although the Court's general policy approach clearly tends to protect employee rights.

SPIJKERS v. BENEDIK ABATTOIR
Case 24/85, [1986] ECR 1119.

[When a company operating a slaughterhouse became insolvent, Benedik bought the assets: "the entire slaughterhouse, with various rooms and offices, the land and certain specified goods." Benedik did not take over the "goodwill" of the insolvent firm, i.e., Benedik did not take over the prior customers. Benedik hired all of the former firm's employees, except for the plaintiff, Spijkers, and one other. Spijkers sued to maintain his employee status. The Dutch Supreme Court asked the Court of Justice whether a transfer of assets to a purchaser who does not take the "goodwill" falls under the "acquired rights" directive.]

8   Mr. Spijkers maintains that there is a transfer of an undertaking within the meaning of Article 1(1) where the undertaking's assets and business are transferred as a unit from one employer to another; it is immaterial whether at the time of the transfer the business activities of the transferor have ceased and the goodwill has already disappeared.

* * *

10   The United Kingdom Government and the Commission suggest that the essential criterion is whether the transferee is put in possession of a going concern and is able to continue its activities or at least activities of the same kind. The Netherlands Government emphasizes that, having regard to the social objective of the directive, it is clear that the term "transfer" implies that the transferee actually carries on the activities of the transferor as part of the same business.

11   That view must be accepted. It is clear from the scheme of Directive No 77/187 and from the terms of Article 1 (1) thereof that the directive is intended to ensure the continuity of employment relationships existing within a business, irrespective of any change of ownership. It follows that the decisive criterion for establishing whether there is a transfer for the purposes of the directive is whether the business in question retains its identity.

12   Consequently, a transfer of an undertaking, business or part of a business does not occur merely because its assets are disposed of. Instead it is necessary to consider, in a case such as the present, whether the business was disposed of as a going concern, as would be indicated, *inter alia,* by the fact that its operation was actually continued or resumed by the new employer, with the same or similar activities.

13   In order to determine whether those conditions are met, it is necessary to consider all the facts characterizing the transaction in question, including the type of undertaking or business, whether or not the business's tangible assets, such as buildings and movable property, are transferred, the value of its intangible assets at the time of the transfer, whether or not the majority of its employees are taken over by the new employer, whether or not its customers are transferred and the degree of similarity between the activities carried on before and after the transfer and the period, if any, for which those activities were suspended. It should be noted, however, that all those circumstances are merely single factors in the overall assessment which must be made and cannot therefore be considered in isolation.

14   It is for the national court to make the necessary factual appraisal, in the light of the criteria for interpretation set out above, in order to establish whether or not there is a transfer in the sense indicated above.

NOTES AND QUESTIONS

1. Most transfers of a business occur through the acquisition of a business entity (purchase of the shares of a corporation or the partnership interests in a partnership) or through the merger of one business entity with another. In both cases, the Transfer of Undertakings Directive clearly applies. The same result would presumably occur in the US by operation of the corporate successor doctrine.

2. An acquisition of assets of an enterprise poses a much more difficult issue. In *Spijkers,* the Fifth Chamber of the Court of Justice did not provide a simple guideline. The fact that the new firm did not take over the old firm's "goodwill" or customers is neither irrelevant, as the plaintiff urged, nor decisive against the plaintiff, as the defendant urged. The Court provides in ¶ 13 what American corporate lawyers would call a "going concern" test, in which the trial court is to weigh all of the relevant factors. If you were the trial court, which way would you decide this case?

US case law on the application of the corporate successor doctrine in an asset purchase of a business is also not very clear. The *Fall River Dyeing* and *Howard Johnson* cases discussed above would seem to indicate that, even though employee relationships are not transferred with the assets, an obligation to bargain with the former entity's union is imposed when a) substantial business continuity is demonstrated and b) it is shown that a majority of the new firm's employees were also employees of the former firm.

FORENINGEN AF ARBEJDSLEDERE v. DADDY'S DANCE HALL

Case 324/86, [1988] ECR 739.

[A Danish court referred two questions to the Court of Justice, one as to whether the transfer of leased business premises was covered by the 1977 directive, and the second as to whether the parties to an employment contract may modify or waive rights granted by the directive.]

3   Mr. Tellerup was employed as a restaurant manager by Irma Catering A/S, which had taken a non-transferable lease of restaurants and bars belonging to A/S Palads Teatret. The lease was subsequently terminated, and on 28 January 1983 Irma Catering dismissed its staff, including Mr. Tellerup * * *. Irma Catering continued to run the businesses in question with the same staff until 25 February 1983.

4   With effect from that date a new lease was concluded between A/S Palads Teatret and Daddy's Dance Hall A/S. Daddy's Dance Hall immediately re-employed the employees of the former lessee, including Mr. Tellerup, to do the same jobs as before. The new management contract concluded with Mr. Tellerup stipulated, however, that his remuneration, which had previously been in the form of commission, would henceforth take the form of a fixed salary. Furthermore, at Mr. Tellerup's request the parties agreed on a trial period of three months during which either side could give 14 days' notice. On that basis Mr.

Tellerup was dismissed on 26 April 1983 with 14 days' notice. The main proceedings concern in essence the period of notice to which the plaintiff was entitled.

* * *

7   In the first question the national court seeks in substance to determine whether Article 1(1) of Council Directive 77/187 * * * must be interpreted as meaning that the directive applies where, upon the termination of a non-transferable lease, the owner of an undertaking leases it to a new lessee who carries on the business without interruption with the same staff, who had been given notice on the expiry of the initial lease.

* * *

9   [T]he purpose of Directive 77/187/EEC is to ensure, so far as possible, that the rights of employees are safeguarded in the event of a change of employer by allowing them to remain in employment with the new employer on the terms and conditions agreed with the transferor. The directive is therefore applicable where, following a legal transfer or merger, there is a change in the natural or legal person who is responsible for carrying on the business and who by virtue of that fact incurs the obligations of an employer *vis-à-vis* employees of the undertaking, regardless of whether or not ownership of the undertaking is transferred.

10   It follows that where, upon the expiry of the lease, the lessee ceases to be the employer and a third party becomes the employer under a new lease concluded with the owner the resulting operation can fall within the scope of the directive as defined in Article 1(1). The fact that in such a case the transfer is effected in two stages, in that the undertaking is first retransferred from the original lessee to the owner and the latter then transfers it to the new lessee, does not prevent the directive from applying, provided that the economic unit in question retains its identity; that is so in particular when, as in this case, the business is carried on without interruption by the new lessee with the same staff as were employed in the business before the transfer.

* * *

12   In its second question the national court seeks in substance to determine whether an employee may waive rights conferred on him by Directive 77/187/EEC if the disadvantages resulting from his waiver are offset by such benefits that, taking the matter as a whole, he is not placed in a worse position.

* * *

14   As was stressed above, the purpose of Directive 77/187/EEC is to ensure that the rights resulting from a contract of employment or employment relationship of employees affected by the transfer of an undertaking are safeguarded. Since this protection is a matter of public policy, and

therefore independent of the will of the parties to the contract of employment, the rules of the directive, in particular those concerning the protection of workers against dismissal by reason of the transfer, must be considered to be mandatory, so that it is not possible to derogate from them in a manner unfavourable to employees.

15 It follows that employees are not entitled to waive the rights conferred on them by the directive and that those rights cannot be restricted even with their consent. This interpretation is not affected by the fact that, as in this case, the employee obtains new benefits in compensation for the disadvantages resulting from an amendment to his contract of employment so that, taking the matter as a whole, he is not placed in a worse position than before.

NOTES AND QUESTIONS

1. In *Daddy's Dance Hall,* a new business operator conducted the same type of business on the same premises and hired the same employees. However, the old and new employers had no contractual relationship whatsoever. The lease was not transferred; indeed, it was non-transferable. Do you agree with the Third Chamber of the Court that this situation nonetheless amounts to transfer of a business, or do you think this goes too far? What is the likely motivation for the Court's approach? Note also the Court's conclusion in ¶ 14 that the transferred employee may not waive any prior employment rights or benefits, because the transfer is "mandatory."

SUZEN v. ZEHNACKER GEBAUDEREINIGUNG

Case C–13/95, [1997] ECR I–1259.

[A German school terminated a cleaning contract with Zehnacker and entered into a new cleaning contract with Lefarth. Zehnacker dismissed all of its seven employees who had cleaned the school. One of them, Suzen, sued to compel Lefarth to take over her employment. The Court began by re-examining the scope of the directive.]

10 The aim of the directive is to ensure continuity of employment relationships within an economic entity, irrespective of any change of ownership. The decisive criterion for establishing the existence of a transfer within the meaning of the directive is whether the entity in question retains its identity, as indicated *inter alia* by the fact that its operation is actually continued or resumed [citing *Spijkers, supra*].

11 Whilst the lack of any contractual link between the transferor and the transferee or, as in this case, between the two undertakings successively entrusted with the cleaning of a school, may point to the absence of a transfer within the meaning of the directive, it is certainly not conclusive.

12 [T]he directive is applicable wherever, in the context of contractual relations, there is a change in the natural or legal person who is responsible for carrying on the business and who incurs the obli-

gations of an employer towards employees of the undertaking. Thus, there is no need, in order for the directive to be applicable, for there to be any direct contractual relationship between the transferor and the transferee: the transfer may also take place in two stages * * *.

* * *

15 [T]he mere fact that the service provided by the old and the new awardees of a contract is similar does not therefore support the conclusion that an economic entity has been transferred. An entity cannot be reduced to the activity entrusted to it. Its identity also emerges from other factors, such as its workforce, its management staff, the way in which its work is organized, its operating methods or indeed, where appropriate, the operational resources available to it.

16 The mere loss of a service contract to a competitor cannot therefore by itself indicate the existence of a transfer within the meaning of the directive. In those circumstances, the service undertaking previously entrusted with the contract does not, on losing a customer, thereby cease fully to exist, and a business or part of a business belonging to it cannot be considered to have been transferred to the new awardee of the contract.

17 It must also be noted that, although the transfer of assets is one of the criteria to be taken into account by the national court in deciding whether an undertaking has in fact been transferred, the absence of such assets does not necessarily preclude the existence of such a transfer.

* * *

19 The United Kingdom Government and the Commission have argued that, for the entity previously entrusted with a service contract to have been the subject of a transfer within the meaning of the directive, it may be sufficient in certain circumstances for the new awardee of the contract to have voluntarily taken over the majority of the employees specially assigned by his predecessor to the performance of the contract.

20 In that regard, the factual circumstances to be taken into account in determining whether the conditions for a transfer are met include in particular, in addition to the degree of similarity of the activity carried on before and after the transfer and the type of undertaking or business concerned, the question whether or not the majority of the employees were taken over by the new employer (*Spijkers*, supra, paragraph 13).

21 Since in certain labour-intensive sectors a group of workers engaged in a joint activity on a permanent basis may constitute an economic entity, it must be recognized that such an entity is capable of maintaining its identity after it has been transferred where the new employer does not merely pursue the activity in question but also

takes over a major part, in terms of their numbers and skills, of the employees specially assigned by his predecessor to that task. In those circumstances, the new employer takes over a body of assets enabling him to carry on the activities or certain activities of the transferor undertaking on a regular basis.

[22] It is for the national court to establish, in the light of the foregoing interpretative guidance, whether a transfer has occurred in this case.

NOTES AND QUESTIONS

1. Advocate General La Pergola's opinion noted his "misgivings" with the application of some prior precedents, notably *Daddy's Dance Hall*, to the present facts. He perceived this contract transfer "in competitive circumstances" to be quite different from the transfers reviewed in prior caselaw and would have flatly concluded that the present case did not fall under Directive 77/187. The Court was certainly influenced by his views in ¶ 16, and by those of the Commission in ¶¶ 19–21. How would you decide the case if you were the referring court receiving this guidance? In your view, would it make a difference if Lefarth, the new cleaner, had an adequate staff to clean the school before getting the contract and hired none of Zehnacker's employees, or if, in contrast, Lefarth needed to hire three or four of the Zehnacker cleaning staff, but didn't hire Suzen?

2. Subsequently, the Court applied the *Suzen* criteria to hold that "in certain sectors, such as cleaning . . . the activity is essentially based on manpower. Thus, an organized grouping of wage earners who are specifically and permanently assigned to a common task may . . . amount to an economic entity." Vidal v. Perez, Cases C–127/96, C–229/96 and C–74/97, [1998] ECR I–8179, at 8231. In consequence, if the new employer "takes over a major part, in terms of their numbers and skills, of the employees specifically assigned by his predecessor to that task," id. at 8233, the provisions of the Transfer of Undertakings Directive should apply.

3. The Court has also held that a transfer of undertakings could occur when an initial contractor's contract was terminated and the new contractor took over the assets and operational infrastructure necessary to carry out the contracting service. Thus, in Guney–Gorres v. Securicor Aviation, Case C–232/04, [2005] ECR I–11237, Securecor, a contractor providing airline security services at the Dusseldorf airport, was replaced by Kotter, an unrelated contractor. The German government provided both contractors with all the security equipment (walk-through metal detectors, baggage screening equipment, etc.) Kotter hired 167 of Securicor's employees, but not the plaintiff and another employee. The Court held that the fact that the new contractor did not own the assets was irrelevant when it made use of them as the sole operational assets for executing the service contract (¶ 41). However, the Court emphasized that a transfer of assets was only one of the criteria the referring court should examine in reaching its decision, citing ¶ of *Spijkers*. If you were the referring court, what would be your ultimate conclusion?

4. Occasionally the issue is what sort of contractual benefits provided by the initial employer must continue to be provided when the second employer

takes over the transferred employee. In Martin v. South Bank University, Case C–4/01, [2003] ECR I–12859, the issue was whether the university had to grant employees of Redwood College the stipulated benefits of Redwood's early retirement scheme after the university had taken over Redwood College. The Court held that the university had to grant the transferred employees the benefits of Redwood's early retirement plan even though they were more generous than those of the university.

3. EMPLOYEE PROTECTION IN EMPLOYER INSOLVENCIES

Because the Collective Redundancies Directive did not cover employees who lose their jobs when the employer becomes insolvent, it was obvious that specific legislation was necessary. Directive 80/987 on the protection of employees in the event of insolvency of their employer, O.J. L 283/23 (Oct. 28, 1980), requires Member States to ensure that "guarantee institutions" provide guarantees for payment of any outstanding employee claims for pay or benefits prior to the onset of insolvency (art. 3). The guarantee institutions must have assets "independent of the employers' operating capital and be inaccessible to proceedings for insolvency," with the assets coming from employers' contributions or from a state agency (art. 5). The directive enables much more rapid and certain payment of amounts due to unpaid employees, and avoids the risk that they would receive only limited recourse as unsecured creditors in an insolvency proceeding. Italy's failure to implement this directive on time gave rise to the landmark judgment on Member State liability in damages, *Francovich,* excerpted at page 369.

Somewhat surprisingly, the 1980 directive did not specify which national guaranty fund is liable for the back pay of employees of a branch in one Member State when the company itself, established in another Member State, becomes insolvent. In Everson & Barrass v. Secretary of State for Trade, Case C–198/98, [1999] ECR I–8903, the Court concluded that the UK guaranty fund was liable for the back pay and benefits of 200 employees of a UK branch of an insolvent Irish shipping company. The Court noted that the employees paid taxes and social security contributions to the UK. Directive 2002/74, O.J. L 270/10 (Oct. 8, 2002), amended the initial 1980 directive principally to insert a new Article 8a which covers such a transnational situation in the manner indicated by the Court.

C. WORKER HEALTH AND SAFETY LEGISLATION

1. GENERIC HEALTH AND SAFETY MEASURES

Adoption of worker health and safety legislation began in the late 1970s and accelerated with the entry into force of EECT Article 118a, added by the Single European Act in 1987. An early example is Directive 77/576, O.J. L 229/12 (Sept. 7, 1977), amended in O.J. L 245/23 (Aug. 26, 1992), which set minimum standards for safety signs at plants and construction sites and required the use of standard symbols that would be easily recognized even by migrant workers who cannot speak the local language. Directive 80/1107 on the protection of workers from risks related to exposure to chemical, physical and biological agents at work, O.J. L 327/8 (Dec. 3, 1980), initiated a procedure for classifying dangerous risk factors, set rules on maximum exposure and monitoring of health, and established a system of emergency health measures. Other significant directives set standards for exposure to noise at work, O.J. L 137/28 (May 24, 1986), and required operational safety standards and prescribed measures for warning the public in the event of serious accidents in industrial operations, O.J. L 230/1 (Aug. 5, 1982) (prompted by the well-known chemical plant explosion in Seveso, Italy).

In Chapter 14D, we learned that the new approach to technical harmonization called for the adoption of "framework" directives to establish general principles, with detailed regulation or specific standards to be provided in later directives for specific fields. A leading example is the "framework" Directive 89/391 on measures to encourage improvements in the safety and health of workers at work, O.J. L 183/1 (June 29, 1989). This directive sets certain generic rules for protection of workers at their principal place of employment, requiring, for example, first aid centers, information and training for workers as to common health or safety risks, and consultation with employee representatives on ways to avoid such hazards.

Also noteworthy is Regulation 2062/94 creating a European Agency for Safety and Health at Work, O.J. L 216/1 (Aug. 20, 1994). This agency, sited at Bilbao, Spain, serves as a center for study and exchange of information.

2. THE PREGNANT AND ADOLESCENT WORKERS DIRECTIVES

Influenced by text in the Social Charter, the Commission proposed directives to protect pregnant workers and working mothers, as well as to protect working adolescents and children. Because both directives focused primarily on the need to protect the health of the workers concerned, they were adopted through use of then EECT Article 118a.

We need only briefly to mention Directive 94/33 on the protection of young people at work, O.J. L 216/12 (Aug. 20, 1994), which was not particularly controversial. This generally forbids employment for children under fourteen, permits young people between fourteen and eighteen to work, but only twelve hours per week during school terms, forbids night work by adolescents, etc. Virtually all the States had to change some aspect of their prior protective legislation for young people.

In contrast, Directive 92/85 on improvements in the safety and health at work of pregnant workers and workers who have recently given birth or are breast feeding, O.J. L 348/1 (Nov. 28, 1992), Document 34 in the Selected Documents, is one of the best-known social action measures. The particular health risks of such workers, both from exposure to chemical, physical and biological agents and from mental and physical fatigue, are to be assessed by the employers, as well as by the Commission on a Community-wide basis. Employers are obligated to reduce the worker's exposure to risks, if necessary by re-assigning the worker to other tasks, or placing the worker on leave (art. 5). Pregnant workers and mothers of newborns are entitled to a minimum of 14 weeks' maternity leave before and/or after confinement, with two of the weeks leave being compulsory (art. 8). Pregnant workers cannot be dismissed during their pregnancy, except for reasons manifestly not connected with their condition (art. 10). During any leave period, the workers are entitled to remuneration calculated to be at least at the level of sick pay required by national law (art. 11).

The UK opposed several aspects of the directive proposal, notably the maternity leave and economic benefits provisions, claiming that they might cost UK employers 100 million pounds annually. After the UK succeeded in having the leave remuneration reduced from full pay to the sick pay level, it abstained when the directive was adopted.

A 1999 Commission report indicated general satisfaction with the implementation and impact of the directive, noting that it had taken action to ensure that Luxembourg ended its ban on night work for pregnant women, without any assessment of whether such work posed a health risk for specific individuals.

The following judgment demonstrates that the Court will usually take an expansive view in interpreting article 10.

PAQUAY v. SOCIETE D' ARCHITECTES HOET

Case C–460/06, [2007] ECR I–8511.

[An architect firm dismissed Paquay after the birth of her child. When she sued for damages for unjust dismissal, the trial court concluded that the firm's alleged grounds for dismissal were insufficient. In view of evidence that the employer had advertized for a replacement for Paquay while she was a pregnant and had otherwise indicated an intention to dismiss her during her period of maternity leave, the Belgian court inquired in a preliminary reference whether Article 10's prohibition of dismissal implicitly banned taking a decision to dismiss during the maternity leave.]

31   [During the maternity leave period,] Article 10 of Directive 92/85 does not provide for any exception to, or derogation from, the prohibition of dismissing pregnant workers, save in exceptional cases not connected

with their condition where the employer justifies the dismissal in writing.

* * *

33 Having regard to the objectives pursued by Directive 92/85 and, more specifically, to those pursued by its Article 10, it is necessary to point out that the prohibition on the dismissal of pregnant women and women who have recently given birth or are breastfeeding during the period of protection is not limited to the notification of that decision to dismiss. The protection granted by that provision to those workers excludes both the taking of a decision to dismiss as well as the steps of preparing for the dismissal, such as searching for and finding a permanent replacement for the relevant employee on the grounds of the pregnancy and/or the birth of a child.

34 As the Italian Government correctly noted, an employer, * * * who decides to replace a pregnant worker * * * on the grounds of her condition, and who, from the moment when he first had knowledge of the pregnancy, takes concrete steps with a view to finding a replacement, is pursuing the objective which is specifically prohibited by Directive 92/85 * * *.

35 A contrary interpretation, restricting the prohibition to only the notification of the decision to dismiss during the period of protection set down in Article 10 of Directive 92/85, would deprive that article of its effectiveness and could give rise to a risk that employers will circumvent the prohibition to the detriment of the rights of pregnant women and women who have recently given birth or are breastfeeding, enshrined in Directive 92/85.

* * *

37 Moreover, regarding the burden of proof applicable in circumstances such as those in the present case, it is a matter for the national court to apply the relevant provisions of Council Directive 97/80/EC on the burden of proof in cases of discrimination based on sex which, under its Article 3(1)(a), applies to situations covered by Directive 92/85 insofar as discrimination on grounds of sex is concerned. It is apparent from Article 4(1) of Directive 97/80 that when persons who consider themselves wronged because the principle of equal treatment has not been applied to them establish, before a court or other competent authority, facts from which it may be presumed that there has been direct or indirect discrimination, it shall be for the respondent to prove that there has been no breach of the principle of equal treatment.

NOTES AND QUESTIONS

1. Do you agree with the Court, or do you think that only an amendment of the directive should prohibit employers from planning to dismiss a

pregnant worker after the end of the maternity leave? The employer contended that it wanted to dismiss Paquay as a secretary because she was incapable of meeting the evolving needs of the firm, but the referring court concluded that the employer did not prove this. If the employer believed this in good faith, do you think planning to dismiss Paquay for that reason should be held to violate the directive? Note that the employer could plan to dismiss Paquay for a legitimate reason, e.g., for theft or insubordination.

2. The Court's first judgment interpreting the directive came in Melgar v. Ayuntamiento de los Barrios, Case C–438/99 [2001] ECR I–6915, where the Court initially held that Article 10's prohibition of a dismissal of a pregnant worker had direct effect, so that Spain had to apply that directive provision even though Spain had failed to implement the directive on time. The Court held, however, that when a fixed term contract ended while a worker was pregnant, the employer had no obligation to renew the contract unless it could be demonstrated that the pregnancy motivated the employer not to renew after successively renewing fixed term contracts previously.

Somewhat in contrast, in Tele Danmark v. Handels–Forbund, Case C–109/00, [2001] ECR I–6993, the Court held that an employer which had hired a pregnant woman for a six month fixed term contract and then fired her upon learning that she was pregnant and would give birth before the end of the six months, was liable in damages. The Court held that the employer was dismissing the employee on grounds of her pregnancy in manifest violation of Article 10 of the directive (¶¶ 26–27), and that the fact that the employer suffers a financial loss because the employee cannot work the full six months but still must be paid, does not change the result (¶ 57 28–29). Tele Danmark argued unsuccessfully that the failure of the employee to disclose her pregnancy before being hired constituted a violation of the duty of good faith which justified the dismissal. What is your view?

3. THE WORKING TIME DIRECTIVE

Directive 93/104 on the organization of working time, O.J. L 307/1 (Dec. 13, 1993) (see Document 35 in the Selected Documents), is undoubtedly the best known and also the most controversial legislation adopted through use of EECT Article 118a. Proposed by the Commission in 1990 to embody rights enunciated in the Social Charter, the draft was warmly supported by France and other liberal governments on the continent, but bitterly opposed by Prime Ministers Thatcher and Major of the UK. The text was finally adopted only with UK-inspired compromise language intended to reduce the scope of some provisions and delay the implementation of others. The UK government contended that it was only trying to protect the interests of millions of UK workers who wanted to work more than 48 hours a week and had no desire to take long holidays.

The principal purpose of the Working Time Directive is to set minimum standards for daily and weekly rest periods and for annual leave. Recitals not only quote the Social Charter's description of these as rights, but declare that these "periods of rest" are essential for worker safety and health, which "should not be subordinated to purely economic considerations." In the substantive provisions, article 3 requires "a minimum daily rest period of 11 consecutive hours per 24–hour period," to which article 4 adds a "rest break" if a work day exceeds 6 hours. Article 6 sets a maximum of 48 hours of work, including overtime, in each weekly period, to which article 5 adds a requirement of a 24 hour uninterrupted period of rest every week (which rest period should "in principle include Sunday"). With regard to annual leave, article 7 requires "paid annual leave of at least four weeks," and forbids substituting added remuneration for any part of the annual leave.

The directive also provides particular protections in the special circumstances of night work. Article 8 sets an 8 hour maximum for night work. Article 9 provides that night workers should receive free health assessments at regular intervals, and states that workers with health problems occasioned by night work have a right to transfer to suitable day work, whenever possible.

Article 17 provides a long list of derogations from some of the usual rules, principally "on account of the specific characteristics of the activity," e.g., in health care in hospitals or custodial care in prisons and residential institutions, for the armed forces, police, and civil protection, for the media and telecommunications, for energy provision and pollution control, and for periodic surges in essential work in agriculture and tourism. A derogation is also granted for managerial personnel. (Note that there is no specific derogation for lawyers, accountants, engineers or other professionals, although there is for persons engaged in research and development.)

Article 15 authorizes States to have rules more favorable to workers, or to permit labor-management collective agreements more favorable to workers. This is common in continental States, which often set 38 or 40 hour maximum work weeks—indeed, the Socialist government of Prime Minister Jospin in France in 1998 reduced the maximum to 35 hours in an apparently successful effort to reduce unemployment. Also, labor-management agreements in some continental States often add a fifth week of paid vacation.

Many of the compromise provisions in the directive relate to exceptions and derogations. Article 1 originally provided a blanket exception for air, rail, road and sea transport, sea fishing, and "the activities of doctors in training." A 1997 Commission White Paper estimated that about 5.6 million workers, 4% of the total work force, was thus excluded, and proposed supplemental legislation. Accordingly, Directive 2000/34, O.J. L 195/41 (Aug. 1, 2000), amended the Working Time Directive to apply it to all the excepted fields, but with additional derogations specific to each field. Subsequently, Directive 2003/88, O.J. L 299/9 (Nov. 18, 2003), codified the directive.

The Working Time Directive became effective on Nov. 23, 1996, but in article 18 the UK obtained a three year extension for a three week paid annual leave instead of article 7's four weeks of leave. The UK also insisted that article 18b provide for a seven year suspension of the maximum 48 hour work week, subject to an employer's obtaining the consent of each worker concerned to work for longer periods.

Over all, the directive provisions stand in sharp contrast to the US, where there is no comparable federal legislation and where collective bargaining agreements customarily provide for rest and vacation periods (e.g., the common 40 hour work week and two weeks' paid vacation), but permit substantial overtime. In September 2001, an International Labor Organization study indicated that in the 1990s Americans increased their average annual working time to a level 15% more than the UK average and 33% more than the German average. Although the US naturally leads the world in productivity per worker, France and Belgium lead in productivity per work hour.

The UK promptly attacked the Working Time Directive in an appeal to the Court of Justice, contending principally that the directive was not properly adopted by use of EECT Article 118a, because it did not in fact protect worker health and safety, and that its provisions violated the principle of proportionality. The Court's judgment rejecting the UK's contentions is excerpted at pages 93 and 164 supra, which should be reviewed at this point.

NOTES AND QUESTIONS

1. In ¶ 15 of the Working Time directive judgment, the Court defines broadly the worker health and safety which EECT Article 118a can be used to protect, holding that it authorizes measures intended only to promote physical and mental well-being, in addition to legislation intended to eliminate or reduce health and safety risks. Do you consider this to be a justified approach?

2. Certainly limits on consecutive hours of work in a day, or upon night work, can be justified on health and safety grounds, but do you consider the 48 hour work week and four weeks paid vacation provisions to be genuinely intended for health and safety or only for a desirable quality of life? Do you agree with the Court view that the Council did not need to have scientific evidence for its precise rules, but could make a general assessment of health benefits?

3. The UK may have lost in advance its argument that the directive violated the principles of proportionality and subsidiarity when it obtained derogations and exceptions in the text, notably the delay in phasing in four weeks of vacation and the 48 hour work week. In that connection, do you consider that workers should be able to agree with employers that they will work on average more than 48 hours, or do you think that governments should not permit this? Also, do you agree with the directive's prohibition of remuneration instead of the four weeks paid leave?

4. Comparable legislation in the US is probably inconceivable, but as a matter of policy, do you think the US would benefit if legislation restricted the length of the work week or set a minimum paid vacation? On the other hand, do you agree with many American economists and European business

leaders who believe that the directive will reduce Community industry's ability to compete in the global marketplace? Or do you agree with those Europeans who believe that the directive provides health and safety and quality of life benefits that outweigh economic considerations?

The Working Time directive's provisions have been interpreted in several interesting cases.

QUEEN v. SECRETARY OF STATE FOR TRADE EX PARTE BECTU

Case C–173/99, [2001] ECR I–4881.

[When the UK Labor government adopted a regulation in 1998 to implement the Working Time Directive, it provided that employees did not obtain any right to annual paid leave until after being "continuously employed for 13 weeks." The Broadcasting, Entertainment, Cinematographic and Theater Union (BECTU) challenged this provision on behalf of its 30,000 members, contending that it deprived many of its members of any form of annual leave because they were customarily employed on short term fixed contracts for less than 13 weeks. The High Court referred questions on the proper interpretation of the Directive.]

43   [T]he entitlement of every worker to paid annual leave must be regarded as a particularly important principle of Community social law from which there can be no derogations and whose implementation by the competent national authorities must be confined within the limits expressly laid down by Directive 93/104.

44   [Moreover,] the directive also embodies the rule that a worker must normally be entitled to actual rest, with a view to ensuring effective protection of his health and safety, since it is only where the employment relationship is terminated that Article 7(2) allows an allowance to be paid in lieu of paid annual leave.

* * *

46   Furthermore, Directive 93/104 draws no distinction between workers employed under a contract of indefinite duration and those employed under a fixed-term contract. On the contrary, * * * the provisions concerning minimum rest periods * * * refer in most cases to 'every worker', as indeed does Article 7(1) in relation to entitlement to paid annual leave.

* * *

50   [The UK rules] are manifestly incompatible with the scheme of Directive 93/104 which * * * makes no provision for any possible derogation regarding entitlement to paid annual leave and therefore, *a fortiori*, prevents a Member State from unilaterally restricting that entitlement which is conferred on all workers by that directive.

51   Furthermore, rules of the kind at issue in the main proceedings are liable to give rise to abuse because employers might be tempted to

evade the obligation to grant the paid annual leave to which every worker is entitled by more frequent resort to short-term employment relationships.

52   Consequently, Directive 93/104 must be interpreted as precluding Member States from unilaterally limiting the entitlement to paid annual leave conferred on all workers by applying a precondition for such entitlement which has the effect of preventing certain workers from benefitting from it.

* * *

[The Court also rejected in ¶ ¶ 57–59 the UK's argument that making the directive apply to short-term employees would pose serious burdens on medium and small enterprises. The Court held that this "purely economic" consideration could not bar compliance.]

NOTES AND QUESTIONS

1.   The Labor government was presumably in good faith in adopting the contested provision, because it generally endorses Community social policy measures. It is certainly plausible to require a minimum period of employment before any right to a proportionate share of an annual paid leave should accrue. The UK noted that other States had similar provisions. Do you agree with the Court's interpretation? As a matter of policy, do you consider that the directive would have been better drafted if it required a minimum period of employment? Do you agree with the Court that the UK's desire to reduce the administrative burden of smaller enterprises constituted only an "economic" justification?

2.   In Sindicato de Medicos v. Conselleria de Sanidad de la Generalidad Valenciana, Case C–303/98, [2000] ECR I–7963, the Court held that the directive contained no express derogation for rules governing medical doctors, as opposed to doctors in training. Accordingly, the Spanish rules on providing primary medical care in rural regions had to be revised, because they permitted doctors to be on call in residence at facilities for excessively long periods of time (the plaintiff association of doctors claimed that doctors could be on call for 31 hours without rest).

Subsequently, in Landes-hauptstadt Kiel v. Jaeger, Case C–151/02, [2003] ECR I–8389, the Court held that a doctor's on-call time had to be considered entirely work-time even though the employer hospital provided the doctor with a bedroom in which to rest during the on-call time and the doctor actually rested about half the on-call time. How to balance the rest requirements for doctors, nurses and other health care providers with the social need for continuous medical care is obviously a difficult issue in many countries (including the US). As a policy matter, do you think the directive should have contained special rules for the medical care sector? Proposals to amend the directive in this regard have been under consideration by the Commission and Council for several years, but without achieving agreement. For an analytical review of these and later judgments, see T. Nowak, The Working–Time Directive and the Court of Justice, 15 Maastricht J. Eur. L. 447 (2008).

Note that in Vorel v. Nemocnice Cesky Krumlov, Case C–437/05, [2007] ECR I–331, the Court reiterated its conclusion in prior case law that on-call duty, where a worker is "required to be physically present on the employer's premises, must be regarded in its entirety as 'working time'" (¶ 27) in applying the directive's rest-time rules. The Court also held that the directive only concerned health and safety, and did not determine the level of remuneration of on-call periods (¶ 33). Presumably Czech law may set the remuneration at less than the normal salary.

3. In Personalrat der Feuerwehr Hamburg v. Leiter der Fuerwehr Hamburg, Case C–52/04, [2005] ECR I–7111, the Court held that the Hamburg fire department could not require firefighters to be on duty for 50 hours a week when the directive requires a maximum 48 hour work week. The Court again held that 'on-call' time had to be included in calculating the work week time. The Court did recognize an exception at times when grave natural technological disasters would temporarily require exceeding the normal work week (¶ ¶ 54–55).

4. In Vicente Pereda v. Madrid Movilidad, Case C–277/08, [2009] ECR I–___ (Sept. 10, 2009), the issue was whether an employee who was on sick leave during the period scheduled by his employer for the paid annual leave was entitled to take the annual leave at another time during the same year. Not surprisingly, the Court held that the employee had an absolute right to take the annual leave at another time (¶ 19), although national law or a collective bargaining agreement could affect the scheduling of the leave (¶ 22). The Court emphasized that sick leave is only given to achieve recovery, while annual leave is to "enable the worker to rest and to enjoy a period of relaxation and leisure" (¶ 21). Accord, with regard to the separate enjoyment of both annual leave and maternity leave, Merino Gomez v. Continental Industrias, Case C–342/01, [2004] ECR I–2605.

D. OTHER RECENT SOCIAL ACTION LEGISLATION

As indicated above, the 1989 Social Action Program produced a series of measures in the 1990s that have significantly enhanced employee rights and affected other aspects of society. Until the Treaty of Amsterdam became effective on May 1, 1999, these were adopted by use of the Maastricht Social Protocol, so that they did not apply to the UK (except for those described in section C that were adopted through use of EECT Article 118a.) After the election of the Blair government in 1997, the UK accepted all of the legislation adopted by use of the Social Protocol.

Space concerns prevent a complete coverage of this active social legislative program. We will only review several measures which have had a major impact on social life in the Union and provide valuable comparisons with US rules and policies.

1.　THE EMPLOYMENT TERMS DIRECTIVE

The first significant measure adopted in the 1989 Social Action Program was Directive 91/533 on form of proof of an employment relationship, O.J. L 288/32 (Nov. 18, 1991), which requires employers to keep on record and provide to employees the written terms of their employment. The terms must specify the job description, the usual daily and weekly period of employment, paid leave, remuneration and social benefits and any applicable collective agreements. As many employers previously did not utilize written agreements, this directive has had a considerable impact. Incidentally, even though its legal basis was ECT Article 94, which required Council unanimity, the directive was adopted because the UK chose to abstain rather than vote against it.

The directive does not expressly cover the subject of overtime work. In Lange v. Georg Schunemann, Case C–350/99, [2001] ECR I–1061, an employee sued for relief after his dismissal for a refusal to work overtime when the subject of overtime was not mentioned in his contract. The Court held that the directive article requiring identification of the usual length of the "normal working day or week" did not implicitly require coverage of overtime, but then went on to conclude that an obligation upon an employee to work overtime whenever the employer requests (as opposed, presumably, to overtime mutually agreed upon) constituted an essential aspect of the employment relationship that ought to have been specified in the terms of employment.

2.　THE PARENTAL LEAVE DIRECTIVE

Directive 96/34 on the framework agreement on parental leave is probably the most innovative social measure of the 1990s. Most States already had legislation protecting pregnant workers and the mothers of newborns before the directive on that subject, but relatively few had legislation granting any form of parental leave rights. The Commission first proposed such a directive in 1983, but it received little support in the Council. The adoption of the current measure is undoubtedly due to a gradual shift in social attitudes concerning the desirability of parental leave.

The Parental Leave Directive is one of those adopted by the unusual procedure of negotiations on a Framework Agreement text between Community-level representative bodies of management and labor, which was then endorsed by the Council under the Social Agreement as a directive effective in 1998. Accordingly, the UK was accordingly not initially bound by the directive, but, as noted above, the Labor government agreed to accept its terms in a supplemental directive in December 1997.

The Preamble to the Framework Agreement refers to the Social Charter's statement that "measures should be developed to enable men and women to reconcile their occupational and family obligations." The

Preamble further declares that "measures to reconcile work and family life should encourage the introduction of new flexible ways of organizing work and time which are better suited to the changing needs of society." It is quite apparent that the Parental Leave Directive is intended to achieve a broad social policy goal.

The directive grants men and women workers a right to parental leave for at least three months to take care of a child, including an adopted child, until a given age up to 8 years, with the age to be chosen by the State and/or by agreement between its management and labor bodies. There is no requirement that the leave be paid, but at the end of the leave the worker has the right to return to the same job, if possible, or to similar work. Member States may opt to make the parental leave subject to the employee having worked for at least one year for the employer, and to a suitable notice period. The State and/or its management and bodies may also opt to protect employers' interests and postpone leave for justifiable reasons, e.g., when a replacement cannot be found within the notice period, or when "a specific function is of strategic importance." The directive also declares that "special arrangements to meet the operational and organizational requirements of small undertakings" can be made.

Apart from parental leave, the directive also requires States to adopt measures to permit leave "on grounds of force majeure," which is specified as meaning "for urgent family reasons in case of sickness or accident." No minimum leave time or conditions are set. Presumably this text grants a right to leave for a reasonable period of time to a worker who needs to care for a spouse, child or other close relative.

An interesting comparison can be drawn between the directive and the US Family and Medical Leave Act, Pub. L. No. 103–03 (1993), the first major legislation in the Clinton administration. The Act grants up to twelve weeks of unpaid leave per year, requiring most employers to grant such leave to employees who desire to meet a variety of family obligations in addition to pregnancy or childbirth.

Because the Parental Leave Directive does not require an employer to pay any remuneration to an employee during a parental leave, obviously such leave is not often requested by employees. In a rare case interpreting the directive, Lewen v. Denda, Case C–333/97, [1999] ECR I–7243, the Court held that an employer was not obligated to pay a Christmas bonus to a worker who was taking parental leave at that time unless the referring court concluded that the bonus represented remuneration for past services, rather than an incentive for future productivity and loyalty (the employer's stated purpose). Similarly, in Gomez–Limon Sanchez–Camacho v. INSS, Case C–537/07, [2009] ECR I–___ (July 16, 2009), the Court held that the Spanish social security system was not required to calculate a disability benefit to a person at the benefit level for full pay rather than the actual lower pay, when the disability occurred while the person had taken parental leave to work at a reduced schedule and accordingly was receiving two-third's pay. The judgments manifestly will not encourage employees to take parental leave.

1. Do you agree with the basic policy behind the Parental Leave Directive, namely that employers should provide short term leave periods for child care to either parent? Would you prefer encouragement of such leaves by subsidies to employers, rather than by binding rules? Overall, do you think the benefit to society from such leaves outweighs the manifest operational inefficiency they represent for employers?

2. The procedural mode of permitting Community-wide management and labor associations to negotiate and draft texts of laws is certainly surprising, from an American viewpoint. The procedure was taken over from the Social Agreement and outlined in ECT Articles 138 and 139, both replicated in the Lisbon TFEU Articles 154 and 155. Some critics have contended that the failure to provide that Parliament must join with the Council in approving an agreement, instead of authorizing approval by the Council alone, represents another example of a "democratic deficit." Would you agree?

3.　THE EUROPEAN WORKS COUNCIL DIRECTIVE

No proposal in the social action field has engendered greater controversy over the years than that to adopt Union measures to harmonize rules on structures, commonly called works councils, to provide operational information from management to workers and to require management-employee consultation on certain issues. Although such rules have long been common in continental States, they varied considerably in scope and operational features. Of course, the whole approach is alien to traditional management-labor relations in the UK and Ireland (and the US). Incidentally, these consultation rules should not be confused with the corporate structure of employee co-determination in management, which requires that corporate supervisory and management boards (corresponding to American corporate boards of directors) must include a certain number of employee members. A variety of corporate co-determination rules are mandatory for companies employing large numbers of workers in Germany, Denmark, Luxembourg and the Netherlands.

Since the 1970s, European unions have urged the creation of works councils to represent all the employees of a multinational corporation with subsidiaries or branches in several States. The Commission endorsed the idea, proposing a draft directive in 1983, but a Council resolution tabled the proposal in 1986. The principal forces in opposition predictably included the UK Government, the European Confederation of Industries, and the subsidiaries of US companies.

The 1989 Social Charter contained a section on "Information, Consultation and Participation for Workers," which called for measures to achieve this goal. After the Social Charter was endorsed by the European Council (except for the UK), the Commission launched a new proposal in 1991. Due to adamant opposition from the UK under Prime Minister Major, the draft was shifted to the procedures set out in Social Protocol, and was adopted as Directive 94/45 on the establishment of a European Works Council, O.J. L 254/64 (Sept. 30, 1994). As noted above, the Labor government elected in 1997 accepted a supplemental Directive 97/74, O.J. L 10/22 (Jan. 16, 1998), which slightly amended the directive to enable its extension to the UK.

The European Works Council (EWC) Directive is intended to ensure that employees of "Community-scale undertakings and Community-scale groups" shall be represented in an EWC with the right to obtain significant operational information and to consult systematically with the "central management." (Note that the EWC directive does not require States to have a general system for works councils for smaller enterprises, nor even for larger enterprises with few or no employees outside of one State.)

To be a "Community-scale undertaking" or "group," the enterprise or group must employ a least 1000 employees (including part-time employees) on average for two years, with bodies of at least 150 employees in two Member States. Obviously, not only large but many medium-sized enterprises will meet these thresholds. Note also that there is no reference to corporate form—limited liability companies and partnerships are encompassed. The concept of a group obviously includes any controlled subsidiary, whether control is exercised by "ownership, financial participation, or the rules which govern it" (art. 3).

Central management and a "special negotiating body" chosen to represent all employees must negotiate an agreement which defines the composition and membership of the EWC, "the functions and the procedure for information and consultation," "the venue, frequency and duration of meetings," and the financial resources for the EWC (which, incidentally, are provided by the central management) (art. 6). EWC members, employee representatives and experts assisting them (e.g., economists, accountants, lawyers) are naturally bound by a duty to keep information confidential (art. 8).

An annex details the scope of the information and consultation rights. Central management must meet annually with the EWC (more often, if "exceptional circumstances," such as the closure of establishments or collective redundancies, are envisaged). The scope of the information and consultation is quite broad:

> "The meeting shall relate in particular to the structure, economic and financial situation, the probable development of the business and of production and sales, the situation and probable trend of employment, investments, and substantial changes concerning organization, introduction of new working methods or production processes, transfers of production, mergers, cut-backs or closures of undertakings,

establishments or important parts thereof, and collective redundancies.''

However, under Article 8, management need not provide information that ''according to objective criteria, would seriously harm the functioning of the undertakings concerned or would be prejudicial to them.''

In May 2009, the initial EWC directives were revised and codified in Directive 2009/38, O.J. L 122/28 (May 2009). Some new rules will become effective in June 2011, notably a clarification of what constitutes consultation, and an obligation to restructure an EWC whenever a merger or acquisition substantially alters workforce numbers. At the time of the codified directive's adoption, the Commission indicated that 820 EWCs had been created, representing around 14.5 million employers, but also observed that over a thousand more groups employing over 1000 workers transnationally ought to have established EWCs.

A recent judgment demonstrates the Court's broad interpretation of the EWC directive's provisions to make it more effective.

GESAMTBETRIEBSRAT DER KUHNE & NAGEL v. KUHNE & NAGEL

Case 440/00, [2004] ECR I–787.

[When the Kuhne & Nagel group's Swiss parent company management refused to create an EWC for its subsidiaries within the EU, the works council of the Kuhne & Nagel subsidiary in Germany sued that company to oblige it to create the EWC. The German company employed 4500 workers in Germany, the largest subsidiary workforce within the EU. The initial German labor court granted the works council's request, but on appeal the German Supreme Labor Court queried whether Germany had the jurisdiction to require subsidiaries outside Germany to provide the information necessary and to participate in the EWC's operations. Questions were accordingly referred to the Court of Justice.]

39   [T]he aim of the Directive is to ensure that the employees of Community-scale undertakings and Community-scale groups of undertakings are properly informed and consulted when decisions which affect them are taken in a Member State other than that in which they are employed.

40   As is clear from the Directive's general scheme, transnational informing and consulting of employees are essentially to be ensured by means of a system of negotiations between central management and the employees' representatives.

44   This special negotiating body and central management must, in accordance with Article 6(1) of the Directive, negotiate in a spirit of cooperation with a view to reaching an agreement on the detailed arrangements for establishing a European Works Council.

45   It is also apparent from Article 11(2) of the Directive that the Member States must ensure that undertakings make available * * * the infor-

mation on the number of employees referred to in Article 2(1)(a) and (c) thereof.

46   Furthermore, the Court has already stated that, if the Directive is to serve a useful purpose, it is essential that the employees concerned be guaranteed access to information enabling them to determine* * * whether a Community-scale undertaking or group of undertakings exists, which is itself a condition precedent for the setting up of a European Works Council * * *.

47   The Court similarly stated * * * that, where information relating to the structure or organisation of a group of undertakings forms part of the information which is essential to the opening of such negotiations for the setting up of a European Works Council, all undertakings within the group are required to supply the information which they possess or are able to obtain to the internal employees' representative bodies requesting it.

* * *

50   Where the central management is situated outside the Member States, its responsibility is assumed, * * * under the second subparagraph of Article 4(2), to the management of the establishment or group undertaking employing the greatest number of employees in any one Member State, that is to say, the deemed central management. * * *

53   [However,] deemed central management is not necessarily in possession of the information concerned [and] not usually in a position to obtain, in the context of legal relations between undertakings within the same group, the information from other undertakings belonging to the group.

54   [G]iven the objective and overall scheme of the Directive and in order that deemed central management can take on the responsibility, and fulfil the obligations, which usually fall to central management, Article 4(1) of the Directive must be interpreted as meaning that deemed central management is required to request the information essential to the opening of negotiations for the establishment of a European Works Council from the other undertakings belonging to the group which are located in the Member States, and has a right to receive that information from them.

* * *

59   [I]n order to ensure that the Directive serves a useful purpose, the other undertakings belonging to the group and located in the Member States are therefore under an obligation [to supply the essential information in their possession] to assist the deemed central management in fulfilling the main obligation.

* * *

61   Finally, under Article 14(1) of the Directive, the Member States must take all the necessary steps in order to be able at all times to

guarantee the results imposed by the Directive. Under Article 11(3) of the Directive, they must provide for appropriate measures in the event of failure to comply with the Directive and, in particular, they must ensure that adequate administrative or judicial procedures are available to enable the obligations deriving from the Directive to be enforced. It follows from the purpose of the Directive that the Member States must take all the measures necessary to ensure that the obligations deriving from Articles 4(1) and 11(1) of the Directive are fully performed.

62   It is none the less appropriate to point out that the Member States, when ensuring that the undertakings belonging to a group comply with their obligations, must be mindful of certain of the undertakings' interests. First, the competent national authorities must ensure that * * * information of a confidential nature is adequately protected. Second, administrative or judicial appeal procedures must be available to those undertakings.

NOTES AND QUESTIONS

1. In order to prevent a recalcitrant central management in a non-Member State (here Switzerland, but it could have been in the US or anywhere else) from blocking an EWC's creation, the Court implies obligations on the largest subsidiary employer to act in its stead, with the cooperation of the other subsidiaries, enforced by State authorities. Do you agree with this approach, or do you think this result should only have been achieved by amending the directive?

2. In several well-publicized cases in the 1980s, a European group in one State closed plants or establishments in other States with little or no warning to the workers laid off and without significant efforts to alleviate the social distress thus occasioned. This partially motivated the efforts to adopt an EWC directive. Do you think that when a group has an EWC, it will promote more balanced treatment of the interests of employees in different States, or not?

3. Consider the various types of information that central management must provide an EWC. Do you think that all the types represent information that employee representatives genuinely need to receive to protect employee interests? Do you think that some EWC members might violate their duty of confidentiality, e.g., by transmitting to union leaders sensitive economic data when contract negotiations are imminent (one of the arguments frequently raised by business leaders in opposing the directive)? Is management's right to withhold sensitive data in article 8 adequate?

4. It is difficult for an American to evaluate objectively the merits or risks of EWCs because the approach is so different from our traditional management-labor policies. Many American economists contend that worker information and consultation rights make European industry less competitive on a global scale, because they occasion ongoing employment costs and delays, and tend to reduce restructuring and rationalization for greater market efficiency. Europeans often respond that these rights facilitate labor peace, reduce the risk of serious management-labor conflicts and strikes, and pro-

mote higher worker productivity. What is your view? In any event, do the rights promote the quality of life for employees?

4. THE 2002 WORKS COUNCIL DIRECTIVE

All the continental States of the Community prior to the Central European enlargement have long had some form of system for employee representatives in enterprise or work councils in large and medium-sized firms. Thus, in France, every firm employing more than fifty persons must have a works council consisting of two or more representatives elected by all employees (not selected by unions, although union leaders may be elected as employee representatives on the works council).

The Works Council Directive was adopted early in 2002. Directive 2002/14, O.J. L 80/29 (Mar. 23, 2002), establishing a general framework for informing and consulting employees, requires all enterprises (including not-for-profit entities) that employ at least 50 employees to enable worker's representatives to exercise information and consultation rights. (A State may opt to lower the threshold to 20 rather than 50 employees.) Most Member States had to implement the directive by March 23, 2005, an easy deadline for those continental States which have long had types of works councils. The UK, Ireland and any other State without a tradition of regular worker consultation procedures were to phase in the directive in stages up to March 23, 2008. The directive is estimated to require consultation procedures in enterprises employing 50% of all workers in the Union.

A works council deals with management on all employee concerns, including the discharge of employees, labor grievances, workers' health, and work conditions. The works council has the right to inspect the annual financial statements and to receive certain relevant operational information. Article 4 of the directive provides that the information and consultation rights must cover the "economic situation" of the enterprise, the "situation, structure and probable development of employment," and any "substantive changes in work organization." Article 4(4) stipulates that the consultation between management and the works council requires meetings between the two, and that the consultation is to be carried out "with a view to reaching an agreement on decisions within the scope of the employer's powers."

Further Reading

C. Barnard, Employment Law (3rd ed. Oxford U.P. 2006)

R. Blanpain & C. Engels, European Labour Law (9th ed. Kluwer 2003)

G. De Burca & B. De Witte, eds., Social Rights in Europe (Oxford U.P. 2005)

S. O'Leary, Employment Law at the European Court of Justice (2d ed. Hart 2006)

P. Watson, EU Social and Employment Law (Oxford U.P. 2009)

CHAPTER 35

EQUAL EMPLOYMENT RIGHTS AND ANTI-DISCRIMINATION POLICIES

■ ■ ■

Like Chapter 6 on basic rights protection and Chapter 16 on citizenship of the Union, this chapter addresses issues of fundamental interest to the people of the European Union. The initial 1957 European Economic Community Treaty only recognized two rights of nationals of its Member States, namely that of non-discrimination on the basis of nationality, treated extensively in a variety of contexts in earlier chapters, and, somewhat curiously, the specific right of equal pay for men and women. Over time, however, evolving Treaty amendments, legislative measures and liberal Court doctrines have combined to accord the people of the European Union extensive rights of equal treatment and protection against discrimination in the context of employment.

This chapter surveys this development, initially reviewing in section A the evolution in Treaty provisions. Section B covers equal pay for men and women, section C the more extensive right of equal treatment in employment for men and women, and section D equal treatment of both sexes in social security and pension plans. In section E, we will examine the recent Treaty provisions, implementing directives and caselaw designed to protect against discrimination in employment on the basis of "racial or ethnic origin, religion or belief, disability, age or sexual orientation."

A. TREATY ARTICLES AND BASIC POLICIES

The 1957 EEC Treaty's Article 117, which mandated equal pay between men and women, only began to have legal force after the famous Court judgment in *Defrenne*, and the Council's 1975 directive intended to implement it, both discussed in section B. After the European Council's endorsement of the 1974 Social Action Program, described in the prior chapter, the Council adopted in 1976 a directive requiring equal treatment of men and women in all aspects of employment. The impact of both directives has been enhanced by their liberal interpretation by the Court of Justice in cases that continue to arise to the present day.

By the time of the Treaty of Maastricht, the political leaders of the Member States had become increasingly sensitive to the need for action to promote gender equality in employment. Article 2 of the EEC Treaty was amended to include "equality between men and women" as a goal of the Community, a phrase reiterated in the Lisbon TEU Article 2.

To enable legislative action to achieve this goal, the Treaty of Amsterdam amended the initial EECT article on equal pay to add a crucial paragraph, then numbered ECT Article 141(3) and now TFEU Article 157 (3):

> 3. The Council, acting in accordance with the [ordinary legislative procedure], and after consulting the Economic and Social Committee, shall adopt measures to ensure the application of the principle of equal opportunities and equal treatment of men and women in matters of employment and occupation, including the principle of equal pay for equal work or work of equal value.

Paragraph 3 authorizes legislation to achieve equal treatment of men and women in all aspects of employment, not merely equal pay. Another Amsterdam Treaty addition, paragraph 4, enables Member States to adopt or keep measures intended to promote equality in employment for the "underrepresented sex" (almost always women), measures often called positive action in Europe, and affirmative action in the US. This topic is discussed in section C2.

We should also note that the Union seeks to promote national policies intended to promote the interests of women. In 2000, the Commission published a Community Framework Strategy on Gender Equality COM(2000)335, which outlines an approach called "gender mainstreaming," aiming to close the equality gap between men and women. It states in part:

> [C]onsiderable progress has been made regarding the situation of women in the Member States, but gender equality in day-to-day life is still being undermined by the fact that women and men do not enjoy equal rights in practice.

> This situation can be tackled effectively by integrating the gender equality objective into the policies that have a direct or indirect impact on the lives of women and men. Women's concerns, needs and aspirations should be taken into account and assume the same importance as men's concerns in the design and implementation of policies. This is the *gender mainstreaming* approach. . . .

In 1994, Commissioner Flynn, responsible for social affairs, incited the Commission to issue a White Paper on Social Policy which proposed Treaty text to combat discrimination on grounds other than gender. The Irish presidency of the Council in late 1996 inserted the proposal into the draft text of the Amsterdam Treaty, and it was accepted in 1997 as part of the new Social Chapter after the election of the UK Labor government of Prime Minister Blair.

The Treaty of Amsterdam thus introduced ECT Article 13:

Without prejudice to the other provisions of this Treaty and within the limits of the powers conferred by it upon the Community, the Council, acting unanimously on a proposal from the Commission and after consulting the European Parliament, may take appropriate action to combat discrimination based on sex, racial or ethnic origin, religion or belief, disability, age or sexual orientation.

Even though ECT Article 13 required the Council to act unanimously, it was able to do so to adopt the two anti-discrimination directives discussed in section E. TFEU Article 10 states the aim of combatting the types of discrimination set out in ECT Article 13. TFEU Article 19(1) then replicates ECT Article 13 and in 19(2) authorizes incentive measures to combat discrimination of the listed types.

B.   EQUAL PAY FOR WOMEN AND MEN

As indicated above, EECT Article 119 mandated the Member States to ensure that "men and women should receive equal pay for equal work." France demanded that this unusually specific article be included in the Treaty because a French constitutional provision required such equal pay, and France did not want its enterprises to be disadvantaged in competing with enterprises elsewhere.

Because EECT Article 119 placed the obligation to achieve equal pay upon the Member States, it was generally believed that the article could not have direct effect. In Chapter 5A supra, we have seen that the Court accorded the equal pay right vertical direct effect in Defrenne v. Sabena, supra page 240, which should be reviewed at this point. Note that in *Defrenne* the Court held that EECT Article 119 had direct effect in cases of "direct and overt discrimination" (¶ 22–23). As we shall see, the Court subsequently held that it has direct effect also to remedy indirect discrimination. The Court also held that EECT Article 119 forbid discrimination in pay by private sector employers as well as by the State as a public sector employer (¶ 39), an application of the relatively rare horizontal direct effect of a Treaty article.

On a comparative note, the Equal Pay Act of 1963, 29 U.S.C.A. § 206(d)(1), forbids sex-based discrimination as to pay, and Title VII of the Civil Rights Act of 1964, 42 U.S.C.A. § 2000e, includes sex-based discrimination as a type of employment discrimination. A large body of caselaw interprets the EPA and Title VII. The US Constitution does not contain any express provision on equality between men and women. An Equal Rights Amendment was proposed to achieve this purpose but was not adopted by a sufficient number of states. However, nine states (including Pennsylvania and Texas) have amended their constitutions to provide for equal rights for men and women.

1.   THE EQUAL PAY DIRECTIVE

The Council adopted Directive 75/117 of February 10, 1975 on equal pay for men and women, O.J. L 45/19 (Feb. 19, 1975) to implement EECT

Article 119. Even after *Defrenne,* the directive remained important because it defined "equal work" and because it created procedures for enforcing rights.

Article 1 of the 1975 directive expanded EECT Article 119's reference to "equal work" by adding "work to which equal value is attributed." This language obviously broadened the scope of equal pay claims. Article 1 of the 1975 directive also required that any "job classification system" be non-discriminatory in character.

Equally important, the directive required Member States to undertake vigorous enforcement of the right to equal pay. Thus, article 3 mandated that States should review their laws, regulations and practices to eliminate any discriminatory provisions. Article 4 obligated Member States to ensure that both collective bargaining agreements applicable to an industry and private employment contracts abide by the equal pay principle. Article 6 required that States generally "ensure that the principle of equal pay is applied" and article 2 reinforced this obligation by mandating judicial procedures to enable enforcement of rights. Article 7 required States to inform employees of their rights "at their place of employment." Overall, this was a powerful package of procedural measures to enforce the right of equal pay.

By way of comparison, the Equal Pay Act of 1963 (EPA), 29 U.S.C.A. § 206(d)(1), forbids any sex-based discrimination as to pay within the same establishment "for equal work on jobs the performance of which requires equal skill, effort and responsibility, and which are performed under similar working conditions." The EPA permits exceptions based on seniority, merit, or objective factors other than sex.

The 1975 directive's inclusion of "work of equal value" was incorporated into the Treaty of Amsterdam's comprehensive ECT Article 141 in its initial paragraphs on equal pay. The text is:

ECT Article 141 (Now TFEU Article 157)

1. Each Member State shall ensure that the application of the principle of equal pay for male and female workers for equal work or work of equal value is applied.

2. For the purpose of this Article, "pay" means the ordinary basic or minimum wage or salary and any other consideration, whether in cash or in kind, which the worker receives, directly or indirectly, in respect of his employment from his employer.

Equal pay without discrimination based on sex means:

(a) that pay for the same work at piece rates shall be calculated on the basis of the same unit of measurement;

(b) that pay for work at time rates shall be the same for the same job.

The 1975 directive itself has been repealed, because its substantive provisions were incorporated into the comprehensive Directive 2006/54,

O.J. L 204/23 (July 26, 2006), which covers equal treatment as well as equal pay. See section C4 infra.

The Court of Justice has often had occasion to apply the Treaty provisions, supplemented by the 1975 directive, in cases continuing to the present. Note that most of the cases have come via preliminary references from courts in Denmark, Germany, the Netherlands and the UK. This presumably reflects a more vigorous enforcement of the directive by the courts and women's rights groups in those States, not more rampant discrimination.

There is no doubt that women's pay overall has significantly increased due to the Treaty articles, the directive, and the liberal Court judgments we will be examining. Nonetheless statistics in 2008 still indicate that women's gross hourly earnings average only about 82% of that of men in the EU (roughly parallel to OECD statistics on US pay levels). This is certainly in part due to traditional stereotypes and behavioral patterns, but also due to the fact that women are heavily employed in low-paying employment sectors (teachers, health care, cleaning services) and represent the great majority of part-time employees.

Before going any further, we should note that the 1975 equal pay directive and Court judgments broadly define what constitutes "pay." It includes base salary, overtime, bonuses and any consideration "in kind." How would you treat commissions based on sales? Christmas or holiday gifts?

Does it include indirect forms of remuneration? In Garland v. British Rail Engineering Ltd., Case 12/81, [1982] ECR 359, the Court held that free or reduced fares given to retired male employees of a railroad constituted a form of pay. The Court defined "pay" as "consideration, whether cash or in kind, whether immediate or future, provided that the worker receives it, albeit indirectly, in respect of his employment from his employer." Id. at 369. The fact that the employer gratuitously provided the lower rail fares did not remove the benefit from the category of pay.

More important is the Court's decision in *Bilka–Kaufhaus*, excerpted below, that an employer's private pension plan (as opposed to state social security) constitutes pay. The Court held an "occupational pension scheme" to be an "integral part of the contracts of employment," noting that it had been in part agreed upon in negotiations with employee representatives.

2. INDIRECT DISCRIMINATION

As we just noted, the Court judgment in *Defrenne* limited EECT Article 119's direct effect to cases of "direct and overt discrimination." The Court soon had to reconsider its initial view.

Most part-time workers are women. Part-time workers are usually paid less, proportionately, than full-time employees. Should lower pay for part-time workers constitute indirect discrimination against female employees? Are part-time workers less valuable to the employer? More exploitable? If there is a salary differential for part-time workers, might it reflect an employer's bias against women, rather than merely more bargaining power in dealing with those individuals who are less flexible in their work hours?

BILKA–KAUFHAUS GmbH v. VON HARTZ

Case 170/84, [1986] ECR 1607.

[The Bilka department store chain provided an occupational (employer's private) pension plan to its full-time employees. Part-time employees were allowed to benefit from the plan only if they had previously worked full-time for 15 years. Ms. von Hartz, a part-time employee, sued for a pension, claiming the plan terms constituted sex discrimination because most part-time employees were women. On appeal, the German Supreme Labor Court referred several questions to the Court of Justice.]

29 If ... it should be found that a much lower proportion of women than of men work full-time, the exclusion of part-time workers from the occupational pension scheme would be contrary to Article 119 of the Treaty where, taking into account the difficulties encountered by women workers in working full-time, that measure could not be explained by factors which exclude any discrimination on grounds of sex.

30 However, if the undertaking is able to show that its pay practice may be explained by objectively justified factors unrelated to any discrimination on grounds of sex there is no breach of Article 119. * * *

33 Bilka argues that the exclusion of part-time workers from the occupational pension scheme is intended solely to discourage part-time work, since in general part-time workers refuse to work in the late afternoon and on Saturdays. In order to ensure the presence of an adequate workforce during those periods it was therefore necessary to make full-time work more attractive than part-time work, by making the occupational pension scheme open only to full-time workers. Bilka concludes that * * * it cannot be accused of having infringed Article 119. * * *

35 ... If the national court finds that the measures chosen by Bilka correspond to a real need on the part of the undertaking, are appropriate with a view to achieving the objectives pursued and are necessary to that end, the fact that the measures affect a far greater number of women than men is not sufficient to show that they constitute an infringement of Article 119.

NOTES AND QUESTIONS

1. The Court's first judgment concerning part-time employers came in Jenkins v. Kingsgate (Clothing Productions), Case 96/80, [1981] ECR 911.

Kingsgate employed roughly parallel numbers of men and women full-time, but five women and one man part-time. Kingsgate paid the part-time workers 90% of the full-time hourly rate. When sued by a part-time woman employee, Kingsgate argued that the differential was justified to encourage greater productivity by workers and to ensure maximum operating time for its expensive machinery. Answering questions referred to it, the Court of Justice held that paying part-time workers less than full-time workers did not represent discrimination so long as the differential was "objectively justified and . . . in no way related to discrimination based on sex" (¶ 11). Do you consider that Kingsgate's arguments show an objective justification?

2. In *Bilka,* the Court shifted the burden of proof: it is the employer who must show "objectively justified economic grounds" to warrant the poorer treatment of part-time employees when a majority are women. In practice, how significant is such a shift?

3. Note Bilka's arguments to justify the higher pay to full-time workers. Bilka also observed that women received 81% of all pensions, even though only 72% of employees were women. The German Supreme Labor Court expressed the view that "in the department store sector there are no reasons of commercial expediency" to necessitate inferior treatment of part-time workers. How would you decide the case on the merits?

4. Compare Corning Glass Works v. Brennan, 417 U.S. 188, 94 S.Ct. 2223, 41 L.Ed.2d 1 (1974), in which the Department of Labor sued Corning because it paid night shift product inspectors more than day shift product inspectors. All day shift inspectors were women, while most night shift inspectors were men. Although the Equal Pay Act was silent as to burden of proof, the Supreme Court held that the employer had the burden of showing objective factors that would justify a pay differential. Since Corning could not show that night work was more difficult or hazardous, the female day inspectors had to be paid the same wages as the night inspectors.

5. A German law requires employers to pay sick pay to employees temporarily unable to work, but states that sick pay is not required for those who do not work 10 hours per week. The majority of German part-time workers are women. Is the German law compatible with ECT Article 119? See Rinner–Kühn v. FWW S–G GmbH, Case 171/88, [1989] ECR 2743. Should mostly female part-time workers be entitled pro tanto to a Christmas bonus given gratuitously by employers to mostly male full-time workers, pursuant to a collective bargaining agreement? See Kruger v. Kreiskrankenhaus Ebersberg, Case C–281/97, [1999] ECR I–5127.

UNION OF COMMERCIAL AND CLERICAL EMPLOYEES v. DANISH EMPLOYERS' ASSOCIATION EX PARTE DANFOSS

Case 109/88, [1989] ECR 3199.

[Pursuant to a collective bargaining agreement, Danfoss paid salary supplements to base pay, calculated on factors such as mobility, special training and length of service. The average wage paid to men was 6.85% higher than that paid to women. When the union claimed sex discrimination, the Danish Industrial Arbitration Board asked the Court of Justice whether the use of such criteria in calculating pay violated EECT Article 119 or the Equal Pay Directive.

Danfoss made the strained argument that "mobility" really meant overall quality. The Court first held that, where a pay system results in a male/female differential and the reasons for the difference are not transparent, the employer has the burden to prove that the system is not discriminatory. It then said:]

19   ... [A] distinction must be made according to whether the criterion of mobility is employed to reward the quality of work done by the employee or is used to reward the employee's adaptability to variable hours and varying places of work.

20   In the first case the criterion of mobility is undoubtedly wholly neutral from the point of view of sex. Where it systematically works to the disadvantage of women that can only be because the employer has misapplied it. It is inconceivable that the quality of work done by women should generally be less good. The employer cannot therefore justify applying the criterion of mobility, so understood, where its application proves to work systematically to the disadvantage of women.

21   [If mobility] is understood as covering the employee's adaptability to variable hours and varying places of work, the criterion of mobility may also work to the disadvantage of female employees, who, because of household and family duties for which they are frequently responsible, are not as able as men to organize their working time flexibly.

22   ... The employer may [nonetheless] justify the remuneration of such adaptability by showing it is of importance for the performance of specific tasks entrusted to the employee.

23   [A]s regards the criterion of training, it is not to be excluded that it may work to the disadvantage of women in so far as they have had less opportunity than men for training or have taken less advantage of such opportunity. Nevertheless, * * * the employer may justify remuneration of special training by showing that it is of importance for the performance of specific tasks entrusted to the employee.

24   [A]s regards the criterion of length of service, it is also not to be excluded, as with training, that it may involve less advantageous treatment of women than of men in so far as women have entered the labour market more recently than men or more frequently suffer an interruption of their career. Nevertheless, since length of service goes hand in hand with experience and since experience generally enables the employee to perform his duties better, the employer is free to reward it without having to establish the importance it has in the performance of specific tasks entrusted to the employee.

NOTES AND QUESTIONS

1. If the factor of mobility connotes an employee's ability and willingness to work overtime or to travel, may an employer reward male employees for this characteristic when female employees may be hampered by family obligations? Contrast Shultz v. Wheaton Glass Co., 421 F.2d 259 (3d Cir. 1970), where the court refused to accept an employer's claim that male packers could be paid more on a factor of "flexibility" when male workers could occasionally work as handymen, while female packers did not do so.

2. Do you agree with the Court's conclusion that supplemental pay for special training can be objectively justified, and that credit for length of service is automatically justified? Note that the Equal Pay Act allows higher pay for employees with greater seniority. Moreover, in Balmer v. HCA, 423 F. 3d 606 (6th Cir. 2005), the Circuit Court held that male workers can receive higher renumeration if based upon higher education or work experience.

3. The Court's decision in *Danfoss* on burden of proof has been formalized in Council Directive 97/80/EC of 15 December 1997 on the burden of proof in cases of discrimination based on sex, now repealed and incorporated in Directive 2006/54, infra section C4. The Burden of Proof Directive introduced a definition of "indirect discrimination": "where an apparently neutral provision, criterion or practice disadvantages a substantially higher proportion of the members of one sex unless that provision, criterion or practice is appropriate and necessary and can be justified by objective factors unrelated to sex."

4. Statistics can provide some evidence of discrimination. When comparing statistics regarding one sex with statistics regarding the other in any given employment scenario, what difference in ratio makes the statistics persuasive evidence? See R v. Secretary of State, ex parte Seymour Smith and Perez, Case C–167/97 [1999] ECR I–623, where the Court held that the statistics must be "valid," covering a sufficient number to be significant, and not "fortuitous or short-term" (¶ 62). Although a plaintiff is not required to introduce statistical evidence in order to succeed in a claim of indirect discrimination, it is obviously helpful to do so.

3. DETERMINING WORK OF "EQUAL VALUE"

Undoubtedly the most difficult issue the Court must examine is what constitutes work of "equal value" under the 1975 directive and ECT Article 141(1) (now TFEU Article 157(1)). The issue first arose in cases concerning the application of job classification systems.

In Commission v. United Kingdom (Equal pay directive), Case 61/81, [1982] ECR 2601, the Commission brought a Treaty infringement proceeding for deficiencies in the UK's implementation of the 1975 directive. The UK law allowed employees to claim equal pay for "work to which equal value is attributed" only if the employer had a job classification system which permitted comparisons by the nature of the work. The UK maintained that a job classification system was a prerequisite to any resolution of disputes and that "the criterion of work of equal value is too abstract to be applied by the courts." The Court of Justice held:

> The Court cannot endorse that view. The implementation of the directive implies that the assessment of the "equal value" to be "attributed" to particular work, may be effected notwithstanding the employer's wishes, if necessary in the context of adversary proceedings. The Member States must endow an authority with the requisite jurisdiction to decide whether work has the same value as other work, after obtaining such information as may be required. Id. at 2617.

Subsequently, in Rummler v. Dato–Druck GmbH, Case 237/85, [1986] ECR 2101, the Court of Justice was asked to appraise a job classification system in the printing industry which permitted higher pay for jobs involving more muscular effort (usually performed by men). The Court held that article 1 of the 1975 directive required that a job classification system "must not be organized, as a whole, in such a manner that it has the practical effect of discriminating generally against workers of one sex." Id. at 2114. Hence, if muscular capacity is considered, then the classification must also consider "other criteria in relation to which women workers may have a particular aptitude." Id. at 2115. What might be examples of such "other criteria"?

US federal courts have authoritatively concluded that the Equal Pay Act and Title VII of the Civil Rights Act do not require employers to make a "comparable worth" evaluation of different job categories, and correspondingly raise the pay of job categories in which women predominate. Employers can justify lower pay to certain job categories by relying upon prevailing external job market pay scales. Spaulding v. University of Washington, 740 F.2d 686 (9th Cir.1984) (female nursing faculty need not be compared with male architecture or pharmacy faculty); Christensen v. State of Iowa, 563 F.2d 353 (8th Cir.1977) (female secretaries need not be compared with male physical plant employees). Only if the employer makes a comparison of the different job categories may relief be granted. Thus, in County of Washington v. Gunther, 452 U.S. 161, 101 S.Ct. 2242, 68 L.Ed.2d 751 (1981), female jail guards sued because they were paid 70% of the male jail guards' salary. The Supreme Court held that, even though there were objective differences in the work performed by male and female guards, the county could not pay the female guards less than what the county itself estimated their work was objectively worth. (Plaintiffs claimed the county had estimated their worth at 95% of the male guards' worth.)

In contrast, in Canada, whose Human Rights Act requires "equal pay for equal value," in a 1999 settlement the Canadian government agreed to pay $2.3 billion dollars to 230,000 present and former female workers in a settlement of their claims. See Equity Case in Canada as Redress for Women, N.Y. Times (Nov. 19, 1999).

The Court of Justice had to directly confront the issue of what constitutes work of "equal value" in the following prominent case.

ENDERBY v. FRENCHAY HEALTH AUTHORITY

Case C–127/92, [1993] ECR I–5535.

[In 1986, Enderby, a speech therapist, sued her employer, a unit within the United Kingdom National Health Service, claiming pay discrimination based on sex. She submitted evidence that senior level pharmacists were paid approximately 40% more than senior level speech therapists, and that the former profession was composed predominantly of men at the senior level, while speech therapists were overwhelmingly women. Before assessing the qualifications required in the two professions, the UK Court of Appeal asked the Court of Justice: 1) who should bear the burden of proof when the plaintiff claims that two different job categories constitute work of "equal value;" 2) whether the use of collective bargaining to set the pay scales for different job categories serves as an objective justification for any difference in pay level; and 3) whether job market factors may justify, in whole or in part, pay scale differences between job categories found to have "equal value."]

13　It is normally for the person alleging facts in support of a claim to adduce proof of such facts. Thus, in principle, the burden of proving the existence of sex discrimination as to pay lies with the worker who * * * brings legal proceedings against his employer with a view to removing the discrimination.

14　However, ... the onus may shift when that is necessary to avoid depriving workers who appear to be the victims of discrimination of any effective means of enforcing the principle of equal pay.

15　In this case, * * * there can be no complaint that the employer has applied a system of pay wholly lacking in transparency since the rates of pay of NHS speech therapists and pharmacists are decided by regular collective bargaining processes in which there is no evidence of discrimination as regards either of those two professions.

16　However, if the pay of speech therapists is significantly lower than that of pharmacists and if the former are almost exclusively women while the latter are predominantly men, there is a *prima facie* case of sex discrimination, at least where the two jobs in question are of equal value and the statistics describing that situation are valid.

17　It is for the national court to assess whether it may take into account those statistics, that is to say, whether they cover enough individuals, whether they illustrate purely fortuitous or short-term phenomena, and whether, in general, they appear to be significant.

18　Where there is a *prima facie* case of discrimination, it is for the employer to show that there are objective reasons for the difference in pay. Workers would be unable to enforce the principle of equal pay before national courts if evidence of a *prima facie* case of discrimination did not shift to the employer the onus of showing that the pay differential is not in fact discriminatory (see, by analogy, *Danfoss*).

19 [Therefore,] where significant statistics disclose an appreciable difference in pay between two jobs of equal value, one of which is carried out almost exclusively by women and the other predominantly by men, Art. 119 of the treaty requires the employer to show that the difference is based on objectively justified factors unrelated to any discrimination on grounds of sex.

20 In its second question, the Court of Appeal wishes to know whether the employer can rely, as sufficient justification for the difference in pay, upon the fact that the rates of pay of the jobs in question were decided by collective bargaining processes which, . . . considered separately, have no discriminatory effect.

21 As is clear from art. 4 of Council Directive 75/117, collective agreements, like laws, regulations or administrative provisions, must observe the principle enshrined in art. 119 of the treaty.

22 The fact that the rates of pay at issue are decided by collective bargaining processes conducted separately for each of the two professional groups concerned, without any discriminatory effect within each group, does not preclude a finding of *prima facie* discrimination where the results of those processes show that two groups with the same employer and the same trade union are treated differently.

24 In its third question, the Court of Appeal wishes to know to what extent—wholly, in part or not at all—the fact that part of the difference in pay is attributable to a shortage of candidates for one job and to the need to attract them by higher salaries can objectively justify that pay differential.

25 [I]t is for the national court, which has sole jurisdiction to make findings of fact, to determine whether and to what extent the grounds put forward by an employer to explain the adoption of a pay practice which applies independently of a worker's sex but in fact affects more women than men, may be regarded as objectively justified economic grounds (*Bilka–Kaufhaus*). Those grounds may include, if they can be attributed to the needs and objectives of the undertaking, different criteria such as the worker's flexibility or adaptability to hours and places of work, his training or his length of service (*Danfoss*).

26 The state of the employment market, which may lead an employer to increase the pay of a particular job in order to attract candidates, may constitute an objectively justified economic ground within the meaning of the case law cited above.

27 If . . . the national court has been able to determine precisely what proportion of the increase in pay is attributable to market forces, it must necessarily accept that the pay differential is objectively justified to the extent of that proportion. When national authorities have to apply Community law, they must apply the principle of proportionality.

NOTES AND QUESTIONS

1. Rather curiously, the "equal work" comparison was made only as between senior level pharmacists and speech therapists. In fact, no issue was raised concerning any differential in pay levels for all speech therapists, 98% women, and pharmacists, 63% women. This may be why the Court in ¶ 17 instructed the referring court to examine further whether the statistics were truly significant. Moreover, the Court never directly held that the two professions provide work of "equal value", but only that the employer has the burden of proof of demonstrating that they do not perform work of "equal value" (¶¶ 14–16).

2. Why isn't the setting of pay scales for different job categories by collective bargaining a solid defense for the employer? To what extent should market factors justify an employer's setting of different pay scales in different job categories? See ¶ 26. Does *Enderby* open floodgates, or can the employer almost always contend that "the market made me do it"? What is the point of ¶ 27?

3. In Angestelltenbetriebsrat v. Wiener Gebiets Krankenkasse, C–309/97, [1999] ECR I–5127, the Court held that the Vienna Health Fund could legitimately pay psychiatrists (medical doctors with specialized training), mostly men, considerably more than psychologists and psychotherapists, mostly women, because of the different training and possible different duties or tasks of the different groups (¶¶ 20–21). Would you agree? Note also in Specialarbejderforbundet v. Dansk Industri (Royal Copenhagen), Case C–400/93, [1995] ECR I–1275, the Court held that a large Danish ceramic producer which employed 1,150 workers producing different types of ceramics could pay certain groups of artisans more if they produced larger quantities of specific types of ceramics, so long as the higher paid groups were not arbitrarily composed principally of men.

Enderby's impact was considerably reduced when the Court had to decide whether work could be considered to have "equal value" if performed for different employers.

LAWRENCE v. REGENT OFFICE CARE

Case C–320/00, [2002] ECR I–7325.

[Employees, mostly women, employed by the North Yorkshire County Council sued for equal pay levels with the employees, mostly men, employed as gardeners and garbage collectors. The plaintiffs won their case after a House of Lords decision concluded that a national job evaluation study in 1987 determined that the different work categories should have equal value. While this legal action was in course, the County Council decided to turn over some cleaning and catering services to private employers. Because these employers paid the women cleaning and catering employees less than the Council had paid, they sued for pay equal to that of the Council's gardeners and garbage collectors. When the plaintiffs appealed an adverse Employment Tribunal decision, the Court of Appeal made a preliminary reference to the Court.]

15 Three features distinguish the present case. First, the persons whose pay is being compared work for different employers, that is to say, on the one hand, the Council and, on the other, the [defendant private] undertakings. Second, the work which the appellants perform for those undertakings is identical to that which some of them performed for the Council before the transfer of undertakings. Finally, that work has been recognised as being of equal value to that performed by the chosen comparators employed by the Council and continues to be so recognised.

17 There is * * * nothing in the wording of Article 141(1) EC to suggest that the applicability of that provision is limited to situations in which men and women work for the same employer. The Court has held that the principle established by that article may be invoked before national courts, in particular in cases of discrimination arising directly from legislative provisions or collective labour agreements, as well as in cases in which work is carried out in the same establishment or service, whether private or public.

18 However, where, as in the main proceedings here, the differences identified in the pay conditions of workers performing equal work or work of equal value cannot be attributed to a single source, there is no body which is responsible for the inequality and which could restore equal treatment. Such a situation does not come within the scope of Article 141(1) EC. The work and the pay of those workers cannot therefore be compared on the basis of that provision.

NOTES AND QUESTIONS

1. Note that the Court is here interpreting ECT Article 141, not the 1975 directive, giving the judgment greater force. Pursuant to ¶ 18, an action claiming that two job categories or professions perform work of equal value can not succeed when the comparison is sought to be made between employees of different employers. The Court does enable suits that might conceivably succeed when the discriminatory pay occurs due to a legislative measure or a collective bargaining agreement (¶ 16), which will certainly have considerable impact.

C. EQUAL TREATMENT FOR WOMEN AND MEN

1. THE EQUAL TREATMENT DIRECTIVES

Defrenne also sued Sabena for damages for discriminatory dismissal. Sabena's policy was to require flight hostesses to retire at age 40, while allowing flight stewards to work beyond that age. When the Belgian Supreme Court asked the Court of Justice whether Defrenne might have a remedy under EECT Article 119, unfortunately for Defrenne, the Court replied that the article covered only discrimination as to pay, not other types of employment discrimination, even when they might have pecuniary consequences. Defrenne v. Sabena, Case 149/77, [1978] ECR 1365.

To provide remedies in circumstances like those of Defrenne, the Council adopted Directive 76/207 on equal treatment for men and women in employment, O.J. L 39/40 (Feb. 14, 1976), Document 36 in the Selected Documents. The Council used EECT Article 235, at the time the "elastic clause" grant of legislative power (now TFEU Article 352), to adopt it by unanimous vote.

Article 1 of the 1976 directive established the principle of equal treatment in hiring, promotion, all working conditions, and vocational training. Article 2(1) prohibited not only direct discrimination on the basis of sex, but also indirect discrimination by reference to "marital or family status."

Article 2 made an exception for three types of discrimination. Two are for the benefit of women: article 2(3) permitted protective treatment "as regards pregnancy and maternity"; and 2(4) permitted "measures to promote equal opportunity ... by removing existing inequalities" (i.e., permitting remedial affirmative action policies). In contrast, Article 2(2) allowed Member States to permit discrimination in "occupational activities" for which workers of only one sex are appropriate. The rest of the Equal Treatment Directive's provisions replicated those of the Equal Pay Directive: Member States must review and reform their own laws and practices, police collective bargaining agreements and individual employment contracts, and introduce systems of judicial recourse (arts. 3–7).

In 2002, the initial Equal Treatment Directive was amended by Directive 2002/73, O.J.L 269/1 (Oct. 5, 2002). Its most important innovation was to prohibit sexual harassment and other forms of harassment during employment or vocational training. A detailed definition of harassment included violation of personal dignity and "creating an intimidating, hostile, degrading, humiliating or offensive environment." Amendments also made more precise the exceptions in article 2 of the 1976 directive, in part to correspond to Court of Justice interpretation. We will refer to these below. The amendments also imposed an obligation on States to carry out gender equality main-streaming policies, described at the start of this chapter, and to impose "effective, proportionate and dissuasive sanctions" for violations of directive provisions. The amended Equal Treatment Directive was repealed and replaced by the comprehensive Directive 2006/54, which retained and slightly improved its substantive provisions. See section C4. For a recent review, see C. Costello & G. Davies, The Case Law of the Court of Justice in the Field of Sex Equality since 2000, 43 Common Mkt. L. Rev. 1567 (2006).

Directive 86/613 O.J. L 359/56 (Dec. 19, 1986), supplemented the Equal Treatment Directive by extending the principle of equal treatment to the self-employed, notably those engaged in business, farming and the professions. Thus, for example, women partners in a commercial, accounting or law partnership are guaranteed rights of equal treatment. The directive has never been the subject of Court of Justice caselaw, and its practical impact is uncertain.

The US analogue to the Equal Treatment Directive is Title VII of the Civil Rights Act 1964, which covers not only discrimination in compensation but also in hiring, dismissal and the "terms, conditions or privileges of employment." It specifically permits "different terms, conditions or privileges of employment" based upon a "bonafide seniority or merit system" or earnings calculated "by quantity or quality of production." Title VII prohibits discriminatory conduct only by employers. It does not parallel the 1986 directive on equal treatment for the self-employed.

2. SCOPE AND APPLICATION OF THE EQUAL TREATMENT DIRECTIVE

An obvious initial issue is whether it covers all employees in all sectors. In Commission v. United Kingdom (Equal treatment directive), Case 165/82, [1983] ECR 3431, the Court held that the UK improperly implemented the 1976 Equal Treatment Directive because it did not forbid discriminatory provisions in collective bargaining agreements and because it created an exception for businesses employing less than five persons, and for private households. As the Court noted, private households can take advantage of the "occupational activity" exception. (Can employers require butlers to be men or women's maids to be women?) Contrast this judgment with Title VII § 701(6), which excludes employers with fewer than 15 employees from the requirements of Title VII. Has the EU gone too far in trying to regulate conduct in small businesses, or has the United States not gone far enough?

Should the basic non-discrimination provision of the directive have vertical direct effect? The leading Court judgment in *Marshall*, supra page 264, held that it does insofar as the State itself is the employer in a public service capacity (the defendant in *Marshall* was the UK public health service). Should vertical direct effect apply when the State-owned entity does not provide a public service? Where should the line be drawn? In Foster v. British Gas PLC, Case C–188/89, [1990] ECR I–3313, 3348–49, the Court provided some guidance, although courts may still have difficulties in applying it:

> [A] body, whatever its legal form, which has been made responsible, pursuant to a measure adopted by the state, for providing a public service under the control of the state and has for that purpose special powers beyond those which result from the normal rules applicable in relations between individuals is included in any event among the bodies against which the provisions of a directive capable of having direct effect may be relied upon.

Finally, another important issue concerning the scope of the Equal Treatment Directive was whether it forbid discrimination against transsexuals and homosexuals.

P v. S

Case C–13/94, [1996] ECR I–2143.

[P, a manager in a UK state educational establishment, underwent surgery to achieve a gender reassignment. Following the operation, P "dressed and behaved as a woman." S, the general manager, dismissed P on this ground only. P sued, claiming a violation of the UK Sex Discrimination Act, intended to implement the 1976 Equal Treatment Directive. The Industrial Tribunal, noting that the UK civil register did not permit a change of a person's gender identification, referred questions to the Court as to the possible application of the Equal Treatment Directive.]

16   The European Court of Human Rights has held that 'the term "transsexual" is usually applied to those who, whilst belonging physically to one sex, feel convinced that they belong to the other; they often seek to achieve a more integrated, unambiguous identity by undergoing medical treatment and surgical operations to adapt their physical characteristics to their psychological nature. Transsexuals who have been operated upon thus form a fairly well-defined and identifiable group'.

17   The principle of equal treatment 'for men and women' * * * means, as Articles 2(1) and 3(1) in particular indicate, that there should be 'no discrimination whatsoever on grounds of sex'.

* * *

19   Moreover, * * * the right not to be discriminated against on grounds of sex is one of the fundamental human rights whose observance the Court has a duty to ensure.

20   Accordingly, the scope of the directive cannot be confined simply to discrimination based on the fact that a person is of one or other sex. In view of its purpose and the nature of the rights which it seeks to safeguard, the scope of the directive is also such as to apply to discrimination arising * * * from the gender reassignment of the person concerned.

21   Such discrimination is based, essentially if not exclusively, on the sex of the person concerned. Where a person is dismissed on the ground that he or she intends to undergo, or has undergone, gender reassignment, he or she is treated unfavourably by comparison with persons of the sex to which he or she was deemed to belong before undergoing gender reassignment.

22   To tolerate such discrimination would be tantamount, as regards such a person, to a failure to respect the dignity and freedom to which he or she is entitled, and which the Court has a duty to safeguard.

* * *

24   [Accordingly,] in view of the objective pursued by the directive, Article 5(1) of the directive precludes dismissal of a transsexual for a reason related to a gender reassignment.

1. The Court was undoubtedly influenced by the carefully reasoned opinion of Advocate General Tesauro. He discussed the caselaw of the European Court of Human Rights, notably the 1992 judgment, B v. France, in which France was required to change the civil status of a transsexual. He also relied upon evolving social views in the treatment of transsexuals in most Member States, citing especially the statutory permission in Germany, the Netherlands and Sweden for a change in the civil register to accord with the new sexual identity. Advocate General Tesauro urged the Court to take a "courageous decision"; one in accord with "social justice."

2. *P v. S* attracted wide, and decidedly mixed, media attention. A useful casenote is L. Flynn, P v. S, 34 Common Mkt. L. Rev. 367 (1997). The chief point of speculation was whether the Court's language was broad enough to cover discrimination against homosexuals generally, and not merely the much smaller group of transsexuals.

When the issue came to the Court in Grant v. South–West Trains, Case C–249/96 [1998] ECR I–621, the Court, not surprisingly, held that this went too far. Grant, a lesbian employed by a UK state railway, claimed sex discrimination in violation of the Equal Pay Directive for refusal to provide fringe benefits for her woman partner when such benefits were accorded to spouses and to persons of the opposite sex with whom an employee had a stable relationship outside of marriage. The Court initially held that under prevailing Member State law, "stable relationships between two persons of the same sex are not regarded as equivalent to marriage," so that employers need not give benefits to same sex partners that they accord to spouses (¶ 35). The Court then held that *P v. S* was limited to gender reassignment, and did not prevent "differences of treatment based on sexual orientation" (¶ 42). The Court specifically noted that the Treaty of Amsterdam, then in the process of ratification, authorized the Council to adopt measures prohibiting discrimination, i.a., on the ground of sexual orientation (¶ 48). As we shall see in section E, the Council has done this in the field of employment.

3. "OCCUPATIONAL ACTIVITIES" SUITABLE FOR ONLY ONE SEX

We turn now to the exceptions expressly stated in Article 2 of the 1976 Equal Treatment Directive. Article 2(2) permits discriminatory treatment for "occupational activities ... for which, by reason of their nature or the context in which they are carried out, the sex of the worker constitutes a determining factor." The 2002 amending directive adds that the determining factor must be "legitimate" and applied proportionately. The US parallel is the exception in Title VII § 703(e)(1) for a "bona fide occupational qualification reasonably necessary to the normal operation of that particular business."

It is common sense to exclude one or the other sex from a few occupational activities. Men usually sell men's suits and women usually sell women's clothes, although that is compulsory only when physical contact is required. Valets are men and nursemaids are women. In contrast, in modern society, women can be police officers, fire fighters, coal miners and construction workers. Do you think that employers tend to exaggerate real difficulties and create imaginary ones in trying to justify single-sex occupations?

JOHNSTON v. CHIEF CONSTABLE OF THE ROYAL ULSTER CONSTABULARY

Case 222/84, [1986] ECR 1651.

[In view of violent civil disorder in Northern Ireland, male police officers of the Royal Ulster Constabulary (RUC) were required to carry arms. Fifty-nine police officers died as assassination targets in the 1970s. In 1980, the RUC concluded that women police officers should not bear arms for various reasons, including a concern that they might then become assassination targets. The number of policewomen was reduced because they were restricted to certain tasks only, such as family welfare work. Although Mrs. Johnston had served satisfactorily as a police officer for six years, her contract was not renewed because of the new RUC policy. Mrs. Johnston sued to require renewal of her contract. The Industrial Tribunal asked the Court of Justice to interpret articles 2(2) and 2(3) of the Equal Treatment Directive, and also queried whether public safety concerns in general could justify the RUC policy.]

Applicability of Directive to Measures Taken to Protect Public Safety

26   [T]he only articles in which the Treaty provides for derogations applicable in situations which may involve public safety are [ECT Articles 30, 39, 46, 55, 296 and 297]which deal with exceptional and clearly defined cases. Because of their limited character those articles do not lend themselves to a wide interpretation and it is not possible to infer from them that there is inherent in the Treaty a general proviso covering all measures taken for reasons of public safety. If every provision of Community law were held to be subject to a general proviso, regardless of the specific requirements laid down by the provisions of the Treaty, this might impair the binding nature of Community law and its uniform application.

27   It follows that the application of the principle of equal treatment for men and women is not subject to any general reservation as regards measures taken on grounds of the protection of public safety.... The facts which induced the competent authority to invoke the need to protect public safety must therefore if necessary be taken into consideration.... in the context of the application of the specific provisions of the directive.

* * *

Article 2(2) Occupational Context

34   [F]irst of all ..., in so far as the competent police authorities in Northern Ireland have decided, because of the requirements of public

safety, to depart from the principle, generally applied in other parts of the United Kingdom, of not arming the police in the ordinary course of their duties, that decision does not in itself involve any discrimination between men and women and is therefore outside the scope of the principle of equal treatment. It is only in so far as the Chief Constable decided that women would not be armed or trained in the use of fire-arms, that general policing duties would in future be carried out only by armed male officers and that contracts of women in the RUC full-time Reserve who, like Mrs. Johnston, had previously been entrusted with general policing duties, would not be renewed, that an appraisal of those measures in the light of [article 2(2)] of the directive is relevant. . . .

35   [T]he Chief Constable [adopted this policy] because he considered that if women were armed they might become a more frequent target for assassination and their fire-arms could fall into the hands of their assailants, that the public would not welcome the carrying of fire-arms by women, which would conflict too much with the ideal of an unarmed police force, and that armed policewomen would be less effective in police work in the social field with families and children in which the services of policewomen are particularly appreciated. [These reasons are] related to the special conditions in which the police must work in the situation existing in Northern Ireland, having regard to the requirements of the protection of public safety in a context of serious internal disturbances.

36   Article 2(2) of the directive, * * *, being a derogation from an individual right laid down in the directive, must be interpreted strictly. However, it must be recognized that the context in which the occupational activity of members of an armed police force are carried out is determined by the environment in which that activity is carried out. In this regard, the possibility cannot be excluded that in a situation characterized by serious internal disturbances the carrying of fire-arms by policewomen might create additional risks of their being assassinated and might therefore be contrary to the requirements of public safety.

37   In such circumstances, the context of certain policing activities may be such that the sex of police officers constitutes a determining factor for carrying them out. If that is so, a Member State may therefore restrict such tasks, and the training leading thereto, to men. In such a case, as is clear from Article 9(2) of the directive, the Member States have a duty to assess periodically the activities concerned in order to decide whether, in the light of social developments, the derogation from the general scheme of the directive may still be maintained.

38   [Moreover,] in determining the scope of any derogation from an individual right such as the equal treatment of men and women provided for by the directive, the principle of proportionality, one of the general principles of law underlying the Community legal order,

must be observed. That principle requires that derogations remain within the limits of what is appropriate and necessary for achieving the aim in view and requires the principle of equal treatment to be reconciled as far as possible with the requirements of public safety which constitute the decisive factor as regards the context of the activity in question.

39 [I]t is for the national court to say whether the reasons on which the Chief Constable based his decision are in fact well founded and justify the specific measure taken in Mrs. Johnston's case. It is also for the national court to ensure that the principle of proportionality is observed and to determine whether the refusal to renew Mrs. Johnston's contract could not be avoided by allocating to women duties which, without jeopardizing the aims pursued, can be performed without firearms.

* * *

Article 2(3): Protection of Women

44 [L]ike Article 2(2) of the directive, Article 2(3), which also determines the scope of Article 3(2)(c), must be interpreted strictly. It is clear from the express reference to pregnancy and maternity that the directive is intended to protect a woman's biological condition and the special relationship which exists between a woman and her child. That provision of the directive does not therefore allow women to be excluded from a certain type of employment on the ground that public opinion demands that women be given greater protection than men against risks which affect men and women in the same way and which are distinct from women's specific needs of protection * * *.

45 It does not appear that the risks and dangers to which women are exposed when performing their duties in the police force in a situation such as exists in Northern Ireland are different from those to which any man is also exposed when performing the same duties. A total exclusion of women from such an occupational activity which, owing to a general risk not specific to women, is imposed for reasons of public safety is not one of the differences in treatment that Article 2(3) of the directive allows out of a concern to protect women.

NOTES AND QUESTIONS

1. Why did the Court refuse to consider public safety as a generic derogation to the directive but admit public safety as a factor relevant to the scope of the "occupational activity" exception of article 2(2)?

2. In ¶ 35, the Court cites several reasons given by the RUC to justify its decision. Did the Court accept these reasons, or was it solely concerned with the risk that armed police women might be assassinated? If that is the Court's rationale, why are women allowed to assume life-threatening risks in other occupations, such as firefighters or mine workers? In its analysis of article

2(3), the Court rules out protection of women in general as a rationale for discrimination. Why does this reasoning not apply to article 2(2)?

3. Is this a 'political' decision? Suppose the Court had found public safety not admissible under article 2(2) to justify exclusion of women from police work in the social field. Might the Court have been influenced by a concern about the North Ireland government's response to a judgment disallowing the RUC's action?

4. *Johnston* is frequently also cited as a major precedent protecting the basic right of judicial review. A Northern Ireland order had purported to give conclusive effect to a certificate of the Secretary of State finding that sex discrimination was necessary to protect public safety. The Court of Justice held that such a provision is "contrary to the principle of effective judicial control laid down in Article 6 of the directive" (¶ 20).

5. In Commission v. Austria (Restrictions on women workers), Case C–203/03, [2005] ECR I–935, the Commission challenged Austria's prohibition of women workers in certain occupations due to health and safety risks. Do you think Austria can exclude women from underground mining or diving which requires pressure safety equipment?

6. The Supreme Court examined the issue whether states must allow women to serve as prison guards in an all-male prison in Dothard v. Rawlinson, 433 U.S. 321, 97 S.Ct. 2720, 53 L.Ed.2d 786 (1977). The Court held that Alabama could exclude women from serving as guards in male prisons because of the risk of sexual assault from aggressive prisoners and a general concern for prison security. The Court so concluded even though, as it held, the bona fide occupational qualification defense was meant to be a very narrow exception to the general anti-discrimination rule. Compare Commission v. France (Prison guards and police force), Case 318/86, [1988] ECR 3559. The Commission accepted that France could restrict guards in male prisons primarily to men and in female prisons primarily to women (¶ 12). As for the French national police force, which has accepted women since 1983, the Court agreed with the Commission that France had not made its rules indicating in which posts women could serve sufficiently transparent, and had not adequately recruited women police officers.

In United States v. Virginia, 518 U.S. 515, 116 S.Ct. 2264, 135 L.Ed.2d 735 (1996), the US Supreme Court held that Virginia's categorical exclusion of women from the Virginia Military Institute denied equal protection to women. A state defending gender-based action must demonstrate an "exceedingly persuasive justification." It must show that the classification serves important governmental objectives and that the means employed are substantially related to those objectives.

Women have traditionally been excluded from any combat role in military services. Several recent cases have issues connected to that exclusion.

KREIL v. FEDERAL REPUBLIC OF GERMANY
Case C–285/98 [2000] ECR I–69.

[Ms. Kreil, who was trained in electronics, applied for a position in the weapons electronics maintenance arm of the Federal German Army (Bundeswehr). Her application was rejected on grounds that the German Constitution prohibited women from holding any military post involving the use of arms. Pursuant to this constitutional provision, secondary legislation in Germany limited women's involvement in the military to medical and military-music services. Kreil brought proceedings in the German Administrative Court claiming that the rejection of her application on grounds based solely on sex was contrary to the 1976 Equal Treatment Directive.]

26　... [T]he refusal to engage the applicant in the main proceedings in the service of the Bundeswehr in which she wished to be employed was based on provisions of German law which bar women outright from military posts involving the use of arms and which allow women access only to the medical and military-music services.

27　In view of its scope, such an exclusion, which applies to almost all military posts in the Bundeswehr, cannot be regarded as a derogating measure justified by the specific nature of the posts in question or by the particular context in which the activities in question are carried out. However, the derogations provided for in Article 2(2) of the Directive can apply only to specific activities.

28　Moreover, having regard to the very nature of armed forces, the fact that persons serving in those forces may be called on to use arms cannot in itself justify the exclusion of women from access to military posts. As the German Government explained, in the services of the Bundeswehr that are accessible to women, basic training in the use of arms, to enable personnel in those services to defend themselves and to assist others, is provided.

29　[E]ven taking account of the discretion which they have as regards the possibility of maintaining the exclusion in question, the national authorities could not, without contravening the principle of proportionality, adopt the general position that the composition of all armed units in the Bundeswehr had to remain exclusively male.

30　Finally, as regards the possible application of Article 2(3) of the Directive, upon which the German Government also relies, this provision ... is intended to protect a woman's biological condition and the special relationship which exists between a woman and her child. It does not therefore allow women to be excluded from a certain type of employment on the ground that they should be given greater protection than men against risks which are distinct from women's specific needs of protection, such as those expressly mentioned.

32　The answer to be given to the question must therefore be that the Directive precludes the application of national provisions, such as those of German law, which impose a general exclusion of women from military posts involving the use of arms and which allow them access only to the medical and military-music services.

NOTES AND QUESTIONS

1.   Where in *Kreil* does the Court draw the line between permissible and impermissible derogations from equal treatment? Is the Court in *Kreil* in effect saying that women can serve in any German army operational unit, so long as it is not actually deployed in combat? May Germany bar women from serving in a peace-keeping operation? *Kreil* is a striking illustration of how the primacy of Union law can be a hard pill to swallow for a Member State.

2.   Shortly before *Kreil*, the Court decided Sirdar v. The Army Board, Case C–273/97, [1999] ECR I–7403, where the issue was whether the UK's Royal Marines may exclude women, even to serve as a chef. The Court accepted the UK's argument that the Royal Marines' military role properly required all marines to be ready and capable for combat as "front-line commandos," so that women could properly be excluded.

Not surprisingly, after *Kreil*, the Court of Justice soon had to evaluate a claim of reverse discrimination brought by a man who contended that Germany's law, based on a constitutional provision, requiring compulsory military service only for men violated the Equal Treatment Directive.

DORY v. BUNDESREPUBLIK DEUTSCHLAND

Case C–186/01, [2003] ECR I–2479.

[The Court first cited its conclusions in *Johnston* and *Kreil* that no Member State public safety or security exception limited the Equal Treatment Directive, so that the only issue was the interpretation of article 2's occupational activity derogation.]

35   Certainly, decisions of the Member States concerning the organisation of their armed forces cannot be completely excluded from the application of Community law, particularly where observance of the principle of equal treatment of men and women in connection with employment, including access to military posts, is concerned. But it does not follow that Community law governs the Member States' choices of military organisation for the defence of their territory or of their essential interests.

36   It is for the Member States, which have to adopt appropriate measures to ensure their internal and external security, to take decisions on the organisation of their armed forces, as the Court observed in *Sirdar* and *Kreil*.

37   The German Government submits that compulsory military service is of great importance in Germany, both politically and in terms of the organisation of the armed forces. It stated * * * that the institution of such service makes a contribution to the democratic transparency of the military, national integration, the link between the armed forces and the population, and the mobilisation of the manpower needed by the armed forces in the event of a conflict.

38   Such a choice, enshrined in the [German Constitution], consists in imposing an obligation to serve the interests of territorial security,

albeit in many cases to the detriment of access of young people to the labour market. It thus takes precedence over the objectives of policies aimed at the work prospects of young people.

39　The decision of the Federal Republic of Germany to ensure its defence in part by compulsory military service is the expression of such a choice of military organisation to which Community law is consequently not applicable.

40　It is true that limitation of compulsory military service to men will generally entail a delay in the progress of the careers of those concerned, even if military service allows some of them to acquire further vocational training or subsequently to take up a military career.

41　Nevertheless, the delay in the careers of persons called up for military service is an inevitable consequence of the choice made by the Member State regarding military organisation and does not mean that that choice comes within the scope of Community law. The existence of adverse consequences for access to employment cannot, without encroaching on the competences of the Member States, have the effect of compelling the Member State in question either to extend the obligation of military service to women, thus imposing on them the same disadvantages with regard to access to employment, or to abolish compulsory military service.

42　In the light of all the foregoing, the answer to the national court's question must be that Community law does not preclude compulsory military service being reserved to men.

4.　PROTECTION OF WOMEN, POSITIVE ACTION AND REVERSE DISCRIMINATION

To what extent can women be favored or protected in employment, either as a class, or when pregnant or caring for young children?

a.　The Scope for Positive (or Affirmative) Action

In the US, legislative or administrative measures intended to promote the interests of disadvantaged minorities are commonly called, 'affirmative action,' while in Europe the term 'positive action' is used. The measures are highly controversial in Europe as in the US. The Equal Treatment Directive's article 2(4) authorized Member State measures to promote equal opportunity for women and men by "removing existing inequalities which affect women's opportunities." This provision was considerably reinforced when the Treaty of Amsterdam introduced ECT Article 141(4) (now TFEU Article 157(4)):

> With a view to ensuring full equality in practice between men and women in working life, the principle of equal treatment shall not prevent any Member State from maintaining or adopting measures providing for specific advantages in order to make it easier for the

under-represented sex to pursue a vocational activity or to prevent or compensate for disadvantages in professional careers.

Note that the Treaty text authorizes measures providing "advantages," rather than the removal of "inequalities," and covers vocational training as well as employment. On the other hand, ECT Article 141(4) deliberately uses the term, "the under-represented sex," which would authorize measures benefitting men in some occupations. Discrimination against men, although rare, can occur. In Mississippi University for Women v. Hogan, 458 U.S. 718, 102 S.Ct. 3331, 73 L. Ed. 2d 1090 (1982) the Supreme Court held that a state vocational training school for nurses could not bar men from studies. Can you think of any other occupations in which men might be "under-represented" and qualify for positive action?

The initial Court of Justice cases naturally only concerned the application of the Equal Treatment Directive.

KALANKE v. FREIE HANSESTADT BREMEN
Case C–450/93, [1995] ECR I–3051.

[In 1990, the German state of Bremen adopted a regulation governing appointments or promotions to public administrative posts in any sector where women are under-represented, which is presumed to be the case if women do not make up at least half of the staff. The regulation provided that "women who have the same qualifications as men applying for the same post are to given priority" in the appointment or promotion involved. Kalanke, a male candidate for promotion to the post of manager in the Parks Department, sued to challenge the choice of an allegedly equally qualified female candidate for the post.

On appeal from the dismissal of his application, the German Supreme Labor Court asked the Court of Justice in a preliminary reference whether the priority thus given to women was in accord with article 2(4) of the Equal Treatment Directive. The German court noted its view that the Bremen rule was in accord with the German constitutional guarantee of equal treatment of the sexes because it did not constitute a strict quota of posts for women regardless of their qualifications. The Court of Justice easily concluded that the Bremen system represented "discrimination on grounds of sex" (¶ 16), and then turned to the harder question of its possible justification under article 2(4).]

18 That provision is specifically and exclusively designed to allow measures which, although discriminatory in appearance, are in fact intended to eliminate or reduce actual instances of inequality which may exist in the reality of social life.

19 It thus permits national measures relating to access to employment, including promotion, which give a specific advantage to women with a view to improving their ability to compete on the labour market and to pursue a career on an equal footing with men.

20   [The Court cited Council Recommendation 84/635/EEC on the promotion of positive action for women which urged governmental action "to counteract the prejudicial effects on women in employment which arise from social attitudes, behaviour and structures" (¶ 20).]

21   Nevertheless, as a derogation from an individual right laid down in the Directive Article 2(4) must be interpreted strictly.

22   National rules which guarantee women absolute and unconditional priority for appointment or promotion go beyond promoting equal opportunities and overstep the limits of the exception in Article 2(4) of the Directive.

23   Furthermore, in so far as it seeks to achieve equal representation of men and women in all grades and levels within a department, such a system substitutes for equality of opportunity as envisaged in Article 2(4) the result which is only to be arrived at by providing such equality of opportunity.

24   [Accordingly, the Directive] precludes national rules * * * which, where candidates of different sexes shortlisted for promotion are equally qualified, automatically give priority to women in sectors where they are under-represented, under-representation being deemed to exist when women do not make up at least half of the staff in the individual pay brackets in the relevant personnel group or in the function levels provided for in the organization chart.

NOTES AND QUESTIONS

1.   In *Kalanke*, Advocate General Tesauro discussed in detail various systems of positive action and cited the leading US cases. He contended that a State may appropriately adopt rules that favor women by eliminating customary barriers to their integration in their workforce, especially the difficulties confronted by working mothers, but concluded that the Bremen rule simply gave priority to women without removing any barriers and therefore could not fall under article 2(4). He noted that his view would be unpopular in some circles, even perhaps in the Parliament.

Indeed, the *Kalanke* judgment provoked a strong adverse reaction in Germany and got quite mixed media commentary elsewhere. See L. Senden, Positive Action in the EU Put to the Test, 3 Maastricht J. Eur. L. 1466 (1996), and the thoughtful casenote by S. Prechal, 33 Common Mkt. L. Rev. 1245 (1996).

2.   In Badeck v. Hessischer Ministerprasident, Case C–158/97, [2000] ECR I–1875, a German state law guaranteed women half the available enrollment places in training courses and half the interview slots for a variety of state employment posts in which women were underrepresented (i.e., constituted less than half of the staff). The Court held that this constituted appropriate action under the Directive's article 2(4). Would you agree? Do you find this an easier case than *Kalanke*?

3.   Perhaps concerned by the level of criticism of *Kalanke*, the Court accepted a German state measure that was considerably more nuanced than

that of Bremen. The regulation stated that in specific civil service brackets, whenever fewer women than men were employed, women should receive an appointment priority over men of equal competence and professional performance, unless in an objective assessment of all relevant criteria some that favored the man "tilted the balance." See Marschall v. Land Nordrhein Westfalen, Case C–409/97, [1997] ECR–I 6363. The Court did not consider the approach to represent the "absolute and unconditional priority" for women invalidated in *Kalanke*. Would you agree, or do you consider mere 'window dressing' to have changed the result?

Some observers considered *Marschall* to have implicitly overruled *Kalanke*. Then came the following case from Sweden, the first in which the new ECT Article 141(4) text was at stake.

ABRAHAMSSON AND ANDERSON v. FOGELQVIST

Case 407/98 [2000] ECR I–5539.

[In an effort to boost the number of female professors in certain universities, Sweden enacted a law adding 30 new professorships in 1995–96, and providing that in choosing the professors, "[a] candidate belonging to an under-represented sex who possesses sufficient qualifications ... must be granted preference over a candidate of the opposite sex who would otherwise have been chosen (positive discrimination) where it proves necessary to do so in order for a candidate of the under-represented sex to be appointed. Positive discrimination must, however, not be applied where the difference between the candidates' qualifications is so great that such application would give rise to a breach of the requirement of objectivity in making appointments." One such university post was offered to Ms. Fogelqvist, even though the selectors agreed that the plaintiff, Mr. Anderson, was more highly qualified.]

45   In contrast to the national legislation on positive discrimination examined by the Court in its *Kalanke, Marschall* and *Badeck* judgments, the national legislation at issue in the main proceedings enables preference to be given to a candidate of the under-represented sex who, although sufficiently qualified, does not possess qualifications equal to those of other candidates of the opposite sex.

* * *

52   It follows that the legislation at issue in the main proceedings automatically grants preference to candidates belonging to the under-represented sex, provided that they are sufficiently qualified, subject only to the proviso that the difference between the merits of the candidates of each sex is not so great as to result in a breach of the requirement of objectivity in making appointments.

53   The scope and effect of that condition cannot be precisely determined, with the result that the selection of a candidate from among those who are sufficiently qualified is ultimately based on the mere fact of belonging to the under-represented sex, and that this is so even if the

merits of the candidate so selected are inferior to those of a candidate of the opposite sex. Moreover, candidatures are not subjected to an objective assessment taking account of the specific personal situations of all the candidates. It follows that such a method of selection is not such as to be permitted by Article 2(4) of the Directive.

54   In those circumstances, it is necessary to determine whether legislation such as that at issue in the main proceedings is justified by Article 141(4) EC.

55   [E]ven though Article 141(4) EC allows the Member States to maintain or adopt measures providing for special advantages intended to prevent or compensate for disadvantages in professional careers in order to ensure full equality between men and women in professional life, it cannot be inferred from this that it allows a selection method of the kind at issue in the main proceedings which appears, on any view, to be disproportionate to the aim pursued.

NOTES AND QUESTIONS

1.   The Swedish government was trying to remedy the radical inequality between the number of men and women at the university rank of full professor. This is a serious problem throughout continental Europe, and has obvious repercussions for women students, who lack mentors and see a 'glass ceiling' in effect. It is hard to deny that Sweden went too far, but what other measure might be effective? Does *Badeck* provide any hints? Could Sweden provide research fellowships, study grants, writing leaves, etc. on a priority basis to younger women academics to help them achieve better professional credentials in order to be promoted to full professorships?

2.   *Abrahamsson* presented the Court with its first opportunity to interpret Article 141(4). Consider the following academic commentary: "The Court declined an opportunity to make a fresh start on positive action in Community law, but rather has woven Article 141(4)EC into the principles already established through its existing case law." L. Waddington and M. Bell, More Equal than Others: Distinguishing European Union Equality Directives, 38 Common Mkt.L.Rev. 587, 602 (2001).What is your view? Do you think the Court could have made a progressive "fresh start"?

3.   Positive action may also justify benefits granted only to women employees. In Lommers v. Minister van Landbouw, Case C–476/99, [2002] ECR I–2891, the Dutch Ministry of Agriculture operated a nursery service to take care of young children of its female employees. Only 25% of the Ministry's employees were women. When a male employee whose wife was employed elsewhere sought to place his child in the nursery, his request was denied. When he sued, the Ministry contended that the nursery benefit constituted positive action to eliminate inequality of women in employment. The Court initially held that providing such nursery care to the children of women employees only could be justified under article 2(4), because it enabled women employees to keep their jobs (¶ 37). The Court then held that the nursery's availability to women employees only was proportionate, because space was limited so that some women employees were on a waiting list (¶ 43).

The Court also noted that the nursery was available to male employees in cases of emergency (¶ 45). Do you agree with the Court's reasoning?

4. In Mouflin v. Recteur de l'Academie, Case C–206/00, [2001] ECR I–10201, the French civil service pension scheme for teachers permitted women to take an early retirement pension in order to cease work to care for a seriously ill or disabled husband. Should EECT Article 119 be interpreted to require that this pension also must be provided to a male teacher who seeks early retirement to care for his wife, suffering from an incurable illness?

5. On a comparative note, the Eleventh Circuit held in Danskine v. Miami Dade Fire Department, 253 F.3d 1288 (2001), that a county fire department could carry out an affirmative action program to recruit women firefighters in 1994–97, thereby increasing their number from 9 to 11.6% of the force. The court noted that the department had excluded women until around 1980, and that the complainants, applicant men not hired in 1994–97, had not proved that the women were not physically qualified to serve. However, the court finally observed that the affirmative action plan had to end at some point, and queried whether the department's goal of 36% women firefighters might be unrealistic.

Affirmative action in employment can be held to violate the Equal Protection Clause of the Constitution. In *Wygant v. Jackson Board of Education*, 476 U.S. 267, 106 S.Ct. 1842, 90 L.Ed.2d 260 (1986), a plurality of the Supreme Court declared that the school board could not constitutionally lay off white teachers with more seniority than minority teachers in order to retain a preexisting percentage of minority teachers, all in an attempt to correct for lack of cultural diversity, to remedy general societal discrimination, and to provide role models for minority school children. Rather, the employer must prove a specific link such as prior discrimination by the government unit involved, and the program must be narrowly tailored to serve the compelling government interest. This analytical model is called "strict scrutiny."

b. Measures to Protect Workers During Pregnancy and Maternity

The 1976 Equal Treatment Directive granted special protection to women during periods of pregnancy and maternity in order better to achieve genuine equality. Article 2(3) of the directive authorizes "provisions concerning the protection of women, particularly as regards pregnancy and maternity." As we saw in the prior chapter, Council Directive 92/85 on measures to encourage improvements in the safety and health at work of pregnant workers and workers who have recently given birth has substantially supplemented this by providing significant health and safety protection and social benefits.

As we have already seen in *Johnston*, the Court has held that article 2(3) does not authorize discriminatory forms of "protection" for women in general, but is limited to measures protecting women with regard to "pregnancy and maternity." As a consequence, the Commission challenged France's implementation of the 1976 directive because France specifically allowed collective bargaining agreements and individual enterprise rules and contracts to contain provisions benefitting only women. Commission v. France (Equal treatment for women and men), Case 312/86, [1988] ECR 6315. The Commission cited as examples a Mother's Day holiday, shorter work hours for women over 59, leave days for female employees when a child is ill or at the beginning of the school year, allowances to mothers to pay for nurseries or child attendants, and daily breaks for women telephone operators or typists.

The Court held that none of these protective measures was justified by article 2(4). Equally important, it construed article 2(3)'s protection of pregnancy and maternity to end within a reasonable period following childbirth, and held that article 2(3) should not be read expansively to cover child care because that is a responsibility of both parents. It would thus appear that if an employer is willing (or obliged by a collective agreement) to grant time off to care for a sick or injured child, or to pay an allowance for nursery or child care, either parent should have a right to claim the benefit.

A US parallel can be seen in Weinberger v. Wiesenfeld, 420 U.S. 636, 95 S.Ct. 1225, 43 L.Ed.2d 514 (1975), which held that social security benefits paid to widows who cease working to care for minor children must also be paid to widowers who do the same thing.

An early Court judgment considered whether the application of the Directive's Article 2(3) might give rise to reverse discrimination.

HOFMANN v. BARMER ERSATZKASSE

Case 184/83, [1984] ECR 3047.

[German law grants working mothers eight weeks' paid leave after childbirth, followed by a further four months of unpaid maternity leave. During the unpaid leave, the mother is paid a daily allowance from a state fund. Mr. Hofmann, father of a newborn, obtained six months unpaid parental leave from his employer, while the mother resumed work as a teacher. Hofmann sued for the daily allowance grant, claiming that a mother's maternity leave after childbirth in fact represented a benefit for child care. In support of his view, he noted that the allowance would be cancelled should the infant die. A German court asked the Court of Justice whether limiting the unpaid leave and daily allowance to mothers was justified under article 2(3) of the Equal Treatment Directive.]

11   According to the plaintiff, the protection of the mother * * * could be achieved by non-discriminatory measures, such as enabling the father to enjoy the leave or creating a period of parental leave, so as to release the mother from the responsibility of caring for the child and thereby allow her to resume employment as soon as the statutory protective period had expired. The plaintiff further claims that the choice between the options thereby created should, in conformity with the principle on non-discrimination between the sexes, be left completely at the discretion of the parents of the child. * * *

24 It is apparent ... that the directive is not designed to settle questions concerned with the organization of the family, or to alter the division of responsibility between parents.

25 [B]y reserving to Member States the right to retain, or introduce provisions which are intended to protect women in connection with "pregnancy and maternity", the directive recognizes the legitimacy * * * of protecting a woman's needs in two respects. First, it is legitimate to ensure the protection of a woman's biological condition during pregnancy and thereafter until such time as her physiological and mental functions have returned to normal after childbirth; secondly, it is legitimate to protect the special relationship between a woman and her child over the period which follows pregnancy and childbirth, by preventing that relationship from being disturbed by the multiple burdens which would result from the simultaneous pursuit of employment.

26 In principle, therefore, a measure such as maternity leave granted to a woman on expiry of the statutory protective period falls within the scope of Article 2(3) of Directive 76/207, inasmuch as it seeks to protect a woman in connection with the effects of pregnancy and motherhood. That being so, such leave may legitimately be reserved to the mother to the exclusion of any other person, in view of the fact that it is only the mother who may find herself subject to undesirable pressures to return to work prematurely.

NOTES AND QUESTIONS

1. Do you agree with the Court's conclusion in *Hoffman*? Should men be discouraged from taking leave to care for a new-born by being denied the paid leave, especially if the mother prefers to resume her own employment? The 1996 Parental Leave Directive discussed in the prior chapter does not affect the outcome in *Hoffman*.

2. In Handels-og Kontorfunktionaerernes Forbund v. Dansk Arbejdsgiverforening, Case C–179/88, [1990] ECR I–3979, Mrs. Hertz, a part-time cashier, was fired after being sick for 100 days. Her illness was due to complications arising from a pregnancy the year before. The Court of Justice held that article 2(3) prevented dismissal of a worker because of pregnancy, as well as dismissal during maternity leave, but did not forbid dismissal for inability to work due to an illness, even if the illness had been originally caused by complications arising from pregnancy. Equal treatment merely required that a woman not be fired for prolonged inability to work due to illness if a man would not be fired in a similar case, whatever his illness might be. Do you agree?

3. May an employer hire a woman who is not pregnant rather than a better qualified pregnant woman in order to avoid the costs of the social benefits provided to pregnant women? Would this violate article 2(1) or 2(3) of the Equal Treatment Directive? See Dekker v. Stichting Vormingscentrum VJV, Case C–177/88, [1990] ECR I–3941.

4. In Mahlburg v. Land Mecklenburg–Vorpommern, Case C–207/98, [2000] ECR I–549, the Court of Justice ruled that the 1976 Equal Treatment Directive precluded a refusal to appoint a pregnant woman to a permanent nursing position, on the grounds that German law (Mutterschutzgesetz) prohibited employers from employing pregnant women in areas in which they would be exposed to the harmful effects of dangerous substances. The plaintiff was employed as an operating-theater nurse on a fixed term contract in a German heart surgery clinic. When she applied for a permanent position in the clinic, she was pregnant. Her employer decided not to appoint her to the permanent post on the basis that German law prohibited employers from placing pregnant women in any position involving exposure to harmful substances. The Court held that the provisions of the German law could not result in unfavorable treatment regarding women's employment. Consequently, it was not permissible for an employer to refuse to appoint a pregnant woman to a post where she might serve for an unlimited time, in circumstances where a prohibition on employment on health grounds would apply only for the duration of her pregnancy.

Compare the US Supreme Court decision, Automobile Workers v. Johnson Controls, Inc., 499 U.S. 187, 111 S.Ct. 1196, 113 L.Ed.2d 158 (1991), holding impermissible under Title VII, as amended by the Pregnancy Discrimination Act, a battery manufacturer's rule barring all women, except those whose infertility was medically documented, from jobs involving certain levels of lead exposure.

5. THE COMPREHENSIVE EQUAL OPPOR-TUNITIES AND EQUAL TREATMENT DIRECTIVE 2006/54

The Parliament and Council, using codecision, adopted Directive 2006/54, O.J.L 204/23 (July 26, 2006), Document 37 in the Selected Documents, to replace the Equal Pay, Equal Treatment, Occupational Social Security, and Balance of Proof Directives, with implementation due on Aug. 15, 2008. Directive 2006/54 retains the substantive provisions of each directive, with some improvements, and consolidates their procedural provisions.

The definitional sections reiterate prior definitions with one innovation. Indirect discrimination is defined in article 2(1) as:

> Where an apparently neutral provision, criterion or practice would put persons of one sex at a particular disadvantage compared with persons of the other sex, unless that provision, criterion or practice is objectively justified by a legitimate aim, and the means of achieving that aim are appropriate and necessary.

The substantive provisions concerning equal treatment in employment are slightly reworded for greater clarity and precision. A new article 3 authorizes States to adopt or maintain positive action measures within the meaning of ECT Article 141(4) (now TFEU Article 157(4)). Article 19 replicates the essential provisions of the Burden of Proof Directive. By article 27, States continue to be permitted to adopt measures "more favourable" to the achievement of equal treatment. Article 29 specifically endorses 'gender mainstreaming' policies.

The procedural and enforcement provisions of the repealed directives have been consolidated and somewhat amplified. A new article 17 requires States to permit private organizations that have a "legitimate interest" in furthering the directive's aims to act on behalf of, or in support of individual complainants in judicial or administrative procedures. Pursuant to article 20, State agencies are supposed to provide support to victims of discrimination, publish reports and execute surveys. As in the prior directives, States must abolish laws and administrative practices, as well as the rules of employer or employee organizations that violate the directive (article 23), provide for adequate administrative and judicial enforcement, and set penalties that are "effective, proportionate and dissuasive" (article 25).

D. SOCIAL SECURITY, PENSIONS AND PENSIONABLE AGE

1. SOCIAL SECURITY DIRECTIVES

Neither the initial EECT Article 119 nor the 1976 Equal Treatment Directive required equal treatment of men and women in state social security plans. To fill the gap, the Council adopted Directive 79/7, O.J. L 6/24 (Jan. 10, 1979), using the implied legislative power provision, EECT Article 235, now TFEU 352.

This State Social Security Directive covers all statutory social security benefit plans, including those for sickness, old age, accidents at work, and unemployment (art. 3). The directive mandates equal treatment as to a) the scope of the plans and conditions for coverage; b) the obligation to contribute and the calculation of contributions; and c) the calculation of benefits and their duration (art. 4). As in the Equal Pay and Equal Treatment Directives, Member States are required to modify their legislation and practices to comply with the directive, and to create a system of judicial recourse (arts. 5 and 6).

The directive contains a number of exceptions to the principle of equal treatment, including special treatment for women on the grounds of maternity. Most importantly, pursuant to article 7, Member States are not obliged to fix the same age for eligibility for old-age pensions for men and women or grant them the same derived rights. The reason is that several States allow women to receive old-age pensions at an earlier age than men. To raise the lower eligibility age for women would be quite unpopular, while to lower the eligibility age for men would be extremely costly.

The State Social Security Directive was supplemented by Directive 86/378 O.J. L 225/40 (Aug. 12, 1986), adopted also by using EECT Article 235. This directive requires equal treatment for men and women in occupational social security schemes (i.e., employer or private sector social benefit plans). Its coverage of types of benefits and the scope of equal treatment parallels most of the provisions of the 1979 State Social Security Directive. The Occupational Social Security Directive forbids different treatment for men and women as to the age at which an employee qualifies to receive benefits (art. 6). However, by a special derogation the directive permits Member States to allow employer plans to parallel different ages of eligibility for pensions set for men and women by the state retirement pension plan (art. 9).

The Occupational Social Security Directive was repealed and its provisions incorporated in the comprehensive Directive 2006/54, with some revision for greater precision. However, the State Social Security Directive remains in force.

2. SOCIAL SECURITY AND PENSIONS CASELAW

The United Kingdom social security system permits women to retire at 60 while men retire at 65. As a corollary, the plan requires men to continue to make contributions when working while aged 60–64. On average, men pay into the state plan for a longer period and receive benefits for a shorter period. In The Queen v. Secretary of State for Social Security, Case C–9/91, [1992] ECR I–4297, the Equal Opportunities Commission claimed that this financial discrimination did not fall under the derogation for different old-age pension eligibility stated in article 7 of the State Social Security Directive. The Court disagreed. It concluded that the derogation for a different pensionable age for men and women was "intended to allow Member States to maintain temporarily the advantage accorded to women with respect to retirement in order to enable them progressively to adapt their pension systems in this respect without disrupting the complex financial equilibrium of those systems, the importance of which could not be ignored." A contrary decision would have created a serious financial and political problem.

A 1995 Pension Act will equalize the UK retirement age at 65 over a period of ten years starting April 2010. Other countries, including Austria, Germany, Italy and Portugal, also plan to introduce a uniform retirement age, to be set at between 65 and 67.

Private employer pension plans frequently also fix different pensionable ages for men and women, customarily using or paralleling the different ages set by the State social security old-age pension scheme. Several important cases have raised the issue whether such private plan discrimination violates Union law.

The first, Burton v. British Railways Board, Case 19/81, [1982] ECR 555, involved voluntary redundancy (dismissal) benefits paid by British Railways to employees taking early retirement. The benefits paid to Mr. Burton were lower than those paid to a woman of the same age, due to the fact that British Railways' private pension plan allowed women to retire at

55 while men could do so only at 60. Burton sued to challenge this discrimination. The Court of Justice first held that the voluntary redundancy plan constituted a work condition and therefore the 1976 Equal Treatment Directive was applicable. The Court then held that when a private employer benefit plan parallels the different pensionable ages for men and women set by the state social security system, the private plan does not violate equal treatment.

After *Burton* came *Marshall* which, as indicated at page 1410 supra, held that the Equal Treatment Directive's prohibition of discrimination between the sexes had vertical direct effect as to the State as her employer.

MARSHALL v. SOUTHAMPTON & SOUTH–WEST HAMPSHIRE AREA HEALTH AUTHORITY

Case 152/84, [1986] ECR 723.

[The Health Authority, a UK state agency, normally required men to retire at 65 and women at 60, paralleling the commencement of UK old age pensions. The Health Authority initially granted Ms. Marshall, a dietician, a two-year extension, but then forced her to retire at age 62. She sued for damages for discriminatory dismissal. The Industrial Tribunal decided in her favor on the basis of the 1976 Equal Treatment Directive. On appeal, the Court of Appeal asked the Court of Justice whether the earlier compulsory retirement age for women violated the Equal Treatment Directive.]

21 [T]he Court of Appeal seeks to ascertain whether or not Article 5(1) of Directive No 76/207 must be interpreted as meaning that a general policy concerning dismissal, followed by a State authority, involving the dismissal of a woman solely because she has attained or passed the qualifying age for a State pension, which age is different under national legislation for men and for women, constitutes discrimination on grounds of sex, contrary to that directive. * * *

32 [This] question of interpretation * * * does not concern access to a statutory or occupational retirement scheme * * * but the fixing of an age limit with regard to the termination of employment pursuant to a general policy concerning dismissal. The question therefore relates to the conditions governing dismissal and falls to be considered under Directive No 76/207.

33 Article 5(1) of Directive No 76/207 provides that application of the principle of equal treatment with regard to working conditions, including the conditions governing dismissal, means that men and women are to be guaranteed the same conditions without discrimination on grounds of sex.

34 [A]n age limit for the compulsory dismissal of workers pursuant to an employer's general policy concerning retirement falls within the term

"dismissal" construed in that manner, even if the dismissal involves the grant of a retirement pension.

35 As the Court emphasized in its judgment in the *Burton* case, Article 7 of Directive No 79/7 expressly provides that the directive does not prejudice the right of Member States to exclude from its scope the determination of pensionable age for the purposes of granting old-age and retirement pensions and the possible consequences thereof for other benefits falling within the statutory social security schemes. The Court thus acknowledged that benefits tied to a national scheme which lays down a different minimum pensionable age for men and women may lie outside the ambit of the aforementioned obligation.

36 However, * * * Article 1(2) of Directive No 76/207, which excludes social security matters from the scope of that directive, must be interpreted strictly. Consequently, the exception to the prohibition of discrimination on grounds of sex provided for in Article 7(1)(a) of Directive No 79/7 applies only to the determination of pensionable age for the purposes of granting old-age and retirement pensions and the possible consequences thereof for other benefits.

* * *

38 Consequently, Article 5(1) of Directive No 76/207 must be interpreted as meaning that a general policy concerning dismissal involving the dismissal of a woman solely because she has attained the qualifying age for a State pension, which age is different under national legislation for men and for women, constitutes discrimination on grounds of sex, contrary to that directive.

NOTES AND QUESTIONS

1. In *Marshall*, the Court held in ¶¶ 34–38 that an employer could not compel a woman to retire between 60 and 64 merely because she could obtain state old age benefits starting at 60. Do you agree with the result? Certainly many, perhaps most women would be happy to retire, but why should those who prefer to continue working be compelled to retire? Does *Marshall* affect the outcome in *Burton*? No, because the employer in *Burton* was only granting a pension benefit earlier to women, which might induce them to retire earlier, but did not compel them to do so.

2. May the Health Authority compel both men and women to retire at age 65? This, of course, is a crucial question that arises with regard to the interpretation of Directive 2000/78 that forbids discrimination, i.a., on grounds of age. See section E infra.

The next Court judgment sent shockwaves throughout the Union.

BARBER v. GUARDIAN ROYAL EXCHANGE ASSUR. GROUP

Case 262/88, [1990] ECR I-1889.

[Guardian Royal granted early retirement pensions to employees dismissed in a collective redundancy (mass lay-off). Its normal pensionable age was 62 for men and 57 for women, paralleling the state social security pension ages of 65 for men and 60 for women. Guardian Royal followed this model in offering early retirement pensions to the dismissed employees at the age of 55 for men and 50 for women. Mr. Barber, dismissed at 52, was therefore not offered an early retirement pension, although women his age were offered one. He sued to claim equal treatment. The Court of Appeal referred questions to the Court of Justice.]

10   In its first question the Court of Appeal seeks to ascertain, in substance, whether the benefits paid by an employer to a worker in connection with the latter's compulsory redundancy fall within the scope of Article 119 of the Treaty and the directive on equal pay or within the scope of the directive on equal treatment. * * *

12   As the Court has held, the concept of pay, within the meaning of the second paragraph of Article 119, comprises any other consideration, whether in cash or in kind, whether immediate or future, provided that the worker receives it, albeit indirectly, in respect of his employment from his employer (see, in particular, Garland v. British Rail Engineering [1982] ECR 359). Accordingly, the fact that certain benefits are paid after the termination of the employment relationship does not prevent them from being in the nature of pay, within the meaning of Article 119 of the Treaty.

* * *

16   [Moreover,] a redundancy payment made by the employer * * * cannot cease to constitute a form of pay on the sole ground that, rather than deriving from the contract of employment, it is a statutory or *ex gratia* payment.

* * *

20   Accordingly, * * * the answer to the first question must be that the benefits paid by an employer to a worker in connection with the latter's compulsory redundancy fall within the scope of the second paragraph of Article 119, whether they are paid under a contract of employment, by virtue of legislative provisions or on a voluntary basis.

21   [T]he second question must be understood as seeking in substance to ascertain whether a retirement pension paid under a contracted-out private occupational scheme falls within the scope of Article 119 of the Treaty, in particular where that pension is awarded in connection with compulsory redundancy. * * *

25   [T]he schemes in question are the result either of an agreement between workers and employers or of a unilateral decision taken by the employer. They are wholly financed by the employer or by both the employer and the workers without any contribution being made by the public authorities in any circumstances. Accordingly, such schemes form part of the consideration offered to workers by the employer.

* * *

29   [In the third question,] the Court of Appeal seeks in substance to ascertain, in the first place, whether it is contrary to Article 119 of the Treaty for a man made compulsorily redundant to be entitled only to a deferred [State] pension payable at the normal pensionable age when a woman in the same position receives an immediate retirement pension as a result of the application of an age condition that varies according to sex [in a manner parallel to] the national statutory pension scheme....

30   [I]t is sufficient to point out that Article 119 prohibits any discrimination with regard to pay as between men and women, whatever the system which gives rise to such inequality. Accordingly, it is contrary to Article 119 to impose an age condition which differs according to sex in respect of pensions paid under a contracted-out scheme, even if the difference between the pensionable age for men and that for women is based on the one provided for by the national statutory scheme.

NOTES AND QUESTIONS

1.   Note that the Court treated the issue in *Barber* as one of equal pay and then resolved it by an expansive interpretation of EECT Article 119. Mr. Barber's claim was not that he should not have been dismissed at all (which was what Ms. Marshall argued), but rather that he was entitled to the same level of severance benefits as women employees of the same age. Do you agree with the outcome?

2.   *Barber* created an uproar in the UK, because many companies had private plans granting women early retirement benefits or allowing them to retire at an earlier age. It was estimated that the Court judgment could cost British employers millions of pounds, since they would have to treat men employees as favorably as women. Perhaps predictably, the practical effect of requiring equal treatment was not to reduce the normal pensionable age of men in employers' benefit plans to the lower one for women but to raise that for women.

3.   Article 9 of the 1986 directive on occupational social security schemes allowed States to permit private employers to set different pensionable ages for men and women corresponding to those set in the State social security plan. The Commission concluded that *Barber* had effectively nullified article 9 and accordingly proposed an amendment to bring the directive into accord with *Barber*. The proposal was adopted in Directive 96/97, O.J. L 46/20 (Feb. 17, 1997).

4. We have previously noted in Chapter 5 that the Court usually gives retroactive effect to any judgment recognizing Treaty-based rights, in this instance equal treatment of the sexes in employment. Occasionally, as in *Defrenne*, the Court is persuaded that this would produce grave economic consequences. The Court in *Barber* decided against giving its judgment retroactive effect to "claim entitlement to a pension, with effect from a date prior to that of this judgment" (which was May 17, 1990). The Member States considered the judgment to have such serious economic consequences that they used the rare device of a Protocol to the Maastricht Treaty to provide that "benefits under occupational social security schemes shall not be considered as remuneration if and so far as they are attributable to periods of employment prior to 17 May 1990, except in the case of workers or those claiming under them who have initiated legal proceedings or introduced an equivalent claim under the applicable national law."

5. The "hundred million pound question" as to how the non-retroactive language of *Barber* would be applied was answered in Case C–109/91, *Ten Oever v. Stichting Bedrijfspensioen fonds*, [1993] ECR I–4879 (the case was filed before the Protocol came into effect on Nov. 1, 1993). When a widower claimed a surviving spouse benefit from a Dutch occupational pension fund whose rules give such a benefit only to widows, the Court first held that a survivor's benefit constituted pay, even though not paid to the employee, because it came from the employer by virtue of an employment relation. However, the Court then explained that its language in *Barber* meant that the amount of the surviving spouse benefit in question could be limited to that "payable in respect of periods of employment subsequent to 17 May 1990."

Ten Oever was greeted with relief in the United Kingdom and other affected States.

E. DISCRIMINATION ON GROUNDS OTHER THAN GENDER

As we noted above, ECT Article 13 (now TFEU Article 19), inserted in 1999 by the Treaty of Amsterdam, significantly expanded the scope for Community action in the area of non-gender discrimination. Armed with this new legislative competence, the Commission wasted little time in proposing two new directives designed to widen the reach of Community non-discrimination law.

Amid growing concerns over the incidence of racism and xenophobia in certain parts of the Union, the Council, acting unanimously, rapidly adopted Directive 2000/43 on equal treatment irrespective of racial or ethnic origin, O.J.L 180/22 (July 19, 2000), Document 40 in the Selected Documents. Shortly thereafter, the Council also unanimously adopted the Framework Employment Directive, Directive 2000/78 establishing a general framework for equal treatment in employment and occupation, O.J. L 303/16 (Dec. 2, 2000), Document 39 in the Selected Documents, addressing discrimination on the grounds of religion or belief, disability, age or sexual orientation.

1. THE FRAMEWORK EMPLOYMENT DIRECTIVE 2000/78

The Framework Employment Directive forbids direct and indirect discrimination on the grounds of religion or belief, disability, age or sexual orientation. Indirect discrimination is defined in article 2(2) as occurring "where an apparently neutral provision, criterion or practice would put persons having a particular religion or belief, a particular disability, a particular age, or a particular sexual orientation at a particular disadvantage compared with other persons unless that provision, criterion or practice is objectively justified by a legitimate aim and the means of achieving that aim are appropriate and necessary." Article 2(3) expressly forbids harassment, defined as "unwanted conduct" that has the purpose or effect of creating "an intimidating, hostile, degrading, humiliating or offensive environment."

In article 3, the directive's scope covers not only employment and working conditions, including dismissals and pay, but also extends to access to employment, recruitment, promotion, vocational training, and membership in unions or professional associations. However, Article 3(4) permits Member States to exclude its armed forces from the bar on discrimination on the basis of age or disability. Implicitly, however, the provisions banning discrimination on grounds of sexual orientation, religion or belief apply to employment in the armed forces. In keeping with the policy established by the 1997 Burden of Proof Directive, article 10 states that where a complainant has established "facts from which it may be presumed that there has been direct or indirect discrimination," the respondent must prove that there has been no discrimination.

Directive 2000/78 contains an "occupational requirements" exception in article 4(1), similar to that in article 2(2) of the 1976 Equal Treatment Directive. The wording is, however, more restrictive, because it requires Member States to show that any difference in treatment is the result of a "genuine and determining occupational requirement" set pursuant to a legitimate policy objective, and proportionate to that objective. Article 4(2) creates an exception for discrimination in "occupational activities within churches" or religious affiliated groups when the discrimination is based upon "religion or belief." Presumably the provision was intended to permit certain churches and religious groups to discriminate on the basis of sexual orientation.

Article 5 states that in order to guarantee compliance with the principle of equal treatment for persons with disabilities, employers are required to provide "reasonable accommodation," if needed in a particular case, to enable disabled employees to become or stay employed, unless providing it would impose a disproportionate burden on the employer.

Article 6(1) is highly important, because it limits possible age discrimination by requiring that it be "objectively and reasonably justified by a legitimate aim, including legitimate employment policy, labour market and vocational training objectives." Note also that a recital states that the Directive is "without prejudice to national provisions laying down retirement ages."

Finally, because the directive lays down only minimum requirements, articles 7 and 8 permit Member States to introduce or maintain provisions, including positive action measures, which are more favorable to equal treatment than those contained in the directive. As in the comprehensive Equal Treatment Directive, article 16 requires States to eliminate discriminatory provisions in their laws and administrative provisions and in collective bargaining agreements, employment contracts, etc.

The Court of Justice has not yet had to deal with questions concerning Directive 2000/78's prohibition of discrimination on the basis of religion or belief. At some point, questions may be posed, perhaps concerning restrictions in an employment context on the wearing of veils or head covering by some Moslem women. Whether employees may claim a right to time-off from work on their religious holidays may also be raised.

For a review of the Directive and initial case law, see E. Szyszczak, Antidiscrimination Law in the European Community, 32 Fordham Int'l L.J. 624 (2009).

2. DISCRIMINATION BASED ON AGE

Whether employers can discriminate against older workers, usually by requiring them to retire, is the most obvious issue arising under discrimination based on age, but there may also be discrimination against younger employees, usually by restricting their access to employment. The Court of Justice has now dealt with both issues.

In Chapter 6 on Basic Rights, we already examined the first prominent judgment, *Mangold*, in which the Court notably held in ¶ 75 that non-discrimination on grounds of age constituted a general principle of Union law, derived from the constitutional traditions common to the Member States. This certainly suggested that the Court would vigorously enforce the right of non-discrimination based on age.

Some Member States set an age that may be invoked by employers to compel employees to retire, usually corresponding to the age at which people may commence receiving state social security benefits. Not surprisingly, the Court of Justice soon had to decide whether a State law which had the effect of setting a compulsory retirement age violated Directive 2000/78.

PALACIOS DE LA VILLA v. CORTEFIEL SERVICIOS
Case C–411/05, [2007] ECR I–8531.

[A 1980 Spanish law fixed 69 as the maximum age for employees, but in 2001 the law was repealed. According to the national court referring questions, the government at that time viewed compulsory retirement as a "burden on the social security system," so that a system of "flexible retirement" was preferable (¶ 15). Although Spain did implement Directive 2000/78 in 2004, in 2005 it adopted a law authorizing collective agreements to set a compulsory retirement age which should be "consistent with employment policy [such as] increased stability in employment, . . . the recruitment of new workers," etc. Cortefiel retired Palacios de la Villa at age 65, the age set by a textile trade collective agreement. Spanish law permitted him to draw 100% of his social security benefits at that age. Palacios de la Villa contested the compulsory retirement as a violation of Directive 2000/78.]

51   National legislation [which provides that when] a worker has reached the retirement age laid down by that legislation [there is an] automatic termination of his employment contract, must be regarded as directly imposing less favourable treatment for workers who have reached that age as compared with all other persons in the labour force.

52   [Under Article 6(1)] differences of treatment on grounds of age * * * will not constitute discrimination prohibited under Article 2 'if, within the context of national law, they are objectively and reasonably justified by a legitimate aim, including legitimate employment policy, labour market and vocational training objectives, and if the means of achieving that aim are appropriate and necessary'.

53   In this case, * * * [the Spanish 2005 law], which allows the inclusion of compulsory retirement clauses in collective agreements, was adopted, * * * as part of a national policy seeking to promote better access to employment, by means of better distribution of work between the generations.

54   It is true, as the national court has pointed out, that that provision does not expressly refer to an objective of that kind.

55   However, that fact alone is not decisive.

56   It cannot be inferred from Article 6(1) of Directive 2000/78 that the lack of precision in the national legislation at issue as regards the aim pursued automatically excludes the possibility that it may be justified under that provision.

57   In the absence of such precision, it is important, however, that other elements, taken from the general context of the measure concerned, enable the underlying aim of that law to be identified for the purposes of judicial review of its legitimacy and whether the means put in place to achieve that aim are appropriate and necessary.

[The Court then noted that Spain's 2005 law was essentially intended to reduce unemployment (¶ 62).]

64   The legitimacy of such an aim of public interest cannot reasonably be called into question, since * * * in accordance with [TEU Article 2 and ECT Article 2], the promotion of a high level of employment is

one of the ends pursued both by the European Union and the European Community.

65 Furthermore, the Court has already held that encouragement of recruitment undoubtedly constitutes a legitimate aim of social policy and that assessment must evidently apply to instruments of national employment policy designed to improve opportunities for entering the labour market for certain categories of workers.

66 Therefore, an objective such as that referred to by the legislation at issue must, in principle, be regarded as 'objectively and reasonably' justifying 'within the context of national law', as provided for by the first subparagraph of Article 6(1) of Directive 2000/78 * * *.

67 It remains to be determined whether * * * the means employed to achieve such a legitimate aim are 'appropriate and necessary'.

68 [A]s Community law stands at present, the Member States and, where appropriate, the social partners at national level enjoy broad discretion in their choice, not only to pursue a particular aim in the field of social and employment policy, but also in the definition of measures capable of achieving it [citing *Mangold*].

69 As is already clear from * * * recital 25 in the preamble to Directive 2000/78, such is the case as regards the choice which the national authorities concerned may be led to make on the basis of political, economic, social, demographic and/or budgetary considerations and having regard to the actual situation in the labour market in a particular Member State, to prolong people's working life or, conversely, to provide for early retirement.

70 Furthermore, the competent authorities at national, regional or sectoral level must [be able to adapt their measures] to changing circumstances in the employment situation in the Member State concerned. The fact that the compulsory retirement procedure was reintroduced in Spain after being repealed for several years is accordingly of no relevance.

71 It is, therefore, for the competent authorities of the Member States to find the right balance between the different interests involved. However, it is important to ensure that the national measures laid down in that context do not go beyond what is appropriate and necessary to achieve the aim pursued by the Member State concerned.

* * *

73 [T]he measure cannot be regarded as unduly prejudicing the legitimate claims of workers subject to compulsory retirement * * *; the relevant legislation is not based only on a specific age, but also takes account of the fact that the persons concerned are entitled to financial compensation by way of a [State] retirement pension at the end of

their working life * * * the level of which cannot be regarded as unreasonable.

74   Moreover, the relevant national legislation allows the social partners to opt, by way of collective agreements—and therefore with considerable flexibility—for application of the compulsory retirement mechanism so that due account may be taken not only of the overall situation in the labour market concerned, but also of the specific features of the jobs in question.

75   In the light of those factors, it cannot reasonably be maintained that national legislation such as that at issue in the main proceedings is incompatible with the requirements of Directive 2000/78.

NOTES AND QUESTIONS

1.   Directive 2000/78 makes no reference whatsoever to an exception permitting a State to require compulsory dismissal on grounds of age. Do you think the Court is justified in relying on the general language of the Directive's article 6(1) to reach the conclusion that the Spanish compulsory retirement age legislation does not violate the Directive? Is it relevant, or not that Spain customarily has high levels of unemployment, around 10% in 2007?

2.   In R. (Age Concern England) v. Secretary of State, Case C–388/07, [2009] ECR I–___ (Mar. 5, 2009), a charitable organization promoting the welfare of older people challenged the UK's 2006 regulation that implemented Directive 2000/78, but authorized employers to retire employees at age 65, or "the normal retirement age" fixed by the employer. Citing *Palacios de la Villa*, the Court held that the UK did not have to specifically justify the compulsory retirement provision on the basis of the grounds set out in the Directive's article 6(1), so long as "other elements, taken from the general context of the measure" provided such justification sufficiently to enable review by the courts (¶ 45).

However, in giving guidance to the national courts that must assess the UK law, the Court noted that States could not rely upon "mere generalizations" (¶ 51), but rather their measures must be based upon a "legitimate aim" achieved by "appropriate and necessary" means (¶ 52). Moreover, because Age Concern England urged that a reviewing court should use "a very high standard of scrutiny" (¶ 54) (reminiscent of the US doctrine of "strict scrutiny"), the Court of Justice, in providing further guidance to national courts, observed that States had "the burden of establishing to a high standard of proof the legitimacy of the aim relied on as a justification" for its measures (¶ 67). How do you think the UK court should decide the case? Is it relevant, or not, that the UK does not usually have high levels of unemployment?

Quite apart from a standard retirement age, State authorities often fix a retirement age for specific job categories, frequently between 45 and 55 for those occupations that require high physical capabilities, such as firefighters or airplane pilots. Can these be challenged as a form of age discrimination?

PETERSON v. BEFUFUNGSAUSSCHUSS FUR ZAHNARTZTE

Case C–341/08, [2010] ECR I–___ (Jan. 12, 2010).

[In 1999, a German local authority set 68 as the maximum age for doctors and dentists who could treat patients in the social security system. Such patients comprise 90% of the customary clientele of doctors and dentists. The authority placed no age limit on doctors or dentists when providing services to private clients outside the social security system. Petersen challenged the regulation as a violation of Directive 2000/78.]

30   [T]he referring court essentially asks whether Article 6(1) of the Directive precludes a national measure setting a maximum age for practising as a [dentist serving social security patients], in this case 68 years * * *.

* * *

38   The referring court mentioned several objectives: first, the protection of the health of patients covered by the statutory health insurance scheme, it being thought that the performance of dentists declines after a certain age; second, the distribution of employment opportunities among the generations; and third, the financial balance of the German health system.

* * *

40   As the Court has previously held, where the national legislation in question does not specify the aim pursued, it is important that other elements, taken from the general context of the measure concerned, enable the underlying aim of that measure to be identified for the purposes of review by the courts of whether it is legitimate and whether the means put in place to achieve it are appropriate and necessary (see *Palacios de la Villa* and *Age Concern England*).

* * *

51   In the case of a measure in the field of health, it should be recalled that, in accordance with Article 152(5) EC, the Member States retain power to organise their social security systems and to adopt, in particular, provisions intended to govern the organisation and delivery of health services and medical care. The Member States must indeed exercise that power in compliance with Community law, but * * * account must be taken of the fact that a Member State may determine the level of protection which it wishes to afford to public health and the way in which that level is to be achieved. Since the level of protection may vary from one Member State to the other, Member States must be allowed discretion.

52   In view of that discretion, it must be accepted that, in the context of Article 2(5) of the Directive, a Member State may find it necessary to

set an age limit for the practice of a medical profession such as that of a dentist in order to protect the health of patients. That consideration applies whether the objective of the protection of health is considered from the point of view of the competence of dentists or the financial balance of the national healthcare system. As regards the latter, it cannot be ruled out that the rising number of dentists [serving social security patients] led to an excessive increase in the supply of health-care, resulting in an excessive level of expenditure to be borne by the State, and that the departure of the oldest of those dentists makes it possible to reduce that expenditure and avert a risk of serious harm to the balance of the social security system. As to setting the age limit at 68, that age may be regarded as sufficiently high to serve as the endpoint of admission to practise as a [social security] panel dentist.

[Noting that the local authority's regulation contained an exception, because it did not prevent dentists from continuing to serve private clients, the Court continued:]

61   A measure to which there is so broad an exception as that for dentists practising outside the [social security] system cannot be regarded as essential for the protection of public health. If the aim of the age limit at issue in the main proceedings is the protection of patients' health, from the point of view of the competence of the practitioners concerned, clearly patients are not protected where the exception applies. The exception thus appears to run counter to the objective pursued. Moreover, it is not limited temporally and, although no figures have been supplied, it potentially applies to all dentists and appears liable to concern a not inconsiderable number of patients.

* * *

63   If, on the other hand, the aim of the measure is to preserve the financial balance of the public healthcare system, the exception does not interfere with the objective pursued. That system belongs to a sphere for which the State has financial responsibility, and by defini-tion does not extend to the private health system. Consequently, the introduction of an age limit which applies only to [dentists providing services to patients in the social security system], in order to control public health sector expenditure, is compatible with the objective pursued.

[The Court considered whether the regulation could be justified as a way of providing opportunities for practice by young dentists entering the profession.]

68   The Court has previously held that the encouragement of recruitment undeniably constitutes a legitimate social policy or employment policy objective of the Member States, and that that assessment must evi-dently apply to instruments of national employment policy designed to improve opportunities for entering the labour market for certain categories of workers (see *Palacios de la Villa*). Similarly, a measure

intended to promote the access of young people to the profession of dentist in the panel system may be regarded as an employment policy measure.

* * *

71 The question arises, however, of whether the application of an age limit is appropriate and necessary for achieving the aim pursued. Where the number of dentists [serving social security patients] is not excessive in relation to the needs of patients, entry into that market is usually possible for new practitioners, especially young ones, regardless of the presence of dentists who have passed a certain age, in this case 68. In that case the introduction of an age limit might be neither appropriate nor necessary for achieving the aim pursued.

* * *

74 However, it is for the national court to ascertain whether such a situation exists.

NOTES AND QUESTIONS

1. Presumably, based on ¶ 63, the authorities can set 68 as the maximum age for doctors or dentists providing services in the social security system, even though based on ¶ 61, they cannot do so based on health concerns. Do you think that is justifiable, or rather that some form of professional capacity test should be employed? Could an administrative regulation forbid architects or engineers from providing services to the state after a given age? In the EU, professors and school teachers customarily must retire at 65, or occasionally 68 or 70. Do you consider this justifiable? What about the argument that room must be made for young people entering a profession?

2. In Wolf v. Stadt Frankfurt, Case C–299/08, [2010] ECR I–___ (Jan. 12, 2010), a German regional authority rule required firefighters to retire at age 60, with a possible postponement to 62. This was not challenged. In order to ensure that firefighters work for a desired number of years, a regulation forbid persons to apply for mid-level firefighter posts after reaching the age of 30. In response to questions referred, the court noted that firefighters needed "exceptionally high physical capacities" which few people over 45 could possess (¶ 41). Consequently, since most mid-level firefighters were required to fight fires and could not be allocated to less physically demanding managerial duties, the Court concluded that the regulation was legitimate and proportionate (¶¶ 42–45). Would you agree? Would this reasoning implicitly permit authorities to set a compulsory retirement age for firefighters, police officers, locomotive engineers, airplane pilots, etc., at some age (between 50 and 60) linked to their physical capacities?

3. Young people can also be subject to discrimination based on age. In Hutter v. Technische Universitat Graz, Case C–88/08, [2009] ECR I–___ (June. 18, 2009), Hutter was paid less as a laboratory technician than a female colleague employed at exactly the same time. The employer claimed

that the pay difference was justified by the female colleague's longer period of apprenticeship training after she reached 18, namely 28 months versus 6 months for Hutter. The employer disregarded Hutter's apprenticeship period prior to the age of 18, contending that this was necessary to prevent discrimination in favor of young people in vocational training before 18 as opposed to those attending school. Since it was undeniable that Hutter's vocational training prior to 18 facilitated his performance of his employment, the Court held that the employer's rule was not justified (¶¶ 47–51).

3. DISCRIMINATION BASED ON DISABILITY

The Court has already provided guidance on the nature and scope of discrimination based on disability.

CHACON NAVAS v. EUREST COLLECTIVIDADES

Case C–13/05, [2006] ECR I–6467.

[Eurest dismissed Chacon Navas after a long absence from work due to sickness. Under Spanish law, dismissal for sickness is not as such considered to be unlawful. However, because sickness is capable of causing disabling conditions, the referring court asked the Court of Justice whether Directive 2000/78's prohibition of discrimination on the basis of disability could cover sickness (without, however, specifying the nature of the complainant's sickness.) The Court initially held that the term "disability" had to be given a uniform Community interpretation in order to achieve the "uniform application of Community law" (¶ 40). The Court then provided its definition.]

43   [T]he concept of 'disability' must be understood as referring to a limitation which results in particular from physical, mental or psychological impairments and which hinders the participation of the person concerned in professional life.

44   [B]y using the concept of 'disability' in Article 1 of that directive, the legislature deliberately chose a term which differs from 'sickness'. The two concepts cannot therefore simply be treated as being the same.

45   Recital 16 in the preamble to Directive 2000/78 states that the 'provision of measures to accommodate the needs of disabled people at the workplace plays an important role in combating discrimination on grounds of disability'. The importance which the Community legislature attaches to measures for adapting the workplace to the disability demonstrates that it envisaged situations in which participation in professional life is hindered over a long period of time. In order for the limitation to fall within the concept of 'disability', it must therefore be probable that it will last for a long time.

[The Court then gave further guidance on the Directive's protection of disabled persons.]

49 According to Recital 17 in the preamble to Directive 2000/78, that directive does not require the recruitment, promotion or maintenance in employment of an individual who is not competent, capable and available to perform the essential functions of the post concerned, without prejudice to the obligation to provide reasonable accommodation for people with disabilities.

50 In accordance with Article 5 of Directive 2000/78, reasonable accommodation is to be provided in order to guarantee compliance with the principle of equal treatment in relation to persons with disabilities. That provision states that this means that employers are to take appropriate measures, where needed in a particular case, to enable a person with a disability to have access to, participate in, or advance in employment, unless such measures would impose a disproportionate burden on the employer.

51 The prohibition * * * of discrimination on grounds of disability contained in Articles 2(1) and 3(1)(c) of Directive 2000/78 precludes dismissal on grounds of disability which, in the light of the obligation to provide reasonable accommodation for people with disabilities, is not justified by the fact that the person concerned is not competent, capable and available to perform the essential functions of his post.

NOTES AND QUESTIONS

1. Most sickness does not cause a disability, although of course severe illness or one of long duration may do so, e.g., severe arthritis may restrict or prevent walking. Do you agree with the Court's conclusion in ¶¶ 49–51? Should the Court have declined to answer the question referred because the referring court did not indicate the nature of Chacon Navas' sickness, as the Commission urged?

2. Do you agree with the Court's clarification of the limit on the protection of the disabled, who can only rely on the directive if they are able to "perform the essential functions of the post concerned" (¶ 49)? The Court is likely to have occasion to decide what constitutes "reasonable accommodation" by the employer. Note also that although article 26 of the Charter of Fundamental Rights calls for measures to ensure that disabled persons are independent and can "participate in the life of the community," Directive 2000/78 is limited to employment and vocational training. Thus, Directive 2000/78 does not require, for example, "reasonable accommodation" for the needs of disabled persons in public or private transport.

3. Does the scope of protection against discrimination cover persons who are caretakers of disabled individuals? In Coleman v. Attridge Law, Case C–303/06, [2008] ECR I–5603, Coleman, the mother and primary caretaker of a severely disabled child, claimed that her employer had discriminated against her in comparison to the employer's treatment of her colleagues with non-disabled children. Allegedly the employer denied her time off to care for her disabled son, called her "lazy" and used abusive language, etc. (¶ 26). In a decidedly liberal interpretative judgment, the Court held that the directive

was intended to "combat all forms of discrimination on grounds of disability" (¶ 38), and hence protected also the caretaker of a disabled person from discrimination (¶ 50). The Commission and two States argued in favor of this approach, while four States argued against. What is your view? For a generally approving casenote, see L. Waddington, 46 Common Mkt. L. Rev. 665 (2009).

4. DISCRIMINATION BASED ON SEXUAL ORIENTATION

While many Member States had legislation prohibiting discrimination on the other grounds specified in Directive 2000/78, few did so with regard to sexual orientation. We previously noted that in *Grant,* supra page 1412, the Court declined to hold that same sex couples could claim the benefit of the 1976 Equal Treatment Directive. The prohibition of discrimination on grounds of sexual orientation accordingly may have a significant impact in many States. The Court's first judgment reverses the result in *Grant.*

MARUKO v. VERSORGUNGSANSTALT DER DEUTSCHEN BUHNEN

Case C–267/06, [2008] ECR I–1757.

[A 2001 German law creates the status of registered life partnerships for two persons of the same sex, with a provision that specifically states that this entitles a life partner to the state widow or widower pension. When Maruko's life partner died, Maruko claimed a survivor's benefit from the VddB, a theatrical organization that provided this benefit to widows or widowers of deceased persons employed in theatrics who had made regular contributions to the VddB's benefit fund. When the VddB refused to pay the survivor's benefit, Maruko sued. In response to questions referred to it, the Court of Justice initially held that the benefit was clearly linked to the deceased life partner's employment as a designer of theatrical costumes for theaters comprising the VddB, and therefore constituted 'pay' (¶¶ 45–46). The Court continued:]

67   [In 2001,] the Federal Republic of Germany altered its legal system to allow persons of the same sex to live in a union of mutual support and assistance which is formally constituted for life. Having chosen not to permit those persons to enter into marriage, which remains reserved solely to persons of different sex, that Member State created for persons of the same sex a separate regime, the life partnership, the conditions of which have been gradually made equivalent to those applicable to marriage.

69   The referring court considers that, in view of the harmonisation between marriage and life partnership, which it regards as a gradual movement towards recognising equivalence, as a consequence of the rules introduced by the [Life Partnership Law], a life partnership, while not identical to marriage, places persons of the same sex in a

situation comparable to that of spouses so far as concerns the survivor's benefit at issue in the main proceedings.

70   However, the referring court finds that entitlement to that survivor's benefit is restricted, under the provisions of the VddB Regulations, to surviving spouses and is denied to surviving life partners.

71   That being the case, those life partners are treated less favourably than surviving spouses as regards entitlement to that survivor's benefit.

72   [Accordingly,] legislation such as that at issue in the main proceedings must, as a consequence, be considered to constitute direct discrimination on grounds of sexual orientation, within the meaning of Articles 1 and 2(2)(a) of Directive 2000/78.

NOTES AND QUESTIONS

1.   Note that although the Court's conclusion will certainly grant same sex life partners equal treatment with married couples with regard to pay or any benefits provided by employers under occupational employment pension plans, it would not entitle them to pensions provided to widows or widowers under State social security systems, nor to the beneficial tax treatment States provide to married couples. Directive 2000/78 only covers the sector of employment.

2.   Furthermore, the Court's holding is limited to same sex couples in a registered life partnership. Germany and a majority of Member States have created forms of registered civil partnerships for same sex couples, but others do not. Do you think that a same sex couple in a State without such civil partnerships who can establish by persuasive factual evidence that they have a long-term durable relationship should also be able to claim benefits accorded by their employers only to married persons?

3.   Remember that article 6 of the directive permits States to exclude the armed forces from the prohibition of discrimination on grounds of age or disability, but not sexual orientation. Most European nations have customarily not barred homosexuals from military service. The UK accepted a famous 1999 decision of the European Court of Human Rights, Lustig–Prean v. United Kingdom, that held the prohibition of homosexuals in military service to constitute a violation of their rights, specifically noting that neither prejudicial views of heterosexual personnel nor alleged concerns regarded shared accommodations could justify the exclusion.

5. THE RACE AND ETHNIC ORIGIN ANTI-DISCRIMINATION DIRECTIVE

Directive 2000/43 prohibits direct or indirect discrimination on the grounds of racial or ethnic origin. In many aspects, the approach taken in the directive is identical to that set out in the Framework Employment Directive. In particular, Directive 2000/43 uses the same concept of indirect discrimination; includes harassment within the concept of discrimination; has a similar derogation for "genuine and determining" occupational requirements; follows the same rule in respect of the burden of proof; and allows Member States to introduce or maintain more favorable measures, including positive action, at national level.

Directive 2000/43 has, however, a much broader scope. In addition to the sector of employment, the directive applies whenever Union law is applicable, notably under article 3 in the fields of social protection, including social security and healthcare; social advantages; education; and access to and supply of goods and services available to the public, including housing. Thus, the directive can be invoked whenever Union rules apply, especially harmonization or incentive measures.

Because all the Member States have legislation (and sometimes constitutional provisions) prohibiting discrimination on the basis of race or ethnic origin, the Court of Justice is not likely to have many questions referred to it concerning the application of Directive 2000/43. The following judgment demonstrates that when the Court has occasion to do so, it will vigorously apply the directive's provisions.

CENTRUM VOOR GELIJKHEID VAN KANSEN v. FIRMA FERYN

Case C–54/07, [2008] ECR I–5187.

[A 2003 Belgian law created a Center for Equal Opportunities and Combating Racism and authorized it to bring judicial proceedings even when there is no private complainant. Following a public statement by the director of Feryn that his enterprise could not employ "Moroccans" because its customers were reluctant to allow them access to the customers' residences to put in place the doors Feryn sells, the Center sued Feryn. The complaint was dismissed for lack of proof of any actual discrimination in hiring or employment. On appeal, several questions were referred to the Court.]

22 It is true that * * * Article 2(2) of Directive 2000/43 defines direct discrimination as a situation in which one person 'is treated' less favourably than another is, has been or would be treated in a comparable situation on grounds of racial or ethnic origin. Likewise, Article 7 of that directive requires Member States to ensure that judicial procedures are available to 'all persons who consider themselves wronged by failure to apply the principle of equal treatment to them' and to public interest bodies bringing judicial proceedings 'on behalf or in support of the complainant'.

23 Nevertheless, it cannot be inferred from this that the lack of an identifiable complainant leads to the conclusion that there is no direct discrimination within the meaning of Directive 2000/43. The aim of that directive, as stated in recital 8 of its preamble, is 'to foster conditions for a socially inclusive labour market'. For that purpose,

Article 3(1)(a) states that the directive covers, inter alia, selection criteria and recruitment conditions.

24 The objective of fostering conditions for a socially inclusive labour market would be hard to achieve if the scope of Directive 2000/43 were to be limited to only those cases in which an unsuccessful candidate for a post, considering himself to be the victim of direct discrimination, brought legal proceedings against the employer.

25 The fact that an employer declares publicly that it will not recruit employees of a certain ethnic or racial origin, something which is clearly likely to strongly dissuade certain candidates from submitting their candidature and, accordingly, to hinder their access to the labour market, constitutes direct discrimination in respect of recruitment within the meaning of Directive 2000/43. The existence of such direct discrimination is not dependant on the identification of a complainant who claims to have been the victim.

* * *

[The Court then replied to questions concerning the Directive's reversal of the burden of proof in Article 8(1).]

31 Statements by which an employer publicly lets it be known that, under its recruitment policy, it will not recruit any employees of a certain ethnic or racial origin may constitute facts of such a nature as to give rise to a presumption of a discriminatory recruitment policy.

32 It is, thus, for that employer to adduce evidence that it has not breached the principle of equal treatment, which it can do, inter alia, by showing that the actual recruitment practice of the undertaking does not correspond to those statements.

* * *

35 The sixth question asks, essentially, what sanctions may be considered to be appropriate for employment discrimination established on the basis of the employer's public statements.

36 Article 15 of Directive 2000/43 confers on Member States responsibility for determining the rules on sanctions for breaches of national provisions adopted pursuant to that directive. Article 15 specifies that those sanctions must be effective, proportionate and dissuasive and that they may comprise the payment of compensation to the victim.

39 [T]hose sanctions may, where necessary, include a finding of discrimination by the court or the competent administrative authority in conjunction with an adequate level of publicity, the cost of which is to be borne by the defendant. They may also take the form of a prohibitory injunction * * * ordering the employer to cease the discriminatory practice, and, where appropriate, a fine. They may, moreover, take the form of the award of damages to the body bringing the proceedings.

NOTES AND QUESTIONS

1. Do you agree with the Court's conclusion in ¶ 28 that the public statement in a newspaper interview would make it unlikely that "immigrants" would apply for jobs at Feryn? Or would you prefer to limit the Directive's protection to complainants who are the subject of actual discrimination in hiring or employment? Note the Court's discussion of possible sanctions in ¶ 39. Which do you consider might be appropriate here?

2. Why do you suppose the Council was willing to ban discrimination based on race or ethnic origin in the fields cited in article 3 of the directive, but limited to employment the prohibition of the other types of discrimination in Directive 2000/78? A directive recital cites a request for priority action to combat racism from the European Council at Tampere in 1999. It is possible that at some point Regulation 2000/78 will be amended to expand its prohibition of discrimination beyond employment.

CHAPTER 36

LITIGATION IN CIVIL AND COMMERCIAL MATTERS

■ ■ ■

Civil and commercial litigation has in the last fifteen years become a highly active arena of EU lawmaking. It was initially doubted that civil justice fell within the Community's sphere of action, and was thus assumed that any cooperation in this field would have to be accomplished, if at all, through the conclusion of separate (i.e., non-Community) conventions among the Member States. Notwithstanding the evident link between Member State practices in the area of civil justice, on the one hand, and the free movement of goods, persons, services and capital, on the other, the Treaty specifically mandated that the Member States enter into negotiations for the conclusion of agreements on certain matters, among them "the simplification of formalities governing the reciprocal recognition and enforcement of judgments of courts or tribunals and of arbitration awards." On the basis of this language, the Member States entered over forty years ago into what became known as the 1968 Brussels Convention on Jurisdiction and the Recognition and Enforcement of Judgments in Civil and Commercial Matters, or simply the Brussels Convention.

The Maastricht Treaty made civil justice a "pillar three" subject, thus bringing it under the umbrella of the European Union, but not the European Community, and authorizing intergovernmental activity only. It was when the Amsterdam Treaty moved civil justice from pillar three squarely into pillar one that it became fully a Community law matter. The institutions were thus able to transform the Brussels Convention into a Regulation proper, popularly known as the "Brussels I Regulation." By the same token they were able to convert other non-Community conventions into directly applicable EU law, another notable example being the transformation of the 1980 Convention on the Law Applicable to Contractual Obligations (the Rome Convention) into a directly applicable regulation (Rome I). The Brussels I and Rome I Regulations are discussed below.

The developments charted in this chapter thus reflect both a heightening of normative activity in the civil justice field and its "mainstreaming" into EU law. (Of course, under the Lisbon Treaty, even the separate pillars are no more.) Currently, civil justice is one of the most dynamic and fast-evolving areas of EU law, comprising a number of significant legislative instruments. TFEU Article 81 (formerly EC Treaty Article 65) empowers the Parliament and Council, by the ordinary legislative procedure, to "adopt measures, particularly when necessary for the proper functioning of the internal market, aimed at ensuring:

(a) the mutual recognition and enforcement between Member States of judgments and of decisions in extrajudicial cases;

(b) the cross-border service of judicial and extrajudicial documents;

(c) the compatibility of the rules applicable in the Member States concerning conflict of laws and of jurisdiction;

(d) cooperation in the taking of evidence;

(e) effective access to justice;

(f) the elimination of obstacles to the proper functioning of civil proceedings, if necessary by promoting the compatibility of the rules on civil procedure applicable in the Member States;

(g) the development of alternative methods of dispute settlement;

(h) support for the training of the judiciary and judicial staff."

By way of exception, Article 81(3) subjects the adoption of "measures concerning family law with cross-border implications" to unanimous voting in the Council upon consultation of Parliament. However, the European Council may decide unanimously to move, even on such matters, to the ordinary legislative procedure.

Note Article 81's authorization of measures, "*particularly* when necessary for the proper functioning of the internal market." This suggests that legislation in the field may likely, but not necessarily, be linked to the goal of market integration. The institutions may presumably legislate on matters of civil justice viewed as a policy area as such.

A. JURISDICTION IN CIVIL AND COMMERCIAL MATTERS

1. THE BRUSSELS I REGULATION: HISTORICAL PERSPECTIVE

Until the adoption in December 2000 of Regulation 44/2001 on Jurisdiction and the Recognition and Enforcement of Judgments in Civil and Commercial Matters (also known as Brussels I Regulation),[1] issues of jurisdiction and the enforcement of judgments in civil and commercial matters were governed by the above-mentioned 1968 Convention. Subject to some relatively minor changes, Regulation 44/2001 largely mirrors that Convention.

The 1968 Brussels Convention, entered into initially among the then six Member States, essentially (1) harmonized the bases on which the

---

1. O.J. L 12/1 (Jan. 16, 2001).

courts of the Member States could assert personal jurisdiction over domiciliaries of another Member State, and (2) obligated Member State courts to recognize and enforce covered judgments rendered by the courts of other Member States (presumably in accordance with the agreed upon jurisdictional rules), provided those judgments did not run afoul of certain additional conditions for recognition and enforcement exclusively laid down by the Convention. Because the Brussels Convention consciously "linked" recognition and enforcement, on the one hand, with the exercise of personal jurisdiction, on the other, it was said to exemplify a "double" convention.

Though plainly linked to Community law objectives, the Brussels Convention was assumed not to represent Community law as such. It was neither a treaty that "constituted" the Community legal order (such as the EC Treaty itself), nor a legislative act taken by the institutions of the Community (such as a regulation, directive or decision). Though foreseen in general terms by the EC Treaty, the Brussels Convention remained an agreement entered into by and among the Member States in their separate sovereign capacities.

Still, the Brussels Convention was not to remain an ordinary international agreement. First, as already noted, the EC Treaty had in a sense mandated it. Second, any State seeking to join the EC was required to accede to the Convention as a condition of membership. Historically, accession negotiations with every new Member State resulted in an obligation to join the Brussels Convention "system," and with each accession the Convention has been appropriately amended.

Then, as early as 1971, the Brussels Convention States entered into a Protocol vesting the Court of Justice with jurisdiction to render preliminary rulings on the interpretation of the Convention[2]. Such rulings are understood to be no less binding on national courts, or authoritative, than preliminary rulings by the Court of Justice under its general preliminary reference procedure. By centralizing judicial interpretation of the Brussels Convention in the Court of Justice, the signatory States sought to ensure not only a uniform meaning and application of the Convention among the courts of the Member States, but also ones that would be consistent with the Convention's and, more generally, the Community's underlying purposes. As the majority of provisions of Regulation 44/2001 are nearly identical to those of the Brussels Convention, the ECJ rulings issued under Protocol 75/464 remain guiding case law.

As the European Community developed closer ties with the EFTA States (some of which were likely accession candidates and others of which would soon join the EC Member States in forming the European Economic Area), it seemed desirable and appropriate for non-EC States to be permitted to join the Brussels Convention system. Accordingly, on September 16, 1988, a separate Lugano Convention was signed, extending the

---

2. Protocol 75/464, O.J. 204/28 (Aug. 2, 1975), republished as amended at O.J. C 27/28 (Jan. 26, 1998).

Convention system to Austria, Finland, Iceland, Norway, Sweden, and Switzerland.[3] (Austria, Finland and Sweden would, of course, upon their 1995 accession to the EU, become parties to the Brussels Convention, leaving Iceland, Norway and Switzerland as the only strictly "Lugano Convention" States.) In declarations annexed to the Lugano Convention, the Member States called upon the Court of Justice, when interpreting the Brussels Convention, to "pay due account" to rulings under the Lugano Convention; conversely, the EFTA States asked their courts to show like respect for rulings by the Court of Justice and the courts of the Member States. The Lugano Convention's Protocol on the Uniform Interpretation of the Convention strengthens this requirement by providing for a centralized system of exchange of information on court judgments interpreting the Convention. Following the replacement of the Brussels Convention by Regulation 44/2001, a new Lugano Convention was negotiated with Iceland, Norway and Switzerland and signed on behalf of the Community on October 30, 2007.

Arguably, the Brussels Convention could have taken the form of Community legislation from the very start. Harmonizing rules on jurisdiction, recognition and enforcement among the Member States could conceivably promote the free movement of goods, persons, services and capital among the States, and thus constitute a proper exercise of legislative authority under the Treaty's general provisions on harmonization in aid of the internal market. It is not implausible that agreement on the bases upon which Member State courts may assert jurisdiction over nationals of other Member States in civil and commercial litigation would facilitate decisions by producers and consumers to participate in cross-border economic activity. The "harmonization case" for recognition and enforcement of "sister-state" judgments is even stronger. A system of mutual recognition and enforcement of judgments offers economic actors an important measure of security in buying and selling, working and hiring, rendering and purchasing services, and investing across borders, if they know that they may rely on other Member States' courts to recognize and enforce judgments rendered in their favor at home and on their own courts to recognize and enforce judgments rendered elsewhere.

With the Maastricht Treaty, the European Union acquired a more solid (albeit non-Community law) basis for the Brussels Convention and like agreements which exemplify precisely the sort of intergovernmental cooperation that lay at the core of the TEU's "pillar three" on cooperation in Justice and Home Affairs. The Amsterdam Treaty, as noted, then went further, shifting cooperation in civil justice from pillar three to pillar one decision-making as an aspect of the EC Treaty's new chapter establishing "an area of freedom, justice and security." Thus was the way cleared both for converting the 1968 Brussels Convention (and indeed also the 1998 Matrimonial Jurisdiction and Judgments Convention) into directly applicable legislation and for enacting fresh legislation on other civil justice matters.

---

3. O.J. L 319/9 (Nov. 25, 1988).

2. BRUSSELS I: AN OVERVIEW

The Brussels I Regulation was adopted by the Council, acting unanimously under EC Treaty Article 65 (now TFEU Article 81), on December 22, 2000. (The Regulation is found in Part VII of the Documents Supplement as document 41.) The Commission had hoped in proposing the measure to replace the Brussels Convention in its entirety with directly applicable and directly effective legislation. Matters were not to be that simple, however, due to the fact that Denmark, Ireland and the UK did not participate fully in the EC Treaty's chapter on "an area of freedom, justice and security" to which the then Article 65 ECT belonged. Ultimately, Denmark opted out of Regulation 44/2001, though the UK and Ireland chose to participate. Consequently the 1968 Brussels Convention, as amended, remained in effect and applicable insofar as questions of jurisdiction between Denmark and the remaining Member States were concerned. In 2007, Denmark revoked its opt-out and the Brussels I Regulation now applies across the board. Upon entry into force of the Regulation, any reference to the Brussels Convention is deemed to be a reference to the Brussels I Regulation.

Regulation 44/2001 begins by enumerating "permissible" jurisdictional bases, i.e. bases that the courts of one Contracting State may assert as against another Contracting State's domiciliaries, and excluding the use of all others, however permissible and even well-established they may be in domestic civil practice. (Courts may of course continue to use the excluded jurisdictional grounds in litigation against domiciliaries of third States). For good measure, the Regulation specifically declares in Annex I that the jurisdictional bases listed there, though customarily used in the respective countries, would be impermissible as against domiciliaries of other Member States. These are the grounds that are generally considered from an international law point of view as being excessive or, to use the more usual term, "exorbitant."

Besides identifying permissible and impermissible jurisdictional bases in civil and commercial actions against domiciliaries of other Member States, the Regulation also lays down rules on other important jurisdiction-related issues, such as the validity of forum selection clauses, *lis pendens*, and the availability of provisional relief in aid of litigation in another Member State. We briefly look at these harmonized rules as well.

Turning to recognition and enforcement as such, the Regulation obligates the courts of all Member States to recognize and enforce fully the final judgments rendered by courts of other Member States in civil and commercial matters. As will be seen, the Regulation does not include lack of personal jurisdiction among these grounds, presumably because Member State courts are presumed to respect the Regulation's limitations on the exercise of jurisdiction.

Though broad in scope, the Brussels I Regulation has its limitations. As its title suggests, it is confined to jurisdiction and judgments in civil and commercial matters. (To reinforce this limitation, the Regulation expressly provides in Article 1 that it shall not apply to revenue, customs or administrative matters.) But the Regulation is also subject to specific exclusions even within the fields of civil and commercial law, namely the status or legal capacity of natural persons, rights in property arising out of matrimonial relationships, wills and successions, bankruptcy and insolvency, social security and arbitration. Certain of these gaps—such as matrimonial matters—are filled by additional, more specialized, EU law instruments on jurisdiction and judgments.

3. JURISDICTION UNDER THE BRUSSELS I REGULATION

In the pages that follow, we explore the main features of the Brussels I Regulation as a framework for both the exercise of jurisdiction and the recognition and enforcement of judgments. Preliminary rulings by the Court of Justice, issued both with respect to the Brussels Convention and the Regulation itself, figure importantly in this chapter. This is because the Regulation, its seemingly straightforward schema notwithstanding, has generated a large number of disputes as to its proper interpretation.

In interpreting Regulation 44/2001, national courts and the Court of Justice alike are guided by the understandings that have developed under the parallel provisions of the 1968 Convention, as well as by the nascent case law under the Regulation. In the following text, where reference is made to the Brussels Convention in relation to a decision of the ECJ, it is with the understanding, unless otherwise indicated, that the findings apply equally under the Brussels I Regulation.

4. BRUSSELS I'S SPHERE OF APPLICATION

A recurring issue in the interpretation of Brussels I is whether, when the Regulation employs a given term, it intends that term to be read in accordance with the various domestic legal systems' understanding of the term, or rather to be given an "autonomous" meaning. For some time, confusion in this regard surrounded even questions of the law applicable to the determination as to whether a particular judgment concerns a "civil or commercial matter," given the absence of an express definition in the Convention.

LTU LUFTTRANSPORTUNTERNEHMEN GmbH & CO. KG v. EUROCONTROL
Case C–29/76, [1976] ECR 1541.

[In an action to enforce a Belgian monetary judgment, a German appeals court asked the Court of Justice whether, for purposes of interpreting the term "civil or commercial matters," reference should be made to the law of the State where the judgment was rendered or to the law of the State where enforcement is sought. The underlying action was a suit by a public aviation safety authority (Eurocontrol) to recover charges payable to it by a private firm for the use of equipment and services.]

* * *

3 It is necessary, in order to ensure, as far as possible, that the rights and obligations which derive from [the Convention] for the contracting states and the persons to whom it applies are equal and uniform, that the terms of that provision should not be interpreted as a mere reference to the internal law of one or other of the states concerned.

[T]he concept "civil and commercial matters" cannot [accordingly] be interpreted solely in the light of the division of jurisdiction between the various types of courts existing in certain states.

The concept in question must ... be regarded as independent and must be interpreted by reference, first, to the objectives and scheme of the convention and, secondly, to the general principles which stem from the corpus of the national legal systems.

4 [C]ertain types of judicial decision must be regarded as excluded from the area of application of the convention, either by reason of the legal relationships between the parties to the action or of the subject-matter of the action.

Although certain judgments given in actions between a public authority and a person governed by private law may fall within the area of application of the convention, this is not so where the public authority acts in the exercise of its powers.

Such is the case in a dispute which, like that between the parties to the main action, concerns the recovery of charges payable by a person governed by private law to a national or international body governed by public law for the use of equipment and services provided by such body, in particular where such use is obligatory and exclusive.

This applies in particular where the rate of charges, the methods of calculation and the procedures for collection are fixed unilaterally in relation to the users, as is the position in the present case....

5 On the basis of these criteria, a judgment given in an action between a public authority and a person governed by private law, in which a public authority has acted in the exercise of its powers, is excluded from the area of application of the convention.

NOTES AND QUESTIONS

1. Do you agree that the Court should insist on a definition of "civil or commercial" that transcends legal usage in any particular Member State? But then what is meant by "the general principles which stem from the corpus of the national legal systems," referred to in paragraph 3 of the judgment?

2. The Court has consistently developed an autonomous understanding of the terms that define the Regulation's scope of application. See, for

example, Préservatrice Foncière Tiard SA v. Netherlands, Case C–266/01, [2003] ECR–I 4867 (the term "customs matters" does not cover a claim by a contracting State to enforce a guarantee contract intended to guarantee the payment of a customs debt, where the legal relationship between the State and the guarantor does not entail the exercise by the State of powers going beyond those governing relations between private individuals, even if the guarantor may raise defenses that necessitate examining the existence and content of the debt); Lechouritou v. Dimosio tis Omospondiakis Dimokratias tis Germanias, Case C–292/05, [2007] ECR–I–1519 (an action by a natural person against a Member State for damages for injury due to acts taken in the victim's State by armed forces of the defendant State is not a civil matter).

3. The Court of Justice has held that a claim for civil damages entertained by a criminal court in conjunction with a related criminal prosecution (a procedure known in France and certain other civil law jurisdictions) falls within the scope of the term "civil matters" within the meaning of the Convention. Sonntag v. Waidmann, Case C–172/91, [1993] ECR I–1963.

5. GENERAL JURISDICTION UNDER BRUSSELS I

The Brussels I Regulation adopts the defendant's domicile as the basis for the exercise of what would be called in US law "general" jurisdiction. According to Article 2, unless otherwise provided, "persons domiciled in a Member State shall, whatever their nationality, be sued in the courts of that State." A person domiciled in a Member State is therefore subject to the jurisdiction of the courts of that State in matters falling within the Regulation's scope, regardless of the links the parties or cause of action may have to some other State (unless, as discussed below, the case falls within the exclusive jurisdiction of another Member State court or is subject to an exclusive forum selection clause designating another Member State court). Article 2 goes on to declare that Member State domiciliaries may also be sued in the courts of another Member State in the circumstances specifically prescribed elsewhere in the Regulation. These are what might be called the Regulation's bases of "special" or, in US parlance " specific" jurisdiction.

To underscore that domicile is the Regulation's presumptively exclusive basis of general jurisdiction over EU domiciliaries, Article 3 (referring to Annex I to the Regulation) explicitly precludes Member State courts from using against such domiciliaries certain specified bases of jurisdiction traditionally considered to give rise to general jurisdiction under domestic law. These are the so-called "exorbitant bases" referred to earlier. The designated bases include, for example Articles 14 and 15 of the French Civil Code (making the plaintiff's nationality a sufficient basis of jurisdiction over a non-national and permitting a French defendant to be sued abroad only by virtue of a forum selection agreement), Section 23 of the German Civil Procedure Code (making the defendant's ownership of property in the jurisdiction a sufficient basis for full *in personam* jurisdiction, even on matters unrelated to the property), and Articles 126(3) and 127 of the Dutch Civil Procedure Code (similar to the French provisions, but making the plaintiff's domicile rather than nationality decisive for jurisdiction over non-Dutch domiciliaries or residents), as well as (for Ireland and the UK) "transient jurisdiction" and (for the UK) the presence or seizure by plaintiff of property belonging to the defendant. EU domiciliaries are thus specifically protected from the assertion of jurisdiction on any of these grounds.

Non–EU domiciliaries enjoy no such protection. Where the defendant is a domiciliary of a non-Member State, Article 4 permits Member State courts to continue to apply their own domestic rules of jurisdiction (including exorbitant ones). Plaintiffs who are domiciled in a Member State may, whatever their nationality, resort to these exorbitant bases against non-EU domiciliaries as fully as may plaintiffs who are nationals of that State.

Returning to domicile as the core jurisdictional basis, there immediately arises the same kind of question that arose in the *Eurocontrol* case. Is the term "domicile," like "civil and commercial," to be determined in accordance with the law of a particular State (perhaps the State in which domicile is asserted) or rather in accordance with a uniform definition? Here, the Regulation itself speaks to the issue: Article 59 calls for a Member State to apply its own internal law to determine whether or not a particular party is domiciled in that State. Once having found that the party is not a domiciliary of that State, the court is then to decide whether the party is a domiciliary of another Member State by applying the law of that other State. Curiously, though, the domicile of a company or other legal person *is* determined by the Regulation. Article 60(1) declares that such a person is domiciled in the location of (a) its statutory seat, (b) its central administration, or (c) its principal place of business.[4] Article 60 thus plainly contemplates the possibility of multiple domiciles. The domicile of a trust is subject under Article 60(3) to still a third approach: the court in which such a case is brought applies its own conflict of law rules to determine domicile.

Does it make sense to you for the Court to have adopted this multiplicity of methods for ascertaining the meaning of "domicile"?

To strengthen the general preference for the defendant's domicile as jurisdictional basis, Article 26(1) of the Regulation requires that, if a defendant who is domiciled in one Member State fails to enter an appearance in a court of another Member State, the court nevertheless "shall declare of its own motion that it has no jurisdiction unless its jurisdiction is derived from the provisions of this Regulation."[5] Thus, for example, a domiciliary of a Member State is not required to appear in the court of another Member State in order to contest the latter's jurisdiction

---

4. Article 60 (2) goes on to define "statutory seat," for purposes of the UK and Ireland, as the registered office and, failing a registered office, then the place of incorporation, and failing both a registered office and place of incorporation, then the place of contract formation.

5. In default situations, Article 26 further directs the court to stay proceedings until it is satisfied that the defendant received notice of the action in sufficient time to enable him or her to prepare a defense.

under the Regulation. He or she may default and assume that the forum will determine its jurisdiction in accordance with the Regulation. Is there not a risk in that strategy, however? In considering the risk, bear in mind that, as we shall see (section 3 infra), the Regulation also recognizes, for certain causes of action, additional "special" jurisdictions (other than the place of domicile) where an EU domiciliary may be sued as a defendant.

The situation is quite different where the defendant makes a voluntary appearance. "[A] court of a Contracting State before whom a defendant enters an appearance shall have jurisdiction," subject only to two exceptions: (1) where appearance was entered solely to contest jurisdiction and (2) where another court has exclusive jurisdiction over the dispute according to Article 22 (discussed in section 9 infra). By appearing without objection, the defendant is deemed to have waived Brussels I's protections.

Does the *plaintiff's* domicile (or nationality) have any bearing on the applicability of the Brussels I Regulation? In Group Josi Reinsurance Company S.A. v. Universal General Insurance Co. (UGIC), Case C–412/98, [2000] ECR I–5925, a Canadian insurance company (UGIC) which was in liquidation brought suit against a Belgian reinsurance company (Group Josi) in the Commercial Court of Nanterre, France, for money claimed under a reinsurance contract between them. When Universal sued Group Josi, Group Josi argued that it could be sued only in the Commercial Court of Brussels where it had its registered office. The Nanterre court upheld its own jurisdiction on the ground that Universal, being a Canadian corporation and having no place of business in the Community, was not bound by the Brussels Convention. On appeal, the Cour d'Appel of Versailles made a preliminary reference to the ECJ, asking whether the Convention rules on jurisdiction apply due to the defendant's having its domicile or seat in a Member State, even though the plaintiff is a non-EU domiciliary.

The Court observed that in certain special cases ("special jurisdiction"), the Convention treats the plaintiff's domicile as an adequate jurisdictional basis. For example, with the aim of protecting the weaker party, Article 14 of the Convention (Article 16 of the Regulation) allows holders of insurance policies and consumers to bring proceedings against the other party to their contract in the courts of the Contracting State in which they are domiciled. Otherwise, however, the Convention and Regulation attach no significance to the plaintiff's domicile. Thus, the nationality of the plaintiff in itself can neither found jurisdiction nor defeat jurisdiction that otherwise exists.

6. SPECIAL JURISDICTION

As mentioned, in addition to establishing general jurisdiction based on the defendant's domicile, the Regulation permits plaintiffs also to bring certain specified categories of disputes against Member State domiciliaries in designated fora, with the result that EU domiciliaries may in the stated circumstances be sued not only in their place of domicile, but in these other places as well, though only on the basis of specific rather than general jurisdiction. These rules of "special jurisdiction" are laid down limitatively in Articles 5 to 21 of the Regulation.

Article 5 recognizes seven instances of "long-arm"-type "special" jurisdiction. These relate to suits in contract (art. 5(1)), maintenance (art. 5(2)), tort (art. 5(3)); civil damages based on a criminal act (art. 5(4)), as well as suits arising out of the operations of a branch, agency or other establishment (art. 5(5)); out of a trust (art. 5(6)), and out of salvage of cargo or freight (art. 5(7)). In this section, we focus on the special contract and tort provisions.

a. Place of Performance in Contract

Article 5(1) of the Regulation establishes specific jurisdiction in contract cases in the courts of the place of performance of the contract. However, unlike its Convention counterpart, the article goes on to presume that the place of performance is the place where the goods were delivered or should have been delivered (in the sale of goods) or the place where the services were provided or should have been provided (in the case of services). In all other cases, place of performance is presumably determined in the way it was under the Convention. In the Convention case of Industrie Tessili Italiana Como v. Dunlop AG, Case 12/76, [1976] ECR 1473, the Court had held that the court where the action is brought should be guided in determining the place of performance by its domestic conflicts of law rules.

14   Having regard to the differences obtaining between national laws of contract and to the absence at this stage of legal development of any unification in the substantive law applicable, it does not appear possible to give any more substantial guide to the interpretation of the reference made by article 5(1) to the "place of performance" of contractual obligations. This is all the more true since the determination of the place of performance of obligations depends on the contractual context to which these obligations belong.

15   In these circumstances the reference in the Convention to the place of performance of contractual obligations cannot be understood otherwise than by reference to the substantive law applicable under the rules of conflict of laws of the court before which the matter is brought.

Is the Court justified in insisting on an autonomous rule for the meaning of "civil and commercial," but not "place of performance"?

Logically perhaps, when a contract provides for multiple places of delivery of goods, more than one court should enjoy special jurisdiction under Article 5(1)b. But, in the interest of consolidating litigation, the Court in Color Drack GmbH v. Lexx International Vertriebs GmbH, Case C–386/05, [2007] ECR I–3699, held otherwise. Positing that, in the interest of efficiency, "one court must have jurisdiction to hear all the claims arising out of the contract" (¶ 38), the Court opted for "the place with the closest linking factor between the contract and the court" and held that place to be, presumptively, the place of the principal delivery, to be determined on the basis of economic criteria (¶ 40). If it is not possible to determine the principal place of delivery, the plaintiff may choose among the places of delivery.

b. Place of Tort

Article 5(3), the fundamental provision on specific jurisdiction in tort, delict or quasi-delict, provides as follows:

> A person domiciled in a Member State may, in another Member State be sued . . . (3) in matters relating to tort, delict or quasi-delict, in the courts for the place where the harmful event occurred or may occur.

HANDELSKWEKERIJ G.J. BIER BV v. MINES DE POTASSE D'ALSACE SA

Case 21/76, [1976] ECR 1735.

[A Rotterdam trial court declined jurisdiction over a suit that a Dutch horticulturalist and Dutch public interest group had brought against a French company for polluting the Rhine River through the discharge of saline waste. It believed that only the courts of France, the place where the discharge took place, had jurisdiction under the Brussels Convention. The Dutch appeals court made a reference to the ECJ.]

13   In the context of the Convention, the meaning of [the] expression ["the place where the harmful event occurred"] is unclear when the place of the event which is at the origin of the damage is situated in a state other than the one in which the place where the damage occurred is situated, as is the case . . . with atmospheric or water pollution beyond the frontiers of a state.

14   The form of words "place where the harmful event occurred," used in all the language versions of the Convention, leaves open the question whether, in the situation described, it is necessary, in determining jurisdiction, to choose as the connecting factor the place of the event giving rise to the damage, or the place where the damage occurred, or to accept that the plaintiff has an option between the one and the other of those two connecting factors.

* * *

17   Taking into account the close connection between the component parts of every sort of liability, it does not appear appropriate to opt for one of the two connecting factors mentioned to the exclusion of the other, since each of them can, depending on the circumstances, be particularly helpful from the point of view of the evidence and of the conduct of the proceedings.

* * *

[19]   Thus the meaning of the expression "place where the harmful event occurred" in article 5(3) must be established in such a way as to acknowledge that the plaintiff has an option to commence proceedings either at the place where the damage occurred or the place of the event giving rise to it.

* * *

[22]   [I]t appears from a comparison of the national legislative provisions and national case-law on the distribution of jurisdiction ... that, albeit by differing legal techniques, a place is found for both of the connecting factors here considered and that in several states they are accepted concurrently.

[23]   In these circumstances, the interpretation stated above has the advantage of avoiding any upheaval in the solutions worked out in the various national systems of law, since it looks to unification ... by way of a systematization of solutions which ... have already been established in most of the states concerned.

NOTES AND QUESTIONS

1. Is the Court consistent in establishing an autonomous definition of place of tort (albeit one that allows a choice), while deferring to forum law on the meaning of place of performance (other than in the sale of goods or provision of services)?

2. In Dumez France SA and Tacoba Sarl v. Hessische Landesbank, Case C–220/88, [1990] ECR I–49, Dumez, the assignee of two French companies, sued a number of German banks in French court in tort for the damage to the French companies caused by the banks' refusal to finance certain property development projects on which the French companies' German subsidiaries were subcontractors. Dumez failed to convince the lower French courts that they had jurisdiction over the German banks, and the French Cour de Cassation made a reference to the ECJ. The Court distinguished the *Mines de potasse d'Alsace* case as a situation in which the damage occurred at some distance from the event giving rise to it, whereas in Dumez's case, the banks, the prime contractor and the subsidiaries which were responsible for the performance of the contract were all established in the same Member State (Germany). The Court considered the harm to Dumez as parent company to be merely the indirect consequence of the losses suffered by the German subsidiaries. It concluded that the place where damage occurred should not be understood as including the place where indirect victims of the damage experienced their own loss.

The exercise of special jurisdiction under the Convention presupposes "the existence of a particularly close connecting factor between the dispute and courts other than those of the defendant's domicile" (¶¶ 17–18). Without this limitation, there could result an unnecessary multiplicity of competent fora and a risk of inconsistent judgments, as well as opportunities for plaintiffs improperly to bring suit in the place of their own domicile, contrary to the Convention's preference. For another example, see Marinari v. Lloyd's Bank plc and Zubaidi Trading Company, Case C–364/93, [1995] ECR I–2719.

3.   In Shevill v. Presse Alliance SA, Case C–68/93, [1995] ECR I–415, the Court allowed the victim of an alleged libel by a newspaper article distributed in several Contracting States to bring suit against the publisher either before the courts of the place where the publisher of the defamatory publication is established (which would have jurisdiction to award damages for all the harm caused by the defamation) or before the courts of each Contracting State in which the publication was distributed and the victim suffered injury to reputation (each of which, however, has jurisdiction solely with respect to the harm caused in the State where the court is located). The existence and extent of the harm are of course governed not by the Convention, but by the substantive law designated by the conflict of law rules of the forum. This enabled the plaintiff to sue in the UK and take advantage of the UK's plaintiff-friendly law of defamation, though only as to injury suffered in the UK.

4.   Since Brussels I's rules governing special jurisdiction differ as between contract and tort, characterization of a given claim can make a jurisdictional difference. In Tacconi v. HWS, Case C–344/00, [2002] ECR I–7357, the Court ruled that claims in pre-contractual liability (*culpa in contrahendo*) are more properly treated as tort rather than contract claims because they do not arise out of obligations freely assumed by one party toward another. This result is consistent with the broad definition of tort in the Regulation ("tort, delict or quasi-delict") as well as the fact that tort in civil law systems is commonly thought of as merely a species of "non-contractual" liability.

7. JURISDICTION BASED ON MULTI–PARTY STATUS

Article 6 of the Brussels I Regulation opens up the prospect of still further additional fora, this time, however, based on certain specified litigation linkages between the defendant and other parties and other claims. It reads:

A person domiciled in a Member State may also be sued:

1.   where he is one of a number of defendants, in the courts for the place where any one of them is domiciled, provided the claims are so closely connected that it is expedient to hear and determine them together to avoid the risk of irreconcilable judgments resulting from separate proceedings;

2.   as a third party in an action on a warranty or guarantee or in any other third party proceedings, in the court seised of the original proceedings, unless these were instituted solely with the object of removing him from the jurisdiction of the court which would be competent in his case;

3.   on a counter-claim arising from the same contract or facts on which the original claim was based, in the court in which the original claim is pending;

4. in matters relating to a contract, if the action may be combined with an action against the same defendant in matters relating to rights in rem in immovable property, in the court of the Member State in which the property is situated.

These provisions for multi-party-based jurisdiction may be quite useful from the plaintiff's point of view. Think, for example, of being able to sue all the many members of a cartel together in the court of the place of domicile of any one of them. But the provisions are also potentially problematic. The plaintiff may, for example, manage to avoid suing the principal defendant in that defendant's domicile by also naming an artificial co-defendant and suing both in the co-defendant's domicile, assuming the conditions laid down in Article 6 (notably the requisite close connection) are met. The Court has held that the plaintiff may do so, even if it joins the defendants in a single action for the sole purpose of ousting the jurisdiction of the courts of the domicile of one of the defendants. Freeport plc v. Arnoldsson, Case C–98/06, [2007] ECR I–8319. (Note that Article 6(2) contains language expressly disallowing use of multi-party jurisdiction to achieve such a purpose. Why should the Regulation—or the Court— disallow use of the multi-party jurisdiction device to avoid suing the defendant in its own domicile in situations arising under Article 6(2), while tolerating it in situations arising under Article 6(1)?)

Of course, if a defendant is sued in the courts of a co-defendant's domicile, without the former having any other connection with that jurisdiction, the assertion of jurisdiction may well be one that a U.S. court would consider as improper for want of minimum contacts. This could well lead a U.S. court eventually to deny recognition or enforcement to the judgment against that defendant.

8. INSURANCE, CONSUMER AND EMPLOYMENT CONTRACTS

Articles 8 through 17 of the Regulation lay down mandatory jurisdictional rules for contracts of insurance and consumer contracts, except where the parties have otherwise agreed and could, by virtue of the Regulation, validly do so. Let us take insurance litigation as the example. Article 9 permits an insurer domiciled in a Member State to be sued either (a) in the courts of its place of domicile, (b) in the courts of the Member State where the policyholder, the insured or a beneficiary is domiciled, or (c), if it is a co-insurer, in the courts of a Member State in which proceedings are brought against the leading insurer. (In the case of liability or real property insurance, the insurer may also, under Article 10, be sued in the place where the harmful event occurred.) Moreover, an insurer that is not domiciled in a Contracting State but that has a branch, agency or other establishment in one of the Member States is deemed, for disputes arising out of the operations of the branch, agency or establishment, to be domiciled in that State. Lastly, Article 11 permits the insurer to be joined, if the law of the court permits it, to proceedings that the injured party has already instituted against the insured. Here we encounter one of the exceptional circumstances in which proper jurisdiction may be based on the domicile of the plaintiff.

The policyholder, insured or beneficiary is also advantaged when it is the defendant rather than the plaintiff. First, under Article 12 of the Regulation, suit by the insurer against any one of those parties may be brought only in the courts of the Member State where the defendant is domiciled (subject, however, to the insurer's right to bring a counterclaim in any court in which a claim has been brought against it). Second, the use of forum selection clauses is curtailed in favor of the policyholder, insured or beneficiary. Article 13 permits a forum selection agreement to be invoked only (1) if it is the policyholder, insured or beneficiary who invokes it, (2) if the agreement was entered into on a post-dispute basis, or (3) under other narrow circumstances. Article 13(5) also permits party agreements relating to certain specified "risks."

The Regulation establishes broadly comparable ground rules for consumer contract litigation. These consumer provisions, according to Article 15, apply to contracts for the sale of goods on installment credit terms, contracts for a loan repayable by installments, or any other form of credit made to finance the sale of goods, and more generally any contract concluded with a person who "pursues commercial or professional activities in the Member State of the consumer's domicile or, by any means, directs such activities to that Member State."

Article 15(1) defines a "consumer" as a person who enters into a contract "for a purpose which can be regarded as being outside his trade or profession." The term has predictably given rise to Court of Justice case law. In Shearson Lehman Hutton Inc. v. TVB Treuhandgesellschaft für Vermögensverwaltung und Beteiligungen mbH, Case C–89/91, [1993] ECR I–139, the Court held that the assignee of the claim of an individual investor against Shearson was not a consumer since it, as assignee, was engaged in trade and professional activities, even though the original investor/assignor was not. According to the Court, only "private final" consumers, not engaged in trade or professional activities, may avail themselves of the advantages of Brussels I's special rules for consumer contracts. It is questionable whether this result comports with the concept of assignment. But the Court buttressed its position with the customary argument that jurisdictional bases designating the plaintiff's domicile as the competent forum should be strictly construed, and in any event applied only insofar as they actually serve to protect the weaker party. "The protective role fulfilled by those provisions implies that the application of the rules of special jurisdiction laid down to that end by the Convention should not be extended to persons for whom that protection is not justified" (¶ 19).

While the Brussels and Lugano Conventions did not contain special provisions favoring employees in employment contracts, the Brussels Regulation introduced a regime to that effect, not unlike the insurance and consumer contract regimes just discussed. Article 18 provides that where an employee enters into an individual contract of employment with an employer which is not domiciled in a Member State, but which has a branch, agency or other establishment in any Member State, the employer shall be deemed to be domiciled in the State of that branch, agency or establishment for purposes of jurisdiction over disputes arising out of the operations of that branch, agency or establishment. Under Article 19, an employer domiciled in a Member State may be sued: (1) in the place of the employer's domicile and (2) in another Member State (a) where the employee habitually carries out his work (or in the last place where he did so), or (b) if the employee does not or did not habitually carry out his work in any one country, then in the place where the business which engaged the employee is or was situated Finally, Article 21 deals with forum selection clauses contained in individual contracts of employment in much the same way as such clauses in insurance and consumer contracts are handled, as described above

9. RULES ON EXCLUSIVE JURISDICTION

Notwithstanding the Regulation's embrace of defendant's domicile as place of general jurisdiction (and its recognition of certain cases of specific jurisdiction), Article 22 exceptionally subjects a small number of disputes to the exclusive jurisdiction of a designated forum—exclusive even of the courts of the defendant's domicile (and, presumably, also of the courts designated in a forum selection clause). Article 22 is reinforced by Article 25, which provides that "where a court of a Member State is seised of a claim which is principally concerned with a matter over which the courts of another Member State have exclusive jurisdiction by virtue of Article 22, it shall declare of its own motion that it has no jurisdiction."

Subject to certain stated limitations, Article 22 provides for exclusive jurisdiction (regardless of domicile) as follows:

1) in proceedings which have as their object rights in rem in immovable property or tenancies of immovable property, the courts of the Member State in which the property is situated,

2) in proceedings which have as their object the validity of the constitution, the nullity or the dissolution of companies or other legal persons or associations of natural or legal persons, or of the validity of the decisions of their organs, the courts of the Member State in which the company, legal person or association has its seat. In order to determine that seat, the court shall apply its rules of private international law;

3) in proceedings which have as their object the validity of entries in public registers, the courts of the Member State in which the register is kept;

4) in proceedings concerned with the registration or validity of patents, trade marks, designs, or other similar rights required to be

deposited or registered, the courts of the Member State in which the deposit or registration has been applied for, has taken place or is under the terms of a Community instrument or an international convention deemed to have taken place.

5) in proceedings concerned with the enforcement of judgments, the courts of the Member State in which the judgment has been or is to be enforced.

In Dansommer A/S v. Götz, Case C–8/98, [2000] ECR I–393, a German court asked whether the rule conferring exclusive jurisdiction in proceedings concerning tenancies of immovable property applies to an action for damage to premises which a private individual had rented for a few weeks' holidays, where the action was brought not by the owner of the property, but by a professional tour operator from whom the person in question had rented the premises. The Court began by observing that the Convention provisions establishing exclusive jurisdiction must be construed narrowly, "since the article deprives the parties of the choice of forum which would otherwise be theirs and, in certain cases, results in their being brought before a court which is not that of the domicile of any of them" (¶ 21). Nevertheless, the Court considered the damage action to be "directly linked to a leasing contract concerning immovable property and consequently to a tenancy of immovable property within the meaning of Article 16(1)(a) of the Convention [Article 22(1) of the Regulation]," this being the only interpretation which would ensure that disputes arising out of tenancies of immovable property are heard in the place best situated to conduct the necessary investigation and to identify the relevant local standards and practices. The Court was uninfluenced by the fact that the suit against the tenant had been brought not by the owner of the immovable property, but rather by the tour operator. Due to subrogation, the tour operator was acting not in that capacity, but as if it were the owner of the property in question.

Each of the core terms in Article 22 is subject, in one degree or another, to interpretation, and thus to dispute. To give just one example, the Court of Justice was asked whether an action to prevent a nuisance in the form of ionizing radiation from a nuclear power plant in a neighboring Member State qualified as an in rem action within what is now Article 22(1) of the Regulation. The Court predictably answered in the negative. Land Oberosterreich v. EZ, Case C–343/04, [2006] ECR–I 4557.

10. FORUM SELECTION CLAUSES

Another possible source of exclusive jurisdiction is a forum selection clause to that effect. Article 23 of the Regulation provides for the exclusive jurisdiction of a court or the courts of any Member State designated by party agreement, provided at least one of the parties to the agreement was domiciled in a Member State.[6] However, a forum selection is not valid or

---

6. Article 23(3) also gives limited recognition to forum selection agreements entered into by parties neither of whom is domiciled in a Member State. In that case, the courts of the other

enforceable if contrary to the Regulation's restrictions on such clauses in insurance, consumer or employment contracts (as set forth above) or contrary to the Regulation's provisions establishing exclusive jurisdiction.

The Regulation deems a forum selection clause to be exclusive unless provided otherwise in the parties' agreement. Such an agreement may apply both to disputes that have arisen and those that may later arise in connection with a particular legal relationship. The agreement may either take written form or simply accord with past practices between the parties or with usage in international trade or commerce.

Forum selection clauses have generated a considerable number of preliminary references to the Court. The question in Powell Duffryn plc v. Petereit, Case C–214/89, [1992] ECR I–1745, was whether the designation of a forum in a company's articles of incorporation constitutes a forum selection clause within the meaning of the Regulation. The party invoking the clause observed that under the law of Germany, where the company in question was incorporated, corporate statutes are considered to be contractual in nature, while the party resisting application of the clause argued that corporate statutes are "normative" and non-negotiable in character, and cannot operate as a vehicle for a forum selection clause.

The Court held that, notwithstanding different national attitudes toward the relationship between companies and shareholders, the question raised by the referring court required a uniform answer which it gave as follows:

16   [T]he links between the shareholders of a company are comparable to those between the parties to a contract. The setting up of a company is the expression of the existence of a community of interests between the shareholders in the pursuit of a common objective.... It follows that, for the purposes of the application of the Brussels Convention, the company's statutes must be regarded as a contract covering both the relations between the shareholders and also the relations between them and the company they set up.

17   [A] clause conferring jurisdiction in the statutes of a company limited by shares is [therefore to be regarded as] an agreement, within the meaning of Article 17 of the Brussels Convention, which is binding on all the shareholders.

The resisting party argued that at the annual shareholders meeting it had voted against inclusion of the forum selection clause in the company's statute and therefore should not in any case be bound by it. The Court considered that fact (as well as the fact that a party became a shareholder after the clause's adoption) to be "immaterial." "Any other interpretation ... would lead to a multiplication of the heads of jurisdiction for disputes arising from the same legal and factual relationship between the company

Member State are without jurisdiction over the dispute, unless and until the chosen court has actually declined jurisdiction.

and its shareholders and would run counter to the principle of legal certainty."[7]

The Court has shown a generally liberal understanding of what constitutes a party agreement on jurisdiction within the meaning of the Regulation. In Coreck Maritime GmbH v. Handelsveem BV, Case C–387/98, [2000] ECR I–9337, the Court was faced with a jurisdiction clause contained in a bill of lading. The Court decided that the clause did not need to specify a jurisdiction in so many words, and that it would suffice if it recited factors sufficiently objective to enable a court to ascertain whether a jurisdiction had been selected or not. Moreover, such a clause, once agreed to by a carrier and a shipper, and appearing in a bill of lading, could be enforced against a third party bearer of the bill of lading who is deemed under the applicable national law to have succeeded to the rights and obligations of the shipper.

11. PROCEDURAL MATTERS

Though concerned primarily with jurisdiction and judgments, and not with civil procedure, the Brussels I Regulation—like the Convention before it—addresses selected procedural matters that have some bearing on those subjects. Among these are *lis pendens* and provisional relief.

a. Lis Pendens

The Brussels I provisions on *lis pendens* (Articles 27 though 30) come into play when duplicative and/or related causes of action between the same parties are filed in the courts of different Member States. According to Article 27, where a second suit is brought on the "same" cause of action, any Member State court other than the Member State court first seized must, of its own motion, stay proceedings until such time as the jurisdiction of the court first seized is established. Article 30 defines when a court is "seised" of an action.[8] Once the jurisdiction of the court first

---

7. The national court also sought to know what was meant by Article 17's requirement that the forum agreement relate to disputes "in connection with a particular legal relationship." The Court of Justice replied:

31   [The purpose of the requirement] is to avoid a party being taken by surprise by the assignment of jurisdiction to a given forum as regards all disputes which may arise out of its relationship with the other party to the contract and stem from a relationship other than that in connection with which the agreement conferring jurisdiction was made.

32   In that regard, a clause conferring jurisdiction contained in a company's statutes satisfies that requirement if it relates to disputes which have arisen or which may arise in connection with the relationship between the company and its shareholders as such.

However, the Court did not itself decide whether the forum selection clause in the dispute at hand did in fact relate to disputes "which have arisen or which may arise in connection with the relationship between the company and its shareholders as such." It also considered the question whether the clause, as drafted, covered the dispute at hand to be a question of contract interpretation and therefore properly for the national court to decide.

8. A court is "seised":

1. at the time when the document instituting the proceedings or an equivalent document is lodged with the court, provided that the plaintiff has not subsequently failed to take the steps he was required to take to have service effected on the defendant, or

seized is established, all other courts must decline jurisdiction in favor of that court. (Article 29 addresses the possibility that the courts of more than one State might assert exclusive jurisdiction over a dispute, pursuant to Article 22. Even then, "any court other than the court first seised shall decline jurisdiction in favour of that court."[9])

The rule is somewhat different for merely "related" causes of action filed in the courts of different Member States.[10] Under Article 28, any court other than the court first seized may (but presumably need not) stay its proceedings. It may also, on application of one of the parties, decline jurisdiction if the law of that court permits related actions to be consolidated and the court first seized has jurisdiction over both actions.

The Court of Justice stated in Tatry v. Maciej Rataj, Case C–406/92, [1994] ECR I–5439, that the *lis pendens* principle is meant, "in the interests of the proper administration of justice within the Community, to prevent parallel proceedings before the courts of different Contracting States and to avoid conflicts between decisions which might result therefrom." Rules for the avoidance of inconsistent judgments are all the more important in the Regulation context since Article 34(3) of the Regulation states as a ground for non-recognition and non-enforcement of a judgment the latter's inconsistency with a judgment in a dispute between the same parties in the State where recognition or enforcement is sought.

Since application of *lis pendens* presupposes an identity between the parties and the sameness (or relatedness) of the causes of action, the Court of Justice finds itself drawn into questions of this sort. This is because, as the Court insisted in the *Tatry* case, the terms "same cause of action" and "between the same parties" have to be given a meaning independent of the meaning they might have in national law. In the result, the Court held in *Tatry* that the *lis pendens* doctrine applied only in part, since the parties were only partially overlapping. As for whether the causes of action were the same, the Court ruled that a suit by the plaintiff to hold the defendant liable in damages for the injury it caused is, for these purposes, the same cause of action as an earlier proceeding that the defendant had brought for a declaration of non-liability for the loss.

The Court has held that an insurer and its insured must be considered as one and the same party for *lis pendens* purposes, where there is such a degree of identity between their interests that a judgment delivered against one would have the force of *res judicata* as against the other. However, the insurer and insured would not be prevented, where their interests diverge, from asserting their respective interests before the

---

2. if the document has to be served before being lodged with the court, at the time when it is received by the authority responsible for service, provided that the plaintiff has not subsequently failed to take the steps he was required to take to have the document lodged with the court.

9. An exception is made for provisional measures. Article 31 allows a court of a Member State to order protective measures pursuant to its own law in a case over which the courts of another Member State have jurisdiction, and even exclusive jurisdiction, as to the merits.

10. For purposes of Article 28, actions are deemed to be "related" where they are so closely connected that it is expedient to hear and determine them together to avoid the risk of irreconcilable judgments resulting from separate proceedings.

courts as against the other parties concerned. See Drouot assurances SA v. Consolidated Metallurgical Industries, Case C–351/96, [1998] ECR I–3075.

The strength of Brussels I's commitment to *lis pendens* was amply demonstrated in the case of Erich Gasser GmbH v. MISAT Srl, Case C–116/02, [2003] ECR I–14693, where the Court ruled that, even when the second court seized had been designated by the parties as the exclusive forum for resolution of their disputes, it still must defer to earlier filed proceedings in another Member State court. The Court's logic is that the latter court is in as good a position as the court second seized to determine whether it has jurisdiction notwithstanding the arbitration agreement—a determination that the first court seized must make in accordance with the rules of the Brussels I, even if that means declining jurisdiction in deference to the arbitration clause. Did the ECJ in *Gasser* wrongly elevate the *lis pendens* doctrine over the principle of respect for forum selection clauses?

NOTE ON *FORUM NON CONVENIENS* AND ANTI-SUIT INJUNCTIONS UNDER THE BRUSSELS I REGULATION

While fully embracing *lis pendens*, the Brussels I Regulation makes no reference to the doctrine of *forum non conveniens*, a common feature of international litigation in the UK. It was widely thought in the UK that nothing in the Regulation, or the Convention before it, inhibited UK courts from applying the doctrine under suitable circumstances. The Regulation, it was thought, *limited* the jurisdiction that Member State courts could assert against EU domiciliaries, but did not *require* them to exercise that jurisdiction in all cases.

The House of Lords nevertheless put the question to the Court of Justice and was told in Owusu v. Jackson, Case C–281/02, [2005] ECR I–1383, that UK courts were precluded by the Convention from declining the jurisdiction that the Convention confers on them "on the ground that a court of a non-Contracting State would be a more appropriate forum for the trial of the action, even if the jurisdiction of no other Contracting State is in issue or the proceedings have no connecting factors to any other Contracting State" (¶ 46):

37   It must be observed, first, that Article 2 of the Brussels Convention is mandatory in nature and that, according to its terms, there can be no derogation from the principle it lays down except in the cases express-ly provided for by the Convention. It is common ground that no exception on the basis of the *forum non conveniens* doctrine was provided for by the authors of the Convention. . . . ,

38   Respect for the principle of legal certainty, which is one of the objectives of the Brussels Convention would not be fully guaranteed if the court having jurisdiction under the Convention had to be allowed to apply the *forum non conveniens* doctrine.

* * *

41   Application of the *forum non conveniens* doctrine, which allows the
      court seised a wide discretion as regards the question whether a
      foreign court would be a more appropriate forum for the trial of an
      action, is liable to undermine the predictability of the rules of jurisdic-
      tion laid down by the Brussels Convention ... and consequently to
      undermine the principle of legal certainty, which is the basis of the
      Convention.

                                * * *

43   Moreover, allowing *forum non conveniens* in the context of the Brus-
      sels Convention would be likely to affect the uniform application of the
      rules of jurisdiction contained therein in so far as that doctrine is
      recognised only in a limited number of Contracting States, whereas
      the objective of the Brussels Convention is precisely to lay down
      common rules to the exclusion of derogating national rules.

44   The defendants in the main proceedings emphasise the negative
      consequences which would result in practice from the obligation the
      English courts would then be under to try this case, *inter alia* as
      regards the expense of the proceedings, the possibility of recovering
      their costs in England if the claimant's action is dismissed, the
      logistical difficulties resulting from the geographical distance, the need
      to assess the merits of the case according to [foreign law] standards,
      the enforceability [in the foreign State] of a default judgment and the
      impossibility of enforcing cross-claims against the other defendants.

45   In that regard, genuine as those difficulties may be, suffice it to
      observe that such considerations, which are precisely those which may
      be taken into account when *forum non conveniens* is considered, are
      not such as to call into question the mandatory nature of the funda-
      mental rule of jurisdiction contained in Article 2 of the Brussels
      Convention, for the reasons set out above.

      In short, the Court viewed the Regulation as conferring on private
parties a right of access to EU courts considered as competent under the
Regulation. The decision was, to say the least, not well received in many
UK circles, either as a matter of law or policy.

      The Court caused further dismay in the UK when it thereafter ruled
in Turner v. Grovit, Case C–159/02, [2004] ECR I–3565, that the Brussels
Regulation also forbade the issuance by UK courts of anti-suit injunction
in cases governed by the Convention:

25   It is inherent in th[e] principle of mutual trust that, within the scope
      of the Convention, the rules on jurisdiction that it lays down, which
      are common to all the courts of the Contracting States, may be
      interpreted and applied with the same authority by each of them....

26   Similarly, otherwise than in a small number of exceptional cases ...,
      the Convention does not permit the jurisdiction of a court to be
      reviewed by a court in another Contracting State.

27   However, a prohibition imposed by a court, backed by a penalty, restraining a party from commencing or continuing proceedings before a foreign court undermines the latter court's jurisdiction to determine the dispute. Any injunction prohibiting a claimant from bringing such an action must be seen as constituting interference with the jurisdiction of the foreign court. . . .

28   Notwithstanding the explanations given by the referring court and contrary to the view put forward by Mr. Turner and the United Kingdom Government, such interference cannot be justified by the fact that it is only indirect and is intended to prevent an abuse of process by the defendant in the proceedings in the forum State. In so far as the conduct for which the defendant is criticised consists in recourse to the jurisdiction of the court of another Member State, the judgment made as to the abusive nature of that conduct implies an assessment of the appropriateness of bringing proceedings before a court of another Member State. Such an assessment runs counter to the principle of mutual trust which . . . underpins the Convention and prohibits a court, except in special circumstances which are not applicable in this case, from reviewing the jurisdiction of the court of another Member State.

The House of Lords later thought that the Court might take a different view where an anti-suit injunction is issued in support of an arbitration agreement, especially inasmuch as Article 1(2)(d) of the Brussels I Regulation excludes arbitration from the Regulation's scope of application. (The exclusion is widely understood as acknowledging the adequacy for recognition and enforcement purposes of the 1958 Convention on the Recognition and Enforcement of Foreign Arbitral Awards (the "New York Convention")). However, the Court of Justice ruled in Allianz SpA v. West Tankers Inc., Case C–185/07, [2009] ECR I–663, that whether a case falls into one of the exceptions depends on the subject matter of the case, i.e. "the nature of the rights which the proceedings in question serve to protect," and that the subject matter of the case at hand was an anti-suit injunction, not arbitration. In any event, the purposes of the Regulation would be frustrated, as would the principle of mutual trust, if the Member State court before which a suit is brought were deprived of the opportunity to determine for itself whether the dispute falls within the scope of an arbitration clause.

The echoes of *West Tankers* are being heard at the national level. Relying on *West Tankers*, the UK Court of Appeal held in the case of National Navigation Co. v. Endesa Generacion SA, [2009] EWCA Civ. 1397 (Dec. 17, 2009), that a ruling by a Spanish court that an arbitration clause had not been incorporated into a contract (and that the court should therefore not decline jurisdiction on account of the clause) was entitled to recognition under the Brussels I Regulation. It therefore barred the UK courts from deciding the point differently (by, for example, compelling arbitration of the dispute). While conceding that the Spanish judgment on whether the arbitration clause was incorporated into the contract was not itself one "on the merits," the Court nevertheless considered it as so tied up with the merits of a contractual dispute (notably a dispute over the terms of the contract) as to fall within the scope of the Regulation and outside of the arbitration exception in Article 1(2)(d).

The Court's treatment in *West Tankers* of the arbitration exception was controversial and has prompted a more general revisiting of the arbitration exception. Concern had independently arisen over the possibility, in the absence of Brussels I, of inconsistent rulings on a common issue in parallel litigation and arbitral proceedings, as when an arbitral tribunal or court in one Member State upholds the validity of an arbitration clause, but a court in another Member State denies it. Neither *lis pendens* nor anti-suit injunctions can be relied upon to eliminate the problem: Due to the arbitration exception, the Brussels I rules on *lis pendens* would not operate to prevent such parallel proceedings and inconsistent rulings. At the same time, the exception, according to the Court in *West Tankers*, does not exempt anti-suit injunctions in aid of arbitration from the Regulation's general bar on anti-suit injunctions.

A Commission "green paper" of April 2009 outlines the problem and possible solutions as follows:

> [A] partial deletion of the exclusion of arbitration from the scope of the Regulation might improve the interface of the latter with court proceedings. As a result of such a deletion, court proceedings in support of arbitration might come within the scope of the Regulation. A special rule allocating jurisdiction in such proceedings would enhance legal certainty. For instance, it has been proposed to grant exclusive jurisdiction for such proceedings to the courts of the Member State of the place of arbitration, possibly subject to an agreement between the parties. . . .

> Next, a deletion of the exception might allow the recognition of judgments deciding on the validity of an arbitration agreement and clarify the recognition and enforcement of judgments merging an arbitration award. It might also ensure the recognition of a judgment setting aside an arbitral award. This may prevent parallel proceedings between courts and arbitral tribunals where the agreement is held invalid in one Member State and valid in another.

> More generally, the coordination between proceedings concerning the validity of an arbitration agreement before a court and an arbitral tribunal might be addressed. One could, for instance, give priority to the courts of the Member State where the arbitration takes place to decide on the existence, validity, and scope of an arbitration agreement. This might again be combined with a strengthened cooperation between the courts seized, including time limits for the party which contests the validity of the agreement. A uniform conflicts rule concerning the validity of arbitration agreements, connecting, for instance, to the law of the State of the place of arbitration, might

reduce the risk that the agreement is considered valid in one Member State and invalid in another. . . .

Further, as far as recognition and enforcement is concerned, arbitral awards which are enforceable under the New York Convention might benefit from a rule which would allow the refusal of enforcement of a judgment which is irreconcilable with that arbitral award. An alternative or additional way forward might be to grant the Member State where an arbitral award was given exclusive competence to certify the enforceability of the award as well as its procedural fairness, after which the award would freely circulate in the Community.

Green Paper on the Review of Council Regulation (EC) No. 44/2001 on Jurisdiction and the Recognition and Enforcement of Judgments in Civil and Commercial Matters, COM(2009) 175 final (Apr. 21, 2009). As of this writing, Brussels I's relationship to arbitration is still under active reconsideration.

b. Provisional Relief

Notwithstanding the Regulation's emphasis on jurisdictional limitations, the drafters of Brussels I (like the Brussels Convention before it) thought it important under proper circumstances to allow access for provisional relief purposes to a court other than the ones designated by the Regulation as competent to decide the case on the merits. And so, Article 31 expressly permits parties to apply for provisional relief to courts of a Member State, even if the latter lack jurisdiction to decide the merits. In its judgment in van Uden Maritime BV v. Kommanditgesellschaft in Firma Deco–Line, Case C–391/95, [1998] ECR I–7091, the Court ruled that Article 31 should be read as conditioning the authority of such a court to grant provisional relief on there existing "a real connecting link between the subject-matter of the measures sought and the territorial jurisdiction of the Contracting State of the court before which those measures are sought."

Enforcement of Article 31 has presented difficulties. First, the very notion of provisional relief may be contested. In St. Paul Dairy Industries NV v. Unibel Exser BVBA, Case C–104/03, [2005] ECR I–3481, the Court of Justice ruled that an order for the hearing of a witness in pre-trial proceedings does not constitute a provisional measure for Article 31 purposes. Then there is the question of establishing reasonable limitations on the availability of provisional relief. In Mietz v. Intership Yachting Sneek BV, Case C–99/96, [1999] ECR I–2277, the Court ruled that access may not be had to a court for provisional relief under Article 31 unless (a) the defendant is guaranteed repayment of any sums provisionally granted against it in the event it ultimately prevails on the merits and (b) the measure of provisional relief sought relates to specific assets of the defendant located within the territorial jurisdiction of the court. Nor will orders of provisional relief issued pursuant to Article 31 qualify as "judgments" for purposes of the obligation to recognize and enforce if these requirements are not met. In Denilauler SNC v. Couchet Frères,

Case 125/79, [1980] ECR 1553, the Court ruled that court orders may constitute provisional measures under Article 31, even if ordered on an *ex parte* basis (i.e. without the opposing party having been heard). But such measures are not necessarily entitled to benefit from the Regulation's simplified recognition and enforcement procedures because fundamental procedural fairness to the opposing party requires a right to be heard at some stage to help ensure that the measures are subject to appropriate conditions. Is this a sound compromise, and is it consistent with the logic of Brussels I?

B. RECOGNITION AND ENFORCEMENT OF JUDGMENTS

The drafters of the Brussels Convention hoped that, having established a uniform framework for the exercise of jurisdiction in civil and commercial matters, they had largely removed personal jurisdiction as a litigable issue at the judgment recognition and enforcement stage. Articles 32 through 56 of the Regulation deal directly with recognition and enforcement.

The basic rule, stated in Article 33(1), requires the mutual recognition of Member State judgments "without any special procedure being required." As for enforcement as such, Article 38(1) states that once a judgment of a Member State court has been recognized and declared enforceable in another Member State, it may be enforced there.[11] There follow more or less technical provisions on such matters as venue and procedures for filing applications for enforcement (arts. 39–40), for the issuance of enforcement decisions and notice thereof (arts. 41–42), and for appeals (arts. 43–46).

Needless to say, Brussels I absolutely prohibits review of the Member State judgment on the merits. (According to Article 36, "[u]nder no circumstances may a foreign judgment be reviewed as to its substance.")

However, the obligation to recognize and eventually enforce is subject to important conditions specified in Article 34. Judgments falling within the Regulation's scope shall not be recognized (1) if manifestly contrary to the public policy of the state of recognition, (2) if there was a default judgment and a defect in service, unless the defendant failed to challenge the judgment when it was possible to do so, (3) if the judgment is irreconcilable with a judgment given in a dispute between the same parties in the State in which recognition is sought; (4) if the judgment conflicts with local laws of private international law on personal and property rights arising out of matrimonial relationships, wills or successions, or (5) if the judgment is irreconcilable with an earlier judgment given in another Member State or third state involving the same cause of

---

11. Article 38(2) continues: "However, in the United Kingdom, such a judgment shall be enforced in England and Wales, in Scotland, or in Northern Ireland when, on application of any interested party, it has been registered for enforcement in that part of the United Kingdom."

action and between the same parties, provided that this latter judgment fulfils the conditions necessary for its recognition in the State addressed. The fact that a judgment is on appeal, or is still subject to appeal, where rendered is not a ground for denying recognition or enforcement. Article 37, however, permits the court in which recognition or enforcement of a judgment is sought to stay proceedings if an appeal against the judgment has been lodged.

Article 35 separately confronts lack of personal jurisdiction as a ground for denying recognition or enforcement. Perhaps surprisingly, the question whether a judgment was rendered on a permissible basis under Brussels I is not ordinarily reviewable by the court where recognition or enforcement is sought. The only exceptions arise in the context of judgments based on insurance or consumer contract claims, or on matters subject under the Regulation to exclusive jurisdiction; in no other case may the jurisdiction of the rendering court be reviewed. And even in those areas, the review that is permitted is limited. The reviewing court is bound under Article 35(2) by the findings of fact on which the rendering court based its jurisdiction; it may only inquire into whether the facts, as found by the rendering court, were properly characterized in legal terms by that court. As to other situations in which an alleged jurisdictional defect is raised, Article 35(3) is clear and categorical: "[T]he jurisdiction of the court of the Member State of origin may not be reviewed." (For good measure, Article 35(3) also precludes a State from applying the "public policy" defense in such a way as to review the jurisdiction of the court of the rendering court.)

Thus, in the great majority of cases, the court where recognition or enforcement is sought is fully bound on the jurisdictional question—not only as to the findings of fact on which the court of the State of origin based its jurisdiction, but also as to the legal characterization to be given to those findings. The Regulation clearly counts on mutual trust among the Member States when it comes to enforcing the Regulation's limitations on the exercise of personal jurisdiction. But suppose a court does not merely err in its interpretation or application of a permissible jurisdictional basis, but instead avowedly employs a forbidden one? As the *Krombach* case below shows, the mutual trust on matters of jurisdiction on which the Brussels I Regulation is built may on occasion (albeit rare) be misplaced. After reading that case, ask yourself whether "full faith and credit" in the EU has been taken too far.

KROMBACH v. BAMBERSKI
Case C–7/98, [2000] ECR I–1935.

[Krombach, a German cardiologist, was the subject of a preliminary investigation following the death in Germany of his 14–year–old French step-daughter. He was suspected of having raped and murdered her. When the investigation was discontinued, Bamberski, the father of the young girl, caused a preliminary investigation to be opened in France. The

French courts based jurisdiction over Krombach on the fact of the victim's French nationality. Following the investigation, Krombach was committed for trial before the Cour d'Assises and, as is permitted under French procedure, Bamberski introduced a civil claim in damages in connection with the criminal proceeding.

Although Krombach was duly notified of the joined criminal and civil actions, he did not attend the hearing. Thereupon, the court set in motion the procedure provided for under the French Criminal Procedure Code which does not permit the person charged with contempt to appear only through counsel, but rather requires appearance in person. In the end, the Cour d'Assises found Krombach guilty *in absentia* of involuntary manslaughter, sentencing him to 15 years. Ruling on the civil claim, it ordered him to pay Bamberski damages in the amount of 350,000 francs.

Upon application by Bamberski, the German court trial court declared the French civil judgment to be enforceable in Germany. Following an unsuccessful appeal, Krombach sought relief in the German Federal Supreme Court, arguing that he had been unable effectively to defend himself in the proceedings leading to the French judgment against him.]

19   The Convention is intended to facilitate, to the greatest possible extent, the free movement of judgments by providing for a simple and rapid enforcement procedure.

* * *

21   So far as [the public policy exception in] Article 27 of the Convention [now Article 34 of the Regulation] is concerned, the Court has held that this provision must be interpreted strictly inasmuch as it constitutes an obstacle to the attainment of one of the fundamental objectives of the Convention.

22   It follows that, while the Contracting States in principle remain free ... to determine, according to their own conceptions, what public policy requires, the limits of that concept are a matter for interpretation of the Convention.

23   Consequently, while it is not for the Court to define the content of the public policy of a Contracting State, it is nonetheless required to review the limits within which the courts of a Contracting State may have recourse to that concept for the purpose of refusing recognition to a judgment emanating from a court in another Contracting State.

* * *

25   The Court has consistently held that fundamental rights form an integral part of the general principles of law whose observance the Court ensures. ...

26   The Court has thus expressly recognised the general principle of Community law that everyone is entitled to fair legal process, which is inspired by those fundamental rights.

* * *

29   [The first question asked is] whether, regard being had to the public-policy clause ... of the Convention, the court of the State in which enforcement is sought can, with respect to a defendant domiciled in that State, take into account the fact that the court of the State of origin based its jurisdiction on the nationality of the victim of an offence.

* * *

31   Under the system of the Convention, [subject to the exceptions set forth in Article 35(1) of the Regulation], the court before which enforcement is sought cannot review the jurisdiction of the State of origin. This fundamental principle ... is reinforced by the specific statement ... that the test of public policy ... may not be applied to the rules relating to jurisdiction.

32   It follows that the public policy of the State in which enforcement is sought cannot be raised as a bar to recognition or enforcement of a judgment given in another Contracting State solely on the ground that the court of origin failed to comply with the rules of the Convention which relate to jurisdiction.

[However, the court went on to hold that, while lack of jurisdiction was unavailable as a basis for defeating enforcement, either in its own right or under the rubric of public policy, public policy may have been seriously offended for a different reason, namely denial of a fair hearing in violation of settled ECJ and European Court of Human Rights case law.]

44   It follows from the foregoing developments in the case-law that recourse to the public-policy clause must be regarded as being possible in exceptional cases where the guarantees laid down in the legislation of the State of origin and in the Convention itself have been insufficient to protect the defendant from a manifest breach of his right to defend himself before the court of origin, as recognised by the ECHR.

. . .

45   [T]he court of the State in which enforcement is sought can, with respect to a defendant domiciled in that State and prosecuted for an intentional offence, take account, in relation to the public-policy clause in Article 27, point 1, of the Convention, of the fact that the court of the State of origin refused to allow that person to have his defence presented unless he appeared in person.

NOTES AND QUESTIONS

1.   Note that the Court considered violation of procedural due process as justifying denial of enforcement on grounds of public policy, but took no note in this regard of the French court's apparent lack of jurisdiction over Krombach under Brussels Convention.

2.   The macabre elements of the *Krombach* case did not end with this judgment. In 1997, following Krombach's conviction, the French authorities

issued an international warrant for his arrest in Germany, where he had received a two-year suspended sentence for sexually abusing a 16–year–old patient after injecting her with anaesthetic prior to surgery. Germany refused to extradite him to France on grounds of lack of evidence and due to his German citizenship. And in 2002, the European Court of Human Rights in Strasbourg issued a judgment against France for violation of Krombach's right to a fair trial, upon which the French conviction was quashed. In 2006 Krombach, having been stripped of his license to practice medicine, was arrested and convicted in Germany for continuing to practice medicine without a license.

Then suddenly, in October 2009, Krombach was found dumped, bound and gagged outside a French court in the city of Mulhouse near the German border. Bamberski, by now a long-retired accountant from Toulouse, made an anonymous phone call to police revealing Krombach's whereabouts, but later admitted it was he who made the call, putting on a "thick Russian accent" to avoid detection. Bamberski admitted that he had received a call from a Croat named Anton who had offered to "deliver" the doctor to France, asking for no money but acting wholly out of sympathy for Bamberski. Anton was subsequently arrested in Austria for having beaten Krombach and transported him over the border in the trunk of a car, and was later extradited at his own request to be tried in France. Meanwhile, Krombach spent the next 5 months in a high security prison in central Paris. In March 2010, the French Cour de Cassation ordered him to stand a new trial, despite the circumstances under which he found himself in France.

As for Bamberski, the German authorities have been demanding his extradition on account of his organizing Krombach's abduction, requests that the French courts have refused. On the other hand, Bamberski was arrested by the French police on charges of kidnapping, though quickly released on bail. He is expected to stand trial in France and could face up to 10 years in jail. Bamberski says he has no regrets about his actions, though his quest for justice cost him, by his account, all he owns and has ruined his life.

3.   Boch, an Italian distributor of agricultural machinery produced by the German company, Solo Kleinmotoren, sued Solo in a Milan civil court, winning a judgment of 48 million lire for wrongful termination. A German court issued an order of enforcement of the judgment and Solo appealed to a Stuttgart appeals court, at which point the parties reached a monetary settlement, coupled with a written understanding that "[a]ll the parties' claims against one another arising from their business relationship are hereby resolved." Boch thereafter instituted suit against Solo in a Bologna civil court for infringement of the trade name "Solo" and for unfair competition, and Boch was eventually held liable to pay 180 million lira. The Bologna court ruled that the settlement reached in the German court did not preclude the second action.

Boch then brought the Bologna judgment to a Stuttgart court for enforcement. Eventually the German Supreme Court made a preliminary reference to the Court of Justice on whether the prior settlement precluded enforcement of the Bologna judgment under Article 27(3) of the Convention (now Article 34(3) of the Regulation).

The Court denied preclusion, quoting the Convention's definition of "judgment" as "any judgment given by a court or tribunal of a Contracting State, whatever the judgment may be called, including a decree, order, decision or writ of execution ..." According to the Court, this wording meant that judgments, for these purposes, must "emanate from a judicial body of a Contracting State deciding on its own authority on the issues between the parties" (¶ 17). "That condition is not fulfilled in the case of a settlement, even if [the settlement] was reached in a court of a Contracting State and brings legal proceedings to an end. Settlements in court are essentially contractual in that their terms depend first and foremost on the parties' intention...." (¶ 18). Solo Kleinmotoren GmbH v. Boch, Case C–414/92, [1994] ECR I–2237.

Do you agree with the Court's characterization? Is it sound in terms of fulfilling the objectives of Brussels I? Note that Article 51 of the Brussels Convention (in language largely carried over in Article 58 of Brussels I) provided that "[a] settlement which has been approved by a court in the course of proceedings and is enforceable in the State in which it was concluded shall be enforceable in the State in which enforcement is sought...." Shouldn't that language have dictated a different outcome in *Solo Kleinmotoren*?

4.   The case of Minalmet GmbH v. Brandeis Ltd., Case C–123/91, [1992] ECR I–5661, raised the question whether Article 27(2) (now Article 34(2) of the Regulation), which ordinarily precludes recognition of a default judgment entered upon allegedly defective service, applies even if the defaulting defendant had become aware of the judgment and failed to exhaust the remedies then still available to him in the courts of the state of origin. The Court refused to engraft a limitation on the exception based on waiver of available national remedies. Is this consistent with the Court's policy of narrow construction of exceptions to recognition and enforcement?

C. OTHER RECOGNITION AND ENFORCEMENT INSTRUMENTS

Though Brussels I provides a general framework for the enforcement and recognition of judgments in civil and commercial matters, it contains important exceptions some of which are addressed through separate instruments on jurisdiction and the recognition and enforcement of judgments.

1. THE MATRIMONIAL JURISDICTION AND JUDGMENTS REGULATION

Best known among these supplemental instruments is the Matrimonial Jurisdiction and Judgments Regulation. The reason offered at the time the Brussels Convention was concluded in 1968 for excluding matrimonial matters was that Member State laws on these matters (notably divorce) were simply too divergent, and that the Member States regarded the scope of review of judgments allowed by the Brussels Convention as simply too limited for such a field. By 1998, however, the Member States were prepared to enter into a separate Convention on Jurisdiction, Recognition and the Enforcement of Judgments in Matrimonial Matters, O.J. C 221 (July 16, 1998). According to the Explanatory Report on that Convention:[12]

> European integration was mainly an economic affair to begin with and for that reason the legal instruments established were designed to serve an economic purpose. However, the situation has changed fundamentally in recent times so that integration is now no longer purely economic and is coming to have an increasingly profound effect on the life of the European citizen, who finds it hard to understand that he encounters problems in matters of family law while so much progress has been made in property law. The issue of family law therefore has to be faced as part of the phenomenon of European integration. We only need to look at the questions put in the European Parliament not only on dissolution of marriages but also on more general aspects of family law (marriage contracts, paternity, child abduction, adoption, etc.). This Convention is a first step, and a positive and decisive one, along this new road and it may open the way to other texts on matters of family law and succession.

To distinguish the 1998 Matrimonial Convention, which likewise was signed in Brussels, from the 1968 Brussels Convention, it has come to be known simply as Brussels II.

The Preamble to *Brussels II* identified as among the Convention's main purposes "to introduce uniform modern standards for jurisdiction on annulment, divorce and separation and to facilitate the rapid and automatic recognition among Member States of judgments on such matters given in the Member States." The Preamble also highlights "[t]he importance of laying down rules of jurisdiction concerning parental responsibility over the children of both spouses on the occasion of such proceedings and therefore simplifying the formalities governing the rapid and automatic recognition and enforcement of the relevant judgments." Therefore, like Brussels I, Brussels II is a "double convention" in that it contains rules of direct jurisdiction linked to rules on the recognition and enforcement of foreign judgments.

The Brussels II Convention has likewise been subsequently transposed into a Regulation, the current version of which is Regulation 2201/2003, concerning jurisdiction and the recognition and enforcement of judgments in matrimonial matters and matters of parental responsibility.[13] The Brussels II Regulation, which largely reproduces the Brussels II Convention, covers proceedings for (i) divorce, legal separation or marriage annulment and (ii) the attribution, exercise, delegation, restriction

---

12.   O.J. C 221/27–64 (July 16, 1998).

13.   O.J. L 338/1 (Dec. 23, 2003).

or termination of parental responsibility. The term "parental responsibility" denotes all rights and duties relating to the person or the property of a child which are given to a natural or legal person by judgment, by operation of law, or by an agreement having legal effect, including custody and rights of access. The Brussels II Regulation seeks to cover much the same ground for matrimonial and parental matters as the Brussels I Regulation covers more generally. Its jurisdictional rules in matters of child abduction are of particular significance as they amend, in relations among the Member States, the provisions of the 1980 Hague Convention on Civil Aspects of International Child Abduction.

Denmark has elected not to participate in Brussels II.

2. THE INSOLVENCY PROCEEDINGS REGULATION

Insolvency is another matter excluded from the Brussels I Regulation but now the subject of its own instrument. Although a draft Bankruptcy Convention had been proposed as early as 1980, agreement on a text was long in coming, and in fact no text was ever opened for ratification. The fact remains, however, that when an undertaking with transnational obligations and creditors becomes insolvent, the proper functioning of the internal market can be significantly affected. More particularly, there was a perceived need to coordinate measures taken in regard to an insolvent debtor's assets. Finally, it was thought desirable to remove incentives for parties to a transaction to transfer assets from one Member State to another in anticipation of bankruptcy proceedings, or to engage in forum shopping so as to obtain relief from liability as a debtor or more favorable rank as a creditor. These concerns resulted in Regulation 1346/2000 on insolvency proceedings,[14] applicable to all debtors, whether a natural or a legal person, and whether a trader or a private party. However, insolvency proceedings of insurance undertakings, credit institutions, investment undertakings holding funds or securities for third parties, and collective investment undertakings are excluded from its scope, presumably because they are deemed adequately covered by preexisting special arrangements.

The Regulation (art. 3) contemplates that main insolvency proceedings will be opened in the Member State where the debtor has its "center of main interests," and will encompass all of the debtor's assets. However, the Regulation also permits the opening of secondary proceedings to run in parallel with the main ones, on the understanding that the effects of such secondary proceedings will be limited to the debtor's assets located in that State. To help ensure coherence and consistency, the Regulation imposes on secondary proceedings mandatory rules of coordination with the main proceedings.[15] Article 18 provides that the powers of the liqui-

---

14. O.J. L 160/1 (June 30, 2000).

15. Under Article 3, prior to the opening of the main insolvency proceedings in the appropriate State, any proceeding opened in another Member State where the debtor has an establishment must be limited to local creditors and creditors of the local establishment or to the situation

dator are to be governed by the law of the State of the opening of procedures, while entitling the liquidator to take certain actions on the territory and before the courts of the other Member States. The Court had an opportunity in Eurofood IFSC Ltd, Case C–341/04, [2006] ECR I–3813, to interpret the insolvency regulation in important respects, including (in ¶ 37) the criteria for determining the "center of main interests" of a subsidiary company. Its ruling also underscored the necessity of affording all parties, notably creditors or their representatives, a fair and equal opportunity to participate in the proceedings.

Except where otherwise provided, the applicable substantive law is the insolvency law (*lex concursus*) of the Member State where proceedings—whether main or secondary—are opened. That law governs all the conditions for the opening, conduct and closure of insolvency proceedings, as well as their effects, both procedural and substantive.[16]

Regulation 1346/2000 seeks to enable every creditor, including tax authorities and social insurance institutions, having its habitual residence, domicile or a registered office within the EU to lodge claims in any or all of the insolvency proceedings pending in the EU which relate to the debtor's assets, with a view to ensuring coordination in the distribution of proceeds and equal treatment of creditors. The transparency and publicity of proceedings is an evident preoccupation of the Regulation.

Invoking the principle of mutual trust, the Regulation calls for immediate recognition by Member States of the opening, conduct and closure of insolvency proceedings in another Member State, as well as of all judgments rendered pursuant to those proceedings (arts. 16 and 17), without review of the assessments on which those decisions were based. As might be expected, available grounds for non-recognition of judgments are drastically curtailed (art. 25). However, the Court underscored in the *Eurofoods* case, supra, that, on a proper interpretation of Article 26 of the Regulation, a Member State may refuse to recognize insolvency proceedings opened in another Member State where the decision to open the proceedings was taken in flagrant breach of the fundamental right to be heard. On the other hand, the Court warned courts not to insist that the proceedings in another State mirror their own, but to assess the fairness of the proceeding as a whole.

3. UNCONTESTED AND SMALL CLAIMS

Still other recognition and enforcement instruments have been adopted in recent years, not so much in consideration of subject matter as in consideration of the size or uncontested character of the claims.

---

in which main proceedings cannot be opened under the law of the Member State where the debtor has its center of main interest. Article 31 mandates cooperation between liquidators in the main and secondary proceedings.

16. Regulation 1346/2000 contains special provisions for rights *in rem* (art. 5), set-offs (art. 6), and payment systems and financial markets (art. 9). At the same time, it seeks to limit the effects of insolvency proceedings on the continuation or termination or employment (art. 10).

The first of these was the European Enforcement Order for Uncontested Claims, established under Regulation 805/2004.[17] Through this instrument, judgments, court settlements and authentic instruments on uncontested claims in civil and commercial matters adopted in one Member State must be recognized and enforced in other Member States, without any intermediate proceedings or any grounds for denying enforcement. The notion of term "uncontested claims" principally covers claims to which a defendant consents or default judgments insofar as these amount to tacit admission of the existence of the claim under the law of the Member State concerned.

The most recent creation of this sort is the European Small Claims Procedure under Regulation 861/2007,[18] designed to ensure that judgments on claims below 2000 euros (excluding interest and costs) are recognized and enforced in other Member States without need of a declaration of enforceability under Regulation 44/2001. This procedure, available since January 1, 2009, significantly simplifies the process of recognition and enforcement.

Neither of these two instruments is applicable in Denmark.

D. FURTHER LEGAL INSTRUMENTS ON COOPERATION IN CIVIL JUSTICE

Using its authority under EC Treaty Articles 65 EC (now TFEU Article 81), the Council has also adopted several regulations governing judicial cooperation in civil matters. In May 2000, the Council adopted Regulation 1348/2000 on the Service of Judicial and Extra Judicial Documents in Civil or Commercial Matters,[19] which was replaced, as of November 13, 2008, by Regulation 1393/2007 on the same subject matter.[20] By this measure, the Member States committed to speedy and reliable methods of transmitting among themselves documents in connection with civil and commercial litigation.

A year later, the Council adopted Regulation 1206/2001 on Cooperation between the Courts of the Member States in the Taking of Evidence in Civil or Commercial Matters.[21] This Regulation in like fashion establishes standardized means of requesting cooperation in the taking of evidence on the territory of one Member State for use in civil or commercial litigation pending or contemplated in the courts of another. Provided the requirements of a valid request, as laid down in the Regulation, have been satisfied, Member States are obligated to provide the assistance requested and to do so expeditiously, unless doing so "is incompatible with the law of the Member State of the requested court or by reason of major

---

17. Amended by Regulation No 1869/2005, O.J. L 300 (Nov. 17, 2005).

18. O.J. L 199 (July 31, 2007).

19. O.J. L 160/37 (June 30, 2000).

20. O.J. L 324 (Dec. 10, 2007).

21. O.J. L 174 (June 27, 2001).

practical difficulties" (art. 10). The requested court must also make available the same coercive measures that are available in analogous domestic litigation circumstances. The Regulation provides certain procedural protections, in the form both of the right of the parties to be present and participate in the taking of evidence, and in the availability of certain testimonial and documentary privileges.

Besides providing for the taking of evidence by the requested court, Regulation 1206/2001 also contemplates the direct taking of evidence by the requesting court in the territory of the other State. Only designated personnel of the requesting State may engage in the direct taking of evidence, and use of this means is limited to situations in which evidence-taking sought can be performed on a voluntary basis, and thus without need for coercive measures. Requests of this type may be refused only if they fall outside the scope of the Regulation, are formally or technically deficient, or are "contrary to fundamental principles of law in [the requested] Member State" (art. 17(5)(c)).

Both of these Regulations, while clearly inspired by two existing multilateral Hague Conventions—the 1965 Convention on Service of Documents and the 1970 Convention on Taking of Evidence, respectively—expressly declare that, within their sphere of application, they take precedence over those instruments (and indeed over other international agreements on the same subjects to which a Member State may be a party). While Ireland and the UK once again agreed to participate in both measures, Denmark did not, and is accordingly not subject to them.

Council Regulation 290/2001[22] codifies the so-called "Grotius" program of incentives and exchanges for legal practitioners, entailing meetings, studies, research, training and exchange programs. Council Decision 2001/470,[23] established a so-called "European Judicial Network in Civil and Commercial Matters." The Network has the general task of facilitating judicial cooperation among the Member States in civil and commercial matters both in areas where existing legal instruments exist (such as the Regulations discussed in this chapter) and in areas where they do not. The Decision contemplates as means to this end the maintenance of information systems and the promotion of contacts between relevant Member State authorities, including periodic direct meetings. (Denmark participates in neither of these initiatives.)

Clearly, cooperation in civil justice has become an area of intense activity at the EU level. It seems reasonable to assume that further legislative steps will be taken to create a "genuine European area of justice."[24] The Commission has for example issued a number of Green

---

22. O.J. L 43 (Feb. 14, 2001).

23. O.J. L 174 (June 27, 2001).

24. The creation of a "genuine European area of justice" is one of the goals outlined in the Communication of May 10, 2005 from the Commission to the Council and the European Parliament. The Hague Programme: ten priorities for the next five years. The Partnership for European renewal in the field of Freedom, Security and Justice (COM(2005) 184 final).

papers covering areas such as succession and wills[25] and maintenance obligations,[26] with a view to eventually proposing EU law instruments on these matters.

E.   CHOICE OF LAW INSTRUMENTS

Last, but by no means least, are a series of new regulations prescribing for Member State courts uniform choice of law rules for use in civil and commercial litigation. Interestingly, these regulations are not limited in their application to litigation involving persons or interests of other Member States. Rather, by these regulations the States have committed to apply the prescribed choice of law rules in *all* cases coming before them, even cases having no link whatsoever with EU law or with any other Member State.

Establishment of common choice of law rules among the Member States has long been seen as complementing and facilitating the mutual recognition and enforcement of judgments. As early as 1980, the Member States had concluded a convention on the law applicable to contractual obligations, opened for signature in Rome on 19 June 1980, OJ C 027, 26/01/1998, which came to be known simply as the Rome Convention. It entered into force on April 1, 1991. As in the case of the 1968 Brussels Convention, the States entered into a protocol vesting the Court of Justice with jurisdiction to interpret the Rome Convention upon preliminary reference from national courts.[27]

1.   LAW APPLICABLE TO CONTRACTUAL OBLIGATIONS (ROME I)

With the Amsterdam Treaty's transfer of civil justice cooperation to the Community's pillar one, work began on transforming the Rome Convention into a directly applicable regulation. The result was Regulation 593/2008 on the law applicable to contractual obligations (the Rome I Regulation),[28] applicable to contracts concluded after December 17, 2009. However, the Rome Convention remains in force and applicable insofar as the United Kingdom and Denmark are concerned, as neither State has adopted the Rome I Regulation.

According to the preamble to the Regulation, "[t]he proper functioning of the internal market creates a need, in order to improve the predictability of the outcome of litigation, certainty as to the law applicable and the free movement of judgments, for the conflict-of-law rules in

---

25. Green Paper: Succession and wills (COM(2005) 65 final—not published in the Official Journal).

26. Commission Green Paper of April 15, 2004 on maintenance obligations (COM(2004) 254 final—not published in the Official Journal).

27. The first two interpretation protocols were signed in Brussels in 1988 and were later amended in 1998. The consolidated versions are published in O.J. C 27 (Jan. 26, 1998).

28. O.J. L 177/6 (July 4, 2008).

the Member States to designate the same national law irrespective of the country of the court in which an action is brought." Subject to stated exceptions, the Rome I Regulation applies to all manner of contractual obligations. In keeping with notions of party autonomy, it allows parties to choose the law applicable to their contract, as well as to change it at any time by mutual agreement, subject to important limitations in the case of consumer and employment contracts and subject to rules of law otherwise deemed mandatory, as defined below.

Absent a choice, and except for consumer and employment contracts in which the need is felt to protect the presumably weaker party to the transaction, the applicable law is the law of the country (even a third country) with which it the contract bears a stated relationship depending on the type of contract in question. In this regard, Rome I moves away from "the most closely connected country" rule that prevailed under the Rome Convention. For example, Article 4 (1) subjects contracts for the sale of goods to the law of the country of seller's habitual residence, contracts for services to the law of the provider's country of habitual residence, and in rem obligations relating to immovable property to law of the country where the property is located. If a contract does not fall within any of the contract types enumerated in Article 4(1), it is governed under Article 4(2) by the law of the country where the party required to effect the "characteristic performance" of the contract has its habitual residence. However, in the interest of flexibility, Article 4(3) provides an escape clause, so that "[if] it is clear from all the circumstances of the case that the contract is manifestly more closely connected with a country other than that indicated in paragraphs 1 or 2, the law of that other country shall apply." Article 5 provides special rules for contracts of carriage, Article 6 for consumer contracts (with the term "consumer" defined exactly as it is in the Brussels I Regulation), Article 7 for insurance contracts, and Article 8 for employment contracts.

Importantly, separate provision is made for the application of so-called mandatory rules of law. Article 9 defines mandatory rules of law as "provisions the respect for which is regarded as crucial by a country for safeguarding its public interests, such as its political, social or economic organisation, to such an extent that they are applicable to any situation falling within their scope, irrespective of the law otherwise applicable to the contract under this Regulation." Mandatory rules of law are not restricted to rules of law of the forum; a court may under stated circumstances also give effect to mandatory rules of law of another country (even a country whose law is not otherwise applicable to the merits under the Regulation).

The Regulation also usefully sets out rules in Articles 10 and 11 for determining the law applicable to the validity—both formal and material—of contracts. Questions of material validity are determined by the law that would have governed the contract under the Regulation if the contract were assumed to be valid. However, when a party disputes having given consent, the law applicable may be that of the country of that party's habitual residence. Subject to certain exceptions, a contract's formal validity is governed either by the law applicable to the substance of the contract or the law of the country where the contract was concluded.

Predictably, Article 21 guarantees respect for the public policy of the forum. Application of the law specified by the Regulation may be refused if, but only if, that would be "manifestly incompatible with the public policy (*ordre public*) of the forum."

2. LAW APPLICABLE TO NON-CONTRACTUAL OBLIGATIONS (ROME II)

Acting on a proposal of the Commission, the Parliament and Council also adopted Regulation 864/2007 on the law applicable to non-contractual obligations (the Rome II Regulation),[29] applicable as of January 11, 2009 in all Member States except Denmark with respect to damage occurring after the date the Regulation came into force, namely August 20, 2007. Rome II applies in principle to all non-contractual obligations in civil and commercial matters, including product liability, competition law, and *culpa in contrahendo*, but is subject to exclusions for revenue, customs and administrative matters, State liability, and matrimonial and family relationships. Like Rome I, the law designated by the Regulation is applicable whether or not it is the law of another Member State or a third country.

As a general rule, the law applicable in tort is the law of the country in which the damage occurs, irrespective of the country in which the event giving rise to the damage occurred and irrespective of the country or countries in which the indirect consequences of that event occur" (Article 4(1)). However, where both the tortfeasor and the injured party are habitually resident in the same country, the law of that country shall apply. Like Rome I, Rome II provides an escape clause for the situation in which a tort is manifestly more closely connected to another country (Article 4(3)).

Parties have a right under the Regulation to choose the applicable law after the liability-generating event has already occurred. If all the parties are pursuing commercial activity, they may also do so by an agreement entered into prior to occurrence of the harmful event. But, again like Rome I, Rome II does not permit the parties to avoid application of the laws of the country where the harmful event occurred if that law cannot be derogated from by the parties.

In the interest of greater predictability, the Regulation establishes specific choice of law rules for specified claims: product liability (art. 5), competition law (art. 6), for environmental torts (art. 7), intellectual property law violations (art. 8), and torts in the labor law field (art. 9). Additional choice of law rules are laid down in Articles 10 through 12 for claims in unjust enrichment, *negotiorum gestio* and *culpa in contrahendo*. Rome II mirrors Rome I in its provisions on mandatory rules of law (art.

---

29. O.J. L 199/40 (July 31, 2007).

16), the formal validity of unilateral acts (art. 21), and forum public policy (art. 26).

3. OTHER CHOICE OF LAW INITIATIVES

The EU has almost certainly not exhausted its appetite for harmonization of choice of law rules. For example, the Commission in 2006 proposed an amendment to Regulation 2201/2003 on jurisdiction and judgments in matrimonial matters to build in harmonized rules on the law applicable in divorce and separation matters.[30] The proposal contemplates a limited role for party autonomy in choice of law.

F. UNIFORM MEMBER STATE LAW

It might well enhance the functioning of the internal market for the Member States to have not only common choice of law rules, but also the same substantive rules of law in certain private law areas, such as contracts and commercial law. Initiatives in that direction—epitomized by a proposed European Civil Code spearheaded by Professor Christian von Barr of Germany—have encountered severe opposition as overreaching by Brussels and an affront to the principle of subsidiarity and, by some, to the values of regulatory competition and the "market" for law.

A fall-back approach is the so-called "Draft Common Frame of Reference" (or "DCFR"). In 2003 the Commission launched an Action Plan for a coherent contract law, the idea being to produce a coherent set of overarching definitions, principles and rules of contract law. An international network of academics labored between 2005 and 2007, under contract with the Commission, to put together a DCFR. The project draws on the above-mentioned European Civil Code project, on the Restatement-like "Principles of European Contract Law" (a project led by Professor Ole Lando of Denmark), and on existing legislation—and, as the multiplicity of sources would suggest, its purpose is less than clear. Professor von Barr describes it as follows:

> A "common frame of reference" ... means a non-binding set of systematically presented rules not unsimilar to the existing national Civil Codes [that could] play a major role in the European Union in its potential influence on national legislation and on the future law-making process at a European level. The second reason for the importance of a reference frame is its potential influence on judgments of the national courts. The third [is] that its scope of application can easily be much broader than that of a binding European instrument. The fourth [is] that in many cases it can in itself serve the purposes of an opt-in model, and the fifth [is] that it will furnish our European universities with a common text for teaching purposes.

---

30. Proposal for a Council Regulation of July 17, 2007 amending Regulation (EC) No 2201/2003 as regards jurisdiction and introducing rules concerning applicable law in matrimonial matters [COM(2006) 399 final—Not published in the Official Journal].

Clearly, the DCFR is driven by a multiplicity of uses. What they have in common is their aim to foster a greater coherence and consistency in European contract law by means short of a binding substantive law instrument.

INDEX

References are to Pages

†